A
DICTIONARY
OF
EUROPEAN LITERATURE

DESIGNED AS A COMPANION TO ENGLISH STUDIES

BY
LAURIE MAGNUS, M.A.

Author of *Introduction to Poetry, English
Literature in the Nineteenth Century, etc.*

41992

LONDON
GEORGE ROUTLEDGE & SONS, LTD.
NEW YORK: E. P. DUTTON & CO.
1926

PRINTED IN GREAT BRITAIN BY HEADLEY BROTHERS,
18, DEVONSHIRE STREET, E.C.2 AND ASHFORD, KENT.

MATRI DILECTÆ FILIUS ORBUS

PREFACE

THE OBJECT of this book is to provide, in a single volume, the information which students require complementary to a history of English literature or to the special study of a part of it.

There are two ways of supplying that information. One is to write, as Dowden suggested many years ago, 'a *General Sketch of European Literature*, somewhat resembling Mr. Freeman's *General Sketch of European History* in its aim and scope and manner of treatment'. But observation confirms my experience of the difficulty, if not the impossibility, of writing this book to that scale. Hallam filled four stout volumes in introducing us to only three centuries, and the 'new Hallam', as Saintsbury would have us call his team of writers of the *Periods of European Literature*, required twelve volumes for their survey. The other and more practical way is to arrange the information under alphabetic headings; and I trust that this *Dictionary of European Literature* will be found to contain what is wanted.

Briefly, it comprises general articles on movements or topics continuous through several centuries and countries; concise surveys of the literary history of the chief countries; critical and biographical accounts, with a minimum of bibliography, of major and minor writers, and definitions of such literary terms as the student or general reader is likely to encounter. America is excluded geographically, and the Orient on the further ground, stated by Saintsbury in the 'new Hallam', that 'no one is likely to succeed in laying down the exact connection between Eastern, Western, and, as go-between, Byzantine literature'. Our own literature is admitted rather fully. The point of view has been European, not insular; but it has seemed clear that a companion to English studies should not neglect the studies which it accompanies. Roughly, and making allowance for the necessary fortunate intrusion of the Ancients, the period covered extends from the twelfth to the twentieth century. But the loops are loosely tied at both ends. There are natural pauses and beginnings, which are not identical in time in the several countries. The only living authors included are Thomas Hardy and Georg Brandes. For the rest, I hope that what is *in* may be judged independently of what is *out*.

I have quoted freely from leading critics ; and, writing in the week of Saintsbury's eightieth birthday, it is a privilege to record a big debt to the many books on this subject which he has written, edited, or caused to be written. Such books, or series of books, as the *Periods* mentioned above ; the twelve volumes of the *Cambridge Modern History* ; the fourteen volumes of the *Cambridge History of English Literature*, the usefulness of which would be much enhanced by the addition of a General Index ; Courthope's *History of English Poetry* ; volumes iv and v of Symonds' *Renaissance in Italy* ; Sandys' *History of Classical Scholarship* ; Saintsbury's *History of Criticism* ; and, among cross-country books, rarer at home than abroad, Lee's *French Renaissance in England* and Herford's *Literary Relations of England and Germany in the Sixteenth Century*, have always proved valuable. But I have found my main authorities in French and German special studies, such as Vogüé's *Roman Russe*, Mornet's *Romantisme en France*, Haym's *Romantische Schule*, Koerting's *Geschichte des französischen Romans im siebzehnten Jahrhundert*, etc., and, more recently, in English and American books of the same class. The growth of this kind in recent years is remarkable and reassuring ; among the latest are G. Scott's *Portrait of Zélide*, Renwick's monograph on *Spenser*, A. F. G. Bell's on *Luis de Leon*, E. H. R. Tatham's *Petrarch* (vol. i), volumes i and ii of *Ben Jonson* by C. H. Herford and Percy Simpson, and the late Miss Lowell's *Life of Keats*. The publications of the British Academy and the English Association are to be mentioned in the same class, and I may refer with gratitude to the weekly *causeries* on books in the leading articles of *The Times Literary Supplement* and by Sir Edmund Gosse in the *Sunday Times*. These are equal to anything in the past, and are surely a notable feature of modern English journalism.

It would be interesting to try to discover from this comparative study a clue to the *future* of European literature. It has made its way through so many inhibitions, ecclesiastical and civil, that the problem of the course it will pursue after the last war of liberation from authority is particularly fascinating. Changing values need not be disappearing values, and the real interest of the lives of Abelard, Dante, Reuchlin, Rabelais, Tasso, More, Corneille, Milton, Heine— to name a few among many,—does not lie in the stones in their path, but in the path which they cut through the stones. The mind of Europe has found expression, despite obstacles and obscurantism, and its greater freedom in the present century will not be strange to the voices of the past. Possibly, the new renaissance will spring in one of the smaller countries, redeemed or restored in recent years. More

probably it will spring in Germany, which, through nearly two generations, has lost or mislaid the key to the stored riches of olden times.
These are matters for the prophet, not the historian of literature.   He
is glad to have spent many years in close communion with the makers
of that mind, whose thought was very little or not at all concerned
with rivalries of rivers and seas ; whose language was competent to
cross the barriers of nationality ; who lead us to Canterbury or Florence,
serene above war and plague ; to rules of gentleness and courtesy,
while Spain and England are in arms ; to a French invasion of English
taste, which the Channel did not resist, and to that later invasion by
Germany, which Charles Lamb greeted so ecstatically on 6th July,
1796. The study of Europe in letters yields other dates, and other
values, than those which we celebrate in politics. The mind of Europe
has sought other modes of more tranquil expression than are contained
in her treaties and her laws ; and those who try to follow the broken
music of that mind in those modes may arrest, among present pleasures,
sounds of the deeper harmony, which ' lends a yonder to all ends '.

This book would never have been written except for the encouragement of my wife, who has turned the labour into a delight.

L.M.

The Athenæum,
    Pall Mall, S.W.

26th October, 1925.

ABBREVIATIONS

C.H.E.L., i-xiv. *Cambridge History of English Literature*, 14 vols.; each volume contains chapters by various authors.

C.M.H., i-xii. *Cambridge Modern History*, 12 vols.; ditto.

P.E.L., i-xii. *Periods of European Literature*, Blackwood, 12 vols.; each volume by a different author.

q.v.—see aforesaid.

s.v.—*sub voce.*

Ordinary common abbreviations are Engl., Fr., Germ., Gk., It., Lat., Span., and so on, for English, French, German, Greek, Italian, Latin, Spanish; lit. for literature; wr. for wrote; crit. for criticism; hist. for history; class. for classical; bk. for book; cent. for century, and others even more obvious.

The title of each article is repeated within the article by initials only.

A study of English Literature alone would give a very false and insufficient idea of the heights attained in the progress of European Literature as a whole.—W. P. KER.

Party politics leave me cold. But the countryside of England and the literature of Europe make me glow.—GEORGE WYNDHAM.

Literature enables nations to understand one another.—WALTER BAGEHOT.

Nationality is something to defend, like life, if it is threatened, but not something to worship because it is strong. When it is not threatened, then we can cease to sing about it, and dream of the Europe that shall be beyond it.—"THE TIMES LITERARY SUPPLEMENT," 20th May, 1915.

It is not at all impossible that, in the immediate or at least the near future, there may be something of a return to that comparative study of European literature, that absence of sharp national divisions, which existed to some extent in the Middle Ages, and was interrupted, partly by ecclesiastical, partly by literary causes, at and after the Renaissance.—GEORGE SAINTSBURY.

The Humanism of the fifteenth century was more literary and artistic than scientific, but it was ready to welcome scientific research, and would in a short time have freed itself from the ecclesiastical shackles which hampered its development. But the outbreak of fierce religious war in the sixteenth century destroyed the hopes of the humanists.—W. R. INGE.

If English literature be connected in our college and university courses with either Greek or Latin, or French or German literature, the thoughtful student can hardly fail to be aroused by his comparative studies to consider questions which demand an answer from philosophy.—EDWARD DOWDEN.

DICTIONARY OF
EUROPEAN LITERATURE

A

Aarestrup, Carl Ludwig Emil (1800-56): Dan. poet. A.'s favourite theme was the 'eternal feminine', and he is the author of many charming love-lyrics (publd., 1838), occasionally too passionate for conventional expression. Brandes (Dan. critic; born, 1842), comparing A. with Winther and Boedtcher (qq.v.), says: 'Whereas Winther stands unapproached, by his far-flung triumphs as a poet of love, in the springtide of our new poesy, and whereas the glowing colours of Aarestrup's muse raised Winther's song to summer heat, we find in Boedtcher this heat tempered, and the air mild and soft, as on a sun-lit day in September'.

Aasen, Ivar (1813-96): Norse philologer, inventor of *Landsmaal* (q.v.), i.e. a national language, formed by selection from living dialects, old Saga (q.v.) speech, etc. A.'s object was to create a Norse literary language, free from Dan., Germ., and Fr. borrowings and contamination; and he wr. a grammar and a dictionary of *Landsmaal* (or Norse-Norse), as well as books in his language. According to champions of A.'s theories, the Norse of Ibsen (q.v.) is a provincial dialect unworthy of the descendants of the heroic age; and the result of the adoption of *Landsmaal* (a question which has occupied Governmental commissions) would be to bring Norse nearer again to Icelandic, and further from Danish. Denmark's influence is strong in Norw. towns, and the problem has political bearings, which do not concern us here; but it is probably correct to say that not 15% of the population are abandoning *Riksmaal* (the colloquial and written language) for *Landsmaal*, which seems to make no headway in the ordinary commerce of life. It is to be noted, too, that the greatest Norse writers, Ibsen and Björnson (qq.v.), did not favour the literary Norse language.

Abbt, Thomas (1738-66): Germ. popular philosopher. Wr. treatises on conduct and ethics, of which the most widely-read were 'Dying for one's country' and 'Merit'. A. succeeded Lessing (q.v.), to whose circle in Berlin he belonged, as joint-contributor to the 'Letters on Literature' with Nicolai and Mendelssohn (qq.v.).

Abelard, Pierre (1079-1142): Fr. theological teacher, whose life was a succession of spiritual and material catastrophes, which he described in an autobiographic *Historia Calamitatum suarum*. Since character is fate, A. was perhaps the author as well as the victim of the calamitous career. After studying dialectic under Wm. of Champeaux at Paris, he disputed his master's doctrine; and, later studying theology at Laon, he became the most frequented teacher of the day, his pupils including, as has been enumerated, one pope, 19 cardinals, more than 50 archbishops and bishops,—Fr., Engl. and Germ. Some of his pupils overwent his own teaching: notably among them the reforming bp., Arnold of Brescia (died, a martyr, 1155), who expanded A.'s principles, one of which may be summarized conveniently as the doctrine that nothing should be believed which has not first been understood, into formulæ of rationalism far in excess of the master's actual words. Still, those words were new enough and bold enough, in the times in which A. taught, and in the circumstances of his life and teaching, to cause him to be suspended, inhibited, and persecuted in his ecclesiastical capacity. But A.'s record as a theologian and an innovator concerns us less intimately than his fame as the tragic lover of Heloïse, niece of a canon Fulbert. The incongruity in that age of passionate love in the flesh with the passion of religion, joined to the taste of that age for tales of chivalric adventure between a man and a maid, have raised the tale of A. and Heloïse into one of the world's great love-stories. It happens to be well documented by A.'s original letters, and it happens, too, that Heloïse was much more than a love-struck girl; she was a woman of fine character and high ideals. Her story (and see s.v. Rousseau, *la Nouvelle Heloïse*), 'was impressed with as entire a self-surrender as ever ravished the soul of nun panting with love of the God-man. There has never been a passion between a man and woman more famous than that which brought happiness and sorrow to the lives of Abælard and Heloïse. Here fame is just. It was a great love, and its course was a perfect soul's tragedy. Abælard was a celebrity, the intellectual glory of an active-minded epoch. His love-story has done as much for his posthumous fame as all his intellectual activities. Heloïse became known in her time through her relations with Abælard; in his songs her name was wafted far. She has come down to us as

1

one of the world's love-heroines' (H. O. Taylor, the *Medieval Mind*, ii, 1).

Abencerraje y la Hermosa Xarifa, Historia del' (Span.) : anon. story of Abencerraje and the beautiful Xarifa, first publd. in the *Inventario* of A. de Villegas (q.v.), 1565 (licensed for publication, 1551), and, later, inserted in editions of the *Diana enamorada* of Montemayor (q.v.). Neither imputation of authorship is admitted by critics to-day.

About, Edmond (1828-85) : Fr. novelist ; journalist ; Alsatian ; developed strong republican views after the Franco-Prussian War, and expressed himself in newspapers and pamphlets. A.'s education was completed in Athens, whence he brought home his *Grèce contemporaine*, a somewhat lively and impertinent volume. He wr. *Tolla*, 1855 (which has a scandalous charge of plagiary tacked on to it) ; *le Roi des Montagnes*, 1856 ; *Trente et Quarante*, 1858 ; *l'Homme à l'Oreille cassée*, 1861, etc. ; and was also a writer of plays ; e.g., *Gaetana*, produced at the Odéon, 1862.

Abravanel, -i. Isaac (1437-1508) : Port. scholar ; descended from an ancient Jewish family in Spain (Abravanel, Abrabanel, or Abarbanel), claiming to trace its origin to king David ; settled at Seville, and, later, in Portugal, where I.A. was born at Lisbon. He held high office at the court, but removed to Toledo, 1483, and to Naples, 1492, at the expulsion of the Jews from Castile. Wr. valuable works in Biblical commentary and exegesis.

-ii. **Judah** (died, 1535) : Span. poet; son of above ; accompanied his father's wanderings, and died at Venice ; known in Span. literary history as Leon Hebreo (Leo the Hebrew). Wr. in Ital. (mixed with Castilian idioms) *Dialoghi di Amore* (' Dialogues of Love '), publd. in Rome, 1535. It is a fine product of Span. genius and neo-Platonic mysticism, and from the traces of it which are found in *Il Cortegiano* it is assumed that Castiglione (q.v.) read the work in MS. It was transld. into Fr. by Tyard (q.v.), and was much appreciated by the poets of the Pleiad (q.v.) ; Montaigne (q.v.) knew it and refers to it (bk. vi, ch. 5) ; and the Castilian versions, of which there were 3, had their influence on the poetry of Camoens and the prose of Luis de Leon (qq.v.). A., who was a physician by profession, enjoyed the acquaintance of Mirandola (q.v.), whose brilliant talents were trained in the same paths as were followed by this Span.-Ital. Platonizing Jew.

Academy : literary club or *côterie*. In this sense the name was first adopted in the era of humanism (q.v.) in Italy ; the most famous A. of that age was founded at Florence by Cosimo de Medici (q.v.) in honour of Plato (q.v.), from whose ' academe ' the name was derived ; Ficino (q.v.) was selected as its original leader, and symposia and discussions were there instituted. The example rapidly spread through Italy in the 16th cent. Mention is due, e.g., to Beccadelli's (q.v.) A. at Naples (see s.v. Alfonso), and, more particularly, to the Accademia della Crusca (grain), incorporated at Florence, 1587, and reconstituted by Napoleon i, 1811, which became proverbial (dellacruscan) for its pedantic classicism. Its chief period of activity was in the notoriously

academic 18th cent., and it published a dict. of the Ital. (chiefly Tuscan dialect) language. The Arcadian A., founded in Italy, 1690, which was one of the most tenacious and remarkable of its kind, is discussed s.v. Arcadia.

The movement spread to France, where the oldest literary society in Europe had flourished since 1323 at the Floral Games (q.v.) of Toulouse, raised to the dignity of an Academy about 300 years later. The younger Baif (q.v.), in the epoch of the Pleiad (q.v.), founded an A. (*académie*) at Paris, with the approval of the court and the university, for the resuscitation of old forms of poetry, and this society was the model for Harvey's (q.v.) Areopagus. Mention is likewise due to the A. founded by, or by the influence of, queen Christina (q.v). of Sweden.

But the leading A. of letters, and the only one which is sufficiently described by that title alone, is the Fr. A. (*l'Académie française*), which, from the normal small beginning of a literary club or *côterie*, has survived to this day in the full vigour of its authority and discretion as the national court of literary arbitrament in France. Other literary academies have risen since, and will rise ; but, for the purpose of literature in Europe, Academy means *l'Académie*. As such, the A. started in the drawing-room, or *salon*, of a certain Valentin Conrart (q.v.), a frequenter of the Hotel de Rambouillet (q.v.). In 1626, when the ' blue room ' of that mansion was at its fullest, Conrart used to invite half-a-dozen of the best known men of letters to informal gatherings at his own house. Perhaps Conrart and his friends were not sorry to be free from the feminine element, despite the gallantry which was the password to the ' precious ' (q.v.) circle ; however that may be, it so happened that it was from Conrart's offshoot of the aristocratic literary set which the marquise de Rambouillet had gathered round her, and not from that gathering direct, that the Fr. A. proceeded. The first eight or ten symposiasts included Conrart himself, Godeau, Gombauld, Maleville, Habert, Chapelain, Desmarets and Serizay. Three years later, card. Richelieu (q.v.) offered the society his patronage and the privilege of royal recognition. The little band was not in a hurry to accept the burden of these honours, but refusal was difficult to word politely, even for such arbiters of polite diction, and on 13 Mar. 1634, the Fr. A., as it had decided to call itself in preference to the suggestions of *Académie des beaux esprits* or *éminente*, or *de l'éloquence*, held the first of its formal sessions. By this time it counted 34 members, the new ones among whom included J. L. de Balzac (who only attended one meeting), Voiture, and Vaugelas (qq.v.). The functions of the A. were so vague that it was not till 10 July, 1637, that parliament advised king Louis xiii to grant its charter of incorporation. In that year the tale of members was fixed permanently at 40. In the reign of the *grand monarque*, Louis xiv, it became the ambition of noblemen and high officials to be admitted to this circle of ' Immortals ' ; but, on the whole, for nearly three centuries, despite the sneer of Voltaire (q.v.) (' the French Academy contains prelates, noblemen, lawyers, professors, and *even some writers*'), the standard of literary qualification has been amply recognized and sustained. It was Patru (q.v.) who invented, 1640, the system of an inaugural discourse, and from the start of the formal Monday meetings of the newly-constituted society, academic harangues were delivered. More and more the A. rose to the level of its responsibilities, and its power in the 18th cent. was supreme. The gradual decline from that supremacy during the 19th cent. to more formal and ornamental functions is due as much to the increase of newspapers and reviews, offering bigger prizes and a wider circulation than the A. could command, as to any more esoteric cause.

Going back to its early history, it is clear that the A. was founded in the atmosphere precisely suited to the genius of Fr. lit. Its founders were the men of trained faculties and logical reason, of refined taste and correct bearing, who were to usher in the great classical age. The worst that can be said of the precious (q.v.) writers (unless we rehearse *les Précieuses ridicules*) is that they were too eclectic and fastidious; but in this they were doing the work of Malherbe in poetry and J. L. de Balzac in prose, and, by anticipation, the work of Boileau (q.v.), who, though late to be elected to the A., quickly made up for lost time in the influence which he exercised. In its early years, again, the A. was doubtless subject to the power of patronage which resided with Louis xiv and card. Richelieu. The latter's jealousy of Corneille's (q.v.) *Cid* (q.v.), and the inadequate tone of Chapelain's final version of the *Sentiments de l'Académie* (1638), upon it are sufficient evidence to this ugly feature. But the unseen presence of de Balzac, and the activity of Vaugelas among its members, proved from the first a source of strength; and, out of several programmes which were proposed as deserving of the attention of the A., Chapelain's scheme of a Dictionary was adopted as the most immediate, and the editorship was entrusted to the competent hands of Vaugelas. He and several successors died before the completion of the enterprise (*Dictionnaire de l'Académie*, 2 vols., Paris, 1694; 7th edn., 1879. A *Dictionnaire Universel* appeared in 1690, Rotterdam, 2 vols., and its author, Furetière, q.v., was expelled from the A. for his action in anticipating its completed labours). It is a matter of history rather than of lit. to add that committees of the A. were appointed by Colbert (Finance-Minister to Louis xiv) in 1663 and 1666, and became the Royal Academy of Inscriptions and Belles-Lettres and the Academy of Sciences respectively; that Napoleon i added an Academy of Fine Arts, and that an Academy of Moral and Political Science was added in 1832. The A. was housed in the Louvre by Louis xiv, but was dissolved in 1793 (under the Revolution), and reformed as the Institut National. The general name of the 5 branches is now the Institut de France, and the oldest and parent society is still *the* Academy in Europe.

The Fr. model was strictly followed in Spain, in the reign of king Philip v, grandson of Louis xiv of France, in the year of the close of the Succession War which broke out when he came to the throne. The *Real Academia Española* (Royal Spanish Academy) was formally founded by a charter dated 3 October, 1714, and the marquis de Villena (q.v.) was its first director. Like its prototype in Paris, the Span. A. undertook forthwith the necessary work of compiling a native dict. which was published in 6 vols., 1726-39 (see s.v. *Diccionario*). A volume on Orthography followed in 1742, and a Grammar in 1771; and works on the Castilian language and on Poetics were projected. The Span. A. has likewise been noted for its *Editions de luxe* of famous works; e.g., for its *Don Quixote* (1780-84). The Academy for Spanish History was founded, 1738, in the reign of the same monarch, Philip v.

Similarly, the Swedish Academy was founded, 1786, by king Gustavus (iii) Adolphus on the model of the Fr.; and M. Arnold's (q.v.) essay, 1865, on 'The Literary Influence of Academies' was a powerful plea for such a limited institution in this country as has since been partially realized in the Royal British Academy.

Finally, and generally on Academies, we may quote the sage remarks of prof. Elton (*P.E.L.*, viii, 426): 'They had, it is true, their dreary and fallacious side, and they were apt to make mediocrity too happy with the sense of company, but they did real service to language, and they were sometimes a refuge of sound sense. They were the casual and official expression of the great struggle of taste to be quit of the weeds that were smothering it. And if the higher forms of art are not born of this kind of joint-stock effort, yet they do not in the end lose by the federal aim; for the instrument of language is cleared of rust and sharpened by long social scrutiny'.

Achery, D', Luc (1609-85): Fr. scholar. Edited *Veterum aliquot scriptorum . . . Spicilegium*, 13 vols., 1655-77; invited Mabillon (q.v.) to collaborate with him in the editorship of the Acts of the Sacred Order of St. Benedict, 1668-1701.

Acosta, de, José (1539-1600): Port. botanist; moralist. Wr. a treatise on the natural history of the Span. Indies.

Acton, John E. E. Dalberg- (1834-1902): Engl. historian; created baron A., 1869; prof. of modern history at Cambridge Univ.; planned the *C.M.H.*, which was completed in 12 vols., 1910, by sirs A. W. Ward, G. W. Prothero and Stanley Leathes: 'Had the great student, who conceived the plan of this work, survived to see its completion, he would not, we think, have been disappointed with his audience' (Pref., vol. xii); or, we may add, with his successors in the editorship. A.'s work was more by influence than by output, and is to be sought now chiefly in 4 vols. of *Lectures*, piously edited by J. N. Figgis and R. V. Laurence, 1906-10. A. was a man of profound learning, and owed, perhaps, partly to his Germ. mother an attraction to, and ability for, Germ. methods of application: 'Across the century', wr. sir A. W. Ward (*C.H.E.L.*, xiv., 119), 'the spirit of the greatest of modern writers on ancient history—Niebuhr (q.v.)—

seems in contact with the spirit of him who had most closely scanned the course of modern history ; and, together, they seem to vindicate the right and duty of the advance made in historical studies and literature during the nineteenth century's course in England and elsewhere '.

Acuña, de, Hernando (16th cent.) : Span. poet, of Port. descent ; Italianate. A.'s first work was in the old style of 10-line stanzas of chivalric court-poetry, and took shape as a versified rendering of a Span. prose version of *Le Chevalier délibéré* by the Fr. poet Olivier de la Marche (q.v.). The ' deliberate knight ' in question was the Burgundian monarch, Charles the Bold, whose daughter, Mary of Burgundy, had been patroness to La Marche and became grandmother to the emperor Charles v. The Span. prose version in question was the emperor's own work, and he put it into A.'s hands to receive its dress of Span. poetry. This royal commission was satisfactorily completed in the *Caballero determinado*, 1553. A. was then free to turn to the Ital. exemplars in which his taste delighted. He followed in the wake of Boscan and Garcilasso (qq.v.) ; wr. sonnets and other slighter verse : transld. a part of Boiardo's (q.v.) *Orlando innamorato* : and even composed a Virgilian poem in blank verse on ' The Contest of Ajax and of Ulysses over the arms of Achilles '. A.'s poetical remains were publd., 1591, by his widow.

Adam de la Halle (*c.* 1240-*c.* 1288) : Fr. lyric poet ; known as the Hunchback (*le Bossu*) of Arras, which fixes the town of his birth. He is said to have died in Italy. A.'s chief distinction, as a *bourgeois* writer in the *langue d'oïl* of the 13th cent. (see s.v. French Literature), lies in his extension of the dramatic potentialities inherent in the old form of the *pastourelle* (q.v.). His *Jeu de Robin et de Marion* was produced at Naples, 1283, and was reproduced with a prologue in dialogue, entitled *Jeu du Pelerin* at Arras a year or two later. It marks the beginning of pastoral-drama, or even of comic-opera, as a literary kind.

Addison, Joseph (1672-1719) : Engl. essayist ; contemporary with Steele (q.v.), with whom he was associated in the foundation of the *Spectator*, 1711, from which he derives his chief title to fame ; wr., too, *Cato*, a tragedy, 1713, which was produced very successfully at Drury Lane ; M.P., 1708-19 ; m. countess of Warwick, 1716.

The excellence of the *Spectator*, in which it is unnecessary to distinguish A.'s part very definitely from Steele's, is twofold : (1) it invented the social *feuilleton* in lit, and (2) it introduced amenity into journalism. A. was the first club-man (see s.v. Coffee-house) in history,—the first man of letters, to whom the epithet ' clubbable ' could be applied. Sir Roger de Coverley, in his circle, whose weekly budget of views and news (chiefly and deliberately, views) delighted *Spectator* readers from week to week, was the ordinary country gentleman of Engld., sitting with his cronies at ease, interested in the funds, the chancelleries, the new bks., the new fashions, etc.— all that was moving on the Rialto,—and seeing it all out of shrewd, kindly, wise, humorous

eyes, with no vehemence of party and no violence of tongue. Out of sir Roger descended colonel Newcome and Mr. Pickwick ; and out of the quiet urbane tone of that little group of middle-class moralists sprang the taste for domestic fiction which Richardson (q.v.) and others were to gratify. The same sobriety and good form governed A.'s writings as a critic. He was largely responsible for repairing public taste in regard to Shakespeare and Milton, and Saintsbury (*Hist. Crit.*, ii, 448), who does not take an enthusiastic view, says that his essay on the *Pleasures of the Imagination* ' is about the first attempt at a general theory of æsthetics (q.v.) in English ; it is a most interesting, and a very early example of that application of commonsense philosophy to abstract subjects which Locke (q.v.) taught to the English 18th century ; and many of its remarks are valuable and correct'. Foreign imitations of the *Spectator* are mentioned frequently in these pages.

Æneas Sylvius Piccolomini. See **Pius ii.**

Æsthetics : Generic name for the theory, science or philosophy of beauty, formulated by laws or principles of taste. With this technical aspect of æsthetics as a branch of knowledge the student of pure letters is not directly concerned. It touches lit. indirectly however, because, as F. Paulsen writes in his monograph on *Kant* (q.v. ; E.T., 17) : ' A transformation in our attitude towards life, and in our general view of the world, always shows itself first in the æsthetic field ' ; and such a transformation, with its earliest signs in the æsthetic field, is expressed in the works of artists and men of letters. They reflect, in the mirror which they hold up to nature, the changes in the mind of man ; and, observing first that the term ' æsthetics ' in its technical sense was the invention of a Germ. critic, A. G. Baumgarten (q.v.), in the 18th cent., we may distinguish two main movements in the history of taste in Europe, initiated and manifested by a transformation in that field. Moreover, there was a likeness, even a curious parallelism (which must not be pressed too far) between the two. The first occurred in Italy in the 14th and 15th cents., and bifurcated out of humanism into the Renaissance and Reformation ; the second occurred in Germany in the 17th and 18th cents. (it owed, and acknowledged, inspiration to France and Engld.), and is known as the *Aufklärung*, Enlightenment or Illumination. Humanism and Illumination in their respective epochs of appearance, showed themselves first in the æsthetic field, and indicated a transformation in men's attitude towards life and their general view of the world. The details and correspondences must be sought s.vv. ; here some names connected with the movement may be mentioned. The first æsthete in Europe in this sense, the first man whose intellectual tastes rebelled against the provisions for men's intellect, and demanded a different kind of food, was Petrarch (q.v.), who was born in 1304. By his devotion to Latinity and his life-long resolve to release thought and conduct from the trammels of an authority which hampered instead of stimulating independence, he and his successors for 200 years, commencing with Boccaccio—the 'escape from Dante', as he has been called,—and ending—only there is no end,—say, with Shakespeare's 'what a piece of work is man', changed the outlook of humanity, or rather, interpreted to the mind of Europe the external changes, of which the discoveries of the Navigators are the most obvious concrete example. Petrarch's appeal to Cicero was an æsthetic revision : it revised the canons of taste, and presented new aspects of beauty to the modern world. 'It was the æsthetic against the ascetic', as lord Acton (q.v.) has said. Then came the Reformation, insensibly altering values. The Roman law of order proved as burdensome as the authority against which it had protested, and Luther, as has been well said, rebelled against Lutheranism, when Winckelmann, q.v., who was born in 1717, 400 years after Petrarch, re-laid the foundations of taste on a direct approach to nature. The 'return to nature' by the teachers of æsthetics was a long and a gradual process, but it started, recognizably, at least, in Germany at the beginning of the 18th cent., when the spade and the foot-rule were used as the tools to prise open the freedom of the classics, in place of Lat., Gk. and Hebr. grammars. The parallelism is very close. 'Pietism and Rationalism', says Paulsen, whose aphorism we quoted above, 'both begin to find their way into Protestant Germany from the Netherlands and France in the second half of the 17th century. . . . As the political friendship between the Renaissance and the Reformation was broken so soon as the common enemy, scholasticism, had been overcome, so the intrinsic opposition between pietism and rationalism passed into open hostility as soon as the old orthodoxy had lost its dominant position'. The æsthetic principles of Gottsched (q.v.) gave way, under the influence of Rousseau (q.v.) and others, to those of the pantheists and romanticists, who prevailed during the 19th cent.

This brief and inadequate account of a field of study difficult to explore and involving philosophy, rhetoric and history, is correct as to the two great movements in the change of the mind of Europe, and may be tested by such a phenomenon as the Pre-Raphaelite Brotherhood (q.v.) in England, whose principles of taste in art and letters heralded social changes in public life. A word of warning is perhaps necessary. Not every new æsthetics is a sure harbinger of new life. There are tentative and imperfect revolts, and wild oats are sown on Parnassus, from which no harvest is reaped. But Paulsen's law is valid to the extent that the æsthetes march before the armies, and that the perception of the Beautiful is the key to the conduct of life.

The technical side of the science—its expression, that is to say, in art—must be studied in special treatises. In modern letters, one of the most famous of these treatises is the fragmentary *Laokoon*, 1766, of Lessing (q.v.), which, though partly indebted to the abbé Dubos (q.v.) and others, had a profound effect on students as different in taste as Goethe and Macaulay. Lessing distinguished clearly the arts of space and time (or of rest and motion), using, respectively, for expression

(*a*) architecture, sculpture, picture, (*b*) dancing, music, poetry.

Afzelius, Arvid August (1785-1871) : Swed. scholar ; folklorist ; edited, with Geijer (q.v.), *Svenska Folk-visor*, 1814-16, and wr. a number of useful works on history and archæology.

Agostino, Antonio (1517-86) : Span. scholar ; archæologist ; archbp. of Tarragona, 1576.

Agricola, Rudolf (1444-85) : scholar's-name of Rudolf Huysmann, Germ. humanist. Studied Gk. at Ferrara under Theodorus Gaza (q.v.) ; taught Gk. and Lat. at Heidelberg and Worms ; wr. *de Inventione Dialectica*, a treatise directed to the reform of philosophical method. Like Müller (q.v.) and others who had enjoyed the advantage of Ital. Renaissance teaching, but lacking the more infectious zeal of leaders like Reuchlin and Erasmus (qq.v.), A., in the brief period before Renaissance and Reformation parted company, is honourably remembered as a pioneer of the new learning at progressive universities in Germany.

Aguilar, de, Gaspar Honorat (1561-1623) : Span. dramatist ; resident at Valencia. Wr. *el Mercader amante* ('The amorous Merchant'), mentioned favourably by Cervantes (q.v. ; *Don Q.*, i, 48), and *Suerta sin Esperanza* ('Unexpected Luck'), a play of no particular merit.

Aguilar, Grace (1816-47) : Engl. novelist ; Jewess, of Span. descent. Wr. pleasant tales of domestic interest, *Home Influence, Mother's Recompense*, etc. ; hist. novels, *The Days of Bruce, The Vale of Cedars* : and essays on *The Spirit of Judaism*, etc.

Aguirre, de, José Saenz (1630-99) : Span. scholar ; card. ; patron of learning. A. publd., 1696, Part i of the bibliographical compilation of N. Antonio (q.v.), 12 years after its author's death, and other works of hist. value.

Ainsworth, Wm. Harrison (1805-82) : Engl. hist. novelist ; edited *Bentley's Miscellany*, (associated with Dickens, q.v.), 1840-2, *Ainsworth's Magazine*, 1842-53, when the *New Monthly Mag.* passed into his hands. Wr. *Rookwood*, 1834, *Jack Sheppard*, 1839 ; *Tower of London*, 1840 ; *Guy Fawkes*, 1841 ; *Old St. Paul's*, 1841 ; *The Miser's Daughter*, 1842 ; *Windsor Castle*, 1843 ; and other romances, mostly illustrated by Geo. Cruikshank (1792-1878), a frequent visitor at A.'s house in Kensal Green, and a busy intimate of the busy London circle of novelists and men of letters.

Akenside, Mark (1721-70) : Engl. poet ; wr. *The Pleasures of Imagination*, and other frigidly conventional poems : 'except in the political kind, he has no passion, and in no kind whatever has he magnificence, or the charm of life' (*C.H.E.L.*, x, 153).

Aksakov, Serge (1791-1859) : Russ. diarist. Wr., from 1840, partly under pressure from Gogol (q.v.), and publd., 1856, his 'Family Chronicle', which properly belongs to the 18th rather than to the 19th cent. This invaluable chronicle of the past (recently transld. into Engl. ; Routledge, Broadway Translns.), takes shape as a record of A.'s daily life in childhood with his grandfather, and 'we see every detail of the life of a backwoodsman of the days of Catherine ii' (q.v. ; Baring, *Russ. Lit.*, H.U.L.). But its interest is not merely social and hist.

' No more perfect piece of prose writing exists ', says the same critic. ' It is impossible to put the narrative down after once beginning it, and I have heard of children who read it like a fairy-tale. One is spell-bound by the charm, the dignity, the good-nature, the gentle, easy accent of the speaker, who was a gentleman by character as well as by lineage, one of God's as well as one of Russia's nobility '. Prince Mirsky, in his Pref. to the Engl. edn. (above) says : ' With due regard to proportion, if I were pressed to name what literary works Aksakov approaches nearest, I would—reluctantly—name the Book of Ruth and the second half of the Odyssey '. A.'s other books include, ' The Snowstorm ', 1834 ; ' Notes on Angling ', 1847 ; ' On Shooting ', 1852 ; ' Tales and Recollections of a Sportsman ', 1855 ; ' The years of childhood of Bagrov the Grandson ', 1858 ; ' Reminiscences of Gogol ', etc. He had two sons, who were well-known in the Slavophil (or conservative) camp, when criticism and lit. in Russia were divided between the supporters of Western and old-Russ. ideals. One of these sons, **Ivan Aksakov,** was a lyric poet of distinction.

Alamanni, Luigi (1495-1556) : It. poet. Born at Florence of noble family, long associated with the Medici (q.v.) ; espoused their cause with Machiavelli (q.v.), and escaped from Florentine factions to France ; returned to Florence, 1527, but was again driven out, and spent most of his remaining years in Paris, as pensioner of kings Francis i and Henri ii, thus adding another name to the long list of proscribed Florentines, of whom Dante (q.v.) is the head. A.'s satires in ' terza rima ' (q.v.) on the corruption of politics and the folly of courts are not altogether unworthy of his greater fellow-exile from Florence. Besides these, he wr. an immense quantity of Ital. poems under the patronage of the Fr. humanist king : among them, the *Coltivazione,* 6 bks. of didactic verse on agriculture, 4 on the farm in each season, one on gardening, and the last a sort of book of days ; Hesiod, Virgil and Varro being all laid under contribution, according to the prevailing taste of his times, which were prolific of bee-poems, garden-poems, and similar imitative georgics. Faithfully to Virgilian example, A. composed this lengthy work in blank verse (q.v.), the released or loose verse (*sciolti versi*) which he adapted to the 10-syllabled line with its feminine ending. The effect is not attractive ; but in France, academically, and in Engld., practically, the experiment introduced by A., with a full sense of its novelty, was quickly recognized and extended. The *Api* of Rucellai (q.v.) was not publd. till 1539, so that A. had no predecessor for his use of this metre in Ital. narrative poetry ; he was cited as the authority for its use in the critical treatise of the Pleiad (q.v.), and he served as model to contemporary poets in Engld. (see s.vv. Surrey, Wyatt) for sonnets, satire, and didactic poetry, and as a link between Petrarch and Sannazzaro (qq.v.).

Alarcon, de, Juan Ruiz (c. 1580-1639) : Span. dramatist ; born in Mexico, but resident in Spain after 1611. From his self-esteem, or some other cause, probably temperamental,

A. was the object of bitter attack by fellow-craftsmen in his day, including Vega and Gongora (qq.v.). An inferior writer, C. S. de Figueroa (q.v.), even abused him on account of a physical deformity. A. was undeterred by jealousy and dislike, and wr. some admirable plays. His *Verdad sospechosa* (' Suspicious Truth ') became *le Menteur,* 1642, of Corneille (q.v.), thus doubling, in the sphere of comic drama, the debt to Spain which Corneille had incurred by his great tragedy, *le Cid,* based on Castro (q.v.). A.'s other plays included ' The Weaver (*Tejedor*) of Segovia ' and ' The Test of Husbands ' (*Examen de maridos*) ; and, ' on the whole, he is to be ranked with the very best Spanish dramatists during the best period of the national theatre ' (Ticknor, ii, 336).

Albert, Heinrich (1604-51) : Germ. poet ; of the Königsberg school of Dach (q.v.).

Alberti, Leo Battista (c. 1407-72) : It. humanist ; architect, musician, artist, mechanic, man of letters ; comparable with Leonardo da Vinci for his versatility of talent, and physical and mental powers. Born at Venice, but is properly accounted Florentine, since his family was exiled from Florence till 1434, when A. returned ; visited and resided at various cities ; died in Rome. A.'s works in other branches of artistic and mechanical production must here be passed by, though they were by no means insignificant, and in some instances proved valuable to later workers ; it is to be noted that he wr. on the theory of several of the arts which he practised, e.g., architecture and painting. He wr. a Lat. comedy *Philodoxius* at 20 years old, vernacular poems, ' novelle ', dialogues and discourses ; and was assigned the important part of champion of Plato and Virgil in Landino's (q.v.) *Quæstiones Camaldulenses* (1480). A.'s principal work in Ital. prose, of which Symonds calls him ' the greatest writer in the 15th century ', was ' The Family ' (*della Famiglia*), in 4 bks., of which bk. 3 (*Economico*), though more prolix, is practically identical with *il Governo della Famiglia* of Agnolo Pandolfini (q.v.), Xenophon's *Œconomicus* was the common source of both treatises, the precise interrelation of which is still doubtful. Authority inclines to the view that A. was the original writer, and that a later version, exalting Pandolfini's family, was adapted and re-issued under the new ascription. The work comprises the whole duty of a family—management, expenditure, domestic life, matrimony, children, and so forth,—and is a not too much elevated commonplace-book in not too excellent Tuscan prose. Its main value at this date lies in its picture of manners in Florence, and of the rise of a type of a Florentine commercial aristocracy. Castiglione's (q.v.) *Courtier* (1514) is a later treatise of similar interest, and the letters of Alessandra Macinghi negli Strozzi (q.v.) supplement the contemporary information contained in the *Famiglia.* A.'s anon. biographer, writing at an early date, makes it clear that his hero was a man whose varied and highly trained powers rendered him a force and an influence in the society of his times, and who was very genuinely a humanist, with intense and keen perception, and with a winning sympathy for old age, children, travel, natural scenery, and similar objects of sensibility.

Albertinus, Aegidius (1560-1620): Germ. student of Span. fiction ; secretary to duke Maximilian of Bavaria ; an industrious translr. of the picaresque novelists. (See s.v. Novel).

Albertus Magnus (1193-1280): Germ. (Suabian) scholar ; Dominican ; count of Bokstadt ; studied at Padua, Bologna, Paris (near the street still called rue de Maître-Albert), and Cologne ; interpreter of Aristotle (q.v.). 'It is our intention', he wr. 'to make all the parts (of the master's *Physics*) intelligible to the Latins'; '*and he did*', adds (in italics) H. O. Taylor (*The Medieval Mind*, ii, 420) who remarks : 'Perhaps the world has had no greater purveyor of a knowledge not his own. He is comparable with Boethius (q.v.), who gave the Latin world the Aristotelian *Organon*. Albert gave his Latin world the rest of Aristotle'. And 'Albert's time was eager'. His writings 'represent, perhaps more fully than those of any other man, the round of knowledge and intellectual interest attracting the attention of Western Europe in the 13th century'.

Alberus, Erasmus (1500-53): Germ. satiric fabulist. Wr. verse-book 'Of Virtue and Wisdom', 1550 ; a Lutheran protagonist.

Albi : Fr. town on the river Tarn, east of Toulouse (q.v.) ; famous in literary history as a stronghold of the Manichean, or dualistic, heretics and freethinkers, who swarmed to the more hospitable regions of the south subsequently to the time and teachings of Abelard (q.v.) in the 12th cent. Before the end of the cent., the Albigenses (Albigeois) had imposed their innovating doctrine on the surrounding country in the counties of Provence and Toulouse. The social and religious ferment stirred the flourishing home of Provençal (q.v.) civilization, and prepared the ever-ready political way for the conquest of *Langue d'oc* by *Langue d'oïl* (see s.vv.) or of southern by northern France. National unity was attained at the cost of the separate culture of the South. Raymond vi was then count of Toulouse and marquis of Provence, and in 1207 he was excommunicated by pope Innocent ii for his anti-clerical policy. In the following year Raymond was deposed, and a crusade was preached against him by the Pope, who thus inaugurated a departure in crusading zeal ; 'in extending the benefits of a Crusade to Christians fighting against Christians, he handed on a precedent which was soon fatally abused by his successors' (Tout, *Empire and Papacy*, 333). King Philip Augustus of France did not actually take any part, but in the 20 years' terror which ensued, count Simon de Montfort assumed the leading rôle under the direction of the papal legate, and, after the battle of Muret, 1213, in which king Peter ii of Aragon lost his life, de Montfort became count of Toulouse in place of Raymond vi, whose son was glad to retain a fragment of his heritage with the title of marquis of Provence. The count's success paved the way for the intervention of king Philip Augustus ; and before the king's death in 1223 the North had conquered the South in a political sense ;

the Albigensian heresy had been stamped out, and Languedocian civilization had been exterminated. Literally, exterminated ; or driven beyond the borders of Languedoc. The poets and thinkers associated with the brief harvest of Provençal culture were scattered through the neighbouring countries—to Catalonia in Spain, to Sicily, to Tuscany to France itself (that is, the northern territories) and even to parts of Germany ; and the cruel and pitiless persecution of the Albigenses by pope Innocent iii spread the light of their brilliant talents into the lands which subsequently became the centres of the Renaissance. The victims were victorious in defeat and exile at last.

Albrecht von Scharfenberg (13th cent.): Germ. romancer. Wr., *c.* 1270, *der jungere Titurel* ('the younger Titurel') in continuation and completion of the court-epos of Wolfram (q.v.) von Eschenbach, and in the manner of the master.

Alcala de Henares : Span. town, not far from Madrid ; celebrated for its university, founded, 1508, by card. Ximenez (q.v.) de Cisneros, on the staff of which was the great humanist, Lebrixa (q.v.). A. is also famous as the birthplace of Cervantes (q.v.).

Alcalá y Herrera, de, Alfonso (17th cent.): Span. novelist, of Port. descent, who used the Castilian language ; a flagrant example of the silly side of *cultismo* (q.v. ; and see s.v. Conceit), since he contrived that each of the 5 tales in his *Varios Efectos de Amor*, 1641, should display the omission of one of the 5 vowels. The Span. Academy cited this book as evidence of the richness of the resources of the language ; and a similar act of violence against style was committed, a little less dexterously, by Fr. de Navarrete (q.v.), who omitted *a* in his tale of 'The Three Brothers', 1641, and by F. J. de Zurita (q.v.), who omitted the same vowel in another story.

Alcazar, del, Baltasar (1530-1606): Span. poet : wr. sonnets, epigrams, etc. ; belonged to the Sevillian or Italianate school of poetry, so called from one of the two centres, Seville and Salamanca, of the tendencies into which Span. poetry bifurcated after the reforms of Boscan and Garcilasso (qq.v.).

Alciati, Andrea (1492-1550): It. jurist, humanist, and epigraphist ; held chairs of jurisprudence at Avignon, 1518, Bourges, 1529, Pavia, 1533, Bologna, 1537, and Ferrara ; was intimate with the leading scholars of his day, including Erasmus (q.v.) ; and has been ranked with Zasius and Budæus (qq.v.) as the third star in the constellation of contemporary jurists. A. was an excellent Latinist, and shared the reaction of Erasmus against a blind Ciceronianism. He wr. a famous book of emblems (q.v.), *Emblematum libellus*, and vols. of misc. scholarship, of legal decisions (*Responsa*), and of footnotes to history. In this last category may be included A.'s studies of hist. inscriptions, of which Mommsen (q.v.) declared, 'not only did he reform jurisprudence, but he founded the science of epigraphy'. His work as a jurist was fragmentary in extent, but intensively it introduced a new method, and established the lines upon which later humanists were to develop that branch of learning.

Aldrete, Bernardo (*c.* 1560-*c.* 1640): Span. antiquary. Wr. a treatise on the antiquities
of Spain, Africa, etc., 1614.

Aleander, Jerome (early 16th cent.): It. Hellenist
in France, reached Paris, 1508; rector of
university, 1512; returned to Rome as
librarian to Vatican, 1517; elected card.;
edited Plutarch, *Moralia*, 1509.

Aleman, Mateo (1547-*c.* 1614): Span. picaresque
(see s.v. novel) novelist. Wr., 1599, 'Part i
of *Guzman de Alfarache*', whose rogue-hero
(see s.v. Lazarillo) enjoyed a popularity
somewhat in excess of his merits. There is
contemporary authority for the statement
that 26 edns. of *Guzman* were required
within 6 years of publn.; and it was
early transld. into other languages, including
Engl. by Mabbe (q.v.), 1622, with a pre-
factory poem by B. Jonson (q.v.), who called
A. 'The Spanish Proteus'. Probably he
meant Protean in the invention of adventures
for Guzman; but there was something
Protean too, or at least something of the
Jekyll and Hyde versatility, about Guzman's
character as well as his adventures. He was
the mouthpiece of his author's didactic
purpose, and thus became 'a composite
monster, at one moment the respectable
Aleman himself, at the next the embodiment
of all that shocks him' (Allen, *Celestina*, xlii).
It is this feature which caused Ticknor (iii, 104)
to write: 'so far from being a moral book,
therefore, it is a very immoral one'; and it
was this feature of 'moralités superflues'
which Lesage (q.v.) omitted in his transln.
of *Guzman*, 1732, which has been frequently
reprinted. But in Spain, at the opening of
the 17th cent., the moral tone was more than
half the attraction. It deeply consoled every
rogue in being and *in petto* (and Spain was full
at that date of knights of industry back from
her wars) to cite Guzman as his authority
that he was a better fellow than he seemed,
more sinned against than sinning, a parasite
for which society was to blame; and A.'s
readers entitled the book 'The Rogue'
(*Pícaro*) *tout court*, regardless of its proper title.
It happened to *Guzman*, as shortly after to
Don Quixote (see s.v. Cervantes), that the
author's genuine Part ii was anticipated and
expedited by a false Part ii, issued, 1602, by a
certain Mateo Luxan de Sayavedra (q.v.), a
pseudonym. A.'s own *Segunda Parte* followed
in 1604, and promised a Part iii, which was
never written. The book has more hist. value
at this date than actual novellistic interest.

Aleria, Bp. of: See **Giovanni Andrea de Bussi**.

Alexander the Great (B.C. 356-323): King of
Macedonia; his exploits passed at an early
date into the cycle of legends which formed
the chief Oriental episode in the romantic
matter of Antiquity ('matière de Rome la
grant'; see s.vv. Bodel, Romance). A Gk.
bk. by a native of Alexandria, known as
pseudo-Kallisthenes, in the 2nd cent., A.D.,
contained the earliest known collection of tales
based on fame and report which had gathered
round the memory of A.'s conquests and
travels. A Lat. version by Julius Valerius
(4th cent.) was epitomized in the 9th cent.;
and this epitome was the basis of a 12th cent.
poem by one Alberic of Besançon in the form

of a *chanson de geste* (q.v.). In this poem A.
was first transmogrified into the likeness of a
feudal monarch, surrounded by his knights and
barons. The next redaction was the *roman
d'Alexandre*, in about 20,000 verses, displaying
for the first time on so extensive a scale the
national metre of verses of 12 syllables. It
had been employed already in an anon.
Pelerinage à Jerusalem in the 11th cent.,
and by Philippe de Thann, 1121, in his
transln. of *Physiologus*; but henceforward this
longer verse, eminently suitable for narrative
poetry, and closely corresponding in effect
with the hexameter of Homer (q.v.), was known
as the **Alexandrine**, and may be regarded as
the last conquest of A. The authors of this
alexandrined *Alexandre* were Lambert le
Tort (li Cors) of Châteaudun, Alexander
de Bernay of Paris, and Peter of St.
Cloud and others anon., towards the close of
the 12th cent. They availed themselves,
additionally, as source-books, of A.'s reputed
correspondence with his tutor Aristotle
(q.v.) and with Dindimus, king of the Brahmins,
and of a certain *Iter Paradisæ*, the legend of
A. in Paradise. A supplementary romance,
the *Vengeance of Alexander*, was added (end
of the 12th cent.) by Jean le Nevelois and Guy
of Cambrai; and the chief Span. redaction of
the Alexandriad is ascribed to Berceo (q.v.)
early in the 13th cent. A.'s Indian campaign
was the subject of a further independent
poem (*c.* 1312) by Jacques of Longuyon, in
which first appeared the triple trinity of
chivalry (3 Christians, 3 Jews, 3 Pagans),
afterwards so popular. By this time, A.'s
identity was completely submerged in the
chivalric accretions to the legend.

Alexis, Willibald. See s.v. **Häring G. W. H.**

Alfieri, Vittorio (1749-1803): It. dramatist;
cadet of a noble Piedmontese family, educated
at the semi-foreign academy of Turin, and
travelled abroad, 1766-72; was thus more
Fr. than Ital. in his upbringing, and had
virtually to acquire a command of his native
language. A. was further removed from the
career of letters, in which he won immense
fame, by his preference for the active over
the contemplative life, in which he resembled
Byron (q.v.), whose influence on him was
considerable and whom he 'overcame, even
to convulsions', it is said, by his tragedy,
Myrrha, 1785. But a good deal went before
Myrrha: his self-dedication to lit. his
intensive study of the masters of his own
tongue, esp. Dante and Tasso, and his
impetuous, brilliant resolve to conquer the
obscurities and archaisms which at first
hampered his style. A. left a vol. of
autobiography, almost as outspoken as the
Confessions of Rousseau (q.v.), from which
the inference has been drawn that he built on
letters, as Wordsworth said of Burns, a moral
redemption of his physical life (' on the basis
of his human life he reared a poetic one ').
However that may be, we may note that A.
was the acknowledged lover of Louisa, countess
of Albany (1753-1824), wife of prince Chas.
Edwd., the Young Pretender, and that
she lived with A., 1780-1803.

It is by his plays that A. is remembered.
A 'monotonous poet' is the description of him

by M. Arnold (q.v.), who found a ' narrow elevation ' in his writings, and this judgment is not unfair to the classical purism of his manner in drama, in which he consistently pruned away all features inessential to the representation of the conflict of the play. ' Of all classical dramatists ', says prof. Vaughan (*P.E.L.*, x, 459), ' he is the most unflinching, perhaps also the most typical ' ; ' he aimed at nervous conciseness ', says R. Garnett (*It. Lit.*, 320), ' and attained it. His plays are such as a Roman poet might have produced if he could more completely have emancipated himself from Greek models ' ; and Seneca, the Roman dramatist who so powerfully influenced Shakespeare's (q.v.) predecessors, was plainly behind him. A. wr. 14 tragedies in 7 years, 1775-82, mainly on subjects from the Gk. : *Antigone, Agamemnon, Orestes, Death of Socrates, Merope,* etc. ; others on later and more romantic themes which he pared down and toned up to the classical stage, *Don Garcia, Saul, Filippo, Mary Stuart, Myrrha,* etc. ; and he wr. hardly less successfully satiric poems and a few comedies. A.'s *Philip ii* had been conned by Schiller (q.v.) before he composed *Don Carlos,* and he is aptly characterized in an Oxford vol. by 4 authors on *Italy Medieval and Modern* (1917 ; p. 352), as a man of adventurous, emotional and vehement disposition, in whom Plutarch's *Lives* invoked ' an enthusiasm for " Liberty ", the " Liberty " of the French philosophers, and a hatred for tyrants, which he embodied in a series of plays. In each of them there is a typical tyrant and an heroic rebel. The rebel declaims with earnest passion against the tyrant, but . . . the plays contain little but declamation. Alfieri hoped to create through his plays an intellectual and moral renaissance, so that " men might learn, through the stage, to be free, strong, generous, transported by true virtue, hating violence, loving their country, conscious of their rights, and be in all their passions ardent, upright, magnanimous." He had little influence in his own age and country ; there was not sentiment in the minds of his Italian contemporaries to respond to his passionate call for regeneration.' Literature is ruthless to such spirits. The man who drives Pegasus against the stream may miss the applause of his own generation and the next, and A., though he composed almost perfect dramas, missed the current movement to Romanticism, which Manzoni (q.v.) was to seize.

Alfonso v and i (1416-58) : Span. king of Aragon and Sicily, and, by conquest in 1442 (after 7 years' fighting), of Naples as Alfonso i ; surnamed The Magnanimous. (The Alfonsos of Aragon should be distinguished from their namesakes of Castile.) This king was a brilliant and liberal patron of letters, and a genuine bibliophile ; his court at Naples rivalled that of pope Nicholas v (q.v.) at Rome, as a centre of learning and rallying-place for scholars, critics, copyists, and wits. He founded the Academy (q.v.) of Naples, with Beccadelli (q.v.) as its leader.

Alfonso x (*c.* 1220-84) : Span. king of Castile ; surnamed The Wise ; succeeded, 1252, his father (saint) Ferdinand iii, and completed the re-conquest of Spain from the Moors. With A.'s wars, civil and foreign, with his policy and his place in history we are not here concerned ; he has justly been compared in these respects with (saint) Louis ix of France (q.v.) and with his own brother-in-law, king Edward i of Engld. But A.'s place in lit. is secure for several causes ; the least among these is his reported statement as an astronomer, that, ' had he been consulted at the creation of the world, he would have spared the Maker some absurdities '. Fontenelle (q.v.), in his treatise on ' The Plurality of Worlds ' records A.'s views on creation, and Bryon (q.v.), *The Vision of Judgment,* ci, refers to them satirically :

I settle all these things by intuition,
Times present, past, to come, Heav'n, Hell, and all,
Like King Alfonso.

Prior to both, Dante had probably intended A. in his reference to ' avarice and poltroonery ' (*Div. Comm., Par.,* xix, 125). Far more serious were king A.'s services to the encouragement of learning in his dominions, and as a practitioner of letters. In these respects, he was the king Alfred of his age and country. He procured Span. translns. of the Koran, the Talmud, and other monuments of Oriental lore ; of works on astronomy and other sciences, and himself participated in the labours which he patronized. If he did not initiate the transln. of the *Tesoro* (' treasury ') of Brunetto Latini (Dante's Latini, sometime Florentine ambassador in Castile), or a dozen other enterprises which legend attributed to the royal zeal for culture, A. is certainly to be credited with the inception of hist. study in Spain, in the unfinished *Grande et general Estoria* (*c.* 1270), which started with *Genesis,* and in the *primera* (' first ') *Cronica general* (see s.v.), or ' History of Spain', composed *c.* 1260-68. More important still was A.'s work in the codification of laws, compiled, 1256-63, and known in the next generation as the *Siete Partidas* (' seven divisions '). There were seven letters in the king's name (Alfonso) and seven subjects of instruction in the old scholastic ordnance-survey of the field of knowledge, viz., grammar, logic, rhetoric (forming the *trivio*), and music, astrology, physics and metaphysics (forming the *quadrivio*). Both these numerical associations helped to determine the form of A.'s code of laws, the chief purpose of which was to unify the various legal systems current in Castile. A. brought to his noble and difficult task a fine literary sense, and a high ideal of government and statesmanship ; his work, too, is of the utmost interest in the reconstruction of the social life of the 13th cent. ; and its influence was deep and abiding. ' It is, in fact, a sort of Spanish common law, which, with the decisions under it, has been the basis of Span. jurisprudence ever since ' (Ticknor, 1, 47). Further, its personal style, as of a king discussing the philosophy and practice of rule, lends the work unique interest, and adds to the debt incurred to A. for his early and great examples of Castilian prose-style. Lastly, A. was a poet. He wr. poems in the conquering Castilian tongue and also in the Gallician and

Provençal (q.v.) dialects ; and he is probably rightly credited with a large share in the authorship of the 420-odd *Cantigas de Santa Maria* : poems chiefly on the Virgin Mary, or otherwise sacred in subject, which have since inspired such followers of A. as Mérimée, Heine, A. A. Procter (*A Story of Provence*), and the late Mr. John Davidson (*Ballad of a Nun*). The great example of king A. was followed by his son and successor, Sancho iv (q.v.) ; but A., surnamed The Wise, has earned this perpetual praise, not merely by his leadership in culture, but also by the breadth of his sympathies and his genuine devotion to learning. It should be added that Bayle (q.v.), in his famous dict., s.v. Castile, spoke less favourably of the king's pretensions, and that Mariana (q.v.), the historian, wrote of him in a well-known phrase : ' He was more fit for letters than for government ; he studied the heavens, and watched the stars, but lost the earth ' (' In vast dreams of Man forgetting men ').

Alfred the Englishman (13th cent.): Aristotelian scholar at Toledo (see s.v. Aristotle).

Aliaga, de, Luis (1565-1626): Span. divine ; inquisitor-general ; confessor to king Philip iii ; lost office at his death, 1621. A. is the reputed author of the false Part ii of *Don Quixote*, publd. under the name of Avellaneda (q.v.), 1614, and eclipsed by the true Part ii of Cervantes (q.v.), 1615. The evidence for the identity of A. with Avellaneda is not conclusive, but ' if we do not like finally to commit ourselves, I think we can at least back Aliaga against the present field, and hope for some further evidence that will bring him home ' (Robinson Smith, *Don Quijote*, 2nd. edn., Routledge, xlix).

Aljama (Span.): Span. term of Arab. orig. denoting ' the self-governing communities of Moors and Jews living under Spanish rule ' (*Jewish Encycl.*, i, 400). More specifically, in relation to lit., *literatura aljamiada* signified works composed in the Span. language but written in Hebr. characters (or in Arab. letters, if by the Moors instead of the Jews). It is to be noted that this early *Aljamia* (Span. lit. in Hebr. or Arab. writing) drew almost exclusively from Western sources for its subjects ; so that, oriental though it was in its appeal to ear and eye, it was properly a part of the heritage of Spain by its vocabulary and by its inspiration. A northern analogue is **Yiddish** (Jew.-Germ.), a dialect of Germ. in Hebr. script, with contributions from Hebr. and Slavonic languages, in which fine much lit. has been written. Reference may be made to Pines, *Hist. de la Lit. Judéo-Allemande*, Paris, 1911, and Wiener, *Hist. of Yiddish Lit. in 19th Cent.*, London, Nimmo, 1899.

Allegory (rhet.): a device of style in lit. by the employment of which the writer conveys a meaning to the reader secondary to the literal meaning of the words or images which he uses. There is always a circumstantial likeness between the outer and the inner, the superficial and the deep, meanings ; and the reader's intelligence will perceive it ; but the imagination and insight of a poet will perceive such likeness more quickly than the ordinary eye : imperviousness to light may be due to a fault not in the material but in the ray. A simile, metaphor or parable may fail to pierce the ear of the mind ; and allegory is, in one aspect, a metaphor worked out in all its relations. Its use by unimaginative writers, more intent upon the correspondence of the parts than upon the appeal of the whole, leads to frigidities and conceits ; while too much imagination in allegorizing may lead to a maze of hidden meanings imperceptible except to mystic seers. The long history of the lit. of Europe supplies examples in both kinds which are noted under their names ; here it is our business to trace the orig. of the device in modern lit. to the Span.-Christian Lat. writer, Prudentius (348-*c*.405), who used it freely in his *Psychomachia* (' Battle of the Soul '). Therein, in a succession of lifelike combats, Faith conquers Idolatry ; Patience conquers Anger ; Shame, Passion ; a combination of the forces of Humility, Hope, Soberness, Honesty, and others fight and vanquish Pride ; finally, victorious Faith builds a temple to Christ. The Lat. language lends itself to such modes of abstract thought, and its example prevailed in the derivative Romance (q.v.)-languages. In such usages, the poetic influence of the Scriptures is obvious, and deeply affected early writers in the vernaculars : thus, the Fr. *débat* was a debate (q.v.) or battle of personified abstractions (see s.v. personification), and was employed, too, for didactic-religious ends. The example of the *Psychomachia* was followed by many allegories of the 12th and 13th cents., and passed with all other medieval methods and resources into the repertory of Guillaume de Lorris in the *Romance of the Rose* (q.v.), an elaborate allegory, with set *débats* and battles, of the quest in the ' garden ' of life for the ' rose ' of love's desire. There was a rapid development of A. in the 14th cent., leading to such famous later works as Brandt's *Narrenschiff* and Bunyan's *Pilgrim's Progress*. Pure A. is rare in modern lit. ; G. Meredith's (q.v.) *Jump-to-Glory-Jane*, though described by the author as a satire, is perhaps the best recent specimen of the kind.

Alliteration (rhet.): repetition of sound for the sake of effect, whether an effect of metre or of style. The sound repeated might be either a syllable or a letter (consonant or vowel) in two or more successive or closely consecutive words. The use of A. in the Hebr. poetry of the Old Testament lies outside the range of the present work, and the history of A. belongs to the technical study of rhetoric far more than to lit. proper. But it may be noted that it was a device with which the Romans were well acquainted, as, e.g., in Cicero's (q.v.) famous line

O fortunatam natam me consule Romam,

and that Virgil (q.v.) employed it with great subtlety and success. It was the basis of the metrical effects of Scandinavian (see s.v.) poetry, of which it has been said that, whereas dactylic verse is measured by the fingers, and iambic by beating the foot, alliteration was blown on the wind through the forests of the north. From Langland and Chaucer (qq.v.) downwards, through the languorous verse of Spenser, the stately manner of Milton, and the masterly melodies of Tennyson (qq.v.), A. has been a favourite ornament of modern European poetry. We may quote a single example from the last-named writer :

Nor ever lowest roll of thunder moans,
Nor sound of human sorrow mounts.

Note here the obvious A. in *moans*, *mounts*, *sound*, *sorrow* ; note the suspended A. in *lowest*, *roll* ; *moans*; *sound*, *human*, *mounts* ; note, most of all the repetition of the open vowel in *lowest*, *roll*, *moans*, *sorrow*, and its variants in *sound*, *human*, *mounts*. Attentive reading of modern verse and prose will reveal infinite harmonies derived from the employment of A.

Almella, de, Diego Rodriguez (*c.* 1426-92) : Span. divine ; chaplain to queen Isabella of Castile ; later, canon of Cartagena. Wr., among other less memorable works, a treatise entitled *Valerio de las Estorias escolasticas*, 'The Valerius of Moral Tales', the idea for which had been suggested (the Valerius of the title was Valerius Maximus, of the 1st cent., A.D., in Rome) by bp. Alfonso de Santa Maria (q.v.). The didactic purpose was pleasantly disguised by a series of illustrative stories drawn from sacred sources and from Span. history.

Almqvist, Carl Jonas Ludwig (1793-1856) : Swed. misc. writer ; novelist, historian, mathematician ; 'his changeful life, which included an accusation of murder, an escape to the United States, and a final return to Norway under an assumed name (Westermann), seems reflected in his works' (Omond, *P.E.L.*, xi, 381). These were certainly mixed and multifarious. The quality common to them all was the sense of Fr. romanticism, which A. derived from his early liking for Rousseau (q.v.). So forceful was this sentiment that A. founded a society devoted to the natural life, and practised that life for some years. The chief outcome was a peasant-wife, with whom he returned to civilization, and a certain restlessness of disposition and inability to concentrate his talents, which prevented him from attaining to the full height of his capacity. A.'s novels and plays are mostly forgotten to-day ; among his poems, the lyrical vol. known as *Törnrosens Bok* and the epical *Arthurs Jagt* are probably the best known. He is notable, too, as a pioneer of the sex-problem (a wife's rights problem) in Scandinavian lit.

Alsted, Johann Heinrich (1586-1638) : Germ. lexicographer. Wr. *Encyclopædia scientiarum omnium*, 1632 ; a Lat. work notable for two causes : it was the first considerable dict. which was called by the name of Encyclopedia (q.v.; there had been a *Cyclopædia* in Basel in 1541), and it was the subject of critical animadversions, directed to its improvement and extension by Leibniz (q.v.).

Althusius, Lat. name of **Johann Althaus** (1557-1638) : Germ. jurist ; burgomaster of Emden. Wr. Lat. treatise on politics, in which the State was represented as the outermost circumference of a number of concentric circles—the family, the tribe, the city, etc. There is a tacit or an express 'contract' (*pactum*) between the sovereign people and the sovereign power, which they confine to one or another sort of rulers. This is virtually the social contract of Rousseau (q.v.), but A., unlike Rousseau, recognized a second pact between the sovereign and the people, a conception common to most political writers and elaborated by Locke (q.v.).

Alxinger, von, Johann Baptist (1755-97) : Austrian poet. Wr. heroic epic poems a long way after the model of the *Oberon* of Wieland (q.v.).

Amadis of Gaul : court-romance of love, chivalry, and adventure, branching off from the cycle of the Arthuriad ; the Gaul (*Gaula*) of its title bearing witness to its hero's descent from the land of faery in ancient Wales, whence, too, the *romans Bretons* (q.v.) took their rise. (See s.vv. Romance, Arthur). The origins of A. are obscure, and Engld., France, Portugal and Spain have disputed the patent of invention. Koerting (*Geschichte des französischen Romans im xvii Jahrhundert* 2nd edn., 1891), rules out the Port. claim, and holds that each of the three other countries has a certain right to regard the romance as a national possession. Whatever Portugal's contribution may have been, the earliest traceable references to A. in the lit. of the Peninsula are found in L. de Ayala (q.v., born 1332) and P. Ferrus (q.v.) towards the close of the 14th cent. Some years later arose the statement of a Port. version of the story, ascribed to a certain Vasco de Lobeira (q.v.). The most probable clues to this much-vexed problem of bibliography may be stated as follows. The original form of *Amadis* was that of a Welsh tale ; thence it passed to the Breton romancers, who transmogrified it, according to their art, into a full-fledged chivalric *roman* ; thence it found its way to Langue d'Oc (q.v.), and, whether through the hands of the Troubadours or direct, it assumed its first written shape in Spain. As corroborative evidence to this theory, it is pointed out that Boccaccio and Petrarch (qq.v.) were unacquainted with A.; it found its way to the Peninsula by the great North road of Romance. Its Span. author was Montalvo (q.v.) who completed his version towards the close of the 15th cent. ('The Four Books of the Virtuous knight Amadis de Gaula', Saragossa, 1508), and composed a new work of his own which was amalgamated with it as continuation. Other Span. continuators went on working at the popular tale, till it attained the respectable bulk of 12 books of printed matter. Among such writers are mentioned Paez de Ribera, Juan Diaz, Feliciano de Silva, and Pedro de Luxan. Meanwhile, it had become naturalized in neighbouring Portugal ; an Ital. transln. appeared in 1546 ; the elder Tasso (q.v.), who had conjectured an Engl. or a Breton orig., composed a new *Amadigi di Francia*, and the romance was known to Fischart (q.v.) and others in Germany, and is said on doubtful authority to have quickened Luther's perception of the need of Church reform. But it was in its Fr. dress and by its adoption into the storehouse of Fr. lit. that *Amadis* entered into its literary kingdom, and became entitled to rank as 'the ancestor of the modern novel'. Welsh by birth, Spanish by adoption, A. is French by resurrection and renown. The incarceration of king Francis i (q.v.) in Spain (1525-26 ;

see s.v. Charles v) is said to have been the starting-point of Fr. interest in the romance ; and at the king's desire, or in consequence of it, Herberay (q.v.) effected a transln. of the first 8 bks., which were publd. (with the remaining 4 by another hand) in Paris, 1540-48. In France as in Spain, there were continuators, who expanded, amplified and adorned the interminable tale of amorous and chivalric adventures, till it finally occupied 25 books. 'Its development marks the birth of the modern political and heroic novel' (Kòerting, *op. cit.*) ; and it will be remembered that Cervantes (q.v.) himself (*Don Quixote, i,* 5) excepted *Amadis* from the bonfire, on the barber's plea that it was 'the very best contrived book of all those of that kind'. Langour, moral changes, and social satire notwithstanding, posterity confirms this plea. Amadis is the illegitimate son of an imaginary king of an imaginary Wales (Gaula) ; he is exposed by his mother, Elisena, and is carried to Engld. and Scotland. In Scotland he meets Oriana, daughter of an imaginary king of Engld., whom he marries in the end. The rest is love, magic and adventure.

The sudden overpowering welcome which Paris extended to A. in the 17th cent. was due largely to the reaction of the aristocratic society of the capital from a long and hateful experience of civil and religious warfare with its attendant evils and brutality. The artificial manners and courtly gallantry of the old 'Amadis' social atmosphere were in a sense deliberately recovered by Fr. social leaders, in open revolt from the stress and ferment of their times. They repaired by choice to Arcadia (q.v.)—to an Arcady of the *salon* and the court, in which no rough word should be heard, no graceless movement be admitted, in which conversation should be more honourable than action, and in which the grace and charm of human life should consist in a noble gallantry, without overmuch regard to its foundation in noble being ; 'cet enchantement de deux coeurs qui s'entretiennent de leur amour et qui oublient le monde entier' (St. Marc Girardin, *Lit. dram.*, iii. 49). The literary affectations of Gongora in Spain and Marini in Italy (see s.vv.) were in time to reinforce this more or less spontaneous retirement to the Hôtel Rambouillet (q.v.) and other fastnesses ; and such part of the element of Celtic magic as had survived the transmutations of A. was transformed once more to the mechanism of incognito, disguised sex, soothsaying, and other devices, thus assisting the passage to modern fiction ; while a more meretricious embellishment was added by resort to the *roman-à-clef* (q.v.). In these ways, A. became the basis on which imitators of Montemayor (q.v.) and his own models, the Ital. pastoral poets, founded a series of novels of manners, of which d'Urfé's (q.v.) *Astrée* was the first. This was the social guidebook of the Fr. aristocracy in the age of king Louis xiv of France, though it sank gradually from that zenith to be a kind of lovers' letter-writer for the lower classes, and passed in the 18th cent. into oblivion. It may be added that the name of *le beau ténébreux,* assumed

by Amadis in his tale, passed through the usage of the *salons* of the 17th cent. into a current term for the taciturn, melancholy, Byronic lover of a young girl's dream.

Ambras : Tyrolean castle where emperor Maximilian i (q.v.) deposited in the royal library a MS. *Heldenbuch* (book of heroes), containing *Gudrun* (q.v.), the *Erec* and *Iwain* of Hartmann (q.v.), and other important specimens of the courtly epic cycle.

Amescua, de, Antonio Mira (*c.* 1578-1644) : Span. dramatist, and, like many fellow-craftsmen, an ecclesiastic. Wr. sacramental *autos* (q.v.) and comedies, excellent for their versification and the ingenuity of their plots. Among these *el Esclavo del Demonio* ('The Slave of the Devil') was utilized freely by Calderon and Moreto (qq.v.), *la Rueda de la Fortuna* ('The Wheel of Fortune') by Corneille (q.v.) and other plays by Rotrou (q.v.) and other French playwrights.

Amfiteatrov, Alexander Valentinovich (19th cent.): Russ. journalist ; affectionately known as the 'Old Gentleman', and famous chiefly for the infamy of his arrest at the hands of official Russia. A more harmless writer never lived. 'Except for this Asiatic barbarism', says Brückner (*Gesch. d. Russ. Lit.*, 301), 'Amfiteatrov and his lucubrations would quickly have been forgotten ; now he is immortalized with the system which had ventured so far'.

Amiel, Henri Francois (1821-81) : Fr.-Swiss diarist ; known to fame by the *Fragments d'un Journal Intime,* publd. posth. as a selection, with an introduction by E. Scherer (q.v.), 2 vols., Geneva, 1883, 8th edn., 1901. These outpourings of a sensitive soul were much praised by the editor himself, by Paul Bourget, Mrs. Humphry Ward (q.v.), and others, and are the subject of a well-known essay by M. Arnold (q.v. ; *Essays in Criticism,* ii). They belong to the intimacies of lit., so much increased and adorned by A. C. Benson (q.v.) in a later day ; and it is interesting to note that Saintsbury (*Hist. Crit.*, iii, 598) holds a high opinion of their purely literary passages.

Amis, Pfaffe ('Papa, parson' Amis): Austrian vagabond priest, invented by the 'Stricker' (q.v.), as burlesque-hero of adventures of wit, cunning, and horseplay, in a poem of the same name, written between 1200 and 1250. A. was a forerunner of the Eulenspiegel and Kalenberg (qq.v.) types of rather later Germ. folk-play. According to his author, Amis was an Englishman in the shadowy lore of his origin ; but his exploits are characteristic of the country and period of his literary appearance.

Amyot, Jacques (1513-94) : Fr. humanist. Born at Melun ; studied Gk. under Danès and Toussain (qq.v) ; patronized by queen Margaret (q.v.), and was, later, appointed successively grand almoner of France and bp. of Auxerre, by his former pupil, king Charles ix. Transld. (1546) *Theagenes and Chariclea* of Meliodorus, and (1559) *Daphnis and Chloe* of Longus (see s.v. Greek fiction) ; earned his title of 'prince of translators' by these works, and esp. by his transln., 1559, of the *Parallel Lives* (Gk. and Rom., in pairs) of Plutarch (*fl.* 60, A.D.), the Gk. biographer, followed, 1572, by his version of Plutarch's *Moralia*. The *Lives* thus became a Fr. bk. (' our breviary ', as Montaigne called it), and, through North (q.v.), the Plutarch of Shakespeare, and the ' begetter ' of works which the world could spare less easily than their original. A. helped to found a prose-style in Fr., which was not only negatively free from the affectations of the ' Rhetoriqueurs ' (q.v.), and from the exaggerations and profuseness of Rabelais (q.v.), but which displayed a simplicity and purity (to employ the epithets of Montaigne's eulogy) as rare in a transln. as they are admirable in themselves. Moreover, A.'s task compelled him to enlarge the Fr. language, by finding and naturalizing such words as ' atom ', ' enthusiasm ', ' panegyric '; and a diligent student of his method of correction discovers that A. had a cultivated ear for the harmonies of prose-rhythm. In all these ways, A.'s contribution to the development of the art of prose in Fr. lit. can hardly be exaggerated.

Anacreon (6th cent. B.C.): Gk. lyric poet; born at Teios. Only fragments of his poetry survive, imbedded in the works of later writers; but a collection of about 60 poems, Anacreontic in style and inspiration, was discovered in a MS. appendix to the Gk. Anthology (q.v.) in 1552 by Henri Estienne (q.v.), and was publd. by him in 1554. Its supreme importance resides in the fact that it exercised a powerful influence on the choice of themes and the attitude towards experience of the Pleiad (q.v.), the central school of Renaissance poetry in France. Belleau (q.v.) transld. Estienne's recovered vol. into Fr. within a year of its first publn., and the wine-women-and-song cult prevailed, and stormed the intellect of Fr. poetry, refashioning it entirely out of its old medieval forms.

Anakreontiker (Germ.): Anacreonticists: imitators of Anacreon (q.v.). Descriptive name of a school of Germ. poetry, otherwise known as the Prussian Poets, which had its headquarters at Halle, Berlin, or Halberstadt, in the second half of the 18th cent., and may be said to have comprised the forerunners of Wieland (q.v.). It arose out of the reaction against the poetic dictatorship of Gottsched (q.v.), and his Saxon supporters: but though parallel to the movement which founded the *Bremer Beiträge* (q.v.) and which established itself chiefly at Zürich, the Anacreontic or Horatian Germ. poetry was more or less independent of actual leadership. It made a good start with Hagedorn (q.v.), and worked its way through Gleim, Uz (qq.v.), and others— Uz was perhaps the most Horatian of them all, —till the great masters, Klopstock, Wieland, and Lessing, revealed the end of all these tentative beginners.

Ancients and Moderns (17th cent.): The Quarrel of the Ancients and Moderns (*querelle des anciens et des modernes*) is the name given to a controversy, peculiarly barren of result and fallacious in its premises, but inevitable at the time of its appearance, in the midst of the *grand siècle Louis Quatorze*. Two contrary (or seemingly contrary) tendencies were at work in Fr. lit. (see s.v.) towards the close of the 17th cent. On the one hand, there was the school of ' good sense ', in

Boileau's (q.v.) terminology, or ' reason ', as Pope (q.v.) adapted it; the school, that is, of Nature (q.v.) ' to advantage dress'd ', of Nature reflected in the mirror of classical antiquity, and supplying models for imitation to readers and writers of the day. This school was invented in the classical revival by Ronsard and the Pleiad (qq.v.), but it corrected the early enthusiasm and undiscriminating classicism (q.v.) of that group of reformers by an eclectic and selective admiration, taught, e.g., by Malherbe and de Balzac and the founders of the Academy (see s.vv.). Racine in tragedy, Boileau in criticism, Bossuet in oratory, La Fontaine in fable, Molière in comedy, but Racine and Boileau above all, were the representatives at the court of king Louis xiv of this methodized and cultivated classicism. All the Nature which they wanted was supplied by the observation of the ancients; their business was merely to frenchify what the classical writers had observed; to naturalize the Pagan classics, and esp. the Lat. classics, in Fr. lit. And on the other hand, there was the school (or there were the schools) of ' precious ' (q.v.) writers: schools of emotion in preference to reason, of women rather than of men, of chivalric and amorous adventure, derived from the lands and times of gallantry and romance (q.v.). And these schools flirted with the theories of Descartes and the Port Royal (qq.v.), with their doctrines of independent thought and of reason reducing art to phenomena. The parties to the quarrel failed to see that they were fighting about abstractions, not realities; and their conflict may be dated from 1657, when St. Sorlin (q.v.) publd. his *Clovis*. This Carlovingian (s.v. Charlemagne) poem was defended vigorously by the author from the attacks of critics who affected to believe that heroic (epic) poetry was inadmissible except with Homeric or Virgilian characters. (Spenser, q.v., it will be remembered, had to meet similar objections to his *Shepherd's Calendar* from Sidney and Harvey, qq.v., in the earlier generation apprenticed to Ronsard and Baïf, qq.v.) St. Sorlin's challenge was taken up by Boileau, who, in his *Art poétique* (canto 3), excluded the Christian religion from subjects suitable to poetic treatment, and even extended his ban to Satan in the epoch of Milton (q.v.) himself. St. Sorlin died in 1676, in a veritable cloud of pamphleteering, and the gage was handed on to Charles Perrault (q.v.). He fluttered the Fr. Academy with a poem (1687), the *Siècle de Louis le Grand*, in which he exalted a crowd of modern writers above the Gks. and Romans; and in 1688 and 1697, he followed up this audacious challenge by a series of clever dialogues, *Parallèles des anciens et des modernes*, in which he sought to prove his case: the moderns, he contended, were later in time, more exact in psychology, better practised in method, and they enjoyed the new advantages of printing, Christianity, and king Louis's patronage. It was a singularly shallow piece of sophistic ratiocination. Fontenelle (q.v.) ranged himself on Perrault's side. La Fontaine (q.v.) replied with his charming ' Epistle ' to Huet (q.v.), one of the few true Hellenists of the age, and La Bruyère (q.v.)

sustained the same cause, and supported it in a discourse at the Academy. Boileau, the protagonist of the Ancients, at first thought to vindicate them by his Pindaric ode ' on the capture of Namur '; but this proved so damaging a defence that he supplemented it, 1694, by his ' Reflexions on Longinus ' (q.v.); even so, his case was weakened by the very modernness, or, at least, the modern appeal, of the authors on whom his case rested—Racine and the rest ; and, happily, Boileau and Perrault were reconciled in 1700, and agreed to compose their differences by admiring what was best in both worlds. The formulation of the grounds of dispute in this noisy and inconclusive quarrel did an ill service to the greater ends of literature. The philosophic basis of Perrault's argument was the Cartesian idea of progress. But a progress away from the ancients was a progress away from art ; and the 18th cent. was to show the danger of a too great reliance on modern thought and inspiration. The quarrel passed into Engld., 1690, with the publication of an essay on *Ancient and Modern Learning* by sir W. Temple (q.v.), who was quite innocent of the storm which he was to raise by a reference to the *Letters* of Phalaris (see s.v. Bentley); its importance lay in the fact that Temple's secretary was Swift (q.v.), who was inspired by it in his *Battle of the Books*.

Andersen, Hans Christian (1805-75) : Dan. poet, novelist, dramatist, traveller, and, above all, writer of fairy tales ; the first vol. of this immortal series appeared in 1835 under the title of *Eventyr*, and a successor was issued at every ensuing Christmastide, the general title being changed to *Historier* in 1852. Faëry or story, it is true beyond dispute that the *genre* created by the Dan. poet is almost unique in its kind and quite supreme in its class. It is the delight and inspiration of every nursery in every land : the delight, for its dramatic and literary qualities : the inspiration, for its tone of unforced piety and of reverent sympathy with the simple virtues of help, self-help, willing service, tenderness, humility, faith. Sir E. Gosse, who first met A. in 1872, wr. at his death three years afterwards : ' In dying he took from among us the most popular of all contemporary writers of the imagination '. Posterity confirms this judgment, and none of the triumphs of imaginative writing recorded since 1875 detracts in the least degree from the fame of this shrewd, shy shoemaker's son. He is the genius of the child's mind, and reigns eternal in that unchanging realm. A. was a constant traveller, and visited Dickens (q.v.) at Gadshill, Boedtcher (q.v.) in Rome, Wagner (q.v.) in Berlin, Rome again in 1861, where he saw Mrs. E. B. Browning (q.v.), and other climes at other times, always bringing away with him some new impressions to be converted to use. His travel-books, ' In Spain ', ' In Sweden ', etc., were notable in their kind, but the best records are contained in his autobiographical ' Fairy-tale of my Life '. In this vol. A.'s naiveté, which was child-like and touching, though, doubtless, a little trying to his contemporaries, and the virginal unworldliness of his character, are fully pourtrayed. ' Like a flaw in a diamond ', says prof. Boyesen, ' a curious

plebeian streak cut right across his nature. With all his virtues, he lacked that higher self-esteem which we call nobility ' (*Essays on Scandinavian Lit.*, p. 178). A.'s novels, poems and dramas need not detain us here, though his comedy of ' The New Lying-in-Room ' successfully challenged comparison with ' The Lying-in Room ' of Holberg (q.v.) : it is as the author of the fairy-tales that A.'s name is literally a household word.

André (13th cent.) : surnamed le Chapelain, the chaplain : Fr. love-jurist (see s.v. woman). A codified in a Lat. treatise, *de arte honeste amandi*, the elaborate rules and etiquette of the Provençal courts-of-love, as practised by the knights of the Round Table, and as obligatory on the aspirants to chivalry under the great ladies of France in 12th and 13th cents., such as queens Eleanor of Poitiers, Marie of Champagne, and Alice (or Adela) of France.

André, Bernard (fl. 1500) : Fr.-Engl. poet. Born at Toulouse ; came to Engld. with king Henry vii, by whom he was appointed tutor to princes Arthur and Henry. A., also known as Andreas, was blind. Wr. in prose and verse ; his poems included *les douze triomphes de Henri vii*, in which the 12 labours of Hercules were adapted to Henry Tudor, who made A. poet-laureate (q.v.) to the Engl. court, thus providing a notable example of the influence of Fr. culture on Engl. letters.

Andreæ, Laurentius (1482-1552) : Swed. reformer ; chancellor to king Gustavus Vasa. Transld. the New Testament into the vernacular, 1526. A. is also known as Lars Andersson.

Angeles, de los, Juan (c. 1536-1609) : Span. mystic ; Franciscan ; wr. spiritual studies of a rare beauty and intensity, including ' Spiritual and Amorous Conflict between God and the Soul ', 1600, abridged from his ' Triumphs of the Love of God ' (1590). Los A. was plainly influenced by Ruysbroek (q.v.).

Angelus Silesius. See s.v. **Sheffler, J.**

Animal-Fable : see **Bestiary.**

Anslo, Roger (1626-69) : Dutch poet ; imitator of Vondel (q.v.), but did not succeed in sustaining the same lofty note of patriotism and piety as his master ; the Dutch homeliness clung to him too closely.

Anthology : Generic name, from the Gk. (*anthos, legein*), for a collection of flowers of verse (or, more rarely, of prose). A variant name is *stephanos*, or garland, used in Gk. by Meleager in the 1st cent. B.C., and in Fr., among many others, by the collectors of the *Guirlande de Julie* (q.v.). But, virtually, in the history of lit., the A. *par excellence* is the Gk. A., or collection of epigrams and other short poems, ranging in time over 1,000 years (from Simonides, 490 B.C., to 6th cent,. A.D.). The chief MS. of the Gk. A. was first discovered, 1607, by the fine Fr. scholar, Saumaise (q.v.) in the Palatine library at Heidelberg, and is hence known as the Palatine A. The MS. was taken to Rome, where it remained for nearly 200 years, and the real *ed. pr.* of the Gk. A. is due to a Germ. scholar, Christian Fr. Wm. Jacobs (1764-1847), who produced an edn. in 13 vols. (text, i-iv ; indices, v ; commentary, vi-xiii), 1794-1814 ; a text in 3 vols., 1813-7, and a selection for use in schools, 1826.

'**Anti-Jacobin**, The, or Weekly Examiner' (20 November, 1797 to 9 July, 1798): Engl. politico-satirical review, founded by G. Canning (q.v.), the statesman, with some Etonian schoolfellows (see s.v. Frere), under the editorship of W. Gifford (q.v.). The editor was no relation to JOHN GIFFORD, 1758-1818, who edited a paper called the *Anti-Jacobin Review and Magazine*, which was publd., 1798-1821, and which was 'inconceivably virulent and dull' (Elton, *Survey Engl. Lit.*: 1780-1830, i, 424). The new *A.-J.* had been announced in the last number of the old, but it was not supported by any of the latter's brilliant staff. The *A.-J.*, which started as a weapon in the Tory campaign against the Revolutionary Whigs, was the sequel, of course, to the *Reflections on the French Revolution* by Burke (q.v.), and to the *Pursuits of Literature* by T. J. Mathias (q.v.). 'There is a pervading form and finish which makes *The Anti-Jacobin* not so much a newspaper as a piece of literature' (Elton, *op. cit.*, 38). The wit was extended to the literary follies of the Whigs, and Erasmus Darwin (q.v.), e.g., 'being a Liberal as well as a bad poet, is slowly and studiously roasted in *The Loves of the Triangles*', a skit on his *Loves of the Plants*, 1789. Among other notable poetic contributions, which seem mostly to have been written in joint authorship, are *The New Morality* (' the last really effective salvo of the old poetic artillery ', Elton, *loc. cit.*, who notes its ' red and hectically pulsing wrath of conviction '), *The Friend of Humanity, The University of Göttingen*, to which Pitt is said to have contributed the concluding verse, and *The Duke and the Taxing Man*, the duke being ' Smithson of Northumberland ',—a mock-Percy ballad. In virtue of the *A.-J.*, Courthope (*Hist. Engl. Poetry*, vi, 134) writes of Canning, its progenitor, as ' the greatest master of English political satire since the days of Swift and Pope ', to whose work the *A.-J.* was the last and not the least brilliant successor.

Antoine de la Salle (c. 1398-c. 1461): Fr. romance-writer, of the age of the decline of chivalry. Wr. *Petit Jehan de Saintré*, a chivalric love-story, founded on fact, and exhibiting in its long-drawn languors the dying affectations of its school. A. has also been credited with the authorship of the famous farce, *Pathelin* (q.v.), and of the collection of fables (q.v.), *Cent Nouvelles Nouvelles*, a valuable source-book mainly from the Italian, and of a brief satire, conventional in the style of the Middle Ages, the *Quinze Joies du Mariage*.

Antonides, Joannes. See **Goes, Van der.**

Antonio, Nicolas (1617-84): Span. Scholar; edu. at Salamanca; resided at Rome as general agent of king Philip iv of Spain (1659-79); collected a valuable library; returned to Madrid at the close of that honourable embassy. A. utilized his considerable bibliographical knowledge to compile a *Bibliotheca hispana*, 1672-96, which founded the study of lit. on scientific lines. Part ii, in dict. form, was publd. first; and Part i, in narrative form, from the age of Augustus to 1500, was issued in 1696 by A.'s friend, card. Aguirre (q.v.). The whole work was written in Lat., and was re-issued in 4 vols., 1787-88, as the *Bibliotheca Vetus et Nova* of A., with notes by P. Bayer, then head of the royal library at Madrid. A. wr., too, *Censura de historias fabulosas*, ed. pr., 1742.

Apollo of Ghesang der Musen (1615): Dutch collection of courtly and popular poetry, the best of the former being by Hooft (q.v.), and of the latter by Bredero (q.v.), the editor of the miscellany, which corresponded to the contemporary collection by Tottel (q.v.) in Engld.

Aquinas, Thomas (c. 1225-74): It. scholar; saint; Dominican; count d'Aquino; pupil of Albertus Magnus (q.v.), at Cologne; the Angelic Doctor; 'brought scholasticism to its highest development by harmonizing Aristotelianism with the doctrines of the Church' (Sandys, *Hist. Class. Schol.*, i, 582); 'the greatest of the schoolmen' (H.O. Taylor, *The Medieval Mind*, ii, 437): ' his way of teaching, his translucent exposition, came to his hearers as a new inspiration '. (See, too, s.v. Aristotle). A. incorporated the scientific approach to philosophy, characteristic of the 13th cent., as John of Salisbury (q.v.) had represented the literary approach in the 12th.

Arber, Edward (1836-1912): Engl. scholar; compiled invaluable aids to Engl. studies by his series of *British Anthologies*, 10 vols., 1899-1901; and *An English Garner*, 8 vols., 1877-96, re-issued in 12 vols., 1903-4; this re-issue was edited by Thos. Seccombe, whose death in 1923 was likewise a grave loss to Engl. studies.

Arcadia: (1) geographically, the Greek Switzerland, whose race of hardy mountaineers was sometimes laughed at for their boorishness, and at other times envied for their simplicity. The tradition of simple manners combined with the musical gifts of the inhabitants, and with tales of their god-haunted hills, to produce the conception of A., prominent in Gk. and Roman poetry, as the home of pastoral innocence and of bucolic happiness. This idea permeates the *Eclogues* of Virgil (q.v.), where A. divided with Sicily the claim to idyllic life: Thyrsis and Corydon are ' Arcades ambo ' (*Ecl.* vii. 4), and the 4th *Eclogue*, with its vision of the golden age (' toto surget gens aurea mundo '), which took the medieval mind by storm, associated the geographical A. with a fabled region of literary romance.

(2) It is this secondary A. which we meet in the lit. of Europe. Nymphs told stories to hunters (the converse is more commonly the fact) in the *Ameto* of Boccaccio (q.v.); and Sannazzaro (q.v.), in 1504, definitely re-invented A. as the refuge of town-tired Neapolitans, anxious to make their escape to the peaceful surroundings of the country. His 12 bucolic eclogues were united by passages of prose, and the rustic illusion was sustained in a vein of sentimental love-making between the shepherdesses and their swains. It was essentially a townsman's country to which Sannazzaro repaired, and it bore no relation to the countryside of the Peasants' Revolt or of Luther's vernacular hymns. But it established a convention which persisted through the Port. *Diana* of Monte-mayor (q.v.), the Span. *Galatea* of Cervantes (q.v.), the Lat. *Eclogues* of Mantuan (q.v.),

and the Engl. *Arcadia* of Sidney (q.v.), not to speak of later developments of the pastoral idea (see s.vv. Pastoral, Nature). Keats (q.v.), in his *Ode on a Grecian Urn*, finely renders the Arcadian atmosphere, and his 'happy melodist, unwearied, for ever piping tunes for ever new' goes straight back to the heart of Arcady through Sidney, *Arcadia* (Bk. iv), with his 'shepherd's boy piping as though he should never be old'. The idea of A. has receded far to-day; possibly through the belief that Arcady, like Heaven, is within us, and that idyllic pictures of the old Gk. mountain-country are inadequate to the happiness at which we grasp. To others, haply, it may seem that the disappearance of the rural illusion, and the displacement of Theocritus, the Sicilian founder of pastoral poetry in the 3rd cent. B.C., are losses to the reality which lit. serves, as was as to the ordeal through which its service is rendered. The repudiation of Sannazzaro's Arcady is to be found explicitly in Crabbe (q.v.), *The Village* (1793), i, 15ff., which is quoted here s.v. Pastoral. It was a perception, traceable as early as Lope de Vega (q.v.; d. 1635), which was bound to arise out of the development of social consciousness, and which was postponed directly by the charm of Arcadian scenery and the opportunities which it afforded of disguising real characters by fiction. (See s.vv. Roman-à-clef, Urfé).

(3) The geographical name had been extended into the literary realm of Arcadia, and the association of this realm, and of its virtual founder, Sannazzaro, was preserved in the title, Arcadia, given to a society, or academy, founded at Rome, 1690, in the garden of the Franciscan fathers on the Janiculum. Originally a memorial to queen Christina of Sweden (q.v.), who had died, 1689, its 14 founders, of whom Gravina (q.v.) was the legitator and Crembisceni (q.v.) became the historian, were united in a resolve to go back to the pastoral convention, and to drive out of Ital. poetry the signs of urban wit and Marinist (s.v. Marini) affectation. It 'probably achieved its unparalleled success as much on account of its follies as on account of its disinterested ambition to purify poetical taste or to amend poetical practice' (Millar, *P.E.L.*, ix, 354). But, though its influence spread throughout Italy, and though it opened kindly doors to young talent, 'Italy became transformed into a breeding-ground for minor poets, who masqueraded as shepherds, and poured forth verses upon the most trivial themes' (*ibid.*), and the time was ripe, 1763, for the bludgeon of Baretti (q.v.). The initial mistake, perhaps, was that none of the 14 founders was born a poet. (The best Engl. account of this A. is in 'Vernon Lee's' *Studies of the 18th Century in Italy*, 1880).

Areopagus: Engl. literary academy (q.v.), founded 1579, by Gabriel Harvey (q.v.), which met at the house of lord Leicester in London, and which counted Spenser and Sidney (qq.v.) among its members. The main propaganda of the club was to promote the substitution of the quantitative metres of classical prosody for the accentual principle of modern verse, which was denounced as a barbarism of the romance (q.v.)-languages; rhyme fell under the same ban. There is no doubt that the A. owed its inception to the similar foundation in Paris, about 20 years before, by J. A. de Baïf (q.v.), and it repeated the fate of its French prototype. Harvey's pedantry, unlike Baïf's, was unrelieved by a genuine sense for poetry, and his harsh and aggressive autocracy could not impose for long on the greater writers, who were junior only in years. The A. came to a natural close; and the attack on rhyme, which was continued into the 17th cent., was refuted by the genius for rhymed melodies of Campion (q.v.), who wr. against them, as much as by the critics who opposed his principles and admired his practice.

Aretino, Pietro (1492-1556): It. satirist, dramatist, and letter-writer; natural son of Venetian nobleman; expelled from his birthplace, Arezzo; resided at Perugia, as bookbinder's assistant; at Rome, at the Papal court; expelled, 1524; accompanied Giovanni de Medici to Milan, where Francis i of France gave him a chain of gold; later, at Vienna, Rome, and elsewhere. Received handsome presents at the papal and other courts, but was refused the rank of card., to which he aspired. Wr. 5 Ital. comedies and a tragedy; many satires and minor verse of outspoken and unrestrained immodesty. His letters have social value. He was a kind of gadfly of the Renaissance in Italy, stinging his impudent way to princes' ears and ladies' bosoms, and tickling the favour of the one by trading the secrets of the other. Ariosto called him 'the scourge of princes', but it must be added that they kissed the rod. A.'s taste and talents were as superb as his standard of conduct was vile, and these gave him his influence at the courts to which he contrived to attach himself.

Argensola, de, -i. Lupercio Leonardo (1560-1613): Span. lyrical and dramatic poet; and

-ii. Bartolomé Leonardo (1562-1631): Span. lyrical poet and historian; brother to above. The chief memorial of these writers is the vol. of *Rimas* (1634), an early example of 'poems by two brothers', publd. after the death of both. It was highly praised by Vega (q.v.), who declared that it seemed as if these poets had been sent from Aragon (their birth-place) for the reform of Castilian verse. The reformers' skill was displayed in their exquisite taste for the harmonies of Horace (q.v.), and their bk. of verse is still held in considerable estimation. Separately, the works of the two brothers are of less significance. Lupercio's plays were lauded by Cervantes (q.v.; *Don Quixote*, bk. iv, 21) as 'three tragedies, written by a famous poet of our kingdom, which were such as delighted, yea, and amazed all the auditors'; but when *Isabella* and *Alexandra* were recovered in 1772 out of the oblivion which seems permanently to have overtaken the third of the tragedies, *Phyllis*, 'they quite failed to satisfy the expectations that had been excited by the good-natured praise of Cervantes' (Ticknor, ii, 68); and more recent critics affirm their disappointment in an ascending scale. The plays were in the old vein of extravagance, and were filled with accumulating horrors ; and, later, 1598, L. L. de A. ranged himself among the reactionary opponents to the ' new comedy ' represented by Vega.—Not much more extended notice is due to the hist. writings of the younger brother, Bartolomé. In 1613, he succeeded Lupercio as historiographer of Aragon, and publd. 20 years later the first part of his annals of Aragon, in continuation of Zurita (q.v.). It is a reputable piece of work, and more notable than his romantic-hist. vol., *Conquista de las Islas Malucas*, 1609.—It is to be added that both brothers enjoyed the patronage of public men of note in Spain and at Naples.

Argenson, d', René Louis de Voyer (1694-1757) : Fr. statesman ; memoirist ; economist ; *marquis* by rank ; member of the Entresol (q.v.) ; foreign minister to king Louis xv, 1744-47. D'A.'s short term of office and his disappointment at not being recalled made him to some extent an opportunist as a political reformer, and deepened the pessimism of his survey of economic conditions in his *Mémoires*. His work on ' the government of France ' was issued posth. in 1764, and was directed to a refutation of the reactionary views of the critical feudalist, Boulainvilliers (q.v.).

Argote de Molina, Gonzalo (*c.* 1549-97) : Span. poet and critic. His verse does not seem to have been of much account ; and he is chiefly memorable to-day for his edn., 1575, of the ' Count Lucanor ' romance of don Juan Manuel (q.v.), with pref. on the succession of the Manuels, including a life of don Juan, and a subsequent discourse on Span. poetry, discussing, as was appropriate at the date, the relative merits of the old school of courtly verse and the new Italianate reforms. (See s.vv. Boscan, Silvestre).

Arguijo, de, Juan (*c.* 1564-1623) : Span. poet. wr. verse in the tradition of Herrera (q.v.), remarkable in its generation for its abstinence from the Gongora (q.v.) affectations, and distinguished by a quiet and delicate sensibility. A. occupies the first place in the *florilegium* of Espinosa (q.v.).

Argyropoulos, Joannes (1416-84) : Gk. teacher in Italy. Arrived 1441, at Padua from Constantinople ; lectured at Florence, under the Medici ; Politian (q.v.) attended his classes ; went to Rome, 1471, where Reuchlin (q.v.) who was among his pupils, 1482, was sped back to Germany by his tutor with the exclamation : ' Ecce, Graecia nostro exsilio transvolavit Alpes ' (Lo ! Greece by our exile hath flown across the Alps). A. transld. parts of Aristotle (q.v.).

Ariosto, Ludovico (1474-1533) : It. poet. Born at Reggio, and spent the greater part of his life in or near Ferrara. From 1503-17, A. was in the service of the card. Ippolito d'Este, whom he abused in his satires and extolled in his romantic-epic. In 1518, A. transferred his services to his patron's brother, duke Alfonso of Ferrara ; he spent a miserable three years (1522-25) as governor of Garfagnana, a wild province across the Apennines. More easeful years at Ferrara ensued ; but A., though dependent on princes' favours all his life, was never comfortable in his dependence, and he was further embarrassed by unceasing

affairs of the heart. He composed satires and love-poems, and wr. several comedies in a Terentian vein, which were produced (1528-33) on duke Alfonso's stage at Ferrara. But A.'s *magnum opus*, a European masterpiece, was the *Orlando Furioso*, begun in 1505, finished in 1515, and constantly repolished. Card. Ippolito is said to have asked A. when he showed the poem to his employer, ' Where on earth did you discover such a farrago of nonsense ? ' and this reception may partly have induced the poet to transfer his services to the duke. It was ungrateful as well as unjust on the part of the patron, for the poem rendered illustrious the origins of the d'Este family and exalted its living representatives. Apart from the motive of flattery, a feature which it is futile to-day either to attack or defend, A.'s *Orlando Furioso* is admittedly a continuation and re-fake (' rifacimento ') of the *Orlando Innamorato* of Boiardo (q.v.). It is also a medley which must have grown out of no clear plan or design ; and it is interrupted by ' novelle ' (in its own metre). But all deductions notwithstanding, the merits of the poem are superlative, and its artistic greatness is undisputed. It sang the Cinquecento (16th cent.) into lit. It served better the interests of Italy in its day than Machiavelli's statecraft or Savonarola's sermons. The positivist and the idealist failed, the one to produce his prince, the other to impose his theocracy. A., with less anxious aim, and with complete indifference to the light, whether of earth or heaven, which guided the builders for the future, took his good where he could find it. His poem, composed in octave stanzas (*ottava rima*, q.v.), which flow with undulating agility, must be read, as it was written, for delight. It had no other end in view, and it is to be judged by no standard but that of pleasure. Engl. Italianate writers, not long after A.'s death, were ready either to read too much into him, or to restrict their own soaring to his flight. In acknowledgment of their deep debt to A.'s example of the romantic-epic, they made the generous mistake of confusing their practical purpose with A.'s artistic aim. Thus, in 1591, sir John Harington, A.'s translr., insisted that *Orlando Furioso* was a mine of moral allegory ; and Edmund Spenser, in a letter to Ralegh, credited Orlando with the qualities of ' a good governour and a vertuous man '. But the *Faërie Queen* overwent its model, and A. was innocent of such sublimities. Italy's 100 years' cult of Humanism had left moral sanctions submerged, and A., who fulfilled its highest hopes, precisely reversed the ideal of Virgil, Dante's guide (*Æn.* vi, 847-53), and of Spenser, fashioning a gentleman. It was A.'s exterior grace which moved the envy and despair of literary Europe, and threatened for a moment to set back the original genius of Elizabethan poetry (cf. Gabriel Harvey's correspondence with Spenser). Hallam, never lavish in praise, described the *O.F.* as ' very rarely surpassed ', and placed A. fourth in succession to Homer, Virgil, and Dante, ' in purity of taste, in grace of language, and harmony of versification ' (i, 314). In the development of lit. in

Europe, these gifts were more valuable than any. New ideas fermenting in great minds were waiting on the means of expression, and A.'s service to the art which Pulci and Boiardo had fostered can hardly be exaggerated. He left the technique of modern verse as perfect as in the best poetry of the ancients. His fluent grace and lucid buoyancy were to be henceforward models for emulation. Petrarch's foresight was satisfied ; his cherished authorities of antiquity had supplied modern Italy with a poet worthy of their example. If A. holds us suspended above ' the fierce confederate storm ' of emotions hardly aroused and aspirations waking to consciousness, he fulfilled his proper part sufficiently. He sang the remembered names of old-time Paladins and Paynims, and raised the ' matière de France ' (see s.v. Bodel) to the summit of its poetic capacity. Amid the distractions of his times, he sat alone on his poet's height, nursing Boiardo's orphaned offspring ; lavishing the riches of his fancy, and the resources of the language which he enhanced, on Angelica and Medoro, whom she crowned king of Cathay, on Bradamante and Ruggiero, the fabled ancestor of Ferrara's dukes, on Rodomonte, the hero of rodomontade, on Astolfo, who journeyed to the moon, and on ' the dames, and knights and arms, and loves, and courtesies, and adventures ', rehearsed in the opening words of his epic of ' Roland, mad '. A.'s irony has been a bone of contention, but in truth it is simply an expression of that insistent search for beauty, and beauty alone, which was the core of Renaissance striving, and which compelled a consistent poet to avoid the extremes of emotion. When passion demanded supreme eloquence, art interposed a cautious reminder of the limits of perfect language.

Aristotle (384-22, B.C.): Gk. (Ionian) encyclopedic philosopher ; born at Stagirus ; exact contemporary of Demosthenes the orator ; came to Athens, 367 (' at that time the Platonic Academy was really the only centre of higher study in Greece '; J. Burnet, F.B.A.), and remained a member of the Academy till Plato's death 20 years later ; went to Asia Minor ; m. in Mitylene ; was tutor, c. 342-35, to Alexander (q.v.), son of Philip, king of Macedon,—an interesting appointment, which was not without effect on the later *romans* of the Orient, but of which no authentic records are available (' we do not really know how long they were together, but it is clear at least that Aristotle never understood his distinguished pupil '; J. Burnet); returned, 335, to Athens, where he laid the foundations of his immortal fame in his Peripatetic (walking up and down) school, held in the gymnasium of the Lyceum. The problem of the chronology of Aristotle's writings is still unsettled, and prof. Burnet, whose lecture, 2 July, 1924, at the Brit. Acad. (*Proceedings*, vol. xi) has been cited above, is of opinion that further research is essential to establish it ; it may be remarked that A.'s treatise *On the Constitution of Athens*, which belongs to this period, was not discovered till 1890. The questions of the relation of A.'s treatises to his lectures, and of the absence in the former of a sense of

style, which is satisfied so completely by Plato (q.v.), are of more special interest.

In an art. on the present scale it is not possible to indicate more than very generally the course of the influence of A. on the thought and lit. of modern Europe, with which alone we are concerned. The rough outline is probably familiar,—how A.'s physics and natural history were poured into the Bestiaries (q.v.) of the Middle Ages ; how his logic and so-called metaphysics (he never used the word himself) passed through Arab. and Jew. translns., and, again, through Lat. translns. from the Oriental, into the possession of the Schoolmen ; and how his treatises on rhetoric and poetics affected the study of letters at the dawn of the Renaissance. We may fill in this outline a little more precisely, first observing (with Spingarn, *Lit. Criticism in the Renaissance*) that 1536 was a memorable year in this story : ' In 1536 Ramus (q.v.) obtained his doctor's degree in Paris by maintaining that all the doctrines of Aristotle were false, thus marking the *decline* of Aristotle's teaching in *philosophy* : but, in the very same year, the dedication of Pazzi's posthumous work (a Lat. transln. of A.'s *Art of Poetry*) declares that " the precepts of poetic art are treated by Aristotle as divinely as he has treated every other form of knowledge ",—thus marking the *beginning* of Aristotle's influence in *literature* ' (Sandys, *Hist. Clas. Schol.*, ii, 133f. ; see s.vv. Vida, Castelvetro). A.'s influence, therefore, has never failed ; and so, as is impressively said by prof. D'Arcy W. Thompson, F.R.S. (*The Legacy of Greece*, Oxford, 1921 ; p. 160) :

' It comes to pass that for two thousand years and throughout all lands men have come to Aristotle, and found in him information and instruction—that which they desired. Arab and Moor and Syrian and Jew treasured his books while the Western world sat in darkness ; the great centuries of Scholasticism hung upon his words ; the oldest of our Universities, Bologna, Paris, Oxford, were based upon his teaching, yea, all but established for his study. Where he has been, there, seen or unseen, his influence remains ; even the Moor and the Arab find in him, to this day, a teacher after their own hearts : a teacher of eternal verities telling of sleep and dreams, of youth and age, of generation and corruption, of growth and decay : a guide to the books of Nature, a revealer of the Spirit, a prophet of the works of God '.

Such is A., the Stagirite, whom Dante (q.v.), brooding in that twilight of time when the theologians of the Middle Ages met the scholars of the Renaissance, counted ' the Master of those who know ' :

All gaze upon him, and all do him honour.
There I beheld both Socrates and Plato,
Who nearer him before the others stand ; . . .
Euclid, geometrician, and Ptolemy,
Galen, Hippocrates and Avicenna,
Averroes, who the great *Comment* made.
(*Inf.*, iv, 131ff, transld. by Longfellow).

With this pen-picture by Dante should be compared an altar-piece by Traini (1345), in the Church of S. Caterina, Pisa (I am indebted for this reference to Sandys, *op. cit.*, i, 582), where Christ in glory is represented among angel-heads at the top-centre of the decorative scheme, with Saints Luke, Matthew and Paul to his left and Moses, Saints John and Mark to his right, St. Thomas Aquinas (q.v.) seated in the centre, with Aristotle and Plato on either side of him, and Averroes below; amid other doctors unnamed. All, except Christ, are holding open books outwards towards Aquinas, and the convergent rays indicate the direction of their teaching.

Before trying to annotate the above passages and picture, with a view to fixing some lines of the influence of A. on Eur. letters, we may perhaps avail ourselves of one more quotation : ' It would not be easy ', says sir Chas. Mallet (*Hist. Univ. Oxford*, i, 76), ' to exaggerate the impression produced in thirteenth century Oxford by the discovery that Aristotle's logic was only part of a larger philosophy, hitherto unknown, and by the translations which made his writings on natural philosophy, metaphysics, and ethics, for the first time familiar to the Western world. It meant a new birth of science. It was the greatest event in the intellectual history of the age '.

How far back shall we go ? Perhaps the most important name in Aristotelian study before the 13th cent. is that of Boethius, q.v., who, in the early 6th cent., aimed at a Lat. exposition of the works of Plato and Aristotle, with a view to demonstrating their substantial homogeneity. Through Boethius, says another ancient writer, Pythagoras, Ptolemy, Euclid, Plato, Aristotle, Archimedes ' learned to speak the Roman tongue ', which became, as we know, the learned language of modern Europe. Boethius transld. into Lat. the *Eisagoge* (introduction) by Porphyry (233-301 A.D., of Alexandria, pupil of Longinus, q.v., at Athens) to the *Categories* of A., and wr. a commentary upon it. In that commentary, Boethius, like Porphyry before him, left undecided the question whether *genera* and *species* are real things existing apart from bodies (Plato), or have no real existence apart from the sensible world (Aristotle). From this started the conflict between (Platonic) Realists and (Aristotelian) Nominalists, whose disputations continued right through the Middle Ages. (Boethius, as the author of the *Consolation of Philosophy*, is discussed in this *Dict.* s.v.).

This conflict belongs to the centuries of Scholasticism, of which V. Cousin (q.v.) remarks : ' On peut dire que la philosophie scolastique est née à Paris et qu'elle y est morte. Une phrase de Porphyre, un rayon dérobé à l'antiquité, la produisit ; l'antiquité tout entière l'étouffa.' We have marked the phrase from Porphyry ; we know how the tide of the Renaissance, bringing all antiquity to the shores of modern Europe, overwhelmed the sandcastles of Scholasticism : it remains briefly to note some features in that deposit. Scholasticism may be defined as ancient philosophy surrendered to ecclesiastical control. The well-understood function of the Schoolmen was to make A. a prophet of the Roman Church. But there were two stages

in the Aristotelian tradition, (1) A.'s logic, separately conserved, and (2) the whole Aristotelian philosophy, as restored to knowledge during the 13th cent. (See the quotation from Mallet, above). Noting the names of Abelard (q.v.; d. 1142) and John of Salisbury (q.v.) in this connection, we observe that the restored and complete Aristotle came from the ' Arab and Moor and Syrian and Jew ', enumerated by prof. Thompson above. Toledo was the centre of Lat. renderings from these sources, *c.* 1150-1250, and prof. Thompson's summary is confirmed by more detailed histories of the passage of A.'s writings from his own library in the 4th cent. B.C. to the Paris Schoolmen in the 13th cent. A.D. We need not pursue this story of bibliography, transln., scholarship, and love of learning, save to observe that, in the process of the transference, the names occur of Averroes (q.v.), the printed edns. of whose commentaries are preserved in a Lat. rendering from a Hebr. transln. from his Arab. orig. ; of Solomon ibn Gebirol (d. 1070), the Span., Jew, known as Avicebron (q.v.) ; of Moses Maimonides (q.v.), of Cordova, another of the learned Jews, whose services to the civilization of Europe are not always adequately recorded by the heirs of the Renaissance. Through these, and others, we pass to Michael Scot, Gerard of Cremona, Hermann the German, Alfred the Englishman, and other translrs. from the Arabic in the 12th and 13th cents. Hermann's *Poetic*, 1256 (*ed. pr.*, Venice, 1481) was the form (taken from Averroes) in which A.'s treatise on Poetry (' than which perhaps no written document in the world, not religious or political, has been the subject of so much discussion ' : Saintsbury, *Hist. Crit.*, i, 31) was transmitted to the busy critics of the 16th cent. and onwards.

The immediate point of interest is the big push which was given to the study of A.'s works as a whole by the great Schoolmen, lecturing at Paris, who inherited this wealth of Lat. learning and extended it. We must be content with mentioning the names, first and foremost, of the greater Dominicans, Albertus Magnus (1193-1280) and his pupil Thomas Aquinas (1225-74) ; next, of Alexander of Hales (Franciscan ; d. 1245), Edmund Rich (archbp. of Canterbury, 1235-40), Wm. d'Auvergne (d. 1249). Robt. Grosseteste (bp. of Lincoln, Franciscan, d. 1253), Vincent de Beauvais (Dominican, d. 1264), Wm. of Moerbeke (or Wm. of Brabant, or Wm. the Fleming ; archbp. of Corinth, 1277-81), and others. These names bring us to the epoch, at the edge of modern learning in Europe, when the ' almost total darkness ' anent A. had been changed by obscure and distant processes to ' nearly perfect light '. We may refer at this point to the researches and writings of Roger Bacon (q.v.), the Franciscan doctor, with his eagerness to encourage the study of A. in Gk., and his belief that ' all the wisdom of philosophy is revealed by God and given to the philosophers, and it is Himself that illuminates the minds of men in all wisdom ' (H. O. Taylor, *The Medieval Mind*, ii, 507, n. 2 ; cf. Sandys, *op. cit.*, 590ff.). But it is time to close this record, brief and imperfect though it be, of the restoration of A.'s philosophy to Europe. Dante* and the Schoolmen and the University of Paris, in all three of whom that restoration culminates, were too devoutly Aristotelian to be aware of the larger forces invading the mind of Europe. 'L'antiquité tout entière l'étouffa': *Vixere fortes ante Aristotelem*, and A. was not all the ancients. The Renaissance, which succeeded Scholasticism, swept other philosophers into its tide.

One word should be added before we quit the centuries of the Schoolmen. Their contact with modern lit. is mainly at two points. First, they helped to introduce system, order, and method into the chaos of ideas. They arranged thought compartmentally. By their grammars and other aids to study they evolved such measure of accurate reasoning as the limits of inquiry allowed. Secondly, they controlled the channels of what we now call chemistry and physics. All investigation of causes, all speculation and research, had lain in the Schoolmen's hands, and every Schoolman, we remember, followed either St. Dominic or St. Francis.

We come back to 1536, and the use of A.'s *literary* influence. He is, says prof. Saintsbury (*op. cit.*), 'the very Alexander of Criticism, and his conquests in this field, unlike those of his pupil in another, remain practically undestroyed, though not unextended, to this day'. Horace (q.v.) was an early extensionist, and among the later ones may be named Robortello, Vittori, Trissino, Castelvetro, Du Bellay, Sidney, Heinsius, Boileau, Pope (qq.v.) and many others, down to S. H. Butcher (d. 1911), who edited and transld. A.'s treatise on *Poetics* (2nd edn., 1898). The famous definition of tragedy, involving the theory of *Katharsis*: the problem of the dramatic Unities (q.v.); imitation, pleasure, and so forth,—the field was mapped out by A., which later critics have surveyed and parcelled out, but in which, as in physical philosophy, he was 'Master of those who know'.

Ari Thorgilsson (1067-1148): Icel. historian; wr. 'Lives of the Kings of Norway', since lost, which served as model to Snorri (q.v.) in his saga-histories of the same name. A.'s sagas, so far as is known, were more scientific in hist. conception than the greater sagas which succeeded his; and he was likewise author of a *Landnamabok*, or history of the Norse Settlement in Iceland—that earliest real vision of Utopia—which was preserved in the collection of a certain Hauk Erlendsson in the 14th cent., and which has well been called 'a Domesday-book turned into literature'.

Arjona, de, Juan (16th cent.): Span. translr. of bks. i-ix of the *Thebais* of Statius, *ed. pr.*, 1855; completed by Gregorio Morillo, died c. 1608.

Arminius (Hermann, Armin or Irmin): Germ. national hero; the alleged liberator of the ancient Germans from the Roman yoke. (See Tacitus, *Ann.* ii, 88). A. became the heroic figure of the patriotic revival in the 18th cent., when native gods and heroes drove out their

rivals from Gk. mythology. (See s.vv. Lohenstein, Klopstock, Kleist, Grabbe).

Arnauld, Antoine (1612-94): Fr. moralist; one of A.'s sisters became the mother of 3 brothers, Le Maître, who were all followers of their uncle's teachings; another sister was Angélique, mother-superior of the convent of Port Royal (q.v.). It was with the fortunes of this nunnery, extended, 1636, into a retreat and hostel for men of pious inclinations, and identified with the religious doctrines of Jansen (q.v.), that A.'s long life is indissolubly connected. He succeeded St. Cyran (q.v.) as its head in 1638, and founded the 'little schools of Port Royal', which, short-lived as they were (they were closed in 1660), effected eminent reforms in the theory and practice of education. The persecution of Jansenism by Church and State has been defined by Ste. Beuve (q.v.), the historian of Port Royal, as a quarrel between the Arnauld family and the Jesuits. A. was censured by the Sorbonne in 1656, and, despite the protection of the duchess de Longueville, was driven into exile 1678. His letters have been publd., and he was part-author with Nicole (q.v.) of the famous *Port Royal Logic*, or 'The Art of Thinking'.

Arnault, Antoine Vincent (1766-1834): Fr. playwright; fabulist. A. founded his plays on Roman history, and wr., 1791, a tragedy, *Marius à Minturnes*, which made his reputation, sustained by *Lucrèce, ou Rome libre*, a revolutionary drama. A. was patronized by Napoleon i, for whom he wr. a drama *Scipion*, but recanted in his *Germanicus* during the Restoration. A. was also active as a writer, like Florian (q.v.), of fables in the school of La Fontaine (q.v.); of these, his *la Feuille* is the best known.

Arndt, Ernst Moritz (1769-1860): Germ. poet and historian; by common consent, the poet-laureate of the War of Liberation. A.'s songs, collected 1818, inspired and celebrated the re-awakenening of Germ. nationalism in its revolt from the Napoleonic yoke. Some of them passed into the permanent lay hymnal of patriotic Germany; among these may be mentioned, 'Der Gott, der Eisen wachsen liess, Der wollte keine Knechte' (A.'s God, it may be interpolated, was always the Hebr. Jehovah, or the Lutheran God of Battles, as was appropriate to the poet's age and aim); 'Es zog aus Berlin ein tapferer Held', and 'Was ist des Deutschen Vaterland?' A.'s devotion to his fatherland was much more than a matter of song-writing, though Tyrtæus is not without honour. But he suffered for what he sowed. In 1807, his bk. on 'The Spirit of the Age' (*Geist der Zeit*)—an anti-Napoleon politico-social treatise (4 vols., 1806-18)—constrained him to retire from the professorship of history at Griefswald, to which he returned in 1813. In 1817, when the univ. at Bonn was founded, he received a like appointment, but was again retired in 1819 on account of his opinions. He was reinstated in 1840 by king Fredk. Wm. iv of Prussia, and retained the chair till his death at a ripe old age. A. was always a busy pamphleteer, and his writings in prose as well as verse were largely instrumental in arousing

* Dante 'thought and reasoned', says H. O. Taylor (*op. cit.*) 'in the terms and assumptions of Scholastic philosophy'.

national sentiment. His sojourns in Sweden, Russia, and elsewhere, during his lengthy periods of enforced leisure, gave him insight into political conditions, which he employed to advantage in several works of history and reflection.

Arngrim Jonsson (1568-1648): Icel. historian; socially, ' the first Icelander who took a family name, calling himself Widalin (Vídalín) from his native place Wididale. All Icelandic Widalins, a goodly race, are descended from him '. (Vigfusson and York Powell's *Corpus Poeticum Boreale*, i, xx; Oxford, 1883). Wr. Lat. ' Short History of Iceland ', 1593; three bks. on the constitution of Iceland, *Crymogœa*, 1610, and *Specimen Islandiœ historicum*, publd., 1643, transld. into Dan., 1782. A. was a diligent collector of MSS., and procured for Worm (q.v.) the MS. of Snorri's (q.v.) *Edda*, still known as *codex Wormianus*, and was the first to ascribe this treatise to Snorri. He is justly known as ' the Learned '.

Arni Magnusson (1663-1730): Icel. philologer; devoted himself to the task of collecting and editing MSS. A part of his collection was burned in the fire in Copenhagen, 1728, but a very valuable remainder was preserved and is still famous under A.'s name. He bequeathed his private fortune for learned purposes, and the Arnamagnian Committee has done very useful work.

Arnim, von, -i. Ludwig Achim (1781-1831): Germ. poet and novelist. A. started work as a student of natural science, but was early attracted into the circle of the Romantic School (s.v. Romance), chiefly through his friend Brentano (q.v.), whose sister Bettina (see *infra*) he married, 1811. After some years of foreign travel, extending to Scotland, which suggested some romantic tales, A. settled, 1805, at Heidelberg (q.v.) and collaborated with Brentano in the collected edn. of Germ. folksong, so stimulating to national sentiment, known by the name of the opening piece as *Des Knaben Wunderhorn*, 1805-8. A.'s novels included, ' The Countess (*Gräfin*) Dolores: Her Poverty Wealth Sin and Atonement ', 1810, and *Die Kronenwächter*, 1817, among many longer and shorter tales.

-ii. Bettina (1785-1859): Germ. Romantic writer; wife of above, and sister to his friend and collaborator, Brentano (q.v.). About 1807, Bettina formed a friendship with Goethe (q.v.), who was always responsive to girlish admiration, and she wr., 1835, a more or less imaginative book of ' Goethe's Correspondence with a Child ' (*Briefwechsel mit einem Kinde*), described by Robertson (*Hist. Germ. Lit.*, 516) as ' one of the most beautiful books of the whole German *Romantik*, and an excellent illustration of the unsophisticated Romantic temperament'. B. v. A.'s *Günderode*, 1840, was inspired by the unhappy Caroline v. Günderode (1780-1806), who committed suicide, the friend of W. v. Humboldt (q.v.). Her *Dies Buch gehört dem König* (' This book appeals to the King ') was a plea for the Silesian weaver against the rising stream of Industrialism. B. v. A., in her widowhood, resided mostly in Berlin, where she devoted herself to good works under the patronage of king Fredk. Wm. iv of Prussia.

Arnold, August Gottfried (1666-1714): Germ. divine; a sweet singer of Pietism (q.v.), and author of an important *Impartial History of Church and Heresy*.

Arnold, Edwin (1832-1904): Engl. journalist, poet, knt.; was for many years on the staff of the *Daily Telegraph*, after employment in India, 1856-61. A. contributed notably to Anglo-Indian studies, by his renderings in verse from the Sanskrit, his chief work being *The Light of Asia*, 1879, the life and teaching of Gautama, which has become a classic in its kind.

Arnold, -i. Thomas (1795-1842): Engl. schoolmaster; historian. Wr., 1838-43, a *History of Rome*, remarkable for its mastery and exposition of military operations, though surpassed in scientific research by the later work of Mommsen (q.v.). A.'s fame rests on his teaching work, which he interpreted as a national function as headmaster of Rugby School, 1828-42. His *Life*, 1844, was written by A. P. Stanley (q.v.).

-ii. Matthew (1822-88): Engl. poet and critic; elder son of above; fellow of Oriel Coll., Oxford; Rugby master; H. M. Inspector of Schools; prof. of Poetry at Oxford, 1857-67, his vols. *On Translating Homer*, 1861-62, and *On the Study of Celtic Literature*, 1867, being the fruits of his tenure of that chair, which Keble (q.v.) had held, 1831-41. A. is characterized by Saintsbury, a safe judge, in the following terms: ' As I rest on my oars, and look back over European criticism for the eighty years which have passed since his birth, I cannot find one critic, born since that time, who can be ranked above or even with him in general critical quality and accomplishment' (*Hist. Crit.*, iii, 516; 1904),—a judgment safer and more generous, since the writer admits that he is ' often in very particular disagreement with Mr. Arnold's critical canons'. Agreement or otherwise matters little, in comparison with the immense benefit conferred on Engl. lit. by A. in what was really a too short life. The crucial word in the above estimate is ' European ', for it was A.'s great merit to insist on bringing criticism in Engld. back from insular to European standards. He was the first comparative critic in the last cent. who admitted to the terms of his comparison not bks. only, but, like Taine (q.v.), the moral forces behind bks.,—conduct, society, general knowledge, and so forth. And, in contrast to the Teutonism of Carlyle (q.v.), and to the patriotic anti-Gallicism of Tennyson (q.v.), A. taught a stiff and ungraceful generation to admire the flexibility and realism of the great Fr. masters. ' It is the fruitfulness of Arnold's method ', says a recent writer (prof. Walker, *Age of Tennyson*, 207), ' that has made the reading of the *Essays in Criticism* (1865; *Second Series*, 1888) an epoch in the lives of many men who have now (1897) reached middle age '. Another generation has passed, and A. is perhaps a little more remote from the needs of the new age, the faults of which are not the same as those which he rebuked so faithfully, and, it must be admitted, with so much cultivated iteration. Still, these *Essays* hold their own, if not invariably for their conclusions, at least for their premises ; and there is present as well as historic interest in the writings in the hinterland of ethics and theology, *Culture and Anarchy*, 1869 ; *Literature and Dogma*, 1873 ; etc.,—which with A. teased the same inquiring minds, which Ruskin (q.v.) was feeding with *Ethics of the Dust, Sesame and Lilies*, etc., Froude (q.v.) with *Short Studies on Great Subjects*, and Mill and Lecky (qq.v.) with their longer works. Certain phrases, too, invented or adopted by A. will not die : his denunciation of the ' Philistines ', his ' criticism of life ', his ' imaginative reason ', his ' ineffectual angel ' (Shelley), his ' grand style ', his ' Wragg ', his ' sweetness and light ', his ' urbanity ', and, among many others, his apostrophe to Oxford : ' home of lost causes and forsaken beliefs, and unpopular names, and impossible loyalties '. But more enduring than A., the critic, is A. the poet. Some of his poetry, too, is criticism, and he was much addicted to the elegiac mood, which suited the half-melancholy and incomplete philosophy of a genius which found no ' shelter to grow ripe ', no ' leisure to grow wise '. The larger spaces and ampler calm of Goethe and Wordsworth (qq.v.) attracted him, but he could not attain to them : the ' strange disease of modern life, with its sickly hurry, its divided aims ', oppressed him. Not for this note, however, is A. destined to live in Engl. poetry, but rather for poems like *Sohrab and Rustum*, 1853, and *Balder Dead*, 1855, where taste and scholarship were combined in narrative verse of rarely high excellence. A.'s letters, too, deserve and enjoy wide esteem.

-iii. **Thomas** (1823-1900) : Engl. critic ; younger son of T. A. above ; held chairs of lit. in various univs. ; entered, left, and rejoined the Church of Rome ; wr. *Manual of Engl. Lit.*, 1862, and other works.

-iv. **Mary Augusta** (1851-1920) : Engl. novelist ; daughter of above ; m., 1870, T. Humphry Ward (born, 1845), editor of the *English Poets*, 1881-1918, to which M. A. above contributed the general introduction. Mrs. Humphry Ward, as M.A.A. was known in all her writings, sprang into fame in 1888 as the author of *Robert Elsmere*, a novel of theological doubt, based partly perhaps on recollections of her father's religious experience, but more directly on her own intimacy with life in Oxford and her reflection on what was occupying thoughtful minds at that epoch. It owed its sudden vogue to the advertised interest of Gladstone, the great statesman, but its reputation is still maintained as the leading novel of its kind in the 19th cent. by a writer second in learning only to George Eliot (q.v.) in her own sex. Her subsequent novels included *David Grieve, Helbeck of Bannisdale, Marcella* and its sequel, *Sir George Tressady*, two very clever pictures of strenuous social and political life, and several others, inferior in interest, but yet displaying the purposiveness, earnestness and creative talent, which were the heritage of a member of the A. family. Mrs. Ward added to the nation's debt to that family by her work and writings during the Great War, 1914-18. (See, too, s.v. Macaulay).

Arolas, Juan (1805-49) : Span. poet. Wr., 1840-42, 2 vols. of ' oriental ' and erotic poetry in the Hugoesque and Byronic school, which by its fire and heat contrasts strangely with his clerical profession.

Arrebo, Anders (1587-1627) : Dan. poet ; bp. of Trontheim, 1607 ; relieved from his see, 1622, in consequence of his unepiscopal share in lay sports and pleasures : it is not every poet-divine who combines as successfully as Herrick (q.v.) the ' Hesperides ' with the ' Noble Numbers '. A. transld. the psalter into Dan. verse, 1623. His chief poetic work was the *Hexämeron*, based on the *Semaine* of Du Bartas (q.v.), composed partly in alexandrine (s.v. Alexander), partly in hexameter verse. It marks a big step in advance in the history of Dan. versification, and brought the Renaissance full-flood into Denmark. There is a Norse feeling in A.'s poetry which earned him the title of the ' Virgil of Norway ', and Germ. critics have not unjustly traced the influence of Opitz (q.v.) in his writings.

Arsenal (Fr.) : The *Bibliothèque de l'Arsenal*, now known as the Mazarin Library, in Paris. The A. became temporarily famous under the direction of Nodier (q.v.), who was appointed librarian by king Louis xviii on 1 Jan., 1824. The *salon* of the Arsenal was the headquarters of the first *Cénacle*, or literary reunion, of the young Fr. romanticists (s.vv. Lyrisme, Romance), including Hugo, Vigny and Musset, who in 1843 replied to a poem addressed to him by Nodier as follows :

Lorsque rassemblés sous ton aile paternelle,
Echappés de nos pensions
   Nous dansions,
Gais comme l'oiseau sur la branche,
   Le dimanche,
Nous rendions parfois matinal
   L'Arsenal.

Art pour l'Art, L' (Fr.) : ' Art for art's sake ': Formula of the naturalistic school, first used by Gautier (q.v.) in the pref. to his novel, *Mademoiselle de Maupin*, 1835. Taking his stand on the plea that he was a man for whom the external world exists (a phrase not very different from Terence's more famous *homo sum, nihil humani a me alienum puto*), G. invented this formula of art, not at all in order to condone (or even admit) the moral improprieties in his novel, but in order to remove the artist's sphere altogether away from the moralist's. The thesis, of course, has done harm, as well as good, in the confusion of human endeavours ; but as a precept of creation it is not assailable. (See, among many references, Cassagne, *la Théorie de l'art pour l'art*, 1906). It should be observed that the phrase, exalting a principle, was formulated after the romantic beginnings of *le lyrisme* (q.v.) in France, 1820-30. Like most formulas, it narrowed, while it expressed, an idea evolved from the examples of writers who practised before the critics theorized. Hugo (q.v.), e.g., never definitely declared for this view ; the most he demanded (*Préface*, 1826) was the right of liberty *in* art (not the freedom *of* art) ; that is, that each should respect the rights of the other. Thus, his claim, whatever its relations to later realistic theorizing, approximated much more closely to the golden word of Goethe, *Nur das Gesetz kann uns die Freiheit geben* (Law alone can give us liberty), which is neither pure classical nor pure romantic, but pure true, underlying both. Gautier's aim in its origin, devised as a protest against rule-of-thumb classicists, served his purpose of emancipation ; and, in discussing the formula *L'art pour l'art*, it is not necessary to defend it from the charges incurred by later extensionists and practitioners. These charges are more properly considered s.v. Realism (q.v.). But one word may be added here ; and, appropriately, it is taken from a work by a countryman of Gautier's. Writing in 1886, the vicomte de Vogüé, an academician, said : ' I am well aware that in assigning a moral aim to the art of writing, I am causing a smile on the lips of the adepts of that honoured doctrine : *L'art pour l'art.* I confess that I do not understand it, at least in the sense in which it is employed to-day. Certainly, morality and beauty are synonymous in art. . . . I do not seek to exclude any class of light literature. A comedy and a novel may be more useful to mankind than a treatise on theodicy. I am solely concerned to protest against the partial view that no moral intention may ever be introduced. Happily, the very writers who defend this heresy are the first to betray it, when they have the heart and the talent. . . . Beyond all variations of taste, human nature does not change at bottom ; it retains its everlasting need of sympathy and hope. He who degrades and mutilates our hope may assuredly entertain us for an hour ; he will not hold us for long ' (*Le Roman Russe*, xxiv-xxxvii ; Paris, 9th edn., 1910). It is well to keep in mind the eternal verities of human nature in all partial discussions of local or temporary canons of art.

Arte Mayor (Span.) : Superior skill ; short title of a Span. verse-measure, known more fully as *versos de arte mayor*, and so called because their composition was deemed to demand a higher degree of poetic art than pre-existing metres. They consist of stanzas in 7 or 8 twelve-syllable lines, with 2 rhymes to each stanza ; and the metre, though not unknown in the old romances, first came into vogue in the 14th cent., and was revived by Cervantes (q.v.). An early attempt to unite *versos de A.M.* was made by P. L. de Ayala (q.v.).

Artemidoro. See **Artieda.**

Arthur : ' flos regum Arturus ' ; leader of the Britons in the struggle (*c.* 450-*c.* 510) between the natives of Britain and invaders from North Germany. A. became the legendary hero of Celtic tradition in the Welsh hills, round whose name grew up an epopee, conveniently known as the Arthuriad, absorbing earlier mythological elements, and admitting constant accretions. The earliest record of the struggle is from the clerkly pen of Gildas (*c.* 540) ; the name of A. first appears in the work of a Welsh annalist, Nennius (10th cent.) who exalts him as the conqueror of the Saxons in 12 battles. Celtic poesy and folklore flourished in the succeeding years of dim history, and the remains of early Welsh prose collections of folklore tales (the *mabinogion*, or lesson-books for apprentices to the bardic craft) indicate that the A. legend formed a part of that poetic quarry ; ' evidently

the medieval story-teller is pillaging an antiquity of which he does not fully possess the secret ' (M. Arnold, q.v., *Celtic Literature :* a well-known passage in a not very valuable bk.) Meanwhile, the Norman conquest of Britain had important literary consequences, and the Arthuriad grew apace. William of Malmesbury (*c.* 1120) wr. a Lat. *de gestis regum :* and Geoffrey of Monmouth (1100-1154) wr. (*c.* 1136) a Lat. *historia regum Britanniæ*, which professed without justification to be transld. from an old Welsh original, and which became the main source for the romantic redactions of the legend. He expanded an episode from Nennius in which an orphan child called Ambrose had predicted to king Wortigern (5th cent.) the Brito-Saxon conflict ; he renamed the child Ambrose Merlin (Myrrdhin was a Welsh sage), and, subsequently, Merlin, and he brought the Merlin-predictions down to his own date, 1135 ; he related the birth of Arthur, son of Uther Pendragon, the treachery of Modred, his nephew, and queen Guenevere, A.'s mortal wound in the last of the battles, and his departure for the happy Isle of Avalon, famous in Celtic faëry lore. The Fr. romancers seized on this quarry, which exactly suited their requirements ; it was rendered into 8-syllabled verse by Gaimar, whose version has been lost, and by Wace (1155), who called his romance *Brut*, after Brutus, the imaginary eponymous founder of the Britons. Wace introduced the Table Round. The lays of Marie of France (q.v.) and other lost Breton lays led to the combination of the Celtic Tristan-cycle with the A.-cycle of tales. Thomas (*c.* 1170) and Béroul (*c.* 1180) were both Anglo-Norman Tristan-romancers ; and Chrétien of Troyes (q.v.) adorned the cycle with a *Tristan*, an *Erec*, a *Lancelot* (*Conte de la Charrette*), an *Ivain*, and a *Perceval*, between 1160 and 1175. (See s.v. Chanson de Geste). By this date chivalric courtesy, in Chrétien's Ovidian manner, had been added to the Celtic magic of the Arthuriad. A further development was introduced by a Fr. romancer, Robert de Boron (q.v.), who, *c.* 1215, wrote a sort of trilogy, *Joseph of Arimathæa, Merlin,* and *Percival.* He and his successors (in prose romances) associated the ' graal ' (grail), a magic vessel of the Celts, cherished for its talismanic virtues, and so treated by Chrétien, with the cup used at the Last Supper, and given by Pilate to Joseph of Arimathæa, the instrument of Britain's conversion to Christianity. Thus, the Grail was promoted out of the region of pagan magic into a sacred emblem of patriotism and faith ; its quest became the symbol of knightly valour under Christ, and an acquired piety of purpose overlay the old boldness of adventure. The Arthuriad, thus extended and transformed, was complete about the middle of the 13th cent. An anon. *Sir Gawayne and the Grene Knight*, contained in the same MS. as *Pearl* (q.v.) is typical of the original tales based on the old material, and is supreme in its kind. In Germany, Eilhart, Hartmann v. Aue, Wolfram v. Eschenbach, Gottfried v. Strassburg, Walther v. der Vogelweide (qq.v.) and other romancers utilized the material before

1300 ; in Italy, Rusticiano of Pisa (q.v.) wr. an important version in 1271 ; in Engld., Malory (q.v.) reduced the whole story from ' a French book ' in the 15th cent. ; it was conned by Milton (q.v.) in the 17th cent. ; and its later history in the *Idylls* of Tennyson (q.v.) is as familiar as it is famous.

For the presumed identity of A. with king Caradoc, or Caractacus, who returned to this country from Rome in the 1st cent. A.D., and was accompanied by St. Paul, see an art. by C. F. Cooksey, in the *Nineteenth Century and After*, June, 1924.

Artieda, de, Andrés Rey (1549-1613) : Span. poet ; soldier. Wr. a play, ' The Lovers of Teruel ', 1581 ; sonnets and other poems, publd., 1605 (' Discourses, Epistles, and Epigrams '), which won the praises of Cervantes (q.v.) a few years earlier. A. wr. under the pen-name of Artemidoro.

Arzamas (Russ.) : Name derived from a tavern and applied to a literary club, or *côterie* at Petrograd, which flourished at the beginning of the 19th cent., and served the cause of romanticism (q.v.) in Russia in much the same way as the Cénacle (q.v.) a few years afterwards was to serve that of *le lyrisme* (q.v.) in France. The A. started as a kind of anti-academy, in opposition to, and in mimicry of, a union for 'lovers of Russian letters ', founded, 1811, under the chairmanship of Derzhavin (q.v.). The young bloods rebelled from the stilted proceedings of this body, and held rival meetings at the A. It was not much more successful ; the soil of Russia was not favourable to associations ; and the A., which was fed at one end by the select graduates—the choice flower—of the Tsarkoé-Sélo (the exclusive *lycée*, founded, 1811, of the Petrograd aristocracy), fed at the other end the higher ranks of the bureaucracy. Out of its circle, too, in which Pushkin (q.v.) was a leader from the start, came some of the hotheads of politics in Russia ; and the ideas which dominated the Decembrist rising of 1824-5, in which the poet Ryleef (q.v.) was one of the victims, may be traced to the debates on all topics at the literary sign of the A.

Asbjörnsen, Peter Christian (1812-85) : Norw. naturalist ; folk-lorist ; travelled on zoological quests in the South, and on anthropological in the North. With the results of the former journeys we are not concerned ; the results of the latter are contained in the *Norske Folkeeventyr*, 1841, which A. publd. jointly with Moe (q.v.), and which have become a household word in this country as the *Popular Tales from the Norse* by sir G. W. Dasent (q.v.). The treasury unsealed by A. has proved of great and growing influence on younger poets, and was of immense importance to his national lit., which he helped to found, after the delirium of Independence in 1814 (see s.v. Syttendemai), on the sure ground of national myth and tradition.

Ascham, Roger (1515-68) : Engl. teacher ; public orator, Camb. Univ. ; Lat. secretary to queen Mary, 1553 ; tutor to queen Elizabeth, 1558. Wr. *The Scholemaster* (unfind. ; publd. posth., 1570), dealing chiefly with the teaching of Lat., and deriving some meretricious fame, apart from the elegances of its style, from its sturdy dislike of foreign, esp. Italianate, affectations. Wr., too, *Toxophilus*, on archery, 1545.

Asselyn, Thomas (*c.* 1620-1701) : Dutch comic dramatist. Born at Dieppe of Fr. parents, who settled at Amsterdam about 1621. Wr. tragic dramas for the *Nil volentibus arduum* (q.v.) stage ; but soon quitted this unprofitable ambition for the production of farces and pleasant comedies of manners, more suited to the country of his orig. His ' Disguised Servant-girl ', 1682, was an excellent picture of Amsterdam life, in the vein of Bredero (q.v.).

Assonance (rhet.) : technical term for a feature common in early Fr. poetry (chiefly in *chansons de geste*, q.v.), consisting of recurring vowel-sounds, indefinite in number, in the final feet of consecutive verses, and preceding the device of rhyme. The same feature is found in early experiments of style in prose, e.g. in the writings of Guevara, Lyly (qq.v.), and others.

Athenæum : Engl. and Germ. literary journals.

The Germ. journal of this name was the organ of Romanticism, founded 1798 (the year of *Lyrical Ballads*), by the brothers Schlegel, Schleiermacher, Novalis, and others, in Berlin. The first number was publd. by Vieweg, a few weeks before the belated issue of the last number of Schiller's *Horen*, from which the Schlegel brothers had broken away. Various names had been proposed and rejected ; among them, *Hercules* (Schleiermacher's choice), *Freya, Dioscuren, Parcæ*, and *Schlegeleum*. The last suggestion, however fanciful, corresponded accurately enough to the plan of the scheme, which was to present the Schlegel point of view without any outside responsible collaborators. The brothers' contributions were always the most important ; no. 2, for instance, which appeared in June, 1798, at a short interval after no. 1, contained Fr. Schlegel's critique of Goethe's *Wilhelm Meister*. The 6th and last issue appeared in 1800. Shortlived though the journal was, it proved of great significance to the spread of the Romantic doctrine at the time and place of its appearance. (See s.vv.).

ii. The Engl. journal of this name was founded in 1828, and was publd. weekly till 1915, when, in consequence of the effects of the Great War, it merged its separate existence. The first editor was Henry Stebbing (q.v.), and the families of Dilke (q.v.) and Francis were associated with the journal as editors and publishers respectively from within a couple of years of its foundation.

The famous Club of the same name was founded in 1824.

Atterbom, Peter Daniel Amadeus (1790-1855) : Swed. poet ; neo-romanticist (see s.v. Romance) ; founded the Aurora League, 1807, at the univ. of Upsala, and was, later, more famous as leader of the Phosphorists, so called after the name of their literary organ, *Phosphorus* (q.v.), which was publd. 1810-15. (Another publication of the same school was the *Svensk Litteratur-Tidnung* (Times) ; see, too, s.v. Hammersköld). The immediate object of the founders of *Phosphorus* was to oppose the Swed. Academy (founded 1786), and to substitute for its Francophil tendencies a sounder and more national strain. But A. and his followers, in avoiding the Scylla of

France, foundered on the Charybdis of Germany; and their Swed. variant of the romantic methods of the brothers Schlegel (qq.v.) and their school was opposed in turn and in due course by the writings of Tégner (q.v.). A. and Tégner had several literary bouts, till Tégner's fine example prevailed. It was a struggle of schools. The Francophil academicians, the Schlegelian Phosphorists, and Tégner, the independent Swed. classicist, were working each against all, though A. and Tégner had common ground in their adhesion to the Gothic league (q.v.), devoted to Scandinavian mythology. In the middle, Swed. poetry went to sleep till Runeberg (q.v.) aroused it to nobler uses. A.'s chief poetic work is 'The Isle of Bliss', an allegory, 1824-27; of more permanent value is his critical vol. on 'Sweden's Seers and Poets'.

Aubignac, d', François Hédelin (1604-76): Fr. critic and playwright; Saintsbury applies the epithets 'native' to the first and 'hard' to the second of these avocations; abbé: supported Richelieu against Corneille (qq.v.) in the dispute which raged about the Cid (q.v.); was a keen champion of the tragic unities (q.v.), which, he declared, were founded 'not on authority, but on reason'. Wr. Pratique du Théâtre, 1657, and other works.

Aubigné, d', Theodore Agrippa (1550-1630): Fr. poet, memoirist, and satirist ('the spirit comes from the Hebrew prophet, and that is perhaps belittled if we call it satire'; Hannay, P.E.L., vi, 306); Gascon seigneur by rank; religious follower of Calvin (q.v.), and as notable in the camp as in the council-chamber of the Huguenots. D'A.'s adventurous life held many romantic episodes; not the least was his oath to his father at the early age of 8 to avenge the violent death of his co-religionists. If he was trained in the stern heroism of the Huguenots on the one part, on the other he was infected with the literary idealism of Ronsard (q.v.) and the Pleiad (q.v.), with whose orig. his birth was contemporary; and his busy, stormy, noble career was devoted to an effort to reconcile the principles of the two. It was the only effort at reconciliation which he ever made; his mood and his muse alike were stubborn and unbending, and he brought, as did Du Bartas (q.v.), the spirit of Hebr. prophecy into the display of classical models in Fr. dress. D'A. wr. Le Printemps, sonnets and lyrics faithful to Pleiad rules; but early passed into his maturer vein in the long poem (Du Bellay, q.v., had asked for long Fr. poems) in 7 bks., Les Tragiques. The nature of the work may be gathered from the titles of the bks.: Misères, the sufferings of the times when religious warfare was at its worst; Princes, the backwardness and folly of the courts; Chambre Dorée, the futile cowardice of authority; Feux, the horrors of the stake; Fers, the terrors of the sword; Vengeances, 'vengeance is mine'; and Jugement, the requital of God. The form was consonant with Du Bellay's requirements; esp. the use of the alexandrine (s.v. Alexander), which Ronsard had not used in his Franciad, added to the claim of that measure, long since admitted and established, to carry the weight of heroic arguments hitherto balanced insecurely on the lighter 8-syllable or 10-syllable verse.

But the spirit was that of the Covenanters, more turbid than Dante's full stream and less sustained in majestic wrath than Milton's, but of the same company and inspiration; 'there is nothing greater in our language', writes Lanson, 'than the concluding pages of Les Tragiques'. This work, composed about 1590, was publd. in 1616, so that D'A., whose active life fell in the 16th cent., was chronologically a writer in the 17th cent., though he never submitted to its new influences. In 1620, when he retired to Geneva, he wrote an Histoire Universelle of contemporary events, and, later, a Vie à ses Enfants, or autobiography written for his children, as well as political pamphlets and satirical romances, with the point directed against the Roman clergy.

Aucassin and Nicolette (c. 1180): Fr. anon. romance, partly in prose, partly in laisses (q.v.) of assonant lines of 7 syllables, and described accordingly as a chantefable or cantefable (song-story). Its theme is a variant on the (originally Byzantine) tale of Flore and Blanchefleur (q.v.), and it is a particularly graceful and charming example of the love-romance so popular in 12th century France, under the rule of Ovid's code of courtly love.

Auchinleck MS. (1330-40): Scot. MS.; a rare and beautiful specimen, now preserved in Advocates' Library, Edinburgh. Its chief contents are verse-romances (Carlovingian, Arthurian, Oriental), and misc. fables, 'débats', sacred pieces, political satires, one 'conte dévot', etc. It is probably typical of the miscellany which would be preserved in one family for private delectation before the era of printed bks.

Auerbach, Berthold (1812-82): Germ. novelist; son of Jew. parents, and wr. his first bk. on 'Judaism and Recent Literature', 1836, followed by a romance Spinoza, 1837, and an edn. of Spinoza's works. A.'s conspicuous success was founded on his peasants' tales, Schwarzwälder Dorfgeschichten, 1843, which came as a welcome relief from the prevailing politics of the times. A. himself had undergone a term of imprisonment for his Radical opinions. Among A.'s later novels, which enjoyed a big reputation in their day—a day of stodgier fiction than ours—were Frau Professorin, 1846; Barfüssele, 1857; Auf der Höhe, 1865. The Black Forest tales, it may be noted, created quite a little school, something like the Kailyard school of Scots novels in Engld. (see s.v. Reuter, F.).

Auersperg, von, Anton Alexander (1806-75): Austrian poet; count (Graf) by rank; wr. under the name of Anastasius Grün. A.'s lifelong activities in Liberal politics were kept separate by this nom-de-guerre from his literary works, which included 'Walks (Spaziergänge) of a Viennese Poet', 1831; Schutt ('Rubble' of the old world) 1835; 'Poems', 1837; 'Folksongs', 1850; 'Robin Hood', 1864; etc. Though not more than a second-class poet, A. was a considerable force in the lyric expression of liberal and pro-German Austria, and his political muse had a real vogue and importance. (See s.v. Metternich).

Aufklärung (Germ.): Illumination: generic name of a period in Germ. history, or, more exactly, a movement in Germ. thought, which started towards the close of the 17th cent., and attained its zenith in the clear thought of Lessing (q.v.), whose critical genius made an end and a beginning of the long years between Luther and Kant (qq.v.). The literal meaning of the word is ' clearing-up ', and it is commonly rendered by Enlightenment or Illuminism ; signifying the clarifying process, the intellectual re-construction and re-awakening of national self-consciousness, which Germany, North and South, underwent after the Thirty Years' War (q.v.) with its grievous experience of disintegration. The light was spread from other countries, chiefly from France, Holland, and Engld., where the liberal doctrines of such thinkers as Shaftesbury, Descartes, Grotius, Spinoza, Bacon, Locke, Hobbes and others inspired the twofold activity of pietists and rationalists. The Germ. pietists, led by Spener (q.v.), sifted the deposit of the religious warfare which had followed the Reformation, and introduced into the dogmas and practice of the Protestant faith a power of personal sublimation and individual responsibility which corrected the harsher and more unlovely features of reform. Similar motives inspired the philosophic rationalists in secular departments of knowledge. Leibniz (q.v.), and C. v. Wolff (q.v.), who popularized the Leibnizian theories, gave a confident and permanent lead to the vague hopes of moral and intellectual regeneration, which, till then, had found no more adequate expression than in the censure of satirists—the one-eyed guiding the blind. Man came now to maturity of self-dependence. The spectral phantoms of superstition, and the cruelties licensed by their terrorism, were banished to the darkness from which they rose. Absolutism was invited to show its credentials. Conduct was submitted to the ordeal of psychology, and was set in relation to individual and social promptings. ' Frederick's title to be called " The Great " is more than half due to his having made room in the world for the *Aufklärung* ' (*C.M.H.*, vi, 725 ; see s.v. Fredk. ii) ; and the undisputed dominance of the Illumination in Germany may be dated from 1740, the year after Fredk.'s accession, when Wolff was recalled to Halle. See Paulsen (*Kant*, 15), who compares the rise of Pietism to that of the Reformation—' Luther rebels against Lutheranism',—and the rise of Rationalism to that of the Renaissance : ' they have a common foe in the dominant system, and a common characteristic in their endeavour after freedom, after the realization of the personal life '.

The spiritual and intellectual guidance of the pioneers of the *Aufklärung*, and the new seeds of action and thought which they sowed on receptive soil, brought Germany within 100 years to philosophic primacy in Europe.

Augier, Émil (1820-89) : Fr. dramatist ; disciple of Ronsard (q.v.) and in the line of descent from Molière. Wr. prose and verse comedies, the former of which only are estimable. They include *Gabrielle*, 1849 ; *le Mariage d'Olympe*, 1855 ; *Ceinture dorée*, 1855 ; *Un beau Mariage*, 1859 ; *les Effrontés*, 1861—all social pieces, comedies of manners written with a social

purpose, after the fashion of Scribe (q.v.). A.'s best plays, which are also the least didactic, and are content to rest their appeal on pure dramatic characterization, are *le Gendre de M. Poirier*, 1854 (the *nouveau riche* and the ruined aristocrat) ; *Lionnes Pauvres*, 1858, and *Maître Guérin*, 1868, which chiefly justifies the reference to Molière.

Augustan (Engl.) : Epithet applied to the type of lit. characteristic of the 18th cent. in Engld. (' our excellent and indispensable eighteenth century ', as M. Arnold, q.v., called it), by analogy with the lit. produced with corresponding characteristics in the period of Augustus Cæsar in ancient Rome. Perhaps the most typical Augustan writer *pur sang* was Horace (q.v.), and the Horatian note is found in the Engl. Augustan epoch in Pope (q.v.) particularly. Strictly, the limits of this period have been defined as from 1700 (death of Dryden, q.v.) to 1726, when Thomson (q.v.) began to listen to natural sounds not always refracted through the mirror of correct taste. But, more generally, as critics have moved further from the romantic reaction from Augustanism, the name is used to cover the 18th cent. as a whole, and the contrary notes are collected as *avant-couriers* of Wordsworth (q.v.), who definitely broke with the Gallo-classic convention. These are all critics' categories, of course, and possess no real significance save for convenience of reference ; and we have the authority of prof. Saintsbury for the more generous limits of A. lit. : see his *The Peace of the Augustans*, 1916, p. 374, n.1 : ' An objection has been made, and may probably be shared by not a few readers, that to take the century " solid " as " Augustan " is a liberty—that about Pope's death a severance was made by some god, and that the star of Anna and the first Georges quailed before the unquiet captain of the dreams and actions of the subjects of George iii '. But, on the whole, the A. characteristics persisted.

Aulnoy, Marie Catherine d' (1650-1705) : Fr. fairy-tale writer, novelist, memoirist ; *née* Sumelle de Barneville ; m. François de la Mothe, comte d'Aulnoy. Wr., in imitation of mme de la Fayette (q.v.), *Les Aventures d'Hippolyte, Comte de Douglas*, and other novels ; *Mémoires de la Cour d'Espagne*, and other memoirs ; and is still famous for her *Contes des Fées*, 1698, with the tales, among others, of the ' yellow dwarf ' and the ' white cat ', to which her delicate and fastidious art gave permanent shape and form.

Aungerville, Richard, surnamed de Bury from his birthplace near Bury St. Edmund's (1281-1345) : Engl. humanist, statesman and bibliophil. Tutor to future king Edward iii, who became patron to Froissart and Chaucer (qq.v.) ; envoy to pope at Avignon, where he met Petrarch (q.v.), with whom he had much in common ; appointed bp. of Durham, lord chancellor, and lord high treasurer. Eager collector of MSS., some by discoveries in monastic libraries, some by purchase ; employed many copyists. Founded library in Durham (later Trinity) Coll., Oxford. Wr. Lat. *Philobiblon*, ed. *pr.* Cologne, 1473, extant in 28 MSS., first collated and transld. from true text by E. C. Thomas (Kegan Paul, 1888) ;

20 chapters, with prologues, on aspects of the love of bks., of real interest and charm.

Aurispa, Giovanni (1369-1459): It. (Sicilian) humanist. Visited Constantinople to study Gk., and brought back with him valuable trove of 238 MSS., now in Laurentian Library, spent quiet and otherwise uneventful life devoted to scholarship and learning.

Austen, Jane (1775-1817): Engl. novelist. Wr. (i.e., publd.; some of her novels were written before the end of the 18th cent.) *Sense and Sensibility*, 1811; *Pride and Prejudice*, 1813; *Mansfield Park*, 1814; *Emma*, 1816; *Northanger Abbey* and *Persuasion*, posth., 1817; also left some unfind. novels: *Love and Friendship*, edited 1922, and *Sanditon*, 1925, deemed by sir E. Gosse (*Sunday Times*, 15 Feb., 1925) to come nearer than any of the extant fragments to the authentic A., and 'the gaiety that sparkled in her life and is vivid still in her letters' (*Times Lit. Suppl.*, 19 Feb., 1925). Miss A.'s *Life and Letters* were issued by W. and R. A. Austen-Leigh, 1913, and Goldwin Smith and others have written special studies of her work and genius. That genius was certainly remarkable: a cameo is commonly invoked to describe the medium of her art, for which she herself spoke of employing 'a little bit of ivory two inches wide'. Within those narrow and exacting limits of early Georgian life in the upper classes ('aristocratic in Aristotle's sense', since 'it rested on a Helotry of labourers and manufacturers'; Omond, *P.E.L.*, xi. p. 3), Miss A. was exquisitely skilful in making every line and dot tell, and the generous praise of sir W. Scott (q.v.) is as famous as it is essentially true: 'The Big Bow-wow style I can do myself like anyone now going; but the exquisite touch which renders commonplace things interesting is denied me' (*Jnl.*, 14 Mar., 1826). J. A. kept nearer to the interior than Miss Burney (q.v.), whose successor in domestic fiction she was, and was a better psychologist than Richardson (q.v.), whose *Pamela* invented the *genre*. Her satire played on her types with a hard and pitiless gaiety, and the types, though constantly repeated in the little circle of country-house society, always revealed new traits in fresh combinations. Her power of observation was supreme, and she possessed a sympathy and humour by which she unfolded her tales, very quietly, very soberly, and quite inevitably, through the interplay of character and environment. Her unwarmed, but not necessarily cold, method evoked situations of the finest human interest out of the commonest incidents of a walk, or drive, or a visit, or dinner-party, or dance. Across this feminine malice playing ironically on the conventions of a nearly effete social organism broke the passion of E. B. Browning, the industrial contrasts of Mrs. Gaskell and Mrs. Craik, and, a little later, the learned revolt of G. Eliot (see s.vv.).

Austin, Alfred (1835-1913): Engl. poet; appointed Poet Laureate (q.v.) a year or two after the office had been vacated by the death of Tennyson (q.v.).

Austin, -i. John (1790-1859): Engl. jurist; prof. of jurisprudence at Univ. Coll., London, 1826; studied in Germany, 1826-28, and lived in Germany again, 1841-43, and later in France. Wr. 1832, *The Province of Jurisprudence Determined*, as a disciple of Bentham (q.v.).

-ii. Sarah (1793-1867): Engl. scholar; *née* Taylor; wife of above; transld. from Germ., Ranke (q.v.), *Popes, Refn. in Germany*, and other works.

Auto (Span.): solemn act (Lat. *actum*); epithet of the acts of faith (*autos de fé*) instituted by the Inquisition (q.v.); but applied technically in lit. to a kind of sacred drama or passion-play, such as has been enacted in modern times at Ober-ammergau. In this sense, the sacramental *a.* date from the 12th or 13th cent. in Spain, and persisted till 1765, when they were prohibited by king Charles iii. They were one-act dramatic representations of the Mystery of the Holy Eucharist, played in the open-air, on Corpus Christi day. They ranged from the simplest performance on the rude stage of humble villagers to the most magnificent masque which Church and State could organize in Madrid; and among the many first-class composers of various allegorical dramas on this subject were Enzina, Vicente and Vega (qq.v.). But the principal Span. *auto*-writer was Calderon (q.v.), who was more careful to collect his *Autos sacramentales, alegoricos y historiales* in 1677 than any other classes of his numerous plays. He composed between 70 and 80 examples, the best, perhaps, being 'The Divine Orpheus'; and the *genre* was precisely suited to his genius, which dwelt securely among abstractions and sublimities. Some of them remind us, 'by their religious extravagance, of the treatment of the gods in the plays of Aristophanes, and others, by their spirit and richness, of the poetical masques of Ben Jonson' (Ticknor, ii, 361); and 'they descended from their highest inspiration after Calderon, who may almost literally be considered their creator' (Kelly, *Lit. espayn.*, 364).

Avellaneda, de, Alonso Fernandez (Span.): name assumed by the author of the *Segundo Tomo del Ingenioso Hidalgo Don Quixote de la Mancha*, publd. at Tarragona, 1614. This was the false Part ii of Cervantes's (q.v.) novel, and a copy would appear to have been in Cervantes's hands late in 1613. The true Part ii by Cervantes himself, with shrewd attacks on A., was issued in 1615. A. has been plausibly identified with Aliaga (q.v.). His bk. was transld. into Fr. by Lesage (q.v.), 1704, and it is to bk. iii, 29, of this version that Pope (q.v.) refers in his *Essay on Criticism*, 267ff.

Avendaño, de, Francisco (16th cent.): Span. dramatic writer. Wr. the *Comedia Florisca*, 1551, in which a play was for the first time divided into 3 acts instead of 5. Some importance was attached to this innovation, the invention of which was claimed by Virues (q.v.) at a slightly later date.

Avenir, L' (1830-1): Fr. newspaper ('The Future') started by Lamennais (q.v.) and suspended by ecclesiastical authority within a year. The editor's views were in advance of his times, and *l'A.* aimed at a kind of democratic theocracy, with a liberal pope at Rome. In 1832, the founder and his associates (Lacordaire and Montalembert) went to Rome, in the vain hope of convincing pope Gregory xvi of the good faith of the programme of *l'A.*; but condemnation awaited them on their return-journey at Munich, and the newspaper could not be revived.

Averroes (1126-98) : Arab. philosopher in Spain ; Abul Wahid Muhammed ibn Ahmad ibn Roshd ; wr. commentary on Aristotle (q.v.), which is a famous work of Arab.-Span. thought, though A. 'may rather be considered an heresiarch in the peripatetic church than a genuine disciple of its founder' (Hallam, *Lit. Eur.*, i, 397). Yet he regarded Aristotle as 'the only man whom God had permitted to attain the highest summit of perfection', and he was the great Commentator approved by Aquinas and Dante (qq.v.). It was due to the Jew. school of Span. philosophers who transld. the works of A., that his Aristotelian teachings, heretical from the Mohammedan point of view, were preserved for the admiration of posterity ; and the 14th cent. is described (*Jew. Encycl.*, i, 348) as 'the golden age of Averroism'. A.'s doctrines attracted disciples as late as Christopher Columbus, who refers to them with respect.

Avicebron (11th cent.) : Solomon ibn Gabirol ; Span.-Jew. poet, philosopher ; born at Malaga ; described as 'the Jewish Plato', and admittedly the philosophic master of Duns Scotus. A. was the earliest and not the least considerable of the Hebr. writers who preserved the treasures of Gk. philosophy in Spain. His chief work in that field was the *Fons Vitae*, transld. from Arab. into Lat. in the middle of the 12th cent. Under his own name A. was the author of devotional Hebr. poetry, an edn. of which, with an Engl. transln. by I. Zangwill, is publd. in the Schiff Classics (Philadelphia, 1923). The editor, Dr. Davidson, writes (Intro., xxxii) : 'For centuries, Gabirol marched through the philosophic schools of medieval Europe, some taking him for a Christian and some for a Mohammedan, none suspecting that he was a Jew. It was on 12 November, 1846, that the learned world was startled by the announcement of Solomon Munk in the *Litteraturblatt des Orients* that the well-known scholastic Avicebron was identical with the still better known Solomon ibn Gabirol'.

Avila y Zuñiga, de, Luis (*c.* 1490-*c.* 1560) : Span. historian ; admitted to the intimacy of the emperor Charles v (q.v.), whom he accompanied to Yuste after his abdication, and who is credited with the *bon mot* : 'My exploits are not equal to Alexander's, but he had not a chronicler like mine'. A.'s work, which evoked this royal commendation, was the 'Commentary on the German War' (the Schmalkaldic war), 1548, and frequently reprinted and transld.

Avila, de Juan (*c.* 1500-1569): Span. moralist ; known as the apostle of Andalusia ; beatified 1894, but already entitled 'saint Jean of Avila' by Hugo (q.v.) in 1830, and recognized as an inspirer of Fr. *lyrisme* (see s.v. Romance) at that date. Wr. 'spiritual letters' (esp. one 'for all estates', *ed. pr.*, 1578), and a paraphrase, 1538, of Psalm 44, which landed A. in an Inquisition prison, but which was later, 1574, taken off the Index. A. added

considerably to the resources of elegant prose style.

Ayala, de, Pedro Lopez (1332-1407) : Span. chronicler and poet ; grand chancellor of Castile, 1398, after various adventures in diplomacy and war ; was for some time prisoner in Engld., 1367, and in Portugal, 1385 ; altogether, a great man in troubled times, and a considerable benefactor to lit. by patronage and example. He transld. a portion of the Roman history of Livy from the Fr. version of Bersuire (q.v.), and added to this admirable apprentice-work a careful study of the *Cronica* of Alfonso (q.v.) the Wise, of the abridgement thereof by Juan Manuel (q.v.), and of the works of his immediate predecessor as chancellor of Castile, Sanchez de Tovar. With this preparation, A. composed the authorized prose chronicle (*Cronica*) of Span. history from 1350 to 1396, comprising the reigns of kings Peter the Cruel, Henry ii, John i, and (part of) Henry iii. Like Commines (q.v.), A. was a statesman writing the history of the events which he had helped to mould ; and a sense of responsibility and participation raised his style to a higher level of the historian's art than the semi-poetic narrative of Alfonso the Wise or the partisan gorgeousness of Froissart (q.v.), A.'s great contemporary. He had acquired from Livy the hint of inserting speeches and letters, invented to heighten dramatic probability ; and critics agree in ascribing to A. a distinct step in advance on the road of hist. writing. His fairness towards king Peter has been called in question ; but no further exception is taken to Ticknor's (i, 165) view in the middle of last cent., that 'it is precisely the cool and patient minuteness of the chronicler, founded on his personal knowledge, that gives its peculiar character to Ayala's record of the four wild reigns in which he lived ; presenting them to us in a style less spirited and vigorous, indeed, than that of some of the older chroniclers of the monarchy, but certainly in one more simple, more judicious, and more effective for the true purposes of history'. Besides the *Cronica* and other prose-works, including a treatise on hunting, A. employed the periods of his captivity and probably some of the leisure of his old age, in writing a poem, or rather a series of poems, now known as *Rimado de Palacio* (Court or Palace Rhymes). The name is due to A.'s nephew, Perez de Guzman ; but neither this, nor Santillana's (q.v.) title, 'The Manners of the Court', nor the more neutral name of 'The Book of the Court', is quite adequate to the form and contents of A.'s really notable work. It has likenesses to the Chaucerian verse of the archpriest of Hita (s.v. Ruiz), but differs from it in its more bitter satire and the deeper and more stately tone of at least the first half of the poem (stanzas 1-706 ; the remaining 903 stanzas are more gentle). This half A. called his sermon, and it rarely departs from the 4-line stanza ; in the second part A. makes more metrical experiments in sacred and secular lyric verse. Doubtless, the criticism of courts and kings, of bishops, lawyers, usurers and merchants, was written by A. as a prisoner, and the more charitable views of life succeeded at the time of his restitution to political power. A. is notable, too, in a generation before the influence of Italy was definitely asserted in Span. lit., for his work as translr. of Boccaccio's *Illustrious Lives* (bks. i-viii; completed, 1422, by other hands) and of Guido delle Colonne's redaction of the Troy-bk. of Benoît de Ste-More (see s.vv.); and his keen literary perception is seen in his reference—which is among the earliest—to the chivalric romance of *Amadis* (q.v.), later so influential in Span. lit., and in his experimental employment of the *arte mayor* (q.v.) versification, then in the first stages of innovation.

Ayenbite of Inwyt (1340): Middle Engl. prose treatise on 'The Remorse of Conscience' (ayenbite = back-bite; inwyt = inner sense), transld. by Michael of Northgate, a monk, from the Fr. *Somme des Vices et des Vertues*, compiled by Lorens, a Dominican friar, for king Philippe le Hardi, 1279. (Caxton rendered the *Somme* into Engl. as the Royal Book). The transln., says Sisam (*Fourteenth Century Verse and Prose*, Oxford, 1921; p. 33) 'is inaccurate and sometimes unintelligible, and the treatment is so barren of interest that the work seems to have fallen flat even in its own day. But linguistically it is one of the most important works in Middle English. It provides a long prose text, exactly dated and exactly localized', —the locality being Kent, since Michael, a lover of bks., belonged to St. Augustine's, Canterbury. (The *A. of I.* must be distinguished from the *Pricke of Conscience*, a didactic poem running to 9,624 verses in Northern Engl., ascribed to R. Rolle, q.v.).

Ayrenhoff, von, Cornelius Hermann (1733-1819): Austrian (-Germ.) playwright; army officer, lieutenant-fieldmarshal. Wr. tragedies and comedies in the classical vein acquired by Gottsched from the example of Boileau and Racine (see s.vv.), and consequently won the approbation of king Fredk. (q.v.) the Great.

Ayrer, Jakob (died, 1605): Germ. playwright. Wr. comedies and tragedies, issued posth. 1618, as *opus theatricum*, under the influence, then paramount, of the Engl. players (see s.v. Englische Comödianten). A. resided at Nuremberg, and has marked affinities with its greater citizen, Sachs (q.v.).

Aytoun, Wm. Edmondstoune (1813-65): Scot. poet; wr. *Bon Gaultier Ballads*, 1845, with sir Theodore Martin (q.v.); *Firmilian*, a dramatic poem, 1854 ridiculing the Spasmodic (q.v.) poets; *Lays of the Scottish Cavaliers*, 1848 (following Macaulay's q.v.; *Lays of Ancient Rome*), etc. A. was a keen admirer of Goethe (q.v.), and collaborated with Martin again in some translns. from him, and was a frequent contributor to *Blackwood's Magazine*.

Azelio, d', Massimo (1798-1866): It. poet and essayist; marquis by rank; son-in-law of Manzino (q.v.), in the wake of whose *Promessi Sposi* d'A. wr. 2 novels: *Ettore Fieramosca*, 1833, and *Niccoló de Lapi*, 1841. He wr., too, political works, in the shape of commentaries on current events, and valuable *Souvenirs*. In 1849, d'A. became a minister of State under king Victor Emmanuel.

Azevedo, de, Alonso (fl. 1615): Span. sacred poet Wr. a 'Creation of the World', partly founded on the *Semaine* of Du Bartas (q.v.), and even more forgotten to-day.

B

Bacon, Francis (1561-1626): Engl. jurist; philosopher, essayist; knt.; 1603; lord chancellor and 1st baron Verulam, 1618; visct. St. Albans, 1621; charged with bribery and deprived of the great seal: the vice of corruption being one to which public men in that age were peculiarly liable, owing largely to the conditions of public life; see, e.g., among several authorities, the *Memoirs of Robt. Cary, Earl of Monmouth*. B. himself wr., in his essay *Of Great Place*, that 'the vices of Authoritie are chiefly foure: Delaies, Corruption, Roughnesse, and Facilitie. . . . All rising to Great Place is by a winding Staire'. We need not discuss this aspect of his career further.

B. wr., while still a young man, with unaffected enthusiasm, to his uncle (by marriage) Burghley, the great statesman: 'I have taken all knowledge to be my province'; and no one to-day disputes his title to that proud proconsulship. It reminds us by its extent of the province of his earlier and hardly greater namesake, Roger Bacon (q.v.), to whom, as was pointed out in an illuminating art. in *The Times Lit. Supp.* (11 June, 1914), 'it may even be said, without much fear of contradiction, that the reformation, the Baconian reformation, in the method of natural science should be referred rather than to the later Bacon. Both

illustrious men', continued the writer, 'made appeal to the reigning powers to the end that learning and research might be fostered; and used the persuasive arts of rhetoric for the furtherance of that purpose. It is in the whole aim and spirit of the two men that true and striking resemblance offers itself'. The whole aim and spirit of B. may be judged from his Pref. to the 'Great Instauration' (*Instauratio magna*, written in Lat., 1620, and forming Part ii, of the *Novum Organum*, of which Part i was *The Advancement of Learning*, Engl., 1605, and Part iii the *de Augmentis*, Lat., 1623; the whole forming a kind of new Aristotle, q.v.). We cite the passage, which is remarkable for a certain direct profuseness, a scorn of calculation and literary accountancy, characteristic of Tudor times.

'Of ourselves we say nothing; but for the matter which is treated, we desire that men should regard it not as an opinion, but as a work, and should be assured that we are laying the foundation not of any sect or theory, but of that which conduces to the use and dignity of man. Next, we desire that, laying aside their jealousies and prejudices, they may fairly consult their own common advantage, and having been rescued by us from the errors and obstacles of their road and furnished with our defence and assistance, they may themselves participate in the labours that yet remain. Moreover, that they may be strong in hope, and not imagine that our *Instauratio* is something infinite and beyond the reach of man, when it is really an end and legitimate termination to infinite error, and is so far mindful of the mortal lot of man that it does not hope to accomplish its work within the period of a single life, but leaves this to succeeding times; when, moreover, it does not arrogantly search for science in the narrow cells of human wit, but humbly in the greater world'.

It is not within the scope of this bk. to evaluate or even to discuss the Baconian reformation in the method of natural science, referred to above. We are fortunate in the fact that B. left us, not only the unfind. edifice of his immense philosophical design, but likewise 'the civil and moral counsels', as he himself called his *Essays*, which were not so much essays in the modern sense, the sense of Lamb or Stevenson (qq.v.), as shorthand notes of a restless intellect, always aiming at definition and line, and at expelling loose thought and false reasoning. 58 *Essays* were collected by B. in 1625 out of previous edns. in 1597 and 1602: they were the 'most current', as he said, of all his works, 'for that, as it seems, they come home to men's business and bosoms'. Many of his splendid sentences have passed out of his commonplace-bk. into proverbial acceptance. Thus: 'Revenge is a kinde of Wilde Justice'; 'In Charity there is no Excesse'; 'Suspicions amongst Thoughts are like Bats amongst Birds: they ever fly by Twilight'; 'Houses are built to live in, and not to look on'; 'Some Bookes are to be Tasted, others to be swallowed, and some few to be chewed and digested'; 'Reading maketh a Full Man: Conference a Ready Man, and Writing an Exact Man'; 'Many a Man's strength is in Opposition'; 'God Almightie first Planted a Garden. And, indeed, it is the purest of Human Pleasures'. And so forth. B., said a Victorian essayist (Alex. Smith, 1830-97, in *Dreamthorp*) 'seems to have written his essays with Shakespeare's pen'. B.'s other works include his *New Atlantis*, a Utopian semi-romance, a *Hist. of Henry vii*, *Wisdom of the Ancients*, etc. Jas. Spedding (1808-81), a friend of Tennyson and Fitzgerald (qq.v.), spent nearly 20 years in editing B.'s works (7 vols., 1857-9) and writing his *Life* (7 vols., 1861-74; abridged, 1878).

Bacon, Roger (*c.* 1214-94): Engl. scholar; pupil of Grosseteste (q.v.); Franciscan; kept in confinement in Paris, 1257-67, on some charge advanced by his Order; wr. 3 famous Lat. treatises: *Opus majus*, *Opus minus* and *Opus tertium*, followed by Lat. compendia of philosophical (1271-2) and theological (1292) studies. Dr. Samuel Jebb (d. 1772) of Cambridge, edited the *Opus majus*, 1733, greatly transforming thereby B.'s 'earlier reputation as an alchemist and a necromancer' (Sandys, *Hist. Class. Schol.*, i., 590); J. S. Brewer (1810-79) edited B.'s works more fully, 1859, and there have been later edns. B. was a critic, and fond of attack. A student of Gk., he attacked the lack of Gk. learning in earlier decoctors of the Arab. or Hebr. Aristotle (q.v.)

into a Lat. Aristotle; he attacked the corrupt text of the Scripture in the Lat. vulgate, thus showing the way to the higher critics of the Bible (q.v.); and he was as eager to extend the frontiers of science as of letters.

Baena, de, Juan Alfonso (15th cent.): Span. anthologist. Collected (*c.* 1450) a vol. known as the *Cancionero de Baena*, containing 576 poems by about 51 writers, of which 78 were by B. himself. The compiler was a converted Jew, secretary to king John ii (q.v.) of Castile, at whose initiative the enterprise was undertaken; the bulk of the bk. was taken up by about 244 pieces representative of the mediocre talent of a certain Alvarez de Villasandino, who died in 1428. (See also s.v. Macias).

Bagehot, Walter (1826-77): Engl. critic,; economist; wr. *Biographical Studies*; *The English Constitution*; *Lombard Street: Physics and Politics*, 1872, and others, partly reprinted from the *National Review*, and all displaying an alertness to impressions, an originality and independence of thought, and a lucidity of exposition, which give B. a high place among the journalist-thinkers of the 19th cent. in the heyday of the periodical press.

Baggesen, Jens Immanuel (1764-1826): Dan. poet; employed Dan. and Germ. languages with equal facility. It is difficult to characterize B. by a single epithet: the Voltaire (q.v.) of Denmark, would be far too big; but there was something of the great Frenchman's versatile genius in B.'s skill in prose and verse, as well as in his hostile theory against the incoming wave of romance. This adhesion to the classical, or neo-classical, tradition was more theoretic than practical; but it involved him after 1806 in a losing controversy with Oehlenschläger (q.v.), ('Schlegelschläger', as he wittily called the greatest Dane of the age), and in 1820 B. finally left Denmark, in a kind of 'soil of my ungrateful country' mood. He had already paid long visits to Paris and Kiel, where he professed immense (though not long-lived) admiration for Kant (q.v.). It was always a roving genius which directed B.'s not too happy life. His *Labyrinthen*, 1789-91, which he left unfinished, was an account of his early travels and experiences, written in an excellent and a witty style. He had already publd., 1785, a vol. of humorous verse, and proved so prolific a writer of satires, epistles, elegies, *vers de société*, etc., during the next 15 years, that, at the century's close, he was accounted a foremost Dan. poet of the 18th cent., and his reputation stood at its height. As sometimes happens by a kind of sentimental fallacy, which was illustrated at the turn of the present cent., B. seemed incompetent to effect with dignity the transition to the 19th cent. He ranged himself with the old guard, and his 'Noureddin to Aladdin' correspondence with Oehlenschläger, whose *Aladdin* had appeared in 1805, lost him much of the influence which he had won. Still, B.'s fame rests securely on his brilliant specimens of light, satiric verse.

Baïf, de, -i. Lazare (1485-1547): Fr. poet; ambassador at Venice; priest. Transld. Gk. plays into Fr.: Sophocles, *Electra*, 1537; Euripides, *Hecuba*, 1544. The translns. were enthusiastically received, and paved the way for the dramatic experiments of the Pleiad (q.v., and see s.v. Jodelle).

-ii. **Jean Antoine** (1532-89) : Fr. poet ; member of the Pleiad constellation ; natural son of above. Like his father, he was a translr. from Gk. and Lat. dramatists, and composed an original Plautine comedy, *le Brave*, 1567, adapted from *Miles Gloriosus*. Wr. collections of sonnets, love-poems, lyric verse, etc., in accordance with the prevailing fashion of Ronsard's (q.v.) brigade, under titles of *Amours* of Méline, 1552, of Francine, 1555, *Mimes, Passe-temps*, and so forth. B. was by temperament a scholar even more than a poet, and his main activity was devoted to the work of an Academy (q.v.) which he founded in Paris, with the approval of the court and univ. Its object was ' de renouveler l'ancienne façon de composer des vers mesurés pour y accommoder le chant pareillement mesuré selon l'art métrique '. The quantitative metres of ancient poetry, to the measures of which modern Fr. lyric verse was to be adopted, according to the pattern of this professional creed, were so wholly unsuited to the genius of the Fr. language, that the founder's principle hardly outlasted its pronouncement, and B.'s Academy was short-lived. Rhyme was added almost immediately to the experiments in Fr. hexameters, elegiacs, etc., which he inaugurated ; and with the return of rhyme the classical principle was given away, and the bottom was knocked out of B.'s argument. The controversy which arose was important, especially in Engld., in connection with the formation of the Areopagus (q.v.) Academy by Harvey (q.v.) on similar lines, and its effect on contemporary poets.

Bailey, Philip James (1816-1902) : Engl. poet ; wr. a philosophical poem, *Festus*, 1839, which challenged comparison with Goethe's (q.v.) *Faust*, and which enjoyed a longer vogue than even its length entitled it to. Perhaps it intimidated our grave fathers, and B.'s habit of continually increasing it (from about 10 to about 40 thousand lines) was certainly formidable. But despite some excellent passages of poetry, computed by Walker (*Lit. Vict. Era*, 347) at a tenth of the tenth which is ' good ', *Festus* is doomed to oblivion. Its repeated revision was as inevitable as fate, and B. was very inconsistently counted among the writers of the Spasmodic (q.v.) school.

Balbuena, de, Bernardo (1568-c. 1625) : Span. poet ; divine ; bp. of Porto Rico, 1620. Wr., 1608, *Siglo de Oro* (' the Golden Age '), a pastoral romance, in the manner of Sannazzaro (q.v.), which was reprinted, 1821, by the Span. Academy. Wr., too, 1624, *el Bernardo*, an heroic epopee in about 45,000 lines, after the model of Ariosto (q.v.), and dealing with the victory at Roncesvalles. Somes of B.'s works were destroyed in the Netherlands, 1625, but his name stands high in the list of the Italianate school of Span. writers.

Balde, Jakob (1603-68) : Germ. sacred lyrist ; Jesuit ; court-preacher at Munich. B.'s verse was composed exclusively in Lat., and had a mystic element of devotion, which was not without influence on the Pegnitz Shepherds (q.v.) and on the stronger imagination of Gryphius (q.v.).

Baldi, Bernardino (1553-1617) ; It. poet. Wr. didactic poem, *Nautica*, in blank verse, of very modest value.

Ballad : A form of lit., common to all countries, defined by prof. Saintsbury (*First Bk. Engl. Lit.*, 258) as ' a short poem, generally with some story in it. The special " ballad "-also called " common "- measure is a four-lined stanza, the first and third lines, which have four iambic feet, being sometimes, and the second and fourth, which have three, being always rhymed together '. There are metrical variations (see s.v. Poulter, e.g.), but the 6-line stanza of Chaucer's (q.v.) *Sir Thopas*, for example, is not strictly a ballad-measure, though sometimes included in that form of lit., but is properly known as the romance-six : its rhyme-scheme is *aab, aab*. W. H. Hudson (*Intro. to the Study of Lit.*, 1910, p. 136) defines the B. as a ' short story in verse ; a form which appears to have arisen spontaneously in almost all literatures, and represents one of the earliest stages in the evolution of the poetic art '. Prof. W. P. Ker, in a paper read at the Royal British Academy, 15 Dec., 1909, admitted at once, that, ' at the beginning one is met by the trouble of definition. " Ballad ",' he went on, ' is here taken as meaning a lyrical narrative poem (all ballads are *lyrical* ballads*), either popular in its origin, or using the common forms of popular poetry, and for oral circulation through the whole of a community '. Still keeping close to the authority of Ker, we may go back to the word ' spontaneously ' (a form which appears to have arisen spontaneously in almost all literatures) in Mr. Hudson's definition above. The great ballad-collections of Europe display many points in common, alike of subject, treatment and metre, and are alike too in concealing the secret of their ' spontaneous ' orig. Like Topsy in the story, they may have ' growed ' ; but ' one of the difficulties about the ballads is that while so much in them seems to be ancient or even primitive, the rhyming ballad verse is comparatively new. Some of the common ballad devices, particularly that of repetition, seem to be as old as anything in humanity, and a large number of ballad subjects are no less widely spread. But the form of verse is not old. In the Teutonic languages, the first appearance of the new rhyming measures can be roughly dated ; they can hardly be older than the eleventh century. How did the folklore themes, the ballad habits of phrasing, find expression before the rhyming stanzas and the new sort of refrains were introduced from France ? Where were the ballads before they were made ? ' (Ker, *loc. cit.*). To this question ' there is no definite answer to be given ', and we must leave it there, noting only ' what is proved by the older Teutonic poetry, especially by the Anglo-Saxon, that an old civilization with an elaborate literature of its own came to an end in the eleventh century, and that there is a great division about that time between the earlier and the later Middle Ages, and great difficulty in understanding the transition.

* The reference is to *Lyrical Ballads*, by Wordsworth and Coleridge (qq.v.), 1798.

Modern poetry, including the ballads, begins about the year 1100 ; we are cut off from the time before that, and from its tastes in poetry, as we are not from any of the rhyming poetry —French, Provençal, Italian, German, English —from that time onward ' (*ib.*).

Denmark is the chief home of the B., as a separate poetical form, ' which can take up any matter, and does not leave the matter as it was before. . . . The ballads' (Ker, *ib.*) ' are not merely a limb of the great medieval body of romance ; they are a separate form ', and the lyrical beauty of the B. is different from the beauty either of epic poetry or of the longer sort of romantic tale. The great Danish collection is by S. Grundtvig (q.v.), whose 5 vols. of *Danmarks gamle Folkeviser*, 1853-90, was continued after 1895 by A. Olrik. The first Germ. authority was Uhland (q.v.), and Engld. possesses in the *Engl. and Scot. Popular Ballads* by F. J. Child, 5 vols., 1882-98, as valuable a collection as any. Count Nigra and others in France, Menéndez de Pelayo in Spain, A. D'Ancona in Italy, with Lockhart's (q.v.) *Spanish Ballads* on the bridge to Engld., are also to be mentioned with honour. (See s.v. Romance, Span.).

The passage from the primitive B. to the artificial B. (or, more strictly, since all extant specimens are artificial, from the primitive to the modern B.) was due mainly to the influence, in Engld. and on the continent of Europe, of the *Reliques of Ancient English Poetry*, 1765, the immense vogue of which is discussed s.v. bp. Percy. The Border ballads of sir W. Scott (q.v.), reviving the Robin Hood cycle in the south, were followed at no long distance by the ballads on various topics of Aytoun, Macaulay, Kingsley, Hawker (qq.v.) and others, down to Mr. G. K. Chesterton in the present cent. They led, too, to the humorous B.-lit. illustrated by Barham (q.v.) particularly ; and the exploration of the material led again to a new kind of lit. in such pieces as *The Revenge* of Tennyson (q.v.) and *Hervé Riel* of R. Browning (q.v.).

Ballade (Fr.): descriptive name of a class of medieval Fr. songs, developed in N. France in the 14th cent. out of models imitated from the Troubadours. The b. consisted of 3 stanzas with, later, an *envoi* (employed, e.g., by Deschamps, but not by Froissart, qq.v.). The last line of each stanza (8 to 11 lines) is the same (refrain), and the rhymes are repeated in sound and order. The b. has been traced back to a certain Nicole de Margival, who wr. a ' dit de la Panthère ' between 1290 and 1328, and it retained its extraordinary popularity and its fixity of form till the end of the 17th cent. in France, where its greatest practitioner was Villon (q.v.). It has been compared in popularity to the sonnet (q.v.), which was the prevailing mode at the Renaissance. Thus, Deschamps (q.v.) is said to have composed as many as 1,374 ballades, and a vol. of 100 *Ballades* was produced at the court of king Charles vi of France. The Pleiad (q.v.) scorned it, and Boileau (q.v.) contemned it. Molière (q.v.) in his *Femmes Savantes*, placed it contemptuously on a level with madrigals and other trivalities : ' la Ballade à mon gout est une chose fade ',

and *fade* it remained till its revival by Theodore de Banville (q.v.) in the 19th cent. The b. has never flourished in Engld., though it was cultivated by Chaucer (q.v.), and there are several hundreds of medieval specimens, —curiously enough, mostly without the *envoi*. There was an artificial *ballade*-cult in the late seventies of last cent. in Engld. by Swinburne, Henley, R. L. Stevenson, A. Dobson, A. Lang and E. Gosse.

Ballanche, Pierre Simon (1776-1847): Fr. wit ; philosopher. Wr. an essay on social institutions, and other works, including prose-poems on Antigone and Orpheus, in which, not unlike Landor (q.v.), he made the old legends the vehicles of his new thought. B. was a welcome guest at the *salon* of mme Récamier (q.v.).

'Ballette' (Fr.): descriptive name of a class of medieval dance-songs, commonly with a love-motive ; the modern ballet is obviously descended from it.

Balzac, de, Honoré (1799-1850): Fr. novelist. B. started life as a notary's clerk and was afterwards associated with a printer's works ; but his genius, applied to business, outran commercial bounds, and B. contracted large debts and even larger ambitions. For some years he wr. novels anon., in the hope of making money ; his first conspicuous success was *les Chouans*, 1829, followed by *Physiologie du Mariage*, to both of which he put his name. From this date B. was launched on the favour of novel-readers and editors of feuilletons, and his output, in the current phrase, was enormous, amounting to 15 or 16 full-size novels, and at least 30 short stories, apart from the stream of journalism, between 1829-33. The critics describe him as a realist, but the vexed question of classification need not concern us overmuch. He was as much and as little a realist as Dickens (q.v.), who had many points in common with B. Both drew types instead of characters, which, technically, is an idealist's trait, and both were realists as towards outward things ; their circumstantial evidence was scrupulously exact. It is true that B. bridges the transition from the romantic Fr. fiction of the 1830 movement to the naturalism of the next generation ; but his grandiosity, his excesses, and his taste belong to the earlier strain. There is something monstrous about B., though he could be pathetic in places, and the monstrous is never natural. His faults and virtues, his physical aspect, his industry, and even his capacity for *amours*, were all built on a Gargantuan pattern. But his care in writing was displayed in the *Contes drolatiques*, a clever but unpleasant experiment in tales after Boccaccio's taste and in the Rabelaisian manner ; and it is plain that he must have used immense pains to produce so many bks. in 20 years. Success and a wealthy marriage released him from toil too late. B.'s ambition is displayed in the general title which he chose (c. 1842) to describe his publd. and to-be written works. He called them *la Comédie Humaine*, and divided it portentously into *Scènes de la Vie Privée* (including *Père Goriot*), *Scènes de la Vie de Province* (including *le Lys dans la Vallèe*), *Scènes de la Vie Parisienne—Politique—Militaire—de Campagne*, and, lastly, *Études philosophiques* ;

an extraordinary edifice which he did not live to construct. B.'s best novels in common opinion are *Peau de Chagrin* and *Séraphita*, and he was a skilful writer of short stories. He is assured of permanent renown for the sake of his marvellous faculty of arresting certain selected aspects in the very life of the Paris of his day, and painting his reflection of them upon his many pages.

Balzac, de, Jean Louis Guez (1597-1654): Fr. essayist; original member of the Fr. Academy (q.v.), at which, however, he only put in a single appearance (during his last visit to Paris, 1636). Owing to his persistent seclusion, which, after a brief diplomatic career, dated from 1624, he was but a late and an irregular visitor at the Hôtel de Rambouillet (q.v.). Richelieu (q.v.) appointed him historiographer of France. B.'s chief works, which were not extensive, consist of his collected 'Letters' (i.e., dissertations), 1624; 'The Prince', 1631; and the 'Christian Socrates' (*Socrate Chrétien*), 1652; further essays were posth. publd. The critics all (and somewhat rarely) agree in calling B. the Malherbe (q.v.) of Fr. prose, so consistently did he devote himself to the science which he placed second only to theology—the science of oratorical prose-composition (*savoir écrire*). In this aim he was a follower of du Vair (q.v.), but it was far more in the deliberate spirit of Malherbe that B. sought to recover for Fr. lit. the sonorous phrase, Ciceronian rhythm, and imaginative dignity of diction, which he handed down embellished and enhanced. Infrequent as were his appearances in Paris, and careless as he was of appreciation, B. was enthusiastically adopted as a tutor and model by the precious (q.v.) stylists, inasmuch as by his own fastidiousness he reached the goal at which they aimed, and drew from the pure wells of the Fr. language the select refreshment of undefiled speech. He made no demands on erudition in his readers; no Grecisms or Latinisms were employed to paint his pages with a show of learning; and yet he introduced a cultured prose-diction, which Desmont (q.v.) had merely to perfect.

Bandello, Matteo (1480-c. 1562): It. writer of *novelle*: bp. of Agen, 1550, when he met and formed a close friendship with J. C. Scaliger (q.v.). B.'s last words are reported to have been *vivete lieti*, 'live merry'; and the report whether true or not, is true to the part which he played in the amusement of his age and of succeeding generations. He wr. several bks. of merry tales, after the Boccaccian model, which it is idle to condemn for their lascivious or licentious tone. In the history of letters in Europe, it is far more important to record that B.'s *Histoires Tragiques*, as they re-appeared, 1565, in the pages of François de Belleforest, and, again, 1567, in the *Tragical Discourses* of Geoffrey Fenton, did so re-appear in a Fr. and in an Engl. dress, and thus popularized and distributed the tales of one of the leading *novellieri* of the *cinque-cento*. 'No other Italian writer of that age had a wider influence outside his own country; none was more popular among Englishmen (though Ascham, q.v., was strongly against his influence). 'All the best stories in the 2nd

tome of Painter's *Palace of Pleasure* were taken from him, whilst Fenton's *Tragical Discourses* is entirely composed of translations of his tales. These "foreign reports", were soon known to all classes of our countrymen' (R. L. Douglas, Introduction to Bandello: *Tragical Tales*, Routledge, 1924).

Banville, de, Theodore (1823-91): Fr. poet; in the wake of Hugo (q.v.), but composed to a more level serenity, which took its emotions at secondhand, and was chiefly exercised with dexterity of craftsmanship. 'This delicate acrobat finished romanticism', says Lanson (*Lit. fr.*, 1059), though he adds, in a later note: 'I do not revise this judgment, but I might express it less harshly. After all, a poet is not compelled to think; and Banville is a genuine artist, whose place is important in the history of versification: that is something'. There is no appeal from this considered judgment, which is not contradicted by Saintsbury's statement (*P.E.L.*, xii, 51): 'There are more Muses than one, and M. de Banville was a favoured servant of more than one or two of the Nine'. B.'s works included: *Cariatides*, 1842; *Stalactites*, 1846; *Odelettes*, 1857, *les Exilés*, 1867; *Gringoire* (prose, 1866); *Ballades joyeuses*, 1873; *Socrate et sa femme*, 1885, etc., and a prose *Petit Traité* on versification, 1872, which is excellent. B.'s revival of ballade (q.v.) from pre-Renaissance Fr. models (e.g., Villon, q.v.) was a happy literary inspiration, which infected several major and minor poets in Engld., including Swinburne, A. Dobson and A. Lang (qq.v.).

Barbaro, Hermolao (1454-93): It. humanist. Friend of Mirandola (q.v.); regarded as foremost Venetian scholar of his day.

Barbauld, Anna Letitia (1743-1825): Engl. teacher and writer for children; *née* Aikin; m. rev. Rochemont B., 1774; started a school for boys at Palgrave, Suffolk; wr. *Hymns in Prose for Children*, and kindred works, including a poem, 1811, on which the New Zealander (in London) of Macaulay (q.v.) was based. Mrs. B., whose 'Eyes and No-eyes' has become proverbial, was a woman of learning, an admirer and imitator of Dr. Johnson (q.v.), a philanthropist and dissenter at a time of rather rigid conventions in thought, and exerted some influence in breaking down social and educational barriers. Manchester Coll., Oxford, the descendant of the Warrington Academy, with which her family were connected, contains a portrait of her in a window in the library.

Barbier, Auguste (1805-82): Fr. poet. B. survived his own reputation, founded (seemingly, imperishably) on his *Iambes et Poèmes*, 1831, which challenged comparison with Lamartine's (q.v.) first vol. of *Méditations*. B. denounced therein, with fierce indignation, the policy and manners of the times, and their devotion to *bourgeois* well-being; later came *Pianto*, inspired by Italy, *Satires et Poèmes*, etc.

Barcelona: Span. town in Aragon; a headquarters of the court; and subject from an early date to the refining influences of Provençal (q.v.) culture, despite the slight barrier of the Pyrenees. The crowns of B. and Provence were united in the 12th cent., and, at the time of the Albigensian crusade in the 13th, king Peter ii of Aragon died, 1213, as a champion of the Troubadours (q.v.). To him succeeded king James, surnamed the conqueror, who enjoyed the benefit of a chronicler, and who raised B. to a capital seat of culture and poetry. Gradually, the Provençal influence declined, under the joint kings of Aragon and Sicily, but John i, who reigned from 1387 to 1395, reverted to the earlier type ; and in 1390 he established at B. a consistory of the Gaya Sciencia (gay science of love ; see s.v. Gai saber), on the model of the Floral Games (q.v.) of Toulouse (q.v.), in accordance with an embassy which he had despatched to king Charles vi of France. Martin i (d. 1410), king John's successor, continued the privileges of B., but they were transferred at his death to Tortosa. But a few years later Ferdinand i, surnamed The Just, became king of Aragon and Sicily, and in his reign the ' consistory of the gay science ' was restored at the height of its splendour. The king himself attended its meetings, and its chief manager was the renowned don Enrique de Villena (q.v.), whose treatise on the *Arte de Trobar* (art of poetry) was intended to spread the institutions of B. through all Castile. B. now became a nest of singing-birds, and contributed considerably to the culture of the monarchy as a whole. Its importance is shown by the fact of its maritime and commercial greatness, and a little grammar, dated Barcelona, 1468, was the first bk. ever printed in Spain. B. finally yielded to Saragossa, and to the influence of Castile and the north of Spain.

Barclay, Alexander (*c.* 1475-1552) : Scot. satirist and translr. ; was largely instrumental in naturalizing certain types of contemporary foreign lit. in Engld. Edu. in Paris ; resided in Engld. ; held church preferments in Ottery St. Mary and Ely. Transld. *The Castle of Labour* from Fr. poem by Gringore (q.v.) ; wr. grammar of Fr. language ; transld. *The Ship of Fools* from Lat. and Fr. versions of the Germ. satire by Brandt (q.v.), employing the Chaucerian 7-line stanza, and extending the poem to more than twice its length in Lat., partly by an increased apparatus of proverbial wisdom and illustrative examples. Wr. *Eclogues*, chiefly from Lat. of Mantuan (q.v.) · and *Tower of Virtue and Honour*, after pattern of the *Temple d'Honneur* by Le Maire (q.v.). B.'s work was of considerable significance in the passage of Renaissance letters from northern Europe to Engld.

Barclay, Jean (1582-1621) : Fr. novelist ; of Scot. descent, and, like More (q.v.) and others, a writer in Lat. His Latinity was praised by H. Grotius (q.v.), and his style has been compared with that of Tacitus. B. resided in Engld. for some time at the court of James i. and is said on insufficient evidence to have grossly attacked that monarch and his predecessors, queen Elizabeth and king Henry viii, in a satire, *Corona Regis* ; more probably, his departure from London to Rome, where he died, was due to religious difficulties. Wr. 1603, satiric novel, *Euphormio*, which he may have lived to regret ; a narrative, 1605, of the Gunpowder Plot ; a school bk., 1614, *Icon Animarum* ; and, 1621, in Lat., his only

masterpiece, *Argenis* : transld., Fr., 1623, Ital., 1625 ; Span., 1626 ; Germ. (by Opitz, q.v.), 1626 ; Engl., 1625 ; Richelieu, Grotius and Leibniz (qq.v.) are named among eminent men who greatly esteemed and admired this work. *Argenis* is, in fact, a political *roman-à-clef* (q.v.), and, while the scene is laid in ancient Rome, and the incidents and adventures are imaginary, the personages can mostly be identified with actual historical characters, and act and talk according to their lights. Mauretania is Engld., Sicily is France, Sardinia is Spain ; Archombrotus is king Louis xiv ; Hyanisbe is queen Elizabeth ; Usinulca is Calvin (anagram of Calvinus), and so forth. Sorel (q.v.) criticized the novel adversely, and with many of his remarks on the anachronisms and the political doctrine a modern critic would be content to agree ; but the success of the work is, after all, the measure of its merits, and as a milestone in the development of fiction from pure romance to ideal character-study it deservedly takes a high rank.

Barditus : Lat. epithet attached by Tacitus to the battle-songs of the ancient Germans : ' They (the Germans) possess, too, a kind of songs, by whose recital, which they call *barditus*, they kindle their courage, and augur the issue of the impending fight from the song itself ' (Tac., *Germania*, iii). The derivation of the word is doubtful, but it is most probably not connected with the term ' bard ', or poet, its confusion with which gives it a place in the later annals of Germ. lit. For Klopstock (q.v.), in his patriotic dramas, assumed this false derivation, and called his plays *Bardiete*, or bardic dramas. These were composed directly under the influence of Macpherson's (q.v.) *Ossian* (Engl., 1762 ; Germ., 1764), and inspired a little crowd of imitators of no permanent worth.

Baretti, Guiseppe (1719-89) : It. journalist ; lived in Engld., 1751-60, and, again, after 1766. During the interval in Italy, B. publd. his *Frusta* (scourge) *Letteraria*, Venice, 1763-65, and Ancona, 1765. It was a periodical founded on the model of the *Spectator*, but far exceeding Addison's (q.v.) limit of the personal, and the objective of B.'s iconoclasm was the Arcadian Academy (see s.v. Arcadia), which survived the attack only in a much attenuated form. B. was a man of vehement character, not unlike in disposition to his friend and constant associate in Engld., Dr. Johnson (q.v.), with whom, too, he travelled in France. Wr. an Ital. and Engl. dict., bks. of travel, etc., and transld. *Rasselas*. In 1769, he was tried for murder at Old Bailey, and acquitted, the victim being a ruffian whom he had killed in self-defence. B.'s portrait was painted by another Engl. friend, sir J. Reynolds, and his name by a pleasant hospitality is included in the *D.N.B.*

Barham, Richard Harris (1788-1845) : Engl. humourist ; author of the *Ingoldsby Legends*, 1840 ; second and third series, 1847. Many had appeared originally in *Bentley's Miscellany* and the *New Monthly Magazine*. Prof. Saintsbury points out the source of the riotous, yet seriously based, fun of the *Legends* in Southey's (q.v.) *The Old Woman of Berkeley* and kindred pieces, and its development in

Hood and Praed, and even in Thackeray (qq.v.). B. ' was an active and by no means unclerical parson, as well as a not very successful novelist, before, at nearly fifty, he found the remarkable vocation which he obeyed, without a sign of impoverishment and exhaustion ', during the last years of his life. (See *C.H.E.L.*, xii, 122). Technically, these mock-ballads reached a high pitch of excellence ; the workmanship, esp. in the handling of rhymes and metres, is constantly surprising ; and pieces like *The Jackdaw of Rheims* enjoyed (and still enjoy) a very wide vogue. But ' there is a hard clank in Barham's verse, and his light is never softened with shade ' (Walker, *Lit. Vict. Era*, 331).

Barlaeus, Caspar (1584-1648) : Dutch Latinist : a distinguished scholar, whose daughter married Constantine Huygens (q.v.).

Barnave, Antoine Pierre Joseph Marie (1761-93) : Fr. revolutionary orator ; victim of the guillotine. Wr. *Discours sur le droit de paix et de guerre*, and took a prominent part in the events and eloquence of the Revolution. B. was one of the deputies of the States-General, charged with the escort of king Louis xvi from Varennes under arrest to Paris.

Barnes, William (1801-86) : Engl. poet ; ' the Dorsetshire poet ' ; son of a farmer ; schoolmaster ; rector of Came, 1862. B.'s importance in Engl. lit. consists in the fact that he was the first Engl. dialect poet (Scot. poetry is of course, excepted). He was an eager student of languages, and wr. a *Philological Grammar*, 1854, comprising no less than 60 languages. Like T. Hardy, q.v., who owed him a manifest poetic debt, B. is chiefly the poet of his own county, and it is likely that Tennyson (q.v.) was directed by B. to composition in rustic dialect. He publd. *Poems in the Dorset Dialect* in 3 series, 1844-58-63, collected, 1879 ; and a true serenity and tranquil wisdom are the pervading characteristics of his muse.

Baro, Balthazar (17th cent.) : Fr. novelist ; friend and secretary of Urfé (q.v.), whose unfind. *Astrée* he publd. as vols. iv and v from the author's MS. remains.

Baron, Michel (1643 or 1653-1729) : Fr. actor and comic dramatist ; more properly written, Boyron. B. was at first a member of Molière's (q.v.) company ; at his death, he joined the company formed, 1680, out of the Bourgogne, Palais Royal and Marais groups, into the Comédie Française (Théâtre Français) ; was a leading actor in his day, and wr., or adapted, or helped to adapt, for the stage several well-known comedies of manners, including *L'Homme aux Bonnes Fortunes*.

Baroque (**Barock**) : Germ. and Engl. critical term transferred from precious stones to architecture, sculpture and poetry. A *barocco* (Ital.) was a pearl of irregular shape, and baroque in the fine arts was used of a style which neglected rules of symmetry and harmony, and depended on surprise for its effects. Grimm (q.v.) defined b. as bizarre, and Germ. poetry in the 17th cent., the essential period of ' Barock ', was primarily bizarre (see s.v. Hoffmanswaldau, e.g.). Recently, however, critical acumen has discovered more than bizarrerie in b. lit., and the style is said to be derived from the painter Michelangelo (q.v.), and to ' represent nothing

less than the necessity of abandoning the struggle for harmony, that longed-for goal of the Renaissance ' (see *Die deutsche Lyrik des Barocks*. By Walther Unus, Berlin, Reiss, 1924). Thus, b. becomes less an epithet than a period and a style, and has an interesting parallelism, awaiting further exploration, with what Dr. Johnson (q.v.) called the ' metaphysical ' (q.v.) style in Engl. 17th cent. poetry : ' The metaphysical poets were men of learning, and to show their learning was their whole endeavour. . . . As they were wholly employed on something unexpected and surprising, they had no regard to that uniformity of sentiment which enables us to conceive and to excite the pains and the pleasure of other minds ' (Essay on Cowley) ; and Dr. Johnson's examples can be fairly matched out of the b. poets of Germany. The subject is too special for discussion in this bk., but we note the recognition by a Germ. critic, D. G. Morhof, writing in 1682, of ' the English practice of employing technical terms as metaphors, as we see in Donne ', which was a feature of the surprise-cult. Material for further study will be found in G. Waterhouse, *Literary Relations of England and Germany in the 17th Cent.* (Cambridge, 1914). See, too, s.v. Gongora.

Barrios, de, Miguel (1625-1701) : Span. poet ; Jew ; Port. by descent ; spent some years in Italy and others in the West Indies as a refugee from religious persecution ; served in Span. army, but retired to Amsterdam, 1674, where he was free to profess his own faith. B.'s works include 3 comedies, of which the best is ' The Spaniard of Oran ' ; poems, *Flor de Apolo*, and *Coro* (choir) *de las Musas*, Brussels, 1672 ; and he had planned a considerable poetic work to be entitled *Harmonia del Mundo*.

Barthélemy, Jean Jacques (1716-93) : Fr. scholar ; *abbé* ; *philosophe* (q.v.) ; employed his scholarship to popularize a knowledge of Gk. antiquity in *le Voyage du jeune Anacharsis en Grèce*, commenced, 1757, publd., 1788. This work took the form of an educational romance in 4 vols., and taught not merely history and sociology, but style, eloquence, and a love of liberty. It enjoyed a long vogue as a school-book.

Bartolus (1313-57) : Lat. name of Francesco Bonacursi, It. jurist ; wr. Lat. treatises important to the progress of juristic studies, ' on the borderland between politics, law, and theology ' (Figgis, *The Divine Right of Kings*, 2nd. edn., 345 ; who adds : ' Now, Bartolus— for we may include Baldus who depends on him—is the channel, or one of the main channels, through which this stream of tendency flowed into the modern life ').

Basedow, Johann Bernhardt (1723-90) : Germ. educationist. B.'s unorthodox writings on religious instruction (*Philalethia* and others) involved him in trouble with the authorities at Altona and Lübeck, but in all his somewhat versatile activities B. was moved by a genuine enthusiasm for a reform of the methods of education, and his ideas were deeply-founded on an intelligent study of Rousseau (q.v.). He succeeded in conciliating the good-natured interest of Goethe and Lavater (qq.v.) and the help of more influential patrons, and collected sufficient funds, 1776, to open a school at Dessau, known as the Philanthropinum, of which the (then revolutionary) principle was to treat children as children. Accounts of B.'s methods (see esp. Quick, *Educational Reformers*, 273ff.) read to-day like an anticipation of mme Montessori; in the manual and technical departments he built for the future. B.'s reign at the Dessau Institute was not long (' I would not trust him with the education of calves, much less of children ', wr. Herder), and he was succeeded by Campe (q.v.). B.'s interest to lit. is enhanced by the new children's bks. which his reforms evoked, and by the practical shape which he gave to the educational theorizing of his time.

Basel: Swiss city; Bâle; humanist centre in 15th cent.; its univ. was founded in 1460, and humane letters were promoted by Froben (q.v.) and other printers during the succeeding decades. Erasmus (q.v.) was attracted to B. by his friendship with Froben, and Rhenanus (q.v.), Erasmus's biographer, lived there till Froben's death.

Basoche (Fr.): the Palace of Justice in Paris, the clerks of which were banded together in an elementary dramatic academy, dating from the 15th cent. At first they confined their activities to morning and evening serenades 2 or 3 times a year before the heads of the court and parliament; later, 16th cent., they were definitely associated for the production of morality-plays. Baude (q.v.) was sent to prison for too much satire in his moral. The B. survived as a dramatic club till the period of the Fr. Revolution, though its functions had been gradually ceasing.

Bassompierre, de, François (1579-1646): Fr. memoirist; marshal of France; courtier; imprisoned by card. Richelieu (q.v.) in the Bastille, 1631-43, where he wr. *Journal de ma Vie*.

Batyushkov, Konstantin Nikolayevich (1787-1822): Russ. poet; ' he had tasted in Europe the fruits of the Tree of Knowledge, and when the Russian Ulysses came back from his wanderings, he did not recognize his Ithaca ' (Brückner, *Russ. Lit.*, 145). It was the fate of all aspiring youth in the Russia of emperor Alexander i, filled with the pestilential doctrine of Metternich (q.v.); and B.'s pessimism and melancholy were not due solely to the influence of Byron (q.v.), whom he transld., or to the slow progress of the painful illness from which he suffered. He was a true poet, and no mere journeyman practitioner, like Sumarokov and even to some extent Derzhavin (qq.v.). B. lived the poetry which he wr., out of a heart full of Ital. music; and in his ' Dying Tasso ' and other works he achieved a really notable advance in the suppleness and responsiveness of Russ. poetic diction before Pushkin (q.v.).

Baude, Henri (1430-95): Fr. satiric poet; wr. *rondeaux* and other verses of acute and penetrating observation. B. was imprisoned on one occasion for the too plainly satiric tendency of a morality-play.

Baudelaire, Charles (1821-67): Fr. poet; visited India: transld. the works of Edgar Allan Poe, and may be said to have derived from the visit his keener sense of touch and smell, to which critics direct attention, and, from the transln.,

the strain of weirdness, noted by Hugo (q.v.), and defined as the gift of ' a new shudder ' (*frisson*). The main *corpus* of B.'s work is contained in his *Fleurs du Mal*, 1857, suppressed for ' some pieces on subjects much better left alone ', and re-issued with additions, 1861. B.'s influence on later Fr. poets of the 19th cent. was considerable; and, while Lanson (*Lit. fr.*, 1060) rightly says that B.'s unique thought and feeling were the thought and feeling of death, Saintsbury (*Fr. Lit.*, 533) writes more analytically, that B.'s ' peculiar and extraordinary charm is due less to the formal merit of his verse, than to its strange expression of a mood, known at all times except the most prosaic, but especially frequent, it would seem, in the centuries immediately before and after the Christian era; . . . a mood wherein the keenest perception of material delights is combined with a constant tendency both to critical and mystical analysis both of passion and thought alike '. Saintsbury compares B. with Lucretius and Donne (q.v.). A nearer analogy may be found in Pater's (q.v.) *Marius the Epicurean*, whose attitude of ' Romantic despair ' towards experience and beyond is precisely in the higher mood of B.

Baudissin, von, Wolf (1789-1878): Germ. critic and translr.; count (*Graf*) by rank. Lived at Dresden in intimate friendship with Tieck (q.v.), and contributed a notable series of translns. of Shakespeare's dramas to the Schlegel-Tieck version. These included *Othello, King Lear, Henry viii, Antony and Cleopatra, Merry Wives*, and others, not comprised in the 17 by A. W. Schlegel (q.v.). Wr., too, ' Ben Jonson and his School ', 1836, and a transln. of Molière's comedies in the new national Germ. decasyllables in place of the Fr. alexandrine.

Baumgarten, Alexander Gottlieb (1714-62): Germ. critic; prof. at Halle (q.v.), the centre of 18th cent. rationalism, and taught under the auspicious signs of Wolff and Breitinger (qq.v.). Thus, B. was ranged on the side of the Swiss opponents to Gottsched (q.v.) at Leipsic, and his Lat. *Aesthetica*, 1750-58, proved a valuable weapon in the armoury of dawning romanticism, and, though unfind., introduced two good things: the naturalization on Germ. soil of the term Aesthetics (q.v.), for the science of the beautiful (he is credited with the invention of the term), and the insistence on sensuousness as a main ingredient of poetry. The treatise was put into Germ. dress by a pupil of B., and it maintained its place till the time of Kant (q.v.); Mendelssohn (q.v.) esp. developed on the psychological side B.'s definition of beauty as a mode of perfection.

Bayle, Pierre (1647-1706): Fr. lexicographer; he lays down in the pref. to his dict. a hard rule for later lexicographers: ' Entertainments, junketings, games, banquets, travelling, visits, recreations necessary to a number of students, according to their own statements, are not my business; I spend no time on them. I spend no time on domestic cares, nor in intrigue of any kind, nor in solicitation, nor in similar matters '. This detached attitude towards the commonplaces of life characterized the philosophy which B. cultivated, and is worth examining a moment in relation to the man and to his times. The epoch of king Louis xiv, in which he grew up, was filled, as we know, with wars of aggrandizement arising out of the wars of religion. To the diplomatists and the fighters, Mazarin and Turenne, for example, this state of existence was satisfactory enough ; by the precious (q.v.) aristocrats in their *salons*, compensation, adequate or ample, according to the degree of their aloofness, was sought in a deliberate obliteration of all that was harsh, and rude, and distracting ; others, such as Boileau and Racine (qq.v.), found their vocation in their art ; and nearer to or farther from the court-centre were the preachers, philosophers, satirists, and letter-writers—Bossuet, La Bruyère, La Fontaine, Sévigné (qq.v.), and hosts of others—who found life livable enough between the extremes of authority and revolt. B.'s place in this company was that of the rather weary spectator, too much exhausted by the clash of arms and opinions to take an active part in the *mêlée*, yet driven by an ardent curiosity for truth to investigate facts, to collect evidence, and, after summing-up with a partial bias towards the Manicheists (from Manes in the 3rd cent., A.D.), who believed in an Evil no less than a Good principle, to leave the jury of his fellow-countrymen to draw their own conclusions. These conclusions were mainly drawn in the 18th cent., of which B. is the most conspicuous forerunner, by a wider jury than the Fr. nation. B. supplied the *materia sceptica*, the philosophic vision of doubt, to Locke (q.v.) in Engld., Frederick (q.v.) ' the Great ' in Prussia, as well as to Voltaire (q.v.) in France, and to the schools and thinkers associated with these names. In the times in which he lived, this detachment, which reminds us of Gibbon (q.v.), was difficult to gain, and difficult to guard. B.'s Protestant orig. was followed by an early lapse to Romanism, from which he reverted to a nominal Protestantism. On these roads of speculation, he delivered himself of various pamphlets, including a letter on the comet of 1680, which supplied some material for the popular science of Fontenelle's (q.v.) ' Plurality of Worlds ' (1686), and two diatribes, 1686, on the revocation of the Edict of Nantes. In these B. maintained a fine attitude of liberal toleration, 3 years earlier than the publn. of the *Letters on Toleration* by Locke (q.v.). About the same time B. was engaged in the sole management of a monthly review, *Nouvelles de la République des Lettres*, 1684-86, which was among the earliest of its kind. Since 1681 B. had found a quiet refuge at Rotterdam, where, though his opinions lost him his State chair of philosophy, he remained till the end of his life. Correspondence was one of the few recreations which he permitted himself. His reputation and universal fame rest on his *Dictionnaire historique et critique*, 2 vols., 1697 (16 vols., Paris, 1820). The prime motive of this great work was to supply the lacunæ and to correct the errors in the dict. of Moréri (q.v.), 1674 ; but B., while he ranks as the founder of scientific biography, in a field where sir Sidney Lee is the latest Engl. exponent, utilized his opportunity to apply the leaven of rational research to the obstructions of superstition and tradition in the branches of science which he encountered in the course of his labours. His art. on David, e.g., earned him a pastoral rebuke at Rotterdam, and, eventually, the loss of his chair ; and if he cannot be called the father of the Higher Criticism (its paternity might even be ante-dated to Roger Bacon, q.v.), B. certainly laid the foundations for the comparative methods which wrought so much destruction and re-construction in the 18th and 19th cents. His last years were much occupied with replies to the criticism and attack evoked by his views and statements. These, it may be noted, were for the most part contained in ample notes to the art. in his *Dictionnaire*, which marks, in one word, the transition from the rambling encyclopedias of the Middle Ages to the standard work of the Fr. Encyclopedists (q.v.).

Beast-Epic : see **Bestiary**.

Beattie, James (1735-1803) : Scot. poet ; philosopher ; met Gray, Johnson (qq.v.) and his circle. Wr. *Original Poems and Translns.*, 1761 ; *The Judgment of Paris*, 1765 ; *Essay on Truth*, 1770 (in reply to Hume, q.v. ; sir J. Reynolds painted B. with this bk. in his hand) ; *The Minstrel, or The Progress of Genius, a Poem*, 2 parts, 1771-4 ; essays, dissertations, religious and philosophic works. We may pass over the polemical and prose writings. In B.'s poetry, it is interesting to observe that, among several Spenserians (see s.vv. Shenstone, Thomson) in the 18th cent., who adopted the winding stanza and archaic diction partly in a spirit of parody, applying their big aims to lowly themes, B. was the first to imitate Spenser ' not in his allegory or antiquated dialect, which, though graceful in him, appears sometimes awkward in modern writers, but in the measure and harmony of his verse and the simplicity and variety of his composition. Antique expressions I have avoided ', he went on, ' admitting, however, some old words, where they seemed to suit the subject : but I hope none will be found that are now obsolete, or in any degree not intelligible to a reader of English poetry. To those who may be disposed to ask, what could induce me to write in so difficult a measure, I can only answer that it pleases my ear ' (Advt. to *The Minstrel*). Byron (q.v.) would have given the same reply : and, though B. did not completely carry out his own Spenserian law, yet he succeeded in using the master as a poets' poet. Saintsbury (*C.H.E.L.*, x, 155) remarks that *The Minstrel* ' has hills and vales and other properties of romanticism *à la Rousseau* ; suggestions of knights and witches and so forth in the manner of romanticism *à la* Percy. But the drawing is all watered-out sepia ; the melody is a hurdy-gurdy strum '.

Beaumarchais, de, Pierre Augustin Caron (1732-99) : Fr. dramatist ; Caron by birth, Beau-marchais by marriage, and *de* by purchase ; author of *le Mariage de Figaro*, produced at the Comédie Française, 27 April, 1784, and remarkable not merely for the gay insolence of its ridicule of the *ancien régime*, and for its supreme qualities of comedy in prose, but also for its meretricious success within 5 years of the Fr. Revolution. B. scandalized the audience which he captivated. All the heavy artillery of the Encyclopedia (q.v.), a large part of Rousseau's (q.v.) attacks on privilege and social inequality, and the ideas germinating in the public mind, were manufactured into bullets and arrows, which exploded and pierced with deadly effect from the lips of the graceless, impudent, witty, sinister Figaro, the valet-hero (see s.v. Gracioso) of the worldly play. B. was well qualified for the task which he undertook. The son of a clockmaker in Paris, with a strong faculty for mechanical invention, he had applied his talents to various financial operations, which landed him in sensational lawsuits. One of these was the occasion of his series of four *Mémoires*, 1773, concerning transactions with mme Goëzman and her secretary for an audience with the court official, Goëzman. The brilliant and scurrilous pasquinades took legal and literary Paris by storm. Finance, law, and aristocratic society were the scenes and subjects of the comedies which were as notorious as they were excellent in comic effect. B.'s first play was *Eugénie*, 1767, founded on an adventure in Spain (it was thus only by accident that Span. influence returned to Fr. drama), followed 1770, by *Deux Amis*. In 1775, appeared the *Barbier de Seville*, the first of the Figaro comedies ; the same characters were introduced in the *le Mariage de Figaro*, and, again, in *la Mère coupable*, 1792. The middle piece of the three was the most successful ; and not the least part of its cleverness was its characterization of the dramatic styles of earlier comedians : Scarron, Molière, Sedaine, Marivaux, Voltaire (qq.v.), and minor writers. B.'s wit united many elements of abundant and fluent humour ; and Brid'oison, the judge, who sings 'Tout finit par des chansons' is nearly as well known as Figaro himself. Both plays, *Barbier* and *Mariage*, have been set to opera ; the latter by Mozart.

Beaumont, Francis (1854-1616): Engl. dramatist; wr. *The Woman Hater*, a comedy, 1607, and other plays, and collaborated in a series of dramas with J. Fletcher (q.v.) between 1607 and 1613-16.

Beaurigout, J. (15th cent.): Conjectural Fr. author of *Journal d'un Bourgeois de Paris*, 1405-49 (q.v.).

Bebel, Heinrich (1472-1518): Germ. scholar of humble birth ; contemporary and friend of Erasmus (q.v.) ; taught at Tübingen. Wr. patriotic poetry, and contributed to the humanistic Lat. of his day. B.'s chief work was 3 vols. of Germ. *Facetiæ*, 1506-08, modelled on Poggio (q.v.).

Beccaria, Cesare Bonesana (1735-93): It. political philosopher ; marquis. Wr., 1764, treatise on 'Crime and Punishment' (*dei Delitti e delle Pene*), which exercised considerable influence on European humanitarian thought. B.'s advice was sought by Leopold, grand duke of Tuscany, in his reform of the criminal law, and the empress Catherine ii (q.v.) of Russia availed herself of B.'s treatise as well as of Montesquieu (q.v.) in preparing her instruction for a new code. His book was transld. into Engl., 1767, when a phrase of his (*la massima felicità divisa nel maggior numero*) was rendered 'the greatest happiness of the greatest number'.

Bentham (q.v.) adopted this formula and made it famous, but ascribed it erroneously to J. Priestley ; as a fact, it had already been invented, with a very slight verbal difference, a few years earlier, by Hutcheson (q.v.), though B. is not likely to have derived it thence. B. was a prominent member of the Societa del Caffè, founded at Milan, 1764, which introduced into Italy the teachings of Voltaire and the Encylopedists (see s.vv.). His daughter m. Manzoni (q.v.).

Beddoes, Thomas Lovell (1803-49): Engl. poet ; son of Thos. B. (1760-1808 ; M.D.) and Anna, sister of Maria Edgeworth (q.v.) ; a very fragmentary writer, but of rare excellence in some of his fragments, and interesting in his reversion to the mentality of the Germ. romanticists (Wackenroder or Tieck, qq.v., for example), acquired probably during periods of medical study (in his father's profession) in Germany. To this imaginative faculty, of which sir E. Gosse has written that B. displayed a ' precocious tendency to a species of mocking metaphysics ', B. wedded successfully a command of Elizabethan diction. A recent editor, Mr. Ramsay Colles (*Poems*, 1907) discovers the biological speculations of Haeckel and Herbert Spencer in passages of B.'s play, *Death's Jest-Book* (completed, 1826 ; publd. posth., 1850) ; but similar finds are made in Tennyson (q.v.) and other young poets of the early 19th cent., and this play may be marked as ' one of the earliest and most remarkable manifestations of the spirit of the rising generation ' (Walker, *Lit. Vict. Era*, 280). Wr., too, *The Bride's Tragedy*, 1819, and a posth. vol. of poems and fragments, 1851. Of B.'s lyric, *Dream-Pedlary* (' If there were dreams to sell '), which is not included in Palgrave's *Golden Treasury*, prof. Saintsbury writes : ' The author of such things attains to that small and disputed class of poets, who, including Sappho, Catullus, some medieval hymn-writers and a few moderns, especially Coleridge, have, by virtue of fragments only, attained a higher position than many authors of large, substantive and important poems '. B. died by suicide at Basel.

Behn, Aphra (1640-89): Engl. playwright and novelist ; *née* Amies or Amis (not Johnson, as stated, e.g., in *D.N.B.*, before the researches of Mr. Montague Summers, in the 6 vol. edn. by Heinemann and A. H. Bullen, 1915) ; m. rich Dutch merchant named Behn, but was left a widow after a year or two, and fell into poverty ; was employed by Engl. court as a spy in Antwerp ; got into debt, and went to prison ; was the first woman to support herself professionally by lit. Transld. Tallemant (q.v.) and others, and wr. some orig. verse in the loose Pindaric ode-structure of the period ; wr. comedies : *Forc'd Marriage*, 1671, produced at Duke's Theatre ; *The Rover, The Good Old Cause, The City Heiress*, etc., all clever, genial, and witty, in the style of the Restoration (q.v.) comedy, but marred by a note of immorality which turned the stomach of a later generation. Scott (q.v.) sent a set of Behn's works to a ' gay old grandaunt,' who returned it with the sage comment : ' Take back your bonny Mrs. Behn and, if you will take my advice, put her in the fire, for I found it impossible to get through the very first novel. But is it not a very odd thing that I, an old woman of eighty and upwards, sitting alone, feel myself ashamed to read a book which sixty years ago I have heard read aloud for the amusement of large circles, consisting of the first and most creditable society in London '. *Autres temps, autres moeurs* : but Mrs. B., in *Oroonoko* and other novels, excited a distinct influence on the fiction of St. Pierre, Chateaubriand, Fielding (qq.v), and later writers, and, despite her grossness of taste, showed a real command of character-study and vividness and reality in story-telling.

Belcari, Feo (1410-84): Florentine writer of lauds and sacred plays, the last-named including ' Abraham and Isaac ' (1449), the earliest *sacra rappresentazione* of which the date can be stated with certainty.

Bellamy, Jacob (1757-86): Dutch poet. Wr. patriotic and erotic poetry ; helped to form a literary society at Utrecht, the *dulces ante omnia Musæ.*

Belleau, Remi (1528-77): Fr. poet ; a star of the Pleiad (q.v.), the chief members of which were his pall-bearers. B.'s earliest contribution to the work of the brotherhood was his transln. of the poems ascribed to Anacreon (q.v.), of which H. Estienne (q.v.) had issued the *ed. pr.* in 1554. The Anacreontic measures and attitude towards experience were enthusiastically assimilated by the young poets. A like modesty distinguished B.'s subsequent work in his school ; his two more ambitious efforts were a comedy, *la Reconnue*, based on an episode in the civil war of 1562, and a rural medley entitled *Bergerie*, which contains one fine song, worthy of Ronsard's (q.v.) colleague, and inspired by the love of springtide, which was a common theme of the Pleiad and their successors.

Bellman, Carl Michael (1740-95): Swed. poet ; court-secretary of king Gustavus iii, but did not take his office seriously, nor did he conform with the Francophil tendencies of Swed. letters in his day. (The Swed. Academy was founded, 1786, on the model of the Fr.). B., ' the Swedish Béranger ' (q.v.), or ' the Swedish Anacreon ' (q.v.), as he has been called, was a lyric poet of wine and love, with the necessary melancholic undernote, and a writer of folksong and folkplays.

Belloy, de, Pierre Burette (1727-75): Fr. dramatist. Wr. the *Siège de Calais*, 1765, which enjoyed a *succès d'occasion*, and won the critical approval of Lessing (q.v.), and other patriotic (and, therefore, romantic) plays, and is memorable for his reform of the scenic appointments of the theatre, and for his anticipation of Mr. Bernard Shaw in his elaborate stage-directions.

Bembo, Pietro (1470-1547): It. stylist ; Ciceronian in his Lat., Petrarchan in Ital. style ; a prince of letters before he became a prince of the Church ; born at Florence ; learned Gk. from Constantine Lascaris (q.v.) and philosophy from Pomponazzi (q.v.) ; resided at courts of Ferrara and Urbino ; went to Rome, 1512, and became papal secretary to Leo x (q.v.); his official correspondence affords models of Ciceronian Latinity (see s.v. Cicero); its lapses into pagan imagery for Christian

theological figures being condoned by Catholic historians as printers' additions. Resided at Padua, 1521-37, when he returned to Rome as card. Meanwhile, B., had devoted his leisure to refined vice and scholarship ; collected MSS., pictures, medals, etc. (the Bembine MS. of Terence he inherited from his father) ; wr. dialogues, elegiac-verse, and other Ital. and Lat. poems, much admired by later humanists, and helped materially by his 3 bks. of *Prose della volgar Lingua*, 1525, to fix the diction of vernacular prose style in Italy. As historiographer of Venice, B. wr. in Lat. and himself transld. into Ital. a *History of Venice*, which was continued by Paruta (q.v.). B.'s name is of interest in lit., too, as one of the dialoguers in the *Courtier* of Castiglione (q.v.), where he talks on Platonic love, the theme of a youthful Ital. work, *Asolani*, 1505, which B. had dedicated to Lucrezia Borgia at Ferrara ; and as the subject of Castiglione's memorial idyl, *Alcon*, which served as model to Milton for his *Lycidas.*

Benedict (480-543): It. saint ; founded Western monachism, and established monastery on Mt. Cassino, near Naples. His *regula monachorum* is important to lit. by its inclusion of directions for the advancement of learning and the encouragement of study. This rule was faithfully followed by the Benedictines of later cents. The first home of the Order in France was at St. Maur, on the Loire, and the old abbey of St. Germain-des-Prés became a famous headquarters of religion and scholarship till it was suppressed, 1792. Its learned members included Achery and Mabillon (qq.v.), who edited the *acta* of the Order, and, incidentally, founded the science of hagiography. The abbey library was afterwards removed to Paris.

Benevieno, Girolamo (15th cent.): It. writer of ' laudi ' and ' novelle ' ; disciple of Savonarola.

Benoît of Sainte-More (12th cent.): Fr. romancer ; clerk ; born at Ste.-More, near Tours. Wr., c. 1160, in rhymed couplets of easy-flowing 8 syllable lines, extending to over 30,000, *Roman de Troie*, dedicated to queen Eleanor of Engld. B. based his romance, not on Homer (q.v.), but on alleged authentic records by Dares, a Phrygian, represented as besieged in Ilium, and Dictys, a Cretan besieger. Lat. versions of these Gk. tales, probably dating from 6th cent., were available with other texts, which B. turned to excellent account. His vast romance was a source-bk. to many writers, and its Lat. transln. by Guido delle Colonne (q.v.) introduced it to Boccaccio, who was followed by Chaucer and Shakespeare (qq.v.) in his use of B.'s episode of Briseis (Criseyde) and Troilus. B. is likewise reputed the author of the romance of Thebes, and was an inferior predecessor of Chrétien de Troyes (q.v.).

Benserade, de, Isaac (1612-91): Fr. poet ; a favourite of the *salons*, and conspicuous among the precious (q.v.) writers. B. began by composing feeble tragedies, but presently specialized in the *ballet*, or masque, which under king Louis xiv laid aside much of its original obscenity and was more or less consistently mythological and gallant. B. composed such *ballets* for about 30 years (1651-81); the best-known are 'Cassandra', 'Night', and 'The Triumph of Love'. He was also the rival of Voiture (q.v.) in a contest of sonnets, which lasted more than a year. B. had written a sonnet on *Job*, and Voiture one on *Uranie*, and the quarrel between the 'Jobelins' and 'Uranistes' engaged the literary factions of city and court, caused an enormous amount of ink and acrimony to flow, was referred in vain to the Fr. Academy (q.v.), and was finally decided in Voiture's favour by referees at the univ. of Caen.

Benson, Arthur Christopher (1862-1925): Engl. poet and essayist ; master of Magdalene Coll., Cambridge, 1915 ; son of Edward White B. (1829-96 ; archbp. of Canterbury, 1882), whose *Life* he wr., 1889. B., who publd. several vols. of poems (collected, 1909), and several critical and biographical monographs, including D. G. Rossetti, E. Fitzgerald, and W. Pater (qq.v.) in the *English Men of Letters* series, *Hugh : Memoirs of a Brother*, etc., and who was associated with second visct. Esher in editing *Selections from the Correspondence of Queen Victoria*, 1907, was chiefly notable for his command of a vein, almost inexhaustible, of pleasant, half-melancholy, reflective, cultivated meditation, displayed in a series of vols. which won him large numbers of readers and friends : *The Upton Letters*, 1905, *The Thread of Gold*, 1906, *From a College Window*, 1906, *At Large*, 1908, may be mentioned by name, but any name would have suited any of the bks., which have a rare and real charm. Sir H. Warren, president of Magdalen Coll., Oxford, writing to *The Times*, 17 June, 1925, drew attention to an important item in the list of B.'s writings : ' Dreamy, mystical, and recluse at times, he was yet the author of one poem which may well outlive all his others and that of many contemporaries. He wr. *Land of Hope and Glory*, to-day the anthem of the Empire '. The music of the anthem is by sir Edward Elgar, O.M. (b., 1857).

Bentham, Jeremy (1748-1832): Engl. jurist ; the first of the so-called Engl. Utilitarians, or ' Philosophical Radicals ', to whom Mill (q.v.), father and son, succeeded, B. being ' the founder and patriarch of the school ' (A. Seth Pringle-Pattison, *The Philosophical Radicals* ; Blackwood, 1907, p. 5). The birth of this school is dated 1769, ' when the conflict between Wilkes and the House of Commons was at its height ' (*ib.*, 9) ; and, in the light of B.'s Fr. studies and mastery of Fr., it is interesting to note that John Wilkes (1727-97 ; M.P., founded the *North Briton*, 1762, with C. Churchill, q.v.) received congratulations from Diderot (q.v.) on his campaign for parliamentary reform. This campaign developed into an attack on the British constitution as a whole, and esp. on the Crown and the House of Lords ; and abroad even more quickly than at home, B.'s schemes for a new penal law and for social re-construction in general found enthusiastic reception. Pierre Dumont (1759-1829), a Fr.-Swiss publicist, acted as a kind of propagandist for B. on the Continent, and D.'s *Traité de Législation de M. Jérémie Bentham*, 1802, carried his fame and name into all countries. B.'s meeting with J. Mill, 1808, led, with the help of sir Francis Burdett

(1770-1844 ; M.P., Westminster), to the foundation, 1824, of the *Westminster Review*, as the distinctively Benthamite organ of the new school. The titles of B.'s writings (11 vols., posth., 1838-43) are less important than their influence on social and political thought : he regarded ' self-interest, properly understood, as the most reliable motive, because he believed that self-interests, properly understood, are harmonious, so that the individual must necessarily be interested in the general welfare even for prudential considerations ' (Höffding, *Brief History of Modern Philosophy* ; E.T., 233). B.'s principle of ' the greatest happiness of the greatest number ' was suggested to him by a phrase in the *Essay on the First Principles of Government*, by J. Priestley (1733-1804 ; theologian and scientist ; his *History of the Corruptions of Christianity* was burnt by the common hangman, 1785) ; the famous phrase was of slightly prior orig., however ; see s.v. Beccaria.

Bentley, Richard (1662-1742): Engl. scholar ; master of Trinity Coll., Cambridge, 1700-42, though twice tried before successive bps. of Ely for despotic encroachments on his statutory powers. B. was a scholar of unrivalled attainments, and was hailed by Grævius (q.v.), with whom he maintained a constant correspondence as *novum sed splendidissimum Britanniæ lumen*. His contributions to classical learning do not directly concern us here : ' his work may be said to have opened a new chapter of humanism ' (Elton, *P.E.L.*, viii, 275) ; ' no greater intellect than his has ever been devoted to the study and elucidation of ancient literature ' (J. D. Duff, *C.H.E.L.*, ix, 340) ; and Sandys (*Hist. Class. Schol.*, ii, 401ff.) recalls that he ' left his mark on the textual criticism of Plautus, Lucretius and Lucan ', that he restored the *digamma* to Homer's text, and that his is ' the greatest name among the classical scholars of Europe in the first half of the 18th century '.

More general interest attaches to other aspects of this bold and great scholar's activities. Late in life, 1732, though several years earlier than his brilliant edn. of Manilius, B. edited Milton's *Paradise Lost*, at the express wish of queen Caroline. It was a task to which, temperamentally, he was as unsuited as his critical method was inappropriate and inadequate : Milton's blindness was not as productive of errors demanding conjectural restoration as the distance in time of classical authors ; and the enterprise is chiefly interesting in illustration of great gifts put to wrong uses. Pope (q.v.), who attacked B., partly on account of the Miltonizing, partly on general principles, as a ' scholiast whose unwearied pains Made Horace dull and humbled Milton's strains ' (*Dunciad*, bk. iv ; 1742), had a personal grievance to avenge, since B. said to him, after the publication of his transln. of the *Iliad*, 1720, ' that it was a very pretty poem, but that he must not call it Homer '. But Pope was right, and B. was wrong, about Milton. More important was B.'s intervention in the controversy about the *Letters* of pseudo-Phalaris, which started in a very modest way. The statesman-bookman, sir W. Temple (q.v.), wrote an essay, 1690, on *Ancient and Modern*

Learning, moved thereto by the contemporary quarrel *des anciens et modernes* in France, in which Boileau, Perrault and Fontenelle had taken part. (See s.vv. and s.v. Ancients and Moderns). Temple espoused the Ancients, and opined that ' the oldest books we have are still in their kind the best. The two most ancient that I know of in prose, among those we call profane authors, are Æsop's *Fables* and Phalaris's *Epistles* '. He remarked that ' several learned men (or that usually pass for such under the name of critics) ' had attributed the *Letters* to Lucian, but he esteemed ' Lucian to have been no more capable of writing than of acting what Phalaris did '. The puff of Phalaris, as it might be called to-day, coming from so distinguished a man (rather like Gladstone with his literary postcards in the 19th cent.) caused a demand for the *Letters*, which were re-edited, 1695, by the hon. C. Boyle (1676-1731 ; afterwards major-genl. the 4th earl of Orrery). Meanwhile, Wm. Wotton (1666-1726) had publd., 1694, a very moderate reply to Temple and his implications, in *Reflections upon Ancient and Modern Learning*, to the 2nd edn. of which, 1697, B. contributed a *Dissertation* on Æsop and Phalaris. B.'s masterly attack on the position which Boyle was holding for Temple aroused the Westminster dons of Ch. Ch., where Boyle had been educated, to the defence of the young scholar : ' though, in point of learning, they were children compared to Bentley, yet they were formidable antagonists at any bar of public opinion. They were wits and men of the world ; they had much influence in literary and academic circles ; and, though their erudition was meagre, they showed a marvellous dexterity in the use of what they had ' (*C.H.E.L.*, ix, 333) : their bk., 1698, bore Boyle's name, but was written chiefly by Francis Atterbury (1662-1732 ; bp. of Rochester, 1713). For some time, the honours lay with the Ch. Ch. faction : Swift (q.v.), resident at Moor Park as secretary to Temple, laughed at B. in the *Battle of the Books* (1697 ; publd. 1704), and sir Samuel Garth (1661-1719), a physician who wr. a poem *The Dispensary*, 1699, ' expressed his agreement with the prevailing sentiment of polite society ' in the couplet :

So diamonds take a lustre from their foil,
And to a Bentley 'tis we owe a Boyle.

But B.'s final *Dissertation upon the Epistles of Phalaris*, 1699, took no account of the sentiment of polite society. ' It is a work which marks an epoch in the History of Scholarship. It is an example of critical method, heralding a new era ' (Sandys, *op. cit.*, 405) ; and it ' showed two qualities besides, which are seen in all he wrote. One in his generalship as a scholar, his Napoleonic power of massing, from the whole of both classic literatures, all that bore on a point at issue. The other was his control of English ' (Elton, *op. cit.*, 276). It crushed the *Epistles*.

Two details of nepotism may be added. (1) The lord Orrery of this Phalaris-controversy was grandnephew to the hon. Robt. Boyle, (1627-91), the natural philosopher, who helped to found the Royal Society, and founded and endowed the Boyle lectures : the 1st Boyle lecturer under this endowment was Bentley himself (1692 ; *A Confutation of Atheism*). (2) B.'s youngest son, Richd. Bentley (1708-82) executed drawings to illustrate the poems of Gray, 1753.

Another Bentley family, descended from Thomas B., a partner to Jos. Wedgwood (1730-95), the potter, and including Samuel B. (1785-1868) and Richd. B. (1794-1871), Paulines, printers, publishers and brothers, was not related to R.B. above.

Benzelius, Erik (1675-1743) : Swed. scholar ; a missionary of humanism, 1697-1700, when he returned with his spoils from foreign univs. to Upsala, where he became librarian and subsequently archbp. Edited, 1708, *Characters* of Theophrastus, and contributed considerable material, afterwards utilized by canon Mangey of Durham (with very inadequate acknowledgment, we are told), for an edn. of Philo. B. founded, 1710, ' the first of the learned societies of Scandinavia ', *Collegium curiosorum* later (1742) under royal patronage *Societas regia Scientiarum Upsaliensis*. This society is to be distinguished from the Swedish Academy of Sciences, founded, 1739, at Stockholm by Linnæus (q.v.), of which B. was an original member.

Béranger, de, Pierre Jean (1780-1857) : Fr. poet ; writer of songs (*chansons*), of which successive vols. were publd., 1815, 1821, 1825, 1828, 1833 ; his posth. poems and biography were publd., 1857, and his letters, 1860. Twice, 1821, and 1828, B.'s songs earned him a fine and imprisonment (3 months and 500 fr. ; 9 months and 10,000 fr.), but on each occasion the prosecution increased his popularity, the second time to a remarkable degree. ' Tout finit par des chansons ' (see s.v. Beaumarchais) was a saying current in France in B.'s age, or a few years before it ; and B.'s function, admirably achieved, was to supply the touching or catching songs appropriate to the thought of his generation. ' In order to understand the songs of Béranger, we must not separate them from the public which sang them ', wr. Lanson (*Hist. Lit. fr.*, 969) in a postscript (11th edn.) to his earlier depreciation of B. as ' mediocre ' and ' irremediably vulgar ' ; a criticism answered (in advance of the recantation) by Saintsbury (*Hist. Fr. Lit.*, 484) : ' Béranger indeed was not in the least a literary poet. But there is room in literature for other than merely literary poets, and among these Béranger will always hold a very high place '. B. has been compared with Burns (q.v.), and there are obvious likenesses ; but a later generation had the opportunity of comparing him more justly with Kipling, who also found depreciation in the words Lanson first applied to B. : ' il a une philosophie et une sensibilité de café-chantant '. A music-hall poet, perhaps ; but there are busy times in a nation's life and thought when the songs to which the ' halls ' supply a chorus wake echoes in statesmen's acts ; and B.'s liberalism and Buonapartism (like the Imperialism of Kipling) had their worthy objects to fulfil.

Berceo, de, Gonzalo (*c.* 1180-*c.* 1247) : Span. poet ; priest ; the earliest known name in the roll of Span. poetry. B. wr. poetic lives of saints and other sacred ' histories ', conscientiously based on definite authorities, and comprising, it is said, about 13,000 lines of verse. Since his restitution to the canon of poetry towards the middle of the 18th cent., B. has been compared with Dante, a comparison as much in excess of his merits as the previous neglect was below them. A *Libro de Alixandre* (see s.v. Alexander) in about 6,000 lines was also ascribed to B., but later critics are disposed to dispute the ascription.

Bergerac, de, Cyrano (1619-55): Fr. romancer. The surname, Bergerac, was taken by Savinien Cyrano from the town in which he was edu.; his personal character, which was striking and effective, was displayed on the stage by M. Rostand, *Cyrano de Bergerac*, 1897; his literary achievement is characterized in the following terms by Lanson (*Lit. fr.*, 388, i): ' One need but examine the eccentric and fantastic work of Cyrano de Bergerac to see how all modes, from the heroic to the burlesque, of falsifying nature can be contained and united in one man of talent '. It should be added that B. died young after a career of wildness and adventure, when his gifts were still immature. He wr. a long-winded comedy in prose, the *Pedant joué*, 1654; a tragedy, or, more strictly, a melodrama, *La Mort d'Agrippine*, and letters, satires, etc. The comedy gave some hints to Molière (q.v.), but B.'s chief work was composed in the realm of Lucianic and Rabelaisian fiction (and perhaps served to inspire Swift, q.v.), and consisted of a series of romances, collected together under the title of *Histoires Comiques des Etats et Empires de la Lune et du Soleil*. The most adequate collation and edn. of these writings is that compiled by P. L. Jacob (Paul Lecroix, 1806-84); Paris, 1858. Campanella, Ariosto (qq.v.) and others may be added to the sources of the fantasy, and Jules Verne (q.v.), among others, to its tributaries; and B. is recognized to to-day as a founder and brilliant expositor of the fiction of planetary travel, with its immense opportunities for satire, humour, and ingenuity.

Berkeley, George (1685-1753): Irish (Engl.) philosopher; edu. Trinity Coll., Dublin; came to Engld., 1713, and associated with leading men of letters of the day; lecturer and fellow, Dublin, again, 1717-24, when he returned to Engld. and visited America, seeking funds for a missionaries' coll. at Bermudas for the conversion of the Indians and the spread of science and art in the West; bp. of Cloyne, 1734-52, when he retired to Oxford, where he died. Wr., among other works, the famous treatise concerning *The Principles of Human Knowledge*, 1710, which aimed at refuting the conclusions of the new science, so far as they were hostile to the conclusions of religion, and by which B. takes a place in the hist. of empirical philosophy in Engld. similar to that of Leibniz (q.v.) abroad. ' He represents a reaction against Locke and Newton similar to that of Leibniz against Descartes, Hobbes and Spinoza, and, like Leibniz, Berkeley, not only represents a reaction, but an advance and further development ' (Höffding, *Brief History Modern Philosophy*, E.T., 98; see also s.vv. ' Childlike piety and acute critical analysis ', adds Hoffding, ' have seldom been so intimately united as in this clear mind '). B.'s polemic

against the Free Thinkers, helping to form a link between Locke and Hume (q.v.), was developed in 2 ' beautiful and ingenious ' (*ibid.*) dialogues : *Hylas and Philonous*, 1712, and *Alciphron*, 1732.

Bermudez, Geronimo (*c.* 1530-90): Span. dramatic poet. Wr., 1577, 2 dramas which he chose to entitle, ' First Spanish Tragedies : Nise the Pitiful (*lastimosa*) and Nise the Triumphant (*laureada*)'; they were publd. under the name of Antonio de Sylva. The *Nise lastimosa* is transld. (with a transparent anagram of the name) from the *Inez de Castro* of Ferreira (q.v.), the Port. poet; and B's own second piece has no further merit.

Bernagie, Pieter (1650-99): Dutch comic dramatist; physician; his plays were acted at Amsterdam for over a cent. with undiminished popularity. B. belonged to the age and the school of Asselyn (q.v.). He was director of the Amsterdam Theatre from 1688 till his death.

Bernaldez, Andrés (fl. 1500): Span. chronicler; curate at Los Palacios, near Seville, 1488-1513. Wr. a chronicle of those years in 144 chapters, entitled ' history of the Catholic kings don Ferdinand and donna Isabella '; chiefly remarkable for chapters 118-131, referring to Columbus (q.v.), who visited B. in 1496 and lent him MSS., of which he availed himself for this work.

Bernard, Claude (1813-78): Fr. physician; professor at the Collège de France. Wr., 1865, *Introduction à l'Etude de la Médecine experimentale*, which had a profound effect upon scientific thought and contemporary philosophy; and, 1878, *la Science experimentale*. B. is to be reckoned among the founders of naturalism (q.v.) in France; his conclusions were utilized by men of letters much in the same way as Darwin's (q.v.).

Bernard, de, Charles, pen-name of Pierre Marie Charles Bernard du Grail de la Villette (1805-1850): Fr. novelist. *Gerfaut*, 1838, is the best-known of his many novels, which are said to have exercised some influence on Thackeray (q.v.).

Berners, lord (1467-1533): John Bourchier, 2nd baron : Engl. translr. B.'s life as diplomatist and statesman was spent chiefly in France, where he was governor of Calais (q.v.) and was present at the Field of the Cloth of Gold. Transld., 1523-25, *Chronicles* of Froissart (q.v.); *Huon de Bordeaux*, *c.* 1530, thus supplying Shakespeare with the fairy-scenes in *Midsummer Night's Dream* (see s.vv. Huon, Oberon); and *Golden Book of Marcus Aurelius*, 1532, from Fr. version of original by Guevara (q.v.). Engl. lit. owed a large debt to B. for his importation of the fruits of Fr. culture, and it is to be noted that, in the prologue to his Froissart, 1524, B. wr. euphuistic prose 5 years earlier than the Span. *Dial of Princes*, 1529, from which Euphuism (q.v.) has sometimes been dated. (See, too, s.v. North).

Berni, Francesco (1490-1536): It. burlesque-poet; gave his name (Bernesque) to the style, not particularly exalted, of which he was master. Wr. a re-fake (' rifacimento ') of the *Orlando Innamorato* of Boiardo (q.v.), which so cleverly hit off the taste of his countrymen for more braggart chivalry than Boiardo's with an

undertone of mockery, that it took the place
of its original in the estimation and memory of
readers (see also s.v. Ariosto, who really
achieved what Berni attempted). Wr. Lat.
verse, including invective launched at Aretino
(q.v.), whose indecencies, however, B.
equalled in his Ital. *capitoli*, in which he is
credited (or debited) with the introduction of
'the snigger into literature' (Saintsbury,
P.E.L., v, 153): a title to fame which we
need not explore further, at least in this early
example of a particularly nasty kind. B.
is in the line of the burlesque-satirists (see
s.v. Pulci, e.g.), from whom the *Beppo* and
Don Juan of Byron (q.v.) descended.

Beroaldo, -i. Filippo (1453-1505): It. Latinist.
Born at Bologna, and held chairs of learning
in several Ital. cities. Wr. love-verse, anticipating Secundus (q.v.), but far behind his successor in depth of feeling and sincerity of
expression; industrious editor of Roman
classics; correspondent of Politian (q.v.).

  -ii. Filippo (1472-1518): It. Latinist;
nephew of above. Publd. at Rome *ed. pr.*
of Tacitus, 1515. Erasmus (q.v.) met both
scholars during his Ital. journey.

Berryer, Pierre, Antoine (1790-1868): Fr. orator;
the 'Cicero of the bar'. B.'s works in 9 vols.
were publd., 1872-78.

Bersuire, Pierre (died, 1362): Fr. early humanist.
Priest; met Petrarch (q.v.) during his visit
to Paris. Transld. extant bks. of Livy, and
effected 'moral' rendering of Ovid's *Metamorphoses*.

Bertaut, Jean (1552-1611): Fr. poet; a disciple
of the Pleiad (q.v.); lived into the era of the
temporary eclipse of Ronsard's (q.v.) star;
bp. of Séez. It has been suggested that B.'s
fame has been unduly exalted by Boileau's
(q.v.) need of a rhyme to 'haut' in lines
129-30 of his *Art Poétique;* 'Ce poète orgueil-
leux, trébuché de ci-haut, Rendit puis retonus
Desportes et Bertaut'; the 'poète orgueil-
leux' of Boileau's epigram was Ronsard
(q.v.), but neither his fall restrained Bertaut,
nor was Bertaut ever aware of it. B. was a
very moderate practitioner of Pleiad lyrical
metres, tending rather to convention than
to originality, and plainly indicating the
cessation of the stream which had its flood-
time at the date of his birth; one of his most
attractive poems is in the 4-line stanza which
Tennyson (q.v.) adopted for *In Memoriam*.

Bertrand, Louis (1807-41): Fr. poet. Wr.
Gaspard de la Nuit, a series of prose-poems,
posth. publd., which testify to the high
imaginative gifts, prematurely closed, of this
writer; his genius had obvious affinities to
that of Baudelaire (q.v.).

Besant, Walter (1836-1901): Engl. novelist;
knt.; wr., in collaboration with Jas. Rice
(1843-82) *Ready Money Mortiboy*, 1872, *The
Golden Butterfly*, 1876, and other successful
novels, and, by himself, chiefly *All Sorts and
Conditions of Men*, 1882, which led to the
foundation of the People's Palace (now E.
London Coll., a school of the univ. of London)
in Stepney. B.'s works on the history and
topography of London also enjoy a partially
unexhausted vogue. Like Dickens and G.
Meredith (qq.v.), B. was a native of Portsmouth.

Beskow, Bernard (1796-1868): Swed. poet;
equally celebrated in his day as dramatist,
critic, biographer, historian and philosopher.
It is in the first of these capacities that B. is
best remembered to-day, by virtue of, chiefly,
his national plays *Thorkel Knutsson*, 1830,
and *Erik xiv*, 1826.

Bessarion (1403-72): Gk. theologian, philosopher
and patron of learning. Attended the Council
of Florence (1439) as archbp. of Nicæa; was
made card. by pope Eugenius iv, and resided
at Rome accordingly, where his palace was a
meeting-house of scholars, and afforded an
early refuge for his learned fellow-countrymen
before and after the fall of Constantinople
(1453). B. upheld the teachings of Plato
against attacks by George of Trebizond (q.v.)
and others, in the long-winded polemic of
the day, and issued *in Calumniatorem Platonis*
(1479); but 'throughout all the tangles of this
complicated controversy a thread of gold is
inwoven by the serene and imperturable temper
of Bessarion' (Sandys, *Hist. Class. Schol.*,
ii, 75). He was an eager collector of MSS.;
edited the Gk. text of Ptolemy, which was
utilized by Regiomontanus (see s.v. Müller),
the eminent Germ. astronomer; and gave
his library (about 600 vols.) to Venice (1468),
where it formed the nucleus of the subsequent
Library of St. Mark's.

Besser, von, Johann (1654-1729): Germ. poet
and critic; an opponent of the Second Silesian
School (q.v.); of the same uninspired and
uninspiring order as Canitz (q.v.); held
appointment of laureate at several minor
Germ. courts.

Bestiary (Bestiaire) Beast-epic: a form of
allegorical or fabulous poetry of the Middle
Ages, satirizing human beings under the guise
of animals; the chief branch was definitely
shaped in 12th and 13th cents. into the various
versions of the romance of Reynard (q.v.)
the fox (*Roman de Renart*). Technical details
apart, it is clear that to observe the habits of
animals and to apply the results of such
observation to the manners of men form an
alimentary exercise of imagination well within
the capacity of the youngest of us, and, therefore of the most primitive people. The slyness
of the fox, the sleekness of the cat, the courage
of the lion, the industry of the ant, have been
available always and everywhere to typify
good and evil qualities. Accordingly, animal-
fables, the basis of literary *bestiaires*, have
been current from the earliest times; in India,
in the 'Buddha Birth-tales', the Fables of
'Bidpai', and the 'Panchatantra'; in
Greece, in the collection made by Æsop, a
Samian slave; in Rome, in the collections of
Phædrus and Babrius, an Engl. version of
whose fables was used by Marie de France
(q.v.) for her vol. called *Ysopet* (little Æsop).
Other source-bks. and derivatives include,
Aristotle (q.v.), the *Natural History* of Pliny
the Elder (fl., A.D. 70), the *Books of Secrets* of
Albertus Magnus, and early poems by Philip
of Taon and William the Clerk. But the main
repository for medieval fabulists in this class
of lit. was the vast series of so-called *Physiologi*, a kind of sacred natural histories, in
which the sacred element took precedence of
the natural, devised to inculcate Christian

virtues through observation of animal life. These collections, probably derived from an Egyptian *physiologus*, were repeated in all parts of the Orient and Eruope, and were reinforced by 'lapidaries', 'volucraries', and 'herbaries', dealing with the moral qualities of precious stones, birds, and herbs; and these diversions of learning—this vast mass of material, allegorizing the non-human universe under the aspect of morality, with the infinite play it afforded to the ingenuity, allusiveness, and mysticism of its compilers—reappeared, through various ascendants, in the *Euphues* of Lyly (q.v., and see also s.vv., Steinhöwel, Gay, Casti).

Beyle, Henri, See **Stendhal.**

Bèze (Beza), **de, Theodore** (1519-1605): Fr. Calvinist scholar; succeeded Calvin (q.v.) as head of Geneva, where his house was for 40 years a place of rest and call for sympathetic visitors and travellers. B.'s drama, *Abraham Sacrifiant*, acted at the univ. of Lausanne, 1551, is one of many similar plays at the transition from mystery to classical drama. More notable and congenial was his *Histoire ecclésiastique des Eglises Réformées*, 1580. His 'Christian Meditations upon 8 Psalms' were transld. into Engl., 1582, and dedicated to lady Bacon by the author, whose relations with Engl. churchmen and scholars were intimate and cordial. He presented a *Codex Bezae* of the Gk. Testament to Cambridge Univ., and sent queen Elizabeth a Lat. epigram on the defeat of the Span. Armada, 1588, which was issued as a broadside in half-a-dozen European languages. Beza, as he is known in this country, was one of the chief of the Huguenots to introduce the psalter to the commonalty. He completed Marot's (q.v.) transln. of the Psalms into Fr. verse, and his rendering, though far less fiery and stately than the master's, was welcomed, alike in France and in the Engl. transln., by the Protestant and Puritan communities. B. was the chief contributor of the words to the Geneva tune-bk. of the psalter, 1551.

Bible: Sacred bk. of Christianity and (in part, of) Judaism, publd. in all known languages, consisting of the Old and New Testaments, which comprise '66 different books by a variety of writers, of occupations as humble as herdmen and as exalted as kings, extending over a period of several thousand years', and dealing with 'history, geography, travel, theology, biology, geology, astronomy, biography, chronology, morality, sanitation, medicine, architecture, poetry, etc., including, it would appear, every conceivable subject under the sun' (F. G. Jannaway, *The Bible and How it came to us*, 12). The place of this vast compilation in a work of this kind is determined solely by its *literary* interest,—by the labours of men of letters in Europe who made it available for readers, and by the use it acquired in other lit. The late prof. R. G. Moulton (1849-1924), in a pref. to *The Modern Reader's Bible* (Macmillan, 1907) wrote: 'Apart from more sacred considerations, even as a phenomenon of literature the Bible is unique. And the best treatment for this literature is to read it'; a recommendation which may be backed by such remarks (one or two among many

hundreds), as Macaulay's: 'A book which, if everything else in our language should perish, would alone suffice to shew the whole extent of its beauty and power'; or Newman's: 'Its vastness like the bosom of the sea, its variety like the river of nature'; or Huxley's: 'By what other book could children be so humanized?' Or, continuing our quotation from Moulton's pref.: 'Scholarship can do much for the Bible, but imagination and literary receptivity can do more'. Reference may also be made to the introductory essays (esp. §1, The Bible as Literature) to *The Literary Man's Bible*, by W. L. Courtney (Chapman and Hall, 1907); to *The Bible for Home Reading*, by C. G. Montefiore, D.D. (Macmillan), to the translns. of both Testaments into modern Engl. by Dr. Moffatt, D.D. (Hodder and Stoughton), and to *The Psalms in Human Life*, by R. E. Prothero, lord Ernle (Murray). The name of bp. Robert Lowth (1710-87), prof. of Poetry at Oxford, 1741-50, is permanently associated with the modern growth of literary interest in the Old Testament in Engld.; his *Lectures on Hebrew Poetry* were publd., 1753.

Approaching the B. in this way, we may turn at once to a particularly discerning art. in *The Times Lit. Suppl.* of 23 Mar. 1911, which discusses the Engl. Jacobean version of the B. as a model in the Romantic style of prose (see s.v. Romance): 'Comparing our literature', says the anon. writer, 'with the one literature in the world with which we can feel pride in comparing it, we may say that, to the Greeks, Herodotus's history held something like the same literary position as our Bible holds with us—an early and inimitable masterpiece of abounding natural grace, whose simple charm set it above the reach of the conscious rules of grammarians, a model which no one who had sufficient taste to admire would attempt to rival.

'"How happy would a man be could he imitate Herodotus" (writes Lucian). "I do not say in all his perfections, for that would be too great a wish; but either in the beauty of his discourse, or in the gravity of his sentences, or in the delicacy of his Ionique tongue, or (to be short) in a thousand other advantages, which make all those that would attempt it, despairing, drop their pens."

'We have even this *delicacy of the Ionique tongue* in our Bible, and one might push the comparison nearer; for Herodotus's book has not been unfairly described as a theistic perspective of accredited events from the Greek point of view—a story of Divine predestiny, making the world's history to culminate in the glory of Athens; just as our Bible is a collection of Christian origins, culminating in the foundation of the Church; and both were historically justified. But our Bible, matching the Greek book in its legendary matter and excursions into old-world history, is much more poetic and varied than Herodotus; and its sources being more original, the documents which it collects are far richer in mental attitudes and literary forms, and have escaped the tincture of one mind. Its inspired elevations above such a mean more than compensate for the immoralities and sophistries that lapse beneath it. And it is not only in poetry and moral inspiration that Herodotus is outmatched, for even in naïvety, wherein he is sometimes thought to have exceeded, he is quite surpassed. There is nothing in literature to compare with that passage in the Creation where it is said that when God had created the animals he, " brought them unto Adam to see what he would call them " '. Thus, Moulton, to refer back to him, urges that ' in the varied types of literature, Hebraic is as rich as Hellenic ', and that ' Biblical culture claims recognition as well as Classical culture '.

We may make one more quotation, this time from the Introduction to *Literary Genius of Old Testament*, by Mr. P. C. Sands (Oxford, 1924). Noting that Mr. Sands places on his title-page the fine dictum of J. R. Green, the historian : ' England became the people of a book, and that book was the Bible ', we may observe that the people of the Book, in ordinary acceptance, is the people whose ancestors wrote it ; and Mr. Sands remarks on the appropriateness of giving some account of the Jewish race which produced the bks. of the Old Testament. ' Books ', he writes, ' have recently appeared upon the " legacy of the Greeks " and the " legacy of the Romans " to the human race. The legacy of the Hebrews is even more important, if religious thought accounts for more than æsthetic ideals or political thought ; the legacy of the Hebrews is the literature represented to us by the Bible ';* and in a series of 18 excellent lessons, Mr. Sands examines that legacy in the prose and poetry of the Old Testament, stating that, while philosophy, comedy (which was incompatible with the serious temperament of the race), and tragic drama are conspicuous by their absence from this national lit., its most striking features are : ' (*a*) *in Prose ; i*. The vividness and dramatic qualities of the stories. *ii.* The sublime descriptions of God, revealing himself to his chosen servants. (*b*) *in Poetry ;* The wonderful imagery and literary figures of the lyrics, and their manner of expressing emotional and devotional experience, both personal and national. But unique in literature,' he adds, ' is the series of Hebrew prophecies, many of which by their rhythm and balance of thought resemble poetry rather than prose, and show the same wealth of imagery, a great power of pleading and invective, and a lofty conception of God '. Perhaps one word of warning may be added. The intense spirituality of these writers, and their habit of seeing all mundane things under the aspect of the divine, led to that ' naïvety ' of which *The Times*' critic spoke. Thus, a Hebr. writer saw no incongruity in the juxtaposition of precepts derived from sanctions so different as ' Thou shalt love thy neighbour as thyself : I am the Lord. Thou shalt not sow thy field with mingled seed, neither shall a garment mingled with linen and woollen come upon thee ' (*Lev.*, xix, 18-19). The literary editors of the B. deal with this anti-climax in their

* *The Legacy of Judœa* has since been added to *The Legacy of Greece* and *The Legacy of Rome*. Oxford Univ. Press, *in prep.*, 1925.

own ways : one by suppressing the linsey-wolsey, another by remanding it to an appendix. The safest way is to recognize that the Hebr. genius was distinct from the Hellenic.

This mode of approach to the literary value of the B. enables us to neglect the Wars of Religion (see, generally, s.v. Reformation), which, breaking out from Germany in the 16th cent., and laying that country bare, extended their devastation through Europe, and were spread into dynastic and territorial wars ; it enables us to neglect the politics, which unfolded from religion like a noxious weed, and to concentrate our attention on the B., in the spirit of the *paraclesis* (summons) of Erasmus (q.v.), the bridge-builder between ecclesiasticism and free thought : ' The mysteries of kings it may be safer to conceal, but Christ wished His mysteries to be published as openly as possible '.

Who first set them open ? The same spirit of Humanism (q.v.) which moved Petrarch (q.v.) in the 14th cent. to search for and toil at Lat. MSS., and to induce Boccaccio (q.v.) to procure a Lat. *Iliad*, was applied at a slightly later date to the study of the Gk. New Testament, which, partly because it was in Gk., preceded the Old Testament in scholars' interest. The new start (for Wiclif, see s.v. and below) was made by Lorenzo Valla (q.v.), whose pamphlet, 1440, on ' Constantine's Donation ', which has since been removed from the Roman Breviary, discredited the papal claim to temporal power by a critical investigation of the alleged authority. ' In the revival of letters and liberty ', says Gibbon (q.v., *Decline and Fall*, ch. 49), ' this fictitious deed was transpierced by the pen of Laurentius Valla, the pen of an eloquent critic and a Roman patriot. His contemporaries of the fifteenth century were astonished at his sacrilegious boldness ; yet such is the silent and irresistible progress of reason, that, before the end of the next age, the fable was rejected by the contempt of historians and poets, and the tacit or modest censure of the advocates of the Roman Church '. Irresistible, indeed ; but we may be permitted to dispute the ' silence ' of the progress of reason in the 15th and 16th cents. Valla's attack on the papal deed ' naturally attracted the notice of the German reformers, and it was first printed in 1715 by Ulrich von Hutten ' (q.v. : the citation is from Sandys, *Hist. Class. Schol.*, ii, 68), famous as the leader of the Erfurt poets who defended Reuchlin (q.v.) from the monks of Cologne. (See s.v. *Epistolœ Obscurorum Virorum*). Similarly, Valla's criticisms, 1444, of the Vulgate version of the New Testament in relation to the original Gk. were first publd. by Erasmus in 1505.

Except for Valla, however, the B. was opened by Humanists, not of the South, but of the sterner North. To Italy was due the spirit of enterprise,—the spirit of an antiquary like Ciriaco (q.v.), who made it his function ' to awaken the dead ' ; the spirit of a mystic like Mirandola (q.v.), in whose vision Socratianity and Christianity were reconcilable in a single revelation ; the spirit described by Sandys (*loc. cit.*), as that in which ' the culture of the classics had to be re-appropriated before the movement of the modern mind would begin ' ; but, though the foundations for the textual criticism of the Scriptures were laid by Roger Bacon (q.v.) in the 13th cent., the real beginning of Hebraic culture was in Germany. For many centuries the Jews themselves had subjected the Hebr. text to close and reverent examination ; the Massorites established a ' standard text ', and the traditional lit., followed by a long line of eminent commentators, established meanings. Among Christians, modern Biblical criticism and Biblical transln., which necessarily went before the appreciation and literary use of vernacular Bibles, began when Reuchlin, the Germ. Humanist, sped home from his Gk. studies in Italy by Argyropoulos, sat down to learn Hebr. from a Jew. The result in 1506 was his Hebr. Grammar, *de Rudimentis Hebraicis*. This event, says Dr. Fairbairn (*C.M.H.*, ii, 696), ' which took the Old Testament out of the hand of phantasy, turned it into an instrument of reform ; for if it is doubtful whether Protestantism would have arisen without the knowledge of the Old Testament, it is certain that without it the Reformed Church would not have assumed the shape it took '. Luther's (q.v.) Bible (Old and New Testament) followed a few years later, 1522-34, and from that date Biblical scholarship was free. Free within limits, indeed, for scholars availed themselves of the freedom at frequent peril even of their lives (see s.v. Dolet, e.g.), as the story of the Huguenots serves, summarily, to prove. But the B. is not to be held responsible for crimes committed in the name of religion,—certainly not the B. as a work of lit., with which aspect we are solely concerned.

Wiclif (q.v.) transltd. it into Engl., 1389, from the Lat. Vulgate of St. Jerome in the 4th cent., revised by Charlemagne (q.v.), 802. Pope Clement vii revised the Vulgate, 1593. Tyndale and Coverdale (qq.v.) in the 16th cent. raised the plant from Wiclif's seed, and utilized the labours of Luther and Erasmus; Coverdale superintended the ' Great Bible ' at Paris, 1538-9, and London, 1539, which became the basis of the Authorized Version, 1611. The Authorized Version still holds its own, despite the Revised Version, 1885. The Bishops' Bible dates from 1568, and was the work of Matthew Parker, archbp. of Canterbury, and of 12 Engl. bps. More popular, because cheaper and smaller, was the Geneva Bible, 1560, prepared by Engl. reformers in exile in that city, and known as the ' Breeches Bible ', owing to the transln. of *Gen*. iii. 7 : ' And they sewed fig-leaves together, and made themselves breeches '. (Wiclif had used the word before). Lefevre and Olivetan (qq.v.) in France ; the polyglot Bible of card. Ximenes (q.v.), contemporary with Erasmus, in Spain ; the critical labours of Beza (q.v.), John Mill (1645-1707), who collated all the readings of the principal extant MSS. for his edn. of the Gk. text of the New Testament, and the Germ. scholars of the following cent., culminating in the great work of Lobegott F. C. von Tischendorf (1815-74) and his successors— these belong to the splendid history of Biblical scholarship, which passes into the higher criticism of the Bible.

We turn back to the B.'s literary influence. The ambition of Erasmus is fulfilled to-day : husbandmen sing it at the plough, and weavers hum it at the shuttle. It is the Bk. of bks., as Heine (q.v.) called it : ' large and wide as the world, based on the abysses of creation, and towering aloft into the blue secrets of heaven. Sunrise and sunset, promise and fulfilment, birth and death, the whole drama of humanity, are contained in it '. Luther's perception of the familiar appeal of homely allocution to the Deity (*du lieber Gott*, etc.) has been justified through the centuries, and the language of the Lutheran B., and of its analogues in Engld. and other countries, has entered into the lit. of every nation. Our proverbs are largely derived from it ; we employ its metaphors and similes ; our sublime and fireside talk is equally drenched in its colours ; and its use at all domestic ceremonies, hallowed by the rites of the church, makes it intimate of our consciousness and hidden thoughts. Much valuable light on this subject, with not a few characteristic shadows, is cast by Matthew Arnold (q.v.), Renan's (q.v.) Engl. disciple, in his *Literature and Dogma* : we may refer, too, to the art. on ' The Bible in the Church ' by prof. Dobschütz, in Hastings' *Encyclopædia of Religion and Ethics*, and to the chapter headings in the same writer's *Influence of the Bible on Civilization*, which include : ' The Bible begins to rule the Christian Empire ', 325-600 A.D. ; ' The Bible teaches the German Nations ', 500-800 ; ' The Bible becomes one Basis of Medieval Civilization ', 800-1150 ; ' The Bible stirs Nonconformist Movements ', 1150-1450 ; ' The Bible trains Printers and Translators ', 1450-1611 ; ' The Bible rules Daily Life," 1550-1850. The expansion of these chapters would make several bks., and we should still not have exhausted the literary influence of the B.

Biehl, Charlotta Dorothea (died, 1788) : Dan. dramatist. Wr. ' Venus and Adonis ', a pastoral, 1757, and ' The Loveable Man ', a comedy, adapted from the Fr. B.'s services to the Dan. theatre after Holberg (q.v.) were considerable, and she merits recognition, too, for her spirited transln. of *Don Quixote* (s.v. Cervantes) into Dan.

Bielinsky, Vissarion Grigorievich (1811-48) : Russ. critic, of humble orig. and self-education, who, despite, or, it may be, because of his disadvantages, exercised an immense influence on the theory and practice of letters in Russia. The hand of the censor was upon B. all this life, and even laid its iron prohibition on the memory of his opinions after death. For B. belonged to, or, more exactly, helped to found, that camp of politico-literary propagandism known locally and temporarily as the Westernizers, in distinction to the Slavophils. He and his party sought to illumine Russ. thought from without, to let in from the enlightened West the splendour and help of new ideas. They were the radicals of literary criticism, while the Slavophils, fastening their hopes on constitutionalism and orthodoxy, were the anti-reform or conservative party. Neither side in the end escaped the shears. The ingenuity of the censorship caught both; and B., it is not too much to say, was really created by the censor; his views and opinions were formed in direct response to the challenges of that authority. So he gave the didactic tone to Russ. criticism, which has remained impressed upon it ever since, and which stamped it definitely and permanently with a journalistic and partizan character. B. strongly assisted the transition from the 'fausse route' of Pushkin (q.v.) to the highway of Russ. realism, commencing with Gogol (q.v.); he switched off the moonlight and colours of the Caucasian poets, and urged that the hour of mature thought must succeed that of heady enthusiasm. And when the thought of Gogol, for example, became too much mixed with pure art for B.'s taste, and too little concentrated on social problems, B. pulled down his own idol, and recanted his praises. His voice was authoritative and final, making and marring literary reputations; and his death at an early age from consumption was a grave loss to the cause which he had sustained. He cannot be accounted a great critic in the sense of M. Arnold or Ste-Beuve (qq.v.); impartiality and objectiveness were lacking; but in his time and place he was a great force in the emancipation of Russ. thought, and in the encouragement of truth and virtue and freedom and hope in Russ. letters. B.'s critical writings appeared in the periodical press: his 'Literary Fantasies, an Elegy in Prose', dealing with Russ. lit. in the 18th cent., were publd. in 1834; his first critiques on Gogol were issued in the Moscow *Telescope*, 1835; 11 essays on Pushkin, 1843-46; and his review of the publications of 1847 was publd. in the year of his death. Not art for art's sake (see s.v. *Art pour l'art, l'*), but Art for life's sake, was the sign of criticism, according to B., if a formula is to be sought for his views.

Bijns, Anna (c. 1493-1575): Dutch poet. Wr. 1528, a 'sweet and sincere little book', as its title-page stated, of sacred song, and continued her poetic activity in the cause of the ancient church till about 1550. The details of her biography are obscure, and it is not quite certain that the Anna Bijns who died at a ripe age in 1575 was identical with the poet of an earlier generation. Her first bk. was the most important of her writings, and was transld. into Lat. verse at Antwerp in 1529. Her verse was outspoken and often coarse; 'everything that was not Catholic was lies'; and in style she affected the older fashions of the rhetorical school (s.v. Rederijkers).

Bilderdijk, Willem (1756-1831): Dutch poet, advocate, and man of letters. Son of a physician; received excellent education in Fr. and Ital., and at 40 years of age won gold medal from Leyden Academy for a poem on *Influence of Poetry*: followed this with another prize-poem on *Patriotism*. Transld., 1779, Sophocles' *Oedipus Tyrannus* into Dutch alexandrines; publd., 1781, vol. of love-poetry, mainly translns. from Anacreon, Theocritus, Bion, and Horace. Pursued his legal career with growing success. Married Katherine Woesthoven, 21 June, 1785, who bore him a daughter, 8 Sept., 1785; the union, thus

contracted, did not prove happy. B. took part in the political happenings of his day; visited Engld., 1795, and was welcomed in London as a 'living encyclopedia'. There he met Katherine Schweikhardt, the young daughter of a fellow-countryman, with whom he joined his life in May, 1797; he and Katherine went to Brunswick, where B. was well received by duke Ferdinand, who granted him a pension, which he celebrated in a poem of that name. At Brunswick, B. called himself von Teisterbaut, and Katherine, who had born him a son in 1798, and a daughter in 1801, was m. to him in 1802, after his divorce from his wife. He effected many notable translns. into Dutch, among them Pope's *Essay on Man*, and a *Fingal*, adapted from Macpherson's (q.v.) *Ossian*. Thereafter, and still under royal patronage, B. composed classical poems in epic and dramatic style, and his last composition in verse was his *Tuvei*, 1811, in stirring alexandrines of a sombre lyrical intensity. The rest of his life was spent in more prosaic pursuits, which included a considerable amount of teaching; and his death, 18 months after that of his devoted (second) wife, was in the nature of a release. B.'s great fault was his lack of taste, which prevented the full expression of his remarkable aptitudes.

Biondo, Flavio (1388-1463): It. humanist and topographer. Less correctly, Biondo Flavio. Native of Forli, but resided long at Rome. Made first copy (1422) of Cicero, *ad Brutum*. Papal secretary to Eugenius iv, Nicholas v, Calixtus iii and Pius ii. Wr. *Romæ Instauratæ libri* 3 (printed 1471), documentary description of monuments of ancient Rome; *Romæ Triumphantis libri* 10 (printed c. 1474), on laws, religion, and other antiquities of the public; *Italia illustrata* (printed 1474), on topography and antiquities of all Italy; and a history *ab inclinatione Romani Imperii*, anticipating Gibbon (q.v.). B.'s works are of little value to-day, but establish his claim as a founder of the study of classical archæology.

Birck, Sixt (1500-54): Germ. Latinist; known by scholar's name of Xystus Betuleius. Born at Augsburg; lived chiefly at Basel as schoolmaster, and imbibed principles of religious and political reform, typical of Germ. humanism, which flourished at those centres. Wr. Lat. dramas in the 'Christian Terence' school, notably *Susanna* (1532), *Judith*, *Zorobabel*, and *Eva* (based on the legend of Eve's dissimilar children, which Melanchthon and Sachs had used; see s.vv.), all characterized by a keen and contructive zeal for a strenuous civic morality.

Biré, Edmond (19th cent.): Fr. diarist. Wr. *Journal d'un Bourgeois de Paris sous la Terreur*, a remarkable piece of history-making, and is conspicuous as a detractor of Hugo (q.v.), or rather, as an iconoclast of the Hugo-legend, in a critical biography, 5 vols., 1883-94.

Bisticci. See **Vespasiano da Bisticci.**

Bjerregaard, Henrik Anker (1792-1842): Norse patriotic poet; one of the three of the Syttendemai (q.v.) voices, which were raised to celebrate the separation of Norway from Denmark on 17 May, 1814. (The two other members of the so-called 'Trefoil' were Hansen and

mysticism in this instance, as in others, was at times an intensely luminous simplicity.

Blank Verse (rhet.) : a metric system for poetic composition, chiefly used in narrative verse, and employing an iambic or a trochaic movement in equal unrhymed lines containing, commonly, 10 syllables. The main skill in the use of the measure resides in the manipulation of the pauses, both within the limits of each line (by cæsura), and within the structure of the paragraph. It may be noted that the Engl. measure of rhymed heroic couplets may tend, in the hands of some practitioners (e.g. Keats, q.v.), to create an impression of blank verse, owing to the poet's skill in building up stately paragraphs of sense, instead of aiming at the epigrammatic effect of sense delimited by the couplet, which occurs so frequently, e.g. in Pope (q.v.). A kind of midway effect between the narrative-poem in heroic couplets and in blank verse may frequently be observed in the work of Crabbe (q.v.). The converse effect of an impression of rhyme conveyed without its use may be found in the poem commencing ' Tears, idle tears, I know not what they mean ', in *The Princess*, by Tennyson (q.v.), the Engl. master-metrist ; there, the devices of alliteration (q.v.) are so artfully employed that the absence of rhyme almost escapes detection.

Blank verse was the almost invariable rule of the Gk. and Lat. poets, even in lyrical poetry ; the Lat. hymns of the early Christian Church departed from this practice ; and the poems composed in the romance- (q.v.) languages confirmed the departure ; even the *chansons de geste* (q.v.) cultivated an assonance, or similarity of sound, in the final foot of every line in a single paragraph. Rhyme-intricacies were a favourite device of the courtly schools of poetry in Provence, Sicily, Spain, Italy, and elsewhere ; and the resources of charm, variety and subtle appeal which this feature of modern verse commands need not be insisted upon here. The honour of re-introducing blank verse is disputed between several claimants ; what is certain is that it was Ital. in its origin. Perhaps its earliest use in narrative poetry was in a transln. effected by Molza (q.v.) of the *Æneid* ; this poem was ascribed to card. Ippolito de Medici, and dates from 1541. Earlier than that year were the blank verse experiments in dramatic composition, of Rucellai, Trissino, and Alamanni (qq.v.) ; and from one or other of these exemplars, so diligently studied in Tudor Engld., Henry, earl of Surrey (q.v.) adopted the measure for his own version of the *Æneid*, and Sackville (q.v.) for his tragic drama, *Gorboduc*. It was introduced in the same period into Spain by the Italianate school of Span. poetry at Naples (see s.vv. Boscan, Navagero) ; but, though successfully practised, it was never fully assimilated by the languages of the Peninsula. It is the Engl. language which responds most successfully to the demands of this noblest of verse-forms, which, when inadequately treated, sinks to a lower level almost than any other, and is hardly distinguishable from prose cut syllabically. Between the two extremes may be set the blocks of blank verse discoverable in the two prose *Canterbury Tales*

of Chaucer (q.v.). The weak (or feminine) endings of Ital. words detract from the dignity of the line, and more than half lead the hearer or reader to expect to find a sound-recurrence in compensation for the want of force in the final sound. The genius of the Engl. language supplies this want ; and Surrey's successors were quick to develop the magnificent qualities of music and strength locked up in the instrument of blank verse, and far surpassing for suitable purposes, in subtlety, sublimity, and distinction, the prettier charms even of the most gracefully turned rhymes. The Elizabethan dramatists, led by Marlowe (q.v.) and gloriously supported by Shakespeare (q.v.) availed themselves freely of the measure, and displayed its grand resources ; Milton (q.v.) for the first time since Virgil employed it in an epic poem ; and Wordsworth (q.v.) modulated it effectively for use in regions of song less remote from human ken than Paradise. These are the writers most immediately associated with the introduction and perfection of blank verse, and by their examples its resources may best be tested ; but all Europe has been converted to its use ; and in modern lit., as in ancient, it is the accepted medium for the message of the greatest poetry.

Blicher, Steen Steensen (1782-1848) : Dan. poet and storyteller ; a native of Jutland, in the folklore and peasantry of which country B. found his chief source of inspiration. The first direction to these studies was imparted to B. by Steffens (q.v.), to whose teaching may be ascribed his transln. of *Ossian*, 1807-09. B.'s early lyric and dramatic verse is not much read to-day ; it was as a parish priest in Jutland that he began the series of folk tales and the later series of tales of peasant-life, on which his reputation justly rests. B. effected in this respect that interpretation and consecration of the commonplace, which was the last and best fruit of the romantic revival, and his tales, whether in verse or prose, belong indisputably to the narrow realm of genius. He was the second Ewald (q.v.) of his own country.

Blumauer, Johann Aloys (1755-98) : Austrian poet. Wr. a travesty of *The Æneid*, ' The Adventures of the Pious Hero Aeneas ', 1784, in which, as in other semi-heroic, semi-comic poems, B. parodied, while he sought to imitate, the airy fancy of Wieland's (q.v.) *Oberon*.

Boccaccio, Giovanni (1313-75) : It. humanist and novelist ; the foster-father of Humanism (q.v.), according to an admirable centenary art. in *The Times Lit. Supp.* (30 Oct., 1913 ; Petrarch, q.v., being of course, its father), and the founder, according to the same authority, and others, of the novel (q.v.) of plot and adventure, the picaresque novel, and the novel of character (though soon surpassed in this last by Chaucer, q.v.). B. was also a scholar and student ; the first Homerist in modern Europe (see s.v. Homer), and a great popularizer of classical antiquity, rather than a monopolist of it, like Petrarch.

B. was born in Paris, as the natural son of a Florentine banker, and a Frenchwoman, known only as Jeanne. He was brought up in Florence by his stepmother and was not happy in boyhood at home. His stern and not sympathetic father apprenticed him first to law and then to commerce, but, like Heine (q.v.), he settled to neither pursuit; love, life, and letters held him by the new humanism's triple cord, and through these he won the goal of self-expression. B.'s inevitable lady—his Beatrice, or Laura, with a difference—was Maria, illegitimate daughter of king Robert of Naples, and wife of a count d'Aquino, from whose family sprang St. Thomas Aquinas (q.v.). Maria's lover called her Fiammetta. He had to wait through several years of mingled idealizing and impatience for his one year's enjoyment of her favours, 1336-37, and the end of their relations is not known. In her likeness, however, or fairly close to it, were conceived the heroines of his earlier works: *Filocolo*, written tediously in Ital. prose round the story of Florio and Biancofiore; *Filostrato* (literally, 'fallen-in-love'), in octave-stanzas, of Priam's son, Troilus, and his Cressida, derived through Benoît de Ste. Moré (q.v.) from the 'matière de Rome' (see s.v. Bodel); *Teseide*, likewise in verse, with the same number of lines as Virgil's *Æneid*, of which, and of Statius' *Thebaid*, this tale of the friendship of Palamon and Arcite and of their love of one mistress is reminiscent; the prose-pastoral, *Ameto*, first in a class to be adorned by Sannazaro, Montemayor, Cervantes (qq.v.); *Amorosa Visione*, in Dante's metre; and, finally, *Fiammetta* itself, 'the first novel of psychology ever written in Europe' (E. Hutton, *Boccaccio*, Lane, 92). Maria d'Aquino died in 1348, by the Black Death which killed Petrarch's Laura, too. Of B.'s compilations of 'illustrious lives' and other industrious bk.-making, much used by later story-writers (see s.v. Lydgate), it is not necessary to say much, save that the concluding bk. of the *Genealogy of the Gods* ranks as 'the first critical treatise of the Renaissance'; generally, these Lat. writings formed a kind of bridge between B., Fiammetta's lover, and B., the lover of humane learning and devoted admirer of Petrarch (q.v.). Literary history contains few examples of friendship so ripe with fruit; Ronsard and Du Bellay is one, Coleridge and Wordsworth is another; Rivas and Frere yet another; (see s.vv.). It was B. who sought out Petrarch; they first met in 1350; and it was always B.'s greatest delight to share a new 'find' in scholarship with his master. We may say that all Petrarch appealed to B., and that only the humanist in B. appealed to Petrarch, who despised the *Decameron* as a scholar's diversion. But then nothing was ever quite as wonderful to B., quite as virginal and unexplored, as Latinity to Petrarch. In 1360, B. received as an inmate of his house at Florence (to which he repaired after Maria's death) a Calabrian scribe, Leontius Pilatus (q.v.), whose business it was to effect a Lat. version of the *Iliad* for the use of Petrarch and B., thus illustrious as the restorer of Homeric study to Italy. One more item of pleasing *personalia* may detain us from B.'s *magnum opus*. In 1373, he was appointed to deliver at Florence the first Dante lectures ever instituted, thus ranking as 'the first Professor of Modern Literature, and incomparably the most distinguished writer who

ever took up with that uneasy trade' (sir W. Raleigh, *Some Authors*, 10). B. had already written a life of the elder poet, thus avenging after 52 years his death in exile from Florence; he had imitated Dante in his early writings, and had praised him enthusiastically to Petrarch who, as Latinist, lent a deaf ear. But B.'s outstanding work, by which he is famous to-day, and in which, as a writer in Ital. prose, he vastly surpassed his greater master, in which too, in the words of prof. Raleigh, he 'might be called the escape from Dante', is his collection of Ital. prose tales, the *Decameron* (Gk. for 10 days; the equivalent Engl. trivial title would be 'The Fortnight'): 'One hundred Novels, or Fables, or Parables, or Stories, as we may please to call them, which were related in ten days by an honourable company of seven ladies and three young men in the time of the late mortal pestilence, as also some canzonets sung by the said ladies for their delectation' (from Proem to *Dec.*). The 10 fugitives from the Plague at Florence (Pampinea, Neifile, Filomena, Fiammetta, Emilia, Lauretta, Elisa, Filostrato, Pamfilo, Dionea; each presided as sovereign of the revels for one day) were frankly seeking distraction from the terror which stalked at noon-day, and which is visibly brought before us with a realistic skill worthy of Zola (q.v.) in B.'s exordium. They had not met for any improving purpose; and this, though a negative description, suggests the clear radiance of the atmosphere of the *Decameron*. It is un-moral; therefore, perhaps, not fully humanized; plumbing romance, but seldom touching poetry. No breath of pity or fear dimmed the brightness of their escape. There are some who object to this attitude as evidence of a debased social consciousness, and of outrage on the principles of religion. (See, on this point, a letter in *The Times*, 17 July, 1911, giving Thackeray's letter to R. Bell, of 3 Sept., 1848, in which the same problem was stated, likewise without solution, in connection with *Vanity Fair*). Others, more fancifully, see an analogy between the flight of the 10 from Florence and the emancipation of thought from medievalism (see J. Owen, *Skeptics of the Italian Renaissance*, 132). The wisest are content to appreciate the value of the *Decameron* as lit., and to share the note of keen personal enjoyment which differentiates it, e.g., from the *Heptameron* of queen Margaret (q.v.). The 100 tales were drawn from all sources known to fable and romance, but their *terminus ad quem* was almost invariably voluptuous or illicit love. The swift, hard strokes of comic irony were driven relentlessly at the women and clergy, who had been the butt of the savagery or wit of Goliards and Reynardists (qq.v.); nor does the evidence of a saint (see s.v. Catherine of Siena) contradict the evidence of the satirist. Friars, monks, nuns, were all included in the attack, which not the soft names invented for the company, nor the ingenious combination of lovers' trickeries, were suffered to mollify or conceal. Licentious, often superficial, but a great pioneer, in the *genre* of the short story; using the medium of a prose-style, complete, complex, and versatile, remarkable for these qualities at the time of its appearance, and not to be repeated in Italy for many years to come; writing like Cicero, as has been said, when he is thinking like Plautus; B., declares sir S. Lee (*French Renaissance in England*, 135), ' was the founder of the novel in the 14th century ' ; and the pious memory of the founder (not less pious, indeed, for his frank exposure of false pietism) must always be held in honour. There were nearly 100 edns. of the *Dec.* in Ital. before the end of the 16th cent. Fr., Germ. and Span. writers drew from it; Engl. poetry, from Chaucer to Tennyson, has been immensely in debt to it (see esp. s.vv. Chaucer, Shakespeare); and collections directly imitating it were made by Bandello, queen Margaret, and others. William Painter, in his *Palace of Pleasure* (1566), transld. many of its tales, and the standard Engl. transln. was effected in 1620.

Boccalini, Trajano (1556-1613): It. satiric historian. Wr. *News from Parnassus*, a journalistic gazette of happenings in the realms of Apollo, which gave the coveted opportunity of a free commentary on politics and letters in contemporary Italy. In a posth. work, 1614, B. launched a more vehement attack on the Span. monarchy, at the moment when Chas. Emmanuel, duke of Savoy, was a kind of Ital. national hero, and B. was further credited with 2 *Philippics*, 1615, against Spain, the authorship of which he repudiated. B. wr. too, *Commentaries on Tacitus*, and it is related (Sandys, *Hist. Class Schol.*, ii, 88) that: ' Early in the 17th century, when a request for permission to publish Boccalini's *Commentaries on Tacitus* was referred to five of the senators of Venice, " it is the teachings of *Tacitus* (they said) that has produced Machiavelli and the other bad authors, which would destroy the public virtue " '. This was probably true; but B., by his example in Parnassian satire, also helped to produce Swift (q.v.) and other good authors.

Bode, Johann Joachim Christoph (1730-97): Germ. translr. Resided at Hamburg, 1757, where he met Lessing (q.v.), and discussed an abortive scheme for setting up in the bk.-trade together. Effected widely-welcome Germ. versions of works by Montaigne, Sterne, Goldsmith, Fielding, and Smollett (qq.v.).

Bodel, Jehan (13th cent.): Fr. romancer. Took part in first and second crusades of St. Louis; contracted leprosy, and took leave of his friends in 42 strophes of a new form of verse since known as *congé*. Wr. *Chanson des Saisnes* (Saxons), and is remarkable as the author of 2 verses which give a masterly summary of the subject-matters of the common stock of Romance (q.v.):

Ne sont que trois matières a nul homme entendant—
De France, et de Bretagne, et de Rome la grant.

' There are but three matters which are at every man's disposal—those of France, of Britain and of Antiquity.' The Fr. matter was the Carolingian cycle; the ' British' was the Arthuriad; and the matter of Rome included the cycles of Troy, Thebes, Alexander, and, briefly, all antiquity.

Bodenstedt, Friedrich (1819-92): Germ. poet; a member of the Schack (q.v.) group at Munich,

in the reign of king Maximilian ii of Bavaria, and, like others in the circle, an excellent translr. of foreign lit. B.'s work in this respect was chiefly devoted to Russia, and he was esp. instrumental in introducing Lermontov (q.v.) to Germ. readers. His Shakespeare translns. were likewise valuable; and, following Rückert (q.v.), B. was addicted to the oriental colours of Goethe's (q.v.) *West-östliche Divan.* His chief original bk. of verse was the *Lieder des Mirza Schaffy*, 1851, chiefly imitations from the Orient, which is still known more widely than his voluminous later writings.

Bodin, Jean (1530-96): Fr. jurist and political philosopher. Wr., 1577, *de la République*, which quickly became a univ. textbk., and which B. accordingly transld., 1586, into Lat. (with extensions), so as to render it more generally accessible. It was an exhaustive inquiry into the theory and practice of government, and exercised considerable influence on 17th-cent. thought. In some minor scientific aspects (e.g., its view of the relation of climate and race to political disposition), it anticipated Montesquieu (q.v.); and Hallam (*Lit.* of *Europe*, ii, 4) compares B., not wholly to his advantage, with Aristotle and Machiavelli. B.'s investigation of the problems of politics was elaborate and comprehensive, and his conclusion favoured the views of the absolutists, though he admitted the right of regicide against a tyrant by usurpation. It is interesting to note, that, in an age when the writings of the Old Testament inspired so much of its poetry and philosophy, B. was supposed to have adopted the Jewish faith, if not openly, at least by conviction. Certainly, his political philosophy is governed by a strong Hebraic bias, and similar criticism may be made of his religious writings. One such treatise was publd. by Herbert (q.v.) of Cherbury in support of deism; and another, the *Heptaplomeres*, was a dialogue between the practitioners of 7 different creeds, including the Jewish, the purpose of which was to demonstrate the underlying likeness of the religious mind, if not to exalt the simple form of monotheism above the rest. B. visited Engld. in the suite of Francis, duke of Alençon, suitor of queen Elizabeth, and his *République*, in use at Cambridge, influenced Hobbes (q.v.) and other writers, and helped to form the ideas of sovereignty in quarters where Hobbes was an unwelcome guide.

Bodley, Thomas (1545-1613): Engl. scholar; diplomatist; knt., 1604; began to form in 1598 the collection of bks. and MSS. (see, too, s.v. Cotton), which constitute the Bodleian Library, Oxford, opened in 1603, and endowed by B., 1611.

Bodmer, Johann Jakob (1698-1783): Germ.-Swiss critic; prof. at Univ. of Zurich, and protagonist in a literary feud between Zurich and Leipsic. This Swiss-Saxon battle of the critics was waged in a personal sense between B. and Breitinger (q.v.) on the one part and Gottsched (q.v.), the dictator of taste at Leipsic on the other. More really, it was the Germ. aspect of the war between the rival schools of Classicism (q.v.) and Romanticism, and the victory was as decisive as the fighting was fierce. Gottsched and the Fr. neo-classics whose rules and principles he sustained were vanquished and routed ; Gottsched himself was deposed from his Johnsonian throne, and fell on a dishonoured old age. The perception of Bodmer and Breitinger, brothers-in-arms throughout the feud, and both, strangely, Johann Jakob by name (they sometimes signed their joint lucubrations ' J.J.J.J.'), that the future of Germ. lit. lay with the romantic sensibilities of Protestant-Germanic Engld., was on the side of time itself. The details of the bk.-war need not detain us. The disputants did not start at any great distance from one another. Neither at Zurich nor at Leipsic in the first quarter of the 18th cent. was there any opinion about poetry which did not accept the rationalizing philosophy of C. von Wolff (q.v.), or which did not wholesomely shrink from the suspicion of Lohenstein's (q.v.) bombast. The first difference probably was that the Zurich professors had taste as well as principles, but the Leipsic prof. principles only. Thus, Bodmer edited Boner (q.v.), and the Minnesinger (q.v.), and parts of the *Nibelungenlied* (q.v.) ; in his ' Painters' Discourses ' (*Diskurse der Maler*, q.v.), the Addisonian paper which he helped to found at Zurich, 1721, he betrayed a leaning to Engl. lit. ; and Gottsched's apprehensions at these signs of Swiss literary heresy were confirmed in 1732 when B. publd. in his journal a prose-transln. of Milton's *Paradise Lost*. A year or two later, Leipsic replied by a new edn. of Gottsched's *Art of Poetry*, in which, while maintaining unimpaired the supremacy of Virgil above Homer, the critic roundly convicted Ariosto, Tasso, and Milton of grave offences against the laws of epos. In 1740, each of the Zurichers entered the field with an *ars poetica* of his own ; and from that date—a crucial date in Germ. lit., for it marked the accession of king Frederic ii (q.v.) of Prussia—the quarrel marched to its inevitable conclusion. To B.'s transln. of *Paradise Lost* was due a part at least of the influence which contributed to inspire Klopstock (q v.) with his epic on the Messiah ; and B. in his turn was so deeply moved by that example that, not only did he write and speak of Klopstock as of a being almost supernatural, but he composed a number of Biblical poems which made him, as Lessing (q.v.) pointed out, as ridiculous as he had rendered Gottsched. Klopstock fell short of the exalted aims, or, rather, of the seraphic qualities, with which B. had credited him ; and B. was yet more bitterly disappointed in his later guest at Zurich, Wieland (q.v.), whose first Klopstockian enthusiasm turned to more worldly ambitions.

Boedtcher, Ludvig Adolph (1793-1874) : Dan. poet ; lived, 1824-35, in Rome, where he formed a little circle or artists, art-lovers and *dilettanti*, including sir Walter Scott, the ex-king of Holland, the king of Bavaria, and Thorwaldsen, the illustrious Dan. sculptor. It was Thorwaldsen's death, and B.'s success in his competition with the king of Bavaria for the reversion of the sculptor's works to Copenhagen in preference to Munich, which brought B. back to his own country in charge of the national bequest. With all his love for Italy, he did not leave Denmark again, but was satisfied, in his easy, pleasure-loving way, to surround himself with a little Rome in Copenhagen. A guitar, some flowers, constant friends, and his own happy detachment of vision sufficiently sustained the illusion. B.'s exquisite lyrical poems were issued, 1856, and form, with later additions, a collection not larger than Gray's (q.v.). Sir E. Gosse, who suggests this comparison, adds (*Lit. of Northern Europe*, 170 ; Kegan Paul, 1879) : ' Almost every one of them is a gem, cut and engraved with the most exquisite precision. He is the most consummate artist in form among the Danish poets. His most characteristic pieces unite a kind of dry sparkle of humour with the intense light and vivid form of antiquity or of Italian landscape '.

Böhl de (y) Faber, -i. Juan Nicholas (1770-1836) : Span.-Germ. scholar ; born at Hamburg, son of a banker at Cadiz, where he lived practically all his life ; married a Spaniard, and adopted the Catholic faith. Is thus to be accounted more Span. than Germ. ; member of the Royal Spanish Academy. Wr., 1820, ' Vindications of Calderon and of the Ancient Spanish Theatre ' against Fr. influences in Span. lit. ; and collected, 1821-25, 3 vols. of Span. lyric and didactic poetry, and, 1832, 24 plays (*Teatro Español*) from the period anterior to Vega (q.v.). These collections are invaluable to the literary historian, and B.'s labours have been considered worthy of mention besides those of Schlegel (q.v.).

   -ii. Cecilia Francisca Hosefa (1796-1877) : Span.-Germ. novelist ; daughter of above ; commonly known by her pen-name, FERNAN CABALLERO, in preference to her patronymic or to the surname of any of her 3 husbands. F.C. wr. her novels in Germ., Fr., and Span. almost indifferently ; the first, *Sola, oder Wahrheit und Schein* (' Sola, or Reality and Appearance ') was publd. in Germ., 1840 ; her first Span. novel, and the bk. by which she is best known, was *La Gaviota*, 1849.

Boehme, Jacob (1575-1624) : Germ. Catholic mystic ; like Sachs (q.v.), a shoemaker by trade, at Görlitz in Silesia. Wr. *Aurora, or The Rising Dawn*, and other works of mystical philosophy, the influence of which has even yet hardly spent itself. His *Mysterium Magnum*, an exposition on the Bk. of Genesis, was transld. into Engl., 1654, and re-issued in 2 vols., 1924. B. gave expression to pantheistic doctrine, marked by a rapt altruism. His method of allegorical interpretation was invaluable in helping to break down the rigid system of his day, though its actual value at the time was more indirect than immediate, inasmuch as it prepared the soil for the seemingly different protest of Luther (q.v.). B.'s mysticism may be said to form a link between Paracelsus and Hegel (qq.v.) : Novalis and Tieck (qq.v) recognized him as a Romantic master, and in Engld. he greatly influenced Wm. Law (q.v.). Dr. Johnson (q.v.), who had no use for the recondite, said that, if B. saw unutterable things, he should not have ventured to utter them.

Böhmer, Auguste (1785-1800): daughter of Dr. Böhmer and his wife Caroline, afterwards wife successively to A. W. Schlegel and Schelling (qq.v.). Schelling had formed an affection for Auguste, and it was the grief at her early death which brought him and her mother more closely together. She was a child of rare precocity, and might have played an important part in the literary side of the Romantic movement, in the personal aspects of which she was destined to fill so unhappy a part. Schelling was attacked by his opponents for having shortened her life by his intemperate doctrines.

Boekler, Johann Heinrich (1610-72): Germ. scholar; tutor at Strassburg; was invited by queen Christina (q.v.), to Sweden, and became prof. of eloquence at Upsala, 1694. B. did not manage to get on either with his colleagues or with his pupils, whom he offended by a reference to the 'leaden-headed Swedes', and returned, 1652, whence he came. The queen appointed him historiographer for life, and he wr. an excellent history of the Dano-Swed. War.

Boendale, van, Jan (c. 1285-1365): Dutch poet; school of Maerlant (q.v.). Wr. rhymed chronicle of the dukes of Brabant; was eye-witness of the expedition against the French, 1338-40, which started from Antwerp under king Edward iii of Engld., and queen Philippa, and wr. its chronicle (van den derden Edewaert), of which about 2,000 verses are extant. B.'s chief work was der Leeken Spiegel ('the mirror of laymen'), one of many 'mirrors', and a masterpiece of didactic poetry. It was contained in 4 bks. and 21,818 verses, and comprised in its octosyllabic couplets a general survey and eschatology of humankind from the creation downwards. Attention may be directed to an early formulation of æsthetic principles in Bk. iii, ch. 15, of the Spiegel, where B. requires of a true poet an honourable life, a knowledge of language and style, and a love of truth. B. was known as John the Clerk of Antwerp.

Börne, Ludwig (1786-1837): Germ. journalist; originally Loeb Baruch, son of a Jew. merchant in the Frankfort ghetto; pupil of Dr. Marcus Herz in Berlin, and fell in love with Henriette Herz (q.v.), his letters to whom were publd., 1861; baptized, 1818, and took an active part in the literary life of his native and other Germ. cities, after the failure of the hopes attached to the War of Liberation. B.'s memorial address on J. P. Richter (2 Dec., 1825) is considered his critical masterpiece. After the July Revolution, 1830, B. settled in Paris, where he wr. his most important bk., Briefe aus Paris, which brought him into conflict with Menzel (q.v.) and other Germ. national-patriots. (B.'s quarrel with Heine was a more personal matter). Treitschke (q.v.) refers to B. (with Heine) as the inaugurator of the Jew. invasion of Germ. culture, but it is full time for controversy to be still, and for B. to be recognized and admired as a brilliant social writer.

Boethius (c. 480-524): Rom. philosopher; Anicius Manlius Severinus B., in his own time, and Boece in the friendly intimacy of European letters in the Middle Ages. B.'s contributions to the study of Aristotle are discussed s.v.; here we note that he was sole consul in 510, and that his 2 sons shared the consulship of Rome in 522. His interest in politics was that of a philosopher, and had been learned from Plato (q.v.); it proved his undoing, and he was condemned by the senate for some crime, unproved and undefended, and put to death, 524. In the 8th cent., B. was venerated as a martyr, and the cult was formally approved in 1883 (see for authorities, Sandys Hist. Class. Schol., i, 252). While in prison, awaiting death, B. wr. the bk., Philosophiæ Consolatio, by which he takes a place in the history of European lit. This poetic dialogue in 39 pieces, interspersed with prose, 'which was his last legacy to posterity, was repeatedly translated, expounded and imitated in the Middle Ages, and these translations were among the earliest literary products of the vernacular languages of Europe,—English, French, German, Italian, and Spanish, among the translators being names of no less note than king Alfred, Chaucer, and queen Elizabeth' (Sandys, ib., 256-7). Dante (q.v.) placed B. in the 4th heaven (Par. x, 124), and paid him the even higher compliment of translating his phrase, in omni adversitate fortunae infelicissimum est genus infortunii fuisse felicem into the well-known lines of Inf., v, 121, to which Tennyson (q.v.) refers in Locksley Hall :

This is truth the poet sings,

That a sorrow's crown of sorrow is remembering happier things.

(Chaucer's transln.—Boece, ii, iv—runs : 'For in alle adversitee of fortune, the most unsely (unhappy) kinde of contrarious fortune is to have been weleful'). More (q.v.), in the Tower of London, 1535, found solace in B.'s Consolatio, whose author was described by Gibbon (q.v.) as 'the last of the Romans whom Cato or Tully would have acknowledged for their countryman.' H. O. Taylor (Class. Heritage of the Middle Ages, 1921) writes : 'In easy, attractive modes of statement, the Consolation of Philosophy sets forth ordinary, universally valid thoughts upon the uncertainty of fortune and the emptiness of its favours. . . . It presented the spirit of Pagan ethics to the Middle Ages, and its office may be compared with that of the Imitatio Christi '. (see s.v. à Kempis).

Boiardo, Matteo Maria (1434-94): It. romancer; wr. Orlando Innamorato, a Carlovingian (see s.v. Charlemagne) romantic-epos, composed in octave stanzas (ottava rima). B. surpassed his contemporary, Pulci (q.v.), in literary power and tradition, and afforded a model to Ariosto (q.v.), whose Orlando Furioso took up B.'s tale, and, by completing, absorbed it. B.'s rank as count of Scandiano, his position at the Ferrarese court, his family connections, and his diplomatic relations as governor of Reggio and Modena, qualified him as a poet of chivalry ; he inherited the tone and glamour, rather than acquired them ; and treated the material of the Chansons de geste (q.v.) in the spirit of the Arthur (q.v.)-legends. In other words, he added a love-motive to the old tales of fighting and adventure, and, by his invention of the romantic heroine, Angelica, daughter of Gallaphrone, king of Cathay, and his introduction of the machinery of romance, adapted the story of Roland to the taste of his ideal audience. Milton (q.v.), whose instinct never failed him, paid a tribute to B.'s creative genius by employing the names of the *Orlando Innamorato* in a simile in *Paradise Regained* (iii, 338-43) :

Such forces met not, nor so wide a camp,
When Agrican, with all his northern powers,
Besieged Albracca, as romances tell,
The city of Gallaphrone, from thence to win
The fairest of her sex, Angelica,
His daughter, sought by many prowest knights,
Both Paynim and the peers of Charlemain.

B. left his poem unfind. at the 9th canto of bk. iii ; later writers (Berni, q.v., e.g.) were good enough to refashion it ('rifacimento' is the Ital. term), but its proper complement is the *Orlando Furioso*, and the successors of B. are Ariosto and Tasso. The less polished style of B., and his avoidance of the more conscious magnificence of the more professional poetry of his time, left his work in comparative obscurity ; though 'in point of novel invention and just keeping of character, especially the latter, he has not been surpassed by his illustrious follower' (Hallam) ; and he eminently succeeded in his aim of combining in a vernacular poem, displaying the true epic unity, the chief resources of humanism and feudalism. More securely than Pulci, B. stands at the head of the 'golden age' which was inaugurated by the labours of the Medici circle at Florence. B.'s next most notable work was *Timono* (c. 1487), a 5-act comedy (of sorts) in Dante's *terza-rima*, which 'must be regarded rather as a Morality than a Comedy' (Symonds, v, 94n.), and which was enacted on a double stage, the higher for heaven, and the lower for earth ; Timon discourses with godlike and allegorical characters (Wealth, Jove, and others) before the introduction of the Athenians who serve as foils to his misanthropy. The play is of interest in the development from 'sacra rappresentazione' (q.v.) to tragic drama.

Boie, Heinrich Christian (1744-1806) : Germ. poet ; a leader of the Göttingen (q.v.) circle, and joint-founder with Gotter (q.v.) of the 'Muses' Almanack' which became the literary organ of the Hain (q.v.), or poets' union, formed, 1772, by ardent enthusiasts for Klopstock (q.v.). B. acted as a kind of mentor to the students who joined in the solemn revels of the brotherhood of worshippers.

Boileau, Nicolas (1636-1711) : Fr. critic and poet ; took additional or alternative surname of Despréaux ; celebrated in his own century—he was almost an exact contemporary of *le grand monarque*, Louis xiv, 1638-1715—as 'the lawgiver of Parnassus', and maintained this celebrity in his own country and outside it through the greater part of the 18th cent., till it succumbed to the Romantic reaction (see s.v. Romance) at the period of the Fr. Revolution. It has gradually lost ground since. B.'s knowledge and his judgment have both been severely scrutinized, and Saintsbury (*Hist. Crit.*, ii, 300) records his deliberate opinion that B. was 'a great man of letters, perhaps ; a craftsmanlike "finisher of the law", and no ill pedagogue in literature certainly : but a great critic ? Scarcely, I think'. B.'s biography need not detain us from the examination of his writings, and of his place in lit. His tastes were literary from the start, and his early apprenticeships,

first to theology and then to law, closed at the death of his father, 1657. Reaching Paris at an early age, he soon found congenial companions in Molière, La Fontaine and Racine (qq.v.), the last of whom served (perhaps somewhat in his own despite) as the constant illustration of B.'s theories of poetics. To this famous quartette were added Furetière, Chapelle (qq.v.) and others, in genial gatherings at taverns (*cabarets*, coffee-houses), and like resorts. Lit. was ripe for law, and the legislator, aided by his keen satiric wit, quickly made his masterful way. He won the favour of Louis xiv, who loaded him with pensions and patronage, and received somewhat lavish flattery in return. In 1677, B. was appointed, jointly with Racine, historiographer-royal, and a few years later the king's direct influence helped him into the Academy (q.v.), despite the enmities which his satires had naturally aroused. La Fontaine's election to that body was made conditional on Boileau's, and king Louis's view of the two poets is told s.v. La Fontaine, and may account for the omission of the Fable (q.v.) from B.'s review of poetic kinds. In late life B.'s health gave way, and his faculties gradually decayed through the first decade of the cent. which he dominated, directly in France, indirectly in Engld. through Pope (q.v.), and in Saxony through Gottsched (q.v.), B.'s works—his powers were at their height in and about 1663—include 9 *Satires* (Horatian in design) ; a 'Dialogue of the Heroes of the *Roman*' (i.e. Fr. prose-tale) ; 9 'Epistles' (*Epîtres*), similarly Horatian ; the famous verse *Art Poétique* (1674), more devoutly Horatian than any ; a Fr. version of Longinus (q.v.), *On the Sublime* : a serio-comic poem in 4 cantos, *Lutrin* ('the Lectern'), composed, like Pope's *Rape of the Lock*, for the sake of proving that the thing could be done ; epigrams against Perrault (q.v.) ; 9 'Reflections on Longinus' ; 3 more 'Epistles', and *Satires* 10 and 11 ; epigrams against the Jesuits, and *Satire* 12 (1710). The *bourgeois* Boileau of Parisian life is best seen in his *Satires* 3, 6 and 10 ; the attacks on living authors, which earned him so much ill-will—his chief victims were St. Amant, Chapelain, Quinault, Scudéry, Théophile (qq.v.),—are to be found in *Satires*, 1, 2, 3, 4, 6, 8 and especially 9 ; the statement of his point of view and the definition of his critical doctrine are the subject of his *Art Poétique*, and his defence of classicism (q.v.) is given in the *Réflexions sur Longin*. There was an industrious factory of anti-Boileau pasquinades from 1666 for more than 20 years ; but with this lit. about lit. we need not trouble ourselves to-day. Chapelain's temporary success in getting B.'s licence revoked for the publication of his works, and the lobbying at the Academy to get his election postponed, were more practical manifestations of resentment.

In attempting to estimate B.'s place in lit., and to strike the just mean between his reputation before and after the end of the 18th cent., there are two facts to be borne in mind : i, B. drew together with true critical skill the threads of taste and philosphy woven into the texture of Fr. life and thought by the writings of Malherbe, J. L. de Balzac,

Descartes, Pascal, and the disciples of Jansen at Port Royal (see s.vv.); ii, this 'return to Nature', as it was represented by the purists, rationalists, and naturalists who practised it, was by the same token a return to art: it was a definite departure along the highways of reason and antiquity from the vagaries and artificialities of the Fr. Precious (q.v.) writers, and from the adventures in Spain of mlle. de Scudéry (q.v.) and her compeers. 'True wit is Nature to advantage dress'd', was Pope's rendering of the creed which he derived from B.: get back to Nature from the false wit of preciosity and conceit, and then, having got back to Nature, aim at the true wit of her most advantageous setting; thus, the return to Nature will become a return to Art. Now, the garb in which B. discovered that Nature was dressed to most advantage was that fashioned by the Lat. authors of antiquity; and here is the true beginning of that long reign of the neo-classic tradition, to the breakdown of which Winckelmann (q.v.) contributed so much by his investigations of form at its source in Gk. sculpture and architecture, irrespective of the rules of Lat. formalists. But in B.'s view, Antiquity (i.e. the ancient writers) was Nature; Nature methodized, not Nature in the rough; and B.'s artistic method was the imitation of the pagan (and, pre-eminently, of the Lat.) classics. To neglect their labours would have meant to go over the same ground (i.e. the imitation of Nature) a second time, with probably worse, or not better, results. The Gk. imitators of Nature, and the Lat. writers who had so successfully rendered them, were themselves models for imitation. They were Nature at one remove; Nature advantageously dressed; and in the study of them lay true wit. But that study was to be governed by 'good sense' (the 'reason' of Pope's prescription) and this 'good sense', obviously akin to the root principle of Cartesian philosophy, and therefore modernist in tendency, replaced the more enthusiastic adoration of the pagan classics which earlier votaries had displayed. Ronsard (q.v.) for instance, in the 16th cent., by discovering Italy for France, had introduced the Fr. Renaissance. But the disciples of what B. called 'good sense', and what a later generation has called 'good form', and what is largely composed of somewhat timid convention, now found Ronsard too undiscriminating in his hospitality to Gk. and Lat. example. He had flooded Fr. lit. and language with a tide of foreign immigrants, and the purists and rationalists from Malherbe to the Fr. Academy did their best to check it and to regulate it. B. aimed at reconciling both streams—classical tradition and modern rationalism; and the old 'servile idolatry' of the classics was to be 'transformed into a reasoned appreciation' (Lanson). There was still the authority of Aristotle, conveyed by a double process of transfusion through Horace and his Ital. commentators (see s.v. Vida); but the Bolæan *Art poétique* did not accept this authority blindfold, nor in a kind of ecstasy of mute adoration. It applied, or sought to apply, the test of reason and commonsense. The petitioners at the court of art and letters—

the forms and diction of the poet's craft—had to submit to a new interrogatory. The credentials of antiquity were not sufficient, as they had sufficed for Ronsard and the Pleiad (q.v.); antiquity had to prove its title at the bar of common consent and by the standard of Cartesian reason. 'Rien n'est beau que le vrai' was the cornerstone of B.'s artistic gospel: Nature is the ultimate truth; and the pagan classics had represented it with the most truthful beauty. If these fundamentals are firmly grasped, the difficulties which surround the changing conception of Nature (q.v.), and its derivatives, contraries and analogues (naturalism, classicism, romanticism, and so forth), are very largely solved. The seeds of neo-classicism, against which Romance (q.v.) and Hellenism (q.v.) both revolted at the end of the 18th cent., will be seen to have been laid up in the theory underlying B.'s *Art poétique*. When the revolt came, it was bitter in the extreme; to the youthful Keats (q.v.), for example, 'the name of one Boileau' was a synonym for anti-poet and anti-Gk., as hateful as anti-Pope to Papists; and, throughout the period which started approximately at the death, 1832, of Goethe and Scott (qq.v.), B. ranked as the archetype of a neo-classicism which laid its dead hand on living lit. The reaction is the measure of his worth. Despite the just detractation which his mistakes and prejudices render necessary, despite, too, his limited imagination and his too great pre-occupation with formalism, B. was the first real critic in modern Europe. He founded certain rules of taste. He released antiquity from the bonds of its worshippers; he undid the frontlet between its eyes and took away the sign upon its hands; he modernized the ancients, in a word, and handed them on for literary purposes, serviceable, reasonable, canonical, not as types of an inaccessible perfection, but as articulated models for imitation. In a sense, the Nature of B. and Pope was the Nature of Rousseau and Wordsworth (q.v.); but the first pair looked at her through the focussing-glasses of the pagan classics, the second pair looked at her with the naked eye, and saw as much as its retina could hold. In this difference lies the clue to that 'quarrel' of the Ancients and Moderns (see s.v. Ancients), in which B. was engaged for five years (1695-1700) with C. Perrault (q.v.), and which did little credit to either. If Perrault had had his way, and had eliminated antiquity from art, he would have eliminated art itself; and the same criticism applies to a later renewal of literary modernism in Walt Whitman, for example. B.'s views of the function of the ancients in modern lit. were sounder, in his day and in ours, and even more conducive to a fair estimate of the living writers, whom, on the whole, he judged with foresight and sanity, than his adversary's defence of the moderns; but the whole quarrel is at present without interest, and is almost as dead as its offspring, the Saxon-Swiss disputation between Gottsched (q.v.) and the Zurichers. Still, these things have a knack of resurrection; and there are signs of the making of a new controversy in the pretensions of 'Futurist' art. B.'s theory, at any rate, was immeasurably better than his practice ; his *Ode sur la Prise de Namur* (alas, for Namur ; always in the wars), 1693, was a very dreary experiment in antique Wardour Street style, and it lent itself easily to a burlesque by Prior (q.v.). Seated on his judgment-stool at the court of the *grand monarque* throughout the period of the *grand siècle*, B. inevitably tended to a degree of dogmatism which made him the terror of his own and the butt of a later generation. But he stands at the head of a school of criticism, with extensive European ramifications, which regularized and standardized the art of poetry, and founded criteria of taste, responsive to reason and consent. This was a great thing done : a point of departure was reached from which the differentiation of kinds, the claims of form, and the fidelity to truth are never likely to go back. Still, it was done at considerable, even excessive, expense ; and this expense had to be liquidated in turn by a *Sturm und Drang* (q.v.) in more countries than that of Schiller (q.v.). B.'s root-error has since been seen to lie in his too strict confinement of the art of letters within its own selected boundaries. The prohibition to stray outside the compound guarded by the tents of the ancients, on the plea that their survey of Nature was so complete as not to require revision, was bound to react unfavourably on later generations, born within the prohibited area. B. confined the art of poetry in a ghetto, and the ghetto-taint of excessive servility and defective enterprise, aptitude and self-help, was bound to display itself in course of time. When and wherever that time arrived, the released children of the ghetto were equally bound to help themselves to more liberty than they could digest. When direct access was given to Nature without, when feeling and colour were re-admitted into the exclusive preserves of Lat. tradition, the Romanticists ran away in the opposite direction, and practised the excesses which we associate with the disciples of Klopstock (q.v.), or which we mark in the coterie of which the brothers Schlegel (q.v.) were leaders. Finally and briefly, it may be said that B. represents a school of criticism, which, though frequently misunderstood, exercised a great influence for good and a far smaller influence for evil on the lit. of the succeeding centuries ; and that the classicism, which we associate with his name, is an inseparable part of every great work of lit. and owes the formulation of many of its highest principles to the perception of the ' lawgiver of Parnassus '.

Not the least of B.'s services to lit. was his restoration of Longinus ' On the Sublime' (see s.v. Sublime) to common uses. Robortelio (q.v.) had transld. the treatise, but B. first utilized it as an authority, and though his *Réflexions sur Longin* deal as much with Perrault as with Longinus, yet there was also the new transln., and the attempt, imperfect but sincere, to get the clue to the meaning of the great Gk. essay in literary criticism.

Boisrobert, de, François le Metel (1592-1662) : Fr. poet ; original member of the Fr. Academy (q.v.). Wr. comedies : *l'Inconnue, la Belle Invisible*, etc., based on Span. models : and supplied at least one scene (from his *Belle Plaideuse*) to Molière, save for whom, it has been averred, we should hardly be aware that B. had written so charming a play. B. was selected by Richelieu (q.v.) as one of his body-guard of 5 poets.

Boissier, Gaston (1823-1908) : Fr. scholar ; wr. *Cicéron et ses Amis*, a brilliant piece of humanistic writing, and other works of Lat. scholarship ; also, a life of mme de Sévigné (q.v.). As successor to a long line of permanent secretaries of the Fr. Academy (q.v.), it fell to B. to write an annual summary of Fr. lit., a task which he discharged with conspicuous skill and tact.

Bolingbroke, Henry St. John, first visct. (1678-1751) : Engl. statesman ; political philosopher ; created visct., 1712 ; impeached for his share in the plans for Jacobite restoration, and name erased from roll of peers, 1714 ; spent some years in France ; pardoned, 1723, but still excluded from House of Lords ; in France, again, 1735-42. B.'s significance lies in 2 directions, one, posth., and the other, contemporary : (1) he deeply influenced the course of democratic Toryism in Engl. politics, and ranks in this respect as a direct precursor of B. Disraeli q.v. ; (2) his two periods of residence in France, with their enforced detachment from current political business, gave him leisure to study the philosophy of affairs, which he employed to excellent purpose. In this sense, B. was a force in the evolution of thought in Europe. Pope (q.v.) deeply admired him, and versified in the *Essay on Man* the system of moral philosophy sketched by B. in a fragmentary manner, *c.* 1730 : the *Essay* is inscribed to B., and starts—
Awake, my St. John ! Leave all meaner things
To low ambition and the pride of kings.
Let us, etc.
B. left his works, publd. and unpubld., to D. Mallet (q.v.), who issued them in 5 vols., 1754. They include *The Idea of a Patriot King*, 1738 ; *The Study and Use of History*, 1735 ; *The Spirit of Patriotism*, 1736, and others.

Bonald, de, Louis Gabriel Ambroise (1754-1840) : Fr. writer on politics ; founded the *Conservateur* with Chateaubriand and Lamennais (qq.v.), and ranked with J. de Maistre (q.v.) as a leader of the anti-revolutionaries ; *vicomte* by creation, but resigned the honour in 1830. B. enjoyed the patronage of Napoleon through Fontanes (q.v.), but maintained a certain admirable independence of intellect, and was instrumental, outside the sphere of journalism, as a legislative reformer (he wr. *Législation primitive*), esp. in connection with divorce-law.

Bonaventura (d. 1273) : It. scholar ; John of Fidanza ; Franciscan ; card. ; saint ; *doctor seraphicus :* interpreter of Aristotle (q.v.).

Boner, Ulrich (died, 1349) : Germ. fabulist ; Dominican monk of Berne. His collection of 100 tales and fables of a moral-didactic tendency was entitled by him *Edelstein* (' precious stone '), and was the first bk. to be printed in Germ. (1461).

Bopp, Franz (1791-1867) : Germ. philologer ; founder of the science of comparative grammar. Wr., 1816, his *System of Conjugation*, which preceded his twenty years' labours at his

masterwork, the *Comparative Grammar* of
Sanscrit, Zend, Gr., Lat., Lithuanian, Gothic,
and Germ., 1833-52; to which he added,
later, Armenian and Old Slavonic.

Borch, Ole (1626-90): Dan. encyclopedic writer;
polyhistor; his 'subjects were theology,
philosophy, philology, poetry, anatomy,
chemistry, and botany'. It was a type of
universal learning satirized by Holberg (q.v.)
in his national comedies, and is mainly interesting to-day as an illustration of the backwardness of the culture which Holberg raised to so
high a level. B.'s name was Latinized to
Olaus Borrichius.

Borja, de, Francisco (1581-1658): Span. poet;
prince de Esquilache by rank; the names
Borja and Esquilache, representing Borgia
and Squillace, testify to B.'s Ital. descent.
He took a high place in the diplomatic service of
Spain, and acted as viceroy of Peru; wr.
several *Obras* (Works) *en Verso*, of considerable
merit.

Borjesson, Johan (1790-1866): Swed. poet. B.
was an early member of the Aurora league and
a contributor to the journal, *Phosphorus*
(q.v.); but he made little impression on his
contemporaries, and is chiefly remembered
to-day by his national tragedy *Erik xiv*,
written late in life, 1846.

Boron. See **Robert le Boron.**

Borovsky (1821-56): Czech publicist. Borovsky's
real name was Karel Havliczek, but he is
commonly known by his *nom de guerre*. His
journalistic activities, in the stormy times in
which he lived, brought him into conflict with
the Austrian Government, 'not only because he
criticized their misrule, but also because he very
ably instructed the Czech public in the elementary knowledge of politics' (Chudoba, *Short
Survey Czech Lit.*, 102). His papers, the 'National News' and the 'Slav', were successively
suppressed, and he was interned in the Tyrol,
his early death being ascribed partly to
political persecution. B. reprinted 2 vols. of
religious, social and political essays; wr.
'Pictures from Russia'; transld. some novels
of Gogol (q.v.), and was a clever writer of
epigrams, chiefly in the manner of Logau
(q.v.).

Borrow, George (1803-81): Eng. travel-writer;
agent for many years to British and Foreign
Bible Society, and employed his journeys in
France, Spain, Germany, Russia, etc., to seek
out the stranger and more nomadic types in
those countries, thus developing a pleasant
taste for folklore, philosophy, and the borderland of romance, satisfied particularly in Wales.
Wr. *The Zincali*, 1841; *The Bible in Spain*,
1843; *Lavengro*, 1851; *The Romany-Rye*,
1857; *Wild Wales*, 1862; etc.; and, though
his contributions to research in the various
sciences which he affected may not have proved
considerable, though his vagrant and exotic
tastes may have been less than fully well
suited to the work in which he was employed,
yet, 'when all is said and done', as was
written in a sympathetic art. in *The Times Lit.
Supp.*, 28 Aug., 1914, 'what fun we have with
him! How rich and mellow is the prose! How
full of light and air the scene! What gaiety!
What a sense of adventure! What relish of the
common things of life!' What a *picaro*, we

may add, peeping up from the travels of a
commis-voyageur!

Boscan, Juan (*c.* 1490-1542): Span. poet;
Catalan (q.v.) by birth at Barcelona (his
Catalonian name was Bosca); Italianate and
Castilian by training and choice; served in
the army, and was at one time tutor to the duke
of Alva. The card. date in B.'s life was the
year 1526, and the event on which it hinged
was his intercourse at Granada with Andrea
Navagero (q.v.), Venetian ambassador to
emperor Charles v (q.v.). B. has left on
record the incidents of this meeting, which
had effects not merely on the direction of his
own talent but on the whole course of Span.
lit.; and the passage (from his letter to the
duchess of Soma) must be transcribed in full:
'As I [Boscan] was discussing with him
[Navagero] matters of wit and letters, and
principally the relative merits of different
languages, he asked me why I did not make an
attempt, in Castilian, at the sonnets and other
poetic forms employed by good Italian authors;
and he did not merely refer to this in passing,
but urged me to devote myself to the experiment. A few days later I had to return home,
and the long and lonely journey gave me the
opportunity of thinking of what Navagero had
said; and so I began to try this kind of
verse. . . . Presently—perhaps because we
grow to be fond of our own creations—it
seemed to me that my experiments were proving
successful, and my taste for them increased little
by little'. This passage, as Kelly remarks,
is 'classic'; and Ticknor (i, 439) rightly says:
'it is rare that any one individual has been able
to exercise such an influence on the literature of
a foreign nation. It is still more rare—indeed,
perhaps, wholly unknown—that the precise
mode in which it was exercised can be so
precisely explained'. What happened was
really analogous to the influence of Ital.
models on the linguistic and metrical reformers
in France, known as the Pleiad (q.v.); B.
was a Fr. Pleiad *in petto*, and Navagero was
his single guide; and the conversion of Span.
verse-forms to the more artistic and artificial
modes elaborated in Ital. had been facilitated
by the political approach between the two
countries after the conquest of Naples by
Alfonso v and i (q.v.) in 1443. The Neapolitan
school of poetry in the latter half of the 15th
cent. had been frankly Hispano-Ital.; and the
Venetian ambassador was sowing on congenial
soil where he dropped his seeds of verse-reform
on B.'s receptive mind. It would be an
exaggeration to say that B.'s personal success
was successful all along the line. The new
style encountered reaction and opposition;
the 'Petrarquistas' were attacked by Castillejo
and Gongora (qq.v.), for example; but, 'seen
at a distance, in the perspective of literary
history, Boscan appears to us as the founder of a
new poetic dynasty, the head of an irresistible
advance-guard' (Kelly, *Lit. espagn.*, 189).
In this aspect, B.'s work is more significant than
his writings, which were publd., 1543, by his
widow at Barcelona, 'with some by Garcilasso
[q.v.] de la Vega', who had been his intimate
friend. This vol., frequently reprinted, does
not contain the transln. of a tragedy by
Euripides, to which reference is made in the

printing-licence ; nor is that play to be found elsewhere. But B. transld. Castiglione's (q.v.) *Cortegiano* at Garcilasso's 'earnest request' (Castiglione was in Spain as ambassador of pope Clement vii, 1525-26, and the three men may have met) ; he wrote an *Historia de Leandro y Hero*, based partly on B. Tasso's (q.v.) paraphrase of the 'Hero and Leander' of Musæus, and remarkable in comparative lit. for its employment of blank verse (q.v. ; and see s.v. Surrey and Trissino), and in Span. lit. for many charming and graceful passages in its (nearly) 3,000 lines ; he wr. an allegory in octave stanzas, largely adapted from the *Stanze* of Bembo (q.v.) ; and he naturalized in Span. poetry the metres of Dante, Petrarch and Ariosto—the sonnet, the *canzone*, the *terza-rima*, the *ottava-rima*—thus achieving with modest capacity a more valuable measure of reform than greater poets might have compassed with more ambition.

Bossuet, Jacques Bénigne (1627-1704) : Fr. divine, orator, and controversialist ; a foremost figure in the great age of king Louis xiv. B. was the son of a provincial magistrate at Dijon, and was edu. in Jesuit schools there and at Navarre. His tastes were early formed, and he received a canonry at Metz, 1652. The town was full of Catholics, Protestants and Jews, and B.'s powers in controversy and conversion were tested and developed. In 1659, he settled in Paris, and entered on ten years' hard work of theological discourses and exposition, preaching several times before the court, and winning favourable opinions from king Louis. The royal favour was practically proved in 1670, when B. was elevated to the bishopric of Condom, and appointed tutor to the dauphin of France (d. 1711). It was this appointment, responsible at any court, and most responsible, perhaps, at the court of the great Bourbon absolutist, which turned B.'s thoughts more directly to methods of study and theological doctrine. The dauphin was an ungrateful pupil, insuperably incurious of learning, and the large schemes devised for him by B., and described in a Lat. letter to pope Innocent xi, were, unfortunately, of none effect ; though, as the son predeceased the father, France did not lose by the royal pupil's inattention nor gain by the tutor's conscientious efforts. In 1679, the tutelage lapsed, and B., who had resigned his former see, was appointed, 1681, bp. of Meaux ; in this capacity, he took the lead in the conferences of 1682 on the liberties of the Gallican Church, directed to the erection of a second, or Western, Rome at Paris. B. received other valuable posts and benefices : almoner to the dauphin, conservator of the univ., etc. ; and devoted himself at the same time to the work of his see, and to his writings a and discourses in the capital. His literary remains include fine specimens of *oraisons funèbres*, preached at the funerals of the two Fr. queens Henrietta of Engld., of Maria Theresa, arch-duchess of Austria, and others ; an *Exposition de la Foi catholique*, written for Turenne, 1668, and publd. 1681 ; *Méditations sur l'Evangile* and *Elévations sur les Mystères*, written in later life for the communities of religious women, in whom he took special interest ; and a *Discours sur l'Histoire Universelle jusqu'à l'Empire de Charlemagne*, composed, among other works, for the dauphin, 1681, which treated the progress of history from the point of view of divine law. The same point of view dominated B.'s *Politique tirée de l'Ecriture Sainte* ('politics drawn from Sacred Writ'), likewise composed for the prince, which owed something to Hobbes and Milton (qq.v.), and affords a text-book for the lost cause of benevolent absolutism. With B. as a controversialist, significant and formidable though he was, we are perhaps less immediately concerned, save in one aspect to be noted. His history of the 'Variations of the Protestant Churches' belongs to the dead ambition of a dead time, and was followed by replies and a 'Defence', and by a long correspondence with Leibniz (q.v.) and others. The most literary of his religious controversies, however, as well as the most embittered, was that which he engaged with Fénelon (q.v.) against the alleged heresy of Quietism. This doctrine, akin to the more specifically Germ. Pietism (q.v.), had been condemned at Rome, but reappeared from Spain in France, where it attracted mme de Maintenon (q.v.), whose governess-instinct was too moderate, however, to allow her to be overwhelmed by her adherence to it, as mme de Guyon, the head of the Quietist Church in France, was overwhelmed, 1695. The chief protagonists disputed for five years, and Fénelon was convicted (March, 1699), shortly after B. had launched the last philippic, *Rélation sur le quiétisme*, 1698, from his terrible armoury. B. was also the author of minor works ; one on 'Comedy', for example, directed against the libertinism of Molière (q.v., and see s.v. *Libertins*) ; but his chief title to fame rests on his supremacy in eloquence, and on the grave, Cartesian sincerity which illuminated everything that he touched. A more difficult matter, which, happily, lies outside the scope of lit., is the evaluation of his moral influence at the court of Louis xiv, and as the tutor of the dauphin. There are those who blame the great preacher for his failure to enlighten the king on the true duties of a ruler, and to save him (and Europe), accordingly, from the war of 1702-13. The reply, is perhaps, that B. made the theory of autocracy, which he found at court, as responsible and as formidable as he could ; and that, if Louis had lived up to B.'s teaching, the worst evils of his reign would have been averted.

Bostrom, Christopher Jacob (1797-1866) : Swed. moral philosopher. B.'s lectures on ethics are publd. in the Royal collection at Upsala, edited by S. Ribbing, 1897.

Boswell, James (1740-95) : Scot. biographer ; son of lord Auchinleck ; travelled in Europe, meeting Voltaire, Rousseau (qq.v.) ; met Johnson (q.v.) 1763, who procured his election to 'the Club' and his life thenceforward was devoted to the influence of his great friend : 'Johnson owes much to Boswell', says the writer in *C.H.E.L.*, x, 190 ; 'but it was Johnson who gave us Boswell'. He was only 23 years of age when he attached himself to J. ; he had formed his steady purpose as early as 1772, and spoke of it to J. a few years later ; his *Life of Samuel Johnson, LL.D.*, . . . *The whole exhibiting a view of* *lit. and literary men in Great Britain, for nearly half a century, during which he flourished*, was ready, in 2 vols., 1791, swallowing up the earlier reminiscences of Mrs. Piozzi (Thrale) and sir John Hawkins (see s.v. Johnson). The 2nd edn., 3 vols., was publd., 1793 ; the *Life* was edited by Croker, 1831 ; G. B. Hill, 1887 ; A. Birrell, 1896 ; R. Ingpen, 1907, among many other edns. and re-issues. Posterity is gradually recognizing B. as one of the greatest among men of letters ; ' foolish, vain, and absurd in every way ', as sir L. Stephens, himself a biographer, describes him, ' he was yet a far kindlier and more genuine man than many who laughed at him. His singular gifts as an observer could only escape notice from a careless or inexperienced reader. Boswell has a little of the true Shakespearean secret. He lets his characters show themselves without obtruding unnecessary comment. He never misses the point of a story. He gives just what is wanted to explain the full meaning of a repartee. Boswell's accuracy is remarkable, but it is the least part of his merit ' (*Johnson*, ' English Men of Letters ', 90). The sum of his merit is this : that, as Macaulay (q.v.). wrote, by B.'s genius for hero-worship, Johnson's ' peculiarities of manner and that careless table-talk, the memory of which he probably thought would die with him, are likely to be remembered as long as the English language is spoken in any quarter of the globe '.

Bouadilla, de, Bernardo Gonzalez (fl. 1587) : Span. pastoralist ; born in the Canary islands ; studied at Salamanca Univ. Wr. ' Part i [there is no known Part ii] of the Nymphs and Shepherds of Henares' (B. acknowledged that he had never visited the banks of the Henares) : a poor experiment in the Montemayor (q.v.) tradition.

Bouilhet, Louis (1822-69) : Fr. poet. Wr. *Festons et Astralages*, 1859, and *Dernières Chansons*, publd. posth. with a pref. by Flaubert (q.v.), 1872. B. belongs to the brief transition from romanticism to naturalism in Fr. verse.

Boulainvilliers, de, Henri (1658-1722) : Fr. historian ; political philosopher ; *comte* by rank. Wr. a ' History of the Ancient Government of France ' and ' Letters on the *Parlement*', both issued posth., in which he maintained that the feudal system, based by the nobles on their victory over the Gauls, was the fundamental principle of just government. The works acquired some importance in the revolutionary era.

Boulevardier (Fr.) : Descriptive epithet of a class of lit., or, more exactly, of its inspiration, which flourished at the period of the Second Empire in France. The word is not readily translatable. The term *boulevard* (street, avenue) has special application to the streets in the central region of Paris, now, as ever, the capital city of Europe. By an extension of meaning, the *esprit boulevardier* signified the mood of the generation of young bloods, pleasure-seeking, material, and mundane, who were to lead Napoleon iii to the disaster of Sedan. The allusion is obvious to the *boulevards*, and to the associations of the *cafés* and *restaurants* with which they are so

frequently studded. Architecturally, that *esprit* found expression in the work of Baron Haussmann, who did so much to build the Paris streets, and in that of the designers and decorators of the Opera House (1861-74), at the junction of 5 principal thoroughfares. In its literary aspect, it was expressed by such writers as Nestor Roqueplan (1804-70), Aurélien Scholl (1833-1902), and the editorial staff of the *Figaro*, who are not further mentioned in this vol. Labiche (q.v.) was the most permanently noteworthy of the circle, though his title to renown as a man of letters may be seriously disputed. But the chief feature of the movement, which was partly a reaction against the excessive idealism of the romanticists, was the vogue of operettas. Their musical director was J. Offenbach, and the two leading librettists were Meilhac and Halévy (qq.v.). The joint products of this trio were as popular and successful in their day as the Gilbert (q.v.) and Sullivan dramas of a rather later day in London ; and Savoyard might fairly be used as a rough equivalent of *Boulevardier*. The *b.* spirit was eminently happy in discharging its function of amusement ; and it did not hesitate to employ the full gamut of the resources of buffoonery, ridicule, irreverence, blasphemy, with a sort of steady undercurrent of commonsense. A characteristic and historic play was the *Grande Duchesse de Gerolstein*, produced by the trio in 1867, the year of the Universal Exhibition.

Bourdaloue, Louis (1632-1704) : Fr. divine. Born at Bourges ; edu. by the Jesuits ; reached Paris, 1669, where he soon established a reputation as a preacher and confessor equal to, if not higher than, that of Bossuet or Massillon (qq.v.). B. was frequently invited to deliver sermons before king Louis xiv, and he was the intimate friend of mme de Sévigné and other leaders of the *grand siècle*. His style of eloquence is usually described as lacking fire and colour ; there is contemporary evidence, however, to the presence of these qualities in the spoken discourses, which were to that extent edited by Père Bretonneau, who publd. (1707-34) B.'s works in 8 vols. In the war between the Jesuits and the Jansenists (see s.vv. Jansen, Port Royal, Pascal), B.'s sermons were an effective weapon to reinforce Bossuet's vigour in controversy.

Bourrienne, de, L. A. Fauvelet de Charbonnière (1769-1834) : Fr. historian ; friend and secretary to emperor Napoleon i. Wr. *Mémoires sur Napoléon, le Directoire, le Consulat, l'Empire et la Restauration*, 10 vols., 1829-31, full of interest, though full, too, of mistakes.

Boursault, Edmé (1638-1701) : Fr. comic dramatist ; wr. *Mercure Galant*, which introduced journalism on to the stage, a rich trove of new manners and models. B. was a popular playwright in his day, and supplied many hints to Vanbrugh (q.v.) ; he was unfortunate, however, in failing to conciliate the good will of Boileau, Racine, and Molière, who, with La Fontaine (see s.vv.), formed a formidable quartette of makers of opinion.

Bracciolini, G. F. Poggio. See **Poggio**.

Bradley, Francis Herbert (1846-1924) : Engl. philosopher ; lived at Oxford ; appointed

O.M., 1924. Wr. *Ethical Studies*, 1876; *Principles of Logic*, 1883; *Appearance and Reality*, his masterwork, 1893.

Brandes, Georg (e Morris Cohen) (born, 1842): Dan. critic; of Jew. parentage, but a free-thinker in all departments of thought; appointed prof. by royal 'patent conferring rank', 1902, in which year, on his 60th birthday, B. received numerous congratulatory testimonials, hailing him as a 'polemical writer of genius', an 'inspired rebel,' and so forth. In early life (1865 onwards), he took a prominent part in the controversy evoked by the speculations of Kierkegaard (q.v.), and was the spokesman of a group of young radicals, whose views he expressed, 1866, in his *Dualism in Modern Philosophy*; J. S. Mill (q.v.) at this time was B.'s personal friend as well as leader. He paid long visits to France, Germany, Engld. and Italy, meeting the chief thinkers and men of letters of the day, and when he returned to Copenhagen in 1871 'he was a mature thinker, a realist, and a literary revolutionist, entirely free from theological ethics, metaphysics, and romantic notions in æsthetics' (*Jew. Encycl.*, iii, 351). In that year he began his lectures on *Main Currents in 19th Cent. Lit.*, which have been transld. into several languages (in Engl., Heinemann, 6 vols., 1901 onwards): 'the central object of this work' is stated in the pref. to be 'the re-action in the first decades of the nineteenth century against the literature of the eighteenth, and the vanquishment of that reaction. The historic incident is of European interest, and can only be understood by a comparative study of European literature'. The method was somewhat that of Taine (q.v.), and no one was better qualified than B. to prosecute it successfully. From 1877-82 he lived in Berlin, and thoroughly acclimatized himself as a German; there he wr. his monographs on lord Beaconsfield and F. Lassalle (each, curiously, a fellow Jew), followed, after his return to Denmark, by his large and valuable study of Shakespeare (E.T., 2 vols., 1898), which, with essays on Holberg (q.v.) Young Germany (q.v.), etc., form the chief contributions to criticism of a writer whose stormy youth was crowned by the title of the grand old man of Denmark. (*Sept.*, 1925).

Brandes, Johann Christian (1735-99): Germ. actor, playwright, and novelist. B. tried his hands at many trades, honest and otherwise, till he found his vocation on the stage, to which he contributed some popular farces. Wr. an autobiography, posth. publd., of some interest in the history of his times.

Brandt, Geraert (1626-85): Dutch historian and poet; preacher. Wr. religious verse in the vein but without the force of Vondel (q.v.); composed, 1646, funeral oration for Hooft (q.v.), which gained a reputation in excess of its merits as a mere adaptation of the similar eulogy pronounced by Du Perron (q.v.) over Ronsard (q.v.). Edited the works of Vondel and Hooft, to which he contributed valuable biographies; and wr. *Life of Admiral de Ruiter*, 1687, and a *History of the Reformation*, 1668-74, which are fine examples of Dutch narrative prose, though in a much earlier stage of development than that of Effen (q.v.).

The biography of the heroic de Ruyter is B.'s masterpiece in prose; selections from it were issued in 1864 by Ten Brink.

Brandt, Sebastian (1458-1521): Germ. satirist; resided at Strassburg. Wr. allegorical-didactic poem, *das Narrenschiff* ('The Ship of Fools'), which cleverly combined 2 motives of popular appeal,—rough fun and fanciful travel; the *Narr* on his *Schiff*. Thus, it took at once a high place in the folly (q.v.) -lit., which it virtually initiated, as a separate branch of European letters. The imaginary voyage had been familiar since Lucian, and satire (tending to horse-play) since Aristophanes; the combination was new. B. counted his fools in the broadest sense of the Book of Proverbs, and herded them on shipboard as indiscriminately as the animals on Noah's ark. Greed, luxury, sciolism, snug foibles and smug pretences, were all alike measured by the standard of self-knowledge, which B. extolled as the test of wisdom; poverty he regarded as the mother of virtue, and contentment as the secret of happiness. (See s.v. Sachs, for a somewhat similar and characteristically old-German ethical point of view). It was by his selection of types rather than by his statement of principles that B. took a step in advance of the old medieval moralists, with their repertory of abstract virtues and vices, and this lead was rapidly developed. B. wr. his poem in the vernacular, and it was publd. at Basel, 1494, with illustrative woodcuts, which helped to popularize the Emblembooks (q.v.) of the 15th and 16th cents. Locher (q.v.) transld. it into Lat., whence it passed into Engl. through Barclay (q.v.).

Brantôme, abbé de; Pierre de Bourdeille (*c.* 1534-1614): Fr. memoirist. Son of a small landed proprietor, young de Bourdeille was granted the abbacy of Brantôme by king Henry ii at the age of 16, and is, and was, always known by its title. An adventurer at heart, he took his fill of fighting in Italy, Scotland, Africa, Malta, etc., as well as in the civil wars of his own country. Was chamberlain to king Henry iii, was exiled from the court, 1582, and, after hesitating as to his place among the various factions, was condemned to inactivity by a fall from his horse. Wr. a series of memoir-studies: 'Lives of Great Captains, Foreign and French'; 'Lives of Illustrious Women'; 'Gallant Women'; 'Adventures in Spain'; 'Duels and Challenges', etc.; nothing was publd. in B.'s lifetime, and the *ed. pr.* appeared in 1665, when the pretext, or sanction, of historical interest began its long work of condonation of the personal and in places scandalous character of much of what B. recorded. 'No writer, perhaps, has ever put things more disgraceful on paper; but no writer has ever written of such things in such a perfectly natural manner' (Saintsbury). B. had the moral standard of his age, and he brought to its lightly-borne burden the eye of an apt observer, the tongue of a ready speaker, and the experience of a soldier of fortune. These gifts unite to make his work one of the most readable human documents in literary history.

Brawe, von, Joachim Wilhelm (1738-58): Germ. playwright. Friend of Lessing (q.v.) at

Leipsic. Wr. classical drama, *Brutus*, in the decasyllabic metre of Engl. plays, in preference to the Fr. alexandrine (see, too, s.v. Schlegel, J. H.).

Brébeuf, Guillaume (1618-61) : Fr. poet. Transld. Lucan's *Pharsalia* into Fr. verse.

Bredahl, Christian Hviid (1784-1860): Dan. poet ; of marked dramatic talent, which did not come to full or mature expression ; B. died in poverty. His 6 vols. of 'Dramatic Scenes', 1819-33, were not intended for enactment ; they are, rather, sketches for plays, laid in an imaginary kingdom of the moon, and rich in humour, satire (sometimes savage), and true pathos. There are Shakespearean qualities in B., whose muse is isolated from the rival schools (Fr. and Germ.) of contemporary Dan. lit. He lacked the stage-instinct, or *flair* for the theatre, and is one of the greatest dramatists *manqués* in literary history. Brandes (q.v.), the eminent Dan. critic, calls B. 'the coarse and wild dramatist of indignation-pessimism', and he is noteworthy as the one Dan. poet with whom Ibsen (q.v.) felt himself in sympathy.

Bredero, Gerbrand Adrianszoon (1585-1618) : Dutch dramatist (comic) and poet ; son of a shoemaker ; edu. as an artist, but drawn early by marked literary talent into the orbit of the Eglantine (q.v.), and was one of the unsuccessful suitors of Tesselschade Visscher (q.v.). 'In Bredero we have the only counterpart in Dutch letters to the Jan Steens and Brouwers of contemporary art' (*C.M.H.*, iv, 718, following Ten Brink, *Geschiedenis der Nederl. Letterkunde*, 378). B. edited *Apollo of Ghesang der Muzen* (q.v.), a kind of Dutch Tottel's (q.v.) miscellany, 1615, and contributed to it many popular songs and verses, not unlike those of Burns (q.v.) in later Scotland. Wr. romantic dramas after Span. and Ital. models, the best parts of which are, admittedly, the comic interludes ; farces ; and two comedies proper, *'t Moortje*, 1617, and *De Spaensche Brabander*, 1618 : the former based on Terence, *Eunuchus*, and the latter on the anon. *Lazarillo* (q.v.) of Span. picaresque fiction. Both are replete with the racy realism of bourgeois life in Amsterdam, and entitle B. to a high place as a comic dramatist ; they have marks of Rabelaisian breadth and Shakespearean humour, and more years might have brought B. better fame. The 3rd centenary of his birth was the occasion of a festival in Holland, 1885. It is interesting to remark in B.'s failure as a romantic dramatist the corresponding imperception of his countrymen to the literary motives which glorified Elizabethan lit. B. lived in the most active dramatic period of 'merry old Amsterdam', as its own historians describe it, when Engl. players brought Marlowe, Jonson, and Shakespeare on the stage of the Chamber theatres ; but he seems to have been most affected by the humorous side of the Elizabethan genius. His *Griane*, 1612, showed traces of the inspiration of Shakespeare's *Winter's Tale*, presented at Amsterdam in the same year.

Breitinger, Johann Jakob (1701-76) : Germ.-Swiss critic and publicist ; teacher at the gymnasium at Zurich, and a protagonist in the literary feud between Zurich and Leipsic. The story is told s.v. Bodmer, the brother-in-arms of Breitinger in the fight, and the better man of letters of the two. (See also s.v. Gottsched, the leader on the Saxon side). B. collaborated with Bodmer in the Addisonian paper which they publd. called 'Painters' Discourses' ; and he issued in 1740 a treatise on poetics by which he definitely ranged himself on the victorious side of Anglo-Germ. Romanticism *versus* the neo-Classicism of Boileau (q.v.) in France.

Bremer Beiträge (1744-48): 'The Bremen Transactions' ; short title of the 'New Transactions for the Delight of Understanding and Wit' (*Neue Beiträge zum Vergnügen des Verstandes und Witzes*), issued at Bremen in the course of the controversy provoked by Gottsched (q.v.). The B.B. was founded on liberal principles and on the anti-Gottsched side, and among its founders was Adolf Schlegel (q.v.).

Bremer, Frederika (1801-65) : Swed. novelist ; romanticist. B.'s first conspicuous success was 'The H. family', 1830 ; her collected *Teckningar* ('Sketches') contain the titles of a variety of stories, familiar to Engl. readers in the versions of Mary Howitt (q.v.) : 'Brothers and Sisters', 'Father and Daughter', 'The President's Daughters', 'Life in Dalecarlia' and 'The Neighbours', are, perhaps, the best known in this country and abroad.

Brentano, Clemens Maria (1778-1842) ; Germ. poet and novelist. Leader at Heidelberg (q.v.) of the younger Romanticists (s.v. Romance), but was somewhat of a thorn in the flesh of the older apostles of the school : 'even in poetry the course of progress did not follow the road which the prophets had laid down. The importunate and eccentric subjectivity of the youthful Brentano began to alienate the friends of the movement at Jena, and there were occasions when Tieck had to protest against his absurd exaggerations, which threatened to compromise the whole school' (Haym, *die Romant. Schule*, 861). However this may be, the seeds were sown by the school, and it was a little indecent of the sowers to object to the scent of the flower. B.'s very life, it has been justly said, 'resembles in many respects a Romantic novel' ; such a novel as the various 'wanderings' of apprentices to practical experience, of which Goethe's *Wilhelm Meister* set the type. He rejected a business career, and spent some time at the univ. of Jena, then a headquarters of Romance, where the heady wine quickly filled him. Many unsettled years succeeded, broken by stays at Heidelberg, Berlin, and Munich, the first at the beginning and the second towards the end of his life. His brief married life with Sophie (Schubart) Mereau (1770-1806), herself a poet and a Romanticist, who was divorced for his sake in 1803, was spent at Heidelberg ; he m. again, but divorced his second wife. In middle life, he entered the Roman Catholic communion. B.'s 1st considerable bk., after a satire on Kotzebue (q.v., the common butt of every budding Romanticist), was *Godwi*, 1801, described by the author as a 'bewildered' (*verwildert*) romance, which is not an uncharitable epithet. It was in the line of *William Lovell* and *Lucinde* (see s.v. Schlegel), but contained some songs which were afterwards extracted for the *Wunderhorn* (see below), as well as a ' Lore ' lay (of the Rhine), later immortalized by Heine (q.v.). ' The Chronicle of a Wandering Scholar ' (*Aus der Chronika eines fahrenden Schülers*), 1803, publd. 1818, was a charming piece of medieval prose-romance ; and shortly afterwards, 1805, B., in conjunction with Arnim (q.v.), who m. his sister Bettina, publd. vol. i of *Des Knaben Wunderhorn*, followed by vols. ii and iii in 1808. This was B.'s most important work, both at its own time and afterwards. Briefly, it took up the revival of the Volkslied (q.v. ; folksong) in a more national spirit than had governed Herder's (q.v.) selection of ' the voices of the peoples ' just a generation earlier. The two Heidelberg poets, as Arnim explained in his introductory essay ' on folk-songs ', were animated by the desire—Romantic in its origin and scope—to assist the new growth of Germ. national sentiment by evoking from the Germ. past the memories, hopes, and inspiration imbedded in popular song. Herder had been a scholar, even an antiquary ; B. and Arnim were patriots first and last. It was for the sake of the call of the ' lied ' to the ' Volk ' that the old Volkslieder were to be revived ; the harp was to be taken down from the willow tree ; the old songs were to be sung in a new land, and, haply, the new would be revealed as merely the old renewed. It was a re-birth of Germany at which they aimed, not merely at evidences to Germ. humanism. The songs which the people had made were to re-make the people, even though the Fr. stranger was within the gates. Thus, the bks. of the *Knaben Wunderhorn* (' The Boy's Cornucopia ', so called from the title of the opening piece) formed a definite and palpable document of Germ. Romanticism, however much anxiety ' young Brentano ' may have caused to the fathers of his school. Goethe accepted the dedication of vol. i, and the work was quickly accepted on its merits as a splendid edition of the old songs, adapted to modern ears and tastes, and as a monument of the Romantic movement.

Bretagne, Breton. See s.vv. Romans bretons, Bodel, and Romance.

Brethren of the Common Lot : Dutch brotherhood of clergy and laity, who, without binding themselves for the whole of their lives, yet lived together in fraternities under a kind of cloistral rule ; founded at Deventer (q.v.) in 14th cent. by Geert (Gerhard) Groot (q.v.) and Florentius Radewyns (q.v.). The object which these semi-mystics set before themselves was to promote the humanistic work of copying MSS. and starting schools in which the moral and religious discipline should be based on the study of Lat. The two schools visited by Erasmus (q.v.)—Deventer and Hertogenbosch (Bois-le-duc)—were among the foundations of the Brethren, though Hegius (q.v.), the great headmaster, was not of their number. Humanism in the Netherlands and in Germany was much indebted to the foresight and zeal of the fraternity (Lat. *Fratres Collationarii* ; Dutch, *Fraterhuis*), which was also significant and influential by the importance which its members attached to the study of the Bible (q.v.) in the vernacular. To the work of these Christian Brethren lit. is deeply indebted,

particularly for the *Imitation of Christ* of Thomas (q.v.) à Kempis, and for the writings of Erasmus. The reforming and educative aims of the B. were more than fully resumed by the leaders of the Protestant Reformation, and a further cause of their decline in that age was the spread of Renaissance theories of education (q.v.) from Italy to northern Europe.

Bristol, Geo. Digby, second earl of (1612-77) : Engl. dramatist ; K.G., 1661. Transld. several comedies of Calderon (q.v.), including *Elvira*, 1667, from *No Siempre lo Poer es Cierto* (' The Worst not always true '). There is no record of this play having been acted, but lord B. was one of several playwrights (though he was more famous as diplomatist and statesman) who domesticated the Span. drama of the cloak and sword (see s.v.) on the Engl. stage.

Brockes, Berthold Heinrich (1680-1747) : Germ. poet ; councillor at Hamburg. Effected translns. from Marino (q.v.), from Fr. poetry, and from Pope and J. Thomson (qq.v.), whose influence, through the *Windsor Forest* of the one and the *Seasons* of the other, was directly instrumental in inspiring B.'s ' Earthly Pleasure in God ' (9 bks. of didactic verse, 1721-48), and, through B., the love of nature and natural description, new at that date in Germ. poetry. This Engl. influence, reinforced by the Fr. influence of Rousseau, was wrought to greater works of native art by Hagedorn, Klopstock (qq.v.) and others.

Brontë, -i. Charlotte (1816-55) : Engl. novelist ; 3rd of 6 children (5 daughters) born to Rev. Patrick (1777-1861) and Mrs. Maria (Branwell, 1783-1821 ; m. 1812) Brontë, the 2 eldest of whom died in 1825. The 4 others were brought up in their father's parsonage at Haworth, Yorks., a lonely moorland parish, which has long been an object of pilgrimage by admirers of the genius of the 3 B. sisters. C.B., the eldest of those who grew to womanhood, was a kind of anxious mother to the rest, and lived even to mother her father with like conscientious anxiety. It was an austere and a difficult home, with a dyspeptic and passionate father, whose deep affection for his children was checked by ideas on education derived from Rousseau (q.v. ; *Emile*) and Thos. Day (q.v.), and by strong views on the virtues of hardiness, which he seems to have failed to qualify by remembering the isolation of his parish, the motherlessness of his children, and their inherited ill-health. C.B.'s *Life*, which necessarily included that of her sisters and brother, has been written for all time by Mrs. Gaskell (q.v.), and has been the subject of writers as distinguished as Swinburne (q.v.) and Mr. A. Birrell : a leading authority and Brontë-collector has been Mr. Clement K. Shorter, whose *The Brontës' Life and Letters* was publd. in 2 vols., 1908. C.B.'s experiences as a governess in Engld., and a student and teacher in Brussels (where her tutor, prof. Constantin Heger was the ' Paul Emanuel ' of her novel, *Villette* : see, particularly, ' Charlotte Brontë's " Tragedy " ; by Marion H. Spielmann, in *The Times*, 29 July, 1913) ; her visits to London after her sisters' death, her shy lionizing by Thackeray (q.v.) and others ; her constant debt to the generous publisher, G. Smith (q.v.) ; her several proposals of marriage, and her final acceptance, 1854, of the hand of her father's curate, Rev. Arthur Bell Nicholls, who survived his eminent wife more than 50 years,—these facts are familiar in literary history, which has seized unerringly on the marvel of so much talent in so little room, so much passion in such narrow circumstances, and so much renown fulfilled in so few years. In 1846, Messrs. Aylott and Jones, 8, Paternoster Row, publd. *Poems by Currer, Ellis and Acton Bell* (Charlotte, Emily and Annie B.), designed by the sisters originally (in a letter from C.B. to the publishers) as ' one 8vo vol., of the same quality of paper and size of type as Moxon's last edition of Wordsworth '. The poems, she wrote, ' are the work of three persons, relatives ; their respective pieces are distinguished by their signatures ', which, as we know, but as the publishers did not know, were *noms de guerre*, chosen to disguise their sex. The reviewer in the *Athenæum* (4 July, 1846) assigned the highest rank of the 3 ' brothers ' to E.B. We must not pause at the details of this biography, perennially fascinating though it be. Literary history records the facts that *Jane Eyre*, C.B.'s 1st novel, and, by common consent, the most permanent contribution of the sisters to polite letters, was publd. (by Smith, Elder and Co.), 1847, and that, though considered rather daring and outspoken, it achieved a success which has been brilliantly maintained. It is a woman's novel from start to finish, a cry out of the heart of unfulfilled and partly inexpressive feminity, cast into the form of domestic fiction, with some of the machinery of the 18th cent., particularly the hidden horror of the lunatic in a secret chamber. *Shirley* followed, 1849 ; *Villette*, 1852 ; the *Professor* (written first, but declined), 1857 ; and *Emma* (unfind.), 1860, in *Cornhill Magazine*.

-ii. **Patrick Branwell** (1817-48) : Engl. author and artist ; brother of above ; a man of inhibited tastes and vicious life (the latter probably due to the former), who caused grave trouble at home. Attempts have been made to credit him with the chief share in writing *Wuthering Heights* (see E.B., below) and, though this theory is untenable, there is no doubt that he possessed great gifts, which he failed miserably to use.

-iii. **Emily Jane** (1818-48) : Engl. poet and novelist (Ellis Bell) ; wr. *Wuthering Heights*, 1847, a curiously morbid and stormy novel, and was the author of the best pieces in *Poems*, 1846 ; sister of above.

-iv. **Anne** (1820-49) : Engl. novelist (Acton Bell) ; wr. *Agnes Grey*, 1847 ; *Tenant of Wildfell Hall*, 1848 ; sister of above.

Even at this distance of time, it is difficult to read without emotion what ' Currer Bell ' wr., in Sept., 1850, of her sisters whom she was soon to follow to the grave : ' Neither Ellis nor Acton ', she wr., ' allowed herself for one moment to sink under want of encouragement ; energy nerved the one, and endurance upheld the other. They were both prepared to try again. . . . But a great change approached ; . . . in the very heat and burden of the day, the labourers failed over their work. My sister Emily first declined . . . she sank rapidly. She made haste to leave us. . . . Stronger than a man, simpler than a child, her

nature stood alone. The awful point was that, while full of ruth for others, on herself she had no pity ; the spirit was inexorable to the flesh. . . She was not buried ere Anne fell ill. . . . she followed in the same path with slower step, and with a patience that equalled the other's fortitude '.

Is E.B. the greatest of the 3 tragic sisters ? ' Examine her work as we may,' says a writer in *The Times Lit. Supp.* (5 Nov., 1908) ' the figure of Emily Brontë becomes more and more of an enigma. One human being, it seems, and that a shy and secluded girl, has been able, without experience of life, without help or even the desire for it, to reach a depth of knowledge to which, for the rest of the world, the way lies only through the lives of others. Emily asked for no share in the lives of others, and she would give none in her own. She held aloof, clasping her liberty, and all it meant to her is more, perhaps, than we can hope to understand '.

Brooke, -i. Henry (1703-83) : Irish novelist ; spent much of his literary life in London, where he made great friends in the circle of Pope (q.v.) and others. C. Kingsley (q.v.) wr. a pref., 1859, to B.'s best known novel, *The Fool of Quality*, 5 vols., 1765-70, which is as true to-day as it was then : ' In that book ', says Kingsley, ' we have the whole man : the education of an ideal nobleman by an ideal merchant prince has given him room for all his speculations on theology, political economy, the relation of sex and family, and the training, moral and physical, of a Christian gentleman '. This last phrase, so reminiscent of the object proposed in the *Faerie Queen* (see s.v. Spenser), accounts for the concluding sentences from the same pref. The wise reader, says Kingsley, ' will irritate himself no more about defects of outward method, but will be content to let the author teach his own lesson in his own way, trusting (and he will not trust in vain) that each seeming interruption is but a step forward in the moral progress at which the author aims. And if he shall have arrived at this discovery, he will be able possibly to regard at least with patience those who are rash enough to affirm that they have learnt from this book (*The Fool of Quality*) more which is pure, sacred and eternal, than from any which has been published since Spenser's Fairy Queen '. It is not meet that the 20th cent. should question the verdict of Kingsley in 1859 on Brooke in 1765 ; a reputation which was revived after 100 years may well survive another century. B. had a mystical vein in his composition, which recommended him to Wesley (q.v.), who deemed *The Fool of Quality* ' one of the most beautiful pictures that ever was drawn in the world '. It must be added that it was drawn in the world of sentiment opened by Rousseau (q.v.), and that B. was an intense believer in the re-ordering of life on a surer moral foundation.

-ii. **Charlotte** (d. 1793) : Irish scholar ; daughter of above (one of the youngest of 22 children, born to him and his ward, Catherine, *née* Meares, whom H. B. m. before she was 15) ; wr., 1789, *Reliques of Irish Poetry*, consisting, like the Loeb Classics of a later day, of the orig. text and an Engl. transln. *en régard*.

-iii. Stopford Augustus (1832-1916) : Engl. (-Irish) critic ; divine ; gr.-gr.-gr.-grandson of Wm. B., of Rantavan, County Cavan, who was the grandfather of H.B., above : born and edu. in Ireland ; held incumbencies in London ; chaplain to princess-royal (empress Victoria) in Berlin ; chaplain-in ord. to queen Victoria ; seceded, 1880, to Unitarian Church. Wr. classic *Life of Frederick Robertson, of Brighton*, 1865 ; sundry theological works of more than temporary importance, and works of literary criticism, including *A Primer of English Lit.*, 1876 (frequently re-issued), which sold more like a popular novel than a text bk., and which was the subject of an ' Essay in Criticism ' by M. Arnold (q.v.). Wr., too, one part of a *History of Early Engl. Lit.*, and enhanced a considerable reputation by his monographs on Tennyson and Browning and his vol. on *Four Poets*. B. received the compliment of a congratulatory address on his 80th birthday.

Brorson, Adolf (1694-1764) : Dan. theological writer ; bp. B.'s poetic reputation rests on his admirable hymnody, in which he surpassed even Kingo (q.v.) in stirring and moving qualities.

Brouwer, Petrus van Limburg (1798-1847) : Dutch novelist and scholar. Wr. a history of Gk. civilization, and a monograph on ' Cæsar and his Contemporaries ', as well as a modern romance of theological import, and modern adaptations of stories from Gk. fiction.

Browne, Thomas (1605-82) : Engl. physician and antiquary ; settled at Norwich, 1637 ; knt., 1671. Wr. *c.* 1635 his most famous bk., *Religio Medici*, which was the first of a fairly long family of individual religious confessions, from Dryden's (q.v.) *Religio Laici*, 1683, to sir Arthur Keith's *Religion of a Darwinist*, 1925, in our own times. One of several MS. copies of B.'s bk. was printed, 1642, without his knowledge, and was made the subject of some critical observations by sir Kenelin Digby (q.v.), to which B. (1) replied, and (2) retorted by issuing, 1643, a true and full copy of the surreptitiously printed works. A certain John Merryweather transld. it into Lat., 1644, in which language it crossed to the continent, and achieved an immense success in France (see s.v. Patin). The faith of a physician in the 17th cent., the compatibility of science and faith, is of less moment to-day, than the delights of B.'s style, into which he rolled, since the style was *l'homme même*, all the curious lore, and the sense of rhythm, and the pot-pourri of colours and conceits, which were partly his Elizabethan heritage and partly his individual equipment. Wr., too, *Pseudodoxia epidemica : inquiries into Vulgar Errors*, 1646 ; and *Hydriotaphia, or Urn-burial* and *The Garden of Cyrus*, 1658, distinguished by an ' utter magnificence of combined rhythmical cadence and imaginative illustration ' (*C.H.E.L.*, vii, 237), which considerably impressed later colourists in Engl. prose-style.

Browning, -i. Robert (1812-89) : Engl. poet ; devoted himself throughout his poetic writings to the study of the drama of psychology, of incidents in operation in the development of the soul of man. And of all formative incidents, compelling the soul to growth, human love was the most powerful and irresistible : ' the removal of love from among Browning's themes would be, original as he was in everything, the removal of his most original, as well as his most massively valuable contribution to our lit. It would have left the poet himself a man without a purpose in a universe without meaning. Love, in the last resort, was the only article in his creed' (sir Henry Jones, *C.H.E.L.*, xiii, 50). This, too, was the real point of contact between R.B. and his poet-wife (see below). ' *The soul in action*—this alone he held worth attention ', is the like statement of prof. Omond (*P.E.L.*, xi, 68).

If we cling to this clue in reading B., we shall learn much more of his meaning, and derive much more help and profit from the discipline, than by consulting all or any of the many text-bks. which have been written round the alleged obscurity of his poetry. The old story may be apocryphal that B. once referred a perplexed reader to the Browning Society for an explanation of one of his poems which he could not understand himself ; but, true or not, it is to be admitted that the extraordinary quickness of B.'s own mental processes caused him to presume too much on a corresponding alertness in his readers. He jumped transitional phrases and conventional pauses in sequent reasoning ; and a jumpy, jerky style is too often the sign of that rapid thinking. The ideas rushed the barriers of language, which were demolished even in course of their erection. But this fact, since it is a fact, merely means that an effort of concentration is required in places to follow B.'s meaning ; and though it is true, as Omond writes, that ' the oracular habit grew on him ' (it may also have been the fact that he hugged, half-unconsciously perhaps, a sense of contrast with his constant friend, and inevitable rival, Tennyson, q.v.), yet the perceptive habit grows on his readers, and is worth intensive cultivation. For B. is a supremely great poet, with real lessons of value to humanity. The Fr. authors of a new *Hist. de Lit. angl.* (Hachette, 1924), are well within the mark when they say : ' He has, everywhere, his inspired moments. Under the impulse of a simpler emotion, as by the magic of an arresting symbol, capable of evoking his eloquence and his imagination, Browning is sometimes, in the most precise sense of the words, *un grand poète*. The flawless specimens are rare, but they have an extraordinarily intense and poignant sound ' ; and reference is suggested to *Evelyn Hope, Love among the Ruins, The Grammarian's Funeral*, the close of *Saul*, and *Childe Roland*. Additions might be made to this list. One admirer at least would wish to add big chunks out of *Cleon* and *Pippa Passes*, the conclusion to the *Statue and the Bust*, and *One Word More*. Perhaps, since they are short, we may quote the essential verses of the latter two :

The sin I impute to each frustrate ghost
Is—the unlit lamp and the ungirt loin,
Though the end in sight was a vice, I say.
You of the virtue (we issue join)
How strive you ? *De te fabula.*

God be thanked, the meanest of his creatures
Boasts two soul-sides, one to face the world with,
One to show a woman when he loves her !

Macpherson's *Ossian*, Shelley and Byron (see s.vv.) are noted among B.'s favourite reading in youth, where he was brought up in London, with his father's big library at his free disposal, and under the inspiring care of his pious half-Scotch, half-Germ. mother; and Italy, as he said, was his univ. Nurtured by these influences and dowered with tastes for painting and music, B.'s genius matured at an early age, and for 55 years—from *Pauline*, anon., 1833, to the *Asolando* vol., 1890 (1889),—he continued to pour out its gleanings, with true Victorian profusion, and to storm the reason of his contemporaries with appeals which, it must be confessed, they received with inadequate gratitude.

Perhaps the greatest of B.'s poems was that which was almost the first,—*Paracelsus*, 1835. The opinion is quoted of J. Forster (afterwards the biographer of Dickens, q.v., and an eminent critic), that ' without the slightest hesitation, we name Mr. Robert Browning at once with Shelley, Coleridge, Wordsworth '. It was a sage perception which posterity confirms, noting that B., like Shelley, was young, being only 23 when this brilliant mono-dramatic poem was publd. The last great speech of Paracelsus is worth special study in this connection, since it contains implicitly all B.'s later thought and manner. It opens with a burst of egoism, traceable straight to the masters of the Ital. Renaissance (q.v.) and recalling particularly the storming individualism of Marlowe's (q.v.) heroes, and, e.g., the ' Moi, dis-je ! et c'est assez ' of the Medea of Corneille (q.v.). Its repetitions more recently by S. Phillips (1868-1915) in his lyric dramas may be remembered.

Paracelsus exclaims :
Yes, it was in me ; I was born for it—
I, Paracelsus : it was mine by right.
Others, declared the physician,
Might seek elsewhere in this blank life of
    ours . . .
To turn the knowledge and the rapture
    wrang,
As an extreme, last born from destiny,
Into occasion for new covetings, . . .
But this was born in me ; I was made so,
Thus much time saved : the feverish
    appetite,
The tumult of unproved desire, the unaimed
Uncertain yearnings, aspirations blind,
Distrust, mistake, and all that ends in tears
Were saved me ; thus I entered on my
    course.

All the course involved immense study ; for B.'s types, unlike Marlowe's, and more like the Faust of Goethe (q.v.) were intellectual, not martial or gubernatorial. Their struggles were set and their triumphs were won in fresh conquests of truth by reason :
           In man's self arise
August anticipations, symbols, types
Of a dim splendour ever on before
In that eternal circle life pursues . . .
. . . They grow too great
For narrow creeds of right and wrong,
    which fade
Before the unmeasured thirst for Good.
This superman (see s.v.) of science learns by suffering

What proportion love should hold with power
In his right constitution ; love preceding
Power, and with much power, always much
    more love ;
Love still too straitened in his present
    means,
And earnest for new power to set love free.

Compare, or contrast, with this revelation (observing that the course of the speech surveys and interprets the new discoveries in physical science which we call Darwinism) the similar and contemporary message of Tennyson in *Oenone*.
Self-reverence, self-knowledge, self-control,
These three alone lead life to sovereign
    power.
Yet not for power (power of herself
Would come uncall'd for) but to live by law,
Acting the law we live by without fear ;
And, because right is right, to follow right

Were wisdom in the scorn of consequence, and something of the bolder outlook, the more courageous confidence, of B. will impress the reader. He will be still more impressed by the fact that Engld. in 1835 was so fortunate as to possess both poets.

B.'s *Strafford, an Historical Tragedy*, 1837, was acted at Covent Garden with Macready in the title part and Helen Faucit (Lady Martin) as Lady Carlisle, but was withdrawn within a week. *Sordello*, 1840 ; *Bells and Pomegranates, Pippa Passes, Dramatic Lyrics*, and others, collected 1846 ; *Christmas Eve and Easter Day*, 1850 ; *Men and Women* (containing *Cleon*, etc.), 1855 ; *Dramatis Personæ*, 1864 ; *The Ring and the Book* (B.'s masterpiece), 4 vols., 1868-9, and 15 further vols. of new poems, down to *Asolando*, with its wonderful ' Epilogue ' (' At the midnight in the silence of the sleep-time ', so close to the other old poet's ' Crossing the Bar '), comprise a part of the list of B.'s lavish gift to his generation.

-ii. Elizabeth Barrett (1806-61) : Engl. poet ; *née* Barrett ; m. R. B. (above), 1846, when the two poets settled at Casa Guidi, Florence. They had met in spirit and correspondence before their actual meeting in 1845, when R. B. came to her father's house in Wimpole Street, and saw ' the little figure, which did not rise from the sofa ' (to which a riding-accident to the spine had condemned her), with her ' pale, ringleted face, and great, eager, wistful eyes '. E. B. had praised R.B.'s poetry in the *Athenæum*, and R. B. had written to E.B. that he ' loved her verse with all his heart'. We must not pause at the romance of their marriage, unique in the annals of literary history. Its passion is poured out in E.B.B.'s 44 *Sonnets from the Portuguese*, which, though unequal in achievement, are unmatched in intensity of feeling since Sappho, the first woman-poet. The sonnet-form corrected the faults of diffuseness and loose structure to which otherwise E.B.B. was liable, and ' the intoxication of her passion helped to secure her against the flatness of the commonplace. . . . It was natural and inevitable that the influence of her love for Browning should transfigure her poetry as well as transform her life ' (sir H. Jones, *loc. cit.*). E.B.B.'s sins against rhyme and metre have become a critics' commonplace, but she was a scholar and a poet, and when Wordsworth (q.v.) died in 1850 her name was suggested as Poet Laureate (q.v.). Among her best known works, besides the *Sonnets*, 1847, are *Prometheus Bound* (transld. from Æschylus), 1833 ; *Aurora Leigh* (a blank-verse novel), 1857 ; *Last Poems*, 1862. Among the best modern writers on the 2 poets may be mentioned Stopford Brooke (q.v.) sir Henry Jones, mme. Darmesteter, Mr. G. K. Chesterton, E. Dowden, C. H. Herford, W. P. Ker, Arthur Symons and J. T. Nettleship.

Brülow, Kaspar (1585-1627): Germ. Latinist. Held chair of Latin at Strassburg, where the tradition of academic drama had been established by Sturm (q.v.), and wr. original Lat. plays which ranked supreme in the so-called Strassburg school of drama, and which have been taken to entitle B. to the fame of the greatest Germ. dramatist before Lessing (q.v.). Historically, the critics can doubtless justify the claim, but B.'s choice of a since dead language for his dramatization of Moses, Andromeda, and other heroes of fate, debars him from the line of modern drama founded so brilliantly in Engld. in his own day.

Brueys, de, David Augustin (1640-1725): Fr. comic dramatist. Collaborated with Palaprat (q.v.) in the classic version of the comedy of Pathelin (q.v.). B. was an abbé, and availed himself of his collaborator to conceal his own share in this and some other plays of the Regnard (q.v.) type.

Brun, Nordahl (1745-1816): Norw. (-Dan.) poet ; by sympathy and geography a Norseman, though politically to be reckoned a Dane till 1814, when Norway achieved independence. Wr. hymns, in worthy succession to Kingo and Brorson (qq.v.), and national odes, and stirred the religious or martial hearts of his fellow-countrymen. These poetic records should be remembered to B.'s credit, when it is re-called —as it always is recalled that he was the author of the notorious Dan. tragedy, *Zarine*, founded slavishly on Voltaire's (q.v.) *Zaïre*, which was produced at Copenhagen, 1772. This play, which was neither worse nor better than others of its kind and time, happened to be the one which was laughed off the stage by Wessel (q.v.) in his burlesque ' Love without Stockings '. Thus B., so patriotic as a song-writer, is associated, by the greater genius of Wessel, with the expulsion of Gothic affectations from the national stage of Denmark.

Brunetière, Ferdinand (1849-1907): Fr. critic ; scholar ; for many years editor of the *Revue des Deux Mondes* : later, associated with the Ecole normale supérieure in Paris ; a devoted disciple of Comte (q.v.) in his Positivist ideas, though reconciled at the end with the Roman Catholic Church. B.'s works included *le Roman naturaliste*, 1883, a valuable introduction to the story of the novel in its transition through Zola (q.v.); *Histoire et Littérature*, 3 vols., 1884-86, etc. His *Histoire de la Littérature française classique* (1515-1830) was publd. posth., and is one of the most notable of his writings. B.'s sympathies were plainly against the 18th cent.: he would not forgive Voltaire (q.v.) for having existed ; but his strong individuality enhances the attraction of his scientific temper in criticism.

Bruni, Lionardo (1369-1444): It. humanist. Born at Arezzo (Petrarch's birthplace) of humble orig., and rose by merit and patronage to posts of papal secretary (1405-15) and chancellor of Florence (1427). Gk. pupil of Chrysoloras (q.v.). Author of Lat. renderings of Gk. classics, and original lives, letters, and commentaries in Lat., much of which is of real value ; ' restored ' missing bk. of Livy in original Lat. vol. on 1st Punic war. Wr. (c. 1405) *de studiis et litteris*, a tractate on education, recommending humane courses of Lat. reading and classical poetry, but not neglecting morals, religion, and social arts of conversation. Wr. Gk. and Lat. vols. on Florence ; Lat. life of Dante, valuable in parts, but vitiated by eagerness to discredit Boccaccio's labours in same field ; and 12 bks. of a projected Lat. ' History of the Florentine Republic ', completed by Poggio (q.v.). ' History mourns, Eloquence is mute ', ran a part of the Lat. inscription on his marble monument in S. Croce, Florence.

Bruno, Giordano (1550-1600): It. pantheistic philosopher ; ' punished with all clemency and without effusion of blood ' by being burned publicly in Rome, 17 Feb., 1600, at the instance of the Holy Office. Cf. too the fate of Galileo, q.v., and read what Symonds (*It. Ren.*, vii, 71) writes, in the wake of earlier historians, of the disillusion in Italy at the close of the 16th cent. of belated sons of the liberties of the Renaissance : ' How much alike in some important circumstances of their lives were these two men ' ! (Bruno and Tasso, q.v.). ' Both wanderers, possessed of that spirit of vagrancy which is the outward expression of an inner vagrancy. The outfrocked friar, the courtier out of service, had no home in Italy. . . . Sufficient justice has not yet been done in history to the Italian wanderers and exiles of this period, men who carried the spirit of the Renaissance abroad, after the Renaissance had ended in Italy, to the extremest verge of the civilized word '. B., like Galileo, chose the dialogue for the conveyance of his brilliant and daring speculations in scientific thought, and he is famous, too, as the writer of a comedy, *il Candelaio*, 1582, and of a set of dithyrambic verses, *gli Eroici Furori*, dedicated to sir Philip Sidney (q.v.), whom B. met during his 2 years' residence in Engld. B.'s philosophy had influence on Spinoza (see sir F. Pollock, *Spinoza*, Duckworth, 1899 ; p. 97) and probably on Descartes, q.v., and attracted Goethe (q.v.) on its pantheistic side (see G. H. Lewes, *Goethe*, Smith, Elder, 1875 ; p. 71) ; Schelling (q.v.) was directly indebted to him, and lit. mourns in him not only the most courageous thinker of his age, but a man, who, in a more fortunate time, would have been one of its chief ornaments in letters.

Brunswick, Heinrich Julius, Duke of (1564-1613): Germ. playwright and patron of drama ; hereditary duke. Enriched his duchy with the earliest court-theatre, for which he composed many tragedies and comedies under the then paramount influence of the Engl. players (see s.v. Englische Comödianten).

Bruun, Malthe Conrad (1775-1826): Dan. pamphleteer ; satirist ; of the same class as

P. A. Heiberg (q.v.), and suffered, like him, a sentence of exile (in 1800), which he spent in Paris. B.'s political songs and newspaper-articles had considerable vogue in the revolutionary period of his youth.

Bryan, Francis (died, 1550) : Engl. diplomatist and scholar ; knighted, 1522 ; cousin to queen Anne Boleyn, and was sent to Rome, 1528, to arrange for papal sanction to the divorce of queen Catherine of Aragon. Wr. poems and translns., including a version of Guevara's (q.v.) ' Courtier and Countryman '.

Brynjolf Sweynsson (1605-75) : Icel. scholar ; ' for ever connected with the old revival of letters, with the Edda MSS., and other treasures which his care preserved for us ' (Vigfusson and York Powell, *Corpus Poeticum Boreale*, i, Intro. ; Oxford, 1883). B., who became bp. of Scalholt, and who preferred to describe himself as Ragnheid's son, after his mother (signing Bryniolfus R.), than as Sweyn's son, after his father, was a diligent student and collector of MSS., among these being the famous MS. of early Icelandic poems, since known as Codex Regius (q.v.). Found in 1642, and hailed almost before its finding as the long-conjectured Elder Edda (s.vv. Edda, Magnus Olafsson), this MS. passed, with others, to the King's Library at Copenhagen in 1662, when bp. B., oppressed by domestic sorrows, was anxious, perhaps, to conciliate the king's favour.

Buchanan, George (1506-82) : Scot. Latinist ; successor in that branch of letters in European reputation to Erasmus (q.v.). Praised by Scaliger (q.v.), lauded by Sidney (q.v.), admired by Johnson (q.v.), despite his Scotophobia, and extolled by Dryden (q.v.), B. does not command to-day either the ecstasies of humanists or the joy of poets ; and the change affords a signal example of the reversal of the secure judgment of *orbis terrarum*. B. resided chiefly abroad, finding in France, Portugal and Italy more congenial surroundings than in his native land to which he returned with his sheaves in 1560. He wr. Lat. tragedies (*Jephtha*, truly Aristotelian and Euripidean, according to Ascham, q.v.), and *John the Baptist* ; a Virgilian poem on the Lucretian subject of *The Sphere* ; a Lat. prose history of Scotland, in the style of Livy or Sallust, but surpassing both in the estimation of many critics ; Lat. satires, elegies, epigrams, letters ; a Lat. treatise on political philosophy, *de jure regni apud Scotos*, composed in the form of a dialogue, and admitting the right (conferred by breach of contract) of regicide by the victims of tyranny ; and, chiefly, Lat. metrical versions of the Psalms, dedicated to queen Mary, under the style of *Nympha Caledoniæ* (1566), which became text-bks. in Scot. and Germ. schools, and twice had the honour of musical settings. That B. was a true poet is a fact beyond dispute ; it is vouched for by Wordsworth (q.v.), who was a good judge ; but, unlike Erasmus, whose Lat. works are still widely read, and should be even more widely, B. missed the note of human appeal which would condone the foreign language for modern ears. It was a vain labour to Latinize the psalms, or to produce Euripidean dramas according to Aristotle in Lat. ; and an age which neglects

the classics is not likely to take its pleasure in Ovidian echoes from the 16th cent. Thus B.'s place in the history of lit. is higher than his place as a man of letters.

Buchanan, Robert (1841-1901) : Engl. (Scot.) poet and critic ; the ' spokesman for a generation rising into manhood when the impulse of the early Victorian poets was beginning to fail, and when their ideals were no longer accepted as all that the heart could desire '. But B. was not strong enough to bridge the transition ; ' he could not fuse the elements of greatness that were in him ' (prof. Walker, *Lit. Vict. Era.*, 585). Wr. *The Wandering Jew*, 1893 (begun, 1866) ; *Undertones*, 1864 ; *London Poems*, 1866 ; *The Book of Orm*, 1870, in order to ' vindicate the ways of God to man ', —a contribution of the Celtic genius to civilization ; *Balder the Beautiful*, 1877 ; *The City of Dream*, 1888 ; etc. B. suffered in repute by his attempt to bring Engl. poetry back to what he believed to be sounder standards of taste, not by the example of his own muse, but by anon. precept. He wr. an art. in the *Contemporary Review* (Oct., 1871), under the name of Thos. Maitland, on ' The Fleshly School of Poetry ', which took shape chiefly as a violent attack on D. G. Rossetti (q.v.). The ensuing controversy has no present interest, and was closed before 1882, when B. dedicated his novel *God and the Man* to Rossetti. B. as a poet stands rather for a moment than for all time, though the mystical strain in his blood and the rare sincerity of his purpose were combined with sometimes magical effect.

Buckle, Henry Thos. (1821-62) : Engl. social historian ; wr. *History of Civilization in England*, vol. i, 1857 ; ii, 1861, and had planned the whole in 14 vols., but died untimely at Damascus. B.'s work is thus but a fragment of a fragment, and needs careful editing and correction. This pious labour was performed, 1904, by rt. hon. J. M. Robertson, who writes, that, all necessary deductions notwithstanding, B., at his best, ' cannot be surpassed in the great qualifications of fulness of knowledge, breadth of grasp, and vivacity and lucidity of presentment. He is fuller of colour than Montesquieu (q.v.), and more abundantly and exactly informative than Voltaire (q.v.), —two early masters of socio-historical exposition, to whom he paid generously just tribute ' (Introduction to Routledge's edn., p. viii).

Budé, Guillaume (1467-1540) : Fr. humanist ; famous under scholar's name of Budæus. Born at Paris, where his father was a wealthy bibliophil ; after a not very strenuous youth, B. applied himself to classical studies, taking Cicero as his model for Latinity, and learning Gk. from Hermonymus and J. Lascaris (qq.v.) ; became secretary to king Louis xii, and visited pope Leo x in Rome on a diplomatic mission ; was present, 1520, at the meeting between kings Francis i and Henry viii on the Field of the Cloth of Gold ; resided in Paris (rue St. Martin) and in the country, tended by the devoted ministrations of his wife, when his strength was gradually impaired by his industry (it is of B. that the story is told : when a fire occurred in his house, without raising his eyes from his bk., he bade the messenger tell his wife, ' for you know that I never concern myself with domestic matters '); prevailed on Francis i to found the Royal Readerships in classical studies, 1530, which were subsequently developed into the Collège de France (q.v.). B. became, and was recognized in his own day as, 'the foremost ornament and monument of letters, by whose greatness France has vindicated the palm of learning' (Calvin), till then held by Italy; and this position he maintained in equal sovereignty with Erasmus (q.v.) from about 1520 till his death. B. was the Hellenist and Erasmus the Latinist in this fraternity; they shared the undivided throne of humanism, impressing their contemporaries almost as much by the rare example of scholars' amity as by the weight of their scholarship. There was a little natural jealousy; but each was too serene and too secure to descend to the abuse which their respective champions affected. B.'s works included annotations to the *Pandects* of Justinian (1508) and a treatise, *de Asse* (1514), pioneer-works in Roman law and coinage; he publd. letters and commentaries; dialogues *de Philologia* (1530); *de Transitu Hellenismi ad Christianismum* (1534), of greater importance in its own time —of Calvin, Rabelais, the reformers and their persecutors—than to-day, for its defence of Gk. philosophy from the imputation of heresy; and (1547; written, 1516), in French, *de l'Institution du Prince*, exalting the study of Gk. Rabelais (q.v.), in his medley, was deeply indebted to B., among other humanists of the age; and the exclamation of Argyropoulos about Reuchlin (qq.v.), 'Greece has crossed the Alps', might be applied with complete accuracy to the transference of the centre of the Renaissance from Florence and Rome, sacked in 1527, to Paris under Budé, and to Northern Europe as a whole under him and Erasmus.

Bürger, Gottfried August (1747-94): Germ. poet. Wr., 1774, ballad *Lenore*, in effect one of the most notable products of the 'Sturm und Drang' (q.v.) period in Germany. 'This ballad did more than any other single work towards calling the Romantic movement to life in Europe' (Robertson, *Germ. Lit.*, 304; 'The eerie tramp of the ghostly horse which carries Lenore to her doom re-echoed in every literature, and to many a young sensitive soul was the poetic revelation of a new world', *ibid.*). William Taylor (q.v.) transld. it, 1795, in the *Monthly Magazine*, and an impression of an impressionable reader may be gathered from a letter of C. Lamb to S. T. Coleridge (qq.v.), 6 July, 1796: 'Have you read the Ballad called "Leonora" in the second Number of the *Monthly Magazine*? If you have !!!!!!!' (*Works*, edn. Lucas vi, 38). Coleridge obviously read it before his *Ancient Mariner* was publd. in *Lyrical Ballads*, 1798; and sir Walter Scott (q.v.) re-transld. it for himself, and 'plunged' into Germ. lit. in its wake. Higher praise no one could desire, and no single poem can be recalled by name which aroused instant enthusiasm and produced permanent influence in like degree. *Lenore*—in 32 stanzas of 8 verses each—was fashioned out of an amalgam of the refrain of an old Germ. folk-song, the patriotic background of the

Seven Years' War, Herder's (q.v.) recent writings on Germ. art, Percy's (q.v.) *Reliques*, and that fiery awakening of genius irrepressibly moved to self-expression for which Goethe (q.v.) in Germany was already finding a vent. The rapidity, passion, and terror of that ballad were exactly calculated to seize both popular imagination and the trained taste of the revivalists of romance. It re-created the freshness of the early morning when the supernatural needed no edging of wonder, because it appealed to the same feelings as the natural; and the local and temporal setting of *Lenore* enhanced the spontaneous effect of its primitive tragedy and truth. This epoch-making ballad first appeared in the *Musenalmanach* at Göttingen (q.v.), 1774, where B. was settled in a teaching capacity. It 'swept, like wild-fire, across Europe', and he followed it up with other ballads, of which the next best is *der wilde Jäger* ('The wild huntsman'). B.'s life, like his muse, was passionate. His marriage to two sisters in succession (1764 and 1774): the early death of his second wife, whom he had desired before and during his first marriage; his third marriage, and its sequel in divorce, are as much a part of his poetic life as the love-affairs of Shelley (q.v.) are of his; and, though we may say of Bürger, as Wordsworth said of Burns (qq.v.), 'on the basis of his human character he has reared a poetic one', yet his love-songs, not unlike Burns', are very intimate of his life, and were severely censured by Schiller (q.v.). The 'Molly' whom he sings is the lady who became his second wife. B. transld., 1786, and fixed the definite text of the famous Bacon Münchausen (q.v.) romance, first issued in the Engl. language by Raspe (q.v.), a fugitive from Cassel.

Buffon, de, Georges Louis Leclerc (1707-88): Fr. natural historian; *philosophe* (q.v.); *comte* by rank; travelling-tutor to an Englishman in Engld. and Italy; transld., 1740, *Method of Fluxions* by sir I. Newton; devoted himself to agriculture and mathematics; member of Fr. Academy of Sciences, and of Fr. Academy (q.v.), 1753. B.'s life work was determined in 1739, when he was appointed keeper of the *jardin du roi*, and concentrated his faculties, accordingly, on natural history. Vols. i and ii of his monumental *Histoire naturelle* appeared in 1749, and the work was completed in 36 4to vols. by 1788. B. was a *philosophe*, in the sense in which the term is used to characterize the contributors to the Encyclopedia (q.v.), but he differed from his colleagues in that undertaking by his single-hearted devotion to the ends of science, without regard to the secondary purposes—moral, religious, and even political—which tinged everything they wrote, including the oriental tales of Voltaire (q.v.), with a sophistical plea for the dominion of reason in human affairs. B.'s antideism was no more than an indifference to the deity which he did not discover in his geological or physical researches; he felt no call to emphasize the fact in the interest of suffering humanity or of the subjects of a monarchy founded on divine right. He was a man of science first and last, and did not compromise his views to suit the colour of the social philosophy of Diderot or Rousseau (qq.v.). The true B. is to be sought in such portions of his natural history as the celebrated *Théories de la terre* and *Époques de la Nature,* which have been aptly compared with the sweeping nature-poetry of Lucretius especially in bk. v of his *de rerum natura.* In his generalizations and some of his hypotheses, B. ranks, through Lamarck, as a precursor of Darwin (q.v.) ; and it is to be noted that he was always more interested in the philosophic and general portions of his great enterprise than in the purely narrative and descriptive matter. The faults in such parts, whether of taste or fact, are his assistants' more commonly than his own ; thus, the peacock and the nightingale were described by Montbeillard (1720-85), and the anthropomorphic swan by the abbé Bexon (1748-84). B. wr., too, as he was well qualified to do, a *Discours sur le style* (his Academy address, 1753), in which occurs the famous maxim, ' le style, c'est [de] l'homme meme '. He quitted Paris soon after his appointment, and lived a scholar's life at Montbard.

Bugge, Sophus (1833-1907): Norw. philologer ; prof. of comparative languages at university of Oslo (founded, 1811). B.'s long life was very active in the field of scholarship, and, apart from purely scientific studies in philology, he wr. a valuable work on old Norse legends, 1881, transld. into Germ. in the following year, and widely criticized and discussed.

Bulgarin, Thaddeus (1789-1859): Russ. novelist, of the old-fashioned moral-historical school, always wearisome and now forgotten. B.'s masterpiece in the eyes of his contemporaries, with whom he was as popular as Pushkin (q.v. ; it was a rivalry parallel to that of Martin Tupper and Tennyson), was *Ivan Vyzchigin,* 1829 ; but it was all very small beer.

Bunyan, John (1628-88): Engl. Biblical romancer. Wr. *Grace Abounding,* 1666 ; *The Pilgrim's Progress from this World to That which is to Come,* Part i, 1678 ; Part ii, 1684 ; *Life and Death of Mr. Badman,* 1680, and other works, in the intervals of preaching and of periods of imprisonment as an unlicensed preacher. He was born and died in Bedfordshire, and was the son of a journeyman brasier.

Reference is made to a Fr. poet of the 14th cent., Guillaume de Digulleville by name, who wr. a *Pélerinage de la Vie humaine,* 1330, and to the obvious source-bks. of Allegory (q.v.), from the *Romance of the Rose* to Spenser's *Faerie Queen* (see s.vv.), which there is no evidence that B. had ever read. But the fact is, that B. cannot be ' placed ' in any of the ordinary categories of writers. He was the product of the Engl. Bible (q.v.), of the Puritan conscience, and of a direct sense of sin and salvation. The dream-motive (s.v. Dream), or vision, was not so rare in such natures as to cause surprise or a search for authorities ; and, with a kind of peasant's vigour of the soil, alike in characterization and in diction, in which B. reminds us of Luther (q.v.), he wr. his lay Bible, as it has been called, of the *Pilgrim's Progress,* with an unrehearsed ease and sureness of touch, which have earned universal acclamation. It was early (1694) transld. into Germ., where the heirs of the

Reformation (q.v.) accorded it a sympathetic welcome, and where its simple, lucent mysticism appealed to Wieland (q.v.) and similar poets. Its supreme call to conduct, its clearness, its dramatic value, its convincing actuality, yet charged with spiritual meaning, have made it the most popular vehicle of the religious sense in lay garb which the world of letters has ever known, and B. stands, if a place must be found for a type of religious genius so unique, between John Knox, the Scot. reformer, and John Milton, the Puritan poet.

Buræus, Johannes (1568-1652): Swed. scholar ; librarian to queen Christina (q.v.) ; tutor to king Gustavus Adolphus and to Stjernhjelm (q.v.), the father of Swed. poetry.

Burchiello, Il (1403-48), Domenico di Giovanni: It. satirist. Son of a barber in Florence. The career of B. is unedifying, but requires a few lines in the history of Florentine manners of his day. His cultivation of coarse speech and rude habits recommended him at first to the notice of the lower ranks of the makers of political faction, and he acquired some force on the side of the Albizzi *v.* the Medici (q.v.) in the struggle for supremacy. Later, he was exiled from Florence by Cosimo de Medici, and opened a shop at Siena (1434). Thence he wandered to Venice, Naples, and Rome, where he finally fell a victim to Cosimo's vengeance. B. wr. burlesque sketches of the passing hour in a jargon which has also passed away ; his sonnets were popular in his own day, and are not without significance in the annals of plebeian verse.

Burke, Edmund (1729-97): Anglo-Irish orator ; statesman ; took a leading part in the impeachment of Warren Hastings and against the Revolution in France ; sat in Parliament, 1765-94. B.'s life and writings have engaged the pens of visct. Morley (q.v.; d. 1923), himself a statesman and man of letters, of A. Birrell, a colleague of Morley's in the Liberal Cabinet of 1906, of Woodrow Wilson, president of the Republic of the United States during the latter years of the Great War, and of other eminent writers. Perhaps we may quote a passage from a prof. who was not a politician, but who shared with B. his nativity in Ireland, E. Dowden (1843-1913). He calls B. ' our highest teacher of political wisdom ' ; he cites from sir Fitzjames Stephen (1829-94) a comparison of B. with bp. Berkeley (q.v.), in the terms that, ' like Berkeley, whose philosophy harmonizes singularly with Burke's writings, and in all probability had powerfully affected his mind, Burke makes duty to God the foundation of everything else ; and also, like Berkeley, he referred to the will and disposition of God all the principal relations between man and man ' ; in this regard, falling into line with the speculations on government of Hooker and bp. Butler (qq.v.). Continuing, Dowden writes : ' With his devout reverence for a Divine order, not fully realized, yet ever present, in human society and human institutions, Burke's imagination co-operated. It is common to speak of him as a great prose poet, and the critics who so describe him commonly cite in illustration some passage brilliant with the colours of a rhetorician's art. In general, Burke's imagery is not for ornament, but for use ; it is, as De Quincey (q.v.) justly observed, not the mere dressing of his thought, but the body in which the thought is incarnated and through which it operates. If we would really bring home to ourselves the power of Burke's imagination, we should think less of this or that passage of resplendent eloquence than of his constant imaginative realization of the greatness and the majesty of social order ' (*Fr. Revolution and Engl. Lit.*, ch. iii). Recalling that B. was the 1st editor of the *Annual Register* started by Dodsley (q.v.), and that he contributed to it till 1788, we note that his most important work in the realm of pure letters was the treatise *On the Sublime and Beautiful*, 1756 (see, too, s.v. Sublime) ; that he was a member of the circle of which Johnson (q.v.) was the centre ; that he was falsely imputed in certain quarters with the authorship of the Junius (q.v.) letters ; and that his literary oratory included *On the Causes of the Present Discontent*, 1770, *Conciliation with America*, 1775 ; *Letters to the Sheriffs of Bristol*, 1777 ; and the *Reflections on the French Revolution*, 1790, which produced a profound effect. Last came the *Letters*, of 1796, to *a Noble Lord* and *on a Regicide Peace*.

Burkhardt, Jakob (1818-97) : Germ.-Swiss historian ; wr. monumental ' History of Renaissance Culture in Italy ', 1860.

Burney. -i. Charles (1726-1814) : Engl. musician ; pupil of T. A. Arne (see s.v. J. Thomson) ; wr., 1776-89, *A History of Music*, 4 vols., and other works.

-ii. Frances (1752-1840) : Engl. novelist ; daughter of above, whose *Memoirs* she edited, 1832 ; m., 1793, general d'Arblay, a Fr. refugee in Engld. ; lived for some years in Paris and Belgium, but returned to Engld. after 1815 ; her *Diary and Letters*, 7 vols., were publd., 1842-6 (edited by A. Dobson, q.v., 1904), and, fascinating throughout, contain a lively description of her discomfort as second keeper of the robes to queen Charlotte, 1786-90. F.B., or mme. d'A.—she is commonly known by her maiden name, was a novelist of manners, who, by her 2 best tales, *Evelina, or A Young Lady's Entrance into the World*, 3 vols., 1778, and *Cecilia, or Memoirs of an Heiress*, 5 vols., 1782, brought the art of fiction very close to the domestic tale of her younger contemporary, J. Austen (q.v.). ' The picaresque scaffolding (see s.v. Smollett), the obtrusive moral (see s.v. Richardson), the deliberate sentiment (see s.v. Sterne) —much more the marvellous and the medievalism (see s.v. Walpole)—of the writers who had immediately gone before her are thrown to the winds. She sets herself to tell a plain story—enlivened, doubtless, with strange adventures, with characters still stranger— and that is all. Yet in this very simplicity is contained a new and, as time has proved, a very fruitful conception of what the novel might achieve ' (*C.H.E.L.*, x, 63). Wr. too *Camilla, or A Picture of Youth*, 5 vols., 1796, and *The Wanderer, or Female Difficulties*, 5 vols., 1814. Mme. d'A. is the subject of an essay, 1843, by Macaulay (q.v.), who opined that ' we owe to her not only Evelina, Cecilia, and Camilla, but also *Mansfield Park* and *The Absentee* ' (see s.vv. Austen, Edgeworth).

-iii. Sarah Harriet (d. 1844) : Engl. novelist ; sister of above ; wr. *Clarentine*, 1796, and other novels.

Burns, Robert (1759-96) : Scot. poet. Since ' on the basis of his human life he reared a poetic one ', in the sympathetic estimate of his younger Engl. contemporary and fellow-craftsman, Wordsworth (q.v.), we need not discuss the amours of this inspired and genial peasant. B., says prof. Elton, ' lived nearer to the brown earth, upturned for sowing and crowded with life, than any other of our poets ' ; and R. L. Stevenson (q.v.), B.'s fellow-countryman, says : ' First, in an age when poetry had become abstract and conventional, instead of continuing to deal with shepherds, thunderstorms and personifications, he dealt with the actual circumstances of his life, however matter-of-fact and sordid these might be. And, secondly, in a time when English versification was particularly stiff, lame, and feeble, and words were used with ultra-academical timidity, he wrote verses that were easy, racy, graphic, and forcible, and used language with absolute tact and courage as it seemed most fit to give a clear impression '. Perhaps the black is too black, owing to a national prepossession, in this account of poetry and its language ; but the white is not too white. An analogy, not more or less inaccurate than usual, might be drawn between B.'s new use of the Scots language and Luther (q.v.) using German for the first time. The conventions and the timidity of the Vulgate Lat. Bible, which Luther exchanged for the vernacular, corresponded to the limitations which B. escaped when his soul of song was expressed in his native language. Luther's sensuous pleasure at approaching the Deity in the homely guise of *du lieber Gott*, instead of in stately and stiff Latinism, was matched by B.'s delight in getting rid of the 18th cent. property box of shepherds and personifications, and going straight to the ' mousie ' and the ' daisy '. This, then, first : B.'s debt to his own soil. Next, he wr. short poems, poems written with his eye on the object. Tennyson (q.v.), no mean judge, praised them for their shape, ' the perfection of the berry ', and for their light, ' the radiance of the dewdrop ' ; and Carlyle (q.v.), who took B. as one of the types of ' The Hero as Man of Letters ', was doubtless thinking of him again, when he wr. in another of the essays : ' Poetry we will call Musical Thought. See deep enough, and you see musically ; the heart of Nature being everywhere Music, if you can only reach it '. So, Wordsworth spoke of B. as ' the great genius who had brought Poetry back to Nature '.

Must we load the tomb of that genius with the critics' burden of the ' return to Nature ? ' They all returned to Nature at the end of the 18th cent., in the works of Rousseau (q.v.), and the Fr. revolutionaries, and who was first in the race seems a matter of accountancy, not of poetry. Mr. Yeats would give first place to Blake (q.v.) : his ' poems mark an epoch in English literature, for they were the first opening of the long-sealed well of romantic poetry ; they, and not the works of Cowper and Thomson and Chatterton (see s.vv.), being the true heralds of our modern poetry of nature and enthusiasm' (*Blake*, edited by W. B. Yeats; 'Muses Library'; Intro.). Maybe. Other readers discover other sources; a chance reference in sir W. Temple (q.v.) is one; and sir W. Watson, a poet of latter days, would refer it to the mood which 'wafted Collins' lonely vesper-chime', and 'breathed abroad the frugal note of Gray' (see s.vv., and s.v. Romance). Who first set open the magic casements is less important than the spectacle revealed; and, in a fine phrase coined by a modern writer, B. saw the daisy ' from God's side ', and not from ' the hither side ' where we dwell. That mystery which we call genius gave him the ' God's side ' view, gave this tiller of the soil, this inspired Faun, as he has been called, that insight into nature which is expressed in song, and in no other language known to man. The thought and the song are one music. The flower perceived by our senses is planted and plucked, lives and dies, is catalogued by the gardener and classified by the botanist, but is never understood. B., in the dawn of the new wonder, wrought with nature to sing her own songs, and his music will vibrate in human hearts as long as the classics of the past. For his verse, finally, is classical in form. Herald of dawn though he was, and child of revolution, he had trained himself in the discipline of Pope, Shenstone (qq.v.) and the poetic masters.

Burton, -i, Richard Francis (1821-90): Engl. scholar-traveller; K.C.M.G., 1885; made pilgrimage to Mecca, 1853, recounted in *A Personal Narrative*, 1855; explored with J. H. Speke (1827-64; his monument is in Kensington Gardens) the sources of the Nile; publd. translns. of Camoens (q.v.), 1880-4; *Arabian Nights* (complete), 1885-8, and other works; a great Orientalist.

-ii. Isabel (1831-96): Engl. scholar; *née* Arundell; wife (1861) of above. Wr. *Life* and edited posth. works of sir R. B., and was the author of several bks. of travel.

Burton, Robert (1576-1640): Engl. savant; ' by profession a divine, by inclination a physician '. Wr., 1621, *The Anatomy of Melancholy*, a prose-medley of humour and satire, as profuse and diffuse in its style as Rabelais (q.v.), and reminiscent of Montaigne's (q.v.) method of approach to its topic, which is, at bottom, an exposure of the folly (q.v.) of men. Attributed by the author to ' Democritus junior ', after the ' laughing philosopher' of Greece, the *Anatomy*, which was publd. in 7 edns. in the 17th cent., and which, though overlooked in the 18th, except by a few *cognoscenti* such as Sterne (q.v.; in *Tristram Shandy*: and see Johnson, q.v., *Vanity of Human Wishes*, 49ff.), was revived by Lamb (q.v.) in the 19th cent., has maintained its reputation since. It took up in the flood of its shrewd humour and winding digressions the deposit of Lucian in antiquity, of Brandt's (q.v.) *Ship of Fools*, Erasmus's (q.v.) *Praise of Folly*, and other modern works, and supplied to La Bruyère and Swift (qq.v.) many texts from which to preach sermons. B., e.g., denounced the folly of war, with ample anecdotes and illustrations, and it is interesting to observe that he found the evil genius of Engld. in her laziness and reluctance to work. All his themes were

adorned, as he said himself, with ornaments pillaged from all quarters, as the Romans pillaged other cities for the beautification of their own, and he loved the sight of epithets in motley, trailing down his long page, and drawn from his scholar's mind, in the fading splendour of the Renaissance.

Bury, Richard de. See **Aungerville**.

Bussi, de, Giovanni Andrea (1417-75): It. humanist; bp. of Aleria. Supervised *edd. pr.* of Cæsar, Aulus Gellius, Livy, Lucan, Virgil, Ovid, and Cicero's *Letters* and *Speeches*—a unique record, even in the busy years, 1465-71, when printing was a new art.

Bussy, comte de ; Roger de Rabutin (1618-93): Fr. memoirist; cousin to mme. de Sévigné (q.v.); army officer, and soldier of fortune. Wr. *Histoire amoureuse des Gaules*, a scandalous piece of court-gossip, for which he was sent to the Bastille, and was sequestrated on his own estates for 16 years. B. never recovered from the blow which he dealt himself. His correspondence has more permanent value, even in his age of busy letter-writers; the letters treat largely of literary taste and fashion, from the point of view, mainly, of the man of the world.

Butler, Joseph (1692-1752): Engl. divine; bp. of Durham, 1750. Wr. *Fifteen Sermons*, 1726, and *The Analogy of Religion, Natural and Revealed, to the Constitution and Course of Nature*, 1736, which was typical of the safety of 18th cent. thought, and is noted as characteristically Engl. by the countrymen of Pascal (q.v.). M. Arnold (q.v.) examined it in 2 discourses to the Edinburgh Philosophical Institute on *Bp. Butler and the Zeitgeist* (re-issued in *Last Essays on Church and Religion*; vol. ix, of his Collected Works), and was controverted by W. E. Gladstone (1809-98), who edited B.'s works, 1896.

Butler, Samuel (1612-80): Engl. satirist. Wr. Restoration-satire, *Hudibras* (in 3 parts, 1663-4-8), directed against the Puritans; founded insecurely on the model of Cervantes, with touches of Rabelais and Scarron (see s.vv.), introduced to adorn the mock-hero of the clever but long-winded poem. It was composed in jolting 8-syllabled verses, and, though king Charles ii is said to have been delighted at the palpable hits at his opponents, he did nothing for the author, who died in poverty and neglect. The name Hudibras was taken from Spenser, *Faerie Queen*, ii, ii, 17; and the poem, which is famous in the somewhat dreary lists of political satire, contains certain brilliant apophthegms, which shine in its waste of verses.

Butler, Samuel (1835-1902): Engl. essayist, critic, romancer; a master of irony (q.v.) in the manner of Swift (q.v.); a disciple of Voltaire and Schopenhauer (qq.v.) in certain aspects of his philosophy and humour, and a product of the age which was breaking the conventions of authority by the light of Darwinism and social reform. This somewhat complex account of a wayward yet austere genius, the full force of which failed to come to expression, indicates at once the experimental character of his writings and their lack of unity in direction. B., a grandson of his namesake (1774-1839; bp. of Lichfield;

schoolmaster, writer of school bks.), whose *Life* he wr., 1896, spent some years breeding sheep in New Zealand ; returning to Engld., 1864, he publd., anon., his famous *Erewhon*, or *Over the Range*, 1872, a kind of *Gulliver's Travels* of Victorianism, which, though not a Utopia (though erewhon=nowhere), criticized with learned irony the intellectual compromises of the age. *The Fair Haven*, 1873 ; *The Way of all Flesh*, 1884 (publd. posth., 1903), and *Erewhon Revisited*, 1901, belonged to the same class of lit. In another class were his *Authoress of the Odyssey*, 1897, a curiously attractive piece of paradox, followed by translns. of the *Iliad*, 1898, and the *Odyssey*, 1900. Nor do these titles exhaust the long list of B.'s writings. 'A heterodox thinker', prof. Walker (*Lit. Vict. Era*, 813) calls him ; ' but a man of wide knowledge and indubitable power. His writings on evolution and his miscellaneous essays prove him to have been a profound student of the problems of his time ; and his works of fiction are just the expression of his philosophy in another form '.

Byliny (Russ.) : Epic songs ; tales of old time. This term, more common in the plural *byliny* than in the singular *bylina*, occurs frequently in connection with the early history of Russ. lit., and is practically the Slav equivalent of the Fr. *chanson de geste* (q.v.), the Scandinavian *saga* (q.v.), and the Germ. *lied* (see s.v. Nibelungenlied). The B. were chiefly associated with the chronicle-cycle of Kiev (q.v. ; see, too, s.vv. Igor, Nestor).

Byron (lord), George Gordon (1788-1824) : Engl. poet ; succeeded his great-uncle, 1798, as 6th baron ; edu. at Harrow and Cambridge ; travelled extensively, bearing, as has been said, ' the pageant of his bleeding heart ' through Europe ; met Shelley (q.v., and cf. *Julian and Maddalo*) in Italy ; died at Missolonghi, from an attack of marsh-fever, contracted on active service with the Gk. insurgents against Turkey ; his memoirs were burned by the undoubted discretion of T. Moore (q.v.), to whom B. had confided them, in the presence and with the consent of his friend and publisher, J. Murray (q.v.).

It cannot be said of B., as Wordsworth affirmed of Burns, that ' on the basis of his human life he reared a poetic one ', with the corollary that the virtues of the latter condone the vices of the former. On the contrary, in B.'s instance, the man and the poet were one : one in their strength and weakness, in their affectation and sincerity, in their moral and intellectual divagations, in their mock heroics and their genuine heroism, in their qualities of heart and head,—the heart, romantic, passionate, democratic ; the head, cool, classical, aristocratic. The facts of that human life are familiar : hardly anyone has been so much written about as B., and his centenary in 1924 produced a fresh spate of Byronica. Though we still do not know the precise cause why his wife, Ada, *née* Milbanke, left him, 1816, after just a year's wedlock, yet we know enough about that episode, about Jane (Clara) Clairmont (see, too, s.v. Godwin), lady Caroline Lamb, comtessa Teresa Guiccioli, and others, to satisfy the utmost calls of legitimate curiosity. The roving, melancholy poet, the type and

apogee of his own heroes, Byronic collar and all complete, is invested with the morbid interest derived from amorous adventures outside the experience of common men. There is evidence that he appreciated the investiture, and wore his reputation like a cloak. Thus, his first sight of a bull-fight in Spain provoked him to flutter the dovecotes of respectable villadom in Engld., and to contrast the ' spruce citizen, washed artisan, and smug apprentice ' faring to Church on Sunday with

> Fair Cadiz, rising o'er the dark blue sea !
> Soon as the Matin bell proclaimeth nine,
> Thy Saint-adorers count the Rosary :
> Much is the Virgin teased to shrive them free
> (Well do I ween the only virgin there)
> From crimes as numerous as her beadsmen be ;
> Then to the crowded circus forth they fare :
> Young, old, high, low, at once the same diversion share.

How wicked, quoth the spruce citizen ; but he turned to the next canto of *Childe Harold* when he got home from Church.

This, then first, that B. struck a new note, a gay note, a laughing note, the note of Pan, in drab lives. He showed the children of a serious generation what fun resided in irresponsibility ; he drew back from our fog-bound island the curtain hiding the southern sun. But there was more in it than this, though this counted for much of the original impetus. *Le Byronisme* in France, *der Byronismus* in Germany, and their equivalents in Italy, Spain, and particularly in Russia, are more than the expression of a release from conventions, of expatiation in the sunshine, of free love and merry quips under a blue sky. The influence of B., esp. on the Continent, is derived not merely, or chiefly, from the ebullience of his life or even from the heroism of his death—both alike startling and ' romantic ',—but is something positive and tangible, something even permanent, to all seeming, in the history of lit. in Europe. Contemporary opinion is often wrong, posterity is sometimes unjust, even after 100 years ; a man may be neglected at home, and yet accounted a prophet abroad. But it seldom, if ever, happens, that contemporaries and posterity, fellow-countrymen and foreigners, are all wrong at the same time together ; and this would be the phenomenon we should have to face if we disputed B.'s poetic genius.

Thus, after 2 years' travel in the Peninsula, the Mediterranean and the Levant (writing the *Maid of Athens* song at Athens during that tour, 1809-11), he came home and published 2 cantos of *Childe Harold's Pilgrimage*, 1812, and ' awoke and found himself famous '. Scott (q.v.), reviewing canto 3 in the *Quarterly Review*, 1816, declared that B. ' was placed pre-eminent among the literary men of his country by general acclamation '. What man of equal standing to Scott has said that since in the *Q.R.*, of a poet of 28 years of age ? Thus, Goethe (q.v.), between 1823-6, in his publd. *Conversations* with Eckermann, declared that no poet in Engld. could be compared with B., that so eminent a poet never existed before him, and was unlikely to exist again ; and so on and so forth. B. dedicated to Goethe, 1821, his tragedy *Sardanapalus*, and Goethe more splendidly replied by allegorizing B. as Euphorion, the offspring of Helen and Faust, in Part ii of his great epic-drama. We must refer more summarily to further evidences. The bibliography of B. (by Messrs. G. A. Brown and J. G. Robertson) occupies nearly 17 large pages of *C.H.E.L.*, vol. xii, and travels through every country in Europe and the U.S.A. Among B.'s biographers, critics and annotators have been T. Moore, sir W. Scott, T. Campbell, lord Jeffrey, S. Rogers, W. M. Rossetti, M. Arnold, W. E. Henley, E. H. Coleridge, R. E. Prothero (lord Ernle), A. Austin, Georg Brandes, Alois Brandl, E. L. Engel, E. Estève, Harnack, V. Hugo, Nodier, Stendhal, A. de Vigny, and many others. As prof. O. Elton writes (*Survey of Engl. Lit.*, 1780-1830, ii, 181 and 419n.) : ' It would take a syndicate of scholars to describe Byron's influence. He has affected the spirit of poetry more than any modern man except Shakespeare and Goethe, and on the whole he has deserved to do so '. Prof. Elton selects 3 traits in this respect : (1) ' his " Titanism ", his rebellious, impassioned self-description and self-assertion. To this instinct, coming straight down from Rousseau and Werther, he gave more potent expression than all other poets put together. This is the lyrical introspective Byron, who made the world his confessional ', and Lamartine, Heine, Leopardi (qq.v.) and the Russian lyrists (see s.v. Russ. Lit.) are in debt to him ; (2) ' Byron the satirist and observer, the Byron of *Don Juan* ' ; and (3) ' Byron, the liberator, . . . the voice of the uprising against the Holy Alliance and the advocate of insurgent nationalities '. And Elton quotes Goethe's song of Euphorion as B.'s most permanent epitaph :

Scharfer Blick die Welt zu schauen,
Mitsinn jedem Herzensdrang,
Liebesgluth der besten Frauen,
Und ein eigenster Gesang.

The ' eigenster Gesang '—the ' very own song ' is true, and it has found no successor.

It is easier to enumerate B.'s creditors than his debtors. It was an Englishman, Frere (q.v.), who first turned his thoughts to burlesque satire, but it was to the great line of Ital. burlesque-satirists, Pulci, Berni, Casti (qq.v.) (esp. Casti, in his *Poema Tartaro* ; see C. M. Fuess, *Lord Byron as a Satirist in Verse*, 1912), that B. was chiefly indebted for the mood and form of *Beppo*, and, particularly, of *Don Juan* (1818-23), in which B. ' attains to the full disclosure of his personality and the final expression of his genius ' (*C.H.E.L.*, xii, 54).

So full, though so short, a life, crowded with such rapid achievement and with so brilliant and profuse improvization, cannot be summarized in a short art. without omissions and gaps. B.'s journalism (*The Liberal*, with Leigh Hunt, q.v., etc.), his letters, and other aspects of his many-sided literary activities cannot be dealt with here. His disputes with Southey (q.v.), his advocacy of Pope, his genius for friendship, his intolerance of criticism, his storming pride, his psychological perversities,—all this, and much else, we must leave. The essential B. is the author of a body of Engl. poetry, exhibiting, in its metrical diversity, its glittering execution, its power of observation, its passion for virile virtues. its rarer softnesses, tendernesses and even sobs, amid satire, frolic, and exhortation, a mastery which is astounding when we remember that the lover, the traveller and the poet was only 36 when he died. ' When the year 1900 is turned ', wr. M. Arnold many years before that now far receding date, ' and our nation comes to recount her poetic glories in the century which has then just ended, the first names with her will be these ' (i.e. B. and Wordsworth). At any rate, the 20th century's distaste for many of the cates that diverted its predecessor has not extended to B.'s poetry.

C

Cabanyes, de, Manuel (1808-33) : Span. poet ; an ' heir of unfulfilled renown ', who did not live to confirm the promise of his *Preludios de mi lira*, 1833.

Cabrera, de, C. A. See s.v. **Saavedra Faxardo**.

Cadalso, Josef (1741-82) : Span. poet ; moral satirist ; soldier ; killed at the siege of Gibraltar ; edu. in Paris, and travelled in various European countries before settling at Madrid, c. 1761. Wr. some plays, which manifested his appreciation of the rules and method of Fr. drama, and became a frequenter of the little circle of literary men who gathered with the elder Moratin (q.v.) at the sign of San Sebastian. Wr., 1772, a prose essay on fashionable pedantry, *los Erudites à la Violeta*, which mocked in a pleasant vein of satire at the affectations of superficial culture ; wr., too, a pleasant vol. of verse, on the occasion of the death of his mistress, *Noches lugubres*

(after the *Night Thoughts* of Young, q.v.) ; and left for posth. publication, 1793, *Cartas Marruecas* (Moroccan Letters), modelled on the *Lettres Persanes* of Montesquieu (q.v.) and Goldsmith's (q.v.) *Citizen of the World*, but slighter and more ephemeral in interest.

Caird, -i, John (1820-98) : Scot. theologian ; principal of Glasgow Univ. ; famous as a preacher through his sermon on ' Religion in Common Life ' before queen Victoria ; wr. *Introduction to the Philosophy of Religion*, 1880 ; *Spinoza*, 1888, etc.

-ii, Edward (1835-1908) : Scot. scholar ; brother of above ; master of Balliol, in succession to Jowett, q.v. ; wr. important monographs on Kant, Hegel, Comte (qq.v.) and Gk. philosophy.

Calais : Fr. coastal town, opposite Dover ; captured, 1558, by France from Engld., who was thus driven, territorially, out of the continent of Europe. Except for a ballad, of which all but the title has been lost, the event, which impressed the name of Calais on queen Mary's heart, passed without literary notice by the losers ; the victors sang it in a hymn by Du Bellay (q.v.), one by Magny (q.v.), a Lat. panegyric by Turnebus (q.v.), and many references in song and drama.

Calderon de la Barca, Pedro (1600-81) : Span. dramatist ; by common consent, the premier playwright in the history of the theatre in Spain ; knt. of the Order of Santiago, 1637. C.'s genius, it is admitted, was essentially Castilian and essentially Catholic ; and he fell short, if he fell short, of universal appeal to the nations only by the sublimity of his expression of the ideals of Catholic Spain in the 17th cent. Modern critics agree in this estimate ; without detracting from C.'s fame, they compute it somewhat more exactly than was the looser habit of the past, and derive it, partly, at least, from local and temporal conditions. They point out that C. enhanced but did not multiply the dramatic forms invented by his predecessors : ' he worked in the lines set by Lope de Vega, borrowing his ideas, his characters, his plots. In fits of laziness he did not hesitate to introduce into his plays complete scenes from certain forerunners' (Kelly, *Lit. espagn.*, 360). His method in this respect may be seen at its best in his transformation of Montalvan's (q.v.) ' Life and Purgatory of St. Patrick ', 1627, into the remarkable religious drama, *el Purgatoria de San Patricio.* Yet C. is far too big a genius to be dismissed as a disciple of Vega (q.v.) and his disciples, nor is there finality in the statement that Molina (q.v.) surpassed him in inventive power. C.'s triumph is supreme, within the limits of his ambition, and he royally liquidated all his borrowings. P. Corneille (q.v.), for instance, was deeply indebted to C., and Dryden's (q.v.) *Evening's Love* and Colley Cibber's (q.v.) *Double Gallant* were derived from Fr. versions of plays by C. Without attempting to draw up a schedule of debtor and creditor account between C., his predecessors, and his imitators, it may be enough to remark that, as recently as the present cent., Dr. Robert Bridges, poet-laureate of Engld., acknowledged an obligation to C. in his *Humours of the Court, Christian Captives,* and other works. C.'s Engl. translrs. include men as eminent as Shelley, E. Fitzgerald, and archbp. Trench (qq.v.). France adopted him enthusiastically in his own cent.; Italy has consistently admired him ; and, in Germany, A. W. Schlegel (q.v.) was among his translrs., and Goethe (q.v.) himself, though he once remarked, not wholly unjustly, that C.'s characters were as alike as tin soldiers, took some hints for his *Faust* from C.'s *Magico prodigioso,* and said to Eckermann, with expert wisdom, that C.'s ' plays are thoroughly stage-perfect ; there is never a feature in them which is not designed to produce a certain calculated effect. Calderon's genius is of the kind which is at the same time the highest talent '. How did that genius express itself, if C.'s characterization tended to be monotonous and his action was sometimes unoriginal ? Kelly distinguishes clearly 3 veins of popular interest, which C. worked with

consummate skill : personal loyalty to the sovereign, absolute devotion to the church, and punctilio, or the national ' point of honour '. Any of these, as a dramatic motive, in the hands of a playwright as ' stage-perfect ' as C. was described by the great director of the Weimar court-theatre, was certain to win the plaudits and to find a straight way to the hearts of audiences in Madrid and other Span. cities, where the dynasty was intensely cherished, where the Church was the very mother of the populace (feared as well as loved), and where chivalry (of the *Amadis,* q.v., type) had handed down to a proud and touchy society the exact code of personal honour. None of the motives was new, and this fact was largely to C.'s advantage ; for, provided only that he had the craftsman's skill, he was able to exploit common national sentiments with a complete confidence in the response of his hearers. The dramatic skill is beyond dispute. The story is told of a member of the guard who sprang forward, sword in hand, to prevent the sale of the Span. heroine to the Moorish infidel in act iii of ' The Love of Gomez Arias ' (*Niña de Gomez Arias* ; a play which was in debt to L. V. de Guevara, q.v.) ; so perfect was the life-illusion which C. produced on his mimic stage. Play after play reveals it, whether in tragedies of horror-breeding jealousy, or in carefully-wrought intrigues of domestic comedy, or in social dramas of the ' cloak and sword ' pattern (see s.v. Capa), or in historic or religious pieces.

It may be noted that C. surpassed Shakespeare in his carelessness about the minor facts of history and geography. He aimed at a dramatist's not an exact scholar's truths : his pagan hero would be the pink of Span. propriety ; his Herodotus would know all about America ; his Jerusalem would be washed by the sea. Like other playwrights, too, Shakespeare among them, C. was not careful to collect his works. His brother, José, published 2 vols. in 1636-37, and a 3rd was issued in 1664 by his friend, Ventura de Vergara Salcedo ; but the booksellers wrought such havoc with his name that it was difficult to identify his compositions or to establish their true text. In 1680, C. sent a list of them to the 7th duke of Veragua, the head of the family of Columbus (q.v.), and on this basis the posth. edn. was published, 1682-91, by Villarroel (q.v.). We count now about 120 plays ; 80 *autos,* and about 20 shorter works (interludes, etc.). Plainly, it would serve no purpose to enumerate this list, or to mention the titles with no account of their contents. A few names may briefly be given : (reference might be made in the first instance to the admirable little study of *Calderon* by Miss E. J. Hasell in Blackwood's ' Foreign Classics for English Readers '). There is ' The Mayor of Zalamea' (*el Alcalde de Zalamea*), for example, indebted, perhaps, for some hints to Vega's *el Cuerdo en su Casa* (' The Wise Man at Home '), which presents an extraordinarily moving story, and gives royal sanction to the doctrine of the sacredness of the poor man's home, and whose heroine was said by E. Fitzgerald to be worthy of the Gk. Antigone : ' If Calderon had consistently maintained this level, he would rank among the greatest masters of all ages and all countries'. There is 'The Constant Prince' (*el Principe constante*), who was, historically, prince Ferdinand of Portugal (a grandson of John of Gaunt), the scene of which opens in Fez, where the prince was a prisoner. A love-story underlies the current of the royal, loyal captive's resolve never to win his liberty at the price of the Christian city of Ceuta : 'it belongs to God, not to me', he tells the Moor. There is 'The Fairy Lady' (*la Dama duende*), a favourite with the author and his audiences, and a brilliant triumph of frolicsome intrigue : in all such plays of social life—the 'cloak-and-sword' (*capa y espada*) plays—it should be remembered that the 'point of honour' was a very real conception, and corresponded more accurately perhaps to social habits and conditions than we imagine to-day. Thus, if a maiden were discovered receiving the visit of a man, her father or brother or other champion was compelled to avenge it in blood. Granting this convention of the punctilio, many of C.'s best plays will be commended more readily to modern taste. Thus, the *Medico de su Honra* ('Physician of his own Honour'; a title taken from Vega) burns its terrible doctrine on our minds, and is pre-eminently typical of the more tragic section in this class. C.'s *Magico prodigioso* we have mentioned in connection with the Faust-legend ; it contains some wonderful lyric verse and a remarkable presentment of the Devil ; Shelley transld. some scenes from it ; Milman's (q.v.) *Martyr of Antioch* was based on the same story, and it is no deduction from C.'s greatness to recall that a *Prodigio de los Montes* had been written a few years before by Castro (q.v. ; another theory is that Castro's reputed play was another name for *la Barbara del Cielo* by Vega). Similarly, the grandeur of C.'s remarkable 'Devotion to the Cross' (*la Devocion de la Cruz*) is not diminished by its debt to Amescua's (q.v.) 'Slave of the Devil'. Schlegel transld. C.'s 'Cross', which Schiller (q.v.) had probably read before he wr. his youthful 'Robbers', and which, whatever its faults of immaturity and imperfect reverence, is among the finest romantic fate-dramas of European lit. It was by such almost abstract studies of the influencce on character of fate that C.'s influence was so deeply felt in the epoch of Germ. romanticism. Space is due, too, to two great tragedies : *Amar despues de la Muerte* ('Love greater than Death'), which is founded on the Granada chronicles of Mendoza and Hita (qq.v.), and introduces such well-known personages as don John of Austria and Lope de Figueroa, who appeared again in 'The Mayor of Zalamea', and who was in command of the Span. troops when Cervantes (q.v.) was serving in Italy ; and *el Mayor Monstruo los Zelos* ('No Monster like Jealousy'), which deals with Herod and his wife Mariamne (from the story in Josephus), and which was a favourite subject of Fr. drama, right down to Voltaire (q.v.).

It would take us too far to extend these notices, but reference must finally be made to C.'s most signal successes in the composition of *autos*. The sacramental *auto* (q.v.), it will be remembered, is a one-act dramatic presentation of the Mystery of the Holy Eucharist, performed in the open-air on Corpus Christi day. It ranged from the humblest performance by devout villagers or peasants to the most maginficent masque and show devised by Church and State in the capital of Catholic Spain. This class of drama, says Kelly, seems to have been invented for the greater glory of C. He had the true instinct for Ober-ammergau ; his very faults as a dramatist were virtues in a composer of *autos*, where sameness of subject, and abstract characterization, and cultivation of allegory were positive qualities of excellence ; and it was in this capacity that C.'s genius expressed itself most completely, and that he consciously found himself most at home. Of his 70-80 *autos*, 'The Divine Orpheus' is perhaps the best, and the best known. He was the regular purveyor of *autos* to Madrid ; and, as Ticknor tells us (ii, 358) : 'There is little in the dramatic literature of any nation more characteristic of the people that produced it than this department of the Spanish theatre ; and, among the many poets who devoted themselves to it, none had such success as Calderon'. C.'s biography, it should be added, was not eventful. He fought in Spain's wars, and he held offices in the Church, and he died, as he said, 'like the swan, singing'. The death of Vega in 1635 left the primacy of the national theatre vacant just at the time when C., whom Vega had lauded in 1622, was ready to assume the fallen mantle.

Calmet, Augustine (1672-1757) : Fr. historian ; theologian ; *abbé*. Wr. 'Universal History', 17 vols. ; 'Commentary on the Bible', 23 vols. ; 'History of the Bible and the Jews', 2 vols. ; and a well known historical and critical 'Dictionary of the Bible', 4 vols., 1722-28 : an industrious record of a useful life.

Calverley, Charles Stuart (1831-84) : Engl. humorous poet ; parodist ; son of rev. H. Blayds, who changed his surname, 1852 ; edu. Balliol, Oxford, and Christ's Coll., Cambridge, where he took a fellowship, 1858. Wr. *Verses and Translns.*, 1862, besides other vols. of light and clever verses, which were always good-humoured and amusing. As a parodist of contemporary authors, he earned a very wide, if somewhat ephemeral, renown. C.'s verse-transln. of Theocritus, 1869, was a brilliant piece of work.

Calvin, Johannes (1509-64) : Fr. reformer and theological writer ; Jean Chauvin, or Cauvin, Latinized to Calvinus. Lit. and religion part company with a curious abruptness in the person of C., whose contribution to the former is on a level with that of Rabelais (q.v.), his religious antitype, and whose contribution to the latter is less than that of his contemporary, Luther (q.v.), whom he surpassed as a master of prose-style. Since C.'s literary influence, unlike Luther's, is almost independent of his religious activity ; since his literary work, in other words, thus differing from the Lutheran Bible, abides for the manner in which he wr. it much more than for its matter, it is not necessary here to discuss the controversial aspects of C.'s life. He was born at Noyon, in Picardy ; played successively at divinity and law ; was at first just enough tainted with reform doctrine to attract the favour of

Francis i, and still more of his sister, queen Margaret (q.v.) of Navarre, but had to quit France, 1534, for Basel; visited Italy under patronage of Renée, duchess of Ferrara, who was always more free than her royal French relatives to receive reformers; settled at Geneva, where he established a kind of one-man theocracy, not as mild or enlightened as Savonarola's might have been, if Medicean Florence had been populated by Mirandolas, but supplying the pattern upon which Scotland cut her future broadcloth of Presbyterianism; was expelled, and restored, and spent his long, dour reign in busy theological politics. His *magnum opus* is the *Institution Chrétienne*, which he wr. first in Lat. (Basel, 1535) and afterwards in French (1541; 1560). Its argument to the doctrine of original sin and its stern anti-Romanism do not affect its literary value, which consists chiefly in its adaptation of Lat. sentence-building and paragraph construction to the Fr. vernacular, without sacrificing the Fr. vocabulary to the vicious Latinism of the ' Rhetoriqueurs ' (q.v.). Rabelais was doing it with all the colours in the paint-box; Amyot (q.v.) was doing it in transln.; C.'s merit is greater by the fact that he attained a gravity and dignity alien to Rabelais's aim in a sphere of composition which demanded hard original thought; though, doubtless, the prior existence of his treatise in his own Lat. version relieved the stress of thought to a large extent, and set him at liberty to concentrate on style. Between the charm of the rambling narrative of Froissart (q.v.) and the grace of C.'s modulated and logical prose there is all the difference between child-hood and maturity; and in this achievement C. stands at the head of a long line of prose-writers, who had the advantage of using the romance-language most direct in descent from the Roman, in which Cicero, so long worshipped and so sedulously imitated, was at last to serve, not as tyrant, but as ancestor.

Camden, William (1551-1623): Engl. antiquary; headmaster, Westminster school, 1593; wr. *Britannia*, 1586; fifth edn., 1600; ninth, enlarged, 1607; comprising a store of valuable information on the history and antiquities of Engld., presented in admirable Lat., and constantly enhanced by further labour and research. Founded C. chair of history at Oxford, 1622; his name has been given to the C. society, and is recognized everywhere as a synonym for learning.

Camerarius, Joachim (1500-74): scholar's name of Joachim Kammermeister: Germ. humanist. Wr. life of Melanchthon (q.v.), and edited (1552) Plautus; a fine example of early textual criticism. Was member of circle of ' poets ' at Erfurt under Eobanus (q.v.).

Camoens, Luis de (1524-80): Port. marine-poet; epicist. Born at Lisbon; received court appointment, but had to leave it on account of an unhappy love-affair. This he deplored in exquisite elegies, which may almost have made it worth while. From thoughts of love C. turned to thoughts of war. He volunteered for service against the Moors; and, having lost his right eye in battle, returned from Africa to the court. His second sojourn at Lisbon was not more fortunate than his first. He

left for the East Indies in 1553, where he took part in constant fighting. A poetical indis-cretion against the home government earned him a harsh sentence of banishment; and disaster by shipwreck was added. C. returned to Lisbon, 1569, to find a visitation of plague; and a fatal expedition against Moors, in which king Sebastian was killed (1578), was the final blow to the stricken poet. So dismal a sequel of calamity has seldom, if ever, pursued a poet as gifted as C. He was haunted all through his life by the melody of the Indian Ocean, which Vasco da Gama and other great com-patriots had navigated. His misfortunes and his unique position as the national poet of Portugal may have exalted him unduly in his own country; but in all countries he is recogn-ized as a powerful Renaissance writer, effecting for Discovery in Portugal what writers more happily placed had effected in Italy and else-where for the Revival of Learning. His epic is called *Os Lusiadas* (' the Lusiads '; i.e., descendants of Lusus, legendary hero of Portugal). In 10 cantos of 8-line stanzas (*ottava rima*), extremely musical and fluent, C. set himself, in long periods of enforced leisure between campaigns, to celebrate the exploits of his countrymen in their heroic age. He utilized resources of travel for his descrip-tions of natural scenery, which reach a high level of art; and he employed the feature, common in humanistic lit., but exotic to modern taste, of introducing Pagan deities to play Homeric parts in Christian battle and debate.

Campanella, Tommaso (1568-1639): It. poet and reformer; ' represents martyrdom for the sake of country ' (R. Garnett, *It. Lit.*, 263); spent the years, 1599-1625, in prison, partly under torture, on an obscure charge of political conspiracy, directed to the release of Naples from the yoke, not only of Spain, but of Rome. C. belongs to that era of the migration of the Renaissance (q.v.) out of its home in Italy to Engld. and France (see, too, s.vv. Bruno, Tasso), and suffered for his opinions accordingly. His vernacular sonnets and other poems were publd. in Germany by his disciple, Tobias Adami, 1622, and republd. by Orelli, 1834. They reveal the essential man more clearly than his vague, Utopian, pantheistic specula-tions, and prove him to have been a poet of deep and powerful imagination, carving a difficult utterance of new poetic truths. Symonds (*It. Ren.*, v. 421f.) discusses these sonnets, translating one, among others, addressed to Bernardo Telesio (1509-85), a similarly-minded anti-Scholastic. Therein, nature (q.v.), distinguished from authority, is hailed as the saint and queen; and ' the spirit communi-cated from Telesio and Campanella to Bacon is the spirit of modern science.'

Campbell, Thomas (1777-1844): Engl. poet; took a leading part in the foundation of London Univ.; rector of Glasgow Univ., 1826-9; buried in Westminster Abbey. Wr., 1799, *The Pleasures of Hope*, inspired by *The Pleasures of Memory*, 1792, of Rogers (q.v.), ' perhaps the last poem of any importance written on the classical model; . . . essentially a glorified prize-poem ' (*P.E.L.*, x, 48); more perman-ently rememberable for his patriotic verses,

Ye Mariners of England, 1800, *The Battle of Hohenlinden*, 1802 ; *The Battle of the Baltic*, 1805 ; his ballad (q.v.), *Lord Ullin's Daughter*, and one or two other pieces. C.'s *Gertrude of Wyoming*, 1809, a narrative ' Red Indian ' tale, has a likeness to Wordsworth's (q.v.) *Ruth*, and is written in the Spenserian stanza of his *Female Vagrant*. C. was, in fact, more addicted to Spenser than Pope (see s.vv.) by temperament, though he clung a little pertinaciously to some critical conventions of the 18th cent. ; his views are to be found in his *Lectures on Poetry*, delivered at the Royal Institution, 1820, and revised in the *New Monthly Magazine*, which he edited, 1820-30 ; and in the introduction to his *Specimens of the British Poets*, 1819, for several generations a favourite and famous gift-book.

Campe, Joachim Heinrich (1746-1818) : Germ. educationist. Succeeded Basedow (q.v.) at the Dessau Philanthropinum. Wr. a children's *Robinson Crusoe* (s.vv., Defoe, Robinsonaden), and a Dictionary of Germ. language. 1807-11.

Camphuysen, Dirk Rafaelszoon (1586-1627) : Dutch poet and preacher (' predikant '). His preaching landed him in the religious troubles of his times, and compelled him to lead a wandering life, though his excellent devotional verse, which included a Dutch version of the Psalms, and which was not dissimilar in kind to the muse of J. Cats (q.v.), might well have served to exculpate him from the charge of Arminian heresy.

Campion, Thomas (1567-1620) : Engl. poet ; musician. Wr. Lat. poems and Engl. experiments in Lat. metres, practice in which was serviceable in perfecting his dexterity in lyric verse. C. has been described as ' one of the last of the Euphuists ' (P. Vivian, *Campion's Works*, Oxford, 1909 ; p. lvii. ; and see s.v. Euphuism), but he possessed a rare faculty of musical notation, and his wit was seldom guilty of deliberate conceits (see s.v.). Wr. *A Book of Airs*, 1601 ; *Observations in the Art of English Poesie*, 1602 ; and other books of airs, as well as Masques which were performed at court. One song from the 2nd bk. of airs (' Never weather-beaten sail more willing bent to shore ') lived as a devotional hymn as late as 1707, and was revived in the 19th cent. by A. H. Bullen, who acted as a pioneer of C.'s works, and ' restored him, as he restored so much else that is good in Elizabethan literature to a grateful and appreciative generation ' (Vivian, *ib.*, lix).

Campistron, de, Jean (1656-1737) : Fr. dramatist ; follower of Racine (q.v.) ; wr. tragedies on classical subjects : *Andronic, Tiridate*, etc. ; his prevailing note was flatness, and he avoided even more timidly than Pradon (q.v.) any contact with a world other than of abstraction and convention.

Campoamor, de, Ramon (1819-1901) : Span. poet ; pamphleteer ; essayist. Wr. dramas and verse, which was much in vogue in the second half of the 19th cent., and for which he invented the descriptive titles *Doloras*, 1846, *Humoradas*, 1886, and *Pequeños* (little) *Poemas*, 1872-74.

Campomanes, Pedro Rodriguez (1723-1803) : Span. economist ; statesman ; count by rank. Wr. political and educational pamphlets.

Camus, Jean Pierre (1582-1652) : Fr. novelist ; bp. of Belley, 1608-29, when ill-health overtook him ; he was awaiting the papal letters appointing him to the bishopric of Arras when he died. C. was a disciple of St. Francis de Sales (q.v.), whose spiritual life-work he nobly commemorated, and with whom he had much in common in his objects. C.'s works, which have been computed to run to nearly 200 vols. and pamphlets, fall into three main classes : narrative (fiction), historical, and didactic (religious). He was a man of vast learning, which he carried easily, and, as is obvious, of rapidity in composition ; and, though his bks. are forgotten to-day, the vigour and fulness of the stream on which his expression flowed reminds his readers of certain aspects of Rabelais and Jean Paul Richter (qq.v.). Among his works may be mentioned, *Elise, ou l'innocente victime*, 1621, *Palombe, ou la Femme honorable*, 1624 ; *Cleoreste*, 1626.

Cancer y Velasco, de, Geronimo (died, 1665) : Span. poet ; dramatist ; wr. a burlesque play, *The Death of Baldovinos*, which was prohibited by the Inquisition, and collaborated with other playwrights in the circle of L. de Vega (q.v.).

Cancionero (Span) : Song-book ; collection of poems. The 15th cent. was a busy time for the compilation of such collections, chiefly at the court of Castile, under king John ii and his children. (See esp. s.v., Baena). The second bk. ever printed in Spain was a collection of prize-poems at Valencia (q.v.) in 1474 ; and in 1492 a C., issued at Saragossa and dedicated to queen Isabella of Castile, gave specimens of the works of 9 recent poets, including Mena (q.v.). Early in the 16th cent. appeared the first C. to which the epithet ' General ' was attached. (See s.v. Castillo). It had considerable vogue, and several successors.

Candamo, Francisco Antonio [de] Bancés (*c.* 1661-1704) : Span. dramatist ; poet. Wr. *el Esclavo en Grillos de Oro* (' The Slave in Golden Fetters '), which had considerable success, and other plays ; and is chiefly remembered for the stimulus which he gave to the *zarzuela* (q.v.), or Span. musical comedietta, or masque, which led to the full-dress opera (q.v.).

Canitz, von, Rudolf (1654-99) : Germ. poet and critic ; an opponent of the Second Silesian School (q.v.) and its extravagances, but a victim of faults as bad as those which he castigated. C. corrected the gospel according to Opitz (q.v.) by the gospel according to Boileau (q.v.).

Cañizares, de, José (1676-1750) : Span. dramatist ; imitator of Vega (q.v.) and other masters ; but one of the most successful in the second class. C.'s *Dominie Lucas* became proverbial for the type of a pretentious and down-at-heels scholar-pedant.

Canning, George (1770-1827) : Engl. statesman. Founded, with Frere (q.v.) and others, the *Microcosm* at Eton, ' a school magazine of such brilliancy that Knight, the publisher, gave £50 for the copyright ' (Courthope, *Hist. Engl. Poetry*, vi, 135), and founded, again with old schoolfellows, the *Anti-Jacobin* (q.v.), 1797, with which his connection with lit. ended. In virtue of that connection, he is adjudged (*op. cit.*) ' the greatest master of

English political satire since the days of Swift and Pope '; he expressed ' the civic genius of the Renaissance '; and ' the gallant gaiety of his parodies make them delightful reading even in a day when all memory of the originals has vanished '. Four lines of Canning's *New Morality* are famous :

Give me th' avowed, th' erect, the manly foe,
Bold I can meet—perhaps may turn his blow ;
But of all plagues, good Heaven, thy wrath can send,
Save, save, oh ! save me from the *Candid Friend* '.

'**Cantatore** ' (It.): A street-minstrel, familiar in Ital. cities, chiefly in 14th and 15th cents. More properly, ' cantatore in banca ' or ' cantore di piazza '. (See s.v. Pucci).

Canter, Willem (1542-75): Dutch scholar. 1st editor of Gk. tragedians ; his (posth., 1579) Sophocles maintained its place for 200 years, and his Euripides (1571) was the earliest to correct the text of the choruses by metrical notation.

Capa y Espada, Comedias de (Span.): Comedies of Cloak and Sword : descriptive epithet of a class of dramas, popular and frequent in Spain, in which the ' principal personages belong to the genteel portion of society, accustomed to the picturesque national dress of cloaks and swords, —excluding, on the one hand, those dramas in which royal personages appear, and, on the other, those which are devoted to common life and the humbler classes. Their main and moving principle is gallantry ' (Ticknor, ii, 207). The first playwright mentioned in this connection is Cueva (q.v.) towards the close of the 16th cent., but the true creator of the type was Lope de Vega (q.v.). Another description may be quoted from *C.H.E.L.*, viii, 130 (by Ch. Whibley) : ' Two ladies, a gallant and his friend, their lovers, a jealous brother or a difficult father, with the attendant servants of all parties ; mistake, accident, intrigue and involvement, honour touched and honour righted—such is the universal recipe '. (See, too, s.vv. Bart of Bristol and Sir Samuel Tuke).

Capponi, Gino (c. 1350-1421): It. historian. Wr. accounts of Florentine history during Ciompi rebellion.

Carducci, Giosue (1836-1907): It. poet ; the most commanding figure, with the possible exception of d'Annunzio, in modern Ital. lit. ; was for many years prof. of Ital. lit. at Bologna, and was awarded the Nobel prize for lit., 1906. His poetry, says a fellow countryman, prof. Segré (*C.M.H.*, xi, 549), ' pointed the rising generation (1860-70) the road of escape from ultra-romanticist affectations and from the fluent versifiers, who sought nothing beyond the empty resonance of metre. " I am proud to own myself inspired by Alfieri, Parini, Monti, Foscolo and Leopardi " (see s.vv.), Carducci once said in speaking of his work. " Through them and with them I arrived at the ancients and commenced with Dante and Petrarch. Upon them my eyes have always been fixed " '. It is like the voice of Petrarch (q.v.) himself, revived from the 14th in the 19th cent., and, in fact, there was much in common between the epoch of the early Renaissance and that of the *Risorgimento* of Ital. liberty. D'Annunzio has called C. ' the mediator between two worlds ',—ancient Rome and modern civilization ; and the persistence of the summons of Rome in Ital. ears is a very remarkable phenomenon. It made C. a classicist in the sense that all through his *Odi Barbare*, starting from 1877, he adapted the Lat. metres of Virgil, Horace and Catullus to the Ital. tongue, which he saved, or strengthened, accordingly : he applied to it, in Saintsbury's epithet, ' an austere and astringent influence ' (*P.E.L.*, xii, 258). But he was Romantic all the time, and ' solved the problem which baffled the Renaissance, of linking strength of thought to artifice of form ' (R. Garnett, *Ital. Lit.*, 398). C.'s poetical works included, 1865, a ' Hymn to Satan ', which may have owed something to Baudelaire (q.v.), and which struck the consciousness of C.'s time and country by its appeal to the genius of revolt, the avenging force of reason.

C. was also a considerable critic, partly in discharge of the duties of his chair, and made notable contributions to the history of his native lit., and to the criticism of individual writers. ' Starting from the concrete study of literary facts, from the analysis of texts, from minute researches in archives and libraries, he rose to criticism of another nature, to æsthetic considerations, to wide and penetrating appreciations in which the artist joined hands with the scholar. He proved by his example, as no one had done before him, that there is not and cannot be any opposition between the æsthetic and historical schools of criticism ' (*C.M.H.*, *ib.*)

Carew, Thomas (? 1589-1639): Engl. poet. After a brief and comparatively futile career at Oxford, C. studied in London for the bar. He subsequently travelled for several years on the continent. So much in favour with king Charles i did he become, that his masque *Cœlum Britannicum* was performed at Whitehall, 1633, achieving a brilliant success. The most trustworthy edn. of C.'s poems, edited by Hazlitt (q.v.), was publd., 1870. An estimate of his work as poet is not easy to arrive at. He was slightly in advance of the Restoration school, but is marred, it must be admitted, by not a little of its coarseness. His songs display however, considerable ease and grace, and he wisely preferred unexacting topics for his light muse.

Carlyle, Thomas (1795-1881): Scot. historian, essayist, and social critic ; born at Ecclefechan, in Dumfriesshire, in which county he lived at a solitary farmhouse in Craigenputtock, 1828-34, when he came to London for the rest of his life. The house where he died in Chelsea is now a C. museum. C. married, 1826, Jane Welsh, and much ink has been spilt over the story of the marriage ; she died, 1866, just after his appointment to the lord rectorship of Edinburgh univ., and, except to record C.'s abiding grief, that story lies outside our ambition. The essential facts for a right understanding of C.'s writings and influence are (1) that, like R. Burns (q.v.), his fellow-countryman, he sprang of Scot. peasant-stock, (2) that, in the reaction from the revolutionary turmoil of the early years of the 19th cent., he fixed his hopes for social regeneration, not on any machinery of government, but on the character and minds of ruling men, and (3) though this may sound fanciful—that the *lacunæ* in his theory, his imperception to some material values, his impatience with other people's accepted axioms, and his eager, even eagle's eye for shams, corresponded with the growth of his style, which displayed similar gaps and leaps, with increasing terror to his readers as years went on. To these 3 points may be added (4), arising out of (2), that C. found the types of his ruling men, his history teaching by examples, first in Cromwell, then in Fredk. the Great of Prussia. Believing passionately that right is might, C. came to believe, or to seem to believe, that might is right, and that the strong man, the 'super-man' (q.v.), was the only saviour of society. The affinity of certain inferences from this conclusion with the doctrine of Treitschke (q.v.), and the Prussian School of historians, combined with C.'s pioneer work in Germ. studies in Engld., chiefly as a hero-worshipper of J. P. Richter (q.v.), to bring about a kind of anti-C. reaction in the period of the Great War (1914-18). Like many war-emotions, it was ill judged, and passed away like a Craigen-puttock mist; but it left some traces behind it, which were added to the deterrent of C.'s later style, and which reduced the measure of his fame, greatest perhaps, in what may be called the Germanophil years of Brit. policy, between 1865-95. What was forgotten in the reaction was the fact that C., however vehement in any cause which he espoused, was at one with the spirit of his time. The recall of rulers to character, and the ensuing, inevitable confusion between the claims of right and might, is found in the polished poetry of Tennyson (q.v.) as well as in the rugged prose of C. 'And because right is right to follow right, Were wisdom in the scorn of consequence', was enjoined by the poet as early as 1833, and persisted through the ruin of the rightocracy, which, finally, emerges from the *Idylls of the King*. There is even a likeness between C. and Bryon (q.v.), his nearer contemporary. 'Carlylism', writes visc. Morley (q.v.) somewhere, 'is the male of Bryonism. It is Byronism with thew and sinew, bass pipe and shaggy bosom'; and a comparison might well be made between C.'s *Lectures on Heroes and Hero Worship* ('The Hero as Divinity')—a splendid book for the young—and Byron's *Childe Harold's Pilgrimage*, 4th canto, xciii and foll. This only means that the ideas were in the air,— the idea of salvation by moral power joined to governing power, as Cromwell and Fredk. had joined them; and the bigger, more impersonal idea that *work* is *power*; 'Close thy Byron; open thy Goethe', we read in *Sartor Resartus* (c. 1830). 'Love not Pleasure; love God. This is the Everlasting Yea, wherein all contradiction is solved; wherein whoso works and walks, it is well with him'. This surpassed Byronism, perhaps, but Byron had died in 1824, and was not the son of a Scot. mason. Yet Byron wr., in the stanzas cited above, that 'France got drunk with blood to vomit crime', and so on, much as Words-

worth (q.v.) had written out of his personal experience on Fr. soil; and so, too, C. wr., in the 6th and last of his *Lectures on Heroes*, 1841: 'We are all born enemies of Disorder; it is tragical for us to be concerned in image-breaking and down-pulling; for a Great Man, more a man than *we*, it is doubly tragical. Thus too all human things, maddest French Sansculottism, do and must work towards Order. While man is man, some Cromwell or Napoleon is the necessary finish of a Sans-culottism'.

So much here for the ideas of this immense purging force in Engl. thought, with his rich spoils from Germ. lit. and Prussian history. One word more may be said about his style, which was too richly interlarded with Germ. terms and Germanisms, imperfectly naturalized at their first landing on Engl. soil, and rendered even more difficult by his devices of capital letters and italic types. The late prof. Mahaffy of Dublin, once wr. (*Hist. Gk. Lit.*, xv) of the 'pregnant obscurity' of Aeschylus, with whose dramatic vision C.'s has been compared in respect to his *History of the French Revolution*, 1837 (vol. i was accidentally burned by J. S. Mill, q.v., who was reading it in MS. in 1835). The phrase might be remembered by C.'s readers, even in these crowded days. His style, though obscure, was pregnant, and his eagle-bark tends to spoil our taste for twitterings. Besides the works mentioned above, and including *The French Revolution*, which established his fame, and *Frederick the Great*, 1858-65 (C. had dwelt in the valley of the shadow of Fredk. since 1851), C. wr. a *Life of Schiller*, 1824, and transld. Goethe's *Wilhelm Meister* in the same year; *Chartism*, 1839; *Past and Present*, 1843; *Life of Cromwell*, 1845; *Life of John Sterling*, 1851; and *Reminiscences*, 1881. He was one of the founders of the London Library. His first biographer was J. A. Froude (q.v.), and C. and his brilliant wife have given cause for shelvesful of bks., of which the great *Life* by D. A. Wilson is the latest.

In 1874, the honour of the G.C.B. was offered to C. by queen Victoria, at the instance of Disraeli (q.v.), the prime minister, whom C. had always treated and described as a 'conscious juggler,' 'a superlative Hebrew conjurer'. The offer was declined, but 'as a proffer of State recognition by a literary man in power to a literary man in (so to speak), permanent opposition, it would be difficult to excel it (Disraeli's letter) either in delicacy or in dignity' (Monypenny and Buckle, *Life of Disraeli*, v. 356).

Carmen Sylva. See **Elizabeth Ottilia Louisa.**

Caro, Annibale (1507-66): It. poet and translr. His verse-rendering of the *Aeneid* is particularly good. C. is esteemed, too, as a letter-writer, and he wr. a comedy, 'The Beggars', 1544.

Caro, Rodrigo (1573-1647): Span. antiquary; poet. C. is now definitely accredited with the admirable stanzas 'To the Ruins of Italy', 1595, formerly ascribed to Rioja (q.v.).

Carrillo y Sotomayor (1583-1610): Span. poet; Italianate. C.'s *Obras* (works) were issued posth., 1611, and include a treatise on 'poetic erudition', which shows traces of the influence of Marino, due to C.'s residence in Italy. It is likely that this work operated in turn to develop the Gongorism of Gongora (see s.vv.).

Carroll, Lewis (1832-98) : Engl. humourist ; *nom-de-guerre* of Charles Lutwidge Dodgson, mathematician, who scrupulously maintained the difference between his two identities. Wr. *Alice's Adventures in Wonderland*, 1865, *Through the Looking Glass*, 1871 ; and other bks. for the delight of children and adults, only less popular than these. The illustrations by sir John Tenniel (1820-1914 ; famous *Punch* cartoonist) added immensely to the success of the orig. edns.

Carvajal, de, Micael (16th cent.) : Span. poet. Wr., *c.* 1530, a dramatic poem entitled ' Josephina, a tragedy ', based on the story of Joseph and his brethren ; and left unfind. a dramatic dialogue on ' the courts of Love and Death ', somewhat after the Dance of Death (s.v. Death) motive ; Hurtado (q.v.) completed this work in 1557.

Cary, Henry Francis (1772-1844) : Engl. scholar ; transld. Dante's (q.v.) *Inferno*, in blank verse, 1805, *Purgatorio* and *Paradiso*, 1812 ; the *Birds* of Aristophanes, 1824 ; Pindar, 1832. C. did work of real value to the revival of medieval studies in Engld. by his spirited rendering of Dante, which was employed by Lamb and Keats (qq.v.), among other romanticists.

Casa, della, Giovanni (1503-56) : It. lyric poet. Wr. sonnets (q.v.) of transcendent merit, with some influence on later lit. His *Galateo*, the conventional treatise on polite manners, earned him the name, we are told of the Ital. Chesterfield (q.v.). But the bulk of his verse is not of much merit.

Casanova de Seingalt, Giacomo (1725-98) : It. adventurer, whose dishevelled *Memoirs*, which he wr. ' in faulty and immortal French ' (sir E. Gosse), are among the curiosities of modern lit. ' A soiled epitome of the Venetian *Demi-monde* ', C. has been called by a writer in *The Times Lit. Supp.*, and a reference to Venice in C.'s day will be found here s.v. Goldoni. C.'s account of his adventures, trickeries and amours in every country of Europe has been transld. into every European tongue ; into English by Arthur Machen, among others ; and, though it belongs in general, and by certain passages in particular, to the class of top-shelf lit., it presents an invaluable picture of the rogue's Paradise in the 18th cent. C. was a scholar and a man of parts, with an enormous gusto for enjoyment. He effected a transln. of the *Iliad* (Venice, 1778), and he was a thorough student and disciple of Horace (q.v.). In his entirely a-moral point of view, he recalls, perhaps, an earlier fellow-countryman, Cellini (q.v.).

Casaubon, Isaac (1559-1614) : Fr. savant ; Huguenot ; born in exile at Geneva, and driven further afield by the tidings (1572) of the massacre of St. Bartholomew's ; returned to Geneva, 1578-96 ; m. daughter of Henri Estienne (q.v.) ; visited Montpellier and, later, Paris, 1600-10, at the invitation of king Henry iv. C.'s religion prevented his appointment to a chair of learning worthy of his attainments ; but he enjoyed his work as sub-librarian in the Royal Library, and deeply regretted the necessity to quit Paris after the assassination of the king, in order to escape the Roman conversionists. C. repaired to Engld.; visited Oxford and Cambridge ; was well received by king James i ; became acquainted with the leading scholars, and, after a few years of too exclusive devotion to the cause of humane learning, was honoured with burial in Westminster Abbey. Edited Theophrastus, Theocritus, Athenæus, Persius, Polybius, and others ; wr. *Letters* and *Ephemerides*, a scholar's diary, and is still esteemed as one of the greatest scholars in modern times. Mark Pattison (q.v.) wr. a life of C. in 1875.

Cascales, Francisco (fl. 1620) : Span. social writer. Wr. letters (*Cartas*) on various topics, esp. *Cartas philologicas*, 1634, which combined pleasantly erudition and gossip ; and *poeticas*, a little more ambitious. C. was among the opponents of the style associated with the practice of Gongora (q.v.), and his animadversions provoked a reply from a certain Martin de Angulo y Pulgar, Granada, 1635.

Castelein, de, Matthew (1485-1550) : Dutch poet and critic ; apostolic notary ; leading member of the Rederijkerskamers (q.v.) of Oudenarde, and a fertile contributor on the dramatic side. Wr. *Const van Rhetoriken* (*Const* = German *Kunst*, art), an *Ars Poetica* of rhetoric, based on Fr. models, and displaying intimate knowledge of such poets as Marot and Le Maire (qq.v.). Of his plays the best-known is *Pyramus and Thisbe* (see s.v. Ovid).

Castellanos, de, Juan (1522-c. 1607) : Span. poet ; soldier, and, later, divine. Wr., in 3 parts, heroic poem entitled ' Elegies of the Illustrious Men of the Indies ', which was really a poetic account of the Span. conquests in America. Part i was publd. in 1589 ; parts ii and iii in 1847 and 1886 respectively. The whole poem runs to nearly 90,000 verses in octave stanzas on the Ital. model ; and its historical interest far exceeds its literary merit.

Castelvetro, Ludovico (1505-71) : It. critic. Born at Modena ; died in exile, in Switzerld., and owing to the Inquisition. Wr. a valuable treatise on Aristotle's (q.v.) *Poetics*, 1576, and other critical works, collected 1727 ; they form the subject of a special study by H. B. Charlton, Manchester, 1913. C. argued, with no little independence (considering the tendency to strict canons of imitation in his day and generation ; see s.vv. Vida, Cinthio, and Unities) that, while the so-called Three Unities are binding on drama, as a condition of stage-management, a poet need not observe them in narrative. The importance of this discovery will be measured more easily if we recall that the main lit. of the time was composed in accordance with the rules of the ancients, reproduced by Ital. critics in Lat. dress. C. was the earliest critic to recall, however tentatively, the study of poetics from technical rules to æsthetic principles. In the gradual emergence of the Unities from Ital. study of Aristotle, it is the Unity of Place with which C.'s reform is chiefly identified.

Casti, Giovanni Battista (1721-1803) : It. satiric poet ; in the line from Pulci to Byron (qq.v.). Quitted priesthood and professoriate successively ; resided at various continental courts, including that of the empress Catherine of Russia, 1778, and recommended himself by his wit, commonly exercised for the entertainment of his royal hosts at the expense of their royal neighbours. Wr. meretricious tales, comic operas, etc.; is pilloried by Ugo Foscolo (q.v.) as the only writer of 'novelle', except Aretino, who cherished ' the deliberate intent of corrupting the morals of his readers ' (*Quart. Rev.*, 1819, vol. 21, p. 488). Wr., 1802, *Animali Parlanti* (' the talking animals '), a late bestiary (q.v), or Æsopian fable, in more than 3,000 six-lined stanzas (*sesta rima*) ; the satire ridiculed all parties, and had a success superior to its merits ; Buonaparte suppressed it when he became emperor. C.'s *Poema Tartaro*, in octave stanzas, was a satire on his Russ. experiences, which had clear influence on Byron's *Don Juan*, esp. in the Russ. cantos. (The dates of C.'s birth and death are variously given 1720-21,-24 and 1803-13, respectively).

Castiglione, Baldassaro (1478-1529) : It. humanist. Born at Casatico ; employed in diplomatic service at papal court ; enjoyed patronage and esteem of emperor Charles v ; resided through most of his life at ducal court of Urbino ; died at Toledo. Wr., *c.* 1508-1516, Ital. prose dialogue, *Il Cortegiano* (' The Courtier ') ; *ed. pr.* at Venice, 1528 ; frequently reprinted and early transld. ; into Span. by Boscan (q.v.), 1540 ; into Fr., 1538, and again, 1580 ; and into Engl. by Hoby (q.v.), 1561. The treatise has been described as the wit's Bible of the Renaissance. It is canonical in authority, and charming in style ; and its provisions for courtesy cover the whole range of knighthood, including particularly the fine arts of music and painting. The duchess of Urbino is among the interlocutors, and the epilogue, spoken by Bembo (q.v.), is written in an exalted strain on the fashionable theme of Platonic love. Bembo, again, was the subject of C.'s Lat. memorial idyl, *Alcon*, which is in the line of ascent to Milton's *Lycidas :* and C.'s Ovidian Lat. verse takes high rank in that class of writings. The prominence of the far from stainless Bembo in the ideal picture of the courtier suggests that the idealist was content to shut his eyes to a part of human conduct ; and the recollection that the *Utopia* of More (q.v.), the *Institution of the Christian Prince* of Erasmus (q.v.), and the unveiled *Prince* of Machiavelli (q.v.) were all dated from the same period at C.'s *Courtier*, suggests an impression of artificiality which is to some extent at least confirmed by attentive perusal. C.'s flattery, for instance, of Ippolito d'Este, though Ariosto (q.v.) was not guiltless in this regard, is less attractive in a discourse on modern courtesy than in a romance of Roland's court ; and Utopia rather than Urbino would seem sometimes the appropriate setting for these scenes of court manners. But, with full allowance for this somewhat fanciful criticism, the fact remains that C.'s *Cortegiano* is a living document of the Renaissance, and that it had considerable influence on the manners of court-iers beyond the confines of polite Urbino, at that time a model of Renaissance ideas. Some of its conditions were reproduced at the court of queen Margaret (q.v.) of Navarre, not merely in the tone and colour of the *Heptameron*, but in the intimacy of the royal circle of talent ; and Rabelais, the greatest of those who fluttered to her court, remembered

C.'s masterpiece in his description of Quint-essence (v. 25). Cervantes (q.v.) in Spain conceived Don Quixote in the very spirit of the ' cortegiano ' ; and, even more obviously, the ' Gloriana ' period of queen Elizabeth in Engld. was governed by the rules of chivalry, as binding on worshippers and worshipped, which C. outlined in his dialogue. Indeed, it may fairly be urged that the practical out-come of this bk. was even greater than its value in lit., inasmuch as the life of sir Philip Sidney (q.v.) was worth more than all the lit. of chivalry ; and Sidney in his life, as Spenser (q.v.) in his *Faerie Queene*, added to C.'s scheme of courtesy the missing, necessary touch of personal devotion to a distant ideal. The framework was supplied by C., to the undying honour of the Ital. Renaissance ; the spirit was drawn from the nobler air of northern virtue and endurance (see also s.v. Court) ; and the late sir W. Raleigh wr., at the close of a brilliant essay (*Some Authors*, posth., Oxford, 1923) on sir Thos. Hoby, C·'s Engl. translr. : ' It is time to remember our ancestry. Our proudest title is not that we are the contem-poraries of Darwin, but that we are the descendants of Shakespeare ; we too are men of the Renaissance, inheritors of that large and noble conception of humanity and art to which a monument is erected in this Book of the Courtier.'

Castillejo, de, Cristobal (*c.* 1490-1556) : Span. poet. C. lived mostly abroad, in the service of Ferdinand, king of Bohemia and Hungary, brother to the emperor Charles v, and, later, his imperial successor ; and his distance from the centre and his gifts of raillery and wit acted on a conservative temperament to make him a keen opponent of the new school of Castilian poets on the Ital. Renaissance models. He proved in places that he, too, could Italianize with the best of them ; but it suited his genius better to ' sport with Amaryllis ' (her local name was Ana) ' in the shade ' of the old courtly verse, in which he laughed at the affectations of the new style. C. sustained a lost cause ; and before 1573, when his scattered pieces were collected, the school of Boscan and Garcilasso (qq.v.) had firmly established its lead. But his loyalty to the old national metres was never without influence and admirers ; and traces of C.'s spirit are to be found in the writings of such poets as Chapelain, Sarrazin and Voiture (qq.v.).

Castillo, de, Diego Enriquez (15th cent.) : Span. history-chronicler ; born at Segovia ; chaplain and historiographer to king Henry iv of Castile. Wr. the *Cronica* of the period 1454-74. C. was captured at the battle of Olmedo (20 Aug., 1467), when his papers, including drafts of his chron-icle, were confiscated by the followers of Alfonso, brother to the king and pretender to the throne, and fell into the hands of Palencia (q.v.), the pretender's chronicler. C., thus deprived of his material, had to trust to some extent to his memory for the events from 1454-67 ; and it would seem that his experience of the tender mercies of the enemy induced a certain obliquity, or, at least, timidity, of vision in his final version of the ' history of king Don Henry iv '. The date of the *ed. pr.* is uncertain ; the earliest extant edn., Madrid, 1787, is described as the second.

Castillo, de, Hernando (fl. 1511) : Span. anthologist ; editor of the first *Cancionero* (q.v.) *General*, or general collection of poetry written at or near the Castilian court in the 14th and 15th centuries. This notable vol., containing 1,115 pieces by 136 writers, was issued at Valencia in 1511, and comprised representative poems by the so called Troubadours of Spain (that is, the Span. poets affected by Provençal influence), devotional verse, songs, ballads, mottoes, madrigals (rustic poems, *villancicos*), questions and answers (*preguntas*, riddle-verses), and, in some later edns., jests provoking laughter (*burlas provocantes à risa*) from a somewhat obscene *Cancionero* publd. separately in 1519. C.'s collection grew in popularity and increased in size, in course of time ; and fresh edns. were rapidly publd. at Toledo, Seville and Antwerp (1557, 1573).

Castillo Solorzano, de, Alonso (*c.* 1584-*c.* 1647) : Span. dramatist ; picaresque novelist. C.'s plays are chiefly memorable by the freedom with which Scarron (q.v.) pillaged them ; 3 tales of his *Roman Comique* were taken from C.'s *Alivios de Casandra*, 1640. Boisrobert (q.v.) transld. C.'s tale of ' The Weasel of Seville : a Hook to catch Purses ', which attained to European celebrity ; and Lesage (q.v. ; in *Gil Blas*) availed himself of other of C.'s tales. It is not necessary to renew for him a reputation independent of his pilferers.

Castro y Bellvis, de, Guillen (1569-1631) : Span. dramatist ; captain of cavalry ; gained a prize at the festival of St. Isidore, the patron-saint of Madrid, at which Lope de Vega (q.v.), his friend, presided in 1620. C. wr. about 40 plays in the Vega manner, with considerable skill in plot-construction and in harmonious versification. Among them are a *Don Quixote*, taken from Part i of Cervantes's (q.v.) novel ; a *Prodigio de los Montes*, reincarnate in the *Magico prodigioso* of Calderon (q.v.) ; and, most importantly, *las Mocedades* (' youthful adventures ') *del Cid*, 1618, (see s.v. Cid.), founded on the national chronicle, and utilized by Corneille (q.v.) in his great tragedy of *le Cid*, which did more than any other single drama to determine for two centuries the character of the theatre all over the Continent of Europe ' (Ticknor, ii, 305). A large share of this determining force was due to the controversy on the *Cid*, within and without the walls of the Fr. Academy (q.v.). When card. Richelieu (q.v.) deemed it worth while to suspend the judgment of the Academy on the question of the adequacy of Corneille's submission to the Unities (q.v.), there was plainly something adventitious (even meretricious) in the vogue and value of the play ; and it is properly pointed out that, though ' Corneille's genius is infinitely superior to Castro's, whom he treats with the utmost liberty, yet all the changes are not improvements ' (Kelly, *Lit. espagn.*, 348). C., indeed, is to be credited with the invention of the most moving tragic departure from the heroic annals of the Cid, *viz.* the conflict between will and fate, passion and duty, in the mind of the heroine, and ' some of the most admired rhetoric of Corneille is nothing but splendid translation ' (from Castro ; Kelly, *ib.*). C. is accordingly to be accounted among dramatic founders in modern Europe.

Catalonia : North-Eastern district of Spain, significant in lit. from the 12th to the 15th centuries on account of the gradual changes in the Catalan, or Catalonian, dialect, which receded further and further from its early affinity to Provençal (q.v.) under the pressure of the conquering Castilian. (See s.vv. Barcelona, Valencia).

Catherine, Saint, of Siena (15th cent.) : It. letter-writer. Her correspondence (publd., Florence, 4 vols., 1860) with popes, princes and less exalted friends, breathes a fervid spirit of religiousness, not unlike the note of the hymn-writers (' laudesi ') of her own day. All the critics agree that she commanded a fine Tuscan diction and an orderly sense of style.

Catherine ii (1729-96) : tsarina of Russia ; patron of letters and arts. Born princess of Anhalt ; m., 1744, grand-duke Peter, Russ. heir-apparent, and became sole autocrat, 1762, by a *coup d'état* which involved assassination of her husband ; thus wearing the name of ' the Semiramis of the North ' with a better title than queen Christina (q.v.) of Sweden. With the empress's reign and policy we are not here concerned, save to note that she herself drew up a document entitled *Nakás*, or ' Instruction', which formed the terms of reference for her commission appointed to prepare a draft for a new code of legislation. C. availed herself freely—to the extent, it has been computed, of nearly two-thirds of the 526 paragraphs of the bk.—of the political writings of Montesquieu and Beccaria (qq.v.), and the liberal views which she affected were considerably edited for consumption, and were modified in her own political action ; so thoroughly, indeed, that the empress withdrew her own bk. from circulation, lest it should do more harm than good. C. was a constant correspondent of Voltaire, Grimm, Diderot (qq.v.), and other eminent foreign men of letters, whom she consulted partly in order to extend the Russ. area of culture, and partly to gratify her natural tastes. The woman and the ruler were always two distinct persons. These tastes also found expression in C.'s *salon*, which was attended by Derschavin and Wisin (qq.v.), and she contributed to a miscellany edited by princess Dashkoff, president of the Academy, in which frank criticism was freely admitted. This was in 1783, but C.'s participation in journalism really dated from 1769, when she had similarly contributed (though with less direct control) to an organ of social criticism. To the journal of 1783, the empress entrusted the publication of her Memoirs (unfortunately only to 1759), and she made it an organ of pedagogy and philosophy for the instruction of her grandson.

C., further, sought laurels on the stage ; and though, as one critic writes, she kept her brilliance for her letters to Voltaire, and did not treat her Russ. audience at the Hermitage theatre to her best wares, yet her comedies, which extended to considerable bulk, qualify her for higher praise than that of a royal dilettantist. For one thing, they were deeds as well as words : ' Her farces directed against freemasonry were not merely the comic attacks of an enlightened writer like Nicolai in Berlin, but they were also the low rumble of a storm, and the threat of an approaching judicial inquiry; behind the actual words was real, unlimited power to act' (Brückner, *Gesch. der Russ. Lit.*, 89; Leipsic, 1905). C. drew generously on Fr. models for her comedies, which were conventional and imitative in construction; and it is to be noted that her wide net was cast across the water to Engld., and that her *Rurik* and *Oleg* had many Shakespearean touches, while she adapted *Timon of Athens* and *The Merry Wives of Windsor* (which became Petrograd, with Falstaff as Polkadov) through Germ. versions of the originals. (See Lee, *Life of Shakespeare*, 629; new edn., 1915). It must be added that, brilliant as was C.'s court, and notable as was the part she herself played in its intellectual aspect, her liberalism (manifest in the *Nakás*) quickly took offence at similar views expressed by countrymen of her own; the warning of the Fr. Revolution may have contributed to the sentence of banishment to Siberia with which Radishcheff (q.v.) was punished for his ' Journey from St. Petersburg to Moscow', 1790, in which he had ventured to describe the condition of the peasants.

Cats, Jakob (1577-1660): Dutch poet, man of business, and statesman; still familiarly known as ' Father Cats ' to his own countrymen; was grand pensionary of Holland for 22 years, and twice visited Engld. on diplomatic missions. C.'s poetry, as his familiar name implies, was of the homely and bourgeois kind better appreciated by Dutchmen than by readers who had been trained under the sign of the Ital. Renaissance. He wr. emblembks. (q.v.) and didactic verse of a moral, quaint, pure and simple kind, not altogether unlike in style to the Germ. poetry of Sachs (q.v.).

Cavalcanti, Giovanni (14th-15th cent.): It. historian. Wr. Florentine history of Albizzi-Medici period.

Cave, Edward (1691-1754): Engl. printer; founded, 1731, under the name of ' Sylvanus Urban ', *The Gentleman's Magazine* (the name ' magazine ' was first employed in this connection), which he conducted till his death. Originally, like the *Grub-Street Journal*, a mere series of edited extracts from other papers, it grew, like the *Review of Reviews* in a later day, into the expression of one man's mind. C. had the good fortune to attract S. Johnson (q.v.) to London, and from 1738 (to 1744) he was ' regularly employed, and the changes gradually introduced were in accordance with Johnson's wishes ' (*C.H.E.L.*, x, 163). The most important of these changes arose out of the denouncement of C. in Parliament for a breach of the privilege of the House of Commons in publishing king George iv's answer to an Address before it had been released for publication. In the result, Johnson took over the parliamentary proceedings in the *Magazine*, in the shape of his *Debates in the Senate of Lilliput*.

Caxton, William (c. 1422-91): Engl. printer; first of his trade in this country. A Kentishman by birth, C. settled in Bruges, 1446-70, where he began his famous transln. of the Fr. *Recueil des Histories de Troye* (see s.v. Troy); he finished it, 1471, at Cologne, and the folio, 1474, which contained the Engl. version, was the first bk. ever printed in the Engl.

language. The printing-press was set up at Bruges, and C.'s second venture was a transln., likewise from Fr., of a bk. on *The Game and Playe of the Chesse*. Thus, printing in Engl. began with war-books: the war of the Gks. and Trojans, and the mimic war of the chessboard. In 1476, C., who had been residing at the court of Margaret, duchess of Burgundy, came to Engld. in the reign of the duchess's brother, king Edward iv; he retained the favour of that sovereign, and of his successors, Richard iii and Henry vii, and the printing-press which he established in Westminster, 1477, was a potent force in the civilization of the times. The first bk. printed in this country (as distinct from the language) was *The Dictes and Sayings of the Philosophers*, transld. from the Fr. by the first earl Rivers; it was followed by about 80 bks. (roughly, 18,000 vols.), many of them C.'s own translns. from Fr., Lat., etc. Malory's (q.v.) *Mort Darthure* is among the most famous. A ' Caxton ' is now, of course, quoted at a very high price for collectors.

Caylus, de, Madame (1673-1729): Fr. memoirist; niece of mme de Maintenon (q.v.). Wr. *Souvenirs*, edited by Voltaire (q.v.), of a more delicate and modest character than the general run of female memoirs of her time.

Cecchi, Giovanni Maria (1518-87): It. playwright; a disciple of Ariosto (q.v.). C.'s *sacra rappresentazione* (see s.v.), ' The Exaltation of the Cross ', was acted in Florence, on the occasion of a wedding at the Medici court. His comedies are said by Symonds (*Ital. Ren.*, v, 161) to ' abound in comical absurdities involving exquisitely realistic pictures of Florentine manners,' and to be invaluable for ' the student of language, no less than for the student of Renaissance life '. But C. is no exception from a zoological law adapted by Symonds: ' The Pegasus of the Italian drama was a mule begotten by the sturdy ass of Latin on the fleet mare of the Italian spirit; and it had the sterility of the mule '.

Celestina: Span. comedy, late 15th cent., of disputed authorship. (See s.v. Rojas). The title *C.*, by which it has been known since the Ital. edn., 1519, is derived from the name of one of its chief characters, an ' old bawd ', as Mabbe (q.v.) plainly called her in his Engl. transln., 1631, corresponding to the ' nurse ' of Shakespeare and to the *trota-conventos* (convent-runner) of Ruiz (q.v.), who was the first to introduce the part into polite letters in Spain. The author, whoever he was, had entitled his play *Comedia de Calisto y Melibea*: a few years later, after expansion, it was re-entitled a *Tragi-comedia*, which not ineptly describes its dramatic purpose. The tragic lovers, Calisto and Melibea, are the literary offspring of Ruiz (q.v.), but they are in the true line of ascent to Romeo and Juliet themselves; and the human comedy is supplied by Celestina and her riff-raff associates. In both directions this Span. prose-dialogue proved of great influence in literary history, apart from the intrinsic interest of its action and character-study. By bringing the romantic *milieu* down from the region of fable and chivalry to the common earth on which men dwell, the *C.*, gave a lead to the national literary movement in Spain which issued in the picaresque (from Span. *picaro*, a rogue) novel (q.v.); contrast *C.* with *Amadis* (q.v.), for example, or with San Pedro's (q.v.) contemporary *Carcel d'Amor*, and we see how big a step was taken by the writer of this comedy towards Lesage, Defoe (qq.v.), and their forerunners and successors. And by combining the elements of the ideal love of the hero and heroine and the realistic criticism of life incorporated in the person of Celestina herself, *lena nequitiarum parens* ('the bawdy mother of naughtiness'), as Vives (q.v.) called her in 1523, the writer took another big step in the development of literary forms, and helped considerably to found the romantic drama of the Elizabethan theatre. Thus, the *C.* has an importance in lit. transcending its merits as a literary composition, which are in themselves by no means slight, and which owe something, as the names of the *dramatis personæ* suffice to show, to the Lat. comedy of Plautus and Terence. But it is due to this secondary importance that many scholars have spent much labour on an investigation, still somewhat inconclusive, into *C.*'s origins and bibliography. There appears to be little or no doubt that a rather older edn. existed than that issued at Burgos, 1499, which we possess as the nominal *ed. pr.* The Burgos edn. and a Seville edn. of 1501 contain 16 acts; later edns. have 21 (and 3 have 22). Thus, three questions arise at once; who wr. the 16 acts? who wr. the 5 extra acts? were the 21 acts written by the same hand? These problems are still not finally settled; but the most recent opinion inclines to the attribution of *C.*, or of the bulk of it, to a certain Fernando de Rojas (q.v.), under whose name, accordingly, we briefly state the evidence in his favour. The chief authorities on the subject are R. Foulché-Delbosc, *Revue hispanique*, 1900 and 1902, and H. Warner Allen, *Celestina*, Appendix ii, Routledge, 1908; the minor question of the precise number of years before 1499 that the *C.* was composed is important in connection with the age of Rojas at the time of his alleged authorship. It should be added that the earlier theories of participation in the authorship of Act i either by Cota or Mena (qq.v.) have since been abandoned. (See, too, s.vv. Urrea, Rastell). Returning from these problems to the bk. itself, it is to be noted that it attained the dignity of a stage-play within a century of its first publication; that for 3 centuries or more it escaped the ban of the Inquisition; that it was highly praised by Cervantes (q.v.); that its style is a model of Castilian prose; that 'the very name of Celestina became a proverb, like the thousand bywords and adages she herself pours out' (Ticknor, i, 240); and that, despite its 'shameless libertinism of thought and language' (*ib.*, 239), it found hosts of imitators, who were attracted by the writer's preoccupation 'with the passions of ordinary men and women, the agonies of lovers, the artifices and perversities of senile vice, the venality and fanfaronnade of rogues, the effrontery of courtesans, and the blind fatalism of the *bourgeois*' (Kelly, *Lit. espagn.*, 168). In this sense the work is of first-rate significance in the comparative lit. of Europe.

Cellini, Benvenuto (1500-71): It. (Flor.) goldsmith, sculptor and artist; author, for the purpose of this record, of a vol. of *Memoirs*, which ranks with Pepys' (q.v.) *Diary*, Rousseau's (q.v.) *Confessions*, Diderot's (q.v.) *Neveu de Rameau*, Casanova's *Mémoires*, and, for a later generation, Marie Bashkirtseff's autobiography, among the few human documents of self-revelation in undress. The standard Engl. translin. of this bk., which 'circulated in MS. and was frequently copied before its first committal to the press in 1730', is by J. A. Symonds (q.v.; 1888, and frequently reprinted), who remarks that 'it is well-nigh impossible to match that vast vocabulary of vulgar phrases and technical terminology. Some of Cellini's most vivid illustrations owe their pungency and special colouring to customs which have long passed out of current usage'. After referring to his 'contemporary Florentine slang', to his 'vehemently ill-conjugated verbs', and his 'breathless and fiery incoherence', Symonds adds that that 'the almost impossible task has to be attempted of reproducing the effect of heedless animated talking'. The man was more deplorable than his style. He was at once artist and bravo, and a typical product, accordingly, of the Ren. in Italy. Vasari (q.v.) describes him as 'in all his doings of high spirit, proud, lively, very quick to act, and formidably vehement; a person who knew only too well how to speak his mind to princes' (cp. Aretino, q.v.). *C.*'s bronze Perseus is a supreme work of art, but his bk. of memoirs is even more remarkable, and is more amusing, as H. Walpole (q.v.) said, than any novel. For Ital. society, as Symonds reminds us, 'admired the bravo almost as much as Imperial Rome admired the gladiator', and 'our artist's frequent homicides and acts of violence were condoned by great princes, who wished to avail themselves of his exceptional ability'. It remains to be added that Goethe (q.v.), who translid. the *Neveu de Rameau*, transld. too, *C.*'s *Memoirs*, and that Comte (q.v.) included the bk. in 'his very limited list for the perusal of reformed humanity'.

Celtes, Conrad (1459-1508): Germ. humanist. Lectured on Gk. and Lat. learning at Erfurt and other univs.; visited Ferrara, Rome and Padua; taught at Cracow; librarian at Imperial Library, Vienna (1497); 'the knight-errant of humanism in Germany' (Sandys, *Hist. Class. Schol.*, ii, 259); known as the German Ovid, from his Lat. Ovidian tales, but is less decent than his prototpye; wr., too, *Ludus Dianæ*, a kind of court-masque or dramatic-pastoral, which was enacted before emperor Maximilian (q.v.), 1501.

Cénacle (Fr.); 'evening meeting': name given to a little society of literary men, which met in 1824 and following years in the *salon* of Nodier (q.v.) at the library of the Arsenal (q.v.). This society formed the nucleus of the Romantic revival in Fr. lit., culminating in the movement of 1830. (See s.vv. Lyrisme, Romance, Fr. lit.). The first *C.* included Vigny and the brothers Deschamps (qq.v.); the second *C.*, which dates from 1829, was more definitely romanticized in membership and aims, and attracted Hugo, Sainte-Beuve, Dumas, the painter d'Angers (David), and the youthful de Musset, who celebrated the gathering in verse. (See s.vv., and s.v. Arsenal). It was a Paris analogue to the Pre-Raphaelite Brotherhood (q.v.) of a later generation in London, and had the same taste for the exotic and the medieval.

Centlivre, Susannah (?1667-1723): Engl. playwright; successfully adapted Fr. and Span. comedies for Garrick (q.v.) and other actors.

Centon Epistolario (Span.): 'Hundred Letters'; title of a vol. of 105 Span. letters, purporting to have been written between 1425 and 1454 by the bachelor Fernan Gomez de Cibdareal, reputed physician to king John ii of Castile. The *ed. pr.* is dated, Burgos, 1499, but is now shown to have been produced, imprint and all, in Italy, *c.* 1630; and the credit of the clever forgery is ascribed to J. A. de Vera (q.v.), on evidence first adduced by Ticknor (iii, App. C.), and successfully sustained against P. J. Pidal and others. The demonstration obviously destroys the hist. interest which was formerly attached to this work, excellent as was the illusion which it created.

Ceo, do, Violante (1601-93): Port. poet; nun. Wr. *Rimas varias*, 1646, and some sacred plays. She used the Castilian language for many of her poems, including an ode on the death of Vega (q.v.); and some of her writings, it is noted, 'are too gallant to be very nun-like' (Ticknor, iii, 26n.). Her surname appears in Span. as del Cielo.

Cepeda, de, Joaquin Romero (fl. 1582): Span. poet; also spelt Zepeda. Wr. 2 plays, the *Comedia Salvaje* (wild), founded mainly on *Celestina* (q.v.), and the *Metamorfosea*, a pastoral drama; and other verse of no great merit, including narratives, drawn from the tales of the Trojan War. C.'s works (*Obras*) were publd. in 1582, but there is evidence that he was still busy as late as 1626.

Cervantes, Saavedra, de, Miguel (1547-1616): Span. novelist; dramatist; 'in close chain with the greatest masters' (Emerson, *Works*, xi, 367). How closely the chain is linked may be judged from the estimate by Hallam, who does not practise hyperbole, of C.'s masterpiece, *Don Quixote*: 'It is to Europe in general', he writes (*Lit. of Europe*, iii, 155), 'what Ariosto is to Italy, and Shakespeare to England; the one book to which the slightest allusion may be made without affectation, but not missed without discredit. Numerous translations and countless editions of them, in every language, bespeak its adaptation to mankind; no critic has been paradoxical enough to withhold his admiration, no reader has ventured to confess a want of relish for that in which the young and old, in every climate, have age after age taken delight'. That the terms *quixotism*, *quixotic*, have become common words in our language, and serve as tokens of exchange in every civilized tongue, is an obvious testimony to the fact, excellently stated by Ticknor (iii, 147), that 'Cervantes has shown himself of kindred to all times and all lands; to the humblest degrees of cultivation as well as to the highest; and has thus, beyond all others writers, received in return a tribute of sympathy and admiration from the universal spirit of humanity'. And Mr. Robinson Smith, C.'s latest biographer and Engl. translr., whose version is used throughout this dict., and to whose *Life* and *Notes* this article is much indebted, adds a more personal touch when he says: 'Cervantes is known and revered all over the world because he forgot himself. One detects no mean streak in him, no running fault, no deplorable side to his nature' (*Don Quijote*, etc., 2nd edn., Routledge, 1914; p. lvii.) It was not till late in middle life (1603-14) that C. struck this universal chord which evoked such instant response. 'Omit those years', writes Mr. Smith, 'and there is left but a clever writer of short stories; include those years, and we have the most imaginative prose-writer of all time'. Still, the man and his bk. are so identic, and all that he learned and suffered from his boyhood to his 55th year is so intimately inwoven in *Don Quixote*, 'the wisest and most splendid book in the world', as it was called in a tercentenary art. in *The Times Lit. Supp.*, 27 April, 1916, that a brief account of C.'s career will assist the understanding of his work. It was an adventurous career, even for a Span. author in the 16th cent., when, as Macaulay (q.v.) says, 'almost every distinguished writer was also distinguished as a soldier or a politician'. Born at Alcalà (q.v.), probably on the saint's day whose name (Michael) he bore, the 4th of 7 children of a not very prosperous physician, C.'s early years (1555-61) were spent at Valladolid, where he visited as a boy the primitive theatre of Rueda (q.v.), of which he gives an interesting description (preface to *Comedias*, 1615; quoted here s.v. Rueda). It is probable, but not certain, that C. went to school at Madrid (under Hoyos, q.v., to whose memorial vol. to queen Isabella of Spain C. contributed some verses), and to the univ. of Salamanca; but his true school and univ. were, like Shakespeare's, life itself. He was launched in it in his 22nd year; and, whether we accept with Mr. Smith (*op. cit.*, xiv) or reject with Mr. Fitzmaurice-Kelly (*Lit. espagn.*, 274) the story of C.'s identity with the Miguel de Cervantes, who quitted Madrid under a warrant of arrest, dated 15 Sept., 1569, and under sentence of 10 years' exile and amputation of his left hand, on account, apparently, of a love-duel (and the balance of evidence is in favour of the identity), at least we know that C. was in Rome in the late autumn of that year. Early in 1570 he was serving as a private in southern Italy, and in 1571 he sailed from Messina in the Marquesa, and was wounded in the chest and had his left hand mutilated ('for the greater glory of the right', as he said in his *Viage del Parnaso*) in the battle of the gulf of Lepanto. He took part in the fights of Navarino and Tunis, and set sail from Naples for Spain in 1575, bearing a letter of commendation from don John of Austria to the king. But on 26 Sept. his galley, the Sol, was captured by pirates off Marseilles, and C. was taken prisoner to Algiers; 'in those days' (Smith, *ib.*) 'a polite name for hell'. He was not ransomed till 1580, when he returned to Madrid (18 Dec.), thus curiously fulfilling the conditions of the sentence pronounced against a certain Miguel de Cervantes in 1569, that he should lose his left hand and be in exile for 10 years. Elsewhere must be sought the record of C.'s detention in Algiers

(1575-80), and of the evidence which is borne to his noble conduct in captivity and to his learning (preface, *Novelas*) of patience in adversity. He had often to apply that lesson in the course of succeeding years, when he was earning a precarious livelihood, partly from literary work, partly from a deputy-collector-ship in the department of naval stores. Here, too, we must abbreviate our narrative, and omit the trials of a tax-collector, whose work was particularly ungrateful in Spain after the Armada. More than once C. was lodged in gaol, pending inquiries into his arrears, and this dreary hand-to-mouth existence went on for about 20 years, only brightened by C.'s happy marriage (12 Dec., 1584) with Catalina de Salazar y Palacios ; till, at last, in Valladolid ' in calle del Rastro, on the first floor, in the year 1603, and at the rate of a chapter or two a week, with but the stump of a left hand to hold down the leaves of his note-book, this middle-aged, silver bearded, weather-beaten soldier and provision-collector wrote the first part of *Don Quijote* and made himself immortal ' (Smith, *op. cit.*, xxix).

What had he written before it ? Chiefly, the *Galatea* (' The First Part of *la Galatea* divided into Six Books '), of which he sold the copyright, 1584, for 1,336 *reale* (about £17). ' It is poor and a pastoral ', says Mr. Smith (*ib.*, xxvi), and Mr. Kelly writes (*op. cit.*, 276), ' He had to please in order to gain a living ' ; a phrase very close to the bitter jest which T. Hood (q.v.) made about himself ; a witty Hood writing for a livelihood. But the *Galatea*, though C. never wr. its part ii, is very appro-priate to its kind (see s.v. Pastoral), and takes its place in the succession of the modern novel (q.v.) from Sannazzaro through sir Philip Sidney (qq.v.). Its success was small, however, and C. turned next to poetry and the stage. He contributed to various verse-collections, and wr. a number of plays (from 20 to 30, he tells us), of which the names of only a few are known. One of these (*los Tratos de Argel*) dealt with Christian slaves in Algiers, and has therefore a personal interest ; another, *Numancia*, dealt with Scipio Africanus and was praised for its versification by Shelley and Goethe (qq.v.) and for its patriotic sentiment by Fichte (q.v. ; in his stirring ' Addresses to the German nation ') and the school of Germ. romance (q.v.). Both plays were printed in 1784, and *Numancia* was revived in 1809 when the French were besieging Saragossa. In 1592, C. contracted with the director of the theatre at Seville to supply 6 comedies at 50 ducats apiece, on condition that they should reach a certain standard of excellence. His-tory does not relate the issue of that contract, and nothing but a few sonnets and other poems now divide us from *Don Quixote*, the great work of C.'s life.

Why did C. write *Don Quixote* ? The bk. is sometimes described as a mere travesty of the chivalric romances, which had obtained so strong a hold on the imagination and the affection of C.'s countrymen. In a sense this statement is true, though far more so of Part i than of Part ii ; and it has the clear authority of C. himself in the opening pages of the novel. Quixote is represented as a victim—a typical

victim, we understand—of the chivalry-bacillus, so readily and fatally communicated by bks. such as *Amadis*, *Palmerin* (qq.v.), and the like ; and the time had arrived in Spain to put off the shining armour and the enthusiasm, and to face the realities of life, with its urgent social and administrative problems, arising out of the conquests in the New World and the defeat of the Armada in the Old. In this aim, C. was the anti-type of sir Walter Scott (q.v.) at a later date. As usefully and as fruitfully as ' the wizard of the North ' revived the spell of a chivalrous past in the hearts and the imagination of his countrymen, so usefully and fruitfully the realist of the South revealed by his disenchant-ing wand the contrast between fact and fiction. There were no more chivalric romances publd. in Spain after 1603 ; the *Amadis* fashion was checked as completely as the taste for hist. romance was created by Scott. ' To Spaniards, it [*Don Q.*] was much more than a witty book ; it was the supreme cry, echoing from the inmost heart of the nation, that the old gods were dead, and that Spain's exalted heroics were now but a laughing stock ' (*C.M.H.*, iii, 547 ; by Martin Hume). But C.'s aim, thus defined, implied a new philosophy of life ; and, in working out his design, chapter after fascinating chapter, he passed beyond the borders of anti-chivalry into a new world of active conduct, with standards for emulation as well as for derision, for imitation as well as for avoidance. ' The famous history of the errant knight ' (Wordsworth, *Prel.* v., 60) is not merely a warning, but an inspiration, and colonel Newcome, for example, is a true descendant of Quixote. Still, the purpose of the bk. was exposure, ' a pitiless exposure of the dead ideal ' (*C.M.H.*, *ibid.*) ; and it is due to this purpose that the bk. wears its extra-ordinary appearance in the trained eyes of a comparative student of lit. Thus, in the notes of Mr. Smith's edn. (1914 ; see above), it appears as a multitudinously pieced mosaic of refer-ences, borrowings, and travesties, to, from, and of the old romances and divers other works. In his list of sources (*op. cit.*, 743), which ' includes only those bks. that have lent phrase, idea, or incident to the *Don Quijote* ', and not those merely mentioned by C., as in the famous ch. (i, 6) of the bonfire of bks., Mr. Smith adduces several hundreds of exact references to over 130 authors ; and he writes (p. viii), ' there are no doubt scores of hits that still remain to be noted '. *Amadis*, Ariosto, Aleman (qq.v.), and Avellandena (q.v., and see below), were perhaps most frequently drawn upon ; but the range of C.'s reading was remarkable. As a feat of memory it was marvellous, more marvellous as a piece of craftsmanship, and most marvellous of all as transmutation. For this happy hunting-ground of literary scholars, this mosaic of the romance of preceding centuries, was trans-formed by the genius of C. into the grandest bk. for men and boys through centuries to come. What reader of a ' Don Quixote for the Young ' cares for the origins of his adventures in the *Orlando Furioso*, the *Morgante Maggiore*, and the rest of them ? How many who smile at quixotic acts remember the acts of chivalry from which they sprang ? For the bk. surpassed its author's intention, and became, like the *Iliad* and *Hamlet*, a bk. for all times and all peoples. Written (most probably) in 1603, printed in 1604, and publd. (by the king's bookseller, Robles) at Madrid in 1605 (2 edns.), 'The First Part' became famous at once, and the typical qualities of Quixote and Sancho were seized in common allusion. In 1606, C. removed to Madrid, where the facts of his life are obscure (we purposely omit the biographers' disputes about his natural daughter, Isabel de Saavedra, who now appears on the scene), till the publication, 1613, of his 12 *Novelas Exemplares* ('Exemplary Tales'; among them *La Tia fingida*, 'The Feigned Aunt', is now reckoned as authentic). Their excellence in humour and characterization may be tested by their use by Fletcher, Middleton, Hardy, Hugo (qq.v.), and others, and by the testimony of masters as supreme as Fielding and Scott; the best of them, by common consent, is the *Coloquio de los Perros*, 'The Dogs' Colloquy'; described by Mr. Smith (*op. cit.*, xlv) as 'incomparably the world's finest short story'. In 1614, C. publd. his poetic *Viage del Parnaso*, a review of contemporary bks., after an Ital. model by Caporali (q.v.); and in the following year he publd. his 'Eight Comedies and eight Interludes' (*entremeses*). Meanwhile in 1613-14 (the precise date is doubtful, though it would be of interest to establish it) a writer calling himself Alonso Fernandez de Avellaneda (q.v.), and most plausibly identified (among other conjectures) with Luis de Aliaga (q.v.), the king's confessor, had issued at Tarragona a (false) *Part Second of Don Quixote*. Whether the publication of this bk. stimulated C. to redeem his promise of writing his own Part ii, or whether Avellaneda's forgery first came into his hands when he had already written 58 chs. (see *Don. Q.*, ii, 59), must be left to exact scholars to settle; Mr. Smith (*op. cit.*, xlix) sums up strongly in favour of the former theory. Anyhow, in 1615, the *Segunda Parte del ingenioso Cavallero Don Quixote de la Mancha*—the genuine Second Part, not the false—was finished and publd. by C., and in the opinion of most judges it is even superior to Part First; more human and universal in its appeal.

The great man's life was nearly over. 'With one foot in the stirrup', as he wr. in a dedication to count de Lemos, adapting the words of an old play to the still older joust with death, he completed, on 19 April, 1616, his last tale, 'Persiles and Sigismonda'; and on 23 April (new style) he died, eleven days after Shakepeare. Engld. and Spain, Protestant and Catholic, queen Elizabeth and king Philip; how vain the old differences appear, in the light of the like and common genius of those two immortal contemporaries. By a confusion of the old and the new calendars, their death is commemorated on the same date, and it was appropriate that the kings of Spain and Engld. should exchange telegrams on the 300th anniversary of that date (23 April, 1916), 'celebrating the two literary glories of Spain and England, another happy tie between our two nations', so unhappily divided 300 years before.

Cesarotti, Melchiore (1730-1808): It. philologer and translr. Wr., 1785, a valuable monograph on *The Philosophy of Language*, which, much in advance of current thought, was a powerful plea for a single literary vocabulary, open freely to extension by contact with daily life and new needs. The plea was in opposition to the pedantry of the Accademia della Crusca (see s.v. Academy), which was hard bound in classical conventions, and which was the author of the standard Ital. dict. As a translr., C. was similarly romantic in his leanings; among other works, he effected 2 versions of the *Iliad*, one literal in prose, the other free in verse; he transld. Gray's (q.v.) *Elegy*, 1772, and Macpherson's (q.v.) *Ossian* at about the same time. This work profoundly affected the course of lit. in Italy, and on no one's imagination, it is noted, did it fasten so firmly as on that of the young Corsican, N. Bonaparte, 'whose constant companion it was from Egypt to St. Helena' (Vaughan, *P.E.L.*, x. 439).

Cespedes y Meneses, de, Gonzalo (c. 1585-1638): Span. novelist. Wr., 1615, 'Tragic Poem of the Spaniard Gerard', which was not a poem but a series of connected tales; and, 1626, 'The Fickle Fortune of the Soldier Pindar', in the same kind; the first more obviously addicted to the style of Gongora (q.v., and s.v. Cultismo) than the second. The *Gerardo* was transld. into Engl. by Digges (1588-1635), and became the basis of Fletcher's (q.v.) *The Maid in the Mill* and *The Spanish Curate*. C. wr., too, a vol. of 'Strange Stories', and Part i of 'a history of king Philip iv', 1631.

Cetina, de, Gutierre (c. 1518-57): Span. poet; Italianate; soldier; died of wounds in Mexico. Wr. pastoral verse in emulation of the reforming school introduced by Boscan and Garcilasso (qq.v.), and directly indebted to their Ital. masters; a Petrarchist of rare dexterity. C.'s madrigal commending *ojas claros serenos* ('eyes serenely clear') is the most commonly quoted of his poems, but he was a skilful artificer of sonnets as well.

Chaadaev, Peter Jacovlevich (1793-1856): Russ. journalist; critic. Wr., 1836, in the *Moscow Telescope*, his famous letters 'On the Philosophy of History', which made an immense stir in contemporary Russ. thought, and brought untoward results to C. himself. His first letter took shape as an uncompromising manifesto of the reform party, in the controversy of the Westernizers *v.* the Slavophils (see s.v. Russ. lit.), which divided critical and creative lit. into two opposed camps in the Russ. 'forties. C.'s argument was that Russ. culture required a renovation from without; a spiritual revolution like that which Ibsen (q.v.) was to demand for Norway in 1870. The isolation of Russia was his main point: 'Solitary in the world', he wr., 'we have given nothing to the world, we have taught the world nothing, we have not poured a single idea into the stream of human ideas, we have contributed nothing to the progress of the human spirit, and anything that has reached us from that progress we have disfigured. There is a principle in our blood, which is hostile and refractory to civilization'. Biélinsky (q.v.) shared these views; 'we are a nation with a mirage for fatherland', he had said, and in circles of liberal thought and truly patriotic outlook they awoke enthusiastic response. But the response of official Russia was proportioned to the enthusiasm. The *Telescope* was suppressed ; the editor was exiled ; the censor, who had passed the article, was dismissed ; and C. himself, by a sentence almost humorous in its solemnity, was ' confided to the care of an alienist physician, who was to visit him every day '. This treatment was kept up for a month. C.'s works (including a 'Madman's Apology ') were ultimately publd. in Paris (4 vols., 1862), and he became the prophet of Herzen (q.v.) and the liberals, who discovered in C.'s spiritual pleadings the source of their own politico-literary propaganda.

Chalcondyles, Demetrius (1424-1511) : Gk. teacher in Italy. Born at Athens ; lectured in various Ital. cities, including Padua (1463-71), and Florence (1471-91), where he worked at *ed. pr.* of Homer (q.v.) printed in Gk., 1488. Retired to Milan after death of Lorenzo de Medici, and issued (1493) Gk. grammar, and *edd. pr.* of Isocrates and Suidas.

Chambers, -i. William (1800-83) : Scot. bookseller ; publisher ; in partnership with his brother, Robert (below), in Edinburgh, where they founded *Chambers' Journal*, 1832, and started the first edn. of their *Encyclopedia*, 1859. C. wr. several bks. of hist. interest, including *A Gazetteer of Scotland*, and received the LL.D. at St. Andrew's, 1872, refusing the honour of a baronetcy, 1883.

-ii. **Robert** (1802-71) : Scot. bookseller and publisher ; brother of above, with whom he was associated in business. Wr. *Traditions of Edinburgh*, 1824, with some help from sir W. Scott (q.v.) ; *Vestiges of Creation*, an important Darwinian work, at first issued anon., 1844 ; *A Book of Days*, a valuable miscellany of antiquarian lore, 1862-4 ; and other works, chiefly Scot. in local interest ; LL.D., St. Andrew's, 1863. His life-story was narrated in his brother's *Memoir of Wm. and Robt. Chambers*, 1872. His son, Robert (1832-88), continued the tradition of the house.

Chamfort, Nicholas (1741-94) : Fr. satiric writer ; moralist. C. was a victim of The Terror in the Fr. Revolution ; for, though he escaped the guillotine, he died from fear of it by his own hand. He is remembered to-day chiefly by his epigrams and maxims, which displayed a mordant brilliancy and wit. His experiments in drama were unsuccessful, and his tales in verse are no longer worth reading. C. eked out a precarious existence, handicapped at the start by obscure birth, in semi-dependence on chance patrons, and doubtless his experience of the rich and great sharpened his satire at their expense. Foremost among his friends was Honoré Mirabeau (q.v.), whose eloquence was often stimulated by C.'s ' electric ' mind. Sparks from that mind included the motto of the revolutionary army, ' Guerre aux palais, paix aux chaumières' (war to the palaces, peace to the cottages), and the transposition of the revolutionary formula, ' Liberté, Egalité, Fraternité ', into ' Be my brother, or I shall kill you ' ; since made famous by a former Germ. Imperial chancellor, prince v. Bülow, as

> Willst du nicht mein Bruder sein,
> Schlag' ich dir den Schädel ein.

Chamisso, von, Adelbert (1781-1838) : Germ. poet, of Fr. descent (the original family-name was de Boncourt), who emigrated during the Revolution, and received a commission (1798) in the Prussian Army. He resigned it in 1806, and spent some *Wanderjahre* in the pursuit of his favourite botanical and zoological studies, ending up (1818) as curator of the Botanical Gardens in Berlin, where he died. C.'s ' Poems ' (1831) are an excellent blend of old lyrical measures with modern diction yielding an extraordinarily fresh effect. His most famous work was the invention of Peter Schlemihl (*Peter Schlemihls Wunderbare Geschichte*, 1814), the man without a shadow. Many ingenious meanings have been read into that fable, which was intended, probably enough, as an allegory of C.'s own experience as a Frenchman in Germany : ' private character must find its complement in public character, and, to this end, private sympathies must agree with public sympathies. Then only can a man cast a true shadow ', (Coar, *Studies in Germ. Lit. in 19th Cent.*, 87) ; and so on. But the story matters more than the allegory, and Peter Schlemihl is constantly delightful, after more than a century of shadowlessness.

Champcenetz, de (1759-94) : Fr. journalist ; *chevalier*. Collaborated with Rivarol (q.v.) in the *Actes des Apôtres* and the *Petit Almanach des Grands Hommes*. C. was one of many talented writers who found the revolutionary epoch too big for their proper display, and he died by the guillotine.

Chansons de Geste (Fr.) ; literally, songs of action, or history (' gesta ', collective plural, whence Fr. singular ' la geste ' and Engl. ' jest ') : generic name of Fr. epical poetry, or epopee, celebrating the heroic era of Charlemagne (q.v.) and his paladins ; commonly said to have taken shape between 1050 and 1360, incorporating older epical traditions, so that the Frankish race has been said to have possessed the epic mind for over five centuries ; shaded gradually into romance (q.v.), and then ceased as separate type ; entered Germany, Engld., Spain, etc., and passed into stream of European lit. through Italy (see s.vv. Pulci, Ariosto, ' Reali di Francia ' ; also s.vv. Boccaccio, Chaucer, and the novel). The c. were composed in blocks of verses, called in Fr. ' laisses ', or ' tirades ', of 5-foot (sometimes 4-foot) iambic lines, with an assonance, or similar vowel-sound in the final words. The number of lines in each ' laisse ' was indefinite. Later the assonance gave place to rhyme, and the 8 or 10 syllables to the 12-syllabled alexandrine (q.v.) ; otherwise, this type of early poetry was rigid throughout its lifetime. The c. was originally sung to a simple musical accompaniment on the Roman lyre or German harp ; the reciter, or singer, was the ' jongleur ' (q.v.), the inventor of the tale was the ' trouvère ', and both were members of the laity. The language was Romance (q.v.). The composition of c. was tireless, and the output enormous ; only a fragment of the class has survived, and not the whole of the fragment is yet available, though it runs to scores of thousands of lines. Gaston Paris (*Littérature française au moyen age*, 44 foll.) has grouped the poems conveniently, as i, national or royal, including Charlemagne's wars against the Saxons; *Aspremont*, fabulous expedition against the Saracens in Italy; *Fierabras*, likewise in Italy; *Enfances* (early exploits) *of Ogier the Dane*: *Pilgrimage of Charlemagne* to Palestine, partly burlesque; *Roncesvalles* or *Roland* (q.v.; the best surviving *chanson*) and other poems of the Spanish campaign; *king Louis* (the Third, against the Normans); *Huon Chapet*, etc.; ii, feudal, dealing partly with the conflict between the barons and the monarchy, partly with the struggles between the barons themselves, and including, chiefly, *Huon of Bordeaux* (q.v.), remarkable for its debarkation into fairyland at Brindisi, the gate of the East, and the first appearance of Oberon, king of faëry, still enthroned after nearly 1,000 years; iii, biographical, distinguished from the national variety by the importance of particular heroes, and leading to the genealogies and ' enfances ', which the ' jongleurs ' invented or combined; and, iv, adventitious, i.e., derived from sources outside national tradition, such as Gk. novels and crusaders' tales. The dividing-line between Fr. epopee and romance cannot be quite accurately determined; *chansons de geste* were composed, in form at least, on other matters than the national ' matière de France ' (see s.v. Bodel), and that material came to be exploited by the romance-writers; but properly this was their inspiration. (See s.vv., Romance, Antiquity, Arthur, and references in those articles, e.g., Alexander, Thebes, Troy, Graal, etc.). In recent years, fresh light has been turned on the orig. of Fr. epopee and on its temporal relations to the *chansons* of the 11th and 12th centuries and the *romans* (s.v. Romance) in which they were absorbed, by the brilliant researches of J. Bédier, whose *Les Légendes épiques : Recherches sur la formation des Chansons de geste* first appeared in 1908, and whose conclusions have gone far to transform all previous theories of scholarship. Briefly, Bédier rejects what may be called the primitive fallacy; he discovers and admits no ground for the arbitrary hypothesis of a body of spontaneous, popular, epical material imbedded in the written documents that have descended to us; and the absence of this hist. substructure does away with the ' mania ' of seeking to identify every hero in the *chansons* with an hist. homonymous original, and of enucleating a fact in history for every dressed-up incident in the *chansons*. On the contrary: Bédier's view, which is winning general acceptance, and which cuts clean through the webs spun by ingenious collators and commentators, is that the age of invention coincided with the age of literary composition in the 11th and 12th centuries; that the tales, as we know them, or very nearly as we know them, were taken by the ' jongleurs ' direct from the lips of the ecclesiastical guardians of the tombs and relics and shrines in the churches and abbeys frequented by crowds of pilgrims; that no one of the three factors employed — clerics, reciters (' jongleurs '), audience—was superior to any other in knowledge of the facts, with, perhaps, a very slight bias in favour of the clerks, due to floating tradition; that the facts as rendered were

created to suit the monuments as seen, and were embellished to please the sightseers, who asked nothing more than attractive stories of the mighty men whose bones were below or whose statues were above the monument associated with their name and place. It is obvious that Bédier's researches in this fascinating field of speculation dispose, once for all, of the old distinction between the primitive and spontaneous epic traditions and the artistic epic poetry superimposed on them. The spontaneity and the art were simultaneous : the tradition and the poem were twin parts of the same response to the credulous curiosity (not for history but for amusement) of the moving streams of pilgrims from sacred spot to sacred spot in those centuries. But no research, however illuminating, can destroy or undo the immeasurable benefit to lit. conferred by Fr. narrative verse in the shape of these *chansons de geste*. Throughout the Christian Middle Ages, their reign and their popularity were undisputed. Their very faults, as they appear to modern eyes—their mediocrity, their compromise, their prolixity,—recommended them to popular taste in an age incurious for accuracy and athirst for the universal appeal of simple incident and obvious emotion. Fiction and history proceeded from the same fertile source of the c.; and the greatest writers in Europe—Ariosto, Rabelais, Cervantes, Shakespeare—were one and all the heirs of their spirit.

Chantefable : song-story; sometimes written *cantefable*, and sometimes mis-written *contefable*, as if the first word were from Fr. *conter*, to tell, instead of *chanter*, to sing. The *chantefable* was a romantic type (s.v. Romance), developed from the *chanson* (q.v.), which took shape as a tale in prose, broken by *laisses* (or, blocks) of verse-*recitatif*. The best example which has been preserved is likewise, by a happy chance, one of the moving stories in fiction, the *Aucassin et Nicolette* (q.v.) of the 12th cent.

Chant-Royal : descriptive name of a form of Fr. verse, which flourished in Northern France during the 14th and 15th centuries, and which was indebted to Troubadour models from Provence. The c.-r. consisted of 5 stanzas, each containing 5 couplets and a refrain, *plus* an *envoi* of 5 lines. The scheme of rhymes in each stanza was as follows : *ab, ab, ce, dd, ed*, and the refrain *e*; the *envoi* resumed it as *dd, ed*, and the refrain *e*.

Chapelain, Jean (1595-1674): Fr. poet and critic; as he halted irresolutely between the two aims, so he has fallen between the two reputations. Yet, in his day and place, C. was something more than a little man deemed great in self-esteem and the opinion of his contemporaries. He exactly fills the interval between lyric and oratory, between the lit. which is overhead and the lit. which is heard, between Ronsard and Boileau (qq.v.) in terms of Fr. writers. He assisted by his mediatising talent the transition of the classical age. C. was eminently *persona grata* at the Hôtel de Rambouillet (q.v.), and had the wit to describe its functions in the social regeneration of Fr. lit. as ' the refuge of the average man ', filled with ' fairies who have more years than sense '. The clear sight and absence of enthusiasm which these two *dicta* reveal are characteristic of C. He was a careful student of Castillejo (q.v.) in Spain; wr. a preface to the *Adone* of Marino (q.v.), and was a purveyor of Marinism to Paris; but the kind of conceit (q.v.) which he affected was intended to enhance the art and dignify the style of Fr. lit.; and it was in the spirit of this ambition, which he sincerely entertained, that C., who was an original member of the Fr. Academy (q.v.), urged on his colleagues in that body that their first and most pressing function was the compilation of a Fr. dict. for 'the embellishment of the language'. Through C.'s direct initiative, the *Dictionnaire*, 1637-94, was put in hand. Another sign of the like zeal for the new correctness, of which, as is shown elsewhere (s.v. Precious), the preciosity of the *salons* was but an aspect, was C.'s attitude towards the unities (q.v.) of tragic drama. He was an early convert to the creed, and had the privilege, 1635, of converting the great Richelieu (q.v.). The bond between Richelieu and C. was always a close one, and the card. depended very much upon the judgment of the poet. C., indeed, was a kind of expert, a 'taster' for Richelieu's literary table; and in the quarrel which raged round the *Cid* (s.v. Corneille), it was C. who at last composed Richelieu's instructions to the Academy to at least a reputable *critique*, 1638. His poetry is much less important than his labours on the road between Marinism and Classicism. His chief work was an epic poem, *La Pucelle* (it was a part of the mechanics of criticism to show how the old forms of poetry should be written !), and he took 20 years in writing it, enjoying meanwhile the same sort of proleptic reputation which Petrarch (q.v.) had claimed for his *Africa*. Unlike Petrarch, however, C. ventured on publication, and the reception of the first 12 cantos, 1656, was so disappointing that the last 12 remained in MS., and were only issued in 1882. Despite this meagre performance, it would be as unjust to C.'s real services to the progress of lit. in his times to dismiss him at Boileau's valuation as it would be to accept him at his own. His letters are of much interest and some importance.

Chapelle, Claude Emmanuel (1626-86): Fr. minor poet; surnamed Lhuillier, but assumed name of his birthplace. Wr., with a certain Bachaumont, a *Voyage en Languedoc*, 1656, which long enjoyed a reputation far in excess of its merits. It had the honour of imitation by Voltaire (q.v.).

Chapman, George (*c.* 1559-1634): Engl. poet; translr.; was a playwright and, like other Elizabethan dramatists, a patcher of other writers' plays, collaborating in that capacity with Ben Jonson and completing Marlowe's *Hero and Leander* (see s.vv.). Meres (q.v.) spoke of C., 1598, as a renowned scholar, tragedian and comedian, and it has been plausibly argued that he was the unnamed 'rival poet' of Shakespeare's (q.v.) *Sonnets* (see *C.H.E.L.*, vi, 30, and sir S. Lee, *Shakespeare*, 1915, pp. 200-5, esp. 204, n. 1). But C.'s poems and plays, even *Bussy D'Ambois*, 1607, and *The Revenge of Bussy D'Ambois*, 1613, which owed much to Serres (q.v.), are insignificant beside his translns. from Homer (q.v.): 7 bks. of the *Iliad* (i and ii,

vii to xi), 1598; bks. i-xii, 1609; the complete *Iliad*, *c.* 1611; *Iliad* and *Odyssey*, 1616, and minor works, 1624; 'the work that I was born to do is done', he said,—how well done, is partly vouched in the famous sonnet by Keats (q.v.). 'There is a grandeur and spirit in Chapman's rendering, not unworthy the original. The long, swinging line of 14 syllables, chosen for the *Iliad*, is the fairest representative of Homer's majestic hexameters, but it is matter for regret that Chapman preferred the heroical distich in his rendering of the *Odyssey*. His version of Homer will ever remain one among the masterpieces of his age and country' (*C.H.E.L.*, iv, 22; by C. Whibley).

Charlemagne (d. 814): Charles, surnamed the Great (Carolus Magnus, Charlemagne) inherited in 768 a narrow kingdom which his father, Pippin, had usurped, and which he was successful in extending by victories in arms from the Danube to the Ebro and from the Elbe to the Po; was crowned Frankish emperor at Rome by pope Leo iii in 800; encouraged architecture and learning; collected old epics of the Franks (whence *Nibelungenlied*, q.v., was formed), subsequently destroyed by his son as heathenish; summoned Alcuin and other scholars to his court; made monasteries centres of classical lore and repositories of MSS. (see s.v. Libraries); founded Holy Roman Empire, though his descendants disputed their shares, and though the shadow of the vaster rivalry between imperial and papal rule (see s.v. Ghibelline) fell across this internecine warfare. The personality of C. endured. He had been a genius among kings in an age when genius and kingship were both attributed to divinity; and his exploits passed into legend, contaminated with pre-existing tales, which inspired the cycle of Fr. epopee known as *chansons de geste* (q.v.). In these forms the paladins of C. were more prominent commonly than their leader. The emperor's old age, doubtless distraught by the conspiracies of friends as well as by the attacks of foes, was a bigger feature than his prowess; Pulci (q.v.), the first of the Italian Carlovingian romantic-epicists, says that 'his beard and his credulity grew long together'; and Roland (q.v.), especially, was more apt at adventures and amours than the old chieftain. A certain burlesqueness which characterized the *chansons* may have owed its orig. partly to the looseness of C.'s private life.

Charlemagnish (Engl.): term invented by Keats (q.v.), to express his sense of the romantic element in medieval life (See s.v. Romance).

Charles i, King of Spain, and
Charles v, Holy Roman Emperor (1500-58): Span. Habsburg; maternal grandson of the Catholic sovereigns of Spain, king Ferdinand of Aragon and queen Isabella of Castile, and succeeded Ferdinand, the survivor of the royal couple, as king of Spain, The Netherlands, Naples, Sicily, and the New World, in 1516; paternal grandson of emperor Maximilian i (q.v.), husband to Mary, daughter of Charles the Bold of Burgundy, and was elected successor to his grandfather as Holy Roman Emperor in 1519; thus attaining at the early age of 19 to an unprecedented magnitude of power;

abdicated, 1556, and was succeeded in Spain by his son (king Philip ii) and in the Empire by his brother (Ferdinand i), thus inaugurating the bitter conflict between the Span. and Austrian Habsburg dynasties, which brought so much woe upon Europe. With this aspect of history we are not immediately concerned, save to note how the position of Charles affected his Span. subjects, and helped to foster that community between the courts of Naples and Madrid, which was one of the chief features of the literary annals of his reign. The sudden discipleship to the leaders of the Renaissance in Italy, which was characteristic of such poets as Boscan and Garcilasso (qq.v.), and which powerfully affected the great soldier-diplomatist, Mendoza (q.v.), was almost directly a result of the political circumstances of the time. C. himself was a patron of art and letters, and may be called the only begetter of Acuña's (q.v.) *Caballero determinado*, for which he supplied his poet-laureate with a version in Span. prose compiled by himself from the Fr. original, *le Chevalier délibéré*, which an earlier laureate, La Marche (q.v.), had written about Charles the Bold to please his daughter, Mary of Burgundy, afterwards grandmother to C. But of far more importance than C.'s literary recreations in Spain, or even his influence on men of letters, were his relations, in his capacity as emperor, with Luther and the Reformation (qq.v.), and with the attitude of authority towards dissent and the seeds of culture which unfolded from it. The momentous results of the Diet of Worms, at which C. presided in 1521, belong to departments of history which cannot be included in this survey, but the dominant personality of the emperor, who triumphed over king Francis i (q.v.) of France at Pavia in 1525, and was crowned by pope Clement vii at Bologna in 1530, is a factor of supreme significance. Though Napoleon thought him a fool for not adopting Protestantism, and founding a united Germany, he took the line inevitable in his age and generation to a Catholic king of Spain and the lay head of the Catholic empire. So far from compromising with reform, C. employed the utmost rigours of the Inquisition, as established in Spain in the reign of his grandparents by card. Ximenez (q.v.), to stamp it out of his kingdom. Even after his abdication, ' from his retirement at Yuste Charles v adjured his son to carry out the work of repression to the uttermost; and Philip replied that he would do what his father wished and more also. He told Carlos de Seso that if his own son were a heretic, he would himself carry the wood to burn him; and in this, as in most other things, he was a typical Spaniard ' (*C.M.H.*, ii, 408 ; by the Rt. Rev. W. E. Collins, bp. of Gibraltar). The effect of this policy of terrorism on Span. humanism and culture was disastrous in the extreme. Though Mr. Hannay (*P.E.L.*, vi, 28) reasonably asks : ' did the Spanish intellect wither because the Inquisition wrapped it in overtight swaddling-clothes ? or did the Spaniard first create and then submit to this repressive institution because he had little tendency to speculation ? ' we shall not be uncharitable in ascribing to C. a habit of tightening the swaddling-clothes

beyond the normal standard of comfort even of an unspeculative lit. And, lastly, we may justly recall the fact that king Philip ii of Spain, the very filial son of his father, was the husband of queen Mary i of England.

Charles d'Orleans (1391-1465) : Fr. poet ; son of Louis, duke of Orleans, and of his wife, Valentina Visconti of Milan ; m., i, Isabella, widow of king Richard ii, next, Bonne d'Armagnac, and, iii, Marie de Clèves. C. was taken prisoner at Agincourt, and spent a long captivity in Engld. In the age of the decline of the chivalric inspiration, this prince in exile, half-Ital. by birth, caught the colours of its sunset in verses tinged with melancholy and regret. His conventional *ballades* and *virelis* (qq.v.) possess the supreme gift of style, and successfully conceal by that grace a paucity of imagination and sincerity.

Charrière de Penthaz, de, Isabella (*c.*1740-1805) : Fr.-Dutch (Batavio-Helvetic, would perhaps be more correct) novelist ; *née* van Tuyll van Serooskerken van Zuylen ; m. her brother's tutor, M. de St. Hyacinthe de C. de P., and spent a curiously inhibited life with him and his maiden sisters at Neuchâtel. Inhibited, because mme. de C. was a Fr. scholar of rare wit and brilliance, an intense lover, yet so severe a self-analyst as never to find satisfaction for her ideals. Her lovers rode away, one after another, from the unconventional, learned, honest girl, who was better to make love to than to domesticate ; and her love-affairs belong to lit. for two male reasons : her lovers included Jas. Boswell (q.v.) at the beginning of her life, and B. Constant (q.v.) towards the end. The former left her for the secure moorings of Scotland and the friendship of Dr. Johnson (q.v.) ; the latter, for the less secure flood of mme. de Stael's (q.v.) eloquence and inspiration. The story of mme. de C.'s life has been told with rare skill and tempered irony by Mr. Geoffrey Scott (*The Portrait of Zélide*, Constable, 1925), and must not detain us longer from her writings. These include *Lettres Neuchâteloises*, 1784 ; *Lettres écrites de Lausanne*, 1785 ; *Caliste*, 1787 ; *Mistress Henley*, 1784 (a self-analytical tale of incompatible temperaments, in which, with characteristic humour, she puts the wife subtly in the wrong, and which her husband, as usual, copied out for her) ; *Trois Femmes*, 1797 ; *Sir Walter Finch*, 1806 ; and others, including a transln. into Fr. of *Sara Burgerhart*, the Dutch Richardsonian novel, 1782, by Wolff and Deken (qq.v. ; the identity of the translr. was first noted by sir E. Gosse, in the *Sunday Times*, 1 Mar., 1925). It remains to add that B. Constant, who was 27 years younger than mme. de C., was the nephew of Constant d'Hermenches, for many years her trusted confidant and correspondent ; that Ste.-Beuve (q.v.), who portrayed her, regarded her, too harshly, perhaps, as Constant's evil genius ; that many of her letters are extant, and that she wr. an early essay on ' The Portrait of Mlle. de Z. ' (uylen), under the name of Zélide.

Charron, Pierre (1541-1603) : Fr. popular philosopher ; friend of Montaigne (q.v.), whom he plagiarized. Wr. *Les Trois Vérités*, 1593 (the truths of God, Christianity,

Catholicism), *Discours Chrétiens*, 1600, and *de la Sagesse*, 1601.

Chartier, Alain (*c.* 1394-*c.* 1450) : Fr. humanist, poet and allegorist. He took Seneca as model for his prose-style. Served as Fr. ambassador in Scotland, and became the hero of a story told by Pasquier and re-told by de Musset (qq.v.) : Margaret of Scotland, first wife of the dauphin, afterwards king Louis xi, kissed C. when asleep in his chair, and explained that she saluted the golden words, not the ugly lips whence they issued. The story, though famous, is now discredited. C. wr. reflective prose on court-life (*le Curial*), and on evils of war (*Quadriloge invectif*), in which the burden of the invective in the title is borne by 4 interlocutors, Nobility, Clergy, Commonalty, and Labour, who join in deploring the hundred years' war. Wr., too, considerable amount of verse (*ballades, rondels*, etc.), composed in the style of medieval tradition, with plentiful admixture of Latinisms ; this last feature, though C. kept it in bounds, caused him later to be regarded as model by the Rhétoriqueurs (q.v.). Caxton (q.v.) issued a transln. of the *Curial*.

Chateaubriand, de, François René (1768-1848) : Fr. imaginative writer ; *vicomte* by rank ; critic, and romanticist (s.v. Romance) by temperament and teaching ; not least, perhaps, by virtue of his sensitive responsiveness to the great public changes which occurred during his long lifetime, including the Revolution, the Empire, the Bourbon restoration, etc. Wr., 1801, an epopee, *les Natchez*, and, 1809, another romance-epic, *les Martyrs, ou le triomphe de la religion chrétienne* ; 1801, *Atala*, and, 1802, *René*, two episodes of romantic love detached from his greatest work, *le Génie du Christianisme*, 5 vols., 1802, on which his reputation rests : *René* remained incorporated in it till 1805 ; 1811, *Itinéraire de Paris à Jérusalem*, travel-notes in which C. collected the local colour and material for his *Martyrs* ; 1826 (but written much earlier) *les Aventures du dernier Abercérage*, a Span. poetic romance ; and, 1849-50 (posth., but composed during previous 30 years) *Mémoires d'Outre-tombe*, 12 vols. Two facts of biography may here be noted : first, C.'s devotion to his sister, Lucile, which had something almost morbid in its intensity, and the motive of which entered into most of his writings, especially into *Atala* and *René* ; and, secondly, the transition, *c.* 1810, from C. as man of letters to C. as man of affairs. After that date, which might even be antedated to Napoleon's execution of the duc d'Enghien in 1804, C.'s interests became more and more political. The execution of his cousin, Armand de C., 1809, as a Bourbon sympathizer ; the prohibition by Napoleon of his Academy discourse in the following year ; these and other events acted upon his idealist disposition to turn him to polemical and political work. He wr., 1814, a pamphlet *de Buonaparte et des Bourbons* : he became minister to king Louis xviii in the following year ; he was created a peer of France ; he founded a newspaper ; he went as ambassador to Berlin and London ; he became minister of foreign affairs, 1823. Under king Charles x, in the following decade, the star of his fortune declined, and he even suffered from financial embarrassments, which compelled him, as he said, to raise a mortgage on his grave, i.e., to sell his *mémoires* on condition that they should not be publd. till after his death. With this period in C.'s long life, we are not otherwise concerned than to note that its episodes fed the devouring pride which was his prominent characteristic. His lofty principles, like Bacon's, were applied in high offices of State ; like Cicero, he came to deem himself indispensable : *s'il n'y avait pas eu de Chateaubriand*, he writes, *quel changement dans le monde*. It may be so ; it is not for a foreigner to pronounce judgment on the politics of those troubled years, nor is this the place for judgment. But we may state with conviction, that, if there had not been a Chateaubriand in Fr. lit., *quel changement dans le monde de lettres* ! Though with sundry harkings-back to outworn forms and themes, C. founded certain traditions, from which lit. marks points of departure ; and, it may be added, the recognition of those departures is due, primarily, to Sainte-Beuve (q.v.) whose *Chateaubriand et son Génie* is authoritative in this connection. Byron, Lamartine, Victor Hugo (qq.v.) are all deeply indebted to C. Romance, melancholy, nature-description, certain aspects of the past and the present, are to be traced to C.'s example ; and he is further to be credited with the invention of the literary use of the Bible (and, less insistently, of Dante and Milton), as a model of style, apart from doctrine. Travel-lit. takes its rise in C., whose voyages in America and the East were undertaken for the sake of romance, in the sense of exploring new skies for strange colours and exotic customs. In the comparative study of literary development, Joseph Conrad (q.v.), a Pole who wr. Engl. novels, and who died in 1924, was a disciple of C. The poisoned arrow of the desert, the primeval forest of the Mississippi, oriental guile and southern passion : C. gathered these in the dawn of the romantic movement ; ' the best and most characteristic part of Byron is only Chateaubriand in English, in verse, and with no crucifixes ' (Saintsbury). For the crucifix is important. C.'s *Génie du Christianisme* appeared in 1802, coincidently with the Concordat between the Fr. Government and the pope of Rome. Its influence on thought was immense : Buonaparte and C. were joining hands to re-establish religion. The purpose of the bk. was to demonstrate that, ' of all religions which ever existed, the Christian religion is the most poetic, the most human, the most favourable to liberty, arts and letters, and that the modern world owes everything to it ; . . . that there is nothing more divine than its morality, nothing more lovable or dignified (*pompeux*) than its dogmas, doctrine, and culture ; . . . that it stimulates genius, purifies taste, develops the virtuous sensibilities, lends vigour to thought, offers noble forms to the writer, and perfect lines to the artist '. Plainly, this programme involved a *critique*, an *ars poetica* : which, not unnaturally, is more valuable than the direct theological argumentation. By the critical portions of the *Génie*, C. is connected in the history of lit.

with the 17th and 18th cents., as well as with the 19th and 20th. The old quarrel of the Ancients (q.v.) and the Moderns; the classical prejudices of Boileau (q.v.); the superficial methods of the German study of mme. de Stael (q.v.); the ideas of nature, medievalism, Gothic art; the literary valuation of the Bible; these threads and others were sorted by C. into a critical treatise, matchless in style and powerful in influence. The *Génie* is a retort on Voltaire (q.v.) from one point of view, as its *René* and *Atala* are enlargements from Rousseau (q.v.) from another; 'but the greatest glory of Chateaubriand is that he is, if not the creator, the first brilliant exponent of what we have called the Critical Imagination— the first great practitioner of imaginative criticism since Longinus (q.v.) himself' (Saintsbury, *Hist. Crit.*, iii, 117).

Chatterton, Thomas (1752-70): Engl. poet. 'The marvellous boy, the sleepless soul that perished in his pride', as Wordsworth (q.v.) called him not many years after his suicide in a London lodging-house, was a native of Bristol, where his family had been employed for several generations at the Church of St. Mary Redcliffe, a well-known Gothic pile. The architecture, the antiquities, the Black Letter Bible, etc., had infected the boy since childhood with a disease the precise nomenclature of which may be determined by psychoanalysts, but the practical expression of which was a series of attempts to impose on the world of letters *Poems* dressed in antique garb and ascribed by C. to a fictitious Thomas Rowley, invented by him to fit his imaginings of the 15th cent. A genuine love of Spenser (q.v.), a brilliant faculty for verse-making, a skill in heraldry, architecture, and kindred arts contributory to heroic verse, were combined with a boyish taste for taking in his elders to land C. in a mesh of deceit, which failed to take in sir H. Walpole (q.v.; C. sent him a forged *Ryse of Peyneteyning* (Painting) *in Englande writen by T. Rowleie* 1469 *for Master Canynge*, a Bristol worthy), and which, when pressed to extremes, were even more easily detected. 'The childhood of Sordello in Browning's (q.v.) poem is the same sort of life at Chatterton's', says the writer in *C.H.E.L.*, x, 236; and the phrase serves to illuminate the waste of this strayed Elizabethan of the 18th cent., who came to typify, as has been said, the symbol of poetic destiny, worsted in an unequal struggle with hostile circumstances.

Chaucer, Geoffrey (*c.* 1340-1400): Engl. poet; romancer. Born in London, the son of a vintner; became page in the household of the duke of Clarence; m. a lady in household of the duchess of Lancaster, wife of John of Gaunt; fought in France, and was prisoner for two months; received rewards and pensions from king Edward iii, who employed him on commercial and diplomatic missions, notably in 1372 to Genoa and Florence, where he met Boccaccio (q.v.) and possibly Petrarch (q.v.), Jusserand (e.g., in *The School for Ambassadors*), being disposed to affirm that this doubtful meeting actually took place. Later on, C. fell into poverty for a while but was compensated by kings Richard ii and Henry iv, and he was buried in Westminster Abbey. C.

made excellent use of his ample opportunities in the age of Engld.'s expansion; he spoke Fr. fluently, and was the foremost Ital. scholar of his day; he knew the Bible thoroughly, esp. the bks. of Proverbs and St. Matthew; read Lat. storytellers (Ovid, q.v., and others) and Lat. fathers, but took his Gk. at secondhand. With this considerable equipment of intellectual gifts and practical experience, C.'s wide and observant talents completed his predecessors' work in so-called Middle Engl. lit., and rounded it to perfection by the example of foreign models. He followed precedent by repairing for his romantic material to the matter of Antiquity, 'Rome la grant' (see s.v. Bodel), in the spirit and sometimes in the letter of Boccaccio, whose example chiefly fired him (though he probably never read the *Decameron*). C. dug low, though he did not always build high. His designs were sometimes vaster than his achievements. He started to translate (very freely) the Fr. romance-quarry poem, the *Romance of the Rose* (q.v.), but stopped short at verse 1,705. Later, he 'left untold the story of Cambuscan bold' (Milton, *Il Penseroso*, 110), i.e., of Gengis (or, more probably, Kubla) Khan, the Grand Khan of Marco Polo's (q.v.) visit. A more serious loss Engl. lit. is partly a matter of conjecture. It is likely that C. had planned an Engl. version of the Troy (q.v.) romance, which possessed (or had acquired) a patriotic interest through the association of the British stock by Geoffrey of Monmouth (q.v.) with an imaginary Brut, or Brutus, a direct descendant of Æneas; C. confined himself, however, to the single Trojan episode of Troilus and Briseis (otherwise Briseida, Griseida, Cressida, Criseyde) which Boccaccio had treated in *Filostrato*: so, too, in his 'Knight's Tale' (*Canterbury Tales*, i), C. treated the same episode of Thebes (q.v.), i.e., the tale of Palamon and Arcite, which Boccaccio had used for his *Teseide*. The treatment differs in both instances; C.'s Troy-tale, particularly, marks an advance in dramatic characterization, so much so that prof. Ker writes, 'Chaucer's *Troilus and Criseyda* is the poem in which medieval romance passes out of itself into the form of the modern novel' (*Epic and Romance*, Macmillan, 367). Again, C.'s *House of Fame*, showing Dante's influence, and his *Legend of Fair Women* were left unfinished. We may say, probably correctly, that C. was constantly preparing for the work which should express his full powers, and sought an outlet through all known channels of poetic art till he found or made his own; his experiments in poetry, one of which at least was surpassing, were incomplete in many thousand of verses, till he fashioned the (again unfinished) *Canterbury Tales*.

The idea of a chain of tales linked by the author's prologues and epilogues was available to C. and Boccaccio from common sources; but, here as so often, C. designed on a larger scale than he attained. The start of the pilgrimage was located at the Tabard Inn, Canterbury, on Tuesday, 16 April, 1387, and each pilgrim was to have told four tales, two going and two returning. This programme was modified to one apiece, but even so the allowance was not reached ; there are more pilgrims than stories. Still, these run to over 17,000 verses, with, additionally, two tales in prose (*The Tale of Melibee* and *The Parson's Tale*. The further interest of these is, that they contain passages of blank verse, q.v., almost inevitable to rhythmic Engl. prose. It were idle to ask for more. For metre C. chose rhymed couplets in heroic verse (q.v.), which, with rhyme royal, the metre of his *Troilus and Criseyde*, he moulded to national possessions, as Petrarch moulded the sonnet (q.v.) in Italy. ' He was as fresh as in the month of May ' (*Canterbury Tales*, Prol., 92) : a recent Fr. critic, Legouis, suggests that this verse is the best description of the poet himself ; ' with him we do not change climate ', he adds ; and it is true that the sunny southern sky, which neither war nor plague could dim, shines as brightly on the Canterbury pilgrims as on the knighthood of Froissart or the garden of Boccaccio's ' ten days '. But C. at his best is more human than either. Not one class of pilgrims, but all manners of men and women, took their parts in the *Tales*, which reflected the active, busy life of Plantagenet Engld., just claiming her place in the sun. The note of stirring in the springtide is struck in the first line of the poem, and its vividness and spontaneity are maintained unimpaired to the end. The sly, shrewd tongue and the keen, kind eye of the story-teller, who was acquainted with all the source-bks. of romance, brighten and illumine this pilgrimage, though the pilgrims are dust long since. We are brought face to face ' with living and breathing men. . . . It is life in its largeness, its variety, its complexity, which surrounds us in the *Canterbury Tales* ' (Green, *History of the English People*, i , 508).

C.'s influence has been deep and permanent. He never passed out of current reading, though he ranked for several generations as a barbarous and uncouth writer. In the revival of medieval studies in the 18th cent., while Dryden (q.v.) and others recognized C.'s poetic genius, it was chiefly Tyrwhitt (q.v.) who found the secret of his style : ' There are few things in English philology more notable than Tyrwhitt's edition of Chaucer ' (*C.H.E.L.*, x, 241 ; by prof. W. P. Ker). So C. stands at the head of modern Engl. lit. ; it got up with him, so to speak, and started its long day's work, and even after its noonday, C.'s genius still commands admiration. He was the first layman in our history who wr. poetry, not to serve the Church, still less to do it a disservice, not to please a mistress or a clique, but to express his own poetic consciousness. He abstracted from reality an ideal picture of common life, and set it in the perpetual sunshine of poets' May.

Chaucerians : 15th-cent. school of Engl. and Scot. poets, who directly imitated Chaucer ; see esp. s.vv. Lydgate, Henryson.

Chaulieu, abbé de, Guillaume Amfrye (1636-1720) : Fr. poet ; a better man of the world than ecclesiastic, though a graceful vein of melancholy runs through his poem *Ecclésiaste*. Wr. occasional verses, including a set to his friend and fellow-poet, La Fare (q.v.), and another, *A la Mort*, on the three ways of dying : the epicurean, the pantheistic, and the deistic. C. was a representative—a very intellectual representative—of the school of *libertins* (q.v.), in its descent from Rabelais and Montaigne to Diderot and Voltaire (qq.v.).

Chekhov (Tchehov), Anton Pavlovich (1860-1904) : Russ. poet and novelist ; son of a serf, who was able to send his son to school and univ. (Moscow), where he trained as a physician. Wr. humorous tales, 1886-90, a successful play, *Ivanov*, 1887, and an unsuccessful play, *The Seagull*, 1895, which was revived successfully, however, at the Moscow Art Theatre, 1898, and was followed by *Uncle Vanya*, *The Three Sisters*, and *The Cherry Orchard*, (produced in London, 1925), the crowning piece of C.'s lit. career. His novels include *The Peasants*, *Ward No. 6*, *My Life*, *The Man in the Case*, etc., and have been transld. into Engl. by C. Garnett (13 vols., Chatto and Windus ; *Plays*, 2 vols., and *Letters*, same translr. and publishers ; lately, 1925, C.'s *Notebooks*, with Reminiscences by M. Gorky, have been transld. by S. S. Kotellansky and L. Woolf, Hogarth Press). A novel, *The Tragedy during the Hunt*, disinterred from a Moscow journal of 1884-5, was first issued in a Germ. transln., 1925. As a novelist, C. is remarkable for creating an atmosphere rather than for delineating character. Prince Mirsky (*Modern Russ. Lit.*, 89), suggests that, in Engld., ' the late Katherine Mansfield was probably the most faithful and at the same time the most original of his disciples ' ; and, remarking on C.'s characteristically Russ. cult of inefficiency—of the Oblomov (see s.v. Goncharov) type,—adds that, ' latterly, and parallel with the great vogue of Chekhov, the cult of Inefficiency and the hate of Vulgar Success has spread in this country (Engld.). There is nothing more Chekhovian, outside Chekhov, than Mr. Lytton Strachey's life of card. Manning, with the pointed contrast between the active and obviously detestable archbp. of Westminister and the gentle dreamer, Newman '. It is a far-sought analogy for the Russ. realist, but it helps to illustrate the subdual of action to a cultivated indifference which Russ. politics helped to develop out of the Russ. lit. of the 'forties of the 19th cent.

Chelczicky, Petr (*c.* 1390-*c.* 1460) : Czech reformer ; wr. *Postilla* (a bk. of interpretations of the Gospels for the whole year) and a smaller work entitled ' Net of the True Faith ' (see *Luke* v, 4-6), the argument of which was that Constantine and pope Sylvester, like two big whales, had broken the net of the humble fishers for Christianity, and that the *roty* (i.e. the ecclesiastical and social hierarchy) had confused and corrupted its unwordlly institutions. Tolstoy (q.v.) ' was astonished to find from a Russian translation of the " Net of the True Faith " that this Czech peasant had preached to his obstinate countrymen the same ideas which he himself disseminated in Russia 450 years after ' (Chudoba, *Czech Lit.*, 38). The Brethren of Chelczice (C.'s native village in Bohemia, from which he took his name) was formed to promulgate his gospel, and spread into the sects of the Bohemian and Moravian Brethren, which took the lead in the

16th cent. in educational and humanistic work.

Chemnizer, Ivan (1744-84): Russ. poet. Wr. 'Fables' (collected, 1779), which take a distinguished place in lit., and are as much better than those of Sumarokov (q.v.) as they were surpassed later by those of Krylov (q.v.).

Chénier, -i. (Marie-) André (1762-94): Fr. poet; Hellenist; patriot; and, by this combination, a precursor of Fr. Romanticism (see s.v. Romance). Born at Constantinople; was brought to Paris as a child; served in the Fr. army; travelled in Switzerland and Italy; resided in Engld., 1787-91, as secretary in the embassy; joined the revolutionary *Société de 1789*, but was presently alienated by the course of events, and quitted Paris, 1793. C. still took part in the more moderate counsels of the constitutional party, and defended Charlotte Corday, 1793; in the following year (two days before the fall of Robespierre, 9th Thermidor), he suffered death by the guillotine. Seldom did that fatal knife server the cord of a more promising life. C. was a scholar born in a turbulent time, and the whirlpool drew his generous spirit to his own hurt. His chief writings were not publd. till 1819. Apart from more ambitious schemes, which he did not live and, perhaps, would never have cared to fulfil, his poetry took shape in idyls, eclogues, elegies, epistles, and odes, by which C. is definitely included among the few poets of modern times who have succeeded in reviving the very spirit of the Gk. anthologists. C.'s *Iambes* are Gk. all through; the writer himself was half a Gk., through his mother, a Santi l'Homaca, and the pure flame and radiant brightness of the 'isles of Greece', so passionately loved a few years later by Byron (q.v.), were in the blood of this victim of Fr. politics. Like Byron, too, C. was a liberationist; the freedom of Hellas was his birthright, no less than the beauty of her seas; so, in his *Jeune Captive*, his *Charlotte Corday*, and other poems, C. became a lyric satirist, and displayed the like force and skill as in his songs of lyric love. *Lydé, l'Aveugle, le Jeu de Paume* (an ode, or hymn, on the oath of the tennis-court, 20 June, 1789): these are a few of the poems which crowned C. with unfading bays. The critics dispute if his name is to be reckoned among the classics or romantics, and disputants seem to settle the question in favour of both claims. By his reflective bias and his naturalism, and his plans for long philosophic poems, he belongs to the generation of Buffon and Diderot (qq.v.); by his fresh outlook on life, his passion, his faith, and his temperament, he belongs to the generation of Chateaubriand and Hugo (qq.v.) By his fate and his achievement, he belongs to the heirs of unfulfilled renown.

    -ii. (Marie-) Joseph (1764-1811): Fr. dramatist; brother to above; a more consistent supporter of the Revolution, and more fortunate in surviving it than André, whom he tried in vain to save. Wr. *Chant du Départ*, 1794, described as 'second only to the *Marseillaise*' (*P.E.L.*, xl, 368; see s.v. Lisle), and was a kind of poet-laureate at the festivals of the revolutionary government. J. C. anticipated the Fr. romantics (and the Romance-movement generally; see s.v. and s.v. Scott)

in his revival of hist. fiction, which he clothed in dramatic form; his *Charles ix*, 1789, *Calas*, 1790, and *Fénelon*, 1793, struck vibrant chords by their choice of subject, and he acknowledged a veneration for Shakespeare, and transld. Gray's (q.v.) *Elegy*. More strictly in the classical tradition were his *Caius Gracchus*, 1792, *Timoléon*, 1795, and other plays.

Chernyshevsky, Nicholas Gavrilovich (1828-89): Russ. critic; condemned on trivial grounds to 7 years' hard labour and 20 years' exile; a petition for alleviation of the sentence was refused, 1881, to an international literary congress. The harsh fate adds to the interest of C.'s early critical writings, 'on the æsthetic relations of art to reality', etc. He was a pronounced materialist, a translr. of J. S. Mill (q.v.), and his subordination of art and beauty to the practical purposes of conduct was precisely the pabulum sought by the half-political, half-philosophical circle of young journalists and doctrinaire critics of the day. C. found eager continuators in Pisarev and Dobrolubov (qq.v.). His one novel, 'What is to be done'? 1863, had considerable influence in the propaganda of Nihilism (q.v.), and he was also author of a work on the 'Causes of the Downfall of Rome', which gave great pleasure to Tolstoy (q.v.).

Chesterfield (Philip Dormer Stanhope) 4th earl of (1674-1773): Engl. statesman and wit; held high offices of state; built, 1749, Chesterfield House, S. Audley Street, later the residence of princess Mary, daughter of king George v, and visct. Lascelles, son of the 5th earl of Harewood; intimate friend of Voltaire, q.v., and profoundly affected by Fr. social thought of the age; patron of letters, in which capacity Dr. Johnson (q.v.) addressed to him the prospectus of the *Dict.*; formed an attachment 1732, with mlle. du Bouchet, who became the mother of his natural son, Philip Dormer Stanhope, to whom he wr., from 1737 onwards, an almost daily letter (in Engl., Fr., or Lat.) of worldly wisdom and advice, followed by a similar series, 1761-70, to a godson and heir-presumptive. The first series were publd., 1774, by the son and addressee's widow, and were early transld. into Fr. and Germ.; the second series were publd., 1819; and together they constitute, with special reference to the *Letters* to his son, C.'s title to a permanent place in Engl. lit. The place should rather be accorded in Fr. lit., and mm. Legouis and Cazamian wr. justly (*Hist. Lit. Angl.*, 875): 'Figure toute française à bien des égards, proche de nous par des affinités, des préférences, écrivant notre langue aussi aisément que la sienne, Chesterfield est bien connu en France'; they add that it is easy to exaggerate his 'immoralisme', and that, 'sous le poli de la culture, son tempérament conserve un grain assez anglais'. He was a master of 'l'art de vivre' in his own rank and time.

Chiabrera, Gabriello (1552-1637): It. poet; native of Savona, in Liguria, to which he retired after spending some years in Rome. C. was a Court (q.v.) poet in the sense, that he composed in a professional manner a large number of stately poems—epic, dramatic, pastoral, sacred-narrative, heroic, etc.,—unillumined by a spark of the wider vision revealed to his greater contemporaries in Spain and Engld., Cervantes and Shakespeare (qq.v.). Perhaps, by virtue of his lyric verse, he may be termed a late Ronsardist in Italy; certainly, he sought to revive, in the barren *Secentismo* (17th century), into which he lived, some of the verse-forms of Pindar and Anacreon, and trusted that inspiration would inform them. In this aim, he strenuously opposed the decadent gorgeousness of Marino (q.v.), and earns respect for his judgment and taste. His lighter songs, intended to be set to music, are still pleasing, and C. was selected by Wordsworth (q.v.), in an article on 'Epitaphs' in *The Friend*, 1810, as having framed his experiments in that class on the model of 'our notion of a perfect epitaph', in which 'what was peculiar to the individual shall still be subordinate to a sense of what he had in common with the species'. Wordsworth himself transld. into Engl. 9 of the poems by C.

Chiari, Pietro (1711-85): It. dramatist; abbot; rival of Goldoni (q.v.) in Venice, as a fertile writer of tales and plays.

Cholmondeley, Mary (died 1925): Engl. novelist. Wr. *Red Pottage*, 1902, and other novels, exhibiting an exactness of workmanship and incisiveness of observation which recall the style and skill of J. Austen (q.v.).

Chrestien, Florent (1541-96): Fr. satirist; converted Huguenot. Contributor to *Satyre Ménippée* (q.v.).

Chrétien de Troyes (12th cent.; 2nd half): Fr. romancer (s.v. Romance); at the court of countess Marie de Champagne, daughter of queen Eleanor (q.v.) and of king Louis vii of France. C. was the chief of many *trouvères*, or romance-writers, whose art and skill were employed in adapting to the conditions of Ovidian love-lit. and to the tastes of sophisticated Norman-Fr. audiences the traditional lore of the *Romans Bretons* (q.v.), built round and over the old Celtic tales. In a sense, C. was a Celtic revivalist, but the revival was not less than a new life. King Arthur (q.v.) emerged from the mists of his ancient Welsh hills as the peer in pomp and exploits of Alexander and Charlemagne (qq.v.), thus ranging the *matière de Bretagne* with the *matières de France et de Rome* (see s.v. Bodel); Arthur became the third in the noble company of Romance-kings; a leader in chivalry, a hero of gallantry, from whom proceeded and to whom, haply, returned the brave and courteous followers of the lure of adventure and quest. To this transformation of the Arthur-cycle, C., working on the narrative 'lays' and other verse of obscurer predecessors, contributed far the greatest share, and handed on several finished romances to continuators in his own country and in Germany (see s.vv. Wolfram, Hartmann, Gottfried). The most famous of C.'s Arthurian romances are the *Percival*, the *Chevalier à la Charrette* (i.e., Lancelot, suggested to him by the countess Marie), the *Chevalier au Lyon* (i.e., Yvain), *Erec et Enide* (closely followed by Tennyson, q.v., in his *Enid*), and the *Cligès*, an Oriental hero who seeks adventures at Arthur's court. C.'s versification of these tales was fluent, dexterous, and attractive, but his undoubted,

even brilliant, talent for narration was combined with—in a sense, it postulated—an imperception to the finer qualities of the Celtic imagination. C.'s blindness was his safeguard. An attempt to render these old tales in the guise of Norman-Fr. gallant romance, and to preserve at the same time the features of natural magic, of vague sympathies and imaginings, of imagery from the supernatural world, and of the myth and mystery with which they came drenched from their native fastnesses, would probably have failed disastrously; and the measure of their failure would probably have been the conscious effort of the romancer to avoid the necessary sacrifice. C. was saved from this effort by his unconsciousness. A Fr. writer, who may be deemed impartial, says a little unkindly: 'Nothing embarrasses him; he clarifies everything, understands nothing, and renders everything unintelligible. His lucid positivism empties the marvellous symbols of the Celtic genius of their contents and of their deep extra-rational sense. . . . This excellent Chrétien . . . is a Bourget of the 12th century, thoroughly *au courant* with the manners of high life, and thus flatters his public' (Lanson, *Hist. de la Lit. Franç.*, 56, 58). Against this somewhat damaging Fr. estimate may be set the views of prof. Saintsbury (*Short Hist. of Fr. Lit.*, 33), that C. 'deserves a higher place in literature than has sometimes been given to him', and of Mr. Lytton Strachey (*Landmarks in Fr. Lit.*, 11), who points out that the transformation of the Celtic myths into artistic Fr. fiction shows 'at what an early date, and with what strength, the most characteristic qualities of French literature were developed'; grace, deftness, and lucidity replaced these 'vague imaginations' with 'the unambiguous elegances of civilized life'. We, at least, have no right or cause to regret the conventions of Romance. The modern novel descends in a direct line from the transmuted ore of C.'s Breton tales, and the mine from which they were dug for his artificer's hand in the 12th cent. is endlessly indebted for the exploitation of its treasures to the Ovidian method of this medieval chivalric court poet. As Lanson urges in extenuation of his criticism, 'the prolix mediocrity of our *trouvères* and storytellers has conquered the world' (*op. cit.*, 63): the 'mediocrity' may have hit the mean.

Christ, Johann Friedrich (1700-56): Germ. humanist; prof. of poetry at univ. of Leipsic, 1734. C. was a leader of the new, as distinct from the old, humanism (q.v.), and aimed, in his archæological studies of gems, inscriptions, architecture, and sculpture, at reconstructing a renaissance of Gk. art which should help to correct the excesses of the Augustan cult of classical forms.

Christina (1626-89): Queen of Sweden; daughter of Gustavus Adolphus; acceded, 1632; abdicated, 1654, in order to embrace the Roman Catholic faith, when, out of compliment to pope Alexander vii, she assumed the second name of Alexandra. The political events of C.'s reign, which included the Peace of Westphalia, largely due to her statecraft, at the close, 1648, of the Thirty Years' War, do not concern us here; her place in lit. is

7

secure, not merely as a patron of men of letters, and as the head of a court of culture (which, unlike other courts, owed its culture to its sovereign alone, and forfeited it, as a fact, at her abdication), but likewise as a writer and a talker, whose accomplishments and gifts made Stockholm for the time being, in a familiar phrase, the Athens of the North. C.'s mind and intellect were masculine, and suited neither the Fr. court which she visited while she was queen, and where she insisted on visiting Ninon (q.v.), nor the Papal court after her conversion. In Rome, as in Stockholm, she was the centre of a circle of wit and learning, and founded an academy which met at her palace (the Farnese). (See, too, s.v. Arcadia). Her collection of MSS. is now in the Vatican, one of her pictures by Coreggio (' Mercury leading Cupid ') is in the National Gallery, London, and other of her valuable possessions are in Stockholm. C. was a genuine scholar ; *elle a tout vu, elle a tout lû, elle sait tout*, was said of her by Naudé (q.v.), and her appreciation of foreign learning led her to try to acclimatize some of its foremost representatives in her northern capital. Grotius came there and Vossius, and Salmasius (see s.vv.), and Milton (q.v.) addressed her in glowing Lat. (See Sandys, *Hist. Clas. Schol.*, 339 f.). Late in his life she drew Descartes (q.v.) to Stockholm, and induced the philosopher to vary his instruction with a ballet called *la Naissance de la Paix* (the peace of Münster) ; his death in 1650 was a real grief to her, and doubtless influenced her opinions on serious subjects.

' Christopher North '. See s.v. **Wilson, J.**

Chrysoloras, Manuel (c. 1350-1415) : teacher of Gk. in Italy. A Byzantine by birth, of noble family, C. came to Venice (1393) as ambassador from Constantinople to solicit aid against the Turks. His reputation as Hellenist had preceded him through Guarino (q.v.) who had studied in his house at Constantinople, and he was prevailed upon by Niccoli, Strozzi, Rossi and Salutati to visit Florence (1396 to 1400), in order to revive Gk. learning. His appointment to the chair of Gk. at Florence ' secured the future of Greek erudition in Europe ' (Symonds). He taught, too, at Pavia, and other Ital. univs. Died during Council of Constance (q.v.). Among his foremost pupils were Bruni, Poggio, Vergerio, and Marsuppini (qq.v.). His chief work was *Erotemata*, a catechism of Gk. grammar, for long the only written introduction to that language, first printed (Venice) 1484, several times reprinted, and abridged by Guarino, with additions (Ferrara) 1509.

Churchill, Charles (1731-64) : Engl. satiric poet ; wr. the *Rosciad*, 1761, which brought him into touch with the *North Briton* periodical of John Wilkes (1727-97). *The Prophecy of Famine, The Epistle to Wm. Hogarth*, and *The Duellist* were among C.'s further politico-personal satiric poems, for which, in their ephemeral and savage futility, time and liking are lacking to-day.

Cibber, -i. Colley (1671-1757) : Engl. dramatist, actor ; poet laureate (q.v.), 1730 ; a player of leading parts in comedy, but a playwright of little value and a poet of less. C. was elevated by Pope (q.v.) to the throne of Dulness in the revised *Dunciad*, 1742, in place of Lewis

Theobald (q.v. ; 1688-1744), editor of Shakespeare ; a change ' to the lasting injury of his poem ', in the opinion of sir L. Stephen (*Pope*, ' English Men of Letters ', 135). ' He dethroned Theobald, who, as a plodding antiquarian, was an excellent exponent of dulness, and installed Cibber in his place, who might be a representative of folly, but was as little of a dullard as Pope himself '. Mr. E. K. Broadus, historian of *The Laureateship* (Oxford, 1921), opines that Pope ' was but putting Cibber in the place which the laureate's odes and a dozen years' jest about them had prepared for him '.

-ii. Theophilus (1703-58) : Engl. dramatist, actor ; son of above ; chiefly remarkable for *not* having written *The Lives of the Poets of Great Britain and Ireland*, 1753, which bore his name on the title-page, but which was mainly compiled by Robt. Shiels, whom Johnson (q.v.) had employed as an amanuensis on his *Engl. Dict.*

Cibdareal, de, Fernan Gomez. See s.v. **Centon Epistolario.**

Cicero, Marcus Tullius (106-43 B.C.) : Roman orator, statesman, letter-writter, and philosopher. In the first and fourth of these capacities, C. took a middle place in the schools and tendencies of his own time. Oratory cultivated two styles, each founded on Gk. models, i, Attic, and, ii, Asiatic. The former, in which Lysias was exemplar, tended towards a chill propriety of diction ; the latter, as its name implies, had an Oriental richness and floweriness. C.'s style happily combined the lucidity of the one with the fulness, or copiousness, of the other. Philosophy, too, was addicted to the tenets of alternative Gk. schools, i, the Stoics, and, ii, the Epicureans ; and here, again, C. steered a safe course, combining the duties of man with his rights of individual opinion and free-will. It was along these two lines that C.'s influence first made itself felt. With the great exception of Quintilian, who ardently defended C.'s style, and made countless converts to his view (' ille se profecisse sciat, cui Cicero valde placebit ', he wr. ; let him congratulate himself on his progress who finds in Cicero his chief delight), Lat. prose mainly vacillated between the unadorned and turgid varieties ; but early in the Christian era, Quintilian's Ciceronianism began to prevail. In the 3rd cent., Christian thought on pagan lit. was divided between the obscurantism of Tertullian, who could find nothing in common to ' Athens and Jerusalem ', and the liberal view of Minucius Felix, who wr. a Ciceronian dialogue, *Octavius*, on the side of free-thought. Later, Lactantius, ' the Christian Cicero ', extolled his model both as orator and philosopher ; and St. Jerome and St. Ambrose in the 4th cent. continued and enlarged the discipleship. Jerome's dream in the Syrian desert of the still, small voice accusing him of being ' Not Christian, but Ciceronian ', is famous ; Ambrose wr. a treatise on Christian ethics based on C., *de Officiis* ; and St. Augustine, later in the same cent., was converted to Christianity by reading C.'s lost work, *Hortensius* ; truly a remarkable tribute to the teachings of a pagan philosopher, who borrowed Gk. thought for Roman readers.

Passing down the changing centuries (and no one can write on this topic without a grateful debt to Zielinski, *Cicero im Wandel der Jahrhunderte*, 1897), we find C.'s influence waning for a while, and that of Virgil (q.v.) waxing, in deference to the medieval practice of submission to authority ; thus, Virgil was Dante's (q.v.) guide and model, and the desire for personal glory, which was a mark of C.'s ideal, was heavily punished in the *Inferno*. On the other hand, C.'s *de Amicitia* helped to console Dante for Beatrice's death ; and pope Silvester ii promoted the study of the rhetoric of C., who was also a favourite author of John of Salisbury and Roger Bacon (qq.v.). By this time, we may say that C.'s philosophy had been merged in the teachings of the Church, and that his sentence-structure, his periods, and his prose-rhythm had found adequate imitators and admirers. We may add that his ' dream of Scipio ', a fragment preserved by Macrobius from C.'s (lost) *de Republica*, became the admitted starting-point of the motive of the dream (q.v.) in medieval lit., which prevailed from the *Romance of the Rose* (q.v.) down to comparatively recent times. But greater influence still was reserved for C., through the medium of his constant worshipper, Petrarch (q.v.) : ' Petrarch was the leader of the New Learning, but who was the leader of Petrarch ? ' (sir J. E. Sandys, *Harvard Lectures*, 149) ; and an answer is given in the same sense as we find it in the Oxford vol. on *Engl. Lit. and the Classics* (131), ' We may therefore say that the Renaissance itself was the work of Cicero's spirit '. Higher influence, personal and stylistic, cannot be affirmed of any writer of antiquity than that of C. on Petrarch ; nor is the consequent debt of the modern world to the ancient greater to any man than to C. Petrarch's discovery of the speech *pro Archia*, and later (1345) of the letters *ad Atticum*, the tone of which fitted in so well with his own sturdy individualism and restless search for glory, set a new moral key to human thought ; and side by side with this growing humanism (q.v.) went the cultivation of the master's style for its own sake. Ciceronianism, like most other -isms in the history of human endeavour, was ridden to death. The schoolmasters dotted the i's and crossed the t's of the scholars, who had been content to write their Lat. letters as scholars and gentlemen, like Petrarch himself and Poggio (q.v.), another diligent searcher for C.'s MSS., not as mere ' apes of Cicero ', in Villani's phrase for Salutati (q.v.), and in the new phase of the cult.

We may perhaps pass over the pro- and anti-Ciceronianism and -Ciceronics of Salutati, Barzizza, Politian, Cortesi (qq.v.) and others in the heyday of Lat. Humanism in Italy, merely noting the high place given to C. in the curriculum of the educationist, Guarino (q.v.). We come in the 16th cent. to the more important names of cardinal Bembo (q.v.) and Erasmus (q.v.). Bembo, as Lat. secretary to pope Leo x (q.v.), was, like Jerome, Ciceronian first and Christian afterwards ; at any rate, in his *History of Venice*, as noted by Sandys (*op. cit.*, 160), ' the Senate even

urges the Pope " to put his trust in the immortal gods, whose Vicar he is on earth " ', and in an official letter the papal secretary represented a bishop ' as calling " men and gods " to witness to the truth of his statement '. These signs and others of excessive devotion to the literal methods of the master moved Erasmus, the greatest humanist of the cent., to write his dialogue, *Ciceronianus* (1528), in which, obediently to the proverb, he protected C. from his friends : part i was a brilliant skit on the seclusion and fasting in which the complete Ciceronian wr. one sentence with the aid of specialist dictionaries ; part ii pleaded more seriously for respect to the requirements of changing times ; and part iii passed in review the writings of 106 Ciceronians. J. C. Scaliger (q.v.) replied intemperately, 1531, and again in 1536, after the death of Erasmus ; and the controversy was taken up by Dolet (q.v.) in Paris, the younger Scaliger (q.v.) and others. Muretus (q.v.) was a Ciceronian in the true sense of Erasmus, and criticized a real dict. of the kind which Erasmus had imagined in *Ciceronianus*, part i. This was the *Thesaurus Ciceronianus* (1535) of Nizolius (q.v.), to whom sir Philip Sidney (q.v.), another true Ciceronian, referred : ' Tully and Demosthenes (most worthy to be imitated) did not so much keep Nizolian Paperbooks of their figures and phrases, as by attentive translation (as it were) devour them whole, and make them wholly theirs. For now they cast sugar and spice upon every desk that is served to the table ; like those Indians, not content to wear earrings at the fit and natural place of the ears, but they will thrust jewels through their nose and lips because they will be sure to be fine '. Towards the end of the 16th cent., when Ascham (q.v.), like Guarino before him, made ' Tully ' (Tullius, i.q. Cicero) the basis of his curriculum, and had the honour of reading his works with queen Elizabeth, the cult of Ciceronian finery began at last to be abandoned. The next stage of C.'s influence in Europe was that of the Christian deists, who went backwards through the Church fathers to the pagan philosopher, who had converted St. Augustine, in order to justify the rational view of religion. (See s.vv., Herbert of Cherbury, Hume, Voltaire). A still later stage was C.'s influence as an orator, esp. on Burke (q.v.) ; and, a little later still, C.'s republican ardour had immense effect on the leaders of the Fr. Revolution, who were fond of citing ' the way of the Romans ' ; it is noted that the enemies of Robespierre used to call him Catiline, and his friends Cicero. Mommsen (q.v.), the great Germ. historian of Rome, allowed C. no virtue but that of oratory ; and it is worth remarking that, with rare exceptions, C.'s fame and influence have been greatest in the nations of the Lat. race to which he belonged. It is hard to believe that the most convinced reformer, who would drive out classical writers from our schools, will find means of stimulating the intelligence as effective as, from age to age, in various aspects of his versatile activity, as champion of individualism, liberty and free-thought, as rationalist, as stylist, and as orator, the study of C. has proved from the time of Quintilian, through the Renaissance and the 18th cent., when 'Tully' was a household name, to the eve of the present day, when we are reminded in a weighty vol. on *The Legacy of Rome* (Oxford, 1923 ; edited by Cyril Bailey), that 'European prose, as an instrument of thought, is Cicero's creation'.

Cid (Span.) : Lord (sidi) ; descriptive title of Ruy (Rodrigo) Diaz de Bivar, *c.* 1040-99, the national hero of Spain, commonly known as *el Cid Campeador* (champion). The hist. personality of the Cid, who achieved his championship in single combat over a knt. of Navarre, is definitely accepted to-day, though attempts to disprove it have been made from time to time. Ruy Diaz in the flesh was a formidable warrior against the Arabs, who laid siege to Valencia in 1092, took it in 1094, and ruled as its lord (*sidi*) till he died. He was m. to a cousin of the reigning king, Alfonso vi, of Castile. So far we accept the statement of his great fellow-countryman, Cervantes (q.v.) : 'That there once lived a Cid and a Bernardo del Carpio there can be little doubt' ; but we agree with him, too, in entertaining 'a grave one as to just what they performed' (*Don Quixote*, i, xlix). We should express the same doubt about the legendary exploits of Alexander, Charlemagne, and Arthur (qq.v.) ; the difference in the circumstances being that Ruy Diaz passed into legend at a date much nearer to his life in the flesh than is the case with any of the other heroes. The Span. *Poema del Cid*, also known as the *Cantore de mio Cid*, was composed in the following cent., probably between 1140 and 1157, and is thus unique in national epos. Fifty years after the hero's death, he had passed out of history into legend. It is not altogether unlikely that between Ruy Diaz and his *Poema* there had been intermediate epopees, traces of which may be conjectured from the prose versions in the *Cronica* (q.v.) *general* of Spain (see, too, s.v. Alfonso the Wise). But such specialist textual researches, which depend on branches of science still comparatively immature, must be sought in separate works. They neither diminish nor enhance the literary importance and interest of the *Poema del Cid* itself. Whether or not it is the last (and consequently the best) of a series of lost predecessors, this sole surviving specimen of the romantic epos of Spain is properly to be compared with the Fr. *Chanson de Roland*, which the Span. writer had no doubt read. It has been preserved in one MS. only, dating from the 14th cent., and is at once anon. and incomplete. The text, as we have it, contains 3,729 verses, but there are many gaps and transpositions, and the metre is almost hopelessly irregular. Still, imperfect though it be, this *Poema* of the 11th cent. Cid is one of the classics of European romantic epopee ; and if Peter Abbat, who appended his name to the MS., was veritably its copyist, posterity will condone his mistakes for the sake of the great poem which he preserved. It should be added that the *ed. pr.* of the *Poema del Cid* was publd., 1779, by Tomas Antonio Sanchez, 1725-1802. There were thus the true Cid of history, and the romantic Cid of epopee. To these was added in course of

time a tragic Cid of drama, and to him, too, a few words are due. It was at the close of 1636, or in the first days of 1637, that *le Cid* of Corneille (q.v.) was played in Paris, and its success raised the dramatist to the height of his great reputation. His play was immediately based on a Span. drama, the *Mocedades del Cid*, 1618, by G. de Castro (q.v.) ; but Corneille's conception of Ruy Diaz was neither the sainted knt. of the Span. stage nor the legendary hero of Span. epopee ; still less, the rude fighter of the 11th cent. The new Cid was a Cornelian hero, exhibiting the immense passions of the Fr. theatre, and representing for all time the conflict between fate and will. And most inappropriate of all to the true Ruy Diaz of the flesh was the scholars' 'quarrel of the *Cid*' which raged about Corneille's play. It was a different kind of fighting from that to which the hero had been bred. Richelieu's coercion of the Fr. Academy to accept the doctrine of the Unities (see s.vv.), Chapelain's (q.v.) mediation between the two, and Corneille's ultimate acquiescence in the 'Sentiments of the Academy', 1638, form a chapter in the story of the Cid, which belongs rather to the curiosities of lit. than to lit. itself. The last considerable work inspired by 'el Cid Campeador' of ancient Spain was the excellent Engl. version of the *Poema del Cid*, effected by R. Southey (q.v.), who was an eminent Span. scholar as well as British poet-laureate.

Cienfuegos, de, Nicasio Alvarez (1764-1809) : Span. poet ; follower of Melendez (q.v.) ; editor of the government gazette at Madrid, and sentenced to death (commuted to banishment) at the Fr. occupation, 1808.

Cifar : Span. hero of chivalric fiction. The *Cavallero Cifar*, or 'history of the Knight of God whose name was Cifar', was begun towards the close of the reign of king Sancho iv (q.v.) of Castile, and was probably written by a priest at Toledo, *c.* 1290. Its main interest lies in the fact that, while its author was plainly familiar with the Breton (q.v.) romances of Marie of France and Chrestien of Troyes (qq.v.), he invented the type of picaresque novel (q.v.), which became so peculiarly characteristic of Span. life. The *Cifar* was printed in 1512, after 200 years' popular esteem, and may have been known to Cervantes (q.v.), and even have influenced his delineation of Don Quixote and Sancho Panza.

Cinthio, Giambattista Giraldi (1504-73) : It. humanist. Born at Ferrara. Wr. tragedies, notably *Orbecche*, which is the earliest of its kind in a vernacular language ever enacted in Europe (Ferrara, 1541) ; its form and language and ingredients of horror were after the example of Seneca (q.v.), and set a model for tragic drama in Italy, and, indeed, in other countries. C. wr., too, *Hecatommithi*, a collection of 'novelle' (tales), adapted, *à la Decameron* and the Plague of Florence, to the Sack of Rome and the escape of the narrators ; some of the tales are re-told by Painter (q.v.), and Shakespeare owed to them the stories of *Othello* and *Measure for Measure* ; also discourses on literary criticism (romance, tragedy, etc.) of considerable ability, and valuable for the development of Aristotelian poetics, and for

C.'s promulgation of the Unity of Time (s.v. Unities).

Ciriaco (de' Pizzicolli) of Ancona (*c.* 1391-*c.* 1450) : It. humanist and antiquary. Sandys calls calls him ' the Schliemann of his time '. though Symonds inclined to the older view of Traversari, Poggio, and others, that he was ' a conceited enthusiast, accepting as genuine what he ought to have rejected '. He was a keen traveller and archæologist, visiting Rome, Greece, and the near East in search of inscriptions, gems, coins, MSS., etc. However, much he may have been imposed upon, or have practised imposition unconsciously, he takes a high place as classical antiquary in the revival of learning in Ital., and supplied a motto for humanism by his reply to an enquiry as to the object of his tours : ' I go to awaken the dead '.

Clapham Sect (end of 18th cent.) : Engl. group of philanthropists and politicians, who, though with no literary bond in their constitution, exercised a powerful influence on the thought of their day : ' they might differ on party issues ; but on any question of religion or philanthropy the voice of the " Saints ", in Parliament or in the Press, was as the voice of one man. It was indeed a unique phenomenon, this brotherhood of Christian politicians. There has never been anything like it since in British public life ' (R. Coupland, *Wilberforce*, Oxford Press, 1923). The chief members —they were all Abolitionists—were Wm. Wilberforce (1759-1833) himself, John Shore, Wm. Teignmouth (1751-1834), Chas. Grant (1746-1823), father of 1st baron Glenelg, Wm. Smith (1756-1835), Jas. Hepburn (1758-1832), Edward Eliot (1759-97), John Venn (1759-1813), Henry Thornton (1760-1815) and Zachary Macaulay (1768-1838). They met at Thornton's house in Clapham, and were united by ties of marriage as well as of opinion.

Classicism (see also s.vv. Romance, Latin, Hellenism). The ' classics ', as a term of literary usage, are the Pagan writers in the golden ages of Gk. and Roman lit., and their influence on modern lit., i.e. the lit. of the Christian era, has been exercised with varying strength at different epochs in its history. We may distinguish at the start four such epochs : i, in the 12th cent., when Ovid, Virgil (see s.vv.), and other story-tellers and love-lorists were ransacked by the manipulators of heroic and chivalric *romans* (q.v.) for the vocabulary and psychology of their craft ; ii, at the revival of learning (see s.v. Humanism), when wandering scholars from the Levant were employed to collect ancient MSS., to translate Gk. texts into Lat., to lecture and teach and copy, and when the example of Petrarch (q.v.) was followed by a host of scholars, who spread the light of the Renaissance (q.v.) from Italy to France and to the North ; iii, in the late 17th cent., when the undiscriminating Classicism of the Renaissance was directed into narrower channels of a reasoned imitation of antiquity, and when Boileau's (q.v.) canons of ' good sense ', ' nature ' (i.q. human nature ; see s.v. Nature), and ' the way of the ancients ' imposed the dead hand of neo-classicism on the lit. of the 18th cent. ; and, iv., in the late 18th cent.,

when Winckelmann (q.v.), e.g., re-discovered for an eager age Gk. art at the back of Lat. formalism, and helped to demolish the cruder doctrine of a progress in art (derived from, or confused with, Cartesianism ; s.v. Descartes), which had proved to be a progress away from art. The æsthetics, art-philosophy, and criticism of the 19th cent. aimed, consistently on the whole, at a reconciliation of the streams which were somewhat violently sundered in France in the *grand siècle* of king Louis xiv : the streams, that is, of the past and the present, or the ancients and the moderns, between whom an academic quarrel (see s.v. Ancients), in which the issues were neither clearly defined nor clearly settled, broke out in Paris in the last years of the 17th cent., with Perrault and Boileau (qq.v.) as protagonists. A fifth stage in the history of classical influence and reaction may be associated with Walt Whitman, whose iconoclastic zeal for democracy would have made a clean sweep of all antiquity as a preparation for Transatlantic art and letters. But, generally, it may be said that the opposition between the ancients and the moderns was merely a passing phase of Classicism, and that a much more obstinate battle has been waged round the standards of Classicism and Romance (or, Romanticism). Here, too, the 20th cent., inheriting the gracious fruits of labourers in both vineyards, is better disposed to see likenesses than differences. There are romantic streaks in Homer and the Homeric Virgil, in Euripides and the Euripidean Seneca, in the Gk. Anthology and in Catullus, in Theocritus and the Theocritean Virgil ; and, therefore, in all the ' classical ' writers of the Renaissance who built their verses on those models. Similarly, it is an exaggeration to speak of an exclusive Lat. classicism even in the writers of the *grand siècle* in France. La Bruyère (q.v.), for instance, went straight back to Theophrastus ; Huet (q.v.) was a Hellenist, and Boileau himself rested his case for his rescript of ' follow the ancients ' on direct ' reflections on Longinus ' (q.v.), even though the tyranny of Horace was excessive from the days of Vida (q.v.) downwards, yet Aristotle was always at his back. The worst sin of classicism was its cult of the letter in place of the spirit ; its deliberate doctrine, taught again by Pope (q.v.), that ' the proper study of mankind is man ', thus excluding from his study all nature that was not human nature. This proscription dates in philosophy from the writings of Descartes, and it was fatal to the cause of truth in art and letters. The reaction came, as we have said, at the epoch of the ' return to Nature ' by Macpherson, bp. Percy, and Richardson (qq.v.), for example, in Engld., by Rousseau (q.v.) in France, and by the Hellenists of the spade and foot-rule, among whom we have mentioned Winckelmann. These discovered that the Classicism of the Lat. grammar, first opened for humane purposes by Petrarch, was very far from the whole spirit of antiquity ; and even if, as Nietzsche has said, Rousseau ' returned to Nature ' *in impuris naturalibus*, yet the joint work of these reformers rescued enough of the ancient spirit from the formal disciples of neo-classicism to correct and temper the excesses of a wild and immoderate Romance. The chief battlefield of this conflict was in Germany, in her unique epoch of culture at the junction of the 18th and 19th cents., when Goethe (q.v.), who lived long enough to represent both schools of thought, wr. his *Wilhelm Meister* for the Romanticists, his *Iphigenie* for the Classicists, and his masterpiece, *Faust*, for both. But the reconciliation can be marked in other writers : shall we call Wordsworth's (q.v.) great *Ode on Intimations of Immortality* classical for the sake of its Platonism, or romantic for the sake of its debt to Pestalozzi and Rousseau (qq.v.) ? And how shall we classify Keats, in his *Grecian Urn* ode, for example ? The fact is, that, despite the convenience of compilers of dictionaries and other compartmentalists, the lure of categories is very perilous. Each invasion of the classics into modern lit. has resulted in colonization (or, even less definitely, in fertilization) rather than in conquest. There have been moments when invaders and invaded faced one another more or less consciously, as in Du Bellay's (q.v.) manifesto of the Pleiad (q.v.), in Perrault's (q.v.) *Parallèles*, in Sidney's (q.v.) *Defense*, and in sundry other works. But the critics analyse the lit. which the men of letters write ; and, though it is obviously correct to name and distinguish the characteristics of such broad literary streams as Classicism, Hebraism, and Romance, it is far more difficult (if not nearly impossible) to apply to any great monument of lit. in any language the method which M. Arnold (q.v.) used so courageously, but so unsuccessfully withal, in his *Celtic Lit.*, of indicating by critical labels the racial origin of single lines or passages. Modern lit. inherits the resources of the Hebr. stream of the Bible (q.v.), directed into the channels of the vernacular by Luther (q.v.), to his undying honour ; it inherits the resources of Romance, descended from the 'invincible knights of old ' ; and it inherits the glorious resources of the Gk. and Lat. classics, for whose sake Petrarch, ' the first modern man ', though Perrault forgot to lay claim to him, counted his Ital. lyric verse as nought. The makers of dictionaries and handbooks quite properly point out that the classical tradition gives us order, logic, reason, form ; the romantic tradition gives us outlook, intuition, mystery, distance. Arnold went so far as to tell us that we are Semitic in our conscience and Hellenic in our consciousness, and advised us to ' Hellenize a little with Free Trade '. All this is true and helpful, if we do not push the distinctions too far ; if we constantly remember that no critic's knife can separate the Classicism of Milton or Bodin (qq.v.) from their Semitism (Hebraism), or the Hellenism of *Faust* from its Romanticism. It is all helpful enough if we remember that Boileau's principles compelled him to pronounce a ban on the appearance of Satan in (' Homeric ' or ' Virgilian ') epic poetry in the very generation of *Paradise Lost* ; and that Harvey's (q.v.) principles led Sidney to denounce the rustic speech of Spenser's *Shepherd's Calendar* as offensive to the dues of eclogue as practised by Theocritus and

Sannazzaro (qq.v.) ; and that Rabelais, Molière, Shakespeare and other giants were content to take the best where they found it. Classicism is a stream which has fertilized European lit. from the 12th cent. downwards, and its function has been most efficacious in places and at times when it has been least assiduously subjected to minute analysis and measured dilution. (For the influence of particular writers see the articles under their names ; e.g., Homer, etc.).

Claude, Jean (1619-87) : Fr. Protestant divine. Wr., 1673, *Défense de la Réformation*, and engaged in frequent controversies with Bossuet (q.v.). His ' Pleas (*Plaintes*) of the Protestants cruelly oppressed in the Kingdom of France ', 1686, just after the revocation of the Edict of Nantes, belongs to history rather than to lit. ; but it was a fine and pathetic piece of writing, and as courageous as it was eloquent.

Claudius, Matthias (1740-1815) : Germ. poet and publicist ; lived at Wandsbeck, where he edited one of the many Addisonian reviews of the age under the name of ' The Wandsbeck Messenger ', 1771-75, to which he contributed poems and critical writings. He was one of the Klopstock (q.v.) worshippers, and was attached to, though never a member of, the Göttingen (q.v.) society of the Hain (q.v.). C.'s songs had the patriotic instinct and the homely key of the school at its best ; and his ' Evensong ' (*Der Mond ist aufgegangen*), his ' Rhine-wine-song ' (*Bekränzt mit Laub den lieben, vollen Becher*), his ' Potato-song ' (*Pasteten hin, Pasteten her, was kümmern uns Pasteten*), and some others, achieved permanent fame *per ora virum*.

Clausen, Henrik Nicolai (1793-1877) : Dan. theologian ; prof. of theology at Copenhagen, where N. F. S. Grundtvig (q.v.) ventured to charge him with heresy, on account of his rationalist tendencies, and was mulcted in damages in a libel action. C.'s chief work, which has importance in the history of opinion in Denmark in the early part of the 19th cent., is ' Reflections on my Life and Times ', 1877.

Clavijo, de, Luy Gonzalez (d. 1412) : Span. travel-chronicler. In the reign of king Henry iii of Castile, relations were established, or instigated, between his court and the courts of the great eastern potentates, including Tamerlane (Marlowe's, q.v., *Tamburlaine*), or Timur-Beg, 1336-1405, the Tartar sultan and conquerer. Two maidens, captives of his sword, had been sent by the sultan to the king ; the praises of one of them is sung by an anon. poet, probably Villasandino (q.v.), in Baena's (q.v.) anthology ; and king Henry reciprocated the courtesy by despatching an embassy to Tamerlane. One member was Alfonso de Santa Maria (q.v.) ; another was C., a courtier, who wr. an account of his mission in the *Historia del gran Tamorlan, e itinerario y enarracion del viaje* (voyage), *ed. pr.* by Molina (q.v.), 1582. The ambassadors started on 22 March, 1403, and reached Samarkand on 8 Sept., 1404, and landed again in Spain, 1 Mar., 1406. It is natural to compare C.'s narrative with that of the Venetian Marco Polo (q.v.) and that of the Engl. Mandeville (q.v.), and it gains by comparison with either. It is trustworthy within the limits of the writer's knowledge : there was a margin for credulity beyond it ; and it is clear and unpretentious ; and his descriptions of Constantinople and other cities and peoples of the east are at once interesting and valuable.

Clenardus, Nicolaus (1495-1542) : Brabant humanist ; his name was Latinized from the Netherlandish Cleynaerts. C. resided mainly in Spain in teaching capacities, and publd., Louvain, 1530, a Gk. grammar, which Hallam (i, 338) described in his 1st edn. as ' the principal basis of those lately or still in use among us ; such as the Eton Gk. grammar ' ; later, he modified this statement, but C.'s work is still characterized as ' excellent ' by Sandys (*Hist. Clas. Schol.*, ii, 159), though it was surpassed by that of J. de Vergara (q.v.).

Climate : A physical factor of national psychology, and, accordingly, a proper object of literary treatment and research by national psychologists, i.e. historians. As such, it did not enter the literary province of history till the time of Fontenelle, Fénelon and Dubos (qq.v.), and, most definitely, till it was admitted by Montesquieu (q.v.) into his ' Considerations on the Causes of the Greatness and the Decline of the Romans ', 1734. The determinism of natural science, in lieu of the determinism of divine providence, is a conception introduced by this great Frenchman into hist. science, as a department of modern letters. From the time of Dante (q.v.) right down to Bossuet (q.v.), Montesquieu's immediate predecessor, who wr. history adapted to the principle of kingship-by-divine-right in which he was training his pupil, the son of king Louis xiv of France, the providential theory had prevailed over the physical, in poetry, history, and philosophy ; and it is due to the critical insight and to the genius for exposition of Montesquieu, that Climate was raised to the rank of a distinct influence in the formation of character, thus resuming its lost place in the conspectus of hist. research. The recovery of this point of view was a minor feature, but still a feature, of the Renaissance (q.v.) ; and lit. goes back to Hippocrates, the ancient Greek physical-philosopher (*fl.*, *c.* 400 B.C.) for the classical analogue to Montesquieu. ' In two productions of the Hippocratic school', we read, ' war was declared against all supernaturalism with extraordinary energy. The first of these passages is to be found in the book " On Water, Air, and Sites ", which forms one of the most remarkable pieces of the Hippocratic collection. We are there listening to a man who had trodden the soil of Southern Russia as well as the valley of the Nile, whose critical eye had surveyed all sorts and conditions of circumstances, and whose thoughtful mind had endeavoured to weave the countless details to a uniform and consistent design. But his many valuable conjectures. . . . were all surpassed by the undying honour that attached to the first attempt to establish a causal bond between the characters of nations and their physical conditions. We may call the writer of this treatise the precursor of Montesquieu ' (Gomperz, *Greek Thinkers*, *E.T.*, i, 311). Montesquieu, too, had travelled

in foreign countries, collecting the evidence for his philosophy ; and no clearer example could be afforded of the re-birth implied in the name Renaissance, and of the relationship of ancient to modern lit., than this comparison between Hippocrates and Montesquieu. The restoration of Climate to its causal place in modern hist. lit., after the long embargo imposed by the medieval supernaturalism, illustrates precisely the general lesson of the Renaissance, that ' nothing moves in this world which is not Greek in its origin ' (sir H. Maine). There are reservations to be made to this statement (see s.v. Hellenism, for example), but the instance of Hippocrates and Montesquieu is crucial.

Clough, Arthur Hugh (1819-61) : Engl. poet ; spent part of his boyhood in S. Carolina ; edu. Rugby and Oxford, where he came under the powerful influence of the Arnold (q.v.) family and Newman (q.v.), and was deeply affected by the Oxford Movement (q.v.) ; resigned, accordingly, 1848, a fellowship gained at Oriel Coll., and travelled for a while, forming friendships with Carlyle (q.v.) and R. W. Emerson. C.'s brilliant *Bothie of Tober-na-Vuolich*, in swinging hexameter verse, was publd., 1848, and was followed, 1849, by another novel in verse, *Amours de Voyage*, and by *Dipsychus*. Much of C.'s lyrical work was marked by an exquisite phrasing, matched by real humour and by high ideals. He died at Florence, on a mission of inquiry on military schools after the Crimean War, having previously held the post of warden of Univ. Hall, London. C.'s gifts might have ripened to even greater effect ; he represented a brief transition of thought, in a reaction from the Anglo-Cath. revival which sought to preserve its romantic qualities in expression. M. Arnold, very appropriately, since his poetry displayed the same features, wr. his elegiac *Thyrsis* in C.'s memory, and J. R. Lowell, the eminent American critic, justly said that C. represented ' the moral and intellectual tendencies, the doubt and struggle towards settled convictions of the period in which he lived '.

Cobarruvias Orozco, de, Sebastian (d. 1613) : Span. lexicographer. Wr., 1611, a *Tesoro*, ' Treasury of the Castilian or Spanish Language ', which had considerable value, and which, as revised by Noydens (q.v.), 1674, became, with the earlier work of Lebrixa (q.v.), the foundation of the *Diccionario* (q.v.) of the Span. Academy (q.v.), of 1726-39.

Cobbett, William (1762-1835) : Engl. political essayist ; wr. *Rural Rides*, *Advice to Young Men*, etc., and conducted a *Weekly Political Register* from 1802 onwards. C.'s enthusiasm for workers' education, his exceptional powers of graphic presentment and nervous eloquence, and his belief in the grammar and the textbook, made him a kind of apostle and forerunner of the W.E.A. ; it is the more appropriate that C.'s *Life* (Collins, 1925) should have been written by Mr. G. D. H. Cole. It was a life of various adventure in soldiering, farming, journalism, agitation, and, at the end, as M.P. for Oldham. There were long periods of residence in America, where he withdrew from prosecution at home, once, in connection with a campaign against flogging in the army, and, another time, in order to escape a libel action. But C.'s heart was always faithful to the southern Engl. countryside, to which he belonged by birth ; he was a peasant by orig., and clung to his own class, following with grave misgiving the change from agrarian to industrial conditions. He is said, like Rousseau (q.v.), to have made the poor man proud, and Engld. is proud of him.

Cochem, von, Martin (1633-1712) : Germ. sacred writer ; Capuchin father. Wr. a life of Jesus and other pious vols. of popular character.

'Cock Lorell's Bote' (c. 1510) : Engl. anon. variant of the *Narrenschiff* of Brandt (q.v.), derived more immediately from a Lat. version by Locher (q.v.) and an Engl. version by Barclay (q.v.). ' Cock Lorell ' was a thoroughly Engl. rogue, a kind of admiral Robin Hood (q.v.), and the motive and theme of the Germ. satire were completely naturalized in this poem, which carried the substitution of types for abstractions a step further in the direction of individualization, and which is interesting, too, for its selection of the tradespeople of town (q.v.)-life as the favourite objects of its satire.

Cockney School (Engl.) : Temporary nickname, invented by Lockhart (q.v.) in *Blackwood's Magazine*, 1818, in order to ridicule the lapses from good taste (and, incidentally, the humble birth) of Leigh Hunt (q.v.), the ' Cockney Homer ', Keats, Lamb, (qq.v.), and other London writers. Lockhart did finer work than this ; indeed, his attack on the London group was particularly ungrateful, since Hunt, Hazlitt and others had rallied to the support of the Lake School (q.v.), of which Lockhart was by residence a member, when they had been attacked by Jeffrey (q.v.) in the *Edinburgh Review*, a few years earlier. Jeffrey had joined the Londoners with Southey, Coleridge and Wordsworth (qq.v.), the leading Lakists, whose cause was championed in the newly-founded *Blackwood's Magazine*.

Codex Regius : Title of MS. 2365 in the King's Library at Copenhagen ; discovered, 1642, by bp. Brynjolf, and sent by him from Iceld. to Denmark, 1662, as a present for the newly-founded royal library, where it has since remained ; commonly known as the Elder Edda. The confusion between the prose *Edda* (q.v.), or *ars poetica*, of Snorri (q.v.), and a conjectural older poetic *Edda*, attributed to Sæmund the Wise, is fully discussed by Vigfusson and York Powell in the Introduction to their *Corpus Poeticum Boreale*, Oxford, 1883. Icelandic scholarship in the 17th cent. was ripe for this second Eddic treasury, surpassing Snorri's in scope and contents ; and a favourite theory in advance of the discovery of the MS. ascribed its authorship to a certain Sæmund, surnamed The Wise, who died in 1133. It was by the name of Sæmund's *Edda* that the learned bp. announced his find ; and the C. R. is still very conveniently known as the poetic or the Elder *Edda*, as distinct from Snorri's treatise in prose.

Coeffeteau, Nicholas (1574-1623) : Fr. theologian ; preacher to Henri iv, whose funeral oration he delivered ; bp. of Marseilles. Engaged in controversy with Du Plessis-Mornay (q.v.).

Wr. *Tableau des Passions humaines*, 1620, and *Histoire Romaine*, 1621, much praised in his own day, but little more than an adaptation from Florus, a Lat. historian of the 2nd. cent. B.C.

Coello, Antonio (c. 1605-52) : Span. dramatist ; reputed (and most likely) author of *le Conde de Sex* (' The Earl of Essex '), a play notable on several grounds, and also because it has been ascribed to the royal authorship of king Philip iv (q.v.) of Spain. Ticknor (ii, 340 n.) decides in favour of C., and points out that this play was the starting-point of that Germ. appreciation of Span. lit., which is honourably associated with the writings of Lessing, Wieland, and the brothers Schlegel (qq.v.). Another play, doubtfully ascribed to C., and alternatively to Calderon (q.v.), has likewise an adventitious interest. It is *los Empeños de seis Horas*, transld. into Engl. as ' The Adventures of Five Hours ' by sir Samuel Tuke (F.R.S. ; d. 1674), and read by Pepys (q.v.) on 20 Aug., 1666, who deemed *Othello* ' a mean thing ' in comparison with it.

Coffee-House : Scene of Engl. literary club-life at the end of 17th and beginning of 18th cents. The first Coffee-house in Engld. was opened at Oxford by a Jew named Jacobs in 1650. Their frequentation by ' idle and disaffected persons ' produced a threat of suppression in 1675 ; but they escaped that peril, and after the Revolution of 1688 were used for more private social purposes. Addison (q.v.) wr., in the 1st No. of the *Spectator* (1 Mar., 1711) : ' There is no place of general resort wherein I do not often make my appearance ; sometimes I am seen thrusting my head into a round of politicians at Will's, and listening with great attention to the narratives that are made in these little circular audiences. Sometimes I smoke a pipe at Child's, and . . . overhear the conversation of every table in the room. I appear on Sunday nights at St. James's Coffee-House, and sometimes join the little committee of politics in the inner room, as one who comes there to hear and improve. My face is likewise very well-known at the Grecian, the Cocoa-Tree, and in the theatres, both of Drury Lane, and the Haymarket. I have been taken for a merchant upon the Exchange for above these ten years, and sometimes pass for a Jew in the assembly of stock-jobbers at Jonathan's. In short, whenever I see a cluster of people I always mix with them, though I never open my lips but in my own club '. If we may annotate this illuminating passage, *Will's* was at the corner of Russell Street and Bow Street ; Dryden (q.v.), who died 1700, used to sit in the cosiest inglenook of the room, the acknowledged chief and referee of all who frequented that resort. Steele (q.v.) in the *Tatler* undertook that articles on poetry should be under the sign of *Will's*, which had changed its character in the few years since Dryden's death. *Button's* was on the other side of the street. *Child's* was in St. Paul's Churchyard, convenient for physicians (from the college in Warwick Lane) and clergymen. *St. James's* was the resort of Whig politicians and officers of the Guard. The *Grecian*, visited by Newton, was the sign of ' learning ' in the *Tatler*. The *Cocoa-Tree*

105

Cochem—Coleridge

was the Tory resort. *Jonathan's* and *Galloway's* in Change Alley were used by stock-jobbers and substantial merchants. Drury Lane Theatre, built by Wren, was opened 1674; Haymarket, by Vanbrugh, 1706. Pepys, q.v., is full of pertinent references. There had, of course, been coffee-houses before this epoch: the *Tabard Inn*, at Southwark, for example, in Chaucer's (q.v.) *Canterbury Tales*; and, more closely analogous, the *Mermaid Tavern*, Bread Street, of which Thos. Fuller, writing in 1662, relates: 'Many were the wit-combats between Shakespeare and Ben Jonson, which two I behold like a Spanish great galleon and an English man-of-war'; and the green-rooms behind an Elizabethan stage were always utilized for literary discussion. But the emergency of the Coffee-House, after it had shaken itself free from the associations of adventurers and spies, and its rise as a distinct home of debate, and as a place where literary opinion was formed, and out of which it was made public, belongs to this later epoch, and is to be associated with the change noted by prof. Courthope: 'Out of the English political spirit was developed in English poetry the classical form'. Lit. became professionalized and standardized, under the sign of poetry at *Will's*, learning at the *Grecian*, and so forth. It assumed social and classical qualities, in contrast to its individual and romantic features in previous generations. The public knew what to expect from the several groups of talkers, who, having established a definite *locale* for the formulation of their views, presently felt the need of definite organs for their expression and distribution. Thus, the beginning of the periodical essay as a separate form of lit., shorter, more personal, and more partisan than a bk., may be dated from the time of the regular frequentation of Coffee-Houses, which became, accordingly, forcing-houses of journalistic activity in the 18th cent.

Colenso, John William (1814-83): Engl. divine; a turbulent priest, in the sense in which rebellion against authority was heretical in the 19th cent. The publication of *Essays and Reviews* by 7 theologians in 1860, the year after Darwin's (q.v.) *Origin of Species*, typified the unrest in the Church to which C. gave expression in his *Critical Examination of the Pentateuch*, 1862-79. It exercised a stupendous influence on opinion, as well as on the career of C., who had been bp. of Natal since 1853, and was now excommunicated by Robert Gray, bp. of Capetown, after the Privy Council had reversed Gray's decision to depose C. from his see. The excitement is dead to-day, though as late as 1925 the teaching of the doctrine of evolution was illegal in Tennessee; but C.'s stand for liberty of thought, and his valuable contributions to Biblical criticism and exegesis are not likely to be forgotten; and he memorable, too, for his *Algebra*, 1841, and *Arithmetic*, 1843.

Coleridge, -i. Samuel Taylor (1772-1834): Engl. poet and critic; described by prof. Saintsbury, never an exaggerative writer, as 'almost may we say that Coleridge was the English romantic movement, Coleridge was the inspirer of nineteenth-century literature'. The evidences, or documents, on which this claim

rests, are exceptionally small. C. 'absolutely revolutionized and restarted English criticism'; his personal influence on any man of letters who come in contact with him was so remarkable that he showed the traces throughout his writings, 'as if Coleridge had touched him with a magic wand'; and yet, C. 'has left us just one finished poem of perfect quality' (the *Rime of the Ancient Mariner*), 'and just one pure work which is (and that not wholly) worthy of his powers' (*Anima Poetæ*. The quotations are from Saintsbury's *First Bk. of Engl. Lit.*, 177. Reference should also be made to the same writer's *History of Criticism*, iii, 230 ff., where the tribute to C. is final and fearless: 'There abide these three, Aristotle, Longinus and Coleridge. . . . For all, I believe, of these later days—certainly for all whose mother-tongue is English—Coleridge is the critical author to be turned over by day and by night. Begin with him, continue with him, come back to him after excursions, with a certainty of suggestion, stimulation, correction, edification'). From the initials (S.T.) of C.'s baptismal names, the epithet Estesian is sometimes applied to his disciples.

C. was a Devonian (Ottery St. Mary, where his father was vicar and schoolmaster) by birth, and was edu. at Christ's Hospital, London, where C. Lamb (q.v.), his constant friend, was a schoolfellow, and where 'the inspired charity-boy', as Lamb called him, was early addicted to poetry, poetics and metaphysics. He went up to Jesus Coll., Cambridge, but quitted the univ. suddenly, 1793, and enlisted, oddly enough, in the 15th Light Dragoons, under the name of Silas Titus Comberback (S.T.C.; Gibbon, q.v., too, had a period of military service), from which he obtained his discharge in the next year, when he returned to Cambridge. He met R. Southey, q.v., when on a visit to Oxford, 1794, and renewed the friendship at Bristol in the Long Vacation, where he made acquaintance with Cottle, q.v., the publisher, and the 3 sisters, Fricker, one of whom, Mary, was the wife of Robt. Lovell, another, Edith, was engaged to Southey, and the third, Sara, became the wife of C. The 3 brothers-in-law were more closely united in a young men's dream of a pantisocracy (an all-equal brotherhood) on the banks of the Susquehanna,—a touch of socialist fever, communicated from the Revolution in France, which was even less long-lived than the domestic happiness of C. in his marriage. Yet another product of the relationship and the times was a tragedy, *The Fall of Robespierre*, of which each brother-in-law wr. one act.

We must pass over the *Poems* (publd. by Cottle), 1796-7, and the lectures in Bristol and elsewhere, and come at once to the cottage at Nether Stowey, in Somerset, lent to C. by Thos. Poole, where he was visited, June, 1797, by Charles and Mary Lamb, and where, at Racedown, in that month, C. and Wordsworth, q.v., first made acquaintance. 'The years 1797-8', says H. D. Traill (1842-1900; an excellent publicist; first editor of *Literature*, later *The Times Lit. Supp.*), 'are generally and justly regarded as the blossoming-time of Coleridge's poetic genius. It would hardly be an exaggeration to say that within the brief period is included not only the development of the poet's powers to their full maturity but the untimely beginnings of their decline' (*Coleridge*, Engl. Men of Letters, 39). The contact with Wordsworth was electric. C. refers to it in ecstatic terms. Writing, 1801, to Godwin (q.v.), he said : ' If I die, and the booksellers will give you anything for my life, be sure to say,—" Wordsworth descended on him like the γνῶθι σέαυτον from heaven ; by showing him what true poetry was, he made him know that he himself was no poet "' ; and of Wordsworth's *Borderers*, 1797, C. declared : ' In Wordsworth there are no inequalities '. Truly Traill (*op. cit.*) may remark that C.'s ' much more receptive nature took a far deeper impression than it made ' ; yet we must weigh this remark against that of Saintsbury (*First Bk. E.L.*, 176) : ' Wordsworth, a strong rather fine nature, was never quickened to his best efforts till he had worked with Coleridge '. The first and most abiding result of that collaboration was *Lyrical Ballads* (Cottle, 1798), more appropriately reserved for discussion s.v. Wordsworth, and representing and formulating, ' for the first time, the imaginative apprehension of experience which lay at the heart of Romanticism, and which was equally profound, though extremely diverse, in the two poets' (Herford, *Age of Wordsworth*, 152 ; and see s.v. Romance). C.'s share in this vol., which has European importance in the history of lit., apart from the poetic beauty of its contents, included the *Ancient Mariner* (' *unum, sed leonem* ', as has been said), and should have included, if C. had been ready (the unreadiness is characteristic), the *Dark Lady* and *Christabel*. Very significant was the authors' statement, that ' the majority of the following poems are to be considered as experiments. They were written chiefly with a view to ascertain how far the language and conversation in the middle and lower classes of society is adapted to the purposes of poetic pleasure '. It is legitimate to argue from the *Ancient Mariner* and *Tintern Abbey*, for examples, that this object was wholly disregarded by the earnest, young poets ; but a further reference to ' the gaudiness and inane phraseology of many modern writers ' helps us more clearly to understand the departure and new beginning in *Lyrical Ballads*, and its place in the transition from one school of poetry to another. C.'s *Biographia Literaria* (publd., 1817) is full of light on this topic, and contains the famous passage describing the initiation of the vol., in which it was agreed, says C., ' that my endeavours should be directed to persons and characters supernatural, or at least romantic, yet so as to transfer from our inward nature a human interest and a semblance of truth sufficient to procure for these shadows of imagination that willing suspension of disbelief for the moment which constitutes poetic faith '. With Wordsworth's part we are not immediately concerned, but we may observe that he was to reverse the process, and ' to excite a feeling analogous to the supernatural ' in the spectacle of common things. Between them, the 2 poets aimed at a reinterpretation of nature, including man, and deliberately not

confining the study of mankind to his own species. *Christabel* and the wonderful fragment, *Kubla Khan*, perhaps the purest single piece of poetry in the Engl. language, likewise belong to this period.

Of C. and the Wordsworths, C. and De Quincey (q.v.), C. and opium-eating and opium-dreams, C. and journalism (*The Friend*, 1809-10, etc.), C. in Germany, C. at Highgate (q.v.), and so forth, the record must be sought in more detailed studies. What is important is the fact of C.'s influence on philosophical and critical thought. From Germany chiefly C. brought home the metaphysical speculation which has profoundly affected the modern mind, and we may cite from Carlyle (q.v. ; *Life of Sterling*) a pen-picture of how this effect was wrought :

' Coleridge sat on the brow of Highgate Hill in those years, looking down on London and its smoke tumult like a sage escaped from the inanity of life's battle, attracting towards him the thoughts of innumerable brave souls still engaged there. His express contributions to poetry, philosophy, or any specific province of human literature or enlightenment had been small and sadly intermittent ; but he had, especially among young inquiring men, a higher than literary, a kind of prophetic or magician character. He was thought to hold—he alone in England—the key of German and other Transcendentalisms. A sublime man ; who alone in those dark days had saved his crown of spiritual manhood, escaping from the black materialisms and revolutionary deluges with " God, Freedom, Immortality ", still his ; a king of men '. So much in this place for the metaphysician, in his *Aids to Reflection* and other works. For the critic, we have already cited Saintsbury, and we may add here the *dicta* of that historian of criticism as to C.'s (1) *Biographia Literaria* and (2) *Anima Poetæ*. Of the former he writes that, if every prof. of lit. were disestablished, and the proceeds of the vacated chairs were applied to ' furnishing the boxes of anyone who goes up to the univ. with a copy of the *Biographia Literaria*, I should decline to be the person chosen to be heard against this revolution ' ; and of the latter he writes : ' for some fifty pages the entries are " diamondiferous ". . . The *yeast* of criticism —the reagent which, itself created by the contact of the critical with the creative, re-creates itself in all fit media—has never been more remarkably represented than here '. It does not seem possible to expand these praises. *Disjecta membra* of C.'s critical writings are to be found in his minor works, and he was emphatically a redintegrator of Shakespeare's fame in his own country.

   -ii. Hartley (1798-1849) : Engl. poet and biographer ; son of above.

Colet, John (*c.* 1467-1519) : Engl. humanist. dean of St. Paul's, 1505. Son of an ex-lord mayor of London ; edu. at Oxford ; pupil of Grocyn and Linacre (qq.v.) who had recently returned from Italy ; visited Italy, 1494, and probably reached Florence (q.v.) at the top of the ascendancy of Savonarola, and after the death of Mirandola and Politian (qq.v.) ; at any rate, his thoughts were always turned to the more distinctively Christian side of humanism, to which his domestic experience of the frailty of life, as the only survivor of a family of 22, may have directed them ; lectured in Oxford, 1496, on the epistles of St. Paul, and struck at once the new note of anti-scholastic learning and man-to-man revivalism which he maintained throughout his clerical career ; 'this new treatment by Colet was, we may say perhaps' (the writer is prof. Foster Watson), 'to the old theological method what the dramatic method was, in the hands of Shakespeare, in comparison with the old method of mysteries and moralities. It was a passage from the artificial to the natural, the assertion of the essentially human as against the merely abstract'. C.'s fame is secure on more grounds than his ardent devotion to truth and hate of theological controversy : i, he founded, 1509-10, St. Paul's School in the shadow of his own cathedral church, and sacrificed his private fortune in order to secure for his 153 scholars (the number of the miraculous draught of fishes) the very best of the spirit of the Renaissance ; ii, he was the intimate friend of More (q.v.), and friend, correspondent, and more than once host of Erasmus (q.v.), and these 3 men of like taste and learning formed a little triumvirate of reformers, generous in zeal, faithful in utterance, beneficent in influence. As to Colet's place in the triumvirate, it would be less than pious on the part of an 'old Pauline' not to quote Seebohm, *Oxford Reformers* (Longmans, 1869, p. 347) : 'It does not often happen that two friends, engaged in fellow-work, publish in the same year two books, both of which take an independent and a permanent place in the literature of Europe. But this may be said of the *Novum Instrumentum* of Erasmus and the *Utopia* of More. Still more remarkable is it that two such works, written by two such men, should, in measure, be traceable to the influence and express the views of a more obscure but greater man than they. Yet, in truth, much of the merit of both these works belongs indirectly to Colet.'

Colin, Muret (13th cent.) : Fr. lyric poet. Native of Champagne, where, as a professional *jongleur*, his *bourgeois* muse tended to the satiric style of the Fable (q.v.).

Collett, Jacobina Camilla (1813-95) : Norse novelist ; sister to Wergeland (q.v.) ; her husband was a prof. of æsthetics. Fru C. was an early fighter in the cause of marriage-law reform and of the rights (then much further to seek than now) of women ; in this respect a fellow-worker with, if not actually a forerunner of, the greater Norw. writers, Ibsen, Björnson and Lie (qq.v.). Fru C.'s first novel, 'The Sheriff's Daughters', 1855, took shape as an attack on such social institutions as forbad a woman to realize her own capacities ; its influence is traced in Ibsen's 'Love's Comedy', even in some details of characterization and expression. A kind of autobiographical work, 1863, was followed by 'Last Leaves', 1868-73, 'The Realm of the Dumb', 1877, 'Against the Stream', 1882, etc. In these tales, the writer's keen sense of wrong found vocal expression, which grew bitterer as her powers and her audience increased.

Colletet, Guillaume (1598-1659) : Fr. poet ; original member of the Fr. Academy (q.v.) ; selected by Richelieu (q.v.) as one of his five poets ; wr. precious (q.v.) verses, and 'lives of French poets', since lost.

Collier, Jeremy (1650-1726) : Engl. divine ; non-juror ; transld. the dict. of Moreri (q.v.) ; wr., 1698, *Short View of the Immorality and Profaneness of the Engl. Stage*, to which Congreve (q.v.) and others replied. (See, too, s.v. Restoration Comedy).

Collier, John Payne (1789-1883) : Engl. scholar, whose genuine contribution to criticism in his *History of Engl. Dramatic Poetry*, 1831, and other works, was ruined by his invention of an imaginary folio of Shakespeare (q.v.) and by further surrenders to the temptations of literary fraud.

Collin D'Harleville, Jean François (1755-1806) : Fr. playwright. Wr. *les Châteaux en Espagne, le Vieux Célibataire*, and other comedies.

Collins, William (1721-59) : Engl. poet ; fell into dejection and intermittent insanity during the latter years of his short life ; wr. *Persian (Oriental) Eclogues*, 1742 ; *Odes* (including his best poems, *Evening, The Passions*, 'How Sleep the Brave', etc.), 1747 ; an *Ode to Thomson*, q.v., on his death, 1748 ; and *Ode on the Popular Superstitions of the Highlands*, 1749, posth. publd. Noting prof. Saintsbury's dictum (*C.H.E.L.*, x, 143) : 'The Collins of the *Odes*, at his best, is the poet of all time in general and no time in particular ; the Collins of the *Eclogues* is everywhere the poetaster of the eighteenth century', and, leaving, therefore, the *Eclogues* to their epoch, we may observe the exquisite taste of F. T. Palgrave, who, in the *Golden Treasury of Songs and Lyrics*, arranged C.'s ode to *Evening* just in front of Gray's (q.v.) *Elegy in a Country Churchyard*. For the 2 poems and the 2 poets belong together : the 2 poems, obviously, because the stanza in C.'s *Evening*,—

Now air is hush'd, save where the weak-eyed bat
With short shrill shriek flits by on leathern wing,
  Or where the beetle winds
    His small but sullen horn,

is akin to the stanza in Gray's *Elegy*,—

Now fades the glimmering landscape on the sight,
And all the air a solemn stillness* holds,
Save where the beetle wheels his droning flight,
And drowsy tinklings lull the distant fold.

  Each 'beetle' recalls Milton's verse in *Lycidas*,—

What time the gray fly winds her sultry horn,
and other likenesses and echoes will be found : likenesses to each other, and echoes of the romantic writers of the past. And the 2 poets because, together, they are the heralds of the revival of Romance (q.v.) in Engl. lit. The *poetic* heralds, observe. Critical heralds accompanied or preceded them (see s.vv. Warton, Temple, Percy), for the movement was in the air ; but later critics, founding their judgment on nearly 2 centuries of experience, concur in linking C. and Gray in this poetic impulse to the growing taste. Thus, sir Wm. Watson, a poet *de nos jours*, wr. in his *Wordsworth's Grave* ;

    * 'Stillness' is subject, ' air' is object.

From dewy pastures, uplands sweet with
    thyme,
A virgin breeze freshened the jaded day.
It wafted Collins' lonely vesper-chime,
It breathed abroad the frugal note of Gray.
And prof. Courthope may be taken as typical
of literary historians, when he writes (*Hist.
Engl. Poetry*, vi, 419) : 'Among the immediate
pioneers of the Romantic movement in English
poetry Gray and Collins alone are entitled to
be considered great constructive artists'.

The C. of these few great *Odes* is the essential
C., and his influence has been profound. But
reverting for one moment to ' the Collins of the
Eclogues ', as distinguished by Saintsbury
above, and remembering that he is recognizable by his stock epithets taken out of contemporary gradues, we may note, purely out of
a love of letters, a remark by prof. Ker
(*C.H.E.L.*, x, 218) on the lines in the ode to
Evening,—

    Or find some ruin midst its dreary dells,
      Whose walls more awful nod
      By thy religious gleams.
This ' nod ', he reminds us, is conventional :
it is a deposit of the ' poetaster of the eighteenth
century ' ; and Ker refers us to a passage in the
brothers Hare (q.v.), *Guesses at Truth*, 1827,
in which they cite instances from Pope (q.v.)
of this *nodding* habit of grave mountains :
' the same piece of falsetto ', they add, ' is
doubtless to be found scores of times in the
verse writers of the same school '. The nodding
wall does not date C.'s *Evening*, but it is a
blemish characteristic of the very taste from
which he and Gray sought release.

Collins, Wm. Wilkie (1824-89) : Engl. novelist ;
friend of Dickens (q.v.), a frequent contributor
to his *Household Words*, and an occasional
collaborator. Wr. *The Woman in White*, 1860 ;
Armaghdale, 1866 ; *Moonstone*, 1868, etc.

Colman, -i. George (1732-94) : Engl. dramatist ;
scholar. Wr. *The Jealous Wife*, 1761, and
other plays ; edited the plays of Beaumont and
Fletcher (qq.v.) ; effected good translns.
from Horace and Terence ; manager of Covent
Garden Theatre, 1767-74.

-ii. George (1762-1836) : Engl. dramatist ;
son of above, and distinguished as the Younger
from the Elder. Wr. *The Heir at Law*, 1797 ;
John Bull, 1803, etc. ; manager of Haymarket
Theatre, 1789-1813 ; wr. comic verse, witty
but coarse, and recommended by his wit
to the favour of king George iv.

Colonna, Francesco (*c.* 1433-1527) : It. allegorical
writer ; Dominican monk at Treviso ; wr.,
1467, *Hypnerotomachia Poliphili*, ' Poliphil's
Strife of Love-in-Dream '. The language is
hybrid ; Italian Latinized to the taste of the
pedants and grammarians among the humanists. Rabelais (q.v.) compared it with
Egyptian hieroglyphs ; but, philologically, it
is interesting in its place in the transition of
Ital. lit. (q.v.) from Lat. to the vernacular.
In form, and subject, too, C.'s prose-allegory
is transitional. It relates the search of
Poliphil for Polia, a nun, in the medieval guise
of dream-adventures through regions peopled
by loquacious abstractions ; but it belongs to
the Revival of Learning by its constant reverence for antiquity, and to the Renaissance in
Italy by its celebration of the nascent fine

arts. A monk's vision of love, it is infused with
the glow of the new dawn breaking on Italy.

Colonna, Vittoria (1490-1547) : It. Latinist and
sonneteer ; daughter of Fabrizio Colonna, and
granddaughter of Fredk., duke of Urbino
(q.v.) ; m. marquis of Pescara (d. 1525) ;
afterwards lived at Ferrara, and, later (*c.* 1538),
at Rome, where she enjoyed the romantic friendship of Michelangelo (q.v.). Admiring beauty
and inspiring admiration for it, learned,
vivacious, and eager for humanism, a devoted
wife and an intellectual woman, Vittoria is
typical of all that was noblest in Renaissance
femininity.

Columbus, Christopher (*c.* 1451-1506) : It.
navigator ; born at Genoa, died at Valladolid ;
entered the service of Ferdinand and Isabella,
and wr. Span. letters to his sovereigns, giving
accounts of his voyages and of his discovery
of the New World. C.'s name belongs to
history by so indefeasible a title, that he can
afford to be contented with the estimate of
his literary merit by Fitzmaurice-Kelly, *Lit.
espagn.*, 173 : ' Certainly, he was not a man of
letters : he was rather a man of genius, for
whom the stirring lines written fourteen centuries earlier by the Spaniard, Seneca, in
Medea, acquired a new and a singularly prophetic significance—

    ' Venient annis secula seris,
      quibus Oceanus vincula rerum
      laxet, et ingens pateat tellus,
      Tethysque novos detegat orbes,
      nec sit terris ultima Thule.'
It is a brilliantly apposite quotation.

Columbus, Samuel (1642-79) : Swed. poet. Wr.
' Swedish Odes ' in vernacular hexameters,
thus increasing the resources of his native
language. C. also employed the Germ.
language, and was a facile writer of Lat.
verse, a medium used exclusively by his elder
brother Joannes C. (1640-84).

Comédie Larmoyante (Fr.) : weeping comedy,
comedy of tears ; a species of Fr. drama, also
described compendiously as *drame*, which was
introduced, 1733, by the production of the
Fausse Antipathie of La Chaussée (q.v.).
This type of play in tragedy was called
tragédie bourgeoise ; and La Chaussée, though
opposed by Voltaire and Piron (qq.v.), was
supported and followed by Diderot (q.v.) and
others, who established the *Com. larm.* about
1750. In its own class, narrowly interpreted.
the record of the dramatic type is not distinguished ; but it stands in clear relationship
of ascent to the human-comedy or problem-play
of the modern stage ; and thus La Chaussée's
innovation has real value and interest. The
' burgherly ' drama of the Germ. stage was a
similar movement towards humanizing comedy,
and seeking its elements neither in horseplay
nor in satire, but in the interplay of common
experiences ; its earliest considerable example
was *Miss Sara Sampson* by Lessing (q.v.).
Self-analysis, psychology, personal responsibility : all these ideas of sentiment and sensibility began to pour into Fr. thought and
philosophy, partly from Engld. (see s.v. Lillo),
partly from the conditions of Fr. life at the
close of the reign of Louis xiv, at about the
beginning of the 18th cent. ; and it was in order
to give full effect to the dramatic value of

these feelings that the domestic drama—neither tragedy nor comedy, and therefore deriving a name from both—found and took its chance of development.

Comella, Luciano Francisco (1751-1812): Span. dramatist, of poor talents and nugatory value. C. is chiefly remembered by the ridicule with which he was assailed in his life-time on the part of Moratin (q.v.) the younger, and others. It is a sorry scandal, and unworthy the dignity of literature.

Comenius. See s.v. **J. A. Komenský.**

Commedia dell'Arte (It.): Improvised comedy; comedy of Masks; the simplest and probably the oldest form of drama, in which the talent of the actors supplied the deficiency of the writers (see Hallam, *Lit. in Europe*, iii, 601). ' A certain quickness of wit, and tact in catching the shades of manner, comparatively rare among us ', Hallam adds, ' are widely diffused in Italy. It would be, we may well suspect, Impossible to establish an extemporaneous theatre in England, which should not be stupidly vulgar. But Bergamo sent out many Harlequins, and Venice many Pantaloons '. Plainly, as Hallam points out in a footnote, ' the pantomime, as it exists among us, is the descendant of this extemporaneous comedy ' (which in his rendering for the *C. dell'A.*), ' but with little of the art and spirit of its progenitors '. Ultimately, that progenitor may be traced to ' the Greek rustics who smeared their faces with wine-lees at the Dionysiac festivals, and from whose improvised songs and gestures Greek comedy was developed.' The peasants of Tuscany and Naples carried on the tradition, and the wine-lees gave way to masks, which necessarily limited the range of characters to a few recognizable types, the rest of the entertainment depending for its success on the cleverness of the actors. Gozzi (q.v.) in the 18th cent. combined the *C. dell'A.* with dramas of faëry. ' Punch and Judy ', still played in the streets of London, is a survivor of this once popular form of comedy, and is derived from the ' Pulcinello ' of Francesco Cerlone, a tailor in Naples, contemporary with Gozzi.

Commines, de, Philippe (*c.* 1447-1511): Fr. historian. A Fleming by descent, C. entered the service of Philip of Burgundy, and of his son, Charles the Bold, 1464-72. In that year, having discharged several missions which took him to London and elsewhere, he quitted the Burgundian duke for the safer service of king Louis xi, and became councillor and chamberlain to the king. He received a munificent pension, and, by his marriage to the heiress of the barony of Argenton (to which the king added other forfeited estates) C. became a rich and important man. Louis xi sent him to Florence in 1478. He took the part of the duke of Orleans, afterwards Louis xii, against the regent Anne, and, though he suffered severely for a while at the hands of Charles viii, he was recalled by Louis xii in 1505, and followed the king to Italy, where he met Machiavelli (q.v.) at Florence. This brief record of a full and busy life, spent in the forefront of politics and diplomacy, is of exceptional interest in connection with the writings of C. Hitherto, historiography had

been one-sided. Villehardouin (q.v.) had written a *chanson de geste* in prose. The sire de Joinville (q.v.) had written the life of a saint whom he had known. Froissart (q.v.) had written feudal annals from the point of view of a feudal knt. C.'s departure from precedent as an historian depended on his activity in public life. He was the first of a long line of opportunists in the higher walks of statesmanship : a Renaissance statesman of the Wolsey type before the dawn of the Renaissance. He was bound to the crumbling Middle Ages by a hundred ties of instinct and style ; but his intellect sought to break the bars. Melanchthon (q.v.) included C. with Sallust and Cæsar in a syllabus for the instruction of princes. Battles, as such, chiefly interested him for their results ; forces, influences, personal factors, were carefully weighed and measured by him, and he commanded a novel power of generalization ; his diplomacy was based on psychology, as well as on an intimate grasp of foreign and domestic policy. He was religious, rather as a Roman of the early Empire, than as a child of the Middle Ages. He was a realist in apprehension, and far too complete an observer and man of affairs to be tempted into the foible of cynicism ; a grave humour was the utmost extent of his wise smile. In all this, we see, first, the relation between C.'s histories and his life : his feudal loyalty to the dukes of Burgundy gave way to his perception of the advantages of an attachment to Louis xi ; his loyalty to Louis xi was affected by his long-sighted view of the coming of Louis xii. Secondly, we see a literary unity between extremes of social difference—between C., the wealthy and influential statesman, and Villon (q.v.) the fugitive felon. These contemporaries in the changing Paris of their day were as distant from each other as the poles, in all material circumstances which operate as links in human life. Yet our social valuation is set at nought by the fact that, after 4 cents., we state, and state correctly, that the two representative men of social and literary France, in the period of transition in the 15th cent., were Villon, the vagabond poet, and C., the grandee historian. Each, according to his opportunity, anticipated the times to be, while each, according to his necessity, was faithful to the times that were passing away. The art of each was founded on medievalism, and reached out towards the Renaissance. C., it should be added, was not more wholly Machiavellian in his intellectualism than Villon was wholly Rabelaisian in his transformation of the medieval formulæ. Both acknowledged limitations, though each was the first of the Fr. modernists in his respective literary sphere. C.'s memoirs have not much dignity of style, and are marred, as hist. writing, by too frequent digressions. It is the man and the subject that attract us, rather than the manner and the bk. His work is contained in 6 bks. of the *Chronique de Louis xi* and 2 bks. of the *Chronique de Charles viii* ; there are, further, 3 vols. of C.'s ' Letters and Transactions ', and a collection of unpubld. papers. It may be permitted to an Englishman to add (more pertinently in connection with Scotland), that another of C.'s claims to fame is his inspiration of Scott's (q.v.) *Quentin Durward*. Writing to Constable, 18 Dec., 1822, Scott said : ' Books of history help me little, except Commines '.

Compagni, Dino (d. 1324) : It. (Florentine) chronicler-diarist. Contemporary of Dante, and took a prominent part in government of Florence from 1280 onwards. Wr. *Cronica* of his own times to 1312 ; ignored till 1640 ; *ed. pr.* in following century ; denounced as apocryphal by Pietro Fanfani, 1858 ; defended as authentic by Fr. critic, Hillebrand, 1862 ; assailed again by Germ. critic, Scheffer-Boichorst, 1874 ; and defended again by signor del Lungo, 1879-80. Opinion is still divided as to the complete genuineness of C.'s work, though hardening in the direction of ascribing to it a considerable authentic nucleus, expanded by copyists in later centuries.

Comte, Auguste (1798-1857) : Fr. philosopher ; founder of the system of moral and social philosophy, known as Positivism, since it claims to rest on positive, as distinct from speculative (or metaphysical) proof. C. began as a disciple of Saint-Simon (q.v.), from whom, though he quickly separated, he derived his two dominating ideas of a synthesis of human knowledge and a religion of humanity. In his chief work, *Cours de Philosophie positive*, 1830-42, C. developed the hist. law of the 3 stages of knowledge—the theological, the metaphysical, and the positive—by classifying the sciences and synthetizing the scientific facts of his own age. C. invented the term ' sociology ', and likewise the social term ' altruism ' ; and he attempted in his later work, *Politique positive, ou Traité de Sociologie instituant la Réligion de l'Humanité*, 1851-54, to found on positivist principles a practical religion which may be described as Utopian romanticism. The whole subject belongs to the history of philosophy, not of lit. ; and C.'s direct followers to-day are neither many nor influential. Moreover, a certain mlle. Clotilde de Vaux turned the master's thoughts into other directions, and her early death crossed his philosophy with a kind of ecstatic feminism. Gradgrind, in Dickens' (q.v.) *Hard Times*, may be taken as an extreme type of the Comtist preceptor, though, naturally, the picture is overdrawn : ' You are in all things to be regulated and governed by fact. . . You must discard the word Fancy altogether ' ; and so severe a regimen of facts has not appealed to educational authorities. Nor has the religion of humanity replaced for more than a very few the older and less demonstrable religions, derived from earlier *strata* of human knowledge. It has been found, on the whole, more satisfactory to adapt these to the conditions of the day than to abandon revelation for positivism, requiring the co-operation of all parts of the social body. But the inventor of sociology can never lack honour and renown, and C.'s fame as a pioneer is secure, above all reconsideration of his conclusions. His influence is to be traced in Mill, Spencer (qq.v.), and other thinkers, and his chief disciple in Engld. was Frederic Harrison (q.v.).

Conceit : Engl. rhet. term (Ital. *concette* ; Fr. *pointe* ; Span. *agudeza*) ; a stylistic device designed to heighten literary effect by an element of rarity and unexpectedness in phraseology or association of ideas. The cult of conceits has been traced to the decadence of lyrical poetry of Italy in the 17th cent. (the ' secentismo ' : see s.v. Ital. lit.). The inspiration of the pure fount of Petrarch had been exhausted, and exercises and experiments in style, and variations in increasing extravagance of far-fetched similes and high-pitched compliments rose from Bembo (q.v.) and the courtly lyrists of the 16th cent. to the more self-conscious and deliberate affectation of Marino (q.v.), latent even in Tasso (q.v.). With Marino at the century's turn (*Rime*, 1602 ; *Lyra*, 1614 ; *Adone*, 1614) the conceits of prettiness, glitter, hyperbole, and analogy reached the height of their vogue in the decay of lyrical love-poetry, and from Marino proceeded the Marinism, which was matched by similar displays of taste in Spain, France, Engld., and even Holland for a time. Gongora, Chapelain, Drummond, Hooft : each of these names may stand as typical of a school of writers in each of the four countries mentioned who were Marinists by assimilation or imitation. Meanwhile it is important to note that, whereas Marino in Italy represented a decadence of lyric inspiration, the daughter-movements in other countries, especially the precious (q.v.) style in France and Euphuism (q.v.) in Engld., were in the nature of an advance. Conceits were invented by Precious and Euphuistic writers in the zeal of their anxiety for refinement and style at a time and in places where these were lacking. They were stepping-stones towards a goal which Italy had reached and abandoned. It should further be noted that the Marinistic conceit and its aftertypes were superficial only ; they adorned the printed page, and tickled the outward ear ; and are thus to be distinguished in rhetorical history from the conceit of thought, of which Donne (q.v.) is the great Engl. exemplar. It would be convenient as well as more correct to reserve *conceit* for the Marinistic verbal variety, and to distinguish the Donne-conceit as *wit*. Johnson (q.v.), following Dryden (q.v.), and discussing such practitioners as Waller and Cowley (qq.v.), described this form of wit-conceit as ' metaphysical ' (q.v.), and the term is far more appropriate, since it indicates the origin in mind and the application to literary content, than the alternative term ' fantastic ' suggested for use by later critics. This metaphysical conceit first appeared in the love-poetry of Europe in the *dolce stil nuovo* (q.v.) of Guinicelli and Dante (qq.v.), and was derived immediately from the Troubadours of Provence (q.v.). It attained its acme in Dante himself, and was always a characteristic of the sonnet (q.v.), when that form of verse was used for the expression of love ; Shakespeare's sonnets, e.g., are filled with metaphysical conceits ; and it is not erroneous to refer this note in modern lit. right back to its ultimate source in Plato (q.v.). The metaphysical conceit is more diffused and less pointed than its verbal variety, and it may be traced in Engl. lit. from Donne and Crashaw (q.v.) in the 17th cent. to Alice Meynell and J. Thomson in the 19th. To resume : there are two distinct classes of conceit in the lit. of modern Europe. The older of the two is Platonic by derivation, and passed through the love-poems of the Troubadours and the love-rapture of Dante and the sonneteers into the metaphysical wit of Donne and his successors. These conceits are ideal ; they are the outer marks of an inward fantastic brooding over the stored erudition of past ages ; founded in scholastic learning and medieval science, they are woven into the garment of modern thought. The second kind of conceits is external only : cultivated and sought out prettinesses and surprises and extravagances of style, lifted above the obvious and the vulgar. They are a part of the movement of the Renaissance (q.v.) towards form and order and beauty ; and, though such conceits were first invented at the period of the decay of the Petrarchan lyric, they acquired the freshness of a new departure when they passed out of Italy into France ; Marinism is a symptom of decadence, but Preciosity a ' malady of growth ', and the same remark applies to Euphuism in Engld., or at least to the signs of it before *Euphues* ; and to Gongorism in Spain, or to some signs of it in the poems of Gongora himself. A famous type of the precious conceit in France is the dagger of Théophile (q.v.), which blushed at its own act of treachery. Rhetorically, the fame is just ; the expression is a conceit of style ; but how far it falls short of, or hits, or overruns the propriety of style is a question of taste and custom. To call it a conceit is not necessarily to condemn it. Thus, Meredith's (q.v.) picture of the valleys at sunset fading from view and ' more and more forgetting ' is precisely an analogous *pointe* ; and every reader will recall his own examples. A blushing dagger or an oblivious valley is a far-fetched, complicated, affected phrase ; but the measure of its propriety is its success ; and this depends upon factors not altogether within the scope of lit. To one class of mind, a dagger is too concrete an object and too readily visualized to admit of an abstraction into vagueness and of a re-presentment with qualities borrowed from another kind of objects, least of all, from human beings. To the same mind, a valley, inasmuch as it is not machine-made and cannot be handled and thrown aside, is more easily subjected to such metaphorical treatment ; to another mind, both objects are, to yet another, neither object is, to be so treated. One mind's conceit may be another mind's propriety of diction ; taste must be true, before a false conceit can be detected. Lastly, it may be suggested that the conceit of one generation may become the commonplace of the next. Literary history is full of experiments which might now be described by the term futurist : Rabelais and the Pleiad were Fr. futurists ; Marino was an Ital. futurist ; Lyly, an Engl. one ; Gongora, a Span. one ; Whitman, an American one, and so forth. Much of their obscurity should be condoned for the sake of the aim which they cherished, however much it may have been crossed with motives less altruistic than the reform and extension of the literary apparatus which they handled. A *conceptista*, or conceited style, is *ex hypothesi* an ugly style, whether it aims at merely verbal or at more subtle metaphysical effects ; (and these

sub-divisions, it may be added, are rather critical conveniences than compartments strictly observed by the stylistic reformers themselves). But ugly though it is, and obscure, and even a ' disease ', as Hallam (iii, 18) calls it, it is a necessary concomitant of the process by which language, or expression, keeps pace with the increase of thought and ideas.

Condillac, de, Etienne Bonnot (1715-80) : Fr. philosopher ; *abbé* ; tutor to duke of Parma, a grandson of king Louis xiv, for whose instruction his works were written ; closely befriended with Diderot (q.v.) and his circle. In the special history of philosophy, C. takes rank as the founder of the doctrine known as sensationalism. He derives all ideas from sensations, on which the mind works ; and his example of the statue endowed with a single sense, and gradually developing its missing senses from the one, and its ideas from the gamut of senses, is famous in lit. (See, too, s.v. Diderot). Lanson (*Hist. Lit. Fr.*, 737) follows Taine (q.v.) in the following brief exposition of C.'s system : ' The operations of thought are an algebra, in which words are the algebraic signs. Judgments are equations, and the collective terms are abstract objects, ideas '. All this, contained in C.'s works, *Essai sur l'Origine des Connaissances humaines*, 2 vols., 1746 ; *Traité des Sensations*, 2 vols., 1754, *Cours d'Études du prince de Parme*, 13 vols., 1769-73, is a little outside the ambit of pure lit. But C.'s place in lit. is assured by the extraordinary lucidity of his style, and by his direct appeal to the common intelligence of edu. men and women. All the *philosophes* (q.v.) of this age—the generation before the Revolution—were reformers first and philosophers after ; and in this sense, without departing in the least from the calm of the philosophic temper, C. was ' le philosophe des philosophes ' : everything he wr. was a missionary effort for the enlightenment and emancipation of the new thought. (See also s.vv. Locke, Mably).

Condorcet, de, Jean Antoine Nicolas de Caritat (1743-94) : Fr. philosopher-mathematician ; *marquis* by rank ; secretary of the Fr. Academy (q.v.), 1777 ; member of the Legislative Assembly and of the Convention in the Fr. Revolution ; was proscribed as a girondist, and took poison in prison. Wr. lives of Turgot (q.v.), his teacher, 1786, and of Voltaire (q.v.), 1787, and other works. His chief work was written in hiding and flight, and ranks high as an account of the tendencies of the philosophic thought of the age which closed in him : *Esquisse* (' Sketch ') *d'un Tableau historique des progrès de l'Esprit humain*, 1794. It was a work of fine confidence and hope, written in troubled times by a victim of the trouble, and it is refreshing for its account of the Machiavellian venality of the British constitution, in reaction from the praises bestowed upon it by Montesquieu, Voltaire, Delolme (qq.v.), and the majority of *philosophes* (q.v.).

Confradia de la Sagrada Pasion (Span.) : Brotherhood of the Sacred Passion ; title of an early Span. dramatic society, founded, 1565, for the production of representations licensed by the Church. The profits were applied to religious or charitable purposes by the proprietor-brotherhood. In such beginnings (see s.v. Rueda) of strolling players with rudimentary stage-properties the Span. theatre took its rise. (See, too, s.v. Confrérie de la Passion).

Confradia de la Soledad (Span.) : Brotherhood of the Solitude ; title of an early Span. dramatic society, founded, 1567, on the lines of the Confradia de la Sagrada Pasion (q.v.).

Confrérie de la Passion (Fr.) : Brotherhood of Passion ; title of an early Fr. dramatic academy, with headquarters in Paris, where their theatre was situated at the Hospital of S. Trinity, 1402-1539. In the earlier period of its activity, the *confrérie*, composed exclusively of laymen largely from the working-classes, confined themselves to the Passion-play and to kindred ' mysteries '. They gradually extended their operations by overtures to the *Enfants-sans-souci* (q.v.), and by force of example from the Pleiad (q.v.), but they cannot be said to have done much for the advancement of drama in France. They paid more attention to stage-furniture and properties than to the actor's or playwright's art ; and the C. sank gradually to its dissolution in 1676 after its installation, 1548, at the Hôtel de Bourgogne. In 1599 its premises were rented by Léconte for the so-called King's comedians, and from that year to 1629 Hardy (q.v.) was the leading dramatist in France, and supplied all the energy in which the C. had conspicuously failed.

Congreve, William (1670-1729) : Engl. dramatist (see s.v. Restoration Comedy) ; ' a spoilt child of life and literature ' (*C.H.E.L.*, viii, 146 ; the writer is Chas. Whibley), and his praises have been sung in more or less extravagant terms by critics as great as Dryden (q.v.) in his own time and Lamb, Coleridge, Leigh Hunt, Hazlitt, Macaulay, Meredith and sir E. Gosse (who wr. C.'s life) in later generations. C.'s comedies include *The Old Bachelor*, 1693, *The Double Dealer*, 1693, *Love for Love*, 1695, and *The Way of the World*, 1700 ; he wr. one tragedy, *The Mourning Bride*, 1697 (' Music hath charms to soothe the savage breast ' is the opening line of this play), but he ceased writing after 1700, when his last and best comedy, in which Peg Woffington played Millamant about 1730, and which was successfully revived in London in 1924, proved a failure. Voltaire (q.v.) visited him in 1726 ; Pope (q.v.) addressed to him the epilogue to his *Iliad* ; Swift (q.v.) was his friend, and he held lucrative offices. He enjoyed the favours of the duchess of Marlborough, wife of Francis Godolphin, and left her £10,000 ; but, though a loose liver, like others, C. was a true poet, and merited his grave in the Abbey. Dryden mentioned him with Shakespeare, and he has more frequently and more justly been placed on a level with Molière (q.v.). He was attacked by Jeremy Collier (q.v.) in the *Short View of the Immorality and Profaneness of the English Stage*, 1698, but C., who was an artist, and no controversialist, was not much ruffled either by failure or attack. The rest was silence, not for those causes, but because he had written his best, and he turned back from letters to life. The heir in his own estimation (as in that of posterity) to Roman Terence and

his Gk. model, Menander, C. practised a ' poetic fastidiousness ', as it has well been called, which was not lost on a later generation, and directly influenced the muse of Collins (q.v.).

Conrad, Joseph (1857-1924) : Engl. novelist, of Polish parentage (C.'s family surname was Korzeniovski) ; edu. at Cracow ; became a sailor before he was 20, and entered British Mercantile Service, acquiring the mariner's master-certificate as well as a complete mastery of the Engl. language during the period of his merchant-service. Wr. *Almayer's Folly*, 1895 ; *The Nigger of the Narcissus*, 1897 ; *Lord Jim*, 1900 ; *Typhoon*, 1903 ; *Nostromo*, 1904 ; *The Secret Agent*, 1907, and other novels, down to *Suspense* (posth. and unfind.), 1925 ; all remarkable, quite independently of the romance of C.'s birth and life, and the charm of his personality, for their delicate interpretation of the moods of men in strange places. C. made ample use of the devices of the hint and pause in style, and his argosies, brought from afar, have the perfumes of the land as well as the salt of the sea.

Conrart, Valentin (1603-75) : Fr. man of letters. C.'s wealth, learning and prestige made him a welcome guest at the Hôtel de Rambouillet, the Saturday gatherings of mlle. de Scudéry (qq.v.), and other social and literary circles, precious (q.v.) or otherwise. In 1626, he established a similar little gathering of his own, confined to the male sex, and select in number. From this modest beginning the Fr. Academy (q.v.) was developed, almost in its own despite, under the powerful protection of Richelieu (q.v.). C., who was the first secretary of the Academy, is said to have been a suitor for the hand of Madeleine de Scudéry. Though so important a figure in the history of the lit. of the 17th cent., C. wr. nothing himself, except, as was said, his own name ; and hence Boileau's (q.v.) well-known verse ' J'imite de Conrart le silence prudent '.

Conscience, Hendrik (1812-83) : Belg. (-Flemish) novelist ; so far, the greatest of the few Flemings who have revived the literary use of their native tongue. C.'s ' Lion of Flanders', 1838, ' Scenes of Flemish Life ', ' History of my Youth ', and other romantic tales and stories have achieved in Fr. and Engl. versions a popularity beyond their native confines. (See too, s.v. Ledeganck).

Conservateur Littéraire (Fr.) : Title of a literary journal, founded in 1819, as a romanticist (s.vv. Romance, Lyrisme) organ. Hugo (q.v.) was its most eminent contributor.

Constance, Council of (1414-18) : With the place of this Council which was opened by pope John xxiii in person, in the history of the papal schism, we are not concerned, save to note that its meetings marked, in the words of Figgis, *From Gerson to Grotius*, 35, a ' watershed between the medieval and the modern world. The principles of Constance ', he continues, ' are the last effort of medieval constitutionalism. Their failure marks the beginning of the modern world. It paved the way for Luther and Machiavelli in the State, for Loyala and Manning in the Church '. Another point of contact with lit. is the eagerness of members of the Council in the cause of the new Humanism (q.v.). Four distinct expeditions for MSS. were made by those who attended it : (i) To Cluni, summer 1415 ; (ii) to St. Gallen, summer 1416 ; (iii) to St. Gallen again, and other monasteries, early 1417 ; (iv) to Langres and other places, summer 1417. The finds of Poggio (q.v.) and others were considerable. See Sandys, *Hist. Clas. Schol.* ii, ch. 3 ; esp. : ' Among Poggio's first discoveries was a complete copy of the *Institutio Oratoria* of Quintilian, a work which Petrarch had never seen except in an imperfect and mutilated form, and which Salutati had vainly hoped to obtain from France. Poggio hastened to send his good news to Niccoli and Bruni in Florence, carried off the MS. to Constance, and copied it himself in 53 days '. See s.vv. Truly, and in a sense bigger than Figgis intends, this Council was a watershed between two worlds.

Constant de Rebecque, Benjamin (1767-1830) : Fr. (Swiss) philosopher ; publicist ; politician ; letter-writer. C.'s family had fled to Switzerland at the time of the revocation of the edict of Nantes, 1685, but C., who was born at Lausanne, resumed his Fr. nationality, served under the emperor Napoleon, and received a present of money from king Louis Philippe. The most interesting facts in his life were derived from his love-affairs. He was obviously a man of brilliant parts, though erratic and unstable in disposition ; and his conversation and personality fascinated successively mme. de Charrière (q.v.), who was many years his senior, and mme. de Stael (q.v.), with whom he travelled in Germany and Italy. He succumbed to the wonder of Germ. romanticism, and transld., 1809, Schiller's (q.v.) *Wallenstein*, with an essay on the subject. C.'s personal letters and those of his correspondents possess considerable and permanent value. Less value is now attached to C.'s heavier writings, meditated through many years and much talk, *de la Religion*, 5 vols., *du Polythéisme romain*, 2 vols., etc., and to the remains of his moral and political work, which displayed the versatility and frequently the opportunism of a journalist. C.'s *Journal intime* was issued in 1895, and reveals him in his letters to his family and friends. He is otherwise chiefly remembered by his psychological romance, *Adolphe*, written, 1816, under the influence of his Germ. period, in which his rapid inductive powers were applied to character-study and analysis.

' **Contes-Dévots** ' (Fr.) : descriptive name of a medieval class of short tales in verse, originally and principally Fr., differing from the fable (q.v.) by their pious tone or sacred subject. They were commonly taken from Lat. sourcebooks, going back to a Gk. or Eastern authority, frequently Jew. or Arab. : e.g., the *Angel and the Hermit*, turned to excellent use by Voltaire (q.v.) in his *Zadig*, and the parable of the true ring, re-told by Boccaccio and Lessing (qq.v.). The type ceased to flourish about the mid-14th. cent.

Cook, Edward Tyas (1857-1919) : Engl. biographer ; journalist ; liberal ; knt., 1912 ; K.B.E., 1917. Wr. *Life of John Ruskin* (see s.v. Ruskin), 2 vols., 1911 ; *Life of Florence Nightingale*, 2 vols., 1913 ; *Literary*

Recreations, 2 series, 1918-9, and other works ; assistant-editor under W. T. Stead of the *Pall Mall Gazette* (q.v.) ; edited the *Westminster Gazette* (evening) from its foundation, 1893, to 1896 ; *Daily News*, 1896-1901.

Cook, John Douglas (d., 1868) : Scot. journalist ; edited the weekly *Saturday Review*, 1855-68 ; and attracted to its staff a very brilliant band of contributors, intent, as stated in no. 1 (3 Nov., 1855), ' by the exercise of commonsense and ordinary perspicacity ' to estop the tyranny of the rule of *The Times*.

Coornhert, Dirck Volkerts (1522-90) : Dutch philosopher and controversialist. Contemporary with Marnix (q.v.), C. was as devoted to the cause of Christian humanism as Marnix to that of Calvinism, and attacked the abuses of the new church as ardently as Marnix those of the old. But while Marnix used the weapons of irony and satire, C. sought to win by dialectic and persuasion. The two were alike in their unlikeness ; both convinced and ardent controversialists, and both great men of letters. C. transld. Cicero, *de Officiis*, Seneca, *Consolation of Philosophy*, and other classical authors, including *Odyssey*, i-xii, from a Lat. version, and 50 tales out of Boccaccio, *Decameron*, from a Fr. version. Wr. Biblical plays, after the fashion of the Rederijkers (q.v.), and anti-Calvinist pamphlets. C.'s chief work was an ethical treatise, based mainly on the teachings of his favourite authors : the Bible, Cicero, Seneca, Marcus Aurelius, Boethius, Plutarch, and Theophrastus. It was designed to inculcate the arts of right living in the spirit of the humanists of the Ital. Renaissance. As such, and as a colleague of Marnix in the foundation of a Dutch prose style, C. merits the praises which he has earned.

Copland, William (15th-16th cent.) : Engl. satirist. Transld. parts of *Eulenspiegel* (q.v.), c. 1528, under the name of *Howleglass*.

Coppée, François (1842-1908) : Fr. poet ; playwright ; disciple of Ste-Beuve and Musset (qq.v.). Wr. *Reliquaire*, 1866 ; *Intimités*, 1868 ; *les Humbles*, 1872, etc., in the ' popular-pathetic ' kind ; and, in drama, *Passant*, 1868 (the year after the Universal Exhibition in Paris, at which C. won a poetic prize), noteworthy for the appearance of Sarah Bernhardt, at the Odéon. C. wr., too, more ambitious plays : *Madame de Maintenon, les Jacobites, Pour la Couronne*, and others. His name stands high in the recent lit. of France.

Copyists : a class of well-paid scribes, employed to make transcripts of MSS. In the early Middle Ages, this work was done in the monasteries, to the chief of which a ' scriptorium ' was attached ; and the best available scholar was deputed to oversee the writers, and to exercise the functions of textual criticism, as it was known at that time, viz., punctuation, orthography, and collation. At the best, the result was meagre ; and, parchment being expensive, the texts were sometimes scraped and overwritten with ecclesiastical works ; such doctored MSS., with upper and lower decks of text, being known as palimpsests. At the period of the revival of learning in Italy, professional copyists were attached to the universities or other centres of learning ; these scribes, though likewise subject to the supervision of censors, were more often than not men of an irritating ignorance. Petrarch, Salutati, Poggio (qq.v). and others bitterly complained of them; and the most enthusiastic humanists preferred the drudgery of making their own copies to the disappointment of paying for inaccurate versions of the cherished texts. Fredk., duke of Urbino (q.v.), kept a staff of 30-40 copyists constantly at work, and a scholar like Niccoli (q.v.) was himself a skilled copyist and an employer of copyists. The industry flourished till the invention of printing (q.v.); and Vespasiano (q.v.), the biggest employer of such scribes at the very time of the decay of their trade, was the most influential of those who sturdily resisted the new-fangled method.

Coquillart, Guillaume (c. 1421-1510): Fr. *bourgeois* poet; lawyer and ecclesiastic. The point of his somewhat heavy satiric verses was directed chiefly at the professional lawyer, at the professional soldier (as distinct from the feudal levies), and at women. It is from a reference in one of C.'s verses to the ' grands rhétoriqueurs ', as descriptive of contemporary writers such as Chastellain (q.v.), that the term (s.v. Rhétoriqueurs) has been applied to the school.

Cordier, Maturin (1479-1564): Fr. humanist; educational reformer. Lecturer in Gk. at Paris, where one of his pupils was Calvin (q.v.), whom he followed to Geneva, where he resided as lecturer, 1536-38, and again 1559 till his death. Wr. Lat. treatise, 1530, against corrupt Latinity of his day, and *Colloquies*, 1564, of marked educational value.

Corio, Bernardino (15th cent.): It. historian. Wr. prose History of Milan.

Corneille, -i. Pierre (1606-84): Fr. dramatist; ' the great Corneille ', by common consent. C.'s life was uneventful; his literary adventures were the events of his life. He studied law and filled an office at the so-called ' marble table ' of justice at Rouen, the Board of Woods and Canals; he was one of the band of 5 poets who discharged the inglorious part of shadows to card. Richelieu (q.v.), but he found the duties as little to his advantage as he later found the resentment at his resignation displayed by the powerful and jealous card.; he occasionally frequented the Hôtel de Rambouillet (q.v.) at Paris, and was a contributor to the *Guirlande de Julie* (q.v.), but for the most part he resided at Rouen, where his first comedy, *Mélite*, was produced, 1629. From that date till 1652, C. wr. steadily for the stage; then seven years of proud and wounded silence followed the failure of his *Pertharite*. C. occupied his retirement with verse-translns.: of the hymnal and of Kempis (q.v.), *Imitation of Christ*: a choice which corroborates other evidence to C.'s purity and devoutness of mind. His return to drama was marked by his *Œdipe*, 1659, and by a further series of plays (closed with *Suréna*, 1674), which failed to satisfy the change of taste which Quinault (q.v.) helped to introduce and which Racine (q.v.) confirmed. C. was conservative of the stage-proprieties which he had learned from classical drama and from Spain. He ' adapted himself awkwardly to the tenderness of Quinault, but he could not compete with Racine. He

became jealous and unhappy. His poverty embittered him less than this glory of a rival, which seemed to him a purloining of his own genius' (Lanson, *Hist Lit. Fr.*, 429). C.'s belief in his genius was as unshakable as it was just: it was the public which betrayed him after his period of retirement; for, except by the inevitable diminution of power which came with increasing years, C.'s dramatic work never changed its character. But this very diminution was fatal, for his work depended on power. The tremendous sincerity of the method contained the seeds of its own decay; and when the strength departed from the master's brain and hand (a departure hastened by the success of a rival method), the shortcomings of the method were revealed. Variety, delicacy, reality; the interplay of characters on one another; humanity's infinite notes of tenderness, pity, hope; the intimate feelings and emotions of living men and women: much, if not all, of this was excluded from the stately procession of clashing will-forces and fate-intelligences which move in a panoply of irresistible reason across the Cornelian stage. When the creative genius began to fail, and C.'s sure reliance on his audience began to waver; when the rhetoric hesitated, and the purpose grew faltering, there was left but a thunder of eloquence echoing round empty abstractions. The paradox of the situation was, that C.'s genius was romantic, while his theatre was classical; the star of Marlowe (q.v.) was hitched to the wagon of Seneca (q.v.); and never did the Senecan tradition, rigidly imposed by Italy upon the tragic drama of modern Europe, operate so unfavourably to the native gifts of a dramatist as in the instance of C. The demonstration of this fact would take us too far; we must be content to register the conviction that the Elizabethan stage of Marlowe, or the later Romantic stage of Hugo (q.v.) would have suited C.'s genius more effectively than the stage of Paris as he found it, with the lifeless Roman tragedies on the one hand and the hackwork of Hardy (q.v.) on the other. C. might have added lustre to Hardy's melodrama; he chose to vitalize the literary drama of Jodelle (q.v.). Thus choosing, he attained to a mastery which he forfeited only to the truer mastery of Racine; but, thus choosing, it is legitimate to believe that his own immensity was limited by the conditions of the art to which he bound himself. C. founded Fr. classical tragedy almost in his own despite; and the best proof of this fact is afforded by an examination of the circumstances which attended his masterpiece, the *Cid*. It was produced in Dec., 1636, or in Jan., 1637. Now, 1637, it must be noted, was the year of the ' Discourse on Method ' of Descartes (q.v.), and the Cartesian method of philosophy made an instant appeal to the rational and enlightened circle of aristocratic thinkers, from whose ranks the new Fr. Academy (q.v.) had just drawn its earliest recruits. The literary formulæ of Malherbe and J. L. de Balzac (qq.v.) and the other fathers of the Academy were resumed and systematized and codified by the great work of Descartes; and, as the Academy, with Richelieu behind it, was the centre and arbiter of taste, and as the theatre, with its classical traditions, was the first hope of the Academy, it is clear that a drama like the *Cid* from the pen of the leading playwright of the hour was something more than just a new play. It was a manifesto, a challenge, a document ; a proof positive of the tenets of the new thought ; and by any means it had either to conform to the views of the thinkers, or else to be outlawed beyond the pale. But it was too successful to be outlawed. C. had been wise enough to go for his *Cid* to the best examples of contemporary Span. drama. A few years before he composed it, Guillen de Castro (q.v.) had produced at Madrid the *Mocedades del Cid* ('Youthful Adventures of the Cid'), in which he had raised the hero of the old Span. chronicle to the height of tragic intensity and passionate power. Castro's play was even superior in some respects to C.'s. It was more free in movement, and less restricted in time, and certainly it had the advantage of priority in its invention of the conflict between desire and fate in which its hero and heroine were involved. C.'s success, therefore, was assured ; and his *Cid* was no sooner launched on the sea of popularity than it was enwrapt in the prevailing atmosphere of abstract literary controversy. It provoked a storm of discussion among the men (and women) of letters, small and big, of the day. Cartesianism descended from the clouds, and folded the *Cid* as with a garment. The storm-centre whirled round the dramatic Unities (q.v.), which Chapelain (q.v.) had just discovered to be founded immovably on that reason which was the basis of the Cartesian universe. Reason, thus exalted, was unreasonable enough to demand the sacrifice of those who denied it. Did C. deny it ? or did he not ? Were the Unities observed by *le Cid* ? or was it an outlaw-drama beyond their pale ? The high-priest of reason was Richelieu, the powerful patron and *quasi* founder of the Academy ; and it is not fair to ask how far literary jealousy on his part reinforced his sense of responsibility as keeper of the Academy's conscience. Even cards have been known to have their weaknesses. Certain it is, that, though the *Cid* had observed all necessary dramatic probabilities, the complete Unity of place was missing. Chapelain, after several attempts, expressed the views of the Academy on this offence in a way which at last met with Richelieu's approval, without absolutely alienating C. ; and the harassed dramatist surrendered at discretion. C. was rewarded a little later by admission to the Academy, and his next play was dedicated to Richelieu. 'The sticklers for rigid principles won the day ; but, from the point of view of lit., the moral of the quarrel about the *Cid* is its illustration of art's revenge upon the artist. For C. had it in him to be greater than the Unities, which the doctrines of reformers like Malherbe, the refinement of the Precious (q.v.) writers, and the epistemology of Descartes, had raised to the dignity of dramatic rules. He had it in him to romanticize the theatre, and to become a Hardy with a style, in other words, the Marlowe of France. But this high, *a priori* art, on the authority of which

Sidney (q.v.) disallowed the *Shepherd's Calendar* of Spenser (q.v.), because it did not conform with the model of Sannazzaro (q.v.), imposed its authority on C., and limited, as we have seen, the full force of his inspiration. Later, when inspiration declined, the method strangled the achievement. There is the other way of looking at it, however, If the rules of the Academy and their application by Richelieu-Chapelain prevented C. from availing himself to the full of the example of Castro, and turned him back from the path which Marlowe followed, after all, it directed him towards Racine. C.'s surrender enabled Racine to conquer the stage for classic drama ; and this is the more consistent view of C.'s contribution to Fr. lit. In a few, at least, of the series of plays with which he adorned the Fr. theatre, C.'s sublime and passionate rhetoric lent an intense vitality to the awful issues of his drama. The insulated will of Descartes spoke with Malherbe's exclusive diction, and was opposed by forces as tremendous and incontaminate as itself. After the comedies of C.'s early period, the grand tragic note was struck in his first tragedy, the *Medea*, 1635, and was sustained through the *Cid*, 1637, *Horace*, 1640, *Cinna*, 1640, *Polyeuctes*, 1643, *The Death of Pompey*, 1643, and *Rodogune*, 1644. This was the period of his masterpieces. His 3rd period extended from *Théodore*, 1645, to *Pertharite*, 1652 ; his 4th from *Œdipus* to *Suréna* (1659-74), including *Sophonisba*, *Attila*, *Otho*, and others plays. It is to be noted that, as C. had founded Fr. tragedy on a Span. tragic drama, so he went 6 years afterwards to a Span. model for the first great comedy of the Fr. stage. His *Menteur*, 1642, is transferred from the comedy, 'Truth Suspected' of Ruiz de Alarcon (q.v.). But it is as a tragic poet that C. is most honoured. He, literally, swept the stage with the tragic grandeur of his characters. The famous 'moi' of implacable and invincible egoism is first sounded as early as in the *Medea*. Medea is asked at the climax of her horrors, 'Dans un si grand revers que vous reste-t-il ? ' and her answer comes with magnificent and indomitable assurance : 'Moi, dis-je, et c'est assez ! ' This Senecan touch, matched by the 'qu'il mourût' in *Horace*, and by many longer outbursts of soul undaunted and unconquerable by Fate, is, to-day, no longer called Senecan, but Cornelian, by virtue of the genius of the Fr. tragedian, who, in sublimity, and purposefulness, has more in common with Milton than with Shakespeare.

-ii. **Thomas** (1625-1709) : Fr. dramatist ; brother to above ; succeeded him as member of Fr. Academy. Wr. tragedies and comedies, and was also active as journalist. A writer of mediocre gifts, he was not only overshadowed by his elder, but he challenged comparison : his *Camma*, 1661, recalled the brother's *Pertharite :* his *Count of Essex*, 1678, the *Suréna*, and so forth. T. C. had a conspicuous success with his *Timocrates*, 1656, and possessed a comfortable little talent of his own, which he tried too hard to assimilate to that of Pierre C. or even of Quinault (q.v.).

Cornwall, Barry. See s.v. **Procter, B. W.**

Corporation of the Royal Readers: Fr. learned foundation, consisting of lecturers, originally 5 in number, in Gk., Hebr., and Mathematics, founded at Paris, 1530, by king Francis i, at the instance of Budé (q.v.), who had made the suggestion in the preface to his *Commentarii*. Budé and J. Lascaris (q.v.) ably supported the royal aim, and the Corporation formed the nucleus of what was afterwards called the Collège of France (q.v.), of which Francis, accordingly, ranks as the founder. Part of its initial success was drawn from the strong opposition of men of learning in Paris in the 16th cent. to the narrow obscurantism of scholars at the Sorbonne, and see s.vv. Danès, Toussain.

Corral, de, Gabriel (1588-1640): Span. pastoralist; resided for some years in Rome. Wr., 1629, *La Cintia de Aranivez*, a verse and prose pastoral romance, in the manner of Montemayor (q.v.).

Corral, de, Pedro (fl. 15th cent.): Span. romance-chronicler. Wr. *Coronica Sarrazyna*, otherwise entitled 'Chronicle of the king Don Roderick, with the Destruction of Spain', *c.* 1443. This work, which the writer attributed to imaginary persons who take part in it (chiefly, Eleastras, chronicler to Roderick), though taken as a serious history of the 8th cent. by March (q.v.) and others, despite its exposure by Guzman (q.v.), is little more than a farrago of chivalric fiction and romantic invention. Ticknor (i, 191), who cites an edn. as early as 1511, throws doubt on C.'s authorship, which is accepted, however, by Fitzmaurice-Kelly.

Cortés, Hernando (1485-1547): Span. conqueror; *el Conquistador*, by right of renown; the hero of the conquest of Mexico, related by Prescott from contemporary historians, and himself the author of official narratives and letters. Titian's portrait gives him the 'eagle eyes' mentioned by Keats (q.v.; sonnet on *Chapman's Homer*), but it was Balboa, not C., who 'stared at the Pacific'. Still, though we deprive him of his right to this reference in the great Engl. sonnet, C. inspired by his career and exploits an immense body of lit.

Cory, William Johnson (1823-92): Engl. poet; Eton master; *né* Johnson. Wr. *Ionica*: *Poems by W.J.*, 1858, charged with 'modern paganism', and succeeding exquisitely in blending the tone of his own age with the style of the Gk. Anthology, or of Hellenism as reflected through Landor (q.v.). The best known of C.'s poems is the (transld.) epitaph: 'They told me, Heraclitus, they told me you were dead'.

Coryate, Thomas (1577-1617): Engl. travel-writer; made a walking-tour, 1608, in France, Italy, Switzerld., Germany and Holland, of which he wr. an account in *Coryats Crudities hastily gobbled up*, 1611, issued with commendatory poems by the wits of the day, including Campion, q.v. The 'thousand-mile shoes', in which C. was supposed to have achieved this walk, were exhibited in the church at his birthplace, Odcombe, Somerset, as late as 1702.

Costanzo, de, Angelo (1507-91): It. poet and historian; not very memorable in either capacity. A follower of Sannazzaro (q.v.) in poetry, but marred in his lyrical composition by the errors of taste against which Bembo (q.v.) protested. C.'s *History of Naples* (1250 to 1486), though lacking judgment and depth of knowledge, has proved serviceable to later students, and is a good type of the work produced by a nobleman writing history out of patriotism and love of letters.

Coster, Samuel (1579-*c*. 1660): Dutch dramatist; physician; intimate friend of Hooft and Bredero (qq.v.), with whom he collaborated as playwright. Was leader in the Eglantine (q.v.) schism, 1615, and was induced to make this breach in the brotherhood of the old Amsterdam Chamber of Rhetoric, chiefly through dislike of the pretensions and of the foreign preferences of Rodenburg (q.v.). The so called 'Coster's Academy', or the 'first Dutch Academy', was founded, 1617; but the quarrel was speedily healed.

Cota de Maguaque, Rodrigo (15th cent.); Span. satirist; born at Toledo; died before 1495; a converted Jew, who became a bitter hater of his former co-religionists, for which he was justly rebuked by Montoro (q.v.); known as 'the elder', in distinction to a junior namesake. C. has been credited plausibly with the authorship of the *Mingo Revulgo* (q.v.), and, less plausibly, with other and more invective anon. satiric poems. He has also been claimed as the writer of the first part of *Celestina* (q.v.), and certainly he possessed considerable latent dramatic talent; but the ascription is discredited to-day. Of the poems known to be from his pen, we may select a burlesque epithalamium (q.v.), addressed to the treasurer royal, to whose wedding C. had not been invited; and a 'Dialogue between Love and an Old Man' (*entre Amor y un viejo*), in 66 9-line stanzas, in which the dialogue and movement were managed so well that the poem ranks properly as a pastoral drama, and was twice utilized by Enzina (q.v.).

Cotgrave, Randle (d. 1634): Engl. lexicographer. Wr., 1611, Fr.-Engl. dict., a notable monument of the influence of Fr. Renaissance studies in Tudor Engld.

Cottle, Joseph (1770-1853): Engl. publisher; author; bookseller in Bristol, 1791-9, during which period he publd. Coleridge's *Poems*, Southey's *Joan of Arc*, and *Lyrical Ballads* of Coleridge and Wordsworth, 1798, entering the portals of Romance (q.v.) by that venture. (See s.vv.). C., whose brother, Amos ('O Amos Cottle! Phœbus! What a name'! Byron, q.v.), was a Cambridge graduate of modest repute in learning, deserves recognition for his enterprise and confidence in the young poets, including Robert Lovell (the 3rd., with Southey and Coleridge, of the lovers of the 3 Bristol sisters Fricker), whose reputation was all in the future, and whose impecuniosity was largely their publisher's charge. C. wr. some fairly useful reminiscences of these early bookselling associations.

Cotton, Robert Bruce (1571-1631): Engl. antiquary; created a knt., 1603, and bart., 1611; sat in parliament; contribued to various learned and hist. works, and befriended the leading scholars of his day; formed a valuable library, from which he presented some MSS. to Bodley's (q.v.) library at Oxford on its foundation. The Cottonian collection was transferred to the nation, 1702, and, after several vicissitudes, was deposited in the Brit. Mus., 1753. (See, too, s.v. Pearl).

Coulanges, de, Fustel (1830-89): Fr. Humanist; wr. *la Cité Antique*, 1864, a brilliant essay in reconstruction, and other works of hist. scholarship.

Courier de Méré, Paul Louis (1772-1825): Fr. Hellenist; pamphleteer; soldier; recalls A. Chénier (q.v.) by his Hellenism and Pascal (q.v.) by his controversial irony. The pity was that C.'s great gifts were expended on less than worthy objects. He fought the Legitimists with his pen, as he had fought for liberalism with his sword; but as he had proved a provincial soldier so he was a parochial pamphleteer. Should villagers dance?; should certain acres be sequestrated for the duke of Bordeaux?; the *Gazette du Village*: these were the topics of a wit trained by the finest models of antiquity to a rare and most effective acumen. C.'s best-known work is his *Simple Discours de Paul-Louis*, 'on the occasion of a subscription for the purchase of Chambord', which took shape as an exquisite satire on the forms and methods of authority, and which earned the author two months' imprisonment. In Florence, on his retirement from active service, C. prepared a Fr. transln. of *Daphnis and Chloe* (see s.v. Greek fiction), and his ironic faculty was first displayed in a controversy with the Laurentian librarian respecting an inkstain on a MS. of Longus. C.'s 'swansong' was a *Pamphlet des pamphlets*, 1824; he was shot in his own grounds on 10 May, in the following year. C. still enjoys the reputation which his learning and his style have earned for him; but it is the artist who is admired, not the uses to which he turned his art.

Court: The influence exercised on lit. by Courts was considerable and practically continuous from Charlemagne to Goethe (qq.v.). We may refer to the literary moulds fashioned in the 11th and later centuries at the courts of the duchies of sunny France, where the names of court William x of Poitiers, of his daughter, queen Eleanor, consort of king Henry ii of Engld., and of her daughter, queen Marie of Champagne, are famous in connection with the love-lore of their courts. In Sicily, after the Albigensian crusade, and on the mainland of Italy, at every centre of learning—Urbino, Florence, Naples, Bologna, Ferrara, Venice, etc., —under the patronage of dukes and princes— d'Este, Sforza, Montefeltro, Medici, and others, —the C. was always the focus of humanistic letters; encouraging, inspiring, remunerating and patronizing artists and poets; 'each city a starlike seat of rival glory'. Later, again, the Germ. princes, carrying on the Carlovingian tradition, were many of them men of culture, eager to welcome men of talent to their courts; the Minnesinger-movement was a courtly one, and it was an elector of Saxony who gave sanctuary to Luther after Worms. In France, king Francis i and his more literate sister, queen Margaret of Navarre, transferred to their own courts the best features of the Renaissance in Italy, as patrons of learning, founders of libraries and univs., and centres of the new

thought. In the Peninsula, though Church influence tended to be more rigid and restrictive, great writers from Camoens downwards were connected with the courts of Portugal and Spain; and in Engld. the legendary influence of Arthur (q.v.) and the hist. influence of king Alfred was repeated in the Renaissance period by king Henry viii and his children, esp. and most notably by queen Elizabeth.

It was in the Elizabethan age that the literary change occurred, about 1588-90, when the national awakening, to which the defeat of the Armada is evidence, made the theatre an organ of the people, and brought men of humble birth into higher honour than the *entourage* of the court. Puttenham (q.v.), writing about 1585, contended that 'the actions of mean and base personages tend in very few cases to any great good example'; but time and revolution added the so-called middle and lower classes to the conventional literary material; and the influence of the C. declined as the self-consciousness of demos grew. In a sense, Tennyson's (q.v.) *Idylls of the King*, with its Albert-Arthur idea of gentleness, may be regarded as the last example of a type of lit. of which Castiglione's (q.v.) *Cortegiano* was, for many practical purposes, the first.

It would be an idle inquiry whether the influence of the C. on European letters has been good or bad. It has been inevitable, which includes both; it has given us Machiavelli's (q.v.) naked *Prince* as well as Spenser's (q.v.) richly-dight knt. It is not possible to conceive of the descent of lit. without its period of court-pageantry; and the functions of verse and prose could never have been developed, or, at least, were not developed (it is the same thing), save by the protection afforded to the arts by the munificence of Renaissance rulers. 'How small of all that human hearts endure, That part which laws or kings can cause or cure', wr. Johnson (q.v.) in the 18th cent.; but the perception belongs to a new and a later revelation, in lit. as well as in social ethics; and the democratic zeal of Whitman, in the middle of the 19th cent., who declared to his American fellow-citizens that 'democracy can never prove itself beyond cavil, until it founds and luxuriantly grows its own forms of art, poems, schools, theology, displacing all that exists, or that has been produced anywhere in the past, under opposite influences', is false to science and fact. There was democratic lit. before Columbus and Cabot set out on voyages of discovery; every age, and the 19th cent. most of all, has profited in increasing measure by the application of moulds and forms devised at the C. to thoughts and sentiments awaiting expression in ruder brains; and the novel (q.v.), now the most democratic of all forms of lit., owed as much to Castiglione and Lyly, the courtiers, in the 16th cent., as to plebeian Richardson (q.v.) in the 18th.

It is not necessary to recount the prevailingly feeble record of the 'Hofpoeten', or court-poets, of Germany at minor duchies in the 18th cent., or of the line of Engl. poets-laureate (q.v.), of whom Wordsworth and Tennyson were successively the greatest. It was at the C. of Louis xiv of France that a king's influence and patronage were most directly exercised for the benefit of national lit. He is, at any rate, the type of benevolent despotism in letters, which is not the same thing as princely patronage. Finally, we may quote an illuminating passage from sir W. Raleigh's essay on sir Thomas Hoby (q.v.), in his *Some Authors* (posth., Oxford, 1923). He had designed, he tells us, in that essay, something in the kind of a history of the lit. of courtesy. The lit. of the Elizabethan age, he says, ' was a literature of the Court, as surely as the literature of the age of Anne was a literature of the Town. The way to political influence, to social advancement, to power and consideration, and fame, lay through the Court, in England as in Italy. Now that the Court has dwindled into a drawing-room, it is perhaps not wholly easy to realize what once it meant to the nation. It was the centre, not of government alone, but of the fine arts : the exemplar of culture and civilization '. He reminds us of the changed conditions presented by Castiglione and lord Chesterfield (q.v.) : ' the Courtier, by an insensible diminution, has become " the man of fashion " '. Then came the Fr. Revolution, and ' the doomed courtier, advancing one stage farther in his degradation, from a man of fashion became a *beau* or dandy '. But ' it is time to remember our ancestry '. ' There was something profoundly sane, after all ', adds Raleigh, ' in the ambitions that built New Place and Abbotsford '—a delightful literary allusion (see s.vv. Shakespeare and Scott), with which to close this literary record of the Court.

Cousin, Victor (1792-1867) : Fr. philosopher ; statesman ; orator ; with Guizot and Villemain (qq.v.), one of the ' triumvirate of the Sorbonne ', who, till 1828, like the Berlin profs. of a later date, turned their professorial chairs into semi-political tribunes. C. succeeded Roger-Collard (q.v.) as a disciple of the Scot. school, and presently widened his outlook after a visit to Germany, 1817, where he made acquaintance with Fichte, Jacobi, Hegel and Schelling (qq.v.). His lectures were suspended in 1821, and in 1824, when in Germany again, he achieved imprisonment in Berlin ; later, he resumed his work with greater *éclat*, and filled several offices of State, including the ministry of Public Instruction. Like the 2 other members of this group of univ. politicians, C. was occupied with popularization rather than with research ; he wr. manuals of the history of philosophy (1826 ; revised, 1840, 1863), of modern philosophy, 1841 ; of moral philosophy in the 18th cent., etc. ; a transln. of Plato, 13 vols., 1825-40 ; ' French Society in the eighteenth century ', 1858 ; works on Pascal and other thinkers ; edns. of Descartes, 11 vols., 1826, Proclus, Abelard, and others. C.'s name constantly occurs in the story of thought and criticism in the great epoch of history in which he lived.

Coverdale, Miles (1488-1568) : Engl. Biblical scholar ; bp. of Exeter, 1551-3 ; rector of St. Magnus, Southwark, 1563-6 ; but spent various terms of residence abroad, under the disturbed conditions of theological thought in his day. C.'s services to the transln. of the Bible (q.v.)

were considerable ; it was probably at Zurich that his Engl. version was first printed, and he superintended the printing of the ' Great Bible ', 1539, at Paris. He transld., too, *Ghostly Psalms, c.* 1540, from Germ. Lutheran hymns, and his last bk., *Letters of Saints*, was publd., 1564. C. was a reformer of immense value to the diffusion of the new religious knowledge.

Cowley, Abraham (1618-67) : Engl. poet ; Spenserian (s.v. Spenser) ; F.R.S. ; buried in the Abbey. Wr. *Poetical Blossoms*, 1633 (the poet, a K.S. at Westminster, blossomed young, it will be observed) ; *Sylva*, 1636 ; and, among other poetic works, 4 bks. of *Davideis*, a sacred epic, 1656. Disappointed, 1663, of the mastership of the Savoy hospital, C. withdrew into the country, and cultivated essay-writing ; ' he praised solitude when he despaired of shining in a court ', said the *Spectator* (q.v.) unkindly ; but his essays *Of Solitude, Of Greatness, Of Obscurity*, and one or 2 more, though much indebted to Montaigne (q.v.), still enjoy and merit esteem. C. was a friend of St. Evremond (q.v.), during his exile in Engld., and probably owed to that genial wit his taste for conversational prose.

Cowper, William (1731-1800) : Engl. poet ; one of the most pathetic and attractive figures in Engl. lit., and a notable link between the schools of Pope and Wordsworth (qq.v.), with a distinct inclination to the latter. ' He broke with Pope, and Johnson, and artifice ', we read (Elton, *Survey Engl. Lit.*, 1780-1830, i, 85) : ' he was inspired by the love of Milton and the love of simplicity, and his real feat is to have found a poetic language that reconciled these two affections '. C. himself wr. of Pope, in *Table Talk*, that he ' made poetry a mere mechanic art ' ; and Ste. Beuve (q.v.), in a *Causerie*, followed by sir L. Stephen (q.v. ; *Hours in a Library*, ii), compared C. with Rousseau (q.v.) for his part ' in bringing about the reaction against the eighteenth-century code of taste and morality '. But there was more in C. than this negative part of reaction ; his style broke away from the classical convention and anticipated in a marked degree the ' natural ' revival of Wordsworth, partly because of his training on the Engl. Bible, partly because of his untaught sensibilities, and partly because, feeling so deeply, he instinctively rejected the adventitious aid of ornament. His unadorned language was emotional, because emotion was his fare in daily life. He was 6 years old when his mother died, and he was sent to a school (1737-8) where he was cruelly bullied. Take, in connection with that experience, his lines composed, 1790, *On the Receipt of My Mother's Picture out of Norfolk* :

Oh, that those lips had language ! Life has pass'd
With me but roughly since I heard thee last. . .
Where once we dwelt our name is heard no more,
Children not thine have trod my nursery floor,

and so on ; plainly, we have here Pope's metre married to an exceptional power in the expression of natural emotion.

C.'s biography must be sought from other records, but 2 facts in it are essential to an understanding of his poetry : (1) his religion, and (2) his madness. They are not necessarily synonyms, though each deepened and intensified the other, and he lived his life on a broken wing. 'His talent', says Taine (q.v. ; *Engl. Lit.*, E. T., bk. iv. ch. ii), 'is but the picture of his character, and his poems but the echo of his life. Affectionate, full of freedom and innocent raillery, with a natural and charming imagination, a graceful fancy, an exquisite delicacy, and so unhappy ! He was one of those to whom women devote themselves, whom they love maternally, first by compassion, then by attraction. He smiled as well as he could, but with effort ; it was the smile of a sick man who knows himself incurable, and tries to forget it for an instant, at least to make others forget it. Poor, charming soul, perishing like a frail flower : the world's temperature was too rough for it ; and the moral law, which should have supported it, tore it with its thorns'. Add to this the pet hares, the garden, the country walks and fireside talks, with which he filled his waking life, and we are ready to read his poetry in the spirit in which it was conceived, as the innocent recreation of a mind distracted by terrors self-evolved. (See, too, s.v. John Newton).

This poetry included *The Task* (in 6 bks. ; bk. i, 'The Sofa ' : lady Austen, a friend, had suggested 'anything' as the subject of a poem, 'this sofa, for example'; and C., accepting 'the task', wr. these 6 bks. of blank verse on domestic, social, and moral topics) ; *The Loss of the Royal George ; Alexander Selkirk ; The Diverting History of John Gilpin ; On a Spaniel Called Beau ; The Castaway*, etc., and a transln. of Homer (q.v.) 1784-91. How famous some of these poems are may be judged by the citation of a few verses, which have passed into current speech :

'I am monarch of all I survey '.
'Toll for the Brave '!
'God made the country, and man made the town '.
'England, with all thy faults, I love thee still ',
'There is a public mischief in your mirth '.
'There is a pleasure in poetic pains '.
'I knew at least one hare that had a friend '.
'He is the freeman whom the truth makes free'.

To these may be added almost the whole of *John Gilpin*, and those pathetic lines from *The Castaway*, which seem to summarize C.'s own experience :

When, snatch'd from all effectual aid,
  We perish'd, each alone ;
But I beneath a rougher sea,
  And whelm'd in deeper gulfs than he.

And, then, there are C.'s letters, 'I live to write letters ', he said on one occasion to a cousin ; and, though he lived to better purpose to write poetry of great moment, his remark is true in a sense of the long, dark period of his life from his 32nd to his 70th year, when successive attacks of religious and nervous melancholia rendered him practically unfit for direct human intercourse. It is true in the further sense that his correspondence remains as a particularly charming memorial of a man whose genial brain was liable to so cruel a disease. Take, for instance, the following extract from a letter to the rev. Wm. Unwin :

' Alas ! what can I do with my wit ? I have not enough to do great things with, and these little things are so fugitive, that while a man catches at a subject, he is only filling his hand with smoke. I must do with it as I do with my linnet ; I keep him for the most part in a cage, but now and then set open the door, that he may whisk about the room a little, and then shut him up again '.

Poor 'whisking wit', poised on a linnet's flight : C.'s ready sympathy with tame, shy things is one of his delightful characteristics. We must not expand these extracts from the lit. remains of a poet, across whose work, as prof. Courthope reminds us, was cast the shadow of the coming individualism in Engld. C., writes prof. Elton (*op. cit.*, 99), ' seems like one of those half-forgotten old water-colour masters of exquisite line, in the dim blue of whose English low skies and blotted distances there is not much sunlight, and whom it may not be best to hang among the Turners ' ; and perhaps we may seek the real C. in a passage from bk. iii of *The Task* :

'I was a stricken deer that left the herd
Long since ; with many an arrow deep infixed
My panting side was charged, when I withdrew
To seek a tranquil death in distant shades.
There was I found by One who had himself
Been hurt by the archers. In his side he bore,
And in his hands and foot, the cruel scars.
With gentle force soliciting the darts,
He drew them forth, and healed and bade me
   live.
Since then, with few associates, in remote
And silent woods I wander, far from those
My former partners of the peopled scene ;
With few associates, and not wishing more.
Here much I ruminate, as much I may,
With other views of men and manners now
Than once, and others of a life to come '.

Crabbe, George (1754-1832) : Engl. poet ; a little older, it will be seen, than Wordsworth (b. 1770), Scott (1771) and Coleridge (1772), and very definitely separated from the romantic (s.v. Romance) approach to phenomena which they represent. Yet he was moved by new ideas to the extent of hearing the call of the countryside : ' so far as Wordsworth and his followers represented the reaction from the artificial to a love of unsophisticated nature, Crabbe is entirely at one with them ' (sir L. Stephen, q.v., *Hours in a Library*) ; and ' he prepared the way for a poet like Wordsworth, who, endowed with a keener sensibility, added lyrism to realism ' (R. Huchon, *George Crabbe and his Times*, E.T., 1907 ; a standard work). But all authorities agree with the view, expressed in the epigram of Horace Smith (q.v. ; joint-author of *Rejected Addresses*), that C. was ' a Pope in worsted stockings ' : in other words, that, taking Pope (q.v.) as his model in versification (though much more diffuse in his employment of the heroic couplet), C. applied Pope's method to sights and scenes which necessarily transgressed, when depicted, the proprieties of the code of the 18th cent. One more quotation may be permitted. Hazlitt (q.v.), a very competent critic, writing while C. was still alive, observed that ' almost all his characters are tired of their lives, and you heartily wish them dead. Crabbe is too much of the parish beadle, and overseer of the country poor. He collects all the petty views of the human heart and superintends, as in a panopticon, a select circle of rural malefactors. With him there are but two moral categories, riches and poverty, authority and dependence. His parish ethics are the very worst model for a state : anything more degrading and helpless cannot well be imagined '. The blame is somewhat overstated, but C.'s pessimism and realism, as a painter of contemporary country life, and his equal distance from the cultivated conventions of Pope and Goldsmith, as from the primary values of the lake poets, may be illustrated from every page of his works. (These include, in an excellent edn. by the late sir A. W. Ward (d. 1924 ; Cambridge, 3 vols., 1905) : *The Village*, 2 bks., 1783 ; *The Borough*, 1810 ; *Tales*, 1812 ; *Tales of the Hall*, 1819 ; *Works*, 7 vols., Murray, 1820, and often reprinted). C.'s rejection of both rustic illusions may be judged by a few verses from *The Village* (i, 40-8) :

But, when amid such pleasing scenes I trace
The poor laborious natives to the place,
And see the mid-day sun, with fervid ray,
On their bare heads and dewy temples play ;
While some, with feebler heads and fainter
    hearts,
Deplore their fortune, yet sustain their parts,
Then shall I dare these real ills to hide
In tinsel trappings of poetic pride ?

From this challenge there was no appeal. These peasants, sweating in public beneath the glare of the noon-day sun, were the first of a long train of witnesses, summoned by C. from the fields and lanes, to rebuke the meretricious pictures of rural peace and rustic innocence which the idea of the country had been employed by town-wits to evoke. C. stands between the old and the new—between nature ' to advantage dressed ' by Pope, and nature interpreted by Wordsworth,—in an almost grim isolation. He rejected the picture of the countryside, carefully swept and garnished for delicate visitors by the idealists of the passing generation, and his positive temperament did not hold the imaginative sympathy which was beginning to re-interpret the real. C. was a botanist who wr. poetry, and a clergyman who wr. satire ; and this imperfection of vision is reflected in the stockiness of his verse.

Craik, Dinah Maria (1826-87) : Engl. novelist ; *née* Mulock ; m., 1864, George Lillie Craik, a partner in Macmillan's publishing business, and brother to right hon. sir Henry Craik (b. 1846), author of *Life of Swift*, *Life of Clarendon*, *Engl. Prose Selections*, etc. Mrs. C.'s chief and rightly famous bk. was *John Halifax, Gentleman*, 1857, which, despite changed conditions, is not likely to lose its classic vogue. It caught the attention of the mid-19th cent. at an interesting stage, to which the Great Exhibition, 1851, in Hyde Park, gave characteristic expression. The industrious apprentice who married his master's daughter, and, succeeding to the headship of the factory, taught a lesson of self-reliance and business management to men older and more highly-born than himself, and impressed the simple virtues of his Christian principles on

underpaid workmen and overfed aristocrats alike, was a type which seized the imagination of readers in all classes,—employed or employers. It arrested in striking form a phase of the industrial movement, and invoked a solution by *character*, which appealed to the sympathy of a generation which read with avidity the treatise on *Character* (with a capital C) by the grave and suave doctor, Samuel Smiles (q.v.). That much of the fault lay at the employers ' doors and that the whole remedy was not in the hands of the employed, was left for writers like Dickens and Mrs. Gaskell (qq.v.) to enforce.

Cramer, -i. Johann Andreas (1723-88) : Germ. poet and publicist ; a member of Gottsched's (q.v.) circle at Leipsic, and was associated with the production of the *Bremer Beiträge* (q.v.). Wr. odes, lyrics, and a verse-transln. of the Psalms. Warmly defended the poetic lead of Klopstock (q.v.) in his paper ' The Northern Spectator' (*Aufseher*), one of the many Addisonian reviews.

    -ii. Karl Friedrich (1752-1807) : Germ. publicist ; son of the above ; prof. of philology at Kiel univ., but was inhibited, 1794, on account of his sympathy with the Fr. Revolutionaries. Went to Paris. Wr. miscellaneously ; his most notable bks. were *Klopstock* and *A Paris Diary*.

Crashaw, Richard (1612-49) : Engl. poet. Wr. *Steps to the Temple*, 1646, in the anon. pref. to which C. was described as ' Herbert's second, but equal ' (see s.v. G. Herbert). It is on the spiritual side that he was indebted to the author of *The Temple*, but C. did not remain in the Anglican communion ; he entered the Church of Rome, and died at Loretto. He was an accomplished Span. and Ital. scholar, deriving mysticism (q.v.) from Spain and Marinism (s.v. Marino) from Italy. C. did not live long enough to give full proof of his powers, which astonish at times by the strength, even to extravagance, of their fervour. He is classified among the metaphysical (q.v.) poets, of whom Donne (q.v.) is the chief, but it was the deeper and more difficult hinterland of thought rather than of expression which C. sought in the loneliness of his religious mood ; and, though his conceits (q.v.) and obscurities are almost universal, they are combined with a warmth of feeling and a lyrical capacity which constantly surprise and attract.

Creasy, Edward Shepherd (1812-78) : Engl. historian ; knt., 1860 ; wr. *Fifteen Decisive Battles of the World*, 1852.

Crébillon, de, -i. Prosper Jolyot (1674-1762) : Fr. tragic dramatist. Wr. *Idoménée*, 1703 ; *Atrée et Thyeste*, 1707 ; *Electre*, 1708 ; *Rhadamiste et Zénobie* (commonly regarded as his masterpiece), 1711 ; and continued composing till quite late in life. In his last years C. was set up by enthusiastic partisans, including mme. de Pompadour, the mistress of king Louis xv, as a rival to Voltaire (q.v.), and he acquitted himself creditably in the competition of tragedies. Opinions vary considerably as to the merit of C.'s plays. Some critics place them as low as the flat, invertebrate tragedies of unassailable correctness by Pradon, Campistron (qq.v.) and others, who followed in the wake of Racine (q.v.), pointing out that C.

depended for his effects on conventional and mechanical devices, such as the *incognito*. Some give him a place between Corneille and Hugo (qq.v.), or recognize, at least, that his poetic power was but little inferior to that of those masters. The truth probably is, that by no genius smaller than Racine's, and in no epoch other than Racine's, was the classical stage-play likely to approve itself as at the same time a moving human drama. Certain conditions met in Racine which were less favourably disposed for C.

-ii. **Claude Prosper Jolyot** (1707-77) : Fr. novelist ; son of above. Wr. *Contes dialogués*, in the school of philosophical fiction, or, more correctly, of fiction which served like ends to those of the *philosophes* (q.v.) : C.'s admirable wit in narrative was marred by salaciousness of taste.

Creighton, Mandell (1843-1901) : Engl. divine ; historian ; bp. of London, 1897. Wr *History of the Papacy* (vols. i, ii, 1882 ; iii, iv, 1887 ; v, 1894), and other works.

Crembisceni, Giovanni Mario (1663-1728) : It. man of letters ; joint founder with Gravina (q.v.) of the Roman Academy of Arcadia (q.v.), 1690, of which C. became 'guardian' (*custode*) and publd. the transactions. He was as little qualified by his poetry as any of the founders, but he wr., 1698, an *Istoria del Volgar Poesia*, part of which is described by Saintsbury (*Hist. Crit.*, ii, 542) as 'a really valuable literary encyclopedia'.

Cretin, Guillaume (15th cent. ; d. c. 1525) : Fr. poet ; verse-historiographer to king Francis i ; virtual leader of the school of aureate artificiality known as the *Rhétoriqueurs* (q.v.) ; even Marot the younger designating C. as the 'sovereign poet'. A *rondeau* ascribed by Rabelais (q.v.) to the 'old French poet', Raminagrobis (*Pantagruel*, iii, 21), was actually written by C., and he enjoyed sufficient reputation for that poem to be used in order to satirize the whole crowd of affected poetasters. C., whose skill in weaving *ballades, chantsroyaux*, and other 'Epiceries', to use the epithet of the Pleiad (q.v.), was not conspicuously superior to that of Molinet, Meschinot (qq.v.) and the rest, has similarly earned the doubtful distinction of lending his name to CRETINISM, as a generic descriptive epithet of the mode. He stands as the synonym of that misplaced ingenuity in arranging rhymes and complicating metres which was brought to an 'art and science' in 3 or 4 textbooks of the age, and which is recognized to-day as the last cry of expiring medievalism when the dawn of the Renaissance broke in France.

Creutz, Filip (1729-85) : Swed. poet ; Finlander by birth ; count by rank. Wr. elegies and idylls, perfect in craftsmanship and impeccable in expression, but with too much of the Watteau-shepherdess and Dresden-china delicacy about them. Still, as the importer of Fr. Arcadian poetry into the North, C. has a distinct place, and enjoyed in his own day a very considerable reputation.

Creuz, Friedrich Karl Kasimir (1724-70) : Germ. poet. His works were written in obedience to the Gottsched (q.v.) code, and included a tragedy *The Dying Seneca*, 1754, recalling by more than its title the master's 'dying Cato'.

Creuzer, Georg Friedrich (1771-1858) : Germ. philologer. Wr., 1810-12, *Symbolik und Mythologie der alten Völker*, 4 vols., a very valuable study of the outward and inner religious life of the ancient, esp. the Gk. and Ital., world ; new edns., 1819-21, and 1837-43. C.'s views on the mystic element in Gk. myth were the object of a violent attack by Voss (q.v.).

Crighton, James (1560-85) : Engl. scholar ; surnamed 'The Admirable' by sir Thos. Urquhart (q.v.), who wr. an account of C.'s career, 1652. It was a career, closed at Mantua in a duel, of promise rather than performance in philosophic disputation and odes to contemporary scholars. C. travelled to Paris, Genoa, Venice, where Aldo Manuzio (q.v.) entertained him, and other centres of learning, and is said to have been master of 12 languages.

Cristo Crucificado, A (Span.) : 'To Christ Crucified' ; title of an anon. sonnet of the late 16th cent., variously attributed to St Theresa, Ignatius Loyola, qq.v., and others, but of uncertain authorship. It is inspired by deep religious fervour, expressed in beautiful language.

Crocus, Cornelius (c. 1500-58) : Dutch Latinist. Wr. Lat. plays, notably *Joseph*, according to the fashion of his days ; but differed from Volder (q.v.) in his loyalty to the Church of Rome, and in a certain austerity of outlook which reacted on his dramatic style.

Croker, John Wilson (1780-1857) : Engl. (Irish) critic ; politician, in which capacity he invented the party-name 'Conservative', 1830. C. was a busy writer, who hit hard and was sometimes hit back. (See Macaulay, q.v., on C.'s edn. of Boswell's *Life of Johnson* ; *Edinburgh Review*, Sept., 1831 ; included in Macaulay's *Essays*) ; a regular contributor to the *Quarterly Review*, and the author, 1818, of the famous review of the *Endymion* of Keats (q.v.), the effects of which on the sensitive poet were much exaggerated.

Cronegk, von, Johann Friedrich (1731-58) : Germ. playwright. Friend of Lessing (q.v.) at Leipsic. Wr. classical tragedy, *Codrus*.

Cronica (Span.) : 'Chronicle' ; the generic term for early works in Span. historiography. There was an industrious composition of chronicles from the 13th cent. downwards in Castile ; and, though there is some obscurity in the relation of these anon. writings, the following order can be traced : i, *Cronica general*, commonly described as *primera* (the first), inaugurated, c. 1260-68, by king Alfonso x (q.v.), surnamed the Wise ; ii, *Cronica general de 1344*, commonly described as *segunda* (the second), and consisting of a revision, with additions, of the *primera* ; iii, a new revision, now not extant ; iv, derived from iii, the *tercera* (third) *Cronica general*, dating from about the beginning of the 15th cent. Another derivative of iii was the *Cronica de Castilla*, from which was derived in turn the *Cronica particular del Cid*, first publd. in 1512, but composed in the previous cent. To the same (15th) cent. belongs the *Cronica* 'of his Most Serene Majesty Don John the Second of his name', first printed in 1517. This valuable work was formerly ascribed to Juan de Mena (q.v.), but later researches have compelled the rejection of this ascription in favour of a multiple authorship, based on the plan of Alvar Garcia de Santa Maria (q.v.), a converted Jew, who died in 1460. The gradual improvement in Span. prose and in the historian's art is traceable in the development of these *Cronica*, of which class of writing Lopez de Ayala (q.v.) was a conspicuous exponent in the 14th cent.

The term *cronica* was extended to cover an immense variety of narrative works, not of general hist. interest. Personal memoirs, chivalric exploits, and even fictitious events were narrated in the chronicle-form, which constituted a definite class of literary activity in Spain during the early centuries, till *c*.1500. 'These old Spanish chronicles', writes Ticknor (i, 194), 'whether they have their foundations in truth or in fable, always strike further down than those of any other nation into the deep soil of the popular feeling and character. The old Spanish loyalty, the old Spanish religious faith, as both were formed and nourished in the long periods of national trial and suffering, are constantly coming out. . . In this vast, rich mass of chronicles, containing such a body of antiquities, traditions, and fables, as has been offered to no other people, we are constantly discovering, not only the materials from which were drawn a multitude of the old Spanish ballads, plays, and romances, but also a mine which has been unceasingly wrought by the rest of Europe for similar purposes, and still remains unexhausted'.

Croxall, Samuel (*c.* 1690-1752): Engl. divine; misc. writer. Wr., 1713-4, 2 verse-satires on the earl of Oxford's administration, entitled respectively *An Original Canto of Spencer : Design'd as Part of his Fairy Queen, but never printed, Now made Publick by Nestor Ironside, Esq.*, and *Another Original Canto*, etc., in the Spenserian stanza; collaborated with sir S. Garth (q.v.) in a transln. of Ovid, *Metamorphoses*; wr. popular paraphrase of *The Song of Solomon* under the name of *The Fair Circassian*, 1720; a version of Æsop, 1722; and other works. Dr. Harko G. de Maar, in a *Hist. of Modern Engl. Romanticism*, i, 85 (Oxford, 1924), says : 'A considerable part of the historic significance that has been ascribed to Shenstone and James Thomson (see s.vv.) should be transferred to Samuel Croxall', whom he describes as 'essentially one of the romantics of an unromantic time. . . . If Croxall succumbed to the popularity of Pope, he had at least shown that he knew how to admire the greatness of romantic poetry, to reproduce it in faint but faithful imitation, and to make it admired by the public'. But C.'s ingredients, it may be submitted, were (1) political satire and (2) provocative sensuousness, and his Spenserian stanza covered a multitude of faults.

Cubillo, Alvaro (17th cent.) : Span. dramatist; is said to have written more than 100 plays. The best among those that have survived are *las Muñecas* (the dolls) *de Marisla, la perfecta Casada* (wife), and *el Señor de Noches buenas* (good nights), which was adapted by T. Corneille (q.v.) in his *la Comtesse d'Orgueil*.

Cudworth, Ralph (1617-88): Engl. scholar; divine; prof. of Hebr. at Cambridge Univ.

from 1645. Wr. *The True Intellectual System of the Universe*, 1678, and a treatise on *Eternal and Immutable Morality*, publd. posth. ; contemporary with Henry More (q.v.), and shared with him the reputation of the Cambridge Platonists of the 17th cent. They were 'Plotinists rather than Platonists', said Coleridge (q.v.); but the distinction must not detain us here, save to note that C. was instrumental in introducing Engl. thought to Ital. interpreters (such as Pico della Mirandola, q.v.), of neo-Platonic philosophy. Martineau's (q.v.) *Types of Ethical Theory* refers at some length to C., whom Dryden (q.v.) criticized.

Cueva, de la, Juan (16th cent. ; d. *c.* 1610) : Span. dramatic poet; the facts of his biography are obscure, except that he attended the school of Mal Lara (q.v.) at Seville, and visited the New World and the Canary Isles. C.'s plays were written to the pattern of his own theories of poetics, contained in his *Exemplar poetico*, 1605, consisting of 3 epistles in Dante's measure of *terza-rima* (q.v.). The 3rd of these epistles commends the choice of dramatic subjects from Span. national history, and the restriction of the number of acts in a play. In both matters C. had been anticipated (see s.v. Carvajal) ; but the enunciation of a principle may be an innovation, whereas practice may be merely experiment ; and C. is properly held to have summoned the drama in Spain to the lines which it was to follow in future master-hands. The 'comedy of the cloak and sword' (see s.v. Capa) was distinctly C.'s invention, though the mailed warrior of Span. history may have trod the stage before he wr. C.'s subjects, accordingly, were taken from the Infants (i.q., princes) of Lara, Bernardo del Carpio, the Sack of Rome (by the emperor Charles v), etc., and were written in various metres ; a vol. was printed in 1583. His play, 'The Slanderer' (*Infamador*) introduced, or adumbrated, the type of libertine afterwards immortalized as Don Juan (see s.v. Molina). As poet, C. is less notable ; he essayed an heroic epopee, 'The Conquest of Bélica', 1603, reminiscent of Tasso (q.v.), but far from successful, and publd. a bk. of poems (*Obras*, works), 1582, which contains but little of permanent interest.

Cujas, Jacques (1522-90) : Fr. jurist ; 'the real juristic coryphæus of the century' (*Great Jurists of the World*, Murray, 82). C., like Alciati (q.v.), in the previous generation, led a wandering life and left a miscellaneous legacy, appropriate to the disturbed public conditions of the day and to the lack of system in juristic study. Its founders in the 16th cent. were more concerned to sift the foundations than to elaborate the structure. But C., 'more than any other single investigator, contributed to the realization of this object. His voluminous publications—a magnificent array of mighty tomes—were nearly all devoted to the exegetic study of the sources' (*ibid.*). He laicized the study of the law, adds the same authority, and thus his liberal and humanistic labours belong to the same class and category as those of Montaigne and Erasmus (qq.v.). The chief seats of C.'s activity as prof. were at Bourges and Valence, where his pupils included Joseph

Scaliger (q.v.), whose life he saved on St. Bartholomew's day, 24 Aug., 1572.

Culteranismo, Cultismo (Span.): The practice of *estilo culto*, or cultivated style, appealing to learned readers, and associated with Gongora (q.v.); hence also called Gongorism. The affectation enjoyed considerable vogue in Spain in the 17th cent., and was responsible for much obscurity and folly. (See, too, s.vv., Marino, Conceits, Euphuism).

Curzon, George Nathaniel (1859-1925): Engl. statesman; traveller; historian; fifth baron Scarsdale; created marquess Curzon of Kedleston, 1921; K.G.; viceroy of India, 1899-1905; Romanes lecturer, Oxford, 1907, and chancellor of the univ., 1907, till his death (see s.v. Milner). Wr., among other works founded on his travels and experience, *Problems of the Far East*, 1894; *Subjects of the Day*, 1915; *Tales of Travel*, 1923. C.'s life has still to be written; a contribution was made towards it by sir Ian Malcolm in the *Quarterly Review*, July, 1925.

Czech, Svatopluk (1846-1908): Czech poet; much influenced in his youth by Byron (q.v.); wr. epics, *Europe* and *Slavia*, lyrical *Morning Songs* and other vols. of verse; epics of hist. and contemporary Czech life, and satiric romances of journeys, to the moon, and to the 15th cent., as well as misc. works, including a large amount of journalism.

Czech Literature: Czecho-Slovakia is a new country, carved into independent existence after the Great War (1914-18), and its lit. is still to be written. A fair beginning has been made, by Karel Čapek, among others, whose play, *R.U.R.*, was successfully staged in London, in 1923. But he and the rest of the young writers whom the new republic is encouraging to create a national art and lit. in the old Czech tongue, are outside the temporal limits of the present vol.; and it is for the sake of former beginnings, interrupted by political causes, that C.L. claims hist. recognition among the literatures of Europe. J. A. Komenský (q.v.; Comenius), for example, whose name has been given to the library of pedagogy at Leipsic, who is the subject of a bk. by prof. S. S. Laurie, of Cambridge, and whom R. H. Quick, another Cambridge teacher, included in his *Educational Reformers*, belongs by birth and faith to the story of C.L. He was expelled from his native country, Moravia (Bohemia), 1628, thus, as Michelet (q.v.) said, losing his country and finding his country, which was the world. He wandered through that larger fatherland, making a temporary home in Poland, Germany, Sweden, Engld. (1641-42), Hungary and Holland, where he died in 1670; but always the exile's heart was in his own land. ' He was the last great author and spiritual leader of the Czech people in the dark period when it lost its independence. As he never abandoned the hope that it would recover the independence again, he prepared the way for its happier future, writing books in which he laid the foundations for the better education of those generations which were to come' (F. Chudoba, *Short Survey of Czech Lit.*, 1924; p. 55). So much so, that, in 1650, in the *Bequest of the Dying Mother of the Unity of Brethren*—the Bohemian Brethren, of whom Komenský

was the last bp.,—he wr.: ' Thee, Czech and Moravian nation, beloved country, I cannot forget. I, too, believe before God, that, after the passing of the storms of wrath, brought down upon our heads by our sins, the rule over thine own possessions shall return to thee again, O Czech people'! These words were quoted by Masaryk, himself a man of letters, in his first message to the National Assembly of the new republic (1918), in order to emphasize the continuity of Czecho-Slovakian history. So, Petrarch (q.v.) linked up the tribuneship of Rienzi with Cicero, or (perhaps, a more auspicious comparison), so Petrarch's ' Ode to Italy ' inspired the makers of united Italy in the 19th cent.

If we go backward from Komenský, we find the new transln. of the Bible, effected (New Testament) by Jan Blahoslav (1523-71), bp. of the Moravian Brethren, in 1564, and (Old Testament) by 9 scholars belonging to the group. This *Bible of Kralice*, so-called from the name of the Moravian village where it was secretly printed, 'influenced the best Czech authors, especially at the time of the National Revival, when they had to learn from older books how to use their mother-tongue correctly, because they could not learn it either in the Germanized schools or in the Germanized society' (Chudoba, *op. cit.*, 47. ' Obliti sunt Romae lingua loquier Latina '). If we go further back, we come to the honoured name of the virtual founder of the Unity of the Brethren, Petr Chelčický (c. 1390-c. 1460), author of ' The Net of the True Faith ', a direct precursor in thought of Tolstoi (q.v.), ' who was astonished to find from a Russian translation of *The Net of the True Faith* that this Czech peasant had preached to his obstinate countrymen the same ideas which he himself disseminated in Russia 450 years after ' (*ibid.*, 38). And yet a few years earlier still, we note that Jan Hus (1370-1415) and Jerome of Prague were likewise Czechs of Bohemia.

Going forward from the epoch of Komenský, we observe that the *Societas Scientiarum Bohemica* dates from 1773, and that, though it availed itself at first of the official languages, Latin and German, it is continuous with the Czech society using the Czech speech at the present day. A little later, we reach the major name of Josef Dobrovský (q.v.), an eminent native philologist, whose *Czech Grammar* (1809) and *Hist. of the Older Czech Lit.* (1818) helped immensely to rebuild ancient foundations. Josef Jungmann (1773-1847) continued the same studies, with his transln. of *Paradise Lost* (1811), and his 5-vol. Czech-Germ. *Dict.*, 1834-39. These pioneers of the Revival were followed by its poets, of whom Jan Kollar (q.v.), 1793-1852, was the first. Of the same generation was Karel Mácha (q.v.), 1810-36, who is counted among the Byronists of the Continent, and who, like Byron, young, was also, like Byron, great. He composed a lyrical epopee called ' May ', and the same title was chosen for a miscellany by a group of young Czech poets in the mid-19th cent., who are known as the Generation of May, and whose chief member was Jan Neruda (q.v.), 1834-91. With the mention of two notable names— J. Vrchlický (1853-1912; poet, critic, and translr., whose work was on a European scale and J. V. Sládek (1845-1912); see s.vv.,—we must bring this brief record to a close, for we must not write of living authors, even in the instance of a nation which has yet to write its national lit. C.L. enters the European comity at a good time, and with fine traditions and hopes to sustain it.

D

Dach, Simon (1605-59): Germ. poet; professor of poetry at Königsberg (q.v.) from 1639, where he was the centre of a little group of writers in the vein of the revival heralded by Opitz (q.v.). D.'s own contributions, though considerable, were composed in a minor key, and he has been contrasted with Fleming (q.v.), his contemporary, as the poet of death rather than of life. But the native inspiration of D. and his circle gave better effect to the Opitz reforms than these had hitherto enjoyed.

Dacier, Anne Lefèvre (1654-1720): Fr. scholar; translr. of Homer. Mme D. came of scholarly stock; her father, Tanaquil Faber (1615-72) was as learned as he was poor, and made an exiguous income by his edns. of Gk. and Lat. authors; her husband, André Dacier (1651-1722) was a member of the recently-founded Fr. Academy (q.v.), and likewise editor and translr.; a Fr. version of Horace was the joint work of himself and his wife. Mme. D.'s Fr. prose rendering of Homer is praised as her masterpiece among much excellent work: it was utilized by La Motte (q.v.) for his verse-adaptation of the *Iliad*. Mme. D., who was a well-known figure in the literary life of Paris in the *grand siècle*, was one of the editors of the famous Delphin Classics (q.v.).

Da Costa, Isaac (1798-1860): Dutch poet; of Port.-Jew. (Sephardic) descent; his mother, Rebecca Ricardo, was connected with the family of the Engl. economist of that surname. Da C. studied under and was befriended by Bilderdijk (q.v.), and their pleasant intercourse and mutual attraction persisted into the period when the pupil began to influence the master. Da C. did not follow Bilderdijk in his sympathy with the philosophy of Hobbes (q.v.) or his admiration of the era of kings Louis xiv and xv, but developed a more romantic leaning to the schools of Camoens, Tasso, Herder and Lamartine (qq.v.). Wr. tragedies after Æschylus (*Persæ*, 1816; *Prometheus*, 1820); warriors' songs (1826); *Five-and-twenty Years : a Song* (1840; frequently reprinted); *Hagar* (1847); and much patriotic verse and prose; also a considerable quantity of religious works; an appreciation (1859) of Bilderdijk as 'man and poet', and a complete edn. of his poems; also addresses on poetical and social topics; also (1848-49) a valuable monograph on *Israel and the Gentiles*; *a Survey of the History of the Jews till our own times*, republd., 1873. An 8th edn. of Da C.'s complete poetical works was issued at Leyden in 3 vols., 1898; and his correspondence (1830-44) was issued in 3 vols. at Amsterdam, 1872-76.

Daguesseau, Henri-François (1668-1751): Fr. orator; held legal office of chancellor in the *parlement*; was exiled, 1718, recalled, 1720, exiled again, 1722, and did not resume the seals till 1737. It fell to D. to grant the *privilège* for the issue of the *Encyclopédie* (s.v. Encyclopedia). D. seems to have been a singularly pure and mild type of reformer, whose chief crime was his opposition to the wild financial schemes of J. Law (q.v.). D.'s experience acted as a warning to similar advocates of moderate views, and the injustice of his persecution embittered the conflict between authority and reform in the generation before the Fr. Revolution. D.'s collected writings were issued posth., 1759-90, and his letters in 1823.

Dahlmann, Friedrich Christoph (1785-1860): Germ. historian; successor to Niebuhr (q.v.); wr. histories of Germany and Denmark.

Dalberg, von, Wolfgang Heribert (1750-1806): Germ. intendant of the court- and national theatre at Mannheim; brother of Karl v. D., ecclesiastical grand-duke of Frankfort. D.'s chief title to fame is his production of the *Räuber* of Schiller, 1781, and the patronage which he gradually extended to the great Germ. dramatic author.

Dalembert (1717-83): Fr. critic and philosopher (the name is also written d'Alembert). D. was a foundling, the illegitimate son of mme. de Tencin (q.v.) and an unknown father, who settled an income on him; christened Jean le Rond by his *bourgeoise* foster-mother. Fortunately, his edu. was adequate to his distinguished talents for lit. and mathematics; and at the early age of 23 he was elected to the Academy of Sciences. He entered the Fr. Academy (q.v.), 1754, and became its perpetual secretary, 1772. In this capacity he won renown, like Fontenelle (q.v.) before him, for his graceful, careful, and elaborate funeral orations on departed members, which gave him congenial occasion for the display of his taste in eulogy and criticism. D.'s disposition seems to have been naturally modest and retiring; he declined, for instance, two lucrative offers, first, to Berlin as president of the Academy of king Fredk. ii (q.v.; and see s.v. Voltaire), and, secondly, to Russia, by invitation of the empress Catherine ii, as tutor to the grand-duke Paul. The same shrinking from publicity is to be observed in D.'s relations with Diderot and the Encyclopedia (qq.v.), by which he earns his place among the *philosophes* (q.v.). D. wr. the preliminary discourse, and many articles for its earlier vols. Among these was one on Geneva, which succeeded by its very moderation in dissatisfying all sections of opinion at once. D.'s love of a quiet life took alarm, and he threw up the job in disgust when the authorities sustained their objections to its publication, which was resumed *consule* (or, rather, *censore*) Malesherbes (q.v.), c. 1770. Late in life, D. joined mlle. de Lespinasse (q.v.) in her home and *salon*.

His personality had considerable attraction, and his name and influence survive the memory of his literary remains.

Dalin, von, Olof (1708-63) : Swed. social writer ; politician. Wr. a Swiftian piece of satire, ' The Tale of a Horse ', in which his country was represented as beridden by successive kings, and adventured also in comic drama and national history. D. was a man of real taste and parts, and contributed considerably to the release of Swed. prose from its old and hampering restrictions ; his main record in lit. is his single-handed conduct for two years (1732-33) of a Swed. imitation of *The Spectator* (q.v.), entitled *Swanska Argus*, which left the pre-existing ' Moral Mercury ' far behind, and the suspension of which is said to have plunged Sweden into national mourning. D. is regarded as the father of modern Swed. lit., with affinities to France and Engld. rather than to Germany.

Damm, Christian Tobias (1699-1778) : Germ. scholar ; schoolmaster in Berlin. Wr. lexicons to and translns. of the works of Homer and Pindar. D. was a believer in the revival of Hellenism, as a 'corrective to the excesses of the Latin Renaissance (see s.v. Humanism), and in this belief he was splendidly supported by his ablest pupil, Winckelmann (q.v.).

Dancourt, Florent Carton (1661-1725) : Fr. actor and comic dramatist ; joined the newly-combined company of the Comédie Française, 1685. Wr. *le Notaire Obligeant*, 1685, *la Désolation des Joueuses*, 1687, *le Chevalier à la Mode*, 1687, *la Lotérie*, 1697, *les Bourgeoises de Qualité*, 1700, *le Galant Jardinier*, 1704, and other plays ; the last two are perhaps the best. D.'s personages ring true, and he was eminently successful in depicting on the stage the shifting characters of the new moneyed *bourgeoisie*, which began to be important in his day.

Danès, Pierre (1497-1577) : Fr. Hellenist ; one of the first two Fr. readers in Gk. in the Corporation (q.v.) of the Royal Readers. Loyola, Calvin, and possibly, Rabelais (qq.v.) were among his pupils.

Dangeau, marquis de, Philippe de Courcillon (1638-1720) : Fr. memoirist. Lived at the court of king Louis xiv, and wr. a detailed chronicle of the royal household and habits, of considerable social value, but of poor literary merit, and marred by an excess of Bourbon hero-worship which may have stimulated the literary faculty of the duc de St.-Simon (q.v.).

Daniel, Samuel (1562-1619) : Engl. poet ; contemporary of Campion (q.v.), with whom he disputed successfully, 1602, in favour of rhyme ; wr. a prose history of Engld., and Masques for the court. Spenser (q.v.) and others were warm admirers of D.'s poetry, which included a sonnet-sequence, *Delia*, 1592 ; a tragedy, *Cleopatra*, 1594, and *Musophilus*, or a defence of learning, 1595.

Dante Alighieri (1265-1321) : It. divine poet ; the first, and in some respects greatest, single figure in the lit. of modern Europe. D. was born at Florence of good stock ; studied philosophy and rhetoric (i.q. Lat. lit.) under Brunetto (died, 1294), from whom he acquired his devotion to Virgil (q.v.) ; visited Bologna and Padua for such natural philosophy as was available ; read deeply in the Church Fathers and the Scholastics ; practised Troubadour poetry with Guinicelli (q.v.) and others ; likewise painting and music ; joined trade-guild to qualify for municipal office ; was employed on various embassies, and attained (1300) to rank of prior of Florence. This appointment led to D.'s material undoing. The Guelf-Ghibelline (q.v.) struggle, in which the imperial Hohenstaufen dynasty had been wiped out at Benevento in 1265, was repeated in bitter party conflicts and family feuds in Tuscan cities ; an outbreak of special virulence occurred in Florence at this epoch, and pope Boniface viii, the most extreme champion of papal claims, intervened in 1302. D. was a victim of the consequent proscription, and was sentenced to exile for life. He reserved for Boniface and his successor the third circle in the eighth trench of Hell (*Inferno*, xix) ; but this refinement of poetic vengeance did not console the exile for his raw patriotic sore and actual physical suffering. The iron entered his soul. It was his least discomfort to learn ' how savoureth of salt The bread of others, and how hard a road The going down and up another's stair ' (*Paradiso*, xvii, 58-60), when he was waiting, e.g., on Can Grande della Scala, captain of the Ghibelline league at Verona ; his main preoccupation was political : the real key to D.'s life and writings is his passion for Italy (' servile Italy, grief's hostelry ! A ship without a pilot in great tempest ' ! *Purgatorio*, vi, 76-7) ; his intense, invincible ambition was to spread the peace of just government across the windy storm of anarchy and faction, and to build on the ruins of politics a true city of God, in which Cæsar should rule his temporalities in the pattern of the divine economy.

D.'s ideal of a united Italy was not realized till the 19th cent., but his urgent, practical belief in it irradiated for Ital. patriots the weary centuries between. He lived to write the world-epic of the human soul, rising through love to the contemplation of Heaven ; but he is first and for ever Italy's poet ; her second Virgil, as he would wish to be known : quite literally, in an old phrase, he created the utterance of her lips. As he was born on the confines of the Middle Ages, so he delivered his message in the consecrated forms of that era : allegory, allusion, personification, are freely employed and extended ; from the first vision of *Inferno* i, to the last vision of *Paradiso* xxxiii, we are rapt in a maze of symbolism ; there is magic even in the number of the stanzas ($33 \times 3 + 1$), and a mystic meaning in each personal experience. D.'s ripe knowledge of philosophy, theology, astronomy, zoology, geography, natural science, antiquity, history and politics, was poured out through old-fashioned vessels, and was linked by imagined bonds to his own spiritual changes.

Thus, D. is often difficult to read, and a whole library of bks. has been written by commentators and interpreters. We may take his simplest writings first. There was, i, the *de Vulgari Eloquentia*, a Lat. treatise on the ' vulgar tongue ', which, in the early morning of its foliation in Tuscany, D. claimed and approved as ' illustrious '. Nationally, he justified abundantly his choice of the vernacular for his epic poem ; and, philologically, amid much else of value, he invented the famous distinction between the *langues d'oïl*, *d'oc*, and *de si* (qq.v.). Saintsbury (*Hist. Crit.*, i, 431), whose ch. on ' Dante ' should be consulted, calls this work ' of intrinsic importance, on a line with that of the very greatest critical documents of all history '. There was, ii, *de Monarchia*, a Lat. treatise which should be read with D.'s letter (*c.* 1309) ' to all the kings in Italy, senators, dukes, and peoples ', and which was composed in the (vain) hope that emperor Henry vii would prove the regenerator and reconciler. In this great imperalist manifesto, D. proved on two lines of argument the immediate responsibility of the emperor to God, without the intervention of the pope ; first, by demolishing the papal pretensions, and secondly by direct proof. ' Even if Dante had written no other work than the *de Monarchia*, it would be hard to refrain from admiration of the mind, which struck out with such force and lucidity the line of argument, which was to remain for centuries the one effectual answer to all claims of the right of papal or clerical inferference with the freedom of secular governments. By its intellectual grasp and breadth of treatment, the *de Monarchia*, despite its scholastic character, is raised far above the great majority of controversial treatises on the same subject ' (Figgis, *The Divine Right of Kings*, 2nd edn. 60). There were, iii, the Ital. *Convito*, or Symposium, with verses interspersed, on themes of virtue and love ; and, iv, the *Canzoniere* (songs), belonging to the poet's youth, in the Cavalcanti and troubadouring period. We come next to the supremely great works : the *Vita Nuova*, or new life, and the *Commedia*, or Comedy, which posterity agreed to call divine (*divina*). Politics lit the fires and froze the ice of D.'s Hell, and no more terrible vision of the tortures of the damned was ever dreamed than he depicted in the *Inferno* (*Div. Comm.*, part 1st) ; but it was love, in the ' sweet new style ' (see s.v. ' dolce stil nuovo),' lyric love most rarely spiritualized, which ' moved the sun and the other stars ' of his *Paradiso* (*Div. Comm.*, part 3rd. See its last line. Part 2nd was *Purgatorio*). For, above all, was D., the ideal lover. Through his marriage, his travels, his hates, his faint hopes, and rarer pleasures, D. followed and sought and cherished one only and one always : the Beatrice of his single adoration. Who she was now signifies little ; whether Bice Portinari (d. 1290), as is likeliest, or another ; nor how much or how little she was to D. in the society in which both moved. It is with the mystical Beatrice that lit. is concerned ; with the heavenly lady of compassion, who took Virgil's place as guide, when the shades of Purgatory were fused in the pure light of inmost Heaven, and Theology (Beatrice), speaking through Reason, resolved the perplexities of experience in an ideal reconstruction of society.

According to the *Vita Nuova*, the prose-poem of love's young dream, D. became love-adept at 9 years old : ' From that time forward, Love quite governed my soul. . . . And albeit her image, that was with me always, was an exultation of Love to subdue me, it was yet of so perfect a quality that it never allowed me to be overruled by Love without the faithful counsel of Reason ' (transld. by D. G. Rossetti, q.v.). ' Incipit *vita nuova* ' : the new life in love's service had begun, and the rest was little more than his soul's espousal, and his subdual to love, purified of all earthly passion. Such love, undreamed-of by the Troubadours, was revealed to the rapturous eyes of the storm-tossed son of Florence. It passed, like the poet himself, an allegory within an allegory, through the ' inferno ' of desire and the ' purgatory ' of patience to the ' paradise ' of self-renunciation. The Beatrice of temporal conditions became the ' beata Beatrix ' of the everlasting habitation of the soul. D.'s Paradise is less definite than his Hell ; supreme anguish is, perhaps, more presentable than supreme bliss. The church-frescoes and paintings, to which the *Commedia* owed some of its word-paintings, were bound by the same limitation. But the impression of light, and colour, and of the pervading radiancy of love is quite wonderfully conveyed. The sixth stanza of the *Hymn to Colour* by G. Meredith (q.v.) just suggests the effect in recent poetry. There are other aspects of D. : his landscape and seascape word-pictures, for example, which Ruskin (q.v.) taught the 19th cent. to appreciate ; his vividness, which inspired sir Joshua Reynolds to paint the Ugolino episode, and which caused Flaxman, the designer, to be called his best translr. ; his sombreness ; his wild bitterness, which offended Voltaire (q.v.), and the taste of the 18th cent., with the exception, as honourable as unique, of Gray (q.v.) ; his Platonism ; his uncompromising individuality ; his dialectics ; his ' beautiful style ' (*Inferno*, i, 85), which he faithfully ascribed to Virgil, the magician and necromancer of the Middle Ages, who was his guide through Hell and Purgatory ; his epic similes, derived from Homer, which he first used in modern poetry, and which reappear, to mention Engl. names only, through Chaucer and Milton (our greatest Dantesque poet ; see s.vv.) to Matthew Arnold (*Sohrab and Rustum* ; see s.v., and see prof. Ker, *Essays on Medieval Lit.*, Macmillan, 32) ; his metre in the *Div. Comm.*, the ' terza rima ' (q.v.), which he nationalized ; his deep foundation of the ideal upon the real, and his passage from actual conditions of life to speculations on theory and problems—all this, and more, is a part of D. ; all this, and more, he would wish ascribed to him as the steadfast worshipper of Beatrice, through whose heavenly translation he was brought to the perception :

Not only does the beauty I beheld
Transcend ourselves, but truly I believe
Its Maker only may enjoy it all.

(*Paradiso* xxx, 29-31. The verse transln. of Longfellow has been used in this article). Outside Italy itself, where, little more than 50 years after Dante's death, Boccaccio (q.v.) wr. a biography of him, and was appointed Dante lecturer in their common Florence, D.'s influence was very small for several centuries. Some aspects of it have been noted above, but no serious Dante revival occurred, till the 19th cent. extended and completed the tentative praises of Rivarol (q.v.) in France and Warton (q.v.) in Engld. in the 18th. Then D. shared in, and, to some extent, governed, the return of Romance (q.v.) to the Middle Ages. Standing at the edge of that time, a ' link between religion and philosophy ', as Coleridge (q.v.) acutely called him, i.e., between the age of faith and the new age of reason, D. became an object of curiosity, and, gradually, of awe and veneration, to men as different in temperament as Shelley and Carlyle. Cary's (q.v.) transln., 1814, stimulated the revival in this country. It was stimulated in turn by Coleridge's lectures on the poet, 1818, the year of Hallam's *Middle Ages*. Leigh Hunt and Shelley were Dante-disciples ; Macaulay's essay on *Milton*, which was virtually on Dante, appeared in 1825, and Carlyle's in 1841. Shortly afterwards, Dante Gabriel Rossetti and the Pre-Raphaelites whom he led spread the Dante-worship more widely ; and, before the century's end, Italy's divine epicist had become a world-poet. To-day, his bibliography is very large in every country of the civilized world, and hosts of readers subscribe to Carlyle's verdict : ' Europe has made much ; great cities, great empires, encyclopedias, creeds, bodies of opinion and practice ; but it has made little of the class of Dante's Thought ' (*Lectures on Heroes*, iii ; and see s.vv.).

Danton, George Jacques (1759-94) · Fr revolutionary. D.'s life belongs to history ; he shares with Mirabeau (q.v.) *fils* the first place among the orators of the revolutionary epoch.

Darley, George (1795-1846) : Engl. (Irish) poet ; wr. *Nepenthe*, 1835 ; *Sylvia*, 1827 ; and edited, 1840, the plays of Beaumont and Fletcher (q.v.). D., a friend of Lamb (q.v.), and a worse stammerer than he, was an early and warm admirer of the muse of Beddoes (q.v.). Carlyle joined him with Tennyson (q.v.), and D. certainly recalls the earlier notes, partly Keatsian, as we know, of the greater poet who outlived him nearly half a century. The *Quarterly* reviewer who pointed out the insincerity of Tennyson's testament, in a poem of 1830 : ' at my headstone whisper low, And tell me if the woodbines blow ', might have found a similar note in D.'s earliest poem :

I'm framed, the fool of sensibility !
I cannot see a young flow'r i' the grass
Smile at my foot which kills it in its prime,
And yet not think of undeservèd death.

The new biology, to which poetry apprenticed itself, had to pass through these jejunities, and D. was among the first of the new school.

Darmesteter, Arsène (1846-88) : Fr. philologer. Wr. *la Vie des Mots*, and collaborated with A. Hatzfeld in a Fr. dict., not as lengthy as Littré's (q.v.), but valuable.

Darwin, -i. Erasmus (1731-1802) : Engl. physician ; correspondent of Rousseau (q.v.) ; resident at Lichfield, 1756-81 ; founded Philosophical society at Derby, 1784 ; publd., 1789, *The Loves of the Plants*, forming a section of his poem, *The Botanic Garden*, completed, 1791, the inception of which was due to Anna Seward (q.v.), a leading member of the Lichfield literary group, including Boswell, T. Day, R. L. Edgeworth (qq.v.). The story is told in her *Memoir of the Life of Darwin*, how D. received,

1779, her little poetic tribute to his collection of aquatic plants with the remark, that ' it ought to form the exordium to a great work. It affords fine scope for poetic landscape. It suggests metamorphoses of the Ovidian kind reversed. Ovid made men and women into flowers, plants, and trees. You should make flowers, plants, and trees into men and women. I will write the notes which must be scientific, and you shall write the verse '. Finally, D. did both. ' The true motive of *The Botanic Garden* ', says Courthope (*Hist. Engl. Poetry*, vi, 38), ' is to be found in the notes, which display the closest observation of Nature and the most ingenious hypotheses about the causes of things. When Darwin had definitely formed his scientific ideas, he began his work of translating them into poetic diction '. That diction was cleverly, even cruelly, but not unjustly parodied by G. Canning (q.v.) and his associates in the *Anti-Jacobin* (q.v.), 1717, by *The Loves of the Triangles*, an ' attempt to enlist the imagination under the banners of Geometry. Botany I found done to my hands '.

-ii. Charles Robert (1809-82) : Engl. man of science ; grandson of above (through Robert, second son of E.D.'s first wife, Mary Howard) ; wr. principally, *The Origin of Species*, 1859 (see, too, s.v. A. R. Wallace), the importance of which to lit. does not lie in its uninterrupted and undiminished scientific value, but in a certain influence which its theories exercised on the thought of the age. Two moments, determining the course of that thought, stand out pre-prominently in retrospect. The first is the Fr. Revolution of 1789 ; the second is the Darwinian hypothesis of 1859. Together, they are parts of a single whole, which, in default of a better name, may be called, in one word, emancipation. The doctrine of political equality preceded the doctrine of the freedom of knowledge—the final stage of the Lutheran Reformation,—and its literary influence may be consulted, among other authorities, in E. Dowden, *The Fr. Revolution and Engl. Lit.*, Kegan Paul, 1897. The doctrine of biological evolution, as applied directly to the conclusions of human knowledge, and acting indirectly on established systems of religion and morals, has proved yet more revolutionary in its consequences, since no parliaments or kings were interposed between the impact of the doctrine and its object ; and the formulae of Darwinian speculation have become categories of thought, which determine the way in which the mind approaches its problems in every field.

-iii. Francis (1848-1925) : Engl. botanist ; biographer ; F.R.S. ; knt., 1913 ; third son of above. Wr. *Life and Letters of Charles Darwin*, 3 vols., 1895, one of the best Engl. biographies, and was eminent, like his great-grandfather, as a botanist.

Dasent, George Webbe (1817-96) : Engl. scholar ; envoy at Stockholm, 1840-5 ; assistant editor of *The Times*, 1845-70 ; prof. of Engl. Lit., 1853, knt., 1876. Transld. *Popular Tales from the Norse*, 1859, from the *Norske Folkeeventyr* of Absjörnsen and Moe (qq.v.), and publd. other valuable studies in Scand. lit.

Dashkov, Ekaterina Romanova (1744-1810) : Russ. writer ; princess by rank ; leading lady

at the court of empress Catherine ii (q.v.) ;
president of the Russian Academy of Sciences ;
largely instrumental in the compilation of its
dict. ; associated with the empress in her
editorial and authorial functions ; and was
herself the writer of an extremely interesting
vol. of memoirs.

Dass, Peter (1647-1708) : Norse poet ; son of a
Scot. immigrant into Norway ; entered the
Church, 1672, and wr. religious and secular
poetry. In the former class are his versions
of Biblical stories and his catechism-hymns ;
in the latter class are ' Norway's Trumpet '
and some folk-tales. Among the peasantry of
Norway, we are told that D.'s name has passed
into legend, so strong was the effect of his
intense national fervour, and his revival of the
nationalism of the North.

Dati, Goro (1363-1435) : It. historian. Wr.
history of Florence (1380-1405), and a confidential diary.

Daudet, Alphonse (1840-97) : Fr. novelist ; a
naturalist in matter, like Zola (q.v. ; and s.v.
Nature) and an impressionist in manner, like
the brothers de Goncourt (q.v.). D.'s debts
to Dickens and Thackeray (qq.v.) have not
yet been fully evaluated, and his habit of
introducing real personages, esp. to their own
discredit, has also to be noted. He stands too
near to modern times to admit of final appreciation, though there is an air of finality in Saintsbury's conjecture, ' that future judgment will
class M. Daudet as the most lamentable failure
of a great novelist that the later nineteenth
century produced ' (*P.E.L.*, xii, 88). D., who
was a native of the south, invented Tartarin
of his own Provence, and immortalized him in
3 good novels, perhaps the best of his writings :
*Aventures véritables de Tartarin de Tarascon,
Tartarin sur les Alpes*, and *Port-Tarascon*.
Other of his novels include *Lettres de mon
Moulin*, 1869 ; *le Petit Chose* (the *David
Copperfield* bk.), 1869 ; *Froment Jeune et
Risler Ainé* (the Thackerayan bk.), 1874 ;
Jack (Dickensian, again), 1876 ; *le Nabab*,
1877 ; *les Rois en Exil* (king and queen of
Naples), 1879 ; *Sapho*, 1884, etc.

D'Avenant, William (1606-68) : Engl. dramatist ;
poet-laureate (q.v.) 1638 ; knighted, 1643,
by king Charles i ; twice imprisoned as
royalist ; took prominent part in restoring
theatrical performances after the raising or
evasion of the ban of 2 Sept., 1642. D'A.,
who is reputed to have been godson to Shakespeare (q.v.), is commonly known as the father
of opera (q.v.) in Engld., by virtue, i, of his
First Day's Entertainment at Rutland Place,
1656, which he himself called by the name of
opera, and which proceeded ' by declamation
and music, after the manner of the ancients ',
the incidental music being supplied by Lawes,
composer of the music for Milton's *Comus*
and others ; ii, of his *Siege of Rhodes*, 1656,
with its ' story sung in recitative music ',
hitherto an ' unpractised ' vogue in this
country. The ' first English opera ', says
C.H.E.L., viii, 118, ' is, dramatically, as absurd
as its species has continued, with certain
exceptions, ever since ' ; but D.'A., who
opened the Cockpit theatre, Drury Lane,
1658, and who received, 1660, the royal patent
for a company of players, did some valuable

work. He produced 2 operas, *The Spaniards
in Peru* and *Sir Francis Drake*, and adapted
to the taste of his generation some of the plays
of Elizabethan playwrights, including Shakespeare. Dryden (q.v.), Shadwell (q.v. ; 1642-
92 ; he succeeded Dryden as poet-laureate),
and others were associated in these adaptations,
which chiefly introduced a lighter tone, new
songs, music, etc. D'A. is properly not of
much account to-day, but he served to bridge
the gulf between Puritanism and the Restoration in their respective attitudes towards the
stage, and modern drama should not ignore his
labours.

David von Augsburg (d. 1271) : Germ. poet and
preacher ; Franciscan mystic. Wr. Lat. and
Germ. tracts of glowing fervour and moral
force.

Davidson, John (1857-1909 ; when he disappeared, 27 Mar., presumably by suicide) : Scot.
poet ; came to London, 1890, after a stormy
and unhappy youth in uncongenial surroundings. Wr. *Fleet Street Eclogues* (2 series,
1893-6) : *Ballads and Songs*, 1894, including
the fine ' Ballad of the Making of a Poet ',
' Ballad of a Nun ', and one or two others,
secure of a place in anthologies and memory.
D. also wr. some plays, and is likely to survive,
less by his mood of revolt in the so-called
' naughty nineties ' of the 19th cent. in London
(see, too, s.v. John Lane), than by his genuine
love of beauty, evinced in a few of his
ballads.

Davies, John (c. 1565-1618) : Welsh (Engl.)
poet. Wr. *Microcosmus*, 1603 ; *The Muses'
Sacrifice*, 1612, containing ' The Picture of
a Happy Man '.

Davies, John (1569-1626) : Engl. poet ; lawyer ;
attorney-genl. for Ireland ; knt., 1607. Wr.
Orchestra, 1594 ; *Nosce Teipsum* (Know Thyself), 1599, on 'The Origin, Nature, and Immortality of the Human Soul ' : a heroic-divine
poem written in 4-line stanzas, like Gray's
(q.v.) *Elegy*. D. wr., too, a series of acrostics
in praise of queen Elizabeth, publd. as *Hymns
to Astræa*, 1599.

Day, Thomas (1748-89) : Engl. social reformer ;
wr. *History of Sandford and Merton*, 3 vols.
1783-9, a curious amalgam of Rousseau's
(q.v.) social doctrines and the more frigid
morality of D.'s friend, R. L. Edgeworth (q.v.),
and in effect a dreary piece of pedagogic fiction,
which afflicted countless nurseries in the first
half of the 19th cent.

Death : a motive of lit., the treatment of which
is derived partly from the example of the
Gk. elegists, partly from the recollection of
such physical and spiritual experiences as the
Black Death (c. 1348) and the teachings of
the Church of Rome on the frailty of mortality.
The Black Death is computed to have carried
off over 25,000,000 victims, including, among
well known literary names, the ladies of
Petrarch and Boccaccio (qq.v.), and its moral
effect must have been tremendous, and must
considerably have emphasized the other-
worldliness of the Church, with its concentration on the life hereafter. The lit. of melancholy, as it is sometimes called, most commonly
took a form which presented a combination of
these motive-forces ; but the more strictly
14th cent. note, associated with the horrid

sights of the Black Death, came to louder expression from time to time. The softer note of melancholy was overborne by the grosser graphical description of physical aspects of death : limbs sundered from the trunk ; decaying human remains ; gravediggers playing with a skull ; grinning skeletons and even dripping entrails. Outside causes assisted this prominence. Thus, in Engld., in the decline of the Renaissance, it attracted the seekers for bizarre effects,—the shock-poets of strange words and surprise emotions ; and, again, after the Restoration, when the social conscience was in revolt from the licentious excesses of that epoch, Blair (q.v.), for instance, was inspired to write his popular poem, *The Grave*, 1743, which was illustrated by Blake (q.v.), and which fed the taste for sombre horror of about two generations of readers. But, on the whole, the Gk. motive prevailed, and there was more melancholy than morbidness in writings on this subject. Modern lit. found in the forms of Gk. elegy and epitaph modes adequate to sorrow and final models for imitation. Burton's (q.v.) *Anatomy of Melancholy*, 1621 ; Milton (q.v.) in *Il Penseroso* and *Lycidas* (the latter based on the ' Death of Daphnis' by Theocritus) ; Shelley (q.v.) in *Adonais*, and Tennyson (q.v.) in *In Memoriam*, though broadly human in their approach to the common theme, were all classical in inspiration. Their poems expressed, not medieval theology, but a theology which had submitted itself to the rule and measure of poetic tradition. The Roman emperor Hadrian's address to his soul, *Animula, vagula, blandula*, which Pope (q.v.) and his contemporaries sought to Christianize, was not different in kind from the death-poems of the greatest Christian poets ; and it was the class of writings, thence derived and enhanced, which led through the graveyard reflections of Edward Young, Thos. Gray (qq.v.) and others, to the *Weltschmerz* at the close of the 18th cent., which, for all its debt to the romanticists and its metaphysical implications, was yet classical by source, and went back from the sorrows of Werther to the sorrows of Virgil, mourning the doubtful doom of human kind.

If we may try to analyse the stages in the 14th cent. view of Death, there are three strands which may be separated : i, the urgent observation of the sudden passing of eminent men and fair women ; the sadness of the disappearance from the assets of humanity of such wealth of fame and beauty. This note, common in lit., may be exemplified from Villon (q.v.), who seized it for ever in his ballad with the refrain, ' Où sont les neiges d'antan ? ' ii, Arising out of this sentiment, is its personal application in the fear of death,—the increasing horror of individual disappearance, of exchanging one's own share of fame or beauty for the putrescent poverty and ugliness of the grave. The mere mood of wistful remembrance, cultivated so assiduously by medieval writers, was not adequate to this lyrical complaint, which, illustrated once more by many poets in the Middle Ages, was rendered with melodious finality by Shakespeare (q.v.), in *Measure for Measure*, iii, i, 118 :—

' Ay, but to die, and go we know not where
To lie in cold obstruction and to rot ;
This sensible warm motion to become
A kneaded clod ; and the delighted spirit
To bathe in fiery floods, or to reside
In thrilling region of thick-ribbed ice ; (cf.
            Dante, q.v., *Purg.*).
To be imprison'd in the viewless winds,
And blown with restless violence round about
The pendent world* ; or to be worse than worst
Of those that lawless and incertain thought
Imagine howling :—'tis too horrible !
The weariest and most loathed worldly life
That age, ache, penury and imprisonment
Can lay on nature, is a Paradise
To what we fear of death.'

iii, The fear of death and the horror of dissolution were exploited for their own sake. There was poetry to be made out of ' worms and graves', which would bring the desired shudder to morbid muscles, and gratify the thwarted longings of hands losing their grasp on worldly possessions. This grim type of *macabre* poetry, as it is called (the derivation of the name is doubtful : it is traced back in France to Jean le Fèvre, 1376 : ' Je fis de Macabré la danse'), left entirely on one side the spiritual associations of Death—Death, the consoler, the healer, the peace-bringer : ' many a time I have been half in love with easeful Death, Called him soft names in many a mused rhyme, To take into the air my quiet breath ' (Keats, ' Ode to Nightingale '),—and concentrated all its powers on the physical apparition, first, of the corpse, once clothed in fame or beauty, now in hideous decay, and, next, by an extension, of Death himself, leading his victims' dance. The Dance of Death, at which we thus arrive, was a favourite subject for brush and pen in the 15th cent., and particularly for the art of the wood-cutter. There was a printer in Paris, Guyot Marchant, whose *Danse Macabré*, 1485, was adorned with woodcuts, probably imitated from the carvings in the cloister, or churchyard, of the Innocents in Paris, dating about 60 years before, and a favourite resort. This Dance was extended from men to women. A *danse macabré* for female corpses was written for Guyot by Martial d'Auvergne (q.v.), whose grim text was only once softened by anything like a human note. He represents a little girl in the dance, led away by Death from her mother, to whom she appeals : ' Take good care of my Doll, my knuckle bones, and my fine dress'. This touch is practically isolated,—so little, as a Belgian critic remarks (Huizinga, *The Waning of the Middle Ages*, ch. xi), did the lit. of the epoch know of child-life ; and he correctly adds that ' living emotion stiffens amid the abused imagery of skeletons and worms '. The Campo Santo at Genoa is full of these stiffened images.

We may leave the Black Death motive here. It was revived by the grotesque school and Robt. Blair for the edification of weary worldliness, seeking release from the flesh, but sober

---

* This passage could take a ream of commentary. The Dantesque hell is noted above. Here we may refer curious readers to the elaboration (over and over again) of the thought and language in these lines by the late Stephen Phillips, a poet much over-praised in his recent generation.

men of letters rejected it in its isolation. Malherbe (q.v.), it has been observed, set it aside (*enfin vint Malherbe*, in this department too) in his slow and deliberate elegiac utterances, and it did not suit the romantic melancholy of the heirs of Milton's tradition. Merely noting that psychical research, though it has produced a technical lit. in its own kind, of which Frederic W. H. Myers (1843-1901 ; characteristically, his favourite authors were Wordsworth and Virgil) was the pioneer, has not yet definitely affected the literary representation of Death, we may conclude by two contrasting illustrations of the treatment of this theme, both taken from one bk. In Thackeray's (q.v.) *Vanity Fair*, at the close of ch. 32, we read : ' Darkness came down on the field and city : and Amelia was praying for George, who was lying on his face, dead, with a bullet through his heart '. This is written in the Gk. tradition, with the restraint and reticence of which we read in Dr. Livingstone's essay on ' Literature ' in the Oxford *Legacy of Greece*. Turn next to ch. 61 of the same novel, ' in which two lights are put out ', and read the *memento mori*, which, more like a medieval engraver, or even a disciple of Blair, Thackeray drew round the death of Mr. Sedley, concluding with the physical contrast between the quick and the dead : ' So there came one morning and sunrise, when all the world got up and set about its various works and pleasures, with the exception of old John Sedley, who was not to fight with fortune, or to hope or scheme any more : but to go and take up a quiet and utterly unknown residence in a churchyard at Brompton by the side of his old wife '.

Debate : ' débat ', ' estrif ' ; medieval form of Fr. verse, mainly of the Northern middle-class, consisting of a discussion or dispute, either between two personifications (summer and winter ; wine and water) ; or between two types of persons (crusader and non-crusader), or, in the religious sphere, between two ideals of conduct (Jew and Christian ; soul and body) ; or, among the troubadours (q.v.), between two poets in alternate stanzas on a point or punctilio of love or courtesy (such a *débat* was known as *tençon* in Provençal, and as a *jeu-parti* in Fr. lit. ; in the latter, the choice of sides was pre-allotted). The importance of the D. in later lit., apart from the charm and interest of many of its specimens, lies in the stimulus which its dialogue gave to the development of drama. *The Owl and the Nightingale* (c. 1220) is an anon. example of the class in Engl. poetry, with filiation to the bestiary (q.v.). The early dialogue was confused with duologue (dyalogue), and when three interlocutors were introduced, as by Wiclif (q.v.), the word ' Trialogues ' was (unnecessarily) invented. The release of the type from the limitation of a dispute between two abstractions, by which it was dominated in medieval lit., was mainly the achievement of Erasmus and Hutten (qq.v.), in their Lat. humanistic writings ; and the Germ. debate or dialogue in the 16th cent., at the time and in the country of its chief cultivation and development, acquired the dramatic qualities, the light touch, and the ease of style, with which it

descended to modern letters, e.g., in the *Imaginary Conversations* of Landor (q.v.).

Décade Philosophique : Fr. newspaper, founded in year 2 of the Revolution, and representative in thought of the school of Locke and Condorcet (qq.v.) ; the editors were keen students of foreign life and lit., and stimulated the study in France of Young, Macpherson, Wieland, Goethe (qq.v.) and others, thus serving the development of Romance (q.v.).

Decembrio : -i. Uberto (1370-1427) ; It. humanist ; studied Gk. under Chrysoloras (q.v.) ; revived his tutor's Lat. version of Plato's *Republic*, continued and completed by

-ii. Pier Candido (1399-1477), his son, who dedicated it to duke Humphrey of Gloucester (q.v.) ; transld. Appian for pope Nicholas v (q.v.).

Decker, de, Jeremias (1609-66) : Dutch poet ; praised by Vondel, in whose afterglow he shone. Wr., 1658, memorial verses to his father ; his best verse, remarks Ten Brink, falls in the category of ' fireside poetry '.

Dedekind, Friedrich (16th cent.) : Germ. Lat. satirist. Wr., 1549, Lat. *Grobianus* in elegiac-verses, the contrast between the elegance of the versification and the ugliness of the subject-matter adding point to the satire, directed at the display of coarse manners (Germ. *grob=* boorish, uncouth), into which Germany had lapsed. The chief cause of the lapse lay in the decay of chivalry and the decline of the German courts. The good side of this social change was the growth of a civic spirit and of a self-respecting and self-conscious burgher-class ; but hungry peasants swarmed over the countryside, making a mockery of the ancient simple virtues ; the worthy burghers had little or no pretence to culture ; the clergy were grossly ignorant, and the folly (q.v.)-lit. of the times is eloquent of the vice and ill-living and low standards which prevailed. D.'s novelty consisted in exalting the practice of bad manners into a cult ; a kind of chivalry turned upside-down, with all the grace and the flower of it spilt. (See also s.vv. Grobian, Scheidt). Later, D. added a *Grobiana* (1552), as a female companion to his original hero. Indecent and unpleasant as his social picture was, it exercised no little fascination over later satirists ; it was transld. into Engl., 1605, as *The School of Slovenry* ; it was imitated in the *Gull's Hornbook*, 1609, of Dekker (q.v.), and as recently as 1739 a new Engl. version, in which ' Grobianus ' was rendered ' Booby ', by Roger Bull was addressed to Swift (q.v.), as the leader of social satire in his age.

Deffand, du, Marie de Vichy-Chamrond (1697-1780) : Fr. literary hostess and letter-writer ; *marquise* by marriage, 1718 ; blind after 1753 ; invited mlle. de Lespinasse (q.v.) to live with her, 1754, and the partnership continued for 10 years, when mme. du D. dissolved it at the discovery that mlle. de Lespinasse was supplanting her in her own house. Mme. du D. was one of the greatest hostesses in a great age, and her *salon* was frequented by Dalembert, Montesquieu, and others, with whom, and with Horace Walpole, Voltaire, and others (see s.vv.) she maintained constant correspondence. The letters from her to Walpole are one of the most valuable possessions of lit. ; 838 are included in the edn. by Mrs. Paget Toynbee, 3 vols., 1912 ; Walpole's to her were destroyed at his particular request. Mme. du D. was supremely witty ; the *mot* most commonly quoted from her is the description of Montesquieu's *l'Esprit des Lois* an *de l'esprit sur les lois*, in reference to its scintillating brilliancy.

Defoe, Daniel (*c.* 1659-1731): Engl. novelist, journalist, pamphleteer ; known in history as the author of *Robinson Crusoe*, vol. i, 1719, and liked to describe himself as the author of *The True-born Englishman : a Satire*, in verse, against opponents of a foreign monarch, 1701 ; son of Foe, a butcher, and changed his name, *c.* 1703. It would be quite defensible, in a work on this scale and of this scope, to wipe out the first 60 years of D.'s life, and to commence, where he nearly ended, with his veracious history, in Lucian's sense, of Alexander Selkirk (1676-1721), the runaway son of a Scot. shoemaker, John Selcraig, whose adventure on the uninhabited island of Juan Fernandez, from which he was rescued, 1709, is the foundation of D.'s literary immortality. *Robinson Crusoe* ' has been translated into every civilized, and into more than one barbarous, tongue. It has had hundreds of imitators of varying degrees of merit. It captivated Rousseau (q.v.), who saw in Robinson the image of the natural man, to that extent that he sanctioned its perusal by the young ; and the book has been almost as familiar a friend in French as in British households ever since ' (*P.E.L.*, ix, 144 ; and for *Robinson Crusoe* in Germany, see s.v. Robinsonaden). The journalist of D.'s earlier period was, of course, apparent in the novelist of later years. He heard the story of Selkirk, not, it is believed, at first hand, but from reports about town, and was quick and clever enough to see what excellent ' copy ' it would make. The genius which turned out the ' copy ' in a plain, straightforward, narrative style, without tall talk or fanciful decoration, and with just enough of the moralizing element to recommend it to the middle class which he knew so well, was D.'s gift,—his difference from the ruck. In this sense, and in this sense only, he is comparable with Bunyan (q.v.) ; and in this sense it is a reasonable exercise in the contrast between good journalism and good lit. to compare *Robinson Crusoe* with R. L. Stevenson's (q.v.) *Treasure Island*. The triumphant journalist in D. is to be marked, again, in his subsequent novels,—a branch of letters, which presumably, he now found lucrative. These included studies of low life : of Jonathan Wild, who was hanged in 1725, and whose exploits were to engage the pen of Fielding (q.v.) ; of John Sheppard, hanged in 1724, whose exploits were to attract Ainsworth (q.v.) ; of John Avery, a notorious pirate, known as the mock-king of Madagascar ; of ' the life, adventures and piracies of the famous Captain Singleton ' ; and, among criminals of the other sex, of *The Fortunate Mistress . . . known by the name of the lady Roxana, in the time of king Charles ii*, and *The Fortunes and Misfortunes of the famous Moll Flanders*. Very close to these journalistic redactions, of which there were several more in the same kind, of narratives from the ' Newgate calendar ' which

adorned a tale even more clearly than they pointed a moral, were D.'s semi-hist. bks. of this period, among which may be mentioned : *Memoirs of a Cavalier ; or, a Military Journal of the Wars in Germany*, etc., 1720 ; *A Journal of the Plague-Year*, 1722 ; *A Tour through . . . Great Britain*, 3 vols., 1724-6, and others enough : the full list of D.'s writings is computed to exceed 250 items, and a bare recital of their titles would not carry us further. ' He was the most practised and versatile journalist and hack-writer of the day, known to publishers as willing to turn every penny ' (*C.H.E.L.*, ix., 21) ; ' he knew exactly what the man in the street and what the man in the shop or in the thieves' crib would find impressive, and nothing could keep him from supplying his customers ' (*P.E.L.*, viii, 294) ; and we note, with Dr. E. A. Baker (Introduction to *Moll Flanders* and *Roxana*, Routledge, p. xviii), that ' one of the most successful books in France at the time when interest in the works of the Naturalist school was particularly absorbing ' was Marcel Schwob's transln. of *Moll Flanders*, who is the direct literary ancestress, by the way, of a long family of like adventuresses, down to the *femme de chambre*, whose *Journal* was written, 1901, by Octave Mirbeau.

If D. had died before writing *Robinson Crusoe*, by which alone he lives popularly to-day, he would be known as a more robust L'Estrange (q.v.). His chief pioneer-work in Engl. journalism was the foundation, 1704, of *The Review*, which he continued to bring out irregularly till 1713, when he started a new trade journal, *Mercator* ; later *c.* 1717, he was associated, though not very honourably, with the *Weekly Journal* of Nathaniel Mist (d. 1717), a printer ; and he was voluminous and industrious as a pamphleteer. There is but little actual interest to-day in enucleating his opinions from his writings, or in trying to test their consistency.

Deken, Agatha (Aagje) (1741-1804): Dutch novelist in collaboration with E. Wolff (q.v.). The literary friendship of these two learned women is unique in the history of Dutch letters, which they enriched with several original novels—the very originality was a novelty in their day (see s.v. Dutch lit.)—of which the best known is *Sara Burgerhart*. A fuller account of the record will be found s.v. Wolff, the greater writer of the two. Aagje survived Betje only a few weeks.

Dekker, John (*c.* 1570-*c.* 1641): Engl. playwright ; pamphleteer ; collaborated on the stage of the day with Ford, Massinger, Middleton, and others, according to the habits of the day ; wr. *Satiromastix*, 1602, in reply to Jonson's *Poetaster*. D.'s *Gull's Hornbook*, 1609, was a species of social satire adapted to London life from the *Grobian* of Dedekind (q.v.) ; his dramatic works were collected, 4 vols., 1873, and Dr. Grosart (1827-99), a busy bibliographer and editor, collated D.'s misc. writings in the Huth Library.

Delavigne, Casimir (1793-1843): Fr. poet, dramatist ; of mediocre talent and achievement. Wr. *Messéniennes* (political odes), and plays, of which the best-known is *Louis xi*, 1832.

Delille, Jacques (1758-1813): Fr. poet. Wr. *les Jardins*, 1782, in stilted and periphrastic verse, which, with his transln. of Virgil's *Georgics*, made him one of the most popular descriptive poets of his day. He belonged to the class of writers who never describe what they see—indeed, who never do see,— but merely make inventories of what should be seen, and his fame has not outlived the passing taste for mannered didacticism. Transld. Milton's *Paradise Lost*, 1805, and Virgil's *Æneid*, 1804, and was frankly indebted to Goldsmith (q.v.) in his original poems, *L'homme des Champs*, *l'Imagination*, etc.

Delolme, John Louis (1740-1806): Fr. (-Swiss) political philosopher. Wr., 1771, *Constitution de l'Angleterre*, which was used as a textbook by the makers of constitutions in the Revolutionary and Napoleonic eras.

Delphin Classics: Fr. 17th-cent. series of Lat. texts, edited with commentary and index, with the engraving of Arion and the dolphin, 'in usum serenissimi Delphini', i.e., the dauphin, son of king Louis xiv of France. The general editor of the series was Huet (q.v.); and it has been pointed out that the prince, in whose service it was organized and who further enjoyed the advantage of tuition by Bossuet (q.v.), 'celebrated the completion of his education by limiting his future reading to the list of births, deaths, and marriages in the *Gazette de France*'; he did not live to succeed to the Fr. throne.

De Morgan, -i. Augustus (1806-71): Engl. scholar; mathematician; prof. in his faculty at Univ. Coll., London, 1828-31 and 1836-66, when he resigned as a protest against the 'intolerance' of the council in refusing to appoint J. Martineau (q.v.) to a chair in philosophic studies. Wr. *Essay on Probabilities*, and other technical works, and, further, a *Budget of Paradoxes*, 1872, consisting of papers publd. in the *Athenæum* (q.v.), and combining the humour of Lewis Carroll (q.v.) with the logic of C. L. Dodgson, Carroll's other self.

-ii. William Frend (1839-1917): Engl. novelist; son of above; a potter by calling, De M. discovered his gift for fiction late in life, and wr. a series of rather lengthy but distinctly attractive novels; of which the first, *Joseph Vance*, 1906, was the best. The vein was biographic, with languorous digressions, and the construction demanded some leisure on the part of the reader; but the dialogue and characterization were clever, with touches of caricature reminiscent of Dickens (q.v.) and of whimsicalness akin to sir James Barrie's.

Denham, John (1615-69): Engl. poet; knt., 1661; wr. *Cooper's Hill*, 1642, a poem in heroic couplets, of which Dryden (q.v.) generously declared, that 'for the majesty of its style it is, and ever will be, the exact standard of good writing'. The standard has changed, but *Cooper's Hill* is still notable as the earliest local poem in the Engl. language; and its celebration of the Thames and its scenery in the neighbourhood of Windsor is famous for the aspiration, extensible, more generally, to the poetic ideal of D.'s age:

O could I flow like thee, and make thy stream
My great example, as it is my theme!
Tho' deep, yet clear; tho' gentle, yet not dull;
Strong without rage, without o'erflowing full.

Denis, Michael (1729-1800) Germ. (Austrian) bardic poet (see s.vv. Barditus and Klopstock). Transld., 1768-69, Macpherson's (q.v.) *Ossian* into Germ. hexameter verse; wr., 1772, 'Songs of Sined the Bard', Sined being Denis written backwards.

Denisot, Nicolas (1515-59): Fr. poet in Engld. Tutor to three daughters of duke of Somerset (the Protector); his pupils wr. Lat. verse-elegies on queen Margaret (q.v.) of Navarre, publd. in Paris, 1550, to the great delight of Fr. friends of Engld.; the vol. was transld., 1551, into Fr., Ital., and Gk., and roused the enthusiasm of Ronsard (q.v.) and other humanists of Engl. sympathy. D., like André (q.v.), was a kind of missionary of the Fr. Renaissance in Engld.

Dennis, John (1657-1734): Engl. critic; pamphleteer; playwright; son of a London saddler; edu. at Harrow and Cambridge (B.A., 1679). D.'s plays were not particularly brilliant; of the 9 actually produced, *Liberty Asserted*, 1704, and *Appius and Virginia*, 1709, alone 'made good.' He was virulently assailed by Swift and Pope (qq.v.), notably by the latter in the *Dunciad* and in a *Narrative of the Strange and Deplorable Frenzy of John Dennis*. It is to Pope's credit, that, in later years, when D. was needy and half-blind, he helped organize a benefit performance for him. D. wr. *The Advancement and Reformation of Modern Poetry*, 1701; *The Grounds of Criticism in Poetry*, 1704; *Three Letters on Shakespeare*, 1711, and defended the stage against the puritanical attack by Collier (q.v.); but his failures and disappointments and bitter disposition would be forgotten, except for the pillory of the *Dunciad*.

De Quincey, Thomas (1785-1859): Engl. essayist; 'it has been said, probably without exaggeration, that there was no writer more popular than De Quincey with clever boys of upper school and lower college age, from about 1855 for twenty or five-and-twenty years onward' (Saintsbury, *C.H.E.L.*, xii, 225),—a sufficiently high record, though it has not been sustained at the same level since 1880. De Q.'s writings, very misc. in subject, were collected, 14 vols., 1853-60; 15 plus 2 vols., 1862-78, and, 4th edn., 16 vols., 1878. A new edn., by Masson, 1822-1907 (q.v., the well-known Scot. scholar of Engl. studies), was publd., 14 vols., 1889-90; the *Confessions of an English Opium-Eater*, 1822, has been issued separately by various editors, and has been transld. into Fr., Germ., and Ital.; hardly less famous is the essay on *Murder as one of the Fine Arts*. De Q. has faults, chiefly of digression; and sir L. Stephen (q.v.), a leading modern biographer, always found in him, 'in regard to biographic and critical questions, gross inaccuracies, and almost always effeminate prejudices and mere flippancies dressed in elaborate rhetoric'. But he found, too, that De Q. 'stands absolutely alone as the inventor and sole performer on a new musical instrument,—for such an instrument is the English language in his hands. He belongs to a genus in which he is the only individual' (*Hours in a Library*, i). It is for the model of this ornate and rhythmical prose, revived from the 17th cent., that De Q. keeps his permanent place in Engl. lit.; and grateful mention is due to his services as a popularizer of Germ. philosophy.

Derzhavin, Gabriel Romanovich (1743-1816): Russ. poet; conspicuous for his facility in the composition of pseudo- (or neo-) classic odes, designed to enhance the splendour of the reign and acts of the empress Catherine ii (q.v.). D. was content, he sang, to live as the empress's echo; and to an ambition of this kind posterity gives an inattentive ear. Yet D. was a greater poet than some of the twittering songsters of his day: e.g., Lomonosov (q.v.) and other imperial cage-birds; he had taste, a severe Horatian training, a feeling for nature, and ability to tear up his verses if they displeased honest critics. Unfortunately, he wr. too easily and too much. 'Feliza' (the title of D.'s ode of 1782), representing Catherine, was a heavier drag on his muse than the 'Eliza' or 'Gloriana' of Engl. Elizabethan bards; and D. survives as Catherine's tame poet, who was most successful when most tame. His services to the language of poetry were comparable with those of Karamsin (q.v.) to Russ. prose.

De Sanctis, Francesco (1817-83): It. critic; described, after the Fr. master who deeply influenced him, as the Ste.-Beuve (q.v.) of Italy. Wr. *Saggi Critici*, 1869, and *Nuovi Saggi*, 1872. Saintsbury (*Hist. Crit.*, iii, 591) finds De S. a little too much attracted by 'the old Italian addiction towards philosophizing. . . . But he did a great, and effectual, and to this day an enduring and admirable work', which was enhanced by the critical writings, contemporary and a little later, of Carducci (q.v.).

Desaugiers, Marc Antoine Madeleine (1772-1827): Fr. lyric poet; manager of a vaudeville-theatre in Paris, for which he wr. songs and dramas; and lived a light-hearted, merry life, largely spent at a club, the Caveau moderne, established by Piron (q.v.).

Descartes, René (1596-1650): Fr. philosopher; spent a wandering life, 'as restless as a hyæna' (De Quincey, q.v.), in the pursuit of ease and knowledge, visiting various countries in Europe; he relates that his central philosophical idea, *cogito, ergo sum* ('I think, therefore I am'), occurred to him, flashlightwise, in Germany; he lay hid two years, 1625-27, in Paris, elaborating his ideas; retired to Holland, returned to France, settled, 1649, at invitation of queen Christina, in Sweden, where he died. D.'s lifework properly belongs to the history of philosophy rather than of letters, though it happened that, in his instance, the two goals were reached along one road. 'As viewed by Descartes', writes prof. E. Boutroux (*C.M.H.*, iv, 784-85), 'science, experience of life, the principles of religious faith, and the good sense of a well-bred man (which was the essence of the style of Malherbe and Balzac, qq.v.), do not merely exist side by side, they co-operate in forming a harmonious whole. Taken by themselves, apart from the mind which sustains them, and considered from an abstract point of view, science, religion, and life may seem in opposition, or even in contradiction to each other. With Descartes, however, they find a common basis in philosophy, which . . . was the necessary mediating power, . . .

and was to accomplish this important function, not by surpassing the other sciences in obscurity and pedantry, but, on the contrary, by assuming the standpoint of the well-bred man towards scholastic subtleties, and by speaking simply and clearly in the common tongue.' Thus, there is a Cartesianism (as his system came to be called) of style as well as of thought, and the aim of Cartesian lit. was the same as that of Cartesian philosophy. In the development of Fr. prose, D. continued the work which Malherbe (q.v.) had begun in poetry, and J. L. de Balzac (q.v.) in prose. It was the work of selection, pruning, eclecticism; of ejecting from the vocabulary of words and the resources of form all the hybrid importations of the Pleiad (q.v.), and all the native and foreign claimants which failed to respond to the test of reason, order, distinction, and logic. It was not an accident of time, but a result of antecedent causes, that D.'s famous *Discours de la Méthode* ('for the right conduct of reason and for the discovery of truth in the sciences') should have appeared in the same year, 1637, which saw the culmination of classical Fr. drama in the *Cid* (q.v.) of Corneille (q.v.); for Cornelian classicism and Cartesian rationalism were woven into one piece out of the strands of thought and experience common to the age in which they lived; and the elements excluded from both, the victims of the proscription which they practised, were re-admitted to lit. and philosophy only at a later date and under changed conditions. It is in Wordsworth (q.v.), for example, that we see a restoration to lit. of those merely sentient and even inanimate witnesses to truth, which a strict application of the principle, *cogito, ergo sum*, had expelled from the rationalist's paradise. Fontenelle (q.v.) e.g., the nephew of Corneille, was more rigidly Cartesian than Descartes, more positively a purist than Corneille. Cartesianism, as Lanson (*Hist. de la Lit. Fr.*, 402) remarks, by its rigorously scientific formula, rules art out: 'there is no Cartesian æsthetic, or, rather, it consists in reducing art to science, and can founding the two'. In a classical lit. governed by Cartesian principles of thought, beauty would be identified with truth; or, rather, truth would be sought without reference to the beauty which justifies it. Art was saved from this hypothesis, however, by the conservatism of the 18th cent., which, while it adopted the rational philosophy of D., never wholly abandoned the cult of antiquity, whence was derived an æsthetic tradition to modify the sanction of pure reason. Thus, the apparatus of style, as provided by D. in his philosophic writings, led to the classic prose—the exactly adequate instrument—of Pascal, La Rochefoucauld (qq.v.) and others, while his thought led to the works of Malebranche, Bayle (qq.v.) and their followers. D.'s chief works in Fr. (he also wr. in Lat.) were the *Discours*, above-mentioned, and a *Traité des Passions*, 1649. The first deals with the biography of thought, and the latter with the theory of will. Together, they founded the principles of modern philosophy; and, though D. himself continued not to force a clash between his teachings and those of the Roman

Catholic Church, he is properly classed as a sceptic ; an adherent to that school of ' honest doubt ', which marked the transition of the Renaissance from medieval to modern thought, from authority to independence. D. answered the ' que sais-je ? ' of Montaigne (q.v.) by his *cogito, ergo sum* ; and, in thus completing the essayist's hints at a system of knowledge, he enhanced the self-dependence of Fr. prose-style.

Deschamps, -i. Emile (1795-1871) : Fr. poet ; transld. some of Shakespeare's plays.

-**ii. Antony** (1800-69) : Fr. poet ; translr. of Dante and the *Cid*. Both brothers were frequenters of Nodier's (q.v.) *salon* at the Arsenal (q.v.), and are to be reckoned as romantic founders (s.v. Lyrisme). ' Vous appelez romantique ce qui est poétique ', was a phrase of E.D. in one of his articles in the *Muse française* (q.v.), which were collected, 1829, under the title of *le Jeune Moraliste du xix* Siècle*.

Deschamps. See s.v. **Eustache.**

Deshoulières, Antoinette (1638-94) : Fr. lyric poet ; *née* de la Garde ; m. seigneur D., who was involved in the political troubles of his day, and fled with his wife to Span. Netherlands (Belgium). Mme. D. returned to France without him. Wr. *Idylles*, madrigals, and other airy verse of a gay and Gallic quality, and long epistles to her constant friend Fléchier (q.v.) ; she was a member of the Precious (q.v.) school, and is mentioned by Boileau (q.v.) *Satire* x.

Desmoulins, Camille (1760-94) : Fr. revolutionary journalist. Born at Guise ; was elected as a deputy for Paris to the Convention, and took a leading part in the sacking of the Bastille and the incarceration of king Louis xvi ; general secretary to Danton, by whose side he perished by guillotine, 5 April, 1794. D. was a born journalist, and possessed the mobile, sensitive temperament, which is the secret of success in the higher walks of that craft. This possession remained through all the bitterness and all the horror which he shared and helped to make ; and, though he was justly execrated by his victims, he was better than the times in which he fought. His writings were partly periodical, *les Révolutions de France et de Brabant* (1789-91) and *le Vieux Cordelier* (1793-94), and included two pamphlets of 1789 ; *la France libre* and *Discours de la Lanterne*. His letters from prison are unique as a human document, and fully worthy of the man and the occasion.

Despériers, Bonaventure (*c.* 1498-1544) : Fr. humanist ; poet. D. was a Gk. and Lat. scholar, and collaborated with Dolet (q.v.) in his philosophical writings. Resided many years at Lyons (q.v.). Became valet-de-chambre to queen Margaret (q.v.) of Navarre, where he met Rabelais (q.v.) and became the friend of C. Marot (q.v.). The queen's powerful ægis protected him from the persecution of free-thought, but we have H. Estienne's authority for the statement that D. escaped the net of Rome by suicide. His best works are not his courtier's poems, nor even his 129 short tales, *Nouvelles Récréations et Joyeux Devis* (ed. *pr.*, 1558 ; the authorship of part of this collection is in dispute). D. is best remembered by his most characteristic work, the *Cymbalum Mundi*, 1538. This consists of 4 parts, and discloses an audacious spirit

seeking to found a liberal philosophy mid-way between the extremes of orthodoxy and reform.

Desportes, Philippe (1546-1616) : Fr. poet ; disciple of Pleiad (q.v.), and represents the decline of the constellation. (See also s.v. Bertaut ; D. and Bertaut are united by Boileau (q.v.) in an epigram quoted s.v. Bertaut). D. was cleric and courtier, and his dual interests are reflected in his poetry, which exhibited, like Herrick's (q.v.), ' divine numbers' as well as courtly verse. D. was a busy sonneteer, and a diligent student of Ital. models, and he became in turn a cherished pattern for Engl. imitators, who honoured him as Ronsard's heir. Thus, sir S. Lee (*Fr. Renaissance in Engld.*, 212) quotes from Lodge (q.v., *Margarite of America*, 1596) : ' Few men are able to second the sweet conceits of Philip Desportes, whose poetical works are for the most part Englished, and ordinarily in everybody's hands ' ; and Daniel, Spenser, and Shakespeare (qq.v.) were all indebted to D. for phrases, sentiments, and ' conceits ' (q.v.).

Destouches, Philippe Néricault (1680-1754) : Fr. dramatist ; ambassador, first in Switzerland, and afterwards in London, 1717-23, where he studied theatrical conditions. D. wr. 17 comedies, of which the best known are *le Philosophe Marié*, 1727, *le Glorieux*, 1732, and *la Fausse Agnès* (publd., 1736 ; performed, 1759). He has been compared with Marivaux (q.v.) in the school of Molière (q.v.), but the deliberate edification at which he aimed ranges D. more properly with the school of Boileau and La Bruyère (qq.v.), if these moralists can be imagined as playwrights. The delineation of character with a view to improving the occasion, as the phrase goes, was more to D.'s taste than pure comedy ; it is observed that he thought laughter vulgar, unless it were a ' smile of the soul' ; which may be good manners, but is obviously bad stagecraft.

Deutsch, Emanuel (1829-73) : Germ. Orientalist ; resided in Engld., as assistant at the British Museum, 1855-70 ; wr., *inter alia*, a valuable study of the *Talmud*, in the *Quarterly Review*, 1867.

Deutsche Rundschau (Germ.) : Title of monthly review of letters, learning, and politics, founded, 1874, by Julius Rodenberg (q.v.).

Deventer : Town in Netherlands, famous in 15th cent. for its humanistic school, revived by the Brethren of the Common Lot (q.v.), and attended, among others, by Agricola and Erasmus (qq.v.). Its great headmaster was Hegius (q.v.), through whose hands passed about 2,000 pupils.

De Vere, -i. Aubrey (1788-1846) : Engl. poet ; second bart., succeeded 1818. Wr. *The Song of Faith*, 1842, and hist. plays.

-**ii. Aubrey Thomas** (1814-1902) : Engl. poet ; son of above ; born in Co. Limerick ; edu. Trinity Coll., Dublin ; fell under the austere poetic influence of Wordsworth (q.v.), and the religious influence of Newman (q.v.) ; was received into the Church of Rome, 1851. Publd. several vols. of graceful and rather stately verse, from *The Waldenses*, 1842, to a series of *Irish Odes*, etc., motivated by his interest in his native country, after 1861. His prose *Essays, chiefly on Poetry*, 1887, still take a high place in criticism.

De Vries, Jan (1819-55): Dutch novelist. Wr., 1844, *The Mysteries of Amsterdam*, in the vein of Sué (q.v.), *Mysteries of Paris*, and Féval (q.v.), *Mysteries of London*. De V. used the pen-name of L. van Eikenhorst.

Diamante, Juan Bautista (*c.* 1630-*c.* 1685): Span. dramatist; imitator of Calderon (q.v.). Wr. *la Judia de Toledo* ('The Jewess of Toledo'), beloved by the king Alfonso viii of Ulloa's (q.v.) play; indebted, too, to a play by Amescua (q.v.); and *el Honrador de su Padre* ('Honouring his father'), 1658, on a legend of the Cid (q.v.), and founded on the *Cid* of Corneille (q.v.). This piece derives an adventitious interest from a mistake in dates by Voltaire (q.v.), who reversed the order of indebtedness.

Diario de los Literatos de España (Span.): Journal of the Men of Letters of Spain; a literary periodical founded at Madrid, 1737. It was the first of its kind, and enjoyed influential patronage; but it was too big, too strange, and too stiff, and it died an early death in its second year (vol. 7). The policy of the *D.* was opposed to the classical tendencies advanced in the 'Poetics' of Luzan (q.v.).

Diaz del Castillo, Bernal (1492-*c.* 1581): Span. conqueror and historian; accompanied Cortes (q.v.) to Mexico, and was an eye-witness of the Montezuma campaign. Wr. from a well-stored memory in 1580 his 'Veracious (*verdadera*) History of the Conquest of the New Spain', *ed. pr.* 1632, in a spirit of righteous indignation against the panegyrical Cortes-first-and-the-rest-nowhere tone of the official *Hispania Victrix* of Lopez (q.v.) de Gomara. Hérédia transld. D.'s history into Fr. in the 19th cent., and a life of D. by Mr. Cunninghame Graham has recently been publd. in this country (Nash, 1915). D.'s blunt, soldierly style was fully adequate to his self-set task of faithfully recording the actual features of the great days which he had shared.

Dibdin, -i. Charles (1745-1814): Engl. writer of songs, chiefly nautical; dramatist; musician. Wr. a *History of the Stage*, 1795; 2 novels, many dramatic sketches, etc.; is memorable particularly for the sea-ditties in his plays, which caught and have kept the public ear.

-**ii. Thomas Frognall** (1776-1847): Engl. bibliophil; nephew of above; wr. *Bibliomania*, 1809, and is well-reputed for his catalogues, notes, etc., in bibliographical circles.

-**iii. Thomas John** (1771-1841): Engl. playwright; son of C.D. above; is said to have composed nearly 2,000 songs and about 200 operas and plays; his song, 'The Snug Little Island', occurred in his *British Raft*, 1797, and he wr. *The Mouth of the Nile* for Covent Garden Theatre, in honour of Nelson's victory, 1798. Wr., too, *The Cabinet*, an opera, 1801; involved in heavy financial loss by the failure of the Surrey Theatre, 1822.

Diccionario de la Lengua Castellana (Span.): Dict. of the Castilian Language; generally known as *Diccionario de Autoridades*. This was the first work undertaken by the Span. Academy (q.v.), after its foundation, 1714, by king Philip v of Spain under the direction of the marquis de Villena (q.v.), on the analogy of the Fr. example in the previous century. The compilers went back to the works of Lebrixa and Cobarruvias (qq.v.), since whom no serious attempt had been made to deal with the changes and accretions in the language. Their work was much needed, and was accomplished with zeal and discretion. The 6 folio vols. appeared at rapid intervals, 1726-39, and an abridgment of the work was issued in one vol., 1780. The discourse on Span. orthography, originally prefixed to the *D.*, was publd. separately by the Academy, 1742.

Dicey, Albert Venn (1835-1922): Engl. jurist; won Arnold prize at Oxford for an essay on *The Privy Council*, which directed his future lines of research; Vinerian prof. of Engl. law at Oxford, 1882-1913; principal of Working Men's College (4th in succession to F. D. Maurice, Thos. Hughes and 1st baron Avebury), 1899-1912; wr. *The Conflict of Laws*, 1896 (constructed out of *The Law of Domicile*, 1879, and dedicated to the great lawyer, Arthur Cohen); *The Law of the Constitution*, 1885, 8th edn., 1915; and *Law and Opinion in Engld.* (based on lectures at Harvard Univ., 1898), 1905.

Dickens, Charles (1812-70): Engl. novelist; by common consent one of the greatest Engl. men of letters. Born at Landport, Portsmouth, in narrow circumstances, reproduced more or less closely in the early chapters of his *David Copperfield*, 1849-50, though D. raised himself out of them with less help and fewer advantages than his David enjoyed; reproduced, again, less directly, in the many scenes of unhappy childhood (Paul Dombey, Little Nell, Oliver Twist, and others), which he drew, with variations on the same theme. D. went as a child to London, and was a truer Londoner, even a Cockney, all his days than many actually born there. He secured reporting work on newspapers, and wr. sketches in the vein of T. Hook (q.v.) and Leigh Hunt (q.v.), whom, later, he rather cruelly, if not deliberately, ridiculed in the character of Harold Skimpole. With the *Pickwick Papers* (edited by Boz, 1836-7, in 20 monthly parts), D. started on the career of popularity and fame, which consumed every ounce of his abundant energies, writing, reading, and reforming, till his burial in Westminster Abbey, 14 June, 1870, his last novel, *Edwin Drood*, left with its mystery insoluble. His *Life* was written by John Forster (1812-76; a *Quarterly* and *Edinburgh* reviewer, and biographer, too, of Goldsmith and Landor, qq.v.), in 3 vols., 1872-4, and ranks as a standard biography; his daughters and his son, sir Henry D., have written about him; Paul Heichen in Germany, P. L. Hervier and André Joubert in France, H. Ibsen in Denmark, and, among many others, F. T. Marzials, G. A. Sala, B. W. Matz, G. K. Chesterton in Engld., have written bks. about him; nearly every man of literary note, including Swinburne, Watts-Dunton, Trollope, Ruskin, A. Lang, F. Harrison, G. Gissing, W. Bagehot, C. S. Calverley (author of the *Pickwick* examination-paper, the prize for which at Cambridge was won by W. Besant, q.v., another Portsmouth novelist), has written essays on him, and there are D. Museums, Dicts., a Boz Club, etc. His works are computed in the *D.N.B.* to have probably had the largest number of readers of any novels in the

Engl. language ; and, outside the Bible, and Shakespeare, and possibly the *Pilgrim's Progress*, D.'s circle of readers is probably the widest.

It is not necessary in this place to enumerate his bks. and writings : the list fills 14 pp. in *C.H.E.L.*, xiii, and the titles of the chief novels are household words, to adopt the name chosen by D. for the periodical which he founded, 1849, subsequently merging it in *All the Year Round*. A descendant of Smollett rather than of Fielding (qq.v.), if these literary filiations are distinguishable, and, through Smollett, of Lesage (q.v.) and the picaresque branch of the Novel (see s.v.), D. reached by sheer genius and exuberance a supreme place in the humour and pathos of character-delineation. He had an extraordinarily exact eye for detail, and an extraordinarily vivid imagination for effect, and the combination was unique : his *real* people had their being in *ideal* (or unreal) surroundings, precisely suited to their temper-amental idiosyncrasies ; and it is this concen-tration on the persons and their requirements, without much regard to dramatic probability, which makes D.'s works rather a gallery of portraits than a collection of tales. Unlike Thackeray (q.v.), his great contemporary, whose characters are developed by circum-stances, and work out their destiny by experi-ence, the characters of D. are placed, full-grown, in niches suited for their display ; and readers know the men and women of D., and remember their characteristics, long after they have forgotten in which novel any one of them appears. For this cause, the *Pickwick Papers* is still, perhaps, artistically, his best bk.

Reference must be made to special studies by D. as a social reformer (of schools, in *Nicholas Nickleby* and elsewhere, of the Court of Chancery in *Bleak House*, and so on) : it was a part of his big, warm heart, which found satisfaction, again, in the *Christmas Books* and stories ; and another, and a duller, special study might be devoted to D. and America, which he visited twice on tours of reading from his own works. But these, though parts of D., are not the best parts of him, whatever flowers of his special sowing were raised from those alien seeds. D. belongs, by nature and inheritance, to the very greatest class of writers in Europe,—to the class which includes Cervantes and Defoe (qq.v.), and from the enjoyment and appreciation of which only those readers are excluded, ' those much to be commiserated people ', as prof. Saints-bury calls them (*C.H.E.L.*, xiii, 311), ' who cannot relish pure fun,—fantastic humour which cares nothing for probability, consist-ency, chronology, and is not in the least afraid of invading those confines of nonsense which Hazlitt proudly and wisely claimed as the appanage and province of every true English-man. For these, of course, nothing can be done '. For the rest, D. will always live.

Diderot, Denis (1713-84) : Fr. *philosophe* (q.v.), dramatist, critic ; founder of the Encyclope-dists (s.v. Encyclopedia) ; the greatest genius of the 18th cent., according to Comte (q.v.) ; ' whoever holds him or his doings cheaply is a Philistine ', according to Goethe (q.v., and s.v. Philistinism.) (See Morley, *Diderot*,

2 vols., 1878). The son of a cutler at Langres, and destined originally for the Church, D. had a hard task to provide the means of liveli-hood for himself, his wife and family, for the subsidiary establishments which he supported, in despite of his philosophic code, and for the lavish hospitality which he dispensed, and which helped him to overcome the slight handicap of his provincial and obscure birth. D. drove his way through Paris society. He was a big, impetuous, masterful man ; fond of good talk, good company, good food ; very hard-working ; inspired by obstacles ; a sojourner in Paris, as he himself said, in the sense that he never felt an obligation to conform to conditions which did not suit him. We are not at all concerned here with the moral problems that have been raised by some of D.'s biographers. Doubtless, it was not consonant with the objects—social, moral and political—of the *Encyclopédie*, that its chief editor should lead an irregular life ; and doubtless British middle-class parents in a later generation were fully justified in quoting this fact when they identified free-thinking with loose living, and atheism (or anti-theism) with free-love. The examples of Byron (q.v.) in England, and of the brothers Schlegel (q.v.) in Germany supplied them with similar argu-ments. But the conclusion is empirical ; and the value of D.'s literary work is independent of the example of his private life. This work was in various kinds. He was a keen critic of the theatre ; and, inspired by this admiration for Lillo and Moore (qq.v.) on the Engl. stage, D. insisted on scenery and sentiment, alike in his dramatic criticism, *de la Poésie dramatique*, 1758, etc., and in his own tearful comedies (s.v. *Comédie larmoyante*), the *Fils naturel*, (1757 ; acted, 1771) and the *Père de Famille* (1758 ; acted, 1761). These pieces were written in prose ; both were transld. into Germ. by Lessing (q.v.), and the latter was the model for the *Hausvater* of Gemmingen (q.v.), and for the development of domestic drama in Germany. Germany, again, was the first home of D.'s dialogue between a cynic and a philosopher on all kinds and conditions of things, and esp. on lit., music and education, known as *le petit neveu de Rameau*. Written by D. in 1773, and circulated in MS., it was brought to Goethe's (q.v.) notice by Schiller (q.v.) in the last year of his life, and was first publd. in Goethe's version as *Ram-eaus Neffe*, 1805. But if some parts of D.'s fame were made in Germany, some parts of his inspiration were made in Engld. We are not speaking here of Shaftesbury and Locke (qq.v.) as the moving spirits of Fr. philosophy in the 18th cent., but rather of Richardson and Sterne (qq.v.), and their influence respectively on D.'s novels, *la Réligieuse*, 1760, after *Clarissa*, and *Jacques le fataliste*, 1773, after *Tristram Shandy*. D. wr., too, an *Eloge de Richardson*, 1761, which is several shades too enthusiastic in its eulogy, and a series of critical art-papers under the name of *Salons*, 1765-67, which contain some of his best work. To his other misc. writings, some of which were posth. publd., very brief notice need be accorded. He achieved the distinction of imprisonment for his *Lettre sur les aveugles*

('blind') à *'usage de ceux qui voient*, 1749, which he followed by similar letters on the deaf and dumb, 1751. The first of these treatises contains the germ of the thought of the one-sense-endowed statue, developed—independently, it is said—by Condillac (q.v.) into a system of sensationalism. 'Thoughts on the Interpretation of Nature', 1754, 'Philosophic Thoughts', 'The Walk (*Promenade*) of a Sceptic', 'Dialogue between Dalembert and Diderot', and a very frankly materialistic 'Dream of Dalembert', were all written during the next few years, though the *Rêve de Dalembert* was not issued till 1830. D. was always a fighter, and his pugnacity, which found expression in various dialogues, or *entretiens* (e.g., *d'un philosophe avec la Marechal de——*, 1777; *d'un père avec ses enfants*, 1773, etc.), was not even kept out of his hist. *Essai sur les règnes de Claude et de Néron*, 1778-82, where he attacked Rousseau (q.v.), who deserted from his standard. The story of the *Encyclopedia* is dealt with in the art. under that name; here a full tribute must be paid to the energy, industry and determination with which D. carried to a successful conclusion an enterprise which far outgrew the original scheme of its promoters, and which was opposed by obstacles which might have daunted less safety-trimming editors than Dalembert (q.v.), who gave way to them. D.'s name and fame are indissolubly linked with this monument of Fr. philosophy, the *Encyclopédie, ou dictionnaire des sciences, des arts, et des métiers*; and, apart from the versatility he displayed in dealing with the sciences and the arts, apart from the tone with which he impregnated the whole undertaking, and apart from the grave vicissitudes of editorship, a line is due to his supervision of the *métiers*, or trades, and to the serious trouble which he took ungrudgingly to acquaint himself with the conditions of wages, employment, and of commerce and manufacture. D. wr. the *Prospectus*, 1750, publd. vol. i, 1751, and got through to vol. vii, 1757, when Dalembert's art. on *Geneva*, followed shortly by the work, *de l'Esprit*, by Helvétius (q.v.), brought about Dalembert's retirement, Rousseau's resentment, and the heavy artillery of the censorship. D.'s recovery from these shattering blows, his rehabilitation of the scheme, his final triumph over opposition, and his completion of the work, undiminished in breadth of design and enhanced in the brilliance of its roll of contributors, till the last of the 35 vols. was placed in the subscribers' hands in 1772: this forms one of the most wonderful chapters in the literary history of modern Europe. When we recall the exiguous salary, averaging £130 a year, which D. received, and which compelled him to teach, write, and talk all through his busiest years, and when we recall, too, the high place of this work in Fr. thought, we recognize that D. truly earned and must always retain the meed of fame which was the sole object of his striving. A line is due to D.'s relations with the empress Catherine ii (q.v.) of Russia, whom he visited once in Petrograd, and who, like her brother-monarch, Fredk. ii (q.v.) of Prussia, was so brilliant a supporter of liberalism—on foreign soil. D. advised the empress on her various schemes of economic and social reform, and the correspondence between the autocrat and the physiocrat sustained the empress in her convictions that her despotism was genuinely benevolent. She invited the encyclopedists to complete their labours in her capital, when Paris proved inhospitable; she bought pictures under D.'s advice (his *Salons* really founded art-criticism); and, best of all, when D. was poor and old, the empress bought his library, and appointed him librarian for life. It is to be added that D. was never elected to the Fr. Academy (q.v.).

Dieze, Johann Andreas (1749-85): Germ. scholar; held a chair at Göttingen Univ., and was devoted esp. to the study of Span. culture. Transld., 1769, Velasco's (q.v.) 'Origins of Castilian Poetry', 'with copious and valuable notes, which more than double, not only the size of the original work, but its worth' (Ticknor, iii, 281n.).

Digby, George. See **Bristol, Earl of.**

Digby, Kenelm (1603-65): Engl. philosophic writer; diplomatist; F.R.S., 1663; knt., 1623; acquainted with Descartes (q.v.); wr. *Of Bodies* and *Of the Immortality of Man's Soul*, 1644, and a critique of the *Religio Medici* (s.v. Browne), 1641. D.'s *Private Memoirs*, 'a production as unreadable to modern generations as a Scudéry (q.v.) romance, which, indeed, in form it very much resembles' (*C.H.E.L.*, vii, 222), were first publd. from the orig. MS., 1827. 'Amadis-Paracelsus' (see s.vv.) is prof. Saintsbury's double-barrelled epithet for D. under these diverse aspects.

Digges, Leonard (1588-1635): Engl. poet. Wr. 2 poems in honour of Shakespeare (q.v.), and transld. *Gerardo, the Unfortunate Spaniard*, from Span. novel by Cespedes (q.v.).

Dilke, -i. Charles Wentworth (1789-1864): Engl. critic; in Navy pay-office, following in the steps of his father, similarly employed in the Dockyard at Portsmouth; continued the *Collection of Old Plays*, by Dodsley (q.v.), 1814-6, and, having established his name as an antiquary, acquired a proprietary share and undertook the editorship of the *Athenæum* (q.v.), 1830-46, raising it to a very high level of lit. interest and influence: his contributions on Junius (q.v.), the writings of Pope (q.v.), and other topics, of special importance, issued posth., 1875. D. edited the *Daily News*, 1846-9.

-ii. Charles Wentworth (1843-1911): Engl. statesman; grandson of above; second bart. Travelled in Australasia and America, and described his experiences in an attractive vol., *Greater Britain*, 1868; M.P., Chelsea; under-secretary for Foreign Affairs; president, Local Government Board; his career in politics was interrupted by private causes. Wr. *Memoir* of his grandfather (above); m., 1885, widow of Mark Pattison (q.v.); wr., 1887, *The Position of European Politics*, a brilliantly reasoned vol. The lit. tradition of the family was preserved by sir Fisher W. D., fourth bart., whom., 1905, Ethel, daughter of William Kingdon Clifford, F.R.S., mathematician, and of Mrs. Clifford, novelist.

Diodati, Charles (d., 1638): Engl. scholar, whose early death was deplored by his friend, Milton (q.v.), in *Epitaphium Damonis*, 1645, as well as in an Ital. sonnet, and Lat. elegies. D.'s father, Theodore D. (d., 1651) was a Swiss-Ital. physician in Engld., and assisted Florio (q.v.) in his transln. of the *Essais* of Montaigne (q.v.).

Diskurse der Maler (Germ.): ' Discourses of the Painters '; title of weekly literary organ founded at Zurich by the Swiss opponents of Gottsched (q.v.); 1721-23; the protagonists were Bodmer and Breitinger (qq.v.). The title was chosen in obvious deference to the famous Horatian tag ' ut pictura poesis ' (*Ars Poetica*, 361 ; and see s.v. Laocoon) ; but the 'painters' were largely painters of manners, 'Sitten-malerei' being the current term for what was later psychology or character-delineation. The main achievement of the *Diskurse*, which played an important part in the period between Gottsched and Lessing, was the firm stand which it was their fixed policy to take against the Germ. Marinism (s.v. Marini) of Lohenstein (q.v.), with its consequences in bombast, galimathias, and word-play, as well as in sumptuary extravagance and Frenchified habits of daily conduct. The national reaction of Klopstock (q.v.) was in part-accordance with the objects of the Swiss campaigners.

Disraeli, -i. Isaac (1766-1848): Engl. bibliophil; son of Benjamin D'Israeli, who settled in Engld., 1748, from Italy, where his family had found refuge from the persecution of the Jews in Spain. Wr. *Curiosities of Literature*, 1791 (anon.) and later series; *Calamities of Authors*, 1812-3, *Genius of Judaism*, 1833 (anon.; he had withdrawn from the Jew. Church, 1817), and other scholarly works. D.C.L., Oxon, 1832.

   -ii. Benjamin (1804-81): Engl. novelist; statesman; twice prime minister of Engld.; created earl of Beaconsfield, 1876 ; K.G., 1878 ; signalized his accession to premiership, 1874, by offering G.C.B. to Carlyle (q.v.) and baronetcy to Tennyson (q.v.). Wr. *Vivian Grey*, 1826 ; *The Young Duke*, 1831 ; *Contarini Fleming*, 1832 ; *Alroy*, 1833 ; *Venetia*, and *Henrietta Temple*, 1837 (when he first entered the House of Commons as M.P. for Maidstone) ; *Coningsby*, 1844 ; *Sybil*, 1845 ; *Tancred*, 1847 ; *Lothair*, 1870, and *Endymion* (his last novel), 1880. Wr., too, burlesques and political pamphlets, and, 1851, *Biography of Lord George Bentinck*, in which he set forth his famous opinions on race and the significance of the Semitic stock in a manner which psycho-analysts might be disposed to refer to the repression of Judaism in his subconscious self. However this may be, the series of brilliant novels publd. by D. in the course of more than half a century, during which the son and type (physical and intellectual) of a despised and persecuted religious community became the hero of the Tory party, the leader of society, the ' friend ' (by queen Victoria's initiative) of his sovereign, whom he crowned as empress of India, and the victor of Bismarck in diplomacy, constitutes a unique record in the hist. of lit. It was unique, too, in another way, since ' of the place of Disraeli in establishing a definite literary *genre* there can be no differences of opinion ' (Speare, *The Political Novel*, 1924 ; cf. 'A quite unique place in the history of English fiction will be universally allowed

to be held by Benjamin Disraeli ',—sir A. W. Ward, *C.H.E.L.*, xiii, 345). Political and social novels took their rise in Engld. out of the changes of which the Reform Act of 1832 may be selected as central, and were written by Trollope, Meredith, Kingsley, G. Eliot, Mrs. Gaskell, Mrs. H. Ward, and others, after D. But D. is properly credited with the initiation of the *genre* (Taper and Tadpole in *Coningsby* are his invention), and, by his expert and intimate acquaintance with the *milieu* in which it moved, he raised it at once to a distinct branch of the art of fiction.

Dixon, William Hepworth (1821-79): Engl. man of letters ; a founder of the Palestine Exploration Fund, and an orig. member of the School Board for London, 1870. Wr. *John Howard and the Prison World*, 1850 ; *Life of Wm. Penn* (q.v.), in answer to Macaulay (q.v.), 1851, and other works in biography and history ; edited the *Athenæum*, q.v., 1853-69. D.'s *Holy Land*, 1865, and *Free Russia*, 1870, were among his best-known travel-books.

Dmitriev, Ivan Ivanovich (1760-1837): Russ. poet, known as the patriarch of Russ. lit., though his claim to literary renown rests a little uneasily on some satires, odes, light verse, and translns. from La Fontaine (q.v.). He was wise enough to build himself on Karamsin's (q.v.) lines, so far as his inferior talents permitted, and certainly he fell short of the sycophancy and exaggeration which Derzhavin achieved as an ode-writer. D.'s correspondence and journals form, perhaps, his most interesting memorial.

Dobell, Sydney Thompson (1824-74): Engl. poet ; critic. Wr. *The Roman*, 1850, a dramatic poem, conveying a passionate plea for oppressed nationalities, which won the attention of many influential friends ; publd. under the *nom-de-guerre* of Sydney Yendys. After a fragmentary and somewhat obscure poem, *Balder*, part i, 1854, D. was inspired by the Crimean war to write a vol. of *Sonnets on the War*, 1855, jointly with Alex. Smith (q.v.), and *England in Time of War*, 1856, a very successful vol. His later life was shadowed by ill-health, aggravated by a fall at Pozzuoli, but his verse reached a very respectable level of fancy and diction, though marred by the irregularities of taste characteristic of the so-called ' Spasmodic ' (q.v.) school.

Dobrolubov, Nicholas Alexandrovich (1836-61): Russ. critic ; materialist. With the quasi-political side of D.'s doctrinaire philosophy we are not directly concerned. His distinction was that his political Nihilism (q.v.) was rooted in a theory of literary criticism, which he owed partly to Chernyschevsky (q.v.), the critic-martyr. D. held that the negative type of character, the anti-social, let-me-be philosophy of spiritual *nirvána* and physical inertia, is the only type true to life, or truly helpful to conduct. And he supported this argument to numbness by an analysis of Russ. fiction. Goncharov's (q.v.) Oblomov, of course, was the sublimation of the type ; but D. found the Oblomov-hero, or constituent parts of him, in most of the famous characters of Russ. novelists : Lermontov's Pechorin, Turgenev's Rudin, Pushkin's Oniégin (see s.vv.), etc. D.'s discovery, which may be compared with a contention once advanced by Mr. Frank Harris that all Shakespeare's male characters are variations of Hamlet, was eagerly seized upon by the youth of Russia as the sanction of anti-idealism, anti-altruism, and materialism.

Dobrovský, Josef (1753-1829): Czech scholar; studied theology, Semitics, and folklore; visited Sweden and Russia in a search for Slavonic MSS.; laid truly the foundations of Czech philology by his ' Detailed Grammar of the Czech Language ', 1809, followed by ' A History of Older Czech Literature ', 1818, and other learned works.

Dobson (Henry) Austin (1840-1921): Engl. poet and critic; the complete bibliography of his writings is of formidable length. D. was a man of shy and retired tastes and of dainty and delicate craftsmanship. His main quarry was the 18th cent., in which he loved the brocades, the furniture, the porcelain, and other evidences of careful work before the epoch of machinery. His *Old World Idylls*, 1883, and *At the Sign of the Lyre*, 1885, were his chief bks. of elegant verse; his *Four Frenchwomen*, 1890, was one of his best vols. in prose, which included studies, admirably executed, of Hogarth, Fielding, Fanny Burney, Goldsmith, and H. Walpole. His *Bookman's Budget*, 1917, is a charming collection from his notebooks, which illuminates the scholar and the man.

Dodd, William (1729-77): Engl. scholar; edited the *Christian Magazine*, 1760-7; held rural livings, and was appointed chaplain to the king, 1763, but was struck off the roll, 1774, for improper solicitation of preferment. D. compiled, among other works, the well-known vol. of *Beauties of Shakespeare*, 1752, and transld. the *Hymns* of Callimachus, 1754. It is a matter for regret to have to add that D. was executed, 1777, after a conviction for forging a bond for £4,200, in the name of his former pupil, the fifth lord Chesterfield.

Dodgson, C. L. See Carroll, L.

Dodsley, Robert (1703-64): Engl. bookseller; publisher; frequently mentioned in memoirs of 18th cent., e.g. Boswell's (q.v.) *Johnson* and Walpole's (q.v.) *Letters*. D. started life as a footman, and wr. his *Muse in Livery*, 1732; he attracted the favourable notice of Pope (q.v.), who lent him £100 to open a book-shop in Pall Mall. The venture succeeded: in 1738, Johnson came to him with an intro-duction from Cave (q.v.), and it was D. who, in 1745, first proposed to Johnson to compile an Engl. Dict. Meanwhile, in 1744, he had set his own mark on letters by his *Select Collection of Old Plays*, now his best-known work. (See s.v. Dilke). He publd. for leading writers of the day, and was a friend of Shenstone (q.v.) and others. In 1759, D. founded the *Annual Register*, and appointed Burke (q.v.) editor and chief contributor. The connection of Burke with the firm was continued after R. D.'s death, under his younger brother, James D. (1724-97).

Dolce Stil Nuovo (It.): ' sweet new style '; phrase employed by Dante, *Purg.* xxiv, 57, and since become the standard description of the new Tuscan stamp impressed on Sicilian court-poetry, chiefly by Guido Guinicelli (q.v.); enlarging the boundaries of Ital. verse-style,

and adapting the language of a clique to the audience of the Renaissance in Florence.

Dolet, Étienne (1509-46): Fr. humanist and printer. Born at Orleans; studied Latinity in Paris and Padua; resided at Toulouse and Lyons, where he planned and issued *Commentarii linguæ Latinæ* in two folio vols., in Cicero's praise. It appeared at about the same time as the new Lat. lexicon of R. Estienne (q.v.), and was epoch-making for the revival of learning in France. Wr., too, handbook of Ciceronianisms, 1539, and Lat. dialogue, introducing sir T. More, on the imitation of Cicero, designed as counterblast to Erasmus's *Ciceronianus* (see s.v. Cicero). As printer, D. produced a Fr. transln. of his favourite Lat. author, a Lat. history of the reign of king Francis i, Fr. translns. of New Testament, of religious works by Erasmus, etc. These last enterprises aroused the jealous eye of the Inquisition, which recalled that D. was a friend of advanced thinkers, such as Marot and Rabelais, who fluttered round queen Margaret of Navarre (qq.v.), and he was convicted of heresy in 1542. A royal pardon prevailed, and, in 1544, D. printed his Fr. renderings from Plato; a fresh prosecution ensued, arising out of a doubt thrown by his version on the belief in immortality, and D. was executed in 1546. This judicial murder—for, like More's, his contemporary's, it was nothing else—has been commemorated by a statue in the *place Maubert* in Paris erected to the ' martyr to the Renaissance '.

Don Juan (Span.): Dramatic character-type See s.vv. Cueva, Molina, Byron. The invention of the type is commonly ascribed to Molina, but the play, *el Bastador de Sevilla* ' The Gay Deceiver of Seville ', 1630, in which it first occurs as a full-length portrait of patrician imperturbability in libertine scoundrelism, may have been the composition of Calderon (q.v.). It was utilized by Molière (q.v.) in his *Festin de Pierre*, 1665, and provided Mozart with the subject for an opera.

Donaldson, John William (1811-61): Engl. scholar. Wr., among other works of first-class significance to classical studies, the *New Cratylus*, 1839, which virtually founded the science of comparative philology in Engld.

Donati, Alesso (14th cent.): It. realistic lyric poet.

Donne, John (1573-1631): Engl. poet and divine; a man of very interesting life, not least because he was brought up in the Roman Catholic faith, but adopted Protestantism, became dean of St. Paul's, 1621, after holding several rectorships, and preached sermons of a rare excellence; as a writer, too, very interesting historically, not least because, though almost an exact contemporary of Shakespeare (q.v., 1564-1616), D. belonged to the autumn of the Renaissance (q.v.) in Engld., and is ranked as a leader of the Metaphysical (q.v.) poets, who, by their parade of learning and abstract treatment of love, had more affinity with Dante than with Petrarch (see s.vv.), and may almost be termed the pre-Raphaelites (q.v.) of the 17th cent. In this sense, as, indeed in others, too remote to trace in a brief survey, there is a likeness, despite vast differences, between D. and Tennyson (q.v.).

Owing largely to these interests, extraneous ultimately to D.'s position as a poet, his bibliography has become somewhat formidable, and continues to grow. It includes, in recent years, the elaborate Oxford edn. of his *Poems*, in 2 vols., by prof. Grierson, who wr. the excellent ch. xi in vol. iv of the *C.H.E.L.* on the subject; Courthope, *Hist. Engl. Poetry*, vol. iii, ch. viii; sir E. Gosse, *Life and Letters of John Donne*, 2 vols.; E. Dowden, ' The Poetry of John Donne ', in *New Studies of Literature ; les Doctrines médiévales chez Donne*, by Mary P. Ramsay, and *A Study of the Prose Works of John Donne*, by Ethel M. Simpson. Reference may also be made to the *Fr. Renaissance in Engld.*, by sir S. Lee, who rates very highly the debt which D. has incurred to Du Bartas (q.v.).

The man himself, in his fascination and versatility, to which virility and unconventionality are to be added, may be seen in the portrait of a contemporary (sir Richard Baker) : ' Mr. John Donne, who leaving Oxford lived at the Inns of Court, not dissolute but very neat ; a great visitor of Ladies, a great Frequenter of Plays, a great writer of conceited Verses ' (s.v. see Conceit). He was a great traveller, too, and it is worth noting that his mother, Elizabeth, was a daughter of John Heywood, the dramatist, and that Elizabeth Heywood's mother was Elizabeth, daughter of John Rastell and Elizabeth, sister of sir Thomas More (see s.vv.). Thus, by descent, by taste and by equipment, D. belonged to the life of wit, in the older sense of that term, which he practised in his eloquent sermons, in his letters, his satires, and his lyric verse. The *Poems*, with elegies on the author's death, were publd., chiefly posth., in 1633, and frequently reprinted, notably by Grosart, 2 vols,. 1872-3. The prose-works include *Biathanatos : A declaration . . . that Self-Homicide is not so naturally sin that it may never be otherwise*, 1648 ; and the sermons include *Death's Duel*, preached at Whitehall before the King, 1630, and known as D.'s own funeral sermon, Thoughts of death, immortality and corruption were closely inwoven with the texture of D.'s thought, and he drew from these thoughts many striking images for his poetry. (The mystic adoration of nature as a symbol of God was common to the ' metaphysical ' poets, and serves to differentiate them from the poets whose effects depended more exclusively on mere verbal conceits. See s.vv. Death, Nature, Mysticism). The philosopher is always behind the poet :

Doubt wisely ; in strange way
To stand inquiring right, is not to stray ;
To sleep or run wrong is. On a huge hill,
Cragged and steep, Truth stands, and he that will
Reach her, about must and about must go,
And what th' hill's suddenness resists win so.
Yet strive so, that before age, death's twilight,
Thy soul rest, for none can work in that night.

The first line suggests a likeness to Tennyson's defence of philosophic doubt ; the second, to R. Browning's hate of the unlit lamp and the ungirt loin ; and the whole passage illustrates at once D.'s attitude to experience and the rough vigour of his verse. ' And as

Donne was at this stage a sceptic in religion ', says Courthope (*loc. cit.*), ' so was he a revolutionist in love . . . The Provençal poets and the female presidents of the *Cours d'Amour* had revised and extended the ancient canons of the art as expounded by Ovid ' (see s.v.) ; ' and, while they tacitly recognized the physical basis of the passion, they disguised it by the elaborate character of the imaginative superstructure they raised upon it. . . This fine Platonic edifice is ruthlessly demolished in the poetry of Donne. To him love, in its infinite variety and inconsistency, represented the principle of perpetual flux in Nature. At the same time, his imagination was stimulated by the multitude of paradoxes and metaphors which were suggested to him by the varying aspects of the passion '. He passed through these stages of experience, alike as theologian and lover ; and he lived to write such excellently clear and arresting verses as :

For God's sake hold your tongue and let me love ;

or

I long to talk with some old lover's ghost
Who died before the God of love was born ;

or

Her pure and eloquent blood
Spoke in her cheeks, and so distinctly wrought
That we might almost say her body thought.

But too often his ' wit ' overreached itself, or, rather overreached its poetic aim ; and, great as D. was in achievement and influence, it is not unlikely that, as bks. accumulate, and the 17th cent. recedes further on the horizon, readers will seek less frequently the beauty and eloquence of D., and will rather be repelled by his habit of ' ransacking his multifarious knowledge to discover new and startling conceits in which to express his bizarre and subtle moods ', (*P.E.L.*, vii, 159).

Dorat, Claude Joseph (1734-80) : Fr. poet. Wr. tragedies (*Regulus*, etc.), comedies (*le Célibataire*, etc.), and misc. verse ; songs, fables, etc.

Dorat, Jean (c. 1502-88) : Fr. Hellenist ; Royal Reader in Gk. at Paris from 1559 (see s.v. Corporation) ; latinized his name (D'Aurat) to Auratus ; tutor to Ronsard (q.v.), who, in gratitude for the world of thought and style opened to him by Gk. learning, included D.'s name in the Pleiad (q.v.) ; wr. prolifically in Gk. verse on all the literary matters of his day, which appealed to the prevailing taste of the learned brigade ; best known as editor of Æschylus. D.'s pupils at the college of Coqueret numbered other members of the Pleiad, among them J. Du Bellay (q.v.), and the teacher's infectious enthusiasm for Hellenism no doubt contributed to the principles adopted by the leaders of the movement ; but beyond this, and beyond poetic eulogies addressed to Ronsard and others, D.'s direct work for the Pleiad was *nil*.

Dorland, Pieter (1454-1507) : Dutch mystic ; reputed author of the Netherlandish ' Everyman ' (q.v.), *Elkerlyck*, a morality-play.

Dostoievsky, Feodor Michaelovitch (1821-81) : Russ. novelist ; in many respects the greatest whom his country has so far produced. ' If one were asked ', says Mr. Maurice Baring (*Landmarks in Russ. Lit.*, 252), ' to sum up briefly what was Dostoievsky's message to his generation and to the world in general, one would do so in two words : love and pity. The love which is in Dostoievsky's work is so great, so bountiful, so overflowing, that it is impossible to find a parallel to it, either in ancient or in modern lit. Supposing the Gospel of St. John were to be annihilated and lost to us for ever, although nothing could replace it, Dostoievsky's work would go nearer to replacing it than any other bks. written by any other man '. A strong statement, but deliberately written, and supported by the reflection, that, throughout his life, D. ' knew what wretches feel, by experience and not by theory, and all his life he was bound by a wheel of fire ' (the allusions are to *King Lear*). We owe, too, to Mr. Baring a quotation from D.'s great memorial speech at Moscow, 1880, in memory of Pushkin (q.v.), expressing his political opinions: ' What is the strength of the Russian national spirit other than an aspiration towards a universal spirit, which shall embrace the whole world and the whole of mankind ? . . To be a real Russian and to be wholly Russian means only this : to be a brother of all men and to be universally human. . . And in the long-run I am convinced that we, that is to say, not we, but the future generations of the Russian people, shall everyone of us, from the first to the last, understand that to be a real Russian must signify simply this : to strive to bring about a solution and an end to European conflicts ; to show to Europe a way to escape from its anguish in the Russian soul, which is universal and all-embracing ; to instil into her a brotherly love for all men's brothers, and in the end perhaps to utter the great and final word of universal harmony, the fraternal and lasting concord of all people according to the gospel of Christ '. This deepens the tragedy of Russia after the revolution. Lastly, of D. as a writer, in the view of the same accomplished Engl. critic : ' His position with regard to Tolstoy, Fielding, and other great novelists is like that of Marlowe with regard to Shakespeare. His genius soars higher and dives deeper than that of any other novelist, Russian or European '. Once more, a strong statement, but supported by the reviewer in the *Times Lit. Supp.*, 9 March, 1916, of Mrs. Garnett's transln. of D.'s ' A Raw Youth ' : ' No one has ever gone so deep into character as Dostoievsky, except Shakespeare in *Hamlet*. . . One can see that it is all conceived and written by one of the greatest writers of the world '.

The invitation to D. should be complete, and it remains briefly to chronicle the list of his novels and the outline of his life. The former include ' Poor Folk ', 1846 ; ' Letters from a Dead House ', 1861-62 ; ' Crime and Punishment ' (his *chef-d'œuvre*), 1866 ; ' The Idiot ', 1866 ; ' The Possessed ' (or ' The Devil ' : these are the parasites of Nihilism), 1871 ; and ' The Brothers Karamozov ' (unfind.), 1880. There were others, but these were the greatest, and on them the estimates are based, in which foreign critics—we may cite the name of M. Vogué—are at one with D.'s own countrymen, who ' gave him a funeral such as few kings or heroes have ever had '.

D. was brought up in a religious atmosphere, and was a wide reader in foreign languages in his youth. In 1849 (see s.v. Russ. Lit.) he was condemned to death by the politicians, and, by a refinement of cruelty, which left permanent effects on a man so young and so sensitive, he was not reprieved till at the last minute of the terrible ceremony. Even then he had to serve 4 years of hard labour in Siberia, and 6 years more in exile.

Douglas, Gavin (*c.* 1474-1522): Scot. poet ; bp. of Dunkeld ; third son of fifth earl of Angus ; died of the plague in London. D.'s great title to renown rests on his transln. of the *Æneid* of Virgil (q.v.) into Engl. decasyllabic verse (*ed. pr.*, 1553), an achievement which, independent of its merits in diction and metre, gives him primacy in the splendid art of Latinity. D.'s rhythm has roughnesses, but he managed his language with a swing, which carried him, too, with success through his 2 allegorical poems : *The Palace of Honour* (written, 1501) and *King Hart* (*ed. pr.*, 1786).

Douglas, William Scott (1815-83): Scot. scholar ; edited the works of his fellow-countryman, R. Burns (q.v.), 6 vols, 1877-9.

Dousa, -i. Janus (1545-1604). Dutch scholar ; governor of Leyden during the siege, 1575 ; first curator of new univ. ; humanist ; editor of plays of Plautus ; known as the ' oracle of the university ', and was instrumental in attracting Lipsius (q.v.) to its chair of history.

-ii. Janus (1571-97): son of above ; librarian at Leyden.

-iii. Franciscus (1577-1606): younger son of same ; editor of Lucilius.

Doyle, Francis Hastings Chas. (1810-88): Engl. poet ; second bart., 1839 ; prof. of Poetry at Oxford, 1867-77. Wr. *Miscellaneous Poems*, 1834 ; *Two Destinies*, 1844 ; *Oedipus, King of Thebes*, 1849 ; *The Return of the Guards*, 1866 ; chiefly notably for an heroic vein. This came to its most enduring expression in the stanzas suggested by the wreck of the transport-ship, *Birkenhead*, 1852 :

What follows why recall ?—the brave who died,
Died without flinching in that bloody surf.
They sleep as well beneath that purple tide
As others under turf.

D.'s *Reminiscences and Opinions* were publd., 1886.

Doyle, Richard (1824-83): Engl. artist; made imperishable contribution to literary appreciation by his illustrations to Ruskin's (q.v.) *King of the Golden River*, 1851, Thackeray's (q.v.) *Newcomes*, 1853-5, etc.

Drachmann, Holger Henrik (1846-1908): Dan. poet and novelist. Wr. several vols. of much-praised verse, which are said to ' establish beyond question their author's right to be named among the few genuine poets of the latter half of the 19th century ' (Boyesen, *Scand. Lit.*, 195 ; Nutt, 1895), and some vols. of short stories, which have won feebler praise.

Drayton, Michael (1563-1631): Engl. poet ; contemporary with Shakespeare (q.v.), but considerably *addictus jurare in verba* and in the manner of the Fr. Pleiad and of Du Bartas (qq.v.). Wr. *Idea : The Shepherd's Garland*, 1593, in which the heroine's name, frequently

on Dramatic Poetry, 1668, defended the employ-ment of rhyme in tragedy. *Annus Mirabilis : the Year of Wonder*, 1666, was written in quatrains, since the subject overflowed the restricting limits of the heroic couplet : but the overflow did not produce *enjambement*, and each stanza is sober and self-contained. His political satires in verse, *Absalom and Achitophel* (2 parts), *The Medall*, and *Mac-Flecknoe*, all belong to 1681-2. The first treats of a topic as dull as the Exclusion Bill, but contains passages as marvellous in their kind as the characterization of Zimri (duke of Buckingham), which the author himself deemed ' worth the whole poem ' :

A man so various, that he seem'd to be
Not one, but all Mankind's Epitome.
Stiff in opinions, always in the wrong ;
Was Everything by starts and Nothing long ;
But in the course of one revolving Moon,
Was Chymist, Fiddler, States-man, and Buffoon,
Then all for Women, Painting, Rhiming, Drinking ;
Besides ten thousand Freaks that dy'd in thinking.

Finally, for the purpose of this brief summary there are the great odes on musical themes : *St. Cecilia's Day*, 1687, and *Alexander's Feast*, 1697.

Brief though the summary is, it may serve to indicate the basis of Dr. Johnson's judgment (*op. cit.*, ' Dryden '), which later criticism has confirmed, that ' Perhaps no nation ever produced a writer that enriched his language with such variety of models. To him we owe the improvement, perhaps the completion of our metre, the refinement of our language, and much of the correctness of our sentiments. By him we were taught *sapere et fari*, to think naturally and express forcibly. He showed us the true bounds of a translator's liberty. What was said of Rome, adorned by Augustus, may be applied by an easy metaphor to English poetry embellished by Dryden,—he found it brick, and he left it marble '. And sir A. W. Ward (*loc. cit.*) concurs, that ' though the work of his life is not marble without a flaw, yet the whole structure overtops the expanse of contemporary English literature like the temple shining from the Sunian height over the sea '.

Du Bartas, Guillaume Salluste (1544-90): Fr. poet and soldier ; Gascon seigneur by rank ; served under king Henri iv ; fatally wounded at battle of Ivry ; religious follower of Calvin (q.v.), and was known as the ' Protestant Ronsard ' (q.v.). Ronsard, the chief star in the Pleiad (q.v.), who had welcomed Du B. at first, resented the implication of equality and withdrew his literary patronage. Partly to this withdrawal, and more largely to the tradition of sectarian bitterness against the Huguenots (q.v.), is due the comparative neglect of Du B. as a poet by his own country-men. It ill becomes a foreigner to attempt to correct an accepted judgment of this kind ; but the Fr. defective appreciation of Du B.'s gifts is particularly obvious in Engld., where the Puritan genius and its consummation in Milton (q.v.) prepare criticism more effectively to recognize its early manifestations. It

was Du B. who, more than any regular member of Ronsard's brotherhood, made experiments in the Fr. epic, which was one of the forms desiderated by Du Bellay (q.v.) in the propagandist-piece of the Pleiad ; and with true Huguenot devotion, he went to the Bible for his subjects. He wr. an epic *Judith*, 1573, designed on the ambitious plan, afterwards realized in *Paradise Lost*, of combining Hellenic form with Hebraic inspiration ; another epic, 1578, on the creation of the world, entitled *la Semaine*, in 7 bks., and he left unfind. *la Seconde Semaine*. The prosodists and philologists note that Du B. followed the principles of the Pleiad in his use of the Alexandrine (q.v.) couplet, which was preserved from the holocaust of the old metres for future development and improvement, as well as in his fertile extension of the resources of the Fr. language by com-pound adjectives and other inventions ; it must be added that in his reliance on the encyclopedias of natural history and philo-sophy, he was distinctly medieval. Thirty editions of the *Semaine* are said to have been sold before its author's early death, but his native fame did not long survive the zest given to Huguenot lit. by reaction from the horrors of St. Bartholomew. Abroad, his fate has been different. Goethe (q.v.) held him in high honour ; but it was in Elizabethan Engld. that Du B. won a reputation even higher than his merits. King James vi of Scotld. transld. one of his epic poems and procured the transln. of another ; he admired the *Semaine* so much that he penned an effusive invitation to Du B. to visit his court. The visit was paid in 1587, and included a reception by queen Elizabeth, and the compliment of warm welcome by sir Philip Sidney (q.v.) ; and it was in consequence of this visit, and of the admiration which Du B. had aroused, stimulated by the news of his heroic death, that Joshua Sylvester (q.v.) commenced in 1592 his transln. of the *Semaine*, completed in 1605. He outdoes the stylistic vices of his original, though he reproduces the best passages effectively ; and the Engl. version was amply praised by Harvey (q.v.) and by the younger poets whom he dominated by his judgment. On the extent of Du B.'s influence on these poets, including Spenser, of his contribution to the metaphysical (q.v.) poetry of Donne (q.v.), and of his affinity even to Milton (q.v.), authorities differ in their estimate. Sir S. Lee (*Fr. Renaissance in Engld.*) is disposed to write the first very high ; but whatever parts of Du B.'s intellectual gifts have passed into the heritage of Engl. poetry, they have now been almost irrecognizably absorbed ; and it is not unjust to the Fr. poet, who has been variously described as a ' Hugue-not Homer ' and a ' Milton *manqué* ', to quote the commentary of another great Engl. writer : ' Who is there that now reads the *Creation* of Dubartas ? Yet all Europe once resounded with his praise ; he was caressed by kings ; and, when his Poem was translated into our language, the *Faëry Queen* faded before it ' (Wordsworth, *Prose Works*, ed. Grosart, 1876, ii, 111). For the value of poetry resides, not in its hist. interest, but in its present appeal.

Du Bellay, -i. Guillaume (1491-1543): Fr. memoirist.

-ii. Jean (1492-1560): Fr. ecclesiastic; card.; constant patron of Rabelais (q.v.).

-iii. Martin (d. 1559): Fr. memoirist. These 3 distinguished men were brothers, and were all moderate in their opinions, and sympathetically inclined to the new learning, to which so considerable a contribution was made by their kinsman (probably a cousin),

-iv. Joachim (1524-60): Fr. poet; member of the Pleiad (q.v.). Fellow-pupil with Ronsard (q.v.) of Dorat (q.v.), and discussed in that congenial atmosphere the principles of linguistic and literary reform. These principles, which provided for the incorporation of the best elements of classical models, were worked out by Du B., shortly after his student-years, in the manifesto of the côterie, issued in 1549: *Défense et Illustration de la Langue française.* The little treatise of 48 pages was written in haste and has been lauded at leisure during three-and-a-half centuries; prof. Saintsbury (*Hist. Crit.*, ii, 115) says that 'Du Bellay preached what Shakespeare practised', and adds (*ib.*, 116, n. 2) that 'its claim lies in its eager eloquence', a remark which is endorsed by a contemporary Fr. critic, Jusserand (*Ronsard*, Hachette, 1913, 36): 'The tone is that of the Commandments; the eloquence is enchanting; it is the interpreter of a god issuing oracles, and if the precepts are obscure or contradictory, the resemblance to oracles is but the more marked'. On this stream of eloquence and patriotism, enthusiastic for the Fr. poetry to-be, which was to depart from medieval limitations, and to outgrow the childish taste for ballads, virelays, and similar 'épiceries' (sweetmeats), Du B. launched his defence of the Fr. language, viewed solely as the medium of Fr. lit. He aimed, and bade his countrymen aim, at an equality with the Gks. and Romans; imitation was to go overboard with limitation, and in this prescription he differed from even so recent a predecessor as Sibilet (q.v.), and still more from Italianate critics of the *Vida* (q.v.) tradition. The new, true Fr. of the society of the Pleiad, of which Du B., as long-sighted as he was short-lived, was at once the prophet and the champion, was to be Fr. for Frenchmen and by Frenchmen. It was to absorb the best elements of other cultures, Ital. and Span. as well as Lat. and Gk.; it was to naturalize the sonnet (q.v.) from modern Italy and the ode from ancient Greece; it was to invent the 'long French poem', worthy of the great history of France, and was not to be content, like Lyly (q.v.) in his *Euphues*, to 'rather lie shut in a lady's casket than open in a scholar's study'. The precise contrary was Du B.'s aim; he dismissed all feebler aspirants 'to the sumptuous palaces of lords and the magnificent courts of princes, where, surrounded by dames and damsels, your lovely and trifling writings, destined to the brevity of your own lives, will be admired and adored; not to the studies of scholars and the libraries of the learned'. We must judge the *Défense* by its aim and its effects even more than by its contents. The enemies of the Pleiad might contend that the defended language needed no 'defence': *non tali auxilio nec defensoribus istis*; that the young critic in a hurry had forgotten more than he had learned; had forgotten Saint-Gelais, and Le Maire, and Marot (qq.v.), and others enough. But we need not fight their quarrel over again. Du B.'s best justification is Ronsard himself, and those who came after Ronsard; and a high place among the Pleiad reformers belongs to the author of their 'poetics'. For Du B. was poet as well as critic. There was even a little coolness between Ronsard and Du B. for the haste with which he rushed into print with a practical example of his principles in a vol. of sonnets to *Olive* (mlle. de Viole, by an anagram), 1549, just prior to Ronsard's *Odes*. Two other collections of sonnets, *Regrets*, and the *Antiquités de Rome*, which Spenser (q.v.) turned into Engl. sonnets, and one or two other works of mark appeared at rapid intervals before the 'Apollo of the Pleiad', as he has been termed, died untimely but not without honour.

Dubos, Jean Baptiste (1670-1742): Fr. historian; *abbé.* Wr. 'Reflections on Poetry and Painting', and an interesting but quite unscientific work on early Fr. history, in which he argued that the invasion of Gaul by the Franks was a matter of arrangement and not of conquest; and in which he propounded some valuable speculations on the influence of climate (q.v.) on habit. Such inquiries, which acquired importance in the academic struggle just prior to the Fr. Revolution, were in a sense signs of that coming time. (See s.v. Boulainvilliers, for example). D.'s æsthetics (q.v.) were part of the material utilized by Lessing (q.v.) in his *Laokoon.*

Du Cange, sieur, Charles du Fresne (1610-88): Fr. lexicographer. Wr. glossaries of medieval Lat. (1678; re-edited in 10 vols. as recently as 1887), and Gk. (1688); edited Joinville and Villehardouin (qq.v.), and contributed notably to hist. study of the Fr. Middle Ages. Du C. likewise edited several of the Byzantine historians, including Anna Comnena (1083-1148), daughter of the emperor Alexius i. The current authority, superseding Du C., but based on his labours, is F. Chalandon, *Essai sur le règne d'Alexis i Comnène*, Paris, 1900; *Jean ii Comnène et Manuel i Comnène*, 1912.

Ducis, Jean François (1733-1816): Fr. playwright; Shakespearean; dramatized *Hamlet, King Lear*, and others, 1769-92, and contributed notably to the enfranchisement of the Fr. stage from the rigours of the classical tradition. The changes which D. made in his adaptations were in the direction of happy endings to the tragedies, and of a high-flown diction and style. It is noteworthy that D. succeeded Voltaire (q.v.) as a member of the Fr. Academy (q.v.), thus symbolizing the change from classicism to romance (q.v.).

Duff-Gordon, Lucy (1821-69): Engl. scholar; daughter of John Austin (1790-1859); m., 1840, sir A. C. D.-G., bt., and became a well-known hostess in London society, before she went to Egypt, 1862, where she died. Transld. various works by Sybel, Niebuhr (qq.v.), and other Germ. historians, and wr. *Letters from Egypt.*

Dufresny, Charles Rivière (1648-1724): Fr. dramatist and novelist; a man of versatile talents, but desultory powers; his marriage with his laundress in order to pay his debt to her is said to have furnished Lesage (q.v.) with a character for the *Diable Boiteux*. D. is chiefly remembered as a writer of comedies, both alone and in collaboration with Regnard (q.v.).

Dumas, -i. Alexandre (1803-70) : Fr. dramatist, novelist ; commonly described as Dumas *père* in distinction from Dumas *fils* below. A.D.'s father was a general of the Revolution ; a reference to his negress grandmother is always suggested in extenuation of D.'s exotic exuberance of matter without form. (A similar strain in Pushkin, q.v., is employed to explain his profusion of formal images). That D. belonged to the romantic founders of the Fr. theatre is indisputable, despite the disclaimer in his preface to *Henri iii* (' je ne me déclarerai pas fondateur d'un genre, parce que, effectivement, je n'ai rien fondé '), and despite the fact that the theory had preceded the practice in critical writings by mme. de Stael, Guizot (qq.v.) and others (see s.v. Lyrisme). The three plays which forced the romantic triumph on the stage were *Henri iii* (11 Feb., 1829), *le More de Venise* (Othello) (24 Oct., 1829), and *Hernani* (25 Feb., 1830) ; the three rebel-authors respectively were A.D., Vigny (q.v.), and Hugo (q.v.). The play which closed this romantic domination was *les Burgraves* (7 Mar., 1843), Hugo's last drama and first failure.

We state these facts at the outset because A.D.'s career as a playwright during the 15 years' dramatic vogue of Hugo represents, in the opinion of most Fr. critics, his chief, if not his only, title to fame. Frenchmen are a little bit biased, or they give this impression to foreign readers, against A.D.'s novels of adventure ; the vast formlessness of his designs and the copious flow of his fancy seem to offend the artistic sense even of those who confess to an unreasoning enjoyment of his works. He made money out of his novels, and is reproached with commercialism in lit. ; while the yet graver charge is brought against him that he had not read all his own bks. He used the labours of others, not merely as pilferer and plagiary, but also in the sense of employing ' shadows ' to write bks. which he revised and fathered. ' Dumas & Co. ', like ' Andrew Lang, Ltd. ' in a slightly later generation, was a term used in contempt. The names of Macquet and Feuillet (qq.v.) are mentioned in this connection. All this is a little beside the mark. No one disputed A.D.'s authorship of his novels, and no one stands as his equal by his side. The countless readers, uncritical perhaps, and unvexed by considerations of style, who frankly enjoy their plunge into the adventurous worlds of *le Comte de Monte Cristo* (12 vols., 1841-45), *les Trois Mousquetaires* (8 vols., 1844 ; who can forget D'Artagnan, Porthos, Athos and Aramis ?) *le Vicomte de Bragelonne, la Reine Margot, le Chevalier de Maison Rouge, Vingt Ans après*, etc., do not inquire too closely into the number of pens which were employed upon their manufacture. One happy, teeming brain directed them : the same brain which directed their author to take his unfortunate part in the revolution of 1848, and which led him to share in the Garibaldi expedition of 1860. It was the brain of a big and busy

man ; and posterity, as time goes on, is likely to cherish the novels, which owed something of their inspiration to Scott (q.v.), far higher than the romantic plays (*Henri iii*, 1829 ; *Christine*, 1830 ; *Antony*, 1831 ; *la Tour de Neste*, 1832, etc. ; *Antony* was the most successful), which owed much of their attraction to their Byronic heroes. If one governing motive may be ascribed to a writer so prolific (he wr., too, a number of travel-books), it may be defined as the ambition to popularize and vivify Fr. history in fiction and on the stage : ' he set himself to exploit the vast collections of chronicles and memoirs which Guizot and others had just published ' (Lanson, *Lit. Fr.*, 976) ; and in this respect, too, A.D. was a romantic founder.

-ii. Alexandre (1824-95) : Fr. dramatist, novelist ; son of above. D. *fils* was romantic, like his father. He started by writing novels, but one of these, *la Dame aux Camélias* (1852), was transformed by him into a play, in which form it was more successful and is better known. It owes something to Hugo's (q.v.) *Marion de Lorme* ; in effect, it is a social play, and it has a long line of descendants, among which not the least direct were the successful plays of sir Arthur Pinero (b. 1855) in the late 19th cent., *the Second Mrs. Tanqueray, The Gay Lord Quex, Iris* (revived, 1925), and others. D. *fils* was fearless in his approach to the more delicate sex-problems of family life ; and, though his purity of motive is undisputed, in his attacks on mercenary marriages, masculine vice, feminine ignorance, maternal selfishness, and so forth, he is not to be absolved from the consequence (for which he was not deliberately responsible) of introducing to the theatre the unpleasant note of sexual relations which made it for many years undesirable for ' the young person '. The moral question does not concern us. D. *fils* in fact was a moral reformer, and he took some part in divorce-law reform in France (1884). Historically, however, the theatre was not benefited as a national spectacle by the series of plays composed by D. *fils* with so much ingenuity and talent. These include, after the *Camélias* lady, *Diane de Lys*, 1853 (transformed from a novel, 1851) ; *Demi-Monde*, 1855 (the name was of A.D.'s invention, and meant, properly, *les déclassés* of both sexes) ; *Question d'Argent*, 1857 ; *Fils naturel*, 1858 ; *l'Ami des Femmes*, 1864 ; *les Idées de mme. Aubray*, 1867 ; *Visite de Noces*, 1871 ; *l'Etrangère*, 1876 ; *Denise*, 1855 ; *Francillon*, 1887. D. *fils* was a student of manners, and his final place in lit. is not yet established. He will, perhaps, tend to lose the place he held, as the ideas for which he strove in the 19th cent. become accepted commonplaces in the 20th. We are not as merciless to-day to the female ' sinner ' as A.D. and his successors taught us to be, or, rather, as they were themselves taught by the harsher conventions of a non-feminist age ; and this gradual re-adjustment of the social code, with its more equal penalties (and veniality) for both partners to the sexual problem is likely to put the plays and novels of D. *fils* out of date, where they may remain without much benefit of literary excellence.

Du Maurier, George L. P. B. (1834-96) : Engl. novelist ; more famous as artist, esp. in book-illustration and for many years on the staff of *Punch*. Wr., 1894 (3 vols. ; new edn., 1895, illustrated by the author), *Trilby*, a romance of 'Bohemian' (*Vie de Bohème*) life in Paris and London, which achieved an immense vogue on both sides of the Atlantic, the name 'trilby' still surviving as an epithet of a particular style of headgear. The novel, which derives a part of its effect from the character of Svengali, with his occult and mesmeric powers, was successfully dramatized. 'The writing is in the kindlier vein of Thackeray (q.v.); the colloquial idiom and confidential attitude are other points of resemblance' (*C.H.E.L.*, xiii, 433). Wr., too, *Peter Ibbetson*, 1891, and *The Martian*, 1897.

Dunbar, William (*c*. 1465-*c*. 1530) : Scot. poet ; believed to have taken the M.A. degree at St. Andrew's univ., about 1479, after which he entered the Franciscan Order ; in that habit travelled in Engld. and France. Much is uncertain concerning his career and works, but his poem *The Thrissill and the Rois*, 1503, in honour of king James iv.'s marriage, has been styled the finest 'political allegory' in the lit. of the age. The earliest example of Scot. printing was the production of several of his poems in 1508. D.'s *Lament for the Makaris* (makers, poets) touched a high level of pathos, just as his *Twa' Marrit Women and the Wedo* was a clever, but coarse, satire. He certainly stood in high favour with the Scot. king, who from 1500 paid him an annual pension, which gradually rose to £80. One story suggests that D. was killed at Flodden Field, in which case he did not write the *Orisone* (1517-18). D., who helps to fill the gap in our literary history between Chaucer and Spenser (qq.v.), was bigger than the members of the Chaucerian (q.v.) school, and struck out original notes both in elegy and satire.

Duns Scotus (d. 1308) : Scot. scholar ; John Dun (Dunne ?), Franciscan, studied in Paris and Cologne ; the most notable Lat. philosopher in Europe at the end of the 13th cent., whose death marks the close of the great era of Scholasticism. D. protested against the intemperate Aristotelianism of the schoolmen (see s.v. Aristotle), and it is by a strange caprice, as Sandys (*Hist. Class. Schol.*, i, 599), following Trench, *Study of Words*, says, that 'the name of one who was celebrated as "the subtle doctor", and was regarded by Coleridge as the only Englishman possessed of "high metaphysical subtlety", has become synonymous with stupidity'. The explanation, of course, is that the new learning referred with contempt to the last representative of the old.

Dupanloup, Félix (1802-78) : Fr. preacher ; prof. of sacred eloquence at the Sorbonne ; bp. of Orleans, 1849. Selections from his literary remains were publd., 1861, 1873, 1888.

Du Perron, Jacques Davy (1556-1618) : Fr. divine ; successively bp., archbp., and card. ; took part in current controversy on the eucharist ; wr., 1586, funeral oration on Ronsard (q.v.), which served as model to G. Brandt (q.v.) on similar occasion for Hooft (q.v.).

Duplessis-Mornay, Philippe de (1549-1623) : Fr. political philosopher and theologian. Wr. a Fr. treatise on the truth of the Christian religion, and is the reputed author of a famous Lat. work, *Vindiciæ contra Tyrannos* (q.v.) which eloquently expressed the Huguenot theory of the limitations and rights of authority in the State, based on Old Testament doctrine. D. forms an important link between the upholders of the divine right of kings (Luther, for example) and the limited monarchists of the type of Locke and Mill (qq.v.) ; while his passionate plea for liberty (with due allowance for the Huguenot view that prayer was the recourse of the 'masses', and that the right of insurrection was reserved to the higher 'classes', or grades, whose members D. called ephors) helped to inspire later revolutionaries, and found a response (again with the above reservation) in the constitution of the United States of America. (For the revulsion of the Huguenots from Machiavellism see s.vv. Gentillet and Machiavelli).

Durant, Gilles (1550-1615) : Fr. poet ; follower of Ronsard (q.v.). Born in the Auvergne, and practised law in Paris, but preferred poetry to law, as many have done since. Wr. considerable quantity of love-verse, of 'an elegant and tender gallantry', and was closely imitated in Engl. by Chapman (q.v.). D. was one of the contributors to the famous *Satyre Ménippée* (q.v.).

Du Ryer, Pierre (1605-58) : Fr. dramatist. Wr. *Alcionée*, 1640 ; *Scévole*, 1647 ; and was most successful in Roman plays with a political interest. Du R. benefited by the example of his far greater contemporary, Corneille (q.v.), and consciously contributed towards the development of the Fr. classical drama. Wr., too, a comedy of *bourgeois* manners in a pastoral setting, les *Vendanges de Suresne*, 1635.

Dutch Literature : The literary history of the Netherlands may be divided into the following periods, to which the appended dates may be taken as roughly corresponding : i, Middle Ages, 1175-1550 ; ii, First Transition, 1550-1600 (Renaissance and Reformation); iii, United Provinces, 1600-1795 ; iv, Second Transition, 1795-1830 (Revolution and Restoration) ; v, Modern Constitution, 1830-present day. It will be observed that the periods are determined by the hist. conditions of the people, whose heroism, independence and self-reliance have been tried by an experience of human and inanimate invaders which would have broken the spirit and demolished the barriers of a less resolute and more sensitive race. Crossing the first two periods is the activity of the Chambers of Rhetoric (see s.v. Rederijkers), extending from about 1450 to 1600, but displaying no features distinguishing them from the medieval character which they shared. The group-system of poetic and dramatic societies has persisted throughout the history of Dutch Literature. In the last two periods we have to reckon with foreign influences, chiefly of Lessing, Scott, and Hugo (qq.v.), which gave occasion for endless translns. ; the break at 1830, which is not more arbitrary than the break of Engl. lit. at 1832, will leave Bilderdijk (q.v. ; d. 1831) on one side of the imaginary line and Da Costa (q.v.) on the other. The prevailing Latinity of (ii), First Transition, does not necessarily diminish the debt of Europe to Holland ;

she must settle her own account with Erasmus (q.v.) and the rest for their preference of the Imperial to the national tongue. (See s.v. Lat.). Taking these periods in order, (i) it would be tedious to examine in detail the various adaptations in provincial dialects of Dutch (Deutsch, German, middle and high) of the romantic cycles of Charlemagne, Roland, Arthur, the Grail, Alexander, Troy (qq.v.), and the rest of the three materials summarized so concisely by Bodel (q.v.), which were a universal manufacture of the age. One name stands out in this record : that of Hendrik van Veldeke (q.v.), who belongs to the end of the 12th cent. By virtue of his orig. at Veldeke in Limburg, that duchy has the honour of first mention in the literary history of the Netherlands. Limburg, with its chief city of Maestricht, and Brabant, with its chief city of Louvain (q.v.), were always important ; and Hendrik's activity added the *Legend of St. Servatius* and an *Æneid*, Fr. by descent and lyrical in treatment, to the early monuments of Dutch letters. A Leyden MS., probably contemporary with Veldeke, contains fragments of native versions of parts of the Carlovingian romances (Roland, Floovent, son of Clovis, etc.). The master in this school was Jacob van Maerlant (q.v.), and see *infra*) who wr. a *Merlin*, a *Graal*, and other tales from the Arthurian cycle (c. 1260) ; and the name of Lodewijk van Velthem (q.v.) is associated with *Lancelot*, etc. Of the ' matter of antiquity ', or the Orient, there were the usual versions of Floris and Blanchefleur and the rest, and mention is due particularly to the Fleming poet, Latewaert (q.v.), who wr. (c. 1350) about 12,000 verses on *Seghelijn*, prince of Jerusalem. It is a characteristic eastern legend of domestic doom, fairy gifts, crusading, and romantic love. But it was in the region of fable (q.v.), and especially in contributions to the bestiary (q.v.) of Reynard (q.v.), that the poets of the Netherlands were notable in this period ; and the poem of a certain Willem, of East Flanders, stands in the direct line of descent from the Fr. versions of the Indian originals to Caxton, La Fontaine, and Goethe (qq.v.). Willem's *Roman van den vos* (fox) *Reinarde* may be dated about 1250. Maerlant, again, editing the works of polyhistors and encyclopedists of an earlier age, was also the founder of a line of moral or didactic poetry, and of its close ally, the rhymed chronicle. Such a chronicle, harking back to the story of the Creation, afforded ample opportunity for the display of theories of society and government, reflected, from the circumstances of the poet's own times ; and if Maerlant had chosen prose instead of verse for his vehicle, Dutch lit. might have produced a Villehardouin and ultimately a Froissart (qq.v.) in the place of her medieval rhymers. The court influences, partly directed by queen Philippa, consort of king Edward iii of Engld., introduced a more romantic strain into the poetry of the 13th-14th centuries, and the *Romance of the Rose* (q.v.) tradition found its way. The last notable writer in this period, combining the didactic method of the moralizers with the erotic sentiment of the fabulists, was Dirc Potter (q.v.) of Loo. The part played by the Chambers of Rhetoric in the Dutch Middle Ages was considerable, wholesome, and social in its tendency (see s.v. Rederijkers). The most celebrated of the older ' rhetoricians ' was the ' excellent modern poet ', Castelein (q.v.) ; and, even in the 1st period of Transition the Chambers of Rhetoric were more industrious in pouring new wine into old bottles than in adapting their consecrated, medieval forms to the needs of the new spirit of the revived classics. This period (ii) is the age of Agricola, Hegius (qq.v.), and the Deventer (q.v.) school, dominated by the world-fame in letters of the great cosmopolite Latinist, Erasmus (q.v.). Smaller than these giants, but still efficient in transln. and preparation for the new age, were scholar-poets of restricted inspiration, such as Ghistele, Houwaert, and Mander (qq.v.). The Reformation combined with the Renaissance to change the character of lit. ; and translns. of the Psalms, after Marot (q.v.), and poems of warfare, religion, patriotism, and martyrology were produced in considerable number, under the inspiring stimulus of the deeds of the ' beggars ' and ' image-breakers ', and other parties to the political strife. (See esp. s.v. Marnix). The ' Eglantine ' Chamber at Amsterdam, which attracted members of the calibre of Visscher and Spieghel (qq.v.), leads us through this 1st Transition to (iii) the golden age of Dutch lit. It was likewise the golden age of Dutch painting : the realism and raciness of Franz Hals and Jan Steen had their counterpart in the fun and humour, in the direct and graphic life-pictures of Hooft, Bredero, Coster, Starter, Cats, and Huyghens (qq.v.). The vogue of Latinity in scholarship (see s.v. Lat.), which is seen in the Latinized names of such notable Dutchmen as Lipsius, Heinsius, Vossius, Grotius, Barlæus (qq.v.), and the rest, and which was due partly to the arrival of foreign scholars in the Netherlands, had one good effect at least : it purified style and language from the affectations of the ' Rederijkers '. When the wedge of Lat. had been driven through the culture of the Netherlands, it was possible for Dutchmen to write Dutch. Merchant and statesman, soldier and poet, all had to learn Lat. first in order to re-learn their own language, and to recover it purged of its falsities, as an instrument fit for the uses to which Vondel (q.v.) was to teach them to apply it. ' With Bredero, Coster, and Starter ' says Ten Brink (*Geschiedenis*, 369), ' we find ourselves in the world of " merry old Amsterdam " ; above all, in the stage-world of 1610 to 1625 '. It was the period of ripe dramatic activity, marked by frequent visits of Engl. players to Amsterdam, with representations of Marlowe, Shakespeare and Jonson, and by the industrious and successful adaptation of Engl., Fr., and Span. tragicomedy by masters of the first rank as well as by more pretentious craftsmen such as Rodenburg (q.v.), who drove Coster (q.v.) to form a new academy (1615) out of the schismatic ' Oude Kamer ' (s.v. Eglantine) of Amsterdam. This great period reached its zenith in the noble life and glorious poetic achievement of Joost van den Vondel, who lived from 1587 to 1679, and who shares with Grotius (see s.vv.) the supremacy among Dutchmen of letters of all time. After his death, a rapid decline marked the last quarter of the 17th cent., and is connected with the names of Vos, Antonides, and others, whose frigidities could not resist the invasion of foreign taste and models. A whole flood of Arcadian romances, picaresque novels, and similar products of Fr. and Span. versions of Gk. fiction drenched the Netherlands in an erotic bath by no means suited to the genius of her people. Simultaneously, the would-be classic stage of the *Nil volentibus arduum* (q.v.) enthusiasts opened the door to the ready imitators of contemporary Fr. drama. The only names which rise above the general level of mediocrity in this period are those of Justus van Effen (q.v.), the genial founder of a *Spectator* in the Netherlands, modelled on Addison's and Steele's, and of the two women-novelists in collaboration, Elizabeth Wolff (*née* Bekker) and Agatha Deken. The influence of Richardson and of the Addison circle was now (iv) to lead to the influence of Germany, France and Engld. in the 2nd period of Transition. No name of note arrests attention in this era of transln. and imitation of sentimental romance and affected epos, with the solitary exception of Bilderdijk (q.v.) ; and we pass to the latest (v) age in the honourable history of Dutch lit.—a history which has achieved greatness against almost overwhelming odds, including a language unsuited to the fine expression of the highest passion and emotion. The names of Da Costa and van Lennep (qq.v.) bring the record so near to modern times that it is legitimate here to conclude the present brief summary of that history. If the Netherlands cannot be said to have been as remarkable in lit. as in art, its lit. counts among its triumphs the works of Erasmus, Groot, and Vondel : three incomparable names, among the most renowned in Europe.

Dyce, Alexander (1798-1869) : Engl. scholar ; publd. *Specimens of British Poetesses*, 1825, and edited works of several Elizabethan playwrights. D.'s *magnum opus* was his edn. of Shakespeare, 9 vols., 1857. His valuable collection of bks. was bequeathed to the nation.

Dyer, Edward (died 1607) : Engl. poet ; knt. 1596 ; friend of sir Philip Sidney (q.v.) and praised by Meres (q.v.) as ' famous for elegy '. The exact identification of D.'s poems has proved difficult, but ' My mind to me a kingdom is ' is certainly one of his lyrics.

Dyer, John (1700-58) : Engl. (Welsh) poet ; artist. Wr. *Grongar Hill*, 1727 ; *The Fleece*, 1757 ; admired by Wordsworth (q.v.).

Dyer, Samuel (1725-72) : Engl. scholar ; translr., friend of Burke (q.v.) ; falsely reputed author of the letters of Junius (q.v.).

E

Eberhard, Johann August (1739-1809) : Germ. critic. Wr. ' Theory of the Fine Arts and Sciences ' and ' Handbook of Aesthetics ' (Berlin, 1803-04).

Ebert, Johann Arnold (1723-95) : Germ. poet. Member of the Leipsic poets' circle who deserted from Gottsched's (q.v.) standard to found the *Bremer Beiträge* (q.v.). Transld. the *Night Thoughts* of Young (q.v.), and wr. original lyric verse which bore traces of the sentimental influence which he helped to spread among his contemporaries.

Ebert, Karl Egon (1801-82) : Germ. poet ; disciple of Uhland (q.v.) ; wr. some admirable ballads, and ' Serious Thoughts of a Worldly Man ', 1859.

Eckhart (d. 1327) : Germ. mystic. Dominican monk of Augsburg ; studied philosophy in Paris ; was summoned to Rome, and received doctorate in theology, whence known as ' Master '. Later, preached in Strassburg and Cologne ; anticipated, so far as his personal mysticism could be reconciled in form and expression with the doctrines of orthodox theology, the spiritual pantheism of much more recent philosophy. (See s.v. Mysticism). Pfleiderer, e.g., a leading historian of philosophy, exalts E. as a pioneer of the movement which culminated in Kant and Hegel (qq.v.).

Edda (Icel.), **-i.** in philology, signifies ancestress, great-grandmother, and thus, by an easy transition, the old universal Mother Earth. In this sense, comprehensively equivalent to Nature ; G. Meredith (q.v.), among modern poets, was chiefly instrumental in employing the word Earth in its remote Icel. signification of Edda.

-ii. in lit., the title of a prose-treatise by Snorri (q.v.), written *c.* 1220, and interspersed with quotations from poems of Icel. heathendom. Snorri's purpose in his E. was to compose a kind of ' Art of Poetry ', and to provide the poets of the 13th cent. with a rational guide to the use of the national myths. ' All Scandinavian thinkers ', says Carlyle (q.v.), ' since the first of them, contributed to that Scandinavian system of thought, in ever-new elaboration and addition, it is the combined work of them all '. Snorri takes his readers right through the poetic region to be surveyed, from the stories of the cosmogony and of the natural powers, Thor, Odin, and the rest, to the myths of Balder and Valhalla, and of the Twilight of the Gods. (This last term, so pregnant with romance for the authors of the Norse revival, is probably Snorri's mistake for the Doom of the Gods : a common term in the older poetry). Snorri's E. reproduces the tone of Christianity superimposed on paganism ; its intention is to show how to preserve the poetry inherent in the myths without committing Christian poets to an acceptance of the divinity of the gods. He is ' amused, ironical, humorous . . . generous to the old gods, and thoroughly interested in their adventures ' (Ker, *Sturla the Historian*, Romanes Lecture, Oxford, 1906) ; and prof. Ker adds that T. L. Peacock (q.v.) is ' the modern author who is most like Snorri in this respect, in this curious combination of levity and romance, so unlike the medieval earnestness on the one hand, the medieval farce on the other '.

-iii. also in lit., the general title affixed to a collection of old Northern poems, made in Iceland towards the end of the 13th cent., and preserved in a famous MS., known as Codex Regius (q.v.), belonging to the King's Library at Copenhagen. In the period of Icel. scholarship and Norse revival in the 17th cent., there was a kind of expectation of a discovery of an Edda older than Snorri's, of which Snorri's was presumed to be an abridgement; and when the Codex Regius was found in 1642, bp. Brynjolf of Scalholt (1605-75) hastened to announce it as 'Edda Sæmundi multiscii', or the Edda of Sæmund the Wise (multiscient): a quite unjustified ascription. This collection is also known as the 'poetic' Edda, in distinction to Snorri's prose-treatise, or, very commonly, as the Elder Edda. Modern scholars agree in rejecting the argument of the 18th cent., but the name is approved as convenient, and as saving a good deal of trouble. (See esp., Vigfusson and York Powell, *Corpus Poeticum Boreale*, i, Introduction, and ii, 514; Oxford, 1883). The Elder E. is an invaluable source-book of the old Northern stock of Teutonic tales, though, unfortunately, the farewell between Sigurd and Brynhild (represented by a prose paraphrase in the Volsung Saga) is missing from the MS.; but, full and varied though it is, Hickes (q.v.), in 1703, and Gray (q.v.), in his rather later Icel. poems, drew from other sources than the *Codex Regius*, and it was another source, again, 'which set up the romantic standard of the ideal Viking' of 19th cent. convention. (See Ker, *P.E.L.*, i, 295).

Edgeworth. -i. Richard Lovell (1744-1817): Anglo-Irish moral writer; mechanician (invented a plan for telegraphy, and was awarded a silver medal by the Royal Society of Arts for a land-measuring contrivance, 1768); friend of T. Day (q.v.) and the Lichfield set (see s.v. Seward); wr. moral and humanitarian bks. of a philosophic-revolutionary kind, mainly under the influence of the Fr. *philosophe*, Marmontel (q.v.).

    -ii. Maria (1767-1849): Anglo-Irish novelist; daughter of above, who 'affected her work very much for the worse, by the admixture of purpose and preachment, which he either induced her to make or (in some cases, pretty certainly) intruded on his own account' (Saintsbury, *C.H.E.L.*, xi, 296). Wr. tales and treatises, stimulated by that influence, derivative from France: *Parents' Assistant*, 1796 (6 vols., 1800); *Practical Education*, 1798; *Early Lessons*, 1801, with its sequels, *Frank*, 1822, *Harry and Lucy*, 1825, etc., 'notable for the fact' (Saintsbury, *ibid.*) that, in them, 'real children, save for a few touches in Shakespeare and still fewer elsewhere, first appear'; wr., too, chronicle-novels of Irish life—*Castle Rackrent*, 1800; *The Absentee*, 1809, etc.,—which directly motivated sir W. Scott (q.v.), meditating like themes in his native Scotland; novels *sans phrase*, such as *Belinda*, 1801, *Leonora*, 1806, and others, which, attractive in themselves, marked a definite advance in the technical development of the kind. (See s.v. Novel).

Education: See s.vv. Arnold, Ascham, Basedow, Castiglione, Deventer, Erasmus, Humboldt, Komensky, Port Royal, Pestalozzi, Rousseau, Soc. of Jesus, Vittorino, Vives, etc. The topic

of E., though many men of letters in Europe derive their claim to that title from educational writings, lies outside the scope of this dict. The epigram of card. Newman may be noted, as a signpost to further study: 'Not a man in Europe now who talks bravely against the Church but owes it to the Church that he can talk at all'; and see Ullmann, *Reformers before the Reformation*, E.T., i, 223: 'The universities of the Middle Ages have all fundamentally an ecclesiastical type, having been instituted under the sanction of the supreme ecclesiastical power, and superintended by an ecclesiastical board'. At the same time, they assumed 'a difference of physiognomy, according as their institution and guardianship were the work of a spiritual or of a temporal prince, or of a free city'. Special reference may be made to R. H. Quick (1831-91): *Essays on Educational Reformers*, 1868 (2nd edn., 1890), who stated in his pref.: 'I have found that on the history of Education, not only *good* books but *all* books are in German or some other foreign language'. This reproach has been largely removed in recent years by the writings of M. Arnold (q.v.), sir Michael Sadler, prof. Foster Watson, and others. A history of the univ. of Oxford has been written (2 vols., 1924) by sir Chas. Marriott, and special reference may be made to the essay on sir Thos. Hoby (q.v.) in *Some Authors*, 1923, by the late sir Walter Raleigh.

Edwards, Amelia Ann Blanford (1831-92): Engl. Egyptologist. Wr. *Pharaohs, Fellahs and Explorers*, 1891, and helped to found the Egypt Exploration Fund, 1882, of which she was hon. secretary. Earlier in life, Miss E. wr. several novels, and her ruling interest was displayed in her bequest of a sum of money to form a chair of Egyptology at Univ. Coll., London.

Effen, Van Justus (1684-1735): Dutch essayist. Visited London on diplomatic business, 1714 and 1727, and came under influence of Addison (q.v.). Transld. Mandeville and Defoe (qq.v.) into Dutch, and started, 1731, *de Hollandsche Spectator* ('The Dutch Spectator'), on the model of the Engl. prototype. E. succeeded, by his adaptability to Fr. and Engl. standards, in raising the dignity of Dutch prose to a level of ease and politeness which it had never reached by its native genius. 120 years later, the title was revived by Marc Prager Lindo (q.v.) in his Addisonian (or van Effenian) letters of the new *Nederlandsche Spectator*, 1851.

Egan, Pierce (1772-1849): Engl. humourist. Wr. *Life in London: or, The Day and Night Scenes of Jerry Hawthorn and his elegant Friend, Corinthian Tour*, in monthly numbers, from 1821. These sketches and sport, etc., under the Regency had considerable success, and encouraged to found *Pierce Egan's Life in London and Sporting Guide*, a weekly newspaper, 1824, which was one of the first to lean on the name of its founder. E.'s son, **Pierce E.**, the younger (1814-80), wr. several novels, and was a pioneer of cheap lit.

Eggert Olafsson (1726-68): Icel. scholar and poet; resident, like so many great Icelanders of the 18th cent. in Copenhagen, whence they laboured devotedly for the renascence of their own country. E. was a purist in Icelandic diction, and as strict in his metrical rules as Pope (q.v.), to whose example he may have been indebted ; and he conferred considerable services on language and prosody. E.'s best-known poem is one on Icel. rural life, in the didactic nature-descriptive vein, written, 1764, and transld. into Dan., 1803. His satire on actual conditions of rural economy in Iceld. is as biting as his patriotic zeal for regeneration is acute ; and, alike as patriot, poet and scholar, E. is not unjustly called the Holberg (q.v.) of Iceld.

Egilsson, Sveinjbörn (1791-1852) : Icel. scholar. Transld. Homer into Icel. verse and prose, 'revealing in his vigorous poetic rendering of the *Odyssey* in particular a perfect consciousness of the kinship between the spirited style of the old Greek Epic and that of the Northern Sagas ' (Sandys, *Hist. Class. Schol.*, iii, 328).

Eglantine (Dutch) : popular name of the *Rederijkerskamer* (q.v.), or Chamber of Rhetoric at Amsterdam, so-called from its blazon-motto ' blossoming in love ' (*in liefde bloeyende*), and also known as the ' oude Kamer ', on account of its antiquity. In 1580, or thereabouts, the E. became one of the most important chambers, chiefly owing to the direction given to its labours by Cornheert, Spieghel, and Visscher (qq.v.), and by the learned and beautiful daughters of the last of this great triumvirate. The leaders in its dramatic activity were Coster, Bredero, Rodenburg, and Hooft (qq.v.), and it was in Hooft's house that its less formal *réunions* were held. The domineering manner of Rodenburg, at the period of his greatest activity in Amsterdam, and his unquestioned lead in the knowledge of foreign languages and literatures, led to a schism in the ranks of the brothers who should have ' blossomed in love '. About 1615, Dr. Samuel Coster led out the revolting dramatists, who formed an independent circle, known as Coster's Academy. The breach was soon healed, however, and the two societies were fused (*c.* 1620).

Eichendorff, von Joseph (1788-1857) : Germ. novelist and poet ; baron ; known in Germany (by Heine's description) as the last knt. of the Romantic movement, to which he was attached as a fellow-student with Arnim and Görres at Heidelberg (see s.vv.), and as a volunteer in the battle of Leipsic, 1813. After demobilization, E. settled down to Government service. His first novel was *Ahnung und Gegenwart*, 1815, one of the many minor Wilhelm Meisters ; his best was *Aus dem Leben eines Taugenichts* (idler), 1826, the picaresque story of a musician, who wanders with his fiddle and his fancies to loveland and Italy. E. was a great lyric poet ; ' in the history of the German lyric, indeed, with the exception of Goethe and Walther von der Vogelweide, there is not another singer, who has brought the national lyric feeling to more exquisite expression than Eichendorff '. (Robertson, *Hist. Germ. Lit.*, 472). E. possessed in an eminent degree the true Germ. wilding spirit, which is not exactly a spirit of adventure, nor a spirit of exploration, such as leads to Spitzbergen or Everest, but is just a love of wandering (*Wanderlust*) for its own sake—a love of nature with a rucksack, not necessarily far

from home. (See, too, s.v. Hain). It was to this spirit that E. gave complete expression in such poems as *Frische Fahrt, Morgengebet, Mondnacht*, and many others.

Eikenhorst, L. Van. See **De Vries, Jan.**

Eike von Repgowe (*c.* 1220) : Germ. jurist. Wr. influential work called the *Sachsenspiegel* (Saxons'-mirror), which was frequently imitated. It has what might now be called a modernist tendency, e.g., in such a dictum as, ' God bestowed two swords on the kingdom of earth for the defence of Christianity, the sacred to the pope and the worldly to the emperor '. The orthodox view was that the pope delegated the worldly sceptre to the emperor ; and it is notable that Maximilian (q.v.) was the first Roman emperor to omit the ceremony of coronation at Rome.

Elbschwanenorden (Germ.) : the order of the Swans of the Elbe ; Germ. literary society founded at Hamburg by Rist (q.v.), in consequence of the movement towards a literary and linguistic Renaissance associated in the first half of the 17th cent. with Opitz (q.v.).

Eleanor (12th cent.) : Fr. patron of romance ; queen ; daughter of William x, count of Poitiers and duke of Aquitaine, and granddaughter of the Troubadour count William ix (q.v.) ; m., i, Louis vii (the Young) of France, who divorced her, 1152 ; ii, Henry of Anjou, afterwards Henry ii of Engld. In lit., queen E., her daughters, countess Marie, wife of Henry of Champagne, and queen Alice (or Adela), king Louis's third wife, were all celebrated as presidents of the chivalrous courts-of-love, which were the centres of poetry in the Midi, or southern France (and, later, by communication, in the north). The *lais* of Marie de France (q.v.) were dedicated to Henry ii, and Marie de Champagne suggested the subject of Lancelot to Chrétion de Troyes (q.v.). Thus queen Eleanor was a central figure in the activity of the art of the Breton romance-writers ; her son, king Richard Cœur-de-Lion, was himself numbered among the Troubadours.

Eliot, George (1819-80) : Engl. novelist and scholar ; pen-name of Mary Ann Evans, who lived for 25 years, 1854-78, under the protection of G. H. Lewes (q.v.), and m., 1880 (8 months before her death), J. W. Cross (d. 1924). The 25 years with Lewes were the central years of her strenuous life, the burden of which deepened towards the close, as the weight of learning increased. G.E. was a novelist on big lines, and was more than usually responsive—it was a common characteristic of Victorian lit.—to the social tendencies of her age. Like Dickens, Kingsley (qq.v.) and others, she emphasized the purpose in her works of fiction with growing insistence, and her later novels are heavier than her first. G.E. first entered letters as the translr. of Strauss (q.v.), *Leben Jesu*, 1846, and Feuerbach (q.v.), *Wesen des Christentums*, 1854. She became assistant editor of the *Westminster Review*, and was one of many young authors who were nursed into fame by *Blackwood's Mag.*, in which parts of her *Scenes of Clerical Life* appeared, 1857. She wr. *Adam Bede*, 1859 ; *The Mill on the Floss*, with its idyl of Engl. childhood, 1860 ; *Silas Marner*, 1861 ; *Romola*, set in Florence in the 15th cent., with extraordinarily intensive perception, after a brief visit to Italy, 1863 ; *Felix Holt*, probably the weakest, 1866 ; *Middlemarch*, probably the greatest of her novels, despite the bad joints in its various stories, 1871-2 ; *Daniel Deronda*, the first Zionist romance, but over-didactic and too philosophic ; poems : *Spanish Gypsy* and *Legend of Jubal* ; and, finally, *Impressions of Theophrastus Such*, 1879, and various essays, including an excellent one on the ' The Wit of Heine '. In the *Etudes sur la Lit. Contemp.* by Edmond Scherer (1815-89), some of which G. Saintsbury transld. (*Essays on Engl. Lit.*, Low, 1891), the great Frenchman, writing in 1861, pronounced G.E. ' the first novelist of England '. Writing again in 1885, after her life by J. W. Cross had been publd., Scherer still placed her ' among the highest class of novelists. The name of Shakespeare ', he said, ' has sometimes been uttered in speaking of George Eliot, an hyperbole which ceases to be shocking if we limit the terms of comparison to the creation of characters. But I had rather endorse, though here also with the necessary distinctions, the judgment of lord Acton, that George Eliot is the most considerable literary personality that has appeared since the death of Goethe '. Beside this judgment we may set that of another great Frenchman, the vicomte de Vogüé, who, in his cassic study of *le Roman Russe*, writes (p. xli) : ' England has the honour of having inaugurated and brought to its highest point of perfection the form of art which corresponds to the new needs of the mind of Europe. Realism, starting with Richardson, reached its most glorious peaks in Dickens, Thackeray and George Eliot. At the time when Flaubert was introducing the doctrine to us (France) in the waning of his intelligence, Eliot was giving it a serenity and a grandeur which none have equalled. Despite my decided taste for Turgenev and Tolstoi, I perhaps prefer to them the magic of Mary Evans ; and if, a hundred years hence, the novels of to-day are still read, I believe that the homage of our descendants will hesitate between these three names '. The criticism turns, it will be observed on the term Realism (q.v.), and G.E.'s courage and honesty in her life and writings, founded on a wealth and breadth of learning very rare in woman's capacity in her time and place, entitle her to a fame which posterity is likely to confirm.

Elizabeth Ottilia Louisa (1843-1916) : Germ. poet ; queen of Roumania ; *née* princess of Wied ; m., 1869, prince Charles of Hohenzollern, king of Roumania, 1881-1914. Queen E. invariably used the pen-name of Carmen Sylva, and was well-known in her adopted country and beyond for the charm and delicacy of her writings. Hers was no royal muse, stimulated and sustained by adulation, but a genuine gift of style and song. Among her works familiar under Engl. titles are : *Thoughts of a Queen*, 1890 ; *Shadows on Life's Dial*, 1895 ; *A Real Queen's Fairy-book*, 1901.

Ellis, George (1753-1815) : Engl. author ; founded, with Canning, the *Anti-Jacobin*, 1797, and had already graduated in political and literary satire as a contributor to the *Rolliad* (q.v.). E. was later associated with the foundation of the

Quarterly Review. He was a friend of Scott (q.v.), and wr., 1778, *Poetical Tales of Sir Gregory Gander* ; 1789 , *History of the late Revolution in the Dutch Republic* ; edited, 1790, *Specimens of the Engl. Poets*, new edn., 1801 ; 1805, *Specimens of early Engl. Metrical Romances*. See, too, s.v. Frere, J.H.

Ellwood, Thomas (1639-1713) : Engl. sacred writer ; Quaker ; travelled with G. Fox (q.v.). Wr. *Davideis*, a sacred poem, 1712, but belongs to lit. more securely by his friendship with Milton (q.v.), whose *Paradise Regained* was started in consequence of a suggestion by E.

Elmsley, Peter (1773-1825) : Engl. scholar ; Camden prof. of Ancient History at Oxford ; associated chiefly with his contributions to the textual criticism of the Gk. dramatists.

Elyot, Thomas (d. 1546) : Engl. scholar ; knt., 1530 ; ambassador to emperor Charles v ; wr. *Boke called the Governor*, 1531, which formed an important contribution to the study of political science, and transld., 1534, from the Gk. orator, Isocrates, *The Doctrine of Princes*, which, apart from its similar value, was notable for its influence on Engl. prose. Some of the features were ' euphuistic ' (see s.v. Euphuism) before Lyly (q.v.). Wr., too, a Lat.-Engl. Dict., 1538, and ranks as an enlightened student of the humane learning of Erasmus (q.v.).

Elzevir : family-name of a dynasty of Dutch printers, among whom may be particularly selected for mention, -i, **Louis** (1540-1617), who left Louvain for Leyden (see s.vv.), in 1580, when he established his famous press, shortly after the foundation of Leyden univ., ; and -ii, **Louis** (1604-70), who founded a press in Amsterdam, 1638, in partnership with Daniel E., grandson of i, (Louis), and son of Bonaventura E., who succeeded his father at Leyden. Both houses began to decline towards the end of the 17th cent., but they achieved an immense and well-merited reputation between 1622-51 for their 12mo. and 16mo. edns. of the Gk. Testament and of various Gk. and Roman classics.

Emblem-Books : generic name of a class of lit., popular in Europe in the epoch of the Renaissance, and characteristic of its temper of melancholy and symbolism. Such a bk. consisted of a selection of proverbs, sayings, fables or reflections, mostly on the vanity of life, the littleness of man, the nearness of death, illustrated by wood-cuts depicting the subject-matter of the text in a manner which was later recalled in Engl. art by William Blake (q.v.). The earliest admitted Emblematist was Alciati (q.v.), but Brandt (q.v.) in his ' Ship of Fools ' (1494) had already provided suitable matter for illustration, and his chapter on ' not foreseeing death ' suggested the wood-cut of the Fool overtaken by skeleton Death (q.v.), which became a regular property of the ' Dance of Death ' group of art and letters. Lat. was the common language and elegiac-verse the common metre of emblem-books, which were a popular feature of Dutch lit.

Emin, Feodor (*c.* 1735-70) : Russ. novelist, if the term may be applied to the wearisome political and didactic romances which E., like his contemporary, Kheraskov (q.v.), imitated somewhat feebly from the Fr. *Miramond's*

Adventures was one; *Letters of Ernest and Doraura* was another, founded on Rousseau's (q.v.) *Nouvelle Heloïse*; *Themistocles* was a third, after the model of Fénélon's (q.v.) *Télémaque*. They were read in Russia in the mid-18th cent., but their savour has departed long since.

Enciso, de, Bartolomé Lopez (fl., 1586): Span. pastoralist. Wr. *Desengaño de Celos* (' Disillusionment of the zealous '), a dreary experiment in pastoral fiction, in which the Arcadian shepherds are carried by the genius of Spain to the reign of the future king Philip iii : a poor performance in the Montemayor (q.v.) tradition.

Encyclopedia : defined in the *New Engl. Dict.* (Oxford) as a ' literary work, containing extensive information on all branches of knowledge, usually arranged in alphabetical order '. In this sense, the word was first employed as the title of a bk. by a certain Ringelberg of Basel in 1541, and, next, by another German, J. H. Alsted (q.v.) in a Lat. *Encyclopædia scientiarum omnium*, 1632, which Leibniz (q.v.) tried to improve. The Engl. *Cyclopædia . . . or, Dict. of Arts and Sciences* by E. Chambers (q.v.) was publd. in 1728, and from that work was derived the name of the Fr. *Encyclopédie, ou Dictionnaire raisonné des Sciences, des Arts, et des Métiers*, to which the name of Encyclopedia (the spelling, -pædia, is often preserved from old-time title-pages) is specially applied in literary history. It is, accordingly, with the *Encyclopédie* that the present art. has chiefly to deal ; and with *the* Encyclopedia in this limited sense must be reckoned the group of Fr. philosophers, thence described as the Encyclopedists (*encyclopédistes*).

There had been cyclopedia-makers before the 16th cent. Roger Bacon's (q.v.) *Opus majus* was a cyclopedia, and the many vast depositaries of learning—universal libraries, and so forth,—collected in the Middle Ages may properly be characterized by that name. But even Gesner (q.v.) called his bk. *bibliotheca universalis*, 1532, within ten years of the invention of the new term, and the true father of encyclopedias is no obscure lexicographer, who chanced to happen on that word, but is Francis Bacon (q.v.), the great Engl. philosopher, to whom Dalembert (q.v.), in his introduction to the *Encyclopédie*, paid a noble and a generous tribute. It was on Bacon's ample plan that the editors projected the Fr. *Encyclopédie*, when the bookseller, Le Breton, who had acquired the Fr. rights in Chambers's Dict., applied, *c.* 1740, to Diderot (q.v.) for assistance and advice. Diderot, then a freelance writer in Paris, with a growing reputation as a man of science and letters, was quick to see how valuable it would be to capture the undertaking for the *philosophes* (q.v.). They were already on the road to capturing the Fr. Academy (q.v.), in the sense that the permanent officers of that society began to be drawn from the ranks of these advanced thinkers (see s.v. Dalembert, e.g.), and the precedent of Bayle (q.v.) made it clear how much influence could be exercised on opinion through the medium of a dict. of this kind. The circumstances in certain features were not unlike those that prevailed in Germany from *c.* 1871 to 1914. There was the same professorial activity ; the same readiness to convert learned offices to the uses of political propaganda. The encyclopedists, or *philosophes*, were devoted to a doctrinal mission, which had political ends in view. They, too, had a culture to preach : the *philosophe* of Paris in the 18th cent. was the *Kultur-mensch* of Prussia in the 19th to 20th ; he aimed through doctrine at action, and the Fr. Revolution towards the century's close was the form which that action assumed. Whether in the club of the Entresol (q.v.), where the physiocrats (q.v.) discussed the single-tax and *laissez-faire*, or in the philanthropy of Voltaire (q.v.), launching his bitter invectives against legal harshness and ecclesiastical tyranny, or in the researches of Montesquieu (q.v.) into the physical causation of national character, or in the constitution-mongering of a score of sociologists, or in the natural philosophy of a score of anti-theists : the same tendency was at work towards simplification, rationalism, materialism, and the propagation of happiness by human right. Plainly, the difference between the *philosophes* and the *Kultur*-professors was that the former were working *against* and the latter *in alliance with* the State. Neither the court of king Louis xv nor the Church authorities of his day were likely to tolerate a campaign directly opposed to the conventions on which they rested ; and the inconvenient martyrdom of imprisonment and exile overtook at one time or another nearly everyone connected with the movement ; while those who survived into the Revolution were mostly despatched under the guillotine. But, with due allowance for the difference in circumstances, the point is that the scheme of the *Encyclopédie*, when it was brought to Diderot about 1740 in connection with the Fr. transln. of Chambers's *Cyclopædia*, appealed to him at once as an opportunity of standardizing and methodizing the liberal ideas of the school of the *philosophes* ; he would turn a more or less neutral dict. into a kind of new Bayle, directly written to spread the creed of the reformers of science, politics, religion, and, indeed, all branches of knowledge. The *privilège* requisite for publication was obtained from Daguesseau (q.v.), an official of singularly equable judgment, in 1746 ; Diderot's *Prospectus* appeared in 1750, and Dalembert was associated with him as joint-editor, and wr. the brilliant *Discours préliminaire* to vol. i, 1751. The editors had collected a large staff of first-rate and second-rate contributors, including Voltaire, Montesquieu, Buffon, Condillac, Turgot, Marmontel, Helvétius, baron Grimm, Holbach, Duclos, J. J. Rousseau (qq.v.) ; and if one view of this society of the encyclopedists is that they were banded together ' to sustain materialism, to destroy religion, to inspire independence, and to foster the corruption of morals ', as one of their persecutors alleged, it will be remembered that similar charges were brought against an earlier *philosophe*, who had to drink the fatal hemlock, and that, in the France of Diderot's day, there was another side to each of these accounts. Reason had its victories to win, and could not be stopped by calling its votaries ugly names. Meanwhile, 7 vols. of the *Encyclopédie* appeared with commendable punctuality, till in 1757 not even the goodwill of Malesherbes (q.v.), then acting censor, could protect the enterprise from its enemies in high places. The most immediate cause of offence was Dalembert's art. on *Geneva*, and the persecutions of Church and State were followed by dissensions in the ranks. The *privilège* was revoked; Dalembert retired; and Rousseau, never an easy yoke-fellow, found cause for quarrel. Through all these difficulties, including the timidity of the printer, Le Breton, who could not be trusted not to improvise excisions, Diderot perserved with indomitable energy, and finally won his way through. Mme. de Pompadour, the king's mistress, and Quesnay (q.v.), her physician, and a physiocrat, were valuable friends at court; and despite police, priests, and warring contributors, vols. vii to xvi were publd. by the end of 1765; vols. xvii to xxviii (containing the plates) were ready in 1772, and 7 supplementary vols. completed the work in 1776. It was a personal triumph for Diderot, and a public victory for the philosophy—moral, physical, and political —since known as that of the Fr. Encyclopedists. It is possible to overrate the importance and the influence of this great work. We may admit that British parliamentary institutions, the foundation of American independence, and the Fr. Republic itself, might all have assumed their actual forms if Diderot had followed Dalembert into the quieter ways; that Montaigne, Descartes, the Libertines and Bayle (qq.v.) had flourished before the Encyclopedists, who did not invent the doctrines which they upheld, but rather popularized them for common acceptation; and that Locke (q.v.) was a philosopher before the *philosophes*. But it is a very narrow criticism which makes isolation a condition of greatness. The greatness of Diderot's *Encyclopédie* lay precisely in the expression which it codified of the progressive thought of his generation: the generation before the Revolution, which altered the ideas of Europe. It is hardly fanciful, indeed it is almost legitimate, to say that the *Encyclopédie* was the *Divina Commedia* of the 18th cent.; certainly, it was the ordered reply of modern thought, gradually filtered through the Renaissance, to the thought reflected by Dante from the scholastic philosophy of the Middle Ages. It taught ' the great counter-principle to asceticism in life and morals, to formalism in art, to absolutism in the social ordering, to obscurantism in thought' (Morley, *Diderot*, i, 5 [1878]).

With encyclopedias after *l'Encyclopédie*, including the Engl. *Encyclopædia Britannica*, the term reverted to the non-specialized use defined by the *New Engl. Dict.* at the beginning of this article. Among names prominently connected with the *Encycl. Brit.* in recent annals are those of **Thomas Spencer Baynes** (1823-87), who superintended the ninth edn., 1873-87; **William Robertson Smith** (1846-94), who joined Baynes as co-editor, 1881, and was dismissed from his chair as prof. of Old Testament exegesis at the Free Church Coll., Aberdeen, in consequence of the advanced tone of criticism displayed in his Biblical art. in the *E.B.*; **John Sutherland Black** (1856-1923),

assistant-editor, 1881, and, later, joint-editor, who wr. the *Life* of Robertson Smith, and was a scholar of very rare attainments; and **Hugh Chisholm** (1866-1924), who was in charge of the tenth—twelfth edns., publd. partly in connection with *The Times* newspaper, of which he had been City editor.

Enfantin, Barthélemy Prosper (1796-1864): Fr. philosopher; disciple of comte Saint-Simon (q.v.); wr. *Doctrine de Saint-Simon*, 1830.

Enfants Sans Souci: Fr. dramatic academy, also known as ' les Sots ', which was founded in Paris in the reign of king Charles vi (1368-1422), and which, later, worked in association with the ' Confrérie de la Passion ' (q.v.). Gringore (q.v.) became its manager in the 16th cent. Its main activity was in the sphere of light farce.

Engel, Joachim Jakob (1741-1802): Germ. miscellanist. Wr. works in popular philosophy, influenced by Lessing (q.v.); a psychological novel, *Herr Lorenz Stark*, 1801, publd. in Schiller's *Horen*; and plays, for which his post as director of the newly-founded National Theatre at Berlin (1786-90) afforded obvious opportunity.

Englische Comödianten: Germ. term for companies of Engl. strolling players who brought to Germany in the 16th cent. the repertory and histrionic skill of the Engl. Elizabethan stage, and thus, through imitation and transln., gave a lead to the development of Germ drama. A collection of the Anglo-Germ. plays appeared in 1620, consisting chiefly of bloody-tragic pieces, and a few comic interludes called *Pickelhering* (q.v.) plays, after the Dutch name of the inevitable fool; ' barbarous pieces ' they are not unjustly called, but they performed valuable service in their time and place.

English Literature*: There is authority as well as convenience in dating the beginning of E. L. among the literatures of Europe from Chaucer's Ital. period, which started about 1372. The convenience is obvious, and among authorities we may quote the scheme for a history of Engl. poetry outlined by Pope (q.v.), which never went further than a rough design, and a passage from the Introduction (p. xx) to *Fourteenth Century Verse and Prose*, edited by K. Sisam (Oxford, 1923): ' In Chaucer we have for the first time a layman, writing in English for secular purposes, who from the range and quality of his work may fairly claim to be ranked among men of letters. His models are men of letters: the Latin poets headed by Ovid, who was Gower's favourite too; French writers, from the satirical Jean de Meung to makers of studied " balades, roundels, virelayes," like Machaut and Deschamps; and the greater Ital. group—Boccaccio, Petrarch and Dante. Keeping such company, he was bound to reject the rusticity of the alliterative school. . . . After his day, even for Northerners who wish to write well, there will be no more " *rum-ram-ruf* by lettre " '—a reference to the Prologue to the Parson's Tale (43) in *Canterbury Tales*:

' I am a Southern man,
I can nat geste *rum*, *ram*, *ruf*, by lettre,
Ne, god wot, rym holde I but litel bettre ';

* The attempt is made to give a brief conspectus of the subject of this art. in place of a detailed summary.

he would not tell tales, that is, in alliterative verse like the Northern singers ('rym'=rhyme). As mariners, exploring the civilized world, sailed westward-ho a few years after, so Engl. poets, acquiring modern measures in the 14th cent., turned the head of their Pegasus to the south. The company which Chaucer kept, in the early morning of Engld. among the nations, determined the course of Engl. lit.; and the models which he rejected were no longer used for imitation. If Petrarch, according to Renan, is the first modern man, Chaucer, who was in Florence in 1373, where he met Boccaccio and possibly Petrarch, was the first modern Englishman of letters.

At the same time, modern Engl. lit. has its springs in a remote past. Courthope, *Hist. Engl. Poetry* (6 vols., 1895-1910; he fulfilled Pope's design), says, in his preface to vol. i: 'We cannot afford to despise the rude art of our forefathers. . . . A modern history of English poetry must deal not only with the progress of poetical invention, but with the more technical question of the development of metrical harmony'; and, if we may cite in this place the 3 best primers of Engl. lit.—the 3 best bks. for students to read *first*,—we note that each of them starts with a chapter on the history before Chaucer, rapidly surveyed by Taine (q.v.) and stratified by Jusserand. These bks. are, in order of date: *Engl. Lit.*, by Stopford Brooke, 1876, and frequently reissued; *Introduction to Engl. Lit.*, by H. S. Pancoast, 1894, etc.; and *A First Book of Engl. Lit.*, by G. Saintsbury, 1914, etc. Following these leaders, we must refer (see s.vv.) to *Pearl* (c. 1375), an elegy somewhat luxuriant in its imagery, by a poet who is also credited with *Cleanness, Patience* and *Sir Gawaine*; to John Barbour's *Bruce* (1375); *Mandeville's Travels* (prose), originally in Fr. (c. 1356), and soon transld. into Lat. and Engl.,—the Fr. writer's claim to be sir John Mandeville is probably a disguise; his name was Jean de Bourgogne;—*Piers Plowman* (see s.v. Langland); the verse transln. of Guido's Troy-book (see s.v. Homer), and other early writings. What went before these is not essential to our story, but a very delightful way of studying a difficult subject is to read the bk. by E. Dale on *National Life and Character in the Mirror of Early Engl. Lit.* (Cambridge, 1907), with its marginal references to orig. sources from the 6th to the 13th cent. This method of approach is so fascinating that the reader is driven to the texts; and the Early Engl. Text Society will supply all that are required.

Dr. Dale's bk. strikes the key-note for the useful study of Engl. lit., as one of the great literatures of Europe. Engl. lit. at its highest has always reflected the nation's life and character. It has always been an open-air lit., never (or never for long) a lit. of the closet or the cloister. All great lit. of course is artificial. (A recognition of this truism dismisses a large part of the old theorizing about the authorship of Homer's epics). But it is not an esoteric art, intended for the few, not the many; and Engl. lit., more persistently than any, has always found its way into the open. With brief and insignificant exceptions, it has been free from the constricting air of a court (q.v.)., which clipt the wings, e.g., of Rabelais, Tasso and Corneille (see s.vv.), and from the tyrannous rules of an academy (q.v.), of which the Fr. Academy, though the chief, was not the first. How free, or, at any rate, how much freer, may be judged, summarily, from the record of G. Harvey (q.v.) alone, on his Areopagus, and of the Euphuism of Lyly (q.v.), which was quickly extended, partly by ridicule and partly by a practical sifting, from the casket in which it was originally enclosed to the common service of every-day writers. The *salon* was never acclimatized in Engld.; the tide of religious persecution, which swept over so much good lit. in Spain and other countries, was likewise much lower in ours; and a result is, speaking generally, yet keeping well within the mark, that Engl. lit. from Chaucer downwards, though deeply indebted to foreign models, and though often placing foreigners in its debt, has at all times been very close to Engl. life.

Chaucer himself illustrates this truth. He travelled in Italy on a commercial mission at the dawn of Humanism (q.v.) in that country. Engld. herself was expanding when Chaucer expanded her letters; and 'in his picture of the Canterbury pilgrimage, with the strength of its public opinion, and its power of regulating its own affairs, we find, what had as yet nowhere else appeared in modern European literature, the image of an organized nation. Poetry was removed from the regions of metaphysics, allegory and theology, and began to be re-animated by the old classical principle of the direct imitation of nature' (Courthope, i, 300). Engl. 'poetry', because of Engl. life. It was impossible that a nation, seeking commercial markets abroad, and negotiating trade-loans from foreign bankers, should not criticize life in its lit. 'by the universal standard of humanity and commonsense', which was to render it supreme in drama and the novel (q.v.). 'Chaucer was the head of the innovating poets, who wrote in rhyme after the French manner. His system proved victorious; and he has therefore justly been acclaimed by Wyatt, Surrey, Spenser, Dryden and Wordsworth, as the founder of the art of English poetry' (*ib.*, 284-5).

Properly viewed, this is, in epitome, the whole splendid history of Engl. lit. Its practitioners have always been ready to write after the Fr. manner, or after any manner likely to polish and make truer the mirror which they held up to nature. There were intervals of dulness, of course,—periods when Engl. writers were precluded, owing to one or another cause, from apprenticeship to foreign models. Such an interval followed the age of Chaucer, when, during, roughly, 100 years, between 1399 and 1485, as many as 7 kings ascended the Engl. throne. It was not till after 1485, when Henry vii, the first Tudor monarch, succeeded to the rival dynasties and kings, and inaugurated the brilliant Tudor epoch, which lasted till the death of queen Elizabeth in 1603, that Engld. looked outward again, and repeated and surpassed the record of Chaucer's Plantagenet period. Then, again, her writers had scope and leisure to employ the resources of progress matured abroad by the humanists, the explorers and the reformers. A host of translrs. brought them to our shores,—Golding, Harington, Hoby, North, Florio (qq.v.), and others ; and a crowd of eager poets and prosemen—Wyatt, Surrey, Spenser, Sidney, Jonson, Marlowe (qq.v.) among the greatest,—turned the accumulated material to national use. The supreme voice of the Renaissance (including the Reformation under that name) was Shakespeare (q.v.), 1564-1616, who, though he held up his mirror to human nature in his own country, and reflected Engl. life in Engl. letters, can be anatomized into European particles as discretely as Chaucer before him.

Milton (q.v.), 1608-74, was a little boy when Shakespeare died. Queen Elizabeth, too, was dead, and less than 50 years after her death, king Charles i was beheaded by his subjects. The ' Gloriana ' epoch was past and irrecoverable ; the last real successor to the Tudors was Parliamentary Government ; and we can imagine Milton's feeling in *l'Allegro* (c. 1635), looking back even before the storm to the time before the clouds had gathered, and listening to ' sweetest Shakespeare, Fancy's child, warble his native wood-notes wild '. The woods of Buckinghamshire, where Milton was then living, sang their notes in vain to his pre-occupied ear. Both Milton and Bunyan (1628-88) were concerned with the new problems of conduct and policy, and with the new thought of the age in which they lived. Our ' sober freedom ' under ' temperate kings ', which Tennyson (q.v.) praised in the middle of the 19th cent., was not a gift from the void, not a *bonus* attached to Engl. citizenship and maturing in due course of time. Undreamed of under the Tudors, it was wrung by an indignant people from the misgoverning Stuarts. As in the parable of Samson—the hero whom Milton emulated—the sweetness came from the strong ; the passionate love of country and the sense of national self-confidence were born from the lion's carcase, from the Tudor autocracy ruined by the misrule of the Stuarts. The period covered by Milton's life contains the seeds of modern Engld. During his life-time, and with his assistance, Engld. passed through a phase of transition and reconstruction. She must have been profoundly dissatisfied with the monarchical theory, when the passing of Elizabeth stripped the romance of the trappings from the Tudor practice of monarchy, and left the theory bare. She must have been equally dissatisfied with the Protectorate experiment, since that violent remedy hardly survived the death of its strong and necessary author. And this double discontent was surely a formative experience in the fifty-odd years which elapsed from Elizabeth's death in 1603 to the Restoration in 1660. When a nation's discontent assumes so strenuous a power in shaping the national destiny, it acquires the quality ' divine '. No nation could pass through this experience without changing its outlook on politics and morals, and on all that makes up its life. Lit. reflected this change. ' A transformation in our attitude towards life, and in our general view of the world, always shows itself first in the æsthetic field ', says Paulsen (*Immanuel Kant*, E.T., 17),

and so it happened in Engld. in the 17th cent. The tinker's son in prison, John Milton in his State Secretary's chair, were alike governed by a passion for purifying faith and restoring God's kingdom on earth.

1660, the year of the Restoration, marks a date in the history of Engl lit. Though Dryden (q.v.) and Milton were contemporaries, in the sense that Dryden, who lived to 1700, was 43 when Milton died at 64, yet, in every other sense, they belonged to different generations. The Restoration had flowed between them, with all that it brought and took away. It brought sedentary criticism ; the Royal society (incorp.. 1665) ; the analytic philosophy of John Locke (1632-1704) and sir Isaac Newton (1642-1727) ; public opinion founded on public responsibility ; the rise of the coffee-house (q.v.), with its issue in news-letters and a periodical press ; and the return to rule and restraint in literary composition, associated directly with the leaders of Fr. lit. (q.v.), and, through these as well as directly, with their authorities in classical antiquity. Individuality tended to disappear, as personal conviction was replaced by general consent : ' out of the English political spirit ', says prof. Courthope, ' was developed in English poetry the classical form '. A form of verse was sought, which should admit the minimum of variation due to individual emotion or caprice, and the maximum of external glitter of a kind which would please the average taste of a cultivated audience ; and the suitable metre was found in Chaucer's rhymed couplets of decasyllabic lines, pointed and painted to suit the new standard, and known as heroic verse. Polish was substituted for colour as an ideal of style. Note that now, again, as in the age of Chaucer, the foreign models for these changes were not so much deliberately imitated as insensibly absorbed, since they responded so accurately to the needs of the times. So we may mention and pass over Waller (1606-87), Swift (1667-1745), Addison (1672-1719), Steele (1672-1729), Defoe, Richardson, Fielding, Pope, and even Dr. Johnson (1709-84), who opposed his dominating influence to the inrush of new ideas, when the Augustanism of the long 18th cent. was drawing to its close. We may pass them over with just two quotations, which help the orientation of the century between the death of Milton, 1674, and that of Johnson, 1784. ' For a whole century ', writes sir E. Gosse, ' the singer that only sang because he must, and as the linnets do, was entirely absent from English literature. He came back at the close of the eighteenth century, with Burns in Scotland and with Blake in England '. Instead of him there were the correct writers, of whom Pope was the chief : ' In no other country of Europe was there an artist so consummate as he, nowhere one in whom the qualities which Waller and Malherbe and Opitz (see s.vv.) had imposed upon taste were developed with so much delicacy, variety and harmony. Pope completed the change which had been silently progressing almost since the death of Shakespeare '. And our second quotation, which will be helpful for what follows, is from Pope himself :

All nature is but art, unknown to thee ;
All chance, direction, which thou canst not see ;
All discord, harmony not understood ;
All partial evil, universal good :
And, spite of pride, in erring reason's spite,
One truth is clear, WHATEVER IS, IS RIGHT.
Essay on Man, i, x.

A complete and well-rounded philosophy of life, but it did not satisfy the new generation. From the mills and workshops of the Midlands came a crowd of factory ' hands ' who were soon to assert their right to be counted as heads and hearts ; from Engld.'s wars in foreign countries her sailors and soldiers came back, claiming the fruit of their exploits in improved colonial administration, with all the consequences it entailed on political life at home ; and the social and economic threads, when they were gathered at last by writers of genius, were woven into new patterns, enlarging the bases of lit. to make room for the accretion of fresh material. Remote from contemporary letters, but close to those hidden fires at which genius is kindled, the new forces were at work. Richard Arkwright, the barber's apprentice, who ended as a knt. of industry ; Matthew Boulton, journeyman-engineer, who supplied machinery to the Mint ; James Brindley, engine-repairer, who constructed the Bridge-water canal ; Abraham Darby, father, son, and grandson, at the Coalbrookdale Ironworks in Shropshire ; James Hargreaves, inventor of the spinning-jenny ; John Kay, inventor of the fly-shuttle ; Thomas Lombe, silk-manu-facturer, who became sheriff of London and a knt. ; James Watt, inventor of the steam-engine ; Josiah Wedgwood, John Wilkinson, John Wyatt—these Johns and Thomases of the workshop were the trustees of Engld.'s expansion at one end of the scale, as knightly and heroic in their way as the captains of the sea under Elizabeth. And ever in the back-ground of their toil is the grim, pathetic spec-tacle of the human continent which they explored. At the other end of the scale was the expansion of Engld. by war ; ' The expan-sion of England in the New World and in Asia is the formula which sums up for England the history of the eighteenth century ', says sir J. Seeley (q.v.). Yet neither industry nor arms affected the outlook of letters from Pope's garden at Twickenham or Johnson's armchair in Fleet Street.

Rousseau (q.v.) was a man of 32, and Kant (q.v.) a student of 20, when Pope died in 1744 ; and to these writers pre-eminently we trace the rise of *le lyrisme* (q.v.), or Romanticism (s.v. Romance), which led to great men and great events in France and Germany in the 18th cent. Signs of the budding and the burgeoning were visible in Engld. and Scotland, too ; but they could not burst the sheath of the heroic couplet. This was the wonder of *Lyrical Ballads*, 1798 : of the poems written ' as experiments, . . . with a view to ascertain how far the language of conversation in the middle and lower classes of society '—we have mentioned some names in the foregoing paragraph—' is adapted to the purposes of poetic pleasure ' ; and Coleridge and Words-worth warned their readers that their verses might give rise to ' feelings of strangeness and

awkwardness '. So that ' the renascence of wonder ' (Watts-Dunton), which dated from that experiment, was within the authors' very intention, and the return to romantic standards was necessarily accompanied by a return to the freer measures of Ronsard, Spenser, Shakespeare, Milton. ' Get order ' had been the text of Pope's gospel ; ' get order ' and all else will follow ; and to the decorous passion for order in all gardens from Twickenham to Eden he offered a willing sacrifice of the allurements of the unknown. Words lost their edging of mystery ; thought, its province of the imagination. The physical frontiers which the Elizabethans explored, the metaphysical boundaries which irresis-tibly attracted the 19th cent.—in Wordsworth's
sense sublime
Of something far more deeply interfused,
Whose dwelling is the light of setting suns,
And the round ocean, and the living air,
And the blue sky, and in the mind of man
(*Tintern Abbey*) ;
in Browning's
future state revealed to us by Zeus,
Unlimited in capability
For joy, as this is in desire for joy,
To seek which the joy-hunger forces us
(*Cleon*) ;
in Meredith's
A wonder edges the familiar face :
She wears no more her robe of printed hours ;
Half strange seems Earth, and sweeter than
her flowers
(*Meditation under Stars*) ;—
all this sublimity, joy and strangeness had been excluded from poetry and its metres. Immense good in compensation had been introduced : in thought, clarity and precision ; in language, the corresponding virtues ; but it was time to restore the lost possessions,—to reinstate in the realm of sentiency, ' dans les années les plus désheritées de la poésie anglaise ', the countless victims proscribed by Descartes (q.v. ; see Legouis, *La Jeunesse de Wordsworth*, 128, 412). The new generation was knocking at the door, opened on unswept interiors by Crabbe (q.v., 1754-1832) ; and was knocking down the doors of those who would not hear.

We need not enter the 19th cent. in their company. The 3 heirs of unfulfilled renown : Byron, 1788-1824, Shelley, 1792-1822, Keats, 1795-1821 (see s.vv.) ; the great octogenar-ians, stretching to our day ; Wordsworth, 1770-1850, Tennyson, 1809-92, Browning, 1812-89, Meredith, 1828-1909, Thomas Hardy, b., 1840 (see s.vv.) ; the novelists, Scott, Jane Austen, Mrs. Gaskell, George Eliot, Dickens, Thackeray (see s.vv.) ; the pre-Raphaelites and the Tractarians ; the histor-ians and the economists : Carlyle, Mill, Macau-lay, and the rest ; the influence of science on the age, with Darwin's *Origin of Species*, falling in 1859,—we need not enumerate the details. It is a century, which, faithful to the traditions of Chaucer, Spenser, Shakespeare, Milton, sought to interpret life in letters : life enlarged from the experience of Plantagenet, Tudor or Restoration Engld. to include humanity at large ; to turn, as F. W. H. Myers said of Wordsworth, ' a theology back into a religion ' ; to ' redeem from decay ', as Shelley said, 'the visitations of the divinity in man;' to reconcile, in Meredith's language, the 'Inner' and the 'Outer', the *I* and the *not-I*; omitting no evidence, ignoring nothing known, fearing nothing seen; to see, as Blake said, 'the world in a grain of sand, and heaven in a wild flower', and, knowing the flower, to seek to know, in Tennyson's words, 'what God and man is'.

Entresol: name of a society of Fr. economists (*Club de l'E.*), founded, 1724, and suppressed by card. Fleury, 1731. It held its meetings at the house of a certain abbé Alary, and its members included Henry St. John (q.v.), at whose instance, probably, it was designated a club, and Saint-Pierre (q.v.), whose tireless activity may have wearied his fellow-members into acquiescence with Fleury's closure.

Enzina, del, Juan (1469-c.1530): Span. poet; pastoral dramatist; reputed founder of Span. drama, by virtue not merely of the form of his compositions but also of the fact that they were acted. E.'s life reflected his tastes. He studied at the univ. of Salamanca; enjoyed the patronage of the duke of Alva; twice visited Rome, where he was preferred to a prebendary stall by pope Alexander and played in the chapel of pope Leo x; was nominated prior of Leon; made a pilgrimage to the Holy Land, which he described in a poor poem, his last work. He is remembered to-day neither for his music nor for his lyric verse, which was fluent and pleasant, but for the dramatic compositions, known as *eglogas* (eclogues; he had graduated by a poetic version of the eclogues of Virgil) or *representaciones* (see, too, s.v. *Sacra Rappresentazione*), which earned him his fame as patriarch of the secular stage. Some were on sacred, others on secular themes; all were simple in form and treatment, dealing with such subjects as Christmas, the Passion, and episodes of rustic life—11 or 12 in all. Some of the pastoral pieces employed a conventional dialect, probably invented *ad hoc*, to represent the speech of the humbler characters; but this affectation was wisely discontinued by E. in his later eclogues. Rojas (q.v.), in the 17th cent., dates the public performance of 'plays' in Castile from E. in 1492, and F. Wolf (q.v.) of Vienna, in the 19th, wr. an admirable account of E.'s life and work. Slight and insipid as his pieces appear to the more sophisticated taste of the present day, they form an important landmark in the development of the history of the stage.

Eobanus Hessus, Helius (1488-1540): Germ. humanist. Prof. of poetry and rhetoric at Luther's univ., Erfurt, 1715-26; during its period of chief illumination, E. presided at the gatherings of the 'poets', from whom the *Epistolæ Obscurorum Virorum* (q.v.) had proceeded; moved later to Nuremberg, then back to Erfurt, which had lost its eminence, and finally to Marburg. Wr. metrical version of *Psalms*, Lat. version of *Iliad* in hexameter verse, and many poems, which won him the title of the 'Christian Ovid'.

Epinay, d', Louise Florence Pétronille (1723-83): Fr. literary hostess; wr. her memoirs, which are interesting; held a *salon* (q.v.) in Paris, where she befriended Rousseau (q.v.) in his schemes of social reform. Later, she was attached to F. M. de Grimm (q.v.), whose correspondence on Fr. lit. with foreign sovereigns mme. d'E. conducted for some time.

Epistolæ Obscurorum Virorum (1514-17): Germ. prose-satire ('Letters of Obscure Men'), consisting of 2 anon. vols. of alleged monks' letters, written in the dog-Lat. appropriate to the pretended authorship, and forming the contribution of the scholars of Erfurt univ. to the Reuchlin-Pfefferkorn controversy (see s.vv.). The authors have been identified as (vol. i) Johann Jäger (Crotus Rubianus), and (vol. ii) Ulrich v. Hütten, and Conrad Muth (Mutian), members of a brilliant inner circle of the univ. known at the time as 'the poets'. The centre of the controversy was the demand, fostered by Pfefferkorn, a Jew. pervert, and backed by the powerful Order of the Dominicans at Cologne, for the suppression, in the cause of Lat. ecclesiastical orthodoxy, of all Hebr. theological lit., except only the Old Testament. Reuchlin, as a leading Orientalist, took the field in defence of Hebr. studies. In the course of this battle of the bks. he publd. a sheaf of testimonials, *Clarorum Virorum Epistolæ*, which eminent men had written in his support; and it was this genuine publication which suggested the mock-letters invented by the Erfurt humanists. Eminent men had supported Reuchlin; his adversary, too, should be supported by letters suited to his merits. The 'obscure men's letters' were ostensibly addressed to the leader of obscurantism, Ortwin Gratius, head of the Dominicans at Cologne. The illusion of genuineness was admirably sustained; and the slipshod, dog-Lat. language, the merciless self-revelation of laziness, ignorance, and licentiousness, unredeemed by any spark of insight, and ignobly content to be obscure, on the part of the supposed writers of the *Letters*, made Reuchlin's mission of culture shine more brightly in contrast. The *E.O.V.* were the reply of Erfurt to Cologne, of Luther's progressive univ. to the forces of darkness and intolerance; and they appeared at the brief moment when Humanism, hot-foot from Italy, and Dissent, quickening in Germany, had not yet parted company. The pasquinade had an immediate success, due as much to its mercilessness as to its brilliance; the taste of the 16th cent. was not delicate, and there was no desire to stint the measure. Whether viewed as satire or lit., the Erfurt *Letters* are superb, and occupy a unique place in the transition from Renaissance to Reformation. (The *E.O.V.* have been edited and transld. by F. Griffin Stokes, Chatto & Windus, 1909).

Epitaph (rhet.): 'An epitaph is a superscription (either in verse or prose), or an astrict pithy diagram, writ, carved, or engraven upon the tomb, grave, or sepulchre of the defunct, briefly declaiming (and that with a kind of commiseration) the name, the age, the deserts, the dignities, the state, the praises both of body and mind, the good and bad fortunes in the life, and the manner and time of the death of the person therein interred'. (From the *Ancient Funeral Monuments*, 1831, of John Weever, 1576-1632, antiquary of Cambridge;

and quoted, 1810, in an essay ' Upon Epitaphs ' in *The Friend*, by W. Wordsworth, q.v.). Wordsworth comments as follows upon the above definition : ' This account of an epitaph, which as far as it goes is just, was no doubt taken by Weever from the monuments of our own country, and it shows that in his conception an epitaph was not to be an abstract character of the deceased, but an epitomized biography blended with description by which an impression of the character was to be conveyed. Bring forward the one incidental expression, a kind of commiseration, unite with it a concern on the part of the dead for the well being of the living made known by exhortation and admonition, and let this commiseration and concern pervade and brood over the whole, so that what was peculiar to the individual shall still be subordinate to a sense of what he had in common with the species, our notion of a perfect epitaph would then be realised ' ; and Wordsworth finds this is the very model upon which the epitaphs of Chiabrera (q.v.) are for the most part framed. Nine of these he transld. into Engl. verse. The epitaph, which is intended to be placed on a gravestone or a monument, is to be distinguished from the elegy, which is a memorial composition not restricted by limitations of space.

Epithalamium (rhet.): Marriage-song (the Gk. word *thalamos* = bed) ; an orig. part of the wedding-ritual, the song was separated and secularized at an early date in the hist. of Gk. lit., and a fine example of the E. jis the 18th idyll of Theocritus imitated in Lat. by Catullus (lxi, lxii), and elsewhere. From these models, the E. passed into Europe in the period of the Renaissance, and many Ital. wedding-songs adorned the masques instituted in honour of such occasions. Puttenham, an Elizabethan critic, in his *Poets and Poesy*, ch. xxvi, defines the E. exactly as ' sung very sweetly by Musicians at the chamber-door of the Bridegroom and Bride, and they were called *Epithalamies* as much to say as ballads at the bridal couch For such as were sung as the board at dinner, or supper were other musics and not properly *Epithalamies* '. Specimens of the E. will be found in many great Engl. poets from Spenser to Shelley (qq.v.).

Erasmus (1466-1536): Dutch humanist ; ' the educator of Europe ' (prof. Foster Watson, *The Nineteenth Century and After*, March, 1916). E. was born at Rotterdam, and became known by the Latinized names (the first being the Lat. equivalent of the second, derived from a bp.-hero of the Netherlands) Desiderius Erasmus Rotterdamus. By birth, he was Gerhard, the natural son of an unknown father, who became a Roman Catholic priest, when the course of his true love for a Brabant maiden, Margaret, went awry. These circumstances cast their shadow over E.'s childhood ; the story is told, with ample borrowings from the writings of E. himself, by C. Reade (q.v.), *The Cloister and the Hearth*. E. received an excellent education at Deventer (q.v.), where Agricola (q.v.) was struck by the lad's promise, and at Herzogenbosch (Bois-de-duc), likewise founded by the Brethren (q.v.) of the Common Lot ; he was ordained in the Augustinian Order, 1492 ; spent some years in the

cloister ; visited Paris (*c.* 1497) in the train of the bp. of Cambrai, and Engld. (1499) in company of lord Mountjoy, a former pupil. E. already enjoyed some repute as a scholar, and received a ready welcome in Engl. centres of learning from the leaders of humanistic thought, and esp. from the Oxford reformers, More, Grocyn and Colet (qq.v.), who became his firm friends. Grocyn taught him Gk. at Oxford, and Colet, the saintliest of students, encouraged E. in his studies. With a view to Biblical erudition, E. devoted himself specially to Gk., in which he lagged behind his great skill in Latinity. He visited Louvain, Paris, and, again, London (1505) ; travelled in Italy, spending some time in each learned centre, and gaining acquaintance with the leading scholars, and returned at last to Engld., 1509. He wrote his *Encomium Moriœ* (' The Praise of Folly '), satirizing the affectations and hypocrisies of ' blind mouths', as the guest of sir T. More in Bucklersbury, and was called to Cambridge in 1511, as prof. of divinity. There, among more monumental labours, he gave lessons in Gk., and wr. textbooks of the Lat. language for the use of Colet's new school of St. Paul's. In 1514, E. removed to Basle, then the world's main publishing centre, which he made his headquarters till he died. There, writes Foster Watson (*loc. cit.*) he ' steadily advanced to a literary dictatorship to (substantially) the whole of Europe '. There he built, in a famous phrase, his bridge from medieval to modern thought, and turned to practical uses the ideal studies of Ital. humanists. The titles and dates of E.'s chief works are : *Adagia* (' Adages ', 1500), a miscellany of extracts and examples, which renewed for the parched intellect of the 15th cent., just turning hopefully to the 16th, all the wisdom and grace of classical antiquity ; *Moriœ Encomium* (mentioned above), an attack, rather too savage for E.'s pen to carry, on sciolism, scholasticism, and clever-seeming stupidity ; a new Lat. version (distinct from the Vulgate) of, and notes on, the Gk. New Testament, 1516 ; *Institutio Christiani Principis* (' Training of a Christian Prince ') 1516 ; *Colloquia* (' Colloquies '), 1516, later expanded ; *Ciceronianus* (see s.v. Cicero), 1528 ; Letters, 1529, and new edn., with additions, 1536 ; a treatise on the correct pronunciation of Gk. and Lat., 1528 ; and an educational treatise, 1529. There were other works, editorial, commentary, occasional, directed by his constant effort ' to arouse the rising generation from the feast of ignorance (*inscitia*—noknowledge) to purer studies ' ; and his main writings, uniformly in Lat. (prof. Saintsbury was haunted by a nightmare, ' if Erasmus had written in Dutch ' !) are the monuments in lit. of the genius of the northern Renaissance. E.'s personal influence and intercourse and his imperturbable scholar's equanimity were hardly less valuable than his learning, as a beacon to the higher ground from which the torrent of the Reformation was receding. In the religious turmoil of this time E.'s sympathy was with reform, but the extremes of Luther (q.v.) attracted him as little as the overtures to Rome held out by his friend and correspondent, pope Adrian vi. Intellectually, he was always a looker-on, a little wayward and whimsical, never pleased except with the best, a dilettante and a connoisseur, generous in appreciation where it was due, but always a little aloof ; a man with a presence ; gifted with irony, whether observing the little things of life—the scolding landlady, and other traveller's impressions,—or, as in his *Ciceronianus*, turning the weapons of Latinity against overbearing Latinists ; beyond comparison, the supreme type of the restless scholar of the Renaissance. It is the *Novum Instrumentum* of 1816, as E. called his Lat. version of the New Testament, which constitutes his chief claim to fame, as his Letters are his chief claim to interest. Modern study of the Bible (q.v.) is dated from that work, which, in the spirit of Colet, humanized and re-spiritualized the sacred narrative. Modern educational methods were derived from E.'s theory of education and from his manuals of Lat. syntax and composition. The false Ciceronianism of his century in Italy was stopped, despite Dolet and the elder Scaliger (qq.v.), by his brilliant restoration of the true Cicero. The 'Erasmian' pronounciation of Gk. replaced the rules of living Gks., imported by Reuchlin (q.v.) from across the Alps ; and, when all this is admitted, and more, we still have not touched the fringe of E.'s real contribution to lit. in his correspondence. and his colloquies. Scott (q.v. ; *Anne of Geierstein*) and Reade (*op. cit.*), are British novelists who have availed themselves of the rich material for scene and story which these Lat. pictures of modern life contain. E. was a ' citizen of the world ' before Goldsmith (q.v.) ; and, though in his lifetime he aroused bitter enmity and attack, as much, perhaps, for what he refused to say, and from the sides which he did not touch, as for what he said and from the sides which he offended, yet posterity leaves the controversies alone, lets alone the evils of the age which provoked them, and recognizes in E. a fine example, in many respects the finest example in literary annals, of erudition with no trace of pedantry, of irony with no tinge of scoffing, of Latinity with no sign of Patavinity, and of humanism without folly or pretence. It is in the ' paraclesis' of his *Novum Instrumentum* (the summons, or preface, to his New Testament, that is to say) that the famous passage occurs : ' The mysteries of kings it may be safer to conceal, but Christ wished his mysteries to be published as openly as possible. I wish that even the weakest woman should read the Gospel—should read the epistles of Paul . . . I long that the husbandman should sing portions of them to himself as he follows the plough, that the weaver should hum them to the tune of his shuttle, that the traveller should beguile with their stories the tedium of his journey '. Watson (*loc. cit.*) calls this passage ' a literary Rubicon. The Middle Ages are on one side ; the modern World on the other '. And it was written, it will be remembered, while Machiavelli (q.v.) was writing his *Prince*. The *Christian Prince* and the professional *Principe* were 2 princes. E.'s ruler and the Utopian hopes of More were the reply of northern humanism to southern experiments

in government. They pointed the true road of the Renaissance to kings and rulers dazzled by false lights. Scholarship, all humanism with all its learning, was not an end in itself, for the most eminent Ciceronian might be still a pagan (this was the burden of E.'s *Ciceronianus*). ' The real pontifex, the bridge-builder across the stream between the science and religion of that age was not one of them, but Erasmus ' (J. H. Lupton, *Life of Colet*).

Erastus (1524-83) : Thomas Lüber, or Lieber, transld. into Erastus ; Swiss theological writer ; physician ; founder of the name, if not of the doctrine, of Erastianism and the Erastians. ' The term *Erastian* has long been a favourite term of reproach in Scotland, and *Erastianism* is now held to mean the doctrine of State supremacy in ecclesiastical matters, or denying the power of the Church to alter any of her own laws without the consent of the State ' (Benham, *Dict. of Religion*, Cassell, 1891). This conclusion from E.'s premises is ' in some respects far broader than anything he seems to have suggested ' (Hallam, ii, 340) ; and the question ' was Erastus an Erastian ? ' is ably argued by Figgis, *The Divine Right of Kings*, 2nd edn., 293 following, who concludes that E.'s main object ' was not to magnify the State, nor to enslave the Church, but to secure the liberty of the subject.' In this aim, if correctly stated, E. contributed to the development of political thought, and has his place in the literary succession through Hobbes and Grotius (qq.v.). His writings, which had involved him in controversy with Beza (q.v.), took shape in 1589 as *Explicatio gravissimæ questionis, utrum Excommunicatio . . . mandato nitatur Divino an excogitata sit ab hominibus.*

Erben, Karel Saromir (1811-70) : Czech poet and folklorist ; keeper of the records at Prague. Wr. the ' Garland of National Folktales ', 1853, comprising in 12 ballads the richest resources of Slav legend ; ' Czech Folk-songs ', ' Slavonic Folktales ', etc. ; and edited with great skill and erudition older works in poetry and prose from early MSS. or printed sources.

Ercilla y Zuñiga, de, Alonso (1533-94) : Span. poet ; a man of heroic adventures which he immortalized in an heroic poem, *La Araucana* ; in 37 cantos in all, publd. in 3 parts, 1569, 1578, 1589-90. It is one of the poems praised extravagantly by Cervantes (q.v.) in the famous chapter dealing with Don Quixote's library of chivalric romances ; and, at a later day, Voltaire (q.v.), in his preface to the *Henriade*, 1726, expressed enthusiastic appreciation of one of the Homeric speeches in E.'s epopee. Apart from these excessive testimonials, E.'s poem, which celebrated his campaign against the Araucans (Arauco was a district of Chili, inhabited by brave and tenacious warriors), has both literary and hist. value, and has maintained its interest to the present day, despite the manifest frigidity of its geographical exactitudes and its classical conventions. E.'s life was full of the romance of the day ; he attended king Philip ii of Spain at his nuptials with queen Mary of Engld. ; he fought, as shown, in South America ; he was condemned to death, and actually imprisoned, in consequence of a dispute at a tournament; he received court appointments, but died in poverty and neglect. E.'s implied depreciation of his leader in the Araucan campaign, Garcia Hurtado de Mendoza, who had been partly responsible for the prison episode, was the occasion of Oña's (q.v.) poem on the same subject.

Erckmann-Chatrian (Fr.): Pen-name of **Émile Erckmann** (1822-99) and **Alexandre Chatrian** (1826-90), joint-authors of a series of hist. novels, dealing with the wars of the Fr. Revolution and of the First Empire, of which their *Contes Nationaux* form a kind of irregular prose-epic. The *Histoire d'un Paysan*, 1868, written last, but the first in hist. order, deals successively with episodes from 1789 to 1802. It has the additional interest of marking the beginning of a decline in E.-C.'s popularity in France; due to the rising militarism of the Second Empire. E. and C. were both Lorrainers, and the setting of their novels was as definitely Alsace as that of Hardy's is Wessex; and the question of Alsace, which culminated in the Franco-Prussian campaign of 1870-1, was not to be settled by the moderate neutrality of such typical border-patriots as these collaborators. Next in hist. order was *Madame Thérèse*, the story of France *contra mundum*; and *The Conscript, The Invasion, The Blockade of Phalsbourg* and *Waterloo* brought the series (comparable, in its insulation, to the Barchester series of Trollope, q.v.) to a conclusion. It was the poor man's experience of warfare which E.C. set out to illustrate, and this point of view was, again, incompatible with the temper of 1870. Outside their block of 1789-1815 romances, E.C. wr. plays, *le Juif Polonais, l'Ami Fritz*, etc., which had considerable success. A generation with a fresh experience of the horrors of warfare may well return to these national tales, exalting the soldier, but hating the harsh necessity of his profession.

Ernesti, Johann August (1707-81): Germ. scholar; prof. of oratory and afterwards of theology at univ. of Leipsic. Editor of Cicero (q.v.). Colleague and supporter of J. M. Gesner (q.v.) in the new Hellenistic humanism.

Eschenburg, J. J. (18th. cent.): Germ. translr. of Shakespeare, 1775-77; superseded by A. W. Schlegel (q.v.).

Escoiquiz, de, Juan (fl. c. 1797): Span. poet. Transld. Milton's (q.v.) *Paradise Lost* and Young's (q.v.) *Night Thoughts*; and wr. heroic poem, 'Mexico conquered', 1798.

Escriva, Juan (fl. 1500): Span. poet; native of Valencia (q.v.), and was one of the last to use his native dialect in poetry; ambassador of king Ferdinand and queen Isabella to the pope. E. contributed 28 Castilian poems to the *Cancionero general* (q.v.), and enjoyed the unique success of having one of his songs quoted by Calderon (q.v., *No Monster like Jealousy*, iii, xi), Cervantes (q.v., *Don Quixote*, ii, 38), and Lope de Vega (q.v.). This is the short poem beginning, *Ven, muerte, tan escondido* ('Come, death, hidden, unaware).' Another title to fame is derived by E. from his dialogue, part-verse part-prose, 'a complaint (*una quexa*) by his lady against the god of Love', which is commonly cited as an early tentative experiment in dramatic composition.

España Sagrada (Span.): Sacred Spain; an encyclopedic history of the Church in Spain, commenced in 1754, and completed in 51 vols., 1879.

Espinel, Vicente (1551-1624): Span. novelist; poet; musician. E.'s life, like that of many men of letters in 16th cent. Spain, was adventurous and varied. He was taken prisoner to Algiers, like Cervantes (q.v.), and entered the church in later life, like Vega (q.v.); chiefly, we gather, for the sake of musical preferment at Madrid. He is said to have added the 5th string to the (later, 6-stringed) national instrument, the guitar; and to have invented the *decima*, or 10-line metre, sometimes called after him the *espinela*. He transld. Horace's *Ars poetica*, included in his *Diversas Rimas*, 1591; but E.'s chief work was a picaresque novel (q.v.), entitled *Marcos de Obregon*, 1618 ('Stories of the Life of the Esquire—*Escudero* —Marcos de Obregon'), a delightful tale of rascally adventures, less broken by didacticism than Aleman's (q.v.) *Guzman*. Voltaire (q.v.), a little maliciously, said that *Gil Blas* was taken entirely from this bk.; but later critics have steadily written down the sum of Lesage's (q.v.) debt to E. The novel has enjoyed a fairly permanent vogue, and among its translrs. was Tieck (q.v.) into Germ., 1827.

Espinosa, Pedro (1578-1650): Span. anthologist. Publd., 1605, a valuable collection of Span. (and Port.) poetry, by dead and living writers, entitled 'Part i of the Flowers of Illustrious Poets of Spain'.

Esplandian: Span. hero of chivalric romance-fiction; son of Amadis (q.v.) and Oriana; invented by Montalvo (q.v.) in his *Sergas* (exploits) *del virtuoso cavallero Esplandian*, c. 1510, in continuation of his version of the *Amadis de Gaula*. Posterity tends to concur with the judgment of the curate and the barber, who, when they went through Don Quixote's library (see s.v. Cervantes), spared the *Amadis*, but declared of *The Exploits of Esplandian*: 'The goodness of the father availeth not the child. Open the window, mistress housekeeper, and lay the foundation of the fire!' (*Don Quixote*, i, 6).

Espronceda, de, José (1808-42): Span. poet; revolutionary. E.'s stormy though brief career hardly belongs to the chronicle of lit., which he adorned with a vol. of lyric verse, *Poesias*, 1840; with *el Diablo Mundo* (containing the *Canto á Teresa*), 1841; and, earlier, an epopee on Pelayo (q.v.). The Teresa of E.'s muse was Teresa Mancha, whom he first met when she was 15 years of age, whom he met again in London when she was married, and with whom he eloped to Paris in 1829. He had already had experience of revolution and prison in Spain, and now took part in the Paris disturbances of July, 1830. He was in Madrid again as an insurrectionist and republican, 1835-40, and ended as secretary to the embassy at The Hague. 'The violence of his temperament and his unabatable artistic egoism lend life and colour to his superb songs, . . . and Espronceda is the most powerful and admirable lyric poet of the nineteenth century in Spain' (Kelly, *Lit. espagn.*, 414; see, too, Kelly, *Modern Language Review*, iv, 1908). It is probably correct to say that,

11

while E. consciously modelled himself on Byron (q.v.), he came more nearly to the Byronic view of life than any other admirer or imitator.

Estampie (rhet.): descriptive name of a class of medieval Fr. dance-songs, obviously accompanied by foot-beats to mark the time.

Estella, de, Diego (1524-78): Span. moralist. Wr. ' Vanity of the World ', 1574 ; ' Meditation on the Love of God ', 1578, the mystical beauty of which fascinated saint Francis de Sales (q.v.).

Estienne, -i. Robert (1503-59): Fr. humanist ; printer and publisher ; known by scholar's name of Stephanus. Publd. 8 *edd. pr.* of Gk. authors between 1544 and 1551, and folio edn. of Gk. Testament ; was prosecuted in connection with printing this text, and retired to Geneva. Wr., 1543, *Thesaurus Linguæ Latinæ*, a kind of exhaustive lexicon, thoroughly revised from an earlier compilation, and popular in subsequent revisions for quite two centuries.

-ii. Henri (1531-98): Fr. humanist ; printer and publisher. Son of above ; travelled in Italy ; succeeded his father at Geneva, 1559 ; issued 18 *edd. pr.* of Gk. authors, starting with Anacreon (q.v.) ; Ronsard (q.v.) paid him a poetic tribute for this gift, and E.'s text maintained its lead for many years ; publd. Plato, 1578, the standard edn. for two centuries ; and others. His greatest work was *Thesaurus Græcæ Linguæ*, a Gk. lexicon in 5 folio vols., which was, as he said, a treasury to others, not himself ; he lost money by the venture, mainly through the sharp practice of an assistant who undersold an abridgement in one vol. It held its ground till quite recent times, and was re-issued in Paris by Didot (q.v.) in 9 folio vols., 1831-65. H.E. spent the last 20 years of his life in visits to Paris and other centres, which he preferred to Geneva, to which his business was attached by his father's will ; partly his travels were due to a need of collecting monies subscribed or promised by powerful patrons, partly to his restlessness of temperament. One of his daughters was married to Casaubon (q.v.).

Estrambot (rhet.): descriptive name of a class of medieval Fr. songs, also called ' estrabot ', of a strongly satirical character.

Eulenspiegel (' Owlglass '): Germ. peasants' jest-book ; first collected, 1483, and since expanded and transld. in many languages and edns. (the latest in *Master Tyll : Owlglass*, Routledge, Broadway Translns.). The peasant-hero, Till or Tyll, who with shrewd and wily mother-wit splits the fat sides of worthy Germ. burghers by his merry malice and homely pranks, has been traced by industrious critics to a genuine prototype at Mölln in the 14th cent. ; and E. is variously explained as a nickname from the proverbial owl (*Eule*) who would not look at its ugly features in the mirror (*Spiegel*), as an actual family-name, and as a surname derived from a polisher's trade (*ul*=clean, *Spiegel*=the mirror !). Apart from these investigations, the real interest of this late 15th cent. prose folk-tale, which became more popular than its humour seems to justify in the town (q.v.) -life of northern Europe (including Engld., where E. was early naturalized by William Copland,

q.v., under the title of *Howleglass*), lies in its evidence to the reaction of taste from the knights and dames of polite lit. according to the courtly convention. Its realistic and plebeian note, and the impact of rustic tricksiness on burgherly complacency, are akin to the outbreak of folly (q.v.) -lit. and to the merging of Minnesong in Meistersong (see s.vv.). Similar qualities, equally broad, characterized the beginnings of native drama (see s.v. Fastnachtspiel), and they corresponded to the lively awakening of social conscience and civic consciousness. Till's mirror was held up to the coarser aspects of town-life in his own day, and the reflection has hist. value in reconstructing the lighter side of that life : its fun, its horseplay, its grosser elements of human comedy, in the busy workshop, the crowded marketplace, the rough drinking-tavern, and other resorts of merry Saxons in those days. The repertory of E.'s jest-book supplied material to jesters in other countries, and notably in Engld., in the Robin Goodfellow cycle and elsewhere ; but Till was racy of his own German soil, and his adventures form a kind of rogue's odyssey in the national satiric lit. of his fatherland. (See also s.v. Stricker).

Euphuism (rhet.): Engl. term of rhetoric, derived by Gabriel Harvey (q.v.), in his *Advertisement for Papp-hatchet*, 1589, from the *Euphues* of Lyly (q.v.), and employed by Harvey and contemporaries, with cognate terms ' euphuing ', ' euphued ', ' euphuese ', ' Euphuist ', etc., to designate a particular feature of vice of Lyly's style, viz. the excessive use and even the deliberate invention of phenomena of natural history and physiology for the purpose of comparison. Originally, the use of the term was limited to denote these strange or counterfeit similes ; a practice which Lyly had affected in a gradually diminishing scale, and to which he was drawn as much by the allurement of his inventive fancy as by the authority and sanction of the reference bks. and wonder-books of his day. Later, the limitation was neglected, and the term E. was more widely applied to the main characteristics of Lyly's style ; inexact critics conveyed by its use vague charges of affectation and preciosity, and more exact scholars denoted by it the marks of antithesis, assonance, alliteration, parallelism, similitude, sentence-balance, etc., which the prose of Lyly displayed. Such features, isolated in this sense under the common name of E., were more or less severely condemned by great writers from Lyly's own time downwards. Sidney (q.v.), for example, spoke of ' honey-flowing Matron Eloquence apparelled, or rather disguised, in a Courtesan-like painted affectation ' (*Apology for Poetry*) ; and Hallam (ii, 197), to skip the centuries, called it ' antithetical and sententious to affectation ; a perpetual effort with no adequate success '. These strictures and the satire of writers as authoritative as Shakespeare and Scott (by the person of sir Piercie Shafton in *The Monastery*) led to a grave misconception of E. as a force and an influence in lit. ; an obstinate view prevailed that Lyly first and expressly ' lifted ' E. from the pages of North's (q.v.)

transln. of *The Dial of Princes* by Guevara (q.v.), and that he trimmed this imported style to the needs of the Elizabethan court-circle, just then searching for a suitable prose-vehicle. It is difficult to overtake old errors ; but E., though originally the name of a feature unduly prominent in Lyly's *Euphues*, may still be restored to proper honour ; and the patient researches of such critics as C. G. Child, *John Lyly and Euphuism* (1894), R. W. Bond, *Complete Works of John Lyly* (1902), A. Feuillerat, *John Lyly : Contribution à l'Histoire de la Renaissance en Angleterre* (1910), and H. Clemens and M. W. Croll, *Euphues* (1916), among others, have rendered clearer its actual services to Engl. prose. Their conclusions, though not identical in all details, are now commonly accepted in the main, and may briefly be summarized. (i) There was E. before Lyly wr. *Euphues* ; E. was not the invention of one man, whether Lyly or another, created by design after a Span. model. (ii) The relation of *Euphues* to E. is that of a finished type to a prevailing fashion. (iii) Similar or analogous types are found in France, Italy, and Spain and proceeded from causes common in Europe. (See s.v. Precious, e.g.). (iv) Among those causes may be mentioned the influence of poetic style (as reformed, e.g., by Marot and Surrey, qq.v.) on the unreformed prose of the vernaculars ; the influence of the Gk. orators, and, esp., in Engld., of Isocrates, and of the consequent study of prose-rhetoric by a dozen teachers active in Lyly's day (see, for instance, s.v. Thomas Wilson) ; the influence of the Bible, esp. of *Proverbs*, with the antithetical genius of the Hebr. language brought out in vernacular versions ; and the need of finding forms of speech better suited to these new perceptions than the long-drawn, formless narration and the ornamental abstractions of medieval prose. (v) The composite resultant of these tendencies has been traced in the Engl. prose of Fisher, More, Elyot, Berners (qq.v.), and other writers ; and the seeds sown in their works by the winds of style from all quarters blossomed to full flower in the *Petite Pallace of Pleasure*, 1576, by Pettie (q.v.), where all the marks of E. are found in overflowing measure three or four years earlier than the publication of Lyly's romances. (vi) Thus, while the Guevara-origin of E. has been abandoned by critics, not least because North transld. from an emasculate Fr. version of *The Dial*, the identity of E. with Lylyism must likewise be rejected, despite the long life it has enjoyed. (vii) It now remains to recognize in E. a combination of very valuable forces which tended to mould and reform Engl. prose-style, and which found its chief practitioners in the 16th cent. These combined forces, which it is misleading but now obligatory to call after the name of the hero of Lyly's stories, included features which were exaggerated by Lyly and which earned the just censure of his critics ; the chief of those was the abuse of the similes from animals, herbs, and stones, drawn from ancient *physiologi* (see s.v. Bestiary), and elaborated by Lyly's fancy. The 17th cent. reacted from such practices, and pruned the exuberance of word-assonance and alliteration which the early Euphuists had affected in Engld., as elsewhere ; but prose-style was immeasurably assisted in its cultivation of balance, harmony, rhythm, metaphor, apposition, paradox, dignity, choice of words, elegance, vivacity, and raciness, by the Euphuistic innovators, and above all, despite his excesses, by the author of *Euphues* himself. If he was not the first of the Euphuists, he was at any rate the particular star by which his successors and even his contemporaries guided their courses to artistic prose ; even a pamphleteer like Gosson (q.v.) was ' euphuized ' (maybe, by the same influences which Lyly felt) ; Shakespeare (in his early comedies, esp.), Lodge, Greene and others, readily yielded to the spell of E., the marks of which are obvious in Macaulay (q.v.), e.g., and are latent in the sentence-structure, word-selection, and ornamentation of all the best writers of Engl. prose. The actual decline of E. as a cult, to be distinguished from its permanent effects on lit. and language, dates from *c.* 1590, and may, summarily, be attributed to the displacement of the court by the stage, and of aristocratic by plebeian writers, which marked the second and greater period of the reign and splendour of queen Elizabeth. A more exact definition of E. is suggested in the edn. of Lyly's *Euphues* by Clemens and Croll (above), and may be quoted here, with the proviso that common literary use does not draw the accurate distinctions which are familiar to professors of rhetoric : ' Euphuism is a style characterized by the figures known in ancient and medieval rhetoric as *schemes* (*schemata*), and more specifically by the word-schemes (*schemata verborum*), in contrast to those known as *tropes* ; that is to say, in effect, by the figures of sound and vocal ornament '. The *tropes* are figures of wit ; the *schemata* are figures of sound ; metaphor is a rhetorical *trope* ; alliteration (q.v.) is a rhetorical *schema* ; and E., despite the many *tropes* which it displays in its Lylyan variety, is primarily a rhetorical schematization.

Eurellus, Gunno (1638-1709) : Swed. poet. Wr. a notable poem in 8-line stanzas, differing from the conventional *ottava rima* by the greater length of its verses, called *Kungaskald* (' King's-poet '), which was alive with patriotic fervour. E., who was ennobled under the name of Dahl-stjerna, achieved in Sweden a position similar to that taken by the writers in the second Silesian school in Germany (see s.v. Germ. Lit.).

Eustache Deschamps (*c.* 1340-1415) : Fr. lyric poet. Surnamed des Champs from the name of his estate, and Morel from his dark complexion. E. was a disciple of Marchault (q.v.), his fellow-countryman in Champagne, and was at one with his master in artificial elegance of diction. He is credited with as many as 1,374 *ballades* (q.v.), and in the year 1392 (perhaps in celebration of the achievement) he wr. an ' Art of versifying (*dictier*) and of making *ballades* and *chants-royaux* ', which is a kind of text-book of rhetoric in advance of the *Rhétoriqueurs* (q.v.). Wr., too, a long poem, ' The Mirror of Marriage ', which has been characterized as the tenth satire of Boileau (q.v.) in the style of the 14th cent.

Evelyn, John (1620-1706): Engl.-diarist; collector; royalist, though distinguished in a circle of lax manners by a singular purity of life and disposition; a founder of the Royal Society, and its secretary, 1672; wr. bks. on various artistic and allied topics, and kept a *Diary* through many years, publd. 1818-19. E. travelled, 1646, with Waller, q.v.

Everaert, Cornelis (1509-33); Dutch dramatist; writer of farcical interludes; a talented 'factor' of the Rederijkers (q.v.), though his broad West-Flanders dialect obstructed the full appreciation of his humour.

Ewald, Herman Frederick (1821-92): Dan. novelist. Wr. novels for the circulating-library, 'the heroines of which were usually models of all the copybook virtues, and the heroes as bloodless as their brave and loyal prototypes in *Ivanhoe* and *Waverley* (Boyesen, *Essays in Scand. Lit.*, 182; Nutt, 1895). A comparison with G. P. R. James (q.v.) would be more appropriate, but the critic is correct in his estimate of E. as a 'feeble successor of Ingemann' (q.v.). His most popular novels are, or were, *The Youth of Valdemar Krone*, *The Swedes at Cronberg*, and *Johannes Falk*.

Ewald, Johannes (1743-81): Dan. poet and dramatist; like Holberg, born in Norway, but accounted Dane in literary history, since politically, Norway was not sundered till 1814. E. was one of the fathers of the Royal Theatre in Copenhagen (founded, 1748), and 'composed, lying on his back in bed, dying, like Heine, by inches, some of the masterpieces of Danish dramatic literature' (E. Gosse, *Lit. of Northern Europe*, 144). He wr., too, the Dan. national anthem, and ranks with Holberg and Wessel (qq.v.) as a foremost poet of his time and country. Among E.'s plays were *Balder's Death*, 1774, and *The Fisherfolk*, 1780.

Ewing, Mrs. See **Gatty**.

Eximinez, Francesch (d. 1409): Span. satirist. Wr. in Catalan (s.v. Catalonia) a 'book of women' (*Libre de les dones*), which enjoyed wide popularity.

F

Fable: a short comic tale in verse, in which it is an almost invariable condition that the subject shall be drawn from common life, and shall imitate nature in its physical, if not in its moral and psychological, manifestations. (The chief recent authorities on the F. in its native country, France, are Bédier, 1893, and Montaiglon and Raynaud, 6 vols., 1872-88. Saintsbury selects the definition of the last-named: 'the recital, for the most part comic, of a real or possible event occurring in the ordinary conditions of human life', and adds that 'it must be in verse, and, with very rare, if any, exceptions, in octosyllabic couplets'). As a definite branch of literary composition, the F. (*fabliau, fableau*, Lat. *fabula*) took its rise in Northern France (see s.v. Fr. Lit.), at the time of the relaxed monopoly of the aristocratic *chanson* and *roman*, and of the emergence of the middle-classes to self-expression and self-esteem. Its writers were mostly anon., and their couplets varied in number from about 20 to several hundred lines in the 200 or more specimens of the genuine F. which have come down to us from its period of florescence, *c.* 1250-1350. Emphasis should be laid on the fact that the F., as distinct from the romances of the *langue d'oil* and from the lyrics of the *langue d'oc*, was *bourgeois*, or middle-class, in orig. It uttered the thoughts, or, rather, the half-formed impressions, of the newly self-conscious *bourgeoisie*: of the merchant, the shopkeeper, the trader, the jolly host, and the clients at his inn; thus illumining a world of the Middle Ages remote from lords' camps and ladies' courts-of-love. The national quality was added by the genius of the race. It was the vehicle of that *esprit gaulois*, that Gallic wit, which, like Attic salt, is native to the soil on which it springs. Fr. wit is inherent in the F., as Celtic magic pervades the Arthuriad, re-fashioned though it was by Breton writers. Geographically, too, the fabliaux were of the centre; 'the most frequent scene of the F.', writes Lanson (*Hist. Lit. Fr.*, 105), 'is situated more or less between Orleans, Rouen, Arras and Troyes, at the very heart of French soil, in Champagne and Picardy, in all the gay towns and villages where no man could escape the society of his neighbour. . . That is the classic land of the *Fabliau*, and there at all times flourish naughty tales, natty quips, impertinent satires, directed at husbands, wives, and priests'. Applied to the experience of daily life, with a kind of grimace at its comic aspects, the gift of quick sight and terse expression led the Fr. fabulist of the 13th cent. to direct his ready mockery at objects most prominent in the public eye, and at the most salient features of those objects. As there was little exquisiteness of selection, so there was little refinement in expression. The language of the F. was frequently marked by a license which would be more offensive than it is, were it not that the delicacy of form corrects the indelicacy of matter. Fr. taste has the deftness to deflect, at the pen's point, as it were, the primary sense of coarseness. In these tales of the 13th to 14th cent., there were a fresh interest in life, a gaiety, a *gaillardise*, which redeemed, while they pointed, the satire on priest and pretence, on smug virtues and snug foibles, and, above all, on women. The haughty, worshipful heroine of romance, who belonged to the lit. of chivalry, gave way to the woman of the people, ready to deceive, ill to be deceived, so familiar throughout Fr. lit.; 'Guillaume de Lorris yields to Jean de Meung' (see s.v. Romance of the Rose). When the F. passed into Italy, Boccaccio (q.v.) drew material thence for his tales, and the *Canterbury Tales* of Chaucer (q.v.) are in the direct line of succession. The Fr. *conte-dévot* (q.v.; a 'pious tale' in its Engl. form) is a kind of Sunday-variety of the F. proper, and is hardly less valuable as a mirror of manners.

Historically, the F. is akin to the Bestiary (q.v.), and the *Ysopet*, or 'little Æsop', of Marie de France (q.v.) forms a kind of link between the *Roman de Renart* (s.v. Reynard) and the *Fabliaux*, the next most important expression of Fr. *bourgeoisie* in the Middle Ages. The F. was developed in Fr. lit. into the ordinary prose-tale, till, in the *Contes* of La Fontaine (q.v.), it reverted, by a brilliant transformation, to the verse-form of its prototype. Collections of *prose*-fables, combined with tales from other sources, furnished the jovial jest-books (q.v.) of Elizabethan lit. ; but it was on the model of La Fontaine that Gellert (q.v.) composed his fables, and that the type was standardized in the lit. of the 18th cent., and found a notable exponent in the Russ. fabulist, Krylov (q.v.).

Fabre D'Eglantine, Philippe (1755-94) : Fr. playwright. Wr. *la Philinte de Molière* and 16 other comedies. The eglantine signified the emblem of victory in the Floral Games (q.v.) of Toulouse. F. perished by the guillotine.

Fabricius, Johann Albert (1668-1736) : Germ. scholar ; author of works on Gk. and Lat. lit., which ' may fairly entitle their author to be regarded as the modern Didymus ' (Sandys, *Hist. Class. Schol*, iii. 2).

Fahlcrantz, Kristian Erik (1790-1866) : Swed. poet ; humourist and satirist. F.'s best-known work is a *Noah's Ark*, 1825-6, attacking follies and excesses in the national politics and lit. of his day.

Fail, du, Noel (*c.* 1520-91) : Fr. social writer ; one of many writers in the 16th cent. who kept a kind of middle way between the exuberant buffoonery of Rabelais (q.v.) and the philosophy of later specialists. F.'s works included ' Rural Topics ' (*Discours d'aucuns propos rustiques, facétieux, et de singulière récréation*), 1547, and *Baliverneries*, 1548 ; both these appeared under the pseudonym (anagram) of Leon Ladufi (Ladulphi), and, after various bibliographical adventures, were reissued, 1878. F.'s *Contes et Discours d'Eutrapel* was first publd., 1585, and gives interesting pictures of country and provincial life.

Falsen, de, Envold (1755-1808) : Dan. popular dramatist. F.'s comedies were for many years performed amid great applause in Copenhagen and Oslo, and his national war songs, fired the martial spirit of Norse patriotism awaiting the ' day ' in 1814.

Falster, Christian (1690-1752) : Dan. satirist and scholar ; transld. the *Tristia* of Ovid (q.v.), and wr. orig. Lat. studies and dialogues.

Fancourt, Samuel (1678-1768) : Engl. bibliophil ; librarian. F.'s life was a continual struggle for subsistence, but, though he failed in every undertaking, he is honourably remembered as the first founder of a circulating subscription library in this country. He opened it off Fleet-street, *c.* 1730, with an entrance-fee of 21s. and a subscription of 1s. a quarter.

Fant, Erik Michael (1754-1817) : Swed. scholar ; Hellenist. Wr. Lat. history of Gk. learning in Sweden to the end of the 17th cent. (completed 1786), and edited an account of Swed. lit. in the middle ages, *Scriptores rerum Suecicarum Medii Aevi*, publd. 1818. F.'s learned researches into the antiquities and archæological lore of his country are very valuable hist. documents.

Faria y Sousa, de, Manoel (17th cent.) : Port. moralist. Wr., 1624, *Noches Claras* (Bright Nights), originally entitled ' moral discourses ' ; and, 1639, a commentary on the *Lusiads* of Camoens (q.v.), in which F. attacked the style of Gongora (q.v.).

Fasting, Claus (d. 1791) : Dan. critic and dramatist, Norse by birth, and a leading member of the Norw. Society (q.v.) founded, 1772, of which Wessel (q.v.) was a founder, and which preceded the national movement, consummated at the time of the independence of Norway, 1814. F.'s most considerable work was his series of *Provincial Papers* (the title is Pascal's, q.v.), issued in Bergen, 1778-81.

Fastnachtspiel (Shrovetide-play) : Germ. mimic composition, displayed by dialogue and drama on a stage, and containing the seeds of future farce and comedy. These artless performances flourished mainly in the 15th and 16th cents., and were developed with the growth of civic consciousness out of the passion-plays (q.v.) which preceded them : the scriptural topic became homely almost to the degree of profanity, or was replaced by motives suggested by current tales, witticisms and proverbs. Itinerant players, known as *mimi* or *histriones*, took a repertory round the towns at the period of the Shrovetide holiday, and a tone best described as ' jolly ' characterized the entertainment which they provided.

Fate-Drama : Generic name of a type of stage-play, the common feature of which is the intervention of a spell, or curse, or other visible or sensible act of destiny, affecting the future of the *dramatis personæ*, usually members of one family, and overwhelming them at last. This idea of Fate or Necessity is, of course, inherent in Gk. tragedy : its distinctive feature, in the comparatively short-lived fate-drama in Europe, was, that Fate took shape as a concrete symbol. Most commonly it took shape as a weapon, and Platen (q.v.), when he satirized the genre, substituted a fork for the conventional dagger. Another concrete form was a fateful date : *February 24th*, in the first of the series by Werner (q.v.), 1810 ; *February 29th*, in Müllner's (q.v.) variant, 1812, and so on. The common source of the F.-D. was Lillo (q.v.), who, in his *Fatal Curiosity*, 1736, ushered in that kind of play, and brought it down from the heights of Gk. tragedy to the bosoms and business of middle-class men and women. Tieck and Schiller (*Braut von Messina* ; see s.vv.), practised the same kind of drama, which died out gradually in Grillparzer (q.v.), and Lillo's influence should also be traced in the allied domestic drama, derived chiefly from his *George Barnwell*, and seen mainly in the *Comédie Larmoyante* (q.v.) of France (and see s.v. Diderot). The Germ. equivalent for F.-D. was *Schicksalsdrama* (*tragödie*).

Fauchet, Claude (1530-1601) : Fr. critic ; of the generation when the science of antiquarianism and philology was cultivated without reference to the art. Wr. *Antiquités Gauloises et Françoises*, 1579-1601, and a work on Fr. language and lit., with biographies and epitomes (*Noms et Sommaires*) of 127 Fr. poets living prior to 1300, which has considerable hist. value.

Fauriel, Claude Charles (1772-1844): Fr. critic, historian ; chiefly memorable for his translns. from Manzoni (q.v.), 1823, containing an article on Goethe and a preface on the Unities (q.v.), which rank among the origins of the Romance (q.v.)-movement of 1830.

Faust : Germ. popular tale (see s.v. *Volksbuch*), founded immediately on an hist. tradition of a learned adventurer, whose conjectural date is given between 1500 and 1530, and more remotely based on the legend of the devil's pact which had been floating in Christendom for 1,000 years. The 1587 *Volksbuch*, publd. at Frankfort-on-the-Main, professed to be based on oral evidence of the ' History of Dr. Johann Faust, the wide-travelled Magician and Black-Artist, how he made a pact with the Devil for a certain period, what strange adventures he encountered and performed during that time, till at last he received his well-merited reward '. In this work the current legends of the doctor of Wittenberg were for the first time collected, and the taste of the times added the moralizing elements which finally brought the devil-possessed alchemist and wonder-worker to hell. The contemporary fame and influence of Luther (q.v.) pointed the moral of F. against the Catholic Church, and represented him as a student at Ingolstadt, the Jesuit headquarters. It was reserved to Goethe (q.v.) in the 18th cent., to interpret the ardent Faust-hunger in terms corresponding more immediately to the universal Faust in man. Prior to Goethe, the legend was treated by Klinger, Grabbe, and others in Germany ; by Marlowe, Greene (*Friar Bacon*), and others in Engld. ; by Calderon (*Il Magico Prodigioso*) in Spain, and frequently in France from Rutebœuf (*Théophile*) downwards. (See s.vv.). It was largely through the influence of the Faust-legend, comprehended in Goethe's drama, that Germany was reputed in Engld. in the 16th cent. as the home of magic and amazement ; and that the ' exciting suspense of a diabolic pact ' was added to the motives of tragic drama. The deep roots of the F.-legend should be noted. His first use of his dearly-bought power was to make blind Homer sing to him, to raise Alexander from the dead, and to take Helen as his bride,—in other words, to win the secrets which Humanism (q.v.) in Italy was to explore with tired eyes and used-up pens (see s.v. Petrarch), and the new apparatus of dictionaries and grammars. ' Faustus is therefore the parable of the impotent yearnings of the spirit in the Middle Ages— its passionate aspiration, its conscience-stricken desire, its fettered curiosity amid the cramping limits of imperfect knowledge and irrational dogmatism. That for which Faustus sold his soul was yielded to the world without price at the time of the Renaissance. Homer, no longer by the intervention of a fiend, but by the labour of the scholar, sang to the new age. The pomp of the empires of the old world was restored in the pages of historians. The indestructible beauty of Greek art, whereof Helen was an emblem, became . . . the possession of the modern world. Medievalism took this Helen to wife, and their offspring, the Euphorion, of Goethe's drama, is the spirit of the modern world ' (Symonds, *Ital. Renaissance* ii, 39. Symonds points his parable with the moral : ' The Renaissance realized the dream of the Middle Ages, and the genius of the Italians wrought by solid toil what the myth-making imagination of the Germans had projected in a poem ').

Favart, Charles Simon (1710-92): Fr. dramatist ; director of the Opera-comique ; born in Paris, the son of a pastrycook. Wr. some excellent comedies, including the *Trois Sultanes, la Chercheuse de l'Esprit*, and a parody of the *Devin du Village* (1752) by J. J. Rousseau (q.v.). F.'s wife was an accomplished actress.

Fazio, Bartolommeo (d. 1457): It. historiographer and moralist. F. was attached to the court of Alfonso (q.v.) v of Aragon and i of Naples, and wr. the chronicles of the prince at the latter capital after its surrender to the Span. conquerer. He is said to have received 500 ducats a year for his literary service, and a bonus of 4,500 ducats at its conclusion. F. was also the author of a Lat. treatise, *dialogus de felicitate vitæ*, 1445, which was adapted in Span. prose by Lucena (q.v.), 1463.

Feith, Rhijnvis (1753-1813): Dutch novelist and poet. F. belonged to the Transition period in Dutch lit. (q.v.), when the Germ. influence of Klopstock, Miller, Wieland (qq.v.) and others, was paramount ; his sentimental romances, *Julia*, 1783, and *Ferdinand and Constantia*, 1785, are deeply indebted to such exemplars, while F.'s prize-poems and dramas show little or no original power.

Femme Incomprise (Fr.): ' Misunderstood woman ' ; a type of character in fiction, first invented by mme. de Stael (q.v.) in her *Corinne*, 1806.

Fénelon, de la Mothe-, François de Salagnac (1651-1715): Fr. orator and divine ; ' the last representative of the seventeenth century ' (Lanson, *Hist. Lit. Fr.*, 610); ' pre-figures some of the sensibility, the liberalism, the expansiveness, of eighteenth century France ' (Elton, *P.E.L.*, viii, 50). Born at the family-seat in Périgord, F. found early expression for his priestly and theological gifts, and he contemplated missionary work in Canada. In 1687, his treatise on *l'Education des Filles* recommended him to the powerful Bossuet (q.v.) and to mme. de Maintenon (q.v.), the governess queen-to-be. Under these auspices, F. was appointed tutor to the duc de Bourgogne, son of Bossuet's ex-pupil, the dauphin, and next heir to king Louis xiv. With the works which he wr. in this capacity we shall deal in a moment ; here, continuing the recital of the bare facts of his biography, he was elected to the Academy (q.v.) in 1693, and was appointed archbp. of Cambrai in 1695. Four years later, he was condemned at Rome. He had gone too far in the Quietist heresy ; farther than mme. de Maintenon was prepared to follow him in her prudent sympathy with the tenets of mme. de Guyon (q.v.), and altogether too far for the most rigid opponent of Quietism (q.v.), F.'s former patron, and the keeper of the king's conscience—Bossuet (q.v.). F., the weaker and more malleable vessel, was overwhelmed by the greater preacher's torrential eloquence, and was confined to his see after 1697. His theological and pedagogic writings hardly interest us to-day. The work on girls' education was fully used by mme. de Maintenon when she started her school of St.-Cyr ; and his treatises on rhetoric, history and other sciences were designed for the use of his royal pupil, who, like his father, the dauphin, predeceased, 1712, his grandfather, Louis xiv. In the same class are to be included the political writings of F., who aimed at training a king of France (a great ambition and a great responsibility in those days of imperial absolutism), who should combine the power of an autocrat with the conscience of a philosopher. He sought to join the statecraft of a benevolent despot with the simplicity of a Homeric captain ; for Rousseau's (q.v.) recall to nature affected F. (by anticipation) as powerfully as the divine right of kings. This duality of outlook, plainly compounded with strong elements of mysticism, this faculty of looking before and after, of reaching into the perfectibility of the future and of resting on the authority of the past, this admixture of Platonism and Machiavellism (or, at least, of Verulamism see s.v. F. Bacon), is the distinguishing mark of F., and renders him in many ways more interesting than his greater adversary, Bossuet himself, and partly contributed to his sequestration. Thus, F.'s ' Letter to Louis xiv ', ascribed to 1699, but not publd. in the author's lifetime, his *Tables de Chaulnes*, or conversations at Chaulnes, dating from 1711, in the interval between the deaths of the dauphin and the duc de Bourgogne, and other political writings, aimed at a system of feudal kingship, peaceful, just, and fraternal, hating vain pomp and luxury, and opposed in every principle except its power (which was modelled on the views of the Stewart no-king James ' iii ') to king Louis xiv himself : the Christian monarch whose weapon was war, and who had caused, or consented to, F.'s disgrace. The chief of F.'s Quietist treatises was his *Explications des Maximes des Saintes*, 1697. More important and better witnesses to F.'s Hellenism (q.v.), which was so rare and welcome an exception to the prevailing Latinity of the Fr. classical school and age, were his ' Dialogues of the Dead ' (1700, 1712), his *Télémaque* (1699), written for the edification of the duc de Bourgogne and for the confusion of the absolutist monarch, his 3 ' Dialogues on Eloquence ' (1681-86 ; publd., 1718) and his ' Letter to the Academy ', 1716, on grammar, rhetoric, poetry, and history, in which, while recommending that the Academy should undertake the regulation of these arts, F. gives us his own impressions of the aims and achievements in each kind, and supplements, while he reinforces, Boileau (q.v.). We must mention, too, his treatise *de l'existence de Dieu*, which anticipated in certain features Chauteaubriand's (q.v.) reconstruction of Christianity after the attacks of Voltaire (q.v.) ; and likewise F.'s vast correspondence, which added notably to the treasures of an epistolary generation. F. had temperament, as his countrymen term it, and this incommunicable gift touched nearly everything which he wr. with a curious and constant attraction. The chief place among these writings belongs to his *Télémaque*, which is commonly chosen, for the sake of its excellent prose, and its not less excellent moral, as the apprentice-book for students of the Fr. language. On the didactic side its influence was considerable, and its tenets were eagerly gathered by the milder social reformers of the 18th cent. Thus, in Russia, it was transld. at least 5 times (see s.v. Kheraskov, e.g.), and gave occasion for several imitations.

Fereira, -i. Antonio (1528-69) : Port. poet. Wr. tragic drama, *Inez de Castro*, characterized by Ticknor (ii, 67n), as ' one of the most pure and moving compositions in the Portuguese language '. (See, too, s.v. Bermudez, G.). F. died of the plague at Lisbon.

   -ii. Miguel Leitao : son of above. M.L.F. is cited as an authority on the bibliographical controversy about the authorship of *Amadis* (q.v.). He consistently ascribed it to Lobeira (q.v.), and asserted that the MS. was in the ducal library at Aveiro, where it may have been destroyed by fire or earthquake in a subsequent century.

Fernan Caballero. See s.v. **Boehl (ii.)**.

Fernandez, Geronimo (16th cent.) : Span. romancer. Wr., 1547, a ' History of the Valorous and Invincible Prince Don Bellanis of Greece ', which was admired by the emperor Charles v (q.v.). That fatherly monarch, however, prohibited the exportation of the vol. to his subjects in the New World, on account of its extravagance and exaggeration.

Fernandez, Lucas (fl. 1514) : Span. pastoral poet. Wr. dramatic dialogues after the manner of Enzina (q.v.), whom ' he resembles so closely that it is impossible to regard him as anything but an imitator, who, like most of his class, falls below his original ' (Ticknor, i, 254).

Ferrier, Susan Edmonstone (1782-1854) : Engl. novelist ; friend of sir W. Scott, q.v. ; wr. 3 notable novels : *Marriage*, 1818 ; *The Inheritance*, 1824 ; *Destiny*, 1831

Ferrus, Pero (14th cent.) : Span. poet ; represented in the anthology collected by Baena (q.v.). Wr. threnody on the death of king Henry iii of Castile (d. 1379), and is of interest to later literary history on account of his reference to *Amadis* (q.v.) : one of the very earliest of such references recorded.

Feuerbach, von, -i. Paul Johann Anselm (1775--1833) : Germ. jurist and writer on criminal law ; partly anticipated the labours of Austin (q.v.) in Engld.

   -ii. Ludwig Andreas (1804-72) : Germ. theologian ; son of above ; contemporary with D. F. Strauss (q.v.), and a writer in the same polemical school. Both applied to theological studies the inquiring method of Niebuhr and Sybel (qq.v.) in history, and L.A.F.'s *Wesen des Christentums* (1841), transld. as *The Essence of Christianity* by Marian Evans (see s.v. George Eliot,) 1854, typified the naturalism and radicalism of the new thought, and proved of permanent influence. F.'s other works, *Principles of the Philosophy of the Future*, 1843 ; *Lectures on the Essence of Religion*, 1851 ; *God, Freedom and Immortality from the Point of View of Anthropology*, 1866, etc., were too extreme to win general assent.

Feuillet, Octave (1821-90) : Fr. novelist ; of the school and manner of G. Sand (q.v.), and, accordingly, of a serious, moral, or purposive tone. In the long history of the development of fiction, F.'s interest was in the higher orders of society, which he pourtrayed with an accuracy approaching to realism, though disguised by the mannered fastidiousness of his style. F.'s chief novels are: *la Petite Comtesse*, 1856; *Roman d'un jeune homme pauvre*, 1858; *Julia de Trécoeur*, 1872; *la Morte*, 1886; *Honneur d'Artiste*, 1890. There is more than a touch of G. Eliot (q.v.) in F., whose place in Fr. lit. has been compared with that of A. Trollope (q.v.) in Engl. F. was supposed, perhaps incorrectly, to have 'devilled' for Dumas (q.v.) *père*, and his *Mémoires* formed an attractive vol.

Feydeau, Ernest (1821-73): Fr. novelist. Wr. *Fanny*, 1858, and was at one time favourably compared with his greater contemporaries, Feuillet and Flaubert (qq.v.). But the stream has moved away from him since.

Feyjoo y Montenegro, Benito Geronimo (c. 1676-1764): Span. scholar; Benedictine monk; did 'more for the intellectual life of his country than had been done for a century' (Ticknor, iii, 274). F. sought to familiarize his countrymen with the results of recent investigation and speculation in France and Engld. He was ardently Francophil: a sympathy far from uncommon in Spain in the reign of the Bourbon prince, king Philip v, who acceded in 1700; and, though it is a gross exaggeration to call him a 'Spanish Voltaire', F.'s careful, learned and well-written works, *Teatro critico universal*, 1726-39, and *Cartas* (Letters) *eruditas y curiosas*, 1742-60, displayed a genuine appreciation of the tendencies of European thought and the needs of Span. intellectualism. F. was opposed (see s.v. Maner), and attacked by the Inquisition; but he found defenders (s.v. Sarmiento), and exerted a real influence for good.

Fichte, Johann Gottlieb (1762-1814): Germ. philosopher; born in humble circumstances, to which he rose superior by his own talents and efforts. After a period of misc. teaching, F. reached Königsberg, where, under the personal influence of Kant (q.v.), he wr. his first bk, the *Kritik aller Offenbarung*, 1792. In the following year, he m. a niece of Klopstock (q.v.), and was appointed to the chair of philosophy at Jena. His lectures attracted large audiences, alike for the boldness of their speculative range, and for the response which they gave to the prevailing tendencies of the time. The sense of oneness, or monism, which had dominated the aim of the early Germ. mystics to establish a communion between man and God, and which was resumed in the teachings of Luther, had been the governing factor in the system of Kant, who completed Luther's work of the liberation of the human mind from fetters. This reconciliation of the outer with the inner, of the external universe with the internal mind, was carried to its extreme power in the doctrine of F., whose theory of the *Ego*, as identical with, or the creator of, the *non-Ego*, was seized upon by storming individualists such as F. Schlegel (q.v.) to build a bridge between the Kantian philosophy and the lit. of Romance (q.v.). These teachings were chiefly contained in F.'s masterpiece, 'The Science of Knowledge'

(*Wissenschaftslehre*), first publd., 1794, and frequently expanded. A few years later, he had to meet a charge of atheism, and, though he defended himself courageously, he was compelled to resign from Jena. A brilliant epoch in the history of its univ. was thus brought to a close. F. went to Berlin, at the invitation of F. Schlegel, and became eventually part-founder and first rector of its new univ. Napoleon's Prussian campaign was the occasion of F.'s 'Addresses to the German Nation', 1808, in which he roused patriotic ardour (so akin to the Romantic perception) by his belief that 'to possess character and to be German are one and the same thing'; another application of monism. This note of moral idealism was eminently Fichtean. To 'realize the pure *Ego*' became the highest moral law; and leaders, seeking regeneration from the foreigner's yoke, might not improperly extend F.'s metaphysical idealism to the regions of conduct and faith. There is a consentaneity in the critics' views of F. which is singularly refreshing. Thus, G. Brandes (q.v.), though no friend of the Romanticists, writes: 'It was the Fichtean doctrine of the *Ego* which gave to the Romantic individuality its character and force' (*Rom. Sch. in Germany*, E.T., 38). Beers declares, 'Fichte's *Wissenschaftslehre* is the philosophical cornerstone of the German Romantic school' (*Hist. Engl. Romanticism in the 19th Cent.*, 137). Robertson says, 'From Fichte the Romantic school drew its most vital ethical ideas' (*Hist. Germ. Lit.*, 403), and Biese (*Deutsche Lit. gesch.*, ii, 324) notes that 'Through Fichte the name *German nation* first regained a meaning and a value.' The responsibility of man for his own destiny was, at bottom, the new thought introduced into lit. and life by F.'s mediation between Kant and the Romantics; the individual *Ego* straining towards the absolute *Ego*, the object at one with the subject, the non-*Ego* limited by the *Ego*: these doctrines are of infinitely less importance than their influence on action and aspiration in the hour of Germany's trial. How the militarists captured the strongholds which the idealists had fortified is a matter of history which F. did not live to see.

Ficino, Marsilio (1433-99): It. Platonist (s.v. Plato) and humanist; selected by Cosimo de Medici to lead his Platonic Academy (q.v.) at Florence, which owed its orig. to the enthusiasm aroused by Gemistos (q.v.), the Gk. envoy to the council of 1439. F. proved thoroughly worthy of Cosimo's conception and selection; his love of the Master was so true that he kept a perpetual lamp before the bust of Plato, as before the image of a saint; the influence of his academy was spread by its notable pupils through Italy and Germany; and F.'s Lat. transln. of Plato was completed at the court of the three successive Medici (q.v.), and was printed in 1482. F.'s introduction to the *Symposium* describes the memorial banquets to Plato, and among the members of the academy were Michael Angelo, Politian, and Pico della Mirandola. F. added a transln. of Plotinus to the Platonic labours, to which he had been devoted since boyhood. He is prominent among the humanists of his age for his combination of Christian piety with the new learning; he sought to reconcile Platonism with Christianity, and was addicted to the former for its mystical and romantic aspects rather than for its ideology and dialectic. In this he was the child, and also the father, of his age; and his treatise on Plato's theory of immortality gave considerable impetus to the studies which his Lat. renderings of the dialogues made available for the brilliant circle of Florentine *savants*, of which he was the centre for many years.

'**Field, Michael**': Pen-name of 2 Engl. poets, -i, Katharine Harris Bradley, *née* Cooper (d. 1914), and ii, Edith Cooper, her niece (d. 1913) Wr. several attractive vols. of verse, between *Callirrhoë*, 1884, and *Wild Honey*, 1908; and successfully preserved their *nom-de-guerre*.

Fielding, -i. Henry (1707-54): Engl. novelist, in which supreme and principal capacity of his busy literary life F. wr. (1) *The History of the Adventures of Joseph Andrews and his friend Mr. Abraham Adams, Written in Imitation of the Manner of Cervantes*; 2 vols., 1742. The motive of *Joseph Andrews* was to parody Richardson's (q.v.) *Pamela* (Andrews), but F.'s novel outgrew the intention of the parodist, and developed, largely by the personality of parson Adams, into a full-blooded original novel of contemporary characters and domestic manners; the 'manner of Cervantes' was imitated in respect to a narrative of adventures, but the manner was more closely that which Bunyan, Defoe and Addison (qq.v.) handed down to their successors in the realm of fiction; (2) *The History of Tom Jones, a Foundling*; 6 vols., 1749. This masterwork ranks incontestably as the first great novel in the Engl. language, and even as the greatest. Evidence to this estimate may be quoted from 2 succeeding great novelists: Scott (q.v.) in 1822, and Thackeray (q.v.) in 1850. The former, in an introductory dialogue to *The Fortunes of Nigel*, wr.: '(*Author:*) There never was a novel written on this plan while the world stood. (*Captain:*) Pardon me — *Tom Jones*. (*Author:*) True, and perhaps *Amelia* also Fielding had high notions of the dignity of an art which he may be considered as having founded. He challenges a comparison between the Novel and the Epic. Smollett, Lesage, and others, emancipating themselves from the strictness of the rules he has laid down, have written rather a history of the miscellaneous adventures which befall an individual in the course of life, than the plot of a regular and connected epopeia, where every step brings us a point nearer to the final catastrophe'. In other words, *teste* Scott, F. developed the novel proper out of the picaresque fiction which preceded it (see s.v. Novel). Thackeray's testimony is contained in his Preface to *Pendennis*: 'Since the author of *Tom Jones* was buried, no writer of fiction among us has been permitted to depict to his utmost powers a man. We must drape him, and give him a certain conventional simper. Society will not tolerate the Natural in our Art'. This brings us up at once against the question of F.'s measure of realism. In ch. i, of *Tom Jones*, he straightly wr.: 'The provision which we have here made is no other than

Human Nature;' and it was 'no other' in a sense unknown to some later realists, who tended to emphasize their naturalism by concentrating on only one aspect of human nature—the sexual,—and thus brought the name realism into evil repute in art. F., more frankly naturalistic, saw human nature as a whole, and Thackeray envied him his independence of the barriers which 'Society' raised against later imperfect realists, who selected a single province for delineation. The evidence of Scott and Thackeray, confirmed by all the major critics and by translrs. into every language, is sufficient to justify the description of *Tom Jones* as the head and fount of Engl. fiction. (3) *Amelia*, 4 vols., 1752, which, though sometimes deemed superior to *Tom Jones*, for its gentler and less boisterous tone, shows signs of failing health and power.

Besides the 3 novels, which constitute F.'s claim to renown, he was a busy dramatist, journalist and pamphleteer, and in his 3rd vol. of *Miscellanies*, 1743, he 'printed the most brilliant piece of work that he had yet achieved, *The Life of Mr. Jonathan Wild the Great*. . . Not even Swift (q.v.) has produced so remarkable a piece of sustained irony, so full of movement, so various, so finely worked in its minutest particulars, or so vivid in its pictures of "low" life' (*C.H.E.L.*, x, 27). F., too, was a magistrate (Westminster and Middlesex), and took his duties very seriously: his charge to the Westminster grand jury, June, 1749, is famous, and he drafted 'proposals for a county workhouse' and an 'inquiry into the causes of the late increase of robbers'. A man of robust stature and fullness of blood, F. was a lover, too, and 'Sophia Western', in *Tom Jones*, and 'Amelia', in the novel of that name are both reminiscent of his dearly-loved wife, who died in 1744; he m. her maid in 1747, and was tended by her till the close of his too short life. He died at Lisbon, on a journey in search of health, and his excellent *Journal* of that last voyage was publd., posth., 1755.

It is not essential to F.'s fame to recall or enumerate his plays or minora opera. It is more appropriate to end as we began by the praise of F. at his highest. We may cite 2 eulogists at an interval of 60 years. Coleridge (q.v.) wr. in 1834: 'What a master of composition Fielding was! Upon my word I think the *Oedipus Tyrannus*, the *Alchemist*, and *Tom Jones*, the three most perfect plots ever planned. And how charming, how wholesome, Fielding is! To take him up after Richardson, is like emerging from a sick-room heated by stoves, into an open lawn, on a breezy day in May'. And prof. Saintsbury in 1893: '*Tom Jones* is an epic of life—not indeed of the highest, the rarest, the most impassioned of life's scenes and phrases, but of the healthy average life of the average natural man; not faultless nor perfect by any means, but human and actual as no no one else but Shakespeare has shown him in the mimic world.' Perhaps, too, we may add at the suggestion of A. Dobson (q.v.; *Fielding*, Engl. Men of Letters, p. 214), 'the compact and penetrating lines which the late James Russell Lowell composed as an inscription for the bust of Henry Fielding at Taunton'—

' He looked on naked nature unashamed,
And saw the sphinx, now bestial, now divine,
In change and re-change ; he nor praised, nor
blamed,
But drew her as he saw with fearless line.
Did he good service ? God must judge, not we.
Manly he was, and generous, and sincere ;
English in all, of genius blithely free :
Who loves a Man may see his image here'.
 -ii. **Sarah** (1710-86): Engl. novelist;
sister of above ; wr. *Adventures of David
Simple*, 1744, to which H.F., wr. a pref.

Fifelfo, Francesco (1398-1481): It. humanist.
Learned Lat. from Gasparino (q.v.), and visited
Constantinople to learn Gk; remained 7
years as secretary of Venetian Legation ; m.
a great-niece of Chrysoloras (q.v.); brought
back valuable trove of Gk. MSS. (a list is given
by Symonds, *Ital. Renaissance*, ii, 195, n. 2).
Lectured at Venice, Bologna, and Florence ;
his migratory habit is explained (*C.M.H.*, i,
554) by the practice of the early humanists of
repeating their exposition of one text in several
cities while working at the elucidation of
another : a habit not unknown to modern
lecturers ; F.'s migration from Florence to
Milan, 1440, was further due to his loss of
Cosimo de Medici's favour. He transld.
parts of Xenophon and others ; wr. Gk. and
Lat. letters, and poems ; took a prominent
part in the tiresome competition of invective
which disgraced the scholarship of his day,
and ' combined the accomplishments of a
scholar with the insidiousness and the brutality
of a brigand ' (Sandys, *Hist. Class. Schol.*, ii,
56).

Figueroa, de, -i. Diego, and **-ii. José** (17th cent.):
Span. dramatists; brothers; wr., c. 1662,
la Dama Capitan, on which Montfleury (q.v.)
founded *la Fille Capitaine*.

Figueroa, de, Francisco (1536-c. 1617): Span.
poet ; included by classifiers in the Salamanca
School of Garcilasso (q.v.). In his own time
and on his merits, F. was a soldier and a gentleman, who spent many active years in Italy,
and whose poems were so pure a recreation that
he gave orders for their destruction at his
death. Between 60 and 80 survive, and
display a pleasant pastoral faculty, with
distinct leanings to Ital. forms and diction,
which F. succeeded in naturalizing more
thoroughly in Castilian poetry. Among his
poems is a *Thyrsis* eclogue in blank verse
(q.v.), and F. figured as Thyrsis (*Tirsi*) in the
Galatea of Cervantes (q.v.).

Filicaja, da, Vincenzo (1642-1707): It. poet ;
a friend of Redi (q.v.), and, like him, a poetic
disciple of Chiabrera (q.v.). Macaulay, in his
essay on Addison (see s.vv.); writes of F.
as ' the greatest lyric poet of modern times ' :
the context denotes the times of Addison, but,
even so, the praise is very excessive. F., who
was governor of Pisa and Volterra, wr. always
less in singing-robes than in robes of state.
He did not forget the governor in the poet,
and this seriousness in his odes became in
places a little pompous. A man of deep
religious feeling, he was moved to majestic
verse by the conversion of queen Christina
(q.v.) and other public events, and his sonnets,
serious or playful, are in the true Ital. tradition.
By far the finest in the former class is his

Italia, Italia, o tu, cui féo la sorte, which ' is
to Italian literature what Milton's sonnet on
the massacre of the Vaudois is to English '
(Garnett, *Ital. Lit.*, 284), and which Byron
(q.v.) transld. in *Childe Harold*, iv, 42-3.

Finkenritter (Germ.) : an adventure-story, dating
from the late 16th cent., known appropriately
in the country of its orig. as *Lügengeschichte*
(lying-tale). It was a caricature of the
romance of chivalry (*Ritter*=knight), and in
form may be described as a kind of ancester of
Munchausen (q.v.).

Finnur Jónsson (1704-89): Icel. historian ; bp.
Wr., 1772-78, Lat. *Ecclesiastical History of
Iceland*, 4 vols., described as the chief work
of erudition produced in Iceld. in the 18th
cent.

Firenzuola, Agnolo (1493-1545): It. poet ; a
busy and bright composer of entertaining tales,
not less licentious because he had at one time
worn the habit of a monk. F. does not lay
claim to any particular measure of originality,
but his direct reflection of the actual talk of
the Florence of his day lends an interest to
his re-cast tales of Boccaccio (q.v.), of
Apuleius, *The Golden Ass*, and others, which
is in really refreshing contrast to the more
precious writers of his generation.

Fischart, Johann (1548-89): Germ. poet and
pamphleteer ; ' the greatest satirist not only
of the sixteenth century, but in the whole
range of German literature ' (Biese, i, 331).
Born at Mayence ; sturdy supporter of
Lutheran reform and hater of Jesuits ; a man of
teeming invention, virile patriotic sympathies,
but unmanageable and ebullient style. Wr.
narrative poem in 8-syllable lines, *das glück-
hafte Schiff von Zürich* (' The Lucky Ship of
Zurich '), celebrating the feat of rowing from
Zurich to Strassburg in 1 day (20 June,
1576) accomplished on a civic festival. The
good relations between the 2 townships,
the fine sportsmanship of the rowers, and the
the events of the day's work from dawn to
sunset, are told in swinging verses full of
patriotic ardour. Popular treatises on marriage
and other social and moral topics, with more
violent excursions into the polemics of church-
satire, in pamphlets with monstrous titles,
were also written by F., whose ready wit and
resourceful prose were freely placed at the
disposal of right and justice, and raised him
high in the rank of workers for humanism.
F.'s most ambitious bk. was also his least
successful ; a free version of the *Gargantua* of
Rabelais (q.v.), in the form of a satirical
romance, *Geschichtsklitterung*, 1575, in which
F. exceeds the excesses of his original with
more than characteristic Germ. thoroughness.

Fitzgerald, Edward (1809-83): Engl. poet ;
transld., 1859 (revised in subsequent edns.)
the *Rubaiyat* of the Persian astronomer-poet,
Omar (q.v.) Khayyám ; wr. *Euphranor*, 1851,
a prose-dialogue on education, and translns.
of 6 dramas by Calderon (q.v.), 1853 ; an
intimate friend of Tennyson (q.v.), and a
personal influence on the lit. life of his times.
The peculiar quality of the *Rubaiyat*, which,
though closer to the original than it is sometimes represented, is yet so deeply pondered as
to rank almost as a new poem in the Engl.
language, is its combination of hedonism and

mysticism,—the melancholy of the mysticism correcting the impressionism of the hedonism. The style of its polished quatrains (a new metre at the time, since employed by Swinburne, q.v., in *Laus Veneris*) made an instant appeal to a generation trained by Keats and the Pre-Raphaelites (qq.v.) to an appreciation of delicacy and music, and many of its slow, long verses of ruminant thought about life and death have passed into current use.

Fitzneal (Fitz Nigel), Richard (12th cent.) : Engl. divine and statesman ; bp. of London ; wr. Lat. treatise, *dialogus de saccario*, on the Treasury, of considerable value.

Flacius, Matthias (1520-75) : Germ. historian. Collaborated with scholars at Magdeburg to forward the cause of the Reformation (q.v.) by critical studies of ecclesiastical history in Lat.

Flamenca (*c.* 1240) : Fr. verse-romance ; triumphant example of Ovidian love-story in the school of Chrétien de Troyes (q.v.) ; of interest, too, for its catalogue (verses 609-701 ; the text is quoted in *Epic and Romance*, by prof. W. P. Ker, Macmillan, 1908 , p. 384) of the contents of the source-books for the 'matières de France, de Bretagne, et de Rome la grant' (see s.v. Bodel).

Flaminio, Marcantonio (1498-1550) : It. Latinist. Visited Ital. centres of learning, but resided chiefly at the Lago di Gardo, ' poring over his Aristotle or writing his Latin poems ' (Sandys, *Hist. Class. Schol.*, ii, 119) ; an attractive type of the virtuous and optimistic scholar who adorned the age, if not the court, of pope Leo x.

Flammarion, Camille (1842-1925) : Fr. astronomer, and an attractive writer on the branch of knowledge which he cultivated ; in the same class as sir Robert Ball (1840-1913), the Irish astronomer, except that F. wr. chiefly in verse, and brought to his myths and marvels of the skies a vivid imagination, always governed by his profound scientific knowledge. His *Mondes imaginaires et mondes réels* and *Dieu dans la Nature* are among his best-known works.

Flaubert, Gustave (1821-80) : Fr. novelist ; by common consent, the unique product of the junction of romanticism and naturalism. A devoted admirer of Hugo (q.v.), and filled with romantic disdain of the so-called *bourgeois* standards, F. passed out of the movement of 1830 on the stream of that punctilious regard for the exact value of words which characterized Gautier (q.v.), for example. This analytical search for truth in expression (depending on a truthful representation, which depended in turn on truth in imagination) formed a bridge which critics utilize for the passage from one school to another : from Dumas *père* to Zola, let us say. But labels are often misleading ; and, as a fact, the impassivity which was alleged of the naturalistic school of fiction was merely another aspect of the intense lyrical subjectivity of the romanticists. There is a way of dwelling so intently on one's own emotions as to view them with a kind of impersonal detachment ; careful readers of Tennyson's (q.v.) *In Memoriam* will know how this can be ; and F.'s ' incurable romanticism rendered his analysis surer and more penetrating '. If we choose to say that he stood sure-footed at the angle of the roads of the two schools, we are merely formulating for criticism a set of principles inherent in art. Thus, F.'s *Madame Bovary*, 1856, is a classical study of the romantic (or sentimental) temperament, set in hostile surroundings ; his *Education sentimentale*, 1869, is the tale of the gradual disenchantment of an impotent lover of life (Mr. W. B. Maxwell's *In Cotton Wool* tells a similar story) ; and F., with a brilliant effort, applied the same methods of detached intentness to distant periods of time. His chief novel in this regard was *Salammbô*, 1862, ' a gorgeous, ghastly dream-panorama of blood, and gold, and orgie, and dim tumultuous horror ; . . . in fact, a sort of novel-nightmare ' (Saintsbury, *P.E.L.*, xii, 75). This was followed by the *Tentation de Saint-Antoine*, 1874, ' one of the great books of the century ' (*ibid.*), which had been written in 1849, and rewritten in 1856, and each time laid aside. The 3 versions are all extant, and it is the 1856 *Tentation* which was transld. into Engl. by René Francis (Duckworth, 1916). F., remarked a reviewer of that transln. in the *Times Lit. Supp.* (27 Jan., 1916), was born with the melagomania of a romantic hero, and his *Temptation of St. Anthony* ' represents his supreme effort to see himself magnificently as a man in whose sufferings should be symbolized those of mankind '. An exquisite artist in style, his magnificent method had considerable influence on the course of Fr. and Engl. fiction. His taste for the monstrous-fantastic and the repulsive-horrible must always alienate sympathy, which is not satisfied by the formula of ' art-for-art's-sake ' ; but he was a sincere worker towards the light of that saving principle, and his reputation, unlike that of some others of the miry school, increases with the lapse of time. It is to be added that F.'s æsthetic aims had their counterpart in the moral aspect. Transferred from style to policy, his search for the right word and his consequently exclusive, fastidious and aristocratic vocabulary involved, in the social sphere, a rejection of the middle class and of the mediocre, and a philosophic attachment, accordingly, to the theory known, later, as that of the Superman (q.v.). The belief in perfectibility of government, in a government by mandarins, as it has been called, proceeded from an impatience of the *bourgeoisie*, which proceeded in turn, in F.'s instance, from the Romantic appetite for stylistic perfection. But his impatience was partly lack of discernment. Brunetière (q.v.) roundly charges him with *sottise* : ' the projection of his own stupidity on to things that he did not understand ' ; and a generation which is growing more and more to sift the foundations of knowledge is likely to move away from F., whose philosophy was insecurely founded on personal prejudice and literary convention.

Flavio, Biondo. See **Biondo.**

Fléchier, Esprit (1632-1710) : Fr. divine and orator ; bp. of Nîmes, 1687. F. learned his eloquence in the school of the precious (q.v.) and great worlds ; in early life he frequented the Hôtel de Rambouillet (q.v.) ; was the intimate friend of mme. Deshoulières (q.v.), and wr. pleasant verses in Lat. and Fr. In

1665-66, he wr. a chronicle, or diary, of the *Grands Jours d'Auvergne* (*ed. pr.*, 1844), i.e. the judicial commission which king Louis xiv appointed to overtake the arrears of justice, and which F. attended as an *abbé* in the train of the judges. His account illuminates an obscure and somewhat seamy side of provincial Fr. lawsuits. His episcopal pronouncements in later life included funeral orations on mme. de Rambouillet, the duc de Montausier, and the great general, Turenne.

Fleck, Conrad (first-half 13th cent.): Swiss-Germ. romancer. Wr. a *Floris and Blanchefleur* (see s.v.), 1220, in a style which indicated the influence of Gottfried's (q.v.) realism on the old unquestioning idealism of the chivalric convention.

Fleming, Paul (1609-40): Germ. poet; edu. as physician; travelled with Olearius (q.v.) in Russia and Persia, penetrating as far as Ispahan, and utilized his rare experience in descriptive verses, and, more fruitfully, in extending the range of poetic vision. A considerable part of his poetry, collected after his death, is in Lat., and it was due to the influence and example of Opitz (q.v.)—more fortunate in this disciple than in some others—that F. added his contribution to the gathering forces of the Germ. Renaissance.

'Fleshly School' (Engl.): See s.v. Buchanan, R.

Fletcher, -i. John (1579-1625): Engl. dramatist; son of Richard F., bp. of London, 1594. A constant frequenter of the theatre-world in Tudor London, F. came nearer than any fellow-playwright to the more modern idea of a studio or academy of dramatic production, in which, with commendable rapidity, play after play was fabricated to suit the taste of the public and the demands of the various companies of actors. He wr. pieces of his own, including *The Faithful Shepherdess*, 1609, *Valentinian* (tragedy), *The Pilgrim* (comedy), etc., and thus supplied a touchstone of his style in dialogue and song, which critics have learned to apply to the many more plays which he wr. in collaboration. For 6 or 8 years, from 1607 onwards, F. was closely associated with F. Beaumont, q.v., and *The Scornful Lady* (comedy), 1610, *The Maid's Tragedy* and *King and No King* (tragedies), 1611, *Philaster* (tragi-comedy), 1609, and *The Knight of the Burning Pestle*, 1611, were, perhaps, the best products of this best period of F.'s activity. The last—the *Burning Pestle*—was a very clever skit, as it would now be called, on what may be described as the stage-mind: it laughed at the contrast between the sedentary liver and the romantic dreams of theatre-goers. Byron (q.v.). was aware of a like contrast in his day; sir James Barrie has dramatized it in our own day, and the satirist of the cinema-mind is yet to arise. F. collaborated with Massinger (q.v.) in half-a-dozen plays of various types, and among others, with Shakespeare (q.v.). On that height, the critics are mere disputators, and we may rely on the authority of sir Sidney Lee (*Life of Wm. Shakespeare*, 437), that, of the 3 plays, *Cardenio*, *The Two Noble Kinsmen*, and *Henry viii*, which 'have been named as the fruits of Shakespeare's co-operation with Fletcher, only in the third case may the association be accepted without

demur'. F.'s charm as a song-writer—they all wrote songs on Tudor bushes—may be judged from the specimen in Palgrave's *Golden Treasury of Songs and Lyrics*, civ.

-ii. Phineas (1582-1650): Engl. poet; cousin to above. His father, Giles F., the elder, was envoy to Russia, 1588, and his travel-book on Russia, 1591, after being suppressed, was partially printed by Hakluyt (q.v.), and publd. in entirety, 1856. P.F., a minor poet, wr. *Purple Island, or The Isle of Man*, 1633, an allegorical poem in 10 bks., in imitation of Spenser, q.v., then, as since, the poet of poets.

-iii. Giles (?1588-1623): Engl. poet; brother of above; known as the younger, in distinction to his father (*supra*). Wr. *Christ's Victorie and Triumph in Earth and Heaven*, 1610, which Milton, q.v., is said to have conned.

Fleury, Claude (1640-1723): Fr. historian; *abbé*; member of Academy (q.v.), 1796. Wr. *Historie Ecclésiastique*, 20 vols., 1691-1720, and other encyclopedic works. He should be carefully distinguished from his great contemporary and namesake, card. André Hercule de Fleury (1653-1743), who was prime-minister to king Louis xv. (See s.v. Entresol).

Floral Games, 'Jeux Floraux' (founded 1323): poetic academy, originally exclusively Provençal (q.v.), the initiation of which at Toulouse by a company of professional Troubadours (q.v.) was due to the same causes as led at about the same time to the formation of guilds of Meistersinger (q.v.), viz. to ensure the conservation of the forms of poetic composition in the decay of the spontaneous activity of its itinerant minstrelsy. The 'sobregaya companhia', or 'very gay company of the seven troubadours of Toulouse', summoned the first meeting of their fellow-craftsmen for May-day, 1324, when the prize of a golden violet was awarded to Vidal (q.v.) for a hymn in honour of the Virgin Mary. The contest became an annual institution, and a silver eglantine and a silver marigold were added as second and third prizes; and presently, 1355, the academy acquired a code of rules, which formed the orig. of the laws of courtly love (see s.v. Woman). The gaiety of the company and of their 'science,' known as the *gai saber* (q.v.) is not wholly appropriate. since the subject of the verse was dominantly religious; but as the meeting formed a May-day holiday, the description is sufficiently accurate. The name most prominently associated with the Games is that of CLÉMENCE ISAURE, a native of Toulouse, to whom a statue was erected in the Town Hall of that city, 1557, though nothing more definite is known of her than is mentioned in the record of her benefactions. The 'science' exercised no little influence on later lit. in France and Spain, and the Games were continued after the disappearance of the *langue d'oc* (q.v.), and were re-organized in a formal Academy (q.v.) in the 17th cent.; suppressed at the epoch of the Fr. Revolution. The revival of the cult by Mistral (q.v.) is a matter of recent history. (See, too, s.v. Barcelona).

Florence (Firenze): City in Tuscany, Italy; associated chiefly, though in company with other cities, in the preparation and spread of the Renaissance (q.v.) in Western Europe.

'If Florence were to disappear from the surface of the globe', wr. C. Yriarte (1831-98 ; Fr. critic), in the introduction to his history of F., ' the archives of human thought would lose their most precious titles, and the Latin race would be in mourning for its ancestors'. Not otherwise wr. S. Rogers (q.v.), in *The Pleasures of Memory* :

Of all the fairest cities of the earth,
None is so fair as Florence. 'Tis a gem
Of purest ray ; and what a light broke forth
When it emerged from darkness ! Search within,
Without : all is enchantment ! 'Tis the Past
Contending with the Present ; and in turn
Each has the mastery.

And not otherwise, again, wr. Robert Bridges (born, 1845), poet-laureate in our day :

Where San Miniato's convent from the sun
At forenoon overlooks the city of flowers
I sat, and gazing on her domes and towers
Call'd up her famous children one by one :
And three who all the rest had far outdone,
Mild Giotto first, who stole the morning hours,
I saw, and god-like Buonarroti's powers,
And Dante, gravest poet, her much-wrong'd son.

In the history of the mind of modern Europe, 2 cities are crowned as queens : Florence, the mother of the Renaissance, and Paris (q.v.), her daughter : behind both is their common mother, Athens ; and the only cities comparable with Athens, in her influence, through Florence and Paris on the history of that mind, are Jerusalem and Rome, the homes respectively of spiritual and civil law. What gave Florence this supremacy, from the date of her independence in 1115, through the lifetime of her exile son Dante (q.v.), and the dynastic succession of her merchant-princes, de' Medici (q.v.) ? ' Something ', says Symonds (q.v.; *Ital. Renaissance*, ii, 118), ' may no doubt be attributed to ethnology, and something to climate ', something, too, to the Florentines' ' sense of the greatness and splendour of Florence. Like the Athenians of old, they had no warmer passion than their love for their city ' ; and M. Yriarte reaches much the same conclusion : ' All is not the result of study, of application ; there is intuition, good fortune, a felicitous something that defies analysis. The softness of the sky, the charm of the atmosphere, the native grace with which everything is imprinted, an inexpressible air of elegance and sympathy, which is the undeniable mark of men and things at Florence, cannot be foreign to so admirable an efflorescence '. It is not within our scope to write a history of F., but it is within our province to refer to the contributions to that history mentioned here s.vv. G. Eliot (*Romola* ; Florence in the time of Savonarola), Vespasiano da Bisticci (most of whose *Illustrious Men* were Florentines), Machiavelli, Ficino, and others ; also s.v. Toscanaggiamento. And perhaps we may conclude on a more modern note. Sir Michael Sadler, master of Univ. Coll., Oxford, in a *Report* to the Education Committee of the City of Liverpool, 1904, wr. : ' The fame and power of Liverpool as a centre of the world's commerce recall a parallel which is apposite in fact, though distant

in date. It will be remembered that the conjunction of municipal and academic interest was also a striking feature of the great period of municipal revival in the Italian cities in the early Renaissance. The origin of all but three of the Italian universities can be traced to the aid or the initiative of the municipality or the ruler of the city. . . The aid thus given to the Italian universities from public funds was not confined to professional or technical studies. At the university of Florence, which was the first to provide academic courses on Dante, the Signoria established, a few years later, a chair for Manuel Chrysoloras, the Byzantine scholar who re-opened in Italy the fountain of Greek learning '. (See s.vv., and also s.v. Boccaccio). Thus, the example of F. still appeals to the 20th cent.

Flores (Florio, Floire, Florence) **and Blanchefleur** (Biancafiore) : episode in the romantic ' matière de Rome la grant ' (see s.v. Bodel), relating the moving tale of 2 youthful lovers, separated and happily re-united after many difficulties and dangers ; conveyed in Fr. 12th cent. redactions from a lost Gk. or Byzantine original ; used by Boccaccio (q.v.) in *Filocolo*.

Flores, de Juan (fl. 1500) : Span. romance-novelist ; Italianate. Wr., c. 1495, a continuation of the *Fiammetta* of Boccaccio (q.v.), and, c. 1521, an imitation of Boccaccio's *Filocolo* entitled *The Story of Aurelio and Isabella*, which was adopted as a lesson-book in Span. schools. To this chance may be partly due its influence on Ariosto (q.v.), G. de Scudéry (q.v.), and J. Fletcher (q.v., in *Women Pleas'd*).

Florez, Enrique (1702-73) : Span. scholar ; Augustinian. F. was engaged in compiling material for the great work of ecclesiastical history, *España Sagrada* (q.v.), and contributed largely to vols. i-xxvi.

Florian, de, Jean Pierre (1755-94) : Fr. poet ; fabulist ; chevalier ; wr. *Fables*, after the model of La Fontaine (q.v.), 1792, a *Galatée*, after the model of Cervantes (q.v.), 1783, and plays : *Numa Pompilius*, 1786, *William Tell*, etc. F. was a nephew of Voltaire (q.v.), but spiritually, a disciple of Rousseau (q.v.) : a somewhat piquant collocation.

Florio, John (c. 1553-1625) : Engl. scholar ; son of an Ital. Protestant refugee ; Ital. reader to queen Anne, 1603 ; compiled Ital.-Engl. dict., 1598 ; transld. the *Essays* of Montaigne, q.v., 1603,—one of the chief monuments of Tudor scholarship.

Folengo, Giralomo (1491-1544) : It. Macaronic (q.v.) writer. Born of noble stock ; studied under Pomponazzi (q.v.) ; was expelled from Bologna Univ. ; joined Order of Benedictine monks under religious name of Teofilo, by which he is often known ; eloped, 1515. Wr. *Macaronea*, 1519 ; *Orlandino*, 1526 ; *Caos*, 1527 ; returned, later, to cloister and pious writings ; assumed pen-name of Merlinus Coccaius. In many important features F. was a Rabelaisian before Rabelais (q.v.), which is, perhaps, not an unfair way of stating the debt which the great Frenchman owed to him. Their common hate of monks ; their common learning, and hate of learning's fads ; their taste for Lucian and other qualities, bring them into a close relationship. But F. was less purposeful than Rabelais, in the sense that his mission was complete when he had bantered with light but masterly burlesque the academic Lat. 'pastoral' and antique 'romance', which, as Pulci (q.v.) had known and shown, was far too remote from the frank, practical genius of 16th-cent. Italy to make a direct appeal. F. stands at the head of a class of writing, which neither began nor closed with him, and he possessed the saving humour which is so frequently lacking to professional humourists. The mixed verbalism of his Macaronic style displays with remarkable success the resources of the satire of adventure, which lends itself readily to linguistic experiments.

Folly : prime object of satiric wit in the Middle Ages, combined by Brandt (q.v.) with the specific Germ. invention of a ship of boon-companions in his famous Ship of Fools (*Narrenschiff*), 1494. This was early transld. into Lat. elegiac verse, and was thus available to cosmopolitan humanists, and inspired a considerable body of lit., of which the 'Praise of Folly' (*Moriæ Encomium*) of Erasmus (q.v.), 1509, dedicated to More (q.v.), and, later, illustrated by Dürer, is the most notable. Bks. thus embellished with wood-cuts illustrating the theme of the text were known as emblem-books (q.v.), and these were chiefly associated with folly-lit.; the graphic skill of the artist supplemented the moral aim of the satirist, and helped to convert the old medieval allegories and abstractions into the pointed wit and definite character-outline, which led eventually to the essay, novel and drama of modern lit.; expanding the medieval gallery of classified scriptural fools into character-sketches of good and evil livers. The *Ship of Fools* was transld. into Engl. by Barclay (q.v.), and was eagerly studied by Skelton (q.v.) and other satirists; and, as folly-lit. started with the court-jester, it was appropriate that its later examples should lie in the field of court-satire. The folly of depending on princes' favours and of seeking wealth at the price of self-respect was a common motive of the poets who bound rods for the backs of fools. In a sense, the sermons of the late card. Vaughan, a direct successor in the 20th cent. of Geiler (q.v.) in the 16th, who preached from the text supplied by Brandt, were folly-lit. in the direct line of descent. The vogue of the fool-satire in the 16th cent. was partly caused by the humanistic reaction from scholastic logic and the obscurantism of such seats of theological learning as Cologne and the Sorbonne school at Paris. Ignorance, luxury, sloth, and other vices, ingrained and acquired, were assailed by the northern humanists with a bitterness and candour which delighted the homely burghers of the busy Germ. towns where Eulenspiegel and Grobian (qq.v.) had their homes; and many a forgotten cargo of folly was borne in cart or ship down the tide of poetic satire to its ultimate goal in the theatre.

Fontaine, Charles (1513-87) : Fr. poet; Marotique (see s.v. Marot). Wr. *Contr' Amie de Cour* ('*Adversus* The Mistress of the Court'), in reply to La Borderie's reply to Héroet (qq.v.).

Fontaines, de, Marie Louise Charlotte (d. 1730) : Fr. novelist; *née* de Givri. Mme. de F. was in the school of mme. de la Fayette (q.v.), and was a friend of Voltaire (q.v.) in his youth. The best-known of her somewhat mediocre romantic stories are *Historie de la comtesse de Savoie* (11th cent.) and *Aménophis*.

Fontanes, de, Louis (1757-1821) : Fr. poet; marquis; negligible as a writer, but of some influence in his own day as the dispensary of Napoleon's patronage to men of letters. As an emigrant to Engld. at the time of the Revolution, F. was always an admirer of Engl. lit. He transld., 1783, Pope's (q.v.) *Essay on Man,* and his poem, *la Chartreuse de Paris* was inserted by Chateaubriand (q.v.) in the *Génie du Christianisme.*

Fontenelle, sieur de, Bernard le Bovier (1657-1757) : Fr. miscellanist; popular philosopher; as such, the historians agree that F. 'vulgarized' science. His mother was a sister of the brothers Corneille (q.v.), whose example turned F.'s early ambition in the direction of drama. The experiment was not a success, and F. incurred at different times in his long life the satire and ridicule of Racine, Boileau, La Bruyère (to whom he sat for the portrait of Cydias the precious, q.v., in the *Caractères*), and Rousseau (qq.v.). Time and an easy disposition were on F.'s side, and he turned from the stage to Lucianic (or, as we should now say, Landorian—see s.v. Landor—) conversations in his *Dialogues des morts* (of the dead), 1683 : Socrates and Montaigne, Paracelsus and Molière, and others, exchange opinions in the Elysian fields ; and the dramatic illusion is admirably sustained. Not dissimilar in scope and purpose was F.'s *Digression sur les Anciens et Modernes,* with which he interposed in the quarrel between Perrault and Boileau (qq.v.; and s.v. Ancients and Moderns) on the modernist side. A large part of his modernism was due to his genuine sympathy with the spirit of scientific inquiry, and there is more than a little scientific value in F.'s *Entretiens sur la Pluralité des Mondes,* 1686, and his *Histoire des Oracles,* 1687. The 'Interludes', or essays, 'on the Plurality of Worlds', particularly, earned F. his doubtful fame as the vulgarizer of learning; if every writer of a bk. has an ideal reader in his mind, F.'s ideal reader was the fashionable woman of the social *salon* (q.v.). He purposely wr. down to her level, and aimed at a delicate parsimony of learning which should neither offend the amateurs nor dissatisfy the studious : 'si j'avais la main pleine de vérités', he declared, 'je me garderais bien de l'ouvrir'. It is not incorrect to add that Montesquieu (q.v.) wr. at first (*Lettres Persanes*) down to the same level ; and it would be in accordance with Montesquieu's leaping generalizations to say that the manner was characteristic of Fr. philosophers in the 18th cent., not excluding Voltaire (q.v.). F. was a prominent member of the Academy (q.v.), of which he wr. the history, and in 1697 was appointed perpetual secretary of the Academy of Sciences. In this capacity he composed the *Éloges,* or eulogies, of its members as they died ; and, as he lived within a month or two of being a centenarian, he had plenty of practice in a task peculiarly congenial to his literary gifts and scientific acquirements. Among these obituary panegyrics are those on Leibniz and Newton, who were hon. members of the Academy. Journalism, esp. in its higher walks, would probably have absorbed the best part of F.'s industry to-day.

Forner, Juan Pablo (1756-97): Span. poet and critic; controversialist; ' knowledge, talent, address, and a despicable character: *voilà* Forner' (Kelly, *Lit. espagn.*, 396). A verse-satire in the worst taste on Iriarte, 'The Erudite Ass', 1782, was unworthy, as were many pamphlets issued under assumed names, of the genuine critical judgment so much misused by this short-lived and violent writer. His poems have merit, and an essay on ' The Obsequies of the Castilian Language ' (which he sought to defend against Francophil and other foreign temptations) is perhaps the best of his prose-works.

Forster, Johann Georg (1754-94): Germ. and Engl. travel-book writer. F. was brought up in Engld., held professorships in Germany, and died in Paris, in an agony of disillusion at the realities of the Fr. Revolution which he had greeted with all the ardour of his Sturm und Drang (q.v.) temperament. In 1772-75, F. accompanied his father and captain Cook on the voyage round the world, and wr. an account of it in Engl., 1777. In 1791-94, he wr. his great work of travel-lit., ' Aspects of the Lower Rhine ' (*Aussichten vom Niederrhein*), ' from Brabant, Flanders, Holland, England, and France '. It is still recognized as a masterpiece of Germ. prose-style, and it displays an unapproachable keenness of observation and facility of descriptive power. F. m., 1785, Therese, daughter of C. G. Heyne (q.v.).

Forster, John (1812-76): Engl. critic; biographer; wr. lives of Landor (q.v.), 1869, and Dickens (q.v.), 1872-4, both of whom were his friends; of Goldsmith (q.v.), 1854, and Swift (q.v.), unfind., 1876; *Hist. and Biog. Essays*, 1858; contributor to *Quarterly* and *Edinburgh* reviews. F. bequeathed his library, etc., to the nation.

Forteguerri, Niccolo (1674-1735): It. burlesque poet; the last link in the chain of Carlovingian epopee, fabricated by Pulci, Boiardo and their successors (see s.vv.). F. worked on the old *matière de France* (see s.v. Bodel) by way of parody and caricature. He was a member of the Arcadia (q.v.) Academy at Rome.

Fortunatus : Germ. popular tale (see s.v. *Volksbuch*) or, at least, a tale popularized in Germany, as a conglomerate of separate deposits of Teutonic legend, Ital. novellistic lore, Fr. romance, etc. The completed tale first assumed shape in an edn. at Augsburg, 1509, comprising (1) the encounter with Fortune, (2) the inexhaustible purse, (3) the wishing hat, and (4) the sons of F., Andelosia and Ampedo, and their final loss of purse, hat, and life. Another Augsburg edn. appeared in 1530, and a Frankfort edn. in 1550; the former has been taken to show traces of a romantic, specifically Span., redaction, but ' its essential ingredients are in the main Teutonic ' (Herford, *Lit. Relations of Engld. and Germany in 16th Cent.*, 206). In its definitive form as a *Volksbuch*, it is a fascinating tale of the wonderful adventures of a

favourite of fortune and his son under the spell of the magic so familiar to current evidence of alchemy and witchcraft. When the story crossed to Engld. (and it is found, too, in the Netherlands and in France), it was treated by Dekker (q.v.), who, here, as in the *Gull's Hornbook*, was directly influenced by Germ. models, and who selected and re-combined the Fortunatus episodes to suit the Elizabethan court; it is likely, further, that the Faust (q.v.) story affected sympathetically this tale, and helped to turn it to an analogous illustration of the vanity of the medieval superman.

Fosforos. See s.v. **Phosphorus.**

Foscolo, Ugo (1778-1827): It. poet, novelist and critic; born at Zante, of a Venetian father and Gk. mother, and spent an agitated life in soldiering, love-making, and writing. At Milan, he met Marini and Monti (qq.v.), to the latter of whom he addressed in 1810 the following well-deserved farewell rebuke : ' Your epitaph will sing your praises; mine will say that, if I had many evil passions, my pen was never soiled with falsehood '; met Alfieri and Niccolini (qq.v.) at Florence, whither his remains were finally brought home, 1871, from Chiswick, where Garibaldi had paid a pilgrimage to his tomb; met Manzoni (q.v.) in Paris, and occupied a chair of rhetoric at Pavia, 1808. Later, the Austrians made flattering overtures to him, which, unlike Monti, he declined, and fled, 1815, to Switzerland. Thence he made his way to Engld., where he was soothed by the devotion of a natural daughter, and where he was much helped (though he somewhat wearied their help) by good friends : his studies of Dante, Petrarch and Boccaccio, and his contributions to the *Quarterly Review*, belong to these latter years.

F. was a true patriot and a great writer; a disciple of Goethe (q.v.) of the *Werther* period, and a forerunner of the romantic epoch of Leopardi, G. Sand (qq.v.) and the men of 1830. His poem, *i Sepolcri*, 1807, meditations in 300 verses at the tomb of national heroes, is a work of genius composed in the tranquil spirit of Gk. elegy, concise in style but rich in imagination. It owed something to the sepulchral muse of Young and Gray (qq.v.), and F. may have seen the fragmentary ' Cemetery ' of Pindemonte (q.v.), to whom *i Sepolcri* was dedicated. But it owed most to F.'s own sense of the greatness of his country and its future. He wr., too, some other odes and lyrics, but his fame rests on his romance *le ultime Lettere di Jacopo Ortis*, 1798, described by Garnett (*Ital. Lit.*, 338) as ' a reminiscence of *Werther* and a forerunner of *René*' (see Chateaubriand). ' With all its debts to Goethe ', says prof. Vaughan (*P.E.L.*, x, 451), ' and in a far less degree to Gray, *Jacopo Ortis* remains a work of striking originality. The denunciation of the wrongs of Italy and of society at large is strangely impressive; and in the more idyllic scenes, which are laid among the Euganean hills, there is wonderful charm '. It is by this bk. that F. survives his unquiet life and times, and dowers the country which he loved and left with a romance worthy of her suffering and aims.

Foulis (orig. **Faulls**), **-i. Robert** (1707-76): Scot. printer; born at Glasgow; attended univ.

lectures of Hutcheson (q.v.); apprenticed to a barber, but was early drawn by the call of learning, and aimed at achieving for Glasgow, then at the height of its intellectual fame, what Manuzio (q.v.) did for Venice at the Renaissance. Visited Oxford, London, and Paris, collecting bks. and book-lore, and became printer to Glasgow univ., 1741. F. loved beautiful bks, and his edns. of Cicero and Homer were particularly famous; the latter, a folio in 2 vols., being used by Winckelmann (q.v.) and Gibbon (q.v.), who declared that 'the poet's sense appears more beautiful and transparent'. F. also ventured on cheap reprints of popular British classics at a shilling. His disputes on copyright with printers south of the Tweed led to the commission to Johnson (q.v.) for his *Lives of the Poets*. F. founded, 1753, an Academy of Fine Arts at Glasgow (half a generation before the Royal Academy in London), but found insufficient support, and was unlucky in his speculations in Old Masters.

-ii. **Andrew** (1712-75): Scot. printer; brother of above. Accompanied R.F. on his youthful quest of bks., and joined his business; was involved in the firm's difficulties caused by the neglect of printing for picture-collecting. The last years of both brothers would seem to have been as unhappy as their earlier efforts to repeat in their native city the old glories of Venice and Florence were public-spirited and generous.

Fouqué, de la Motte, Friedrich Heinrich Karl (1777 -1843): Germ. poet and novelist; baron by rank. F., a soldier and country gentleman, not dependent on letters for a livelihood, found and retained high rank in the literary group in Berlin at the beginning of the 19th cent. Like Oehlenschläger (q.v.) before him, and Wagner and, to some extent, W. Morris (qq.v.) after him, F. sought his quarry from the sagas (see s.v. Scand. lit.), and wr. a *Sigurd*, a *Sintram*, a *Thiodolf*, and other romances, in rapid succession. His chivalric romance, the *Magic Ring*, 1813, made a strong appeal to the national sentiment of that year (battle of Leipsic). H.'s best known and best work is *Undine* (1811), the story of a nixie, or sea-fairy, who gains a soul by marriage with a mortal, and kills him with a kiss on his betrayal. A modern Undine, the Rautendelein of G. Hauptmann's *Versunkene Glocke* (1897), testifies to the unchanging genius of Germ. romance in creating these half-fey, half-human characters. (The baroness de la M.F.—Caroline, *née* v. Briest, 1773-1831—was also an author, and wr. numerous second-rate romances).

Fouquet, Nicholas (1615-80): Fr. statesman, financier; vicomte de Vaux and marquis de Belle-Isle; superintendent of finance under card. Mazarin, king Louis xiv's great minister; was thwarted in his ambition to succeed Mazarin, 1661, when he was arrested on charges of peculation, and, after a long trial, was condemned to imprisonment for life. F. is among others who have been wrongly identified with Louis xiv's famous prisoner, 'the man in the iron mask'. F.'s importance to lit. is derived from the correspondence seized at the time of his disgrace, which compromised many pretty women and some eminent men.

He was a generous host and patron of letters in his prosperous days, and figures prominently in all the memoirs of the period. La Fontaine (q.v.), with notable fine feeling, wr. his *Élégie aux nymphes de Vaux* to deplore the fall of F., who had shown him many kindnesses.

Fourier, François Marie Charles (1772-1837): Fr. social writer; in mental descent from Rousseau (q.v.) and akin to C.H. de Saint-Simon (q.v.). F.'s chief work, 1822, was re-edited, 1841, under the name of *Théorie de l'Unité universelle*, and contained the generous but wild philosophy of economics out of which social ethics have gradually been sifted. F.'s periodical *Phalanstère*, or *Phalange*, was publd., 1832-4, and, again, 1836.

Fox, George (1624-91): Engl. nonconformist; founded Society of Friends of Truth (nick-named quakers). F.'s life of missionary travel and adventure was related by him in a *Journal*, publd., 1694.

Foxe, John (1515-87): Engl. martyrologist; tutor in the families of sir Thos. Lucy, of Charlecote, and Henry Howard, earl of Surrey; Protestant preacher, pamphleteer; retired to Strassburg *regno* queen Mary, and issued Lat. 'Commentaries on things done in the Church', later (1563) reissued in Engl. as *Actes and Monuments*, and popularly known as *The Book of Martyrs*; canon of Salisbury, 1563; preached famous sermon 'On Christ Crucified' at St. Paul's Cross, 1570. 4 edns. of the *Bk. of Martyrs* were called for during F.'s life-time, and a memoir (of doubtful authenticity, attributed to his son) appeared in a posth. edn., 1641. John Strype (1643-1737), a painstaking and voluminous ecclesiastical historian, availed himself of F.'s papers, which were bought by Edwd. Harley, 2nd earl of Oxford, and are now in the British Museum. F. had 2 sons, —i, **Samuel** (1560-1630), whose *Diary* was appended to Strype's *Annals of the Reformation*, 1709-31; and ii, **Simeon** (1568-1642), president of the Coll. of Physicians, 1634-40.

Fracastoro, Girolamo (1483-1533): It. Latinist; physician. Born at Verona; studied philosophy under Pomponazzi (q.v.); resided at Padua. Wr. Lat. medico-didactic poem, *Syphilis* (1530), dedicated to Bembo (q.v.), which commands admiration by its vigorous style and skilful and fearless handling of a topic important at its time, and allegorically represented as a stroke inflicted by the sun on a shepherd; also Lat. dialogue, *Naugerius*, so called from Navagero (q.v.), who sustains the chief part in the discussion of Horatian poetics.

France, Anatole (1844-1924): Fr. novelist; satirist. F.'s baptismal name was Jaques Anatole François Thibault, but he habitually used, and was known by, the surname employed by his father, a bookseller and bibliophil, who signed himself, 'France, libraire'. F. started as a poet, writing *Poèmes dorés*, 1873, and *les Noces Corinthiennes*, 1876, but his true field was that of the novel and short story, and his genius displayed itself in irony and humour. 'Court jester for the court of Heaven' and a 'saintly Devil's advocate' were among the epithets attached to him by his biographers, who mourned in him the greatest Fr. author of his generation, and the intellectual descendant of Voltaire (q.v.). Wr. *le Crime de Salvestre Bonnard*, 1881; *Thaïs*, 1890 (a tale of ancient Alexandria); *la Rôtisserie de la Reine Pédauque*, 1893 (introducing the abbé Jerome Coignard, a favourite character with F.); *le Lys Rouge*, 1894, and others. During these years, too, F. acted as literary critic to *le Temps*, and in 1897 he became a member of the Academy (q.v.), having already been awarded the Nobel prize for lit. F.'s later works included *l'Histoire Contemporaine*, 1897-1901, the hero of which was M. Bergeret, the Dreyfusard prof. of Lat.; in this bk., F., who had displayed himself a convinced supporter of Zola (q.v.) in *l'affaire Dreyfus*, poured scorn on clericalism, anti-Semitism, Orleanism, and other-isms which he deemed dangerous to his country. His wit became more mordant with increasing years, in *Crainquebille*, 1904, *l'Ile des Pingouins*, 1908, and *la Revolte des Anges*, 1914. F. was a master of Fr. style in its most characteristic features of precision, order, irony, and resourcefulness. 'Master of the Laugh' Saintsbury has called him, recalling Rabelais (q.v.), his literary ascendant, who declared that 'le rire est le propre de l'homme'. He owed much in diction to Racine (q.v.), among native masters, but his style was his own, and he was secure enough in the admiration of his age (and of posterity) to permit himself a certain amount of repetition.

Francis, Philip (1740-1818): Engl. publicist; pamphleteer; civil servant; K.C.B.; reputed author of the *Letters of 'Junius'* (q.v.).

Francke, August Hermann (1663-1727): Germ. theologian. Not sufficiently orthodox for Erfurt (q.v.), F. became prof. in the newly founded univ. at Halle, which he helped to raise to the rank of the Wittenberg of the Aufklärung (q.v.). He was one of the leaders of the Northern movement of Pietism, which wrought for the religious revival of Germany after her long period of warfare what Rationalism (q.v.) under Leibniz (q.v.) wrought on the scientific side.

Frankenburg, von, Abraham (1593-1652): Germ. Catholic mystic; pupil of Böhme (q.v.) and friend of Sheffler (q.v.), who owed much to his advocacy and companionship.

Franzén, Franz Michael (1772-1847): Swed. poet; born in Finland; bp. of Hernösand, 1834. F., unlike Runeberg (q.v.), whom he lived to welcome as the national Finnish poet, did not rise fully above the unhappy politics of his country. The annexation of Finland to Russia, 1809, was not a *fait accompli* in F.'s youth, which was passed in the Francophil days of king Gustavus iii (q.v.), founder of the Swed. Academy, 1786. In 1797, F. won the Academy prize with an 'Ode to Creutz' (see s.v.), and this success confirmed him more strongly in the conventions of the Gustavian age. Thus, his early lyric poems were full of promise of more perfect performance than his later works were to fulfil; and his poetry is like a springtide nipped by a sudden frost.

Fraunce, Abraham (fl. 1587-1633): Engl. poet and translr.; M.A., Cambridge, and member of the circle of Harvey (q.v.), whose experiments in classical prosody he supported.

Transld. into Lat., under title of *Victoria*, Ital. comedy *Il Fidele* by Pasqualigo (q.v.), which, through A. Munday's (q.v.) Engl. version, was a part-source of Shakespeare's (q.v.) *Two Gentlemen of Verona*. F.'s attachment to Harvey brought him into contact with Sidney and Spenser (qq.v.), in whose *Colin Clout's come home again* F. figured as Corydon; he wr. songs in Sidney's *Astrophel and Stella*, and publd., 1591-92, Engl. hexameter poems, *The Countess of Pembroke's Emanuel* and *The Countess of Pembroke's Ivychurch*; was associated with T. Watson (q.v.) in translating the *Aminta* of Tasso (q.v.), and wr. a verse-paraphrase of some of the Psalms.

Frederick ii (1712-86): king of Prussia; succeeded his father, king Fredk. Wm. i, 1740; surnamed 'the Great'. With the great monarch's reign and policy we are not here concerned, save to note how completely he identified himself with what he deemed to be the welfare of his country; more truly even than the other absolutist, Louis xiv of France, he could say 'l'Etat, c'est moi'. But F.'s interest in and influence upon lit. were considerable, indirectly even more than directly. His own Fr. bk. on Germ. lit., and, generally, his devotion to the Fr. language, to Fr. taste and models and men—Voltaire, above all, and D'Alembert (qq.v.),—all followed lines which mistook the vital tendencies in the literary spirit of his own subjects in his own day. That he recalled Wolff (q.v.) to Halle, and that he reversed the contemptuous, if not insulting and suspicious, attitude of his father towards the forces making for enlightenment, stands to his credit and to his country's gain; but not even if we add to this the military muse of Gleim and Kleist (qq.v.) and the acceptable incense of Ramler's (q.v.) odes, do we explain the oft-quoted dictum of Goethe: 'The first true and higher self-consciousness came into German poetry through Frederick the Great and the Seven Years' War.' It was rather by the hold on the nation's imagination which that war and its leader seized, that F. affected literary tendencies in despite of his own predilections. He it was who made Germany a nation, in the sense that 'Deutschland found Prussia; a solid and living State round which the Teutonic people should consolidate itself' (Carlyle, q.v., *Hist. Fredk. the Gt.*, xx, 13: a consolidation completed after a hundred years,—with what issues in more recent days is well known). National lit. was then possible in Germany, and the fact that it could be written was due to king F.'s policy and life. Nor should lit. ignore the debt which it owes to F. through Carlyle (q.v.). Schiller (q.v.), who planned a 'Fredericiad', wr. in familiar lines:

Von dem grössten deutschen Sohne,
Von des grossen Friedrichs Trone,
Ging sie schutzlos, ungeehrt,

the 'she' who went 'unprotected and unhonoured 'from the Frederician presence and throne being the Germ. muse. But F. made his country so great, or so conscious of her potentiality for greatness, that the authors of *Wallenstein* and *Faust* fought and won in his name, and despite his Francophil tastes, their long war against foreign influences in Germ. lit.

12

Freidank (13th cent.) : name or *nom-de-guerre* (signifying, not inappropriately, free-thought) of a Germ. poet, who is otherwise unknown except that he accompanied emperor Fredk. ii on the crusade of 1228, and brought back with him a reflective poem called *Bescheidenheit*. The modern meaning of this word is modesty, but formerly it conveyed a stricter sense of the governing virtue of sanity-in-judgment (*scheiden*=to decide), or power-of-insight. F.'s work is a collection from the wisdom-lit., proverbs and tales of former and contemporary times, arranged without definite order, but dominated by personal observation, ripe experience, and a definite philosophy. These qualities ensured it enduring fame and later generations honoured it in Germany as a kind of worldly Bible.

Freiligrath, Hermann Ferdinand (1810-76) : Germ. poet. Intended for a commercial career, F. fell early under the influence of foreign Romantic poetry, and effected translns. from Byron and Hugo (qq.v.). In his first vol. of *Gedichte*, 1838, written while he was supposed to be applying himself to business, he followed those masters in their flight to the East for the liberty of colour and licence of sentiment which he sought. The infection caught, and confirmed F.'s choice of a poetic career. Herwegh's (q.v.) poems of 1841 stimulated F.'s steadier muse, and he espoused the cause of the growing Revolution (1848), and established his home in London. His vols. of political verse included the *Glaubensbekenntniss*, 1844, *Ça ira*, 1846, *Die Toten and die Lebenden*, 1848 (whence a prosecution for *lèse majesté*, which resulted, however, in the poet's acquittal), and *Neuere politische u. sociale Gedichte*, 1849-50, probably the finest flower of the revolutionary muse in Germany. 1871 found F. in Germany again, celebrating the union of his fatherland, though it had been accomplished otherwise than he had sung, and he contributed some lyrics to the poetry of victory. His long residence in Engld. lent him, with his poetic sensibilities, a rare skill in transln., and he added very effective renderings from Tennyson and others, including, esp., Burns, to his early exercises in transln. Political verse is always in danger of losing its first temporary vogue, and F.'s does not escape. But his earlier romantic poetry proves the genuineness of his inspiration, and it is partly a matter for regret that he was swept into the storms which raged round 1848.

French Literature : *Omnis Gallia in tres partes divisa est* ; but in literary France, at the beginning of the 12th cent., when the Romance (q.v.) languages had foliated from Lat., Cæsar's ancient survey has to be revised. The former landmarks were submerged, and France, the most graceful and fruitful of the heirs of the culture of Rome, France, who, like Greece of old, conquered her conqueror by her arts, was divided into two parts instead of three. The dividing-line was the river Loire, and a chief mark of the division was linguistic. The vernacular Lat. speech had developed in different forms North and South of that line ; and there were two distinct Romance-languages in sunny France. The Franks had spread in the North, the Burgundians and Visigoths in the South. To these tribal influences were added a strain of Norman blood and a Celto-Breton sympathy in the North ; a Moorish sympathy in the South, which was naturally buoyant and blithe. And over the whole of the country the warlike habits of the crusades and the manners of the code of chivalry imposed their canons of taste and refinement.

The Northern language is known as *langue d'oïl*, and included several dialects (Picard and Norman, for example), over all of which that of French (*Français*), spoken in the centre-province, predominated. The Southern language is known as *langue d'oc*, a descriptive term often used geographically, and it likewise, included several dialects (Périgord and Limousin, for example), with that of Provence (*Provençal*) predominating. *D'oïl* and *d'oc*, from Lat. *illud* and *hoc*, were called after the respective words for *yes*, and were employed by Dante (q.v.) to characterize the languages to which they belonged. Thus, Fr. lit. in the 12th cent. is in two distinct kinds, French in the North, and Provençal in the South (see s.v. Prov. Lit.) ; and though, in the 13th cent., the crusade of pope Innocent iii against the so-called heretics of Provençal Albi (q.v.) broke up the fair peace of Provence, interrupting its ' dance, and Provençal song, and sunburnt mirth ', and scattering its seeds of culture East and West ; though the blossoms, thus ruthlessly shattered, withered on their native soil, despite brave attempts to revive them, extending even to the 19th cent. (see s.vv. Toulouse, Mistral) ; though Provençal lit. declined, that is to say, and was absorbed in neighbouring literatures ; yet a recognition of its contemporary beginning, and of the exquisite lyric forms which it produced, is essential to a study of Fr. lit.

We start, then, with the Troubadours of Provence. The love which they sang and codified was sublimated by Sicilian imitators into the love-lore of Dante and Petrarch, and of the poets attached to the Petrarchan tradition. Kings and rulers became courtly makers, and queens were the poets' nursing-mothers. Richard Cœur-de-lion in Norman Engld., Fredk. Barbarossa in Germany, Alfonso ii of Aragon, were Troubadours all. Every court and camp in those days was a factory of chivalric love-poetry. Across the river Loire, in Northern France, the Troubadour, still synonymous with love-minstrel, was known as Trouvère. There, his function was a little more professionalized ; it was his part to find (*trouver*) for the *Jongleur* (q.v.), or reciter, the material for the tale (in verse or prose, *roman*), or for the song (*lai*), which was to conjure gold or gifts in kind from the audience. This ready audience of the 12th cent. was sought at the shrines of saints, in the halls of nobles and dames, sometimes in the camp, and, later, in the marketplace ; and the subjects found (*trouvés*) by the *roman*-tellers, at first for oral recitation, and, afterwards, for written composition—their repertories, in a word—were retrieved from everywhere and nowhere. Inscriptions on memorials and tombs ; hints of place-names and dates ; floating tradition and repute ; pre-existing song and story ; the fertile fancy of the clerical guardians of sacred

relics, supplemented by the quick invention of
the Trouvère with his living to earn : all were
utilized for the purpose of increasing the
immense mass of romantic lore. The outcome
was the huge collection of Northern Fr.
chansons de geste (q.v.), and the main cycles
on which these *chansons* turned were, i, the
exploits of Alexander (q.v.) in antiquity, ii,
of Charlemagne (q.v.) in Frankish legend,
and, iii, of Arthur (q.v.) in Celto-Breton legend.
The romantic redaction (see s.v. Romance)
of these heroic tales was the work of the literary
men of the 12th to 14th cent., whose
aristocratic audiences required more skilful
and more sophisticated versions of the old
tales of fighting and adventure than had
satisfied a generation prior to the conventions
of chivalry. Rude love had to adapt itself to
the code of chivalrous lovers ; rude war had
to suit itself to the manners of knightly
warriors ; and, though none of the passion
was spilled either from love or war, each
submitted to the literary forms (even the
formalism) devised by the Troubadours of the
South ; and this new narrative lit. of the
aristocracy of Northern France, which enriched
every duchy and county with Breton *romans*
and chivalric *chansons*, proved the fruitful
mother of later history and fiction. Among
these courtly makers, many of whom are
anon., we may mention the greater name
of Chrétien de Troyes (q.v.) ; and, among the
later writers in France who drew variant forms
of composition from that exhaustless fount,
we may select for mention here Villehardouin
(q.v.), who wr. a *chanson de geste* in prose, and
who, since he was a statesman, became the
earliest chronicler of Fr. history.
   The heroic spirit decayed. There came a
time when the lords of chivalry condescended
to be amused at the point of view of the
victims of militarism. There came a time, too,
when the middle-classes, the busy merchants
and manufacturers, emerged to wealth and
self-esteem, and when the Trouvère found it
worth his while to stock his repertory from
their storehouse. Thus, a *bourgeois* lit., as
it is called, came to expression in the 13th
cent., and filled the old forms of romance with
the new contents of middle-class invention.
This non-chivalric or even anti-chivalric lit.
was consummated in two great kinds, which
had gradually grown to maturity : i, the
Roman de Renart (see s.v. Reynard), and, ii,
the *Fabliaux* (s.v. Fable). The romance of
Reynard the fox was a reflection of the
chivalric romances in the distorted mirror of
the *bourgeoisie*. The lion, Charlemagne or
another, was outwitted by the nimble fox,
as, doubtless, many a knt., home at last from
his wars, was outwitted by a crafty steward or
a greedy tradesman from the town ; and this
allegory was almost endlessly elaborated for the
entertainment of the market, and, presumably,
for the edification of the court. The Fables
were short pieces with a like tendency; and
the whole body of this lit. took shape as satire
and ridicule, partly lyrical, partly dramatic,
directed at all kinds of institutions, and esp.
at priests and women. The most famous
name among such lyric satirists is that of
Ruteboeuf (q.v.), whose muse is dated midway

between the unequal halves of the *Roman de la
Rose* (q.v.). This greatest storehouse of Fr.
poetry in the Middle Ages was begun *c.* 1237
by a certain Guillame de Lorris and was completed *c.* 1277 by a certain Jean de Meung. The
first wr. at the zenith of the chivalric romance,
the second in the period of its decline, when the
middle-classes were coming into their own.
Together, their collection of tales comprises the
main repertory of romance, and illustrates the
two-fold methods of its manipulators ; and the
Roman de la Rose became the main source of
later inspiration, and was transld. into Engl.,
e.g., at the time of (and partly by the hand of)
Chaucer.
   We have dwelt at some length in the portals
of Fr. lit., because France, above all other
countries, was the inventor of forms of verse
and prose. Her Chrétien and other romancers,
her Reynardists and other fabulists, and her
Romance of the Rose, set models for universal
imitation, and gave France from the first age
of modern history her proud primacy in the
lit. of Europe. We come next to a period of
transition. In the late 14th and early 15th
cents., Fr. lit. was feeling its way through
vague hints of humanistic learning, through
the affectations of art for art's sake, and through
experiments in criticism and social satire, to its
discovery of Italy and the Renaissance.
   In the last twilight of that dawn, we reach
the names of one poet and of one prose-writer,
who, together, open the modern and close the
medieval period. These are Villon and Commines (qq.v.), the former a felon and a vagabond,
the latter a statesman and a grandee ; separate,
therefore, in their paths by every material
condition, yet united in the history of lit.
by a common genius which sets at nought the
tokens of social valuation. Villon released
in his poems the sealed springs of lyrical
inspiration ; Commines opened in his chronicles
the methods of comparison and psychology,
which had been closed alike to the saintliness
of Joinville (q.v.) and to the feudalism of
Froissart (q.v.) ; accordingly, Villon is still
a living poet, and Commines a living historian.
Meanwhile, the school of poetry, aptly known
as the *Rhetoriqueurs* (q.v.) poured out a turgid
stream of verse, marred by allusiveness, false
sentiment, and affectation, sometimes described
as Cretinism, after the name of the rhetorical
Crétin (q.v.), whom Rabelais thought it worth
while to laugh at. From the 15th cent., too,
date various dramatic societies, which provided
stages for future playwrights (see s.vv. Basoche,
Enfants sans Souci, and Confrérie de la Passion),
and one good farce, *Pathelin* (q.v. ; *c.* 1480),
which is in the line of ascent to Molière.
   And so we come to the epoch of the Fr.
Renaissance, which was a recovery of the pagan
classics through Italian humanists.
   Briefly, the 16th cent., in the chronology of
Fr. lit., lies between the lives of C. Marot (1463-
1523) and Malherbe (1555-1628). With Marot
the Renaissance began ; with Malherbe, its
effects were absorbed in the national lit. of
France.
   This cent. of apprenticeship and craftsmanship includes the reign of king Francis i of
France (q.v. ; *regn.*, 1515-47), who, whatever
his record in history, sought deliberately to

reproduce the example of Italian princes, and to re-found Florence in Paris (s.vv.). His term of captivity in Spain was turned to advantage, too, by the taste which he acquired and spread for Span. romantic fiction. (See s.v. Amadis, e.g.). The pattern of the Medicean court was even more graciously followed by the king's sister, queen Margaret (q.v.) of Navarre, who was less subject to restrictions of high policy in the protection which she royally afforded to erring Catholics and persecuted Calvinists, and who herself wr., or partly wr., the *Heptameron*; and a break in the century is marked by the reign of king Henry iv of France and Navarre (*regn.*, 1594-1610), when Fr. lit. may be said to have passed from its Renaissance-apprenticeship to its classic self-dependence. The patriotic labours of Ronsard and Du Bellay (qq.v.) to found, under the sign of the Pleiad (q.v.), a Fr. literary edifice on a scaffolding of Greco-Roman forms are the foremost product of the Italianate movement, which spread through France like a flood. At or near this central stream of lyric, epic and dramatic verse and criticism were speculations in applied art (by Palissy), in agriculture (by Serres), in morals (by Vair), in economics (by Montchrétien), in law (by Bodin). Protestant writers, such as Du Bartas and D'Aubigné (qq.v.) extended the classical formulæ to subjects of Biblical inspiration. Calvin (q.v.), prince of Protestants, imposed a classical style on the sacred topics of his Fr. prose ; Amyot (q.v.) caught from his originals (particularly Plutarch) the master's touch in the pagan classics which he made Fr. ; and the authors of the *Satyre Menippée* (q.v.) practised a defter note in the discussion of the art of government. Above all, there were the laughter of Rabelais (q.v.), ' broad as ten thousand beeves at pasture ', and the sly, shrewd smile of Montaigne (q.v.). Rabelais laughed men free ; laughed them free of the phantoms of the Middle Ages, at the edge of which he stood in his new strength, fearlessly fronting the dawn. He did not live to see the full Renaissance ; still less, to see the shades of superstition gather about its setting sun, when other Frenchmen, Voltaire and Diderot, the joint Rabelais of the 18th cent., were to hail a new Renaissance, which opened in revolution. *Felix opportunitate mortis*, Rabelais died with the morning laughter on his lips. And the *essais* of Montaigne are the smile of the Renaissance. He invented the name of Essay, as Montchrétien, who also wr. tragedies, invented the name of Political Economy from his observation of its action on Engl. soil ; and the philosophy which Montaigne taught, and which profoundly affected future thought, was faithful to two main principles : i, to make the most of the opportunities of life, and, ii, not to expect too much from them ; loyal enjoyment and honest doubt. For Montaigne, too, like Rabelais, reverted from medieval self-submission to a recognition, however limited, of the rights of man in nature.

Malherbe, critic and grammarian, was also of the new time. He cleansed the apparatus of the Pleiad of its foreign and affected forms, and sought to modernize and nationalize the literary resources of his countrymen. It was the fault of his imagination, not of his knowledge, that, valuable as his labours were in transmitting to the 17th cent. the humanistic acquisitions of his own age, he was a scavenger and not a creator. As a poet, his achievement fell below the useful work of Alexandre Hardy (q.v.), who, with no concern for the formal pedantries of Malherbe and the Pleiad, wr. acting-dramas for a business-manager.

The total effect of the Italianate period in Fr. letters was to form public taste ; and an impetus was given to this aim by the retirement of fashionable Paris from the weary controversies of politics and religion. Malherbe was right : it was better to discuss style than to take part in faction and feud ; Montaigne was right : it was better to enjoy the good than to slay the dragon of evil ; and d'Urfé (q.v.), for example, hit off the prevailing mode in his admirable *Astrée*, which was a picture of social Paris in the guise of a pastoral romance. At the Hôtel Rambouillet (q.v.) and in other centres, the *literati* practised the life which d'Urfé painted. They became fastidious in their choice of words, and careful of their manners. They looked at everything through a polished mirror, and the Fr. Academy (q.v.). itself was, at its inception, at least, the meeting-place of the witty ladies and gallant gentlemen who wr. long-winded romances, art-epopees, political novels, and much extravagant trash in a very exquisite style. This was the period of the Span. school in Paris, and of the influence of Vega, Calderon, and the lesser lights of their constellation on Scarron, Boisrobert, Montfleury, and the greater Fr. masters themselves. In the event, the civilizers (*los cultos* of Spain ; see s.v. Gongora) succeeded in their aim. The writings of Descartes (q.v.) and the foundation of the Academy (whatever toll of sycophancy was exacted by card. Richelieu) were the chief marks of the first half of the 17th cent., and they sum up the various movements, at court, in society, and in the middle-classes, towards a central authority of taste, a definite standard of practical morality, and a canon of lit. and language. And these movements were consummated in two writers, Corneille and Pascal (qq.v.), who may both, since dates are useful landmarks, be placed before 1661, when king Louis xiv of France took the reins of government into his own hands, and divided the 17th cent. by beginning the *grand siècle*. In Corneille, sweeping the stage with types of indomitable vigour matched by inexorable fate, Fr. verse found its noblest expression ; in Pascal, rationalist and moralist, finest product of the doctrines of Port Royal (q.v.)., Fr. prose found its true Attic maker. Together, they brought to full expression the higher motives of life and thought, which had been gathering strength since the Middle Ages. They stood at the threshold of the *grand siècle*, and handed to the masters of that age the finished instruments of prose and verse, which had been fashioned by precious (q.v.) writers in the academic schools after the Italian models of the Pleiad. ' The union of ancient art and modern reason in high literary intelligences produced a marvellous fecundity ' (Lanson, *Hist. Lit. Fr.*, 474).

Having followed the course of Fr. lit. to the border of the great age of Louis xiv, it is not within the scope of the present sketch to examine its master-pieces in detail. Versailles is still famous as a resort for pilgrims at the shrine of art and letters ; the ghosts of the gay or grave company, who composed the court of the *roi Soleil*, at the noon of his splendour and in the more sombre colours of his setting, still haunt the corridors and gardens, from which the laws of taste, empire and faith were dictated by France to the civilized world. The letters of mme. de Sevigné ; the moving tragedies of Racine ; the critical canons of Boileau ; the human comedies of Molière ; the brilliant fables of La Fontaine ; the lucid magnificence of Bossuet, the preacher ; the penetrating maxims of La Rochefoucauld ; the moral reflections of La Bruyère : these were some of the productions of the transcendent genius of Fr. lit. in its classical or Attic Age. And, appropriately enough, it is as the monarch at whose court this glory rose (and we have left out many lesser stars), that Louis xiv is remembered, now that his palace is a show-place, and his kingdom a republic, and his statecraft a name of shame.

Louis xiv died in 1715 ; in 1714, Voltaire (q.v.) made his début. The contrast is striking between the 17th and 18th cents., and yet they are intimately and closely bound together. The 17th founded the principles ; the 18th drew the conclusions ; and the 19th put them into practice. There is a chain, or concatenation, which links Montaigne to Descartes, Descartes to La Bruyère, La Bruyère to Bayle, Bayle to Fénelon, Fénelon to Montesquieu, Montesquieu to Voltaire, Voltaire to Diderot, Diderot to Rousseau, Rousseau to the Revolution, and the Revolution to the 20th cent. The speculative philosophy of the 17th cent. became positive, practical, revolutionary ; and the zeal of the reformers and propagandists who wr. the *Encyclopédie* was communicated from the financial disaster and the social decay caused by the wars of the *grand monarque* and the taxes levied to pay for them. The shadow of his great grandson's guillotine is to be sought in the eclipse of Louis xiv. Like the 17th, the 18th cent. is divided, for the purpose of Fr. literary history, into two clear halves : 1715 (death of Louis xiv) to 1750, and 1750-1789 (Fr. Revolution) ; The middle year is the date of the Encyclopedia (q.v.) and of the so-called *philosophes* (q.v.), who included such diverse talents as those of Turgot and Buffon. The greatest name in the century is Voltaire's, and he lived till 1778, within a few years of the Revolution. Nor did he merely live : he represented his age till he died. He was still active in the year of his death ; and he reflected in his writings the deepened philosophic tone which prevailed after *c.* 1750. Once more, we must evade the task of discussing details in this sketch. Quite summarily, the chief writings to be studied are those of Voltaire, Lesage, Diderot, Rousseau ; the last esp., for the sake of his new notes of sentiment, democracy, nature-worship, and individualism, which found such potent exponents in the life and thought of Europe and the United States. Respect should be paid

to the memoirs and the social tradition of Saint-Simon, and the contrast should be marked with Beaumarchais, who, in his wonderful comedy, *le Mariage de Figaro* (1784), touched the brilliant fabric of society with the mocking finger of imminent revolution.

Rousseau and Voltaire both died in 1778, and the next greatest name in Fr. lit. is that of Chateaubriand, whose *Génie du Christianisme*, 1802, is significant in several directions. It is the retort to the Voltairean precept of *écrasez l'infâme* (q.v.). Its aim was to prove that Christianity is the most human and humanizing of religions, and that it distinguishes favourably the products of modern as compared with ancient thought. Thus, this bk., which was publd. coincidently with the concordat between Napoleon and the Pope, reversed the conclusions of pre-Revolution philosophy, and contributed a notable part to the development of the new ideas of the Romantic Movement. It formed a stepping-stone from 1778 to 1830. Further, in itself, and in its separate episodes of *René* and *Atala*, and in other of Chateaubriand's writings, it continued and enlarged the work begun so ably by Rousseau. It freely availed itself of the avenues opened out by that original nature-worshipper and individualist, and showed the way to Byron and Victor Hugo in adventure, local colour, and foreign travel. Lastly, Chateaubriand was a critic, and the first critic truly gifted with imagination. He dealt with truths and faiths, instead of with rules and theories ; and, while he destroyed the foundation of much of the 18th-cent. sciolism, he built the surer foundations of 19th-cent. imagination. With Chateaubriand is to be mentioned mme. de Staël, whose German studies, however superficial, were sincere and novel in their time ; and we have to note, too, the social changes involved by the closure of the *salons* and the rise of political journalism. True, oratory and journalism, too, were discouraged in their turn by Napoleon ; but, meanwhile, the transition was effected which Beaumarchais had hinted at in his play.

So we come to 1830, the crucial year of *le lyrisme* in France, as the romantic triumph of modern Fr. lit. The movement, so rich with changes which were to mould the thought of the new century, was ushered in by foresightful newspapers. The *Conservateur littéraire* was active in 1819. The *Globe* appeared in 1822, and quickly attracted Sainte-Beuve to its staff. The *Muse française* was definitely literary, and it issued a kind of annual supplement, *les Annales romantiques*, from 1823 onwards, with a brilliant list of contributors drawn from the ranks of the new writers. Foremost among these was Victor Hugo, poet, dramatist, humanitarian, and the leading man of letters of the century. Hugo's *Odes* and Lamartine's *Méditations* inaugurated that revolt against convention, and against the restrictive and dead hand of classicism, which was consummated on 25 Feb., 1830, when Hugo's *Hernani* was produced at the Théâtre Française. The new gods of Romantic drama expelled the old gods in the temple of Racine. A renovated Alexandrine metre, a more elastic poetic vocabulary, a more subjective and personal psychology, a relaxation of every rule except the rule of pleasure, were among the signs which were greeted with so much enthusiasm by Gautier (in his symbolical red waistcoat) and by the rest of the Hotspurs of revolt.

We cannot follow this movement in detail. It included the criticism of Ste.-Beuve ; the romantic fiction of Dumas *père* ; the novels of Balzac, George Sand, Mérimée ; the poetry of Gautier, de Vigny, de Musset ; the ' new shudder ', as Hugo called it, of Baudelaire. It was at once artistic and natural ; and it led to developments in both kinds : to the literary impressionism of a Guy de Maupassant, and the vigorous realism of an Emile Zola, with many exponents of the sensational school between. The result was a regeneration of Fr. speech and a renewal of the Fr. spirit, comparable to the romantic movements of the 12th cent. and of the Renaissance. How the renewed spirit will avail itself of the enlarged capacities of language in the present century, our children will see. And, seeing, they will be glad that, among their fathers, there were some who were faithful and who foresaw :

The mother who gave birth to Jeanne : *
Who to her young Angelical† sprang ;
Who lay with Earth and heard the notes she sang,
And heard her truest sing them ; she may reach
Heights yet unknown of nations ; haply teach
A thirsting world to learn 'tis ' she who can'.

She that in History's Heliaea‡ pleads
The nation flowering conscience o'er the beast ;
With heart expurged of rancour, tame of greeds ;
With the winged mind from fang and claw released ;—
Will such a land be seen ? It will be seen ;—
Shall stand adjudged our foremost and Earth's Queen. . . .

The devotee of Glory, she may win
Glory despoiling none, enrich her kind,
Illume her land, and take the royal seat
Unto the strong self-conqueror assigned.
The poet-prophet who wr. this in 1898 appeals triumphantly to the custodians of the genius of France, renewed by the baptism of the Great War.

Frere, John Hookham (1769-1846) : Engl. poet, translr., and statesman ; minister at Lisbon and Madrid ; friend of Canning, and fellow-contributor to the *Anti-Jacobin* (q.v.; 1797-98) ; F.'s contributions consisting of most of the *Loves of the Triangles* and parts of the *Friend of Humanity*, etc. Wr., 1817, a small vol. in *ottava rima* (the Ital. 8-line stanza), with the eccentric name of *Prospectus and Specimen of an extended National Work, by Wm. and Robt. Whistlecraft, of Stowmarket in Suffolk, Harness and Collar Makers, intended to comprise . . . Particulars relating to King Arthur and his Round Table*, publd. by Murray.

Joan of Arc.
† The Heavenly Lover (1789).
‡ Court of Justice.

Society was surprised to discover both the nature of the poem and its author. It was an imitation of the *Morgante* of Pulci (q.v.), and it served as model to Byron (q.v.) in *Beppo* and *Don Juan*. A second part was publd. in 1818, when the cumbrous title was changed to *Monks and the Giants*. F. did not persevere in this vein, but years afterwards he inspired another Romantic poet by his influence in Paris on the Spanish duke de Rivas (q.v.). F's translns. from Aristophanes have proved of permanent value, and, with his *Theognis Restitutus*, 1842, were publd. originally at Malta, where he spent years of elegant leisure in retirement. He was a founder of the *Quarterly Review*, and not the least remarkable of his poems was a ' War-Song upon the Battle of Brunanburh ', which he wr. as a schoolboy at Eton, and which was included by G. Ellis (q.v.) in his *Specimens of the Early English Poets* (2nd. edn., 1801), with an editorial note stating that ' it was intended as an imitation of the style and language of the fourteenth century. The reader will probably hear with some surprise that this singular instance of critical ingenuity was the composition of an Eton schoolboy '. Scott (q.v.), who met F. in later life, much admired this poem. F.'s works in verse and prose were publd. in 3 vols. by his nephew, sir Bartle Frere.

Fréron, Elie Catherine (1719-76) : Fr. critic, journalist. F. founded, 1754, after one or two previous experiments, the *Année Littéraire*, which he kept going through the rest of his life against the active and passive resistance of Voltaire and the Encyclopedists (qq.v.). Voltaire attacked F. as *frélon* (' hornet ') in *l'Ecossaise*, and F. retorted on the play in the *Année*.

Frese, Jakob (1691-1728) : Swed. poet ; Finlander by birth. Wr. ' religious soliloquies ' of rare sweetness and devotional feeling. F. died too young to measure his full strength, but his *Spring Thoughts in Sickness*, written in suffering and faith, have undeniable beauty of thought and diction.

Freytag, Gustav (1816-95) : Germ. novelist. F. began his long and successful career as a playwright, and his *Journalisten*, 1862, is described as one of the best Germ. comedies of the 19th cent. But he quickly found his real *métier* in fiction, and *Soll und Haben*, 1855, established him on a level of achievement which he hardly reached again in his remaining 40 years. It may be termed the *John Halifax, Gentleman* (see s.v. Muloch) of Germany, and belongs to the same generation of the gospel of work (*Arbeit*), industrialism, and the rise of the middle-class. F. essayed a more ambitious task in a series of hist. novels, *Die Ahnen* (' The Ancestors '), 1872-80, based on his studies for his ' Pictures from the German Past ', 1859-62.

Friedrich von Hausen (d. 1190) : Germ. Minnesinger (q.v.) ; an early example of a noble kind. F. died in a crusade against the Turks.

Frimann, Claus (1746-1829) : Norse poet ; wr. unpretentious, popular songs, of the life of sea and field under the open skies of Norway, which won considerable renown : a worthy successor to Dass (q.v.).

Frischlin, Nicodemus (1547-89) : Germ. Latinist. Held chair of Lat. at Tübingen, but was drawn into whirlpool of religious strife and perished by violence after long captivity. In his happier years F. was typical of the free, plain, hard-drinking, brilliant scholars who retained the tradition of student-days and student-ways throughout their subsequent academic career, and who flourished at Germ. univ. centres. Characteristically, he transld. Aristophanes into Lat., and the spirit of the old Gk. humourist dominated the original masques and comedies which F. wr. in Lat. verse, for the entertainment of the minor court and of the common-room. His best play was *Julius Redivivus*, in which Julius Cæsar is revived with Cicero to visit the German heirs of their physical and intellectual empery.

Froben, Johannes (1460-1527) : Germ.-Swiss printer ; established his press at Basel (q.v.), 1491, and attracted Erasmus (q.v.) to that city at 3 periods of his life, including the last 2 years. F. received several kindly epistolary references from the great Dutch humanist.

Froissart, Jean (1337-c. 1410) : Fr. chronicler ; ' je suis un historien ' is his own just claim. His birth coincided with the outbreak of the Hundred Years' War between Engld. and France, and diplomacy and arms went to his making. Wr. poetry as a youth, *virelis*, *ballades*, and *pastourelles* (qq.v.), in melodious and dainty numbers, and kept his lyre in tune all his life to recommend himself to ladies in high places. His talents were quickly called to more central and serious affairs. The destruction of a Fr. fleet at Sluys, the defeat of a Fr. army at Crecy, the surrender of Calais, the victory of the Black Prince at Poitiers, and the contemporary revolt of the Fr. peasantry, known as the *Jacquerie*—these were successive events, occurring before F. was 20, which no young man of genius could witness with sluggish blood. The Peace of Brotigny, 1360, gave F. an opportunity to visit Engld., where he was welcomed by queen Philippa, his countrywoman, at the court of king Edward iii ; travelled in Engld., Scotland, and, later, in Italy and Belgium ; and spent most of his full and busy life at the courts of princes or in their atmosphere. It is fruitless to ask how far the favour of princes in the changing fortunes of war was an excellent equipment for an historian. Certainly, F. was not impartial, if by that quality is meant, scrupulous in sifting evidence, skilled in calculating its weight, and unbiased by emotion in judgment. These are later conventions of historians, alien to the romantic spirit, trained in the method and style of the Fr. *Chansons de geste* (q.v.). Other than it, and not less honourable, is consistent faithfulness to a man's own sympathies. This quality F. displayed in a pre-eminent degree. ' His one-sidedness ', says a recent critic (Snell, *P.E.L.*, iii, 347) ' gives a sort of unity to his work ' ; and the sort of unity which it gave may be gathered from an older critic, Scott (q.v.), who said of F., through the mouth of Claverhouse (*Old Mortality*, xxxv) : ' With what true chivalrous feeling he confines his beautiful expressions of sorrow to the death of the gallant and high-bred knight, of whom it was a pity to see the fall,

such was his loyalty to the king, pure faith to his religion, hardihood towards his enemy, and fidelity to his lady-love ! How he will mourn over the fall of such a pearl of knighthood. . . . But, truly, for sweeping from the face of the earth some few hundreds of villain churls, who are born but to plough it, the high-born and inquisitive historian has marvellous little sympathy '. Time has been on the side of the churls : the peasants' rising, Wat Tyler's revolt, the decimation of plague and war, are social facts of more urgent import to the modern science of history than all the glamour of chivalry. But F.'s preoccupation with the picturesque is not always or necessarily superficial. He was a chronicler of a race of court-chroniclers : Villehardouin and the sire de Joinville (qq.v.) had preceded him ; he was born and nurtured in chivalry ; a Fr. aristocrat, he saw Fr. arms, first, defeated, and, later, avenged ; he moved freely among the great personages to whom fighting-men were pawns, and he told magnificently what he saw. To him, the writing of chronicles was the prose-art of a poet or old romance. Further, he wr. of what he knew. Even in old age he was ready to make a long journey in order to seek a new fact or to correct an old impression. He re-wrote more than once the earlier portion of his *Chroniques* (to 1378), bringing to it the light of fresh evidence, or of novel points of view derived from discussion or suggestion. Its first version had been based upon, even paraphrased from, the narrative of Le Bel (q.v.), F.'s immediate predecessor, whose accounts at first hand of the surrender of Calais, the death of the Bruce, and other incidents, are still among the finest portions of the bk. But F. adapted it in later life to his own more expansive and confidential style. Briefly, his Chronicles fall into 4 parts (or bks.) : 1325-78, 1378-85, 1385-88, and 1388-1400. Moving from court to court, watching the drama of war and peace unfold itself under different aspects, F. would obviously wish to revise and even to rewrite. Hence, there are variant MSS. What had seemed true in London in 1360 might seem misleading 10 years afterwards, when F. was attached as secretary and laureate at the court of duke Wenceslas of Brabant. It is as a storyteller that F. was supreme, as a shrewd travelled man of letters, with unrivalled powers of observation, a keen eye for the striking details, a prodigious memory, and a constructive imagination, which he employed, with a talent that mellowed as he grew older, in Herodotean narrative by conversation. His prose was worthy of its romantic descent ; and, doubtless, its resources were supported by F.'s early and bright experiments in light verse of the so-called rhetorical variety (see s.v. Rhétoriqueurs). He preserved in his prose the atmosphere of Fr. chivalry, and extended its literary tradition with a skill fully equal to Malory's (q.v.). The language is rich and noble ; not too swift to be pictorial, nor too slow to be vivid ; and the new prose weapons of paragraph and pause are admirably effective. (The standard Engl. transln. is that of lord Berners, q.v., in the Tudor period, 1523-25). F. also wr. at great length through many years a verse-romance, *Méliador*, one of the very last poetic compositions in the old Arthur (q.v.)-cycle.

Fromentin, Eugène (1820-76): Fr. painter, critic. F., famous in another sphere of art as the interpreter by brush of the beauties of Algeria and the East, is the author of travelbooks on the countries which he depicted, and of a novel, *Dominique*, 1863, as striking in its way and day as the *Trilby* of our Engl. artist, du Maurier (q.v.). Wr., too, *les Maîtres d'Autrefois*, 1876, on the Dutch and Flemish schools of painting.

Froude, -i. Richard Hurrell (1803-36): Engl. theologian ; pupil of Keble (q.v.) ; joined the Oxford Movement (q.v.) ; travelled in Italy with Newman (q.v.), and contributed 8 poems, signed B., to Newman's *Lyra Apostolica*, 1836 ; wr., too, nos. 9, 59, 63, and, possibly, 35, of *Tracts for the Times*. R.H.F.'s *Remains*, 2 vols. were edited, 1838, by Keble, and are said to have ' alienated many supporters (of Tractarianism), alarmed those ignorant of history and turned the mass of the public into bitter opponents ' (*C.H.E.L.*, xii, 259), by their intransigent attitude towards the Reformation.

-ii. James Anthony (1818-94): Engl. historian ; brother of above. Wr. life of Neot for Newman's *Engl. Saints*, and, 1849, *The Nemesis of Faith*, a propaganda-bk., a copy of which was publicly burned by Wm. Sewell, White's prof. of moral philosophy at Oxford. J. A. F., turned from religious controversy to history, and became a fervent admirer and disciple of Carlyle (q.v.), who appointed him sole literary executor. In this capacity he publd. Carlyle's *Reminiscences*, 1881, and wr. various memoirs, etc., of the master and his wife, which aroused storms of more or less personal controversy in the last decades of the 19th cent. J.A.F., was editor of *Fraser's Mag.*, 1860-74, and wr. a *History of Engld.* (from Wolsey to the Armada), 12 vols., 1856-70. Of more permanent value are the essays, chiefly on Reformation topics, collected in 4 vols. of *Short Studies on Great Subjects*.

Later, he visited Australia and the West Indies, and was regius prof. of modern history at Oxford, 1892-4, in succession to E. A. Freeman (1823-92). The chief product of his chair was a vol. on Erasmus (q.v.), 1894. J.A.F., was a brilliant writer, with a particularly sympathetic style.

Fuller, Thomas (1608-61): Engl. historian ; divine. Wr. *Church History of Britain*, and other works ; most notably, The *Worthies of Engld. and Wales*, which enlarged the resources and increased the suppleness of Engl. prose. Take, e.g. the following extract from F.'s sketch of ' The Good Sea-Captain ' : ' In taking a prize he most prizeth the men's lives whom he takes ; though some of them may chance to be negroes or savages. 'Tis the custom of some to cast them overboard, and there's an end of them : for the dumb fishes will tell no tales. But the murder is not so soon drowned as the man. What, is a brother of false blood no kin ; a savage hath God to his father by creation, though not the church to his mother, and God will revenge his innocent blood. But our captain counts the image of God nevertheless his image, cut in ebony as if done in ivory '.

Note the power of ' dumb fishes ', ' innocent blood ', ' ebony . . . ivory ', etc., and it will be seen how quickly Engl. prose style has moved since Lyly (q.v.) borrowed some of his ornaments from abroad.

Furetière, Antoine (1620-88): Fr. novelist and lexicographer ; member of Fr. Academy (q.v.) 1662-85, when he was expelled for having outstripped that society by publishing his own *Dictionnaire universel*, afterwards wellknown as the *Dictionnaire de Trévoux*, in anticipation of their *Dictionnaire de l'Académie*. The precise measure of his offence has been a matter of dispute in after-days. F., who was friend and boon-companion to Boileau and Racine (qq.v.) in their youth, wr. also, 1666, *le Roman bourgeois*, a kind of *Sketches by Boz* (s.v. Dickens) of the 17th cent., more photographic than artistic.

G

Gärtner, Karl Christian (1712-91): Germ. publicist. Associated with the fortunes of the *Bremer Beiträge* (q.v.).

Gai Saber, el : the gay science of the Provençal Troubadours (s.vv. Fr. and Provençal lit.), in the early period (about the beginning of the 13th cent.) of the decline of their art from its first spontaneous efflorescence. This science, which every poet was supposed to have at his fingers'-ends, was the science of poets'-love,— that sweet passion of poetry which had its particular form of expression for every mood and tense of lovers' madness. Every approach and recoil, every move in the well-understood game, tender, or bold, or coy, had its place and proper expression in the scientific apparatus of the craft. Ovid and Virgil had been ransacked (see esp. s.v. Ovid) by these codifiers of the ' art of love ', and the works of the earlier

romancers, with their endless glorification of chivalric manners, supplemented the examples and the rules. The gay science flourished at the Floral Games (q.v.) of Toulouse, and its lovelore spread into Barcelona and the ' Gaya Sciencia ' of Spain, and eastwards through Sicily and Tuscany to Dante, Petrarch, and the Elizabethan sonneteers.

Galahad : hero of grail-episode in romance-cycle of Arthur (q.v.) ; represented at first as a direct descendant of Joseph of Arimathea (see s.v. Grail), thus ensuring for him a degree of purity adequate to the holy quest ; in this version Lancelot (q.v.) was G.'s sponsor at Arthur's court. Later, Lancelot was endowed with G.'s paternity. G. finally emerged from the unwieldly redactions of the legend in Fr. verse and prose (see s.vv. Chrétien de Troyes and Robert de Boron) as the single hero of the hallowed Grail, and, as such, his part was sifted through the fine selective process of Malory (q.v.) to the modern revival of the romance in Tennyson (q.v.). A certain Walter Map, of Oxford (d., *c.* 1209) was long credited with the invention, or first clear redaction, of this branch of the Breton tales, but the evidence for his share in it is uncertain.

Gale, Theophilus (1628-78): Engl. scholar. Wr. *The Court of the Gentiles*, 1669, and later parts, the aim of which ' is to prove that all heathen philosophy, whether barbaric or Gk., was borrowed from the Scriptures, or at least from the Jews '. G. is commonly reckoned with the Cambridge Platonists (see s.v. Plato), but Hallam (*Lit. Europe*, iii, 304) adds a little coldly : 'It is not likely that Plato would have acknowledged such a disciple '.

Galiani, Ferdinando (1728-87): It. economist and letter-writer ; attached for many years to the Neapolitan Legation in Paris, and identified himself with the life of the country of his diplomatic adoption, using the Fr. language and accepting Fr. title of *abbé*. Wr. *Dialogues sur les blès* (agricultural), which delighted Voltaire (q.v.). G. was famous in his own day as a talker and in ours as a letter-writer ; and was thus an idolized frequenter of the *salons* (q.v.) of literary-feminine Paris, which he tried to naturalize in Naples on his return. G. likewise enjoyed esteem as a student of numismatics.

Galilei, Galileo (1564-1642): It. astronomer, critic, letter-writer. It is in the last two capacities alone that G.'s name is included in this dict.: the rest belongs to the splendid history of science and, *tanto quanto*, to the shameful history of religious persecution. The facts are well known. G. constructed a telescope, 1609, and used it to observe the stars. His observations brought him into disagreement with the axioms of scholastic astronomy, and he was haled by the Inquisition to Rome (pope Paul v, 1616 ; a Renaissance pope might have proved more amenable). His plea that Holy Scripture taught salvation, not astronomy, was accepted, on condition that he ceased to touch the doctrine of Copernicus. But in 1632 he sinned again, in a dialogue *delle nuove scienze*, in which two advocates of the Copernican system win an easy victory over a Ptolemaist, who is named Simplicio, and in whom the pope (Urban viii) was induced to recognize some likeness to himself. G. was again summoned before the Holy Office, and was sent to prison in 1633, a solemn ceremony of recantation being a condition precedent to that ' mild ' penalty. It is said that, rising from his knees, G. mattered *Eppur si muove* (yet it—the earth—moves), but the story is a later invention, though not therefore less characteristic. The action of the Church was defended in an art. by W. G. Ward (1812-82), himself a Roman Catholic and a mathematician, publd. in the *Dublin Rev.*, 1871. G., who was the son of a Florentine musician, wr. essays on the *Inferno* of Dante, on the comparative merits of Ariosto and Tasso, with a strong preference for the former, original verse and other works, including some illuminating letters, publd. with those of his favourite daughter, Marie-Céleste, who died at the time of his greatest sufferings. He became blind, 1636. As controversialist, G., like Huxley in the 19th cent., had a clear and truly literary style, with the vivaciousness and picturesqueness native to Florentine writers.

Galland, Antoine (1646-1715): Fr. scholar ; Orientalist ; traveller ; prof. of Arabic. Transld., 1704-17, the *Arabian Nights' Entertainments* into Fr. (*Mille et Une Nuits*), thus introducing the eastern work into European lit., and satisfying and increasing the romantic appetite of the *grand siècle Louis quatorze*.

Gallego, Juan Nicasio (1777-1853): Span. poet ; patriot. Wr. odes and elegies ; attached to the Salamanca (q.v.) school of poetry.

Galt, John (1779-1839): Scot. novelist and miscellanist ; settled as a young man in London ; wr. about sixty bks., the most rememberable of which is one of several novels of Scot. rural life, *Annals of the Parish*, 1821. G. travelled with Byron (q.v.) in the Mediterranean, 1809, and later in life visited Canada on a financial land-company venture. The town of Galt in Ontario is named after him.

Gamez, de, Gutierre Diez (*c.* 1379-1450): Span. biographical chronicler. Wr. charming and hero-worshipful account of the life and adventures in love and war of Pero Niño (q.v.), *ed. pr.* (incomplete), 1782.

Garcilasso de la Vega (1503-36): Span. poet ; ' the prince of Spanish poets ', in the estimation of posterity ; born of noble ancestry at Toledo, where every stone, as Gongora (q.v.) said, in his monument. The family of Lasso de la Vega traced its descent from the age of the Cid (q.v.) ; and G.'s maternal grandfather was Fernan Perez de Guzman (q.v.). G. proved himself worthy of his forbears ; and his brief, illustrious career recalls, in more than their common fate of heroic death, the record of sir Philip Sidney (q.v.) in our own history. Like Sidney, G. wielded the sword and the pen (*Tomando ora la espada, ora la pluma*, as he wr.) ; and the wonder is how he found time, in the intervals of an active life, to write even the few but very perfect poems, which his contemporary and admirer, Boscan (q.v.), prepared for posth. publication, and which were piously included by Boscan's widow in the volume of her husband's remains, 1543. G. achieved what Boscan had attempted, at the instance of Navagero (q.v.), viz. the Italianization of native Span. verse-forms. The Renaissance of Span. poetry was the joint work of Boscan and G. ; but if Boscan was the pioneer, G. was the finished artist. He served the emperor Charles v, and fought in his wars. Once he incurred the royal displeasure (in consequence of a nephew's secret marriage to a maid of honour of the empress), and was imprisoned for three months. His happiest times were spent at Naples, the centre of Hispano-Ital. culture ; but wherever he went he took with him the beauty of a very gentle spirit ; and his heroic action at the assault of Muy (he died at Nice three weeks later from the effects of his wounds) was as genuine a poem of the Renaissance as any of the 38 sonnets, 3 pastoral eclogues, 5 odes, 2 elegies, and one epistle (in blank verse, q.v.), which form the bulk of his poetical remains. Rarely has so slight a harvest enjoyed so constant a renown. We may admit that his blank-verse experiment was foreign to the genius of the Span. language, and that he did not create a following for his scheme of interior rhymes; and it is true that he freely imitated Petrarch, Bembo, Ariosto, Sannazzaro (qq.v.), and their own masters, Horace and Virgil; but it was his mission and purpose as a poet to distil the essence of pastoral and eclogue into the Castilian tongue, and his rare failures merely emphasize the consummate success which he achieved. The insight of his country-men was not at fault. From the first they greeted him as a supreme artist in verse; 'the famous poet', as Cervantes called him (*Don Quixote*, ii, lviii); the head of the so-called 'learned poets', the Renaissance School of Castile, whose contact with the living Ital. masters of poetic style enabled them to attempt *in petto* the same work of reform and innovation which the Pleiad (q.v.) accomplished in France. Unfortunately, the after-history of Span. lit. (q.v.) proved the imperfect assimilation of the reforms of Boscan and G. A sort of bifurcation occurred, and Seville became the nominal centre of the more strictly Italianate School of the followers of the re-formers, while Salamanca was the centre of the more consciously national school. It should be added that G. was unlucky in his editors; or, rather, in the jealousies which pursued them. The squabbles are unedifying, and brief references are made to them s.vv. F. Sanchez and Herrera.

Garnier, Robert (1545-1601): Fr. dramatist; disciple and exemplar of the Pleiad (q.v.). More than any other dramatic writer of this epoch, not excepting Jodelle, Grévin, and La Taille (qq.v.), G. fulfilled the aspiration of Du Bellay (q.v.), the prophet of the Pleiad, to restore classic dignity to native drama, which farces and moralities had usurped. G.'s work in this direction was confined, or very nearly confined, to tragedy: his last play, *Bradamante*, as we shall see, was a comedy in its happy ending, and was described on its title-page as ' tragecomedie '; but within the sphere of tragedy, G.'s contribution to classic drama in France was of high importance, and had its influence not only on Corneille (q.v.) but likewise on the Elizabethan stage. G.'s earlier plays, *Porcia, Cornelia, Mark Antony, Hippolytus, The Troad*, and *Antigone*, were all, as their names indicate, drawn from the subject-matter of the ancients, with special reference to Euripides and Seneca; but within this group, conventional as it was, two significant observations are to be registered: i, G. perfected and standardized the employ-ment of the alexandrine metre (s.v. Alexander) in drama; ii, in his tragedies dealing with Roman subjects (*Porcie, Cornélie*, and *Marc-Antoine*), he made fuller use than had been made before of the writings of Plutarch, whom Amyot (q.v.) had just transld. Thus, ulti-mately, G.'s Roman tragedies were lit by the same light which North (q.v.) poured on that of Shakespeare (q.v.). G.'s personal influence on the Engl. stage was neither strong nor permanent; his merit lay in his guidance and direction; and it is to be noted that G. was a member of the academy of Baïf (q.v.), and

was commended, accordingly, to the school of Harvey (q.v.) in Engld. Sidney's (q.v.) sister, the countess of Pembroke, transld., 1590, G.'s *Mark Antony* into blank verse, and Kyd (q.v.) transld., 1594, his *Cornelia*; and others continued the endeavour to transplant Fr. classic drama to Engl. soil. The experi-ment only gradually declined before the fiercer onset of the romantic convention. Later, 1580, G. produced two other plays, *Sédécie, ou les Juives* (' Zedekiah, or the Jewesses ') and *Bradamante*, differing, one from the other, and both from his earlier vogue. The first was a sacred play of the victory of Nebuchadnezzar over Zedekiah, king of the Jews; and the Jewesses of the title-rôle formed the chorus. Dramas of this kind had been common in Lat., on the themes of Judith, Jephthah, the Prodigal Son, and so forth (see s.vv. Buchanan, Lat.), and G. was continuing here an innova-tion started by Jean de La Taille (q.v.). In *Bradamante*, founded on a plot from Ariosto (q.v.), G. made a further departure; the story was neither classical nor scriptural, and the Senecan (ex-Gk.) feature of a chorus was for the first time abandoned on the Fr. stage. The result was that the action of the chorus had to be distributed among the *dramatis personæ*, and thus the person of the ' confidant ' first appears. G. seems to have been somewhat diffident of the success of his theatrical percep-tion, for he warned managers that they must supply a chorus if the play were staged; but the experiment is notable, and the mixed character of the drama, which aimed at representing the human comedy, in the Dantesque sense of the word, not at relieving tragedy by comic interludes, marked a real advance in composition, and adds fresh bays to the wreath with which the work of the Pleiad is crowned.

Garrick, David (1717-79): Engl. actor; Shake-sperean; pupil of Dr. Johnson (q.v.) at Edial, and came with him to London, 1737; manager of Drury Lane theatre; designed Shakespeare festival at Stratford, 1769; his portrait painted by Reynolds, Gainsborough, Hogarth; was a leading figure in the literary, dramatic and club-life of the times; buried in West-minster Abbey.

Garth, Samuel (1661-1719): Engl. poet, physician; M.D.; physician to king George i; knt., 1714; pronounced a Lat. oration over the body of Dryden (q.v.) at the Coll. of Physicians, 1700; wr., 1699, *The Dispensary*, a satire on a medical controversy of the day, which enjoyed con-siderable vogue. G. was a friend of Addison and Pope (qq.v.), who contributed to his edn. of a transln. of Ovid, *Metamorphoses*.

Gascoigne, George (1525 (or -35) -77): Engl. poet; wr. prose-comedy, *Supposes*, 1566, after the *Suppositi* of Ariosto (q.v.), and blank-verse tragedy, *Jocasta*, in the same year, adapted from the *Phoenissæ* of Euripides. These two dramas formed the second chapter in the history in the story of dramatic art in this country (for the first chapter, see s.vv. Sackville, Udall). They were both included in G.'s *Posies* (1573 and 1575), ' gathered partly (by translation) in the fine, out-landish gardens of Euripides, Ovid, Petrarch, Ariosto, and others; and partly by invention, out of our own fruitful orchards in England '; the edn. of 1575 contained *Certain Notes of Instruction concerning the Making of Verse or Rhyme in English*, which was again, a pioneer work in its kind, followed presently by the critical treatises of W. Webbe and R. Puttenham (qq.v.) Wr., too, *The Glasse of Government*, 1575, described as a ' tragical comedy '; *The Steel Glass*, a satire, 1576, etc., and was a transitional writer between Chaucer and Spenser (qq.v.), of considerable influence in his own time.

Gaskell, Elizabeth Cleghorn (1810-65): Engl. novelist; *née* Stevenson (her father, Wm. Stevenson, 1772-1829, a nonconformist minister in Manchester, the ' Drumble ' of *Cranford*, being a compiler of the *Annual Register*); brought up at Knutsford, the ' Cranford ' of the famous novel, by an aunt; m., 1832, Wm. G., another Manchester nonconformist minister, who became a prof. at Owens Coll. (now incorporated in the univ. of that city), and a contributor to the *Hymnal* of J. Martineau (q.v.), and who d., 1884. Mrs. G.'s associations and talents brought her into pleasant contact with Dickens, Carlyle, Thackeray, C. Brontë (qq.v.), and other leading men and women of the day; and it is a fairly safe conjecture of the present writer that Samuel Bamford, who was the subject of her correspondence with Tennyson (q.v.), through the medium of John Forster, in 1849, was the original of ' Mr. Holbrook ' as a Tennysonian (in *Cranford*, ch. iv; see *Alfred Lord Tennyson : A Memoir*, 1897; i, 283-6; Tennyson called it ' the highest honour I have yet received '). Mrs. G.'s acquaintance with C. Brontë led to her writing the *Life*, 1857, of that author, included, 1905, in the definitive edn. of the works of the Brontë (q.v.) sisters, and described by Mr. C. K. Shorter, in his introduction to the vol. in that edn., as a classic, which contributes to ' solidify the reputation ' of both women novelists. It may be added that the friendship between them, begun in 1850, was cemented by an exchange of visits at Manchester and Haworth; that George Smith (q.v.), the publisher, provided a meeting-ground for both, and that the first edn. of the *Life* had to be withdrawn, owing to objections taken to certain references to living persons.

Among Mrs. G.'s novels, some of which appeared in *Household Words* and other magazines, may be mentioned *Mary Barton*, anon., 1848; *Ruth*, 1853; *Sylvia's Lovers*, 1863, which struck a more distinct social-political note of radicalism than any, and some others, including the unfind. *Wives and Daughters*, republd. from the *Cornhill Magazine* after the author's death, 1866. Much the best by common consent is *Cranford*, a short tale of feminine society in the suburb of a big commercial town, full of pathos, charm, and careful observation, ' in that style of domestic miniature-painting, which, after being sketched by Addison before the dawn of the novel proper, was brought to unsurpassable perfection by Miss Austen ' (see s.vv.; Saintsbury, *P.E.L.* xii, 125).

Gasparino of Barzizza (*c.* 1370-1431): It. humanist. Early specialist in the so-called *ars familiariter scribendi*, or Ciceronian Latinity

in letter-writing. The art became a cult, and declined into an affectation, but it was of great importance in the dawn of the Renaissance, not only as a bond between scholars, but as a discipline in style. G.'s *liber epistolarum*, was the first bk. ever printed in France (Paris, 1470).

Gassendi, Pierre (1592-1655): Fr. philosopher; prof. of mathematics at the *collège royal*, Paris. G.'s chief writings were in the sciences of physics and astronomy, and his works were written in Lat. On both accounts, his name, eminent in the history of Fr. philosophy, has hardly a place in that of Fr. lit. He was an opponent of Descartes (q.v.) and the Cartesian school. Wr. lives of Copernicus, J. Müller (Regiomontanus) (qq.v.), and others; *Institutio Astronomica*, 1647, etc.

Gato, Juan Alvarez (*c.* 1430-96): Span. poet; attached to the courts of king John ii of Castile and his children, and wr. poems on public affairs as well as the polite love-verse of his age, of which he was a deft and practised representative.

Gatty, -i. Margaret (1807-73): Engl. writer for children; daughter of rev. A. J. Scott (1768-1840), chaplain of the Victory, Nelson's flagship at Trafalgar; m. Alfred G., 1837, with whom she wr., 1842, the *Life* of her father. Founded *Aunt Judy's Magazine*, 1866, and is best known by her charming *Parables from Nature*, 1855-71.

-ii. Juliana Horatia (1841-85): Engl. writer for children; daughter of above; m. major Alex. Ewing, 1867, gave her (nick) name to *Aunt Judy*, which she edited with her mother; wr. soldiers' tales, and, particularly, *Jackanapes*, which is a classic of child-literature, too rarely exemplified in Engld.

Gautier (Pierre Jules) Théophile (1811-72): Fr. poet, critic, novelist; essentially a dilettante, and yet, though too indolent to found schools or propaganda, ' the greatest recent master of the ornate style of French ' (Saintsbury, *Hist. Fr. Lit.*, 518). G. was smitten early with the romantic spirit, and even more with the romanticist affectations (see s.vv. Lyrisme, Romance); and, at the *Hernani* production (s.v. Hugo) in Feb., 1830, he led the tumult against the classicists in the Théâtre français, and attracted the attention which he sought by his long hair and symbolical red waistcoat. Hugo, who ' tolerated red waistcoats, but did not wear them ' (Catulle Mendès), admitted the young rebel to his circle, where he became a right-hand man to the master, and a leader of the men of 1830 (see s.v. *Mil-huit* etc.). G.'s first wish had been to become a painter, and his romantic sense of word-values was assisted by a natural talent for observation and description,—practised, it must be added, in an age when this concentration on beauty in form did not seem quite proper to some tastes. *L'art pour l'art* (q.v.), the principle of art for art's sake, was a phrase of G.'s own invention; and those who followed it most loyally, such as Baudelaire (q.v.), G.'s disciple, did achieve a kind of art which was at least independent of moral restraints. The emancipation of the subject and the cultivation of style in lit., which were consummated in the 19th cent., owe much to G.'s battle for romanticism; and his talents were assisted by his experience of travel in Spain, 1840, Italy, 1850, Constantinople and Athens, 1852, and Russia, 1858. The ' marvellous times ', as he called them, of Scott, Goethe, Shakespeare, Chateaubriand, Lamartine, Hugo, entered into this poet's young blood. At the same time, G. was a journalist, and lazy. He was content to write from day to day for the *Artiste*, the *Moniteur* and the *Presse* ; and one of his best-known works, consisting of studies of 17th-cent. eccentrics, was reprinted from the first of these journals under the title of *les Grotesques*. In all, his works fill about 300 vols. The most characteristic, perhaps, are the poems, collected as *Emaux et Camées*, 1852, a title (' enamels and cameos ') which expresses exactly his method of elaborate word-painting and -engraving. *Mademoiselle de Maupin*, 1835, was a novel which anticipated the method of Flaubert (q.v.), and helped to build the bridge of picturesque natural description on which romanticism passed to naturalism : Hugo to Zola, in other words. *Les Jeune-France*, 1833, was more in the early Byronic manner, with mingled prose and verse satire. Other works included *Poésies*, 1830, *Albertus*, 1832, *Contes et Nouvelles*, travel-books, dramatic criticism, etc., and a kind of new Lesage and Honoré Balzac (qq.v.) romantic-comic mixture, entitled *Capitaine Fracasse*, 1863.

Gawain : hero of the romance-cycle of Arthur (q.v.), and in earlier redactions hardly second to Arthur himself in noble and knightly qualities ; ' the flower of courtesy '. The chief authority is the poem, *Sir Gawain and the Green Knight* (c. 1370), an anon. Engl. verse-romance of exceptional merit ; edited at Oxford, 1925, by Tolkien and Gordon. (See, too, s.v. Pearl).

Gay, John (1685-1732) : Engl. dramatist, fabulist; friend of Pope (q.v.) and Swift (q.v.), who collaborated with him in *Trivia*, 1716, a mock-heroic poem on the dangers of the streets of London, and suggested to him the theme of *The Beggar's Opera*, 1728. This play, which satirized the Ital. opera (q.v.), and which is described as a Newgate pastoral, was the one conspicuous success of G.'s lit. life, and has been successfully revived after 200 years. As a librettist, G. gave hints to sir W. S. Gilbert, the Savoyard of the 19th cent. ; as a writer of *Fables*, 1727 and 1738, he enjoys good repute, and some of his songs have permanent vogue. He took a part, at Pope's instigation, in the reaction against the pastoral verse derived by A. Philips (q.v.) from Spenser.

Gaza, Theodorus (1400-75) : teacher of Gk. in Italy. Fugitive from Thessalonica, G. first lectured at Ferrara, where his pupils included Rudolf Agricola (q.v.). He became prof. of Gk. at Rome, and made transcripts of the *Iliad*, still preserved at Venice and Florence. Wr. Gk. grammar, used by Budé and Erasmus (qq.v.), and Lat. translns. of parts of Aristotle (q.v.).

Gebauer, Jan (1838-1907) : Czech scholar; colleague of Masaryk (b. 1850 ; later, first president of the new republic of Czecho-Slovakia) at the restored Czech univ. at Prague. Wr. monumental ' Czech Grammar on Historical Principles ', and is accounted a leader of the

positive and national movement, which was to have important consequences in politics as well as in art and letters. G. was one of the chief scholars who exposed the forgery of the so-called MSS. of *Králové Dvůr* (q.v.) and *Zelená Hora*, dating from *c.* 1817.

Geel, Jacob (1787-1862) : Dutch critic ; bookseller. Transld. Sterne's (q.v.) *Sentimental Journey* and Scott's (q.v.) *Lady of the Lake*. Wr. essays on style and diction which prepared the way for the school of romantic hist. fiction.

Geibel, Emanuel (1815-84) : Germ. poet ; studied philology in Berlin, where he met Chamisso (q.v.) and his circle ; travelled in Greece, where he pursued his archæological researches ; received a pension from king Fredk. Wm. iv. of Prussia, and was invited to Munich by king Maximilian ii of Bavaria, where he led the literary movement ; returned to Prussia, 1868, and greeted the union of Germany in his *Heroldsrufe*, 1871. G. was a facile writer of patriotic lyrics, who won royal favour by his opposition to Herwegh (q.v.), and whose sympathy with Freiligrath (q.v.) did not extend to F.'s revolutionary verse. He may, perhaps, be called a fashionable poet, and the fashions have changed, in epic, dramatic and lyric poetry. But his influence was considerable, esp. in Munich ; his sweetness, if sometimes cloying, was genuine, and his name is likely to live.

Geijer, Erik Gustav (1783-1847) : Swed. historian ; sociologist. G.'s ' History of the Swedes ' and his treatise on the Poor Law were both transld. into Engl. in the first half of last cent., and he collaborated with Afzelius (q.v.) in the editorship of the periodical *Svenska Folkvisor*, 1814-16.

Geiler, Johann, of Kaisersberg (1445-1510) : Germ. divine. Resided at Strassburg, where his sermons attracted immense audiences. Preached a series of 112 discourses on the *Narrenschiff* of Brandt (q.v.) ; his style departed from that of the mystics (s.v. Tauler), and returned to the older, cruder, and more sledge-hammer style of Berthold of Regensburg (d. 1272), the most famous preacher of his age.

Gellert, Christian Furchtgott (1715-69) : Germ. fabulist ; dramatist. Studied at Leipsic univ., where he became prof. of rhetoric. His lectures attracted large audiences and much enthusiasm. Deserted Gottsched's (q.v.) standard to help found the *Bremer Beiträge* (q.v.), with other members of the forward school. His reputation spread far beyond univ. circles, and his genial intelligence and brilliant talents recommended him to readers in all classes : a letter is quoted in which G. wr. that his highest ambition was to serve the largest number of intelligent readers rather than a narrow circle of scholars ; his *Letters*, with an essay on the epistolary art, were collected, 1751. As Ebert (q.v.) was influenced by Young (q.v.), so G. was influenced by Richardson (q.v.) ; or perhaps it is more correct to say that the softer graces of Engl. lit. at this date availed to correct the dogmatism of the purely rational point of view introduced by the Aufklärung (q.v.) in Germany. G.'s *obbligato* Richardsonian novel was entitled ' The Life of the Swedish Countess of G—— ', 1747-48, and was a quaint amalgam of the humdrum morality of his Engl. master and the romantic decadence typified by Lohenstein (q.v.) ; still it ranks, where it is remembered, as a pioneer-work in Germ. domestic fiction. Still less memorable to-day were G.'s comedies and pastorals, composed in the Gottsched tradition ; and he lives chiefly as a writer of fable (q.v.). His verse *Fables and Tales,* 1748, became a model for his successors, and were themselves founded on the model of La Fontaine (q.v.). With Rabener's (q.v.) satires, they comprise the best product of native Saxon talent in this age. King Fredk. the Great of Prussia (q.v.) praising all things classic in 1780, declared that ' only in the little class of Fable have we had a Gellert to rank with Phædrus and Æsop ' ; and Goethe (q.v.) wr., *àpropos* the fables, ' to believe in Gellert, virtue, and religion is one and the same thing with our public '. There is a simple charm in these compositions which has the quality of permanence. Wr., too, treatise *de comœdia commovente,* 1751, i.e., the comedy of manners (See s.v. *comédie larmogante*) as opposed to the comedy of types of Molière, e.g. ; thus, G.'s plays indicated a prospect of genuine advance from the standards of Gottsched towards those of Lessing.

Gelli, Giovanni, Battista (1498-1563) : It. writer of dialogues, known as the learned tailor of Florence. G. combined a store of classical knowledge with his native Florentine wit, and his *Circe,* 1549, is an amusing tale of the efforts of Ulysses to persuade his companions to resume human shape ; they all, with one exception, prefer the forms imposed by the enchantress, and Dryden's (q.v.) *Hind and Panther,* may owe something to this spirited dialogue. In 6 disputations, *Capricci del Bottaio,* 1546-8, between Giusto and his soul, G. touches with spontaneity and wit on problems of religion, morality and letters.

Gemistos, Georgios ; Plethon (1356-1450) : Gk. neo-Platonist; stimulated learning and humanism in Italy. Born at Byzantium ; settled at Mistra (Sparta) in the Peloponnese, where he held a magistracy under the moribund Empire, which fell finally just after his death ; was also engaged in teaching, and embodied in a Gk. work called *The Laws* a new system of philosophy and politics. Profound scholar though G. was, he was over 80 years old before his influence was communicated outside the Morea. In 1439 he attended the Council of Florence, and ancient and modern writers vie with one another in their descriptions of the effect produced upon the eager humanists of Italy by the old man eloquent from Greece. Thus Ficino (q.v.), who was a boy at the date of the Council, wr. in after-life of the fervour breathed by G., and of how it inspired Cosimo de Medici with the conception of a Florentine academy (q.v.). This was duly founded in course of time, with Ficino as its teacher of Platonism, and it proved of immense value in stimulating the cause of Hellenism and culture in the Florentine republic. Thus, bp. Creighton (*History of the Papacy*), writes : ' Instead of attending the council, he [Gemistos] poured forth his Platonic lore, and uttered dark sentences to a circle of eager Florentines ' ; and thus Symonds (*Ital. Renaissance,* ii, 149) :

' hanging upon the lips of the eloquent, grave, beautiful old man, who knew so much that they desired to learn, they called him Socrates and Plato in their ecstasy '. He indulged their fancy by using the name Pletho (Plethon) in lieu of its synonym Gemistos, for the sake of its likeness to Plato (q.v.), of whom he became the foremost exponent and champion, in opposition to the traditional Aristotelianism of the Church. Lit. is not much interested in the ensuing controversy, the good of which was the extended study necessarily devoted to both authors, but the evil of which was the immoderate tone of personal invective which was employed. G. returned to Mistra in 1441, where his last years were embittered by the polemic waged against his *Laws,* and its doctrines, by Gennadios, afterwards patriarch of Constantinople. He was buried at Mistra, but his remains were removed to Rimini in 1455. As a mystic and neo-Platonist, as the *causa causans* of the Academy of Florence, and as a Hellenist in the dawn of humanistic zeal, G.'s name is always memorable in Europe.

Gemmingen, von, Otto (1755-1836) : Germ. playwright ; associated with the national theatre at Mannheim, where Schiller's *Räuber* was produced, under the direction of Dalberg (q.v.). Wr. a family-drama, *der deutsche Hausvater* (cf. Diderot, *Père du famille*), which had some influence on the stage of his day.

Generation of May : Czech school, or group, of poets, dating from the middle of the 19th cent., and attached by their own choice to the protection of Mácha (q.v.), whose vol., *May,* supplied the title for their collected miscellany and for their school. Their chief representative was Neruda (q.v.), and, passing over lesser members of the group, we may mention here Karolina Světlá, the pen-name of Johanna Mužáková (1830-99), whose novels, partly under the influence of G. Sand (q.v.), were the first feminist novels in Bohemia.

Gentillet, Innocent (16th cent.) : Fr. jurist ; Huguenot. Wr., 1576, *Discourse on the Means of well governing and maintaining in Good Peace a Kingdom or other Principality ; divided into Three Parts ; against Nicholas Machiavel, Florentine.* This tractate included a selection of maxims from Machiavelli's (q.v.) *Il Principe,* directed to blacken its writer's reputation, and long original excursuses were added. The attack produced a great effect, esp. in countries with experience of masterful rulers, and the *Discourse* served as a text-book of psychology to dramatists representing such rulers on the stage (cf. Shakespeare's *Richard iii* ; G.'s treatise was transld. into Engl., 1577, by Simon Patericke). The orig. of ' Machiavellism ', in the sense of an unscrupulous lust for power, as a moral and political concept, may be dated from G., who attributed the massacre of St. Bartholomew (1572) to the spread of that pernicious doctrine.

Gentz, von, Friedrich (1764-1832) : Germ. critic ; transld., 1793, Burke's (q.v.) *Reflections on the Revolution in France,* and was on the patriotic side of Arndt and Fichte (qq.v.) ; gradually leaned, however, to the policy of Metternich (q.v.), and made his home in Austria.

Geoffrey of Monmouth (12th cent.); Welsh historiographer. Born at Monmouth, nephew of archdeacon of Llandaff; succeeded to his uncle's position, and died at St. Asaph's, 1154, as bp. of the see. Wr., c. 1136, Lat. *historia regum Britanniæ*, which had an immense influence on contemporary romancers (s.v. Romance), by colouring the early annals of Britain for the glorification of her Norman conquerors with the stolen lustre of a storied past. G. professed to rely on the authority of an old Welsh bk., but it cannot be denied that he was an early and audacious specimen of literary impostor. He established Brut (Brutus, descendant of Aeneas of Troy) as progenitor of the British; and contaminated the lore of king Arthur (q.v.) out of all likeness to Celtic legend. He combined Merlin (q.v.) with Ambrosius, a 5th-cent. prophet, mentioned by Nennius, and confused both with Myrrdhin, a Welsh sage; thus naturalizing the predictions of Arthur's victories, death, and return. G.'s 'history' had an immediate success, as is testified by the fact that 35 MS. versions of it are in the British Museum Library alone; and some legendary tales in the Arthuriad, such as those of Cymbeline, Lear and Locrine, familiar to Shakespeare, for example, might have been mislaid or misprized except for G.'s inventive skill. It will be observed that G. may be described either as a romancer or an historian; and there is an epoch in every nation's history where the two parts coalesce. Noting this, prof. G. S. Gordon, writing on *The Trojans in Britain*, 1923, said that he would ' like to see the Fables of the Britons restored to their place in the first chapter of our histories '.

Geoffrin, Marie Thérèse Rodet (1699-1777): Fr. literary hostess; her *salon* in Paris, was one of the most famous in the 18th cent., and was frequented by Stanislas Poniatowski, among others, later, king of Poland, and, later still, the victim of the first partition of Poland, 1772. Mme. G. was a singular example of a devout woman of learning, who entertained the Encyclopedists (q.v.) as well as their adversaries with equal hospitality.

George of Trebizond (1395-1484): Georgius Trapezuntius; Gk. scholar and copyist. A native of Crete; pupil of Vittorino (q.v.); reached Venice, c. 1430. Became a papal secretary, and was employed by pope Nicholas v in translg. Gk. classics into Lat., his share including Plato's *Laws* and Aristotle's *Rhetoric*. He took a not particularly enlightened part in the not particularly enlightening controversy, which crossed into Italy from Greece about mid-15th cent., between the champions of Aristotle and Plato; joined Gaza (q.v.) in an attack on Plato and Plethon (s.v. Gemistos), but far exceeded his leader's brief. Bessarion, (q.v.) replied *adversus calumniatorem Platonis*, 1469. G.'s writings on rhetoric were publd. at Venice in 1522.

Gerhardt, Paul (1607-76): Germ. sacred lyrist; of the Luther type, and by general consent not surpassed by his master in the composition of pure church-hymns, directed to the immediate heart.

German Literature: It is not within our scope to explore the obscure beginnings and the confusion of tongues in which Germ. lit., as we know it, and as covering the German-speaking peoples, took its start. Scholars have divided the early period into three main epochs, designated respectively the Old High German, prior to the 11th cent., the Middle High German, commencing about 1050, and the New High German, dating from about 1350. Into these philological distinctions, and into the remoter regions of comparative philology, mapped out by Bopp (q.v.) and the brothers Grimm (qq.v.), we need not enter here; nor shall we pause at the theory of W. Scherer (1841-86), as to a periodic law in Germ. lit., with productive times at intervals of 600 years. According to this hypothesis, there would have been a florescence about 600 A.D., anterior to the flowers which were gathered at about the years 1200 and 1800. But the lay of Hildebrand (8th cent.) is the only survival of such Old High Germ. fecundity; and the limits of the present vol. preclude an examination of this famous heroic ballad.

The truth, is, that Germ. lit. has had an interrupted and spasmodic life, owing to social and political causes which operated adversely to art; and Scherer's periodic law was probably invented *ex-post-facto*. We may distinguished here 7 stages in the development of our subject: (i) From the earliest times to Charlemagne (q.v.); (ii) from Charlemagne to the opening of the 12th cent., covering the defeat of paganism by Christianity, and the dominance of the church in lit.; (iii) the blossoming of Chivalry from 1100 to about 1320; (iv) Guild-verse, or the rise of civic lit. (see s.v. Town); (v) the Reformation, from 1500 to about 1625; (vi) Academic lit., and the period of apprenticeship to foreign models, from 1625 to about 1750; leading to the *Geniezeit* or *Sturm und Drang* (q.v.; say, 1767-87), included in (vii) Modern Germ. lit., from 1750 to 1832 (death of Goethe), or a little later. As to the lit. since that later date, we may quote the statement of prof. Courthope *Life in Poetry, Law in Taste*, 1901; p. 276): ' It is certainly a striking fact that the establishment of the German Empire has not been followed by a period of characteristic creation . . . in the arts of Painting and Poetry. . . . Of what is passing in the poetical imagination of the German people, as distinct from the mind of the German State, we know nothing, for in poetry the German soul is at present silent '.

Of these 7 periods, (i) and (ii) lie outside the scope of the present survey. In (iii), the period of chivalry—court-epic and love-lyric (' Minnesong ', q.v.)—with its centre at 1200 or thereabouts, we come to the names of Veldeke (q.v.), who is counted as a son of the Netherlands; of Wolfram (q.v.) of Eschenbach, who raised the story of Parzival (see s.v. Percival), long afterwards re-animate in Wagner's opera, ' now by phrase, now by verse effect, now by the indefinable magic of sheer poetic handling, out of ordinary ways into ways that are not ordinary ' (Saintsbury, *P.E.L.*, ii, 255), and who introduced a deep spiritual meaning into the old-time adventurous tales; of Hartmann (q.v.) of Aue, who gilded the ' golden legend ' (q.v.), and of other romancers and songsters. The most notable among the singers, was undoubtedly Walther (q.v.) von der Volgelweide, ' Walter of the Birds'-Meadow ', by common consent, the greatest lyric poet of medieval Europe. His was really a remarkable age, in which the inalienable mystery and magic of Germ. river and wood, immemorially clinging to the legends refashioned during this era in the *Nibelungenlied* (q.v.), brought a new but permanent and characteristic change, in the direction of sentiment and seriousness, into the tales of chivalry and gallantry acquired by Germany from France, esp. from Chrestien (q.v.) de Troyes. But, great as the achievement was, in Wolfram's stories and Walther's songs, Germ. genius, in retrospect at any rate, seemed to rush through the period ; and already in Gottfried (q.v.) of Strassburg, whose *Tristan* is among the major works, a note of transition is discerned.

That note took two main directions, each more realistic in its tendency. While the old lilt of the courtly lyric was retained, instead of knightly passions the poets sang more openly of village amours. The peasant in his cottage was preferred to the knt. and dame of Troubadour tradition. Thus, Minnesong was assimilated to folksong, and the court-epos began to merge in novelette and historiette. (See s.vv. Neidhart, Wernher). At the same time, the towns were becoming centres of busy works and days, and more mechanical verse fashioned by workmen in their guilds displaced the spontaneous gush of simple delight in flower and song. So Meistersong was developed out of Minnesong. (See s.vv., and also s.vv. Court, Town). Both aspects of the change illustrate what a Germ. historian describes as the sapping of *Sinnlichkeit* (sensuousness) by *Sittlichkeit* (consciousness). It was perhaps a combination of the two qualities which made Germany a fertile soil for lay and religious mysticism (q.v.), culminating in Thomas (q.v.) à Kempis.

The transition to the new period (iv) gives occasion for a good deal of ' tall ' writing in the works of Germ. historians. Thus, we read of the springing of the strings of the lyre, and the close of the reign of the goddess Fancy. A simpler explanation of a change which was gradual and natural has been found in the substitution of foot-soldiery for horsemen, and consequently of pedestrian for chivalric deeds and songs. Prof. Ker (*Epic and Romance*, 1908, p. 4) writes that ' the victory of the Norman knights over the English axemen [at Hastings] has more than a fanciful or superficial analogy to the victory of the new literature of chivalry over the older forms of heroic narrative ' ; and the decaying chivalry was superannuated in its turn and displaced in industrial Germ. cities by more sober and burgherly measures. Anyhow, whether this explanation be deemed over-fanciful or not, we may select Frauenlob (see s.v. Heinrich von Meissen) as a type of the transition.

One word about Meistersong in general, Frauenlob and others were Meistersinger in the primary sense of that term. They were bound, that is to say, to compose *in verba magistri* ; to take a master-Minnesinger (Walther, Wolfram, or another) as their model. But presently this obligation was weakened,

and the master-title gradually acquired a new trade-qualification. By the time that the Meistersinger-guilds were fully flourishing in the 15th cent., the Meistersinger meant a master-tailor, or master-weaver, and so forth, who was also at the head of a craft-school of song. The value of these schools was more indirect than immediate. Except only Sachs (q.v.), they fathered no great men of letters ; but they spread a love of letters among little men which only awaited the magic of impregnation. Moreover, the commercial links between Germ. and Ital. cities brought Ital. culture into Germany through the poetic activities of her manufacturing classes. This, too, was the period of the *Volkslied* (q.v.), or popular song, or ballad (q.v. ; the art-ballad, not its presumptive heroic ancestor of that name), treating the common themes of bird, and leaf, and bud, of a man's way with a maid, as well as of the old heroic tales, the local battles (Sempach, 1386 ; Näfels, 1388, etc.) and sea-fights of the day, and the sacred themes of *Gottesminne* (the desire for God). Lastly, we have to note the development of Germ. prose by translators of the romantic tales, and the stimulus given to humanism (q.v.) by Gutenberg's invention of printing (q.v.) in the middle of the 15th cent.

So we reach the labours of the humanists. Writing mainly in Lat., they began to spread the glory of Gk. learning from a date which may be fixed (for convenience) at 1348, when king Charles iv founded the univ. of Prague. Soon, they swarmed at Germ. schools and universities, and scholars as universally respected as Celtes, Pirkheimer, Muth (and the fiery, young Erfurt ' poets '), Wimpheling, Reuchlin, Agricola (qq.v.), and others, led, by their concentration on the new learning and its criticism of the old sacred writings, to (v) the period of the Reformation, with Martin Luther (q.v.) at its head.

Luther's work as a hero of the Germ. nation rested partly on the labours of the mystics and humanists who were his predecessors and contemporaries, and was aided by, though it overshadowed, the scholarship of such lieutenants as Hutten and Melanchthon (qq.v.). Briefly, apart from purely theological writings, and from the less pure lit. of controversy, with which theology was so helplessly confused, Luther's contribution to letters consisted in his new transln. of the Bible (q.v.), effected, not, as previously, from the Lat. Vulgate, but from the Hebr. and Gk. originals ; in his magnificent additions to sacred popular song (hymns) ; and in his standardization of a common Germ. language. So strong was the influence of his personality that Germ. lit. of the Reformation-era means little more than the works of Luther, his supporters and opponents ; and it is to be remarked at once that it was really not till the 18th cent. that the nation was able to throw off the pre-occupying burden of religious problems. The evidence to this fact may be drawn from every department of lay letters, in which the bias of theology prevailed. Thus, Fischart, (q.v.), the leading satirist of the 16th cent., hated the Jesuits too bitterly to do full justice always to his great gifts ; and, generally, the popular consciousness, somewhat suddenly released in consequence of the social disintegration, expressed itself more coarsely and more narrowly than happier times might have approved, or than less distraught peoples actually achieved. Folkbook, farce, satire and folly—in *Faust, Fortunatus, Grobian, Eulenspiegel* (qq.v.) and their like—flourished and multiplied. Advance was marked in dramatic composition, particularly in Lat. school-plays. Outside the politico-theological arena, or, at least, as far removed from it as possible, men of science, such as Copernicus and Kepler, were adding to the knowledge of mankind. But the seamy side of Germ. letters was turned upwards. ' It was not in her casual and fitful wooing of beauty that Germany caught the attention of the world, but when she grappled with ugliness, plunging breast-high in the slough and derisively impaling its creeping population of foul things ' (Herford, *Lit. Relations between Engld. and Germany in* 16*th cent.*, xxviii ; prof. Herford's dictum is, of course, not to be read as applying more widely or to a longer period of time than its actual context admits) ; and the more gracious movements, shading into the next period, towards a true Germ. Renaissance, on the lines of Engl. drama and Fr. lyric, and not merely a partially Hellenized Reformation, were interrupted by the Thirty Years' War, 1618-1648, appalling alike in the preparation for it, in the course of it, and in its effects. This catastrophe, which is compared by native historians to the earlier invasion of the Huns and the later invasion of Napoleon, put back the clock of Germ. culture for nearly 2 centuries.

It was due to the consequences of this war on the capacity and character of the Germanic peoples that, in our next period (vi), Academic lit., no more striking personality appeared to take the lead in lit. than Opitz (q.v.), who was, at best, a Ronsard (q.v.) *manqué*. The chief merit of Opitz resides in the stimulus which he gave to the formation of literary societies ; for these, though they exaggerated their zeal for linguistic and metrical reform, were serviceable on the whole to the cause of a purer taste. It is to be remarked that, with the foundation of these academies, the centres of lit. began to shift from the south to the north of Germany. War and peace estopped the honourable lead of Nuremberg and Strassburg, and brought Hamburg and Königsberg, for instance, more prominently to the fore. The so-called Silesian Schools (q.v.) likewise took their rise in this epoch. It is a time which cannot be reviewed without a sense of poignant regret at the mournful fate of what should have been a powerful nation. The wars of religion, merging in territorial wars, and in what was almost worse, territorial treaties, withered culture in its bed. The winds were not tempered to it, nor might it expand in the sun. No fit or full opportunity, equal to the nation's capacity, was afforded for the union of the beauty of the southern Renaissance with the strength of the northern Reformation ; and Germany was abandoned to the melancholy contemplation of the comparative decay of her own powers in the ignobleness of a Gryphius and a Grimmelshausen (qq.v.), at the very time that Tasso, Cervantes,

Shakespeare and Molière were born of that union in other countries. The period was marked by imitative fiction, borrowed from Fr. translns. of the Span. ; by some genuine indignation of satirists, such as Logau, at the obsequiousness of the Germ. nation to foreign manners, but by little new, little true, and still less great.

It is good to get away from such performances and to reach the strenuous, heroic epoch of reconstruction and self-esteem in the first half of the 18th cent. The impetus came from isolated thinkers. There was no focus of German thought, and its brief period of national power was independent of central guidance. The patronage of letters exercised by Fredk. (q.v.) the Great of Prussia, who acceded in 1740, belongs more to the history of Fr. lit. (q.v., and see s.v. Voltaire), than of Germ. But the wind blew where it listed ; and cleansing breaths of rationalism from Engld. and Holland and of individualism from France blew their wholesome influences across the sky of a future puissant people, and enabled them to prepare the splendour which illumined that sky before the century's close ; and we may concur with the verdict of a native historian of Germ. lit. : ' How powerful and rapid must the development have been which produced a Goethe and a Schiller within a bare hundred years of the tumid bombast of a Lohenstein' (Biese, i, 429). The time of this change is known in Germ. history as the *Aufklärung* (q.v.), and no better term can be found to describe the signs of clearing-up, brightening, and enlightenment, associated with the names of Leibniz and Spener (qq.v.) on the twin lines of rationalism and pietism. To the philosophic influence was added the poetic. Pope's *Pastorals* and Thomson's *Seasons* gave a lead to Germ. nature-poetry, and Brockes inaugurated the new spring. The bleak winter went out in storm. The literary feud between the Swiss and German schools, so-called from their headquarters respectively at Zurich and Leipsic, though it took too personal and critical a form, was really a feud between the forces of Lat.-Fr. neo-classicism and Engl.-Teutonic sensibility to the nascent romantic movement. The leader of the Leipsic group was Gottsched, the Saxon Boileau, a heroic defender of the breach, and a pathetic figure in old age, by virtue of his obstinacy in resistance and of his gradual loss of following. This war of critics and reviewers, while it was marked by little creative power, cleared the air from the gathered miasma of alien dust and native dirt, and introduced the giants of the 18th cent. in period (vii) of our preliminary survey. Klopstock's high and mighty line, pealing the organ-notes of conduct through the stately hexameters of the *Messias* ; Wieland's fancies and faery, and his sensuous response to the ' wood-notes ' of Shakespeare's orchestra ; Bürger's borrowings from Percy, and his restorings in over-running measure to Coleridge and Scott : the Ossianic return to nature ; the Richardsonian fiction of psychology ; the Rousseauan breach with the ordnance-surveyors of Parnassus , the extraction of a purer Hellenism from the decadent neo-classicism, in Winckelmann's revelation of Gk. art : all this action, reaction, and interaction of new passion, new sentiment, and new feeling, led through Herder and Lessing to the Germ. world-literature, to the age of ' heaven-storming ' genius, to the classic heights to which Goethe and Schiller rose, and to a sudden flowering of romance in the desert of dreariness which the Reformation had ultimately introduced. Kant and his successors in philosophy ; Schiller, the Schlegels, Novalis ; but, above all and before all, Goethe : the Goethe of *Götz* and *Werther* in the 18th cent., of *Tasso* and *Iphigenie* on the border, and of *Faust* across the border, of the 19th ; the Goethe of *Dichtung und Wahrheit*, the most remarkable self-revelation of any age. The administration of the Court Theatre at Weimar by Goethe and Schiller from the date of their reconciliation in 1794 till Schiller's death in 1805 is a period of poetic production as great, within its brief duration, as any in modern history ; nor is the impression diminished by acknowledging the lavish debt which was owed to Fr. example, and esp. to Voltaire and Rousseau ; and Goethe's *Faust, Part i*, 1808, is one of the greatest single poems which the lit. of Europe has produced. It is an epic-drama of heaven and hell, as Dante's *Comedy* and Milton's *Paradise Lost* are dramatic-epics of the same regions ; and the humanity of Goethe's poem fully matches that of the epicists. Out of the old folk-tale of Faust, who made his pact with the devil, is wrought an immense tragic history of human longing and human disillusion ; and we may subscribe to the opinion of a Germ. critic, that ' there is no other philosophical poem of equal poetic power ; there is no other masterpiece of poesy of equal depth of thought ' (R. Meyer, *Goethe*, 1898 ; 451, 453). In Germ. lit., this masterpiece is supreme ; but its reconciliation of the warring hosts of reason and faith—or of Rationalism and Pietism, to give them their secondary names,—its transformation of thought, which consummated, while it corrected, the world-wide effects of the earlier Reformation, was, philosophically, the concurrent work of Kant, the Luther of the late 18th cent. He it was, who, by making every man's mind a seat and throne of the moral law, helped to restore that national self-consciousness and that sense of personal responsibility for the dignity of mankind, which inspired Goethe and Schiller in their great years of common work at Weimar, and which communicated to the creative powers of Europe a stimulus as quickening as, if not more quickening than, that of the contemporary Fr. Revolution.

The exploration of antiquity by Herder, Winckelmann, and Lessing, and the classical revival associated with lit. at Weimar, led by normal stages to the cultivation of Romance (q.v.) ; and a prominent intermediate voice between Kant's philosophy and the lit. of the Early Romanticists was that of J. G. Fichte. He was the author of *The Science of Knowledge*, 1794, and of the stimulating doctrine, more defensible as stimulus than as conclusion, of what the mystics teach us to call the creation of the Outer by the Inner, or what metaphysicians call the creation of the *non-Ego* by the

Ego. Observing the distinction, emphasized by R. M. Wernaer (*Romanticism and the Romantic School in Germany*, New York, 1910), in modification of Heine (*die Romantische Schule*, 1832) and of G. Brandes (*Main Currents*, ii, E.T., 1902), between the earlier and later exemplars of the Romantic movement in the 19th cent. in Germany—the *Früh-* and *Spätromantik*—, we may note the first centre of the Romance-movement in Berlin, where the brothers Schlegel started their *Athenœum* in 1798, the year of *Lyrical Ballads*. Thenceforward, in differing ways and in various cities—Jena and Heidelberg, for instance,—the Schlegels, Tieck, ' Novalis ' (Hardenberg), ' Jean Paul ' (Richter), Hölderlin, Wackenroder, Schleiermacher, Schelling, and others, handed on the torch of Romance to the younger group, Brentano, Arnim, Kleist, Uhland, Hoffmann, and others, including Heine himself, whom neither cynicism nor Paris could make other than a German Romanticist. The development of thought in Hegel and Schopenhauer, and the decline of the Romantic attempt to create a new Inner of the spirit, and to reconcile it with the new Outer revealed by science, with its consequent lapse into narrower by-ways of affectation, belong to a later period. Before we reach it, two factors should be noted, which characterized the Romantic triumph in Germany. One was the dominance of women, and the other was the revelation caused in Germany by new acquaintance with Shakespeare. Such women as the wives of the brothers Schlegel (Caroline and Dorothea), with their tragic adventures and their brilliant gifts ; the women beloved by Goethe at every stage of his long career, and others in literary history at this time, exercised an influence which extended beyond the homes and *salons* which they adorned. It made itself felt in the lit. itself, and the sensuous note of feminity which such a romance as *Lucinde* (by F. Schlegel)—one among several—gave to the *ego*-motive of Goethe's *Wilhelm Meister*, was Romantic by association rather than by descent. It adds little to the dignity of the Romanticists. It expressed a selfish detachment from the large affairs of human life which is difficult to extenuate or to defend. The re-birth of Shakespeare in Germany at the end of the 18th cent. (1797-1801), was almost wholly the single-handed work of A. W. Schlegel and his accomplished wife ; and the influence which the new Germ. Shakespeare exercised, as the prime exemplar of the critics' principles, is hardly to be exaggerated. We might dwell at very great length on this time of the flowering of Romance, and of the influence communicated by Germ. thought, through mme. de Staël and Heine in Paris, through Coleridge, Carlyle, and others in Engld. Many vols. have been written on this subject ; the best, perhaps, is that by Haym (*die Romantische Schule*, 2nd. edn., 1906). But the essential point to note is the difference before and after the War of Liberation (1813-14). The early Romantics had tended towards the precipice of *ego*-mania ; the later Romantics were taught by Napoleon and anti-Napoleonism to sow their whimsy with wheat. H. von Kleist (q.v.), though he died by his own hand, did not perish *apraktos* in this sense. He turned into a more fertile channel the stream of Romantic thought; he diverted it from its narrowing bed into the ways that led to the open sea. An altruistic purpose consecrated the conclusions from the doctrine of individualism. It was as though the 'blue flower' of Novalis—the poet's self-possession in the poetic life—were changed for the 'white flower of a blameless life,' worn nobly in the public eye. The Romantic method, in a word, was made the servant instead of the master of its practitioners. This period, into which Goethe survived with his vigour still unabated, is distinguished chiefly by the name of Arndt (q.v.), with whom may be named the brothers Grimm, Brentano, Uhland, Heine, Grillparzer, and others. In this phase, it perished untimely. Royal reaction, ministerial disfavour, and the official suspicion of liberal ideas—the more abominable at headquarters, because of the recent example of the Fr. Revolution,—stifled the young shoots of lit., and scattered its seeds abroad. Metternich (q.v.) was virtually dictator in Germany, and his hand was heavy. Grimm, e.g., was dismissed from his professoriate, and Heine was an exile from his dear 'fatherland'. The momentary promise of a national lit. was ground under an iron heel, which gradually extended its hold.

We shall not pursue this sketch beyond the first quarter of the 19th cent. The revolution of 1848, the wars of 1864-71, the military rule of 1871-1914, comprise a period of political changes inimical on the whole to art and letters. The ideals of Kant and Goethe, cleansed of the grosser accretions which had gathered round the work of Luther, did not flourish under the new conditions. Richard Wagner at the beginning of the Empire, Sudermann and Hauptmann towards its close, are not enough to redeem it from ineffectiveness, or from an addiction to foreign models. We think in Engld. alone of Dickens, Browning, Tennyson, Ruskin, Meredith, as great imaginative writers, and we find no names to compare with them in Germany. Scholarship, commentary, research: these were Germany's gifts to the literary culture of the 19th cent., since the brief but glorious epoch when the stimulus of foreign invasion lent national expression to her native resources of pietism and romance. But her rulers, ignoring and deliberately modifying the simpler and nobler aptitudes of the nation, deflected by professorial precept and by political practice the proper channels of the Germ. genius. It was always a genius independent of the politicians. Luther was not a politician; it was his fate to see his idealism submerged in a turbid rush of politics. Goethe and Kant, the twin-Luther of a later age, were similarly not politicians. The one at Weimar, the other at Königsberg, sought to impose their ideas on a peaceful and peace-loving community; for there was always an element of Hans Sachs in the lit. of the Germ. people. The Teuton note, in other words, had always a homeliness in space. The cement of blood and the girders of iron which welded the new Empire together did not provide for lit. and art; material aims absorbed the new Imperialists, and Germ. lit. in the 19th cent. has had no great man since Goethe died. 1832, his death-year and Scott's, is a *terminus a quo* in Fr. and Engl. letters; in Germ. letters, it is a *terminus ad* Goethe; and the overthrow of the Empire destroyed no power which the culture of Europe need regret. On the contrary, lovers of Germ. lit. may hope that, from the fall of the idol in the shattered temple of *Weltpolitik*, the true heart of Lutheran Germany will turn again to the ideas for which its greatest thinkers have always striven, and the mind of the Germ. people will express itself independently of Germ. rulers.

Gerson, de, Jean Charlier (1363-1429): Fr. theologian; chancellor of Gerson, in Navarre, represented the king of France and the univ. of Paris at the Council of Constance (q.v.), 1414. Formerly, G. was among the candidates for the then disputed authorship of the *Imitation of Christ* (see s.v. Thomas à Kempis). His sermons attracted large audiences at Paris, and, as a conscious disciple of Ciceronian prose, G. is numbered among the early humanists.

Gerstenberg, von, Heinrich Wilhelm (1737-1823): Germ. poet; typical of the transition from the brief bardic movement (see s.vv. Barditus and Klopstock) to the Sturm und Drang (q.v.). In the earlier category fall his Ossianic 'Poems of a Skald'; in the latter his Dantesque tragedy *Ugolino*.

Gesner, Conrad (1516-65): Germ. (-Swiss) naturalist and scholar; 'a man of prodigious erudition' (Hallam, *Lit. Eur.*, i, 355); resided at Zurich, where he formed a botanical garden, and first classified plants according to their organs of fructification; is said to have been acquainted with the properties of tobacco (Hallam, *ibid.*). Scholarship looks back to G. as the first student of comparative languages; bibliography looks back to him as the first compiler of a 'universal library' (*bibliotheca universalis*), in the form of an encyclopedia of Gk., Lat. and Hebr. lit., with a critical estimate of the bks. catalogued. But perhaps his most interesting title to fame, at least from the literary point of view, was his susceptibility to mountain scenery; he climbed the Alps once a year, 'partly to learn the mountain flora, partly to strengthen my body and refresh my soul. . . . How it stimulates worship, to be surrounded by the snowy domes'. Thus G. may be said to anticipate Rousseau's attitude to Nature (see s.vv.), though his voice in the 16th cent. was more lonely than Rousseau's in his own. (Petrarch's (q.v.) much earlier susceptibility to mountain-scenery should not be forgotten).

Gesner, Johann Matthias (1691-1761): Germ. humanist; prof. of poetry at new univ. of Göttingen, 1734. Edited various classical texts, and is notable as a pioneer of the new aims of classical study, directed less to verbal and stylistic imitation than to the use of the spirit of Gk. culture in the conduct of modern life. G. anticipated Heyne (q.v.) 'in introducing the principles of taste into the interpretation of the Classics' (Sandys, *Hist. Class. Schol.*, iii, 6; who quotes, in a footnote *in loc.*, J.E.B. Mayor, *Journal Class. and Sacred Philology*, ii, 279; 'By rejection of encyclopedic articles and of barbarisms, by many insertions, and particularly by interpretations of vexed passages, Gesner's *Novus Linguæ et Eruditionis Romanæ Thesaurus*, 1749, did very much towards enlarging and simplifying the science '). ' The age of Winckelmann, Lessing and Goethe ' (see s.vv.), adds Sandys, ' was approaching, and Gesner was its prophet and precursor '.

Gessner, Salomon (1730-88): Germ. (-Swiss) idyllist, copper-engraver, and landscape-painter. Born at Zurich; lived in Berlin. G.'s *Idyls* are little fancy-pictures of a little fancy-countryside of his own, or, rather, of a state of rural bliss abstracted from Ital. and Fr. variants of Sicilian pastoral poetry. He wore the spectacles of the Anacreontic school (s.v. Anakreontiker), but his artist's eye was better trained, and he cultivated a kind of porcelain prose, which is not unattractive. Wr., too, narrative idyl, *The Death of Abel*. G.'s fragile labours in the shadow of Klopstock (q.v.) would hardly be worth recording, save for his fame in his own day, when his idyls were transld. into nearly all European tongues, and have been particularly well liked in France.

Ghasel (Rhet.): Oriental form of verse, brought to western poetry by the late Romanticists, chiefly Rückert and Platen (qq.v.) in Germany. The G., though admitting variety, consists of a short poem, of 10 or 12 to 20 or even 30 lines, opening with a rhymed couplet, the rhyme of which is repeated in each even line, while the odd lines remain unrhymed,—thus : —*aa ba ca du eu fu*, etc. Any type of verse is permissible. The effect is somewhat artificial, but has a charm and subtlety in its own kind.

Ghistele, van, Cornelis (1558-80): Dutch scholar; member of the Antwerp chamber of Rhetoric (see s.v. Rederijkers). G. was faithful to the traditions and words of medieval diction consecrated by the cult of the chambers, and his loyalty in that regard detracts from the value of his work. Despite the dawn of Renaissance humanism, and despite his own occupation with 'rhetorical' renderings from Ovid, Virgil, Horace and Terence, G.'s scholarship was marred by an inability to master the forms as well as the vocabulary of Gk. and Lat. lit.

Gibbon, Edward (1737-94): Engl. historian; edu. at Westminster School and Magdalen Coll., Oxford, and expressed a stately, if just, disdain for both seats of learning; lived at Lausanne, 1753-8, where his tutor, Pavillard, a Calvinist, drew him back from a temporary attachment to the Church of Rome, and where he met his ' first and only love ', mlle. Suzanne Curchod, afterwards mme. Necker (q.v.); wr., in Fr., in which he was thoroughly proficient, an essay on the study of lit., 1761, and, after service in the Hants militia, and long premeditation on various topics of history, visited Rome, 1764. In that year, on 15 Oct., ' as I sat musing ', he recorded, ' amidst the ruins of the Capitol, while the bare-footed fryers were singing vespers in the Temple of Jupiter, the idea of writing the decline and fall of the city first started to my mind '. The city was extended to the empire, Montesquieu's (q.v.) *Considérations sur les causes de la Grandeur des Romains et leur décadence*, 1734, being, perhaps, an incitement to this extension (see *C.H.E.L.*, x., 304, by sir A. W. Ward); vol. i was publd. 1776, vols. ii and iii, 1781, vols. iv-vi, 1788; and G. has recorded

the close of the great enterprise, with the same precision as he recorded its inception. It was at Lausanne, ' on the day, or rather night, of the 27th June, 1787, between the hours of 11 and 12, that I wrote the last lines of the last page in a summer-house in my garden. After laying down my pen, I took several turns in a berceau, or covered walk of acacias, which commands a prospect of the country, the lake, and the mountains. The air was temperate, the sky was serene, the silver orb of the moon was reflected from the waters, and all nature was silent. I will not dissemble the first emotions of joy on the recovery of my freedom, and perhaps the establishment of my fame. But my pride was soon humbled, and a sober melancholy was spread over my mind by the idea that I had taken an everlasting leave of an old and agreeable companion, and that whatsoever might be the future date of my history, the life of the historian must be short and precarious '. G. had just cause for pride and joy : *The History of the Decline and Fall of the Roman Empire* (edited by Milman, 1838; by J. B. Bury, 1896-1900; transld. into Fr., 1777-95, into Germ., 1779, and into Ital., 1779-86, in each instance by a leading scholar) was recognized from the first, and has maintained its position to the present day, as a work of transcendent and luminous excellence, at once a monument of learning and a model of prose-style. ' His power of narrative ', says sir A. W. Ward (*loc. cit.*), ' is at least equalled by this gift of argumentative statement ', and, noting, as others have noted, G.'s occasional want of terseness and proportion, his tendency to an *obscénité érudite et froide*, and his subdued or ' sub-cynical ' (F. Harrison's, q.v., epithet) irony, the critic, who was also an historian, adds : ' Gibbon, then, has much of the magnificence of Burke, of the incisiveness of Hume, and of the serene humour of Fielding, in addition to the ease and lucidity of the French writers who had been the companions of his youthful studies '. It would take us too far from our proper province to discuss the controversy on G.'s 15th and 16th chs. (dealing with the origins of Christianity), which engaged the pens of scholars and divines till the end of the 18th cent., and which affords to-day corroborative evidence to his early fame. He became a member of Dr. Johnson's Club, 1774; sat in the House of Commons, 1744-83; formed an intimate friendship with J. B. Holroyd, first earl of Sheffield (1735-1821), who acted Boswell to G.'s Johnson, and edited (partly with the help of his daughter, Maria Josepha, afterwards lady Stanley of Alderley) G.'s *Miscellaneous Works* and his famous *Memoir of My Life and Writings*, 1796-1814 (newly edited, 1896, by John Murray), one of the most fascinating pieces of autobiography in existence.

Gifford, William (1756-1826): Engl. critic. Like sir Henry Stanley, the explorer, in a later day, G. had a hard fight against ill-fortune in early life, and met good-fortune, when it arrived, with a certain sense of having got less than his due share. His occasional truculence as a reviewer may, perhaps, be traced to harsh experience. G. conciliated the patronage of lord Grosvenor, and his first works were 2 verse-satires, the *Baviad* and *Mæviad*, 1794-5, in the kind adapted by Boileau (q.v.) from ancient Rome, and used in Engld. by Pope (q.v.) with more consummate skill. The *Baviad* modernized the first satire of Persius. Both satires suffer from an excess of spleen and a defect of appropriateness : ' his violence is such that some of the absurdity he derides recoils on himself when he treats his victims as criminals and lepers ' (Elton, *Survey Engl. Lit., 1780 to 1830*, i, 36). The victims, it may be added, were mostly Whigs. The *Mœviad* was directed against contemporary drama, and possesses some hist. interest. G.'s translns. from Juvenal and Persius are of more permanent value, and formed the background of the busy years in which he edited the *Anti-Jacobin* (q.v.) for Canning (q.v.) and his Tory circle. Canning, again, and Scott (q.v.) were associated with the John Murray of that day in the foundation of the *Quarterly Review*, as Tory counterpoise to the *Edinburgh*, and G. served as its editor from its first number in 1809 till 1824.

Gilbert, Nicholas Joseph Laureut (1751-80) : Fr. poet. Wr. satiric and lyric verse, the former comprising *le XVIIIéme Siècle, le Poète malheureux*, and other pieces, inspired by an eloquent opposition to the *philosophes* (q.v.). G. was very far from a great poet, but his religious poems contain hints of the reaction against formalism, which was to grow into the romantic counter-movement.

Gilbert, William Schwenk (1836-1911) : Engl. dramatist, librettist; knt. G. began to write for the stage in a comic and vulgar vein, derived from the *fiabe* of C. Gozzi and the fairy-plays of Planché (qq.v.). His extraordinary metrical facility and his sense of proportion (or contrast, or humour) were displayed in his *Bab Ballads*, 1869, and came to even riper expression in the songs, joined to a kind of story placed in a comic situation, which formed the basis of the series of comic or satiric operas, which delighted play-goers at the Savoy in the third quarter of the 19th cent., and are still revived with success. These included *Trial by Jury*, 1875 ; *The Sorcerer*, 1878 ; *H.M.S. Pinafore*, 1879 ; *Iolanthe*, 1881 ; *Pirates of Penzance*, 1882 ; *Patience*, 1884 ; *Princess Ida*, 1885 ; *The Mikado*, etc. The music of sir Arthur Sullivan was half the secret of the great success of G.'s productions. His pleasant vein of social satire, rarely offensive, and wisely superficial, owed much to the example of Gay (q.v.).

Gillot, Jacques (16th cent.) : Fr. satirist ; advocate. Contributor to *Satyre Ménippée* (q.v.).

Giordani, Pietro (1774-1848) : It. critic ; letter-writer ; devoted his great talents untiringly to the creation of a single Ital. prose style, out of the rivalries of Rome and Tuscany, and to the growth of a united Italy. G. espoused the cause of Napoleon, and was one of many who suffered from the persecution of Austria. He was a wise counsellor of younger men of letters in his day, who ' resorted to him for ideas ', says Dr. Garnett (*Ital. Lit.*, 370), ' as English authors resorted to Samuel Rogers for breakfast, and neither went away empty '. G.'s correspondence is his main literary monument.

Giovanni, di, Domenico. See **Burchielli.**

Giovio, Paolo (1483-1552) : It. Latinist ; Paulus Jovius. Wr. Lat. verse ' eulogies ' of

scholarship and scholars (chiefly Ital. Latinists, like himself), with whose ' images '. he adorned his villa on lake Como ; lost part of his library in the sack of Rome, 1527.

Giraldi, Lilio Gregorio (1478-1552) : It. Latinist. Born at Ferrara ; resided at Rome, where he lost his library in the sack of the city, 1527. Wr. Lat. dialogue *on the poets of our times*, ranging with rather rare impartiality through writers of all countries and in all styles, but tending to an inevitable preference for the Lat. humanists of his own country.

Giraldus, Cambrensis ; Gerald, or Giraud, de Barri (*c.* 1147-*c.* 1223) : Welsh historiographer ; of princely descent ; served in diplomatic appointments under kings Henry ii and Richard i. Wr. Lat. works on Welsh history and topography, much used by later romancers.

Girondins (Fr.) : Party of moderate Republicans, 1792, during the Revolution, so called from the place of orig. (department of Gironde) of many of the members. They were overthrown, 1793, and suffered the common fate of the guillotine. Mme. Roland (q.v.) was the moving spirit of the party, which thus has a name in lit. as well as in history. The G. were also distinguished by the oratory of some of their members (s.v. Vergniaud, for example). It was with the G. party that Wordsworth (q.v.) would have thrown in his lot.

Gissing, George (1857-1903) : Engl. novelist ; struck a sombre and pessimistic note, derived from the new inquiries current in the last quarter of the 19th cent. into the life of the denizens of ' slums ' in great cities. Wr. *Demos*, 1886 ; *New Grub Street*, 1891, and others ; the last of which was a pleasant series of *Private Papers of Henry Ryecroft*.

Giusti, Giuseppe (1809-50) : It. satirist ; ' fills a place by himself ' (*P.E.L.*, xi, 358) ; ' the gallantry with which Giusti, living under the absolute government of Tuscany, itself wholly subservient to Austria, launched shaft after shaft against the oppressors of his country is paralleled by the boldness of the literary innovation he made in discarding the time-honoured forms of blank verse and *terza-rima*, and conveying satire in easy and familiar lyric ' (R. Garnett, *Ital. Lit.*, 366). G.'s satires, some of which have been transld. into Engl. by W. D. Howells, were circulated in MS. between 1833-47, and a complete edn. was publd. in 1852. Affinities with R. Browning (q.v.) are noted by Garnett, but G.'s work is necessarily ephemeral, despite the originality of his genius in a limited and temporary vogue.

Gleim, Johann Wilhelm Ludwig (1719-1803) : Germ. poet ; Anakreontiker (q.v.) ; studied at Halle and Berlin, and settled at Halberstadt, thus boxing the compass of the Prussian or Anacreontic school. His best bk. of verse was the ' Prussian War-songs of a Grenadier ', which went straight to the hearts of the subjects of Frederick (q.v.) the Great, and were collected, 1758, with a foreword by Lessing (q.v.). Otherwise G.'s poetry has little to recommend it except a complete apparatus of the tags and devices of his classical and Fr. models. His long poetic activity was instrumental in attracting to Halberstadt a line of adherents to his school of poetry well on into the first quarter of the 19th cent.

Globe, Le (Fr.) : Title of a Paris journal, founded, 1824, which quickly assimilated to its Liberal politics the Romantic ideas which found a focus in the new literary circle of the Arsenal (q.v., and s.vv. *Lyrisme*, *Romance*). Its influence was considerable on the ideas of 1830, and it was Goethe's (q.v.) favourite journal ; a preference doubtless due to its good fortune in securing the services of Ste.-Beuve (q.v.) as literary critic.

Gnapheus, Gulielmus. See **Volder, W.**

Godeau, Antoine (1605-72) : Fr. poet ; one of the founders of the Fr. Academy (q.v.) ; a frequenter of the precious (q.v.) set at the Hôtel de Rambouillet (q.v.), where his small stature and his attentions to his hostess' elder daughter won him the name of ' Julie's dwarf '. G., who was a bp. and a man of erudition, blossomed with a poem on *Saint Paul*, 1654, on the dead branch of the art-epopee, and qualified by his shorter poems for the fame which he enjoyed and has since lost.

Godfrey of Bouillon (11th cent.) : Crusader ; central hero of the cycle of heroic legends known as the *chanson d'Antioche*, compiled from Lat. chronicles nearly contemporaneous with the actual events. A later *chanson de Jerusalem* was collated from oral tradition gathered from the crusading forces, and the romantic-cycle (s.v. *Romance*), incorporating every probable and improbable invention and collection of the art of the *trouvères*, grew out of and around the noble figure of G., whose genealogy, thus enlarged, included the exploits of the knt. of the swan (s.v. Lohengrin).

Godwin, -i. William (1756-1836) : Engl. social philosopher ; novelist. Married (1), 1797, Mary Wollstonecraft (see below) ; and (2), 1801, Mary Jane Clairmont, mother of Clara M. J. Clairmont, whose name occurs in Byron's (q.v.) biography. Wr., most notably, *Political Justice*, 1793 (frequently reprinted, at first with considerable alterations), and, in fiction, *Caleb Williams*, 1794, *St. Leon*, 1799, *Fleetwood*, 1805, and *Cloudesley*, 1830. Wr., too, a creditable *Life of Chaucer*, some excellent essays, and a considerable amount of forgotten hackwork. The tractate and the novels help to illustrate one another : the latter contained psychological types, based largely on the abstractions conveyed by the former,—in one instance (*St. Leon*), there was a deliberate admission that human nature in the concrete should be guided by less rigid conceptions of correct conduct than the abstract philosopher had dictated. But, though *Caleb Williams* still finds readers for its story's sake—the final justification of a novel,—it is as the author of *Political Justice*, and of the writings which it inspired, that G. is permanently recognized, as ' a focus of radical speculation in England during the last years of the eighteenth century ' (Elton, *Survey Engl. Lit.*, *1780-1830*, i, 269). The limitation to Engld. is important : for the true home of this kind of bk. was France, where Rousseau, Condorcet, d'Holbach (qq.v.), and like writers, and the supreme event of the Revolution and its consequences, formed its source and fount. And more important to Engld. than the source or the stream were some

of its tributaries. Some of the younger revolutionaries of G.'s day, infected by the example of Fr. action and thought, forgot, if we may say so, God in Godwin, and substituted an idealized Man for real, human, suffering men and women. A long and painful process of social reconstruction was required, in order to found the true socialism on the false, and ' il serait aisé ', says prof. Legouis, in his brilliant study of *La Jeunesse de Wordsworth* (1896, p. 316), ' de montrer Wordsworth recontruisant, un à un, par l'observation des humbles, les sentiments dont Godwin avait dépouillé l'homme idéal ' ; or, as Elton (*op. cit.*) remarks : ' Into the poets, many of Godwin's hopes and conceptions passed, not unlike some stark lump of jelly on the shore that is cast into the sea, and flowers into lovely shape and lucent colour when beheld through the dream of the water '. Thus, G., who became Shelley's (q.v.) father-in-law, was intellectually, if more remotely, related, as the author of *Political Justice*, to the author of *Prometheus Unbound*. G.'s political ideal was a society founded on rational perusasion, when every one would seek ' with ineffable ardour ' the good of all, and where government would cease to function, because all the objects of government would be governors. Into the mere doctrinaire conclusions from this creed, as into G.'s experiment as a bookseller off the Strand, his disagreeable habit of handing round the hat, and other traits of vanity and self-esteem, it is not necessary to enter. *Political Justice*, derived from Fr. *philosophes* (q.v.), had an immense influence on the social idealists of its day, and was not without influence on J. Mill (q.v.) and the founders of the *Westminster Review*.

-ii. Mary (1759-1797) : Engl. feminist ; m., 1797, W. G., above ; *née* Wollstonecraft ; attempted suicide in despair of the unfaithfulness of her lover (1793-95) G. Imlay, whose *Letters* from her were publd. 1879, by C. Kegan Paul. Wr., 1792, *Vindication of the Rights of Woman*, a pioneer bk. of its kind. M.G. was very far from the ' hyena in petticoats ', as Horace Walpole (q.v.) impolitely described her, and, though an early reformer of women's education, was careful to limit women to self-expression in ' their own sphere ', without laying claim to ' equality ' with men.

-iii. Mary Wollstonecraft (1797-1851) : daughter of William and Mary, above ; m., 1816, P. B. Shelley (q.v.), as his second wife ; step-sister of Clara Clairmont, mother of Byron's (q.v.) Allegra.

Gockingh, von, Leopold (1748-1828) : Germ. poet. G. was a member of the Hain (q.v.), founded at Göttingen to spread the gospel of Germ. poetry according to Klopstock (q.v.), but his writings, which included verse-epistles of literary charm and value, went back to the older standards of Logau (q.v.), the epigrammatist, and of the First Silesian School (q.v.).

Görres, von, Jacob Joseph (1776-1848) : Germ. publicist. As a man of letters, G.'s activity was largely governed by political sympathies, or, more precisely, antipathies. He visited Paris at the time of the Fr. Revolution, and, like others, was disillusioned ; but his Liberalism survived the experience, and found expression in the political organ, *die Rheinische Merkur*, which he edited, 1814-16. Exile and mysticism tempered the national zeal of his earlier years, in which his scholarship led him to further the Romantic aim of a study of old Germ. lit. In this aspect G. belongs to the Heidelberg (q.v.) group, of which Brentano and Arnim were leaders; he lectured there, 1806-08, and edited 'The German Folkbook', in emulation of the revival of folksong (see s.v. Volkslied).

Goes, van der, Jan Antoniszoon (1647-84): Dutch poet; later called himself Johannes Antonides. 'The reading of Hooft and Vondel made him a poet' (Ten Brink), whence, perhaps, it follows that he was not born one. G. Brandt (q.v.) ascribed to Vondel 'a tender, not to say fatherly, affection' for G., who shows full traces of the elder poet's influence. Wr., 1671, *Ystroom* ('The River Y'), a graphic description of life in Amsterdam; joined, 1669, the new poets' society, *Nil Volentibus Arduum* (q.v.), but seceded in the following year, and opposed the incoming influence of France, which Dutch lit. was too much enfeebled to resist and not strong enough to mould to its own uses.

Goethe, Johann Wolfgang (1749-1832): Germ. poet, dramatist, romancer, and critic; the greatest Germ. personality since Luther, whose claim to the title of liberator (eleutherios) G. emulated; ranking by common consent with Dante in the 14th, and Shakespeare in the 16th cent., as a force and influence in European letters. The bibliography of G., in the brief period since his death, is becoming as formidable as theirs. One remark may be made at the outset. G.'s life was exceptionally long and exceptionally active; it was also exceptionally well placed. It was a more fortunate experience for a creative genius to be alive from 1763—the year of G.'s earliest poem—to 1831, when he finished *Faust, Part ii*, than to start, like Wordsworth, about 1796, or, like Carlyle, about 1832. The greatest blessing of length of years is that they should coincide with variety of experience. Germany's period of *Sturm und Drang* (see s.v.) stretched at most over the quarter of a century from 1765 to 1790; G. lived in it and survived it; he lent it colour as he passed through it; and for 40 years afterwards he composed its storm to calm. 'Ueber alle Gipfeln ist Ruh', he wr. in 1780, in one of the loveliest songs of lyric longing which the whole *corpus* of Germ. poetry contains; and those who know G. and Germ. history (as well as the passage in Lucan—*Pharsalia*, ii, 273; 'Pacem summa tenent' —of which the stanza is reminiscent) are aware that the peace which he expected ('Warte nur, balde ruhest du auch') was literary as well as literal. G. not merely lived in 2 centuries; that is the fate of most of us to-day (1925); but he lived in 2 *different* centuries, and was the representative poet of each. In this sense, his experience was unique, as was likewise his equipment. 'Never was there a life so rich as his. Not only did he lead German literature through the stormy days of *Sturm und Drang* to the calm age of classical perfection; not only does he form

the end and goal of the movement of 18th cent. thought, which had begun in England [e.g., in Richardson], and had become Europeanized in France [e.g., in Rousseau]; but he was able to understand, as no other man of his generation, the new time. He was the spiritual leader of the Romantic movement, and he encouraged all that was modern and healthy in the literatures of Europe, which sprang up under the influence of Romanticism. He looked on life, it is true, with the eyes of eighteenth century humanitarianism, but, at the same time, he showed an understanding for modern conflicts, for modern ethics, for modern ideals in art and literature, which made him, in the fullest sense, a poet of the nineteenth century'. (Robertson, *Germ. Lit.*, 456-57). More eloquence has been spent on Goethe-criticism, but rarely more wit than in this passage. What was the achievement of G., who was born while Dr. Johnson (q.v.) was writing his *Engl. Dict.*, and who died in the year of Tennyson's (q.v.) first *Poems*? His life falls into well-defined periods, marked by the places of his residence, and by the ladies whom he loved; for G., no distant worshipper of a Beatrice or Laura, was always dependent on women's society and a keen student of their psychology. He distilled the passions which he aroused into exquisite lyric or deeply-wrought drama, and passed thence to a fresh object of love and study. It is to be added that these studies began, like many great and good men's, with his mother, who was only 18 years older than her son and 21 years younger than her husband.

G. was born at Frankfort-on-the-Main, and lived at home till 1765, when he went to Leipsic univ. His boyhood included an eager acquaintance with fairy-tales and stories of adventure, a remembered impression of the Lisbon earthquake (1755), of the Seven Years' War, and of the consequent Fr. occupation of Frankfort (1759-61), which brought a busy circle of soldiers, actors, and artists to his father's house. It included, too, the episode of Gretchen, the cellarman's daughter, through whose pretty eyes 'a new world of the beautiful and good opened' to him. G.'s anxiety at discovering that his Gretchen, who passed into *Egmont and Faust*, was connected with a family of forgers, and his resentment at her treating him as a child, brought on an illness, for which the distraction of Leipsic proved a successful cure. It was the Leipsic of the decline of Gottsched's star, of Gellert, and of the Saxon theatre; and G. quickly corrected his provincialisms by the standard of that centre of fashion and learning. There he wr. a one-act pastoral play, *Die Laune des Verliebten* ('The Lover's Caprice'), in the manner of the Saxon school; a melodrama, or comedy, die *Mitschuldigen* ('The Accomplices'), and a quantity of lyrical verse: *juvenilia* all, and all composed under the influence of a certain Annette, daughter of a merchant, Schönkopf, to whom he had transferred his affections. Another illness occurred, and brought him home to the influence of fräulein v. Klettenberg, a friend of his mother's, the 'beautiful soul' of his subsequent *Wilhelm Meister*. In 1770-1 he completed his studies at Strassburg, where he fell more seriously in love with Friederika Brion, daughter of the pastor of Sesenheim, whose family, to G.'s delight, was like a real-life reproduction of the Primrose family in *The Vicar of Wakefield*. Friederika was Sophia. To this attachment, closed in agony, we owe a little bk. of love-songs, and a deeper note in dramatic characterization. Strassburg brought G. into contact with Herder (q.v.), who introduced him to the circle of Engl. idolatry for Shakespeare, Sterne, 'Ossian', and Richardson, as well as to the beauties of Gothic architecture, as exemplified in Strassburg Cathedral. (It was Herder—the Herder of the *Fragments*—who expounded *The Vicar of Wakefield* to an admiring young audience). Here, too, at the end of the student-years, it is appropriate to note that, desultory as G.'s reading had been, and however unsatisfactory to his father's ambition to make him a successful lawyer, he was proficient in many branches of science, in lit., art, theology ; and, above all, in a joy of life and a knowledge of men and things, by which his innate genius was fed and fired. From 1771-75, when he first went to Weimar, at the age of 26, G., was principally at Frankfort, nominally practising law; actually, love and letters. There was a brief visit to Wetzlar in 1772, followed by a journey up the Rhine ; and these wonderful early twenties included his passion for Charlotte Buff, the 'Lotte' of *Werther*, and again, for Lili (Schönemann), a wealthy banker's widowed daughter. They included his stimulating friendship with the scientific visionary, Lavater (q.v.), to whose studies of physiognomy he contributed ; his discipleship to 'Mephistopheles' Merck, a mocking spirit of the *Sturm und Drang*, who ran a paper in its interests ; his acquaintance with young Jerusalem, who killed himself in love's name, and with Kestner, 'Lotte's' betrothed ; and his friendship with minor poets of the *Sturm und Drang*, Goethe-satellites, as they rank to-day, such as Lenz and Klinger (qq.v.). It was a period of immense productivity. Herder inspired his eulogy on the builder of Strassburg Cathedral, which was publd. in Merck's Frankfort journal under the title of 'German Architecture', 1722 ; and in 1773 G. issued his drama, *Götz von Berlichingen*, which he had begun 2 years before, which 'young Germany greeted with stormy acclamation', and which fixes a date for the *terminus a quo* of the lit. of the storm and stress. G.'s Götz of the Iron Hand was born in 1480, and became a robber-chief of the 16th cent., and a leader of the lawless barons who waged war for freedom against the emperor Maximilian (q.v.). Thus, G.'s dramatization of his hero's career took shape as an hist. play. Scott (q.v.) transld. it in 1799, and we have Lockhart's authority for the fact that it helped directly to inspire Scott's own hist. romances of similar warfare on the Border. The exaltation of right and liberty, the splendid scenic variety—Shakespearean, as it was called even in Scott's day,—the rapidity of action, the vivid colouring, and the careless prodigality of characterization, all contributed to the immediate success of *Götz*. It was followed, 1774, by a work in another kind, quite as closely connected with the *Sturm und Drang*, even more intimate of G's own feelings,

and even wider in the popularity of its reception. This was the famous Rousseau-Richardsonian Charlotte-Buff-and-Jerusalem epistolary-romance entitled 'The Sufferings of Young Werther' (*die Leiden des jungen Werthers*). Werther, the tender lover, trained by Ossian and Homer to a sensibility for passion too immense for his body to withstand, is so human as to have convinced Napoleon, and so attractive as to have created a vogue. We must pass over some plays and plans (*Clavigo* and *Stella* among the first ; a *Mahomet*, a *Prometheus*, and a *Socrates* among the latter) to note that this period included the first version of *Faust*, as well as lyrical poems, occasional verse and prose, and the usual flow of illuminating letters. It was ended by the Lili episode, from which her lover fled to Weimar, 1775, in pursuance of a standing invitation from the young duke, Karl August, his duchess, Louise, and his mother, the duchess Anna Amalia. Henceforward, Weimar was G.'s home ; the remainder of his life divides itself into 2, or perhaps 3, periods : 1774 to 1805, at the death of Schiller, with a break at 1794, when his friendship with Schiller began, and 1805 to 1832. Out of these full and busy years we must be content to select the salient features and works. Two women chiefly influenced him : Charlotte von Stein, wife of duke Karl's Master of the Horse, a lady seven years his senior, whose attraction, always more intellectual than that of other women in his life, began to wane about 1786 ; and Christine Vulpius, 1788, a girl of more sensuous appeal, whom G. m. in 1806, to the scandal of a society already scandalized by the long irregular liaison. The date, 1806, coincided with G.'s attraction by a bookseller's daughter, Minnie Herzlieb, who inspired his 'Elective Affinities' (*Wahlverwandschaften*), but Minnie and her sacrifice must not detain us here. It is more important to note that the interval between the two mistresses, 1786-88, was filled by the journey in Italy (the *Italienische Reise* of his later diary), which steadied his maturer mind to purpose and reflection, in much the same way as Herder had affected his youthful genius. The Götz-stormer, the enthusiast for Gothic architecture, was recomposed (like Wordsworth in France) to a nobler and more catholic sense of beauty, freedom and truth. Once more, as so often in the long history of the Renaissance, the soil of Italy acted as a baptism, or a purgation, on the receptive mind of her visitor from the north. G.'s first 10 or 12 years at Weimar were devoted to the service of the duke ; to consolidating his position at the theatre and in public life ; to travel (*Harzreise im Winter*, 1777 ; and *Briefe aus dem Schweiz* from a Swiss tour with the duke, 1779, publd., 1796) ; to dramatic and lyrical writings ; to the gradual enlargement of his subjective point of view and to the partial preparation of works which he brought home with him in a more or less finished state from Italy. These included *Egmont*, 1788, an hist. play of the Netherlands revolt against Alba, with a demonic (G.'s own epithet) hero, and with Clärchen (a new Gretchen of Frankfort), revealing G.'s intimate knowledge of the way of a maid with a man ;

Iphigenie auf Tauris, 1787, 'devilish human', as he called it, transforming and spiritualizing by Gk. grandeur his emotional relations with frau v. Stein ; *Torquato Tasso*, 1790, in which Tasso's poetic agony at the court of the d'Este at Ferrara was raised to the height of drama from G.'s own experience at Weimar ; and *Faust, a Fragment* (the witches' kitchen scene). 1790. Herr Müller, the *nom de voyage* of his excellency von Goethe (the duke had ennobled him in 1782), resumed his emoluments at the ducal court on his return from Italy, without the corresponding obligations which he had discharged before his departure ; his main public activity, to which we shall refer in the Schiller period, was his directorship of the Weimar theatre from 1791 to 1817. Meanwhile, he produced his hexameter version of the low-Germ. *Reineke Fuchs* (s.v. Reynard), 1794 ; he wr. his *Roman Elegies*, 1795, chiefly inspired by his 'forest blossom' Christine ; his *Venetian Epigrams*, 1796, his *Campaign in France* (publd. 1822), on which he had accompanied the duke in 1792 ; and his *Wilhelm Meister's Lehrjahre* (i.e., apprentice-years) 1795-96. This romance had been started in 1777, as a novel of theatrical life (*Wilhelm Meisters theatralische Sendung*) based on G.'s youthful experiences ; it ended as a romance of the conduct of life, in which the apprentice learns the lesson that 'life is real, life is earnest'; and it is not fanciful to say that, despite the incoherency of the parts of the bk., G.'s reflections in Italy are plainly interposed between the stage-struck idealist at the beginning and the more responsible pietist at the end. The transition is marked by the episode, 'Confessions of a Beautiful Soul', to which reference was made above in connection with fr. v. Klettenberg. The exquisite creation of Mignon, imitated in Fenella in Scott's *Peveril of the Peak*, and the romantic harper, partly reproduced in the *Lay of the Last Minstrel*, and the lovely lyrics interspersed, redeem the early bks. of Wilhelm Meister from the charge of vulgarity, noted by Carlyle (' no gentleman, we hear in certain circles, could have written it ; . . . no real lady should profess having read it at all ': the same strictures have been passed with far more justice upon Rabelais, q.v.), and due to the low life of stage society ; the different tone in the closing episodes was the result of Schiller's influence and counsel. For we reach now the wonderful years of the friendship between the two poets. Schiller (q.v.) was living at Jena, and the previous mutual distrust between him and G. (probably founded on jealousy) was reconciled in 1794. Schiller invited G. to contribute to his reviews, the *Horen* and the *Musenalmanach*, and an acquaintance, deepening to friendship, and rich with significance for both poets, was built upon their differences and likenesses. The effect on *Wilhelm Meister* has been noted ; and their *Xenien*, or critical epigrams (the title was borrowed from Martial), which expressed their negative dissatisfaction with current standards of poetry, led each to a positive production of excellence : Schiller, in his *Wallenstein* trilogy, and G. in *Hermann and Dorothea*, 1797. This epic hexameter poem (the metre

of *Reineke Fuchs* and of the *Luise* of Voss, q.v.) was composed in the Homeric manner, and offered a solution of the problem, then occupying both the Germ-poets, how to clothe a theme of common life with the mantle of Gk. calm and dignity. G. adopted his plot from an incident of the Salzburg emigration of 1731 ; he modernized it, and gave it the background of the Fr. Revolution ; and thus raised a provincial tale to a type of the conflict between the things that endure and the things that restlessly change. The record of G.'s administration at the Weimar Theatre is so largely the story of Schiller's plays that we need not repeat it here ; nor can we pause at the lesser works of these busy years in G.'s life. His masterpiece was *Faust, Part i*, completed in 1808 under the beneficent influence of Schiller's friendship and sympathy. Five hundred years had elapsed since Dante, in the *Divine Comedy*, had measured the height of Heaven and fathomed the depth of Hell; and never in the intervening centuries, with all their varied experiences, had a poet arisen till Goethe to write the 'divine comedy' of human life ; transforming the old Germ. folk-tale of Faust's pact with Mephistopheles into an epic-drama of the soul's temptation and repentance, of yearning infinite and disillusion bottomless, of the furies of good and evil warring eternally in the mind of man :

Alles Vergängliche ist nur ein Gleichniss ;
Das Unzulängliche, Hier wird's Ereigniss ;
Das Unbeschreibliche, Hier ist's gethan ;
Das Ewig-Weibliche Zieht uns hinan.

There is little to add to this survey. Shakespeare's total achievement surpasses G.'s, if comparison is admissible on Olympus ; but G.'s *Faust* divides with Milton's *Paradise Lost* the claim to rank as the greatest *single* poem which the genius of modern Europe has produced. It is the drama of man, thus sufficiently distinguished above even the greatest dramas of men. Schiller's death, 1805, evoked the magnificent verses, *Epilog zu Schillers Glocke*, with the conclusion so dear to M. Arnold's (q.v.) heart :

Indessen schritt sein Geist gewaltig fort,
In's Ewige des Wahren, Guten, Schönen,
Und hinter ihm, in wesenlosem Scheine,
Lag, was uns alle bändigt, das Gemeine.

In 1811, 1812, 1814, 1821, 1830, 1831, G. publd. the 4 parts (the fourth in 3 instalments) of his reminiscences, *Dichtung und Wahrheit* (' Fable and Fact '). In 1808-19 came his 'Elective Affinities', referred to above ; in 1814, *Shakespeare und kein Ende* ('and no end '), and (1814-19) the 12 bks. of the *Westöstliche Divan* (' West-Eastern Divan ', transld. by E. Dowden ; Dent, 1914), the occidental's interpretation of the spirit of the orient ; in 1816-29, his ' Italian Journey ' in 3 parts (*supra*), and his ' Art and Antiquity ' in 17 parts (an eighteenth was publd. posth.) ; in 1821 (revised, 1829), *Wilhelm Meisters Wanderjahre*, continuing the *Lehrjahre* (*supra*) ; in 1830, a prologue to Carlyle's *Life of Schiller* ; in 1831, *Faust, Part ii*. And this summary record omits the remarkable scientific writings : ' The Metamorphoses of Plants ', 1790 (rendered into a poem, 1797), which anticipated the leading principle of the science of morphology ;

works on colour, optics, philosophy, and on osteological discovery ; it omits the immense body of writings, comprising fragments of great poems, and perfect small ones—ballads, love-lyrics, etc.—as well as letters (innumerable), pamphlets, and so forth. It is, finally, as the author of *Werther* and *Faust*, of *Iphigenia* and *Tasso*, and as the dictator of dramatic reform at Weimar, that Europe honours eternally the greatest man in the history of Germ. lit. His last recorded utterance was ' more light ! ' (*mehr Licht*).

Göttingen : Germ. headquarters of school of poetry, founded *c.* 1769, in order to perpetuate the example of Klopstock (q.v.) as a national idealist, and to resist the perilous call of Wieland (q.v.), in his second period, to sensuousness and lightheartedness. The leading members of the movement were Voie, Gotter, Voss, Hölty and Bürger (qq.v.) ; their organ was the *Göttinger Musen-almanach*, called after the Fr. *Almanac des Muses* ; and in 1772 they formally banded themselves together and swore eternal friendship in a grove (*Hain*) of oaks, whence their union was known as the Hain (q.v.). The actual contribution of the Göttingen school to the poetry of the age was far smaller than the sum of the separate con-tributions of its members. When they came seriously to their work, they were very vari-ously observant of the Hain aims and ideals. The univ. of Göttingen was founded in the second quarter of the 18th cent., and its prof. of poetry and oratory was J. M. Gesner (q.v.), a humanist of the new school, who preceded Winckelmann and Lessing (qq.v., and see s.v. Laocoon) in changing the direction of classical studies from the letter to the spirit. The Royal Society of Sciences, the second of Germany's learned societies, was founded at Göttingen, 1751. A little later, Bürger (q.v.), the passionate author of *Lenore*, was settled at Göttingen, somewhat astray among its men of learning ; and he and Heyne (q.v.) were united in exercising an early influence on A. W. Schlegel (q.v.), the great Romantic critic and the father of Shakespeare in Germany.

Götz, Johann Nikolaus (1721-81) : Germ. poet ; Anakreontiker (q.v.) ; wr. light verse in easy metres with somewhat fatal facility.

Gogol, Nicholas Vasilievich (1809-52) : Russ. novelist ; commonly described as the Russ. Dickens (q.v.), an epithet due to the vagabond humour of G.'s masterpiece, *Dead Souls*. Vogüé (*Roman Russe*, 130) places this novel midway between Cervantes and Lesage (qq.v.), and, when posterity has become as familiar with the strange world of Chichikov in *Dead Souls* as we are familiar with the world of Don Quixote and Gil Blas, the comparison will be found to be just : G.'s romance of the road in Russia entitles its author to a rank, as Merimée (q.v.) declared, ' among the best European humourists '. It is to be noted, too, that G. himself, in acknowledging the encouragement which he always received from Pushkin (q.v.), says that Pushkin based this encouragement on the example of Cervantes, who had written several minor works before he made a hit with *Don Quixote*. G. took the hint almost literally, for there is a certain likeness between (1) Don Quixote, Sancho and Rosinante, and (2)

Chichikov, Selifan and the three nags ; and G.'s bk., which, though classified as a novel, was described by its author as a poem, and is divided by him into cantos, may be described by whatever epithet is found most suitable to *Don Quixote*. Canto i was publd., 1842 ; canto ii was burnt by G., 11 Feb., 1851, shortly before his death, either in an access of despair at its inadequacy to design, or for some cause unknown, and was printed posth. from a rough copy, rudimentary and incomplete ; part iii was never written.

So much by way of anticipation. For G., though his drama, *The Revisor* (or *Inspector*) is the only Russ. comedy fit to rank with Griboye-dov's (q.v.) *Gore ot Uma* (' Learning makes Trouble ') was, like Griboyedov, essentially a man of one bk. It is as the writer of *Dead Souls* that G. is compared with Cervantes, Balzac, Lesage and Dickens. It is by that bk. that G. heads the realists of Russ. fiction, fulfilling and completing the half-tones which Lermontov (q.v.) reached in his ' Hero of our Days '.

Retracing the steps we have anticipated : G. was a Little Russ., and was born in the Ukraine, or frontier, country of untamed Cossacks and wide plains, of long shadows and deep imaginings. In early manhood he came to Petrograd, with the big hopes common to genius and youth. These turned slowly to disillusion in the course of his grey exper-ience as a minor Government official, a private tutor, and a prof. of history. He endured it all till 1835, writing ' Evenings in a Farm on the Dikanka ', 1832, a beekeeper's tales of his old home ; *Mirgorod*, 1834, a second series in the same vein, containing, among others, the grand Cossack epic of *Taras Bulba*, the fan-tastic tale of *Viy*, and the simple, moving story of a South Russ. Darby and Joan (or Philemon and Baucis) entitled ' old fashioned Land-owners ' ; ' Arabesques ', 1834, and ' Tales ', 1836, in which the Poë-like fancy receded, and the nymphs and naiads retired to their woods and streams, while the new humour and pathos of the commonplace, the harvest of a quiet eye, were more and more powerfully represented. Esp. the tale of ' The New Cloak ', longed-for through shivering years by Akaky Akakievich, a clerk in the civil service, bought at last and worn for the first time, and stolen on the very day of its first wearing, is always referred to as the source of all the realism of Russ. novelists. ' We all derive from " The New Cloak " of Gogol ' was said, in the same sense as Swin-burne (q.v.) called Villon (q.v.), the ' head of all our quire '. The tale of the overcoat was the first, the play of the inspector general (the *Revisor*) was the second blow dealt by G. at the bureaucratic wheel on which he had been broken. This comedy was performed in Petrograd in 1836, and was specially franked through the terrors of the censorship by the emperor Nicholas, who had read it with huge amusement ; and this ' Köpenick '-comedy of Russia has drawn big audiences ever since. Its hero is a resourceful liar who happens to arrive at a country-town just when the ' revisor ' is expected, and who readily takes the great man's part. In a corrupt and tyrannous civil service, the opportunities for satire are obvious, and G. fully availed himself of them. It was his last thrust at the conquest of the capital. He went to Rome in 1836, and was rarely seen again in the north before his long illness terminated fatally. On the personal side of G.'s last years, which, like Tolstoy's (q.v.), were marked by inward struggles, there is little need to dwell ; the word mystical has been used to describe them, but its meaning is somewhat too definite for the altruistic and ascetic longings for direct communion with righteousness which marked G.'s pathway to the grave. His *Dead Souls*, in its second and third parts, was intended to express his spiritual conviction of the superiority of renunciation over great possessions. But it was left unfind., as we have seen, and these more personal messages have to be gleaned from G.'s ' Letters ', 1847, and from sundry ' confessions ' and other writings.

Part i of *Dead Souls* must be taken as it stands : it was the story of Chichikov in search of a fortune, and seeking to build his fortune on the brilliant perception of a loop-hole for fraud in the Russ. land-laws of the pre-emancipation era. The magnificent idea is this : Every Russ. landlord paid a poll-tax on the male adults among his serfs. The census was revised at intervals of 10 years. In the meanwhile, the serfs (or souls) might die, migrate, or otherwise be depleted, and the landlord would continue to pay on them till the new census. G.'s new rogue of the road, his Gil Blas *de nos jours*, proposed to buy up these ' dead souls ', and to deposit the nominal roll as security for cash in a distant bank which would regard it as a list of names of living serfs whose labour could be mortgaged. The humours of the road were infinite ; and the touch of Chichikov which is common to all of us responds with illumination and delight to the record of his adventures. There were the simple who sold their ' souls ' for nothing, glad to be rid of the tax, the contentious who argued it out, the thief-catch-thief who suspected a trick ; and the whole rural population of that era lives for ever in G.'s pages. For Chichikov is one of the immortal company of the *picaro*, and *Dead Souls* wrought more freedom for Russ. fiction than even Pushkin had won for Russ. poetry ; setting it free from the trammels of the grand style, and opening the common way of realism as a new force in European letters. ' How sad a country our Russia is ', was Pushkin's remark to G. after the first reading of *Dead Souls* ; and this revelation of the underlying sadness, renewed, from G.'s ' New Cloak ', by Dostoievsky's ' Poor Folk ', and from G.'s 'Evenings in a Farm ', by Turgenev's (q.v.) ' Sportsman's Sketches.', was a potent method of social reform in Russ. life in the middle of the 19th cent. Views, opinions, criticism ; these were non-existent in Russ. lit. ; the censor forbad them and prosecuted them ; but a detailed realistic survey of actual conditions in humble life proved a more efficacious method of argument than dreary remedial proposals ; and G. laying bare the sadness as well as the resistent, persistent cheerfulness of his countrymen, is properly numbered among the makers of better times.

Golden Legend, The : Popular name early given to the *Legends of the Saints*, first collected in Lat. by Voragine (q.v.), afterwards archbp. of Genoa, and transld. into Fr. by Vigney (q.v.) and into Engl. by Caxton (q.v.). Longfellow, in re-telling one story from this great treasure-house of legends, called his poem *The Golden Legend* (1851), because the particular tale, derived secondarily from Hartmann (q.v.) von Aue, seemed to him more purely golden than any in the collection.

Golding, Arthur (16th cent.) : Engl. translr ; friend of sir Philip Sidney (q.v.) and other leading humanists ; transld. Ovid's (q.v.) *Metamorphoses*, 1565-7 (first Engl. version ; rendered into ballad metre) and Cæsar's *Commentaries*, 1565. G.'s Ovid is his most famous work, and his long lines are most successful when Ovid himself is at his best. Shakespeare's debt to this transln. is incalculable ; or, more exactly : ' In one or other of Shakespeare's plays there are allusions to every one of the fifteen books of the *Metamorphoses*. Similarity of language proves that Shakespeare frequently used Golding's noble and melodious translation ' (S. G. Owen, ' Ovid and Romance ', in *Engl. Lit. and the Classics*, Oxford, 1912 ; p. 185).

Goldoni, Carlo (1707-93) : It. comedian ; a native of Venice, the Venice of carnival, masquerade, gambling, intrigue, and, it must be added, iniquity, which G. was too easy a moralist to denounce and too indulgent a contemporary to see in perspective. ' Goldoni, good, gay, sunniest of souls ', R. Browning (q.v.) apostrophized him, and added that he reflected ' half Venice ' in his mirror of verse (as M. Arnold wr. with equal truth of Wordsworth, that he averted his eyes from half of human fate) : the reflected half was ' the shade and shine of common life ', the omitted half was the ' grandeur and gloom '. Precisely (or, partly) on account of that omission, the description of G. as ' the Molière of Italy ' (ascribed without evidence to Voltaire) is false and misleading. Voltaire (q.v.) never said it, though lesser men did, and though G. himself aimed at achieving for Italy the creation of a type of drama similar to that of Molière (q.v.) in France. G., says a Fr. writer, ' n'est pas Molière mais il est quelque chose ', he adds generously, ' que Molière n'a pas été non plus ' ; and this recognition of difference—of G. being G., and M. being M.—is a truer reply to the old, false comparison than such statements as R. Garnett's (*Ital. Lit.*, Heinemann) : ' we may term Goldoni a halved Molière '. There was nothing half-way about G.'s achievement. He succeeded in creating for the Ital. stage a type of comedy which it had not known before, and which has never been so successfully repeated since. He broke away from the prevailing *commedia dell 'arte* (q.v. ; the comedy of masks and intricate plot), and from the amalgam of that type with the faëry of Gozzi (q.v.), and in their place he produced the more normal European comedy of manners and character. As it happened, there was not room for both types in Venice, and G. betook himself to the more hospitable stage of Paris, 1762, where he remained till the end of the chapter. But it is an error to call G. a dramatic reformer. 'There was nothing of the missionary about him. He wrote one kind of plays, Gozzi was writing another, and each made good in his own line'. And, as Addington Symonds says of G.: 'One of the best theatres in Venice is called by his name. His statue stands almost within sight of the Rialto. His comedies are repeatedly given by companies of celebrated actors'. In France G. wr. in Fr., and his *Memoirs*, 1787, were composed in the same language. The Convention revoked the pension which had been granted under the monarchy, and the proposal to restore it was made (by a curious coincidence) on the day after G.'s death; it was in the proposer's speech that the Voltaire-legend of the Ital. Molière was started. We need not enumerate G.'s plays, some of the best of which were written in the Venetian dialect. They include *La Locandiera*, in which Duse appeared in London; *Il Burbero Benefico*, *La Bottega del Caffé*, *Il Vero Amico*, etc. A new life of him was written in 1915 by an American author, Dr. Chatfield-Taylor (Chatto and Windus).

Goldschmidt, Meyer Aaron (1819-87): Dan. critic and journalist; a leader of the liberal movement, and, like Brandes (q.v.), his successor, of Jewish parentage. G. founded *Corsaren* ('The Corsairs'), a weekly organ of lit. and liberalism, which flourished from 1840-46, and the shafts of whose wit and satire pierced the philistines of art and letters and the absolutists of politics. The *Corsaren*, which served as model for *Kladderadatsch*, of later fame in Germany, fell foul of Kierkegaard (q.v.), among others; and G. became dissatisfied with the notoriety associated with the publication. Accordingly, he severed his connection, and founded, 1847, another journal 'North and South', which he ran till 1859. His position in Copenhagen at this period has been compared with that of Holberg (q.v.): G., as a Jew, and Holberg, as a Norw., having both imposed a foreign culture on the conservative Dan. capital. This view is supported by the novel, 'A Jew', 1845, in which G. forcibly depicted the alien-native problem so frequently represented by distinguished members of his race. His Jew. tales evoked the epigrammatic protest of Brandes against 'perpetually serving up one's own grandmother with *sauce piquante*'. Other novels of psychological interest succeeded this first experiment, and a vol. of thoughtful reflections on the events and results of his lifework concluded, in 1877, a brilliant, if somewhat isolated, career.

Goldsmith, Oliver (1728-74): Engl. novelist, playwright, essayist; Irish by birth; of the circle of Johnson (q.v.), who deemed G. 'a very great man', touching many kinds of lit. and none that he did not adorn. Posterity confirms this verdict more and more. G. lived in Ireland till 1752; then, after various adventures on the Continent, including a visit to Voltaire (q.v.)—the French experiences are important—practised medicine, teaching and reviewing in London. His *Citizen of the World* appeared, 1762, as a series of 'Chinese Letters' in the *Public Ledger*. About this time, G. first met Johnson, who sold for him

his *Vicar of Wakefield*, 1766, 'an irregular novel which became popular all over Europe' (Saintsbury); the proceeds saved him from arrest for debt. Wr. school bks., including an Engl. history, and next turned to the stage. His *Good-natured Man* was produced, 1768, and *She Stoops to Conquer*, 1773. There were also the verse-essays, *Traveller*, 1764, and *Deserted Village*, 1769, in both of which Johnson had a hand. ('When Johnson prunes or interpolates lines in the *Traveller*', says sir Leslie Stephen in his monograph on the former writer, 'we feel as though a woodman's axe was hacking at a most delicate piece of carving'). Delicacy of touch and sensibility were certainly main characteristics of the 'excitable Irishman of genius', whose short life was so full of hackwork, Grub Street scenes, and permanently brilliant achievement. G.'s debt to France must not be overlooked. He was dominantly original in talent, and characters like the Vicar and Tony Lumpkin are new, Engl., and unique. But, technically, G. owed much to Fr. example: his *Chinese Letters*, e.g., to Montesquieu and the marquis d'Argens (qq.v.); his *Good-natured Man* to le *Legs* of Marivaux (q.v.), who is also found in the *Vicar* (e.g., ch. 20, esp.), and he owed not a little, too, to Voltaire, of whom, in despite of Johnson's aversion, G. was a consistent admirer. It has been said of Goldsmith by Austin Dobson (q.v.), that he represented a 'halfway attitude between the poetry of convention and the poetry of nature—between the gradus-epithet of Pope and the direct vocabulary of Wordsworth'. Neither judgment is quite fair to either poet (see s.vv.), but G. belonged to an age of transition between 1688 (the Revolution) and 1832 (the Reform Act) in Engld., and something transitional in his style (which was the man) was inevitable.

Golias (9th cent.): a bp., whose ribald speech and indecorous conduct survive in the so-called Goliardic poems, written anon. from about 1220 onwards in familiar Lat. verse. A well-known item in this collection is the *Confessio* ascribed to Map (q.v.), and preserved in the 13th cent. MS. (known as Benedicto-buranus) of the *Carmina Burana*, formerly in a Benedictine monastery in Bavaria, and now at Munich. G.'s character and reputation correspond to the 'Philistine' (q.v.) qualities denounced in the 19th cent. by M. Arnold (q.v.), and Goliardic verse embodies the earliest outspoken experiments in popular satire in Europe; Rabelais (q.v.) has been called the last of the Goliards.

Gomara, de, F. de Lopez. See Lopez de Gomara.

Gombauld, de, Jean Ogier (1576-1666): Fr. poet and novelist; an original member of the Fr. Academy (q.v.), and a welcome guest at the Hôtel de Rambouillet (q.v.). G.'s place in the development of fiction was won by his allegorical-romance, *Endymion*, 1624, which grew out of his 'respectful and a little absurd admiration' (Grierson, *P.E.L.*, vii, 265), less politely called his 'Schwärmerei' (Koerting), for the queen-mother, Marie de Medici. It is an incoherent piece of writing on the whole, innocent of character-study, and almost mechanical in its floods of oratory. G. also wr. pastoral verse (*Amaranthe*, 1631), and a more notable quality of lyrical compositions.

Gomberville, sieur de ; Marin le Roy (1600-74) :
Fr. novelist ; original member of the Fr.
Academy (q.v.). which sometimes met in his
house ; a valued member of the precious
(q.v.) set at the Hôtel Rambouillet (q.v.),
where, among more illustrious services to the
aims of the school, G. engaged with Voiture
(q.v.) in a mimic warfare against the literary use
of the Fr. particle *car* ; later in life, he became an
adherent to the tenets of Port-Royal (q.v.).
(By an obstinate error, probably due in the first
instance to a misprint, the date of G.'s death
is commonly mis-stated as 1647). G.'s minor
works in prose and verse (he publd., *ætat.* 14 !
a poem on the ' Happiness of Old Age ') are
insignificant in comparison with the experiment he undertook of converting the erotic-
adventurous hero of the *Amadis* (q.v.) type
into an heroic-gallant knt., for the imitation
of society in the 17th cent. ; the *parfait amant*
into the *honnête homme*. The endeavour
remained an experiment ; G. commanded
neither the talent nor the industry to make
his design effective : 2 of his 4 novels were left
unfind., and the 2 others halt imperfectly
between the confusion of aims. But G.'s
place is secure as a pioneer in the development
of modern fiction, say, from Urfé to Sand
(qq.v.). His chief work is *Polexandre*, 1632
(complete in 5 vols., 1637) ; and its departure
lies in the fact that, despite its prolixity and
involution, and despite the conventional
machinery of *Amadis* and Gk. fiction (q.v.) and
their Ital. and Span. imitators, G. devised for
his Mexican lovers an atmosphere of hist.
verisimilitude, which corresponded exactly to
the needs of the times and created the desired
illusion.

Gomez, Antonio Enriquez (1602-*c.* 1662) : Span.
picaresque novelist. Wr., 1644, ' The Pytha-
goric Age and The Life of Don Gregorio
Gaudaña ', which opened with a series of satiric
sketches based on the Pythagorean theory of
metempsychosis, and which included the prose-
tale (' Life ' etc.) of the rogue (*pícaro*) -hero
Gaudaña. Other works of less interest are
attributed to G., who appears to have taken
refuge in France and Holland, *c.* 1636, and to
have been burned in effigy at Seville, 1660,
on account of religious troubles. G. is said to
have been of Port. Jewish descent, and was
also known in Spain as Enrique Enriquez
de Paz. Among his friends in the Netherlands
may have been a companion in misfortune,
Barrios (q.v.).

Goncharov, Ivan Alexandrovich (1812-91) : Russ.
novelist. G. presents an interesting contrast
to his slightly younger contemporary, Turgenev
(q.v.). He came of honourable merchant
stock, not of the landed gentry, like Turgenev.
He wr. only three bks. of mark, in distinction
to Turgenev's prolific list ; and he strictly
confined himself to the time of the Russ.
'forties, thus avoiding Turgenev's fate of
failing in sympathy with the new order after
1861. Yet there is an underlying likeness,
which makes it worth while to institute the
comparison. Both novelists alike are psychologists, keenly interested in the development
of character ; and their reciprocal interest
lies in the transference by G. of Turgenev's
people from the country into the town.

' Accept ', she says : ' it is not hard In woods ;
but she in towns Repeats, accept ', writes
Meredith somewhere ; and acceptance of the
conditions of nature in the country life delineated by Turgenev became a more urgent and
a more difficult problem in the city surroundings depicted by G. This is the essence of the
problem of *Oblomov*, 1858 (one chapter publd.,
1849), whose eponymous hero has passed into
the proverbial philosophy of Russia. One
critic, Dobrolubov (q.v.), indeed argued
forcibly enough that every hero in Russ.
fiction was a part of Oblomov : Lermontov's
Pechorin, Turgenev's Bazarov, Griboyedov's
Chatsky, Pushkin's Oniégin (see s.vv.), and
the rest. A far more reasonable contention
than this Hamlet-obsession is that the Oblomov-
type, and Oblomovism, if the term may be
coined, is inherent in the Russ. temperament,
which finds refusal and negation and abstinence easier than spontaneous and volitional
acceptance, whether ' in woods ' or ' in towns '.
Krylov (q.v.) was said by contemporaries to
have been an Oblomov in real life ; Hardenberg (q.v.) was another, and Harold Skimpole
may, perhaps, be taken as a parody of the type
in Engl. fiction : ' He was a mere child in the
world, but he didn't cry for the moon. He
said to the world, Go your several ways in
peace !. Wear red coats, blue coats, lawn-
sleeves, put pens behind your ears, wear aprons ;
go after glory, holiness, commerce, trade, any
object you prefer ;—only let Harold Skimpole
live '. (Dickens, q.v. ; *Bleak House*, 1853,
ch. 6). So, G.'s Oblomov lay on his sofa, ' the
incarnation of what the Russian calls *Khalat-
nost*, the quality of dressing-gownness '
(prince Mirsky, *infr.*), and the great winds of
power passed him by, and Stolz, his Germ.
friend, failed to rouse him, and Olga fell in
and out of love with him, and left him on his
sofa, and married Stolz (there is a subtle
suggestion that she chose the lower way,
though irresistibly driven to it), and in the end
he marries his housekeeper, and dreams of
laziness for ever. ' It is ', says prince Mirsky
(*Mod. Russ. Lit.*, Oxford, 1925 ; p. 34), ' the
life-story of a Russian gentleman, who is made
to be the incarnation of sloth and conscious
inefficiency, coupled with no mean amount of
intellect and talent. The gradual growth of
the inevitable doom of the *unfit* man is developed
with a cunning and unerring hand '. (See,
too, s.v. R. Browning, on the crime of the
' unlit lamp and the ungirt loin '). Which
is right—right for heaven, if not for earth ?
Acceptance or negation, strenuousness or ease,
toil or the lotus ? Part of the greatness of
G.'s *Oblomov* resides in the lack of a complete
answer to these questions, knocking so urgently
at the door of Russ. thought and conscience in
the 'forties. The whole conflict of Westernizers *v.* Slavophils (see s.v. Russ. Lit.) was
typified by Oblomov's sofa. G.'s two other
novels of significance were ' A Common
Story ', 1847, of the young Aduyev from the
country, acclimatized gradually to the conditions of town-life, and weaned from his
provincial romanticism, under the tutelage of
the elder Aduyev, like another Pendennis
(s.v. Thackeray) by his uncle ; and ' The
Precipice ', 1868, originally entitled ' The

Artist '. This novel, though inordinately long, is one of the finest examples of objective realism in Russ. fiction. Its hero, Rasky, is again a recurrent type, and is to be found, e.g., in Herzen's (q.v.) Beltov.

Goncourt, de, -i. Edmond (1822-1896) and **-ii. Jules** (1830-1870): Fr. novelists, miscellanists; ' les deux Goncourt '; brothers. They may lay claim, or at least they formulated the claim, to three several inventions : Japanese art, the cult of the 18th cent., and naturalism in lit. (see Lanson, *Litt. fr.*, 1081). The first claim is based on their collection, and on sundry monographs in connection with it, which need not occupy us here. The second claim rests on such bks. as their *Femme au xviiie Siècle*, 1862, *Portraits Intimes du xviiie Siècle*, 1857-58, etc., which are not different in kind, though more original in date, than the many memoirs of personal history which have succeeded them. A Pompadour always attracts a writer with a taste for curios. Tho brothers' third claim has more interest, and their novels, *Soeur Philomène*, 1861, *Renée Mauperin*, 1864, *Germinie Lacerteux*, 1865, *Manette Salomon*, 1867, etc., certainly indicate those tastes for detailed descriptions of aspects of low life, which is characteristic of the school of which Zola (q.v.) was head, of which Flaubert (q.v.) was joint-founder, and which is the outcome of, rather than the reaction from, romanticism. That the G. brothers inaugurated this class of fiction in France may be affirmed, without too much emphasis. More precisely, they exhibited in their manner of writing characteristic signs of literary impressionism, and by this innovation in style they undoubtedly exercised great influence. After the death of the younger brother, Edmond G. continued to write novels, ' fatiguing ', in Ste-.Beuve's (q.v.) epithet : but his most important work was the publication of the *Journal des Goncourt* (9 vols., 1887-96), consisting of the literary diary of the brothers during their long social reign in Paris. It is a quite unpleasant bk., which violates the decencies of a diarist ; but its storehouse of scandalous tales and literary foibles lends it a value which has elements of permanent interest. E. G. used to invite Sunday gatherings of literary people to his house, and he bequeathed his fortune to a new Goncourt Academy, with an annual prize for a realistic novel of artistic merit. The whole record of the brothers G., whose collaboration is somewhat unique in lit., is on the verge of the egotistic and the exotic.

Gongora y Argote, de, Luis (1561-1627): Span. poet ; of marked genius in thought and expression ; founder of a style in poetry (later, extended to prose : see s.v. Paravicino) known by its founder's name as Gongorism, and also as *cultismo* (or *culteranismo*), from its appeal to the *culto* (Span.; educated or learned) man. Gongorism, in fact, was an intellectual cult or affectation, derivative from the reforms of Garcilasso and Boscan (qq.v.), the original Italianates of Spain, and akin to the Pleiad (q.v.) movement in France, to Euphuism (q.v.) in Engld., and, most of all, to Marinism (s.v. Marino) in Italy. Indeed, a little treatise on ' poetic erudition ', publd.

in the *Obras* (' Works ') of Carillo (q.v.), 1611, who had come under the influence of the Ital. futurist—for all these movements alike were aspects of what we now call futurism—was among the motives of G.'s second style. His second style specifically, because the verse of G.'s first poetic period was singularly pure and unaffected ; so much so, that Cascales (q.v.), in the critics' storm to which the new gospel gave rise, avowed that there were two Gongoras : one, an angel of light, and the other, an angel of darkness ; a sort of Jekyll and Hyde of poetic style. As in most futurist movements, there was good and evil in Gongorism : good theory and evil practice ; and the evil predominated. But G. preceded Gongorism, and we may come back to the poet himself. G. was born at Cordova, edu. at Salamanca univ., and, after a brief apprenticeship to the law, decided to enter the church. His poetic talents were early apparent, and were praised by Cervantes (q.v.) in his *Galatea*, though G.'s verses for the most part were circulated in MS. only. He was represented in the *Romancero* (q.v.) of 1600-04, and in Espinosa's (q.v.) *florilegium* of 1605, and was notable in both as the author of moving ballads of war and love. [See s.v. Romance (Span.)]. As a metrist he is to be reckoned the chief disciple of Herrera (q.v.), and his Armada ode ' to the armament of Philip ii against England ' is an admirable example of lyrical power. G. was also a writer for the stage ; and the collection of his plays and poems, very casually issued in his lifetime, is due to the labours of his friend Vicuña (q.v.), who publd. all that he could find, with almost supererogatory zeal, under the title of ' Works in Verse of the Spanish Homer ', 1627. The recent and definitive edn., by the modern scholar, Foulché-Delbosc, gives, with dates of composition, 420 pieces from G.'s pen (about 23,000 lines), and enables the reader to trace the development of his rare and brilliant gifts. The point to be noted in that development is the change which occurred about the year 1609, when G.'s second style succeeded to, and gradually replaced, his first. The ' Panegyric to the duke of Lerma ', the ' Fable of Polyphemus and Galatea ', the ' Pyramus and Thisbe ', and the ' Solitudes ' (*Soledades*), are longer poems which all display the deliberately cultivated mannerisms of style which had affected in a lesser degree some of his earlier sonnets and lyric verse. The Span. concettists (see s.v. Conceit) of this epoch made their most effective play with the ideas which words convey ; G.'s more contagious vice was to play with the words themselves : to introduce strange words ; to invent new ones ; to employ old ones in new surroundings ; to invert the order of words ; to use forced constructions ; somehow, and, ultimately, anyhow, to cause surprise by unexpectedness, and thus to attain to a style so obscure, so allusive, and so much involved, as to perplex even the learned audience of cultivated linguists to whom his poems were addressed. What was the object of it, in the first place ? Plainly, no poet of genius would practise Gongorism out of sheer malice ; and G.'s purpose was clearly enough to supple and diversify the resources of the literary language of Spain. It was capable of extension and enlargement; of Grecisms, Latinisms, Italicisms; of borrowings of vocabulary and construction from languages which had proved themselves capable of more perfect lit. than Spain had yet produced. In a sense, Meredith (q.v.) was a Gongorist, as Rabelais (q.v.) had been before him; and though all obscurity is not Gongorism, all Gongorism is obscure. Every great writer who is dissatisfied with the powers of the language which he uses, who finds some words worn by use and others inadequate for emphasis, and who tries to supply such shortcomings by new formations or new combinations, is doing work which will bear future fruit, however much ridicule it may arouse in the present by its more or less violent breach with current usage. A Gongorist is strictly an altruist, though his conscious motives may be mixed. He is risking contemporary misunderstanding, even personal obloquy, for the sake of enriching the inheritance which he administers in his generation. G. was no exception to this rule; his immediate success was considerable; he founded a school of Gongorists, who, naturally, exceeded his excesses; but he encountered much enmity and opposition, and more harm was wrought in his name than he ever dreamed or intended. Lope de Vega (q.v.), though not guiltless of flirting with Gongorism, undertook to train a *culto* poet in 24 hours: a few inversions, six Lat. words, and three or four formulæ, and the thing was done. But Vega was too consistent a hunter after popularity not to try to conciliate G., who did not take his strictures at all meekly, and G.'s triumph, though not long-lived, was complete. In a wider sense, Span. lit. owes to G. an example, which, strained and over-ambitious though it was, undoubtedly served a good end, and which, like similar movements before and after, must be accounted as a necessary concomitant of the process by which expression keeps pace with thought. There was a voluminous polemic *pro* and *con* Gongorism in Spain. (See s.v. Pellicer, Jauregui, Ledesma, Liñan, Villamediana, Quevedo).

Gonzalez del Castillo, Juan Ignacio (1763-1800): Span. dramatist. Wr. a tragedy, *Numa*, 1779, but soon turned to comedy and farce, and developed as a second and somewhat inferior (Ramon de) la Cruz (q.v.).

Googe, Barnabe (1540-94): Engl. poet; translr.; employed in Ireland, 1574-85, by his kinsman, sir Wm. Cecil. Wr. a vol. of eclogues, epitaphs and sonnets, 1563 (reprinted, 1871), and transld. works from Lat. and Germ., including a satire by Kirchmayer (q.v.) and *Four Bks. of Husbandrie* by C. Heresbach (1509-76), a statesman and scholar of the Low Countries.

'Gorboduc.' See s.v. **Sackville**.

Gosson, Stephen (1554-1624): Engl. poet; critic; praised by Meres (q.v.) for his pastoral verse, and wr. plays, now not of any account. G. is chiefly remembered as the author of a critical treatise, 1579, *The School of Abuse*, directed against 'poets and pipers, and such peevish cattle'. This was dedicated without permission to sir Philip Sidney (q.v.), whose *Apologie for Poetrie* (and similar essays by

Puttenham and Webbe; see *Documents illustrating Elizabethan Poetry*, Routledge, 1906) was to some extent provoked by it. G., who cited Plato's authority for excluding poets from the ideal Commonwealth, and whose invective was launched chiefly at the theatre, declared that 'we have robbed Greece of gluttony, Italy of wantonness, Spain of pride, France of deceit, and Dutchland of quaffing'. See, too, s.v. Ascham.

Gothic League (Swed.): Name of a Society devoted to the revival of native themes, mainly drawn from Scand. mythology, in Swed. letters. The league was founded early in the 19th cent. in opposition to the Swedish Academy. founded, 1786, by king Gustavus iii, on the Fr. model and in the Francophil spirit inherited from queen Christina (q.v.). The G.L. united men as different as Atterbom and Tegnér (qq.v.), though the one favoured and the other rejected the neo-romantic style of writing. The chief organ of the league was *Iduna*.

Gotter, Friedrich Wilhelm (1746-97): Germ. poet; a leader of the Göttingen (q.v.) school, and joint-founder with Boie (q.v.) of the 'Muses' Almanack', which became the literary organ of the poets' union, founded, 1772, under the name of the Hain (q.v.), for the purpose of expounding the gospel of Germ. poetry according to Klopstock (q.v.). G. was succeeded in the editorship by Voss (q.v.), and his writings are of no present worth.

Gottfried von Strassburg (fl. 1210): Germ. romancer. G. is always contrasted with his contemporary, Wolfram (q.v.), as representing the decadence of the court-epic, which Wolfram raised to the height of its powers. Nothing is known of G.'s life, except an inference from his title of 'Meister' to his burgherly orig. Wr., 1210, *Tristan*, in the Arthur (q.v.).-cycle of romance, founded on Fr. models; G. left it unfind., and it was completed later in the same century. Though G., as is clear, was less deeply imbued with the sense of the permanence of chivalric institutions than other composers of court-epos in his day, he surpassed them in his exaltation of the 'Minne' (q.v.)-idea—in the delineation, that is, of the pure passion out of which noble deeds were done. The sheer, sweet love between man and maid was sung by G. as by no poet before him.

Gottsched, -i. Johann Christoph (1700-66): Germ. critic and publicist; born at Königsberg or near it, but migrated, 1724, from his post at its univ. in order to escape the enrolment in the king of Prussia's grenadiers due to his stature of six feet; reached Leipsic, where his literary tastes suited the prevailing taste in the poetic academy, of which he became president; was appointed to the chair of poetry at Leipsic univ., a post which he held till his death; issued weekly literary organs, after the *Spectator* (see s.v. Addison) pattern: 'The Intelligent Faultfinding-women' (*Tadlerinnen*), 1725, and 'The Honest Man' (*Biedermann*), 1727; neither particularly successful. Wr., 1730, a manifesto for the neo-classic school poetry (see s.v. Boileau), of which Saintsbury says, that G. 'is an apostle not so much even of classicism as of that hopeless *prosaism* to which classicism lent itself but too easily' (*Hist. Crit.*, ii, 555). If we may imitate Saintsbury in disdaining to analyse this Germ. variant of a Fr. perversion of more ancient theories, a reference at least is due to the battle of bks. (or of pamphlets and newspapers) which G.'s *ars poetica* provoked. Leipsic armed against Zurich, Saxony therefore against Switzerland, in G.'s newly-imbrued area of the perennial warfare between the classicists and romanticists. The Swiss protagonists were two professors, Bodmer and Breitinger (qq.v.), *arcades ambo*, and Johann Jakob both, so that they sometimes signed a joint brochure with the initials ' J.J.J.J.' Bodmer's ' Discourses of the Painters ', which was the fanciful name of the literary review which he had founded at Zurich, opened the fray about 1721, and it burst with fresh virulence round the publication in 1732 of Bodmer's transln. of *Paradise Lost* ; for Milton was a sinner against the light according to G.'s mechanic laws of heroic poetry. Each J. J., Bodmer and Breitinger, issued an *ars poetica* of his own c. 1710 ; and the stream of publications, periodical and permanent, swelled to considerable dimensions. Like other battles of the bks., it is dreary to follow in its details, some of which are given in Saintsbury (*op. cit.*), and more of which are to be found in Braitmaier's Germ. *History of Poetic Theory and Criticism from the ' Discourses of the Painters ' to Lessing* (1889). The public effect of the quarrel between the Leipsic and the Zurich schools were inevitably a victory for the Swiss ; it cleared the air once more, by a final and decisive *Aufklärung* (see s.v.) for the triumph of Klopstock (q.v.) and his successors. The exhaustive and exhausting investigation into the canons of correctness in poetry made the road smoother for the coming poets ; and G. may at least have the credit of having collected the obstructions for removal. The personal effect of the quarrel was disastrous to G. in his life-time, and he has hardly been restituted since. He was deposed from the eminence of dictator of taste which he had created for himself at Leipsic. As he grew older, the younger men deserted his standard, and flocked to the hated Zurichers ; and at last even the youthful Goethe, who saw him at Leipsic, laughed at his learned wig. He outlived his reputation so completely that, though it had been greater than that of Opitz (q.v.), it was quite forgotten in his old age ; and, though he was a fighter till the end, he died in dishonour and neglect. It was life itself, with its quickened movement, which passed him by. Yet even for his industry he is memorable. To be busy was the keystone of his teaching, and he produced a long row of textbooks, pamphlets, journals and libraries ; of these a treatise on the Germ. language, 1748, and his materials for a history of Germ. drama, 1757-65, are perhaps the most valuable. G.'s dramatic labours were not confined to history. He attempted a reform of the stage, in the sense of creating a taste for Fr. classical drama, or, rather, for Germ. plays after Fr. models ; and his attempt was so far justified that he paved the way for the long-due reunion of lit. and stage in Germany. In this work

at Leipsic he was aided by the actors Neuber and his wife, of whom the latter (Frederika Karoline, 1697-1760) was the more talented and valuable coadjutor. G. provided plays for his stage in 6 vols. of ' The German Theatre according to the Rules of the Ancient Greeks and Romans ', and to this repertory of translns. and adaptations he contributed a tragedy of his own, ' The dying Cato ' (*der sterbende Cato*), which owed nine-tenths of its existence to Deschamps and Addison (qq.v.).

   -ii. Luise Adelgande (1713-62): Germ. playwright ; wife of the foregoing ; *née* Kulmus. Wr. *Das Testament* and other original comedies of merit for her husband's theatre at Leipsic, and contributed translns. to his repertory, ' The German Theatre,' 1740-45.

Gournay, de, Jean Claude Marie Vincent (1712-59): Fr. political economist ; free-trader ; advocate of the single tax (*impot unique*) on land, and the practical man among the Physiocrats (q.v.). To de G. is due the precept, *laissez faire, laissez aller*.

Gournay, de, Marie (1566-1645): Fr. woman of letters ; met Montaigne (q.v.) in Paris, 1588, and was adopted by him as his daughter. Edited his *Essais*, 1595, from the author's annotated copy. Mlle. de G. was always an advocate of the lyrical as opposed to the oratorical school ; of Ronsard, e.g., as against Corneille ; and, while much esteemed in her generation, was the centre of certain lit. controversies, and developed some eccentric habits.

Gower, John (*c.* 1325-1408): Engl. poet ; contemporary with Chaucer (q.v.), who dedicated to him *Troilus and Criseyde* ; ' O moral Gower, this booke I direct To thee ' (v, 266). The epithet, which has stuck, may have been due to the didactic tone of G.'s *Vox Clamantis*, a Lat. poem, dealing, not unlike *Piers Plowman's Vision* (s.v. Langland), with social evils and divine remedies. Wr. too, *Speculum Meditantis* (*Mirour de l'Omme*) in Fr., which was lost till G. C. Macaulay's Oxford edn., 1899-1902 ; and Fr. love-ballads on old Provençal models ; also a Lat. ' Tripartite Chronicle ', and other works. G.'s only Engl. work of note was his *Confessio Amantis*, tales and moralizings of love in octosyllabic couplets. As a linked sequence of stories it anticipated the formal device of the *Canterbury Tales*, and a jealousy is said to have sprung up between G. and Chaucer, whose name occurred in the first version of the *Confessio*, 1390—

    ' And greet well Chaucer when ye meet,
      As my disciple and my poete '

but disappeared in the final version, 1392-3. There is little original in G., but he enhanced the Fr. and Italianate reform of Engl. poetry, and may be termed ' correct ' rather than ' moral ' by the historian. Particularly interesting is the example he affords in his writings of the double influence on the modern Engl. language of Lat. and Fr. G.'s equal facility in all three is symbolical of the tributaries which flowed into the stream. G. still enjoyed a reputation among the Elizabethans ; his story of Apollonius of Tyre in bk. viii of the *Confessio* was the immediate source of

Shakespeare's *Pericles*, which G. enters in Act i:

> 'To sing a song that old was sung,
> From ashes ancient Gower is come'.

Gozzi, -i. Gaspare (1713-86): It. journalist; founded (1) the *Gazette Veneta*, 1760-61, and (2) the *Osservatore Veneto*, 1762, a weekly journal of manners and letters on the model of Addison's (q.v.) *Spectator*. G.'s wife was the poet, Luisa Bergalli, whose 'Pindaric' system of housekeeping led to domestic ruin, and G. had to support his children by the proceeds of his pen. He won success without losing the good-humour, which marked his native Venetian wit.

-ii. Carlo (1720-1806): It. dramatist; brother of above. After an adventurous youth, C.G. returned to Venice in the period of the dramatic quarrel between Goldoni and Chiari (qq.v.), and sought to pour ridicule on both camps, and, at the same time, to revive the national glory of the decadent *commedia dell'arte* (q.v.) by giving it a fresh lease of life. To this end, in which he was backed by the excellent journalist, Baretti (q.v.), he blended the old masks with the magic and mystery of eastern fairy-tales, and in 4 years, 1761-65, composed 10 of these romantic contaminations, known in Italy as *fiabe*. Their immediate success in Venice was extraordinary, and led to Goldoni's retirement to new pastures in Paris. But the vogue declined into a compound of fancy, vulgarity and irony, which found more popularity in Germ. adaptations than in G.'s native city or country. G's *Turandot*, e.g., in Schiller's (q.v.) version, has become a Germ. classic, and was produced in that language at the St. James's Theatre in London. Others were the 'Three Oranges', 'Blue Monster', 'Green Bird', etc. J. R. Planché (q.v.) had something of the kind of genius in Engld., and it is akin, though inferior, to that of W. S. Gilbert (q.v.), which adds a point to the perception of J. A. Symonds, who admirably transld. G.'s *Memoirs*, that the *fiabe* would make excellent material for operatic libretti.

Gracian y Morales, Baltasar (1601-58): Span. moralist; Jesuit; rector of the coll. at Tarragona; flourished at the height of the *cultismo* introduced by Gongora (q.v.), and helped to infect Span. prose with the conceits and obscurities of its style. This dis-service has caused more neglect of G.'s thoughtful and sometimes brilliant writings than is altogether just, though his *Oraculo Manual y Arte de Prudencia*, 1647, had the distinction of being transld. by Schopenhauer (q.v.), and, possibly, of inspiring some of the maxims of La Rochefoucauld (q.v.). More recently, it was made accessible in an Engl. transln. by J. Jacobs (Macmillan, *Golden Treasury*). A more ambitious work than this 'art of worldly wisdom' was G.'s *el Criticon*, issued in 3 parts, 1651-53-57 (spring and summer, autumn, winter, of life), an allegory of a ship-wrecked Span. nobleman, Critilo, who meets an untutored savage on his desert island (St. Helena, of later fame). They contrive to exchange ideas in Span., and later travel together, and discuss all kinds of topics with real and imaginary personages. It has been suggested, from the obvious likeness in some circumstances, that Defoe (q.v.)

derived hints for *Robinson Crusoe* from this bk.; Ticknor (iii, 223) compares it with an even greater Engl. classic: 'the *Criticon* is to the Catholic religion and the notions of life in Spain during the reign of Philip iv what Bunyan's fiction is to Puritanism and the English character in the age of Cromwell. But there is little vitality', he adds, 'in the shadowy personages of Gracian'. Many of G.'s writings may have been lost; his position in the Jesuit Coll. rendered publication distasteful to him, and it was a friend, Lastonosa, who issued several under the name of Lorenco Gracian. *El Discreto*, 1646, was anon., and consists of misc. prose, including some letters; there were also 'The Hero', 1637, a sort of specification for the heroic likeness of *el politico don Fernando el Catolico*, 1640; and, more importantly, an 'Art of Rhetoric' (*Aguzeda y Arte de Ingenio*), 1648, which was a kind of manifesto of Gongoristic style, displaying 'vast reading, extreme sublety, and—in places —good taste' (Kelly, *Lit. espagn.*, 379).

Gracioso (Span.): Generic name of the shrewd, presuming, confidential servant, who was a stock character in Span. comedy. The part was really invented in the *Serafina* of Naharro (q.v.), but the definitive shape which was given to it by Lope de Vega (q.v.) entitles that 'prodigy of nature' to rank more permanently as its father. From Vega the *G.* was adopted by the playwrights of Spain and France; Calderon's (q.v.) buffoon was drawn with a heavier hand than Vega's, but fresh emphasis was laid on the part in the comedies of Moreto (q.v.). The *G.* of Molière (q.v.) was given a generic name, and figures as Sganarelle in several of his plays; he reached, perhaps, the height of his powers in the Figaro of Beaumarchais (q.v.).

Graevius (Graeve, Greffe), Johann Georg (1632-1703): Dutch scholar and antiquary. Held chair of eloquence at Deventer and Utrecht, where most of his life was spent; edited Cicero's *Letters*, and other works, including compilations ('Treasuries') of antiquarian research. G. and Bentley (q.v.) were constant correspondents, 1692-1703.

Grail: Magic vessel in the Arthuriad (s.v. Arthur); by extension, object of spiritual quest. The literal meaning of grail (Lat. *gradalis*) is dish or chalice, and Celtic tales of the exploits of Perceval (q.v.; the Peredur of the Welsh *Mabinogion*, or tales for the young) included, as an isolated episode, his search for a mysterious vessel which he had seen in an enchanted castle during his many wanderings. If he found the vessel he would release the castle and its inmates from the spell. Thus, the grail, so far as it can be traced clearly to its first home in Celtic folklore, was a magic dish, represented in a single episode of the Perceval Breton-cycle ('matière de Bretagne'; see s.vv. Bodel and Arthur), and had no further connection with any other part of that many-branched legendary lore. But there was another grail. In sacred Christian legend, Joseph of Arimathea had caught in a dish the blood that flowed from the body of Jesus Christ at the Crucifixion. This dish was brought into association with the pagan dish of Celtic lore by the legends of the conversion of Britain to Christianity through the missionary zeal of the same Joseph. He came to Britain with a sacred grail; he found a magic grail in British story; it was natural to confuse the two in the tales of Joseph and the Breton heroes among whom he walked. The *Perceval* (or, *conte du Graal*) of Chrétien de Troyes (q.v.) does not throw much light on the subject; but Robert du Boron (q.v.), not long afterwards, designed a romantic redaction of the chivalric and ecclesiastical grail-stories, which brought them together for all times; and Wolfram von Eschenbach (q.v.) made brilliant use of the material. Later in the 13th cent., the dominance of the sacred relic deposed Perceval in favour of Galahad (q.v.), as the purest flower of knighthood (see also s.v. Lancelot). The grail-quest was extended and adorned in verse and prose; Glastonbury Abbey, by its connection with the relic, and early Engld. as a whole, were venerated as shrines of Christian story; the grail became the symbol of knightly service under the Cross, and brought the Celtic magic of the Arthuriad into intimate relation with the most sacred aspirations of religious life. (See s.vv. Rusticiano, Malory, and Tennyson).

Gram, Hans (1685-1748): Dan. scholar; historiographer, archivist, and prof. of Gk. at univ. of Copenhagen, which was rebuilt, 1732, during his term of office. G. was active, too, in the foundation of the Kongelige Danske Selskab (the Royal Danish Society of Sciences) under king Christian vi, 1742. Apart from his official posts and duties, G. has no considerable claim on posterity: his writings, which won him the fame of the greatest man in Denmark, are 'buried in a number of minor lucubrations, and he was only too apt to lose himself in mazes of minute detail' (Sandys, *Hist. Class. Schol.*, iii, 314); they included a Dan.-Lat. and Lat.-Dan. dict., *Nucleus Latinitatis*.

Grammont, de, Philibert (1621-1707). Fr. adventurous gallant, at the courts, successively, of kings Louis xiv of France and Charles ii of Engld., and in exile; *comte* by rank; m., Elizabeth, sister of A. Hamilton (q.v.); and is celebrated in lit. for his *Mémoires*, publd. anon., 1713, by Hamilton, his brother-in-law and fellow-adventurer. The Engl. transln. was edited by H. Walpole (q.v.), 1772, and sir W. Scott (q.v.), 1811; and the memoirs comprise the best picture of the corrupt and frivolous Stuart court.

Grasso Legnaiulo, Il (15th cent.): It. novella; 'the stout Carpenter'; ascribed to Antonio Manetto (1423-1497); written in Florentine prose. This type of tale was more commonly versified. The G.L. turns on a practical joke of the usual farcial kind, based on a question of identity between Manetto, the good fellow ('grasso' has a moral as well as a physical connotation), and a certain Matteo, who is heavily in debt. Symonds (*Ital. Renaissance*, i, 219) describes it 'as the finest extant specimen of homespun Tuscan humour'.

Gratius, Ortwin (1491-1541): Germ. ecclesiastical scholar; head of the Dominicans at Cologne; Ortuinus. Selected as typical butt of medieval

dog-Latinity and scholasticism by the Reuchlinite-humanist authors of the *Epistolæ Obscurorum Virorum* (q.v.).

Gravina, Giovanni Vincenzo (1664-1718): It. jurisprudent; wr. *Origines Juris Civilis*, 1701-8. G. was one of the 14 founders of the Roman Academy of Arcadia (q.v.), in memory of queen Christina (q.v.), and, in token of his legal eminence, he drew up its tables of law. His qualification was not poetry, but the criticism of it, and Saintsbury (*Hist. Crit.*, ii, 538) calls him 'a critic of remarkable shrewdness, who wrote excellent things on tragedy, and thought his own bad tragedies excellent. . . . The total effect is, as with most other eighteenth century critics, a conclusion that the writer has not found his way: though he is nearer to it than some others writing later.' G. was the patron and adoptive father of Metastasio (q.v.).

Gray, Thomas (1716-71): Engl. poet, scholar, letter-writer; his 'influence upon subsequent literature was largely in excess of the volume of his published works' (*C.H.E.L.*, x, 116). Dealing, first, with the publd. works of this accomplished Etonian, they comprised (1), anon., 1747, *Ode on a Distant Prospect of Eton College*; (2) *An Elegy Wrote in a Country Church Yard*, 1751, (3) *Odes*, 1757; (4) *Poems*, 1768, and (5) *Ode performed in the Senate-House at Cambridge*, 1 July, 1769. 'The frugal note of Gray', sir Wm. Watson, a poet *de nos jours*, has called it, and the epithet is just; but there is justice, too, in a remark in the paper on G. in Johnson's (q.v.) *Lives of the Poets* (1779-81; shortly after G.'s death): 'In 1757 he publd. *The Progress of Poetry* and *The Bard*, two compositions at which the readers of poetry were at first content to gaze in remote amazement. Some that tried them confessed their inability to understand them, though Warburton (1698-1779; critic; friend of Pope) said that they were understood as well as the works of Milton and Shakespeare, which it is the fashion to admire'. The passage is illuminating, since it shows that G., who was one of the most learned men in Europe at that date, was working his solitary way back to the Middle Ages, as the phrase went, i.e. to an appreciation of the older tradition in poetry represented by Chaucer and Spenser, Milton and Shakespeare. He was teaching himself to change the fashionable admiration and conventional appreciation of those writers into an intelligent and reasoned knowledge of their permanently admirable qualities. The romantic (s.v. Romance) revivalists were restoring the past, and therefore building for the future: sir Wm. Temple (q.v., died 1699) had treated Icel. song as a constituent element in the progress of poetry; bp. Percy (q.v.; *Five Pieces of Runic Poetry*, 1762) and T. Warton (q.v.) had doubled the parts of antiquaries and poets; and Macpherson (q.v.) had gratified the taste of Home (q.v.) and others by discovering (*i.q.* inventing) the romantic magic of the Northern Celts. Taliesin of Wales, Ossian of Ireland, and the rest were coming into their own again, and G.'s odes from the Norse or Welsh (*The Fatal Sisters*, *The Descent of Odin*, etc.) were on the road of that long journey, which led at last to a new perspective of poetry, and to the reflorescence of romance.

The *Elegy*, which is the chief monument to G.'s genius, is written in the 10-syllabled quatrains of Dryden's (q.v.) *Annus Mirabilis*, and belongs to a series of poems which depend for their appeal on the associations of death (q.v.), melancholy and the grave. Young, Collins, Thomson (qq.v.) and others were alike moved by the same sentiment, which was stirred by that reaction of poetic taste from the mixed hedonism and fatalism of the 18th cent. to the fiercer questioning of a less acquiescent age. When all is said and done, when every allowance is made for the correctness of G.'s taste and the sobriety of his diction, we yet feel, in reading this stately *Elegy*, with the added experience of nearly two centuries, that G. was sensibly enlarging the moral boundaries of poetry, and was making way for the expression of humble and obscure lives. These 'annals of the poor', this 'village-Hampden' and 'inglorious Milton', this 'rustic moralist' with his 'unlettered Muse', these voiceless, disinherited, unhonoured sons of unfulfilled renown,—surely the lonely tombstone in the churchyard at Stoke Poges, where G. lived for a short time with his widowed mother, cries its *siste, viator*, from one age to another, and arrests, in G.'s melodious stanzas, less simple in diction than a first reading reveals, the transition of Engl. lit. from Pope to Wordsworth and his successors. The perpetual appeal of this *Elegy* is indicated by the fact that ten acres of land surrounding the country churchyard were acquired by the National Trust, and dedicated to the public for ever, in order to preserve the scene from vandalism, on 5 May, 1925, visct. Grey of Fallodon, K.G., presiding.

It remains to note that G. was a friend of H. Walpole (q.v.) : that he was appointed prof. of Modern History at Cambridge, 1768 ; that he was offered, and refused, 1757, the poet-laureateship bestowed on Wm. Whitehead (q.v., and see s.v. Rolliad), and that his 'letters are an excellent guide as a survey of continental literature '. In France, Germany and Italy, G.'s poems produced notable influence on the rising romanticism of the day, and his *Elegy* particularly has enjoyed the admiration of successive generations of readers in the U.S.A.

Grazzini, Antonio Francesco (1503-83): It. writer of tales (*novelle*), burlesques, and comedies, in reaction against the prevailing classicism of his name. Known as *il Lasca* (the roach), in accordance with the fashion of the Florentine Academy *degli umidi* to call each member after the name of a fish. G.'s tales are particularly notable for the impetus which they gave to dramatic and novellistic composition. But everything which he wr. is fatally marred by the common faults of the school (for it was hardly less) of Aretino and Berni (qq.v.), viz. unpleasantness and nastiness for its own sake, without the relief of bigness.

Greek Fiction : The late Gk. writers of stories, devoted to love and adventure, flourished from very early in the Christian era till the 12th and even the 13th cent. With the unique exception of the *Filocolo* of Boccaccio (q.v.), however,

this class of lit. did not exercise any considerable influence upon the development of European letters until a comparatively late date. It served as a kind of extra source to the writers of *romans* and *chansons* in the first period of Romance (q.v.) : thus, Chrétien (q.v.) derived his *Cligès* from an eastern original, and Beaumanoir (q.v.) traced his *Manekin* to Byzantium ; and other tales, more or less famous, were drawn from sources outside the great cycles. At the time of the beginning of the Renaissance (q.v.), however, and right away to the end of the 17th cent., the inspiration of Gk. fiction, as distinct from the employment of story-plots (e.g., in Shakespeare, *Cymbeline* and doubtful *Pericles*), was utilized by pastoralists and novelists in Spain, Italy, and France. France caught the infection last, though her reaction at about 1610 from civil and religious warfare to a deliberate cultivation of a literary atmosphere (see s.vv. Fr. lit., Rambouillet, Precious) rendered her particularly liable to the appeals of the Gk. novelists. The one competing influence was the popularity of *Amadis of Gaul* (q.v.), which supplied most of her wants for the time being. But busy translrs. soon got to work, and their labours were swiftly followed by a train of admirers and imitators. It suited the genius of the *grand siècle* to retire from the stress of public life into the *milieu* and manners depicted by amorous Arcadians. Among the more famous writers included in lists of *Erotici Græci* are : i, Longus, reputed author of *Daphnis and Chloe*, and therefore as definitely the father of prose-pastoral as Theocritus (q.v.) of pastoral poetry ; ii, the author of *The Golden Ass*, probably Lucius of Patras, who served as model to Apuleius ; iii, Heliodorus, author of *Theagenes and Chariclea*, transld., 1549, by Amyot (q.v.), whose version was dedicated to king Francis i (q.v.), and frequently reprinted ; this romance fascinated Racine (q.v.) ; iv, Achilles Tatius, author of *Leucippe and Clitophon*, transld. by Belleforest (q.v.), and among the sources of the *Astrée* of Urfé (q.v.) ; v, Charito of Aphrodisia, author of *Chaereas and Callirrhoe*, ed. pr., 1750 ; vi, Photius, patriarch of Constantinople, 857 A.D., who, though not a novelist himself, made summaries of bks. which he had read, and thus preserved in outline some works not otherwise extant ; vii, Iamblichus (preserved in Photius), author of *Babylonica*, a prime authority for the romance of heroic gallantry, utilized in a *Sophonisbe, histoire Afriquaine*, formerly ascribed to Scudéry (q.v.), of which the *Rasselas* of Johnson (q.v.) is a good enough example of many similar derivatives from the prototype ; viii, Antonius Diogenes, who is said to have written 24 bks. of imaginary travels (*Incredible Things from beyond Thule*), parodied by Lucian (*Vera Historia*), whose influence on Rabelais (q.v.) is a matter of common knowledge. It was precisely this connection between fiction and history, between the unreal and the actual, and this mode of describing the improbable in terms of narrative prose, which attracted so powerfully the Fr. novelists of the 16th and 17th cents. They aimed at an illusion themselves ; at a reconstruction of lit. on a social basis, and at imposing on a distracted generation the authority of an aristocratic *côterie*; and they found in these old Gk. art-tales the tone and the style which they sought, and the verisimilitude essential to their design. It is to be added that Gk. fiction is more often than not unpleasantly indecent. (See, too, s.v. Novel).

Green, John Richard (1837-83): Engl. historian. Wr. *Short History of the English People*, 1874 (and often reprinted), which by its charm of style and imaginative insight maintains its place in hist. lit. G. was a founder of the *Engl. Hist. Review*. His widow, Mrs. Alice (*née* Stopford) G., assisted and has continued his labours.

Green, Thomas Hill (1836-82): Engl. philosopher; pupil of Jowett (q.v.), master of Balliol; edited the works of Hume (q.v.), 1874-5, and then and, later, in his *Prolegomena to Ethics*, 1883, opposed the utilitarianism of the school of J. S. Mill (q.v.). G. was the 'Mr. Gray' of *Robert Elsmere* by Mary Ward (s.v. Arnold)

Greene, Robert (*c.* 1560-92): Engl. poet; pamphleteer; one of the Tudor univ. wits, with experience of travel on the Continent, who led a roystering life among the young bloods of the green-rooms in London. Harvey (q.v.) dubbed him 'the ape of Euphues' (see s.v. Lyly, whose *Euphues* G. continued in his *Censure to Philautus*, 1587). Wr. plays and tales, of no great worth or moment at this day, though his *Triumph of Time*, 1588, suggested to Shakespeare the fable on which he wr. *The Winter's Tale*; and G. likewise had a part in the original draft of the three parts of *Henry vi*, which Shakespeare twice helped to recast; this fact alone, says sir Sidney Lee (*Life of Shakespeare*, 1915; p. 121) 'can account for Greene's indignant denunciation of Shakespeare as "an upstart crow, beautified with the feathers" of himself and his fellow-dramatists'. The famous phrase occurs in G.'s autobiographical *Groatsworth of Wit bought with a Million of Repentance*; his last and now his best-known piece of writing.

Gresset, Jean Baptiste Louis (1709-77): Fr. poet and dramatist. Wr. one good poem and one good play, after which he retired to a monastery (it was a return as well as a retirement), and drew down upon himself the facile epigrams of Voltaire and Piron (qq.v.) for his desertion of the stage. The good poem was *Vert-vert*, 1733, on a parrot, a particularly charming trifle; and the good play was *le Méchant*, 1745, a satire of manners, directed against the would-be man-of-the-world. It contains many excellent verses, and is remarkable for its attack on Parisian life in his day. A like moral bias inspired G.'s inferior drama, *Sidney*.

Greville, Charles Cavendish Fulke (1794-1865): Engl. memoirist; clerk to the privy council, 1821-59. Wr. political and social diary in 3 parts, 1817-37, 1837-52, 1852-60, publd. respectively 1875, 1885 and 1887, under the competent editorship of H. Reeve (q.v.), and constituting a valuable authority for the inner history of the times.

Grévin, Jacques (*c.* 1540-70): Fr. poet, dramatist; Calvinist by faith, and follower of Ronsard (q.v.) in letters. A tragedy, *La Mort de César*, founded, as Shakespeare's after him, and as Jodelle's (q.v.) contemporarily with him, on Plutarch, and 2 comedies survive, and some graceful minor verse. A lesser satellite of the Pleiad (q.v.) galaxy.

Griboyedov, Alexis Sergievich (1795-1829): Russ. dramatist; wr. a rhymed comedy, *Gore ot Uma*. ('Woe from Wit' or 'The Misfortune of being Clever', as prince Mirsky and the hon. M. Baring respectively translate it; publd. 1825), which 'is the first revelation of that wonderful power of character-drawing which struck the Western reader when he first discovered the Russian novel' (Mirsky, *Modern Russ. Lit.*, Oxford, 1925, p. 11), and which may be compared in intention and effect with the *Mariage de Figaro* of Beaumarchais (q.v.). G., though not implicated in the Decembrist rising of 1825 (that brief political effusion of mystic and masonic fellowship), which cost Ryleef (q.v.) his life, was near enough to it in sentiment to find insuperable difficulty in gaining publication for his play. He wr. it before 1820: in 1823-4 he gave readings from it in select circles at Petrograd, where it aroused immense enthusiasm, and where extracts were publd. in a literary almanack, 1825. The whole play enjoyed wide circulation *per ora virorum* before it was surreptitiously staged, 1831, and printed, 1833. So hard was it in Russia for a dramatist to hold up the mirror to life. The play was classical in its respect for the unities (q.v.), and was written in the irregular iambic verse which Krylov (q.v.) had employed for his fables. The plot of the drama is of the simplest: Chatzky, the hero, returns to Moscow after three years' residence abroad; and, like Batiushkov (q.v.) in real life, he does not recognize his Ithaca. The peaceful Germ. penetration of thought and society in Moscow have made it more foreign than the city which he left, in an access of home- and love-sickness; and his soliloquies and tirades against the superficiality, the falsehood, the folly, the idle and empty apishness of the new régime at Moscow account at once for the esteem of sympathizers and the anger of authority. In diction and characterization alike G.'s comedy stands on a pinnacle supreme in the history of Russ. drama; its social satire is fully equal to the diction of W. S. Gilbert (q.v.) at his best, and its characterization is as excellent as Sheridan's (q.v.). Pushkin (q.v.), who relates how he met the funeral chariot of G. on the road from Teheran to Tiflis ('Journey to Erzerum'; G. was assassinated in Persia, where he held the post of Russ. minister, by a troop of bandits), lost in this one-play dramatist the only serious rival whom he might have feared.

Grigoriev, Apollon Andreyevich (1822-64): Russ. critic; the founder in his own country of the so-called organic criticism, as distinct from the æsthetic. A work of art, in G.'s view, was to be explained as an organic product of the national genius at a given moment of history, and Gogol (q.v.) served him admirably as an example. He divided mankind into 2 classes: birds of prey and their dovelike victims, and, though his critical repute was too temporal and local to win him a mention in Saintsbury's *History of Criticism*, it had considerable

influence on the fiction of Dostoievsky (q.v.).
G. liked to call himself the last of the Romanticists, and his idols in poetry were Pushkin
and Byron (qq.v.).

Grillparzer, Franz (1791-1872) : Germ. dramatist.
After some experiments and successes in lyric
verse, and after the production of *Die Ahnfrau*
in Vienna, 1817,—a fate-tragedy (q.v.) in
trochaic metre,—G. completed, 1818, his
second play, *Sappho,*- which was followed,
1819-22, by ' The Golden Fleece : a Trilogy '
(*Der Gastfreund, Medea* and *Die Argonauten*),
likewise based on the Greek. Though G.'s
' field is not wide, and his influence was not
great ' (*P.E.L.*, xi, 300), his plays are fully
in the big tradition, and, while they look back
on the romantic past, they are set on the forward
lines that arose in France in the decline of
the Romantic movement. He wr. another
drama on a Gk. theme, that of Hero and
Leander, and next turned in *Ottokars Glück
und Ende*, 1825, to a theme of national history,
king Ottokar of Bohemia's vain struggle
against the Habsburgs ; this play was not
composed without reference to the contemporary rise and fall of Napoleon, who dominated
every stage, not only G.'s. Besides these
best known dramas G. wr. comedies and
Biblical plays, and ' The Jewess of Toledo ',
from a drama by Lope de Vega (q.v.), whose
fame G. helped to restore from the excessive
depreciation of the Calderonists in his critical
studies of the theatre in Spain. Lastly,
mention is due to G.'s delicately fanciful prose-
tale, *der arme Spielmann*, 1848. G.'s plays
are still performed on the Germ. stage, and his
place in Germ. lit. may perhaps be defined
as that of one of the authors whom no gentleman's library can omit. It is notable, too,
that dramatic talent was rare in his age, and
that he possessed it in a unique degree.

Grimald, Nicholas (1519-62) : Engl. poet. Contributed to the *Miscellany* of Tottel (q.v.),
which he probably helped the publisher to
compile. Wr. Lat. plays, and translns. from
Lat. authors. It is to be noted, though no
explanation of the fact is forthcoming, that out
of 40 poems by G. in the first edn. of Tottel's
Miscellany (June, 1557) quite 30 were omitted
in the second edn. in the month following,
when his full name was reduced to his initials.

Grimm, -i. Jacob (1785-1863) : **-ii. Wilhelm**
(1786-1859) : Germ. folklorists ; founders of
Germ. philology ; Romanticists ; brothers. J.
was the greater scholar, W. the greater writer
of the two, but, biographically, the brothers
are inseparable. Together, they learned law
under Savigny (q.v.) ; together, contributed
to a Heidelberg Romantic journal (*Zeitung
für Einsiedler*, founded 1808 ; afterwards
called *Tröst Einsamkeit* ; short-lived) ; together, were librarians, first in Cassel, then in
Göttingen ; together, settled in Berlin, 1841,
and became members of the Academy of Sciences
and univ. lecturers. Together, too, less
pertinently to lit., they exemplified in their
lives that ' naïve heart of the German people '
(Robertson, *Hist. Germ. Lit.*, 461), which
Arnim and Brentano (qq.v.) had embalmed
in the Heidelberg collection of folksong, *des
Knaben Wunderhorn* (1805-08). These great,
tender, gentle brothers poured into the

national revival all the mingled resources
of their scholarship and sensibilities. Just
a year before the battle of Leipsic, which liberated Germany from Napoleon, and which should
have liberated Germany's spirit from the
bondage of *das Gemeine*, W.G. wr. in his
Preface to the ' Fairy Tales ' (*Kinder-und
Hausmärchen*), which was the brothers' chief
bounty to European letters (18 Oct., 1812) :
' There lives in these tales the same purity
which makes children seem so wonderful and so
blessed (*selig*) to us. . . . The sphere of this
world is limited : kings, princes, faithful
servants, honest craftsmen, above all, fishermen, millers, charcoal-burners and shepherds,
all the folk who live nearest to Nature appear
in it ; what lies beyond is strange and inhuman '.
The ' nearest to nature ' and ' the blessed '
(' Ye blessed Creatures, I have heard the call,
ye to each other make ', Wordsworth, q.v.,
Nature's neighbour, was singing by the Eng.
lakes) : these are the key-notes of the perception, which the brothers G. and their Romantic
fellows sought to recover for re-awakening
Germany ; and if we remember that the
Germ. word *selig* and the Engl. word *silly* are
the same word, we see at once the height and
the depth of Germ. Romanticism, so completely
realized in the brothers' works and lives. So,
Hänsel and Gretel, and Schneewittchen and
Briar-Rose, and the dwarf, and the princess,
and the rest of the old, sweet company of
Germ. forest and field, came out in their artless
charm, at the summons of the folklorist-poets,
to recall all rulers and their subjects to truer
values of conduct. The *Kinder- und Hausmärchen* (1812-15) and the *Deutsche Sagen*
(1816-18) are the most famous, most widely
distributed, and most permanently established
of the brothers' bks. : no nation, so brilliantly
as Germany, has placed men's learning at the
service of children, or has cultivated so assiduously a child's heart as the people's most
precious possession. There is, of course,
more than a touch of the brothers' naïvety
and whimsicalness in some of the faëry of sir
Jas. Barrie, O.M. How deep was the learning
which went to the decoction of these simple
' Fairy Tales ' out of the mass of ancient,
native myth and legend, may be judged from
the brothers' other bks. These include J.'s
Deutsche Grammatik (4 vols. ; i, 1819, iv,
1837), in which he formulated ' Grimm's
Law ' of consonantal philology, and similar
works on German antiquities and mythology ;
W.'s *Deutsche Heldensage* (1829) ; and, jointly,
the great *Deutsches Wörterbuch* (1852 and
following), which they did not live to complete.

   -iii, Hermann (1828-1901) : Germ. poet
and critic ; son of W. above. Wr. dramas and
tales, and a well-reputed monograph on
Goethe.

Grimm, de, Frédéric Melchior (1723-1807) : Fr.
critic ; letter-writer ; of Germ. descent ; born
at Ratisbon, died at Gotha. G. was one of
several authors of what may be called a Paris
letter to foreign princes. The chief recipient
was the duchess of Saxe-Coburg ; and, among
other royal personages to whom the bulletin
was circulated were the empress Catherine ii
(q.v.) of Russia and the kings of Prussia and
Poland. It was through G.'s letters that these

monarchs were kept so thoroughly well-informed of the progress of the Encyclopedia (q.v.), and other matters. G. conducted the *Correspondance* from 1753-73 ; later, Diderot and mme. d'Epinay (qq.v.) often took his place. The journal was intimate and strictly private, and was not made known till 1812 : the best edn. is that of Tourneux, 1877, and later.

Grimmelshausen, von, Christoffel (1625 (or 1610)-75) : Germ. picaresque (i.q., rogue-) novelist. The facts of his biography are obscure, but his patronymic was probably Christoffel, and after some desultory experience of active warfare he seems to have been received into the Roman Catholic Church, and to have died in the odour of sanctity as bailiff to the bp. of Strassburg at Reachen in the Black Forest. Apart from some translns., satires and amorous fiction, exceeding the bad taste of Zesen and Lohenstein (qq.v.), G. wr., from 1668, onwards, a series of heroic-gallant bks. of adventure, which comprise the most successful Germ. romance of the 17th cent., in the vein of the Span. rogue-vogue, then beginning to become popular in Germ. versions. It is known by its short title, *Simplicissimus*, but its full title smacks of Fischart's (q.v.) Rabelaisian humour, and ran as follows : ' The adventurous Simplicissimus Deutsch ; that is, The Description of the Life of a remarkable vagabond, called Melchior Sternfels von Fuchshaim, viz. where and how he came into the world, what he saw, learned, experienced and exploited therein, also why he voluntarily quitted the same. Abundantly merry and variously advantageous to read '. The picaresque element was crossed with a stronger vein of native romance, and the course of Simplicissimus's career recalls the *Parzival* of Wolfram (q.v.) more immediately than the Span. *Lazarillo* (q.v.), recently transld. by Albertinus (q.v.), or the ' dreams ' of Quevedo (q.v.). ' despite its trafficking in waste places ', says Biese (*Deutsche Littgesch.*, i, 414), ' there is wafted through this most German of German books a breath of the Teuton forest and of that old-time longing for reconciliation with all mother Nature ' ; and perhaps the universal note which G. undoubtedly introduced into the individual record of his rogue-hero was partly due, as in Goethe's *Wilhelm Meister* and Dickens's *David Copperfield*, to the transformation of personal experience ; for Simplicissimus, like his creator (and Melchior Sternfels von Fugshaim (=Fuchshaim) is an anagram of Christoffel von Grimmelshausen), was carried away to the wars from his father's cottage, and had to work out his destiny and philosophy of life, from the level of a soldier of fortune. His final abandonment of adventure and return to the simple woodman's life, even after swaggering in Paris as ' beau alman ' (*allemand*), related by G. in *der stolze Melcher*, 1673, teaches the moral not of his age only but of all ages. G. has been described as a Defoe (q.v.) before his time, partly because a bk. vi of *Simplicissimus* represented its hero as cast away on a desert island ; and the realistic note, which he struck so firmly, and in which he was a direct forerunner of his fellow-countryman, Gerhart Hauptmann (b. 1863), is perceived even more

clearly in his sequel to *Simplicissimus*, the *Courasche*, or camp-follower. ' The Simplician writings,' says Dr. Wm. Rose (*Simplicissimus*, Broadway Translns., 1924), ' present an incomparable picture of a period of which Grimmelshausen was the only German writer of the century to appreciate the literary value '. But the lit. value was not very great.

Gringore, Pierre (1478-1544) : Fr. publicist. G.'s name was later spelt Gringoire, and his dates are variously given as 1475-1534. The uncertainties correspond to the circumstances in which his life was spent, and are likewise reflected in the description, publicist, which best expresses his varied literary activity. He belonged to the rout of Raminagrobis (Crétin, q.v. ; see Rabelais, *Pantagruel*, iii, 21), i.e., to the ranks of the Rhétoriqueurs (q.v.), who tried to give the forms of rhetoric to the waning shadows of the allegorical verse-tradition. On this style he grafted a satiric faculty, which found expression in his *Folles Entreprises*, a kind of politico-theological dramatic monologues, which prof. Saintsbury characterizes as ' a groping after journalism in the most awkward and inappropriate form ' (*Short History Fr. Lit.*, 189). G., who was also a strolling actor, became manager of the ' Enfants sans Souci ' (q.v.), and wr. ' sotties ' (q.v.) and farces in the rudimentary morality-style. A social critic in the dawn of drama, is perhaps the true description of this writer, whose name and fame as a pamphleteer for king Louis xii have been praised more highly than they deserve.

Grobian : Germ. satiric type of sloven, lout, gowk, booby, Mohock ; first invented by Brandt (q.v.), in an incidental reference to ' saint Grobianus ' in a chapter on *grobe Leute* (coarse folk ; Germ. *grob*=boorish) in his *Narrenschiff*, 1494 ; later, 1538, subject of an anon. short treatise on the rules of behaviour of G. at table, the commonest *milieu* for the display of his greedy, selfish and dirty habits ; later, 1549, promoted by Dedekind (q.v.), in his Lat. *Grobianus*, into a ' Cato turned wrong side outwards ' (sub-title to *School of Slovenry*, by R. S. Gent ; transld., 1605, from Dedekind), or the hero of a complete manual of the etiquette of inverted manners. This work was transld., 1551, from Lat. into Germ. by Scheidt (q.v.), and Dedekind availed himself of the Germ. version for his expanded *Grobianus and Grobiana*, 1552, The name ' caught on ', and originated the quality and practice of *grobianisme* in France and of *grobianism* in Engld., both equivalent to gross slovenliness of speech, attire, behaviour, etc. Dekker (q.v.) in the *Gull's Hornbook*, 1609, first saw that this vein of satire could be extended from the ' Grobian ' of slovenry to the ' Grobian' of hyper-civilization ; out of the German he fashioned an Englishman, and naturalized G. in London, as the type of the young fop about town, whose idea of good form was a pushful self-assertiveness and an ostentatious defiance of his neighbour's rights and feelings. The relation of this conception to the satiric mood of Swift (q.v.) is obvious ; and the last Engl. version of Dedekind's work (*Grobianus, or the Compleat Booby*) was inscribed to Swift by Roger Bull, 1739. Thus the type prevailed in northern lit. for more than 200 years. It began in the decline of Germ. court-life at the close of the Middle Ages, with the transition from Minnesinger (q.v.) to Meistersinger (q.v.), with the corruption of the clergy, the upheaval of rural life, and the conscious growth of the burgher-spirit. It survived to paint the satire of the age of Pope (q.v.) against an insolent exaggeration of town-talk and civic wit.

Gronovius, -i. Johann Friedrich (1611-71): Dutch scholar. Born at Hamburg; studied at Leyden, where he succeeded D. Heinsius, (q.v.), and distinguished himself as editor of Gk. and Roman classics, in accordance with the prevailing tradition of the men of learning of his country and generation.

-ii. Jakob (1645-1716): Dutch scholar; son and pupil of above. Held chair of Gk. at Pisa, and, later, at Leyden; lived to some extent on the reputation of his father, whose works he revised, and added to them critical edns. and manuals of his own; was engaged in disputes with Bentley (q.v.), who held his talents in mean esteem.

Groot, Geert (Gerhard) (1340-84): Dutch mystic; known as Gerhardus Magnus; founded the 'Fraterhuis' at Deventer (see s.v. Brethren of the Common Lot), which influenced considerably the development of humanism (q.v.) in the Netherlands and Germany and the study of the Bible (q.v.).

Grossi, Tommaso (1791-1853): It. novelist; friend and follower of Manzoni (q.v.). Wr. romantic drama, *Ildegonda*, 1820, and a prose romance, *Marco Visconti*, 1834, dedicated to Manzoni.

Grosseteste, Robert (c. 1175-1253): Engl. scholar; bp. of Lincoln; chancellor of Oxford univ.; Franciscan. Wr. a classified account of the sciences, *Compendium Scientiarum*, and effected various translns. from Aristotle (q.v.) and others. Gower (q.v.) called him a 'great clerk'; R. Bacon (q.v.) his greater pupil, lauded him as 'perfect in all wisdom', and, with a contemporary, the 'greatest clerks in the world'; and Matthew Paris (d. 1259), the chronicler, noted some interesting traits in the following character-sketch: 'He had been an open rebuker of pope and king, the corrector of bishops, the reformer of monks, the instructor of the clergy, the support of scholars, the preacher of the people, the persecutor of the incontinent, a careful reader of the Scriptures, the hammer of the Romans, whom he despised'. G. wr. *Château d'Amour*, in *romanice* (i.e. romance-Fr.; see s.v. Romance), which was transld. into Lat. and Engl., besides his numerous learned works.

Grote, George (1794-1871): Engl. historian; banker; M.P., city of London, 1832-41; a founder and vice-chancellor (1862) of the univ. of London; declined a peerage, 1869. Wr. *History of Greece*, 8 vols., 1846-56; a work of permanent value, which has been transld. into Fr. and Germ.

Grotius, Hugo (1583-1645): Dutch scholar; statesman; one of the greatest men of letters in the whole range of European lit.; of Fr. extraction on his father's side, and inherited the intellect and humanism of that great nation. Born at Delft; studied law at Orleans

and Leyden, and rose rapidly to be leader of the bar at The Hague. In 1613, G. was Dutch ambassador in London; but his intimate association with Barneveldt (beheaded, 1619, by decree of the Council of Dordrecht, in the politico-religious Arminian controversy) led to his condemnation to the harsh sentence of imprisonment for life. He spent a period of this sentence in the undistracted pursuit of learning, aided by his wife and by G. J. Vossius (q.v.), who was permitted to send him bks. in large boxes. In one of these G. effected his escape. He took refuge in Paris, 1622, where he issued his *Apologeticus* in Dutch and Lat. He was punished by the vindictive sentence of exile for life for an attempt to return to Holland; and entered the service of queen Christina (q.v.) of Sweden as her ambassador to France (1635-45). He died, after shipwreck, on recall. G.'s vicissitudinous career, so eloquent of the perils which attended learning in his day, was as remarkable in achievement as it was chequered in experience. He wr. 1601, a Lat. sacred drama, *Adamus Exsul*, to which Milton (q.v.) owed more in *Paradise Lost* than to Vondel (q.v.), though neither debt was very heavy: he added weighty tomes to the ever-growing library of translns.; he edited classical texts with even more than the wonted elegance of Dutch scholarship in this age; he composed original Lat. verse; he wr. theological works; he narrated in a Lat. history the events of the revolt of the Netherlands—an account which is still authoritative; and, above all, he wr., 1623-24, and issued, 1625, his celebrated masterpiece, *de iure Belli et Pacis*, which laid the foundations of the study of international law, and ranks as an epoch-making work in its own department of knowledge. G.'s advocacy of the law of nations as a binding principle in war was urged with all the weight of his immense erudition and humanism against the terrible experience of Germany's conduct of the Thirty Years' War; and a great jurist of last century, sir W. Rattigan (1842-1904) writes that G., 'in the midst of a cruel and devastating war, was the first to discover a principle of right and a basis of society which was not derived from the Church or the Bible, nor in the insulated experience of the individual, but in the social relations of men'. In the generation of the sack of Magdeburg and the extrusion of the Calvinists from Heidelberg by the savage troops of Maximilian of Bavaria, G. was the prophet of a new gospel of international law, which still awaits ratification 3 centuries afterwards.

Grundtvig, Nicolai Frederik Severin (1783-1872): Dan. poet; divine; known as bp. G. by much the same right as the first head of the Salvation Army was known as general Booth: 'he was an old Pagan at heart', says sir E. Gosse (*Lit. of Northern Europe*, 165), 'a Viking—baptized, indeed, and zealous for the faith, but dim on all crucial questions of dogma'; he used himself to remark that he was not as Grundtvigian as the Grundtvigians: not an uncommon experience of pioneers. G. was cousin to Steffens (q.v.), whose romantic influence c. 1803 dovetailed into G.'s own devotion to the study of Icel., Germ. and Engl.

(the *sagas*, Goethe, Shakespeare) at the univ. of Copenhagen. On top of these came the influence of Oehlenschläger (q.v.), the heroic Dane, whose ' younger brother ' G. has been called. It is this aspect of his genius which has most attraction to-day, when his heretical opinions, his theological law-suit (s.v. Clausen), and his ecclesiastical ban have lost present interest and urgency. Even his visits to Engld. are more significant for his literary studies than for his watching brief in the Oxford movement. G.'s works from first to last are too misc. for permanent value : they include ' The Mythology of the North ' ; lyrical and patriotic poetry ; social, educational, and religious writings and addresses, Dan. versions of Snorri, Saxo (qq.v.) and *Beowulf*, and a collection of religious verse in 5 vols. G.'s name is also well known in connection with his educational foundation of what is called in this country the polytechnic movement.

Grundtvig, Sven (1824-83) : Dan. folklorist. G.'s greatest work, which he unfortunately left unfind., was his monumental collection of Dan. ballads (*Danmarks samle Folkeviser*), which he began in 1853.

Gruter, Janus (1560-1627) : Dutch Latinist. Born at Antwerp of an Engl. mother ; edu. at Norwich and Cambridge ; resided from 1592 at Heidelberg, where he became prof. and librarian ; the Palatine Library (as well as his own private collection of bks. and MSS.) was scattered or destroyed, 1622, at the capture of Heidelberg, and its chief treasures went to the Vatican, where the *codices* are still known as *Palatini* ; G. spent his last years in quiet retirement. He had produced valuable edns. of and commentaries on Gk. and Roman classics, but is to-day chiefly rememberable for his ' *Delitiae* (Delights) of 200 Illustrious Italian Poets of the present and the past age ' (1608), followed by similar collections of Fr., Germ. and Belgian Lat. poets, to which we owe the preservation of so much of the 16th cent. Latinity. It may be noted that G. invented the present chapter-divisions of Livy's history.

Gryphius, Andreas (1616-64) : Germ. dramatic poet ; his name was Latinized from Greif. G.'s early manhood was shadowed and impoverished by domestic bereavements, to which his real sense of art rose superior, and, in a country more fortunate than the Germany of the Thirty Years' War, G. might have achieved results more commensurate with the inspiration of the Renaissance. His lyric verse consisted chiefly of hymns, Lutheran in everything but their form, which acknowledged the sway of Opitz (q.v.). His dramatic work was more important, and owed something to the influence of the Engl. Comedians (q.v.), then bringing their wares to Germ. courts, and more perhaps to his residence at Leyden and the opportunity which he enjoyed of familiarizing himself with the genius of Vondel (q.v.), and of Engl. drama through Dutch spectacles. Wr. blood-thirsty tragedies, mostly based, like the Comedians' plays, on Ital. *novelle*, but including a dramatization of the recent tragedy of *Charles Stuart, King of Great Britain* ; and more successfully, comedies : among others, *Herr Peter Squeuz,*

reminiscent of the Shakespearean *Midsummer Night's Dream*, and *Horribilicribifax*, an up-to-date farce of his own times.

Guarino da Verona (1374-1460) : It. humanist and teacher. Learned Gk. from Chrysoloras (q.v.) at Constantinople (1403-08) ; brought home Gk. MSS., and quickly took rank as first Gk. scholar of his day ; prof. of rhetoric at Florence ; lectured in Venice, where he started first humanistic school (1414), with Vittorino (q.v.) among his pupils ; returned to Verona (1419-29) ; and finally settled at Ferrara (1429-60), first, as tutor (1429-34) to Lionello, son of the reigning marquis d'Este, and afterwards as prof. and teacher. Transld. Strabo, and 15 *Lives* of Plutarch ; edited numerous classics ; revised and abridged Gk. grammar of Chrysoloras. G. had many loyal pupils from all countries, both women and men, including his son, **Battista** (1434-1513), whose treatise (1459), *de ordine docendi et studendi*, is authoritative on his father's methods, and is one of the earliest manuals of educational theory and practice. G. was notable as attaching equal importance to Gk. scholarship as to Latin, in which he regarded Cicero's *Letters* as the best discipline in style.

Guazzo, Stefano (1530-93) : It. moralist. Wr. *la Civile Conversazione*, 1574, a practical manual of good manners, which enjoyed some esteem in the 16th cent., when other nations went to school in Italy. George Pettie (1548-89 ; compiler of *A Petite Pallace of Pettie his Pleasure*, 1576, modelled on *The Palace of Pleasure* by W. Painter, q.v.), transld. 3 bks. of G.'s treatise into Engl., 1581, and bk. 4 was added by B. Young, 1586. Recent evidence, adduced chiefly by sir E. Sullivan, who edited the treatise, 2 vols., ' Tudor Translations ', 1925, shows that Shakespeare (q.v.) was among the writers who owed G. a very considerable debt.

Gudrun : Germ. national epic poem (*Volksepos*) or lay (*Lied*), composed in Austria about 1200, and based on a tale to be found in the so-called Younger Edda, or Icel. saga-cycle of Snorri Sturluson (q.v.). The motive of the tale is the rape of a bride, Hilde, daughter of Hilde and Hagen, by Hetel, a Scand. king. Gudrun is the daughter of Hetel and the second Hilde, and is wooed by several suitors, of whom Hartmut, son of king Ludwig of Normandy, carries her off, while her lover, king Herweg of Seeland, is warred upon by yet another competitor. Plainly, there is ample scope for the romantic and heroic compiler, who drew together in the 13th cent. the threads of these stories of love and fighting ; and, though the *G. lied* is inferior in workmanship to the *Nibelungenlied* (q.v.) which preceded it, its rank and interest in its class are high.

Guelfs and Ghibellines : Party-names, transferred from the rival houses of Altorf in Swabia and Weiblingen in Bavaria respectively to a wider sphere of political differences in the Middle Ages. They were extended to denote the two parties to the conflict between the emperors in the North and the popes in the South for supremacy in temporal and spiritual affairs. The papal cause (Guelf) tended to become identified with the theory of rule by right of merit, and the imperial (Ghibelline) with that of rule by right of birth. Thus, dynastic and political differences were embittered by an opposition, or class-warfare, between aristocrats and democrats. In the city-states of Italy esp., where the command of trade and commerce raised the middle classes to self-esteem, and in Florence (q.v.) above all, these names acquired fatal significance. Thus, Dante (q.v.), in 1302, was proscribed (and exiled from his native Florence for life) through a feud between the White and Black Guelfs, minor factions of the main parties to the long conflict. The varying fortunes of empire and papacy are primarily a matter of history, but they touch lit. at several points, and are essential to the understanding of Dante's writings, owing to his personal experience, and to his intense participation in national events prior to his own day. The rival names and cries first entered history when the Hohenstaufen dynasty acceded to the imperial crown in the person of Conrad in 1138. His successor, Frederic i, Barbarossa, a descendant of both houses, hoped to compose their differences, and aimed at reviving the world-empire of Charlemagne. He went to aid pope Hadrian iv (Nicholas Brakespeare, the only Engl. pope) against Arnold of Brescia, and received the crown at the pope's hands in Rome. His grandson, Frederic ii, The Magnificent, was the infant ward of pope Innocent iii, whose crusade against the heretics of Albi (q.v.) drove the men of letters out of Provence into Sicily and Northern Italy, thus sharpening the weapons of his opponents and assisting the Ghibelline policy of the emperor in his manhood. But the final defeat of the Ghibellines at the battle of Benevento (1266) wiped out the Hohenstaufen dynasty, and destroyed, beyond revival even by the idealism of Dante, the hopes which had animated Barbarossa when he crossed the Alps in 1154. The Guelf victory brought the papacy face to face with France, under her strong Capet king, Philip iv (1285-1314); and in 1309, when Dante was 44 years of age, pope Clement v, king Philip's nominee, assented to the removal of the papal see to Avignon, where it remained in virtual captivity for 70 years. History, at the Renaissance, moved away from the idea of metropolitan Rome, whether papal or imperial, so long associated with these names, and, though they survived till the end of the 15th cent., esp. in family feuds and class rivalries in the Tuscan cities, their original distinction, so vivid in Dante, expired in factious cries of public men and in the recriminatory or adulatory verses of kept poets.

Günther, Johann Christian (1695-1723): Germ. poet; Silesian by birth. His way of life estranged him from his father, and he died in penury and misery, one of the heirs of unfulfilled renown; 'he could not tame himself', wr. Goethe (q.v.) of him, the Goethe whose achievements he might have emulated; 'and so life and poetry ran away from him'. The epitaph is just and noble, and he wr. of himself in like terms: 'Fortune and Time forbade the fruition of his poet's art'; but even within his short span G. established his claim to rank as the first voice of the new era which was dawning on Germ. poetry, distracted by the imitation and feebleness of Optiz (q.v.) and his disciples. As a lyric poet he struck the note of deep and pure sensuousness and sincerity which recalls the art of the Minnesinger (q.v.) and anticipates the art of Klopstock (q.v.).

Guérin, de, Maurice (1810-39): Fr. prose-poet. Wr. *le Centaure*, a fragment of poetic prose, eloquent and meditative, reminiscent of Chateaubriand (q.v.) and fore-running Leconte de Lisle (q.v.). It was publd. posth. (by G. Sand, q.v.) in the *Révue des deux Mondes*, 1840, and was republd., with other literary remains, and with a critical notice by Ste.-Beuve (q.v.), 1860. M. Arnold (q.v.) devotes two well-known essays (*Essays in Criticism*, i) to M. de G. and to his sister, **Eugénie** (1805-1845), whose 'soul had the same characteristic quality as his talent—*distinction*'. So they found their audience, 'fit, though few'.

Guevara, de, Antonio (*c.* 1480-1545): Span. romancer and moralist; Franciscan monk; was promoted in the employ of the Holy Office of the Inquisition; became preacher at the court of the emperor Charles v (q.v.), and bp. of Guadix and Mondoñedo, 1537, successively. G. has enjoyed a reputation somewhat in excess of his merits, and is characterized, fairly enough, by Kelly (*Lit. espagn.*, 212) as 'a clever romancer doubled with a wit (*un plaisant*), who amused his contemporaries, and whose influence has been exaggerated'. The exaggeration has been heaped particularly on the influence of his style, which, with its learning, vivacity, alliteration, allusiveness, and occasional involution, has been held to be the basis (through sir Thomas North, q.v.) of Engl. euphuistic prose. The subject is discussed s.v. Euphuism, and need not detain us here, save to note that the characteristics of Guevara-prose were 'in the air' at the time, and are to be traced to the examples of Latinity, newly revealed at the Renaissance, and of the Bible, newly transld. into the vernacular languages at the Reformation. 'The most that we can say', writes Feuillerat (*John Lyly*, Cambridge, 1910; 460, n.1), 'is that Guevara had success in England, because his style displayed *some* of the features which were desiderated in English prose'. G.'s writings included, chiefly, 'The Golden Book of Marcus Aurelius' and 'The Dial of Princes' (*Relox de Principes*), 2 parts of one work; the former passing itself off as hist., and alleged to be founded on a (non-existent) Florentine MS.; the latter, frankly didactic fiction, or moral romance. The former had been publd. twice in 1528 and 3 times in 1529 without G.'s assent; in 1529 he issued an authorized edn., entitled 'The Book called Dial of Princes, with which is incorporated the very famous Book of Marcus Aurelius' (the fame being Florentine). This title was presently shortened to 'The Book of the Emperor Marcus Aurelius, with The Dial of Princes.' It was a work full of eloquence and striking phrases in the artificial and antithetical style so familiar in Lyly (q.v.), and it was transld. into Engl. (from the Fr., by lord Berners, q.v., 1534, and by sir T. North, 1557) into Fr., Ital., Germ., Lat., Dutch, and even

Armenian. Ticknor (ii, 15) cleverly compares it with the *Cyropædia* of Xenophon, and it was plainly in the line of the *Cortegiano* of Castiglione (q.v.), in its aim at setting before the emperor a final model of princely virtues. Its hist. pretensions were severely attacked by Rhua (q.v.) in G.'s lifetime, and Bayle (q.v.) in his Dict. is a very hostile critic. Still, the popularity of the *Reloz* has been undoubted and not much less honour was paid to some of G.'s subsequent writings : *Decada de los Cesares* (' Ten of the Cæsars '), 1539, transld. by Hellowes, *Tenne Emperors of Rome.* 1577 ; ' Familiar Epistles ', 1539-42, transld. into Fr. under the name of ' Golden Epistles ' (by which they were known to Montaigne, q.v., *Essais*, i, 43), and several times into Engl. ; a treatise on favourites (*privados*) and courtesans (see also s.v. Santillana) ; another piece of rhetorical moralizing, transld., 1548, by sir Francis Bryan (q.v.) under the title of *A Dispraise of the Life of a Courtier* (the Span. was briefer, *Ménosprecio de la Corte*) *and a Commendation of the Life of the Labouring man* ; and other works. The influence of Guevara on La Fontaine (q.v.) is well-known, and special reference is made to the *Paysan du Diable* ; there were usually Fr. intermediaries, however, and La Fontaine is infinitely more readable.

Guevara, de, Luis Velez (*c.* 1579-1644) : Span. dramatist. Wr. about 400 plays, with a facility almost equal to Vega's (q.v.), of which about 24 survive. Some had a patriotic motive, such as *Mas pesa el Rey que la Sangre* (' Loyalty is thicker than blood ', or ' King before Kin ', as Ticknor renders it), which finely presented the spirit of passionate loyalty that characterized the great age of Span. history. Others had a spiritual purpose ; and mention is due particularly to his *Diable conjuelo* (lame), 1641, which had its influence in the making of the *Diable boiteux* of Lesage (q.v.).

Guicciardini, Francesco (1483-1540) : It. historian. Served on several diplomatic missions, including an embassy to Spain, where, under Ferdinand of Aragon, ' even an Italian might discern deeper reaches of human depravity' (Symonds, *Ital. Renaissance*, i, 233). His training and experience deprived him of every moral illusion in his contemplation of the causes of human action ; like Pomponazzi and Machiavelli (qq.v.), his contemporaries, he took an objective view, and his writing displays an unrelieved fatalism and indifference. His chief work was a ' History of Italy ' carried down to his own times, and first issued in 1564 ; *edd. pr.* of other works, including a ' Constitution of Florence ' and a separate ' Florentine History ' were first publd. in the 19th cent. His positive outlook pruned his style of all superfluous ornaments, and he ranks as the earliest exponent in Italy of the art of hist. prose.

Guidi, Alessandro (1650-1712) : It. poet ; compared by his contemporaries with Pindar, but remembered more appropriately by posterity for his use of the unrhymed strophe in the *canzone*, which afforded a model to Leopardi (q.v.) in a latter age. G. enjoyed the patronage of queen Christina (q.v.).

Guidiccioni, Giovanni (1500-41) : It. poet. Wr. sonnets (q.v.) and pleasant Petrarchan verse of no high quality of distinction.

Guido delle Colonne (fl. 1270-87) : Sicilian Latin-romancer. Judge at Messina ; turned to authorship at the invitation of the archbp. of Salerno. Wr. Lat. *Historia destructionis Trojæ*, based on Benoît (q.v.) de Ste. More's poem, with additions from Virgil and Ovid. This work, though vastly inferior to the Fr. romantic poems, became very popular, and was a source-book for Lydgate (q.v. ; *History, Siege and Destruction of Troy*, c. 1412 ; printed, 1513) and others.

Guillaume de Lorris (13th cent.) : Fr. romantic poet. Author of the first and shorter part of the *Romance of the Rose* (q.v.).

Guillen de Segovia, Pero (1413-c. 1474) : Span. poet ; native of Seville, though he described himself as de Segovia. Wr. verse-transln. of the 7 penitential psalms (preserved by Castillo, q.v.), and other poetry still unpubld. ; proclaimed himself a disciple of G. de Manrique (q.v.).

Guinicelli, Guido (*c.* 1230-c. 1276) : It. poet. Native of Bologna, and identified by his verse and by Dante's praise of it with the Tuscanization (see s.v. ' Toscanaggiamento ') of Sicilian court-poetry, and its adaptation, accordingly, for the larger audience of the Florentine Renaissance. Wr. philosophical love-poetry of the Troubadour-*cum*-Plato kind, in which he attained great success, as e.g., in the stanzas *Of the Gentle Heart*, beautifully rendered into Engl. by D. G. Rossetti (q.v.). The ' dolce stil nuovo ' (q.v.), attributed to G. by Dante, who called him ' father of me and of my betters ', and foretold that his dulcet lays would ' make for ever dear their very ink ' (*Purg.* xxvi, 97, 112), must not be mistaken to mean that the style is easy to follow. It is still erudite, symbolical, and complex ; but the diction marks the transition from Sicily to the mainland. (See s.v. Ital. lit.).

Guirlande de Julie (Fr.) : Title of a vol. of verse (' Julie's Garland '), consisting of 63 madrigals, composed by the most eminent Fr. wits of the mid-17th cent. in Paris, and written by hand on 29 folio leaves of vellum, each one ornamented with a hand-painted floral design ; presented to mlle. Julie de Rambouillet (q.v.) on 1 Jan, 1641, by her lover, the duc de Montausier, who ' sighed ' for her for 14 years. 16 of the poems were composed by the duke himself, and Corneille (q.v.) was a contributor to the garland. The G. was at one time in Engl. possession (at a cost of 30,000 francs), and is now owned by the duc d'Uzès, on Fr. soil, as is appropriate. It is a monument of the precious (q.v.) school.

Guittone of Arezzo (1230-94) : Sicilian court-poet. Notable in the transition of Ital. verse from Sicily to Florence by his rude attempts to address a larger public than the courtly audience.

Guizot, François Pierre Guillaume (1787-1874) : Fr. historian ; statesman ; orator ; with Cousin and Villemain (qq.v.), one of the ' triumvirate of the Sorbonne ', who, like the Berlin historians of a later date, used their professorial chairs as tribunes of political influence. G.'s chair was history, and the too sweeping range of his teaching caused his lectures to be suspended at one time. Like his colleagues, G. was occupied rather with

Hahn, Johann Friedrich (1753-79): Germ. poet ; a member of the Hain (q.v.) brotherhood at Göttingen, who were banded together to spread the gospel of Germ. poetry according to Klopstock (q.v.).

Hain : Germ. short title of a Bund or union of poets, founded, 1772, by Voss, Boie (qq.v.) and others, with its headquarters at Göttingen (q.v.), and the *Göttinger Musenalmanach* as its organ. The word *Hain* is Germ. for grove, or coppice, and the name was selected in honour of the circumstances of the foundation of the union : ' We sallied ', wr. Voss, ' in the dusk to a neighbouring village. The evening was bright, and there was a full moon. We gave ourselves over entirely to the influence of the lovely surroundings. We took a draught of milk in a peasant's hut, and then repaired into the open country. Here we found a little oak plantation, and forthwith it occurred to us all to swear the bond of friendship under those holy trees. We garlanded our hats with oak-leaves, laid them beneath the tree, took one another's hands, danced round the lonely trunk, and called the moon and the stars to witness to our eternal friendship '. The Grove-brothers' idol was Klopstock (q.v.), and none dared mention Wieland (q.v.) at their festive gatherings, so repugnant was the breath of Epicurus to these enthusiasts for national idealism. On Klopstock's birthday, 1773, writes Voss again : ' We drank in Rhine-wine to Klopstock's health, to Luther's and Hermann's immortal memory. We spoke of freedom, of Germany, of the songs of youth, and finally burned the likeness of Wieland'. The Pickwickian note did not endure very long; and the best work of the Göttingen poets, such as Bürger (q.v.), was not achieved in the pattern of the *Hain* aims and ideals.

Hakluyt, Richard (*c.* 1552-1616): Engl. imperialist ; contemporary of Shakespeare (q.v.), and infected, similarly to him, with a sense of the wonders of the deep, and the greatness of Engld.'s destiny on the sea ; clergyman ; chaplain to Engl. ambassador at Paris, 1583-8, where he compiled the first collection of his *Principal Navigations, Voyages . . and Discoveries of the English Nation made by Sea or over Land to the Remote and Farthest Distant Quarters of the Earth, . . within the Compass of these 1500 Years*, 3 vols., 1598-1600. The 300th anniversary of H.'s death was celebrated in 1916, in the midst of the Great War, when ample tribute was paid to the splendid spirit of the old scholar-epicist in prose, who would have appreciated as well as any the unbroken faith displayed under the ordeal to the tradition of the sea-captains of queen Elizabeth. H. left a large number of MSS., which were edited by Samuel Purchas (d. 1626), in *Purchas, his Pilgrim*, 1619, and similar works.

Halevi, Jehudah. See s.v. Jehudah.

Halévy, Ludovic (1834-1908): Fr. comic librettist ; joint-author with Meilhac (q.v.) of *la Grande Duchesse de Gerolstein*, produced in the year of the Universal Exhibition, 1867, and of other musical plays, designed, successfully, to keep Paris amused. The musical director was Offenbach (Lévy), and the trio exactly rendered the mood which is described as *boulevardier* (q.v.).

Hall, Joseph (1574-1656): Engl. satirist ; divine ; bp. of Norwich, 1641. Wr. satires (*Virgidemiarum*, 3 bks., 1597, 3 bks. 1598) in his youth, and sermons in his old age, and considerably suppled the resources of Engl. prose. An extract from his sketch of ' The Happy Man ' may be cited in illustration : ' It is his trade to do good, and to think of it his recreation. He hath hands enough both for himself and others, which are ever stretched forth for beneficence, not for need. He walks cheerfully the way that God hath chalked, and never wishes it more wide or more smooth '. Note, so shortly after Lyly's (q.v.) prose-reforms, the exact balance of ' trade . . . recreation , ' do good . . . think of it ', and the metaphor and alliteration in ' walks cheerfully . . . way chalked '.

Hallam, Henry (1777-1859): Engl. historian ; wr., among other learned works, *Introduction to the Lit. of Europe in 15th, 16th and 17th Cents.*, 1837-9, which, though lacking the breadth of knowledge of lord Acton (q.v.) and the wide sympathy of prof. Saintsbury, must be piously as well as gratefully acknowledged in this dict. H. enters lit. again as the father of Arthur Henry H. (1811-33), the subject of Tennyson's (q.v.). *In Memoriam*, 1850. Mrs. Henry Hallam was an Elton of Clevedon, ' where he in English earth is laid '.

Halle : centre of Germ. intellectual movement at the close of 17th cent. (See s.v. Aufklärung). Its univ. was founded, 1694, by Thomasius (q.v.) with the help of Spener (q.v.), the Pietist, and Francke (q.v.), the Erfurt theologian ; and it took a place in Germ. life similar to that which Wittenberg had occupied in the age of Luther and the Reformation; a Prussian headquarters of Germ. thought. (See also s.v. C. von Wolff).

Hallenberg, Jonas (1748-1834): Swed. historian ; successor to Lagerbring (q.v.), and still accounted among the most trustworthy authorities on Swed. history and antiquities.

Haller, von, Albrecht (1708-77): Germ.-Swiss poet and man of science. Born at Berne ; travelled ; taught anatomy, botany, and other branches of learning at newly-founded univ. of Göttingen, 1736-53, when he returned to his native country ; achieved eminence in both walks of life, and was the leading physiologist of his time. His poetry, which chiefly interests us, though he also wr. historico-political romances, belonged really to neither of the contending schools in his day (see s.v. Gottsched). While it marked a departure from the Second Silesians ' (q.v.) extravagances, and gave a lead to younger writers wearied of critics' disputations, it was inspired by a naturalist's love of nature, and was strengthened in its expression of such feelings by H.'s reading of Pope and Thomson (qq.v., and see s.v. Brockes). Publd., 1732, a vol of *Poems*, containing one on the ' Origin of Evil ', and the yet more famous *Die Alpen* (the Alps). This poem marks a definite step in the advance of sensibility to mountain-scenery between, say, Gessner (q.v.), H.'s countryman, and Rousseau (q.v.), the fountain of natural magic. The ' renascence of wonder ' in a well-known phrase, is clearly found on Germ. soil in this poem, in such verses as, ' Whoso compels to truth through the wide regions of the world that noble sense which is quickened by art and wisdom, he will not fail to see in every spot a wonder which bids him pause and search '.

Hallgrím Pjetersson (1614-74): Icel. poet; enjoyed the powerful patronage of bp. Brynjolf (q.v.); lived, 1630-8, at Copenhagen, where he married a ransomed victim of a Turkish sea-raid on the Northern coast; he died blind and poor. H. was a poet of very considerable power and talent, and his religious verse still reflects honour on the lit. of his country; his *Passion-songs*, particularly, are famous not only at home but abroad. There are 50 of these songs in all, and in consecution and homogeneity they have genuine epical force. ' The text of Holy Writ is almost verbally reproduced, but between the versified words of the text the poet introduces the emotions and temperamental associations evoked by the Biblical phraseology' (Schweitzer, *Scand. Lit.*, ii. 166). The full value of H.'s work can only be appreciated by his own countrymen, owing to the national style and rhyming-scheme of his verse and diction; but its excellence and influence are beyond dispute.

Hallgrimsson, Jonas (1807-45): Icel. poet and novelist: one of the first champions of the national sentiment of Iceld. in the 19th cent. Wr., too, prose-tales of ample promise, unfortunately interrupted by H.'s early death.

Hamann, Johann Georg (1730-88): Germ. neo-humanist. H. led too unsettled a life to be otherwise than desultory in his writings; but his brilliant intuitions, his fertile fancy, and his flashes of original genius lent his works considerable influence on the writers of the *Sturm und Drang* (q.v.), of which he may be called a fore-runner. He spoke of himself as the ' Magus of the North ', and he found a complementary talent in Herder (q.v.), who brought many of his seeds to flower. (Cp. Hamann's aphorism ' Poetry is the mother-tongue of the human race ' with the argument of Herder's *Fragmente*, 1767, the starting-point of the *Sturm und Drang*). H.'s style was obscure, mainly because his thought was tentative and in the making, and his works were mostly fragmentary. They included *Socratic Memorials*, 1759; *A Philologer's Crusades*, 1762, and other chips from his Germ. workshop.

Hamilton, Anthony (*c.* 1646-1720): Irish adventurer in France; *comte* by rank; governor of Limerick, 1685; fought at the Boyne, 1690, and thereafter followed the fortunes of the exiled Stuart at St. Germain-en-Laye. He was bilingual, and wr. Fr. verse, and *contes de Féerie* (fairy-tales, with a worldly undermeaning); and, most notably, the Fr. *Mémoires du Comte de Grammont*, which were publd. anon., 1713, were transld. into Engl. in the following year, and were edited by sir Horace Walpole (q.v.), 1772, and by sir Walter Scott, 1811. Grammont (q.v.) married H.'s sister, and his memoirs of amorous intrigues and scandal are the most valuable extant document of the manners of the court of king Charles ii. H.'s *contes*, it may be added, are

full of piquant phrases; one of them, particularly famous, recommends a speaker to ' commencer par le commencement '.

Hammersköld, Lorenzo (1785-1827): Swed. romanticist; founder of the ' Friends of Literature ' society, 1803-05, and of the literary journal, the *Lyceum*, 1809. H.'s activities were confined mainly to occasional writing in the new critical journals (see s.v. Phosphorus), common in Sweden at this date; and he has not unfairly been called the A. W. Schlegel (q.v.) of his own country; certainly, he was a worthy forerunner and colleague of Atterbom (q.v.).

Hansen, Mauritz Christopher (1794-1842): Norw. patriotic writer; one of the three (with Bjerregaard and Schwach, qq.v.) of the Syttendemai (q.v.) voices, raised to celebrate the separation of Norway from Denmark, 17 May, 1814. He kept his poetry for these occasions, and tedious enough it was. A little higher esteem is due to his novels, in which he sought the hidden springs of romance in the rustic life of his countrymen.

Hardenberg, von, Friedrich Leopold (1772-1801): Germ. Romanticist (see s.v. Romance); employed *nom-de-guerre*, **Novalis**, which has been explained as *nov-*(Lat., new), equivalent to *hard* (first syllable of Hardenberg: Germ. *hart*, hard, new or virgin, soil; see, too, s.v. J. Thomson). However, this may be, H. or N. certainly struck new soil in his writings, in which, according to Haym (*Romantische Schule*, 324), ' he set the lines of the movement, and by the wealth and originality of his genius did more than anyone else to give definiteness, character and self-consciousness to the Romantic school. He is the prophet of Romanticism '. Heine (q.v.), the author of an earlier *Romantische Schule*, took a less enthusiastic view; and prof. C. E. Vaughan (*P.E.L.*, x, 312), writing of H.'s romantic romance, *Heinrich von Ofterdingen*, says that ' it is the quips of Heine that alone save it from oblivion '. It is very difficult, at our present distance from the conventionalized medievalism of Tieck, Schlegel (qq.v.) and their circle, to strike a correct balance between the conflicting views of H.'s services to Germ. lit. and universal thought. The official Germ. view before the Great War, 1914-8, was not friendly to his genius. Kluge, e.g., in his textbook on Germ. national lit., which was (and probably is) very widely used for educational purposes, complained quite properly of the lack of principle, the intangible mysticism and the purposeless unreality in H.'s writings, despite ample beauties which are frankly recognized; and Francke (*Hist. Germ. Lit.*, 1901; p. 428), expressing the same official view of a teacher of militant Prussian youth, remarked: ' In studying these fantastic ravings of an eccentric and uncontrolled imagination, one understands how a generation, whose reason and will had been benumbed by their influence, should have become unfit for discharging the simple duties of the citizen and patriot; one comprehends Napoleon's contempt for these " German ideologists "; and one sees the inner justice of the political humiliation of Germany in 1806 '. Unfortunately for the moral of this criticism, the sub-title to *Tess*, which gave occasion for an author's pref., dated July, 1892, to the 5th and later edns. of that classic novel. There were reviewers, said Mr. Hardy, who revealed ' an inability to associate the idea of the title-adjective [pure] with any but the artificial and derivative meaning which has resulted to it from the ordinances of civilization. They ignore the meaning of the word in Nature, together with all æsthetic claims upon it, not to mention the spiritual interpretation afforded by the finest side of their own Christianity '. But the occasion had passed in 1895, when, in another pref., Mr. Hardy, wr. : ' Some of the critics who provoked the reply have " gone down into silence ", as if to remind one of the infinite unimportance of both their say and mine '. We shall not break that silence. In the same pref., Mr. Hardy accepted his readers' identification of certain places described under fictitious or ancient names, ' as at least an indication of a real and kindly interest in in the scenes '. They are as follows : Shaftesbury, ' Shaston '; Sturminster Newton, ' Stourcastle '; Dorchester, ' Casterbridge '; Salisbury, ' Melchester '; Salisbury Plain, ' The Great Plain '; Cranbourne, ' Chaseborough '; Beaminster, ' Emminster '; Beer Regis, ' Kingsbere '; Woodbury Hill, ' Greenhill '; Wool Bridge, ' Wellbridge '; Harfoot Lane, ' Stagfoot Lane '; Hazelbury, ' Nuzzlebury '; Bridport, ' Port-Bredy '; Maiden Newton, ' Chalk Newton '; Sherborne, ' Sherton Abbas '; Milton Abbey, ' Middleton Abbey '; Cerne Abbas, ' Abbot's Cernel '; Evershot, ' Evershead '; Taunton, ' Toneborough '; Bournemouth, ' Sandbourne '; Winchester, ' Wintoncester '.

To some, the creator of *Tess* and *Jude*, children of tragic destiny ; to others, the author of *The Dynasts*, one of the most ambitious canvases ever filled by a history-chronicler, or epic-dramatist, in verse, has the more enduring title to renown. We shall not attempt to judge between these opinions. The right attitude is of gratitude that such high endowments were bestowed on one great Englishman in the 19th cent. He has enhanced the study of human character, in various dramatic phases of its awe-inspiring conflict with fate ; he has utilized his wide antiquarian lore—hist. and architectural—to rehabilitate and repopulate an ancient kingdom of Engld. ; and he has commanded, throughout his 50-60 years of authorship, a strength and delicacy of expression, alike in nature-description and character-delineation, which never fail to give delight. He has been faithful, too, like Meredith (q.v.), his slightly older contemporary, and other makers of modern thought, in interpreting the Outer to the Inner—the universe to the mind of man,—with due regard to reverence for the past and to the influence of present knowledge on future conduct. (*July*, 1925).

Hare, -i. Augustus William (1792-1834) : Engl. essayist ; divine; and

-ii. Julius Charles (1795-1855) : Engl. essayist ; archdeacon of Lewes ; chaplain to queen Victoria ; brothers ; joint-authors, 1827, of *Guesses at Truth*, a series of annotations to history and philosophy, which display

the classical erudition, theological knowledge and profound culture of the sons of **Francis Hare-Naylor** (1753-1815), who lived at Bologna and Weimar, and wr. a valuable *History of Weimar,* and the grandsons of **Francis H.** (1671-1740), bp. of Chichester, 1731, who was complimented on his preaching by Pope (q.v. ; *Dunciad*, iii, 204), and who was accounted equal with Bentley (q.v.) in Lat. scholarship (See Sandys, *Hist. Class. Schol.*, ii, 409).

Haren, van, -i. Willem (1710-68) : Dutch poet and statesman. Wr., 1740, epic poem in 10 bks. ; 1741, *Leonidas*, urging under guise of the Gk. story the duty of the Netherlands towards the empress Maria Theresa, when Prussia seized her province of Silesia. ' I raised 20,000 men by 3 pieces of verse ', was his own boast. His best poem was written in 1760, on *The Life of Man*. Van H.'s private life was the reverse of exemplary.

-ii. Ouno Zwier (1713-79) : Dutch poet ; brother of above, and even less reputable in moral character. Wr. epic verse and dramas.

Haro, de, Luis (d. 1532) : Span. poet ; soldier. Very little remains of his verse, and what remains is meagre in interest and old-fashioned in style. Presumably, parts have been lost, since Castillejo (q.v.) bracketed H. with Boscan (q.v.) and others among the pioneers of Italianate models in Span. verse.

Harrison, Frederic (1831-1922) : Engl. critic, philosopher ; founder and president, 1880-1905, of Engl. Positivist Committee, designed to give expression in this country to the philosophic and political doctrine of Comte (q.v.). H., who was an eminent liberal, though he took no active part in politics, and was an intimate friend of visct. Morley, sir L. Stephen (qq.v.), and other great Victorian writers, will perhaps live rather as an influence than as an author. He wr. many bks. in his many years : chiefly, *The Meaning of History*, 1862 (enlarged, 1894) ; *Victorian Lit.*, 1895 ; *Byzantine History in the Early Middle Ages*, 1900 ; *Among my Books*, 1912. H. was a busy editor in the prosperous days when publishers were better able to afford to retain the services of distinguished scholars in that capacity, and contributed to Macmillan's ' English Men of Letters ' (*Ruskin*), ' Twelve English Statesmen ' (*Cromwell*), etc.

Harsdörffer, Georg Philip (1607-58) : Germ. poetaster ; founder of Nuremberg literary society known as Pegnitz Shepherds (q.v.). As an extreme follower of Opitz (q.v.), an example of the blind following the one-eyed, H. surpassed in his poetic practice the mechanical principles of his master. Wr. a guide to Germ. poetizing ' without recourse to the Latin language ' and an early and popular ' every woman's book ', *Frauenzimmer Gesprech-spiele* (see s.v. Klaj).

Hartmann, Moritz. See s.v. **Alfred Meissner.**

Hartmann von Aue (*c.* 1170-*c.* 1215) : Germ. romancer and Minnesinger (q.v.) ; a Swabian by birth ; attached to the service of the lord of Aue (on the river Neckar) ; joined the crusade of 1196. Wr. love-poems in the familiar style of the *débat* (q.v.) ; and, later, several court-epics of merit and importance. The first of these was *Erec*, the earliest considerable contribution to the Arthur (q.v.)

-cycle on Germ. soil ; this was followed some years afterwards by *Iwein*, both tales being much indebted to Chrestien (q.v.) of Troyes ; and the two Arthurian epics were balanced by two courtly redactions from monastic legend, *Gregorius* (St. Gregory, who m. his mother unwitting, and after long penance was ordained pope) and *der arme Heinrich* (' poor Henry '), the best and most famous of H.'s writings, and one ' of the simplest, most direct, and most touching of medieval poems ' (Saintsbury, *P.E.L.*, ii, 250). H. may have taken the story from the family records of his patron, the lord of Aue, for ' the poor Henry' is one Heinrich von Aue, who is stricken with leprosy at the zenith of his fortunes, and in the end marries the maiden who is willing to sacrifice herself to save him. H. narrates this old legend in swift and melodious octosyllabic couplets, and with a true poet's appreciation of its sentiment and nobility of feeling. Robertson (*Germ. Lit.*, 89) calls it ' an idyl rather than an epic ', and notes that ' it is the first example of that class of poetry which in New High German literature culminates in *Hermann und Dorothea* ' (see s.v. Goethe). Longfellow retold the story of ' poor Henry ', which seemed to him ' to surpass all other legends in beauty and significance ', in his *Golden Legend*, 1851, so-called by using the name of the whole for a part (see s.v. Golden Legend).

Hartzenbusch, Jean Eugenio (1806-80): Span. dramatist. Wr., 1837, romantic drama on the theme of ' The Lovers of Ternel ', which had been utilized by Tirso de Molina and other earlier playwrights. It had a considerable success which H. failed to repeat in his later plays.

Harvey, Gabriel (c. 1545-1630): Engl. critic ; poetaster ; spent a long and busy life in a somewhat pragmatical opposition to native metres and moods in Engl. poetry. H.'s importance was purely contemporary, and was derived from his influence, rarely for good, on much greater writers than himself, such as sir Philip Sidney and Spenser (qq.v.). He was the centre of a little *côterie* which used to meet at Leicester House in a club known as the Areopagus (q.v.), in order to recall poetic practice from the employment of rhyme back to the classical measures, and esp. the hexameter, which has never been successfully used in Engl. poetry. Sidney was so far prevailed upon as to blame Spenser (in *Apologie for Poetrie*) for letting his shepherds in the *Calendar* talk in the rustic language of their class instead of in Sannazzaro's (q.v.) artificial diction ; and even Spenser, whose Hobbinol in the *Shepherds' Calendar* was intended for H., was temporarily seduced away from rhyming. His correspondence with H. on these topics was publd., 1579. H. promoted an inelastic classicism (q.v.), unaware that the true value of Gk. and Lat. culture is to liberate, not to bind, the mind and pen ; and, despite his precepts and examples, he failed to stop the flowing tide of the Renaissance.

Hauch, Johan Carsten (1790-1872): Dan. poet and playwright ; born in Norway, studied in Copenhagen, and was as eminent in philosophy as in poetry. H.'s early lyrical dramas were not conspicuously successful, and he abandoned poetry for some years in favour of travel and nature-study. An inner psychological crisis, in which H.'s thoughts had turned to suicide, brought him back to the cultivation of the muse, and a romantic tale, *The Hamadryads* marked the transition from his first to second period. A series of Shakespearean dramas, *Bajazet, Tiberius, Don Juan*, etc., was produced in rapid succession from 1828 onwards, but proved too scholarly and academic to win general esteem. An hist. romance, *Vilhelm Zabern*, 1834, was more successful, and was followed by other novels : *Robert Fulton, A Polish Family*, etc. H. essayed the stage again in later years, and achieved his most striking success by a play on the national subject of the Dan. astronomer, Tycho Brahe, 1852. His ' Lyrical Poems and Romances ', publd. at about the same time, established his high reputation as a poet of deep feeling, sincere conviction, and ripe imagination ; and he succeeded Oehlenschläger (q.v.), 1851, in the chair of æsthetics at the univ. of Copenhagen.

Hauksbók (Icelandic): Hawk's book : Collection of MSS. of early Icel. prose and verse, ' a perfect magazine of antiquities ', made by Hauk Erlendsson (d., 1334) at the beginning of the 14th cent. Among other monuments, it contained the *Landnáma*, or the history of the colonization of Iceland (see s.v. Scand. Lit.), first issued by bp. Thord (q.v.), 1688-89, at the period of the revival of Old Icel. studies.

Havliczek, Karel. See Borovsky.

Hawes, Stephen (c. 1470-1524): Engl. poet ; Chaucerian. Wr. *The Example of Virtue*, which owed a part of its rhetoric to *Le Temple d'Honneur* of Le Maire (q.v.), his contemporary ; and *The Pastime of Pleasure, or Graund Amour and La Bel Pucel*, a rhetorical allegory, with the crumbling wooden machinery of its kind, plainly indebted to Fr. patterns, and possibly to a definite model now lost. Though the mechanical features of H.'s poems looked backwards to the medieval tradition, and though the new lights of Surrey (q.v.) had not risen on his horizon, still it is clear that he was alive to the potential value of allegory in his own times, as interpreted in Engld. by Barclay (q.v.) in his transln. from Gringore (q.v.) ; thus forging a link in the chain from Chaucer to Spenser (qq.v.). Anthologists are grateful to H. for the lines, ' For though the day be never so long, At last the bell ringeth to evensong '.

Hazlitt, William (1778-1830): Engl. critic ; sought at first to develop his romantic talents as a painter, and was an acute judge of the painter's art, even anticipating Ruskin (q.v.) in his admiration for Turner ; but turned to lit., as a flower to the sun, partly in consequence of a visit, in the spring of 1798, to Coleridge (q.v.) at Nether-Stowey, where he met Wordsworth (q.v.), when *Lyrical Ballads* ' were still in manuscript, or in the form of Sybilline Leaves ' : the record of this experience is contained in H.'s essay, one of the most charming in the Engl. language, on *My First Acquaintance with Poets*. It reads like a prose variant of Keats's (q.v.) sonnet on opening Chapman's *Homer*. H. built his style (in Buffon's sense of *l'homme même*)

15

The univ. of H. was founded, 1385, and took a kind of middle line between the extremes of reaction and reform represented by Cologne and Erfurt. Later, at the close of the 18th cent., the univ. of H., which had been comparatively obscure during the previous 100 years, became again an intellectual centre. Eminent scholars were attracted to its chairs, and the publication at H. of *des Knaben Wunderhorn* by Arnim and Brentano (qq.v.), 1805-08, gave it a definite and leading rôle in the story of the development of Romance (q.v.) in Germany. The organ of the young Romanticists at H. was the *Einsiedler-Zeitung* ('Settlers' Gazette'), founded 1808, which, though short-lived, like so many of its literary contemporaries, counted among its contributors J. P. Richter, Uhland, and the brothers Grimm, besides the 'settlers' (Brentano and others) themselves. Thus, H. has been hospitable in lit. both to Renaissance and to Romance. It may be added that the castle of H. is an unique example of Renaissance architecture in Germany.

Heine, Heinrich (1799-1856): Germ. lyric poet. 'Rightly to understand Heine's work', says Omond (*P.E.L.*, xi, 302), 'we must have some idea of the world into which he was born', and that idea, to be complete, must be gathered from (1) his nation, and (2) his religion. H. was born of Jew. parents in Düsseldorf during the period of the Fr. occupation, after Napoleon's victory at Jena, 1806, Thus, (1) his boyhood was spent in an epoch of national awakening and reconstruction. The statesmen, poets and philosophers (see, e.g., s.vv. Fichte, Humboldt, Arndt, Körner) were seeking to revive the national spirit, and their splendid devotion and patriotism were rewarded in 1813 by the defeat of the invader at Leipsic. But the spirit of the nation in defeat was not maintained after victory. 'For a year or two statesmen as well as poets [and H. was a poet from boyhood] thought that this patriotic enthusiasm might find permanent expression in a free, independent and national German State. The quarter of a century which followed the War of Liberation [say, from 1815 to 1840, when H.'s health became definitely shattered] was, however, a period of disillusionment, of hopes belied, promises broken, and reforms deferred' (prof. A. F. Pollard, in *C.M.H.*, x, and see s.v. Metternich). The causes belong to Germ. history, not Germ. lit., but we may note that 'those moral effects of the War of Liberation, from which so much had at first been hoped, now seemed to have been lost utterly and for ever' (Bryce, *Holy Rom. Empire*, 398). This moral disappointment fell particularly heavily on (2) a Jew, who had looked forward to the liberal triumph to provide him with a road out of the ghetto,—to provide his ardent youth, unfitted for any of the trades to which members of his faith were restricted, with liberty to range as an equal among his fellows of similar tastes and culture. His personal training had fostered the hopes which the national experience had encouraged. He learned his early lessons at what was practically a Fr. *lycée*, under one of Bonaparte's schoolmasters (the *abbé* Schall-

mayer) at Düsseldorf; the *Code Napoléon*, in force during the occupation, had alleviated the separateness of the Jews; and H.'s mother, to whom 'Harry' was bound by a very close tie of love (pathetically expressed in later life by the deceptive brightness of his letters to her from his bed of suffering in Paris), contrived to modify in his favour the less imaginative affection of his more orthodox and ordinary merchant-father. It was, accordingly, by a doubly harsh fate that H. grew into manhood in this period of national disillusionment, of broken promises of freedom, and of liberal reforms deferred. He lived it all intensely in his own experience: 'The régime of Metternich', we read, 'had resurrected the dead, . . . and the Jew fell back into the circles of the social outcast' (J. F. Coar, *Studies in Germ. Lit. in the 19th Cent.*, 158; reference should also be made to a very clever sketch of H. in I. Zangwill's *Dreamers of the Ghetto*). Thus, thrown back on two lines at once, H.'s muse was Young Germany's (q.v.) authentic voice; and, though he became an apostate from Judaism (1825), and an exile from Germany (1831), an unchanging love of both may be read between his mocking, melodious lines. Take the following, for example:

Ich hatte einst ein schönes Vaterland.
Der Eichenbaum
Wachst dort so hoch, die Veilchen nickten sanft.
Es was ein Traum.
Das küsste mich auf deutsch, und sprach auf deutsch
(Man glaubt es kaum
Wie gut es klang) das Wort : ' Ich liebe dich ! '
Es was ein Traum.*

So H., the pariah from his country, the pervert from his fathers' faith ; and as a dream when the sleeper awakeneth was his life as a Christian and in Paris. And he awoke to bodily torment. For eight years he lay on a 'mattress-grave', unconscionably long a-dying ; so long, that, one day, when the doctor sought to reassure him, after a specially bad paroxysm, that the end had not yet come, 'Don't tell my wife', he said, with his inscrutable smile on his lips,—the *grisette* wife, who loved him so devotedly, yet who was so remote in education and taste, and wholly ignorant of the language in which his Fatherland whispered 'I love'. Was it his pain or her vigil that he intended by the deep, droll irony of the prohibition ? Germ. Romantics practised irony (q.v.) as a cult ; H., like Cervantes (q.v.) in the wake of Romanticism, was irony incarnate. Like Cervantes in one aspect ; like Rabelais and Byron (qq.v.) in others : like Rabelais, in his mixture of droll and earnest (frivolity, H.'s serious countrymen call it, but raillery is a better name), derived, partly, from like experience of fleeing from the authority which he flouted ; and like

---

* Once I possessed a lovely Fatherland.
The oaken-tree
Grew there so tall, the violets peeped soft.
It was a dream.

It kissed me German-wise, and German spoke
(You'll scarce believe
How good it sounded), saying ' I love thee ! '.
It was a dream.

Byron, in the more outward feature of his recourse in his poems to oriental imagery. We need not follow the details of H.'s sad, brilliant life, which has attracted many biographers (Strodtmann, Elster, Marpeles, lady Duff Gordon, principessa della Rocca, baron v. Embden, and others): his 3 years on a bank-clerk's stool with rich uncle Solomon at Hamburg; his love-affair with cousin Amalie; his studies (1817-24) in law and philosophy at Bonn, Göttingen and Berlin; his *Wanderjahre*, in Engld. (1827), Italy (1828), and on the North Sea (1829-30), where he found his sea-voice; his duels; his migration to Paris, after the July-revolution (1830); his marriage to Eugénie Mirat ('Mathilde'), who survived him many years; his interdict from Germany (1835), which he visited twice by stealth; his increasing paralytic disease, till he lay, helpless and blind, awaiting reluctant death. It is more important to enumerate the bks. produced by this wayward, wilful genius, always pursuing an elusive ideal, and mocking its shadow in his empty hands. In hist. criticism, he wr. 'Contributions (*Beiträge*) to the History of the new Belles-lettres (*schönen Litteratur*) in Germany' (1832); 'Philosophy and Literature in Germany' (1834), a work which contains such epigrams as that on Goethe, 'the Spinoza of poetry', on Kant, 'the executioner of Deism', on Luther's hymn (*ein feste Burg*), 'the *Marseillaise* of the Reformation', etc.; 'The Romantic School', 1836, a veritable source-book and authority on the subject; and others. In polemical criticism, we may mention his bk. (1840) on Börne (q.v.); in travel-books his series of *Reisebilder* (1826-31); and, in general letters, his correspondence to French newspapers, for which they called him *spirituel Allemand*. But, first and last, H. was a lyric poet, in some respects the greatest among Germans, since he doubled the parts of 'a brave soldier in the war of the liberation of mankind' (*Reisebilder*, iii, 31) with those of a Parisian by adoption and a Jew by descent. The combination, as we have seen, had its drawbacks: H. was a child of environment and destiny, and was often as passionate, as intractable, and as irrational as an ill-bred child. But, at his greatest, he was unsurpassed, and sang himself into the hearts of men. 'Nach Frankreich zogen zwei Grenadier'; 'Lorelei'; 'Du bist wie eine Blume'; 'Ein Fichtenbaum steht einsam'; 'Sei mir gegrüsst, du ewiges Meer'; 'O Deutschland, meine ferne Liebe'; and a score more from each successive *Buch der Lieder*,—untranslatable incomparable, inimitable, the lyric verse of H. survives time. He went down, fighting, to the grave, in a foreign land, with a foreign faith, and a foreign wife, racked with suffering, physical and intellectual. Yet he never uttered a complaint. Only on the wings of his poetry were occasional flecks and stains, confessing the dust of the journey through which he had to drag them to the upper air. 'Dieu me pardonnera', he said at the last; 'c'est son métier': and 'shall we leave to Him for ever', it has been finely asked (by lady Magnus, *Jewish Portraits*, 51), 'the monopoly of His *métier*'?

Heinrich, Julius, Duke of Brunswick (Braunschweig): See s.v. **Brunswick**.

Heinrich von Meissen (c. 1250-1318): Germ. poet of the transition from Minnesong to Meistersong (see s.vv.); founded a craft of poetry at Mayence, which ranks as the earliest of the Meistersinger schools. H. enjoyed a great reputation in his own day for his skilful distillation of common themes of the town into the exquisite moulds of courtly lyric. His, too, was the day of poetic contests, and in one of these H. sustained a defence of the Germ. term *Frau* (=woman, wife) in preference to the alternative *Weib* (=wife, woman); to this contest, in which he is said to have been opposed by Walther (q.v.) von der Vogelweide, H. owes the name of Frauenlob (Praise of Women) by which he is commonly known.

Heinse, Johann Jakob Wilhelm (1746-1803): Germ. novelist; a product of the Sturm und Drang (q.v.) and an extreme example of its universal fire-eating propensities. H. was a follower of Wieland (q.v.), and outwent his master in sensuousness raised to the power of sensualism. He effected prose-translns. from Tasso and Ariosto, and wr. some minor works, before his chief original romance, *Ardinghello*, sub-titled 'The Fortunate Islands', 1787. It is a tale of a painter-visionary, who recognizes no law but his own will, and no limits except those set by his own power; finally, he founds an ideal kingdom. Even more unrestrained in tone was H.'s *Hildegard von Hohenthal*, 1795, in which the painter was replaced by a musician.

Heinsius, -i. Daniel (1580-1655): Dutch scholar. Edited, 1611, Aristotle's (q.v.) *Poetics*, and wr. Lat. treatise on *Tragedy*, which had considerable influence on dramatic writing, and the theory of drama throughout Europe.

 -ii. Nicolaas 1 (1620-81): Dutch scholar and diplomatist; son of above; lived abroad, Italy, Sweden, etc., 1641-71; wr. Lat. verse, and publd. edns. of Roman poets, evincing marked talent in criticism and textual emendation.

 -iii. Nicolaas II (1656-?): Dutch picaresque novelist; son of above; 'the vagabond descendant of a line of scholars'; wr., 1695, 'The Sportive Adventurer', and, 1697, his adaptation of Du Verdier's *Chevalier Hypochondriaque*, under the title of *Don Clarazel de Goutarnos*. The date of his death is uncertain. He was a physician by calling, and he romanced under the initials N.H.

Helgesen, Paul (15th-16th cent.): Dan. theological polemical writer. H.'s name constantly recurs in the early history of the Reformation in Denmark. He transld. Luther's 'book of prayers', and likewise addressed a remonstrance to Hans Mikelsen (d., 1532), who had transld. the New Testament into the vernacular. H. stood between parties in his activities, but leaned to the reformers in his views.

Hellenism: Hellenic or Gk. culture; the content and influence of ancient Gk. spirit and forms. A distinction with a difference is drawn between the manner of applying these vast resources of antiquity to European art and letters before and after the 18th cent. 'We are all Greeks', wr. Shelley (q.v.) in his pref. to *Hellas*. 'Our laws, our literature, our religion, our arts have their root in Greece'. But lit., our special concern, descended from Greece through Rome ; and, broadly speaking, it was not till the 18th cent., that Hellenism was definitely sought at the pure wells of ancient Greece undefiled by Lat. transmitters and intermediaries. For Classicism (q.v.), though it should signify the cultivation of the ancient classics, both Gk. and Lat., meant from the 14th to the 18th cent. pre-dominantly Lat. alone, or, at least, Lat. first ; and the faults and evils which it engendered of the neo-classic and pseudo-classic types were to be cured, homœopathically, by a fresh infusion of Classicism : if the evil was Latinism in excess, the remedy was a dose of Hellenism. This prevailing Latinity in Classicism is readily demonstrable. In epos, Virgil was intermediary between Homer and Dante. In drama, Seneca intervened between the Gk. tragedians and Corneille ; Terence between Menander and Molière. In lyric verse, Horace interposed the example of his brilliant execution between Sappho or Anacreon and Ronsard with his Ital. forbears and Engl. heirs. In criticism, Horace once more was interpreter of Aristotle to Vida, and again to Boileau, and their respective successors. In pastoral writings, Virgil's *Eclogues* afforded a model to Sannazzaro and his followers for their Theocritean idyls ; and Ovid was the direct source of the European romance of antiquity. Even Pindar, in the later fashion of the Pindaric ode, was partly reflected through Horace ; and the orators and historians repaired to the fountains of Demosthenes and Thucydides along the streams of Cicero, Sallust and Livy. These facts, which are to be taken as only broadly correct, may be dated from the direction given to the revival of learning in Italy, when Petrarch, despite his anxiety to read Homer in Gk., identified Classicism with Latinity, in consequence, partly, at least, of his historic sense of Italy's descent from Pagan Rome. (Further information should be sought s.vv. Humanism, Petrarch, Latin, etc., and the classical, esp. Lat., writers, whose names are mentioned here). How far this secondary Hellenism—the cult of the Gk. spirit at secondhand—made the Renaissance less fruitful than it might have been, is an impertinent question to-day. European culture was baptized in Latinity, and Lat. preceded Fr. as the common language of scholarship, diplomacy, and polite letters. It is less irrelevant to ask with Locke (q.v.) if the consequent primacy of the Lat. grammar in the curriculum of modern schools is defensible to-day, or is more than an hist. survival of the movement quickened by Petrarch ; but. however this question be answered, two facts may here be adduced. First, though Lat. was always the scholars' language, Hellas was unveiling her story. Gk. learning made progress almost *pari passu* with Roman. The recovery of Gk. MSS. was not less welcome than of Lat. ; the new printing-presses poured out Gk. texts almost as rapidly as Lat. ; commentators, editors, and grammarians laboured at both languages with like industry, in the schools, universities, academies, and libraries, founded by the missionaries of

culture who continued Italy's example beyond the Alps. Secondly, the classical tradition and style in lit. became, in the Augustan age of Europe, so pedantically deferential to the rules derived from Lat. imitators of Gk. critics, that the vogue defeated itself. The orthodoxy of Classicism was a Lat. cult, and exceeded the rigour of its masters. This so-called classic correctness, which was only half-classic by direct derivation, was impelled by its inherent principles to oppose, and, if it could, to dam, the rising flood of romantic inspiration and of romantic indifference to mechanic laws. The name of Gottsched (q.v.) at Leipsic, whose rule of prosaic taste was the very negation of the classical spirit which he caricatured from Boileau's caricature, serves to illustrate this opposition. The end of this battle was inevitable. It was engaged in Paris in the famous quarrel between the Ancients and the Moderns, with Boileau on the side of antiquity. But it was fought out even more thoroughly in Germany than elsewhere. It was there that the Engl. romantic movement of bp. Percy and Macpherson (qq.v.) found untrammelled expression in the ballads of Bürger (q.v.) ; it was there that Klopstock's (q.v.) mighty line fused the harmonies of a Milton in the church-music of a Bach, and made his name a new synonym for sensibility in the generation of Goethe's Werther ; and it was there, where Gottsched and Bürger were warring at opposite poles of Latin-French classicism and English-Teutonic romanticism, that the Hellenic angel of reconciliation sped on his mission of peace. The true Hellenism, as distinct from Gk. culture refracted by Roman echoes, or reflected through Lat. edns. of Gk. texts, may be dated from the first works, 1755, of Winckelmann (q.v.), who took his compass and footrule, and rediscovered the secrets of Gk. art. (He described its characteristics as ' a noble simplicity and a quiet grandeur '). Not Fr. laws, derived from Lat. writings, and codified anew by Germ. critics, but the actual measurements of Gk. statues formed the basis of Winckelmann's conclusions on painting and sculpture ; the only rules which he laid down, and which became, later, the inspiration of Flaxman, the Engl. sculptor, and Haydon, the painter, of Elgin marbles fame, were rules of proportion and design, revealed by the measure and the level. Lessing and Herder (qq.v.) succeeded Winckelmann : Lessing, continuing in his *Laocoon* (q.v.) the investigation of the spirit of Gk. art ; Herder, opening in his *Fragmente* not only the epoch of Sturm und Drang (q.v.) but also a reasoned revolt against the dominance of the Lat. grammar, one of the three symbols of the Renaissance introduced by the Ital. pioneers. Winckelmann, whom Herder appreciated even more highly than Lessing, inaugurated a new epoch of the Renaissance. Like a new Columbus, he explored another hemisphere. He stands in the line of advance of Rousseau and Kant in philosophy, of Goethe, Schiller, Landor, Keats, Byron, Shelley, and even Wordsworth, in lit. Hellenism, recovered by Winckelmann and Lessing (the ' emancipated classic ', as he has been called) from the decay of that imitative pseudo-classicism, which Herder deplored, has been skilful to reconcile the differences between the classic and the romantic schools. It has taught Classicism a strange and a forgotten beauty, and Romanticism a difficult and an ordered truth. ' The aim of a right criticism ', writes W. Pater, (q.v.), a humanist of the later 19th cent. in *The Renaissance*, 240, ' is to place Winckelmann in an intellectual perspective, of which Goethe is the foreground. . . That note of revolt against the eighteenth century, which we detect in Goethe, was struck by Winckelmann. Goethe illustrates a union of the Romantic spirit, in its adventure, its variety, its profound subjectivity of soul, with Hellenism, in its transparency, its rationality, its desire for beauty,—that marriage of Faust and Helena, of which the art of the nineteenth century is the child. . . . Goethe illustrates, too, the predominance in this marriage of the Hellenic element ; and that element, in its true essence, was made known to him by Winckelmann '.

Hellowes, Edward (16th cent.) : Engl. scholar. Transld. various works of Guevara (q.v.).

Helps, Arthur (1815-75) : Engl. essayist ; K.C.B., 1872 ; revised writings by queen Victoria. wr. *Friends in Council*, 1847, and subsequent series ; *Companions of my Solitude*, 1851, etc.

Helvétius, Claude Adrien (1715-71) : Fr. philosopher ; farmer-general, 1739 (a fiscal appointment under the Crown) ; chamberlain in the queen's household ; a man of moderate talent, social charm, and benevolent disposition, whose wife, formerly de Ligueville, was a noted leader of a *salon* (q.v.). H. wr., 1758, a moral treatise *de l'Esprit*, followed, 1772, by 2 vols. *de l'Homme*. Each had a more fiery reception than its merits appear now to justify, the former being burned by the public hangman (after which conviction for immoral doctrine H. travelled abroad for some years), and the latter being attacked even by the leader of the *philosophes* (q.v.), Diderot (q.v.) himself. It is the tendency of these bks. which is significant, far more than their actual contents. H.'s ethic was founded on physical first principles : man, and his progress and his civilization, is what his organs make him ; and, to this extent, H., however tentatively, may be regarded as a precursor of Comte (q.v.) and the Positivist philosophy, and he exercised marked influence on Bentham (q.v.).

Hemans, Felicia Dorothea (1793-1835) : Engl. poet ; *née* Browne ; m. capt. A. H., 1812, but separated from him, 1818. Her works, collected in 7 vols., 1839, have not worn as well as her contemporary admirers expected ; but popular taste was sound, as prof. Walker (*Lit. Victorian Era*, 363) agrees with prof. Saintsbury (*C.H.E.L.*, xii, 125f.) in remarking, in its admiration of certain of Mrs. H.'s sentimental poems, for the sake of their universal appeal. *England's Dead, Casabianca*, ' The Boy stood on the Burning Deck ', ' They grew in beauty side by side ', etc., are more than ordinarily good, even though too much water is mixed with the lyrical element (derived from Moore, q.v.) in their composition.

Hemmingsen, Niels (1513-1600) : Dan. theologian and jurist. Wr. Lat. *de lege Naturæ*, by which H. is accounted among the direct predecessors of Grotius (q.v.), and *Syntagma*, 1574, a treatise on dogmatic theology, which raised the intellectual status of the univ. of Copenhagen, where H. held successive chairs of Gk., Hebr., and theology.

Henley, William Ernest (1849-1903) : Engl. poet ; critic ; spent many months in a hospital at Edinburgh, where he was attended by baron Lister (1827-1912), the great surgeon, and formed a friendship with R. L. Stevenson (q.v.), who dedicated to him *Virginibus Puerisque* ; came to London ; engaged in journalism ; exercised considerable influence on the Press by his editorship of *The Outlook, The Scots* (later, *National*) *Observer*, etc. ; wr. plays with Stevenson, but is chiefly memorable for several vols. of brave, ardent and aspiring verse : *In Hospital* ; *The Song of the Sword* ; *London Voluntaries* ; *For England's Sake* ; *Verses in Time of War*, 1900, and others ; publd. *Lyra Heroica*, a bk. of verse for boys, 1892, and, in prose, *Views and Reviews*, 1890, and an essay in the centenary edn. of Burns, q.v., 1901. There is always strength in H.'s poetry ; in the brief ' Out of the Night that covers me ', for example, which is almost everywhere famous ; in ' England ! my England ' ! and many others, and notice is due to the fact that H. was one of several successful practitioners of the artificial ballad-measures from across the channel (see s.vv. Banville, Ballad), in which A. Dobson, A. Lang (qq.v.) and sir E. Gosse were equal masters : the effect in lightening and brightening Engl. verse at that date was brilliant and considerable. The strength was sometimes a little violent, or so it seemed to some liberal politicians in the years 1901-14 between the third Boer War and the Great War : ' By his very personality in literature ', said a writer in the *Nation* (20 June, 1908), ' Henley helped to propagate those tricks of violence and unreal boasting that became such a plague in the days when guns coughed and generals barked and pens put on khaki. . . . The mood of Henley, the *National Observer*, and Mr. Kipling is over now '. Six years later, pens put on khaki again, and the value of H.'s infectious courage was more justly and is now more permanently appraised.

Henryson, Robert (*c.* 1425-*c.* 1500) : Scot. poet ; schoolmaster at Dumferline ; Chaucerian (q.v.). Wr. 13 *Moral Fables of Æsop the Phrygian*, in the *ababbcc* stanza, of which prof. Gregory Smith writes (*C.H.E.L.*, ii, 246) : ' The merit of his *Fables* is that they can be enjoyed independently and found self-satisfying, because of the contemporary freshness, the unfailing humour, and the style which he weaves into familar tales. The old story of the sheep in the dog's skin has never been told in such good spirits ; nor is there so much " character " in any earlier or later version of the Town and Country Mouse as there is in the *Uponlandis Mous and the Burges Mous* '. (See, too, prof. Smith's definitive edn. for the Scottish Text Society, 1906). Wr., too, *The Testament of Cresseid*, for which he turned (Smith, *loc. cit.*), ' for fireside companionship, on a cold night, to the " quair "

' Writtin be worthie Chaucer glorious
Of fair Cresseid and lustie Troilus ',

and the text of which, in 85 stanzas, is contained in *Chaucerian and other Pieces*, by W. W. Skeat, q.v., forming vol. vii of his Oxford Chaucer. Skeat dates the poem *c*. 1460, and considers it the 'best piece' in his vol. of Chaucerian imitators and continuators. H., who wr., too, some minor works, and has touches in common with his greater fellow-countryman, Burns (q.v.), stands as high as king James i (q.v.) among Scot. Chaucerians.

Herbart, Johann Friedrich (1776-1841): Germ. educationist; pupil of Pestalozzi (q.v.). Wr. treatises on general pedagogy, 1806, and similar branches of his faculty, and was described in *School* (J. Murray, Feb., 1904) as a 'high authority in the educational world to-day, owing to his encyclopedic width of view, his complete absence of one-sidedness, and the sureness and sanity with which he treats all that he touches'.

Herberay des Essarts, Nicholas (d. *c*.1552): Fr. humanist; translr. of *Amadis of Gaul* from its Span. original (see s.v. Amadis), thereby conferring an enormous benefit, not merely on the court of king Francis i (q.v.), which was seized by the fascination of the chivalric and amorous Spaniard, but likewise on the development of idealistic romance in France through Scudéry to Sand (qq.v.). H.'s translr. included bks. i-iv., *Amadis de Gaule*, v, *Esplandian*, vi, *Perion et Lisuard de Grèce*, and vii and viii, *Amadis de Grèce*. The complete translr. of 12 bks., the last 4 by another hand, appeared in Paris, 1540-56. (See, too, s.v. Munday).

Herbert, -i. Edward (1583-1648): Engl. philosopher; historian; poet; created baron Castle-Island in the peerage of Ireland, 1624, and baron Herbert of Cherbury in the peerage of Engld., 1627; both baronies became extinct, 1691. Lord H. wr. his own *Life* (to 1624), the *ed. pr.* of which was printed by sir H. Walpole (q.v.) at his Strawberry Hill Press, 1764. Walpole refers to it in several of his *Letters* (29 Dec., 1763; 16 July, 1764; and 16 Dec., 1764, to Geo. Montagu: 'The thing most in fashion is my edition of lord Herbert's *Life*; people are mad after it, I believe because only two hundred were printed'). This edn. was reprinted 1770, 1809, 1826. It was re-issued by sir Sidney Lee, 1886 (reprinted, Routledge, 1906), with a critical introduction and a continuation of the Life from 1624-48. A quotation from the last paragraph of that introduction may be permitted: 'I have endeavoured', wr. sir S. Lee, 'to place before the reader a just estimate of lord Herbert's character in all its contradictory aspects: to make manifest that the light-hearted vain-glorious man of the world was a poet and a subtle-souled psychologist'. He reminds us that H.'s 'complicated character does not stand alone in his own age' (see s.v. F. Bacon, e.g.), and that 'ideas that sprang from modern and from ancient Italy, from classicism and medievalism, from base and pure forms of Christianity, all sought at once, in the late sixteenth and early seventeenth centuries, to gain the mastery over Englishmen's minds'. H's Lat. treatise, *de Veritate* (Paris, 1624; London, 1645), which Descartes (q.v.) praised, but Locke (q.v.) and others disputed, is distinguished as the first purely metaphysical work

written by an Englishman. In 1663, at Amsterdam, appeared his second great Lat. treatise, *de Religione Gentilium*, which treated of comparative religion, and of which an Engl. translr. was publd., 1709. The 'common notions' of religion which he discovered therein determined the characteristics of Engl. deism—a subject of acute theological controversy in the first half of the 18th cent.,—and were as follows: (1) that there is a supreme Deity; (2) that He ought to be worshipped; (3) that virtue and piety form the chief part of divine worship; (4) that men should repent of their sins; (5) that reward and punishment follow from the goodness and justice of God, both in this life and after it. These were H.'s 5 points, the charter of deism, as they have been called. H. wr., too a *Life of Henry viii*, 1649, and he was the author of a not inconsiderable quantity of Lat. and Engl. verse, issued posth. by his brother (*infra*), and edited, 1881, by prof. J. Churton Collins (1848-1908). The Engl. verse recalls the allusive and subtle manner of Donne (q.v.), and prof. Collins remarks in the introduction to his edn. the skill displayed by H. in his effective employment of the metre adopted by Tennyson (q.v.) for his *In Memoriam*. It affords in places really a remarkable anticipation.

-ii. George (1593-1633): Engl. poet; divine; brother of above; public orator, Cambridge univ., 1619-27; entered the Church at the instance of Nicholas Ferrar (1592-1637), of Little Gidding, and became rector of Bemerton, Wilts., 1630. Wr. *The Temple; Sacred Poems and Private Ejaculations* (Cambridge, 1633; Ferrar prepared it for press, and fresh edns, were publd., 1633-4-5-8-41, etc.), which king Charles i read in prison, and which won at once and has retained wide repute. The *Life* of H. was written by I. Walton (q.v.), 1670, and his *Works*, together with the *Life*, were edited by S. T. Coleridge (q.v.), 2 vols., 1835; by A. B. Grosart, 3 vols., 1874, and by Geo. Herbert Palmer, 3 vols., 1905. Reference should be made to *C.M.H.*, iv., 766-9 (by A. Clutton-Brock) and to *C.H.E.L.*, vii, ch. ii. *The Temple* is a sacred poem in the same school of wit to which Donne and Vaughan (see s.vv.) belonged, and the excesses of which were stigmatized as 'false wit' by Addison (q.v.) in the *Spectator*, 7 May, 1711. (See, also, s.v. Metaphysical Poetry). His genius, which was true and deep, found its best expression in personal poems of religion.

Herder, Johann Gottfried (1744-1803): Germ. critic, poet, and philosopher; gave a brilliant lead to Germ. thought; 'the gate-keeper of the nineteenth century' (J. G. Robertson, *Hist. Germ. Lit.*, 293). Born in East Prussia in humble circumstances, H. contrived to attend the univ. of Königsberg, where he enjoyed the advantage of tuition by Kant (q.v.), and where he came in contact with the versatile genius of Hamann (q.v.), whose infectious and magnetic humanism proved an abiding influence in his life and writings, and introduced him to Shakespeare and *Ossian* (qq.v.). H. was a voluminous writer, and a man of strong individuality. His circumstances were not always happy, and he did not possess the faculty of taking good fortune at the flood. He found a devoted wife, but did not live amicably with her in later years; and those years, whether from a sense of neglect or from some kink in his disposition, were marred, too, by conflicts of opinion with Kant, Schiller, and Goethe (q.v.), with the last of whom, esp., he had been united through many years of intimacy at Weimar. But, while his writings differ in value according to the mood of the writer, H.'s contributions to Germ. lit. belong in the main to the highest rank, and he holds a secure place as a pioneer of the romantic revival (s.v. Romance). The aspects which particularly attracted him were, i, the primitive poetry of the nations, ii, the philosophy of history, and, iii, exotic verse. In these departments, each so typical of the curiosity and reverence for tradition which distinguished the movement, H. publd., among other works, *Volkslieder*, 1778-79, a collection of early poetry, later known as *Stimmen der Völker in Liedern* ('Voices of the Nations in Song'), mainly transld. by himself; *The Spirit of Hebrew Poetry*, 1782; *Ideas towards a Philosophy of the History of Mankind*, 1784-91, a real landmark in the science of history; a transln. of the *Cid* (q.v.), 1802-03 (publd., 1805), one of the chief treasures of Germ. ballad-literature; and other treatises, poems, and essays, in or near the period of the Sturm und Drang (q.v.). H. belonged, and, indeed, may be said to have inaugurated, the new interest of the Germ. people in their own storied past, and the sciences of philosophy, folklore and history were naturally grouped round H.'s investigation of the nation's songs, prompted probably by bp. Percy's (q.v.) *Reliques*, and described by prof. C. E. Vaughan as 'one of the crucial works of early German Romanticism' (Warton Lecture, British Academy, 1913). Akin to that romantic temper was the passion for Hellenism (q.v.), as distinct from an excessive Lat. Classicism, by which H. is linked, despite his differences, with Winckelmann and Lessing. If any one man may be credited with the achievement of breaking down the tyranny of the Lat. grammar, established since Petrarch's day as an instrument of the Renaissance (q.v.), this is due in the first instance to H., in virtue of his *Fragmente über die neuere deutsche Litteratur* ('Fragments on recent German Literature'), 1767 (ostensibly, discussions of Lessing's *Letters on Literature*), his 'Thickets of Criticism' (*Kritische Wälder*), 1769, and his *German Art*, 1773. H.'s conviction of the obstruction to the Hellenic spirit which the reign of Latinity, unflanked by Hellenism, had caused in Germany, was supported by his appreciation of Homer (q.v.) and by his renderings of nine odes of Pindar. 'With Greece the morning breaks', he declared at the opening of an eloquent passage, instinct with the fervour of true Hellenism, in his 'Ideas towards a Philosophy of History'; and the brightness of a new Gk. morning at the dawn of liberal thought in Germany illumined H.'s best work throughout his life. 'He is peculiarly interested in Homer', says sir J. Sandys (*Hist. Class. Schol.*, iii, 34). 'He was in fact one of the first to elucidate the general character of the Homeric poems. He finds in them

the fullest illustration of the idiosyncrasy of national poetry'. H. dealt in aphorisms, where Lessing dealt in arguments; he moved in ellipses, where Goethe followed a straight line; but he belongs to the same order of genius as Lessing and Goethe themselves. He, too, was a son of the generation in which Rousseau, bp. Percy, and Macpherson (qq.v.) were fathers, and he, too, sought to mould the new ideas to the purposes of religion and history—to pantheistic and pantisocratic beliefs. It was always H.'s misfortune to seem less great than he was; his work was too fragmentary and, perhaps, too diffuse to win direct recognition, and its influence has been vaster than its reputation. But in comparative philology and comparative lit., in anthropology, in æsthetics, in theology, and in history, H. was at once a pioneer and a scholar. The torches he kindled were borne by others to triumphs which he failed to achieve; his mantle had fallen on another prophet before he died at Weimar in 1803; yet Goethe, in many of his activities, was H.'s disciple as well as his heir.

Heredia, de, José Maria (1842-1906): Fr. poet; wr. *Trophées*, a collection of sonnets, publd. 1803, and belongs by poetic affinity to the school of Gautier (q.v.).

Hermann the German (13th cent.): scholar at Toledo, then the centre of Aristotelian studies. Transld. from the Arabic the commentary of Averroes (q.v.) on the *Ethics* of Aristotle (q.v.), and transmitted to medieval Europe all that it knew of the master's treatise *On the Art of Poetry* till the full text was publd. by Aldus (q.v.) at Venice, among the *Rhetores Graeci*, 1508-9.

Hermes, Johann Timotheus (1738-1821): Germ. novelist. Wr. romances, moral in tone and didactic in purpose, directly under the influence of Richardson (q.v.). Among the best-known of these novels are: *History of Miss Fanny Wilkes, as good as transld. from the English*, 1766; *For Daughters of Good Family*, 1767; and *Sophia's Journey from Memel to Saxony*, 1760-73.

Hermonymus, Georgius (15th cent.): Gk. lecturer in Paris. Born at Sparta; copyist by trade; taught Gk. to Erasmus and Budæus, who found him an incompetent scholar.

Hermosilla, José Gomez (1771-1837): Span. critic; held a chair at the coll. of S. Mateo, Madrid. Wr., 1826, 'The Art of Verse and Prose', which enjoyed considerable esteem for its thoroughness and correctness.

Herodotus (d. 425 B.C.): Gk. (Ionic) historian; born at Halicarnassus; travelled in Upper Egypt, Babylonia, etc.; resided at Athens for some years, contemporaneously with Sophocles, the great tragic poet; retired later to Thurii, near Sybaris. Wr. *History* in 9 bks., narrating the conflict of the Gks. and barbarians, 'in order that their causes may be known, and that the glorious exploits on neither side may be forgotten'. He chose, says prof. J. P. Mahaffy (*Hist. Gk. Lit.*, ii, 23) 'the great shock of East and West, of liberty and despotism, which has lasted in many Protean phases up to the present day'. Thus, his work was important to posterity for its matter, and it was also important for its manner, as to which we may quote from a notice in the *Times Lit. Supp.* (27 Nov., 1924) of *Herodotus*, by T. R. Glover (Cambridge Univ. Press). 'Herodotus was one of the first people ', we are correctly reminded, ' who wanted to *talk* to future generations. The opening of his bk., in which he tells us that Herodotus of Halicarnassus has desired to tell the result of his inquiries, so that the great deeds connected with the war between Gks. and Persians may not be forgotten, shows a new and epoch-making movement of the human mind. It was a step of immense importance, when men began writing bks. in prose. It marks the passage of the mind from childhood to manhood. For the most primitive utterance is not in prose, but in poetry—an expression of imagination and feeling nearer to the mind of childhood. Prose aims at being the statement of things as they are, without that transfiguring halo. That Herodotus wr. in prose means that in him Hellenic rationalism was already coming to prevail, though there remained still so much of the charm and freshness of the child. Men in an earlier age, stirred by the memories of the great national struggle, might have sung or chanted things for later generations to hear ; but Herodotus wants to talk to these generations in the voice of ordinary conversation, to talk to them as he might if they were present before him, and tell them just what he had found out by his inquiries. And so, while the songs of ages older than Herodotus still sound in our ears, the voice of Herodotus is the first talking voice which comes down to us through the ages : the first voice which tries, not to stir our feelings and imagination by the magic of poetry, but to tell us quietly and conversationally just what the facts were, so far as he could find them out '.

The above passage, admirably lucid, conveys the value of H. to the modern world, as an exemplar of hist. method, and ' the author of the most perfect masterpiece of the historical art, which will delight the heart of man till the end of time' (Gomperz, *Gk. Thinkers*, E.T., i, 258). It remains to note that his *History* was transld. (partially) into Lat. by L. Valla (q.v.), 1454-5 ; that the *ed. pr.* of the Gk. text was printed at Venice by Aldus Manutius (q.v.), 1502 ; that Barnabe Rich (d., *c.* 1620) transld. the *History* into Engl., 1584, anticipating the modern transln. by H. F. Cary (q.v.) ; and among recent scholars, Germ. and Engl., who have elucidated the text and meaning, mention is due to Joseph Wm. Blakesley (1808-85), who edited H., 1852-4, for the sake of a second literary association : Tennyson (q.v.) referred to him as ' Clear-headed friend ! ' in his early stanzas *To ——*, and said of him (*Memoir*, i, 38), 'He ought to be lord chancellor '.

Heroet, Antoine (1502-68): Fr. poet ; contemporary of Marot (q.v.), and member of literary circle of queen Margaret (q.v.) of Navarre. Wr. *La Parfaite Amie* (' the perfect mistress '), printed, 1542, by Dolet (q.v.). The poem was composed in a Platonizing vein of mystic sentiment, and obtained a little vogue in its own day (see s.vv. La Borderie, Fontaine).

Herrera, de, Antonio (1559-1625): Span. hist. Wr., among other less valuable works, a general history of the Indies, 1601, from the discovery of America to 1554. H. utilized in this work the writings of Las Casas (q.v.).

Herrera, de, Fernando (1534-97): Span. poet ; scholar ; belonged to the Seville school of poetry, as distinct from that of Salamanca ; i.e., to the more definitely Italianate branch of the art as reformed by Garcilasso (q.v.), and H. duly accounted that writer the first of Span. poets. He settled at Seville *c.* 1565, and devoted himself to letters ; his profession was the Church. He wr. a life of sir Thomas More (q.v.), 1592 ; a collection of poems, 1582 ; and a commentary on the works of Garcilasso, 1580. This last very elaborate undertaking offended the friends of F. Sanchez (q.v.) at Salamanca, who had issued an edn. of the same works in 1574, and whose name H. did not mention. We need not pursue the squabble through all the ink that was spilled ; H.'s commentary, though inordinately long, is proof positive of his critical gifts, and of his real appreciation of poetry ; and, though his discipleship to Ital. models and to the Latinity upon which they were securely founded, led him to a certain degree of exaggeration, not wholly free from signs of the coming pedantry of Gongora (q.v.) he thoroughly merited the high esteem of Cervantes (q.v.) and other good judges. Moreover, in poetry itself, as distinct from its criticism, H. was to win renown. His love-verse was addressed to ' Eliodora ', who has been identified with Leonor de Milá, wife of the count of Gelves, a grandson of Columbus (q.v.). It is uncertain if H. was merely experimenting in the Petrarchan style, or if his experience of passion was genuine ; the one would be more creditable to his ecclesiastical cloth, the other to his poetic singing-robe ; and the epithet ' innocent immorality ' has been applied to the suggested *liaison* between the countess and the priest. However this may have been (and the problem of sincerity has also been posed in reference to the sonnets of greater erotic poets), H.'s love-poems ring true, and are supreme works of art in their kind. And no question of ethics or sincerity touches the instant appeal of H.'s patriotic poetry. His ode on the battle of Lepanto, which inspired so much fine Span. verse, and at which Virués (q.v.) was wounded, has the real prophetic fervour, and the great word ' sublime ' is not inappropriate to the best examples of H.'s lyric verse.

Herrick, Robert (1591-1674): Engl. poet ; divine ; a Londoner by birth, but surveyed affairs from a remote vicarage on Dartmoor, thus affording a striking contrast to Milton (q.v.), whose death occurred in the same year as his. Wr. *Noble Numbers, or Pious Pieces*, 1647, and *Hesperides*, 1648 ; the two (*Works, both Humane and Divine*) being issued together in the latter year ; edited by A. B. Grosart, 1876, by A. W. Pollard (pref. by Swinburne, q.v. ; 2 vols., Muses Library), 1891, by prof. Saintsbury (Aldine Poets, 2 vols.), 1893, and L. Magnus (Temple Classics, 2 vols.), 1899. H., as a lyrist, was a late Elizabethan, with a considerable debt to Horace (q.v.), Catullus and Martial, whom he imitated, too, in too many coarse and gross epigrams. He sang of daffodils, cherry-blossom, lilies, pansies, violets, gillyflowers, carnations; he tuned his lyre to Julia, Perilla, Perenna, Silvia, Electra, Lucia, or, comprehensively, ' to his mistresses '; he even invited Anthea to ' bid me die, and I will dare E'en Death, to die for thee '; he saw a flower in every face, and heard a bell in every flower; but he heard no sound of the great events which turned Engld.'s epic poet into a Lat. secretary to the Protector. Neither in his light or noble numbers—in his *allegro* or *penseroso* mood—whether alone in Devonshire or on a visit to London and his friends, did H. feel the sweep of real emotion; and, delightful though he is in song, it is a little doubtful, perhaps, if his revival since the end of the 18th cent. has not passed its highest point.

Hertz, Henrik (1798-1870): Dan. dramatist; of Jew. parentage; ' he has the distinction of having influenced Ibsen (q.v.) more directly than any other writer ' (*C.M.H.*, xi, 699; by sir E. Gosse). H.'s plays appeared anon. till 1832; as soon as he doffed his incognito, he took his place beside, or hardly behind, Heiberg (q.v.), as the leading Dan. playwright of the age. For Heiberg's success, writes the same Engl. critic in another place (*Lit. Northern Europe*, 152; Kegan Paul, 1879). ' combined with it that of his intimate friend Hertz, whose southern imagination and passion flowed out in plays that brought an element of richness and colour into Danish dramatic art that had always been lacking before '. And ' Heiberg and Hertz ', a Germ. critic tells us (Schweitzer, *Skand. Lit.*, iii, 88), ' were concerned to bring poetry back out of the romantic past to a romantic view of the common life of the present day at home. Their *vaudevilles* and comedies, even their romantic dramas, such as Heiberg's *Hill of the Elves* and Hertz's *Svend Dyring's House*, which had recourse to popular life in the Middle Ages, treated it as far as possible realistically, and subserved the same end. Further, they aimed at preserving the purity and beauty of form and the *esprit* of matter, which threatened to vanish in the clouds of poetic romance '. H. wr. (after the Germ. pattern, it should be added) comedies and romantic dramas, among which may be mentioned, in the former class, *Herr Burihardt* and *Moving Day*, and, in the latter, *Svend Dyrings Hus* (transld. into Engl. by sir T. Martin, q.v.), *Ninon*, and *King René's Daughter*. There were also lyrical poems, vaudevilles, novels, etc.; and his *Poetic Epistles from Paradise*, 1830, publd. anon., in the manner of Baggesen (q.v.), aroused immense contemporary interest. The eminent Dan. critic, G. Brandes (q.v.), explains that : ' the powerful impression produced in its day by Henrik Hertz's *Svend Dyring's House* is to be found in the fact that in it, for the first time, the problem was solved of how to fashion a metre akin to that of the heroic ballads, a metre possessing as great mobility as the verse of the *Nibelungenlied*, along with a dramatic value not inferior to that of the iambic pentameter ' (*Critical Studies, E.T.*, 88). It was this skill which Ibsen acquired from

H., turning it to admirable use in some of his national plays, and in the metre of *Brand* and *Peer Gynt*.

Hervas y Cobo de la Torre, de, Jose Gerardo (d., 1742): Span. critic. Wr. a scathing ' Satire on the bad writers of his time ', which was publd. in vol. vi of the *Diario* (q.v.), the first literary journal of Spain. H. espoused the cause of Luzan (q.v.) and was a disciple of Boileau (q.v.); he wr. under the names of Jorge Pitillas and don Hugo Herrera de Jaspedos.

Hervás y Panduro, Lorenzo (1735-1809): Span. philologer; Jesuit. Wr., 1800-05, *Catalogo de las lenguas de las naciones conocidas* (cognate); of great value in comparative philology, of which science H. ranks as a founder.

Hervey, James (1714-58): Engl. divine. Wr. *Meditations and Contemplations*, 2 parts, 1746-7, and *Theron and Aspasio; Dialogues and Letters*, 3 vols., 1755. H.'s *Meditations among the Tombs* and *Contemplations on the Night* fell in with the contemporary vogue of Young's (q.v.) *Night Thoughts* and Blair's (q.v.) *Grave*, and illustrate ' the descent of popular taste in the darkest period of English letters ' (*C.H.E.L.*, x, 366). See, also, s.v. Death.

Herwegh, Georg (1817-75): Germ. revolutionary poet; wr. *Gedichte eines Lebendigen*, vol. i, 1841; ii, 1844; was received by king Fredk. Wm. iv of Prussia, but was banished from Prussia shortly afterwards, and plotted in Switzerland to convert Germany into a republic. ' Had he been less of an agitator, or had he lived in less stormy times, he would have been a truer poet '. (J. G. Robertson, *Hist. Germ. Lit.*, 546).

Herz, Henriette (1764-1847): Germ. *femme savante; née* de Lemos; m. Marcus Herz, a physician, and was one of the few women who acclimatized the literary *salon* in Berlin; a Jewess. Among the frequenters of her *salon* were Schleiermacher, the Humboldts, Börne, the Schlegels (qq.v.), and others; F. Schlegel met his wife, D. Veit, at her house, which became a centre of Germ. Romanticism, transposed from Heidelberg (q.v.) to the Prussian capital. H. H. destroyed her ample correspondence, but some letters to her from Börne were publd. (1861).

Herzen, Alexander (1812-70): Russ. critic, novelist, memoir-writer. Son of a Russ. father, Jakovlev, and of a Germ. mother, whose surname he bore, as his parents' marriage had not been legalized in Russia. Despite name and maternity, however, H. was always Francophil in sentiment, and belonged by the fullest strength of his conviction to the left wing of politics in Russ. lit. (q.v.), the Westernizers as opposed to the Slavophils. He was a follower of Biélinsky (q.v.), and exceeded his master's lead in the direction of atheism and socialism, developing, in fact, in his latter years into a full-fledged socialist in exile. He graduated in physics and mathematics, and, after minor conflicts with authority, left Russia permanently in 1847, by which time he was already well-known as a misc. writer under the pseudonym of Iskander. His dramas, etc., need not detain us; more notable was his novel, *Who is to Blame ?* Beltov, its hero, is a familiar figure in Russ. fiction, an artist of the ' *bourgeois* Hamlet' type, as Vogüé (*Roman Russe*) calls it, recurrent in Goncharov's (q.v.) *Precipice* and in several of Turgenev's (q.v.) novels. *Who is to Blame?* was partly autobiographical, and the resemblances between Beltov and H. himself were matched by other portraits drawn from life in a popular and realistic style. From 1847-52 H. was immersed in pamphleteering and journalism, with his headquarters in Paris and his heart in the new Russia of his social dreams. These contributions to socialism (or nihilism) belong to the annals of Russ. history ; their literary value is to be sought in the memoirs, 'Memories and Thoughts' (*Byloje i Dumy*), which he wr. in London, 1852-55. A human document of the first importance, reflecting with brilliant and subtle wit all the happenings and feelings of eventful and thoughtful years, this work was completed in 5 parts, of which the final section (dealing with ' Natascha ', the wife of his youth's romance) was withheld from publication ; as it stands, his readers agree that these memoirs are more fascinating than a novel, and that H.'s accounts of life in Russ. towns during the stirring ' forties of the 19th cent., of revolutionary movements in Paris and London, and of the great and little men and women who moved across the busy stage, are enhanced by ' the wonderful precision, the French clearness and French *esprit* of his style' (Brückner, *Gesch. d. Russ. Lit.*, 288). We must leave to historians the record of *Kolokol* (' The Bell' ; no. i, 1 July, 1857 ; at first monthly, then weekly), which H. edited in London for international socialists, and which rang itself into silence about 1863. The violent methods by which revolutionaries sought to give effect to H.'s ideals were always remote from his sympathy, though, not altogether unjustly, he had to bear a part of the responsibility for them ; and, sincere though his attitude was, it is no sufficient defence that assassination, bombs and other horrors were actually detested by the idealist who sought the end while he repudiated the means. Reference to these political aspects is made in two arts. (the second being a rejoinder to the first) in the *Quarterly Review*, Jan. and April, 1920.

Hesse, landgrave of, Moritz (1572-1632) : Germ. patron of drama and playwright ; hereditary ruler. Like the contemporary duke of Brunswick (q.v.), he maintained a stage at his court for the performances of a company of ' English Comedians ' (q.v.), to whose strolling activity in Germany of the Reformation era the native drama was indebted for a stimulus which was unfortunately interrupted by the 30 Years' War (q.v.).

Hewlett, Maurice (1861-1923) : Engl. novelist and poet ; wr. works of rather rarely imaginative power, drawing his subjects from the annals of medieval Italy and Engld. H.'s romances include *The Forest Lovers*, 1898 (his first and still, perhaps, his best), and his poems include *The Song of the Plow*, a metrical narrative of the Engl. countryside.

Heyne, Christian Gottlob (1729-1812) : Germ. scholar. Born in humble circumstances, out of which he raised himself to important positions in the univ. and literary life at Göttingen (q.v.), where he settled, 1763. Some of his early experiences, not uncommon in Scot. as well as Germ. rustic homes of learning, recall the search for bks. and the passion for scholarship of the Humanists of the 14th cent. in Italy. H. edited various classical texts, including Virgil, and was praised by Gibbon (q.v.) for his scholarship, and by Carlyle (q.v.) for his example : ' let no lonely unfriended son of genius despair'. He is described by Sandys (*Hist. Class. Schol.*, iii, 42). as ' the founder of the scientific treatment of Greek mythology', and, though inferior to Winckelmann (q.v.) in enthusiasm and artistic penetration, and to Lessing (q.v.) in critical and philosophical acumen, ' surpassed both in a full and accurate knowledge of antiquarian details and in a trained aptitude for historical methodical investigation'. Later, *c.* 1797, H. was engaged in controversy with F. A. Wolf (q.v.), Herder (q.v.) intervening, as to priority in the Homeric question. raised by Villoison's (q.v.) edn. of the *scholia* to Homer (q.v.), and by R. Wood's *Essay on the original Genius of Homer*, 1769. H.'s many pupils included A. W. Schlegel (q.v.), the later leader of Romantic criticism, and H.'s daughter, Therese, became the wife, successively, of J. G. Forster and L. F. Huber (qq.v.).

Heywood, Thomas (d. *c.*1650) : Engl. dramatist ; reputed on his own showing to have written or patched more than 200 plays. Among his orig. dramas are the 2 parts of *Edward iv, The Four Prentices of London* (laughed at by Fletcher, q.v., in *The Knight of the Burning Pestle*), *The Rape of Lucrece, The Golden Age, The Late Lancashire Witches*, and *A Woman killed with Kindness*. The last, a domestic drama, acted, 1603, is much the best, and goes far to explain C. Lamb's (q.v.) description of H. as ' a kind of *prose* Shakespeare '. H.'s plots were always laid in Engld., and he liked to delineate the Engl. country gentleman ; hence Symonds (q.v. ; in *Shakespeare's Predecessors*, 210) writes of ' Heywood's mossgrown manor-houses. '

Highgate (Engl.) : Suburb (north-west) of London ; celebrated in lit. as the place of residence (from 15 April, 1816, to his death, 25 July, 1834) of S. T. Coleridge (q.v.). He made his home at the house of a Mr. and Mrs. Gillman, whose influence was partly efficacious in reducing his opium-habit and in restoring his mental and moral equilibrium. Coleridge's *Biographia Literaria* appeared in 1817, and the house at H. became a resort and even a shrine for the many admirers of the poet-philosopher and his conversation ; so that the name of H., otherwise chiefly known for its cemetery and for Dick Whittington's stone, has acquired an allusive meaning, derived esp. from the associations of the ' Thursday evenings ' at which (from 1824) Coleridge gathered his friends under the Gillman roof.

Hiller, Philip Friedrich (1699-1759) : Germ. sacred poet. His ' noble numbers ' still enjoy high esteem in his native country, and a new edn. was publd., 1844.

Hippel, von, Theodor Gottlieb (1741-96) : Germ. miscellanist. The epithet is appropriate both to his life and to his writings. He rose by merit and hard work to be burgomaster, police-president and military-councillor at Königs-berg ; accumulated a fortune, and obtained the coveted patent of nobility (*von*). But his public career contradicted his private tastes, which affected a humorous cynicism, not alien to dean Swift's (q.v.), at one time, and a deep sensibility at another. His writings were for the most part anon. ; a precaution wisely observed on the part of a civil official who advocated in his bks. women's rights and revolutionaries' visions. Wr. ' On Marriage ', 1774 ; psychological novels, of which ' Ways of Life on the Upward Grade ' (*Lebenslaufe in aufsteigender Linie,*) which is partly auto-biographical, is best-known ; and left copious diaries and note-books, issued as his biography, 1801.

Hita, Archpriest of. See s.v. **Ruiz.**

Hita, de, Ginés Perez (*c.* 1545-*c.* 1610): Span. hist. novelist ; served in the campaign against the Moors ; resided at Murcia after 1597. Wr., *c.* 1604, a work of fiction known as ' The Civil Wars of Granada ', the chief value of which consists in the vivid picture of life in Granada in the period prior to its fall. H. took the unpopular side of the infidel enemies of his country, and represented the Moors in the brilliant colours of their exotic civilization ; interspersing his narrative, for the first part of which he cited native authorities, with vivid and attractive ballads. See s.v. Romance (Span.). The work did not win much way in Spain : public sympathy was against it ; but a few years later it became the rage at the Paris circle of the Hôtel de Rambouillet (q.v.), and helped to inspire the *Almahide* and *Zaide* romances of Scudéry, Lafayette (qq.v.), and their circle. It is to be added that Scott (q.v.) is reported to have said, that, if he had seen the ' Wars of Granada ' earlier in his career, he would have utilized some parts of it in romance.

Hjarne, Urban (1641-1724). Swed. physician ; F.R.S. ; celebrated as one of the most learned men of his age. H.'s place in lit. is deter-mined by an early tragedy, *Rosimunda*, which assisted the transition *via* Fr. example to national drama in Sweden.

Hobbes, Thomas (1588-1679) : Engl. philosopher ; author of *Leviathan, Or the Matter, Forme, and Power of A Commonwealth Ecclesiasticall and Civil,* 1651 (in 4 parts ; i, of Man ; ii, of Commonwealth ; iii, Of a Christian Common-wealth ; iv, Of the Kingdom of Darkness). Wr. too, other important works in Lat. or Engl., including *de Corpore Politico,* 1640 ; *de Cive,* 1642 ; *Humane Nature,* 1650 (consist-ing of chs. i-xiii of *The Elements of Law, Natural and Politic,* 1640 ; first publd. completely, 1889 ; *de Corpore Politico* consisted of chs. xiv to the end) ; *Government and Society,* 1651 (H.'s own Engl. version of *de Cive*) ; replies to various critics ; *Behemoth : The History of the Civil Wars in Engld.,* 1679, and, more fully, 1682 ; together with, in another class, *The Peloponnesian War,* from the Gk. of Thucydides, 1629 (H. was attracted by the bias against democracy), and the *Iliad* and *Odyssey* from the Gk. of Homer, 1673, and, complete, 1676. Even this list is incomplete, for H. was busy and active till past 90 years of age. He spent many years (1628-31, 1634-7, 1641-52) in France, partly owing to the commotion of politics at home, and met Gassendi, Descartes (q.v.), and other men of equal learning ; in 1647, he was appointed mathematical tutor to the prince of Wales (later, king Charles ii), when the Court was in exile in Paris, and he enjoyed the patronage of the house of Caven-dish, to one or two of the scions of which he had acted as tutor in earlier years. His opinions involved him in considerable controversy, with which it is convenient to deal at this point : John Bramhall (1594-1663 ; bp. of Derry, 1634) led him to discuss *Liberty and Necessity,* 1654 ; he was in dispute with John Wallis (1616-1703), the eminent mathematician, from 1655-71, and so on ; and ' the views on human nature set forth in the book (*Leviathan*) became, for generations, the favourite battle-ground for contending philosophies ' (*C.H.E.L.,* vii, 287 ; by prof. Sorley). Among more immediate critics were James Harrington (1611-77), in *Oceana* (—Engld.), 1656, and Thos. Tenison (1636-1715 ; archbp. of Canterbury, 1694), in *The Creed of Mr. Hobbes Examined,* 1670.

This is not the place to expound or discuss the mechanical philosophy and the conse-quent view of human nature with which H. is identified, and opposition to which came from the idealists and Platonists, whose principles were at variance with his scheme. The natural law of *bellum omnium contra omnes* (war of all against all), the artificial contract correcting natural selfishness, and the political conclusion to an enlightened despotism, such as was dominant in several States in the 18th cent., lie outside the scope of this dict. What may be noted, however, is H.'s constant and consistent endeavour ' to bring within the bounds of exact science the problem of man in society ' (H. Morley), so obvious in the political experience of his long day. We may note, too, the concurrence of two modern writers as to the dependence of H. on Erastus (q.v.), anent the relations of Church and State : ' his theory is Erastianism pushed to its extremest limits ' (Sorley, *loc. cit.,* 296) ; and Dr. Figgis, *Divine Right of Kings* (second edn., 1914), after pointing out that, ' alone among the men of his time, Hobbes realized that politics are not and cannot be a branch of theology ', writes of ' his un-relieved Erastianism '. We must leave here the political theory of this great and learned philosopher. It is more appropriate to our proper sphere to quote (from prof. Sorley again ; *loc. cit.,* 289) an appreciation of him as a master of Engl. lit. : ' Hobbes ', we read, ' is one of a succession of English writers who are as remarkable for their style as for the originality of their thought. Bacon, Hobbes, Berkeley and Hume—to mention only the greatest names—must be counted among the masters of language, wherever language is looked upon as conveying a meaning. And, in each case, the style has an individual quality which suits the thought and the time '. After mentioning Bacon's (q.v.) ' Wealth of imagery and allusion ', Berkeley's (q.v.) ' musical eloquence ', and Hume's (q.v.) ' unimpassioned lucidity ', Hobbes, he says, ' differs from all three, and, in his own way, is supreme. There is no excess of imagery or allusion, though both are at hand when wanted. There is epigram ; but epigram is not multiplied for its own sake. There is satire ; but it is always kept in restraint. His work is never embellished with ornament ; every ornament is structural and belongs to the building. There is never a word too many, and the right word is always chosen. His materials are of the simplest ; and they have been formed into a living whole, guided by a great thought and fired by the passion for a great cause '.

Hoby, Thomas (1530-66) : Engl. scholar ; diplomatist ; knt., 1566. Transld., 1561, the *Cortegiano* (Courtier) of Castiglione (q.v.), with permanent effects on Engl. lit. and Engl. character. A fine essay on H. in sir W. Raleigh's (q.v.) posth. *Some Authors* (Oxford, 1923) should be read by every student.

Hölderlin, Friedrich (1770-1843) : Germ. poet. Visited Tübingen univ., where Schelling and Hegel were among his fellow-students, and became an ardent admirer of Kant and Schiller (see s.vv.), with whom, and in whose circle, he spent a congenial year, 1794. H.'s working years were otherwise not happy. He earned his bread by writing and teaching, and had the misfortune to contract a passion for the mother of one of his pupils. Moreover, his health broke down, and from 1806 till his death he was under restraint in an asylum. H. was a Hellenist by sympathy, and a Pan-worshipper in advance of his times : ' love learnt I among the flowers ', he wrote ; ' in the arms of the gods I grew to man's stature '. His chief poems were lyrics in classical metres, and even more distinguished than his lyric verse was his prose-poem, *Hyperion, or The Hermit in Greece*, an unfind. romance told in letters.

Hölty, Ludwig Heinrich Christoph (1748-76) : Germ. poet. As a member of the Göttingen (q.v.) brotherhood, banded together in the name of Klopstock (q.v.), H. danced round the oak-tree on that autumn evening, 1772, when the Hain (q.v.) was constituted ; but he did not live to express the music that was in him. His poems, collected posth., show a genuine lyrical power, tinged by a melancholy reflected from the impact of his deep sense of beauty on the doom of his own early death, which his state of health made plain to him.

Höpken, von, Johan (1712-89) : Swed. orator ; count by rank ; co-operated with Linnæus (q.v.) in founding the Academy of Sciences ; has been called the Tacitus of Sweden, and is chiefly notable for his funeral orations on the great dead of his day, in the style of the Fr. *oraisons funèbres* (q.v.).

Hoffmann, August Heinrich (1798-1874) : Germ. poet and philosopher ; commonly called H. von Fallersleben, after the name of his birthplace, A meretricious interest attaches to H. to-day as the author, 1841, of the song ' Deutschland, Deutschland, über Alles ', and those who have had cause to object to its sentiment may be interested to learn that H., in his own day, was a bit of a revolutionary, and was dismissed from his univ. (Breslau) in consequence of his 2 vols., 1840-41, of *Unpolitische Lieder*. Thereafter, he led a wandering life, ' like a

Spielmann of the Middle Ages '. Francke (*Social Forces in Germ. Lit.*, 520 *n.*) contrasts ' the unreflecting joyousness of patriotic feeling ', revealed in the *Deutschland, Deutschland* lines, with the pathos of Heine (q.v.), *In der Fremde.* H.'s studies in philology also led him to write folk-songs.

Hoffmann, Ernest Theodor Wilhelm (1776-1822) : Germ. Romantic (s.v. Romance) novelist and musician ; adopted Christian name of Amadeus, after Mozart. Carlyle (q.v.) in Engld. wr. a well-known essay on H., and Balzac (q.v.) in France declared that he was the poet, ' de ce qui n'a pas l'air d'exister, et qui néanmoins a vie '. As a romanticist, he displayed a morbid humour, ' dealing in corpses and spectres instead of nymphs and fairies ' (*P.E.L.*, x, 291), but he was always responsive to the sensibilities of the era of Germ. national revival and he exercised a potent influence on Schumann (1810-56), the composer, besides giving direction to the novel in France. Wr. *Lebensansichten* (Life and Opinions) *des Katers Murr*, a fantastic medley, fairly autobiographic, in the form of memoirs of a ' philistine ' cat, supposed to be written on the proof-sheets of an idealist musician's love-romance (2 vols., unfind., 1821-22) ; *Serapionsbrüder* (4 vols., 1819-21), stories, connected by friends' conversation, called after a real brotherhood of literary men (Chamisso, Fouqué, qq.v., and others) in Berlin, where Hoffmann settled, 1814, after various wanderings, musical and theatrical ; *Phantasiestücke* (4 vols., 1814-15), tales and essays, frankly in the manner of a Fr. grotesque 17th.-cent. artist, Callot, for which J. P. Richter (q.v.) wr. the Pref., and which made H.'s reputation. Among the contents of this bk. was *Kreisleriana*, or biographical fragments of a music-director Kreisler, partly H. himself, partly quarried from a character in Wackenroder's (q.v.) *Herzensergiessungen*, and revived as the author of the proof-sheets in *Kater Murr* above. ' The Devil's Elixir ' (1816) is probably the best-known of H.'s tales, many of which have been translated into Engl. ; it is described by Robertson (*Germ. Lit.*, 482) as ' an attempt to adapt the " Gothic " tale of terror to the Romantic novel, . . . possibly suggested to H. by Lewis's *Monk* ' : its hero, indeed, is a Capuchin monk. Francke (*Germ. Lit.*, 467) writes more scornfully of H.'s age of political coercion, in which it was consequently ' no wonder that the hollow phantasms of a spiritualistic dreamer like Amadeus Hoffmann were admired as marvels of poetic fiction ' ; but even he, despite his political bias against the ' reactionary ghosts of the palmy days of Metternich ' (q.v.)—and nights, we might add in H.'s instance—conceded to H. a mastery in realistic description and psychological analysis.

Hoffmann, Heinrich (1809-74) : Germ. physician ; author of *Struwwelpeter* (' Shock-headed Peter '), 1847, written to entertain his own children, and the delight of children in many families and countries beyond. H.'s other ballads, humorous poems and satires are of inferior interest.

Hoffmannswaldau, von, Christian Hoffmann (1618--79) : Germ. poet ; of the so-called Second

Silesian School (q.v.). The 'elegant and gallant' style which he professed to practise was too full of similes and other affectations to prove either valuable or popular. H. was brought up in the atmosphere of Opitz (q.v.) -worship, and complicated that perilous tendency by the admiration which he acquired in his Ital. travels for the art of Marini (q.v.), whose *Pastor Fido* he transld. H.'s chief work was *Heldenbriefe* ('heroic epistles') in verse and prose, which earned him the sounding name of the Germ. Ovid. The headquarters of his school was Hamburg, the earliest home of Germ. opera.

Hogg, James (1770-1835): Scot. poet; known as the Ettrick Shepherd; employed as a boy at a farm at Willanslee by the father of sir W. Scott's (q.v.) amanuensis, Wm. Laidlaw (1780-1845). Thus, made Scott's acquaintance—a valuable asset for the rustic lad of mother-wit,—and supplied material for his *Border Minstrelsy*. Later, made friends with Wordsworth, Southey (qq.v.), and others, including John Wilson (q.v.; the 'Christopher North' of *Blackwood's Magazine*), who partly caricatured and partly idealized H. in *Noctes Ambrosianæ*. Publd. several vols. of ballads and other verse, and prose-tales (notably, *Kilmeny*), and enjoyed a high reputation as a practically self-taught genius.

Hojeda, de, Diego (c. 1570-1615): Span. sacred poet. Wr., 1611, *la Christiada*, which has been favourably compared with the *Messiah* of Klopstock (q.v.).

Holbach, d', Paul Heinrich (Henri) Dietrich (Thiry) (1723-89): Fr. *philosophe* (q.v.) of Germ. birth; *baron* by rank. Born at Hildesheim, but lived and died in Paris; wr. in Fr. language, and was a wealthy host in the circle, and in keen sympathy with the aims and ideas, of Diderot (q.v.) and his friends. Wr. *Christianisme dévoilé* ('unveiled'), 1756, and other anti-deistic works, and was a champion of the physical, as superior to the metaphysical, laws in social, and, by extension, in political, organisms. D'H. is credited with the authorship, or, more probably, with a leading part, in the authorship of *Système de la Nature* (q.v.), 1770, which drove the materialist argument to the utmost confines of theology and metaphysics, and profoundly influenced opinion at the time. Rousseau (q.v.) was in bitter conflict with d'H. and the Holbachian positivist morality.

Holberg, Ludvig (1684-1754): Dan. playwright; historian; Latinist; by common consent, a leading man of letters in his own country and beyond. 'Denmark owes to Holberg what rank she has succeeded in attaining' (sir E. Gosse, *Lit. of Northern Europe*, 140; Kegan Paul, 1879). 'One notable man, the very embodiment of the classical, reasonable age, in its critical and liberating function—yet going far beyond it in his loud, genial laughter and grasp of common life—suddenly, without precursors and without disciples, initiated Denmark into the art of writing and the current thought of the world' (O. Elton, *P.E.L.*, viii, 366). His work, says Brandes (q.v.), the Dan. critic, is 'genuine Renaissance invention, reminding us of the greatest masters, Shakespeare, Cervantes and Rabelais';

and he is spoken of too, as 'the Molière of the North'. It is high praise, and a chorus of praise, but it is to be conceded as defensible, particularly in Denmark, partly on the individual ground of H.'s own genius, but chiefly on the hist. ground of his departure from Dan. obscurity into the company of European men of letters. He saved—almost violently and savagely—the lit. of his country from the invasion of Germ. style and models; and, though Pedersen (q.v.) is properly accounted the father of Dan. lit., H. is its saviour and champion, who transmitted to Oehlenschläger and Andersen (qq.v.) the fount of Dan. genius undefiled. H., too, went abroad for inspiration. Critics compute in an ascending scale his debt to Steele and Addison (qq.v.) and the Augustan atmosphere in Engld., where he resided for 2 years (after 1706), finding most of his friends in Magdalen Coll. (though it is not certain if he was acquainted with Addison, q.v.) and supporting himself by teaching. To France, too, he incurred obligations, though the Molière influence is less deep than superficial, and the Ital. theatre, and Vega and Moreto (qq.v.) in Spain were also tributary to his stagecraft. But his way was his own; his invention was original and facile; and he struck a blow for the liberty of Dan. thought and for the cosmopolitan quality of Dan. lit., which his countrymen gratefully acknowledge, and which other countries recognize and applaud. As prof., at first without a chair, later, by rotation, of metaphysics and rhetoric, and, at last, 1730, congenially, of history, at the univ. of Copenhagen, H. was the author of a number of learned works,—a *History of the Danish Kingdom*, the first experiment in its kind since Saxo (q.v.), a *History of the Jews* (a topic demanding a liberal mind in those days), a *Church History*, etc. His *Heroes* are Plutarchan, his *Epistles* are Addisonian, and his Lat. *Niels Klim* or *Klimins*, or 'Subterranean Journey', 1741, is Lucianic, Utopian, and Swiftian. But the true genius of H. was revealed in his poems and dramas. To his biography it merely remains to add that he lived an adventurous youth, that he was created a baron in 1751, and that, like many Dan. writers before 1814, he was Norw. by his birth at Bergen. *Peder Paars*, H.'s mock-heroic epic, was publd. in instalments under the name of Hans Mikkelsen, 1718-20, and the satire and humour of these poems in rhyming alexandrines brought Copenhagen back to a sense of national consciousness. Much dramatic stuff was wrapped up in the epic, and H. was the heart and soul of the management of the national theatre, which became the Royal Theatre of 1747 to this day. A company of Germ. actors had long been established at the court, but were dismissed in 1721, and on 23 Sept., 1722, the first Dan. company of comedians opened its first season. It passed through various vicissitudes, including the Puritan suspension of the stage during the reign of Christian vi (1730-46). But H. re-opened it with his earlier successful drama (*The Pewterer Politician*), and it has not looked back. The conscience of comparative lit. (if so recent a branch of study has acquired so ancient a burden) may be tranquillized with the reflection that the Germans, whom H. drove from the Dan. stage, repaired to him for encouragement and example, when Lessing (q.v.) descended from heaven to teach dramaturgy on earth. H.'s first hero, *The Pewterer Politician*, was the 'muzzy politician who is deceived into thinking himself a functionary ' (Elton, *op. cit.*, 372), founded, perhaps, on the *Tatler* paper on the political upholsterer ; and, properly to dramatic purpose, the supposititious Burgomaster of Hamburg is delighted to turn tinker again. *Jeppe o' th' Hill* (a Christopher Sly motive play) and Jeppe's son, *Rasmus Berg* or ' Erasmus Montanus ', the Latinized student returned to his native soil, are two similar comedies, expressing the playwright's patriotic passion against snobbery, coxcombry, and foreign apishness. *Ulysses in Ithaca, Witchcraft, The 11th of June*, are titles of other of H.'s plays, which still hold their own on the Dan. stage, and many of which have been acclimatized in foreign repertories. If it is true, as it probably is, to say, that, without H., there would have been no Ibsen (q.v.) in the North, it must be affirmed, at the same time, that H. was a somewhat stockish and sluggish playwright, who, lacking love in his life, missed passion in his plays, and that his greatness—for he attained it—was on the middle level of dramatic achievement.

Holcroft, Thomas (1745-1809) : Engl. playwright ; actor ; miscellanist ; an interesting figure in lit. annals, gifted with a touch of genius. Contrived, by organising relays of memorizers, to convey *le Mariage de Figaro* (see s.v. Beaumarchais) from Paris to London, where he produced his version, *The Follies of a Day*, at Covent Garden Theatre, 1784, His *Road to Ruin*, 1792 (9 edns. in the year), made him famous. His fame was enhanced, 1794, by an indictment for high treason, from which he came out with colours flying. H., who was a friend of Hazlitt, Godwin (qq.v.), and others, kept an interesting diary, and wr. novels, comics operas, and translns.

Home, John (1722-1808) : Scot. dramatist and historian ; sometime tutor to the prince of Wales ; his *Douglas*, founded on an old Scot. ballad, was produced in Edinburgh, 1756, and at Covent Garden, 1757. ' Its native background, and its atmosphere of brooding melancholy, invest it with something of the romantic atmosphere of his friend Collins ' (q.v. ; *C.H.E.L.*, x, 87) ; but it is chiefly remembered to-day for the once famous quotation (Act ii, sc. i) :

My name is Norval ; on the Grampian Hills
My father fed his flocks.

H.'s later plays proved less successful. Of *The Siege of Aquileia*, a tragedy, produced at Drury Lane, 1760, sir H. Walpole (q.v.) wr. that it pleased him ' less than Mr. Home's other plays. In my own opinion, *Douglas* far exceeds both the other ', and posterity confirms this contemporary judgment. H. wr., too, a *History of the Rebellion of* 1745. See, too, s.v. Macpherson.

Homer : Students of European letters are not directly concerned with the debated question as to the orig. of the old Gk. epic poems, the *Iliad* and the *Odyssey*, attributed to a writer known as Homer, and dated about the 9th cent. B.C. They are concerned with the influence of those poems on the lit. of Europe, and with the course of European scholarship by which acquaintance of them was recovered. For H., like other classical authors, was unknown, or very imperfectly known, in Europe until the period of the discoveries of Humanism (q.v.). He was seen through a cloud or belt of smoke, known as ' Dares ' and ' Dictys ', after the reputed names of two writers, one from Phrygia, and the other from Crete, who were supposed, possibly incorrectly, to have compiled prose epitomes of the Greco-Trojan War (the martial topic of the *Iliad* ; Ilion was Troy), from the Trojan and Gk. sides respectively, some time between the 4th and 6th cents. A.D. Reference to these reputed authorities is found in a passage of the *Gest Hystoriale of the Destruction of Troy*, freely rendered into verse, *c.* 1375, from the Lat. prose *Historia Trojana*, finished in 1287 by Guido delle Colonne (de Columna) in Sicily. This passage, says K. Sisam (*Fourteenth Century Verse* and *Prose*, Oxford, 1923 ; p. 69), ' is a curious example of the pseudo-critical attitude of the Middle Ages. Homer is despised as a teller of impossible tales, and a partisan of the Greeks,—for Hector is the popular hero of the medieval versions. The narratives of Dares Phrygius and Dictys Cretensis, products of the taste for fictitious history that spread westward from Greek-speaking lands in the fourth and succeeding centuries, are accepted as reliable documents ; and Guido de Columna as their authoritative literary interpreter '. Students should also refer to *Homer : The Origins and the Transmission*, by Thos. W. Allen (Oxford, 1925).

Another screen, reflecting H. to modern eyes, several centuries later than Dares-Dictys, was fabricated by Bénoît (q.v.) of Ste.-Maure, the Norman-Fr. trouvère, whose verse-redaction of their Troy-books formed the basis of Guido's history (above), though, oddly enough, Bénoît is not mentioned by Guido's Engl. translr., and it is from Bénoît's verse-narrative that the Trojan tale passed directly into the Homer-repertories of the story-tellers of the 14th cent. as a part of the *matière de Rome* (see s.v. Bodel).

The real study of H. in Europe began with Boccaccio and Petrarch (qq.v.), who received a MS. of H. from Sigeros of Constantinople, on his visit to Avignon, 1353. Petrarch, in one of his ' Epistles to Dead Authors ', told H., his imaginary correspondent, that those who ' knew and loved ' him at that date numbered only 4 or 5 in Florence, 2 in Verona, one each at Bologna, Mantua and Solmona, and none at Rome. It is worth remembering (1925) that this is still less than 600 years ago, and that H., for practical purposes, is as recent an author as Chaucer, and only 200 years older than Shakespeare. The greater honour is due to the early scholars who rescued him from the dust of ages.

In 1360, Leontius Pilatus (q.v.) a rare and precious but somewhat boorish Gk., was brought from Venice to Florence by Boccaccio, who entertained him for three years, and set him at work to translate H. into Lat. for the use of Petrarch and himself. Thus, (1) Boccaccio justly ranks as the first Homerist in Europe, and (2) the first Homerists were compelled, for lack of a Gk.-Ital. dict., to restore a Lat. H. to aspiring Hellenists. Among several Homerizing humanists, may be mentioned Politian (q.v.), known as *Homericus juvenis*, alike for his Lat. rendering of five bks. of the *Iliad*, and for his *Ambra*, in Lat. hexameters, which was a critical panegyric on Homer.

Things moved more quickly in the 15th and 16th cents. The *ed. pr.* of H. was printed at Florence, 1488, by Demetrius Chalcondyles, a Gk. lecturer in that city and in Padua. The *ed. pr.* of the *Scholia* on the *Iliad* was printed in Rome, 1517, at the Gk. press on the Quirinal, by Janus Lascaris, another Gk. exile, who afterwards sought the hospitality of king Francis i in Paris. Aldine edns. (see s.v. Aldo) were publd. in Venice, 1504 and 1517. The earliest essay in Homeric commentary was that of Joachim Camerarius (q.v.), 1538, which was extended and completed at Frankfort, 1584, thus commencing the Germ. study of H., which has been exceptionally valuable to criticism. The 17th cent. was busy with Homerica, in Florence, Venice, Paris, and other cities, and mention is due to the edn. 1710, of Joshua Barnes, some time prof. of Gk. at Cambridge and to that, 1729, of Samuel Clarke, a pupil of Isaac Newton.

A new departure in Homeric study was marked by the work of Villoison (q.v.), who publd. at Venice, 1788, the *ed. pr.* of the ' Scholia of A,' i.e. of the Marginalia of the MS. of the *Iliad* known now as Codex Venetus A (no. 454, St. Mark's Library, Venice). This contains the epitome, compiled *c.* 200-250 A.D., of critical treatises on H. by four scholars of antiquity, including mainly Didymus, who has preserved all we know of Aristarchus (*fl. c.* 160 B.C.), described by sir R. Jebb (1841-1905), the Cambridge Hellenist, as ' the greatest scholar and best Homeric critic of antiquity '. Villoison's recovery of Didymus-Aristarchus marks the beginning of textual criticism of the *Iliad*. The MS. corresponding to Codex Venetus A. in relation to the *Odyssey*, is Harleianus, no. 5674, British Museum.

The ' Homeric question ' next occupied modern scholars. Two main aspects are distinguished : (1) external,—how artistic works were in existence at the opening of a national (Gk.) lit., and (2) internal,—how inferior or discrepant parts had entered into otherwise complete wholes. Casaubon, Bentley, Vico, R. Wood and others touched on the Homeric question before it became actual at and after 1788. Herder (q.v.) in Germany ' was one of the first to elucidate the general character of the Homeric poems ', as recently, observe, as 1773, 1795 and 1803 (*Homer u. das Epos*): ' he finds in them the fullest illustration of the idiosyncrasy of national literature ' (Sandys, *Hist. Class. Schol.*, iii. 34). But the true beginner of scientific Homerizing was the Germ. specialist, F. A. Wolf (q.v.; 1759-1824), whose *Prolegomena*, publd. at Halle, 1795, is first identified with a critical theory as to the authorship and composition

of the Homeric poems, with arguments from textual criticism, and other apparatus of exact scholarship. Was H. the earliest (Wolf) and more (G. J. Hermann, another learned Germ.) or less (Lachmann) supreme poet of a dynasty ; or was he the master-epicist, subsequent to the epoch of short lays (Nitzsch and Grote ; anti-Wolf) ? So, discussion grew into controversy, as has been the way of scholars with their bones in all ages, and was continued through the 19th cent. by Christ, Kirchhoff, Niese, Fick, and others. Interest in the subject has died down a little in the present cent., which is disposed to the anti-Wolf view of a single as distinct from a multiple H. ; but Homeric scholarship will always be a distinct and many-ramified branch of classical learning and taste.

Translrs. of H. have been legion. The most famous of the Germans is J. H. Voss (1751-1826), whose early version of a fragment from the *Odyssey* was approved by no less competent a judge than Klopstock (q.v.). His complete *Odyssey* was publd., 1781, and ' surpassed ' (Sandys, *op. cit.*, 62) ' all previous attempts to render the original in German verse '. It was followed by the *Iliad*, 1793. In Engld. we may mention Chapman, Pope, Cowper, 14th earl of Derby (see s.vv.), and the more recent prose versions by A. Lang, S. H. Butcher and others. John Flaxman (1755-1826) won renown by his drawings illustrating H.

The influence, direct and indirect, of H. on European lit., is a topic for a bk., not for the close of a brief art. of this kind. Winckelmann and Keats (qq.v.), each of whom was a discoverer of H.'s secret, must be consulted on the point, and the author of the ch. on ' Literature ' in *The Legacy of Greece* (Oxford, 1921) directs us sagely to that consultation : ' Hellenism ', he writes (it is Mr. R. W. Livingstone), ' is one of the forces which are continually being buried and re-found, and which, like talismans, have a disturbing power when they fall afresh into human hands. Those who read the lit. of the age which rediscovered Gk., will see that it brought above all a sense of liberation and expansion. At the Renaissance as in the eighteenth century, Greece found the world in chains, and broke them and threw down the prison walls. The fetters of the two epochs were different, but freedom was brought, at the Renaissance partly, and in the age of Winckelmann entirely, by the vision of beauty which Greek exhibited '. This generalization is worth a crowd of particular instances ; but reference may be made to Schiller's (q.v.) essay, 1795, *ueber naive u. sentimentalische Dichtung*, or poetry based on observation (naive) and reflection (sentimental), in which the model of the former class was H. (and which really proved very little more than that H.'s genius was objective) ; to the lectures on *Our Debt to Antiquity*, delivered in 1903 by prof. Zielinski at what was then the univ. of St. Petersburg (E.T., Routledge, 1909 ; see esp. ch. v) ; to M. Arnold's (q.v.) essay *On Translating Homer* ; and to ch. i of *Introduction to Homer* by sir R. C. Jebb (q.v.)

Hood, Thomas (1799-1845): Engl. writer of comic genius and tragic experience ; a lively Hood writing for his livelihood, as he expressed it himself; the tragedy consisted of ill health, poor pay, and financial struggles due to the failure of his publisher; lived abroad for some years: Coblentz, 1835-7, and Ostend, 1837-40. Edited *Comic Annual*, 1829; *New Monthly Magazine*, 1841-3; *Hood's Magazine*, 1844, etc.; wr. *Eugene Aram's Dream*, a fine poem, in the *Gem*, 1829; *The Song of the Shirt* in *Punch*, 1843; *Miss Kilmansegg*, and other well-known sets of verses. H., apart from his punning fame, was a master of wistful emotion, and his verses commencing 'I remember, I remember, The house where I was born', strike a note of deep appeal to human sympathy. See, too, s.v. Praed.

Hooft, Pieter Cornelis (1581-1648): Dutch humanist; historian, dramatist, and poet. Travelled abroad for some years, studying poetry and philosophy in Italy and France. Appointed, 1609, governor of Muiden, on the Zuyder Zee, with an official residence which he made the literary centre of the celebrated 'Muiderkring' (q.v.), a circle comparable to the Parisian Hôtel Rambouillet (q.v.). H. effected for Holland what Spenser (q.v.) effected for Engld., as a disciple of the Renaissance: he acclimatized, that is to say, the best products of Ital. and Fr. culture on his native soil. His love-poems, sonnets, and pastorals, and, in a less degree, his dramas, in which he took Garnier (q.v.) as model, are the pure fruit of Petrarchism in the Netherlands, and constitute a chief splendour of its golden age. But greater and more permanent than his plays and lyrics is H.'s masterpiece in Dutch prose, the unfind. *Nederlandsche Historien* ('History of the Netherlands'), covering the period from 1555-87, which he began in 1628 and issued in a folio in 1642. This is H.'s real monument: 'he did for the seventeenth century what Macaulay, Ranke, and Taine did for ours' (Ten Brink); and tradition relates that he prepared himself for his task by reading Tacitus 52 times through, besides translating his works into Dutch. The title of 'the Dutch Tacitus' was amply earned by these labours. Thucydidean and Tacitean was H.'s fondness for the imaginary conversation by which to bring out the drama of events; and, whether regarded as history or lit., this great work is an ornament of Dutch letters. H. was one of the leaders of the revolt of the dramatic members of the Eglantine (q.v.) into the new and short-lived Coster's Academy, later merged in the Amsterdam Academy, and doomed to the easeful fate of those who took as their motto 'nil volentibus arduum' (q.v.). His house was always open to talent; his correspondence was extensive and interesting; and his name is one of the most famous in the history of the Netherlands which he served so well.

Hoogstraten, Van, Samuel (1627-78): Dutch painter and novelist. Pupil of Rembrandt. Wr. romances based on Fr. recensions of Gk. fiction (q.v.), of little artistic value, and interesting chiefly as an indication of the decline of literary taste in the Netherlands towards the close of the 17th cent. (See s.v. Dutch Lit.).

Hook, Theodore Edward (1788-1841): Engl. novelist, whose father, James H. (1772-1828;

dean of Worcester, 1825), and grandfather, James H. (1746-1827; organist at Vauxhall Gardens, 1774), were both men of letters; edu. at Harrow; a member of the prince of Wales's 'set', and famous for his practical jests and ready wit. H.'s irregularities as accountant-general at Mauritius (1812) and his subsequent imprisonment, 1823-5, are less interesting to lit. than his direct influence on Dickens (q.v.), in the period of *Sketches by Boz* (see *C.H.E.L.*, xiii, 307), and his indirect influence as the Lucian Gay of B. Disraeli's (q.v.) *Coningsby* and the Mr. Wagg of Thackeray's (q.v.) *Vanity Fair*. Edited *John Bull*, a tory review, 1820, and the *New Monthly Magazine*, 1836-41; wr. a number of novels, mostly forgotten to-day, *Sayings and Doings* (3 series), *Gilbert Gurney*, etc.

Hooker, Richard (1554-1600): Engl. divine; wr. *The Laws of Ecclesiastical Polity*, planned in 8 bks.: 4 publd., 1594, and 1 in 1597; the epithet attached to him of 'the judicious' was inscribed on his tombstone at Bishops-bourne, nr. Canterbury. Hallam (*Lit. of Europe*) calls him the 'knight of romance among caitiff brawlers', and H. expressed his own aim in the words: 'not to provoke any, but rather to satisfy all tender consciences'. The theological value of his *Eccles. Polity* lies outside the scope of this vol., but it is pertinent to note the modulation and dignity of H.'s style in prose, of which he ranks as a master. Take, e.g., the following passage from Bk. i:

'He that goeth about to persuade a multitude that they are not so well governed as they ought to be, shall never want attentive and favourable hearers, because they know the manifold defects whereunto every kind of regiment is subject, but the secret lets and difficulties, which in public proceedings are innumerable and inevitable, they have not ordinarily the judgment to consider. And because such as openly reprove supposed disorders of state are taken for principal friends to the common benefit of all, and for men that carry singular freedom of mind, under this fair and plausible colour, whatsoever they utter passes for good and current. That which wanteth in the weight of their speech is supplied by the aptness of men's minds to accept and believe it. Whereas, on the other side,' etc.

It is impossible to construct rules for excellence in prose, nor is it as easy to recognize the elements of prose-style in practice as in the instance of poetry. But here we note not merely the admirable choice of words, which give dignity and weight; the swing and balance of the sentences, and the rhythm of the movement: we note further the element of reasoned argument, the shaping of which may be traced by the phrases of logical transition, 'because', 'whereas', etc., above, 'but also', 'albeit', 'yet', and so forth, in the succeeding clauses. This is new in Engl. prose. Lyly (q.v.) and the early Elizabethans, had necessarily attended more to the manner of their prose than to the matter, for they lacked an urgent topic. Therefore, they chiefly imitated the most 'mannered' writers of former times or other countries, and they even exaggerated such mannerisms. H., absorbed by his subject, was less consciously concerned with his style. See, too, s.v. Hobbes.

Hopkins, John (d. 1570): Engl. divine; rector of Waldingfield from 1561. H. was associated with archbp. Parker (q.v., and see s.v. Bible) in the metrical version of the Psalter, which enjoyed extreme popularity for about 150 years (1563-1698). Among H.'s personal contributions is said to have been the famous ' Old Hundredth '.

Horace (65-8 B.C.): Quintus Horatius Flaccus; Roman poet; after Homer and Virgil (qq.v.), one of the most influential makers, among the classics of antiquity, of modern European lit. His influence was exercised mainly in 3 directions; (1), by his *Ars Poetica* (B.C., 19; ' The Art of Poetry '), to the theory and practice of literary composition; (2), by his Odes and Epodes, to lyrical measures and diction; and (3), by his *Sermones* (*sermo*= talk), or conversational verse-satires and epistles, to what is known as *vers de société*, a poetry touching in a light, reflective vein on the passing follies, fashions and opinions of the day. H.'s cultivated attitude to experience, derived from Gk. stoic philosophy, of a humorous, patient, tolerant, easy acceptance of things as they are, appealed particularly to the minds of Englishmen in the 18th cent., reacting from extravagance of adventure and extremes of individuality.

H.'s debts to earlier writers, whether Roman or Gk., and whether debts of style or thought, are a matter for special students of Horatian origins, not for the general student of European lit. Among such writers may be mentioned, summarily, Archilochus, Sappho, Pindar, Lucilius, for whom, says prof. Tyrrell (*Lat. Poetry*, 1895, p. 168), ' Horace seems to have done very much what Pope did for the coarse tales of Chaucer, for the rough philosophizing of Dr. Donne, and even for the epistles of Horace himself '. Nor need we be concerned with the inquiry how far H., in the seclusion of his Sabine farm, was a true lover of the country for its own sake. The townsman in the country is a familiar figure in Engl. social life, and ' although Horace often dwells on the simplicity of his life at the Farm, he was comfortable enough in his well-built house, where he loved to entertain his friends, now the wealthy Maecenas, now humble and less well-known guests. We can imagine him the perfect host, with a chosen companion, sitting by his fireside, beside the piled-up logs, and, as they quaffed the homely Sabine, bringing up from the treasure-house of his mind things old and new, touching all with his incomparable ease and modesty and wisdom ' (G. H. Hallam, *Horace*. Harrow School Bookshop, 1922). It was that incomparable quality, that inimitable felicity of diction, which chiefly impressed Ronsard (q.v.) and his Pleiad (q.v.), seeking from H.'s *Odes* a model for the lyrical note in France; as the *Ars Poetica*, drawn from various Gk. sources, including, mainly, Aristotle (q.v.) and a lost treatise by Neoptolemus of Parium, impressed the critics of the 17th cent. by its ' crisp, rememberable phrases. The few hundred lines of the little piece ', continues prof. Saintsbury (*Hist. Crit.*, i, 226), ' are positively " made of

quotations " ', and he notes at least 7 familiar tags in the first 25 lines; ' the proportion ', he adds, ' is well maintained throughout '. Though Lat. studies are unfortunately declining, and the House of Commons no longer smiles approval to arguments clinched by a Horatian phrase, we cannot refuse admiration to a Roman author of nearly 2,000 years ago, who said better than anyone has said since the moving, obvious, universal truisms of human observation and experience.

When did H. reach modern Eruope ? He was known to Alcuin, at the court of Charlemagne (q.v.) in the 8th cent., and was named by Abelard (q.v.) among the pagan philosophers. In the long cents. before the Renaissance, he was more familiar in France and Germany, in the shadow of Charlemagne's revival of learning, than in Italy, and was better known by his satires and epistles than by his lyric verse.

Petrarch (q.v.) possessed a copy (now in the Laurentian Library) of H.'s works, and preferred the odes to the *sermones*. The oldest extant MS. is the *codex Bernensis*; another *codex*, known as *Blandinius*, was burnt in a monastery library at Ghent, and our knowledge of it rests on the labours of J. Cruquius, of Bruges, who edited, 1565-78, H. from that MS., which he had borrowed for the purpose. The *ed. pr.* was printed at Venice, c. 1471; Navagero (q.v.) edited H. for Aldus (q.v.) early in the 16th cent., and the great edn. of that cent. was by Lambin (q.v.), to whom J. Bond (1550-1612) was much indebted for his commentary, 1600. Eminent among later editors were Bentley (q.v.), 1711, and Pieter Burman (1668-1741), of Utrecht and Leyden. The influence of H. on Vida (q.v.) and other Horatian-Aristotelian critics of the 16th cent. is discussed s.vv. The critical labours of J. Caspar Orelli (1787-1849; *Horace*, 1837-8), Jas. Tate (1771-1843; *Horatius Restitutus*, 1833), John Conington (1825-69; complete verse transln.), Gaston Boissier (1823-1908), and many others, belong to the hist. of scholarship rather than of letters.

We may close this brief study of H. in Europe with the words of prof. Mackail in *The Legacy of Rome* (Oxford, 1923; p. 350): ' His *Odes* became a sort of Psalter of secular life; his *Satires* and *Epistles* have been, for the whole European world, the great handbook of good sense, good temper, and practical wisdom. No one has done more to spread, and fix, and make attractive that spirit of " humanity ", which, like its name, is of Latin creation. He gave mankind the type of the man of the world and the gentleman; he showed how it is attainable without birth or wealth, without anxiety or ambition, without either high intellectual gifts or unattainable saintliness of life. From the great idealisms and the deeper passions he keeps himself apart. He never touches what are called " problems ", whether social or individual. His thought and feeling are both, in the literal sense of the word, commonplace; but, in both, he is plumb on the centre. Just for this reason, what he gives us is of a kind to which the human mind instinctively and immediately responds '; and we gather from this passage how H.

served to inspire the Lovelaces and Sucklings of a later day, composing their mundane psalter to the measures of the poet, in whom Petronius, leader of fashion at the court of the emperor Nero, 54-66 A.D., was the first to discover the faculty of a *curiosa felicitas* in diction.

Horne, Richard Henry (1803-84): Engl. poet, of adventurous and eccentric character, and somewhat rapidly fading reputation. Wr. tragedies : *The Death of Marlowe*, 1837, and others, which never held the stage, and an ambitious epical allegory, *Orion*, 1843, which, as a gesture of contempt for the public, he issued at a farthing. Several large edns. were sold, and it was extravagantly praised in places. H. collaborated with Elizabeth Barrett (Browning, q.v.), 1844, and others, in a vol. of essays, *The New Spirit of the Age*, which, despite real talent and immense energy, H. somehow failed to seize. He emigrated to Australia for gold, but spent his last years in Engld., when he changed his name Henry to Hengist, a fact of biography which no one explains.

Hostrup, Jens Christian (born, 1818): Dan. playwright ; a notable leader of the liberalizing movement in univ. circles ; rose from composing students' farces to writing comedies for the King's theatre in Copenhagen.

Hotman, François (1524-90): Fr. jurist ; successor to Cujas (q.v.) as prof. of law at Bourges ; Huguenot ; after the massacre of St. Bartholomew, 1572, withdrew to Geneva. Wr. commentaries on Cicero (q.v.), and composed, 1560, Fr. political pamphlet addressed to, and entitled, *Le Tigre* (i.e. the card. of Lorraine), modelled on the Catiline orations. A philippic against queen Catherine de Medici, who was regarded as responsible for the massacre, was also, perhaps incorrectly, ascribed to H., who certainly wr., 1573, a Lat. treatise, *Franco-Gallia*, as a reasoned plea for liberal institutions. It consisted chiefly of illustrative passages from early Fr. history, brought together, to prove the inherent right of the people to take part in their own government. 'Like Locke and Rousseau (see s.vv.), he will allow omnipotence to no administration, and would apparently, like Rousseau, regard all forms of constitution as liable to change at the will of the sovereign people. The basis of the argument, where it is not historical, is utilitarian, and Hotman has frequent recourse to the maxim *salus populi suprema lex* ' (Figgis, *The Divine Right of Kings*, 2nd edn., 119). H.'s writings on political theory exercised great influence in his day, and inspired the works of such men as Du Plessis and Gentillet (qq.v.), who sought to found the principles of government on conceptions of popular right as distinct from monarchical might.

Houwaert, Jan Baptista (1533-99): Dutch poet ; nobleman ; active in political events of his age. Wr., 1578, a kind of allegorical poem on those happenings, dedicated to the prince of Orange, and adapted from an episode in Guevara's (q.v.) *Dial of Princes*, thus anticipating the Dutch transln. of that famous work in 1586 ; this poem, entitled *Milenus*, after the name of the character in Guevara whose mission it was to travel from the Danube to carry the fatal tidings to the Roman Senate, was written in the conventional verse of the Rederijkers (q.v.), to one of whose chambers H. was closely attached. He, like Ghistele (q.v.), his contemporary, was a medievalist surviving into the Renaissance ; so strong was the force of the tradition of the rhetoricians' guilds ; indeed, his masterpiece was described on its title-page as 'poetically invented and rhetorically composed'. This work consisted of 16 bks. of didactic, moralizing verse, under the general name of *Pegasides*, reminiscent of the *Romance of the Rose* (q.v.), and of H.'s own countryman, D. Potter (q.v.). H. was greeted in his own day as the Brabantian Homer, and every kind of honour was rendered to him ; but we see him so steeply fastened in the manner and tone of the Middle Ages that he is best characterized as a disciple of Castelein (q.v.).

Houwald, von, Ernst (1778-1845): Germ. dramatist. Wr. fate-dramas (q.v.) of even less convincing horror than those of Müllner (q.v.). Thus his ' Picture ', 1821, and his ' Light-house ', 1824, were themselves the unconscious instruments of the transmitted spells. Wr. other plays of no particular merit, more sentimental in taste, and a farce which ridiculed the fatalism which he imitated in his tragedies.

Howitt, -i. William (1792-1879): Engl. miscellanist ; wr. many bks. of a popular character, ephemeral in type : *Rural Life in Engld.*, *Visits to Remarkable Places* ; *Homes and Haunts of the Poets*, etc.

-ii. Mary (1799-1888): Engl. translr. ; wife of above, whom she m., 1821. Transld. some works of F. Bremer and Hans Andersen (qq.v.) ; wr. some children's bks., and collaborated with her husband in some popular bookmaking. M.H. received a civil list pension, 1879, and both she and W.H. died in Rome.

Hoyos, de, Juan Lopez (16th cent.): Span. humanist. Compiled, 1568, ' The True History and Narrative of the Illness, Most Happy Passing, and Sumptuous Obsequies of the Most Serene Queen of Spain, Donna Isabel de Valois ', third consort to king Philip ii. To this memorial vol. Cervantes (q.v.) contributed an elegy of 199 lines, and other verses, including, possibly, a sonnet. H. speaks of Cervantes as his ' dear and beloved pupil ', and it is likely that he acted in 1561-64 as his schoolmaster at Madrid.

Hoz y Mota, de la, Juan Claudio (d., 1714): Span. dramatist ; knt. of the order of Santiago, 1653. Wr., among other plays, *el Castigo de Miseria* (' The Punishment of Avarice '), based on a story of Zayas (q.v.), on which Scarron (q.v.) likewise founded a drama, *Châtiment de l'Avarice*.

Huber, Ludwig Ferdinand (1764-1804): Germ. publicist ; edited the *Allgemeine Zeitung* and wr. two not notable dramas. H. enters literary history through his wife more directly than through his works. He m., 1794, Therese, widow of J. G. Forster (q.v.) and daughter of C. G. Heyne (q.v.), and had already sacrificed for her sake his chances of promotion in the diplomatic service of Saxony.

Huarte de San Juan (c. 1530-c. 1591): Span. philosopher. Wr. *Examen de Ingenios para* *las Sciencias*, a treatise on the association between physical and mental fitness, *ed. pr.*, 1575, and frequently reprinted. The work enjoyed exceptional vitality, and was transld. into Engl. by R. Carew, 1594, and into most other European tongues, including Germ. by Lessing (q.v.), who compared H. to 'a spirited horse, that, in galloping over the stones, never strikes fire so brilliantly as he does when he stumbles' (see Ticknor, ii, 220 n.).

Hudson, William Henry (died, 1922): Engl. naturalist; spent his boyhood in the Great Plains of South America, where he acquired his love and intimate knowledge of fauna and flora. Wr. *The Naturalist in La Plata*, 1892, preceded by *The Purple Land*, a novel, 2 vols., 1885. H.'s most famous bk. is *Green Mansions: a Romance of the Tropical Forest*, 1904, which displays to the full his rare command of a kind of so-called Celtic magic in his birdlore and beastlore. He is commemorated by a birds'-sanctuary in Hyde Park, opened in 1925 by Mr. Baldwin, prime-minister, and containing a symbolic sculpture by J. Epstein.

Huerta, de la, Vicente Garcia (1734-1787): Span. poet; dramatic writer. Wr. *Raquel*, a poor Racinian (s.v. Racine) tragedy on the old story of the Jewess of Toledo (see s.v. Diamante); *Poesias*, collected poems, 1778, after old Span. metrical models; and publd., 1785-86, an extensive *Teatro Hespañol* (14 vols.), or library of Span. plays, which, by its omission of Vega and Molina (qq.v.) and other exhibitions of bad taste, gave rise to considerable discussion on the part of Iriarte, Jovellanos, and others. The controversy is said to have affected H.'s brain.

Huet, Pierre Daniel (1630-1721): Fr. scholar; managing-editor of the Delphin Classics (q.v.), and tutor to the Dauphin, son of king Louis xiv, for whose benefit the series was inaugurated, later, bp. of Avranches. La Fontaine (q.v.) addressed a verse-epistle to H., which is valuable for our knowledge of both great men.

Hughes, Thomas (1822-96): Engl. social worker, principal of Working Men's Coll., 1872-83. Wr. *Tom Brown's School-days*, 1856, which enjoyed and enjoys an immense vogue as a story of Engl. public school life. The school was Rugby, and the headmaster T. Arnold (q.v.). H. wr. a sequel, *Tom Brown at Oxford*, and lives of Alfred the Great, and others. His work brought him into close association with Kingsley and Maurice (qq.v.).

Hugo, Victor Marie (1802-85): Fr. poet, novelist, critic, dramatist; leader of the Romantic (s.vv. Romance, Lyrisme) revival in France, and the centre of the movement revolving round the 'men of 1830'. H. has been the subject of extravagant eulogy and exaggerated dispraise in the generation, or more, which has succeeded his death; in a sense, and unlike Goethe (q.v.), he lived too long in a world, which, in his own country esp., underwent very rapid changes during his four-score years. Of the eulogists, we may cite Catulle Mendès (1841-1909), a leader of the Parnasse (q.v.) group, who wr. (*Mouvement poétique français*), that H. *is* 1830, and that 1830 is to Fr. lit. what 1789 is to Fr. politics; that H.'s Pref. to his *Cromwell* (see below) is the

Oath of the Tennis Court of the literary revolution; that H. was the Danton of the Fr. ode, and the Napoleon of the Fr. epopee; and, summarily, 'qu'il y a dans Victor Hugo toute l'Humanité; il contient aussi tout l'univers, visible et invisible. Il est les mers, les montagnes, les ciels, le ciel; et dans tout ce qui existe, il offre asile a tout ce qui vit'. Praise could not be more sweeping. Of the detractors, we may cite Edmond Biré, whose monumental work, *V. Hugo avant 1830* (1 vol., 1883), *V. Hugo après 1830* (2 vols., 1891), and *V. Hugo après 1852* (1 vol., 1894), though indispensable and documentary, is described as 'pitiless' by Saintsbury, and is admitted by Lanson (*Lit. fr.*, 1051, n.2) to have warped his own judgment for a while. Time is confirming H.'s fame, and repairing the moral reputation which Biré in places tore to tatters; the work outlives the man; and, though Hugo-worship is partly at least a matter of temperament and even of climate, the testimony of Swinburne (q.v.) should not be forgotten by his countrymen, esp. in the present century of a Franco-British *entente*: 'There is but one thing under heaven to which a man should bow—genius; and but one to which a man should kneel—goodness. And while reverence endures for either, the veneration of all times will cherish the memory of Victor Hugo' (*Studies in Prose and Poetry*, 192). We may leave it at that; smaller men will disinter smaller views of H.'s vacillations in politics (his mother was a royalist, his father a republican general under Bonaparte), of his imperfect intellectual synthesis, of his egoism, his vanity, his complacency, of his intuitional reasoning and symbolical argumentation, and of the hundred and one excellent causes why he should not have been the great man he was. 'At worst as at best', says Saintsbury (*P.E.L.*, xii, 43), who describes H.'s effect as intoxicating, 'Hugo never lacks greatness. He is not only by far the greatest poet of France, but he is the first poet who, in his own words, gave France *toute la lyre*'. And 'poetry never leaves him'. H. began to write in 1819, when, with his two brothers, he collaborated at the literary journal, *le Conservateur littéraire* (q.v.); he went on writing for 60 years, when his *l'Art d'être grand-père* appeared in 1877, and his *Quatre Vents de l'Esprit* revived in 1882 the colour and wonder of his own earlier poetry. And, through all these years, and through all the changes in social and political surroundings which occurred in the passage of these years, H., however, 'childish' his politics, however 'visionary' his social reform, stamped on the changing features of the times the impress of his own personality: of his passionate hate of wrong, his infinite pity for suffering, his deep sympathy with the poor and needy, his invincible optimism, his essentially simple faith. He was a great commander of language, as impetuous almost as Rabelais (q.v.) in guiding his torrent of words, as skilful as Tennyson (q.v.), his contemporary, in selecting and combining their resources. He refused to be bound by rules, and this was his link with the Romanticists, to whose bondage, however, in the heyday of *Lyrisme* (1820-30; see s.v.), he never directly committed himself. Others took up the romantic gage, which the exuberant genius of H. had thrown down in his poems, plays, and prefaces (to *Cromwell*, 1827 ; to *Hernani*, 1830). It was of a piece with the childish seriousness of the age, and of Romanticist heresy in particular, that the crime of crimes committed by H., in his breach with the Racinian (s.v. Racine, and see also s.v. Boileau) rules of neo-classicism was not contained in his precepts but in his examples. It was not primarily for his breach with the dramatic unities (see s.v.), in which, as a fact, he had been anticipated by Manzoni (q.v.), but for his separation of *escalier* from *dérobé*, its epithet, at the end of one line and the beginning of another, in the opening scene of *Hernani*, that H. not merely brought down the house on the historic first-night, 25 Feb., 1830 ; he brought down the last defences of classical drama, and confounded the ' last ditchers ' of that convention. The bks. live, the battles are forgotten ; and happy is the present generation which may admire both H., the iconoclast, and Racine, the outraged idol. But, though the battle has been won so completely that its episodes have lost their vital importance, the meed of the victors is yet immense. The sartorial symbols are ridiculous : the red waistcoat of Gautier (q.v.), and other affectations to attract notice, to which H. himself was not always superior. Far from ridiculous, however, are the meanings signified by these symbols, and esp. at the present day, the fight for a literary language undefiled by the rules of schools. Proscribed hosts of words were re-admitted to the franchise of the literary republic by the fiat of H. and his abettors. Base and noble merged their distinctions in his purely artistic vocabulary, and the common ceased to be vulgar. Pedantry, clique-ism, purism, were banished at last, and it was no disrespect to the shade of Malherbe (q.v.) to recognize that his work was finished, and that the dead hand of the dictionary-makers had to be removed from living verse and prose. H.'s extension of the franchise to words corresponded to the extension of the literary horizon as a whole. South and East had been brought very near by Napoleon's audacious campaigns, and the exotic was becoming familiar to the generation after Waterloo. The barriers of the arts, too, were fused ; music, painting and poetry pursued the same subjective ends ; and to a great intuitionist of H.'s range there were hardly any limits to the capacity of language in its metrical and pictorial effects. The misc. poem (cf. Tennyson's *Princess : a Medley*), in Saintsbury's phrase, replaced the poem determined by its kind. By variety in the cadence of the Alexandrine (q.v.) it was possible to alter the theory of dramatic propriety.

It should be easier now to follow the course of H.'s writings, and Biré's divisions of his career at 1830 and 1852 are helpful in arranging them. But one word more, by way of warning. Fr. history, as we have said, had many changes in the course of H.'s life ; *nos et mutamur in illis*, and the evil was, not that H. changed his political opinions, but that he tried from time to time to gyrate round an imaginary consistent principle, and doctored his works accordingly. To this weakness of genius we need not recur. H. won the prize at the Jeux Floraux (q.v.) at Toulouse in 1819, was acclaimed by Chateaubriand (q.v.) as ' enfant sublime ', joined, as we have said, the staff of the *Conservateur*, frequented Nodier's (q.v.) *cénacle*, and publd. his first bk. of *Odes* in 1822. This was followed by *Odes et Ballades*, 1826, and by *Orientales*, 1829, distinctly rebellious in tendency ; the eastern subjects were *tabu* to the classicists, and the lyrical measures were all lyric and no measure. The *Feuilles d'Automne*, 1821, may also be included in the first of Biré's 3 periods, among the first-fruits of romantic poetry. But it was not in lyric verse alone that the reform of lit. was to be consummated. The novel and the stage had also to be captured (see, too, s.vv. Scott, Stendhal), and H.'s early experiments in fiction included *Han d'Islande*, publd. anon., a kind of skit on the classical convention, 1823, and *Bug Jargal*, 1826. His first tragedy, *Cromwell* (' an Attila ', he said, ' made by Machiavelli ') was publd. in 1827, and, though never staged, derived added importance from its Pref., which defined a critical position afterwards identified as romantic. ' All that is in nature is in art ' was a proposition, enunciated by H., and directly opposed to the classicists (see s.v. Nature), which obviously contained the seeds of naturalistic extravagance and decadence ; but the principle was sound in its place and time, and the derivation of poetry (ode, epic, drama) from the triple springs of Bible, Homer and Shakespeare was a truth of universal interest. It must be admitted, however, that H., as a dramatist, brought more of Byron than of Shakespeare to his theatre. His plays are lyrical melodrama, and achieved no conspicuous success : *Hernani* (or Castilian Honour), 1830, had the *succès de scandale* to which reference has already been made, and seldom, if ever, has an important movement been associated with a less memorable piece ; it was followed by *Marion de Lorme*, 1831, *le Roi s'amuse*, 1832, *Lucrèce Borgia*, 1833, *Marie Tudor*, 1833, *Angelo*, 1835, *Ruy Blas*, 1838, and *les Burgraves* (a failure) 1843. Romance did not capture the stage, though its experiments undoubtedly availed to break down many hampering restrictions ; and, despite the beauty of H.'s plays, general opinion would probably assent to the remark of Lanson (*Lit. fr.*, 980) : ' The Greeks and Turks of Racine are much nearer to us, by their acts as well as by their sentiments, than the Spaniards and Frenchmen of Victor Hugo '. It was far different with his novels. He wr. *le Dernier Jour d'un Condamné*, as a plea against capital punishment, and this was followed, 1831, by *Notre Dame de Paris*, by *Les Misérables*, 1862, *les Travailleurs de la Mer*, 1866, *l'Homme qui rit*, 1869, and *Quatre-vingt-treize*, 1879. H. was exiled, it is to be remarked, after 1848, for his opposition to the Second Empire, and for the social-democratic principles which he avowed, despite the peerage which he had accepted from king Louis Philippe. These episodes matter less than the local colour and the sympathy with the poor which he assimilated during his residence in the Channel Islands, where he spent some years of his banishment. Readers of his hist. romances will recognize the value of this experience. He was enabled to return to Paris, after the Franco-Prussian War, and, with the exception of one ebullition of political temper, lived tranquilly at home till the end. His funeral, 1885, was an occasion of national mourning. It remains briefly to enumerate the greater poetical works on which H.'s enduring fame rests most securely. These include *Chants du Crépuscule*, 1835, *Voix intérieures*, 1837, *les Rayons et les Ombres*, 1840, *les Châtiments* (written in exile; brilliant satire), 1853, *Contemplations*, 1856, *la Légende des Siècles* (i), 1859 (the most magnificent of all his works), *Chansons des mers et des bois*, 1865, *la Légende des Siècles* (ii), 1877, and *les quatre Vents* (see above), 1882. Nor must the misc. contents of *Toute la Lyre*, 1888, be forgotten, in appraising the extraordinary lyrical gifts of the author of the *Châtiments* and the *Légende*. It has been noted that H., ' when he was at his best, was almost always writing by the sea '; and it was as sea-lover, perhaps, that H. appealed most powerfully to the sympathy of the great Engl. sea-poet, Swinburne : ' il est les mers ', we were told ; and as sea-lover and Shakespeare-lover (a *William Shakespeare*, 1864, was his chief bk. of prose-criticism), H., the immortal child of art, must always appeal to Swinburne's country-men. ' France et Angleterre sont pour moi ', he wr. (to Tennyson, 1877), ' un seul peuple, comme Vérité et Liberté sont une seule lumière '. It is a noble sentiment, finely expressed, and, among those who strove for truth and freedom through all the flashlights and will-o'-the wisps of the 19th cent., H.'s name stands serene and high, beckoning both peoples to one aim in the generation now opening before them. So, in the highest sense, H.'s cause prevails ; and it is satisfactory to add, that, in the minor polemics of literary history the cause of the Romanticists *versus* Classicism was won, when they carried the fortress of the Academy (q.v.) by H.'s election to it in 1841, eleven years after *Hernani*.

Hugo von Montfort (1357-1423) : Germ. poet ; nobleman by birth, in token of which he pre-served the tradition of the Minnesinger (q.v.) in his lyric verse, which was suffused with a sense of the decay of the courtly inspiration.

Hugo von Trimberg (*c.* 1300) : Germ. moral poet. Wr. medley in about 25,000 octosyllabic couplets entitled *Renner* (runner, ' because it shall run through the land '), exalting the Bible as the source of all wisdom and decrying the chivalric romances.

Humanism : humane studies, or *litteræ humani-ores*, comprised, first, Lat., then Gk., and, next, Hebr. ; but H., in its broadest aspect, as a factor of European progress was more than a method or curriculum of studies ; it may be defined as a rule of life directed to the recovery for modern use of the standards of ancient culture. The Revival of Learning, which is another name for H., was also to be a renewal of a temperament : ' it was recog-nized that there had been a time when men had used all their faculties of mind and imagination without fear or reproof ; not restricted to certain paths or bound by form-ulas, but freely seeking for knowledge in every field of speculation, and for beauty in all the realms of fancy ' (*C.M.H.*, i, 532 ; the writer is sir R. Jebb, a distinguished humanist of the 19th cent.). And another recent definition runs : ' Humanism is the effort of men to think, to feel, and to act for themselves, and to abide by the logic of results ' (G. Scott, *The Architecture of Humanism*, Constable, p. 191). In this aspect, H. was one of 3 roads—the other 2 were Discovery and Dissent, associated respectively with Da Gama and Luther—by which men emerged from the Middle Ages ; from the ' dark forest ' of the second line of Dante's *Inferno*, at the edge of which the Rabelaisian laughter rent the morning sky of the Renaissance. The triple symbol of the Renaissance (q.v.) are a Lat. grammar, a sailing-ship, and an open Bible, and of these three the Lat. grammar was the special sign of the humanists. It was first sought in this spirit, as the key not to a language but to a life, by Petrarch (q.v.) at the beginning of the 14th cent. in Italy. All the authorities warn us not to ascribe too much to one man, but all agree, that this instance is exceptional ; and that a movement, or impulse, or perception, which has directed and dominated culture through 8 centuries of history, is definitely traceable to Petrarch, ' the first modern man ' (Renan ; see also s.v. Latin). The earliest bearers of the seeds of H. were the migratory scholars from the East, who, even before the fall of Constantinople (1453), found refuge, welcome, and honour at the courts of patrons of learning and in the homes of ardent disciples. Merchant-princes and princes by blood employed secretaries and agents to enrich their libraries with new MSS., and the decipher-ment, collation, and multiplication of these treasures gave employment to an endless tribe of scribes, librarians and editors, and, later, to the newly-invented printing-presses. It was a part of the great work of the humanists to found schools, universities, libraries, and academies ; and such a ruler as Lorenzo the Magnificent at Florence was surrounded by a circle of scholars devoted to the spread of H. (See s.vv. Medici, Politian). The Ital. centres of learning were visited by students from other countries, and these returned as missionaries to their own. Lascaris (q.v.) was tempted to Paris by Budé (q.v.) ; Argyro-poulos (q.v.) sped ' Greece across the Alps ' in the person of his pupil Reuchlin (q.v.) ; the Netherlands proved a refuge for many persecuted thinkers, and repaid the debt munificently by giving Erasmus to Europe ; Grocyn, Linacre (qq.v.) and others brought their harvest home to Engld., and gradually the light which rose in Italy was spread across the face of every country within the pale of learning. That Italy's cult of Latinity retarded the golden age of her own lit. ; that Germ. humanism was deflected too soon from the pure scholarship of teachers like Agricola (q.v.) to the polemics of the Erfurt (q.v.)-poets and the bitter conflicts which started from Luther (q.v.) ; that much good effort was wasted in translating Gk. into Lat. ; that of select inner circle of self-styled 'poets' at Erfurt univ., the seat of progressive studies in Saxony, where Luther was student. Associated with authorship of vol. ii (1517) of *Epistolæ Obscurorum Virorum* (q.v.), Erfurt's contribution to the Reuchlin-Pfefferkorn controversy (see s.vv.), which took the form of mock-letters of alleged monks : a brilliant pasquinade intended to show up the evils of obscurantism and to advance the cause of the new learning. Was also brilliant poet ; received the bay from Maximilian (q.v.), 1517 ; and ranks almost equally with Erasmus (q.v.) as modernizer of the old debate or disputation, developing it into the discourse, or dialogue, which was midway to the essay. H. wr. chiefly in Lat., and commanded a style remarkable for its qualities of boldness and raillery.

Huygens, -i. Constantine (1596-1687) : Dutch poet and statesman ; private secretary successively to 3 princes of the House of Orange, to whose service his long life was devoted ; visited Engld. on diplomatic missions and received honour of knighthood ; was a brilliant member of the Muiderkring (q.v.) ; composed music as facilely as poetry, which he wr. as easily in Fr. and Lat. as in Dutch ; effected elegant translns. from Guarini, Marini, Donne (qq.v.), and from Span. aphorists ; his Dutch verse was in more familiar vein and treated more homely themes than his statelier Lat. or more courtly Fr. poems.

-ii. Christian (1629-93) : Dutch mathematician and man of science ; son of above. Inventor and philosopher of the highest order of genius, but only incidentally to be included in a record of European letters.

Huxley, Thomas Henry (1825-95) : Engl. natural philosopher ; wr. many scientific works, and was busily engaged in controversy with theological and other opponents ; invented the name and—virtually—the idea of 'agnostic' ; publd. *Collected Essays*, 9 vols., 1893-4, and is notable, among scientific men, for his command of an Engl. prose-style of rare lucidity and flexibleness ; successor in this respect to the big four, Bacon, Hobbes, Berkeley and Hume (qq.v.). H. was active, too, as a member of the original School Board for London, 1870-2, and left his impress on the educational system of Engld. His *Life and Letters* were issued (2 vols., 1900 ; 3 vols., 1903) by his son, Leonard H.

Huysmann, Rudolf. See s.v. **Agricola.**

Hviezdoslav (1849-1921) : Slovak poet. H.'s real name was Pavol Országh ; he belonged to the poorer gentry of Slovakia, and, despite his Magyar schooling, retained his national consciousness, and became a member of the first National Assembly, 1918, of the new republic of Czecho-Slovakia. Wr. epic and lyric verse, including 'Sonnets written in Blood' (1914-15), and notable translns., which greatly assisted the revival of his country's humanism after the Great War.

I

Ibsen, Henrik (1828-1906) : Norw. dramatist ; by common consent one of the greatest men of letters of the later 19th cent., when in all countries of Europe, a spirit of criticism and even rebellion succeeded the high notes of romance, optimism, enthusiasm, and the worship and quest of beauty. (See, summarily, a paragraph by sir Stanley Leathes, *C.M.H.*, xii, 13-4 ; and cf. Sonnet 50 of *Modern Love* by G. Meredith, q.v. :

Ah, what a dusty answer gets the soul
When hot for certainties in this our life !).

Omitting for the moment the catalogue of I.'s plays and other writings, we may refer at this point to his predecessors in his native country : Kierkegaard (q.v.), the philosopher of doubt, Hertz (q.v.), the playwright, who, *teste* sir E. Gosse (*C.M.H.*, xi, 699) 'has the distinction of having influenced Ibsen more directly than any other writer' ; and Oehlenschläger (q.v.), the master of them all. We may refer, too, to I.'s great contemporaries in Europe : : Nietzsche (q.v.) in Germany, Zola (q.v.) in France, Dostoevsky (q.v.) in Russia, and T. Hardy (q.v.) in Engld., all of whom, with sundry important differences, and moving with minor satellites (G. Gissing, q.v., in Engld.) in their wake, were affected by a pessimism and an instinct to revolt, similar to those which affected I. in Norway. We may refer, again, to I.'s direct influence—as distinct from parallel likenesses—on such playwrights as Sudermann and Hauptmann

(b. 1862) in Germany, sir A. Pinero (b. 1855) and Mr. Bernard Shaw in Engld. A writer for whose full understanding so many countries and minds have to be visited is not properly to be dismissed as parochial. Yet this is the epithet applied to him by our leading authority on European lit., prof. Saintsbury (*P.E.L.*, xii, 320-6) : 'There is genius in Ibsen', he admits ; 'but it is difficult to think that much of Ibsen's work will retain, in the calm judgment of posterity, a very high place in literature'. And, again (*ib.*) : 'He is not for all time. He is parochial, and not of a very large or a very distinguished parish. He is, in that parish, a frequenter of the hospital and the asylum'. This dispraise, though excessive perhaps, is true to the extent that I. deliberately sought some of his characters from those places. But he must be judged by intention as well as act ; and if it was his belief that the dramatic presentation of such characters would help to empty the hospitals and to close the asylums, he is to be accounted, with Crabbe and Dickens (qq.v.), among those who have used the art of letters for purposes of social reform. Chiefly, his zeal in reform was directed towards the status of women in relation to sex-problems and matrimony. In the late 19th cent., as in the 17th, a new curiosity in physical science 'extended itself to everyday life ; men and women were experimenting in social things ; they were trying to rationalize human relationships' (B. Dobree, *Restoration Comedy*, 20 ;

see s.v., and also s.v. Woman) ; and if, on the stage of both epochs, some decorum, beauty and strangeness were shattered with the shams, conventions and hypocrisies, yet the evils which I. struck at by rapier-thrusts and hammer-strokes have been slowly repaired, and women at any rate in the 20th cent. should light a candle in I.'s honour. Cruel and restless some of his plays were ; local and occasional, in a sense ; but they exercised an immense influence on the social conscience of Europe, and even on the technique of the theatre in many countries. The most that can be said in depreciation is that I. is a little like the policeman who holds up his hand to regulate the traffic. The traffic is rolling on by his directions, but he is left, *planté là*, with his hands raised to no obvious purpose. His moment, in other words, is past.

With this brief but, we believe, fair exordium, and giving full weight to prof. Saintsbury's opinion, we may cite some witnesses on the other side. Sir E. Gosse, writing in 1879—and contemporary valuation is important,—described I. as a dramatic satirist : ' a typical modern European, a soul full of doubt and sorrow and unfulfilled desire, piercing downward into the dark profound, Promethean ' (*Lit. Northern Europe*, 36). G. Brandes (q.v.), the Danish critic, wr. in 1882 : ' At one time or another during the battle of life, a lyric Pegasus must have been killed under him ', meaning that the dramatic satirist was also a lyric poet ; and a writer who knew I. well, commenting on this passage* in the *Times Lit. Supp.*, 13 Feb., 1913, conjectured, that ' the lyric Pegasus merely had a master, who, on grounds partly of policy, partly, it may be, of self-distrust, kept him locked in the stable '. Similarly, ' Ibsen is a poet ' are the opening words of a very sound little monograph (*Four Lectures on Ibsen*, 1892) by Mr. Philip Wicksteed, who was trying in the years of growing reaction from the hospital and asylum atmosphere of I.'s problem-plays to bring the disciples of prof. Saintsbury back to the tracks of the fallen Pegasus.

What were the conjectural ' grounds of policy ', which turned I. from lyric poetry to social drama, and, incidentally, which caused him to quit Norway, in 1864 and to live in Germany and Italy till 1893 ? We find a key to this biographical problem (and it is just worth finding even at this date) in I.'s demand, 1870, for a ' revolution of the spirit of man '. It was Norway's great refusal to join Denmark's war against Prussia, which turned I., the great Norse poet, from lyric verse to satiric drama, and from his homeland to alien soil ; and it was his reflection on the causes of that refusal which moved I. to shake on the stage the settled conventions of conduct.

Prior to the war, 1864, in which his country did not join, I. had edited a newspaper similar to the *Germ* of the Pre-Raphaelite Brotherhood (q.v.), with Vinje (q.v.) among

---

* The passage occurs in Brandes, *Ibsen and Björnson* (E.T., 47). The Ibsen portion was written in 3 instalments, at intervals of 16 years, and represents 3 stages in the development both of the great critic and of the great playwright.

his colleagues, and had directed the theatre at Bergen, where Björnson succeeded him in 1857, and at Oslo, 1857-9. He had written an apprentice-play, *Catilina*, 1850 ; some patriotic dramas, *The Banquet at Solhoug*, *Fru Inger at Osterrad*, and *The Warriors of Helgeland*, culminating, 1862, in *Kongsemnerne* (Royal Rivals ; see s.v. Oehlenschläger), based, like the others, on an old saga (q.v.), and bringing the rivalry between king Hacon (q.v.) and duke Thule into relation with modern politics.

Love's Comedy, 1863, marked I.'s transition to his second period. It was the first satiric drama in the new style, and it ' rises by degrees into a tongue of lashing, scathing fire that bursts all bounds of decorum ' (sir E. Gosse, *op. cit.*, 40). The topic, of course, is love and marriage ; passionate love and conjugal convention, whence the element of ' comedy ' in this ' burning ' drama, of which only the setting is ' parochial '. *Brand*, 1866, and *Peer Gynt*, 1867, are the 2 next poetic dramas, which I. sent to his native country from his place of sojourn in Rome. They preached one crusade from two ends : Brand is the priest without stain, Peer Gynt is the mean and stained worldling, and each is in conflict with his environment. Both are written in a short lyric measure, and they attain—the latter esp.—a high level of artistic workmanship. The butterfly-song in *Brand* and the death-bed scene of Peer Gynt's mother are famous in literary records. *The League of Youth* (or ' The Young Men's Union '), 1869, is a prose-comedy with its scene in a small town, in which Stengaard, an ambitious lawyer-politician, was supposed to have been drawn with an eye on Björnson ; it was followed (by desire) in 1873 by a double-drama, *Emperor and Galilean*, which went away from the local interest of the previous plays. With many merits, it was not as successful, and the choice of prose as the dramatic vehicle is curiously inappropriate from I.'s pen for a play dated, 4th cent., A.D.

So we reach the series of social or problem-plays, which appeared at regular intervals of 2 years, in the third period of I.'s activity, and which are specifically, ' Ibsenitish ': *Pillars of Society*, 1877 ; *A Doll's House*, 1879 ; *Ghosts*, 1881 ; *An Enemy of the People*, 1882 (I.'s personal experience under the guise of a physician whose remedy was voted worse than the disease) ; *The Wild Duck*, 1884 ; *Romersholm*, 1886 ; *The Lady from the Sea*, 1888 ; *Hedda Gabler*, 1890 ; *The Master-Builder*, 1892 ; *Little Eyolf*, 1894 ; *John Gabriel Borkman*, 1896 : we can but enumerate these plays, and leave the judgment to posterity. At least, I. was never a ' limp doubter ', such as Skule in his play, *Kongsemnerne* : all his desire was the boon of ' King's-thought ', and thus seeking, he is never out of date.

Iffland, August Wilhelm (1759-1814) : Germ. playwright and actor. I. was engaged at the Mannheim theatre, 1779-96, during the period of Schiller's connection with it through the production of his *Räuber* under Dalberg's management (see s.vv.). Later, he went to Berlin, as director of the Prussian National theatre, which he raised to supreme importance. His own plays were well received, and sustained a high level in the domestic vein ; their place in dramatic lit. is about equal to that of Mrs. Henry Wood's novels in fiction.

Iglesias de la Casa, José (*c.* 1750-*c.* 1790) : Span. poet ; follower of Melendez Valdés (q.v.).

Igor Svyatoslavich (1151-1202) : Russ. chieftain ; prince of Novgorod ; directly descended from Rurik (d., 879) the Norse Viking who invaded Russia, 862, occupied Novgorod, and founded the commercial greatness of Kiev (q.v.) ; hero of a little epic prose-poem (a *bylina*, q.v., or tale of old-time), written, obviously, by an eye-witness of the foray which he happened to be inspired to relate. How I. ' led his brave hosts to the land of Polovtsy (Hungary), for the sake of the land of the Russians ' ; how he started on Thursday, 23 April, 1185 ; how he was taken prisoner by the pagan nomads, and how he escaped : all this is told in the *Igor*-idyl, and ushers in the history of Russ. lit. (q.v.). It contains *in petto*, says one critic, all the lyric poetry of the 19th cent. in Russia, and the praise, though high, is not above the charm of its epic-lyric note. It possesses the additional bibliographical interest, that the MS. was lost for many centuries, being rediscovered, 1795, by count Musin-Pushkin, an antiquary, who publd. the *ed. pr.* in 1800. Many critics, taught to be sceptical, were inclined to cry ' Ossian ! ' (see s.v. Macpherson) ; but the genuineness of the 14th cent. copy of the MS. was beyond dispute ; and another copy was discovered, 1864, among the archives of the empress Catherine ii (q.v.). The lay of *Igor* was edited and transld. into Engl. by L. A. Magnus (Oxford, 1915).

Ihre, Johan (1707-80) : Swed. philologer ; wr. in Lat. a Swedo-Gothic lexicon, 1769, which enjoyed a European reputation. I.'s works are marked by a certain brilliance and vivacity, very characteristic of the man, and by a purity and grace of diction somewhat rare in scholarly writings.

Immermann, Karl Leberecht (1796-1840) : Germ. playwright and novelist ; fought at Waterloo, 1815 ; tried his hand at many forms of romantic lit., including an early fate-tragedy, and other not very notable dramas. The best of these was *Merlin*, 1832, described by the author as a tragedy of negation or contradiction, and by Robertson (*Hist. Germ. Lit.*, 497) as ' the last of many attempts which the German *Romantik* made to win for its ideas the great secular mysteries associated with the Reformation Faust and the medieval legends of the Holy Grail '. Platen (q.v.) lashed out at these plays in his *Romantic Oedipus*, and it is to be noted that I. was always a close friend of Heine (q.v.). Passing over I.'s *Tristan and Isolde* 1812, an unfind. epical experiment after Gottfried (q.v.) v. Strassburg, we come to his romance-novel, *Die Epigonen*, 1836, which places him, as it were, as a ' late-born ' in his own times. He defines therein the evil of the age : ' We are ', he writes ' if all the misery were to be expressed in a word, *Epigoni*, and bear the burden that is always the fate of an afterbirth '. It was probably a correct diagnosis of the disinherited sons of the War of Liberation. (See s.v. Metternich). Goethe's

Wilhelm Meister was the model (perhaps its last appearance in that capacity) for the *Epigonen*, which had the social change from agriculture to industry as background. More fantastic and confused in its top layers was I.'s next satiric novel, *Münchhausen*, partly based, so far as the titular hero is concerned on Raspe and Bürger's (see s.vv.) original. It was publd. in 1838, and contained the episode of *der Oberhof*, recognized as I.'s best work. This is a picture of an old Westphalian peasant, Hofschulze, whose simple, faithful rustic character is in striking contrast with the social corruption outside ; it has been described as ' the finest short story of peasant-life that was written before the middle of the nineteenth century '. Between 1835-38, I. took a prominent part in the direction of the theatre at Düsseldorf.

Imperial, Francisco (15th cent.) : Span. poet ; born at Genoa ; resided at Seville ; and displayed in his verse the growing Italianate taste of Castilian poetry in this age. I. was also acquainted with Arabic and Engl. He wr. a poem on the birth of king John ii (q.v.), and minor verse, of which Baena (q.v.) preserved some examples.

Ingelow, Jean (1820-97) ; Engl. poet ; publd. several vols. of verse, and is best remembered by her masterpiece, *High Tide on the Coast of Lincolnshire*. Wr. one or two novels and stories for children, notably *Mopsa the Fairy*.

Ingemann, Bernhard Severin (1789-1862) : Dan. poet ; dramatist ; novelist ; an acknowledged leader of the romantic revival of the first quarter of the 19th cent., of which Oehlenschläger was the risen sun, Schack v. Staffeld and others the attendant satellites (see s.vv.), and Germany the land of morning. I.'s early lyrics were filled with the glamour and moonshine of the Tieck and Wackenroder (qq.v.) convention ; from these, which were well received for the sake of their implicit power, he passed to fairy-plays and dream-dramas, which the critics found, not unreasonably, too remote from the common requirements of the theatre. His *Fairy-tales* of 1820 marked a distinct step in advance, and a further big step was taken in his verse and prose romance-histories, drawn from Denmark's storied past. Walter Scott (q.v.) is not too great a name to compare with I. as the redintegrator of the heroic middle-ages of his own country, and as the narrator of the romantic exploits of the Ottos, Erics, Waldemars, and Margarets, who adorned it. These tales are still ' the favourite reading of such part of the Dan. public as prefers enjoyment to criticism, and they are still one of the means of educating the women and children of Denmark to a patriotism ready in sacrifice and strong in deed ' (Schweitzer, *Skand. Lit.*, iii, 60). I.'s *Village Children*, 1852, and similar tales, idealized from common life, have also to be noted, with recognition of the esteem which they enjoy ; and, lastly, his reputation rests securely on the ' noble numbers ', as Herrick (q.v.) would have entitled them, of his maturer muse : the hymns and psalms which he wr. out of his own childlike faith for the children of Denmark's new generation.

Iriarte, de, Tomas (1750-91): Span. poet; fabulist. Wr. a poem of 'Music', 1780, which was praised by Metastasio (q.v.); and *Fabulas literarias*, 1782, adapted mainly from La Fontaine (q.v.) and other sources, which enjoyed a long vogue of edification and instruction. (See, too, s.v. Samaniego). I. was a member of the little company of men of letters, whom the elder Moratin (q.v.) gathered round him at the sign of S. Sebastian in Madrid; and he was busied with small literary controversies (see s.v. Forner).

Irony: The technical employment of this word in a limited literary sense starts from the meaning of 'dissembling' connoted by its Gk. original, and was a common usage in Gk. drama. Attic tragedy in its golden age dealt with plots and characters familiar to the audience, and derived from the matter of national legend. Thus, it was possible for the dramatist to invent situations, the dénoûment of which was known to the spectators, but was unknown or insufficiently known to the actors in the characters which they represented and at the point which the action had reached. Speeches and words, accordingly, might carry their face-value on the stage, but be fraught at the same time with another and a deeper meaning for the audience. Such a situation was aptly termed ironical, and this was the limited meaning of tragic irony in Gk. drama. An extension was given to the use of the word by what is known as the Socratic method. Socrates, in his sophistical capacity, elicited information by interrogation, and conquered his opponents by a self-conviction of ignorance or error. His interrogatories were couched in the ironical manner: to his opponent they came as genuine questions, posed from a desire for information; to his audience or readers they were clearly in the nature of a cross-examination, carefully framed with the object of entangling his victim in a mesh of confusion or contradiction. The philosophic irony of Socrates was added to the tragic irony of the Gk. tragedians; and in this sense the Gk. word passed into common European acceptation. Like most technical terms, it tended in course of time to lose its strictness of limitation; and irony was and is employed to denote a sarcastic intention, or even a sardonic intonation, when one speaker veils by selected words, but does not withhold, his opinion from the other. But in France and Germany in the 18th cent., men of letters again seized the term, and sought to enlarge it to their own purpose. Voltaire (q.v.) employed an extended irony, and the term acquired a technical meaning in the sense in which it was employed by the leaders of the Romantic Movement in Germany (see s.v. Romance). The writer who, above others, called in Irony as trite, and fashioned it anew for fresh use, was Friedrich Schlegel (q.v.), author of *Lucinde*. This Irony of Germ. *Romantik* had likewise 'dissembling' at its root; and the particular dissimulation which it fostered was that of the *Ego* confronted by the *non-Ego*, according to the teachings of Fichte (q.v.). Fichte's especial province was to provide a bridge between the philosophic system of Kant and the literary ideals of Romance, with the brothers Schlegel at its head. His method consisted in a direct application of the emancipating ideas of Rousseau, Kant and Herder to the individual himself: the individual *Ego*, he taught, had the power of creating its *non-Ego*; the Outer is a condition of the Inner. This plenary individualism worked like magic in the brains of a generation eager to assert itself against the absolute domination of Napoleon. Every man could be his own Napoleon. It was a heady doctrine for the age, and admirably efficacious; and its romantic value was found in the detachment of the writer from his work, or, more precisely, in his regulation of the proportions between the reality of the mind under the restraint of expression, and the unreality (leading to destruction instead of creation) of the external world in which it moves. Expression should be carried *bis zur Ironie*, up to the breaking-point of Irony; that lurking, mischievous elf which lies in wait to interrupt and overthrow the harmonious structure erected in the artist's truce between Inner and Outer. Thus, Irony, in F. Schlegel's sense, has affinity with Humour, or the Comic spirit. 'If the Comic idea prevailed with us', wr. G. Meredith (q.v., *Essay on Comedy*), 'the vapours of unreason and sentimentalism would be blown away before they were productive'; and it is precisely this interruption to the creative process of self-expression which occurs, in the Schlegelian doctrine, at the Irony-point, the point at which the *non-Ego* mocks at the conscious *Ego*, and the outside world breaks down the artist's structure. Death with his bodkin bores through the castle-wall. In the development of the doctrine under Tieck (q.v.) and others, Irony came to be used, not only as a means of detection, but as an end in itself. The destructive irony of satire was more serviceable to literary effect than the constructive irony of restraint; and the deliberate literary irony of many of the Romanticist tales and dramas, in which characters and audience take each other into mutual confidence, became, first, an entertainment, and then a trick. And the trick retrograded the term, which Schlegel has rescued from ignoble use. This excess of Irony, used neither as trick nor entertainment, but as a kind of drug, under the stimulus of which the *Ego* forgot the *non-Ego*, is seen in the dreamland of Novalis (s.v. Hardenberg). An Engl. example of the whimsical Irony of *Romantik* is to be found in the short concluding paragraph of Thackeray's (q.v.) *Vanity Fair*; its spirit permeates the household tales of Andersen (q.v.), and a modern master of it on the stage is sir James Barrie.

Isla, de, Josef Francisco (1703-81): Span. satirist; Jesuit; expelled with members of his Order, 1767. I.'s two most important works were, i, a satiric romance, *Friar Gerund* (part i, 1758; ii, 1770), publd. under the name of Francisco Lobár de Salazar; and, ii, a transln. of Lesage's (q.v.) *Gil Blas*, publd. posth., 1787, with a continuation transld. from the Ital. of Monti (q.v.). Each work requires a brief commentary. The object of I.'s *Fray Gerundio* was to cover with ridicule the high-falutin style of pulpit-oratory, with which the *cultismo* (q.v.) of

Gongora (q.v.) had infected the style of Paravicino (q.v.), for example. Thus, the *Gerundio* is correctly described as the *Don Quixote* of ecclesiastical lit. The justice of the satire may be judged from an instance of a preacher's affectation cited by Kelly (*Lit. espagn.*, 390): 'The divine Adonis, Christ, enamoured of the unique Psyche, Mary'. I. did his task with humour and discretion; so successfully, indeed, that, though the Inquisition condemned the bk. in 1760, and forbade discussion upon it, they found it impossible to stay its popularity and its distribution by private means. Part ii was less successful; but *Friar Gerund* may fairly be called a brilliantly executed piece of work, which was thoroughly efficacious in cleansing the pulpit of its Gongoristic monsters. I.'s *Gil Blas* had also an object; less praiseworthy, however, than that of his original romance. Taking his cue from a reference to a supposed Span. original of *Gil Blas*, advanced by Voltaire (q.v.) in his *Siècle de Louis xiv* (*second* edn., 1775; the reference is not found in the 1751 edn.), I. purported to 'restore the book to its own country and language' from the Fr. plagiarist or thief. That Lesage was much indebted to Espinel (q.v.) and others is well known; but there is no ground whatever for Voltaire's gratuitous imputation, which was revived in the 19th cent. by A. de Llorente (q.v.), the historian of the Inquisition. Still, I. produced an admirable and a spirited version, cumbered unnecessarily with the Monti addition, which satisfied the pride of Span. readers in the Fr. writer's choice of a Span. hero for his romance. I.'s other works included *Sermons* (6 vols., 1792-93); *Cartas* (Letters) *Familiares* (1785-90); and a poem in octave stanzas, called *Cicero*, written in exile in Italy, and taking shape as a satire on the follies and vices of Spain.

Italian Literature: For the purposes of the Engl. student, and, indeed, for all students except specialists, there is authority as well as common-sense in dating the *terminus a quo* of Ital. Lit. from Dante (q.v.; 1265-1321). True, there was Ital. poetry before Dante. He speaks himself of two of his predecessors:

So has one Guido from the other taken
The glory of our tongue, and he perchance
Is born, who from the nest shall chase them
    both.
      Purg., xi, 97-9; Longfellow's transln.

The 'he perchance' is Dante himself, modestly meditating his *de Vulgari Eloquentia*, described by Saintsbury (*Hist. Crit.*, i, 418) as 'a document of the very highest value: the first critical treatise on the literary use of the vernacular, at exactly the point when the various vernaculars of Europe had finished, more or less, their first stage'. The two Guidi are of Calvalcanti and Guinicelli, both of the 13th cent.; both are Tuscans of the Sicilian tradition in poetry, characterized by Dante (*Purg.*, xxiv, 57; the exact reference is to Jacopo da Lentino) as *dolce stil nuovo* (q.v.); and both came into D. G. Rossetti's (q.v.) debt for some excellent renderings in modern Engl. verse. Dante was aware, by the insight of genius, that the Sicilian nest of singing-birds, vocal at the court of emperor Fredk. ii (d., 1250), and joined by a flight of migrant birds

from the stricken nests in Provence (see s.vv. Albi and Provençal Lit.), as well as by wandering troubadours from Northern France, was destined to be surpassed by the native notes in the Tuscan 'vulgar tongue', which he was founding by his critical studies and his own magnificent example. We may leave these beginnings, accordingly, merely noting that the course of I.L., which was comparatively late in its independent rise, had been retarded by (1) the absence of a common centre; the removal, 1309, of the papal see to Avignon is indicative; (2) the incessant rivalry of the city-states, and (3) even within each city-state, of the rival parties of Guelfs and Ghibellines (q.v.); (4) the struggle between Lat. and the vernacular, which foliated most slowly in the native country of the ancient Roman tongue; and (5), allied with (4), the absence of local Ital. story-matter more recent than the *matière* (see s.v. Bodel) of antiquity. There was further (6) the fact that, owing partly to colour and climate, the genius of Italy is expressed in painting even more brilliantly than in letters.

Dante broke through these various obstructions. But it was of the essence of Dante's dream of Ital. salvation and regeneration that the medieval structure of society should be preserved. 'During the years when Italy was like "a riderless horse", bereft of either temporal or spiritual sovereign, it seemed to Dante that the whole hope for the future lay in the revival of the medieval system in its entirety. He looked forward to the day when man should be guided "by the supreme Pontiff in accordance with the theological virtues to eternal felicity, and by the emperor according to the moral virtues to temporal felicity"' (*Italy, Medieval and Modern: A History*; Oxford, 1917, p. 158). Dante 'looked forward' backwards, that is to say; his dream, like that of Henry vii, king of the Romans, 1308, 'was the revival of the imperial power and the initiation of a reign of universal peace, unmarred by national rivalries or party factions'. The dream of Italy's men of letters had a rude and a centuries'-long awakening. I.L. is largely enmeshed in the tangled web of Ital. politics; and of Dante the paradox is true, that he is at once the greatest poet in his own country—one of the greatest in any country—and yet the last of medieval statesmen, inextricably fixed in a system of political theory and belief which was passing away even in his own day. As a reformer of the Ital. language, we have already spoken of him; as a politician, in the *de Monarchia*, we need not discuss him here; as the love-adept of Beatrice in the *Vita Nuova*, he was a prosepoet and a lyrist of supreme charm; as the author of the 3 bks. of the *Commedia*, afterwards termed *divina* (the *Inferno*, the *Purgatorio*, and the *Paradiso*), Dante is a poet unsurpassed in imagination, whether of darkness and terror or of colour and light; he is the very fountain of the Sublime (q.v.) in modern lit., a profound interpreter of the learning of Church and Schoolmen, and an inventor—for it amounts to no less, despite its Platonic origins and affinities—of a conception of human love, so completely irradiated by heavenly beams, and so intensely refined by that searching experience, as to fuse desire and will with the love that moves the sun and other stars. Poets after Dante, down to Shelley (q.v.), in *Epipsychidion*, have attempted to rise to this height, but Dante outtops them all ; and, to his own countrymen particularly, the close bond between him and Virgil (q.v.) is a further sign of exceptional greatness.

Dante's service to the Ital. language was quickly seized by his successors. Leaving his Beatrice of theology aside, they wooed his Beatrice of lyric verse ; and, leaving aside the demonology of Virgil, they approved the transfusion of his style for vernacular use. When Petrarch (q.v. ; 1304-74) succeeded to Dante's heritage—and he was a lad of 17 when Dante died,—he approached the same problems from a different angle. ' The dawn began to reappear ', says Macaulay (q.v.) in a famous passage in his essay on Machiavelli (q.v.), ' before the last reflection of the preceding sunset had faded from the horizon ' ; and Petrarch, the first modern man, as Renan (q.v.) called him, heralded the dawn at the medieval sunset. He, too, like Dante, was a politician, and an ardent aspirer for a united Italy. His *Ode* to Italy still rings true, as it rang true in the ears of Machiavelli (1469-1527), a century and a half after Petrarch's death, when that great philosopher-statesman articulated the anatomy of a ruler (*Il Principe*), who, in the distracted Italy of that day, should be trained to avoid the chances of princely weakness and to cultivate a princely infallibility. The *virtù*, or courage, of the earthly ruler was to be founded in the example of ancient Rome, where Petrarch was crowned laureate on the Capitol, and where he hoped too much from the pinchbeck dictatorship of Rienzi (1313-54) ; and, inevitably, this conception of *virtù*, as it descended through centuries of imperfect human experiment, became almost irrecognizably transformed from the theory of Petrarch and the practical counsels of Machiavelli. But though political experience transformed these political dreams, the dreamers are still to be applauded ; and Petrarch stands at the head of a long line of reformers, who actually culminated in the Reformation (q.v.), and in its sequel of weal and woe for humankind.

We cannot follow the movement in detail. Our articles on Humanism and the Renaissance, summary names of successive stages in the movement, should be consulted at this point, and reference should be made, too, to the art. on Cicero. For the intense Roman feeling of Petrarch and his keen sense of oneness with the Lat. past made him view the restoration of Cicero as the revelation of an oracle to modern Italy. This attitude did not lack authority. Even before 1300 Cicero's had been a name of marvel. He had seduced saints from their orisons. His essay *de Amicitia* had consoled Dante when Beatrice died. His *Somnium Scipionis* had been a powerful motive in medieval letters. And now he entered on a fresh stage of influence. Humanism, or the revival of learning, was a revival of much more besides. By its outlook on life, it was philosophy ; by its Ital. origin, it was patriotism ; by its sense of form, it was beauty ; by its freedom of knowledge, it was truth. But it was a revival of Cicero's spirit first. ' Humanism ', says a recent writer, ' is the effort of men to think, to feel, and to act for themselves, and to abide by the logic of results '. We may accept the definition for Petrarch. The first man to make this effort was the poet-antiquary of Vaucluse and Arqua, who died in his library in 1374. He loved learning as a patriot, and Italy as a scholar ; and as the Renaissance was the work of Cicero's spirit, so Petrarch ushered in the Renaissance.

' The Renaissance,' says sir J. E. Sandys (*Hist. Class. Schol.*, i, 610), ' generally associated in its early stages with the name of Petrarch, was a gradual and protracted process, and not a fixed and sudden event with a fixed and definite date '. It is to be followed through the writings of Boccaccio (1313-75), with his brilliant improvisation of the short story in the ten-days' revels of the *Decameron* ; and its progenitors in Italy may be re-visited in the pages of Vespasiano da Bisticci (1421-98), who left over 100 biographies of the leaders of the movement who had been personally known to him. The movement spread, as we are aware. It crossed the Alps in several directions, when the missionaries of the new learning went home from their studies in Florence, Rome, and other city-states, and planted abroad the seeds of humane culture. It is always the glory of I.L. to have been not only national, but international. It had mission-stations in France, Holland, Spain, Germany, Engld., and other countries. If the peoples of Europe to-day were to be bidden, in the words of Dante's Virgil, *antiquam exquirere matrem*—to seek the mother-country of their art and letters across 6 or 7 centuries of history, —they would go back to the Renaissance source in Italy. ' On that classic soil ', says Sandys (*ibid.*), ' the Renaissance was slowly called into life by a variety of causes, by the prevailing spirit of intellectual freedom, by the social and political condition of the country, by the continuous tradition of the Latin language, by the constant witness to the existence of Greek in the region once known as *Magna Graecia*, by the survival of the remains of antique sculpture, and by the abiding presence of the ruins of ancient Rome, which aroused the enthusiasm, not only of unnamed pilgrims of the tenth and twelfth centuries, but also of men of mark such as Petrarch in the first third of the the the thirteenth '. So, with Dante, Petrarch, Boccaccio, and the Humanists, who sowed the Renaissance on that classic soil, the course of I.L. is set.

With Luigi Pulci (q.v. ; 1432-84), author of *Morgante Maggiore*, began the half-serious, half-burlesque epic, which Byron (q.v.) was to bring to perfection. With Sannazzaro (q.v. ; 1458-1530), author of *Arcadia*, began the line of pastoral fiction, which has enjoyed an almost uninterrupted vogue. The Ital. court-epos of the *Faëry Queen* (s.v. Spenser) type passed through the master-hands of Ariosto (q.v. ; 1474-1533) and Tasso (q.v. ; 1544-95), whose contemporary, Galilei (1564-1642), like F. Bacon (q.v.) in Engld., was a master of Ital. prose. They were pioneers, these Italians of the 15th-16th cents. Though, owing to the backwardness of the ' vulgar tongue ', released by Dante from its Lat.-matrix, they began late, yet they flourished quickly. They were assisted by the very cause which had retarded them. Latinity aided the vernacular. The Ital. language was mature from the start. The conscious and constant aim of its practitioners was to equate it with the language of the concurrently practising Latinists. It had thus a standard to appeal to, which other vernaculars lacked in their childish days. Ital. and Lat. were spoken and written side by side, and princely patrons such as Lorenzo de Medici (q.v.) encouraged the literary use of the younger speech, which was suppled to the flexibility of the older. So, Tasso's *Jerusalem*, for example, was veritably the *Iliad* or *Æneid* of the modern world : ' the great epic poem, in the strict sense, of modern times. It was not the theme of a single people, but of Europe ', says Hallam (q.v.) ; and the language of this epic of the Crusades was as classic as that of Virgil. We need not enumerate here the critics, grammarians and printers—the noble tradition of scholar-printers has survived—who facilitated by their labours the transition from Rome to Rome, from the Rome of the Cæsars to the Rome of the popes ; still less need we detract from these records of strenuous and enlightened labour by referring to any of the excesses committed in the name of scholarship. The disputes of learned men were often unedifying, however accurate the Latinity of their invective ; and the 17th cent. was marked by an exaggerative stylisticism, or by a search for extravagant beauty in diction, of which Marino (q.v. ; author of *Adone*, 1623), the

father of the ' metaphysical ' (q.v.) poets, is the prime example and chief offender. How Chiabrera (q.v.; 1552-1638), whom Dryden and Wordsworth (qq.v.) appreciated, resisted the tide of Marinism ; how Filicaja (q.v.; 1642-1707) was inspired in his great *Odes* to sing the gaudy notes away ; and how a new Arcadia (q.v.) was founded and broken up (see s.v. Baretti, 1719-89), must be sought in the separate articles. The greatest single name in all this period was that of Metastasio (q.v.; 1698-1782), who first succeded in raising the theatre in Italy (see s.vv. Sacra Rappresentazione and Trissino) to a high place in the drama of Europe.

So we come, in the middle of Metastasio's career, to the *Risorgimento*, commonly dated by Ital. historians from the Treaty of Aix-la-Chapelle, 1748. Goldoni (1707-93) and Alfieri (1749-1803), qq.v., comic and tragic dramatist respectively, dominate I.L. in the 18th cent., and Manzoni's (q.v.) *Promessi Sposi*, 1827, praised by Goethe and Scott, among others, as the greatest novel of the age, was a belated product of the same era. With Leopardi (q.v.; 1798-1837) and Carducci (q.v.; 1836-1907), we span the 19th cent., and reach the eve of the present day. ' We owe a large part of the New Italy to our poets ', is a saying ascribed to Garibaldi. The dictum would apply to Ital. history throughout the whole of the modern period. And with no less truth it may be said, in Engld. and in other countries, that we owe a large part of modern Europe to the poets of Italy, —the conscious heir of the splendour that was Rome.

Iwain : typical hero of the romance-cycle of Arthur (q.v.) ; and the subject of the best surviving poem by Chrétien de Troyes (q.v.).

J

Jacobsen, Jons Peter (1847-85) : Dan. novelist ; botanist by profession, and translr. of Darwin (q.v.) into Dan. Wr. *Mistress Marie Grubbe*, 1876, which is not easy reading, despite its elaborate design ; *Mogens and Other Stories*, 1852 ; and *Niels Lyhne*, 1880, transld. into Engl. under the name of ' Siren Voices '. Saintsbury (*P.E.L.*, xii, 331) follows Brandes (q.v.), the eminent Dan. critic, in a eulogy of J., who was certainly ' advanced ', in the esoteric sense, and confessed the mastership of Flaubert and Turgenev (q.v.). Boyesen (*Scand. Lit.*, 193 ; Nutt, 1895) is a little less enthusiastic. ' The studious avoidance of the commonplace ' in J., he writes, causes the reader to begin ' to feel the sympathetic weariness which often overcomes one while watching acrobatic feats '.

Jacobsen, Peder Wilhelm (1799-1848) : Dan. playwright. His *Trolddom*, 1847, is the best-remembered of his hist. dramas, and deservedly won admiration for its stage-management and historic grasp.

Jakobi, -i. Johann Georg (1740-1814) : Germ. poet ; studied and taught at Halle and Halberstadt, headquarters of the Prussian or

Anacreontic school (s.v. Anakreontiker), to which he was affiliated, partly through his friendship with Gleim (q.v.). J.'s light, lyrical verse helps to bridge the distance between the pygmies and the giants of the 18th cent.

-ii. Friedrich Heinrich (1743-1819) : Germ. philosopher ; brother of above ; president, 1804, of the Royal Academy of Sciences at Munich. J. was a friend of Goethe (q.v.), and wr. two sentimental-didactic novels, which were much read in his own day. His more permanent work consisted in his influence on a host of pupils, directed against materialism and fatalism. Wr. letters to M. Mendelssohn (q.v.) on the teachings of Spinoza (q.v.), and other philosophical treatises. There was always something feminine in J.'s constitution, which expressed itself spitefully or sentimentally. He said of himself that he was Pagan at head and Christian at heart, and Schelling (q.v.), who met him at Munich, described him as luke-warm.

James i (1394-1437) : Scot. Chaucerian poet ; third son of king Robert iii ; captured by Engl. ship on his way to France, 1406, and detained in Engld. till 1423 ; crowned king of Scotland,

1424, and reigned with benefit to his country till his murder at Perth by sir Robt. Graham. Wr., c. 1423, *The King's Quair* ('The King's Book'), a poetic allegory of love in a dream (q.v.), in 197 stanzas (rhyming *a b a b b c c* ; 1,379 lines), and based on the royal author's study of Chaucer (q.v.) and his masters, esp. the writers of the *Romance of the Rose* (q.v.), during the period of his imprisonment in Engld., and his wooing of lady Joan Beaufort, daughter of first earl of Somerset. *The King's Quair*, the only extant MS. of which is in Bodley's (q.v.) library at Oxford, was first publd. at Edinburgh, 1783, by Wm. Tytler (1711-92), W.S., a Scot. historian, father of Alex. Fraser, lord Woodhouselee (1747-1813 ; judge of session, and likewise an historian). Tytler's edn., from an indifferent transcript, held till 1884, when W. W. Skeat (q.v.) edited the definitive text for the Scottish Text Society. Reference should also be made to D. G. Rossetti's (q.v.) poem, *The King's Tragedy*, founded on the love-tale of J. The *quair* is commended by the king to his masters, Chaucer and Gower, and prof. Gregory Smith (*C.H.E.L.*, ii, 243) remarks that 'this means more than the customary homage of the fifteenth century. . . *The King's Quair* represents the first phase of Scottish Chaucerianism, in which the imitation, though individualized by the genius of its author, is deliberate and direct'.

James, George Payne Rainsford (1799-1860); Engl. novelist ; historian ; and, combining the two parts, historical novelist ; served as consul at Massachusetts in Virginia, and, later, at Venice, where he died ; historiographer royal to king William iv (see s.v. Poet-Laureate). J. was a prolific writer of hist. romances, and suffered from what is now called his rapidity of output. Thackeray (q.v.) burlesqued his style in *Barbazure*, one of the series of *Novels by Eminent Hands*, which starts : ' It was upon one of those balmy evenings in November which are only known in the valleys of Languedoc and among the mountains of Alsace, that two cavaliers might have been perceived by the naked eye threading one of the rocky and romantic gorges that skirt the mountainland between the Marne and the Garonne. The rosy tints of the declining luminary were gilding the peaks and crags which lined the path, through which the horseman wound slowly ; ' and these two nameless horsemen winding slowly down a romantic path of history became rather cruelly proverbial of J.'s style in fiction. As a fact, his bks. are better than they are reputed : they include *Richelieu*, 1829 ; *Philip Augustus*, 1831 ; *The Huguenot*, 1838 ; *Henry of Guise*, 1839 ; *The King's Highway*, 1840 ; *Agincourt*, 1844, etc.

James, -i. Henry (1843-1916): Engl. (-Amer.) novelist ; second son of Henry J. (1811-82 ; Amer. theologian, and writer on Swedenborg, q.v.) ; born in New York ; naturalized as British subject, 1915 (in the course of the Great War), ' because of his having lived and worked in Engld. for the best part of 40 years ; because of his attachment to the country and his sympathy with it and its people ' ; O.M., 1916. Wr. *A Small Boy and Others*, 1913, and *Notes of a Son and Brother*, 1914, containing records of his father and brother (below). H.J. was subject to the influence of Turgenev (q.v.) in Russia and of Hawthorne in his native country, on whom he wr. a monograph in the ' English Men of Letters ' series. His novels dealt chiefly with studies of the effect of the discovery of Europe by cultured Americans (and esp. by the cultured Amer. girl) in the third quarter of the 19th cent. They were renaissance-studies in the New World, and his style had something of the leisureliness, of the great vocabulary, and the humane splendour of Renaissance writers in the 16th cent. None of his novels was popular or sought popularity ; *Daisy Miller*, 1878, came nearest to it ; but the rich luxuriance of his themes and treatment may be judged better by *The Portrait of a Lady*, 1881, or *What Maisie Knew*, 1897, or *The Ambassadors*, 1903, to name only three out of about 30-40 vols.

-ii. **William** (1842-1910) : Amer. philosopher ; brother of above. Wr. works on psychology, and *Pragmatism : a New Name for some Old Ways of Thinking*, 1907.

Jamyn, Amadis (1540-85) : Fr. poet ; disciple of Ronsard (q.v.) ; reached Paris at the height of the literary success of the Pleiad (q.v.). J. was a distinguished Gk. scholar, and effected a verse transln. of *Iliad*, xiii-xxiv ; wr. poems after the new Fr. models, including sonnets in which a likeness has been traced to passages in the Shakespearean sonnet-sequence.

Jan i (1252-94): Dutch poet ; duke of Brabant. Wr. songs of love and chivalry.

Jansen, Cornelius (1585-1638) : Dutch theologian ; Roman Catholic bp. of Ypres ; founder of a heresy known as Jansenism, which dropped like balm on the austerities of the Jesuits, and obtained a strong hold in France, through the Port Royal (q.v.) and its greatest offspring, Pascal (q.v.). J. preached predestination and grace, and wr. a work entitled *Augustinus* (issued posth., 1640), in which his doctrine, which had affinity with Calvin's (q.v.), was based on the teachings of St. Augustine. The rehabilitation of the old nunnery at Port Royal, its extension into a retreat for men of pious inclination, and the foundation of the Port Royalists' schools, with leaders as eminent and devout as St. Cyran, Arnauld, and Nicole, lent to Jansenism, which still has adherents in Holland, a brief, though troublous, period of glory from 1636 to 1660, when the schools were definitely closed, or till 1710, when Port Royal was demolished. The glory belongs to the disciples rather than to the eponymous founder. The Port Royal system of education, its logic, its rhetoric, and, above all, its Pascal, are, arguably, nobler fruit than J. was ever conscious of sowing. But the seed was geniune all the same. It was from J.'s *Augustinus* that the famous Five Propositions, or Articles, were derived (they were implicit, not explicit), on which Port Royal stood and fell ; and the grandeur of Jansenism lay wholly in its moral teaching, and in its noble austerity of conduct and its liberal attitude to learning, which pervaded its schools for boys and girls. Its influence was out of all proportion to the tale of its adherents ; it was the leaven to the worldliness of a mme. de Sévigné, to the

tragic drama was symbolically 'sacrificed' to Bacchus, and this parade of delight was seized by the already jealous guild of the Confrérie (q.v.) as a pretext for attacking J. on the ominous charge of atheism. The comparison between J.'s *Cléopâtre* and Shakespeare's *Antony and Cleopatra* must be left to special students of the drama; the common dependence of both plays on Plutarch is as obvious as that Amyot preceded North (see s.vv.) as his translr. J.'s last experiment in drama was a tragedy, *Didon*, written throughout in Alexandrines (s.v. Alexander), henceforward the regular metre for Fr. dramas. Thus, J.'s innovations were in the forward line, and he notably advanced the patriotic aims of the literary revolutionaries who were united in the 'learned brigade' of Dorat's (q.v.) pupils at the collège de Coqueret. Naturally, his successors surpassed him (see s.v. Garnier, particularly), but to J. belongs the credit, enthusiastically extended to him in his brief, unhappy lifetime, of naturalizing classic drama on Fr. soil.

John ii (1404-54): Span. king of Castile; succeeded his father, king Henry iii, 1406, under the regency of his mother, queen Catharine (daughter of John of Gaunt) and her brother, the king's uncle, Ferdinand, afterwards (1412) king of Aragon. With the difficulties and complexities of king J.'s effective reign we are not here concerned; our immediate business is to note that the king's natural proclivities and the policy of the constable of Castile, Alvaro de Luna, turned his attention to the patronage of learning and the cultivation of letters, and made his court one of the nests of singing-birds, such as those of Sicily and parts of Germany in the same age. Contemporary chroniclers inform us that king J. 'was a good musician; sang, played, danced, and wrote good verses', some of which, in the lyrical vein, survive; and his name is justly commemorated at the head of his tuneful court. (See s.v. Villena, e.g.).

John of Salisbury (1120-80): Engl. philosopher; disciple of Abelard (q.v.); traveller and man of letters; served on frequent diplomatic missions; friend of Nicholas Breakspear, the only Engl. pope (Adrian iv); bp. of Chartres, 1176. Wr. Lat. prose treatises, *Polycraticus*, a work of great learning, defending the the pleasures of intellectual life, and *Metalogicus*, on the study of logic, based on Aristotle's (q.v.) *Organon*. His writings had great influence in medieval schools.

Johnson, Samuel (1709-84): Engl. lexicographer; writer of biographies, etc., and the subject of the best biography (see s.v. Boswell) in the Engl. language. J. was the son of a bookseller at Lichfield, and was at Pembroke Coll., Oxford, as a commoner 1728-9, where he distinguished himself by a translin. of the *Messiah* of Pope (q.v.) into Lat. verse (Pope himself said that posterity would be puzzled to know which version was the original), but left without taking his degree. He draw up plans, which came to nothing, of an Engl. edn. of Politian (q.v.), with a history of Lat. poetry in the 14th and 15th cents. After a period of schoolmastering, and an adaptation and extension, 1734-5, of *A Voyage to Abyssinia*, from the Fr.

of Lobo, a Port. Jesuit, in which may be discerned the future author of *Rasselas*, J. m., 1735, Mrs. Elizabeth Porter, the widow of a friend at Birmingham, and set up 'a private boarding-house for young gentlemen' at Edial, near Lichfield. The enterprise failed, and in March, 1737, J. proceeded with Garrick (q.v.), one of his pupils, to London, thenceforward his home. He brought with him his tragedy, *Irene* (produced by Garrick at Drury Lane, 1749), an immense enthusiasm for lit., an unrivalled quickness and capacity for work, and an introduction to the *Gentleman's Magazine*, the first of its kind to use the name 'magazine' (see s.v. Edward Cave). J.'s contributions were various and valuable, and included the 'Debates in the Senate of Lilliput', 1738-44, which replaced, with extraordinary skill, the reports of proceedings in Parliament, found to be a breach of the privilege of the House of Commons: 'they are Johnson's own debates on the political questions of the day, based—and only based— on the debates in parliament. There is more of Johnson than of Pitt in the famous speech about "the atrocious crime of being a young man". And two speeches entirely written by him appeared, to his amusement, in the collected works of Chesterfield' (q.v.; *C.H.E.L.*, x, 164; by D. Nichol Smith). The *Life of Mr. Richard Savage* (q.v., afterwards included in the *Lives of the Poets*), 1744, and congenial work on the collections of the first earl of Oxford (Harley), bring us to the *Plan for a Dict. of the Engl. Language*, addressed to the earl of Chesterfield, 1747; to the free imitation of Juvenal, satire x, in *The Vanity of Human Wishes*, 1749; to the *Prologue* (by J.; *Epilogue* by Garrick), spoken at the opening of Drury Lane theatre, 1747, and to the foundation of *The Rambler*, publd. Tues. and Sat. between 20 March, 1750, and (No. 208) 14 March, 1752, 3 days before the death of Mrs. Johnson.

These do not exhaust the bibliography of J.'s writings during those busy years in London; but they indicate the kind of life which he was leading, and his poem on the *Vanity of Human Wishes* and his essays in *The Rambler* sufficiently express his character and views. And apart from the Juvenal-imitation, which contains such well-known tags as

Survey mankind from China to Peru.

There mark what ills the scholar's life assail, Toil, envy, want, the patron and the jail.

He left a name, at which the world grew pale, To point a moral, or adorn a tale.

Superfluous lags the Vet'ran on the stage.

Counts death kind Nature's signal of retreat; the true philosophy of J. is most surely to be found in the lines which he added at the close of *The Traveller* of his friend Goldsmith (q.v.).

How small, of all that human hearts endure, That part which laws or kings can cause or cure!

Still to ourselves in every place consign'd, Our own felicity we make or find:

With secret course, which no loud storms annoy,

Glides the smooth current of domestic joy.

To men remote from power but rarely known, Leave reason, faith, and conscience all our own.

'He was no pessimist', says prof. Smith (*C.H.E.L.*, *ib.*). 'The sense of vanity may keep us from thinking that things are better than they are, but it need not make us think that they are worse. He would maintain in talk that the world was not half so wicked as it was represented to be, that there was very little gross wickedness in it, and very little extraordinary virtue'.

It was a typical Engl. philosophy, and in the *Dict.*, 2 vols., 1755 (4th edn., 1773); frequently reprinted and re-edited, J. took an Englishman's view of the structure and use of his own language. He became his own Fr. Academy (q.v.). His quotations, which he was the first lexicographer to employ systematically, were intended to illustrate the author as well as the word, and his definitions were clear, logical, and simple. For a one-man job, this 8 years' labour is unique in literary history. There followed the *Idler* (Sat., 1758-60), a supplement to the *Univ. Chronicle or Weekly Gazette*; the new *variorum* edn. of Shakespeare, 8 vols., 1765 (see s.v. Boyle for J. and the 'Unities', q.v.); *The Prince of Abissinia: a Tale*, 2 vols., 1759, re-issued, 1787, and subsequently known by the name of its prince, *Rasselas* (transld. by Baretti, q.v., and into all European languages); *A Journey to the Western Islands of Scotland*, 1775; and, 1777, his engagement by London booksellers 'to write little Lives and little Prefaces to a little edition of the English poets' (J., in a letter to Boswell, 3 May, 1777). The booksellers concerned were 36 in number, and included such well-known names as Strahan, Rivington, Payne, Caslon, Longman, Dodsley, Baldwin, Cadell, Nichols, Evans, Murray, and others (see C. Knight, *Shadows of the old Booksellers*, app. 1); their *Works of the Engl. Poets*, 68 vols., were publd., 1779-81, with J.'s *Prefaces* contained in vols. i-iv, 1779, and v-x, 1781; these were separately re-issued in 4 vols., as *The Lives of the Most Eminent Engl. Poets; with Critical Observations on their Works*, 1781; new edn., 1783, and frequently re-issued (by G. Birkbeck Hill and H. S. Scott, 1905). Apart from its editorial origin,' it is even more important to remember' (*C.H.E.L.*, x, 183), 'that this great body of critical opinion—perhaps the greatest in the Engl. language—was written on invitation and in conformity with conditions controlled by others'. Despite these conditions, says prof. Saintsbury (*Hist. Crit.*, ii, 486), 'in very few cases have task and artist been so happily associated'. Making allowance for the criticisms of the critic, particularly in his *Lives* of Gray, Milton and Cowley, 'on the whole, it may safely be said that, however widely a man may differ from Johnson's critical theory, he will, provided that he possesses some real tincture of the critical spirit himself, think more and more highly of the *Lives of the Poets* the more he reads them, and the more he compares them with the greater classics of critical literature'; and we may commit ourselves to the safe judgment of that authority.

The rest of the story is Boswell's, who met J. in 1763. 'It was a supreme fortune', we are told, 'that gave Johnson the friendship of Reynolds and Boswell'. Sir Joshua painted him 4 times, and Boswell (see s.v.), writing his life, wr. one of the great bks. of Engl. lit. Mrs. Hester Piozzi (1741-1821), *née* Salusbury, who was the wife of Henry Thrale, and at whose house at Streatham, 1765, J. became almost domesticated—her second marriage, 1784, which took her to Italy, was a bitter grief to J.,—wr., *Anecdotes of the late Samuel Johnson*; and sir John Hawkins (1719-89), who drew up J.'s will, publd. his *Life and Works*, 1787-9. These served as material for Boswell, in whose pages the true J. of Fleet Street, of talk, and of 'The Club' (founded by him, with Reynolds, 1764), lives for ever in the guise of a true Englishman. What talk it was! No extracts can do justice to it, though the judicious reader may be commended to ch. iv (' Johnson as a Literary Dictator ') in the *Johnson* in 'English Men of Letters' (Macmillan) by sir L. Stephen (q.v.), himself a biographer of repute. There will be found the letter to Macpherson (q.v.) of *Ossian* fame ('I hope I shall never be deterred from detecting what I think a cheat by the menaces of a ruffian '), the letter to Mrs. Thrale on her marriage, the 'patriotism is the last refuge of a scoundrel' epigram, and many other of the purple passages. It belongs to Boswell, rather than to J., to add, in the words of sir L. Stephen : 'In him adoration never hindered accuracy of portraiture. "I will never make my tiger a cat to please anybody", was his answer to well-meaning entreaties of Hannah More (q.v.) to soften his accounts of Johnson's asperities. We should not do justice to Johnson's intense tenderness, if we did not see how often it was masked by an irritability pardonable in itself, and not affecting the deeper springs of action. To bring out the beauty of a character by means of its external oddities is the triumph of a kindly humourist. To see this required an insight so rare that it is wanting in nearly all the biographers who have followed in Boswell's steps'. So, through Boswell's unrivalled work, we see, in Macaulay's (q.v.) words, 'the gigantic body, the huge massy face, seamed with the scars of disease, the grey wig with the scorched foretop, the dirty hands, the nails bitten and pared to the quick. We see the eyes and mouth moving with convulsive twitches ; we see the heavy form rolling ; we hear it puffing ; and then comes the "Why, sir"! and the "What then, sir ?" and the "No, sir "! and the "You don't see your way through the question, sir!"'

It only remains to add that J., who received the LL.D. from Dublin, 1765, and from Oxford, 1775, never used the title of doctor, by which he has since become universally known.

Johnsonese (Rhet.): Epithet derived from the name of Dr. Johnson (q.v.), to describe a style in prose, which like other kinds of style, may be said, after Buffon, to have been *l'homme même*. It is characteristic of the man and his time ; and, despite a tendency, lending itself to parody, to ' use ', as he said of himself, ' too big words and too many of them ', ' he was the dominating influence in English prose throughout the second half of the eighteenth century. The lesson of discipline required to be taught, and it was learnt from him by many whose best work shows no traces of his manner ' (*C.H.E.L.*, x, 189). That manner consists, not merely in the bigness of the words, but in ' a peculiar love of putting the abstract for the concrete, of using awkward inversions, and of balancing his sentences in a monotonous rhythm ' (sir L. Stephen, *Johnson*, 168).

Johnstone, Charles (? 1719-1800): Engl. novelist. Wr., 1760-5, *Chrysal, or The Adventures of a Guinea*, a series of stories within a story; after the manner of the *Diable Boiteux* (see s.v. Lesage, and see, too, s.v. Heiberg), employed to satirize social manners somewhat savagely.

Joinville, sire de, Jean (1224-1319): Fr. sacred historian (hagiographer). Born at the castle of Joinville, and brought up as an orphan at the court of the count of Champagne, his guardian and suzerain; hereditary seneschal of Champagne; started, April, 1248, on disastrous crusade; met king (saint) Louis ix at Cyprus in the Sept.; remained in Egypt and Syria till 1254; on his return, enjoyed the close confidence of the king. Years afterwards, queen Jeanne of Navarre, wife of Philip iv of France, applied to the aged seneschal of her own county of Champagne for a true account of the crusade; and J. in 1305 revived his memories of more than half a century ago to write his prose *Histoire de Saint Louis*; the queen, too, had died, when he inscribed it, 1309, to her son, afterwards Louis x. Such is the story of the man and the bk; and the haze of the distance interposed between the action and its chronicle, between the old man eloquent in 1305 and the young man active in 1250, increases, rather than diminishes, the interest and value of the writing. The history of a crusade, such as Villehardouin (q.v.) might have written it, becomes the life of a saint, in the line of descent of religious lit.; and the dialogues, the descriptions, the touches of humanity, the humour, the personal intimacy of the links between the chronicler and the king, the radiance, the sympathy and the imagination, raise this record of 'emotion recollected in tranquillity ' to a high level of positive attainment. J.'s *Histoire* has been transld. into Engl. by E. Wedgwood (Murray, 1906).

Jón Eiríksson (1727-87): Icel. scholar; librarian of the Royal Library, Copenhagen; one of several erudite Icelanders in Denmark who worked with zeal and enthusiasm for the enlightenment of their native country. This group of scholars included Jón himself, Haltdán Einarsson (d. 1785; author of a Lat. history of Icel. lit.), Skúli Thorlacius (d. 1815), Gunnar Pálsson (d. 1791), bp. Jón Arnason (d. 1743), Bjorn Halldórsson (d. 1794; author of an Icel.-Lat.-Dan. lexicon, issued by Rask, q.v., 1814), Jón Olafsson von Svefney (1729-1811; author of a history of Northern poetry, 1786), and others. They did not write any bks. of outstanding merit, but they were associated in journalistic and antiquarian activities, designed to stimulate a revival of the Old Icel. spirit and to renew it in their own generation. The Royal Fine Arts Society of Iceld. was founded by their exertions, and did admirable work between 1779-95, with its headquarters in Copenhagen.

Jongleur (Fr.): Technical name, now passed into common acceptance, for the reciter, singer, or poet, of a tale drawn from the epical material (epopee), arranged in poetic form by the *trouvère*, or inventor. The tale, thus completed, is known as a *chanson de geste* (q.v.). The golden age of the J. comprised the 11th and 12th cents., when it was his main business to acquire by purchase or otherwise a stock of suitable narratives, to alter and embellish them as skilfully as he could in order to satisfy the taste of his various audiences, and to recite them at fairs, weddings, feasts, sacred shrines, and at the resorts of pilgrims, etc., —anywhere, in fact, where lucrative business could be done. The tradition that the *Chanson de Roland* (s.v. Roland) animated the warriors at the battle of Hastings may or may not be true; but, generally speaking, it was in times of peace and for the entertainment of leisure that the professional J. sought to attract the gifts and ears of the crowd. His success would be the measure of his reward; and success in his job was won by a constant and even a cumulative power of arousing the interest and retaining the attention of his audience. He had to grip them. New incidents and fresh sensation taxed his powers of invention and combination. The hypothesis of a primitive basis of hist. facts, around the epical rendering whereof the J. wove his increasing *chansons*, has been discredited in recent years by the researches of Bédier (*les Légendes epiques*), who practically identifies in time the primitive and the artistic invention. Further, the epic simplicity—the characteristically Homeric note of epos—was gradually, even swiftly, disused under the strain of the demand for novelty; towards and after the close of the 12th cent., the heroic style was merged in the romantic (s.v. Romance), and the J. composed the *romans d'aventure*, which, originally, at any rate, are a ' bad counterfeit ' of epopee. The J. was commonly anon., but sometimes (see s.v. Bodel, e.g.) he signed his name, and at all times he exercised authoritative (not to say, arbitrary) rights over the work of his predecessors. There was no consecrated text of a Fr. epopee, corresponding to Homer's text of the Gk. Every J. was a Homer *in petto*, and in his own estimation; the matter was more or less fixed, but the J. had a free hand with the manner. Assonantal rhyme was varied with consonantal; 10 syllables were stretched to 12 (the *chanson* of Alexander, q.v., first employed the thence-named alexandrine metre); the blocks (*laisses*) of verses were broken up into short stanzas; the desuetude of the J.'s musical accompanist, who had helped his memory in recital, led to more elaborate versification; and the spread of reading gradually brought about a change from verse to prose, and (15th cent.) the beginning of prose-romances. It is not necessary to discuss other aspects of the industry of the J. in the period of the decline of heroic poetry; the cyclical re-combination of his material from the point of view of genealogy and family is a salient feature in this kind. We first hear of the J., accompanying the *trouvère's* songs on his viol, or violin, as early as the 9th cent., and the name, as written now, has descended through *jougleur, jougleor*, from *jogledor* (Lat. *joculator*) and *jogler* (Lat.

jocularis). At the period of the street-collection trade of the itinerant J., it was a favourite occupation of the blind, and the street-singer of to-day is the sorry and faded representative of the itinerant novelist and entertainer of the brighter days that are dead.

Jonson, Ben (1573-1637) : Engl. dramatic and lyric poet ; 'the first, and, in some ways, the greatest of English literary dictators' (*C.H.E.L.*, vii, 3) ; 'rare Ben Jonson' of a chance admirer's inscription on his grave in Westminster Abbey ; friend and eulogist of Shakespeare (q.v.) as 'not of an age, but for all time'. In the person of this literary dictator, there was, by contemporary evidence, a rather curious likeness between J. and his later namesake, Dr. Johnson (q.v.). Thus, T. Fuller (q.v.) wr., 1662, referring to encounters at the Mermaid tavern : 'Many were the wit-combats between him (Shakespeare) and Ben Jonson, which two I behold like a Spanish great galleon and an English man-of-war ; Master Jonson, like the former, was built far higher in learning, solid but slow in his performances. Shakespeare, with the English man-of-war, lesser in bulk, but lighter in sailing, could turn with all tides, tack about, and take advantage of all winds by the quickness of his wit and invention'. And these gatherings at the Mermaid were matched by the 'lyric feasts' recalled by Herrick (q.v.), so much indebted to J. in his classic epigrams, at a later period of his life :

> Ah Ben !
> Say how, or when
> Shall we, thy Guests,
> Meet at those Lyrick Feasts,
> Made at the Sun,
> The Dog, the triple Tunne ?
> Where we such clusters had,
> As made us nobly wild, not mad ;
> And yet each Verse of thine
> Out-did the meate, out-did the frolick
> wine.

So, prof. Moorman could write of him (*C.H.E.L.*, vi, 1) : 'Huge of body, bibulous and brawling, he yet loved Latin as heartily as canary, and would write the tenderest epitaph as well as the grossest epigram'. Among the verses for which he is chiefly remembered is the song in the vol. of poems, *The Forest*, 1616 : 'Drink to me only with thine eyes' (not less orig. because it is a free transln. from the Gk. of Philostratus), and 'It is not growing like a tree, In bulke, doth make men better be' (a strophe out of an ode in *Underwoods*).

But the past dictatorship of J. and even his present literary interest are far from the sum of his hist. achievement. It is necessary to say a word about the learning, referred to by Fuller in 1662, referred to again by Milton (q.v.), in a similar contrast with Shakespeare :

> Then to the well-trod stage anon,
> If Jonson's learned sock be on,
> Or sweetest Shakespeare, Fancy's child,
> Warble his native woodnotes wild.
>   *Il Penseroso*, 131-4,

and, again, in the epithet by J. A. Symonds (q.v. ; *Shakespeare's Predecessors*, 210) : Engl. drama 'donned that ponderous sock, and trod the measures of *Volpone*'. We owe to a Span. playwright (see s.v. Torres-Naharro)

a distinction between plays founded on knowledge (*a noticia*) and on fancy (*a fantasia*), and this distinction is true of the difference, glibly defined in stage-law by Polonius (*Hamlet*, ii, 2), between 'the law of writ and the liberty', or classical and romantic drama. Writers *a noticia*, whether their knowledge was poured into elegant masques and pageants, or into plays in the Lat. tradition, appealed directly to the court and its wits, while playwrights *a fantasia* had to carve their own way by psychology and emotional power. Very broadly, the *fantasia* was Shakespeare's way, the learning or *noticia* was J.'s.

There were several distinct periods in J.'s literary career, during a part of which he was unofficial poet-laureate (q.v.) to kings James and Charles. His additions to the famous *Spanish Tragedy* are noted s.v. Kyd. More significant were his early comedies : *Every Man in his Humour*, performed at the Globe Theatre, 1598, with Shakespeare in the lord chamberlain's company of players ; *Every Man out of his Humour*, 1599, and others. These had direct influence on later playwrights, and they are significant, too, as 'the beginning of a revolutionary movement in dramatic methods and the institution of a new species, the comedy of "humours". It is an important turning-point in the course of the Elizabethan drama' (*C.H.E.L.*, vi, 3). 'Humours' in this context was more or less a medical metaphor, derived from the physicians' categories of phlegm, blood, choler and melancholy, and the transference from physiology to mentality may perhaps be compared with some of the conclusions of the psycho-analysts of the present day.

Leaving J.'s masques and his satire-dramas, which involved him in a very dull quarrel with Thos. Dekker and other contemporary playwrights and pamphleteers of small account, we come to his finer plays : four comedies, *Volpone*, 1606 ; *The Silent Women*, 1609 ; *The Alchemist* (founded on *il Candelaio*, by G. Bruno, q.v.), 1610 ; and *Bartholomew Fayre*, 1614 ; with *Catiline*, a tragedy, 1611. These are genuine character-plays, displaying a real command of drama, as arising out of character rather than out of situation ; and the great novelists from Fielding (q.v.) downwards have profited by J.'s studies of manners in action. Thus, Dickens (q.v.), it is interesting to note, once played Bodabill in *Every Man in his Humour* and some of his comic characters are Jonsonese. J., who received the M.A. degree at Oxford, 1619, and whose name was considered for the honour of knighthood, enjoyed the rare distinction of a collected edn. of *The Workes of Benjamin Jonson*, 1616 (folio). To his plays and poems were added a transln. of Horace (q.v.), *Ars poetica*, an *English Grammar*, and a commonplace-book, *Timber, or Discoveries*, rather extravagantly praised by Swinburne (q.v. ; *Ben Jonson*, 1889), and displaying very wide misc. reading. A new edn. of *Ben Jonson*, in 10 vols., by C. H. Herford and Percy Simpson (vols. i and ii, 'The Man and his Work', 1925), is publd. by the Clarendon Press, Oxford.

Jon Thorlaksson (1744-1819) : Icel. poet ; chiefly famous for his series of verse-translns. from the works of Tullin and Wessell (qq.v.), Pope's (q.v.) *Essay on Man*, Milton's (q.v.) *Paradise Lost* and Klopstock's (q.v.) *Messias*. A Germ. historian of Scand. lit. admits that J.'s version of Klopstock ' excels and enhances the German poem by its old-Icelandic force '. The services which J. rendered in this wise to the renascent literary genius of his own countrymen cannot be too highly estimated. Most of his days were spent in poverty and a struggle for sub-sistence ; but honours came to him in old age, and Dan. and Engl. admirers procured him the much-needed pensions, granted for the first time to an Icelander.

Joseph of Exeter (12th cent.) : Engl. writer of epopee ; wr. *de bello Trojano* in Lat. hexa-meters, and another poem on the siege of Antioch, in a passage of which occurred the famous epithet ' flos regum Arturus ', prefixed by Tennyson (q.v.) to his *Idylls of the King.*

Joubert, Joseph (1754-1824) : Fr. moralist. J.'s *Pensées* and Letters were collected, 1842, and reveal the intense, fine, ineffective passion of the artistic temperament which he cultivated. He was a friend of Fontanes (q.v.), the useful dispensary of Napoleon's patronage ; and ' there is probably no writer in any language who has said an equal number of remarkable things on an equal variety of subjects in an equally high and unbroken excellence of style and expression ' (Saintsbury, *Fr. Lit.*, 441). In his power of vivifying abstract thought— the aspect which particularly attracted M. Arnold (q.v.)—J. contributed to the new movement of Fr. romance (q.v.) in 1830 ; and, appropriately enough, Chateaubriand (q.v.) edited his literary remains. Naturally, J. was an opponent of Fr. 18th cent. thought and of its outcome in the Revolution.

Jouffroy, Théodore Simon (1796-1842) : Fr. philosopher ; assistant to Roger-Collard and Cousin (qq.v.) at the Sorbonne ; a disciple of the Scottish School. Wr. treatises on natural law (1835-42) and æsthetics, 1843, and *Mélanges philosophiques*, 1833, 1842.

Journal d'un Bourgeois de Paris (1405-49) : Fr. ' Journal of a Citizen of Paris, 1405-49 ' ; anon. ; publd., 1876, by the Historical Society of Paris, with conjectures as to authorship (ascribed to J. Beaurigout) by Auguste Long-non ; and again 1881. The authorship is still conjectural ; but the *Journal*, whether by a parish priest, or whether the work of several hands, is remarkable and fascinating for its garrulity, puerility, ingenuity, pathos and grandeur. The name has stuck, and Biré (q.v.) publd. a *J. d'un B. de P. sous la Terreur*, and a similar publication ensued at the beginning of the Great War, 1914.

Jovellanos, de, Gaspar Melchior (1744-1811) : Span. poet ; patriot ; statesman. Originally destined for the church, J. accepted a judicial appointment at Seville, 1768, and remained thenceforth in the service of the law. For about a year, 1797-98, he was minister of justice, but the political disturbances of the times (it was the period of the premiership of Godoy, the queen's lover) drove him into exile at Majorca, 1801-08. In the reign of the Bonaparte king Joseph, ' next to the punish-ment of Godoy, what all men most desired was

the release of Jovellanos ' (Southey, *Penin-sular War* ; quoted by Ticknor, iii, 325) ; but restitution came too late. J.'s prose works fairly indicate the high motives which actuated his career, and his patriotic writings (e.g., *Defensa de la Junta Central*, 1810) were widely esteemed. He is remembered to-day chiefly, however, as a poet ; and, particularly, as a dramatic poet, and a shining light in the Salamanca (q.v.) circle associated with the name of Melendez Valdés (q.v.). In this category, J.'s best play was *el Delinquente honrado* (' The honourable delinquent '), 1774, a prose piece which owed something to Richardson and more to Diderot (qq.v.). His verse-tragedy, *Pelayo*, 1769, was not acted till some years later.

Jowett, Benjamin (1817-93) : Engl. scholar ; Hellenist ; master of Balliol Coll., Oxford, 1870-93 ; regius prof. of Gk. at the same univ., 1855, but deprived of the emoluments of the chair for 10 years owing to his alleged heretical opinions, the suspicion of which was increased by his essay on ' The Interpretation of Scrip-ture ' in *Essays and Reviews*, 1860. Wr. very valuable translns. of Plato, 1871, Thucydides, 1881, and Aristotle's *Politics*, 1885. J. grew into a kind of legend of Oxford, owing to his influence on his pupils, and a certain wayward whimsicalness in dealing with problems of conduct.

Juan de la Cruz. See s.v. **Yepes.**

Juan Manuel (1282-1348) : Span. romancer ; prince ; nephew to king Alfonso the Wise (q.v.) ; commonly known as don Juan (John) ; regent of Castile during the minority (1312-22) of king Alfonso xi ; afterwards implicated in wars and intrigues, with which we are not here concerned. Don J.'s pen was mightier than his sword ; and, while he was the author or ' begetter ' of treatises on various subjects, including an abridgment of his uncle Alfonso's *Cronica general*, his masterwork was the ' Count Lucanor ' (*Libro de los Enexiemplos del Conde Lucanor et de Patronio*), written between 1328-35, and first printed, 1575. This work, divided into 4 parts, of which part i, consisting of 51 chs., is the most important, is described (by Kelly, *Lit. espagn.*, 61) as ' the Castilian equivalent of the *Arabian Nights Entertainments*, with Patronio as Scheherazade and count Lucanor (i.e. Juan Manuel himself) as caliph ' ; and, like the *Decameron* of Boccaccio (q.v.), which it anti-cipated by about 20 years, or like the *Canter-bury Tales* of Chaucer (q.v.), Don John's *Count Lucanor* drew on the source-books of Eastern fable, and achieved in the region of prose-narration the same triumph of individual mastery as Ruiz (q.v.), his contemporary, was achieving in vernacular verse. The *Enexiemplos* of the title means ' stories ' or ' apologues ', and don John collected his tales from all quarters, and supplied material in turn to Shakespeare (*Taming of the Shrew*, but probably indirectly), Calderon, Lesage (qq.v.), and others. J.M.'s other bks.—12 in all—need not detain us ; it is as the founder of Span. prose fiction that his renown is fixed in the lit. of his country and beyond.

Jungmann, Josef (1773-1847) : Czech scholar and translr., in which capacity his chief work was a version, 1811, of *Paradise Lost* (s.v. Milton), on which he spent great pains. Wr. too, a students' handbook on poetics, a history of Czech lit., and, most notably, a dict. of the Czech and Germ. languages (5 vols., 1834-39), which proved of immense service to the new learning.

Jung-Stilling, Johann Heinrich (1740-1817): Germ. pietist. Born in humble circumstances, Jung, commonly called Stilling, worked his own hard way by tailoring and school-mastering up to the rank of univ. prof. of medicine at Heidelberg and Marburg. He belonged to that region of the Rhineland esp. associated with the teachings of Paracelsus and Böhme (qq.v.), and displayed in all his writings the simple faith and devout mysticism of his orig. At Strassburg in 1770 J.-S. made the acquaintance of Goethe (q.v.), who procured the publication (1777) of his autobiography, vol. i, entitled 'Heinrich Stilling's Youth' (*Heinrich Stillings Jugend*); 5 further vols. followed, the last in 1817. The Stilling-worshippers formed a kind of cult, and were actually enrolled in his name, and Goethe pays him a high tribute in *Dichtung und*

Wahrheit, ii. J.-S.'s other works include a romance, *Heimweh*, 1794, drenched in spiritualism, which enjoyed wide popularity.

Junius: Engl. anonymous pamphleteer, who contributed a series of political letters to the *Public Advertiser* from 1768-73. The *nom-de-guerre* was very strictly guarded, and as many as 46 names, including even that of E. Gibbon (q.v.), have been conjectured for the authorship. The problem, except as a curiosity of lit., has little interest to-day, though the *Letters of Junius*, 2 vols., 1772 (frequently reprinted), have been the occasion of a fairly voluminous lit. of their own, and reached a very high level in a very low class. J., says a writer in *C.H.E.L.*, x, 406, ' was the most perfect wielder of slanderous polemic that had ever arisen in English political controversy. Not lack of rivals, but eminent ability, made him supreme. Direct invective, lucid irony, dry sarcasm mingle with one another in the smooth-ranked phrases'. J. is almost certainly to be identified with sir Philip Francis (1740-1818), a War Office clerk, who received an appointment in India, and sat in Parliament, 1784-1807.

K

Kaestner, Abraham Gotthelf (1717-1800): Germ. epigrammatist; prof. of mathematics at Göttingen; attached to the Gottsched (q.v.) circle, and possessed a stinging wit and exceptional neatness of expression.

Kalenberg, Pfarrer von (Germ.): ' The Parson of Kalenborow'; eponymous hero of South-Germ. jest-book (q.v.), written in rhymed octosyllabic couplets, and compiled, probably in Vienna, from earlier sources, towards the end of the 15th or beginning of the 16th cent. This folk-tale hero, whose exploits are on a plebeian level of horse-play, rough humour, and irreverence, has been identified with a certain Weigand, who was attached to the court of Otto, duke of Austria, about 100 years before his *geste* and the accrued legends received the honour of collection; and the village of Kalenbergersdorf still bears its name. The Pfarrer's wit, which was thoroughly one-sided, played its tricks and catches and practical jokes with varying degrees of audacity on duke, bishop, and peasants; and is clearly akin to the contemporary humour of Eulenspiegel (q.v.). An Engl. prose version, under the title above, was effected about 1510, and the bk. maintained its vogue with 3 or 4 generations of admirers. (See also s.v. Amis).

Kant, Immanuel (1724-1804): Germ. philosopher. Born and died at Königsberg, in Prussia, and never quitted his native province. K.'s life was bound up with the univ., where he began to lecture in 1755, and became prof. of logic and metaphysics in 1770. In the brief reactionary reign of king Fredk. Wm. ii (1786-97), who sought to undo the work of the Aufklärung (q.v.), which had reached its zenith in the year, 1740, K. was threatened in a cabinet order (1 Oct., 1794) with ' unpleasant consequences'

unless he ceased his researches into natural and revealed religion. The ageing *savant* acquiesced, in compliance with ' a subject's duty ', and did not resume publication of the offending work (*Religion within the Bounds of Pure Reason*) till after the king's death. With this solitary interruption, K.'s life is marked by the establishment of his philosophical primacy in Europe. He was writing all his life: his chief works are *die Kritik der reinen Vernunft* ('The Critique of Pure Reason'), 1781; *Prolegomena zu einer jeden künftigen Metaphysik die als Wissenschaft wird auftreten können* (' Prologue to every future Metaphysic that will be able to appear as Science'), 1783; *Idee zu einer allgemeinen Geschichte in weltbürgerlicher Absicht* ('Sketch of a Universal History from a cosmopolitan point of view'), 1784; *Grundlegung zur Metaphysik der Sitten* '(Foundations of a Metaphysic of Morals'), 1785; *Metaphysische Anfangsgründe der Naturwissenschaften* ('Metaphysical Elements of the Natural Sciences'), 1786; *Kritik der practischen Vernunft* (' The Critique of Practical Reason '), 1788; *Kritik der Urteilskraft* (' The Critique of Judgment'), 1790; *Religion innerhalb der Grenzen der blossen Vernunft* ('Religion within the bounds of pure Reason'), 1793; *Metaphysik der Sitten* (' The Metaphysic of Morals ') 1797, and *Logik*, 1800. Of these, the most important are the 3 Critiques, of Pure Reason, Practical Reason, and Judgment. An immense body of philosophical lit. has grown up during the last hundred and more years round the Kantian system, and is associated in this country with the names, chiefly, of Fr. Max Müller, J. P. Mahaffy, A. Seth, and E. Caird. It is with the influence of K.'s teaching, and with its relations to other departments of life and thought, that we are here principally concerned ; with the revolutionizing effect of his demonstration that the Reason of 18th cent. dogmatists is not a tyrant but a servant of the mind, and that the experience upon which it acts and the knowledge resultant from its action are both alike necessary to its operation, and that it cannot operate independently ; and, further, with the consequent elevation and the binding character of the moral law. K.'s 'categorical imperative '—so act that your maxim may be capable of becoming the universal natural law of all rational beings, —by restoring the human mind to the usurped throne of the Creator, shattered the pretensions of the Fr. *philosophes* (q.v.), and coincided with the national re-birth of Germ. self-dependence, of which the *Faust* of Goethe and the dramas of Schiller were purely literary expressions. In this aspect, K. acknowledged the inextinguishable debt which he owed to the inspired teachings of J. J. Rousseau (q.v.), whose moral revelation he compared to the physical revelation of Newton ; and, admitting the Fr. leadership of K.'s thought, it is commonly and truly said that K. was the successor of Luther (q.v.), and that, after his appearance, the dreary centuries between the two great liberators were as if they had not been. 'Luther, by combining in himself the Mystic and the Humanistic movement, revolutionized the medieval church. Kant, by combining in himself both the empiricism and the idealism of his predecessors, revolutionized modern thought' (Francke, *Hist. Germ. Lit.*, E.T., 328) ; and Paulsen declares even more luminously : 'The great influence which Kant exercised upon his age was due just to the fact that he appeared as a deliverer from unendurable suspense. . . . Voltaire and Hume had not written in vain. Science seemed to demand the renunciation of the old faith. On the other hand, the heart still clung to it. Pietism had increased the sincerity and earnestness of religion . . . At this point Kant showed a way of escape from the dilemma. His philosophy made it possible to be at once a candid thinker and an honest man of faith. . . . It was a deliverance similar to that which the Reformation had brought to the German spirit a century or two earlier. Indeed one may in a certain sense regard Kant as the finisher of what Luther had begun ' (*Kant*, E.T., 6-7). The Reformation, then, we may say, was completed by this Transformation, which Rousseau in education and government, Kant in philosophy, Winckelmann and Lessing in æsthetics, Goethe and Schiller in pure lit., each acting and reacting on each, so far as was possible in time, wrought at the close of the 18th cent. in the outlook of man on experience. Together, they effected a reconciliation, which has been shaken but never undone, between reason and faith (Rationalism and Pietism, to give them secondary names) ; and if K. had not founded that peace in the sanction of conduct, its literary and æsthetic expression would have been robbed of more than half its influence. He communicated to the creative force of European thought a stimulus hardly less quickening than that of

the contemporaneous and similarly derived Fr. Revolution.

Kantemir, Antiochus (c. 1700-44) : Russ. satirist ; Roumanian by birth ; prince by rank ; ambassador in Paris. K. was a dilettante in lit., the practice of which in his age and generation was deemed unbefitting his station ; and his most memorable work was never publd. in his lifetime. This was his collection of satires, after the manner of Boileau (q.v.), some in verse, three others in prose, issued first in a Fr. translm. K., who was a student of Horace (q.v.), was filled with the spirit of the reforming zeal of Peter (q.v.) the Great, and poured the wine of the new ideas, didactic and enlightened, into the old forms of epistles, epigrams, and so forth. He takes his place with Prokopowich (q.v.) as a pioneer of the new lit. to come.

Kapnist, Basil (1756-1823) : Russ. dramatist. Wr. comedies, of a satiric tendency, after Fr. classic models, and achieved a contemporary reputation second only to that of Visin (q.v.). K. is credited with the bold enterprise of representing Russian judicial procedure realistically, and the ban pronounced on some of his plays is accordingly not contrary to expectation.

Karamsin, Nicolai Michaelovich (1765-1826) : Russ. historian : 'the first Russian man of letters of genuine cultural influence on the entire reading world' (Brückner, *Gesch. d. Russ. Lit.*, 113), and so epoch-making in his generation that the period 1790-1820 is sometimes called after his name, which became a kind of cult or religion to his followers. There were a warmth and a personality in K.'s writing, which assured it admiration and welcome. In the two schools of Russ. letters at this date, those of Petrograd and Moscow, or those of Fr. neo-classicism and of Germ. individualism and romance, K.'s choice and temperament led him to Moscow. Macpherson's (q.v.) *Ossian*, Sterne, Haller, Gessner, Kleist, Richardson, Young and Thomson (see s.vv.), were the masters to whom he went to school ; he shared their sentiment, their naturalism, and their sense of values in lit., if not in life. Of the two great Fr. thinkers of the 18th cent., K. followed Rousseau, not Voltaire (qq.v.). And his powers rose to his perceptions ; the man made the style. The Petrine grammarians and philologers (s.v. Peter the Great) had shown how the Russ. language should be made literary ; K. wr. Russ. lit. : ' to European thoughts and feelings European expression attached itself' (Brückner, *ib.*, 115). K. was the great reformer of Russ. speech, working not by precept but by example. He did not start as an historian : the objective, impersonal point of view came later in his life ; his early reading and efforts in transln. (among them, Shakespeare's *Julius Cæsar*) pricked him, like Chaucer, to pilgrimage, and in 1789-90 he travelled to Königsberg, Weimar (where, it is noted, he visited Herder and Wieland, qq.v., not Goethe), Switzerland, Paris, London, and back by sea. His impressions were gathered in the *Letters of a Russian Traveller*, publd. in his own *Moscow Journal* (1791-2) ; and, though he had to deal warily with what he saw in revolutionary Paris, and even to some extent in free Engld., his letters reveal a fresh, human observation and a tender feeling for men and nature. Their appeal, it is pointed out, was to the heart; a new note in Russ. lit.; and this note was struck even more clearly, and with a more direct ring of response, in K.'s two tales, *Poor Lisa* and *Natalia*. Their success, judging by the flattery of imitation, was immense; sorry Maschas, unhappy Margarets, and frail Henriettas succeeded one another in the likeness of K.'s characters; but the Egyptian darkness of the empress Catherine's literary censorship (see s.v. Radishchev) spread itself over K.'s soul, and, though his sensibility did not diminish, he sought personal safety in silence or other fields. First, in silence about present conditions and the things that he saw around him; then, by a happy development of his genius, in a narrative of Russia's past history. Leaving unfind. his romance, *A Knight of our Times*, K. turned to the times that were gone. He publd., 1818, the first 8 vols. of his *History of the Russ. State*, adding vols. 9 and 10 in 1824. The publication was 'the first colossal success of a prose work'; K. 'revealed their own history to the Russians, as Columbus discovered America' (Pushkin, q.v., cited by Brückner, *ib*, 157). His human outlook, his love of truth, and his gradually acquired control over the language which he had modulated to literary uses, made K.'s *Russian State* a classic in its own country, and a work admired and esteemed abroad. We distinguished above between K.'s new sense of values in lit. and in life. In this connection, Vogüé (*Roman Russe*, 28) quotes two illustrative passages. In one K. writes of country life in the full-blown strains of Rousseau's idealism; in the second he complains in a private letter of the difficulty of 'buying a decent cook'; and the reader is invited to listen to the growl of the wolf in the sheepfold. The implied criticism is not wholly just. K. affected some of the virtues which he praised, and reformed himself while he reformed others. The more honour to him, accordingly, that he reversed the saying of the cynic, and that, while he saw the worse, he applauded and followed the better.

Karsch, Anna Luisa (1722-91): Germ. poet; known by the feminine termination as Karschin, according to the fashion of the times; Silesian peasant by birth; the 'German Sappho' in the kindly estimation of Gleim and Ramler (qq.v.), and even of Lessing (q.v.). Her poetry was imitative of Gleim's songs of a Prussian grenadier, and formed a section of the voluminous verse inspired by the Seven Years' War. It has little permanent value.

Katkov, Michael Nikoforovich (1818-87): Russ. scholar; journalist. K. originally attached himself to the circle of Herzen (q.v.), and sacrificed his chair of philosophy in order to plead reform in the newspapers, as editor of the *Moscow News*. Events narrowed his sympathies and showed him the practical dangers of doctrinaire Nihilism (q.v.), and K. was found at a later date at the head of the reactionary Nationalist movement.

Keats, John (1795-1821): Engl. poet. The facts of K.'s life are familiar: they were related first by Richard Monckton Milnes (q.v.), first baron Houghton, in the *Life and Letters of John Keats*, 1848 (following his *Poetical Works, with a Memoir*, 1834); secondly, by sir Sidney Colvin, in the 'English Men of Letters' series, 1887, and in an edn. of K.'s *Letters*, 1891; and, thirdly, by Miss Amy Lowell, a brilliant American writer (1874-1925), in *John Keats* (2 vols.; Cape, 1925), who 'made Keats, the man, at least in his earlier years, real to the reader as no biographer has done before' (*Times Lit. Supp.*, 19 March, 1925). We need recall but one or two essential facts: (1) K. was one of the group of 3 Engl. poets slightly younger than Wordsworth and Coleridge (qq.v.),—the 2 others were Byron and Shelley (qq.v.),—who were born in the new liberal age of the Fr. Revolution, of Fr. *lyrisme* and Germ. romance, and whose cultivation of beauty and liberty and other stirring and enfranchising abstractions of revolutionary thought emancipated Engl. poetry from 'the proper study of mankind' in man himself. In their ardent extension of the boundaries of poetry they were even suspect of impropriety: Byron, by his subjects; Shelley, by his opinions; and Keats, by his style. Byron was the only one of the 3 who passed his 35th year. (2), Still within the terms of this comparison, Byron was the son of a peer, Shelley of a country baronet, and K. of a livery stableman in Moorfields, London, by whom he was apprenticed to a surgeon. (3) Despite this difference in circumstances—a school at Enfield instead of Harrow (Byron) or Eton (Shelley),— K.'s call to poetry was irresistible. Among his schoolfellows was Charles Cowden Clarke (1787-1877; later, an author and publisher), whose father, John Clarke, introduced him to Leigh Hunt (q.v.), and lent him Spenser's (q.v.) *Faerie Queen* to read: 'he went through it', said Clarke, in famous words, 'as a young horse through a spring meadow ramping. Like a true poet, too, he specially singled out epithets; he hoisted himself up, and looked burly and dominant, as he said,—" What an image that is, *sea-shouldring whales* "'. (4) Spenser, the poets' poet, as he is called, led K. to other Elizabethans, esp. to Chapman (q.v.), who inspired K.'s great sonnet, 1816, *On first looking into Chapman's 'Homer'*. The young Enfield scholar knew no Gk., but the initiation into the Elizabethans was an initiation into Hellenism as well. (5) Abandoning surgery about this time, K. met at Hunt's cottage, in Hampstead, Haydon, the painter, Hazlitt (q.v.), the critic, Shelley, and others, and had his being at last among men of his own stamp. His first vol. of *Poems* was publd., 1817, but, despite Shelley's help and Hunt's support, its success was inconsiderable. (6) There were only 4 more years to run: they included the publication of *Endymion: a poetic romance*, 1818; and of *Lamia, Isabella, The Eve of St. Agnes, and other Poems*, 1820. Among the 'other poems' were the great *Odes* and the yet greater *Hyperion*, of which a second version, or fresh draft, was issued by lord Houghton (*supra*), 1856. These short years included, too, a visit to the Isle of Wight, a walking-tour, the sad love-story between K. and Fanny Brawne, symptoms of illness, increasing consumption, the final dragging visit to Italy, and the poet's death in Rome, 23 Feb., 1821. His monument in the Protestant cemetery was designed by his constant friend, Joseph Severn; his memorial was written by Shelley in *Adonais*; his immortality is in his poetry.

Before coming to that poetry, to the influences that made it, and to the influence which it has made, and which has increased with the growing years, we may justify this discussion by citing a few of the judgments that have been passed on K.'s work. MM. Legouis et Cazamian, for example, write (*Hist. Lit. angl.*, 1924; p. 1014): '*Hyperion* is an epic poem, in which Keats, emulating Milton on equal terms, attempted a recital of the celestial revolutions of Pagan mythology, as Milton recounted those of the Christian cycle of *Paradise Lost* and *Regained*. The attempt of Keats is bolder and more dangerous, since the elements of interest afforded him by his material are of a yet more austere and less human order. But his imagination, not less forceful than his precursor's, displays a more plastic quality. . . . *L'oeuvre est d'une grandiose majesté*'. Mr. Robert Bridges, poet-laureate since 1913, in an essay written in 1894, and reprinted as an introduction to the Muses' Library edn. of K.'s *Poems*, writes of a quality in the poet ' that is the very seal of his poetic birthright, the highest gift of all in poetry, that which sets poetry above the other arts; I mean the power of concentrating all the far-reaching resources of language on one point, so that a single and apparently effortless expression rejoices the aesthetic imagination at the moment when it is most expectant and exacting, and at the same time astonishes the intellect with a new aspect of truth. This is found only in the greatest poets, and is rare in them; and it is no doubt for the possession of this power that Keats has often been likened to Shakespeare, and very justly, for Shakespeare is of all poets the greatest master of it'. Prof. C. H. Herford (*C.H.E.L.*, vii, 84ff.) says, in words echoed by the Fr. writers above: ' In the story of *Hyperion* he found a theme equal in its capacity for epic grandeur to that of *Paradise Lost* ', and he ' was not at all points at a disadvantage in his bold rivalry with Milton. . . . It would be rash to say what in poetry would have been beyond the reach of one who, at twenty-five, compels the comparison with Shakespeare and Milton, and yet, deeply as he came under their spell, was lifted by their genius only into more complete possession of his own '. And sir Sidney Colvin (*op. cit.*, 219) rather under-estimates than otherwise the influence of K. on later poetry when he writes, that Tennyson (q.v.) was ' the heir of Keats and Wordsworth in almost equal degrees. After or together with Coleridge, Keats has also contributed most, among English writers, to the poetic method and ideals of Rossetti and his group. Himself, alike by gifts and training, a true child of the Elizabethans, he thus stands in the most direct line of descent between the great poets of that age and those of our own day' (written in 1887).

One more note in explication is necessary, *Hyperion: a Fragment* (3 bks., unfind.;

357 + 391 + 136 lines) was publd., as we saw, 1820; *The Fall of Hyperion: a Vision* (2 cantos, unfind.; 444 + 62 lines), all in blank verse, was publd., as we remarked, by lord Houghton, the first biographer of K., in the *Miscellanies of the Philobiblon Soc.*, vol. iii, 1856. It was reprinted in the second, 1867, edn. of Houghton's *Life and Letters* of the poet, with the words, ' I have no doubt that it was the first draft ' of *Hyperion*; and this opinion held for 20 years, when sir S. Colvin successfully disputed it in the vol. quoted above. The MS. of the *Fall* is not extant, but a transcript made in 1833-4 was discovered, 1904, in the library of lord Houghton's successor, lord Crewe, and was used by prof. E. de Sélincourt in his edn. of K.'s *Poems*, 1905. The fact that the *Fall* is a revision of *Hyperion* is now established beyond dispute. K. was engaged in remodelling the poem in Nov. and Dec., 1819; and, though ' it betrays the impending failure of his powers, it is of surpassing interest as an index to the ways of his mind. There is little doubt that, from Milton, he had passed, during 1819, to a renewed study of Dante (in Cary's transln.). In the pregnant symbolism of *The Divine Comedy*, he found a mode of expressing ideas more akin to his own than Milton's austere grandeur. . . . Though the *Fall* does not approach *Hyperion* in sustained splendour, and diverges from it, in the passages common to both, mostly for the worse, yet it contains some lines which he never surpassed; and his attempt to charge the myth with a richer and deeper import . . . justifies the surmise that, had his powers not failed, he might have given to England a poem more nearly comparable than any other with Goethe's *Faust* ' (Herford, *C.H.E.L.*, xii, 86). So, this consumptive son of a London ostler, who started life as a surgeon's apprentice, and who died before he was 26, crowned European lit. with poetry, which commands the admiration, and demands the study, of readers of Dante, Spenser, Shakespeare, Milton, Goethe, Wordsworth, Tennyson and Rossetti.

There is little to add to this preparation for K. *Sleep and Poetry*, 1817, was remarkable for its revolt from the disciples and ' name of one Boileau ' (q.v.), selected as typical of the standards of the 18th cent., and for the young poet's resolve to pursue the chariot of Apollo:

There ever rolls
A vast idea before me, and I glean
Therefrom my liberty; thence too I've seen
The end and aim of Poesy.

Endymion, ' the stretched metre of an antique song ' (Shakespeare, *Sonnet* xvii), as K. called it, was inscribed by him to the memory of Chatterton (q.v.). It is complete in 4 bks. of heroic couplets and occasional songs (992 + 1023 + 1033 + 1003 lines), and, while it was roughly reviewed, in the *Quarterly Review*, for example, K. himself, in a letter of 9 Oct., 1818, proved his own best critic: ' My own domestic criticism ', he said, ' has given me pain without comparison beyond what *Blackwood* or the *Quarterly* could inflict. . . In *Endymion* I leaped headlong into the sea, and thereby have become better acquainted with the soundings, the quicksands, and the rocks, than if I had stayed upon the green shore, and piped a silly pipe, and took tea and comfortable advice. I was never afraid of failure; for I would sooner fail than not be among the greatest '. This is the full reply to the half-political attitude of Lockhart (q.v.) towards the Cockney (q.v.) School of Poetry, and disposes finally of the old tradition, fostered partly by Byron, that K. was killed by the *Quarterly*, ' so savage and tartarly '. The opening verse of *Endymion*, by the way, is the familiar line : ' A thing of beauty is a joy for for ever '. It is by his shorter poems, rather than by *Lamia, Isabella* (a story from Boccaccio, q.v.), *The Eve of St. Agnes*, or even *Hyperion* itself, that K. lives in the hearts and on the lips of his countrymen : by the great odes, *To a Nightingale, On a Grecian Urn, To Autumn* and *On Melancholy* ; and by the great sonnets, such as ' When I have fears that I may cease to be ', ' Standing aloof in giant ignorance ', ' Fame, like a wayward girl, will still be coy ', ' To one who has been long in city pent ', ' Much have I travelled in the realms of gold ', ' The poetry of earth is never dead ', ' Good Kosciusko, thy great name alone ', etc. But this most Shakespearean of our poets deserves and receives the amplest study. The philosophy of the art which K. taught by practice is best expressed by prof. J. A. Stewart, in a noble passage in the Introduction to his *Myths of Plato* (1905 ; p. 35). There he writes : ' The chief end of poetry is to induce Transcendental Feeling in the Poet's patient by throwing him suddenly, for a moment, into a state of dream-consciousness, out of a waking consciousness which the Poet supplies with objects of interest ; the sudden lapse being effected in the patient by the communication to him of images and other products of the Poet's dream-consciousness through the medium of language'. This is the effect of K.'s poetry at its height, and K., like Spenser before him, is accounted among poets' poets for his vision through the

> Casement ope at night
> To let the warm Love in !
> *Ode to Psyche* ;

—one of the

> magic casements, opening on the foam
> Of perilous seas, in faëry lands forlorn.
> *To a Nightingale.*

Keble, John (1792-1866) : Engl. poet and divine ; fellow, 1811, and tutor, 1818-23, of Oriel Coll., Oxford, a hive of religious revival ; prof. of Poetry, 1831-41, his lectures in the chair being delivered in Lat. K.'s famous vol. of verse, *The Christian Year*, was publd. anon., 1827, but its authorship was no secret, and it achieved and retains immense success. Newman (q.v.) ' once laughingly said that it was the *fons et origo mali* ' (*C.H.E.L.*, xii, 264). The *malum*, of course, was the Oxford Movement (q.v.) to Anglo-Catholicism, which went Romewards with Newman himself, and which came from France (see s.v. Chateaubriand), from Germ. romanticism, and from its influence on Scott (q.v.), with his deep interest in the Middle Ages. Its Engl. start was in Oxford, 1833, where K., on 14 July, preached the Assize sermon on ' National Apostasy ', denouncing the liberal and Erastian (s.v. Erastus) tendencies of the age. ' I have ever considered and kept the day as the start of the religious movement of 1833 ' (Newman, quoted in Walker, *Age of Tennyson*, Bell, 145). In the following Sept. began the *Tracts for the Times* (hence, Tractarian epithet), of which K. wr. seven. Wr. too, *Lyra Innocentium, Life of bp. Thomas Wilson*, etc. A true poet and a man of saintly vision, K. is correctly said by prof. Walker (*loc. cit.*) to have stepped into his historic position at the head of the Anglo-Catholic movement by ' little more than an accident : He was like a child who by a thrust of his hand sends a finely-poised rock thundering down a hill '.

Keller, Gottfried (1819-90) : Swiss novelist. Wr. *der grüne Heinrich*, 1855, largely autobiographic ; ' the type of novel which began with *Agathon* and *Wilhelm Meister*, and passed through the hands of the Romanticists, seems to have reached a close with *der grüne Heinrich* ' (Robertson, *Hist. Germ. Lit.*, 581). This type of novel, in its passage from Goethe (q.v.) to K., played a large part in the development of national Germ. fiction. Later, K. specialized in short stories (*Novellen*), writing the *Zuricher Novellen*, 1878, and *Sinngedicht*, 1882 ; he ranks as a master in that very exacting kind.

Kellgren, Johan Henrik (1751-95) : Swed. poet and arbiter of poetry ; right-hand man to king Gustavus iii (q.v.), in the Fr. revival of Swed. letters. (The Swed. Academy was founded, 1786). K. assisted his royal master in his dramatic ambitions ; but his own work in poetry was mainly lyrical. His great authority was exercised through the medium of the *Stockholm Post*, which he edited from 1778, and which speedily became the leading literary organ in Sweden. K.'s death before he was 45, and in the midst of the transition from Fr. Voltairean to Fr. Rousseauan influences, was deeply deplored.

Kemble, -i. Roger (1721-1802) : Engl. actor ; progenitor of a large family, whose association with the stage did much to enhance appreciation of Engl. dramatic lit.

-ii. **John Philip** (1757-1823) : Engl. actor ; eldest son of above ; manager of Drury Lane theatre, 1788-1802 ; Covent Garden, 1803-8 ; and, again, after its rebuilding, 1809, when he raised the prices of seats, with consequent riots. J.P.K. adapted many Shakespearean plays for the modern stage, and was a chief founder of the declamatory school of acting.

-iii. **Sarah** (1755-1831) : Engl. actress ; sister of above ; m. Wm. Siddons, 1773 ; her chief part was lady Macbeth.

-iv. **George Stephen** (1758-1822) : Engl. actor ; brother of above ; wr. *Odes, Lyrical Ballads*, and *Poems*, 1809.

-v. **Charles** (1775-1854) : Engl. actor ; brother of above ; played Norval in Home's (q.v.) *Douglas*, and many comic parts, including Falstaff.

-vi. **John Mitchell** (1807-57) : Engl. scholar ; son of above ; studied philology under J. Grimm (q.v.), and made important contributions to Anglo-Saxon history and lit.

-vii. **Frances Anne** (1809-93) : Engl. actress ; sister of above ; Fanny Kemble ; m. P. Butler, 1834 ; played Shakespearean parts, and gave Shakespearean readings.

-viii. **Adelaide** (d. 1879): Engl. singer; memoirist; sister of above; m. E. J. Sartoris, 1843; wr. *A Week in a French Country House*, 1863, etc.

Ker, Wm. Paton (1855-1923): Engl. critic; held chairs of lit. at various univs., but was very far, in his charm, magnetism and versatility, from the conventional type of a prof. Wr. *Epic and Romance*, 1896; *P.E.L.*, i, 1904; *Essays on Medieval Lit.*, 1905, and other works of rare brilliance and distinction.

Kerner, Andreas Justinus (1786-1862): Germ. poet. K. was a physician by calling (though blindness in late life compelled him to abandon his profession), and a mystic by taste. An intimate friend of Uhland (q.v.), a member of the so-called Swabian school, and, like Uhland, attracted to poetry through folksong, K. was more sentimental-romantic by temperament, and some of his *Gedichte* (1826; enlarged, 1854) strike a very clear note of true poesy. 'Wohlauf! noch getrunken' is a favourite lyric. Another favourite is the one beginning 'Poesie ist tiefes Schmerzen', which may be paralleled from Heine (q.v.), and may be compared with the concluding stanzas of Tennyson, *In Mem.*, xix,—a genuine recurring lyric note. In 1826, K. treated a villager for somnambulism, and the case appealed to his interest in the borderland of sense-perception. Out of the case-paper he constructed his strange, famous *Seherin von Prevorst* (1829), 'the Seer (witch) of Prevorst: Investigations into the Inner Life of Man and the Intrusion of a Spirit-World into our own'.

Kheraskov, Michael (1733-1807): Russ. poet and novelist; freemason; composed odes, dramas, novels, etc., more distinguished by quantity than by quality, and provided the new lit. of his country with two specimens of the Fr. neo-classic epic poem (epopee) in his *Rossiad*, 1779, and his *Vladimir*, 1785. From internal evidence of careful construction on the model of Voltaire's (q.v.) *Henriade*, and from the external evidence of the gap filled by this experiment, it is clear that K. approached his task with a certain conscious sense of supplying a felt want. Other kinds of lit. had been constructed; it was time that Russia, too, should begin to epicize. The *Rossiad* is the better performance of the two, and Karamsin (q.v.) had nothing finer to bring to Lavater's (q.v.) notice as representing contemporary Russ. lit. Still, as Brückner writes (*Gesch. d. Russ. Lit.*, 118): 'a couple of proper names in it are Russian; all the rest is Voltaire, Tasso, and Virgil'. K. tried his hand, too, at novels, of a very languid and wearisome sort, based on the example of Fénelon's (q.v.) *Télémaque*, of which several Russ. versions had been issued. The first of these was *Numa Pompilius*, 1768, followed by *Cadmus and Harmonia*, 1786, and *Polydore, Son of Cadmus*, 1794. The mystic element deepened in K.'s later works, and his freemasonry (so offensive to the empress Catherine, q.v.) brought him into disfavour; but his name is always to be remembered among the fathers of modern Russ. lit.

Khomyakov, Aleksey Stepanovich (1804-60): Russ. poet; leader of the Slavophil, or conservative camp, as opposed to the Westernizers, or reformers. (See s.vv. Russ. lit.; Herzen). Wr. theological tractates, and was a debater of unrivalled skill, whose services were freely at the disposal of the orthodox. Wr., too, tragedies of no note, and lyric verse of real feeling and musical power, inspired by a sane and genuine patriotism.

Kielland, Alexander (1848-1906): Norse novelist. Wr. *Little Novels*, 1879, which contained all the promise of delicate satire, restrained humour, and clever character-drawing, which was realized in full measure in his subsequent single novels: *Labouring People*, 1881; *Skipper Worse*; *Poison*; *Snow*; *St. John's Eve*; *Jacob*, etc. There is more than a touch of Daudet's (q.v.) exquisite style in K., and he conferred high services on the Norw. language, which he used more skilfully than many as a medium for fiction of the Fr. type. It should be added that K.'s social satire, though not less keen than that of the contemporary greater masters, Ibsen and Björnson (qq.v.), was directed more steadily at its objective, and never swamped observation in didactic purpose.

Kierkegaard, Sören Aaby (1813-55): Dan. philosopher; in sheer force of thought, the greatest Dane of the 19th cent. We are not here concerned with any comparative estimate of K.'s contributions to philosophy; though it is within our province to note that his influence, undervalued in his lifetime, became effective in later years, when the zest of patriotism and nationality, the strength of the individualist perception, and the wars for right and freedom brought K.'s deeply-wrought speculations into higher relief. He belongs to that little band of fastidious and twice-refined thinkers, who, like Pascal (q.v.) in the 17th cent., and like Renan (q.v.) in the 19th, cleared the air at successive epochs in France. And, like Renan, K. may be charged with a share in the making of the doctrines which Nietzsche (q.v.) brought to maturity. These matters do not belong to lit., but we should add that the close of K.'s life was marked by bitter controversy on the subject of Christian ethics. His first and perhaps his best work was *Enten-Eller* ('Either-Or'), 1843, publd. under the pen-name of Victor Eremita, in which the rival claims of ethical and æsthetic principles of conduct were explored and contrasted; a series of aphorisms, or loosely connected prose-poems of rare beauty in diction, was prefixed to the æsthetic exposition. A second work in the same kind, as distinct from more definitively philosophical writings, was *Stadia on Life's Way*, 1845, publd. under the pen-name of Hilarius Buchbinder. In the following years, K. acknowledged the authorship of these masterworks, which he used in connection with his later polemical and theological writings.

Kiev: first capital of Russia; as such, founded by the Norse invaders of Western Russia, who arrived effectively in 862, under Rurik the Viking. They came on a roving mission of trade and conquest, and gave names and rulers to the Slavs. From the 10th to the 13th cent., at the time of the Mongolian (Tartar) incursion, when Kiev was destroyed, 1240, the struggle for the possession of that city and of the waterways of commerce which it commands on the Dnieper, is the key to medieval Russ. history. Thus, K. ' was the mother of Russian culture '. Like another Troy, battles innumerable raged around it, till the Vaerings, Varangians, or Northmen, were merged in the Slavs. Chief of the most interesting relics of medieval K. are the Chronicle of Nestor (q.v.) and the prose-poem of the raid of Igor (q.v.), written by a contemporary of that prince of Novgorod, 1185-7. After 1240, K. gradually declined and sank into a kind of torpor till the 17th cent., when its system of education, based on the teachings of the Society of Jesus (q.v.), and its Lat.-Polish culture attracted the attention of more backward cities in Russia, and K. was invited to send its missionaries of culture to the new capital, Moscow. The more cosmopolitan Europeanism of the emperor Peter the Great closed the second period of K.'s primacy.

King, Henry (1592-1669): Engl. poet; divine; bp. of Chichester, 1642. K.'s poems are included in the *Caroline Poets* by prof. G. Saintsbury, who sums him up as a Donne (q.v.) *in usum vulgi*, and they have recently been edited by Mr. John Sparrow (Nonesuch Press, 1925). The gold in the dross, though of true quality, is very slight in quantity.

Kingis Quair. See s.v. **James i.**

Kingo, Thomas (1634-1704): Dan. sacred poet; half Scot. by descent. Wr. the *Spiritual Choir* in two parts, 1674 and 1681, and contributed many metrical versions to the national psalter of Denmark, which is named after him. K.'s verses, says prof. Elton (*P.E.L.*, viii, 357) ' are part of the Danish soul. His buoyant lines belie his favourite mood of penitence, and his tide of energy, fed from the heart, bears him up from his ashes into a superb flight of triumph '.

Kingsley, -i. Charles (1819-75): Engl. poet, novelist, social reformer; curate (later, rector) of Eversley, Hants, 1842; canon of Westminster, 1873; prof. of modern history, Cambridge, 1860-9; joined his ' dear **Master** ', F. D. Maurice (q.v.) and the Christian Socialist group, 1848, when he was lecturer in Engl. lit. at Queen's Coll. for Women, Harley Street, London; wr. as ' Parson Lot ' in *Politics for the People* and the *Christian Socialist*, displaying prominently in these writings (and likewise in *Yeast* below) a powerful influence derived from Carlyle (q.v.) in his prophetic mood; engaged in controversy with Newman (q.v.), whose *Apologia*, 1864, was a reply to K. In pure lit., K. is best known as the author of *Water Babies*, 1863, and of the hist. novel, *Westward Ho!* 1855. Each is a masterpiece in its kind, and K.'s other bks. group themselves round these excellent examples of his interest in natural and human history, combined by a moral purpose for instruction and entertainment. They include *The Saints' Tragedy*, a drama, 1842; *Yeast*, 1848; *Alton Locke*, 1850; *Hypatia*, 1853; *Glaucus, Wonders of the Sea-shore*, 1855; *Two Years Ago*, 1857; *Hereward the Wake*, 1866. An art. in *The Times* newspaper (23 Jan., 1925, the 50th anniversary of K.'s death) analysed his gifts very skilfully, and, incidentally, disturbed the judgment which had insisted too

much on his ' muscular Christianity '. ' Kingsley was too full of thought for his fellow-men to be interested in his own courage and gaiety. He had all the sensibility of a poet. One of his best and most famous poems, " Three fishers went sailing away to the West ", was born of the turmoil which shook him after he had been publicly rebuffed by a brother clergyman. A poet he was. Perhaps baron Bunsen and others of his friends were right; if he had kept to poetry he might have been a great poet ! But he did not believe that any art was his proper means of giving the world of his best. The sensibility of the poet he turned to the service of the afflicted; the wonder of the poet he indulged in his studies of natural science. This attitude of mind had its effect also upon his novels. Parish priest, poet, sportsman, professor of history, theologian, novelist, naturalist, he was an eager worker in all these fields. He was supreme in none of them, because all of them seemed to him contributory to a higher task. That task was social service '.

-ii. George Henry (1827-92): Engl. traveller and scholar; brother of above, who drew him as Tom Thurnall in *Two Years Ago*. Wr. *South Sea Bubbles*, 1872.

-iii. Henry (1831-76): Engl. novelist; brother of above. Wr. *Geoffrey Hamlyn*, 1859; *Ravenshoe*, 1861; and 14 others; war-correspondent (at Sedan), 1870-71. H.K. was less successful in his appeal to the public than his eldest brother, but, in the opinion of some critics, his was the more original talent and the higher artistic power of the two.

-iv. Mary Henrietta (1862-1900): Engl. traveller and author; daughter of G.H.K. above. Wr. *Travels in West Africa*, 1897, a very fine and stimulating travel-record of observation of primitive habits, esp. in the moral sphere; died of enteric fever, contracted as a nurse in third Boer War.

Kinkel, -i. Johann Gottfried (1815-82): Germ. poet and critic; condemned to imprisonment for life after the revolutionary rising in Baden, but escaped, 1850, from the fortress of Spandau with the help of Karl Schurz, subsequently an agitator in America. K. took refuge in London, where, as later at Zurich, he taught the history of art. His epical *Otto der Schütz*, 1846, was a ' best seller ' in its day, but the day has passed, and ' his talents were hardly in proportion to his popularity '.

-ii. Johanna (1810-1858): Germ. novelist, *née* Mathieu; wife of above; wr. *Hans Ibeles in London*, an excellent story of Germ. refugees in Engld., of whom there was a large colony after 1848. The husband and wife publd. a vol. of stories jointly (1850).

Kinker, Johannes (1764-1845): Dutch critic and philosopher. Wr. some notable parodies of the romantic-sentimental school of Germanizing novelists, and was instrumental in spreading the study of Kant (q.v.) in the Netherlands.

Kirchmayer, Thomas (1511-63): Germ. Latinist; known as Neogeorg. Pastor of Sulza, in Thüringen, 1536-44; took prominent part in religious wars, and ranked, after Hütten, Murner (qq.v.) and other front-rank leaders, as firebrand and freelance of Protestant

Reformation ; twice withdrew from Germany, and died outside its frontier. Wr., 1553, *Regnum Papisticum* (' The Papal Realm '), a colossal piece of polemical verse, transld. into Engl. by Barnabe Googe (q.v.) ; *Agricultura Sacra*, 1560 (a ' Book of Spiritual Husbandry '), also famous in Engl. version, discussing the cultivation of the soul in the style of Virgil's *Georgics* on the cultivation of the soil (note his Lat. name, Neogeorg) ; best known as writer of Lat. plays, according to the fashion of his times : *Pammachius, Pyrgopolinices, Mercator, Haman, Jeremiah, Judas Iscariot.* The general characteristic of these dramas is strength, even vehemence, in the delineation of good and evil qualities ; unlike Birck (q.v.), whose genius was constructive, and sought to repair for his contemporaries the pattern of civic virtue, K.'s aim and genius were destructive, and were directed against the papal Antichrist and the misrule of Rome. As a powerful, bitter, and combative champion of these ideas, K.'s dramas exercised great influence on the formation of Lutheran thought in Northern Europe, including Engld., where they were speedily produced. The taste for theological stage-spectacles and argument is dead to-day, and should, perhaps, bury its dead ; but, historically, and, in a less degree, dramatically, a high place in lit. is claimed by the Protestant fighting-drama, *Pammachius*, which K. inscribed to the archbp. of Canterbury and which ' is in a sense the representative drama of the Reformation era ' ; pope Pammachius, Antichrist, allies himself with the Infernal Powers, as a protest against the policy of ecclesiastical persecution, which the emperor Julian renounces. Again, *Pyrgopolinices* was directed against duke Henry of Brunswick (q.v.). K., like other and great masters, is particularly effective in the presentation of Satan and his associates. But the most dramatic touch in the drama was, perhaps, Act v, described as the second coming of Christ. As this advent remains unaccomplished, K. merely told his audience to expect no fifth Act.

Klaj, Johann (1616-56) : Germ. poetaster. Associated with Harsdörffer (q.v.) in the foundation of the Pegnitz Shepherds (q.v.), literary society at Nuremberg ; applied the mechanic arts of Opitz (q.v.) with dire results to the Passion-plays.

Kleist, von, Christian Ewald (1715-59) : Germ. poet ; Pomeranian ' Junker ' (country squire) by birth, and Prussian officer by profession. K. was drawn into the literary circle so congenial to his character and temperament through the intervention of Gleim (q.v.). He planned a long poem, ' The Love of the Land ' (*Landlust*), of which only one part, ' Spring ' was completed, and which follows the lines of nature-description adapted by Brockes and Haller (qq.v.) from Thomson (q.v.). The Seven Years' War, in which he fought as major, inspired him with his *Ode* to the Prussian Army, 1757 ; a fine soldier's cry of honour or death. He met death on the field of honour 24 Aug., 1759, twelve days after the battle of Kunersdorf. And his character is drawn (at least as closely as John Wordsworth's in his brother's *Happy Warrior*) as Tellheim in Lessing's (q.v.) *Minna von Barnhelm.*

Kleist, von, Heinrich (1777-1811) : Germ. dramatist and novelist. The recognition of K.'s great gifts as a patriot-poet of his Fatherland (' the most original dramatist that North Germany has ever produced ', says J. G. Robertson, *Hist. Germ. Lit.*, 434) came too late to reward him in his lifetime. Even some of his most notable masterpieces were not issued till ten years after his death, when Tieck (q.v.) publd. his literary remains. His own temperament was against him, and the spirit of the age in which he lived. A poet by disposition, fate made him a soldier, and his finest soldierly qualities were broken and wasted on the barren rock of Napoleon's rule in Prussia : ' he, too, no less than the thousands who died on the fields of Leipsic and Waterloo, must be numbered among the martyrs for freedom and right ' (Francke, *Social Forces in Germ. Lit.*, E.T., 484) ; and, in the bitter end, missing national glory and personal renown, he shot his mistress and himself on a November day at Potsdam. His three greatest plays were *Käthchen von Heilbronn, Die Hermannsschlacht*, and *Prinz Friedrich von Homburg. Käthchen* (' Little Katie '), 1810, was a Ritterdrama (q.v.) of the medieval-fighting type. Katie loves a knight, Wetter von Strahl, with simple, uncompromising devotion, tried even by ordeal of fire, and since she is finally recognized as the daughter of the Kaiser, she is wedded to her knight. The pathos and charm of the piece are of a very high order. *Hermann* (see s.v. Arminius), 1808, publd. 1821, was the common quarry of Germ. patriotic revivalists, and K. used the old setting of Varus in the 1st cent. to point the moral of Napoleon in the 18th ; it was by audiences after the Franco-Prussian war of 1870-71 that the appeal of this tragedy was most fully admitted. ' The Prince of Homburg ', 1810, publd. 1821, was Kleist himself, a kind of Hamlet-figure of indecision, in the hist. surroundings of the Great Elector of Brandenburg in the second half of the 17th cent. It is by this play esp. that K. takes his place in the first rank of hist. dramatists. His other works included romances, of which *Michael Kohlhaas* is the most powerful and realistic ; a village-interior comedy, ' The Broken Jug ', produced without success by Goethe at Weimar, 1808 ; *Amphitryon*, 1807, a comedy after Molière ; *Penthesilea*, a tragic drama ; patriotic hymns, poems, etc. K.'s genius was really in advance of the response of his countrymen to his call.

Klinger, von, Friedrich Maximilian (1752-1831) : Germ. dramatist and novelist. Till 1780, K.'s interests were mainly theatrical, and he worked his way up from very humble circumstances to friendship with Goethe (q.v.) at Weimar. After 1780, his interests were mainly military, and he attained high rank in the Russ. army and war office, and died at Petrograd. K.'s early writings belong to the Sturm und Drang (q.v.) movement, to which he had the privilege of acting as godfather, in virtue of his storm-play, *Wirrwarr, oder Sturm und Drang* (' The Whirl, or Storm and Stress '), 1776. This was a tale of lovers' passion, placed in the appropriate *milieu* of the American War of Independence, and displaying the *obbligato* signs of dialogue broken by emotion, and emotion itself without a bridle. Even more genial of the movement was K.'s tragedy, *The Twins*. Later, at the distance of his new experiences, K. moderated his ecstasies. He wr. two Hellenic dramas in pure prose on the Medea legend, and a series of novels (after 1790), of which the best-known are *The Faust of the East* and *Story of a German of Modern Times*. In these romances K.'s preoccupation with the problem of reality and the ideal was attuned to a finer sense of the universal appeal of his theme.

Klopstock, Friedrich Gottlieb (1724-1803): Germ. poet. Born at Quedlinburg; edu. at Schulpforta and Jena; went to Leipsic, 1746; visited Bodmer (q.v.) at Zurich, 1750; was invited, 1751, by king Fredk. v of Denmark, to Copenhagen, where he resided till 1770; retired to Hamburg, where he died. It was at Hamburg that he received the reverent visit of Coleridge and Wordsworth during their Germ. tour, 1789. When we add that, in 1748, midway between his arrival at Leipsic and his visit to Bodmer, K. publd. the first 3 cantos of his religious epic 'The Messiah' (*Messias*) in the *Bremer Beiträge* (q.v.), it will be clear (see also s.v. Gottsched) that he had definitely ranged himself with the Swiss faction against the Saxon, or, in literary terms, with the Engl. Protestant romanticists against the Francophil neo-classicists in poetic taste. But in truth, K.'s appearance on the horizon marks a pause or a close to these conflicts, domestic and personal as they largely were, and is the date of a new departure in Germ. lit. Whatever K.'s shortcomings, and they are various, he was at least a whole poet, not the partisan adherent to a school of verse; and a perception of this innate superiority was probably, even if not always consciously, at the bottom of the enthusiasm and adulation with which the author of the *Messias* was greeted, when the *Bremer Beiträge* issued its first portion. Bodmer wr. to Gleim (q.v.) that Milton's spirit rested on the new poet; Wieland (q.v.), weeping tears of joy, extolled the new Milton above Homer and Virgil (it is to be added that this extravagant eulogist was then but 15 years of age and lived to alter his view); others called K. an embodied seraph; and there is the famous passage in Goethe's youthful work, where the spectacle of a thunderstorm from the window causes Werther and his Lotte to call on the name, not of Nature, or Romance, or the Almighty, but, simply and sufficiently, of 'Klopstock', as the complete expression of their mood of exalted feeling. Time has moderated these transports, and has referred the inspiration of the *Messias* to its proper source in *Paradise Lost* (transld. by Bodmer, 1732), and to the current melancholy and sentimentalism reflected in Gellert (q.v.) and other Germ. writers from Thomson, Young and Richardson (qq.v.), and has ranged it more definitely with the oratorios of Bach and Händel than with the epic of poesy. The praises, too, have been abated with the recognition that the epic setting of the *Messias* lacks the action and the characterization without which the form is null. K.'s instinct and temperament chose the way of theology and pietism instead of that of anthropology and dramatic insight. But despite the deductions of time, the detractations of critics, and the incontrovertible weariness of modern readers, this epic, which K. meditated as a schoolboy (wavering, like Milton, between the sacred subject and a subject founded in national tradition), and which he did not complete, in its 20 cantos and about 20,000 lines, till 1773, is a great work in its place and in all places. The choice of metre alone was epoch-making, or, in the milder Germ. phrase, *bahnbrechend*, road-breaking. K. abandoned the Fr. alexandrine for the classical hexameter verse; and, at least, he started with a swing—

Singe, unsterbliche Seele, der sündigen Menschen Erlösung,
die der Messias auf Erden in seiner Menschheit vollendet.

Sing, O spirit immortal, of sinful mankind's redemption,
Which the Messiah on earth in his garb of manhood accomplished.

The intensity and sublimity of the first 3 cantos of the poem were hardly sustained till the last; but the ardour and grandeur of the design lifted Germ. reflective poetry on the powers and rights of man to a new level of ambition and endeavour below which it could never sink again. K. wr., too, patriotic odes in the rhymeless classical metres in which Pyra and Lange (qq.v.) had experimented; and the example of Macpherson's (q.v.) *Ossian* (Engl., 1762; Germ., 1764) inspired this great Germ. patriot to revive on Germ. soil the gods and heroes of old Germania. To this end he wr. a prose trilogy of bardic dramas (s.v. Barditus,) revolving round the heroic figure of Hermann (s.v. Arminius). Some Biblical plays complete the tale of his writings. In a sense K. survived his own fame; or, rather, the tendencies of Germ. lit. moved on more quickly than he followed them; and the societies founded in his honour made plain the need of a clearer gospel (see s.v. Hain). But he stands at the close of the long period of preparation since Luther's day, and at the head of the harvesting-time into which his own life extended.

Knapp, Albert (1798-1864): Germ. sacred poet; wr., chiefly, *Christliche Gedichte*, 1829, 'in which religion for once does not overpower poetry' (*P.E.L.*, xi, 301).

Knigge, von, Adolf (1752-96): Germ. novelist and popular-philosopher. Wr. 'Story (*Roman*) of my Life' and other Richardsonian fiction, and a work on social intercourse (*über den Umgang mit Menschen*, 1788), which was frequently reprinted and still possesses sociological value.

Knight, William Angus (1836-1916): Scot. scholar; entered Free Church ministry, but cut the knot of ecclesiastical controversy, in connection, severally, with Colenso, Tyndall and Martineau, by resigning his pastorate. K. was appointed, 1876, to the chair of moral philosophy at the univ. of St. Andrews, where he lectured, too, on political economy; but his renown rests on his Wordsworthian studies. Wr. *Life* and edited *Poetical* and *Prose Works* of Wordsworth (q.v.); wr., too, *English Lake District* (where K. himself resided many years and died), *Dove Cottage*, etc., and lived to issue a vol. of war-verse, *Pro Patria et Rege*, 1915. K. was, perhaps, rather an industrious than an accurate or a brilliant editor, but students of Wordsworth unite in acknowledging a deep debt of gratitude to his almost pioneer labours.

Knolles, Richard (*c.* 1550-1610) : Engl. historian. Wr. *General History of the Turks*, 1604 ; frequently republished. Transld. *Commonweale* from Fr. of Bodin (q.v.), 1606 ; provided early example of excellence in prose style in Engl.

Knowles, James (1831-1908) : Engl. publicist ; edited *Contemporary Review*, 1870-77 ; founded *Nineteenth Century Review*, 1877, and edited it till his death ; K.C.V.O., 1903. At the turn of the century, the words *And After* were added to the title of the *Review*. K., who was brought up as an architect, and designed Aldworth for Tennyson (q.v. ; Tennyson inaugurated the *Review* with a prefatory sonnet, written 'in this roaring moon of daffodil and crocus '), proved a brilliant editor, and the *Nineteenth Century* was for many years a great force in periodical lit. It was particularly K.'s aim always to have one or more very eminent names in his contributors' list, and Gladstone, Huxley and others were frequently drawn upon. K.'s name occurs, accordingly, in most of the biographies of the day. A kind of inner circle (a *Cénacle*, q.v.) was formed by him in the Metaphysical Society (q.v.), which he founded, 1869, and served as secretary till 1881.

Kock, de, Paul (1794-1871) : Fr. novelist ; of ' the seamy side of lower middle-class life in Paris ' ; a writer to be avoided, though he accumulated a fortune by his bks.

König, von, Ulrich (1688-1744) : Germ. courtpoet ; succeeded Besser (q.v.) as laureate to Frederic Augustus ii at Dresden, an extravagant and luxurious ruler whom K. eulogized in obsequious terms. K. opposed the excesses of the Second Silesian School (q.v.), but his mediocre talent did not restore Germ. poetry to healthy conditions.

Königsberg : Germ. city of literary fame, and, geographically, as a key to the East, of political importance. K. first came to literary significance at the time of the comparative decline of the southern cities during the Thirty Years' War (q.v.). Dach (q.v.), prof. of poetry, 1639-59, founded its literary society, and attracted many disciples. K. and its univ. were later famous as the home and the seat of the teaching of Kant (q.v.).

Körner, -i. Christian Gottfried (1756-1831) : Germ. publicist ; a loyal, intimate and self-sacrificing friend of Schiller (q.v.), and a talented member of the circle of art and letters. K.'s correspondence with Schiller is his best literary monument.

    -ii. Karl Theodor (1791-1813) : Germ. poet ; son of above. K. was a man of great promise and of happy surroundings and disposition, whose gallant death in the ranks of Lützow's volunteers at Gadebusch, where he had rejoined his comrades after an imperfect recovery from a wound, has added a halo to his fame which his actual work can hardly carry. Wr. comedies and tragedies ; the best-known of the latter being *Zriny*, 1812. His

fiery patriotism found expression in verse collected posth. by his father under the title *Lyre and Sword*. It is good, ringing stuff, and K. would have done better.

Kollár, Jan (1793-1852) : Czech poet ; appointed late in life to the chair of Slavonic Archæology in univ. of Vienna. Wr. part-elegiac, part-erotic poem, 'The Daughter of Sláva ', 1824, which enjoyed immense esteem in its own day, and still appeals to the national sense of K.'s countrymen, as an expression in stirring and often emotional verse of the idea of Slavonic solidarity. A specimen may be submitted, in the spirited version of Mr. Paul Selver :

From the treacherous Elbe o'er the plain to
    the Vistula faithless,
    From the Danube until Baltic's insatiate
      foam,
Where the mellifluous tongue of the sturdy
    Slavs once resounded,
    Now it, alas ! is still, silenced by onslaughts
      of hate.
Who has committed this theft, that cries for
    vengeance to Heaven ?
Who has upon one race outraged the whole
    of mankind !
Blush thou for shame, O envious Teuton, the
    neighbour of Sláva,
Many such sins have thine hands often
    committed of old.
Ne'er has an enemy yet shed blood—or ink—
    so profusely,
    As by the German was shed, compassing
    Sláva's decay ;
Worthy of freedom is only he who values all
    freedom,
    He who puts captives in bonds—he is a
    captive himself.

Koltsov, Alexey Vasilievich (1808-42) : Russ. poet ; of peasant orig. and a singer of peasant life, in southern Russia esp. His verse, says Baring (*Russ. Lit.*, ' H.U.L. ', 125), has ' the dignity and truth of Jean François Millet, and his lyrical cry is as authentic as that of Burns ' (q.v.). K.'s range, says Brückner (*Gesch. d. Russ. Lit.*, 221), ' is naturally limited, if there are limits to the steppes which he embraced. But the homeland, the savour of the crops, the swelling of the seed, the harvest-home, are turned into poetry by Koltsov only ; his are Russian idyls, and the artistry of the poets sought their expression in vain '. K. anticipated in folk-verse of romantic texture the note of realism and ruralism which the novel (q.v.) of the next generation was to introduce.

Komenský, Jan Amos (1592-1670) : Czech educational writer ; commonly known as Comenius ; the last bp. of the Unity of the Bohemian Brethren (see s.v. Czech Lit.) ; born in Moravia, where he married, but driven out by Spaniards, 1621, and lost his MSS., and, later, his wife and child. In 1628, K., with the remnant of the Brethren, had to flee his country for ever. He wandered from Poland to Germany, Holland, Engld., Sweden, Hungary, Poland again (where, for the second time, he lost his bks. and MSS., including a Czech and Lat. dict., on which he had worked for many years), finally settling at Amsterdam, where he died. Wr. 1631, *Janua Linguarum reserata* (The Gate of Tongues unlocked), 'which made him and the little Polish town where he lived (Lesno) known throughout Europe and beyond it' (Quick, *Educational Reformers*). It was transld. 'even into Mongolian'. In Engl., 1641-42, K. arrived at one of the rare moments when Parliament was interested in education, and S. Hartlib, a Pole on his father's side, and a friend of Milton (q.v.), tried to seize the moment, in order to institute a coll. of learned men to give effect to the objects of K.'s *Reformation of Schools*. But 'the rumour of the Insurrection in Ireland', says K. (quoted by Masson, *Milton*, iii, 224; reproduced by Quick, *op. cit.*, 127), 'and the plentiful signs of the bloody war about to break out disturbed those plans, and obliged me to hasten my return to my own people'. His *Orbis Sensualium Pictus*, which surpassed and outlived the *Janua*, was publd. in 1657, and belongs to the history of education; 'he struck the key-note to the science of education', we are reminded. The educational reformer was also a prophet-patriot, and K.'s vision in 1650, fulfilled in 1918, of the resurrection of his country is quoted s.v. Czech Lit.

Konrad, von, Würzburg (d. 1827): Germ. romancer; akin to Gottfried (q.v.) of Strassburg, rather than to the first school of chivalric epos (e.g. Wolfram, q.v.), which was more immediately under the spell of the Fr. courtly convention. K. was a fertile poet, of pleasing fancy and graceful style, who showed himself sensible of the appeal of the real world and its actual conditions in contrast to the ideal world of knightly romance. He wr. his epics with the best of them: an unwieldly *Trojan War*, after Bénoît (q.v.); a *Parthenopeus and Meliur* love-story, after another Fr. model; and religious legends, *Alexius*, *Silvester*, etc.: but his chief works were verse-tales, novellistic in form, and realistic or partly hist. in character. *Otto with the Beard* is one, the *Herzmäre*, a folk-tale of the lover's heart, served up to the lady he had loved and left, in another; and the best, perhaps, is *der Welt Lohn*, in which the poet is converted from the world (*Welt*) by seeing her beautiful in front but loathsome behind.

Kortum, Karl Arnold (1745-1824): Germ. satirist. Wr., 1784, comic epic entitled, *The Life, Opinions, and Deeds of Hieronymos Job, candidate*. The by no means kindly ridicule of the sufferings of the candidate in theology under the hands of his examiners, and the exposure of his genius turned to ignorance, are very cleverly hit off, and the poem, popularized as the *Jobsiad*, enjoyed a long vogue.

Kosegarten, Ludwig Theobul (1758-1818): Germ. minor poet; resided many years as pastor in the island of Rügen. Wr. rural idyl, *Jukunde*, 1808, which is the best-known of his well-forgotten writings.

Kotzebue, August von (1761-1819): Germ. playwright. K. is said to have written as many as 211 plays, besides satires, biographies, and other works. He was a native of Weimar, and resided there, 1801-04, not altogether to the delight of Goethe and Schiller (qq.v.). He had acted as theatre-manager in Vienna, and had spent several years in Russia, where he attained high rank in the diplomatic service,

and survived some political adventures. The reputation of these pursued him, and it was partly as a suspected spy and partly as a confessed pro-Russian, and anti-patriot, as young Germany interpreted patriotism, that K. was assassinated at Mannheim by a student Karl Sand. This misdeed had important consequences on the treatment of univ. clubs. and of the liberal movement as a whole, during the reaction, encouraged by Metternich, from the ardour of the Prussian War of Liberation. The ill-fame of K.'s literary anti-patriotism rested briefly on his burlesque of the Romantics in 'The Hyperborean Ass', 1799, directed against the *Lucinde* of F. von Schlegel (q.v.), and others. It rested, too, on K.'s cynical preference of popularity to principle, which marked his writings throughout. His tragedies are forgotten to-day; *Menschenhass und Reue* enjoyed a long vogue, and was familiar in Engld. as 'The Stranger'; among his comedies, by far the best was *die deutschen Kleinstädter*, 1802 (the *Petite Ville* of Picard, q.v., preceded it by a twelve-month), a clever study of Germ. provincial manners, which enriched the language with the name of Krähwinkel (q.v.); but K.'s place in the development of dramatic technique is far higher to-day than his place as a dramatist. His 'name has now passed into a byword for all that is flashy, hollow, and sentimental' (Vaughan, *P.E.L.*, x, 315), and even the eulogistic and pro-Prussian Biese is moved to regret, 'that so gifted and versatile a writer offended the instincts of the public merely for the sake of passing success' (*Deutsche Lit. gesch.*, ii, 285).

Krähwinkel: type of Germ. provincialism; generalized from a character in the drama, *die Deutschen Kleinstädter*, 1802, of Kotzebue (q.v.).

Králové Dvůr: Town in Bohemia, in the church of which a certain Václav Hanka alleged, 1817, that he had discovered a parchment MS. of old Czech poems, dating back to the 13th cent. Later, Hanka and a friend, Linda, similarly discovered another MS. at Zelená Hora (a Bohemian castle), containing fragments of epic from the 9th cent. The alleged finds fitted the needs of research in Czech lit. at the beginning of the 19th cent., and Dobrovský (q.v.) was inclined to accept at least one of them as genuine. The Chatterton (q.v.) of Bohemia enjoyed the esteem of these discoveries for some years, but Gebauer (q.v.) and Masaryk (first president, 1918, of the Czecho-Slovak Republic), at the univ. of Prague, demonstrated finally that both MSS. had been forged by Hanka or his accomplices.

Krasicki, Ignatius (1735-1801): Polish novelist and polyhistor. bp.; 'the true Polish Voltaire' (q.v.), he has been called, 'by the volume and variety of his works as well as by his grace of happy phrase and massive boldness of free thought'. K. was a shining light in the Warsaw circle of men of letters in the 18th cent., and enriched the resources of his native lit. with the first encyclopedias of universal knowledge and universal literary history. He effected a verse transln. of Macpherson's (q.v.) *Ossian*, and wr. several political satires ('Battle of the Monks', 'Battle of the Mice and Rats', 'The Organ', etc.), not of much interest to-day, but valuable in their time and place, in the Voltairean vein. These were inspired by a genuine and fervid patriotism, which found more positive expression in lyric poems, one or more of which are in every school child's poetry-book in Poland. K.'s novels include ' The Adventures of Mr. Nicholas Experience ', which is said to combine effects derived from Defoe (q.v., *Robinson Crusoe*) and Rousseau (q.v., *Emile*), and he was also a prolific author of satires, epistles and fables, based on Lat. exemplars (Juvenal, Horace) : ' among good friends, the dogs devoured the hare ', is one of several of K.'s proverbs which have passed into the folklore of Poland, so apposite was it to political conditions in his much-partitioned country.

Krasiński, Sigismund (1812-59) : Polish poet ; wr. philosophical dramas on history and society : the *Undivine Comedy* and the *Iridion ; Psalms of the Future*, etc. The national preoccupation of the chief men of letters of Poland is illustrated by K., a young aristocrat of high idealism, in an intense degree.

Kretschmann, Karl Friedrich (1738-1809) : Germ. bardic poet (see s.vv. Barditus and Klopstock). Wr., 1769, ' The Song of Rhinegolf the Bard, when Varus was defeated ', followed by the same bard's ' Lament ', which Goethe declared to belong to the rank of Germ. poetry only for the sake of the Rhine and its local names.

Krüger, Johann Christian (1722-54) : Germ. actor and playwright. Friend of Lessing (q.v.) at Leipsic.

Krylov, Ivan Andreevich (1768-1844) : Russ. poet ; dramatist ; fabulist, after the model of La Fontaine (q.v.) ; ' with a rough and popular *bonhomie*, as distinct from the suave *bonhomie* of his exemplar ' (Vogüé, *le Roman Russe*, 25). The final edn. of K.'s fables was publd. in 9 vols., 1843, and they were (and are still to a large extent) the object of enthusiastic admiration. Pushkin (q.v.) described K. as ' le plus populaire de nos poètes '. K. acclimatized the fable (q.v., and see s.v. Gellert) on Russ. soil, and re-equipped old Æsop's happy satire with new and original shafts of wit directed at the foibles and follies of his own place and time.

K.'s laziness or apathy has become proverbial, and he is the type of a character which is itself a type created by a Russ. novelist. The ' Oblomov ' who is the hero of the novel of that name by Goncharov (q.v. ; d., 1891), and who is as well-known in Russia as ' Tartufe ' in France or ' Harold Skimpole ' in Engld., and who, like Skimpole, lived in dressing-gown and carpet-slippers, is commonly identified with K. This, by the way ; more germane to the great fabulist's writings is the high eulogy of an Engl. critic, who says that K. ' has the talisman which defies criticism, baffles analysis, and defeats time : namely, charm ' (Baring, *Russ. Lit.*, 42 ; see, too, the same author's *Landmarks in Russ. Lit.*, 29 ; and *Oxford Bk. of Russ. Verse*, Introduction).

Kyd, Thomas (?1558-1594) : Engl. tragic-playwright and translr. ; a writer of great interest to scientific historians of lit., though not so interesting to the æsthetic critics. K. might be left out altogether from a history by a writer in the latter class, without serious or even obvious loss, yet a writer in the former class would have to invent him, if he were not there. Indeed, for many years (practically, for more than a century after 1602), in a sense, he was not there, and he was invented as author of the *Spanish Tragedie* under the name of ' Smith ', his real name being recovered by a mention of it by Heywood (q.v.), in a quotation of three lines from that play in the *Apology for Actors*. Further, K.'s fame has been overlaid by two contrary imputations, (1), the ' Additions ' by Ben Jonson (q.v.) to the *Span. Tragedie* (in the 4th quarto, 1602, and onwards), which gave the play a fresh lease of life, and probably suggested to Shakespeare a similar redaction of the (lost) *Hamlet* play (see below), and (2) the foisting on the *Span. Tragedie* of a fore-piece (1605) entitled *The First Part* of *Ieronimo, or the Warres of Portugal*, which is little more than a burlesque (by an unknown writer), and of which K. had long to bear the ill-repute. The latest authorities are quite definite as to this false ascription. Prof. F. S. Boas (Oxford edn., 1901) says, that, though there was in 1592 a fore-piece to the *Span. Tragedie*, presumably from the hand of K., the answer to the question whether this quarto has preserved it, ' must, in my opinion, be an unqualified negative . . . Apart from *a priori* assumptions, this quarto of 1605 contains internal proofs of having been written after the seventeenth century had begun '. (K.'s death in 1594 is fixed by a renunciation of probate by his parents, 30 Dec., 1594, discovered by Schick, *Shakespeare Jahrb.*, xxxv ; the *D.N.B.*'s date, ?1595, was anterior to this discovery). K.'s fame has further been injured by the circumstances—obscure and now unimportant—of his arrest (and torture) on a charge of atheism, 1593, which involved proceedings against Marlowe (q.v.) ; but, more pertinently to lit., K. is deprived of just renown by the loss of a *Hamlet*-play, which he may confidently be stated to have written. (See s.v. Ur-Hamlet). If this play were ever recovered (and Boas, *op. cit.*, liii, writes : ' The Ur-Hamlet was written by Kyd, probably in the latter part of 1587, and resembled the *Spanish Tragedie* in style and technique '. See, too, prof. Gregory Smith, in *C.H.E.L.*, v, 159 : ' Kyd's authorship of a *Hamlet* which served as the basis for the Shakespearean *Hamlet* is more than a plausible inference '), K. would come into his own again, and we should learn ' more of Shakespeare's " mind and art " than we could learn from the unravelling of all his collaborated plays ' (prof. Smith, *loc. cit.*) So far, chiefly, what K. is not, or what we cannot write of K. What we know of him is his *Span. Tragedie*, which became ' perhaps the most popular of Elizabethan plays ' (Boas), and which exhibits affinities in construction and plot (even allowing for what was common in that age to Senecan tragedians ; see s.v. Seneca) to the Shakespearean *Hamlet*. It was probably the first of the type, which the greatest dramatist was to make supreme : ' none could exhibit more clearly, and on a broader scale, the union of national and foreign elements than *The Spanish Tragedie* ' (Boas, *ibid.*) ; ' Kyd is the first to discover the bearing of episode and of the " movement " of the story on characterization, and the first to give the audience and reader the hint of the development of character which follows from this interaction. In other words, he is the first English dramatist who writes dramatically ' (Smith, *op. cit.*, 163). We have, too, K.'s transln., of Tasso's (q.v.)

Padre di Famiglia, under the title of *The Householders Philosophie*, and of Garnier's (q.v.) *Cornelie*, under the title of *Cornelia*, 1594, anon., reprinted 1595, after the translr.'s death, ' by Thoma(s) Kid '. Future years are likely to increase the value of K.'s posth. repute.

L

Labé, Louise (1526-66): Fr. poet; ' la belle Cordière ' ; of the Lyonese School (s.v. Scève), and a direct follower of Marot (q.v.). L.'s poems reach a high level of lyrical passion and sincerity, and ' have in places a singular approach to the ring of Shakespeare's sonnets and minor works ' (Saintsbury, *Fr. Lit.*, 152). The comparison with Sappho is safer, and, therefore, more common.

Labiche, Emile (1815-88): Fr. comic dramatist; operettist; leading *boulevardier* (q.v.) of the Second Empire. L.'s earliest characteristic play was the *Chapeau de Paille d'Italie*, 1851 ; this was followed by a long series of frankly entertaining foolery, with a strong undernote of commonsense, correcting and ridiculing the excessive romanticism of the Hugo (q.v.) tradition. Among L.'s better-known pieces may be mentioned : *le Voyage de M. Perrichon*, 1860 ; *l'Affaire de la rue de Lourcine*, 1861 ; and *la Cagnotte*, 1864, which still arouses peals of laughter.

La Boétie, de, Etienne (1530-63): Fr. poet and political philosopher. Wr., 1548 (first publd., 1578) prose-treatise, *de la Servitude volontière*, commonly known by its short title *Contr' Un*, expounding liberal conceptions of government, based on study of Lat. orators ; also poems of no little merit. La B. was fortunate in winning the admiration and friendship of Montaigne (q.v.), through whose good offices he is chiefly remembered to-day. La B. was a Catholic, but his sentiments appealed to the champions of liberty in the Huguenot camp, and Hallam (*Lit. of Europe*, ii, 37) describes him as ' almost a single instance of a thoroughly republican character till nearly the period of the Revolution '.

La Borderie (16th cent.): Fr. poet ; Marotique (see s.v. Marot). Wr. *L'Amie de Cour* (' the mistress of the court) ', defending worldly love in reply to the mystical sentiment of Héroet (q.v.).

La Bruyère, de, Jean (1645-96): Fr. essayist ; character-writer. Was recommended by Bossuet (q.v.), 1684, as tutor in the family of the prince de Condé at Chantilly ; elected to the Academy (q.v.), 1693 ; wr. *Dialogues on Quietism*, in support of his patron, Bossuet ; is famous as the translr. of the *Characters* of Theophrastus (Lesbian philosopher, contemporary of Aristotle, 3rd. cent., B.C.), and as author of similar sketches from his own times. This work, *Les Caractères de Théophraste, traduits du grec, avec les Caractères ou les Moeurs de ce siècle*, was first publd., 1688, and was in its eighth, much enlarged, edn. in 1694, within a few years of which date the epoch of Louis xiv reached its appointed

close in the wars of Marlborough and queen Anne, 1702-13. La B.'s pages, says a recent writer, contain the epitaph of this great age. The portrayal of character in prose, as a separate class or kind of lit., was an obvious development of Montaigne's (q.v.) essay, and formed an easy step from the memoir, the maxim, the personal letter, and the *roman-à-clef* form of fiction, which were all fashionable and current in the *grand siècle* of king Louis xiv. Thus, Theophrastus, who served La B. as model, and whose precedent admitted his disciple to the ranks of the faithful classicists, according to the canons of Boileau (q.v.), was a crutch rather than a staff to his translr. La B., that is to say, did not introduce character-sketches into Fr. lit. because Theophrastus had written them in Gk. ; rather he found in Theophrastus a serviceable example of a class of writing for which Fr. lit. had already prepared itself ; and, in an epoch of conflict between Ancients and Moderns (q.v.), it was as well for an innovating ' Modern ' to appear from behind the screen of an ' Ancient '. The characters or manners of his age, observed from the vantage-ground of the prince of Condé's palace at Chantilly, where La B., when his tutorship was ended, remained as a kind of useful pensioner, enjoyed a double success, ' de scandale ' as well as ' d'estime '. Without the penetration of a maxim-maker, such as La Rochefoucauld (q.v.), who was also a man of the world, La B. had a pointed wit, keen sight, and subtle expression, and his *Caractères* have survived many longer bks. of the period which they helped to mirror. La B.'s classical tastes endowed him with refinement of style, the fault of which lay in the direction of an over-exquisiteness in the search for the adequate and right word. La B. exposed the follies and weaknesses which he observed without any missionary or reforming purpose ; and, though he may rightly be classed among the pessimists, he is remarkable for the depth and tenderness of his outlook on life and death.

La Calprenède, Sieur de ; Gautier de Costes (1609-63); Fr. novelist ; Gascon by birth ; m., 1646, an heiress, Madeleine de Lyée ; was employed at court and on diplomatic missions abroad, and died after a fall from a horse. Wr. from 1635 onwards 10 tragic dramas, which, in the opinion of competent critics (e.g. Koerting, *Geschichte des franz. Romans im xvii Jahrh.*, i, 245), have been unduly eclipsed by Corneille (q.v.) and deserve to be rescued from oblivion. La C.'s fame rests meanwhile on his heroic-romances : *Cassandre*, 10 vols., 1642-45, which the author himself characterized as 'sufficiently long-winded' (*travail d'assez longue haleine*), and which has been computed to be more than 1,000 pages longer than Gomberville's (q.v.) *Polexandre*; even so, La C. recommends his readers to pursue the after-story of his heroine, Statira, Darius' daughter (afterwards, Cassandra), in the historians of antiquity, Plutarch and Q. Curtius, on whom he drew very freely; *Cleopatra*, 12 vols., 1647 (an Elzevir edn. appeared at Leyden, 1648-58), the actual heroine of which is not the Cleopatra of Jodelle, Garnier, Shakespeare (qq.v.) and others, but her daughter of the same name, who is represented as one of 3 children born to the queen by her marriage with Antony after Cæsar's death; La C.'s hist. authorities for this romance included Josephus as well as Plutarch, Suetonius, and the rest; *Faramond*, 7 vols., 1661-63, vols. 7-12 (the completion of the work by Vaumor-ière, q.v.), 1667-70; this work, which dealt with early Frankish legend, was inscribed to king Louis xiv. Despite the inordinate length of La C.'s novels of heroic gallantry (a fault more apparent to-day than in the inter-vening centuries), he occupies an important place, in succession to and by the side of Gomberville (q.v.), in the development of fiction from the *Amadis* (q.v.)-worship of a previous generation to the psychological character-study of later times. The restrain-ing influence of the hist. characters and true background was efficacious in producing a verisimilitude, more or less consistently pursued through all the confusing adventures of the loquacious personages; and La C., even more than his contemporaries, respected the unities (q.v.) of place and time. His works are not read to-day, but he had his reward in the unstinted admiration of La Fontaine, Rousseau (qq.v.), and other great fellow-countrymen; in transln. and imitation by Germany and the Netherlands; in his influence on the Engl. stage, and on such a writer as Mrs. Aphra Behn (q.v.).

La Chaussée, de, Pierre Claude Nivelle (1691 (or 1692)-1754): Fr. dramatist; first writer of *comédie larmoyante* (q.v.), or *drame*, so-called, as distinct from the unmixed dramatic kinds of tragedy and comedy. La C.'s *Fausse Antipathie* was staged in 1733, the year after the *Glorieux* of Destouches (q.v.), which had included scenes of tenderness and sensibility. The motive of the tender or 'weeping comedy' is explained s.v.; here it is enough to point out that La C.'s philosophic experiment had an immediate success, and that, though his plays are deservedly little read to-day, they contri-buted considerably to the development of Fr. drama from the lines of ridicule and satire to those of sentiment and pathos. It was a timely purification of interest to which La C. devoted his talents. He was laughed at by Piron (q.v.), and attacked by Voltaire (q.v.; but Voltaire, wr. comedies of mingled tears and laughter in his *Enfant prodigue* and other plays), and he had affinities to the dramatic work of Lillo and Moore (qq.v.) in Engld.; and by fastening the interest of playgoers on moral problems in domestic circumstances he was obviously making dramatic progress. In 1731,

La C. wr. an *Epître de Clio* against the anti-poetic theorizing of La Motte (q.v.); and his *Fausse Antipathie* was succeeded by *Préjugé à la Mode* (serio-comic, and indebted to the *Philosophe marié* of Destouches, q.v.), 1735, *Mélanide* (wholly pathetic-drama), 1741, *L'Ecole des Mères*, 1744, *la Gouvernante*, 1747, and *l'Homme de Fortune*, 1751.

Laclos, de, Choderlos (1741-1803): Fr. novelist. soldier and man of fashion; stationed, 1769-75, at Grenoble, where, according to Stendhal (q.v.), he had every opportunity of meeting the types immortalized in his novel, *Liaisons dangereuses*, 4 vols., 1784. This novel is written in letters, after the Richardsonian tradition, and, though Baring and Saintsbury differ as to its value (Saintsbury's adverse opinion should be consulted in Pref. to vol. i of his *History of the French Novel*, Macmillan, 1917), it must be accounted an extraordinarily clever specimen of a very salacious type. Written in the age of reason, it precisely represents the logic of the polite art of seduction. Granted these unpleasant premises, the execution by L. of his task is a masterpiece in psychological analysis; and its occasional apophthegms 'would make quite a little sheaf of *Maximes et Pensées*, to stand on that side of La Roche-foucauld which is more remote from Pascal' (see s.vv.; R. Aldington, Pref. to his transln. of *Liaisons*; Routledge, 1924).

Lacordaire, Jean Baptiste Henri Dominique (1802--61): Fr. orator, preacher; accompanied Lamennais (q.v., and see s.v. *Avenir*) to Rome, 1831, and is so far to be accounted a Mennaisian, but readily submitted himself to the authority of the pope, and entered the order of St. Dominic, 1840. L.'s sermons (*conférences*) at Notre-Dame, 1835 and 1843-51, were famous, and he carried the ardour of his spirit to various centres of Catholic France; he was elected to the Fr. Academy (q.v.), 1860, and is to be included among the new makers of romance (q.v.), spreading its outlook to the pulpit.

La Cruz, de, Juana Inez (1651-93): Span. poet; nun. Wr. sacramental *autos* on Calderon's (q.v.) model, and 3 vols. of sacred poetry, showing deep traces of the style of Gongora (q.v.).

La Cruz y Cano, de Ramon (1731-94): Span. playwright; dealt disdainfully with the tedious rival pretensions of the old-Castilian and new-French schools of dramatic art, and wr. plays to tickle the ears of the groundlings; at once frankly and successfully. La C. collected his *Teatro* in several vols., 1786-91, and remarked in his pref., 'Truth dictates, and I hold the pen'. His chief success was scored in short farces, known as *sainetes*; he likewise popular-ized the *zarzuela* (q.v.), or musical comedietta, and kept Madrid smiling for about 30 years. La C. held the stage against all attacks from the champions of correctness; and, when the elder Moratin (q.v.) tried a fall with him, La C. retorted by putting him into a play. 'Bourgeoisement jovial' is Kelly's epithet, and it hits the mark.

La Fare, Marquis de (1644-1712): Fr. poet and memoirist; a friend of the abbé de Chaulieu (q.v.), and, like him, an intellectual representa-tive of the school of *libertins* (q.v.), or free-thinkers, from Rabelais and Montaigne to

Diderot and Voltaire (qq.v.). Unlike Chaulieu, La F. did not know so well where to stop ; or, at least, his sceptical vein was not crossed so happily by epicureanism, and he made a less fortunate venture of his life. Wr. poem to Chaulieu on *la Paresse* (idleness), of which La F. is unkindly, if truthfully, said to have been a master, and memoirs of the *grand siècle*, in which he gave expression to his dissatisfied and critical talents.

La Fayette, de, Marie Madeleine (1634-93) : Fr. novelist ; *née* Pioche de la Vergne, daughter of governor of Havre ; edu. by Ménage, Rapin, Segrais (qq.v.), and others, and grew to charming and intellectual womanhood ; m., 1655, to *comte* François de La Fayette, a man of insignificant character, whose death after some years left her with 2 sons ; later, *c.* 1665, mme. de La F. formed her lasting friendship with the duc de La Rochefoucauld (q.v.), who honoured her as the most ' vraie femme ' of his acquaintance, and of whom she wr., that he gave her ' de l'esprit, mais j'ai réformé son coeur ' (from *Segraisiana* ; see s.v. Segrais, who became secretary to the comtesse, 1672, and lent his name for some of her title-pages). Mme. de La F. was a frequenter of the Hôtel de Rambouillet (q.v.), and a leader of precious (q.v.) society and taste ; she held a *salon* of her own in the rue de Vaugirard, and was *persona grata* with king Louis xiv. Her correspondence with Huet and others has value and literary interest, and she wr., too, two memoirs, i, *de Henriette d'Angleterre*, first wife of Philip, duke of Orleans, and ii, *de la Cour de France*, 1688-89 ; the latter was publd. posth. by her son, 1720. But mme. de La F.'s reputation rests upon her series of novels : *Mademoiselle de Montpensier*, 1660 ; *Zayde*, 1670 ; and *la Princesse de Clèves* (her master-piece), 1677. Her impulse to romance was derived from her admiration of mlle. de Scudéry (q.v.) ; her aim as a novelist was to abbreviate the portentous bulk of that writer ; she stuck very closely to the triangular plot of the husband, the wife, and the wife's lover ; and the result, wholly unforeseen, was to substitute the La Fayette model for the Scudéry model, and to originate (no smaller claim is adequate) the psychological character-novel which was to descend through Lesage, Prévost and Richardson (qq.v.). *Zayde, histoire espagnole*, in the school of Moorish fiction founded in Spain by G. P. de Hita (q.v.), which was issued under the name of Segrais, but was attributed by him to its true author, is less of a departure from the style and school of heroic gallantry than the *Princesse de Clèves*, similarly fathered on to Segrais, and ascribed by one lexicographer to Segrais, mme. de La F. and La Rochefoucauld jointly. The false attribution enabled the true author to discuss the bk. in her letters, and in one of these she wr. (quoted from *Révue des deux Mondes*, Sept., 1880, by Koerting, *Geschichte des franz. Romans im 17ten Jahrh.*, i, 486, n. i) : ' Above all, I find in it a perfect imitation of life at court and of the mode of living there ; there is nothing romanesque or forced about it ; it is not a novel ; it is properly memoirs, and I am told that this was the title first chosen for the volume '. As such, it was attacked by Bussy (q.v.) in his scandalous chronicle *des Gaules*, and it found other detractors ; the more readily, since the scene was placed at the court of king Henri ii, and the author may even have known some old people whose parents may have met the living characters in her hist. romance. Moreover, several of those characters were recognized as drawn from modern life (the duke and the author were among them), in accordance with the prevailing fashion of the *roman-à-clef* (q.v.). A more distinctly literary criticism notes that the *Princesse de Clèves* represents the transposition of a Cornelian (see s.v. Corneille) tragic motive to fiction ; and its realism, if we regard it, not with the weary eyes of the 20th cent., but with eyes that still had not opened to Lesage, Defoe (qq.v.) and the rest, is an indisputable title to fame.

La Fontaine, de, Jean (1621-95) : Fr. poet ; writer of fables ; of middle class orig. and aristocratic tastes ; unable to settle to business or domestic habits, La F. acquired (and, possibly, cultivated) a reputation which may best be characterized as a mixture of what used to be called Bohemianism and ' Harold Skimpole '-ism. In this connection, it is worth noting that La F. styled himself the ' butterfly of Parnassus '. The term is apt in several senses. He fluttered from one flower of fashion to another : the duchesse de Bouillon, madame de Montespan (afterwards mistress to king Louis xiv), and, most assiduously, to madame de La Sablière. He fluttered from one class of writing to another : drama, satire, light verse, romance, etc. ; and his easy and careless habits gave rise to various legends, among which his alleged failure to recognize his son in later life probably grew out of the authentic fact of his abandonment of his wife. At the same time, he was capable of loyalty and attachment, as is proved by his relations with Fouquet (q.v.), the powerful and ambitious minister, whose disgrace in 1661 involved many smaller men (and women) in his downfall. La F., whom Fouquet had pensioned, wr. an ' elegy to the nymphs of Vaux ' (a title of Fouquet's viscounty) after his patron's fall. More literary interest belongs to the quartette of genius in Paris composed by the friendship of Molière, Racine, Boileau and La F. This was commemorated by La F. in his romance, *Psyche*, 1669, where the four friends are represented by Gelaste, Acante, Ariste and Polyphile, in the order mentioned just now. Nor was this friendship interrupted by the episode of 1684, when Louis xiv delayed the election of La F. to the Academy (s.v.) till room had been found in it for Boileau. Happily, a second vacancy occurred, and the king signified his assent in the following terms : ' Your selection of monsieur Despreaux (Boileau) is very agreeable to me, and will meet with universal approval. You may now add La Fontaine to your body : he has promised to behave himself ' (*d'être sage*). The implied rebuke was perhaps due to the licentious tone of La F.'s writings. The ' butterfly of Parnassus ' had sipped his honey from Boccaccio, Ariosto, Rabelais, and others, and his unmoral (rather than immoral) tendency was later the subject of severe comment by Rousseau, for example, and other moralists. At the time, king Louis's attitude may have caused the omission of La F., and, indeed, of the class of writings which he adorned, from Boileau's *Art poétique* ; and La F.'s promise to 'behave himself' may have been observed by his ceasing to compose poems in that particular class. The class in question was the Fable (q.v.), in which, and in the *conte* (or verse-tale), La F. won his undying fame. His *Fables* (1668, 1678) were epicurean, no doubt, but they were only so far licentious or immoral as the passing shows of the human comedy which he dramatized (in a drama of a hundred scenes) displayed these qualities to the spectator. The human-animals in his tales of beast-life are irresistible in their individual truth and in their universal appeal. He took his fables whence he could : from all the fabulists from Æsop to Marot ; but he reflected through their medium the life of Paris in the *grand siècle*, and each fable was etched with unerring skill. La F. was a witness, not a judge or a legislator ; and if he bore witness to self-interest, egoism and guile, this was the fault of the times, not of the fabulist ; of the spectacle, not of the little mirror. The *Fables* and *Contes* of La F. are supreme in the narrative poetry of the 17th cent. for the brilliance of their diction, the high polish of their art, the brevity of their wit, and the success of their lyrical achievement.

Lagerbring, Sven (1707-87) : Swed. historian. His works on the history of his native country, publd. 1769 and 1772, were for many years the classic authorities on the subject.

Lagerlöf, Petrus (1648-99) : Swed. poet and Latinist ; prof. at univ. of Upsala ; historiographer of Sweden. Wr. mainly in Lat. ('Introduction to Swedish Poetry', etc.), his chief writings being first publd. as late as 1780. Among L.'s vernacular poems, the pastoral *Elisandra* is most liked.

La Grange-Chancel, de, François Joseph (1677-1758) : Fr. dramatist. Wr. tragedies in the wake of Racine (q.v.) on classical subjects, characterized by a dead flatness and an avoidance of concrete reality. Wr., too, satires directed against the then duc d'Orleans.

La Harpe, de, Jean François (1739-1803) : Fr. critic and dramatist ; wr. tragedies of little merit, and, later, as member of the Fr. Academy (q.v.), and as prof. of lit., became a somewhat formidable critic on the model of Boileau (q.v.). His chief work in this class was the *Lycée, ou Cours de Littérature, ancienne et moderne*, 1799, which had considerable vogue ; his commentaries on the drama of Racine (1807) and Voltaire (1814) were posth. publd. La H. was imprisoned during The Terror, but was quickly cured of his republican sympathies.

Laisse : Fr. technical term for a block of verses, indefinite in number, of 8 or 10 syllables each (4 or 5 iambic feet), distinguished by a recurring identic vowel-sound in the final foot of each, or, later, by rhyme ; and confined in use to the *chansons de geste* (q.v.). The 'laisse' was also called 'tirade'.

Lake School (Engl.) : Descriptive epithet (Lakers, Lakists, etc.) invented by lord Jeffrey (q.v.), editor of the *Edinburgh Review*, to designate (and deride) a group of poets, including, chiefly Wordsworth, Coleridge, and Southey (qq.v.), who resided from time to time in the lake district in Cumberland. Jeffrey, writing in his own review, Oct., 1802, distinguished a 'sect of poets', displaying the 'anti-social principles of Rousseau' (q.v.), the 'simplicity and energy of Kotzebue and Schiller' (qq.v.), the 'homeliness and harshness' of Cowper (q.v.), 'interchanged occasionally with the innocence of Ambrose Philips or the quaintness of Quarles and Dr. Donne' (see s.vv. ; the immediate occasion of this critique was Southey's *Thalaba*). Byron (q.v.) joined in the attack, which was countered in *Blackwood's Magazine*, by C. North (q.v.), himself a resident at the Lakes, who was supported by Hazlitt, Lamb, Leigh Hunt (qq.v.), and others, for the defence. These Londoner champions of the Lakists whom Jeffrey had lumped in one group, despite their geographical distance, were ungratefully repudiated by Lockhart (q.v.) in *Blackwood*, and were re-distinguished by the name of Cockney (q.v.) School ; but by that time the title of Lake School had been turned from a name of contempt to a name of honour, and it is still in use.

La Marche, de, Olivier (1425-1502) : Fr. court-poet. Wr. *le Chevalier délibéré*, in celebration of Charles the Bold, at the instance of his daughter, queen Mary of Burgundy, to whose court La M. was attached. Queen Mary became the grandmother of the future emperor Charles v, who effected a version of La M.'s heroic poem into Span. prose, and entrusted this to Acuña (q.v.) to render into Castilian poetry as *el Caballero determinado*, 1553. (See, too, s.v. *Teuerdank* and Maximilian i, the husband of queen Mary).

Lamartine, de, Alphonse Marie Louis Prat (1790-1869) : Fr. poet ; statesman ; Prat by birth, de L. by inheritance from a maternal uncle ; a romantic founder (see s.vv. Romance, *Lyrisme*), and, incidentally, a distinguished politician ; he 'seemed to unite the favours of genius and fortune' (Omond, *P.E.L.*, xi, 231). Critics have gradually written down the extravagant estimates of L.'s nearer contemporaries ; and Saintsbury (*Hist. Fr. Lit.*, 487) is probably correct in his more measured judgment : 'he is quite of the second order of poets—sweet but not strong, elegant but not full, not imitative but at the same time not original, not insincere but also never intense'. Still, first or second in poetic rank, L. enjoyed in the greater part of the 19th cent. a reputation only inferior to that of Hugo (q.v.), and his initiative in poetry and statesmanship merits permanent recognition. It was the meditative note which he introduced, or, more precisely, which he transferred from the prose of Rousseau and Chateaubriand (qq.v.) into the lyric poetry of his country. He was Byronic, but he was Wordsworthian too ; and L.'s undertone of gentle tenderness, though it may degrade him to the 'minor' poets, as has been alleged, was so far new in Fr. poetry and was so far desiderated and due that L.'s *Méditations poétiques*, 1820 (the very title implied a new intimacy), achieved an immense and a sudden success, of the kind which was sought by Wordsworth and Coleridge in *Lyrical*

Ballads, 1798. *Nouvelles Méditations* followed in 1823, together with a Platonic narrative *Mort de Socrate*, and the *Dernier Chant de Childe Harold*, 1825 ; the *Harmonies poétiques et religieuses*, 1830, completed this period of L.'s activity. He had married in 1822, was elected to the Academy (q.v.), 1829, and had held diplomatic posts in Florence and Naples, where he dispensed magnificent hospitality. In 1832 he set out on his *Voyage en Orient*, a stately tour poetically described ; and on his return in the following year, when he was chosen as a deputy, his political career began. It lasted till the year of storm, 1848, when for a brief time L. was head of the provisional government ; an access of power too great for his capacities, and due to his fame as an orator. His last 20 years were spent in comparative retirement and retrenchment ; and his works of that period included *Histoire des Girondins*, 1847 ; *Confidences* (two series), 1849, 1851 ; novels, *Raphael, Geneviève, Graziella* ; literary criticism, *Portraits*, etc. ; L. wr., too, a tragic poem, *Jocelyn*, 1836, and an ambitious Byronic poem, *La Chute d'un Ange*, 1838, among other less known works ; and it is satisfactory to learn that his many eminent services were rewarded, 1867, by the vote of the annual income derived from a funded pension of half-a-million francs. The sure reward of national gratitude has crowned this solace of his old age ; and the centenary of L.'s first volume of 'meditations' found him firmly established in the heart and mind of his fellow-countrymen.

Lamb, Charles (1775-1834): Engl. essayist ; poet ; edu. at Christ's Hospital, where he formed his constant friendship with S. T. Coleridge (q.v.) ; employed at India House, 1792-1825 ; the centenary of his release from his clerkship was celebrated, 1925, by a memorial dinner. L.'s life was marred, yet adorned, by domestic tragedy ; his sister, Mary (1765-1847), was subject to mental attacks, in one of which she killed their mother with a table-knife. L. devoted himself to her during his lifetime ; and his courage, and charm of disposition (emphasized by the familiar stutter), have won him friends, admiration and esteem. Keeping more strictly to his literary record, L. wr., 1798, a little vol. of verse, which contained, among other pieces, the delightful *Old Familiar Faces* ; he wr., 1807, with his sister, Mary (whose long, lucid intervals displayed touches of the genius which is akin to madness), the famous *Tales from Shakespeare*, which is still the children's gate to Shakespeare's plays ; he edited excellently selections from the Elizabethan dramatists ; and wr., 1820-5, the *Essays from Elia* (first series, 1823 ; *Last Essays of Elia*, 1833), on which his reputation most permanently rests. (Elia was just the name of a fellow-clerk in the India Office). A. Ainger (canon, 1837-1904), in a previous generation, and E. V. Lucas, more recently, are the editors chiefly associated with the works, lives and letters of C. and Mary L. ; and, while some of C.L.'s writings may not survive a second full and busy century, canon Ainger justly claims that ' it is the man, Charles Lamb, that constitutes the enduring charm of his written words. It is this humanity that gives to his intellect its flexibility and its deep vision, and that is the feeder at once of his pathos and his humour '. Among the essays, the chief favourites are the *Dissertation on Roast Pig, Imperfect Sympathies*, and *Dream Children*. Readers of L. are reminded of Addison (q.v.) in the *Spectator*, and of sir Thos. Browne (q.v.).

Lambert, de, Anne Thérèse (1647-1733): Fr. literary hostess ; m. *marquis* de L., 1666 ; widowed, 1686. The *salon* of mme. de L. in Paris was more than any other the successor to that of mme. de Rambouillet (q.v.) in the previous century, and was frequented by most of the eminent men and women of letters, including Marivaux, Houdar de La Motte, Montesquieu (qq.v.) and others. Wr. *Lettres sur la véritable éducation* (Paris, 1727 ; Amsterdam, 1729) ; *Réflexions nouvelles sur les femmes* (Paris, 1727 ; The Hague, 1729) ; and other works, distinguished, in the judgment of Fontenelle (q.v.), ' par le ton aimable de vertu qui y règne partout '. Mme. de L. is discussed by Ste.-Beuve (q.v.), in his *Causeries*.

Lambin, Denys (1520-72): Fr. scholar ; Royal Reader, first in Lat., then in Gk., at Paris from 1561 (see s.v. Corporation) ; latinized his name to Dionysius Lambinus ; studied in Italy ; edited Horace, 1561 ; Lucretius, 1564 ; Cicero, 1566 ; Nepos, 1569 ; and was engaged on the works of Plautus when the shock of Ramée's (q.v.) death cut short his own distinguished career. L.'s name gave rise in France to a new term in the vocabulary of scholarship, the injustice of which is best characterized by H. A. J. Munro (1819-85), who edited Lucretius 300 years after L. (1864). L.'s ' thankless countrymen', he there remarked, ' thinking however more perhaps of his Horace than his Lucretius, have made *lambin* or *lambiner* classical terms to express what is diffuse and tedious '.

Lamennais, de, Hugues Félicité Robert (1782-1854): Fr. romantic (s.v. Romance) writer on politics and theology. L.'s early years were spent in religious musings and preparation, which found expression, 1817-24, in his famous essay in 4 vols. *sur l'Indifférence en matière de Religion*. The ' indifference ' which he attacked was in three sorts : the political atheism of governors, who think religion necessary for the people ; the so-called natural religion of 18th-cent. deists ; and Protestantism ; all three, forms of individual religion as distinct from the ultramontanism of Rome. The essay was brilliant and eloquent, in the school of Chateaubriand and J. de Maistre (qq.v.) ; but L., despite his fear of private judgment and tolerance, was equally averse from the principles of legitimism, and his experience in revolutionary Europe of the conservative tendencies of Rome led him to seek a deeper basis for the theocratic liberalism at which he aimed. In 1824 he went to Rome, and pope Leo xii offered him a cardinal's cap ; but in 1832 he was condemned by pope Gregory xvi. L.'s opinions had matured in the interval. In 1830 he had founded (with Montalembert and Lacordaire) a newspaper *l'Avenir*, which was suspended in the following year; and the personal attempt of the eager reformers to convince the pope of their good intentions broke on his holiness's chilling reception, recounted by L. in his *Affaires de Rome*, 1836. L.'s greatest work was his *Paroles d'un croyant*, 1834 (how many believers have written bks.), which is really a lyric poem in prose paragraphs, and which, while it completed L.'s rupture with authority, produced a huge sensation in wide circles of public thought. Apocalyptic is the epithet commonly applied to this profession of democratic faith and catholic piety, 'anticipating in some ways the English Tractarian Movement' (*P.E.L.*, xi, 201), and dissolved in the revolutionary romanticism of the era 1830-48. L.'s later bks. and later newspapers, with which he struggled against tides stronger than his own, were inferior to his masterpiece of 1834, and he succeeded neither as prophet nor as politician. L. was the type of visionary who is greater by his failures than by success; and, though he died without becoming reconciled with the church, he was sustained by the consciousness of his own consistency to an ideal in advance of his age, preserved in the Mennaisian School which was called after his name.

La Mettrie, de, Julien Offray (1709-51): Fr. *philosophe* (q.v.); wr. *L'homme-machine*, 1748, *L'homme-plante*, 1749, the titles of which place them in the school of materialistic determinism, which was a part of the preparation for the reign of Reason in the Fr. Revolution.

La Motte, de, Antoine Houdar (1672-1731): Fr. miscellanist; commonly linked in reputation with Fontenelle (q.v.), to whose talents and their application the record of La M. bears distinct likeness. They were friends, too, and allies in the cause of modernism *versus* the ancients (q.v.), and exercised a kind of joint supremacy as arbiters of polite taste, in the period of the decadence of the *salons* and of preparation for the 18th cent. La M., like Fontenelle, began with drama, and, though his anti-classical theories (or heresies) were attacked by Voltaire (q.v.) in a pref. to *Oedipe* (2nd edn.), he achieved a conspicuous success with his *Inès de Castro*, 1723; he publd. *Odes*, 1707, *Fables*, 1719, and his chief work, an adaptation of the *Iliad* in Fr. verse, 1714. La M.'s theory was to re-write the poem in the form in which Homer would have written it, if he had enjoyed the advantage of living in the 17th cent., and of sharing the triumphs of progress which had been made since his day. Progress, transferred from the scientific sphere of Descartes (q.v.) to the sphere of poetry and the arts, was the chief argument employed by the modernists (see s.v. Perrault) in their dispute with the champions of classicism; and, whether they relied on theory or on practice, as in this modernist *Iliad*, art itself, indifferent to the stages by which mechanical invention marks its progress, defeated their best intentions. La M.'s Gk. was not his strong point, and he availed himself of the prose transln. by mme. Dacier (q.v.), thus embroiling himself in a double controversy, first, as to his theory, and secondly as to his execution. He defended himself with considerable ingenuity in his *Réflexions sur la Critique*, 1716.

Lancelot: a hero of the romance-cycle of Arthur (q.v.), surnamed 'of the Lake', since he was brought up by a fay, or lady of the lake. When king Richard i was detained as prisoner at Vienna by duke Leopold of Austria (1194), an Anglo-Norman knt. (de Morville) was sent as hostage for his release, and took with him a lost Fr. Lancelot-poem. This survives in a German transln. effected by Ulrich von Zatzikhoven, and formed the basis of a romance by Chrétien de Troyes (q.v.), called *conte de la charrette* (cart), from the [cart in which L. had to ride on one occasion contrary to the dignity of chivalry. Fr. prose-versions of the legend followed, and, in some of these, L. is the hero of the quest of the grail, replacing Perceval (q.v.) and replaced in turn by Galahad (q.v.). But the chief Lancelot-episode in the cycle is his rescue of queen Guenevere from Meleagant, king of the country whence no one returns (i.e. the netherworld; an old pagan myth). The guilty love of L. for the queen, which led to the dissolution of Arthur's realm, and the wonderful nobly-imagined close, became, as gradually elaborated, a main part of the Breton 'matière' (see s.v. Bodel). Dante's reference is ever-memorable (*Inferno*, v, fin.): the tragic lovers, Paolo and Francesca, on whom S. Phillips wr. a play, 1900, recall their past reading of the tragic fate of the lovers of old story, Lancelot and Guenevere; and from Dante to Tennyson (qq.v.) the appeal has been irresistible in European lit.

Landino, Christofero (1424-1504): It. humanist. Born and resided at Florence, where he became a leading member of the Platonic Academy; was attached to the Medicean court, at first as a tutor of Lorenzo the Magnificent, whom he survived; prof. of Lat. till his death. Transld. Pliny's *Natural History*, lectured on Virgil and Horace, and is noteworthy for his attention to Ital. native letters in lectures on Petrarch (1460) and commentaries on Dante (1481). His chief work was Lat. *Disputationes Camaldulenses*, Camaldolese Discussions, in 4 bks. (1480), dedicated to duke Fredk. of Urbino (q.v.). Cicero's *Tusculans* served as model for this graceful and celebrated dialogue on the comparative values of the active and contemplative life. Alberti (q.v.) sustains the argument in favour of the theoretic, and Lorenzo de Medici of the practical ideal; and other portions of the dialogue are entrusted to the great leaders of thought of L.'s day. Alberti presents the stronger case, and supports it with a wealth of illustration drawn by L. from his long and devoted labours in the study of Plato and Virgil. (See s.vv.).

Lando, de, Ferrant Manuel (14th cent.): Span. poet. Italianate disciple of Imperial (q.v.); represented by 31 pieces in the collection of Baena (q.v.).

Landon, Letitia Elizabeth (1802-38): Engl. misc. writer; m. Geo. Maclean, governor of Cape Coast Castle, 1838, and died from overdose of poison 2 months after her arrival at Cape Coast. Wr. poems (*Rome*, 1820, etc.) and novels (*Ethel Churchill*, 1837, etc.), and was a frequent contributor to the fashionable albums of the day over the familiar signature, L.E.L.

Landor, Walter Savage (1775-1864): Engl. essayist, poet; a Hellenist by taste, though reputed not an exact Gk. scholar ; Swinburne (q.v.), an ardent admirer, wr. of him :

Through the trumpet of a child of Rome
Rang the pure music of the flutes of Greece,

and the epithet ' pure ' has been called in question as a qualification of L.'s scholarship. But a love of the Gk. classics is the dominant note in the writings of his long life. By modern readers he is chiefly memorable for a few brilliant epigrams in verse, and for the series in prose of *Imaginary Conversations* : 2 vols., 1824 ; vols. 3 and 4, 1828 ; 5, 1829 ; complete edn., 1853. His epical *Gebir*, 1798, never won many readers (De Quincey, q.v., described himself as a ' mono-Gebirist ', in the sense of its solitary reader) ; and, though its blank verse contains many beautiful lines and passages, L. was right in his self-criticism : ' I shall dine late, but the room will be well lighted, and the guests few but select '. The ambition was dignified, if chilling ; and prof. Saintsbury, in an admirable ch. of the *C.H.E.L.* (vol. xii, ch. ix), quotes a remark by prof. Lewis Campbell (1830-1908 ; classical scholar) as to L.'s ' aloofness and unreality '. His *Conversations* afford models of ornate prose.

Landstad, Magnus Brostrup (1802-80) : Norw. folklorist ; divine. L.'s chief services to his national lit. were the collection of popular songs, 1853, ' too clumsy for common use ', and of religious poetry, in a psalm-book, produced at Government expense, ' on a scale so huge as to be quite unfit for the use for which it was intended ' (E. Gosse, *Lit. of Northern Europe*, 21).

Lane, John (1854-1925) : Engl. publisher ; closely associated with a movement, in which Aubrey Beardsley (1872-98) was the chief representative in art, and Oscar Wilde (q.v. ; 1856-1900) in letters. It was a kind of late shoot of pre-Raphaelitism (see s.v.), and, while it owed a large debt to contemporary Fr. example, it was likewise a reaction against the conventional Victorian standards, *circa* 1890. A wiser reaction is represented by Thos. Hardy (q.v.), in *Jude the Obscure*, for example ; but the revolting juniors did good work, and credit is due to L. for his enterprise in encouraging them. The *Yellow Book* (vol. 1, 1894) was a main channel for their expression, and another of L.'s ventures was the apolaustic *Anglo-Saxon Review*, no. i, June, 1899, edited by lady Randolph Churchill.

Lang, Andrew (1844-1912) : Scot. critic ; poet ; folklorist ; a voluminous writer, whose charm and skill kept pace with his really remarkable industry. He collaborated with prof. S. H. Butcher (1850-1910 ; author of *Some Aspects of the Greek Genius*) in a prose translu. of Homer's *Odyssey*, and with F. W. H. Myers (q.v.) and Mr. Walter Leaf in a similar version of the *Iliad*. He regularly issued a *Fairy-Book*, designated by a special colour, during many years between 1889-1907, and he was the author of a *Life* of Scott's (q.v.) biographer, Lockhart (q.v.), and admirably edited the Border edn. of the Waverley novels. L.'s *Ballads and Lyrics of Old France*, 1872, and *Ballads in Blue China*, 1880, link him with the modern ballad (q.v.)-revival by A. Dobson (q.v.), sir E. Gosse, and others ; and he wr.

valuable treatises on Scot. hist., *Custom and Myth*, 1884, and kindred topics.

Langbein, August Friedrich Ernst (1757-1835) : Germ. miscellanist. Wr. novels, sketches, and light verse, in a fluent and an attractive vein.

Lange, Samuel Gotthold (1711-81) : Germ. poet ; studied at Halle. Wr., with Pyra (q.v.), ' Songs of Friendship ' in the rhymeless verse of classical metres, thus ranking with the Anakreontiker (q.v.) ; effected a transln. of the *Odes* of Horace, which was severely criticized by Lessing (q.v.).

Langebeck, Jacob (1710-75) : Dan. historian. Wr. *Scriptores rerum Danicarum medii œvi*, a Lat. account of medieval Dan. annals, which was continued by various hands, and, though not as indispensable as it was, still of considerable documentary value. L. founded, 1745, the Royal Dan. Society ' for Patriotic History ', and the early vols. of the organ of the society, *det Danske Magasin*, are full of his contributions.

Langen, Rudolf von (1438-1519) : Germ. humanist. Founded a school of new learning at Münster (1498), and belonged to the circle of scholars who adorned the brief period before Renaissance and Reformation parted company.

Langendijk, Pieter (1683-1756) : Dutch comic dramatist. L. worked under the influence of Cervantes (q.v.), but his last play was perhaps his best ; it was a comedy of manners, resting on the old motive of the antagonism between fathers and children, older than *King Lear*, and doubtless to be renewed in *Milestones* to come. L.'s play was called *Spiegel der vaterlandsche Kooplieden* (' the merchants' mirror '), and achieved and merited a great success.

Langland, William (*c.* 1330-*c.* 1400) : Engl. poet. It must be stated at the outset that the surname Langland or Langley and the forename William or Robert are alike disputed, and that the authorship of the allegorical poem of the 14th cent., *The Vision of William concerning Piers the Plowman*, attributed to this conjectured writer, is one of those problems of literary scholarship which each age settles anew on seemingly probable evidence. Thus, prof. J. M. Manly of Chicago, who was entrusted with the ch. on this subject in *C.H.E.L.*, ii (1908), decides against the earlier conclusions of Skeat (q.v.) and Jusserand, and in favour of 5 several authors, of whom one only is certainly known to the bare extent of his name John But. Prof. Snell (*P.E.L.*, iii, 1899) was still content to accept the one-author view ; Courthope, in vol. i of his *History of Engl. Poetry* (1895 ; 208), agrees that L. ' left in his poem an anagrammatical clue to his own identity in the line

' " I have lived in *Londe*," quod I, " my name is *longe Wille* " ',

which is, further, typical of the scheme of metre and alliteration ; but he adds, ' For my part I do not think it desirable to introduce even the appearance of scientific reasoning into what must necessarily always remain a region of nebular hypothesis ; ' while A. Lang (q.v.), in his brilliant little *Hist. Engl. Lit.* (Longmans, 1912 ; 99), deferred to the new criticism sufficiently to write, ' this author is generally supposed to have been named ' etc.

The general supposition is convenient, and will not be lightly surrendered for popular as distinct from exact and scholarly purposes; and the author of *Piers Plowman*, whether single or composite, will here be referred to as Langland. Two things are certain in the welter: first, that, as Skeat has shown, there were three periods of composition in the poem (as in the composition of the chronicles of Froissart, q.v.), if not three or more pens at work. The first, or 'A' version dates from 1362, and from the neighbourhood of the Malvern Hills in Worcestershire. Its political motive is inspired by the ravages of the plague (the Black Death) and by the social disturbance of the Fr. war concluded by the Peace of Bretigny, when the demobilized soldiery returned home; a great tempest (15 Jan., 1362), which devasted the countryside, also helps to fix the date. The 'B' version is attributed to *c.* 1377, and it considerably expanded the allegorical hints in 'A'; and 'C', dated 1380-90, or even a year or two later (Jusserand says, 1398-99) continued this process of poetic allegorizing in a more deeply mystical vein. Noting that the author of 'C', according to Manly (*loc. cit.*), 'seems to have been a man of much learning, of true piety, and of genuine interest in the welfare of the nation, but unimaginative, cautious, and a very pronounced pedant', thus differing from the style of the author of 'A', which, according to the same critic, 'is always simple, direct, evocative of a constant series of clear and sharply-defined images of individuals and groups', we may pass to our second certain point, which is the more important of the two. It is that *The Vision of William* (who, according to Lang, was a kind of early Carlyle, q.v.), *concerning Piers the Plowman* is in existence for the delight of posterity, albeit for the confusion of commentators. For 'the poem is the thing', as Saintsbury says (*First Bk. of Engl. Lit.*, Macmillan, 1914; 29), 'and a very remarkable thing it is, written in the new-old alliterative manner, and giving the best examples of that manner, though showing also its limitations and its defects'. Piers himself, Peter, the church, who starts in the character of the just man, is gradually allegorized into Christ; the original dream in the Malvern Hills slides, as dreams are apt to do, into visions within visions, expounding the nature of virtue through the counsels of Dowel, Dobet and Dobest (do well, do better, do best); and the social outlook of the poem in its opening is more and more overlaid with moral and literary reflection. Langland, it is true, was not a Lollard, but he (or his continuators) deepened in religious tone as years advanced. The marriage of Meed in 'A' may be selected as a kind of purple passage, or at least as a test-piece of the literary value of the whole. Meed (=reward) is either God's recompense to man, or man's recompense (=bribe, corruption) to his brother; and the marriage of the maiden Meed with Fals (False-hood), which was brought about by Favel (? Duplicity; *fabula*; there is a Fr. *Roman de Fauvel*: see Snell, *op. cit.*, 381), is forbidden by Theology. But note that L.'s Theology plays a far less important part than the

Beatrice (=Theology) of Dante's *Commedia*. 'Dante's constant guide is Theology, while Langland's favourite abstraction is Conscience' (Courthope, *op. cit.*, i, 256); and this difference, which is manifest in the manner of the 2 poems, is inherent in the temperament of the poets: the Italian, spiritual, scholastic, metaphysical, remote; the Englishman, practical, scriptural, social, close to fact; 'in all this Langland shows himself a thoroughly representative Englishman' (*ibid.*). So they go to London, and appeal to the king, as is the right of all good Englishmen. And the king seeks to marry Meed to Conscience, who has his own objections, and Reason, when asked to mediate, forbids the banns 'till all lords and ladies love Truth, and clerks and knights are courteous, and priests practise what they preach'. Were I king, he urges, 'no wrong should go unpunished or get grace by bribes, and love should rule all'. Satire in allegory and reform in vision is the key to these—the best—portions of the poem, which 'supplies a picture of contemporary England, and unfolds to us the moral and religious ideas of an educated layman' (Snell, *op. cit.*, 384): a *religio laici* before Dryden (q.v.). Of the influence of Dante (q.v.) on the visions, and of Ruiz (q.v.) on the tone of L., comparative students of lit. rightly dwell; the whole poem is suffused with that style of visionary moralizing which the contemporary *Romance of the Rose* (q.v.) was imposing on a reflective age. 'It is the age of desire, and satiety seems well-nigh impossible. The Englishman would know all the sciences under the sun, and all the subtle crafts; and in his quest for new ideas he is indefatigable, turning over and over the contents of the Latin, French and Italian literatures, and making their thought his own. . . . As in Chaucer's pages we have the life of the people portrayed, so in Langland's we have the ripening conscience. . . . Langland shows Peace pleading before Parliament against wrong, his oppressor. . . . The scales are falling from the Englishman's eyes. At last he has reached the point where he can perceive, and strive to remove, the evils of his race. . . . We see him in the tall, gaunt figure of Langland, passing through the jostling crowds of London streets to pray for rich men's souls, and yet living his life in a world apart, a world of ideals of what ought to be, where rank, fine clothes and jewels go for nothing, where even theology, as then understood, is a vain help. He stands the harbinger of the Reformation to come' (E. Dale, *National Life and Character in the Mirror of Early Engl. Lit.*, Cambridge, 1907; 271, 273, 297, 319; quoting *Piers Plowman*, xv, 48; Prol., 20; iv, 48). This is the importance to life and thought of this great, imaginative poem, or series of poems, of the 14th cent.; and mention only is due to L.'s shorter and more pragmatic poem (in one of the 'B' manuscripts), which has no title of its own, but which was entitled by T. Wright (q.v.) *A Poem on the Depositions of Richard ii*, and by Skeat, its next editor (1873 and, again, 1886), *Richard the Redeless*: there is some evidence that its author called it *Mum, Sothsegger* (Silence, Truthteller). A poem, *Piers Plowman's*

Creed, dated by Skeat not long after 1393, and a long *Plowman's Tale*, probably compiled in the 16th cent., and then wrongly attributed to Chaucer, belong to the L. cycle but not to the original L.

Langue d'oc and Langue d'oïl (Fr.): Languages spoken respectively North and South of the river Loire in France, before the assimilation of both to *Français*, or French proper, the central dialect of the northern provinces. The names were taken from the particle of affirmation (*yes*) in each language, *oc* being derived from Lat. *hoc*, and *oïl* from *illud*. The *langue d'oc* was nearer to Lat. in its inflection and vocabulary, and is principally famous as the language of Provençal lit. (q.v.), from which the influence of the Troubadours was poured through Sicily, Portugal and Italy after the crusade against the Albigensian heresy, which pope Innocent iii started in 1208. Dante (q.v.), in his treatise ' On Vulgar Eloquence ', discusses the relative claims to priority in rank of the *langues d'oc, d'oïl*, and *de sì* (Ital.).

Langveldt, von, Georg (c. 1475-1558): known by scholar's name of Georgius Macropedius: Dutch Latinist; schoolmaster. Inspired by example of Reuchlin (q.v.) to write Terentian dramas, of a type midway between the broad farce of native Germ. wit, as displayed in Eulenspiegel, Grobianus and the Shrovetide-plays (see s.vv.), and the semi-sacred character of the edifying prize-day school-dramas (see s.v. Latin), which were a feature of Teuton Latinity at this date. The chief play of Macropedius was *Rebelles*, a sufficiently amusing comedy of school-boys, mothers, and birch-rods, with a moral which Solomon would have approved.

Lannel, de, Jean (17th cent.): Fr. novelist. Wr., 1624, *le Roman Satirique*, which attempted imperfectly to combine the new rationalism of modern speech and conduct with the old romantic idealism and apparatus. Its success, which was considerable, was due in part to its interest as a *roman-à-clef* (q.v.), and partly, it may be conjectured, to the obscenity and salaciousness of its satire. In a second edn. 1625, L. transposed the scene from Sirapis (Paris) in Galatia (France) to India, and changed the name to *Roman des Indes*; but the first and more transparent nomenclature was, later, restored.

Lannoy, de, Juliana Cornelia (1738-82): Dutch poet; *baronne* by rank. Wr. several tragic dramas, and a poem, *Het Gastmaal* (' The Dinner '), which has outlived her more ambitious work, and which sheds a pleasant light on the social side of the life of a Dutch noble in the 18th cent., not without a touch of intentional satire or caricature.

La Noue, de, François (1531-91): Fr. soldier-statesman. Fought through the religious wars on the Protestant side; was taken prisoner by Alva, in Flanders, 1580-85; served at Arques, Ivy, and the siege of Paris and fell at the siege of Lamballe, 4 Aug., 1591. La N.'s *Discours politiques et militaires*, which include his memoirs, were publd., 1587, and were addressed with ardent patriotism to both sides of his divided countrymen; he had the felicity of commanding the respect of both, as a moderate

Calvinist, a brave soldier, and a pacifist in political philosophy.

La Noue, Sauve (1701-61): Fr. dramatist. Wr. *Coquette Corrigée* and other plays of no special merit, though La N. enjoyed the patronizing esteem of Voltaire (q.v.).

Laocoon: Title of an unfind. (Germ.) treatise by Lessing (q.v.), *Laokoon, or the Limits of Painting and Poetry*, 1766, in which the actual topic selected for discussion and illustration, inspired by Virgil (q.v.), *Aeneid*, ii, 199 foll., is a group of sculptured marble, figuring L. and his sons in the folds of a serpent. This sculpture, which was probably executed at Rhodes, had a place at the Baths of Titus in Rome, and was buried in the ruins of the ancient city. The group was disinterred in 1506, and at once aroused the interest of archæologists at the papal court. The earliest work of real importance produced in Europe on the subject was *Thoughts on the Imitation of Greek Works of Art* by Winckelmann (q.v.), 1755. Starting from a consideration of Horace's æsthetic formula ' ut pictura poesis ' (*Ars Poetica*, 361), and traversing it more dogmatically than the picturesque poesy of the Pre-Raphaelites (q.v.) would admit, this essay in criticism contributed to the deLatinization and progressive Hellenization of the classicism of the Renaissance. The movement initiated by Petrarch (q.v.) had declined in the intervening centuries into a kind of pseudo-classicism, a base thing of rules and formulæ, lifeless and unreal and flat; and the sole satisfactory means of restoring it to its proper uses was to introduce into the study of antiquity the Gk. spirit of order and method and patient inquiry and proportion. The only way, it began to be recognized, of employing the classics profitably for modern culture was to cease worrying Virgil and Horace into systems of formalism and legalism, as the Rabbis in medieval studies had worried the Hebrew Scriptures into Talmudical commentaries, and rather to seek them afresh, and to inaugurate a new era of humanism. The scholarship of the spade and the footrule, of spirit-level and the compass, took the place of the scholarship of grammar and metre. The old cry of ' follow Virgil ', which Vida (q.v.) had bequeathed to the Pleiad (q.v.), and which dominated the genius of the Augustan (q.v.) period, was improved into a cry of ' trace Virgil ', which was to lead to the new Romantic movement (q.v.). Virgil was not consequently deposed, but the ideas which governed Virgil's art, and caused it inevitably to assume its forms, were exalted immeasurably above the codification of laws of composition to be drawn from the finished forms themselves. Not the external result, but the internal cause was investigated. The pioneer of these methods in the limited field of Gk. sculpture was Winckelmann, and it was on the basis of his writings that Lessing raised his structure of *Laokoon*, which founded the new and truer Hellenism taught by Goethe to Europe. ' Lessing scoured the clogged and stagnant channels of Neo-Classicism by recurrence to the original fount ' (Saintsbury, *Hist. Crit.*, iii, 40); and the simplicity and grandeur of Gk. art, searched-out by the evidences of construction, were applied to moral uses—to the purposes of character—by thinkers such as Herder and Kant (qq.v.), and established a new literary convention. Thus, this buried piece of Greco-Roman sculpture enjoyed a glorious exhumation. (See s.v. Humanism).

La Peruse, de, Jean Bastier (16th cent.): Fr. poet and dramatist; of the school of the Pleiad (q.v.); died young, after producing a *Medea* in the classical style of tragedy and a number of Ronsardist lyrics.

Laprade, de, Victor (1812-83): Fr. poet; philosopher, in the sense that he steadily subordinated feeling to thought, apart from (or, more correctly, in conformity with) his tendency to Platonic and mystical speculation. Wr. *les Parfums de Madeleine*, 1839, and *Psyche*, 1841, 2 vols. of thoughtful verse; and was a convinced opponent of the Second Empire. L. was elected to the Fr. Academy (q.v.) in succession to de Musset (q.v.).

Larivey, Pierre (*c.* 1540-*c.* 1611): Fr. comic dramatist; son of an Ital. printer, who had settled at Troyes, and, being naturalized in France, changed his name from Giunto to l'Arrivée. As Garnier (q.v.) may be said to have realized most completely the hopes of Du Bellay (q.v.) and the Pleiad (q.v.) for the future of Fr. tragedy, so L. may be reckoned the most conspicuous exponent of the new school in the allied sphere of comedy, and a notable forerunner of Molière (q.v.). L.'s 12 plays, of which 9 survive, were freely adapted from originals in Italy, the country of his own orig., and have been traced to Pasqualigo (q.v.) and other dramatists, who derived them from Lat. sources. At each stage of derivation, native features and developments were added; and L.'s most obvious contribution is the punning, sharp-pointed dialogue, which passed again, through Fraunce, Munday (qq.v.) and other translrs., into the pedantic pleasantry of Holofernes (*Love's Labour's Lost*) and other characters of Lyly's and Shakespeare's comedies.

La Salle (La Sale), de, Antoine. See s.v. **Antoine.**

La Rivière, de, Mercier (1720-94): Fr. political economist; member of the Physiocrats (q.v.). Wr., 1767, *L'Ordre naturel et essentiel des Sociétés politiques,* in which the very benevolent despotism of the empire of China was taken as his prime model of social order.

Laroche, von, Sophie (1730-1807): Germ. novelist. Wr. *The Story of Fräulein von Sternheim*, in the form of letters imitated from Richardson (q.v.), but L. cultivated a more erotic style, acquired partly from her friend, Wieland (q.v.).

La Rochefoucauld, duc de, François vi (1613-80): Fr. moralist and memoirist; his family belonged to the highest nobility of France, and La R. was known before his father's death as prince de Marcillac. He lived at first an active and ambitious life, as befitted his rank and talents; he was eager to play a part in the great world, and found scope for display in the troubled politics of his age. He joined in the intrigues against Richelieu and Mazarin successively; he paid court to mesdames de Chevreuse, de Longueville, and de La Fayette successively, and was intimate with mme. de Sévigné (see s.vv.). But neither the *salons* of the *marquises* nor the ante-rooms of the cardinals

brought peace or happiness to La R. His temperament was not made for success. As a soldier, he was more reckless than courageous; as a diplomatist, he was more impulsive than prudent; as a man, he was more wilful than resolute; and his last years, burdened by increasing illness, were spent in partial retirement, in the lap, so to speak, of mme. de La Fayette (q.v.). La R.'s *Mémoires*, which are interesting, but not wholly trustworthy ('he composed his person for posterity', says one critic) had a curious bibliographical history; one unauthorized edn. was issued in his lifetime, and another shortly after his death; and it was not till 1817 that the genuine text was collated out of family archives. More important in the history of lit. are La R.'s *Réflexions et Sentences, ou Maximes Morales,* commonly known as *Maxims* (first edn., 1665; fifth edn., 1678; to this and the previous edn. the characteristic maxim was prefaced as motto: ' Nos vertus ne sont le plus souvent que des vices déguisés '). Maxim-making was one of the pastimes at the fashionable and precious (q.v.) *salons* of the day; and none brought the art to higher perfection than the reflective, disillusioned great nobleman, who had sampled all the fruits of the tree of life, and was left with a bitter taste in his mouth. His 500-odd compressed 'sentences' (*sententiæ*; cf. sententiousness) contain the packed wisdom of a retired man of the world: ' Virtues lose themselves in interest, as the rivers are lost in the sea '; ' Self-love is the greatest of all flatterers '; ' How can we expect another to keep our secret if we have not kept it ourselves ': these are types of the concentrated worldly wisdom which La R.'s delicate wit fashioned with a keen edge of style out of his experience of men and things. They make fascinating reading; and if they reveal a Wolsey's remorse after his fall from power, we recall 2 maxims out of the collection which may have consoled La R. in his old age: ' The mind is always the dupe of the heart ', and ' Youth is a continual *ivresse* '.

Larra, de, Mariano José (1809-37): Span. satirist: journalist. Wr., 1832, *el Pobrecito hablador,* and, 1834, *Revista española.*

Lascaris, Constantine (1434-1501): Gk. scholar-exile; grammarian. Wr. grammar of his native language, which was the first bk. ever set with Gk. types (Milan, 1476).

Lascaris, Janus (1445-1535): Gk. scholar-exile; librarian; relative of above. Assisted Lorenzo de Medici (q.v.) in his collection of MSS. Resided at Rome, under pope Leo x (q.v.), Lorenzo's younger son; and, later, at Paris, under king Francis i (q.v.), whom he helped at the foundation of the Royal Library at Fontainebleau. Thus, L. formed an important link between the Renaissance in Italy and France, where he enjoyed the unique distinction of teaching Gk. to Budé (q.v.), by common consent the foremost Hellenist of his age.

Las Casas, de, Bartolemê (1474-1566): Span. historian; controversialist. LC. is chiefly remembered by his 6 voyages across the Atlantic—no mean feat of travel in those days —in order to follow in the footsteps of Cortes the Conqueror, and to plead the cause of the just treatment of the native Indians of America.

He wr. a 'History of the Indies' and an *Apologetica Historica*; but his principal work was a *Brevissima Relacion*, or 'Very Brief Account of the Destruction of the Indies', 1552, which had a striking success, and was transld. into 7 languages. 'But history gave place in it to polemic. . . . Las Casas was a partisan, let us hasten to add a partisan of reason and of justice; and if in his polemical writings his philanthrophy led him to exaggerate, he was honesty personified. When he writes of Columbus (whose papers were put at his disposal), or of any events of which he was an eye-witness, his authority is conclusive' (Kelly, *Lit. espagn.*, 216); his attitude was as honourable to his character as it was almost unique in his age.

Lassalle, Ferdinand (1825-64): Germ. socialist; founder of the Labour party in Germany, and of 'that form of Socialism which, for better or for worse, has transformed European politics' (from a centenary art. in *The Times* newspaper, 11 April, 1925). With L.'s economic writings, his triumphal progresses through Germ. cities, 1862-4, his love-affair with a countess Hatzfeldt, and the later love-affair through which he lost his life in a duel in Switzerld., we are not here concerned. L., who was a Jew by birth, and a man of rare eloquence and handsome bearing, enters lit. by a side-door as the hero of *The Tragic Comedians*, 1880, by G. Meredith (q.v.), and his portrait forms the frontispiece to that novel in the memorial edn., 1910, of Meredith's works.

Lasso de la Vega, Gabriel Lobo (1559-1615): Span. poet. Wr. romantic ballads and elegies, and a collection of verse which was praised by Cervantes (q.v.).

Lasso de la Vega, Garci. See s.v. Garcilasso.

La Taille, de, -i, Jean (1540-1608), and **-ii, Jacques** (1541-1562). Fr. poets; brothers; satellites in the Pleiad (q.v.) galaxy. Jean wr. sacred tragedies of some note, and a satiric poem, *le Courtisan retiré*, 1574, imitative of Du Bellay (q.v.), and not unmindful of Guevara's (q.v.) *l'Aviso de Privados y Doctrina de Courtesanos*; Jacques, who died very young, is chiefly memorable for his epigrams.

Latewaert, Loy (14th cent.): Dutch romancer. Wr. long poem of nearly 12,000 verses, entitled *Seghelijn van Jherusalem*. The hero, Seghelijn, was the son of a Saracen prince, whom, in order to save from death at his father's hands, his mother placed with poor fisherfolk. Later, he went crusading, and L. reproduced the familiar conjunction of ecclesiology and thaumaturgy, and combined it with an element of sentimental love.

Latin: After the foliation of the romance (q.v.) languages with which European lit. properly begins, the Lat. language was still employed, as a convenient substitute for backward vernaculars, as a medium of communication between humane scholars, and, finally, as an elegant exercise, till within a quite recent date. The Lat. works of Dante (q.v.) were rather a conscious concession to the inadequacy of the 'illustrious vulgar tongue', in which he composed his great works, and the use of which he strenuously defended, than a willing tribute to the rights of antiquity. The first real impulse to such a revival of ancient Lat. in modern lit. was given at the instance of Petrarch (q.v.), who affected to despise his Ital. lyric verse, by which modern readers justly set more store, and who based his claim to the gratitude of posterity on his Lat. epic, letters, and moral treatises. It went against his grain as a Roman patriot (and it is to be added in Petrarch's praise that he was an original Lat. writer, never slavishly addicted to the style of any old master, whether Cicero or another) that Boccaccio (q.v.), his friend, spent time on Ital. prose *novelle* which might have been given to the study and imitation of the ancients. The recovery from monastic libraries (q.v.) of MSS. of treasured classical writers, the importation of MSS. from the East before and after the fall of Constantinople (1453), and, briefly, the whole course of humanism (q.v.) conspired to further Petrarch's dream—at one wild moment of politics nearly realized by Rienzi—of renewing in Italy, the most Lat. of all the heirs of Lat. blood, a living lit. in the dead tongue. So Cicero (q.v.) became a model, even a snare, to papal secretaries and princes' envoys; the style of Horace's *Ars Poetica* was combined with Aristotelian precepts and the example of Virgil (qq.v.) to produce poetic treatises on poetry which dominated the art in Italy and France; and, though a native verse lit. was fostered at the court of Lorenzo de Medici (q.v.), and flowered, through Pulci and Boiardo, in the epic-romance of Ariosto at Ferrara (see s.vv.), though Castiglione (q.v.) wr. the *Courtier* and Machiavelli (q.v.) wr. the *Prince* in Ital. prose, though Rabelais (q.v.) made Fr. his vehicle, and Luther (q.v.) wr. Germ. hymns and transld. the Bible into the vernacular, yet Lat. throughout the 16th cent. was the chief language of scholars and humanists: Erasmus (q.v.) employed it exclusively; More (q.v.) used it for his *Utopia*; Dedekind (q.v.) for his *Grobianus*; Locher (q.v.) transld. Brandt's (q.v.) *Narrenschiff* into Lat. hexameters; Bembo (q.v.) was more Ciceronian than Cicero himself; the Erfurt 'poets' employed monkish dog-Latin for their *Epistolæ Obscurorum Virorum* (q.v.); and Lat. was the universal passport for many years before it became the fashionable recreation of writers in the 18th cent. Especially was Lat. the language of scholarship and learning. The lectures of Politian (q.v.) at Florence were adorned by original Lat. poems on his favourite authors and influences; the magnificent contributions to learning of men like Calvin, Bodin, Bacon, Scaliger, Grotius, Casaubon (qq.v.) were invariably composed in Lat.; and the Renaissance passion for education (q.v.), from Vittorino (q.v.) downwards, was distinguished at every stage not merely by text-books, treatises, and commentaries in the Lat. tongue, but, further, by compositions which formed new classes of lit. in themselves. An important specimen of these classes was the Lat. drama of the 16th cent., which had its orig., in northern Europe at least, in schoolmasters' plays for their pupils. Since boys would be boys, even in days when teaching meant birching, the wise schoolmaster, instead of banning the theatre, made play-going a part of his curriculum. (School speech-days, esp. at Westminster, still conserve this tradition). Wimpheling (q.v.), the eminent educationist, is credited with an early experiment in this kind ; Reuchlin (q.v.) is known to have tried his hand at it ; and, a very little later, came the really great series of Lat. plays by two Dutch schoolmasters, Langveldt and Volder (qq.v.) ; the plays of Birck, Kirchmayer, Buchanan, Frischlin (qq.v.), and many others, which display as a rule the motive, either directly or by variation, of the improving moral story of the prodigal son (q.v.). In many of the chief Germ. towns in the 16th cent., there was an interchange of plays between the schoolhouse and the council-chamber, where the play was possibly presented with a less severe eye upon the moral. Partly, the persistence of Lat. was due to the cosmopolitanism of scholarship : Budé, Erasmus and More (qq.v.) could have met on no other common ground ; partly, too, it was due to the outdistancing of the resources of the vernaculars by the learned writers of the Renaissance. Men trained to an exact appreciation of the logical arrangement, flexile expressiveness, and other rhetorical capacities of authors as perfect in their art as Cicero, Virgil, Horace, and Tacitus, could not be expected to acquiesce in the limited literary vocabulary, the unco-ordinate sentence-construction, and the allegorical apparatus of ornaments, which their own backward languages displayed. What was partly an affectation of Ital. humanists was a genuine handicap in Engld., Germany, Holland, and France, where Rabelais's lively vigour did so much to supple the vernacular which Froissart and Commines (qq.v.) had employed. Poetry was better off than prose, which availed itself of the Lat. alternative till a comparatively more recent date ; the aids of rhyme and metre made it easier to devise rules and to cultivate the practice of pauses, in all of which uses vernacular prose was so defective. The Meistersinger (q.v.) did admirable work in popularizing the vernacular in Germany, and the Fr. poets, Marot and Ronsard (qq.v.), acquired from Petrarch and his successors and taught to France, Engld. (see s.vv. Wyatt, Surrey) and Holland excellent counsels of form and style. Even as late as Newton and Leibniz (qq.v.), who held the Lat. language, as it were, in reserve, Lat. maintained its honourable primacy as the tongue in which scholars spoke to scholars. Its gradual conquest by Fr., the conquest of a mother by a daughter (' matre pulcra filia pulcrior '), was due to several causes, among which may just be mentioned the influence of the Fr. court, the emigration of Fr. refugees, and the intellectual cosmopolitanism of Fr. thought. But Lat., even when it ceased to hold undivided sway, was a potent influence for good on its successors. The ' imperial tongue ' was a fertile founder of style in the daughter-nations, as will readily be seen from the works of Guevara (q.v.) in Spain, Pettie and Lyly (qq.v.) in Engld. The growth of this art, and the gradual displacement of Lat. in favour of Fr., have led to the more or less complete desuetude of Lat. for all purposes of earlier use ; it survives in physicians'

prescriptions to pharmacists ; and a need may be said to have arisen consequently of re-considering the curriculum of modern humane education. Meanwhile, it is not impertinent to note some of the drawbacks to European culture due to the excessive cult of Lat. One such evil is obvious (though in a diminishing degree) in the humanists' practice of introducing the gods and rites of Roman mythology into the lit. of Christian countries. Bembo, though a card. of the church, was a prominent offender in this respect ; and our colloquial apostrophe, 'by Jove', has descended direct from Europe's Lat. centuries. Further, the ornaments of poetic diction, such as ' Phoebus ' for ' sun ', ' nymph ' for ' maid ', and so forth, which obstructed so long the pure wells of modern languages undefiled, were imposed so heavily on lit. that it has only recently found relief. But a more important consideration than the incidental tyrannies of Lat. was the tendency to identify Latinity with classicism, which led to the neo-classic excesses of the Augustan age in Europe. Rome gave her name to the Romance languages, but the romantic outlook to which in their turn they gave a name became opposed to the classical outlook of those who echoed the speech of ancient Rome. Rome was the mother of classicism, and Rome was the mother of romanticism, at different times in the life of the ' eternal city ' ; and her offspring, grown to maturity, met and quarrelled in the 18th cent., and even to-day they are not completely reconciled. The descent of humanism in Italy's Lat. tongue ; the transln. of Gk. texts into Lat., and their interpretation by Latinizing humanists ; the approach to Homer through Virgil, and Virgil's Dante ; the regard for Horace, ' Stace ' (Statius) and Ovid, in preference to Sappho, Callimachus, and Alcæus ; for Cicero, in preference to Demosthenes and the Gk. orators and philosophers ; Seneca, to the Gk. tragedians ; Terence and Plautus, to the Gk. comic dramatists ; Phædrus, to Æsop ; Sallust, to Thucydides ; Horace, as critic, to Aristotle ; Virgil, as pastoralist, to Theocritus : all this, and much more, was at work to exalt the Lat. side of classicism above its Hellenic ancestry. The restoration of Gk. culture to Europe (see s.v. Hellenism) was largely due to the labours of Winckelmann, ' the last fruit of the Renaissance ' (Pater) ; and the Hellenists' revolt against Latinism in excess was no less valuable to the romantic movement than the progress of romance itself, in Richardson, Rousseau, Percy, Bürger, and their literary heirs. But though, at certain epochs and in certain senses, there has been too much deference paid to Lat. in Europe, whether in the practice of the language, or in the assimilation of the secondary and derivative culture of the Lat. race, still the debt is incalculably larger than any deductions that can be made from it. Elegy, satire, oratory, epigram, epistle ; these are of Lat. orig., almost *pur sang*. The gravity of Cicero, the curious happiness of Horace's diction, the romantic quality of Ovid's heroic tales, the moral ardour of Lucretius, the undernotes of Virgil, the passion of Catullus : Europe could have found no masters of a nobler or a more exacting sort, whether for lyric love or epic romance, whether for troubadour, allegorist, or cavalier. ' Greece has flown across the Alps ', declared Reuchlin's tutor at Rome when his pupil returned to Germany ; ' we are all Greek ', declared Shelley in his pref. to *Hellas* ; but between Reuchlin and Shelley in the history of the Renaissance in the North lay the centuries of Lat. culture in Europe. It is to Herder (q.v.), as much as to any one writer, and to his ' Fragments towards a German Literature ', 1767, which stands at the head of the Sturm und Drang (q.v.), that modern Europe looks back as the champion of release from the Lat. yoke, and as the first to restore the true balance of classicism, deflected, since Petrarch's day, by a too great esteem for the Lat. grammar. We may add that the first competition between Lat. and Fr. for primacy in scholarship and letters occured about 1670, when a small library was filled with big bks. on both sides of the dispute. The scene was Paris ; the time was the *grand siècle* of Boileau (q.v.) and his contemporaries ; and the occasion was an inscription for a triumphal arch. The contest had points of contact with the wider quarrel between the Ancients (q.v.) and Moderns ; and, though La Bruyère, Fénelon, Malebranche (qq.v.) and others were Hellenists as well as Latinists, there is no doubt that the excessive Latinity of the neo-classicists helped to avenge itself by the adoption of Fr. instead of Lat. as the medium for communication in polite society.

La Torre, de, Alfonso (15th cent.): Span. scholar ; native of Burgos ; a member of the coll. of St. Bartholomew, Salamanca, 1437. Wr., *c.* 1440, *Delectable Vision of Philosophy and the other Sciences* ; a kind of encyclopedia (q.v.), in the medieval sense, composed in the learned diction of his own day, which the poets and satirists were suppling for commoner uses. The work was compiled at the request of Juan de Beamonte, prior of the Order of St. John of Jerusalem, and La T. seems to have been diffident of his powers to achieve it satisfactorily. Still, it enjoyed esteem in the 15th and 16th cents. ; ' but the taste for such works passed away in Spain, as it did elsewhere ' (Ticknor, i, 377), and an Ital. version, 1556, masqueraded as an original work, and was actually transld., as such, into Span. by Caceres, a converted Jew at Antwerp in 1663. *Habent sua fata libelli !*

La Torre, de, Francisco (*c.* 1534-*c.* 1594): Span. poet ; of the school of Garcilasso (q.v.) at Salamanca. Wr. Italianate sonnets and love-poems, frequently adapted or transld. from Ital. originals. The collection was publd. by Quevedo (q.v.), who was at one time mistaken for its author.

Laube, Heinrich (1806-84): Germ. novelist and playwright. Wr. *das junge Europa*, 1833-37 ; *der deutsche Krieg*, 9 vols., 1865-66,—both in the vein of hist. fiction ; *Struensee*, 1847 ; *die Karlsschüler* (see s.v. Schiller, at the Karlsschule in Stuttgart), 1847, and *Graf Essex* (queen Elizabeth's favourite), 1856,—his 3 most successful plays ; and was also director of theatres in Leipsic and Vienna, and author of several sound treatises on the stage.

Laude (laud): It. sacred song, dating from early times. Such hymns tended to differ little, except in the object of their devotion, from love-songs of secular orig. ; the same tunes, the same amatory expressions and equal passion are found in both. The *laudi* by natural gradation acquired features of dialogue and action, and produced *divozioni* in Umbria in the 13th, and *sacre rappresentazioni* in Florence in the 15th cent. There are numerous collections, or song-books, of *laudi*, and the type was popular in the dawn of the Renaissance as a channel of vernacular verse.

Laurenberg, Johann (*c.* 1588-1658): Germ. humanist and satirist ; settled in Denmark, 1623, and was the author of satires in the Dan. tongue, which formed part of the inspiration of Holberg (q.v.) in the next cent. L. wr. much Gk. and Lat. poetry, some Germ. comic dramas, and, most memorably, ' Four Absurdities ' (*Scherzgedichte*), in which he smartly satirized the ' à-la-modish ' affectations in dress, speech, lit., etc., characteristic of his times. The epithet and point of view were Logau's (q.v.) ; but L. was far from imitating Logau's pointed epigrams and neat rhymes. He deliberately chose the Low Germ. dialect (*Platt-deutsch*) of his lowland home at Rostock : the language of the early Bible and of the popular *Reinke Vos* (s.v. Reynard) ; thus emphasizing his repudiation of the aims of Opitz (q.v.). L.'s 4 poems achieved the success which they merited in a High Germ. transln. He wr., too, a Lat. *Antiquarius*, a dict. of archaisms, 1624.

Lavater, Johann Kaspar (1741-1801): Germ. (-Swiss) poet, preacher, and philosopher ; more notable for his Christian life than for his science and poetry. L. was an early worshipper at the shrine of Klopstock (q.v.), and was admitted, later, to the intimacy of Goethe (q.v.). He takes a prominent place in the Sturm und Drang (q.v.) movement, and his description of genius (*Genie*), which gave its name to the period (*Geniezeit*), is characteristic of the aims of the movers and of the nature of the movement. L. calls it ' the torch of the universe, the salt of the earth, the substantive in the grammar of humanity, the image of divinity, creator, destroyer, revealer of the secrets of God and men, guide of nature, prophets, priests and kings'. Genius, he says, is ' super-Nature, super-Art, super-Learning, super-Talent, self-life. Its way is the way of lightning, or storm-wind, or eagle. We gaze with amazement at the path of its passage ; we hear its rush, or see its majesty ; but we know not the whither or whence of its going, and no man findeth the print of its feet '. This intense, intractable individualism seized Germany's poetic youth like strong wine ; stronger than wine, its influence endured, and permeated with the radiance of its faith the philosophy of a Kant and the vision of a Goethe. L.'s own contribution to the new thought was contained in his *Physiognomical Fragments towards the Advancement of Human Knowlodge and Human Love*, 1775-78, a work in which Goethe is said to have collaborated, and which, despite its large admixture of pseudo-science, stands in the line of advance towards a better comprehension of man in his environment. L. wr., too, a Messianic epos; a biblical play, *Abraham and Isaac*; hymns and patriotic songs: the last, *Swiss Melodies*, 1767, forming the worthiest memorial of the recreations of this Zurich parson.

La Vega, de, Alonso (d. 1565): Span. dramatist; member of the strolling company of Rueda (q.v.); his 3 prose dramas (one of which was dramatized from a *novella*—ii, 44—of Bandello, q.v.) were issued by Timoneda (q.v.).

La Vega, de, Bernardo (fl. 1591): Span. pastoralist; resided in the New World, where he became a canon at Tumman in Peru. Wr. the *Pastor de Iberia*, a poor performance in the manner of Montemayor (q.v.).

La Vega, de, Garcilasso (*c.* 1540-1615): Span. historian; said to be a cousin of the famous Vega (q.v.), and, through his mother, an Inca of Peru. He served in the Span. South American campaigns, and wr. some picturesque chronicles of Peruvian history.

Law, John (1671-1729): Scot. speculator. Fled from London to Amsterdam in consequence of a duel, 1694; studied credit-banking, but failed to convince the Scot. parliament of the value of his paper-currency proposals on his return to Edinburgh, 1700; carried his schemes to Paris, where he and his brother, Wm. Law (1675-1752), started a banking business, 1716. Two years later, the regent of France consented to the transformation of L.'s business into a national bank; in 1719, he floated a scheme for reclaiming lands in the Mississippi valley, and in 1720 he reached the dizzy altitude of controller-general of Fr. finances. It will be remembered that king Louis xiv had died in 1715, after the close, 1713, of his war of the Spanish succession. Public want and economic distress had attained terrible dimensions, and the extravagance of the regent's court, in the minority of Louis xv, did not tend to redintegration. L.'s bubble burst, of course, and his importance to lit. is contained in the fact that his financial operations, conducted on so vast a scale of disastrous speculation, gave occasion for the economists, physiocrats (q.v.), *philosophes* (q.v.), and others to back their theories of political reform, in the age which closed in revolution, with arguments directly drawn from immediate circumstances within public knowledge. L. served as a drunken helot to the purists of political science, newly released by historians and philosophers from the trammels of sacrosanctity, with which tradition and authority had surrounded it during the absolutist monarchy of Louis xiv.

Law, William (1686-1761): Engl. divine; tutor to the father of Gibbon (q.v.), the historian; wr. brilliant polemic, 1723, against B. Mandeville (q.v.), author of the *Fable of the Bees*; publd., 1728, his *Serious Call to Devout and Holy Life*, which was at once logical and mystical, and deeply impressed Wesley (q.v.) and others.

Layamon (fl. 1200): Engl. verse-chronicler; wr. *Brut* in unrhymed alliterative verse, based on the existing chronicles in Fr. and Welsh. L., who was connected with the church of Areley Regis (Ernley), Worcs., is known only by references in his own chronicle.

Larazillo (Span.): 'Little Lazaro', rogue-hero of *La vida* (life) *de Lazarillo de Tormes*, the

first formal picaresque novel (q.v.). Its authorship and date are uncertain. The earliest ascertained edns., were issued, 1554, at Alcala, Burgos and Antwerp, and the authorship was formerly ascribed to Diego de Mendoza (q.v.), an attribution since abandoned. The word L. occurs in Span. romance before 1554, and some of the incidents in the *L. de T.* have been traced to older tales and jest-books. But no priority of invention in detached phrases or adventures detracts from the originality of the anon. *L. de T.*, which is the coherent autobiography of little Lázaro. Born on a bank of the river Tormes, and starting his career of wit as a blind man's leader, after serving various masters, such as a miserly priest and a vendor of indulgences, he finished up ' on the pinnacle of fortune' as town-crier at Toledo. *L.* was happy in the time of its appearance; the realities of empire and the disillusioning costs of conquest were beginning to bring home to some of the more thoughtful minds in Spain the artificial structure of the ideals, fed so luxuriously on the diet of the chivalric romances of the *Amadis* and *Palmerin* (qq.v.) type. That his realism was a little in advance of its age is shown by the comparative non-success of an anon. sequel to *L. de T.*, 1555; and perhaps the fear of the Inquisition, which dealt fairly lightly with Lázaro himself, may have acted as a warning to his successors. But the tone of mockery and cynicism, and the substitution of the sordid *chevalier d'industrie* for the knight of gallantry and adventure, were in the line of advance of fiction; and *L. de T.* marks an important point of departure, the course of which is to be traced in Bredero, Aleman, Dekker, Cervantes himself, Lesage, Fielding, Dickens (qq.v., and see s.v. Novel). As such, and apart altogether from the intrinsic merit of the romance, with its cold and objective cynicism, *L.* stands at the head of a new movement in fiction; and it is significant of the creative forces at work in the 16th cent. in Span. life and lit.—the pivotal date in 1492, when Granada fell, and the New World was discovered, and Spain expelled her Jews,— that, alike in chivalry and in anti-chivalry (the type and the anti-type of ideal fiction), the motive-power should have come from Spain: in the anon. *Amadis* of the last decade of the 15th cent., with its immense influence through France; and in the anon. *L. de T.* of 60 years after, when the glow was fading, and the laurels were withering, and the nation was waiting for *Don Quixote* to dissolve its memories in laughter.

Lazarus, Moritz (1824-1903): Germ. philosopher; held chairs at Berne and Berlin; a distinguished member of the Jew. community. Wr., 1898, *Ethik des Judenthums*, *i*, and edited, with Steinthal (q.v.) *Zeitschrift für Völkerpsychologie*.

Lear, Edward (1812-88): Engl. nonsense-writer; artist; traveller; in the second of these capacities, he exhibited at the Royal Academy and gave drawing-lessons to queen Victoria, 1845; in the second and third, he wr. and illustrated some travel-books of Italy, Greece, and Corsica; in the first and second, he wr. and illustrated the delightful *Book of Nonsense*, 1846 (10th edn., enlarged, 1863, and often re-issued),—inimitable, except for its successors from L.'s own pen and pencil. That the 'limerick' of newspaper competitions (why so called we do not know) is commonly required to be composed in the metre employed by L. does not detract from enjoyment of his verses. They conveyed sense in nonsensical form, and sequent reason in verbal *non sequiturs*. L. was a genuine humourist, and he and Carroll (q.v.) help to establish an Engl. claim to divide the literary kingdom of nonsense with Germany alone among the nations.

Le Bel, Jean (14th cent.) : Fr. chronicler ; canon of Liège. Wr. out of his own experience, in simple, direct, romantic prose, an hist. *Chronique* of the period 1326-61. This served as a model and an exemplar to Froissart (q.v.), whose Bk. i, in its earlier versions, was little more than a paraphrase from Le B., weakened by the necessary substitution of the third for the first personal pronoun. Le B.'s affluence, deep reading, and wide travel lent him considerable importance in private life and in public affairs ; he liked pomp and pageantry and the display of great state, and practised in his writing the art of picturesque narration descended from chivalric romance.

Lebrixa, de, -i. Antonio (*c.* 1455-1522) : Span. scholar ; Italianate ; received his education in humanistic letters at the coll. of St. Clement, Bologna, founded in 1364 by the then archbp. of Toledo for the benefit of Spaniards in Italy. L. is known by the scholar's-name of Nebrissensis. On his return to Spain in 1473, he brought back the fruits of learning, as a kind of missionary of culture, and became prof. of grammar at the univ. of Salamanca. L. took charge of the Gk. text of the great polyglott Bible (q.v.), organized by card. Ximenez (q.v.), and wr. dictionaries, including one of Span., important in the history of the development of Castilian as the leading language among the Span. dialects ; and grammars of Lat. (*Introductiones Latinæ*, 1481), Gk., and Hebr. It has been pointed out that L. anticipated Erasmus (q.v.) in the theory of the correct pronunciation of Gk., and he ranks among the greater humanists of the age.

-ii. Marcelo (16th cent.). Span. poet · son of above. Wr. a dramatic medley (*Triaca*) in 3 parts, ' of the soul ', ' of love ', and ' of sorrow ', which is rather reminiscent of the age of the songbooks (s.v. *Cancionero*) than anticipatory of the era of Span. drama.

Le Brun, Ponce Denis Escouchard (1729-1807) : Fr. poet. Wr. so-called Pindaric odes, which earned him the surname of ' Le Brun Pindare ', and an unfind. didactic poem, *la Nature*. Le B. was a noted writer of epigrams, at that time a serious diversion ; and was fortunate enough, in a troubled age, to compose verses in celebration of king Louis xvi, the Revolution, and the emperor Napoleon i successively, earning a pension from the last.

Lecky, Wm. Edward Hartpole (1838-1903) : Engl. (Irish) historian ; O.M. (an orig. member of the Order). Wr. *History of Engld. in the 18th Cent.*, 8 vols., 1878-90, a work of permanent importance ; preceded by more special studies, which, valuable as they are, did not win universal acceptance : *History of the Rise and Influence of the Spirit of Rationalism in Europe*, 2 vols., 1865, and *History of European Morals from Augustus to Charlemagne*, 2 vols., 1869. L.'s later works included *Democracy and Liberty*, 2 vols., 1896 ; *The Map of Life*, 1899, etc. L. was M.P. at Westminster for Trinity Coll., Dublin, 1895-1903. In his attraction to the broad canvas, the big map, and the sweeping range, L. was a disciple of H. Buckle (q.v.) and, less immediately, of Comte (q.v.), and he ranks with Burke (q.v.) as an intellectual Irishman enriching Engl. lit. and public life.

Ledeganck, Karel Lodewijk (1805-47) : Belgian (-Flemish) poet. Wr. *Bloemen mijner Lente* (' Flowers of my Spring '), 1839, and ' The Three Sister-Cities ' (Ghent, Bruges, Antwerp), 1846. L.'s name is important as the first— Conscience (q.v.) being the greater second —who revived the native Flemish of Belgium as a literary language independent of the French.

Ledesma Buitrago, de, Alonso (1552-1623) : Span. poet ; reputed founder (with a certain Alonso de Bonilla) of the so-called *conceptismo*, conceited style, as distinguished from the *cultismo* (q.v.), or *estilo culto*, learned style. The difference lay between the verbal play of the concettists (see s.v. Conceits) and the play with ideas of Gongora (q.v.) and the cultists ; but both alike led to affectation and obscurity, and L.'s innovation, in his ' Spiritual and Moral Conceits ', 1600-12, and his ' Chronicle of the Fanciful Monster ', 1615 (variously ascribed to Bonilla), failed to establish a school. (See, too, s.v. Quevedo).

Le Fanu, Joseph Sheridan (1814-73) : Irish novelist ; grandson of Alice Sheridan (q.v.), sister of the greater dramatist and orator. Wr. *The House by the Churchyard*, 1863 ; *Uncle Silas*, 1864 ; *In a Glass Darkly*, 1872 ; and other novels, and is generally ranked next to Lever (q.v.) in the history of fiction in Ireland. Mr. A. P. Graves, himself an Irish poet, in *C.H.E.L.*, xiv, 310, adds that Le F.'s verse and, notably, his drama, *Beatrice*, are likewise memorable for their fine qualities : ' our (Irish) literature can ill afford to lose lyrical dramas with such a stamp of appalling power upon them as is impressed on *Beatrice*, or old-world idylls so full of Gaelic glamour as *The Legend of the Glaive*, or so terrible a confession . . . as *The Song of the Bottle*, and such stirring Irish ballads as *Shamus O'Brien* and *Phaudrig Crohoore* '.

Lefèvre, d'Etaples, Jacques (1455-1537) : Fr. humanist ; theologian ; commonly known as D'Étaples from his birthplace at Étaples, and Latinized as Faber Stapulensis. L.'s Biblical zeal almost passed the limits of orthodoxy, as it was interpreted in the early 16th cent., and may be said to have anticipated, in his speculations of 1512, the coming Lutheran Reformation (q.v.). But the very novelty of his views as to right of research into texts and origins served to disguise their bold departure, and L. was tutor to the younger son of king Francis i. Suspicion grew more active shortly after the publication, 1523, of the first part of L.'s new Fr. scholarly transln. of the Bible which the Sorbonne condemned. Queen Margaret (q.v.) of Navarre extended her ægis to the enterprise, which was completed, and issued, 1530, at Antwerp. It became the authorized version of the Fr. Catholic Church, and was adapted to Huguenot use by Olivetan (q.v.).

Lefèvre-Deumier, Jules (1797-1857): Fr. poet; a founder of *lyrisme* (q.v.); a member of the first *cénacle* of Nodier (q.v.), and was ranged on the side of Vigny and Hugo (qq.v.) by his vol. of romantic verse, 1823.

Leibniz, Gottfried Wilhelm (1646-1716): Germ. philosopher. Son of prof. of moral philosophy at Leipsic, where he visited the univ.; later, resided in Paris, where he met Huyghens (q.v.), and London, where he met Boyle (q.v.) and others; returned to Hanover, and afterwards to Berlin, where he founded, 1700, the society (Academy, 1744) of Sciences (*der Wissenschaften*). It is not relevant to lit. to discuss all the many-sided activities of ' the first of the great German thinkers '. His criticism and completion of the systems of Descartes, Spinoza, and Hobbes; his doctrine of monads, substantial units or primal substances; his correspondence with Bossuet; his dispute with Newton for the discovery of the infinitesimal calculus; these and other facts of L.'s illustrious career as a mathematician and metaphysician must be sought in histories of those sciences. His importance to lit. is twofold: first, though he himself wrote mostly in Fr. or Lat., he strenuously advocated a scientific revival of Germ. speech and manners among his countrymen; secondly, and more significantly, L.'s towering figure marks the height of the Aufklärung (q.v.) movement, directed to the reconstruction of national thought after the disintegration of the Thirty Years' War (q.v.). He brought into Germany from France, Engld. and Holland a note of spiritual and intellectual rationalism, which permanently raised the level of culture, and makes a landmark in its history between Luther and Lessing. In his idealism and his mental power he is the most like Plato among Germ. philosophers; and, deeply as he was indebted to Descartes for the inspiration of his thought, it took the colour of his own optimism and was enriched by his native Teuton qualities.

Leipsic : Centre of Germ. intellectual activities in Saxony. Its univ. was founded, 1409, and its fairs were important early in the 15th cent. Under the influence of Celtes (q.v.), L. and Deventer (esp. the former) were prominent in the new art of printing (q.v.); and, though these various humanistic paths were blocked by the devastation of the Thirty Years' War (q.v.), L. became a great trading community and has been the leading city in the Germ. bk. trade since the 18th cent. The *Leipsic Acts*, a periodical review of international learning, commenced publication, 1682, ' but, being written in Latin, with more regard to the past than to the growing state of opinions, . . . and with an absence of anything like philosophy or even connected system in erudition, it is one of the most unreadable books, relatively to its utility in learning, which has ever fallen into my hands ' (Hallam, *Lit. of Europe*, iii, 551; the present writer can merely repeat this at secondhand). L. is famous as the home of Gottsched (q.v.), who

held his throne there as the dictator of taste during his period of ascendency, and whose personality brought the univ. into prominence, as one of the combatants in the feud between the Swiss and Saxon schools, with Zurich as headquarters of the former. At L., too, was founded the poets' union, which deserted Gottsched's standard, and started, 1744, the *Bremer Beiträge* (q.v.) at Bremen, as the organ of their craft. Round them were gathered many of the short-lived writers, who kept the feud alive for a few years (see, too, s.v. Lessing).

Leisewitz, Johann Ariton (1752-1806): Germ. dramatist. Wr., 1774 (publd., 1776), a tragedy, *Julius of Tarentum*, with which he had hoped to win a prize offered by Schröder (q.v.); it was won by Klinger (q.v.) with his drama, *The Twins*, which dealt with the same theme of two brothers. L.'s was really the better play, though less explosively violent, and less well suited, accordingly, to the prevalent taste of the Sturm und Drang (q.v.) movement. His disappointment went deep, and no other work of any note was produced by him, though his genius showed affinities with Lessing in its restraint and with Schiller (in his early period) in its power.

Le Maire de Belges, Jean (1475-1524): Fr. poet; historiographer to king Louis xii; nephew of Molinet (q.v.). (Belges, or Bavia, is in Hainault). Le M. is sometimes accounted the father of the Rhétoriqueurs (q.v.), and he displays in his poems their tendencies to allegory and Latinizing. His work was valuable in the literary development of the Fr. language, and his chief prose-work, *Illustrations des Gaules*, has antiquarian interest and a picturesqueness of style. Wr. allegorical poem, *Le Temple d'Honneur et de Vertu*, 1503, an elegy in memory of a member of the Bourbon dynasty.

Lemercier, Népomucène (1771-1840): Fr. poet; playwright. L.'s tragic *Méléagre* was played at the Théâtre français as early as 1788, and won instant success; his *Pinto* (1800) was a first example of hist. comedy on the Fr. stage (L. invented the name *comédie historique*). But it is by his *Panhypocrisiade*, 1819, a dramatic-satiric-epic poem designed on a colossal scale, that L. is chiefly to be remembered; for the work, though far from completely successful, is extraordinarily vigorous and clever. L. would have been happier if he had written a few years later, after the linguistic and metrical reforms of *le lyrisme* (q.v.) in France; he was too much constricted by the classical tradition to express his new thought with genuine spontaneity.

Lemierre, Antoine Marie (1723-93): Fr. poet and dramatist. In the latter capacity, wr. *Hypermnestre*, 1758; *Guillaume Tell*, 1766; and other plays; and in the former wr. misc. verse, imitative of the prevailing fashion of Young and Thomson (qq.v.) in Engld.

Lemon, Mark (1809-70): Engl. humourist; wr. plays, novels, and misc. works, and is always famous as a founder and first editor of *Punch*, from 17 July, 1841, till his death.

Lemos, de, Conde (c. 1576-1622): Span. patron of letters; Pedro Hernandez de Castro, count of Lemos, marquis of Sarria; viceroy, 1610, of

Naples, where his court was a centre of literary and artistic culture. Cervantes (q.v.) dedicated to L. his *Persiles and Sigismunda* a few days before his death ; Vega (q.v.) acted as L.'s secretary, and his patronage or influence was extended to most of the prominent men of letters of his age.

Le Moyne, Pierre (1602-72): Fr. poet; ecclesiastic. Wr. *Saint-Louis*, an epic poem, on the model supplied by Du Bartas (q.v.), in 18 cantos, 1651-58 ; adversely criticized by Boileau (q.v.).

Lena, de, Pero Rodriguez (15th cent.): Span. official secretary to king John ii (q.v.) of Castile. Wr. *Libro del Passo Honroso defendido por el excelente cavallero Suero de Quiñones* ; a chronicle of chivalry. (See s.v. Passo Honroso).

L'Enclos, de, Anne. See **Ninon**.

Lenngren, Anna Marie (1754-1817): Swed. poet; *née* Malmstedt. Fru L., whose verses were favourably known to king Gustavus iii (q.v.), publd. many of her poems anon., and they were ascribed variously to Kellgren, Leopold (qq.v.) and others. Her muse was domestic, but not cloying in its sentiment ; her attitude towards family-life being not unlike that of Patmore (q.v.) in a later generation. 'A Few Words to my dear Daughter' is the title of one of her best-known poems.

Lenz, Jakob Michael Reinhold (1750-92): Germ. poet ; critic. L. reached Strassburg in 1771, and joined the young circle of the Sturm und Drang (q.v.), of which Goethe (q.v.) was the leader. He founded his writings and even his mode of life on Goethe's model ; so much so, that, when he followed his leader to Weimar, in 1776, the duke called him Goethe's ape. The ape could not refrain from monkey-tricks, and he made himself impossible at Weimar by his references to the Goethe and frau v. Stein *liaison*. A year later, L.'s unbalanced brain gave way, and he gradually declined. L.'s so-called Shakespearean dramas (Shakespeare was the rallying-point of the Sturm und Drang), 'The Master of Ceremonies' (*Hofmeister*), 1774, 'Soldiers', 1776, etc., mark an advance from the level of the Saxon comedies, and are full of the wild and strenuous features associated with the green wood of the young Germ. movement. More notable was his performance in the field of lyric, in which he successfully emulated Goethe's love-songs, and took up the dropped threads of Goethe's passion for Friederika Brion (see s.v. Goethe). More notable still were L.'s critical writings : *Remarks on the Theatre*, 1774, which he appended to his transln. of *Love's Labours Lost*.

Leo x ; Giovanni de Medici (1475-1521): It. statesman ; patron of learning ; pope of Rome, 1513. Second son of Lorenzo, The Magnificent (see s.v. Medici); succeeded pope Julius ii, in whose papal reign 'the zenith of Renaissance culture falls' (*C.M.H.*, ii, 11). L.'s relations to Rafael and Michelangelo, in contrast with the munificence of his predecessor, cannot detain us here ; nor are we concerned with the politico-religious policy of his papacy, respect for which may be said to be diminishing as the researches of historians grow more exact. But deductions from L.'s fame as patron of art and as head of the Church correspond to a less favourable

view than was formerly held of his place in the lit. of Europe. The so-called 'golden age of Leo', which was hailed with such ample expectation, and which Erasmus (q.v.) praised so abundantly, is seen to have reflected at its opening the glitter of the reign just closed, and to have failed to keep it undimmed through the ensuing years. If we may employ an allusion strictly within the four walls of lit., we should say that L. was rather the hope of Ariosto than of Luther, both of whom (qq.v.) were his contemporaries ; certainly, he was more susceptible to the cultured overtures of flattery than to the menacing demands of reform. Want of money was largely responsible for the decline of papal patronage ; but even this, though partly due to L.'s generous gifts to the poor, was also caused by his lavishness to favourites and sycophants, even of so base a type as Pietro Aretino (q.v.). Thus, Janus Lascaris (q.v.) was summoned at the beginning of L.'s reign to lead a school of Gk. at Rome, but was allowed (1518) to transfer his talents to Paris ; similarly, L. founded the univ. of Rome, but was compelled in the same way to reduce its establishment a few years later. Still, as son of The Magnificent, as an apt pupil of the eminent scholars who had been attracted to his father's court at Florence, as a true Hellenist and a discriminating *virtuoso*, and as the much-admired head of a luxurious and pleasure-loving court, to which intellect and talent naturally gravitated as a centre, L. is conspicuous among popes as patron and leader of Renaissance ideals, second only, if second, to Nicholas v (q.v.).

Leon, de, Luis Ponce (*c.* 1528-91): Span. poet ; a Church brother (*fray*), and commonly known by that title. In the departments into which critics divide and subdivide the realm of lit., L. belonged to the Salamanca school of Span. poetry, as distinct from that of Seville ; i.e., to the more definitely national, and not to the more definitely Italianate direction taken after the reforms of Boscan and Garcilasso (qq.v.). L. was born at Belmonte, and, like some other great men of Spain, was partly of Jew. orig., through his great-grandmother, Leonor de Villanueva, who was burnt, 18 April, 1512, 20 years after the expulsion of the Jews. L. was edu. at the univ. of Salamanca, and became an Augustinian monk in 1544 ; and the habits of monastery and univ. were his dower through life. He occupied chairs of scholastic theology and sacred scripture at Salamanca, and it is pointed out by Ticknor (ii, 76) that L.'s rapid professorial promotion over the heads of rival candidates aroused the jealousy of some of these, who numbered among them members of the Dominican order, which controlled the weapons of the Inquisition. It may here be recalled that it was the Dominicans at Cologne who persecuted Reuchlin (q.v.), and against whom was launched the philippic of the *Epistolæ* (q.v.) *obscurorum virorum*. Inasmuch as Reuchlin was attacked in consequence of his Hebraic humanism, the two cases are further analogous ; for L.'s lectures on the Vulgate Bible in 1569 were denounced as sympathetic with the Lutheran heresy of favouring interpretation by the

Hebr. text and rabbinical commentary; the suspected taint of Jew. blood was an aggravation of L.'s offence. Starting with an academic dispute between the professors, the matter was deemed of sufficient moment to call for the intervention of the inquisitors; and on 27 March, 1572, L. was removed from Salamanca to Valladolid, where he was kept in prison till 28 Sept., 1576. The *gravamen* of the charges against him was his transln. of Solomon's canticle (*The Song of Songs*) from the original Hebr. into Castilian verse. After this 4½ years' detention in the secret prisons of the Inquisition, L.'s 7 judges at Valladolid voted, 4 for 'moderate' torture, 2 for public rebuke, and one doubtfully. The verdict was referred to the supreme tribunal at Madrid, who acquitted L., 7 Dec., 1576, after admonishing him and confiscating his offending transln. of the canticle. On the 30 Dec., L. returned to Salamanca, where a provisional chair was created for him, and where he is said to have resumed his lectures with the phrase 'dicebamus hesterna die' (we were saying on the previous occasion); the story is too fine not to be retold, but it is now said to be an invention dating from 1623. Later, L. filled the chairs of moral philosophy and of the Bible successively. His experience of the tender mercies of the Inquisition was not unique in his age, and tolerance, despite the defence of the Inquisition in the opening chapters of *Luis de Leon : a study of the Spanish Renaissance*, by Aubrey F. G. Bell (Oxford, 1925), was least indigenous to Spain of all countries. Still, the life-history of this pious poet, with the 5 years blocked out by the religious censors of learning, affords valuable evidence, accumulated in Italy, France, the Netherlands, and Germany, to the travail of humanism in the 16th cent. L.'s more strictly theological writings included a prose-dialogue on 'The Names of Christ' (*de los Nombres de Cristo*), 1583-85; an 'Exposition of the Book of Job', with a verse-transln., composed in prison, but not publd. till 1779; 'The Perfect Wife' (*la perfecta Casada*), 1583, composed in connection with *Proverbs*, xxxi, and suggested, perhaps, by Vives's (q.v.) *de Christiana femina*. His poetical writings, restricted in inspiration by his clerical habit, gained in depth what they lost in breadth; and Kelly (*Lit. espagn.*, 247) notes that they reveal in places a 'majestic and serene simplicity not found again till Wordsworth' (q.v.). Reference is esp. due to his ode on a 'serene night' (*Noche serena*). 'Leon had a Hebrew soul', writes Ticknor (ii, 87, 89); 'while his religious odes and hymns, beautiful in their severe exactness of style, rank him before Klopstock and Filicaja, his prose, more rich and no less idiomatic, places him at once among the greatest masters of eloquence in his native Castilian'. L.'s poetical works, including translns. from Horace, Virgil, and other masters, were publd. in 3 vols. by Quevedo (q.v.) in 1631, and have frequently been re-issued and transld. A definitive edn. of L.'s work is still to seek, but valuable bibliographies, etc., are included in the vol. by Mr. A. F. G. Bell mentioned above.

Leon, Hebreo. See **Abravenel.**

Leopardi, Giacomo (1798-1837): It. poet, essayist, scholar; count by rank; the greatest name in Ital. pure lit. since Petrarch (q.v.). L., like Heine (q.v.), was an invalid from youth upwards; unlike Heine, he was deprived of the chief comfort of a suffering child,—the close sense of his mother's sympathy; for the countess L., little Giacomo's mother, saved what her husband spent, and this sense of dependence on his wife embarrassed the father of the family in his relations to his children, of whom the poet was the eldest. The ménage was probably not very different (just a little more accentuated, perhaps) from that of many impoverished aristocrats, struggling to pay off mortgages; but L.'s sensitive, studious childhood was deeply embittered by his mother's lack of sympathy, and her hardness was partly responsible for his grave and increasing ill-health. He suffered from a spinal disease, which affected his eyesight, wasted his frame, and racked his nerves. With his shrunken limbs and sallow face, and with his voice which he could not raise above a whisper lest he should spit blood, L.'s physical life was a wreck, the more tragic in contrast with the vigour of his intellect and spirit, which survived his body's decay, and which found expression in the rarely sweet smile remarked by everyone who knew him. L. made friends, and escaped from the 'prison' which was his home at Recanati. He met and attracted Manzoni, Viesseux, Niebuhr (qq.v.) and others; he was devoted to a political rebel, Giordani, whose intimacy seems to have obstructed the efforts of several friends to find him permanent employment as a prof. or an official; and his latter years were soothed by the attentions of a young Neapolitan, Antonio Ranieri, who stood to him somewhat in the relation of Theodore Watts-Dunton to Swinburne (qq.v.). In search of health, and love, and work, and change, he resided from time to time at Florence, Bologna, Pisa, etc., and finally at Naples, varied by periods of exile at home at Recanati, where he was at last recognized as a prophet, and where a statue has since been erected to him. His biography included love-passages of peculiar passion and poignancy, into which this brief record need not enter, but which prove the poet's superiority to the weakness of the flesh; and a last word is due to the Milanese publisher, Stella, a kind of Cottle of Bristol in generosity, who used to pay L. so many *scudi* a month for hackwork at anthologies, etc. The best product of this employment was his edn. of Petrarch.

We come back, where we began, to that master's name. The influence of Cicero on Petrarch is noted here s.vv. The same influence, transmitted through Petrarch, was exercised on L. His great patriotic odes were Petrarchan; and between the *canzoni* of the early 14th and those of the early 19th cent., there were 500 years of Ital. history, but no similar odes to Ital. unity. Particularly we may select in this context the ode to the 'ardent Italian', Angelo Mai, 'upon his discovery of the MS. of Cicero's *De Republica*'. It takes us straight back to the pioneer of humanism, with his virginal joy over the Roman master, in whose likeness the Renaissance was imagined : ' O famed Discoverer ', cried L. to Mai, ' be

Unresting : wake the dead,
Since the quick sleep ; bid the old heroes rise
And scourge us with their tongues, until this vain
And rotting age, revitalized, shall rush
To emulate their deeds, or learn to blush '.*

Of the very essence of Petrarch, again, nay, of Italy herself embalmed, is the verse in the same ode, *Ahi dal dolor comincia e nasce L'Italo canto ;* ' Alas, of suffering aye was born Italian song ' (cf., perhaps unhappy Heine's ' Aus meinen grossen Schmerzen Mach' ich die kleinen Lieder ') ; and this *canzone*, together with those *To Italy, On the Monument of Dante* and the *Ginestra* (' Broom '), are among the noblest, if not actually the noblest, expressions of the Ital. muse, as they are undoubtedly among the finest and most letter-perfect compositions in the Ital. tongue. For L. was philologer as well as poet, ' and it is his signal distinction to be the only Italian poet and one of the only poets of modern Europe to have completely acquired the Greek style at its simplest and clearest, *while at the same time retaining his own world of ideas* ' (Bickersteth, *op. cit.* ; author's italics). ' As Shelley is a Greek by his pantheism, Keats by his feeling for nature, Platen by the architectonic of his verse, so is Leopardi by his impeccability ' (R. Garnett, *Ital. Lit.*, 359.) Remember that L. was contemporary with all 3, and actually met von Platen—for whom, see s.v. at Naples. We may borrow one more quotation from Bickersteth : ' Dante first taught modern Europe how to *think* passionately, but it was reserved for Petrarch to teach it the art of passionate feeling ', and ' Dante was not better pleased to meet Virgil ' than was L. to come upon Petrarch ' at a critical moment in his life both as man and artist '. It is not surprising that L.'s great patriotic verse responded to the same test as Wordsworth's (q.v.),—that of instant revival in the Great War (1914-18). Indeed, as has been remarked, there is a deep and ultimate resemblance between these 2 poets, different as they were in circumstances and experience. Both looked beyond the appearances of things, beyond the illusion of human progress, to ' what man has made of man ' ; both found ' thoughts that do lie too deep for tears ' in the study of nature's lore : Wordsworth in the primrose, L. in *la ginestra*. In this sense, L.'s pessimism, emphasized by M. Arnold (q.v. ; see *Essays in Criticism, Second Series* : ' Byron '), and marked afresh by prof. Segré (*C.M.H.* x, 127), a fellow-countryman of the poet, is resumed in the ampler consolation of him who ' hath kept watch o'er man's mortality ', and who despairs not of man, but of men. L.'s chief prose work, besides his letters and his various scholarly writings, were the *Operette Morali*, 1827, a collection of essays illustrative of his mastery of Gk., Lat., Hebr. and modern languages, and students of style

take delight in his constant choice of the ' inevitable' word. Hauvette (*Lit. Ital.*, 436) asks if L. is ' classique ou romantique ? ', and the answer, despite L.'s place in the age of the Romantic triumph (see *P.E.L.*, xi ; L. was born in the year of *Lyrical Ballads* and Schlegel's Athenæum, and could read both Engl. and Germ.), is—neither and both : ' Classic by his conception of his art, he is at bottom far more romantic than Manzoni ; he evades all critical categories, and dominates them from the height of his genius '. And a last word about L.'s Hebraism. There is no Ital. Bible, in the sense in which the Engl. or Germ. vernaculars are *Engl.* and *Germ.* classics of lit., quite apart from their religious significance (see s.v. Bible). Thus, L., in his sacred hymns, was an original Hebraist, not a derivative Hebraist, like many authors of versions of the Psalms. He drew his Hebrew from the pure wells undefiled ; and, though a student of *Paradise Lost*, L.'s Puritan vein, as we may call it, was unique in an Ital. poet.

Leopold, Carl Gustav (1756-1829): Swed. poet ; patronized by king Gustavus iii (q.v.) and an original member of his academy. L., who adhered, though not blindly, to the Fr. school of Swed. letters, wr. erotic and sentimental verses and plays, satires, and didactic poetry : none of it of much present interest.

Lermontov, Michael Jurevich (1814-41) : Russ. poet ; second only to Pushkin (q.v.) in national esteem ; like him in the tragedy of his death in a love-duel, and, even more consistently than Pushkin, a disciple of Byron and romance (s.vv.). A third point of similarity between the two poets is their naturalization in Russ. lit. of the Caucasus, to which L. was exiled in 1838-39 and again in 1841 : and a fourth is the record of their stormy youth, orgiastic, showy, Byronic. Thus, L.'s early love-tales in verse and prose, *Monyo, The Fête at Peterhof*, etc., have a certain wild beauty of lyric and subjective force, reminiscent of the author of *Beppo* and *Don Juan*, but they have not much besides. It was in the later years of his short life that L., as an army-officer, and with a consciousness of the Scot. strain (Learmonth) in his blood, developed a deeper tone of romantic longing and idealism ; and that, finding no relative reply to the protests which he had hurled at the absolute, he became the poet of pessimism and doubt. Yet despite the Caucasian colour in the background of much of the scenery of his tales, and despite the *Weltschmerz* (the woe of the world) in his soul, L.'s romanticist flight was checked by the tuggings of Russ. realism. He was ' true to the kindred points of heaven and home ' ; and a certain ' homelessness in desert air ', or rather, in the gorgeous scenery of the Caucasus, pulled him back to the native simplicities which adorn Russ. style in its best and most characteristic manifestations. Splendid, indeed, he often was ; his ' Ode on the Death of the Poet ' (Pushkin) is most frequently cited in witness ; but L.'s ' poetic world, compared with Coleridge's, is solid fact beside intangible dream ' (Baring, *Russ. Lit.*, ' H.U.L.', 117), and in this little monograph and in his *Landmarks of Russian Literature* (Methuen, 1910 ; 28), and, again, in his *Oxford Bk. of Russ. Verse*

* ' Wake the dead' ; see s.v. Ciriaco. The transln. is from the Cambridge Press edn. of *The Poems of Leopardi*, by G. L. Bickersteth, M.A., Ch.Ch., Oxford, to which every student of the poet is immensely indebted.

(1924, xxvii-ix), Mr. Baring quotes L.'s poem, *The Testament*, in which the words ' are the words of familiar conversation, and yet the effect in the original is one of poignant poetical feeling and consummate poetic art '. ' What Matthew Arnold said about Byron and Wordsworth is true about Lermontov—there are moments when Nature takes the pen from his hand and writes for him ' ; and ' his diction is far more like that of everyday life than that of Wordsworth, and yet his verse is never prosaic '. Plainly, this effect is not reproducible in transln. Its interest is personal to L.'s fame ; and it is interesting, too, as a mark of the Russ. literary temperament, which was to find complete expression in fiction. Appropriately, therefore, one of L.'s masterpieces, *A Hero of our Days*, 1839, is a novel : the first of a line which was to found a new school in the lit. of Europe. The hero, Pechorin, is L. himself, but the subjectivity enhances rather than diminishes the value of the psychological study. Of L.'s poems the most important is *The Demon*, completed in 1841, but prohibited by the censorship for another 20 years. The demon again is L. himself, a wanderer, and a stranger between men and God ; the epic story is the conventional one of the demon's love for a mortal, who is seduced by her pity for the fallen angel (Vigny's, q.v., *Eloa* is the nearest analogue), and the epic setting is, again, the gorgeous Caucasus ; the heroine's name, Tamara, betrays it ; but the paradise sought by L. is not the lost paradise of Milton but the heaven on earth denied to ardent Russians. (' When will Russians become Russians ? ' L. had asked in a youthful drama). L.'s verse-tale of the Circassian convent-novice, *Mtsyry*, and his Erl-könig's dream of the silver voices of the fishes, is a glowing and moving poem, at the height of his lyrical powers. ' The temperament of a Thackeray with the wings of a Shelley ' is a description in Engl. literary terms which not inadequately characterizes L.

Leroy, Pierre (16th cent.): Fr. satirist. Contributor to, and probably editor of the *Satyre Ménippée* (q.v.).

Lesage, Alain René (1668-1747): Fr. novelist and dramatist ; a realist and satirist, who adapted Span. models to Fr. conditions. L. was born in poor circumstances, was apprenticed to law, married in 1694, received a modest pension from the abbé de Lyonne, but was otherwise honourably distinguished by his independent and hard-working livelihood at the practice of letters, from which he retired in 1743 to the canonry of his second son. His profession, which thus absorbed him, involved a certain amount of hackwork for the booksellers, and his stories, translns., anthologies, and other pot-boilers need not detain us here. L. had the journalist's instinct : to know something of everything, and everything of something ; and the subject which he had thoroughly mastered was Spain, as reflected in Span. lit. Picaresque fiction (see s.v. Novel), and all that it required in a knowledge of Span. travel and history, were at L.'s fingers' ends ; and he found his special study, picked up from bks., available partly by the kindness of the abbé of Lyonne, of immense help in obtaining

a hearing for his original writings as well as in supplying publishers' wants. After some years of hacking Span. authors, L. wr., 1707, *le Diable boiteux* (' The devil on two sticks '), the idea and title of which were borrowed from Guevara (q.v.), but which develops on wholly original lines. It is in essence a gallery of satirical portraits, more vivid and keener, if less profound, than the contemporary *Caractères* of La Bruyère (q.v.), but in the same class of inspiration ; and the amusing procession defiles rapidly before our eyes, linked, character to character, by the shrewd and not unkind wit of the showman-spectator of roguery. Two years later, 1709, in the midst of the war of the Span. Succession, in which Louis xiv tempted fate for the last time, L. produced his comedy, *Turcaret*, at the Comedie-française. It was a cruel and bitter piece of satire on the financial basis of society, and neither was his theatre strong enough to stomach it nor was his reputation equal to the attack. *Turcaret* ranks in lit. as one of the few comedies of high merit between Molière and Beaumarchais (qq.v.), but, in effect, it estopped L.'s dramatic ambitions ; he had to think of his livelihood before his art. The success of the *Diable boiteux* was repeated and extended by L.'s picaresque novel (or succession of novels) *Gil Blas*, 2 vols., 1715, vol. 3, 1724, vol. 4, 1735. It was again a series of characters, again a triumph of realism, and again a Fr. dress over a Span. model. L.'s debt to Vicente Espinel (q.v.), author of *Marcos Obregon*, has been gradually written down during the last two centuries, and, except for his general obligation to Span. originals, the search for the alleged *Gil Blas* of Spain has now been abandoned. It is recognized as L.'s own creation ; and L., accordingly, has the credit—and a very considerable one it is—of writing the novel, which ' is the immediate parent and pattern of that of Fielding and Smollett (qq.v.) in England ' (Saintsbury, *Short Hist. Fr. Lit.*, 390) ; indeed, Smollett, who transld. *Gil Blas*, directly admits the debt. The novel of manners, or character-delineation, which has prevailed over all other types, was a French creation before L. (See s.v. Sorel, whose *Francion* was ' the ancestor of *Gil Blas* '). Since the *Marianne* of Marivaux (q.v.) helped to form the *Pamela* of Richardson (q.v.), the novel, which proved so great a force in Engl. letters in the 19th cent., is thus due largely to Fr. example. The dates of publication of *Gil Blas* have some importance to its contents. Vols. 1 and 2 were written at the close of the reign of Louis xiv, vol. 3 during the regency of the duke of Orleans—a time of cynical reaction from the regal state and Versailles manners of the *grand monarque*,—and vol. 4 in the effective reign of Louis xv, which was to that extent a monarchical restoration. The public changes are reflected in the novel, which, though disjointed and occasional, displays real unity in its consecution ; and the glimpses afforded by its low adventures behind the scenes of great houses vary with the variations of government. *Gil Blas* is a fine, brave bk. ; its rogue-hero is realistically conceived, and its ease of style conceals its art. Lanson

(*Hist. Lit. Fr.*, 672) acutely remarks that *Gil Blas* lacks what is called 'difference', or personality and identity in his character; a criticism not improbable in a novel written over a course of 20 years. It remains one of the world-novels, and the chief work of a writer who added nothing more considerable to his list than a *Guzman d'Alfarache*, 1732, after Aleman (q.v.), and one or two similar adaptations. It should be added that the *Diable boiteux* supplies a classic instance of the linked-narrative of successive adventures, familiar in all ages from the *Arabian Nights* to *Sherlock Holmes*, and that L. reverted to its use in his *Valise Trouvée*, 1740.

Lescurel, de, Jehannot (14th cent.) : Fr. lyric poet Wr. *ballades* and *rondeaux.*

Leskov, Nikolai Semenovich (1831-95) : Russ. novelist; acquired a wide outlook and some acquaintance with conditions outside Russia by his work as agent to an Englishman, named Scott, who was chief steward of a large landed estate, and also from an Engl. Quaker friend of the family; wr. a novel, 1876, which has been transld. into Engl. (by I. F. Hapgood; John Lane) as *Cathedral Folk*, but which is deemed not typical of L.'s genius, so that the epithet of the Russ. Trollope (q.v.), which is sometimes applied to him, is not appropriate. For L. was, above all, a story-teller, 'in fact the greatest of Russian story-tellers', says prince Mirsky (*Modern Russ. Lit.*, 40), and has 'a wider and fuller knowledge of the Russian character than any other single Russian writer'. His range of language, humorous and colloquial, was co-extensive with his range of character-study, and 'in a better understanding of Leskov there lies much promise of a revival of Russian fiction ' (*ib.*, 42). Late in life, L. came under the influence of Tolstoy (q.v.), and wr. would-be moral stories of early Christian life, suffused, however, with a glow of pagan colour which tended to drench the moral.

Lespinasse, de, Julie Jeanne Eléanore (1731 or 1732-1776): Fr. literary hostess and letter-writer; of noble, but illegitimate birth. Lived, 1754-64, with mme. du Deffand (q.v.), where Dalembert (q.v.), a chief frequenter of their *salon*, was faithful to mlle. de L. when the two hostesses separated through jealousy. Their quarrel was due to mme. du Deffand's discovery that mlle. de L. was taking advantage of her blindness to wean the most eminent frequenters of her *salon* to a new *salon* of her own. The situation is treated in Mrs. Humphry Ward's (q.v.) novel, *Eleanor*. Mlle. de L. is remembered by her love-letters, addressed to a certain count de Guibert, and marked by genuine fervour and true feeling. That the writer was about 40 -years of age when she wr. them, and that she had never been beautiful, are facts which add to the real greatness of these literary remains.

Lessing, Gotthold Ephraim (1729-81): Germ. critic; playwright; leader of the Aufklärung (q.v.); 'beyond all dispute, the first critic in Europe' (Macaulay, *Addison*), and a critical practitioner of pure letters, in the sense that his plays and poems subserved his principles of criticism. These had limits, as Saintsbury (*Hist. Crit.*, iii, ch. 2) points out, and the limits

were not always co-terminous with the frontiers of lit. Thus, he considered Aristotle's *Poetics* ' as infallible as the *Elements* of Euclid ', but his own survey in the *Hamburgische Dramaturgie*, of the function and methods of tragedy excluded, or practically excluded, the lessons to be drawn from the examples of Æschylus and Aristophanes. Predilections other than purely literary affected his own infallibility as the Germ. Aristotle (q.v.) of criticism. His battle with Gottsched (q.v.) and the neo-classical school, of which his play, *Miss Sara Sampson*, was an expression; the side-issues of this frontal attack, which caused him to praise Shakespeare for his classical and to blame La Fontaine for his romantic aspects; the theological pre-occu-pation, which gave lit. *Nathan der Weise*, but which may have robbed it of even greater benefactions : it is these considerations and others that bring the historian of criticism to the impartial conclusion that L. 'is grand-duke of not a few critical provinces which, somehow or other, he never can consolidate into a universal monarchy of critical wit' (Saintsbury, *ibid.*). The exact truth would seem to be that L., though removed as far as possible from the taint or suspicion of sciolism, was so universal or ' enormous ' a scholar (the epithet is Goethe's) that he was enabled, as smaller men cannot, to select from each field of knowledge the particular sanctions which he sought for his system of literary criticism. Art lent it the quality of Gk. order; philosophy, the analytic temper; theology, the passion for freedom; archæology, the reverence for tradition; and the result was less a system than a combination of intuitions of culture, unapproached in its range of obser-vation and in its purity of inspiration. Historically, in the development of Germ. and European thought, L. is called an ' eman-cipated classic '. He broke away from the classical thraldom, and acknowledged a debt to Fr. and Engl. influences, but he did not throw right forward into the Sturm und Drang (q.v.), of which Herder (q.v.) was the prophet, Bürger (q.v.) the apostle, and Goethe (q.v.) the reconciling genius in Germany. Even more justly L. might be called the eman-cipating romantic, for, though both Herder and Winckelmann (q.v.), from whatever different points of view, found causes of dispute with L., yet the romance of the one and the Hellenism of the other were fed at L.'s spring. The critic of the transition from neo-classicism to romance forged the one indispensable link by which the lit. of Chateaubriand, Scott and Coleridge was to be connected with that of Lillo, Rousseau, and bp. Percy (qq.v.). The new lit. underwent a Germ. cure, and returned like a giant refreshed. These general considerations may help to explain the place which L. takes in the history of letters. In 1746 he entered the univ. of Leipsic, then under the sign of the *Bremer Beiträge* (q.v.), before Klopstock (q.v.) had written his *Messias*. Without definitely submitting himself to the waning influence of Gottsched, L. turned eagerly to the theatre which that dictator of taste supported, and he wr. some early comedies in the prevailing fashion of taste. The taste did not pay, and L. was involved in the financial failure, and repaired, 1748, to Berlin, where, save for a visit to Wittenberg, he remained till 1755. Then came a second period in Leipsic, 1755-58, and again a return to Berlin. 1760-65 L. spent in Breslau, as secretary to the governor of Silesia ; shortly afterwards, he accepted an appointment as director of the newly-founded National Theatre at Hamburg, where he remained till 1769. Early in 1770 he became librarian to the duke of Brunswick, and made Wolfenbüttel his headquarters till his death. In 1775 he accompanied prince Leopold of Brunswick on an Ital. tour, and in 1776 he married Eva König, who died in Jan., 1778. L. survived her only 3 years. The first Berlin period was devoted to dramatic writings and dramatic criticism. The former included the *Freigeist* (freethinker) and the *Juden* (Jews ; anticipating *Nathan*), and the latter included a short-lived quarterly review, edited by Mylius (q.v.) and L., and book-reviews for the newspaper since known as the *Vossische Zeitung*. A book by Lange (q.v.) was one of those thus reviewed, and the censure led to a little literary battle in which L. was first enabled to display his great critical gifts. This period was marked by L.'s friendship and collaboration with Mendelssohn and Nicolai (qq.v.) ; by his earliest excursions into theological controversy (*Rettungen*= rescues, i.q. of unappreciated thinkers), and by his ' domestic tragedy ' (*bürgerliches Trauerspiel*) *Miss Sara Sampson*, 1755. Lillo supplied the type, and Richardson the tears for this play, and L. himself supplied the dramatic theory from Fr. models of *comédie larmoyante* (q.v. ; and see s.v. La Chaussée) ; and since Sara Sampson and her lover perished by violence on the Frankfort stage the weeping heroine of everyday life has dominated the social-problem drama. The second Leipsic period was marked by L.'s friendship with E. v. Kleist, Brawe, Weisse, and Cranegk (qq.v.), all of whom, except Weisse, died young. In his second Berlin period L. resumed his association with Mendelssohn and Nicolai, and collaborated with them in the occasional ' Letters concerning recent literature ', commonly known as *Litteraturbriefe*. L.'s place in the triumvirate was taken, 1760, by Th. Abbt (q.v.). L.'s contributions to these letters form his most serious title to critical fame ; they contain his reasoned vindication of the Engl. Shakespearean stage, and his mature judgment on current Germ. schools, based on his perception of a national awakening after the Seven Years' War. This period was, perhaps, the most concentrated in L.'s career : he was working at lit. all the time ; and if much of it was the bread and butter work of transln. and annotation, it all tended to consistent effort. At Breslau, L. wr. the *Laokoon* (see s.v.) and the comedy of manners, *Minna von Barnhelm*, thus definitely challenging supremacy as the restorer of Hellenism (q.v.) to æsthetics and as the founder of a national type of Germ. drama. The *Laokoon* was left unfinished, but L.'s residence at Hamburg in connection with the earliest experiment at nationalizing the stage in

Germany was the occasion for a continuation of the same line of thought in his *Hamburgische Dramaturgie*. His *Emilia Galotti*, 1772, formed his next contribution to stage-plays, and was a better example than *Miss Sara Sampson* of the social-tragedy type. Antiquarian and theological controversies filled a part of his Wolfenbüttel years. He had been effecting for lost leaders of learning the resuscitation which his earlier *Rettungen* had attempted more definitely for theologians, and he became involved in a single-handed fight with the champions of orthodox thought, among whom J. M. Goeze, the chief pastor at Hamburg, took the lead. L.'s last masterpiece was *Nathan der Weise*, 1779, the drama of free-thought, or, more exactly, of freedom to think. It was based on a fable of Boccaccio (q.v. ; the three rings), and it ranks as the latest and greatest document of the European Illuminism (s.v. Aufklärung), by its insistence, through the exaltation of Nathan the Jew, that the question for religion to pose to humankind is not ' what do you profess ? ' but ' what are you ? ' The long, grand, terrible sequel of Luther's Reformation was closed by L.'s Enlightenment ; and the philosophy of Kant, Fichte and Hegel (qq.v.) followed as naturally as the poetry of Goethe on the critical work of this truly noble thinker. His furrow turned up the soil, and his right hand scattered the seed ; and in his final work on ' The Education of Mankind ' (*Die Erziehung des Menschengeschlechts*, 1780), he strained his forward-beaming eyes to a vision of the sower's harvest-home : ' Is not all Eternity mine ? '

L'Estrange, Roger (1616-1704) : Engl. journalist and scholar ; Tory pamphleteer ; M.P., Winchester ; knt., 1685 ; was once or twice imprisoned, and was condemned to death for his royalist activities during the revolution, and is notorious as the writer of *No Blind Guides*, an attack on Milton (q.v.) with an inhuman reference to his disability. But L'E. was a greater man than the politics of his time contrived to make him. He was licensee of the press, 1663, and ranks among the pioneers of journalism in Engld., esp. in virtue of his *Observator : In Question and Answer*, 1681-6, issued in the guise of a dialogue ; Addison's (q.v.) *Spectator* developed this convention, and Defoe (q.v.), though he rejected it, had the advantage of watching L'E.'s experiments. L'E. was also something more than a useful translr., though his work in this field was done for profit ; he was an accomplished master of foreign languages, and issued the *Visions* of Quevedo (q.v.), 1667 ; *Five Love Letters* of a Portuguese nun (q.v.), 1678 ; Tully's *Offices* (see s.v. Cicero), 1680 ; Seneca's *Morals*, *Colloquies* of Erasmus (q.v.), Terence's *Comedies*, *Works* of Josephus, etc., including 2 vols. of the *Fables* of Æsop, 1692 and 1699.

Letourneur, Pierre (1736-88) : Fr. scholar ; poet ; translr. of Shakespeare (q.v.), and notable, accordingly, as a precursor of Romanticism in France (see s.v. Romance). L., who was assisted by 2 collaborators, publd. his transln. in 1776 ; the subscribers included the empress Catherine (q.v.) of Russia, the king of France, Diderot, Turgot, Holbach (qq.v.), and others, and the readiness of the fashionable and philosophic worlds of lit. to greet the rising sun of Shakespeare in France in L.'s transln. and in the adaptations of Ducis (q.v.), aroused the champion of classicism in Voltaire (q.v.), who wr. on the occasion a famous 'Letter to the French Academy', which Dalembert read with zest on 25 Aug., 1776. L.'s romantic proclivity was likewise shown in his translns. of Young's (q.v.) *Night Thoughts*, 1769, and of Macpherson's (q.v.) *Ossian*, 1777.

Lever, Charles James (1806-72): Irish novelist; wr. *Harry Lorrequer*, 1837; *Charles O'Malley*, 1840, and others; collected, 1876, and still enjoying a deserved reputation.

Levin, Rahel. See **Varnhagen von Ense.**

Levy, Amy (1861-89): Engl. poet; novelist; of Jew. parentage. Wr. *A London Plane-Tree*, 1889; *Reuben Sachs*, 1888, etc., and 'gave occasional evidence of a passionate and almost triumphant intensity not common' (*C.H.E.L.*, xiii, 181; by prof. Saintsbury).

Lewes, George Henry (1817-78): Engl. critic; Positivist (see s.v. Comte); wr. *Psychology of Common Life*, 1859-60; a *Life of Goethe*, 1855, which was for many years the standard biography; and philosophical works inspired by his master, Comte. L. enters the history of letters again as the companion, 1854 till his death, of Mary Evans (see s.v. George Eliot), the novelist, whose tastes he guided and fostered. He was the founder, and editor, 1865-6, of the *Fortnightly Review*.

Lewis, Matthew Gregory (1775-1818): Engl. novelist; commonly known as Monk Lewis, in virtue of his shock-novel, *The Monk*, 1795, which, boy though he was, instantly made him famous. He had always had a taste for witchcraft and the supernatural, and had learned to read Germ., with its treasury of magical lore. All these sources were combined in this story of accumulated horror and wonder, which took our ancestors *fin de siècle* by storm. Wr., too, *Tales of Horror*, 1799, and others, and had some influence on the genius of sir W. Scott (q.v.). L. had estates in Jamaica, and died on his way home from a voyage to inquire personally into the condition of the slave-trade in that island.

Leyba Ramirez, de, Francisco (Antonio) (1630-76): Span. dramatist. Wr. *la Dama Presidente*, and other comedies.

Leyden: Seat of learning in the United Provinces (proclaimed, 1579, aiter revolt from Spain) of the Netherlands; its university, founded in memory of the siege, 1575, and distinguished by the names of scholars and professors of European repute, became the northern counterpart to that of Louvain (q.v.), founded 1426, in the southern, or Span. Netherlands. L. was famous, too, for its Elzevir printing-press, which swiftly followed the foundation of the university.

L'Hermite, François Tristan (1601-55): Fr. novelist and playwright; commonly known as Tristan. Wr., 1636, *Marianne*, a tragedy, which became very popular on the stage, and rendered its author in some degree a rival to Corneille (q.v.); in colder light, the play has little except some rhetorical polish to make it superior to the play of the same name by Hardy (q.v.). Nearly 20 years after, Tristan wr. a comedy, *Le Parasite*, 1654, which also had a great success, and which introduced the type of the parasite from Ital. comedy to the Fr. stage, where Molière (q.v.) established it more firmly in his *Illusion Comique*. Between the two, and among some minor plays, T. wr. his novel, *le Page Disgracié*, 2 vols., 1642-3, which has the charm of autobiography in the guise of fiction, though the style is by no means attractive.

L'Hôpital, de, Michel (c. 1505-73): Fr. statesman and orator. L'H., whose life belongs to history, became chancellor of France in 1560, and fell into disgrace in 1568. His political orations, as publd., include chiefly the 'Harangue to the States of Orleans', 1560, and the 'Memorial to the King on the Object (*But*) of War and Peace', 1568. L'H. was an ardent reformer of justice and advocate of peace, and he commanded the arts of eloquence as fully as Burke (q.v.) in a later day.

Libertins (Fr.); 'Libertines'; epithet attached in the late 17th cent. to a contemporary school of thought, which included individuals and groups of men and women of letters. They differed in most other characteristics excepting only their common vein of licence, free-thought, or epicureanism: a kind of easy and temperamental indifference, hardening sometimes to hostility, towards faith and pragmatic religion. The attitude (for, at its best, it was little more) ranged from an open scepticism to a hardly formulated preference for the elegant and leisurely side of life, and included the 'idleness' of La Fare (q.v.), who addressed a poem on that topic to Chaulieu (q.v.), as well as the 'philosophy' of St. Evremond (q.v.), and even the drama of Molière (q.v.), whom Bossuet and Bourdaloue (qq.v.) assailed with that charge. Their type of libertinism, if such diverse manifestations of a mental tendency can be typified, was reactionary and decadent at the epoch of its appearance; but historically, it connects the writings of Rabelais and Montaigne (qq.v.) with those of Diderot and Voltaire (qq.v.). Its best historian is Ste.-Beuve (q.v.) in his *Causeries*.

Libraries: The collection and storage of bks. before the invention of Printing (q.v.) was a much more enterprising affair than thereafter. Apart from internal work, such as cataloguing, arrangement, etc., it consisted mainly of 2 functions, (i) the multiplication of MSS. by hand-copying (see s.v. Copyists), and (ii) the discovery and acquisition of new MSS. This period lasted, roughly, 100 years, from Petrarch's find of Cicero *ad Atticum* (1345) to Aurispa, who brought 238, and Fifelfo, who brought about 50 MSS. from Constantinople (see s.vv.). Dr. L. Pastor, S.J. (*History of the Popes*, E.T., Kegan Paul, i, Intr.), writes that 'Monasteries founded and protected by the Popes rendered valuable service in guarding the intellectual treasures of antiquity'; and to this fact, fully as it is admitted, a footnote must be added that the guardianship might in places be somewhat perfunctory. Thus, Poggio (q.v.), on his visits (1415-17) to the abbey of St. Gallen, near Constance, found the abbot and monks quite indifferent to learning, and the 'intellectual treasures' in a state of miserable neglect; so, too, Boccaccio was moved to tears at Monte Cassino, where ' the grass was growing on the window-sills, and the dust reposing on the books and bookshelves '; and similar tales are told by other eager retrievers. When the early monastic libraries had thus yielded up or been rifled of their contents, the second period began with the collection and housing of these MSS. at wealthy courts of culture and scholarship, where they enjoyed the advantages of custodians, editors, and expositors. This movement, too, rose in Italy, though the names of bp. Aungerville de Bury (1281-1345 ; q.v.), and Humphrey, duke of Gloucester (1391-1447; q.v.), occur honourably as early donors of book-collections to the univ. of Oxford. Humphrey's contemporary, Cosimo de' Medici (1389-1464), who gave his commercial agents a free hand in the acquisition of artistic and literary treasures for Florence, ' had a proclivity, one must almost call it a passion, for building libraries ' (Sandys, *Harvard Lectures*, 119) ; the famous Medicean collections went to form the Laurentian Library (1571). The Library of St. Mark's at Venice was definitely founded by Bessarion (q.v.), in 1468. King Mathias Corvinus, in Hungary (1443-1490); king Francis i, in France (1494-1547), who had the assistance of Janus Lascaris (q.v.), formerly librarian successively to Lorenzo the Magnificent at Florence and his son pope Leo x at Rome, ranks as founder of the Royal Library at Fontainebleau, of which Budé (q.v.) was the head, and which is now the National Library in Paris ; king Christian iii of Denmark (1533-1559), who extended more ancient foundations ; pope Nicholas v (1398-1455 ; q.v.), at the Vatican Library, which he so thoroughly re-organized as to be reckoned its true founder ; cardinal Bembo (1470-1547 ; q.v.); duke Fredk. of Montefeltro (1422-1482 ; q.v.), at Urbino ; the agents, Vespasiano, Strozzi, Niccoli (qq.v.), and others ; king Philip ii, in Spain (1527-1598); sir Thomas Bodley (1545-1613 ; q.v.), at Oxford ; Antonio Magliobechi (1633-1714 ; q.v.), at Florence— these are among the names, too many to enumerate at length, of learned patrons, pious founders, or generous builders of the great libraries of Europe. The humanist name for librarian was *armarius*, and no better authority can be consulted than J. W. Clark's essay on the development of libraries and their fittings from the earliest times to the end of the 18th cent., *The Care of Books*, (Cambridge Univ. Press). Turning to Engld., the British Museum Library began as a royal collection in the reign of king Henry vii, and was presented to the nation by George ii (1757). The Act entitling it to a copy of every book published was passed in 1662, and was first enforced by Richard Bentley (q.v.), keeper of the Royal Libraries, 1694. Rich collections were added to it by bequests from sir Robert Cotton (q.v.), d. 1631, Robt. Harley (q.v.), d. 1724, sir Hans Sloane, 1753, and others to the present day. The chief Libraries of the United States were founded at Harvard Univ., 1638, at Yale Univ., 1700, at Washington (Library of Congress), 1800, and at Albany (New York State Library), 1818. The names of the late

Samuel Elliott, John Jacob Astor, and of Dr. Carnegie are as eminent in this connection in America as is the name of the late John Rylands in Manchester, England, among modern benefactors of lit., emulating the noble ' passion ' of Cosimo de' Medici in the 15th cent. Lastly, the free Public Library may be traced back to the chained Bible in churches, and the circulating Subscription Library is plainly a commercial convenience, derived from a very early monastic practice ; Aungerville (q.v.), for instance, wr. a chapter on lending books in his *Philobiblon* ; and we know that, in 1342, Paris booksellers (before the age of printing) were bound by law to lend MSS. on hire to poor students. The modern circulating L. dates in Engld. from the 17th cent. (see s.v. Fancourt); Mr. Mudie opened his shop in Bloomsbury in 1840.

Lichtenberg, Georg Christoph (1742-99) : Germ. popular-philosopher ; satirist and humourist ; and eminent as a physicist at Göttingen univ. It is generally agreed that L. might have taken a leading place either in the science or the lit. of his age (' he might have been a German Swift ', Robertson, *Germ. Lit.*, 292), if, in his own striking phrase, he could have ' opened canals in his head to promote the inland trade of his thought-supplies '. As it is, his collected writings from periodicals and reviews include brilliant observations on the acting of Garrick and the engraving of Hogarth, but little else of permanent value.

Lichtwer, Magnus Gottfried (1719-83) : Germ. writer of fable (q.v.); jurist. Follower of Gellert (q.v.) as fabulist, and accounted by some as even superior to his master.

Liddell, Henry George (1811-98) : Engl. scholar ; dean of Ch. Ch., Oxford, 1855-91 ; joint-author of Liddell and Scott's *Gk.-Engl. Lexicon*, 1843, and often reprinted ; new edn., Oxford, 1925.

Lidner, Bengt (1757-93) : Swed. poet ; patronized at first by king Gustavus iii (q.v.), but forfeited the royal favour by the profligacy of his private life as well as by the tendency of his muse. For L., in his short career, represents the reaction (which was almost simultaneous with the rise) against the neoclassic Francophily of the Swed. court. L.'s masters were Rousseau (again a Frenchman, but anti-Fr. in his opposition to the Voltairean school), and the Goethe of *Werther* (see s.vv.). He wr., chiefly, lyric verse, of a musical and passionate order, which displayed for the first time in Swed. poetry, an immediate sense of natural feeling.

Lie, Jonas Lauritz Edemil (1833-1908) : Norse novelist ; poet ; a lawyer by profession, and was involved in the financial crisis of 1867-8, when, like another Scott (q.v.), he tried, though not successfully, to redeem his obligations by the work of his pen. L. was granted stipends from public funds (a distinction previously confined to Björnson and Ibsen, qq.v.), and spent much of his later life abroad, principally in Paris. Referring to L.'s Finnish descent on his mother's side, Boyesen (*Scand. Lit.*, 125 ; Nutt, 1895) wr., in L.'s lifetime : ' Truth to tell, if it had not been for the Norse Jekyll in his nature, the Finnish Hyde might have run away with him altogether '. The figure is the more appropriate since L. (on his Finnish side) had a curious sixth sense for the eerie and terrible, not unlike that of Stevenson (q.v.), the author of the Jekyll and Hyde fable. It is said that L.'s happy marriage saved him from the worse consequences of his secondary character. L.'s poems, 1867 (revised, 1889), have not been transld., and are described as intelligible only in their own language, and not easily so in that; it is as a novelist that, with several failures and a curious lack of effective self-criticism, he at last won the fame which he deserved by his considerable and exceptional talents.

The chief novels were *Den Fremsynte* ('The Visionary'), 1870, which expresses the Finnish, or romantic, side of his nature; 'The Barque Future', 1872; 'The Pilot and his Wife', 1874; and, after several somewhat halting experiments, due, perhaps, to the responsibilities of the income voted for his maintenance by parliament, 'Rutland', 1881, the first of a series of conspicuous successes. *Gaa Paa* ('Press On') followed, 1882; *Livsslaven* ('The Life Prisoner'), 1883 (not unlike Dostoievsky's, q.v., 'Crime and Punishment', and not less dreary), 'The Family at Gilje', 1883, L.'s admitted masterpiece; and several others. L.'s works have been transltd. into many languages and posterity is confirming the reputation which he won in the last quarter of the 19th cent.

Ligne, de, (prince) Charles Joseph (1735-1814): Austrian general; field-marshal, 1808; Fr. memoirist. The prince, whose works, *Mélanges*, were publd. in 34 vols., 1795-1811, was a friend and correspondent of king Fredk. ii of Prussia, of Voltaire, Rousseau, mme. de Staël, and enjoyed the favour of Maria Theresa, the great archduchess of Austria, and of empress Catherine ii of Russia (see s.vv.). He was a typical example of the cosmopolitan man of culture, who gravitated inevitably to Paris, the intellectual centre of learning in his age; and, in a literary sense, the prince de L. is to be accounted as a Fr. writer.

Lillo, George (1693-1739): Engl. playwright; son of a London jeweller, to whose trade he was brought up. 'Introduced prose domestic tragedy' (*C.H.E.L.*, x, 79), and by this signal act of introduction is better known as an usher than an author. His line, 'A London 'Prentice ruin'd is our theme', from the Prologue to *George Barnwell*, produced at Drury Lane, 22 June, 1731, marks the substitution of 'the actions of mean and base personages' (Puttenham, q.v.) for those of personages of more exalted orig. as the subjects of dramatic delineation. Domestic drama was not new on the stage, but L. made more effective, more 'aggressive', use of the more domestic milieu. In this respect his aim may be said to anticipate that of Crabbe (q.v.) in pastoral poetry. Barnwell, the idle apprentice, goes back for his plot to an old ballad, and the treatment of the plot suggests the method of Hogarth, L.'s contemporary, in his plates. The change of milieu corresponded to a change of language, and, though L., in his prose, could not shake off the old shackles of verse—even of the grandiloquent verse, which was appropriate to the 'grand manner' of acting—he did succeed in showing the way which

Ibsen (q.v.) and others were to make perfect. In *Fatal Curiosity*, 1736, with a Prologue by Fielding (q.v.) ('From lower life we draw our scene's distress'), L. pursued the domestic vein, though he wr. the play in blank verse, and this drama particularly inspired a series of fate-plays on the German stage (see s.v. Fate-Drama), known as *Schicksalstragödien*. The first was *Blunt*, 1781, by K. P. Moritz; the next, *der Vierundzwanzigste Februar*, 1810, by Werner (Schiller's *Braut von Messina* came between the two); the next, 'The 29th February', by Müllner, and so on to the last of the kind, Grillparzer's *die Ahnfrau* (see s.vv.). But the fate- or destiny-play was not the chief kind of drama ushered into Europe by L. The domestic drama was to enjoy a longer vogue, still, of course, unfind. and flourishing Germany called it *bürgerlich*, or middle-class, in token of the stratum of society from which its characters came, and Lessing's (q.v.) *Miss Sara Sampson*, 1755, which dissolved the sentimental pittites into tears, was derived almost directly from L. The tears are a part of the tradition, and the *drame domestique*, or *sérieux*, or *bourgeois*, of France in the 18th cent., was soon unified into the *comédie larmoyante*, due very largely to Diderot's (q.v.) Lillo-worship. Marivaux and Destouches (qq.v.), to whom O. Goldsmith (q.v.) was so much indebted, were already in the field, but the English influence of L. and Richardson (q.v.) brought floods of tears on the Fr. stage. L., unlike Gay (q.v.), is not likely to find revival in his own country, where his true successor was E. Moore (q.v.). But his name is of permanent importance as a pioneer and an innovator.

Linacre, Thomas (*c.* 1460-1524): Engl. physician and scholar; king's physician; first president of Roy. Coll. of Physicians; practised in London, with card. Wolsey among his patients; a pioneer of the Renaissance (q.v.) in Engld., who infused into the study of medicine the spirit of the New Learning, and in some ways ranks as a precursor of the Baconian philosophy; studied Lat. under Politian (q.v.) in Florence, and built an altar 'to Italy' on the top of an Alpine pass on his return journey. Erasmus (q.v.) was among his pupils. L. effected translns. from the Gk., esp. from the medical works of Galen, and wr. 3 Lat. grammars: (1) for St. Paul's School in 1512, rejected in favour of Colet's (q.v.), founder of the school; (2) *Rudimenta Grammatices*, 1523, written for a royal princess to whom he was tutor, and transld. into Lat. by Buchanan (q.v.); and (3) *de emendata Structura Latini Sermonis*, 1524, recommended by Melanchthon (q.v.) for use in Germ. schools.

Liñan y Verdugo, Antonio (fl. 1620): Span. social writer. Wr. a 'Guide and Handbook for Strangers', Madrid, 1620, consisting of 14 tales, told by 2 men of the major Pendennis type, in order to familiarize a younger man with the perils of fast life at court. It was an attractive vol., by a writer of whom nothing more is known, and it contained a spirited plea against Gongorism (s.v. Gongora), or affectation, in Span. prose style.

Lindsay, David (1490-1555): Scot. poet; Lyon king of arms, and knt., 1529; compiled

Register of Arms of the Scottish Nobility and Gentry, 1542, *ed. pr.* 1821 ; ambassador at the court of emperor Charles v, 1531 ; wr. *Ane Pleasant Satyre of the three Estates*, 1540, a dramatic dialogue between ' Experience and a Courtier ', which was characteristic of L.'s constant sympathy with the laity and commonalty, and his abuse of the clergy and nobles. He was thus a supporter and precursor of the Reformation of the Scot. church, though he adhered, at least nominally, to the church of Rome. L.'s other poems included *The Complaynt to the King* (James v of Scotland), 1529, and *The Testament and Complaynt of our Soverane lord's Papyngo* (Parrot), 1530. His works enjoyed wide popularity and esteem, as much for their genuine poetic quality as for their outspeaking hate of vice and hypocrisy in high and sacred places ; new edns., each in 3 vols., were issued by G. Chalmers, 1806, and D. Laing, 1879.

Linton, Eliza Lynn (1822-98) : Engl. novelist ; misc. writer ; *née* Lynn ; m. Wm. Jas. L. (1812-98 ; wood-engraver ; international political reformer), 1858 ; contributor to *All the Year Round* and the *Saturday Review* ; a sturdy opponent of the feminist movement ; wr. *A Girl of the Period*, 1883, and several novels, including *Joshua Davidson*, 1872, and *Christopher Kirkland* (autobiographical), 1885.

Lipsius, Justus (1547-1606) : Belgian humanist, resident in Netherlands. Born at Issche ; student at Louvain (q.v.) ; visited Rome and Vienna ; held professorship at Jena, where he formally joined Protestant church ; repaired to Louvain, owing to disturbed politics in central Europe ; was invited by J. Dousa (q.v.) to quit Span. Netherlands for new United Provinces, and to aid by his learning the newly-founded univ. at Leyden (q.v.) ; resided there as honorary prof. of history, 1579-91 ; visited Mayence on leave of absence, and was readmitted into Roman church ; returned to Louvain in following year, 1592, as prof. of history. Like Scaliger (q.v.), whom Dousa appointed to his vacated chair at Leyden, and others, L. was hampered in his career of scholastic distinction by the grave political and religious warfare and differences in his times ; nothing, indeed, is more remarkable, or more creditable to the force of the love of learning, than the record of these persecuted profs., whose whole interest in happier times would have been spent in the cause of humane letters, to which, despite such difficulties, they devoted themselves so enthusiastically. L.'s *magnum opus* was his edn. of Tacitus, furnished with a critical apparatus and with profound hist. and antiquarian exegeses ; he issued other works in Lat. scholarship, and a treatise, inscribed to Sidney (q.v.), on Lat. pronunciation.

Lisandro y Rosella (Span.) : ' Lysander and Roselia ', a tragi-comedy of unknown authorship (sometimes attributed to Sancho Sanchez de Muñon, who died as late as 1601) ; imitative of *Celestina* (q.v.). Its date is 1542.

Liscow, Christian Ludwig (1701-60) : Germ. publicist. L., who commanded an elegant style, took part in the Swiss-Saxon battle of the books provoked by Gottsched (q.v.) at Leipsic ; his contribution was in the form of a satire on criticasters, which Gottsched's opponents took care to direct to the address of their adversary. L.'s genial irony does not make for popularity, but he is not unworthy to be counted among the Baptists who went before Lessing (q.v.).

Lisle, de, Leconte (1820-94) : Fr. poet ; born in the tropics ; brought home with him a fertile fancy for exotic images and flowers of diction. L. was a scholar and translr., whose Hellenic purism in the transliteration of Gk. names led Gautier (q.v.) to remark, ' It would have been simpler to write in Greek ' ; but L.'s services to the renewed appreciation a Homer and the tragedians were considerable and important. His intellectual interest was devoted chiefly to the religious beliefs of antiquity and of the period known as the twilight of the gods. His method was not lyrical, but processional ; his poems are like a series of bas-reliefs, such as are seen in the remains of temples, and the epithets ' statuesque ' and ' marmoresque ' are constantly applied to it. L.'s works include *Poèmes antiques*, 1853, *Poèmes barbares*, 1859, *Poèmes tragiques*, 1884, *Derniers Poèmes*, 1895 ; and his mastery was attested by his place at the head of the so-called Parnassian school of Fr. poetry (see s.v. Parnasse), which arose in the wake of Hugo (q.v.) as a kind of sequel to the movement of 1830.

Lista, Alberto (1775-1848) : Span. poet ; canon of Seville ; held a chair at the college of S. Mateo, Madrid ; friend of Blanco White (q.v.). Wr. divine odes (e.g. ' The Death of Jesus ') and other poems.

Littré, Emile (1801-81) : Fr. lexicographer. Wr., 1863-9, the famous Fr. dict., *Dictionnaire de la Langue française*. L. was an ardent disciple of Comte (q.v.) in his Positivist opinions, but was reconciled on his deathbed to the Roman Catholic Church.

Livio, Tito (15th cent.) : It. humanist ; of Forli. Included in circle of Humphrey (q.v.), duke of Gloucester, as his ' poet and orator ' ; wr. life of king Henry v.

Llaguno y Amirola, de, Eugenio (18th cent.) : Span. dramatic author ; disciple of Luzan (q.v.), whose *Poetica* he republd., 1789, with, it is probable, some omissions and alterations, tending to emphasize Luzan's Francophil sympathy. Ll. transld., 1754, the *Athalie* of Racine (q.v.) into blank verse. He was secretary to the newly-founded Academy (q.v.) of History at Madrid.

Llorente, Juan Antonio (1756-1823) : Span. historian ; secretary to the Inquisition, 1789 ; was entrusted with the archives on its suppression in 1809. Resided at Paris ; wr., 1817-18, his *Histoire critique de l'Inquisition d'Espagne* ; and, 1822, his *Portrait politique des Papes*. The bias displayed in these books procured his expulsion by the clerical party and Ll. retired to Madrid, whence he sustained a controversy, 1822, with the Fr. Academy on the authorship of Lesage's (q.v.) *Gil Blas*. Ll. argued for a Span. orig., which he ascribed to Solis (q.v.). The question, revived from Isla (q.v.) in the previous cent., is as nugatory as the Bacon-Shakespeare discussion of some years back. Ll.'s ' History of the Inquisition ' is a valuable and a standard work.

Lobeira, de, Vasco (14th cent.) : Port. knt. ; reputed author or translr. of the famous chivalric romance of *Amadis* (q.v.) ; but his claim and fame are mentioned in a diminishing scale of affirmation by special students in recent years. These tend to the conclusion that, though the great romance may have existed in a Port. version, it was really through Spain (see s.v. Montalvo) that it passed back to France (see s.v. Herberay) in the 16th cent. on its road to the origins of modern fiction. L. received the accolade in 1385, and is said to have died in 1403 ; his romance should, accordingly, be dated *c.*1390, which is rather late for the references to it in the lit. of the Peninsula (see s.v. Ayala, e.g.). But the statement of a Port. version of the tale, prior to the Span. version, persisted till the 18th cent., and Ticknor (i, 200) conjectures that the mysterious MS., whether of L. or another, must have perished in the earthquake of 1755. On the whole, the evidence is in favour of L., as the fount of the chivalric tale which so profoundly impressed itself on Fr. fiction in later generations, and which passed into the stock of the novel, is too slender to be maintained.

Lobo, Eugenio Gerardo (1679-1750) : Span. poet ; soldier ; a good metrist ; but his verses belong to the period of decadence after the Span. Succession Wars, and ,' if anything like poetry appears in them, it is at rare intervals ' (Ticknor, iii, 257).

Locher, Johann (fl. 1500) : Germ. Latinist. Wr. Lat. spectacular poems, notably one expressing the current hate of the Turks ; transld. *Narrenschiff* of Brandt (q.v.) into Lat. elegiac verse, thus helping to popularize it among learned readers, and to exalt it to the realm of scholarship, in which it enjoyed so considerable and so long a vogue (see s.v. Folly). The Engl. version of Barclay (q.v.) owed less to the original than to L., who altered Brandt's order of material, and brought the voyage of the ship more immediately into relation with its crew.

Locke, John (1632-1704) : Engl. philosopher ; writer on politics, theology and education. Wr. Lat. *Letter for Toleration*, tranld. into Engl., 1689, and followed by second *Letter*, 1690, and third, 1692 ; *Two Treatises on Govt.*, 1690 (transld. into Fr., Germ. and Ital., early in 18th cent.) ; *An Essay concerning Human Understanding*, L.'s most important work, publd. in abstract, 1688, in Leclerc's *Bibliothèque universelle* ; first complete edn., 1690 ; second, 1694 ; third, 1695 ; fourth, 1700 (tranld. into Fr., 1700 ; Lat., 1701 ; Germ., 1757) ; *Some Thoughts concerning Education*, 1693 (transld. into Fr., 1695, Germ. and Ital.) ; *The Reasonableness of Christianity*, 1695 (transld. into Fr., Germ., etc.) ; vindicatory and controversial papers consequent on the foregoing works, and *opera minora*. Complete edns. of L.'s writings have been issued at various dates, and his views, which produced a profound influence on European thought, have been discussed by writers as eminent as R. H. Quick, T. H. Green, sir F. Pollock, Leibniz, M. Ferrari, and others.

Leaving these details of bibliography, we have to note the deep debt of Kant (q.v.) to

' the most important figure in English philosophy ' (*C.H.E.L.*, viii, 328). L.'s treatise on *Human Understanding*, which he worked at for nearly 20 years (1671-89), really founded the science of epistemology, or the investigation of the method of apprehension and the nature and validity of human knowledge. Bk. i criticized the doctrine of innate ideas, in the form advanced by lord Herbert (q.v.) of Cherbury ; Bk. ii proved the origin of all ideas in experience, and resolved composite ideas into their elements ; Bk. iii discussed the influence of language on thought, and Bk. iv investigated the ideas of self, God and the universe, and defined the kinds and limits of knowledge. L. was edu. at Westminster and Ch. Ch., Oxford, and paid a pious tribute to his father's training in his essay on *Education* ; he was a student of Descartes, Hobbes, Bacon and Gassendi (qq.v.), a trained physician, and a tutor and friend in the family of A. A. Cooper (1621-93), first earl of Shaftesbury ; he travelled in Holland and other countries, and he retired, 1691, to Oates, in Essex, where he made his home with sir Francis and lady Masham (dau. of R. Cudworth, q.v.). As a thinker whose prime aim it was to disprove the current and (as he said) the indolent doctrine of innate ideas, and to show that the human mind might be likened to a *tabula rasa*, on which such impressions only were inscribed as were received through the senses, L. was bound to attach the utmost importance to education in moulding the intellect and will. Rousseau (q.v.) was to some extent his disciple, and he anticipated the views of Ruskin (q.v.) on the importance of manual training. The necessity of arousing children's interest in their work was always present in L.'s mind, and the most valuable of his thoughts on education follow directly from his psychology, and give his treatise scientific value. He preceded Spencer (1820-1903) in the doctrine that ' to prepare us for complete living is the function that education has to discharge ', and, in his time and place, he is notable for his statement : ' I know not why anyone should waste his time and beat his head about the Latin grammar, who does not intend to be a critic or make speeches and write despatches in it '. It is interesting to observe that L. was directed to his 20 years' labours on *Human Understanding* by a talk, in 1670, with a few friends on the principles of morality and revealed religion. L. undertook to set down his views, like a statesman-philosopher of our day (first earl of Balfour) on a half-sheet of note-paper, so ' little did he realize the magnitude of the issues which he raised ' (*C.H.E.L.*, *ib.*). It is not within our province to measure the magnitude by the results. The repercussion of L.'s thought on the 18th cent. is the subject of a careful analysis by F. D. Maurice (q.v.) in vol. ii, ch. viii, of his *Moral and Metaphysical Philosophy* : ' Englishmen ', he says, in opening ch. ix, ' must always feel a certain suspicion of themselves when they assign a very prominent position to a philosopher of their own land or race. But the evidence of Germans and Frenchmen has, we think, sufficiently justified us in putting Locke at the head of the period which we have just been considering. So early as the year 1707, we have found Leibniz according to the *Essays on Human Understanding* the authority almost of a text-book, the principles of which it behoves him, learned student as he is, with a wide European fame, only to arraign with great caution and diffidence. His successor, Wolff, consciously or unconsciously adopts many of Locke's decrees into his system, and Voltaire builds the new philosophy upon the Lockian basis'. (See s.vv. Leibniz, C. Wolff, Voltaire, from the last of whom Maurice quotes a long and important passage—from a letter *sur M. Locke,*—in the course of which Voltaire says that ' Locke has discovered the human reason to man, just as an excellent anatomist explains the springs of the body '). But the ascendency of L. ended with Voltaire : ' The lively Parisian stooped to the sober sage of Wrington ' (in Somersetshire ; L.'s birthplace) ; ' but he stooped to conquer. From the middle of the (18th) century Voltaire's acknowledged reign commences ' (Maurice, *ibid.*). It remains to add, that, despite the Voltairean reign succeeding and even superseding L.'s, recent philosophy remains in debt to the prior investigations of the ' sage of Wrington '. Thus, in a work on *The Meaning of Meaning* (by C. K. Ogden and I. A. Richards ; intro. by J. P. Postgate ; Kegan Paul, 1923), we are told (pp. 105-16), that ' the work of Locke is in all that concerns language much in advance of its age ' ; that subsequent writers have unduly neglected Bk. iii of *Human Understanding*, which remains ' all-important ', and that Condillac (q.v.) ' was another of the prominent 18th century writers who were influenced by Locke, and one of the few who endeavoured to develop his treatment ' ; and Condillac was a few years junior to Voltaire. For L. in another aspect was Bentham's (q.v.) precursor, and, in the words of A. L. Smith, (1850-1924 ; master of Balliol after 1916) : ' The headlines of Locke's bequest to the 18th century are indicated by the words Individualism, Reason, Utility, Toleration, Property ; all of which words might be summed up in the first of them. No wonder that the century witnessed in England the use of a gospel of self-interest which made the wealth of a nation consist in setting the individual free ; and in France that titanic evolution of the pent-up forces of the individual which made the French Revolution so epoch-making' (*C.M.H.*, vi, 815). So, European lit. touches the polity of Europe.

Locker-Lampson, Frederick (1821-95) : Engl. poet ; successor to Praed (q.v.) as writer of *vers de société*. *Né* Locker ; m., *en secondes noces*, dau. of sir C. M. Lampson, bt. (L.L.'s dau., Eleanor, by his first marriage, m., i, Lionel, son of Alfred, lord Tennyson, q.v., ii, rt. hon. Augustine Birrell, and d. 1915). Wr. *London Lyrics*, 1857, mainly collected out of various newspapers ; *Lyra Elegantiarum*, 1867 ; *Patchwork*, 1879 ; *Confidences*, posth., 1896. His library at Rowfant was catalogued by him, 1886, and has been the topic of essays by his son-in-law, Mr. Birrell (*supra*).

Lockhart, John Gibson (1794-1854) : Scot. critic ; novelist ; wr., 1838, the *Life* of sir Walter Scott (q.v.), whose dau., Sophia, he had married,

1820 ; transld. some of Schlegel's (q.v.) lectures, and publd., 1823, a vol. of *Ancient Spanish Ballads*, by which, with his biography of his great father-in-law, he is chiefly remembered to-day. In his own day, L. was famous as an orig. contributor to *Blackwood's Edinburgh Magazine*, founded 1817, where he fought the Cockney (q.v.) school and refused the help of the Lake (q.v.) poets,—all somewhat barren controversy now ; he edited the *Quarterly Review*, 1825-53 ; wr. a *Life of Burns*, 1828, and several novels, including *Adam Blair*, 1822.

Lodge, Thomas (*c.* 1558-1625) : Engl. dramatist ; poet ; son of a lord mayor of London ; edu. Trinity Coll., Oxford ; studied medicine and law, and practised the latter in Lincoln's Inn ; preferred lit. to either, and wr. a reply to Gosson (q.v.) in defence of the stage. L. was a friend of Greene (q.v.), with whom he wr. 1594, *A Looking-glass for London and England*, and was the author of sundry other plays. L.'s most memorable works are his prose-romance, *Rosalynde*, which is said to have been written on a voyage to the Canaries, and to have inspired much of Shakespeare's *As You Like It*, and his vol. of verse, *Phillis honoured with Pastorall Sonnets*, etc., 1593. L. was also an industrious translr. from Seneca, Josephus, and others, and wr. a *Treatise of the Plague*, 1603.

Lönnrot, Elias (1802-84) : Swed. (-Finn.) poet ; folklorist. Transld. and edited the *Kalevala* (1835 ; revised, 1847 ; new edn., 1862) ; ' whatever scholars may say as to the fidelity of this version of the ancient epic, Lönnrot's edition made it celebrated through Europe, and probably suggested to Longfellow the metre of *Hiawatha* ' (Omond, *P.E.L.*, xi, 382). L.'s chief work was a Finnish dict., and he was likewise an editor of native folksongs.

Lo Frasso, de, Antonio (16th cent.) : Span. pastoralist ; Sardinian by birth. Wr., 1573, *Ten Books of Fortune and Love*, remarkable for a literary accident, though not for any merit of its own. In a famous chapter (1, vi) of *Don Quixote*, Cervantes (q.v.) dealt faithfully with its extravagant pretensions in a vein of ironical humour ; many years later, Pedro de Pineda, a Span. Jewish refugee in London, mistook the irony for earnest, and cited Cervantes as his authority for a highly eulogistic introduction to a new edn. in 2 vols. (London, 1740) of this tasteless work. ' Hardly any other of the Spanish prose-pastorals is so absurd as this, or contains so much bad verse ' (Ticknor, iii, 86 n.).

Logau, von, Friedrich (1604-55) : Germ. satirist, of real genius and notable power, revealed to the admiration of his countrymen mainly through the perception of Lessing (q.v.) in 1759. The comparative imperception of L.'s own and succeeding generations has been amply atoned for since, and L. is recognized to-day as a master of the epigram in the front rank of the cultivators of that difficult kind. His work marked a great advance on prevailing or preceding models. He learned from Renaissance (q.v.) teachers to substitute the example of Catullus and Martial for the diffuse and turgid style in satire which had made its vulgar appeal. Gradually, therefore, the finished and polished epigram replaced the coarser lit. of farce and folly, and the long neglect of L.'s less blatant vein of satire may, perhaps, be due to this change. He publd., 1654, a vol. of 3,000 *Sinngedichte* (epigrams), ascribed to Solomon von Golau ; the first name, the king's of wisdom-literature and the second, Logau re-spelt. The variety and dexterity of these poems are remarkable ; they range from a couplet on the month of May, ' a kiss which Heaven bestows on the Earth, to make her a bride to-day and a mother to-morrow ', to the bitter, patriotic trumpet-calls to his fellow-countrymen, composed, be it remembered, in the midst of wars ; especially, and properly, Germ. patriotism is grateful to L. for the ridicule which he poured on frenchified Germans ; ' *à-la-mode* dress, *à-la-mode* thought ; as one's outward wearing, so one's inward bearing '. L.'s contempt for this affected ' alamodishness ' (he introduced a Germ. word into the language) was at once timely and appropriate to future use.

Lohengrin (fict.) : hero of the Teutonic cycle of the Arthuriad (s.v. Arthur) ; represented as the son of Percival (Parzival), and a knt. of the Grail (q.v.). The first Germ. redaction of this branch of the romance was composed in Bavaria in the 13th cent., and Wagner's opera made it world-famous in the 19th. The essential feature of the story is L.'s love for the countess Elsa of Brabant, whose country he reached in a boat drawn by a swan ; he performed mighty exploits in the wars of emperor Henry i against Hungary and the Saracens, and returned crowned with victory to Elsa. She loses her lover by yielding to fatal curiosity, and L. departs in his swan-boat to his own land. (See, too, s.v. Wartburg).

Lohenstein, von, Daniel Caspar (1635-83) : Germ. dramatic poet ; of the so-called Second Silesian School (q.v.) ; disciple of Hoffmannswaldau (q.v.). Wr. several plays of little merit, and a novel *Arminius*, which is praised more highly than his imitative dramas, on account of its patriotic feeling, overlaid though this feature was by the tall and tropical writing which his school had acquired from foreign models of gallantry in fiction. The turgid style became known by L.'s name, and was the counterpart of Marinism (q.v.) elsewhere.

Lomonosov, Michael (1714-65) : Russ. ' metallurgist, geologer, chemist, electrician, astronomer, political-economist, statistician, geographer, historian, philologist, critic, poet ' (Brückner. *Gesch. d. Russ. Lit.*, 81). It is a long list of accomplishments, even in an age innocent of specialization, but L. had more right than Sumarokov (q.v.) to boast that his ' odes, orations, chemistry, physics and history redounded to the glory of his country '. Æsthetically, the odes are negligible ; the majority are merely formal complimentary pieces addressed to members of the ruling dynasty, and even those on religious or abstract topics bear the marks of the labour of the file. But, historically, they are of importance as marking the beginning of a literary faculty in Russia. ' Our literature starts in 1739 ', says one writer, ' at the appearance of the first ode of Lomonosov '. It is the ' Let there be light ' of Creation ; the ' Enfin Malherbe vint ' of Boileau (q.v.) in France. Of far more

permanent value were L.'s addresses, as public orator at the Moscow academy ; and his *Russian Grammar*, 1755, was authoritative for many years, and was only a part of L.'s considerable and valuable services to the cause of the literary as distinct from the ecclesiastical language in vocabulary, orthography and style. In these ways and others L. ably aided the reforming genius of Peter (q.v.) the Great, who was the object of his genuine veneration, and in whose honour L. wr. a would-be national epopee, *The Petriad*. The furtherance lent by L. to the foundation of the univ. of Moscow, 1755, would in itself entitle him to the gratitude of scholarship and learning. It should be added that L. was of peasant origin, and that his education was acquired by that rare self-sacrificing determination, characteristic of the Scot. and Russ. rural populations.

Longinus, Cassius (died 273) : Gk. scholar ; reputed author of treatise on *the Sublime* (rhet.) ; settled at Palmyra, under queen Zenobia, who, ' like Christina of Sweden, our own Elizabeth, and Mary queen of Scots, delighted in literature and in the society of scholars ; what Salmasius, Ascham and Buchanan were to them, Longinus became to the queen of Palmyra ' (*Quarterly Review*, Oct., 1900). A pupil of L. has left on record that ' Longinus was a kind of living library and walking encyclopedia '. The treatise on *the Sublime* was first transld. by Robortello (q.v.), 1554 ; then by Boileau (q.v.), 1674, and so passed into Engld. It was edited at Cambridge by prof. Rhys Roberts, 1899, and transld. again into Engl. by H. L. Havell (Intr. by Andrew Lang), 1890. Its contents and influence are examined s.v. Sublime.

Longolius, Christopher (1488-1522) : Fr. scholar ; Ciceronian. Drawn to Rome (1517) by the magnet of Latinity ; patronized by Bembo (q.v.), and praised by Erasmus (q.v.) in his *Ciceronianus* for his skill in the epistolary art.

Lope de Moros (12th cent.) : Span. (reputed) author of *Razon de Amor* (q.v.), the earliest example of Span. lyric verse. It is more probable, however, that the words *Lupus me fecit de Moros*, which occurs at the close of the poems, refer, not to its writer, but to a copyist.

Lopez, Alonso (fl.c. 1600) : Span. poet ; critic ; commonly known as Pinciano. Wr., 1596, *Philosophia antiqua poetica*, a Lat. treatise in pleasant, epistolary form on the poetics of Aristotle (q.v.). L. ranged himself on the side of the classical tradition against the Castilian school of Vega (q.v.). His theory, though well stated and documented, was not more popular than his practice, as displayed in a dreary verse-epopee, *el Pelayo*, 1605.

Lopez de Ayala, Adelardo (1829-79) : Span. dramatist. Wr. *un Hombre de Estado*, 1851 ; *Rioja*, 1854, etc.

Lopez de Corella, Alonso (16th cent.) : Span. physician. Wr., 1539, ' The Secrets of the Philosophy of Medicine ', after the model of Villalobos (q.v.), and in the form of questions and answers, well-known in early Span. lit. by the name of *preguntas*. L. publd. a second edn. in 1546, which is more frequently cited than the first, and is called ' Three Hundred

Maffei (qq.v.); he returned to Spain, 1733, and occupied himself with transln., adaptation, and original verse; his translns. included versions of Milton's (q.v.) *Paradise Lost*, of Ital. dramas for the Span. stage, and an abstract of the Port Royal (q.v.) *Logic*. From 1747-50, L. was secretary to the Span. embassy in Paris. L.'s chief work was a treatise briefly known as his 'poetics', or 'Art of Poetry', and entitled *la Poetica, o Reglas de la Poesia en general, y de sus principales especies*; it was publd., 1737, out of his material for 6 lectures prepared for the academy of Palermo, and Saintsbury (*Hist. Crit.*, ii, 547) remarks that Muratori and Gravina (qq.v.) were L.'s masters rather than Boileau and le Bossu (qq.v.). Whatever the immediate derivation of his critical theories, L. was a more or less consistent neo-classicist, and 'argued Spain's poetry away far more actually than Cervantes had ever laughed away her chivalry' (*ibid.*). Naturally, he gave rise to controversy, and some Span. men of letters started the first lit. review of Madrid (see s.v. *Diario*), 1737, in order to confute his views. (See, too, s.v. Feyjoo). L. was the leading figure in the *Academia del Buen Gusto* (good taste), founded on the lines of the Rambouillet (q.v.) circle in Paris; it used to meet at the house of the comtesse de Lemos, 1749-51.

Lydgate, John (*c*. 1370-1421): Engl. Chaucerian (q.v.) poet; consistently described himself as Chaucer's disciple. He enjoyed the patronage of Humphrey, duke of Gloucester (q.v.), and was set poetic tasks by him and other royal employers. L. was a monk at St. Edmondsbury abbey, and is often referred to as the monk of Bury. Though his work was very voluminous, he was really at his best in unambitious pieces, or occasional verse for civic or court functions. Wr. a *Fall of Princes*, after Boccaccio's *de casibus illustrium virorum*; a *Troy-book* from Guido delle Colonne (q.v., and see s.vv. Troy and Caxton; Chaucer had stopped short in this department of romance at his masterly *Troilus and Criseyde*); and a *Story of Thebes*, in attempted continuation of the *Canterbury Tales*. It must be admitted that L. was a dull writer, though his services to versification and diction are, historically, important.

Lyly, John (*c*. 1554-1606): Engl. dramatist and (rudimentary) novelist. Edu. at Oxford (Magd. Coll.), but missed success there and at Cambridge, where his also studied; entered the service of the seventeenth earl of Oxford (E. de Vere), thus attaching himself to one of the most brilliant members of queen Elizabeth's court, to the aggrandizement of which, as a centre of refined speech and letters, L.'s ambition directed his great gifts. Wr., 1579, *Euphues, the Anatomy of Wit*, followed, 1580, by its sequel, *Euphues and his England*, a prose-romance in 2 parts; plays: *Campaspe*, 1584, *Endimion*, 1591, *Midas*, 1592, and others, with charming lyric poems imbedded in them; a pamphlet, 1589, *Pappe with an Hatchet* (a proverbial phrase, *à la* soup with a fork) as a contribution to current theological polemics; and other prose and verse. L. is chiefly and justly remembered for his *Euphues* vols., the title of which he took from a description by

Ascham (q.v.) of the complete gentleman (Gk., *euphues*). Several causes contributed to the popularity of these vols. in their own day, and to their fame in after-days. They displayed a perfect mastery of the style, since known as Euphuism (q.v.), towards which tentative endeavours had been made by Berners (q.v.) and others, and of which the best example before L. was contained in Pettie (q.v.), *The Palace of Pleasures*, 1576. The main marks of this style, which corresponded to similar tendencies in vernacular prose-narration in France, Italy and Spain (see s.vv. Marini, Guevara), and which was at one time uncritically alleged to have been founded directly by L. on North's (q.v.) transln. of a Fr. version of Guevara's *Dial of Princes*, were suppleness, vivacity, raciness, crafty sentence-building, metaphor, alliteration, word-assonance, clause-antithesis, parallelism, rhythm, harmony; all the features, in fact, which are still recognized as distinctive of eloquence in prose. To the cultivation of this style L. brought the native gifts of insight into character, a vivid imagination, a sense of form (doubtless partly transferred from his poetic perception of the formal merits of Marot and Surrey qq.v.), and a vigorous desire to supply the courtly circle in which he moved with a medium of sentimental expression more modern and up-to-date than the traditional language of figurative abstractions bequeathed by Chaucer and Malory (qq.v.). All this was to the good, and it places Engl. lit. under a considerable debt to L. But there were vices in his practice, and his qualities tended to excess. Especially, he let himself go in the multiplication of similes and analogies drawn with a lavish hand from the reference-books of his own day, which went back in their turn to more ancient sources of bestiary (q.v.), lapidary, volucrary, and, summarily, *physiologi*. The 'unnatural natural history' which vitiates L.'s pages seriously detracts from his merits, and to this feature was added a habit of piling-up antitheses, of forcing word-plays and letter-hunts, and of exaggerating his effects in general, which earned for him, and for the Euphuism identified with him (although he was its most cultivated practitioner, not its author), the ridicule of great writers from Shakespeare (q.v.) to Scott (q.v.), and the condemnation of great critics from Sidney (q.v.) to Hallam (q.v.). The Euphuism proper was sound rhetoric; its excesses should be recognized as Lylyism. But, while the existence of these faults is undeniable, modern criticism tends to recognize more and more fully that L.'s benefits to Engl. prose-style, which he found inchoate and formless and left ordinated and artistic, counterbalance and outweigh the excesses into which he was betrayed. He filled, and filled adequately, a gap between the decline of the courtier and the rise of the popular poet; between the lit. written for the court by men like Surrey, Vaux, Harvey, Churchyard, Sidney and Ascham, and the lit. written for the populace by greater men like Marlowe and Shakespeare; and, though Shakespeare, the greatest of all, laughed at euphuistic follies, yet his Jaques in *As You Like It* was 'simply Euphues

Redivivus' (Bond, *Lyly*, i, 167). Similarly, Greene, Lodge and others euphuized, or Lylyized, as consciously as the dames at court learned to 'parley Euphuism'. The decline of L.'s direct influence was rapid, and a cause is to be sought in the change, which occured about 1588-90, in the social centre of Engl. life. The introspective lover, anatomizing his emotions, disillusioned before he is 25, with whose careful, if languid, delineation L. founded the novel of psychology, vanished in his bloodless excellence before the human men and women of Elizabethan drama ; but he played a notable part in his place and time ; he was necessary to Shakespeare's development ; and L.'s romance and L.'s style are both of supreme importance in the history of the Renaissance (q.v.) in Engld., and of the delatinizing of literary prose. And L. himself is at the same time an important factor in the development of prose-fiction (see s.v. Novel).

Lyons : headquarters of Fr. lit. in 16th. cent ; the Florence of France, as it has been designated, as famous as Venice for its printers and merchants, and rival to Paris in learning ; ' the head of Celtic Gaul, and flowering like a second Ilion ', in the words of one of its own poets. It was the home of Marot (q.v.) and the ' Marotiques ' : the literary côterie over which queen Margaret (q.v.) reigned, and in which Scève (q.v.) was recognized as spokesman among many voices, strong and sweet ; and it was the best-loved city of Ronsard (q.v.), prince of poets. In June, 1564, L. was the scene of Anglo-Fr. fêtes to celebrate the Treaty of Troyes (6 years after the capture of Calais, q.v.), and the *entente* on that occasion was sung by Ronsard himself.

Lyrisme (Fr.) : ' Romantisme ' ; Romantic movement ; descriptive epithet current in France for the anti-classical reaction and neoromantic revival in drama, pure lit., and art, characteristic of the second decade of the 19th cent., and culminating in 1830, the year of Hugo's (q.v.) *Hernani*, whence its practitioners are often known as the men of 1830. L. is a part, and only a part, of the general movement of individualism common in Europe at this time (see s.v. Romance) ; the *lyric* note specifically attached to it is the individual's voice in the new universe, revealed to the enchanted gaze of the young men who were growing up in France in the generation after the Revolution. ' Le vers de Lamartine et de Hugo *chante* ', writes Lanson (*Lit. Fr.*, 945) ; and the spontaneous song which went up from the lips of these younger poets was bound by no rules and prescribed by no schools, but was insistent, self-expressive, free. France had found herself in those days ; 1815 was the date of a new beginning ; the Bourbon restoration was a redintegration ; the glory without the terror of the *grand siècle*. Note, too, that, apart from the removal of the overhanging destiny of Napoleon, other restrictions were removed in the special sphere of lit. The boundaries of painting and poetry had been merged by Diderot (q.v.) ; the *salons* (q.v.), with their rigidities, had been broken up ; Napoleon had brought the Orient into fashion ; the universities had lost their authority.

Thus, the old ways were being closed on every side ; and the young men of letters utilized their opportunities. Declamation, formalism, rhetoric, rule, were replaced and relaxed at the option of the poet's personal sentiment and taste ; and the most obvious concomitant of the romantic revival in France is that reform of language and metre by which the innovators sought to enlarge the capacity and to extend the range of literary expression. In this respect, their work resembled that of the Pleiad (q.v.) in a former age ; and it is not to be denied that they took a certain malicious pleasure in shocking the literary susceptibilities of the classical school, whose patent was derived from Malherbe (q.v.) in the 16th cent. The technical aspects of their reforms on the stage, and in the ballad, ode, and other modes of poetry, and in the scansion of the alexandrine (s.v. Alexander) and other measures, are too complicated to detain us here. Hugo's pref. to *Cromwell*, 1827, and his famous *l'escalier dérobé* in the opening lines of his *Hernani* (25 Feb., 1830 ; the revolution consisted in placing *escalier* at the end of the first and *dérobé* at the beginning of the second line), are still authoritative. The point is, that colour, variety, surprise and the principles of tolerance and freedom were superimposed on the classical forms, and that these novelties were chiefly due to the enlarged vocabulary of poetry, which now refused to admit a class-distinction in words, and treated the ' base ' and the ' noble ' as of one literary value. The practice of Kipling in our own time has illustrated this principle in an extreme degree, and John Masefield and Rupert Brooke display the same romantic verbalism in their poetry. It was not (and probably is never) a mere inverted pedantry. Poets depend on causes outside their art. They do not sit down and say, Now let us neologize, shock, and innovate. This may come at a later stage, but the first impulse is from without ; and in France at this date it was given by the adventurous career of Napoleon, which closed in 1815, and by the bright hopes founded on the Bourbon restoration. These external events introduced the unrest and upheaval, the sense of movement and of colour, which found expression in new words and changing forms. Foreign influences contributed to the romantic impulse ; esp. the influence of Goethe, communicated partly through mme. de Staël, who introduced the name *romantique* to France ; Scott, Byron, Shakespeare, and the Span. romances (qq.v.). Constant was writing about Schiller, Fauriel about Manzoni and modern Greece, Nodier about *Faust*, Deschamps about Dante, Guizot about Shakespeare (see s.vv.), among many other translrs. and commentators at this receptive epoch in Fr. lit. and thought. The painters added their quota, and the Bible (q.v., and see s.v. Chateaubriand) was explored in the same direction. The resulting *lyrisme*, or romantic style, may be dated from about 1820, the year of Lamartine's *Méditations ;* Vigny's *Poèmes*, Stendhal's *Racine et Shakespeare*, and Nodier's *salon* at the Arsenal (see s.vv.) all followed by 1823, the year of the *Muse française* and the year before the *Globe* (qq.v.). The vogue of *L.* in the theatre where he was studying law. He was engaged to be married, and had just publd. his poem, *May*, on which his reputation rests. This is, undoubtedly, a Byronic poem, but it contains the promise of much more than imitative secondhand Byronism, and M.'s countrymen judge rightly in the homage which they pay to the memory of the young poet. A generation after his death, the name *May* was given in his honour to the first-fruits of a group of writers (see s.v. Neruda), who even called themselves the Generation (q.v.) of May, with special reference to M.'s poem.

Machault, de, Guillaume (*c.* 1290-1377) : Fr. lyric poet ; musician ; born in Champagne ; secretary to John of Luxembourg, king of Bohemia ; later in the service of Fr. court. M. was an industrious composer of *ballades*, and his ingenuity in inventing new and complicated variations of metre and rhyme entitles him to be considered as the founder of the Fr. *rhétoriqueurs* (q.v.), the school of poets which regarded poetry as a branch of rhetoric. M. had nothing, or next to nothing, to say ; and he contrived to say it elaborately in a number of artificial and elegant poems, extending in all to several scores of thousands of verses.

Machiavelli, dei, Niccolo di Bernardo (1469-1527) : It. statesman and political philosopher. Born at Florence of a distinguished family ; served in high offices of state, and undertook important missions to Paris, Rome, Vienna, and elsewhere, thus acquiring valuable first-hand knowledge of contemporary rulers and inner methods of government and diplomacy. These he turned to account in his masterly writings on statecraft. In 1512, M. was expelled from Florence, after suffering incarceration on suspicion of conspiring against the Medici (q.v.) after their return from political exile. Later, he was partially restored to the favour of the ruling family, a member of which, Giovanni, had become pope Leo x. M. now turned his ripe experience to the use of history and political philosophy, in which he displayed the resources of an expressive and a vigorous prose-style, unique in Ital. lit., and exactly suited to the positive genius of this class of writing. At the same time, these works were doubtless intended to win him back to active diplomacy. They included a *Florentine History* in 8 bks. ; *Discourses on Livy's Histories*, delivered to a distinguished audience in the Rucellai (q.v.) gardens in Florence ; a treatise in 6 bks. on *The Art of War* ; a short life of Castruccio Castracani, of Lucca, who 'was in every way a prince', and minor political studies. But the *magnum opus* of his life, and the one by which he is for ever famous, is his *Il Principe* (The Prince), which, in clear and concise expressiveness, in mastery of arrangement and subordination, and in economy of verbiage and ornament, marks a very considerable advance in skill ; M. said himself (*Prin.*, ch. 15) 'It being my intention to write a thing which shall be useful to him who apprehends it, it appears to me more profitable to follow up the real truth of a matter than the imagination of it'. As to the character and contents of the treatise, 2 preliminary notes may be made : one, internal ; the other, external. First, the conclusion of the *Prince* strikes an eloquent chord of idealism (ch. 26), to which it is not unfair to state that M. intended to direct his whole argument : 'Let Italy at last see her liberator appear. He would be greeted with love throughout her provinces. . . . May the prophecy of Petrarch be fulfilled under the illustrious standard of the Medici : "Courage shall take up arms against blind fury ; the ancient valour of the Italian heart is not yet dead " '. Secondly, the Italy of M.'s date was distracted by anarchy and corruption, and base bargains with foreign invaders. The government of Florence was a shuttlecock between Savonarola's theocracy and his opponents' schemes for the restoration of the Medici. Both sides, gospellers and humanists, though seemingly so bitterly opposed, are revealed in the perspective of history as allied engines of reform ; but Dante's dream of a united Italy was not realized till the 19th cent., and, meanwhile, neither prince nor monk, neither Medici nor Savonarola, read the signs of the times aright. There was too much native force in each for a violent revulsion to the other. Into this welter of politics, M. drove the hard philosophy of his prince to-be, who should succeed in making Italy one nation in the 16th cent. which he knew. He wr. for the new prince, for the prince who has to impose his will ; and the tragedy of his statecraft was, that neither the prince nor the strategist was forthcoming. If M. was the Bismarck of his period, he lacked both a Wilhelm and a Moltke. ' Of all princes, it is impossible for the new prince to avoid the imputation of cruelty, since new states are full of dangers' (ch. 17) ; 'our experience has been that those princes who have done great things have held good faith of small account' (ch. 18) ; but experience likewise shows that a prime minister, or even a grand vizier, does not formulate such principles before his prince, or tyrant, has arrived. History has recorded in United Italy and United Germany, and, even more recently, in Russia, affirmations of a national sentiment which enunciates its own code of ethics ; and, while much of the hostility to M., and to the ' Machiavellism ' (see s.v. Gentillet) of which he became the eponym, is directly traceable to the Church which employed and banned him successively, and which condoned in the name of religion acts of torture, bad faith, and violence, far worse than his ' prince ' might commit in the name of stable government, much, too, is due to the fact that he drew up his code of princely ethics in advance of the coming of the ruler. Everything depended on that factor ; if the prince to-be, for whom M.'s treatise was composed, had proved himself a capable ruler, M. might have saved distracted Italy from several centuries' agitation. So much, at least, is due to the sagacious statesman's conception. The reply, which he could not foresee, comes from history itself. A Machiavellian State, such as the Germ. Empire of 1871, in which the prince (king William of Prussia) responded to the statesman's summons, is liable to perish by the means by which it was raised. When

Bethmann-Hollweg, the Germ. chancellor, pleaded the sanction of 'necessity' for tearing up the 'scrap of paper' on which was inscribed his prince's guarantee for the neutrality of Belgium (August, 1914), he destroyed the Machiavellian edifice of Bismarck in the authentic spirit of M.'s *Il Principe*. Machiavellism failed in Florence because no prince was forthcoming; its subsequent failures have been due to its inherent violation of right.

The controversy that has encompassed this bk. is without parallel in literary history; and perhaps we may say that the bk. takes colour, chameleon-like, from its controversialists. To a Borgia or a Buonaparte, it is one thing; to the children whom they orphan, it is another. In lit., too, *The Prince* is important as a source (through Gentillet's *Anti-Machiavel*) of the type of villain-hero of Elizabethan drama (see s.v. Marlowe; and cf. Shakespeare's *Richard iii*), and for its sensible enhancement of the influence on tragedy of the Senecan models of antiquity. This added influence is to be found in the heroes of tragic drama in Corneille (q.v.), and in the memoirs of such a Corneille-like character as cardinal de Retz (q.v.) in France. M. also composed prose comedies, the *Andria* (from Terence), *Cligia*, and *Mandragola*: contemporary studies of Florentine manners, to which Ben Jonson (q.v.) and other dramatists repaired for situations in their plays.

Macias (14th cent.): Span. poet; celebrated as *el Enamorado*, the *Lover* of poetic history, on account of the sensation created by his unhappy life and death. Traditions differ as to details, but he seems to have been killed by the dart of a jealous husband who overheard him singing to his mistress behind the bars of his prison at Arjonilla. Whether genuine or not, the romantic tale appealed to a romantic age, and M.'s immortality was assured more permanently than is warranted by such fragments of his poetry as survive in the collection of Baena (q.v.) and elsewhere. His name became proverbial as a tragic lover in Santillana, *Celestina*, Vega (qq.v.), and right down to the 19th cent., in the *Macias*, 1831, of Larra (q.v.). (See also s.v. Rodriguez de Padron).

Mackenzie, Henry (1745-1831): Scot. novelist; lawyer; Tory pamphleteer. Wr. *The Man of Feeling*, 1771; *The Man of the World*, 1773; *Julia de Roubigné*, 1777; chairman, 1805, of the committee which reported on the *Ossian* of Macpherson (q.v.). M.'s reputation and memory rest to-day on his first novel, which was written in the manner of Sterne (q.v.), and which seized the moment of sentiment in Engl. fiction. But his third novel, in that short period of productivity, was, artistically, the best; it is smaller, less elaborate, and simpler in idea and construction than the other 2, and places M. in the direct line of descent from Richardson (q.v.), and of ascent to Scott (q.v.) and others. M. was one of the first to praise Burns (q.v.), and was an early admirer of Lessing and Schiller (qq.v.).

Macpherson, James (1736-96): Scot. antiquary, poet; historian; edu. at Aberdeen univ., and became schoolmaster in Ruthven, his native parish; was early interested in Scots antiquities, and wr. a poem, the *Highlander*, 1758; collected *Fragments of Ancient Poetry in the Highlands*, 1760, and met, while he was preparing that vol., J. Home (q.v.), author of *Douglas*, 'who was full of the romantic interest in the Highlands, which he passed on to Collins, and which was shared by Thomson' (see s.vv.; *C.H.E.L.*, x, 230, by prof. Ker). M. was already steeped in these studies, and produced in successive years, 1762-3, *Fingal: an Ancient Epic Poem, in six books; with several other Poems translated from the Galic language*, and *Temora, in eight books*, similarly sub-titled. Home was delighted, and Dr. Hugh Blair (1718-1800), regius prof. of rhetoric and belles-lettres at Edinburgh, and leader of a circle which included Hume, Adam Smith, and others, wr. a 'critical dissertation', 1763, which gave these 'translated ancient epics' their academic send-off. How far they were sent, or travelled, by their own impetus and velocity, we shall see immediately; here we note, as Home and Blair failed to note, chiefly because M. gave them exactly what they were looking for, that the orig. 'ancient poems in the Galic language' were conspicuous by their absence. The advt. to *Fingal* stated that 'there is a design on foot to print the Originals as soon as the translator shall have time to transcribe them for the press; and if this publication shall not take place, copies will then be deposited in one of the public libraries, to prevent so ancient a monument of genius from being lost'; the design on foot, it will be observed, was even then represented as unlikely to be accomplished. What ground was there for believing that *Fingal* and *Temora* were faithful translns. from ancient epics at all? It was known, or, at any rate, it is known now, largely through the researches of Kuno Meyer, that, in the vast complex of old Irish prose sagas, probably representing the deposit of a vanished era of civilization, the Ossianic cycle revolved round the persons of the chieftain Finn MacCumhall and his son, Ossin. It is known as Ossian's cycle, or the Fenian cycle (from *fainne*, the royal bodyguard), or, locally, as the Leinster cycle; and, in Scotizing this Gaelic Finn MacCumhall into a Caledonian Fingal, M. satisfied the Highland pride of Home and his friends, and successfully glorified his own country: 'In the glory of Ossian', says prof. Ker (*C.H.E.L.*, loc. cit.), 'the Irish have only by courtesy a share'. That these alleged ancient Gaelic epics were neither ancient nor Gaelic, but were a poetic antiquary's view of what the Ossianic epics ought to supply to romantic Scotsmen in the 18th cent. ('both nations'—Caledonian and Irish—'were almost the same people in the days of Fingal', declared M.), does not in the least detract from the brilliance of M.'s achievement; nor would the form of publication, or even the pretence that the originals existed, be a very serious literary hoax, if M. had not pursued it too far. Unfortunately, and probably very much to M.'s own confusion, Irish scholars and Engl. enthusiasts insisted on his producing the goods; and, 'twenty years after his triumph, he had to sit down in cold blood and make his ancient Gaelic poetry. He had begun with a piece of literary artifice, a practical joke; he ended with deliberate forgery, which, the more it succeeded, would leave to him the less of what was really his due for the merits of the English Ossian' (Ker, *ibid.*).

On M. the forger, so termed by poetic justice, we need not dwell to-day, nor on Malcolm Laing (1762-1818), who exposed the forgery in his *Poems of Ossian*, 1805, nor on the *Report*, in 3 vols., of the Committee (of which H. Mackenzie, q.v., was chairman) of the Highland Society of Scotland appointed to inquire into the nature and authenticity of the Poems of Ossian, which was publd. in Edinburgh in the same year, nor on the masterly art. by sir Walter Scott (q.v.) in the *Edinburgh Review*; July, 1815. For literary history, the really important thing is neither the fact of the forgery nor its exposure, but the extraordinary vogue of M.'s Ossianic epics, and the exceptional skill of their construction. We see now how much they owed to the language of the Bible (q.v.), to genuine study of Erse sources, and to M.'s own romantic sensibilities and his sense of what the public wanted. His vogue was even greater on the Continent than at home. 'The questionable translation', remarks prof. Vaughan (Brit. Academy, fourth Warton Lecture; Oct., 1913), 'spread like wild-fire over the face of Europe'. It was transld. into Fr. by no less a man than Turgot (q.v.); Cesarotti (q.v.) transltd. it into Ital., and in that version it was the constant companion of Napoleon all the way from Egypt to St. Helena: thus, the literary forger of Kingussie helped to shape the history of the world. 'But perhaps the greatest of Macpherson's triumphs' (Vaughan, *ibid.*) 'was the capture of Goethe' (q.v.), who proclaimed his capture unequivocally at the close of *The Sorrows of Werther*. Ossian, as these epics are briefly known, is one of the monuments of the Romantic movement in Europe. Though not obtrusively medieval in style, it fitted in with the return to studies of the Middle Ages, which Gray, Scott himself, and others were encouraging; and M., in close association with bp. Percy (q.v.), the more modest and honest revivalist of Icelandic (see s.v. Scandinavian lit.) sources of poetry, helped immensely to inspire the sense of mystery, wonder, terror, and adventure, which thrilled every lit. in Europe, 'ending with things so remote from us as the tragedies of Ozerov (q.v.) in Russia' (Vaughan, *op. cit.*; the same writer notes, as significant, that the great prince Bismarck's sister, born 1827, was given the Ossianic name of Malvina). We may cite the first notice by Blair (*supra*), quoted in *C.H.E.L.*, x, 227: 'The description of Fingal's airy hall and of the ascent of Malvina into it deserves particular notice, as remarkably noble and magnificent. But above all, the engagement of Fingal with the spirit of Loda cannot be mentioned without admiration. The undaunted courage of Fingal, opposed to all the terrors of the Scandinavian god; the appearance and the speech of the awful spirit; the wound which he received and the shriek which he sends forth, are full of the most amazing and terrible majesty, that I know no passage more sublime

in the writings of any uninspired author'. That M., working on such slender material, should have attained the sublimity of an inspired writer in his style, and should have produced the glamour of Gaelic legend and the machinery of the Celtic underworld, is a feat not to be depreciated by the tricks of authorship which he played on his generation.

M. became secretary to a West Indian governor, 1764-6; wr., 1773, a prose transln. of the *Iliad*, and, 1775, a *History of Great Britain, from the Restoration in 1660 to the Accession of the House of Hanover*, for which he received £3,000; was M.P. for Camelford, 1780-96, and was buried in Westminster Abbey.

Macropedius, Georgius. See **Langveldt, G.**

Madvig, Johann Nicolai (1804-86): Dan. scholar; prof. of Lat. at univ. of Copenhagen from 1829; minister of education, 1848-51; chiefly eminent for his work on Livy and Cicero (q.v., thus linking the humanism of 5 centuries with Petrarch): his edn. of the *de Finibus* is described as 'one of those standard works which instruct and stimulate the student not only by the knowledge they impart but also by the way in which they impart it' (Sandys, *Hist. Class. Schol.*, iii, 320). M.'s *Lat. Grammar*, 1841, achieved a European reputation. In the course of his long life. M. helped to train most of the rising scholars of Denmark, who paid him due honour in his old age. A 'sound humanity' is discovered by Henry Nettleship (1839-93) to be M.'s chief characteristic.

Maerlant, van, Jacob (1235-?1300): Dutch poet; his works are 'a mirror of the thirteenth century' in the far from extravagant estimate of his last editor, Dr. Jan te Winkel (Ghent, 1892), and in versatility, fluency, and well-directed talent M. takes a leading place in the early history of letters in the Netherlands. He was romancer, didactic moralist, and polyhistor; he relied, as was obligatory in his age, on the labours of predecessors, without critical discernment; but he succeeded in impressing a clear character upon the works which he transld. and adapted. These included a *Gests of Alexander*, a *Graal*, a *Merlin*, a *Torec*, and a *Troy-History*, founded on the obvious models sought in Fr. and Anglo-Norman versions. Two short poems on dreams and precious stones (both full of meaning in medieval thought) gave M. better opportunity of displaying the moral vein which he worked out to such excellent effect in his three *Martin*-poems. The Martin of these poems was an unknown friend of M., to whom he opened his heart on all the problems of his day—theological, political, and social. Composed in long strophes of rhymed octosyllabic verses, the Martin pieces reflect the conditions of 13th cent. life and ideas, and they are especially notable for a feature which is permanent in Dutch lit., viz., respect for the middle-classes. The *Sachsenspiegel* of Eike (q.v.) and the *Vision* of Piers (q.v.) may be compared with these 3 poems of M. Other works followed rapidly, and form parts of the *Spieghel Historiael* ('mirror of history') MS. at Leyden. They include chronicles from the scriptures, from eastern legends, and from the physiologists, and they were all written in verse ; had M. chosen prose as his medium, Holland, too, would have had her Villehardouin (q.v.).

Maffei, Scipione (1675-1755) : It. scholar ; count by rank. Born at Verona, where he discovered, 1713, a number of Lat. MSS. His investigation of this trove enabled him to complete the researches of Mabillon (q.v.) into Lat. palæography (q.v.), by inventing the distinction, since accepted as the basis of scientific classification, between the Majuscule, Minuscule and Cursive forms of Roman handwriting. Wr. *Verona Illustrata*, 1732, and other antiquarian works. Besides his distinction as a scholar, M. was the author, 1713, of the only Ital. tragedy of any note before the dramas of Alfieri (q.v.). He chose the familiar Gk. subject of Merope, and, as metre, 11-syllabled blank verse.

Magalotti, Lorenzo (1637-1712) : It. man of science and general culture ; secretary of the Accademia del Cimento (of experiment), founded, 1657, by Viviani, the biographer of Galileo (q.v.), and publisher of its transactions. Wr. series of epistles on philosophic doubt, and transld. parts of *Paradise Lost* and other foreign *opera majora*.

Maggi, Carlo Maria (1630-99). It. poet ; an Arcadian before the Arcadia (q.v.) Academy, in the sense that M. represented a protest against the wit and conceits (q.v.) of the Marinist (s.v. Marini) writers. Wr. several comedies in the Milanese dialect, but was too intent on simplicity to avoid platitude.

Magliabechi, Antonio (1633-1714) : It. bibliophil. Learned goldsmith at Florence, where he became librarian to Cosimo iii, grand duke of Tuscany ; founded a library, to which he bequeathed his collection of 30,000 vols., and which was afterwards absorbed in the grand ducal Palatine Library (founded, 1815), known since 1862 as the National Library.

Magnin, Charles (1703-1862) : Fr. critic. Wr. *Histoire des Marionettes*, 1854, and collected vols. of his contributions to the *Globe* and the *Révue des deux Mondes : Origines du Théâtre*, 1838, and *Causeries*, 1842.

Magnus, -i. Johannes (1488-1544) : Swed. humanist ; student at Louvain, Cologne and Perugia, which at that time ' supplied the link between certain scholars of Sweden and the Italian humanists ' (Sandys, *Hist. Class. Schol.*, iii, 332). J.M. became archbp. of Upsala, where the univ. had been founded, 1477 ; but, as a Catholic prelate, the dawning Protestant controversies drove him into exile, 1526. He wr. a Lat. history of the kings of the Goths and Swedes, which is characterized by Sandys as ' a still more uncritical performance than the elaborately written and curiously illustrated *History of the Northern Nations* ' by his brother (below).

　-ii. **Olaus** (1490-1568) : Swed. humanist ; brother to above. His *History of the Northern Nations*, characterized by Sandys (*supra*), was issued in Rome, 1555, where the 2 brothers were living in exile.

Magnus Olafsson (1574-1636) : Icel. scholar. Edited the *Codex Wormianus* (see s.v. Worm), or MS. of the *Edda* of Snorri (q.v.), rearranging its contents into tales and index, in which form it has since been most popular. M. was

responsible for the theory of an earlier *Edda* than Snorri's, and was thus prominent in the controversy as to the authorship of the miscalled Elder Edda at the revival of Old Icelandic lit. in the 17th cent.　(See s.v. Edda).

Magny, de, Olivier (died c. 1560) : Fr. poet ; ardent follower of the Pleiad (q.v.) ; began writing 1553, at an early age, though the date of his birth is uncertain, and died young. His poetry was composed in the letter, even more perhaps than in the spirit, of the principles enunciated by Du Bellay (q.v.). It comprised *Amours, Odes*, including one of jubilation, couched in tones of modest gratitude, at the capture of Calais (q.v.), *Gaietés* and *Soupirs* ; and the level attained was full of promise and of no mean performance in the new schools of modern Fr. (and French-inspired) verse.

Maimonides (1135-1204) : Span.-Jew. scholar ; philosopher ; Moses ben Maimon ; author of *The Guide for the Perplexed* ; born at Cordova ; died in Cairo, where he was chief rabbi. Wr. Arab. work, transld. into Hebr., 1204, under the title of *Moreh Nebukim*, and into Lat. (Paris, 1520, and Basle, 1629), and, later, into Ital., Fr., Engl., Germ., etc. The standard Fr. version is that by S. Munk, *Guide des Egarés* (3 vols., Paris, 1856-66), issued in Engl. by M. Friedländer, *The Guide for the Perplexed* (second edn., Routledge, 1904, 700 years after the author's death) ; a new Germ. transln. by Dr. Adolf Weiss was publd. at Leipsic ; 3 vols., 1924. Apart from the special Jewish interest of the *Moreh*, as an elucidation of Talmudic commentaries, the spirit of rational philosophy which permeated the work made M., who aimed at a ' reconciliation of Aristotelian philosophy with Jewish theology ' (Sandys, *Hist. Class. Schol.*, i, 564 ; and see s.vv. Aristotle, Scholasticism), a forerunner and master of the Schoolmen, such as Duns Scotus and Thomas Aquinas.

Maine, de, Anne Louise (1676-1753) : Fr. literary hostess and patron of letters ; *née* de Bourbon, through her grandfather, prince de Condé, and m. a Bourbon prince, Louis, duc de Maine (1670-1736), son of king Louis xiv and mme. de Montespan ; the young duke was brought up by mme. de Maintenon, q.v., and won her devoted maternal affection as well as the distinguished praises of mme. de Staël (q.v.). But the duke, who bought the château of Sceaux (q.v.) in 1711, was eclipsed at its revels and in its hospitality by his more brilliant wife, who raised it to a kind of minature Versailles, and kept it going after Versailles had been hushed by the death of the *grand monarque*, 1715. The memoirs of mme. de Staal (q.v.), *femme-de-chambre* to the duchess, are a chronicle of Sceaux, to which reference is made by Ste.-Beuve (q.v.), *Causeries du Lundi*, iii. Mme. de M. wr. in verse a vol. of *Divertissements de Sceaux*, and many of her letters have been publd.

Maine de Biran, François Pierre (1766-1824) : Fr. philosopher ; characterized by Cousin (q.v.) as ' the greatest metaphysician who has adorned France since Malebranche ' ; psychologist and anthropologist. The boundary-line between philosophy and lit. is difficult to draw, but we may follow in this instance the safe lead of the distinguished writer of the standard *Hist. de la Lit. Fr.* (Lanson, p. 907) : ' En philosophie, il nous faut prendre Cousin, et laisser Maine de Biran '.

Maine, Henry Sumner (1822-88) : Engl. jurist ; regius prof. of Civil Law at Cambridge, 1847-54 ; K.C.S.I., 1871 ; Corpus prof. of jurisprudence at Oxford, 1869-78 ; master of Trinity Hall, Cambridge, 1877, and Whewell prof. of International Law at that univ. from 1887. M., who was a contributor to the *Saturday Review* in the brilliant days of its foundation in 1855, wr. *Ancient Law ; its Connection with the Early History of Society and its Relations to Modern Ideas*, 1861 ; *Village Communities*, 1871 ; *Early History of Institutions*, 1875 ; *Early Law and Customs*, 1883 ; and was one of the first scholars to apply the hist. method to the study of ' political ' or communal-social institutions. As a pioneer in this field, M.'s writings have permanent value, and he is said by sir F. Pollock (*Oxford Lectures*, 1890, p. 158) to have forged ' at one master-stroke a new and lasting bond between law, history, and anthropology '. The new ethnology, as developing in the 20th cent., a tentative bibliography of which is appended to *Givers of Life*, by prof. M. A. Canney (Black, 1923), is thus largely indebted to the earlier investigations of M.

Maintenon, de, Françoise (1635-1719) : Fr. letter-writer ; legal consort, 1685, of king Louis xiv of France ; *marquise* by title ; *née* d'Aubigné, grand-daughter of the Huguenot poet (s.v. Aubigné), and orphaned at 15 years old ; m. 1652, Scarron (q.v.), the crippled poet, to the astonishment of Paris society in that day ; Scarron's death, 1660, reduced his widow to the poverty from which he had rescued her, and she supplemented the small pension which his writings had earned by teaching and by social service, for which her gifts and disposition particularly fitted her, Her apppointment, 1669, as governess to the 2 sons of king Louis xiv and mme. de Montespan (see s.v. Maine) brought her, not merely a change of fortune, and the title and estates of the marquisate of Maintenon, but also brought her into the ambit of Fr. history ; her private marriage to the king, 1685, is a fact of history rather than of lit. We are not here concerned with her cold, if wise, conduct in that exalted rank, nor with her characteristic foundation, 1686, of a girls' home at St. Cyr, to which she retired 1715. She had a genius for teaching and for letter-writing : as a teacher she was a disciple of Port Royal (q.v.) ; and her correspondence, which ranks hardly, if at all, lower than that of mme. de Sévigné (q.v.), reveals a calm temperament, a grave outlook, and a sure constancy, which her difficult experience at court could never deeply embitter or impair. (See, too, s.v. Racine).

Mairet, de, Jean (1604-86) : Fr. dramatist. Wr. tragi-comedies : *Sylvie*, 1626 ; *Silvanaire*, 1629, a pastoral on Ital. models, reissued, 1631, with a pref. in which for the first time was formulated the classic theory of the Fr. dramatic Unities (q.v.). An Italiante comedy, *les Galanteries du duc d'Ossone*, followed in 1632, and, 2 years later, an important date, came M.'s *Sophonisbe*, the first regular

tragedy on the new classic stage. The subject was a favourite one (see s.vv. Trissino and Marston, with the latter of whom M. has been compared) ; and M.'s dramatic theory and practice lent him rank and esteem in the busy disputations of the time. He took part in the battle about the *Cid* (q.v.) of Corneille (q.v.), whom he accused of plagiary, but the fact is that Corneille's success spelt M.'s eclipse, and his pref. to *Silvanaire* is to-day his chief title to recollection.

Maistre, de, -i. Joseph Marie (1754-1821) : Fr. moral and political writer. Retired to Lausanne, 1792, when Savoy, where he had been a senator, became French, and to Petrograd, 1802-16, as ambassador of the king of Sardinia. Wr. *Soirées de Saint-Pétersbourg*, 2 vols., 1821, the sub-title of which was *Entretiens* (Discussions) on the temporal government of Providence ; *Considérations sur la France*, 1796 ; *du Pape*, 1819 ; and, among others, a treatise on the Gallican church in relation to the sovereign pontiff. M. was a dour logician, no doubt because he found facts intractable, and his doctrine of government tended to a somewhat bare absolutism both for Church and State, the direction of which, in reaction from the thought of the 18th cent., he would have committed to the joint keeping of pope and king ; but in private life M. was most lovable, affectionate, and full of the sensibility of the age.

   -ii. Xavier (1763-1852) : Fr. idyllist ; brother to above, whose politics and wanderings he shared. Wr. 1794, *Voyage autour de ma Chambre*, a charming piece of light fiction, in the manner of Sterne (q.v.), but without Sterne's salaciousness. Wr., too, among other tales, *la jeune Sibérienne*, and *le Lépreux de la Cité d'Aoste*, in a similar vein of grace, fancy, and pleasantry.

Maldonado, de, Gabriel Lopez (fl. 1586) : Span. poet. Wr. ballads [see s.v. Romance (Span.)], and publd. a *Cancionero*, 1586, which was a prized possession in the fictitious library of Don Quixote (s.v. Cervantes).

Malebranche, Nicolas (1638-1715) : Fr. divine ; an exact contemporary of king Louis xiv, whose reign he adorned with the writings of his humane and cultivated Platonism. M. was a Platonist by temperament, and is duly mentioned in connection with the Cambridge Platonists (see s.v. Plato) by prof. J. A. Stewart (*Myths of Plato*, Macmillan, 501), whose analysis of dream-consciousness (*ibid.*, Introduction) exactly applies to M.'s poetic vision : ' the vision of all things in God '. But by mental training M. was a Cartesian (s.v. Descartes), and a disciple of the *Discourse on Method*, and of all the logical ratiocination which it implied. The combination makes M. as fascinating to read for his speculation and his lucidity as it made him liable to attack from the orthodox and the sceptics at the same time in his own controversial generation. Fénelon (q.v.) was put up by Bossuet (q.v.) to reply to M.'s *Treatise on Nature and Grace*, 1680, before the Quietist controversy a few years later separated the great Bossuet from his henchman. But the conflict was continued and extended by the militants of Port Royal (q.v.), including Arnauld (q.v.) and others, and led to the work of Bayle (q.v.). M.'s greatest and most enduring treatise was *de la Recherche de le Vérité* ('The Search for Truth'), 1674-75, which ranks among the supreme pieces of philosophical writing. M. was a member of the Oratory all through his life, and is still known as the Fr. Plato of the cloister.

Malesherbes, de, Chrétien Guillaume de Lamoignon (1721-94): Fr. statesman; member of the Academy (q.v.); misc. writer on agricultural and financial topics (*Oeuvres Choisies*, 1809). M.'s significance in lit. is derived from the office which he filled as press-censor under king Louis xv. He administered it in a spirit of liberalism and tolerance, so far as was compatible with the spirit of the times. Thus, M. removed the ban from Montesquieu's (q.v.) *Esprit des Lois*, when he took office in 1750, and the licence to publish the *Encyclopédie* (q.v.), was due to him. He was dismissed in 1771, probably as too righteous a judge, was recalled by Louis xvi, 1774, and 20 years later suffered death by the guillotine for his defence of that monarch.

Malherbe, de, François (1555-1628): Fr. poet and literary reformer of the relaxed taste and style of the disciples of Ronsard (q.v.). *Habent sua fata libelli*, and the fate of the Pleiad (q.v.) arrived in the 16th cent. 'Enfin Malherbe vint', wr. Boileau (q.v.), in a mood as nearly apocalyptic as the strict canons of his classicism permitted, and M., in the sense of Boileau's welcome, has been called 'the tyrant of words and syllables' (J. Balzac), 'regent of Parnassus', 'philological legislator', 'a grammarian in blinkers', etc. His domestic life was not happy; he was separated from his wife; his daughters died in his lifetime, and his only son, recently pardoned after sentence to death for one duel, was killed in another, 1626. On the other hand, M. was fortunate in his material circumstances; he enjoyed the favour of the court, and was appointed poet-laureate to king Henri iv and treasurer of France to Louis xiii at the nomination of card. Richelieu. M. was a grammarian, a pedant, as his adversaries said, before he was a poet; and his real poverty of poetic imagination had the unfortunate result that he was never moved to invent the forms of verse suited to his principles. Perforce of defective invention, he was content to express his inspiration through the current forms of lyrical measures, though every instinct of his intellect and all the talent that was in him cried out for a less subjective medium. Almost (if not quite) deliberately, certainly by a powerful instinctive choice, M. rejected the very motives to lyric verse which might have fired his muse. Thus, his own children's death failed to move him; but he wr. an ode on the death of Rose Du Périer, the daughter of a friend; and in the more objective contemplation of a sorrow detached from personal emotion he struck out the beautiful line :

'Et rose, elle a vécu ce que vivent les roses.' It is said that M. intended to write an ode of consolation for a widower, and that, when it was ready, the bereaved husband was a bridegroom; and the tale, even if not true, illustrates the slow process of composition and perfection

which replaced the sudden pangs of inspiration. M.'s contemporary, A. Hardy (q.v.), though he cannot be mentioned in the same breath as a scholar, gentleman, or artist, was, practically, M.'s superior, for the simple reason that Hardy used the drama for the purpose for which M. misused the lyre. The transition to the classical 17th cent. was prepared and surveyed by M.; he effected an ordnance-survey of Parnassus; he liquidated the affairs of the previous age; he put the house of letters in repair for the succession of oratory to lyricism, for the new tenancy of the poetry which is heard in place of the poetry which is overheard (to adopt a fine distinction from John Stuart Mill, q.v.); but he did not enter it himself. He wr. some admirable verse, in the *Larmes de Saint Pierre*, 1587, inscribed to king Henri iii, and in his later more excellent odes to Du Périer, 1599, to Marie de Medici, 1600, 'to the king starting for Limousin, a Prayer', and others on other public occasions, never altogether free from sententiousness and convention. But M.'s great and abiding work was in the domain of language and style. In the striking phrase invented by J. L. Balzac, M. 'degasconnaded' the Fr. language; he released it from the insupportable burden of the neologisms and licenses imported by such Gascon squires as Du Bartas, D'Aubigné (qq.v.) and the rest; he purged it of the Pleiad's borrowings which it had not been able to assimilate. His constant and conscious aim was restoration, not impoverishment; simplification, not pedantry; commonsense and reason, not adventitious ornament. Everything irregular and meretricious in vocabulary, metre, and prosody, was to be driven out of use by the same literary force which had introduced it. The principles of the Pleiad were repealed, though the best results of their practice were made welcome. It was to standardize the living tongue, without recourse to the plausible classicism of dead times or foreign exemplars, that M. devoted his zeal as reformer. He found his detractors, and he made his mistakes; but on the whole his selection was just, and his rejection of hiatus, inversion, 'enjambement', cacophony, want of caesura, etc., was in the forward line of classical Fr. style. He perceived that poetry was an art, with a technique as exacting as it is indispensable; so that 'he rendered literature the greatest service that it was possible for him to render; he revealed to it the cost of truth and of perfection'. In a sense, his aims may be compared to those of Goethe (q.v.) in his classic period: M.'s aims, even his service, be it noted, not his achievement. For M., too, saw the evil of the excesses of too much liberty of choice; he, too, saw the need of peace and discipline and order in lit., as in politics. He, too, sought, though he might not exemplify, that 'peace on the heights', which Goethe, in a famous stanza, transferred from the hills of nature to the heights of classical verse. And M.'s services, though they were interrupted for a while by the Precious (q.v.) school which arose in Paris, were destined to prevail in the language and lit. which he loved with so whole-hearted a devotion. He cleared the way for the pure style of the 17th cent., and his salvage from the Pleiad's super-cargo was selected with inestimable discretion and a real care for the future of Fr. letters. This care, it should be added, included thought for the beauty of lit. as well as for its truth. It is an inadequate account of M.'s services to classical taste to represent him as merely the Descartes (q.v.) of æsthetics ; ' Cartesian æsthetic would reduce art to science '. What was wanted in France in M.'s day was not science (that was to come with the Academy, q.v.), but the preliminary spade-work of observation and selection. ' Not in his own verse ', says sir E. Gosse (Taylorian lecture, 1920), ' but in that which his doctrine encouraged others to write, and not in verse only, but in prose, and in the very arrangement and attitude of the French intellect, Malherbe's influence was wide-spreading, was potent, and will never be wholly superseded. He found French, as a literary language, confused, chaotic, no longer in the stream of sound tradition. He cleared out the channel, he dredged away the mud, and cut down the weeds ; and he brought the pure water back to its proper course '. We should add that M.'s theories of poetics have had to be collated from various sources ; chiefly from his own marginal annotations to the works of the ' monstrous ' Desportes (q.v.).

Mal Lara (Malara), de, Juan (c. 1525-71) : Span. dramatic writer ; humanist ; schoolmaster at Seville. ML.'s dramas have all been lost, but he is said to have been a prolific and popular playwright. His collection of proverbial philosophy, or, rather, one part of it, *la Philosophia vulgar*, 1568, is extant, and belongs to a class of lit. which was at once abundant and attractive in Spain.

Mallarmé, Stéphane (1842-98) : Fr. poet ; contemporary with and comparable to Verlaine (q.v.) ; a so-called symbolist poet, representing a type, the final value of which has not yet been determined, and will, perhaps, be found not much worth determining.

Mallet (Malloch), David (?1705-65) : Engl. dramatist. See s.v. J. Thomson, with whom M. wr. a masque, *Alfred*, containing the national ode, *Rule, Britannia*. M. was lit. executor to H. St. John, visct. Bolingbroke (q.v.).

Mallet du Pan, Jacques (1749-1800) : Fr. journalist. Born at Geneva ; contributor to the *Mercure* of Panckoucke (q.v.), and a member of the constitutional party. M. emigrated in August, 1792.

Malleville, de, Claude (1597-1647) : Fr. poet ; original member of the Fr. Academy (q.v.) ; a favourite in the Precious (q.v.) set at the Hôtel de Rambouillet (q.v.). Wr. occasional verse, including 9 ' flowers ' for the *Guirlande de Julie* (q.v.) ; M. was pitted against Voiture (q.v.) in one of the sonnet-tournaments of the school, the subject being *la Belle Matineuse*. (M.'s name is variously spelled, Maleville).

Malloch, Wm. Hurrell (1849-1923) : Engl. essayist ; nephew of the brothers Froude (see s.v.) ; wr. 2 *romans-à-clef* (q.v.) : *The New Republic*, 1887, and *The New Paul and Virginia*, 1893, each a successful satire, with characters disguised from real life, of current aspects of political, religious and social thought. M. was a busy publicist in the Victorian age.

Malon de Chaide, Pedro (c. 1530-96) : Span. didactic writer ; Augustinian monk. Wr. *The Conversion of the Magdalen*, 1588, frequently reprinted ; in 4 bks. : introductory, the sinner, the penitent, the saint. The combination of moral severity with a wide license of discourse on the sumptuary laws makes a curious impression, but may account for the attractiveness of the work to increasing numbers of readers. M. regarded the Lat. poets, and the Span. poetry of Boscan and Garcilasso (qq.v.) founded on those models, as deleterious to the Christian life.

Malone, Edmund (1741-1812) : Engl. (Irish) critic ; wr., 1778, *Attempt to ascertain the Order in which the Plays attributed to Shakespeare were written*, and edited the plays, 10 vols., 1790. This edn., together with M.'s notes in MS., formed the basis of the *Third Variorum* edn., 21 vols., 1813, by Jas. Boswell (1778-1822), son of his namesake (q.v.), the biographer. It is commonly known as ' Boswell's Malone ' ; and M., *teste* sir S. Lee (*William Shakespeare*, 582) ' threw abundance of new light on Shakespeare's biography and on the chronology and sources of his works, while his researches into the beginnings of the English stage added a new chapter of first-rate importance to English literary history '.

Malory, sir Thomas (died, 1471) : Engl. romancer ; author of *Morte Darthur*, a coherent Engl. prose-narrative, reduced from the unwieldy material of Norman-French and Breton poets and chroniclers ; completed ¦by M. in 1469, and ' divided into twenty-one books, chaptered, and imprinted, and finished in the Abbey Westminster, the last day of July, the year of our Lord, 1485 ', by William Caxton (q.v.). M. refers 56 times to the ' French book ' on which his romance was built ; and critics (chiefly, Dr. Oskar Sommer, 2 vols., Nutt, 1889-90) have been at pains to distribute M.'s version of the tales among his precursors : 4 bks. to one source, 7 to another, and so forth. The partition is ingenious, but is pushed too far if it omits M.'s own share in what Caxton rightly called this ' noble and joyous book . . . of the birth, life, and acts of the said king Arthur, of his noble knights of the Round Table, their marvelous enquests and adventures, the achieving of the Sangreal, and in the end of the dolorous death and departing out of this world of them all '. Such is the high argument of the *Morte Darthur*; and, though Geoffrey of Monmouth, Chrétien of Troyes, Walter Map, Robert de Boron, and others, had reaped in the same vineyard, yet that M.'s vintage is mellow while the rest are crude is a judgment confirmed by 4 centuries and 2 continents. The first Arthuriad in Engl. prose is at the same time the final form of the old ' matière de Bretagne ' (see s.v. Bodel). All that followed it was drawn from it. One other question has been raised. Roger Ascham (q.v.) objected to the *Morte Darthur* that it was full of ' open manslaughter and bold bawdry ', and Tennyson (q.v.), who owed so much to it, described Arthur, its hero, as ' touch'd by the adulterous finger of a time that hover'd between war and wantonness '. Neither the schoolmaster nor the idyllist is quite fair. M.'s business, like

Boccaccio's, was to tell a story ; and if the 'bold bawdry' of an adulterous time was a part of the story which he found, he could not away from his facts. 'Do after the good and leave the evil', was Caxton's precept to his readers ; and the idealism of bk. xviii, ch. 25, is an adequate reply to critics. The *Morte Darthur* is the epic of chivalry ; and that means, as we are apt to forget, that it is the picture of manners in an age which is to our own as childhood is to manhood. By a happy chance, it is written in Engl., not in the Norman-French of our common ancestry ; the prose is flexible and modulated, in a rare and excellent degree ; M., like Chaucer (q.v.), had acquired the art of composition and arrangement from Boccaccio chiefly, and handed it on to the Elizabethans and their successors ; and grave lessons of 'old gentleness and old service' and of the burgeoning of love in May are for all time to be drawn from M.'s pages. Sir E. K. Chambers (Engl. Assn., pamphlet no. 51 ; 1922) selects 3 points in illustration of M.'s admirable prose : (1) 'the constant use of vivid words, which have now gone out of the language' ; (2) 'his adventures are hung about, like English sport, with outdoor sights and sounds' ; and (3) 'a trick of dialogue. . . . Brevities of speech are Malory's nearest approach to humour'.

Mander, van, Karel (1548-1606) : Dutch scholar and artist ; Franz Hals was among his pupils at Haarlem. Visited Italy to study painting, and made acquaintance with the works of Ariosto, Castiglione, Sannazzaro (qq.v.). Wr., 1604, *Het Schilder-Boeck* ('the book of Painters'), reprinted, 1618, with a life of M., an account of the art, with lives, of celebrated artists. Wr., too, Biblical plays : *Noah, David*, etc. ; transld. Virgil's *Eclogues* and *Georgics* into Dutch verse, which strove to break with an iambic movement the conventional 8 syllables of the rhetoricians' metre (see s.v. Rederijkers) ; transld. the first 12 bks. of the *Iliad* from a Fr. version of Homer, for, like Petrarch 250 years earlier, M.'s humanism was confined to Latinity ; and wr., 1604, a kind of handbook of classical mythology, as a commentary on Ovid's *Metamorphoses*. (See s.vv.).

Mandeville's Travels (*c.* 1356) : Fr. travel-book in 2 parts, (1) of the Holy Land, and (2) further Asia. The writer makes 2 pretensions, neither of which has withstood modern criticism : (*a*) that he writes from personal observation, whereas he was probably compiling from definite sources which have been traced, as well as, generally, from existing encyclopedic works ; (*b*) that he is sir John Mandeville, of St. Albans, whereas he has been confidently identified with a certain Jean de Bourgogne, sometime physician at the court of the sultan of Egypt. The Engl. transln. is taken mainly from 2 MSS., of which one (Titus C., xvi) was in the Cotton (q.v.) collection. This version is known as *The Voiage and Travaile of sir John Maundeville* ; it was first printed at Westminster, 1499, and Halliwell re-issued it, 1839, from the 1725 edn. It has been rendered into Lat., Germ., Dan., Dutch, and other languages, and Snell (*P.E.L.*, iii, 362), who claims that the bk. in its Engl. form is a

distinctive work in Engl. prose, aptly describes it as 'the culmination of the literature of pilgrimage'.

Mandeville, Bernard (*c.* 1670-1733) : Dutch-Engl. moralist ; born in Holland, but settled in Engld., where, like Erasmus and Conrad (qq.v.), he was bi-lingual. Wr., 1705, a didactic poem, *The Grumbling Hive*, re-issued, 1714, with a long, defensive prose-commentary, and again, 1729, with a supplementary dialogue ; the bk. is commonly known as *The Fable of the Bees, or Private Vices—Publick Benefits*, and was edited under that name, 1925, by F. B. Kaye, 2 vols., Oxford. As the sub-title suggests, the cynicism in M.'s social philosophy was derived from La Rochefoucauld (q.v.), and handed on ideas to Voltaire and Adam Smith (qq.v.). Briefly, the *Fable* and attendant essays attack pleasant shams in ethics and economics, and, while M. deeply offended the idealists, and was controverted by bp. Berkeley (q.v.) and others, he effectively stimulated thought, and anticipated some conclusions of the Utilitarian school in the 19th cent.

Mañer, Salvador José (died 1751) : Span. scholar. Wr., 1729-31, an *Antiteatro critico*, in the hope of denouncing the errors in the *Teatro critico* of Feyjoo (q.v.). His work is nugatory, and is forgotten to-day.

Manetti, Antonio (1423-97) : It. reputed author of prose 'novella', *Il Grasso legnaiuolo* (see s.v. 'Grasso').

Manetti, Giannozza (1396-1459) : It. humanist. Intended for commerce, but devoted himself to humane letters at Florence. Member of Marsigli's academy of S. Spirito. Ranked as Christian as distinct from Pagan humanist. Learned Hebr. from Jew. housemate. ; and wr. *Contra Judæos et Gentes* in polemical theology. His powers of rhetoric earned him odium at the Florentine court of erudite jealousy, and he was taxed into exile, according to the genial policy of Cosimo de Medici, who 'used taxation like a poignard'. M. retired, at first to Rome, where pope Nicholas v (q.v.) made him Lat. secretary and commissioned him to effect new renderings from Hebr. and Gk. of the Old and New Testaments, and afterwards to king Alfonso's court at Naples. There he completed his controversial writings ; wr. life of Nicholas v, and a literary history of Dante, Petrarch, and Boccaccio.

Mangan, James Clarence (1803-49) : Irish poet ; translr. ; a man of unhappy life and intemperate habits, who, 'under favourable circumstances, would have left a great name in literature. As it is, he is likely to be remembered only by a few pieces which well deserve, and which, it may be hoped, will receive more frequently in the future than they have received in the past, a place in the anthologies' (Walker, *Lit. Victorian Era*, 360). Among such pieces are *My Dark Rosaleen*, and *Soul and Country*. Wr. *Anthogia Germanica*, 1845, a valuable contribution to Germ. studies.

Manning, Anne (1807-79) : Engl. hist. writer. Wr. 1849, *The Maiden and Married Life of Mistress Mary Powell*, which appeared orig. in *Sharpe's Magazine*, and has been frequently reissued ; *The Household of sir Thomas More*, told in the form of a diary kept by

More's daughter, Margaret, and other works of delicate charm and imagination.

Manrique, de, -i. Pedro (died 1440): Span. soldier; figures largely in the chronicles of the age of king John ii (q.v.) of Castile ; opposed the royal favourite, de Luna (q.v.), constable of Castile, but was worsted in the conflict ; his hereditaments, of which he had been deprived, were restored to his sons at the intervention of count Haro, the hero of the Seguro (q.v.), or Truce, of Tordesillas. The descendants of this stout old warrior rose to eminence in literary history as well as in affairs of State.

-ii. Gomez (c. 1415-90): Span. poet ; son of above ; largely represented in Castillo's (q.v.) collection. Wr. a long ' Lament (*Planto*) of the Virtues and of the Muse for the marquis of Santillana ', M.'s uncle, and other allegorical and conventional verse of no great merit, though some of it has enjoyed high esteem. G.M. is chiefly to be remembered for his novel experiments in primitive dramatic composition, which have historic as well as literary interest. His ' Representation of the Birth of our Lord ', composed for a convent in which his sister was mother superior, introduced saints Joseph, Gabriel, Michael and Raphael, the Virgin Mary, an angel, and 3 shepherds as interlocutors, and was followed by a Passion-week play ; the 2 forming the earliest specimens of sacred drama in Castile, analogous to the Sacre Rappresentazione (q.v.) in Italy. In secular poetry, too, G.M. adopted the dramatic method in 2 instances.

-iii. Rodrigo (c. 1416-76): Span. commander ; poet ; brother to above ; was instrumental in the overthrow of his father's enemy, de Luna ; and is represented by at least one poem in Castillo's collection.

-iv. Jorge (c. 1440-79): Span. commander; poet ; son of above, and nephew, accordingly, to Gomez M., whom he eclipsed in renown. Of this intrepid and chivalrous fighter, who died in battle, about 50 poems are preserved in the *cancioneros* (q.v.) of the age. The best of these by common consent is that composed in 1476 ' for the death of his father ', and known simply as *Coplas*—(stanzas), of which there are 42 (about 500 verses). It is without reserve a fine and moving composition, which ' has won for its author an immortality, surviving all changes of taste, as assured, apparently, as that of Cervantes ' (Kelly, *Lit. espagn.*, 124). Lope de Vega (q.v.) said that the *Coplas* should be reproduced in letters of gold ; they have been set to music, transld. into Lat. verse, and into Engl. by Longfellow.

Mansfield, Katherine (1889-1923): Engl. novelist; pen-name of Mrs. Middleton Murry, *née* Beauchamp ; wr. *Bliss and other Stories*, 1920, and had earned in her too short life an enduring reputation for insight into character and precision of detail, to a degree in which she is described by prince Mirsky (*Mod. Russ. Lit.*, 89) as ' probably the most faithful and at the same time the most original of Checkhov's (q.v.) disciples '. (Mr. M. Murry wr. a life of Dostoevsky, q.v., 1917).

Mantuan (1448-1516): pen-name of Johannes Battista Spagnolo ; It. poet. Head of a Carmelite priory in Mantua, whence he derived his pen-name. Wr. Lat. poems, including 10 Virgilian eclogues (Virgil, q.v., too, was a Mantuan), 1498, which enjoyed an extraordinary vogue of popularity, esp. in 16th cent., when the Virgil-worshippers in Italy divided his throne with M., and Scaliger (q.v.) even noted that some teachers preferred the Virgilian to the authentic Virgil. The eclogues were used as a reading-book in St. Paul's (see s.v. Colet) and other schools (cf. Shakespeare's *Love's Labour Lost*, iv. 2, 97) ; they were transld. into Engl. by Tuberville (q.v.), 1567, and were put under contribution by Spenser (q.v.) in the *Shepherd's Calendar*, 1579, esp. in the sections on July, Sept., and Oct. The last line of Milton's (q.v.) *Lycidas* is an echo of M.'s ' coge pecus melioraque pascua quaere '. Of the present value of M.'s verse it is difficult to speak, the whole pastoral cult being a matter of the long past ; but Shakespearian scholarship in America provided a new edn. of the *Eclogues* by prof. W. P. Mustard (John P. Hopkins Press), 1911, and M. still enjoys the aftermath of his earlier fame.

Manuzio, Aldo (1449-1515): **Aldus Manutius**: Venetian printer ; founder of the famous Aldine Press, whence he issued *edd. pr.* of 96 works of 27 Gk. authors ; started Hellenic Academy at Venice, and by his own example helped immensely to popularize the cause of learning in Italy.

Manzoni, Alessandro Francesco Tommaso (1785-1873): It. critic, dramatist, poet and novelist, in an ascending scale of excellence and success. ' We cannot refrain ', wr. a reviewer of M.'s tragedy, *The Count of Carmagnola*, 1820, in the *Quarterly Review* of Oct. in that year, ' from making known to our readers the most noble piece of Italian lyric poetry which the present day has produced, and which occurs as a chorus at the end of the second act of his drama ; and we confess our hopes that the author will prefer, in future, gratifying us with splendid odes, rather than offending us by feeble tragedy '. M. did not gratify this testy reviewer. In 1822, he published another tragedy, *Adelchi*, which, however, was likewise remarkable for its magnificent choric odes ; and in 1825-7, he publd. his novel *I promessi sposi* (the betrothed) which Scott and Goethe (qq.v.) agreed in praising, and which raised its author at once to the front rank in European letters. And, thereafter, though he lived to be 88, he wr. no other work of imagination. Moreover, though he founded a small school of dramatists (Niccolini and Pellico, qq.v., may be named), M. had no real successor in Italy either as playwright or novelist. He was unique as he was supreme.

A very exact and careful writer, taking infinite pains in research and revision, M., like Scott himself, went to the history of his country for his subjects. *Carmagnola* is placed in the 15th cent., *Adelchi* in the 8th, and *I promessi sposi* in the 17th. In each, the history is greater than the story : there are feeblenesses, as the *Quarterly* reviewer said at the time, in the plays, and there are *longueurs* in the novel (a feature not entirely unknown in Scott) ; but the songs in the plays, and the sentiment in the novel, and the hist. interest in all 3, place them among the masterpieces of fiction. The plays exhibit the further feature that M. anticipated V. Hugo (q.v.) in rejecting the yoke of the dramatic unities (q.v.). Nurtured on a generous diet of Shakespeare, Goethe, and Schiller, M. boldly broke with the hampering stage-convention of one place and one time for the action of his plays. Late in life, he defended his position in critical writings, which included one on Ital. dialects.

M.'s other works need not detain us. His lyric verse (*Imni Sacri*, 1812), and his ode on Napoleon's death, *The 5th May*, 1821, which Goethe transld. into Germ., possess many characteristics of great verse, and prepare us for the choruses in the plays ; but it was *I promessi sposi* which won M. his honours in his lifetime and his reputation after death, and by which, finally, he survives. He belongs to and virtually founded the Romantic school in Italy, not merely by his technical breach with the classical unities in drama, but by his political opinions and his lyrical genius. M.'s mother, a daughter of C. Beccaria (q.v.) left her husband for the protection of C. Imbonati, to whom, on his death, 1806, M. addressed an elegy of much merit.

Map, Walter (*c.* 1140-1210): Norman-Welsh occasional writer ; archdeacon of Oxford. Wr. Lat. *de nugis Curialium* (' Diversions of Courtiers '), which was part of the sub-title of *Polycraticus* by his friend, John of Salisbury (q.v.), and in which M.'s moral attitude was closer to Chaucer's than to Gower's (see s.vv.) ; he added to it a treatise against marriage which became very popular, and was known to Chaucer (cf. *Wife of Bath's Tale*). M. was credited, till recent scholarship rejected the ascription, with a considerable work on the grail (q.v.) portions of the cycle of Arthur (q.v.) ; and also (similarly discredited) with the composition of goliardic (satirical) verse, giving dramatic reality to the ribald person of bp. Golias (q.v.) as an ecclesiastical type in the Middle Ages of the qualities described as Philistine by M. Arnold (q.v.) in the industrial age.

March, Auzias (*c.* 1397-1459): Span. poet ; ' a great troubadour and a man of very lofty spirit ', in the estimation of his contemporary, Santillana (q.v.). Resided at Valencia, and wr. love-poetry on the model of Petrarch (q.v.), whom he imitated even in the detail of the meeting with the lady of his affections on a Good Friday and in church. M.'s poems enjoyed a great esteem, due to their grave and moral tone of feeling, and were transld. into pure Castilian by Montemayor (q.v.), 1562.

Mareschal, André (17th cent.): Fr. novelist. wr., 1627, *La Chrysolite, ou le Secret des Romans*, which Koorting (*Gesch. d. fr. Romans im 17ten Jahrh.*, ii, 134) does not hesitate to describe as, ' the first French psychological novel, and in form and contents alike one of the completest and most remarkable products of the century ; a product with which, in maturity and depth, we can compare—in contemporary fiction, nothing ; in contemporary poetry, only the masterpieces of Molière '. It is high praise for a writer in the vein of mme. de Lafayette (q.v.) half a century before her appearance ; but, though the Gk. nomenclature and the great length of the work are deterrent, M. certainly succeeded in working

out the effects of experience on character, in the extreme infancy of the problem-novel.

Margaret of Angoulême and Valois (1492-1549) : queen of Navarre ; sister to king Francis i (q.v.) of France ; married, i, 1509, the duke of Alençon (d. 1525), and, ii, 1527, Henri d'Albret, king of Navarre ; mother, through her daughter, Jane, of Bourbon kings to be ; patron of letters ; founder of the univ. of Nimes, and writer of ' novelle '. The court-idea of the Renaissance, which Castiglione (q.v.) typified in his writings and sir Philip Sidney (q.v.) in his life, and the positive foundation of which had been stripped by Machiavelli (q.v.) of every rag of illusion, was exemplified at the minor court of M., who inspired a devotion in her courtiers which anticipated on a small scale the spirit of the Gloriana period of queen Elizabeth in Engld. M. extended protection to many free-thinkers of Reformation or Huguenot tendencies, and once at least had herself to invoke the more powerful ægis of king Francis ; though in gifts of statecraft and diplomacy, in her more limited field for their display, the sister was superior to the brother. Rabelais (q.v.) took shelter with her from the monkish spite and storms which he provoked, and among the more permanent retainers intimately associated with the queen were Despériers, Le Maçon, De la Haye and Clement Marot (qq.v.). M. was an author on her own account, and her *Marguerites de la Marguerite des Princesses* (i.q. daisies of the pearl of princesses) reproduced in its title and contents the artificer's skill of the ' rhétoriqueurs ' (q.v.), with its fanciful and frigid conceits. But the great masterpiece of her court was the collection of tales, the *Heptameron*, originally known as *Stories of Fortunate Lovers*. That it is commonly ascribed solely to M. herself does not mean that no other pen was employed on it. Le Maçon was Boccaccio's translator ; Despériers had already publd. Fr. ' novelle ' ; and Marot's proved pith as a fabulist was always at the call of his mistress. It was a court which loved the lights of Colet and Erasmus better than Luther's austerity or the rigour from which Rabelais fled ; and queen M.'s *Heptameron* was exactly representative of her circle. The prose-tales treat mainly of love, and are related in turn by a group of narrators, brought together by a travellers' mischance. The separate persons are clearly distinguished, and the episodes between the tales, in which they play their own parts, link the participants in the adventure by a kind of novel *per se*. The name *Heptameron* is a misnomer, though unquestionably a happy one. It was invented by a certain Claud Gruget, who republished the stories in 1559, and the editor of course had in mind Boccaccio's *Decameron*. But, apart from the technical objection that ' hepta ' means 7, and that an eighth day's story-telling is started, the likeness of the one-bk. to the other is rather accidental than real. M.'s are true travellers' tales, without the background of the plague at Florence. It is true that the occasion is not joyous. There had been ' such extraordinary rains that it seemed as though God had forgotten the promise He made to Noah '. Lives are lost, and

Solomon, the wisdom-king of the Old Testament. The character appears in variant forms and disguises, chiefly in Fr. and Teutonic redactions of the questions and answers, humorous in an increasing degree, of the riddling king and his companion.

Marlowe, Christopher (1564-93): Engl. dramatist of rarely great achievement; son of a shoemaker at Canterbury. M.'s surname is variously written Marley, Marlyn, Marlo, Morley, etc., and an almost equal amount of variation has been admitted into his biographical records. He was edu. at the King's school in his native city, and at Bene't (now Corpus Christi) Coll., Cambridge, where he proceeded not long after Christmas, 1580, and where he held a scholarship for 6 years, a length of tenure which seems to imply that the holder was intended for holy orders. But after 1586, M. had lost favour at the univ., and was settled in London, where he was associated with persons engaged in secret service work, and earned, partly on the evidence of Kyd, q.v., another pre-Shakespearean playwright, an evil reputation for atheism and loose living. He met his death by violence, 30 May, 1593, at the house, or inn, of Eleanor Bull, a widow, in Deptford Strand. In *The Death of Chr. Marlowe*, by J. Leslie Hotson (Nonesuch Press, 1925), the name of M.'s assailant was for the first time identified as Ingram Friser, who obtained a conditional pardon for slaying him in self-defence. Whether M. fell in a quarrel about the reckoning, as the contemporary story was told, or whether, as the records of the party suggest, Friser, Robert Poley and Nich. Skeres were concerned in getting rid of an inconvenient secret servant, is a question still awaiting further investigation, in connection with sir Thomas Walsingham (1568-1630), patron of poets and 'master' of spies. Reference may be made to an art. by Eugénie de Kalb, in the *Times Lit. Supp.*, 21 May, 1925 (p. 351), but Mr. Hotson's researches are too recent for present decision. An interesting detail is found in the consequent new light on Shakespeare's *As You Like It* (1599), iii, iii, 12 : 'When a man's verses cannot be understood, nor a man's good wit seconded with the forward child, understanding, it strikes a man more dead than a great reckoning in a little room'. This reference is now assumed to be to M., from whose *Hero and Leander* a verse is quoted later in the same play :
Dead shepherd, now I find thy saw of might:
'Who ever loved that loved not at first sight?'
Passing from M.'s troubled life and violent death to his immortal work, and starting at the end with *Hero and Leander* (in heroic couplets ; publd. posth., 1598, with continuation by G. Chapman, q.v.), we note that the story was founded on the Alexandrian poet Musæus, of the 5th cent., whom Marot (q.v.) had been content to follow fairly literally, in transmitting it from the Gk. to the Fr. But M., characteristically, was not content to translate : he added to the simple and natural tale of love a medieval attack on women's frailty and a pagan enthusiasm for masculine beauty. There is a sensuousness, even a sensuality, in M.'s version of the tragic idyl,

which recalls the manner of Ariosto or even of Aretino (see s.vv.) ; 'a pure and graceful theme is changed into a tale *mi-satirique, mi-aphrodisiaque*' (Legouis-Cazamian, *Hist. Lit. Angl.*, 1924 ; p. 309). Not otherwise was M.'s method in his plays. And, first, of his blank verse. He found (in Surrey's *Æneid* and Sackville's *Gorboduc* ; see s.vv.) models of this metre in narrative and dramatic verse ; but where he found a succession of even lines of 10 syllables apiece, each more or less complete in itself—blank verse on promotion from the heroic couplet,—he left a paragraph of music, broken by variations in pause and accent, and freed for ever from the trammels of the false analogy of scansion by weak and strong syllables. Engl. blank verse (q.v.) after M. is scanned by accent, not by quantity, and Shakespeare, Milton and Wordsworth (qq.v.) followed M.'s magnificent lead. The 'Marlowe touch' is as recognizable as the 'Nelson touch', and his 'mighty line' and mighty desire reach up to the triumphs of the greater playwright who succeeded him.

The metre passes into the manner. The passionate declamations of M.'s characters 'co-operated with the victory over the Armada, and the pride of conquests overseas, to inspire his countrymen with a sense of the intoxication and exuberance of force. Like the discoveries of the navigators, they helped to push back the limits of the possible. Marlowe's plays exalted, one by one, the infinite capacity of military power, of science, and of wealth', i.e., in *Tamburlaine, Faustus*, and *The Jew of Malta* (Legouis-Cazamian, *op. cit.*, 401 ; and cf. the present writer's *General Sketch of European Lit.*, 1918, p. 335 : 'Marlowe's ornaments of style arose out of construction, because the inspiration which he drew had been communicated from the gallery to the green-room. The pages of Hakluyt and Ralegh and similar writers in England and Spain leaped with the waves of the sea, and shone with the light on the waves. Men talked like the knights of king Arthur and fought like the Australians at Gallipoli, and the combination made the rich music of English and Spanish drama'.

We must not pause at these 3 great plays ; nor at (the troublesome reign and lamentable death of) *Edward ii*, 1594, which was M.'s contribution to the chronicle-play, developed immediately by Shakespeare ; nor at his *Massacre of Paris* (St. Bartholomew's day, with horrors enough even for M.), nor at his *Dido* (with T. Nash), 1594. We must be content, too, merely to mention here that M. drew his knowledge of Tamerlane from a transln. of the (Span.) life of him by P. Mexia (q.v.), and his wide-flung geography in the play from a Flemish antiquary, Ortelius (1527-98 ; see Ethel Seaton, 'Marlowe's Map', in Engl. Association *Essays and Studies*, vol. x) ; that Mr. Percy Simpson has investigated the 1604 text of *Doctor Faustus* in vol. vi of the same Association's *Essays* ; that a certain David Passi has been conjecturally identified as the prototype of the rich *Jew of Malta*, Act i of which is a finer rehabilitation of the Jew than Shakespeare attempted a few years later in the *Merchant of Venice*.

The special studies of M. by sir E. K. Chambers and other scholars are yielding ever fresh results, increasing knowledge and appreciation. One final remark is due here. M. first brought Machiavellism (see s.v. Machiavelli) into Engl. lit. and onto the Engl. stage. In the prologue to his *Jew of Malta* occur the ominous verses :

Albeit the world thinks Machiavel is dead,

Yet has his soul but flown across the Alps, and, in the words of Ascham (q.v.), the school-master, the new Ital. missionaries were bring-ing,—' for religion, Papistry, or worse ; for learning, less, commonly, than they carried out with them ; for a policy, a factious heart ; for experience, plenty of new mischiefs never known in Engld. before '. *The Prince* had recently been transld., and M. saw dramatic possibilities in the villain as hero (see, if avail-able, *The Villain as Hero in Elizabethan Tragedy*, by C. V. Boyer, Routledge, 1914) of which he was not to be robbed by any censor of national morals. He visualized his Machiavellian hero, and brought him alive upon the stage.

I count religion but a childish toy, he wr. further in the Prologue to the *Jew of Malta* (was this the ' Papistry or *worse* ' of Ascham's bitter indictment ?); and then he announced the central dogma of the Machia-vellian creed, the central motive of the Machiavellian drama—

Might first made kings, and laws were then most sure

When, like the Draco's, they were writ in blood.

A 'mighty line ' Ben Jonson (q.v.) called M.'s; and ' might is right ' was his rule for staged kings. But his dramatic moment was short-lived ; Shakespeare, indebted to M. at so many points, confounded this philosophy at a touch : ' Within the hollow crown ', etc. (*King Richard ii*, III, 2).

Marmontel, Jean François (1723-99): Fr. critic, dramatist, *philosophe* (q.v.) ; ' one of the most eminent professional men of letters of the second class ' (Saintsbury, *Short Hist. Fr. Lit.*, 430), ' universal and mediocre ' (Lanson, *Hist. Lit. Fr.*, 735). Where experts agree so well, it is not necessary to advance much evidence. M. wr. hist. tales, *Bélisaire* and *les Incas*, of excellent moral tendency, which had its influence on R. L. Edgeworth (q.v.) ; light comedy, as in *l'Ami de la Maison*, and became editor of the *Mercure*. At the founda-tion of the Encyclopedia (q.v.), M. was appointed its chief contributor of the minor articles on literary subjects, and collected these in a readable vol., *Eléments de Littérature*, 1787, interesting today as an indication of 18th cent. taste in criticism. (See, too, s.v. La Harpe). M.'s *Mémoires* form, not un-naturally, the most valuable of his bks. for the present day.

Marnix, van, Philip (1538-98): Dutch poet, soldier and statesman ; controversialist ; son and brother of successive seigneurs of Toulouse, and himself seigneur of Mont St. Aldegonde. His mother-tongue was Fr., but his father sent both sons to Geneva, where his tastes and talents were trained. Here M. studied under Beza (q.v.), learned Lat., Gk., and Hebr., and

attended the public discourses of Calvin, who coloured his outlook on all life ; he recognized no truth outside Calvinism. Visited Italy, 1559-60 ; on his return to the Netherlands wr. pamphlets in Dutch and Fr. on the religious events of 1566 ; composed, 1568, the great patriotic song *William of Nassau*, which was instantly adopted by the fighting burghers as ' the palladium of their young liberties ', and as a national anthem of victory, comparable to and even surpassing in moving power the *Marseillaise* (1792) and the *Wacht am Rhein* (1870). Its appeal has endured at all the great moments of Dutch national annals. M. took an active part in the politics and fighting of his own day, was at one time a prisoner of war, and at all times true to his motto—' répos ailleurs '. His chief controversial work in prose was the celebrated *Biënkorf*, or ' Beehive of the Holy Roman Church ', publd., 1569, reprinted 15 times in his lifetime and 18 times since (to 1878), transld. into Engl., 1578, and into Germ., 1579, by Fischart (q.v.), the Rabelais-ian. There are notes of Rabelais and Hutten (qq.v.) and of Rabelais' prototype, Lucian, as well as touches of Erasmus of the *Colloquies*, in this bitter, clever satire, which was greeted with enthusiastic applause by the whole Protestant community of Europe. In our day, its appeal fails ; but we recognize there-fore even more clearly the yeoman service rendered by M. to the backward prose-style of his country.

Marot, -i. Jean (1463-1523): Fr. rhetoriqueur (q.v.). Wr. verses in the aureate and artificial style of that school.

-ii. **Clement** (1497-1544): Fr. poet, son of above. His education in the Crétin (q.v.) tradition served to train his early facility, which he displayed by editing the poems of Villon (q.v.) and the *Romance of the Rose* (q.v.), in the new principles of philology and criticism, recently imported from Italy, and manifest in the *Instructif de la Seconde Rhétorique* and other Fr. works ; wr. *The Temple of Cupid* in that vein of medieval allegory ; became secretary to (c. 1519) and, later, pensioner of queen Margaret (q.v.) of Navarre, whom he doubtless assisted in the *Heptameron* ; enjoyed her protection and that of king Francis i, but was still suspect of the heresy of a love of humane letters, and did not escape the con-sequences of his liberal theology. M.'s free handling of the psalter and other acts of alleged impiety brought him 4 times into conflict with Rome, acting through the subordinates whom Rabelais likewise found so vigilant ; was once in prison, where he wr. poem, *L'Enfer* ; once fled to Ferrara ; once to Geneva, which he found too sombre ; and died in temporary refuge in Piedmont. M., who had admired Crétin excessively, lauding him as ' the sovereign Fr. poet ', and whose own early works were written in the vein of his father's generation, gradually sang himself free, however, from excessive aureation. The vol. of his early verse entitled *Adolescence Clémen-tine*, was in the fanciful style of the *Rhétori-queurs* ; but his critical faculty and classical learning sought simpler modes of expression, and he sought to avoid the hard, stiff rocks of the rhetorical poetasters. He rounded the cape perilous of artifice with a deft, light touch upon the helm ; his metrical versions of the Psalms, his ballads, epigrams, rondeaux, and songs for music have qualities of charm and skill which made M., especially in the later period of reaction from the Pleiad (q.v.), a model to younger Fr. poets whose ambition did not overleap his modest standards. His true successor is La Fontaine (q.v.) ; and if the best Fr. poetry is light verse, M.'s old fame as the father of Fr. poetry is not undeserved. He at once founded a school of ' Marotiques ', which for some time had to meet the factious rivalry of the long forgotten ' Sagontiques ', so-called after a certain François Sagon (q.v.), who upheld the rhetorical tradition. M. likewise claims a large share in the fatherhood of Engl. poetry, through the influence of his style and kinds of poetry on his contemporaries, Wyatt and Surrey (qq.v.). It was partly, even chiefly, by M.'s mastery that Paris became at this date ' the chief mission-station of Renaissance culture ' on its northward road from Italy. (See s.v. Paris).

Marquez, Juan (1564-1621): Span. politico-theologian. Wr., 1612, polemical treatise on *The Christian Governor*.

Marryat, Frederick (1792-1848): Engl. writer of sea-tales ; sailor by profession. Wr. *Frank Mildmay*, 1829, and about 30 other stories, including *Mr. Midshipman Easy*, 1836, which is perhaps the best of a good series. M.'s humour is sometimes a little broad, as is the sea, and there is a hint of monotony about both ; but as a marine novelist on straightforward lines of vigour and vivacity M.'s supremacy is still unchallenged.

Marseillaise, La (Fr.) : national song of France ; the music and words were composed by Rouget-de-l'Isle (q.v.), who called it *Chant de Guerre pour l'Armée du Rhin*, when war was declared between France and Austria at the close of the 18th cent. It ' caught on ' in Marseilles (whence its name), and was sung by the volunteers from that port when they marched on the Tuileries in Paris, 10 Aug, 1792 ; thus deriving its association with the revolution-aries. The song was forbidden by the restored Bourbons, but played its part in the July revolution of 1830 and again in the revolution of 1848. Napoleon iii preferred Laborde's (q.v.) *Partant pour la Syrie*, which has a vogue of its own ; but since 1870 the M. has held undisputed sway in the hearts of gallant Frenchmen and Frenchwomen.

Marston, John (c. 1575-1634): Engl. dramatist ; satirist ; left lit. for the church, 1616. M. exchanged, or bandied, satire with Ben Jonson (q.v.), in reply to whom he wr. (with T. Dekker) *Satiromastix*. Collaborated, after the fashion of the times, with Jonson and other playwrights, in several half-forgotten comedies ; wr. *Sophonisba*, a tragedy, 1606 (see, too, s.v. Mairet) ; *What You Will*, a comedy, 1607 ; and, probably, *The Insatiate Countess*, a tragedy, 1613. Symonds (q.v.), in *Shake-speare's Predecessors*, selects M.'s ' pointed sentences ' as his characteristic.

Marston, -i. John Westland (1819-90): Engl. playwright ; critic. Wr. *Strathmore*, 1849 ; *Marie de Méranie*, 1850 ; *Hard Struggle*, 1858 ; *Donna Diana*, 1863 ; contributor to the

Athenæum (Engl.), q.v. ; notable for his practical support to the vogue of poetic drama.

-ii. Philip Bourke (1850-87) : Engl. poet ; son of above ; blind from the age of 3 years ; friend of Rossetti (q.v.) and Swinburne (q.v.), who indited a sonnet to his memory. P.B.M.'s vols. of poetry included *Song-Tide*, 1871 ; *All in All*, 1875 ; *Wind Voices*, 1873 ; 3 vols. of his more misc. writings were publd. posth.

Marsuppini, Carlo (c. 1399-1453): It. humanist. Born, like Petrarch and Bruni, at Arezzo ; came early to Florence to study Gk. ; intro-duced by Niccoli to Medicean court ; became papal secretary, and succeeded Bruni (1444) as chancellor of the Republic. Distinguished as Latinist, Hellenist, and lecturer ; transld. parts of Homer and Aristophanes. Com-memorated, like Bruni again, by fine monument in S. Croce.

Martial, surnamed d'Auvergne or de Paris (c. 1430-1508): Fr. poet. Wr. *Vigiles de la Mort de Charles vii*, who died in 1461, a long and long-popular memorial epopee, divided into 9 ' psalms ' and 9 ' lessons ', composed in the short and rather breathless metre of quatrains of 5- or 6-syllable lines ; and other verse and prose of an attractive and a graceful simplicity. This Fr. pattern of the short line, with its gay and quick effect, was early transferred by Skelton (q.v.) and other Engl. contemporary poets from its virtual founder in France.

Martin, -i. Theodore (1816-1909): Scot. poet ; biographer ; translr. ; K.C.B., 1880. Collab-orated with Aytoun (q.v.), whose *Life* M. wr., 1867, in the famous *Bon Gaultier Ballads* ; and effected very useful translns. from Horace, Dante, Goethe, Heine, and others. M. was a trusted lit. adviser of queen Victoria, whose travel-notes, etc., he helped to edit, and was entrusted with biographies of the prince consort, 5 vols., 1874-80, and of princess Alice, 1885.

-ii. Helen (1820-98) : Engl. actress ; *née* Faucit ; wife of above. Wr. an attractive study of *Some of Shakespeare's Female Characters*, 1885.

Martineau, -i. Harriet (1802-76) : Engl. economist and philosopher ; wr. bks. on taxation and kindred subjects, which brought her into contact with official circles when she came to London from Manchester about 1834 ; travelled in America, Egypt, etc., and wr. bks. inspired by her travels ; transld. Comte's (q.v.) *Positive Philosophy*, 1853 ; contributed to *Edinburgh Review*, *Daily News*, etc. ; wr. *Deerbrook*, a novel, 1839, and an autobiography, publd. posth.

-ii. James (1805-1900) : Engl. theologian ; brother of above ; unitarian divine in Bristol, Liverpool, etc. ; prof. of philosophy and political economy at Manchester New Coll., 1840-57 (removed to London, 1853) ; principal, 1869-85. Wr. *Seat of Authority in Religion*, and other works, including 2 collections of *Hymns*, and was a busy contributor to *National* and other reviews.

Martinez de Toledo, Alfonso (c. 1398-c. 1470) : Span. satirist ; native of Toledo ; resided at Barcelona ; later, arch-priest of Talavera ; chaplain to king John ii (q.v.) of Castile. Wr. chronicles and lives, but is chiefly known by an early prose-work, 1438, of which 6 or 7

edns. were issued between 1495 and 1547, satirizing the foibles of women. Various titles are given to it. In 1498 it was known as *el Corbacho*, on the analogy apparently of *il Corbaccio* by Boccaccio (q.v.); the precise connotation of this word (the raven), as applied to the common subject of the 2 bks., is obscure; other names were 'Reprobation of worldly love', 'Treatise against women', etc. It is now commonly known as 'The Archpriest of Talavera'. M. had plainly read the anti-women bk. of Eximinez (q.v.) and some of the writings of Ruiz (q.v.), and he produced a powerful and bitter piece of sententious invective, which supplied hints to later writers; among them, the author of *Celestina* (q.v.). As a popularizer of prose, even apart from the vigour of his expression, M. has real significance in literary history.

Marvell, Andrew (1621-78): Engl. poet and satirist; often known as A.M. the younger, out of respect to his father, Andrew Marvell (d., 1642) the elder, master of the Charterhouse and a preacher of repute. M. *fils* was known in his own day as an ardent politician on the republican side; and his friendship with and admiration for Milton, to whom he was able to be of some assistance after the Restoration, and whom he had assisted in his work as Lat. secretary to the Protector, have both political and literary interest. Wr., 1650, *Horatian Ode upon Cromwell's Return from Ireland*; anon. pamphlet, 1677, on *The Growth of Popery and Arbitrary Government in Engld.*; but is chiefly rememberable as a man of letters to-day by 2 or 3 songs and lyrics, preserved in Palgrave's (q.v.) *Golden Treasury* of that name. Thus, Palgrave describes the *Horatian Ode* as 'beyond doubt one of the finest in our language'; M.'s *Thoughts in a Garden* he properly regards 'as a test of any reader's insight into the poetical aspects of Poetry. . . In imaginative intensity Marvell and Shelley are closely related'; and he includes in the same anthology M.'s moving *Song of the Emigrants in Bermuda*.

Mascaron, Jean (1634-1703): Fr. divine; bp. of Agen; court-preacher; one of several preachers of funeral sermons for Turenne, marshal of France, d. 1675.

Masdeu, Juan Francisco (1744-1817): Span. scholar; Jesuit. Wr., 1783-1805, a *Critical History of Spain and of Spanish Culture*, 20 vols., which still has some use and value. M.'s writings displayed a strong tinge of 18th cent. scepticism.

Mason, William (1724-97): Engl. poetaster (*Musœus*, 1747, a monody on the death of Pope; odes, elegies, etc.); biographer and close friend of T. Gray, q.v., whose *Life and Letters* he publd., 1774.

Mass (Theol.): 'On the 3rd of December, 1521, when mass was going to be sung in the parish church (of Wittenberg), several of the students and younger burghers came with knives under their coats, snatched away the mass-books and drove the priests from the altar. . . . The prince called upon the university to pronounce an opinion on the mass in general. A commission was accordingly chosen, of which Melanchthon was a member, and which decided for the entire abolition of the mass,

not only in Wittenberg, but throughout the country, be the consequences what they might' (Ranke, *History of the Reformation*, iii, i). With this decision and its consequences we are not immediately concerned; but interest attaches to the lit. of the Mass, to which these changes, violent and otherwise, in the ritual gave rise. Manuel and Kirchmayer (qq.v.) contributed to this satiric *genre* in Germany, in dialogues on the sickness, death, and testament of the personified Mass; they were imitated by two Englishmen in Germany, Roy and Barlow, in *Rede me and be not wroth*, or *The Burial of the Mass*, 1528, and a later little flood of like satires rose in Engld. about 20 years after, chiefly at the instance of William Turner (died 1568; dean of Wells), more famous as a botanist than as divine.

Massey, Gerald (1828-1907): Engl. poet; of humble orig.; patronized (in the old, honourable sense) by F. D. Maurice and C. Kingsley (qq.v.). Wr. poems collected, 1889, in a vol., *My Lyrical Life*.

Massillon, Jean Baptiste (1663-1742): Fr. divine; prof. of rhetoric; of philosophy (at Vienna); was summoned to Paris as preacher, c. 1696; bp. of Clermont, 1717; elected to Academy (q.v.), 1719. M. preached the Lenten sermons (*Petit Carême*) before king Louis xiv, 1701 and 1704, and before Louis xv, 1718, and the funeral sermons for the dauphin of France, 1711, and for Louis xiv, 1715. As court-preacher, he was a great success, though it is to be noted that Louis xiv did not invite him again after 1704 (that M. preached at his funeral cannot be counted as the king's own invitation), and said that, while other preachers made him contented with them, M. made him discontented with himself. M. was unquestionably a fine orator, of the school of Bossuet and Bourdaloue (qq.v.), and he enjoyed an exaggerated fame in the era of Voltaire (q.v.), into which he survived, owing to his preference of persuasion to dogma; he was known as the Racine of the pulpit.

Massinger, Philip (1583-1640): Engl. dramatist; *A New Way to Pay Old Debts*, 1632, is probably his best-known play. Like other Elizabethan playwrights in those days of busy production, he wr. freely in collaboration with others, including Fletcher (q.v.), in *Two Noble Kinsmen*, 1634, and *Henry viii*, 1613, in connection with both of which Shakespeare (q.v.), too, is mentioned as part-author.

Masson, David (1822-1907): Scot. scholar; edtd. *Macmillan's Magazine*, 1858; prof. of Engl. lit., Univ. coll., London, 1852; Edinburgh univ., 1865. Wr., among other important contributions to Engl. studies, *Life of Milton*, 6 vols., 1859-80, a comprehensive history of the man and his times.

Masuccio of Salerno (1420-c. 1476): It. novelle-writer. Tommaso dei Guardati, commonly called after his estate at Salerno, resided at the court of Naples, where he acquired local colour for his tales. Wr., 1476, *Novellino*, a collection of 50 tales, in the vein of Boccaccio (q.v.), with traces of Juvenal's satiric purpose. Each *novella* has a dedication and an epilogue; and the bk. is marked by a vigorous, even Rabelaisian, hate of licentious and dissolute clergy, and by a keen power in depicting the follies and humours of high and low life.

Matarazzo or **Maturanzio, Francesco** (15th cent.) : It. prose historian. Wr. *Annals of Perugia*.

Mathias, Thomas James (?1754-1835) : Engl. satirist ; Ital. scholar ; librarian at Buckingham palace ; edited, 1814, the works of T. Gray (q.v.), an undertaking on which he lost heavily ; lived in Italy from that date, and contributed to the ' comfort and amusement ' of sir W. Scott (q.v.) in Naples, 1832. Wr. *Pursuits of Lit.*, 1794-7 in 4 satiric dialogues in verse, which ' may be taken as a faithful mirror of the dominant literary taste of English society during the war with revolutionary France ' (Courthope, *Hist. Engl. Poetry*, vi, 128). Something was due to Pope (q.v.) in his *Seventeen Hundred and Thirty-eight*, and the point of view was that of Burke (q.v.) ; but M. was an orig. satirist, and was justly praised by Canning (q.v.) in the *Anti-Jacobin*, which was founded to represent the same position. Wr., too, *Runic Odes imitated from the Norse Tongue in the Manner of Mr. Gray*, 1781, and translns. from and into Ital.

Matos Fragoso, de, Juan (1608-88) : Port. dramatist, resident in Madrid ; publd. 1 vol. of dramas, much indebted to the labours of his forerunners, esp. of Vega (q.v.) ; whose ' Peasant in his Inglenook ' (*Villana en su Rincon*) became M.'s ' Wise Man in Retirement and Peasant at his own Fireside ', and whose ' Prince's Downfall ' (*el Principe despeñado*) became M.'s ' Revenge and Downfall of the Tyrant of Navarre ', and passed through his play into the *Punizione nel precipizio* of Gozzi (q.v.).

Matthias Corvinus (1443-90) : king of Hungary from 1458 ; son of crusader, John Hunyady ; illustrated by his real example the qualities of Machiavelli's ideal prince ; patron of learning ; collected MSS.; founded univ. and Corvina Library at Buda. During Turkish occupation of Buda in 16th cent., the collection was partly burned and partly scattered, Vienna acquiring the most for its Imperial Library, founded (1440) by emperor Frederick iii (1415-1493).

Matthisson, Friedrich von (1761-1831) : Germ. poet ; wr. nature-poetry of the sentimental-descriptive kind, which won considerable respect in his own day, even from a judge as scrupulous as Schiller (q.v.).

Maturin, Charles Robert (1782-1824) : Irish playwright ; novelist ; of Huguenot descent. M.'s novels were written in the ' terror ' school, cultivated by M. G. Lewis (q.v.), and included *The Fatal Revenge*, 1807 ; *The Milesian Chief*, 1812, which sir W. Scott (q.v.) is said to have imitated in *The Bride of Lammermoor* a few years later ; and, chiefly, *Melmoth, the Wanderer*, 1820 ; his plays included *Bertram*, a tragedy in verse, produced at Drury Lane, 1816, at the recommendation of Byron (q.v.). M.'s direct influence was felt in France, in the dawn of the new *Lyrisme* (q.v.), more directly than at home.

Matz, Bertram Waldrom (1865-1925) : Engl. critic, associated particularly and very honourably with the cult of Dickens (q.v.). ' No one, living or dead ', wr. sir Hall Caine in *The Sunday Times*, 19 July, 1925, ' can have done so much to promote the popular appreciation of Charles Dickens. For 33 years, to my personal knowledge, this was his chief aim in life '. M. lived to see the opening of the Dickens Museum in the house in Doughty Street, W.C., where the great novelist spent the early years of his married life ; he founded the Dickens Fellowship, edited the National edn. of his works, and the Memorial edn. of Forster's (q.v.) *Life* of him, and wr. various bks. for the extension of his fame and influence.

Maucroix, de, François (1619-1708) : Fr. poet ; a member of the Precious (q.v.) set ; friend of La Fontaine (q.v.) ; transld. certain dialogues of Plato ; epicurean, or ' libertin ' (q.v.).

Maupassant, de, Guy (1850-93) : Fr. novelist ; disciple and godson of Flaubert (q.v.). Saintsbury, (*P.E.L.*, xii, 95) cleverly calls him ' the Marcellus of Naturalism,' in reference to the Virgilian Messianic prophecy, ' tu Marcellus eris ' ; but it may be questioned if M. completely fulfilled his destiny. His *Une Vie*, 1883, and *Bel Ami*, 1885, have established a reputation of skilled workmanship in the school of his master ; *Pierre et Jean*, 1888, stands on a different, even a higher, level ; but it is not easy now to say if the morbid tendency in M.'s writings was a sign of the mental decay which killed him or a genuine gift of the artistic temperament.

Maurice, Frederick Denison (1805-72) : Engl. divine ; founded the Apostles' Club with John Sterling (1806-44, whose *Life* was written by Carlyle, q.v., 1851), and had taken a leading part in the theological controversies of his day, when he was asked to resign his chair of Engl. Lit. at King's Coll., London, 1853, after the publication of *Theological Essays*. M. helped to found Queen's Coll., London, 1848, and the Working Men's Coll., 1854, of which he was chosen principal ; prof. of Casuistry and Modern Philosophy at Cambridge, 1866 ; Cambridge preacher at Whitehall, 1871. M., who had once acted for a brief time as editor of the organ of the Christian Socialists, exercised a profound and wholesome influence on the liberal thought of the period, and is, perhaps, better known by the inspiration of his noble life than by his written works : among these is a stately and academic history of *Moral and Metaphysical Philosophy*, 2 vols., 1862.

Maury, Jean Siffrein (1746-1817) : Fr. orator ; member of the French Academy (q.v.), and laureate to that body. Emigrated during the revolutionary turmoil ; returned to Paris, 1804 ; archbp. of Paris under Napoleon i.

Maxim (16th cent.) : Gk. scholar in Russia ; reached Moscow from mount Athos, 1518, after a sojourn in Florence, |where his acquaintance included Aldo Manuzio, Savonarola and Pico della Mirandola (qq.v.). It was a tragic change from the Florentine circle of eager humanists to the chilling atmosphere of obscurantism in Russia ; and very truly might M. have exclaimed, with the Gk. tutor of Reuchlin (q.v.), ' lo ! by my exile hath Greece flown across the Alps '. In Moscow, M. helped to found schools, to introduce the art of printing, and to surround himself with the curious scholars, few in number, who had the courage to wish to learn. Unfortunately, he was before his time and persecution swiftly overtook him. ' We kiss your chains, as if they were a saint's ', said the head of the Moscow church to him, ' but we are powerless to help you ' ; and M.'s cruel term of 30 years' imprisonment made him the first martyr of learning in Russia. Still, his influence was considerable, esp. in the direction of the textual criticism of Holy Writ.

Maximilian i (1459-1519): king of the Romans (1486) ; Roman emperor (-elect, 1493, on the death of his father, Frederic iii. His coronation at Rome never took place ; the ceremony fell into desuetude after his reign, and the formal title ' elect ' lost its meaning) ; m., 1477, Mary of Burgundy, daughter of Charles the Bold ; a leader of Germ. Renaissance. It is with this last capacity, and not with M.'s life and influence as ruler, warrior, and statesman, that we are directly concerned. He was an illustrious patron of music and other arts, esp. the art of wood-engraving as practised by Dürer (1471-1528), and in the allied art of lit. he was practitioner as well as patron. Wr. *Teuerdank*, in halting verse, assisted by admirable wood-cuts, disguising under the chivalric adventures of a knight of that name M.'s own wooing of Mary of Burgundy ; projected various other works, some of which have been edited posth. in sumptuous forms. Apart from these literary ambitions, the Germ. Renaissance owed M. a considerable debt for his consistent encouragement of humanistic learning, and for his educational zeal, displayed at the univs. of Freiburg and Vienna, where direction was given to his wishes by Celtes (q.v.), among others. M. is known as ' the last knight of chivalry ' in an age when his subjects were rapidly disusing its virtues.

Mayans y Siscar, Gregorio (1699-1781): Span. scholar. Wr. a life of Cervantes, 1737, and was a busy editor of the writings of other famous men of Spain. Wr., too, a *Rhetorica*, 1757, too long to be useful then or readable to-day, and even more academic than the *Poetica* of Luzan (q.v.). M. was an industrious critic, more notable for his intentions than his achievements.

Maynard, de, François (1582-1646): Fr. poet ; disciple of Malherbe (q.v.). M. hastened the decline of lyric verse, so conspicuous between Ronsard and La Fontaine (qq.v.), by his rigid compartmental method of closing the sense at the end of each stanza or strophe ; and, eloquent as many of his verses are, the effect is epigrammatic rather than lyrical ; by the same sign, he was not sufficiently a devotee to the cult of conceits (q.v.) to recommend himself to the precious (q.v.) stylists. Thus, his fame has fallen between 2 stools, though his poetry deserves to be mentioned with that of Malherbe and Racan (s.vv.).

Mazarinades (1648-50): Fr. series of political pamphlets, squibs, pasquinades, and satires, directed by members of the Fronde (the revolting *parlement* and press) and their supporters against card. Mazarin (1602-1661), Richelieu's pupil and successor as chief minister to king Louis xiii, and to the regent Anne during Louis xiv's minority. The anti-Mazarin lit. was a busy industry for about 2 years, and then died down rapidly.

Megerle, Ulrich. See **Santa Clara.**

Medici, de (It.): eminent Ghibelline (q.v.) family of merchant-bankers in Florence (q.v.), who,

by financial and commercial operations, by matrimonial alliances, honourable dealing, and political sagacity, rose to the highest offices of state, and founded ruling dynasties. The successive heads of the family during the period of its chief prosperity were **i, Giovanni** (1360-1428), who left a huge fortune to his sons, and excellent maxims and example as to moderation in seeking and displaying power. His son **ii, Cosimo** (1389-1464) was appointed *gonfalionere*, head of the governing body of the Florentine republic, and consolidated his position. He received and munificently entertained guests at the Council of Florence, 1439 ; was a devoted student of Plato (q.v.) ; founded the famous Platonic Academy, with Ficino (q.v.) as its leader ; invited eastern scholars and copyists to his court, and inaugurated the future Medicean Library (see s.v. Libraries) ; entitled *pater patriæ* by public decree, 1464. Succeeded by his son **iii, Piero** who died 1469, and was overshadowed even in his brief reign as head of government by his son **iv, Lorenzo** (1448-1492), surnamed The Magnificent. Lorenzo's place in lit. and art is determined, not so much by his original work, which in bulk and quality was not great, as by the impulse which he gave and the patronage which he extended to writers and artists like-minded with himself. During his period of rule, he made Florence the centre of Renaissance art and letters. Ital. lit. (q.v.), as it was re-formed out of the broken dreams of Petrarch, owed its new birth to Lorenzo, and was conceived at his brilliant court. How illustrious a court it was which gathered at banquets of the Platonic Academy and at less formal symposia, how splendid in pageantry, how tireless in scholarship, how richly dowered in taste and enthusiasm, must be sought in Lorenzo's biography by Roscoe (q.v.) and elsewhere. A few names may just be set down : Michelangelo was there, and Ficino, and, later, Pico della Mirandola ; Fifelfo, Valla, Politian, Pulci, Sannazzaro, and many others ; including a numerous train of librarians, secretaries, and teachers from the east. The urgent task which Lorenzo set himself in lit. was to recall Tuscan speech to literary use. Adequate material had to be found for the display in the vernacular of the graces recovered by the Humanists. To graft classic style on popular stock, and so to re-create a national lit., modifying and justifying at the same time the direction given by Petrarch to the culture of his countrymen, was the problem which presented itself in a uniquely definite shape to the Florentine sons of Latinized Italy. They had obeyed the Virgilian precept, *antiquam exquirere matrem*, and the exquisite heritage of forms had now to be endued upon new bodies. Lorenzo's Carnival songs, his Petrarchan sonnets, and his other decorative or amatory verse, always sensuous and objective, were a by-product of his full career ; but the lit. which he fostered and encouraged may be accounted to him almost equally with his own. His death occurred in the period of the growing ascendancy of Savonarola (q.v.), which was not resisted by his son **v, Piero ii** (1471-1503), who was expelled from Florence, 1495, and died in exile. Few members of Lorenzo's circle survived the ferment of these changes and counter-changes ; Boiardo, Politian and Mirandola all died in the year—1494—of the invasion of Italy by Charles viii of France ; Mirandola, indeed, on the very day (17 Nov.) of his un-opposed entry into Florence. Another son of Lorenzo, **Giovanni** (1475-1521) became pope Leo x (q.v.), and was cousin to pope Clement vii, another grandson of Piero i. Later, in 1512, the M. dynasty was restored at Florence in the person of Piero ii's son **vi, Lorenzo ii** (1492-1519), known as duke of Urbino, 1516, the disappointing repository of the hopes of Machiavelli (q.v.), who had dedicated to him *Il Principe*. His natural son **vii, Alessandro,** who is variously stated to have been the son of pope Clement vii, m. a natural daughter of emperor Charles v, and was created duke of Florence, 1532, thus closing the republican era and the untitled primacy of his family. Lorenzo ii's only daughter, **Catherine,** was m., 1533, to Henry, son of Francis i of France, and is notorious in Fr. history for her share in the Massacre of St. Bartholomew. Descendants of another **Lorenzo,** second son of Giovanni i, likewise came to eminence in genealogy, but the great days of the M. dynasty were over before the blood of the fine old merchant-prince of Florence was lost in that of the royal families of Europe.

Meilhac, Henry (1832-97) : Fr. comic librettist ; a leading *boulevardier* (q.v.) of the Second Empire ; collaborator with Halévy (q.v.), and one of the trio (completed by Offenbach), who kept Paris amused in the years before Sedan. Among the joint musical comedies may be mentioned *la Grande Duchesse de Gerolstein*, 1867, of the year of the Universal Exhibition, and the topical *Vie Parisienne*, 1866.

Meissner, Alfred (1822-85) : Austrian poet and novelist ; a native of Bohemia, and a champion of the national cause of the Czechs, in which he was assisted by his fellow-countryman, Moritz Hartmann, a Jew (1821-72), for many years editor of the Vienna *Neue Freie Presse*, which he made a power in Euorpe. Meissner wr. Byronic *Gedichte*, 1845, an epic *Ziska*, 1846, and a succession of undistinguished novels.

Meissner, August Gottlieb (1753-1807) : Germ. miscellanist. Wr. sketches (14 vols.), dealing with history, romance, art, etc., in the light vein of Wieland (q.v.), and novels (*Alcibiades*, 1781-88, and others) of no particular merit.

Meistersinger : Germ. schools of poetry (' Meister-gesang '), founded by master-workmen, or members of trade-guilds, at first chiefly in the towns of the south and midlands. The movement rose at the time of the decline of the Minnesinger (q.v.), when the social centre shifted from the courts to the cities, and the *bourgeoisie* became the repositories of the poetic craft in place of knightly dependants on princes' favours. The earliest of these schools of master-song is said to have been established at Mayence by one Heinrich von Meissen, who died in 1318, and who was definitely ' addictus jurare in verba magistri ', or, at least, to cultivate the art of a master-Minnesinger. Later, the ' master ' title was

merged in the trade-qualification, and lost its older and nobler meaning. The Meistersinger were master-singers in the sense that, as master-smiths, -tailors, or -weavers, they took part in the direction of a school of singers. The vogue spread rapidly, and reached its summit of popularity in the 16th cent. ; the Mayence guild was not dissolved till 400 years after its foundation, and some schools were still flourishing in the 19th cent. Shortly before and for some time after the Reformation, sacred subjects were commonly selected by the fratern-ities, though they were often treated in very homely fashion (see s.v. Sachs). There were 5 classes of membership, graded according to proficiency : the apprentices, who had to study the rules, known as the ' Tablatur ' ; the initiate, who had mastered this scheme of composition and metre ; the singers, who could sustain a part ; the composers, who could set new words to existing tunes ; and, at the top, the masters, who invented new songs to new melodies, The committee was elected from the masters, and appointed its body of officers, including a marker (critic), assisted by four assessors, whose business it was to guard the rigours of the ' Tablatur ' ; ornamental prizes—chains, medals, wreaths—were awarded by their judgment. Practice was held after work-time in beer-gardens, etc., and on Sunday afternoons the town-hall and the churches were the scene of master-song displays. It is obvious that the movement provided opportunities not merely for healthy recreation and for the cultivation of the musical talent which is of native growth on Germ. soil, but also for the development of the club-spirit and of mutual help among the members, and between the singers of different towns.

Melanchthon (1497-1560) : grecized *nom-de-guerre* of Philip Schwartzerd (black earth= melan-chthon) : Germ. humanist and reformer. The name was invented by Reuchlin (q.v.), whose grand-nephew M. was, and by whom, as by Erasmus (q.v.), M.'s brilliant gifts were early recognized and pushed. He was appoin-ted, 1518, prof. of Gk. at Wittenberg univ., where he influenced Luther (q.v.), his senior, in the direction of humane studies, and became in turn an ardent advocate and a brilliant supporter of Lutheran reform. Wr. treatises on Renaissance education, and philological works which became standard schoolbooks in Germany. M. was a student and lover of folk-song and story, and among the legends which he revived was that of ' Eve's Dissimilar Children ', afterwards dramatized by Sachs (q.v.).

Melendez Valdés, Juan (1754-1817) : Span. poet ; founder of the so-called school of Salamanca (q.v.), which was a kind of reconciler of, and intermediary between, the extreme groups of foreign and native (or, Francophil and old Castilian) writers, who divided Span. taste in the mid-18th cent. M. owed his training to Cadalso (q.v.), and acknowledged the noble influence of Jovellanos (q.v.), who was his senior by 10 years. *Obra suy tuya*, ' I am thy work ', he wr. to Jovellanos ; and the statement was figuratively true in regard to M.'s official and literary career. With the vicissitudes of the former in the age of the Bourbon and Bonaparte kings of Spain we are not here concerned, save to note that the times were too exacting for M.'s somewhat modest and frugal muse. His was a linnet's, not an eagle's, note ; and his *Poesias*, 1785, were better in intention than in execution.

Meli, Giovanni (1740-1815) : It. (Sicilian) poet ; cut off by his dialect from the mainland of Ital. lit., but entitled to his place on it as fully as the Sicilians of the 13th cent., who went to the making of Dante (q.v.). Wr. lyric verse and idylls, in conformity with the island tradition, which exhibited a love of natural beauty and a sense of scenic values, in advance of the romantic revival ; his sketches, too, of native life in Sicily are lively and convincing.

Mello, de, Francisco Manoel (1608-*c.* 1666): Port. historian ; the innocent victim of a series of heroic misadventures, which render more extraordinary the high level of his many bks. He was ship-wrecked in 1627 in a storm disastrous to the Port. navy ; he was rival in a love-affair with king John iv of Portugal ; was imprisoned on a charge of murder subsequently proved false, 1644 (till a date unknown ; probably, 1653), and was exiled in Brazil, 1659. All the time, he was a voluminous writer, both in Span. and Port., and 'is, in both languages, admitted to the honours of a classic writer' (Ticknor, iii, 194 ; cf. Kelly, *Lit. espagn.*, 374). M.'s chief work was the 'History . . . of the War of Catalonia', Lisbon, 1645, written partly in prison, and first publd. under a pseudonym.

Melville, Andrew (1545-1622): Scot. scholar ; studied and taught in Paris and Geneva, 1564-73, where he met the leading humanists of the day. On his return to Scotland, conferred immense benefits on the Presbyterian church and on the univs. of Aberdeen and St. Andrews ; rector of the latter, 1590, after visits to Oxford and Cambridge. Confined in the Tower of London, 1607-11, for his advanced opinions, and was the author of many works in theological controversy. Wr. Lat. poems of a high order of excellence. M.'s nephew, James M. (1556-1614) was prof. of Hebr. and Oriental languages under his uncle at St. Andrews ; wr. poems, and kept a *Diary*, which was first publd., 1829.

Melville, James (1535-1617): Scot. historian ; page to Mary, queen of Scots ; knt. Wr. *Autobiography*, valuable for the history of his times, lost till 1660 ; publd., 1663, and again, 1827.

Mena, de, Juan (1411-56): Span. poet ; born at Cordova, travelled in Italy, and became Lat. secretary to king John ii (q.v.) of Castile, where he formed a friendship with the powerful marquis de Santillana (q.v.), and rose to great eminence as a court-poet. M. dedicated to the king his long allegorical poem, *The Labyrinth of Fortune* (*c.* 1444), originally called *The Three Hundred*, from the number of its stanzas (now 297). It is reminiscent of Dante and the *Romance of the Rose*, and, despite its tediousness and excessive display of erudition, it is full of sonorous and effective verses. Another poem, *The Coronation*, is an imaginary journey to Parnassus, where Santillana is crowned by the Muses and Virtues. M.

enjoyed a great reputation, and exercised considerable influence, and 'would have accomplished much more if he had attempted much less' (Kelly, *Lit. espagn.*, 99 ; who adds that M. was 'the head of a school of poetry, the indisputable master of the verse of *arte mayor*', q.v.) ; and it is further to be remarked that M.'s writings considerably strengthened the resources of the Castilian tongue, however pedantic was his own use of it in places. See, too, s.v. *Cronica*, where the view of M.'s authorship of the 'Chronicle of the Reign of John ii' is shown to be disproved ; and see s.vv. *Celestina* and Rojas, where his participation in the authorship of *Calisto and Melibea* is shown to be likewise completely discredited.

Ménage, de, Gilles (1613-92): Fr. scholar. Wr. *Menagiana*, in 4 vols., Lat. literary miscellanies and anecdotes ; *Poemata*, pleasantly reminiscent of Ovid and Tibullus ; a Lat. history of women philosophers, and other works. M., who was a member of the Academy (q.v.), and a member of the Precious (q.v.) circle at the Hôtel de Rambouillet (q.v.), survives by his critical *obiter dicta* rather than by his more serious works, and is immortalized as 'Vadius' in the *Femmes Savantes* of Molière (q.v.) and as the 'Pedant' in the *Caractères* of La Bruyère (q.v.).

Menard, Louis (1822-1901): Fr. poet ; Parnassian (s.v. Parnasse). Wr. *Rêveries d'un païen mystique*, 1870 ; a title which exactly expresses the genius of this poet and of his sympathizers, midway between the passion of the romanticists and the objective realism of later writers. M.'s inspiration was too complex to find full satisfaction in any medium of merely human art.

Mendelssohn, Moses (1729-86): Germ. critic and philosopher. Born of humble Jew. parents at Breslau ; trudged as peddler to Berlin, where he worked his way through social and racial disadvantages to the literary circle of Abbt, Nicolai, and Lessing (qq.v.). The acquaintance with Lessing 'soon ripened into an intimate and life-long friendship, which gave to Mendelssohn, the Jew, wider knowledge and illimitable hopes of the outer, inhospitable world—which gave to Lessing, the Christian, new belief in long-denied virtues ; and which, best of all, gave to humanity those "divine lessons of *Nathan der Weise*", as Goethe calls them, for which character Mendelssohn sat, all unconsciously, as model, and scarcely idealized model' (lady Magnus, *Jew. Portraits*, Memorial edn., 1925, p. 114). M.'s writings included a dialogue on immortality under the Platonic title of *Phaedon*; a vol. of letters on *Sensibility* ; Hebraic works ; a joint-treatise with Lessing on *Pope a Metaphysician !* ; and contributions to the triumvirate's *Letters on Lit.*, 1759-65, later (1765-1806) continued under the style of the *Allgemeine deutsche Bibliothek*. Many of M.'s most valuable writings were identified only after his death. He was an illuminating commentator on Shakespeare, and brilliantly expanded the critical work of Baumgarten (q.v.) in his labours to found the principles of a national literary taste. M.'s significance to the history of æsthetic theory has been generously recognized by recent Germ. writers. Lessing, Schiller and Kant brought his work to completion, the first by his treatise, *Laocoon* (q.v.), the second by his treatment of the naive and of the sublime, and the third by his critique of judgment. 'But Mendelssohn it is who laid the foundation for all this' (Braitmaier, *Poetische Theorie und Kritik*, ii, 279; Saintsbury, *Hist. Crit.*, iii, 33, regards Braitmaier's estimate as a little too favourable to M.). M.'s daughter, Dorothea, became the wife of F. Schlegel (q.v.), and a leader of Romanticism in Germany.

Mendoza, de, Diego Hurtado (1503-75): Span. statesman, scholar, poet, historian; great-grandson of the marquis of Santillana (q.v.); fifth son of the governor of Granada, where he was edu. M. was intended for the church, but chose diplomacy and arms; he fought at Tunis with Garcilasso (q.v.); was ambassador extraordinary to Engld. on a royal marriage project, 1537, and ambassador to Venice during the next 10 years; he represented emperor Charles v at the Council of Trent, and remained at Rome till 1554, when the accession of king Philip ii put a stop to his public career. M.'s motto was *étudions*, and his devotion to learning and humanism found a profitable field at Venice, where he worked in intimate association with Manuzio, Bessarion (qq.v.), and others, and was a diligent collector of MSS., the most highly prized (and highly priced) *objets de vertu* of the age. Wr. poetry, at first in the older Castilian measures of chivalric court-verse, and, later, experimentally, as a convert to the Italianate reforms of Boscan and Garcilasso (q.v.), to the former of whom he addressed an epistle in *terza-rima* (Dante's metre). The truth seems to be that his native taste responded more spontaneously to the old models, while his Renaissance training in Italy made him a ready disciple of the new school; and his practice in that school became an example and a model to future poets. Late in life, 1568, a breach of decorum in the royal palace at Madrid earned M. a sentence of exile to Granada from the punctilious monarch, Philip ii; and he spent his last few years in arranging his library and family papers, especially in relation to his father's Moorish campaigns and subsequent governorship of Granada; and in composing his *Guerra de Granada*, or history of the Moors' rebellion, 1569-70, against the oppression of Philip ii, which was publd. at Lisbon in 1627. Ticknor (i, 480) points out that M.'s conspicuous fairness to 'the hated enemies of his faith and people' was so scrupulously just, that his work could not be issued till the Moors had been expelled from Spain; and Kelly writes (*Lit. espagn.*, 268): 'he had the qualities of a great historian; knowledge, impartiality, narrative faculty, insight, and dramatic eloquence'. M. took Sallust as his lit. model, and at least one famous passage (in bk. iv) is closely imitated from Tacitus (*Ann.*, i, 61-2); but the greatness, almost the majesty, of M.'s *Guerra de Granada* lies in the fact, that he successfully combined a narrative of events within his own cognizance and observation with an hist. style based with pure objectivism on the most

stately masters of Lat. antiquity. It was really a unique achievement, by a poet-statesman descended from a line of soldier-administrators and trained at the courts of Ital. Renaissance princes. It should be added that the attribution of *Lazarillo de Tormes* to M., which was doubtfully accepted by Ticknor, is now universally abandoned. (See s.v. Lazarillo).

Mendoza, de, Iñigo (15th cent.): Span. poet; Franciscan friar; patronized by queen Isabella of Castile, and attached to the circle of Gomez de Manrique (q.v.). Wr. a 'Life of Christ' in stanzas (*por coplas*), 1482, which transferred to the sphere of devotional verse the note of popular romance displayed in the secular ballads (s.v. *romancero*) of the age.

Menéndez y Pelayo, Marcelino (1856-1912): Span. scholar; of recent date, but assured of permanent reputation. European scholars are indebted to M. for his *Calderon and his Theatre*, 1881; his *History of Æsthetic Ideas in Spain*, 1883-91; his brilliantly edited anthologies of Span. and Span.-American poetry; and his classic edn., 1890-1902, of the works of Lope de Vega (q.v.). M. did not complete all that he began; in this respect, he fell short of the achievement of G. Saintsbury, his contemporary and congener in this country; but in purity of taste and expression, in sympathy and insight and learning, M. founded a standard of excellence which has proved and is proving a source of inspiration at home and abroad. Foremost among his immediate pupils has been Ramon Menéndez Pidal (born, 1869).

Menzel, Wolfgang (1798-1873): Germ. critic; literary editor (1826-48) of the *Morgenblatt*, wherein he attacked the reformers in politics and letters, including Goethe. Wr., in several vols., a *History of Germ. Lit.* which has passed through many edns. M. is spoken of as 'the intellectual father of modern (i.e. 19th cent.) German anti-Semitism'.

Menzini, Benedetto (1646-1704): It. satiric poet; disciple of Chiabrera, friend of Redi, and protegé of queen Christina (see s.vv.). M.'s Odes, *Ars poetica*, and satires enjoyed esteem in their day, but did not rise above a respectable mediocrity.

Mercier, Louis Sébastien (1740-1814): Fr. dramatist and romantic critic. Wr. plays according to the canon of Diderot (q.v.), domestic dramas, that is to say, of which we may mention as typical his *Jenneval*, 1768, founded, like many others, on Lillo's (q.v.) *George Barnewell*. Wr., too, *Essai sur l'art dramatique*, 1773, and a later treatise on (mainly dramatic) lit., *de la Littérature et les littérateurs*, 1778, which imagined 'the prose of Rousseau on the French stage', and which more generally anticipated many features of the romantic revival of the following generation (see s.v. Romance). M.'s Shakespearean adaptations are in the same line of reform; and the 50 years from 1778 to 1828 constitute the period of the triumph of romance over classicism on the Fr. stage. At the beginning of that period is M.'s treatise on dramatic lit.; at the end, is Hugo's (q.v.) pref. to his *Cromwell*; the one 'marks the first stage of the assault upon classical Tragedy, as the other is the blare of trumpets which heralded its triumphant conclusion '. (C. Vaughan, Warton lecture, British Academy, 1913; Vaughan distinguishes 3 heads in M.'s indictment of the classical Fr. drama: its monotony, its mechanical character, and its sacrifice of everything to elegance of style).

Meredith, George (1828-1909): Engl. novelist; poet; born at Portsmouth, son of a naval tailor in the High Street, and grandson of Melchisedec M., whom M. immortalized in *Evan Harrington*; edu., 1842-4, at the Moravian School in Neuwied, and was absorbed in journalistic and literary pursuits almost immediately after his return to Engld.; m., 1849, a widowed daughter, (Mary Ellen Nicholls) of T. L. Peacock (q.v.), to whom he dedicated his *Poems*, 1851, which included the first version of *Love in the Valley*. The marriage lasted till 1858, when a separation was agreed upon; Mrs. M. died, 1861; 3 years later, after occasional residence with Rossetti and Swinburne (qq.v.) in Chelsea, M. m. Marie Vulliamy, who died 1885. He lived, 1865 till his death, at Flint Cottage, Box Hill, Dorking, and received, among other honours, the O.M., 1905. M. was reader to Messrs. Chapman and Hall, publishers, 1860-95, and acted as editor, 1867, of their *Fortnightly Review*.

Passing over the early contributions to *Chambers' Journal*, *Once a Week*, etc., and noting only the exceptionally early age at which M. assumed the responsibilities of a wage-earner,* we may enumerate at once the list of vols., in which M.'s works are contained. These include, in poetry: *Poems*, 1851; *Modern Love*, 1862; *Poems and Lyrics of the Joy of Earth*, 1883; *Ballads and Poems of Tragic Life*, 1887; *A Reading of Earth*, 1888; *Odes in Contribution to the Song of French History*, 1898; *A Reading of Life*, 1901; in fiction: *The Ordeal of Richard Feverel*, 1859; *Evan Harrington*, 1861; *Sandra Belloni* (*Emilia in Engld.*), 1864; *Rhoda Fleming*, 1865; *Vittoria*, 1867; *Harry Richmond*, 1871; *Beauchamp's Career*, 1876; *The Egoist*, 1879; *The Tragic Comedians*, 1880; *Diana of the Crossways*, 1885; *One of Our Conquerors*, 1891; *Lord Ormont and his Aminta*, 1894; *The Amazing Marriage*, 1895; in criticism: *On the Idea of Comedy*, 1877; and some short stories and misc. verse.

It is easy to say the obvious things about M.: that he owed something, or has some likeness in temperament, to lady Morgan (q.v.); that the poem, *Modern Love*, should be collated, or read side by side, with the novel, *The Egoist*; that the metre of *Love in the Valley* is the same as that of G. Darley's (q.v.) *Serenade of a Royal Martyr*, and that ' the leg ' of the hero of *The Egoist* may have stepped out of Darley's *Becket*; that ch. 3 of Björnson's (q.v.) *Absalom's*

Hair should be compared with ch. xv. of *Richard Feverel*; that *Sandra Belloni* is founded on the idea of progress in Mazzini; that *The Tragic Comedians* tells the story of F. Lassalle (q.v.); that the comic spirit is the cosmic spirit; and so on. Hardly less obvious are (1) M.'s gallant Gallic sympathy, in which he and Swinburne were at one, and which was in striking contrast to the prevailing Teutonism of the age, derived partly through Carlyle (q.v.), and consonant with the tone of the Victorian court; (2) M.'s reaction to a kind of shagginess of diction from the elegance of Tennyson (q.v.): a feature to be remarked, too, in R. Browning (q.v.); and (3) M.'s response to advanced liberal thought—J. Morley and F. Harrison (qq.v.) were regular contributors to the *Fortnightly Review*, displayed particularly in his treatment of feminism, which became a dominant social problem in the very year of M.'s death.

These points of appreciation are fairly obvious, but they do not take us very far in the study of M. as novelist and poet. For M., as is said by the writer in *C.H.E.L.*, xiii. 443, ' envisaged afresh the whole area of life— natural, human and universal,—and aimed at ensuring the truth of his delineations of particular characters and incidents by their consistency with this wide survey. The full purport of his novels is not, therefore, to be grasped except in the light of such poems as *The Woods of Westermain*, *Earth and Man*, *The Thrush in February* and *The Test of Manhood* '; and, as the present writer has said elsewhere: ' Meredith, as poet, even more than as novelist, belongs to the class of pioneers, to the men in the line of advance,* whose full greatness awaits recognition till the advance is completed and the novelty has become commonplace. The identity of Faith with Reason, the Real as the basis of the Ideal, society reanimated by love of Earth, and not shivering with dread of the things that are —not clinging to the customary and the sentimental,—for these ideas Meredith strove in the worst years of the divorce between knowledge and belief, fulfilling the vision of Wordsworth in the new era of democracy, raising to impassioned contemplation the milder curiosity of Tennyson, and surpassing by a deeper transcendentalism the human harmonies of Robert Browning. Meredith breaks through the thicket of words, using images as lanterns and shaping swords to pruning-hooks, till those that win with him to the other side, panting and a little breathless, forget which was lantern or sword, which was image or metaphor, in the glad greeting of a goal to which none other could have led them. It is for his supreme reconcilement of " the external world " with " the individual mind " in Wordsworth's programme, of the " outer " with the " inner " in his own, that Meredith is accounted among the maker-poets. He offers the revelation sought in the morning of the nineteenth century, and

* The present writer was associated formally with the publication, 1907, of Mr. Arundell Esdaile's *Bibliography of Meredith*, a copy of which he sent to Mr. Meredith. In a letter dated 13 April, 1907, from Box Hill, Dorking, Mr. Meredith wrote: ' The little book is presented in good form, but I cannot conjure in my mind a purchaser. . . . Some months back I received from Rome 6 copies of the *Nuova Antologia*, containing the translation of my *Diana of the Crossways*. . . . I see no other omission, and I can see more than it pleases me to recall.' An author in his old age would gladly exclude three parts of his work from the knowledge of men.'

* ' The deepest thinker is not really—though we often use the phrase—in advance of his day, so much as in the line along which advance takes place ' (sir L. Stephen, q.v.; *Engl. Lit. and Soc. in the 18th Cent.*, 17).

he rests it on no divorce between flesh and spirit, on no antagonism between reason and faith, on no compromise disguised by association, but on a real union of the two ' (*Engl. Lit. in 19th Cent.*, 291). It is in this mood of thought that we may enter the woods of Westermain. In this mood, M.'s portrait-gallery of characters should be examined— he is particularly successful with his boys,— his aphorisms should be pondered, and ' the meaning of Earth ' in M.'s philosophy must be elucidated. As to the style of this forward-striving author, its difficulty cannot be denied, though it was much exaggerated by some contemporaries : if we allow for compression, allusion, and rapid imagination, there is nothing wrong with his sanity and psychology. 'The army of human thought ', wr. Mr. G. M. Trevelyan (see s.v. Arnold) in 1906, ' is advancing in two bands : one marches along the high road under the bright hard light of science ; but the other is straggling into the dimmer shades of intricate psychology, into " haunted roods ", the birthplace of new aspirations, prophecies, and religions, which can find no expression in dogmatic statement, but only in the inspired language of beauty, suggesting the undefined, and making the unseen felt. Mr. Meredith has long been a leader in this direction ', and it is becoming to acknowledge his lead.

Meres, Francis (1565-1647) : Engl. critic. Wr., 1598, *Palladis Tamia* (' Treasury of Wit '), otherwise unimportant except for a passage anent Shakespeare (q.v.) giving a list of his plays, and referring to him as ' mellifluous and honey-tongued ' (see s.v. Ovid) and to the distribution of his ' sugred sonnets among his private friends '.

Mérimée, Prosper (1803-70) : Fr. novelist, playwright, letter-writer ; the most finished artist in Fr. prose of the 19th cent., which, since a new epoch commenced in 1871, his life may be said to have spanned. M.'s work is a practical illustration of the theory of art for art's sake (see s.v. *l'Art pour l'art*), and neither the romanticists nor the realists can claim him wholly for their own. He was both or either, as it suited the artistic purpose which he was following. M.'s activity as an author extended from 1825 to 1847 ; under emperor Napoleon iii he became a somewhat reluctant courtier, the link with the court being the (Span.) countess Montijo, mother of the empress Eugenie. With Napoleon's studies of Julius Cæsar and with the other interests of M. at court we are not more closely concerned. M.'s first work combined two romantic motives : mystery and exoticism. It was entitled *le Théâtre* (i.e. the plays) *de Clara Gazul*, and purported to be dramas written by a Span. actress. Next, 1826, he publd. a vol. called *la Guzla* (the change of letters was a characteristic piece of cynicism), which transferred the interest to Dalmatia, and reproduced the best elements in current Slavonic lit. His next works were purely Fr. : *la Jacquerie*, 1828, and the *Chronique de Charles ix*, 1829. They were romantic in the sense that they revived the historic past ; they were realistic in the details of their representation ; and they may be compared

with the *Contes drôlatiques* of Balzac (q.v.) in their uncompromising, unfaltering and cold brilliance of imagination. M.'s later works were mainly novels and short stories : *Colomba, Matteo Falcone, Carmen*, and others ; unrivalled in their delineation of human character, and in their chaste excellence of diction. M.'s hist. essays and papers and his services to Russ. and Span. letters should not be overlooked ; and, on the personal side, his deep obligation to Stendhal (q.v.) is a commonplace of criticism and biography.

Merlin : originally, Myrrdhin, Welsh bard and necromancer, earlier than first period of romance (q.v.) ; passed through the transforming manipulation of Nennius (10th cent.), Geoffrey of Monmouth (12th cent.), and others (see s.v. Arthur) into an intimate association with the ' matière de Bretagne ' (see s.v. Bodel), centring round the Celtic legends of the Arthur-cycle. In the Fr. verse-romances of Robert of Boron (q.v.), M. was raised to a pivotal place in the assimilation of the various semi-independent sections of the cycle; and his (Welsh) mysterious birth became an (ecclesiastical) demonic birth : later in the Middle Ages, he rivalled, and was even confused with, Virgil (q.v.) as a magician. M.'s fame as prophet survived in Engld., both in lit. and in common parlance. Malory (q.v.) selected the most striking episodes in his romance, and handed them on eventually to Tennyson (q.v.).

Mesa, de, Christobal (1559-1633) : Span. poet : Italianate ; addicted to national themes, including, 1607, the ' Restoration of Spain '. He transld. Virgil, 1615, and Homer (still unpubld.).

Meschinot, Jean (c. 1420-c. 1509) : Fr. poet ; one of the major or minor *rhétoriqueurs* (q.v.), who infested the courts of kings Charles viii and Louis vii, making them a nest of mechanical singing-birds. M.'s musical works were as complicated as any of the school, and were entitled *Les Lunettes des Princes*.

Messenius, Johannes (1579-1637) : Swed. historian and playwright. M., who spent the last 20 years of his life in prison expiating a sentence for treason, combined his 2 chief studies in a series of hist. plays, designed to illustrate Swed. history on the stage. It had been said that the scheme was Shakespearean and the execution on a par with Hans Sachs (q.v.). The plays belong to that curious product known as academic or students' drama, written for edification and for performance in coll. halls. See s.v. Kirchmayer, for example.

Metaphysical Poetry : Engl. descriptive epithet, first applied by Dryden to the poetry of Donne (qq.v.) : ' Donne affects the metaphysics, not only in his Satires, but in his amorous verses, where Nature only should reign ' (*Dedication to Juvenal*, 1693), and made famous by Dr. Johnson (q.v.), who extended it in his essay on Cowley (q.v. ; in *Lives of the Poets*, 1781) to a whole group of poets, as follows :— ' The metaphysical poets were men of learning, and to show their learning was their whole endeavour ; but, unluckily resolving to show it in rhyme, instead of writing poetry they only wrote verses, and very often such verses as stood the trial of the finger better than of the ear ; for the modulation was so imperfect, that they were only found to be verses by counting the syllables. . . . Their thoughts are often new, but seldom natural ; they are not obvious, but neither are they just ; and the reader, far from wondering that he missed them, wonders more frequently by what perverseness of industry they were ever found. . . . From this account of their compositions it will be readily inferred that they were not successful in representing or moving the affections. . . . Their wish was only to say what they hoped had been never said before '.

It will be observed that Dryden used the term in its strict sense of beyond-Nature : Donne's love-verse, he said, used beyond-natural language, where Nature only should reign. Johnson, by his definition and his examples, proved that he used ' metaphysical ' in the sense merely of *unnatural* in poetry, unsuitable, far-fetched, or fantastic : a use by no means remote from that of the verbal conceit (q.v. ; the whole question is discussed at greater length s.v.). Accordingly, the Dryden-Johnson epithet has never taken thorough hold on Engl. critics, and is gradually being dropped. Southey (q.v.) objected to it in 1814, when, in an art. in the *Quarterly Review* (no. xxxiii), he wr. of the ' metaphysical poets, as they have been improperly called. . . . The appellation is peculiarly unfit ' ; and Saintsbury objected to it in 1914 (*First Book of Engl. Lit.*, p. 111) : ' What has been rather unfortunately called " metaphysical " poetry '. The late Mr. A. Clutton-Brock, in *C.M.H.*, v, ch. 26, called these writers the ' Fantastic School ' of Engl. poetry : ' Their extravagances and incongruities, ' he said, ' both of style and of thought, reflect the extravagances and incongruities of an age of transition and revolution, an age violent and uncompromising both in action and in ideas. But . . . the Fantastic Poets in their conflicts of thought produced beauties, " things extreme, and scattering bright ", to quote the words of Donne, which cannot be paralleled in any other period of our literature '.

The metaphysical school, wr. Southey (*loc. cit.*), ' which marred a great poet in Cowley, expired in Norris of Bemerton ' (q.v. ; 1657-1711 ; clergyman and philosopher); and, since the school died young and obscurely, the safer course is to look for the unparalleled beauties in Donne, Herbert, Vaughan, Traherne, Crashaw, Cowley, and the rest, and to leave critics to dispute as to the precise epithet to be attached to their triumphs in strange ways of speech, reporting the flotsam of the encyclopedias, and reflecting the rich colours of the autumn of the Renaissance. If the name ' metaphysical ' be dropped, the name ' learned ' will probably be found adequate to express the parade of learning and the abstract treatment of love, which are 2 main characteristics of this group of poets, and the second of which was derived from, or may be paralleled in, the *dolce stil nuovo* (see s.v.), which Dante (q.v.) brought into the Ital. mainland from Sicily. And the learning, too, goes behind Dante, whose philosopher was St. Thomas Aquinas, to Lucretius, the Roman poet, whose philosopher was Epicurus. If metaphysical poetry is learned poetry, Lucretius and Dante are the 2 ruling metaphysicians in classical and modern verse. Sir S. Lee (*Fr. Renaissance in Engld.*, 354) tells us that ' the so-called metaphysical vein which is usually said to have been inaugurated in English poetry by Donne, is entitled to rank with Du Bartas's legacies to this country ' (see s.v. Du Bartas),—a debt written down to some extent by prof. Grierson (*Donne's Poems*, Oxford, vol. ii, Introduction). The whole subject, which is really critical, and literary only in a secondary degree, is discussed scientifically in Courthope, *Hist. Engl. Poetry*, vol. iii, ch. viii.

Metaphysical Society (Engl.) : An assembly of leaders in philosophy and letters, founded, 1869, by sir James Knowles (q.v.), who officiated as secretary till 1881, when the society gradually dispersed.

Metastasio (1698-1782) : It. melodramatic poet, in the sense of a writer of operatic plays (see s.v. Opera). M.'s life contained a double romance. He was the son, Pietro Bonaventura, of an old papal soldier, Trapassi, who kept a tallow-chandler's shop in Rome, where the small boy of attractive appearance used to exercise his talent for improvisation in the public streets. There in 1709, Gravina (q.v.) heard him one day, and put him to school, and finally adopted him, the name M. being the Gk. form of his patronymic. The youth justified his patron's favour, and publd. an early vol. of verse, 1717. Gravina died in the following year, and left M. a fortune. The second romance was of love. M. quickly ran through his money, and articled himself to an advocate, Castagnola, at Naples, who had the bad taste, but the good legal instinct, to shy at a poetic clerk. M.'s *Endymion* and his *Gardens of the Hesperides*, 1722, written by command of the viceroy of Naples, had to be issued anon., but the *prima donna*, who took the part of Venus in the *Gardens* (' Orti '), Marianna Bulgarelli, known as ' la Romanina ', found the not too bashful librettist, who lost his job with Castagnola, but gained other joys in compensation. He entered the society of his kind, under the wing of Romanina, and his first melodrama, *Dido abandoned*, 1724, proved an immense success in every Ital. city. Dido was more modern than would be approved by a more sophisticated generation, but she delighted her audiences in the 18th cent., and M. exhibited from the start his rare *flair* for the operatic stage, with its minimum of psychology and its maximum of sentiment and action, lending themselves to musical expression. *Dido* was succeeded by 6 or 8 more melodramas, *Artaxerxes*, *Cato*, etc., which were produced in Naples, Venice and Rome, where M. had followed la Romanina, and there, in 1730, the invitation reached him to replace Zeno (q.v.) as court-poet to emperor Charles vi in Vienna. This was due to the good offices (we need not inquire for a further motive) of another Marianna, widow of count d'Althann, and la Romanina was left behind. A year or two later she died, and made M. her residuary legatee, a post which the lover of the countess d'Althann renounced in favour of the signor

Bulgarelli. Was it all as simple as it sounds ? 'Vernon Lee' sums it up as follows : 'Thus ended the romance of Metastasio's life, and with it his youth, and soon after his hope and his genius'.

The genius prevailed till 1740, the year of the emperor's death, and of the outbreak of the war of succession ; and it is likely that the genius was unequal to these martial and political events, which interrupted the enter- taining flow of M.'s facile and even plays. Among these may be named *Demofoönte, la Clemenza di Tito, Achille in Sciro, Temistocle,* and *Attilo Regolo* (written, 1740 ; postponed till 1746) : they all had a wide vogue and a great success, which they earned by their real charm and sense of music and rhythm.

Metternich-Winneburg, von, Clement Lothar Wenzel (1773-1859) : Austrian statesman ; chancellor ; prince by rank. M., as a literary craftsman, has no claim to a place in this lexicon, but his influence on Germ. lit. was so important and immense that a few lines are necessarily devoted to him. Refer- ence should be made to *C.M.H.*, vol. x, ch. xi, by prof. A. F. Pollard, and to *Periods of European History,* viii, by prof. Alison Phillips, *passim,* for the hist. events of the long epoch, from the Congress of Vienna (1815), during which M. was supreme. The following quotations, which indicate the course of his policy, and its direction in intellectual affairs, are selected from one or other of those authori- ties. 'In the character of the Austrian Empire lay the explanation, if not the justi- fication, of the system which Metternich had imposed upon Europe. . . . To a State such as Austria all change was dangerous. There- fore, all change must be prevented, whether without or within. . . . The result was that the policy of stability became the policy of slumber. . . . As Woden walled round Brynhild with fire, so Metternich guarded the sleep of Austria with a ring fence of censors and customs officers'. So, in Austria ; next, anent Prussia : 'Hardenberg's best days were over ; in 1819 Metternich declared that he was "morally as well as physically in a state of weakness bordering on childhood". The decay of Hardenberg's influence deprived the Prussian Government of all unity of direction. Fred- erick William himself, whose chief active mental trait was, according to Metternich, "the repressive", came more and more under the reactionary influences. . . . The heroes of the War of Liberation became suspects of the Government. . . . Liberalism, moreover, has always been an exotic on Prussian soil. . . . The explanation is not far to seek ; nature, it is said, did not foresee Prussia, and Prussia in the work of man's hands. . . . The net result of the movement for constitutional progress was a bitter disappointment to that portion of the German people which took an interest in public life. . . The intellectual atmosphere of Germany was indeed charged with electricity, but it was the repressive conduct of Governments which gave a political direction to the storm. . . . Whatever the cause, the effect was to remove the only barrier against repression in Europe, to bring Russia and consequently Prussia into line with Austria,

and to assure to Metternich a dominant position in Europe and almost a dictatorship in Germany'. So far, the pure historians. A final quotation may be made from Kuno Francke, a Germ. at Harvard, who revised in 1901 his *Hist of Germ. Lit. as determined by Social Forces* (a queasy topic, *teste* Saintsbury, but admissible, if in any national lit., in that of Germany). In the last ch. of that bk., 'we come to the days of the Holy Alliance and of Metternich, to the time of reaction against the very spirit which made 1813 possible, to the proscription of liberty, to the blighting of hope. What a singular and astounding spectacle ! Here is a people just recovered from centuries of political misery, having just regained the full sense of its power, just risen with one accord to vindicate its honour and independence ; and the very moment that the foreign enemy is vanquished, . . . this same people again falls a victim to its hereditary lack of common consciousness. . . . Public opinion was again reduced to naught. . . . Even the best minds of the nation were affected by this universal repression of public activity'. And, lest there should seem too much Harvard, and too little Germany in this Americanized Germ. professor's outlook, there is the contemporary evidence of the bitter apostrophe of count Auersperg (q.v. ; Anastasius Grün) to M., at the very zenith of that statesman's rule :

Oestreichs Volk ist's, ehrlich, offen, wohler- zogen auch und fein,
Sieh, es fleht ganz artig : 'Dürft' ich wohl so frei sein, frei zu sein ? '

Austria is it, honest, open, on her best behaviour,—See !
Sir, she asketh, Prithee, may I make so free as to be free ?

Meurs, de, Jan (1579-1639) : Dutch antiquary ; his name was latinized to Johannes Meursius. Prof. of Gk. and history at Leyden univ., 1610-25, when he accepted the chair of history at Soroë, in Denmark. Wr. exten- sively on Gk. monuments, mysteries, and antiquities.

Mexia, Hernan (15th cent.) : Span poet. Wr. a satire on women.

Mexia, Pero (*c.* 1499-1551) : Span. romancer and historian ; knt. of Seville ; is plausibly identified with the 'Caballero cesareo', who contributed ballads to the *Romancero* (q.v.) of Sepulveda (q.v.), 1551. Wr. a *Silva de varia lecion,* 1542, a moral and hist. miscellany, on the lines of the *Apophthegmata* of Erasmus (q.v.), transld. into many languages, including Engl., 1571, and, again, 1613. Wr., too, *Dialogos Eruditos,* 1545 ; and *Historia imperial y Cesarea,* a biographical history of emperors from Julius Cæsar to Maximilian i (q.v.). M.'s history of the reign of Charles v (q.v.) was left unfind. His life of Tamerlane was read in transln. by Marlowe (q.v.) before writing his play on that hero.

Meynell, Alice (died 1922): Engl. poet; essayist ; *née* Thompson. Wr. slim vols. of *Poems* and *Later Poems* ; and slim vols. of essays : *The Rhythm of Life ; The Colour of Life,* etc. ; edited 2 anthologies ; practised throughout her distinguished lit. career a parsimony of production which corresponded to a rare delicacy of thought and phrase. Mrs. M. suffered at first (in the 'nineties of the 19th cent.) from an excess of adulation : suffered, not in self-esteem, but in the esteem of readers outside her circle, which seemed a bit precious to the uninitiate. But, since the circle included men of judgment as sound as that of E. Dowden, C. Patmore (q.v.) and Ruskin (q.v.), who agreed in ranking Mrs. M.'s sonnet, ' Renouncement ', e.g., among the great poems of modern lit., it is probable that opinion will come back with increasing appreciation to her careful, even exquisite, muse ; and that, like some of the older writers whom she studied so well, she will take a permanent place, for the sake of one or two poems and essays, in future anthologies of verse and prose.

Mézeray, de, François Eudes (1610-83) : Fr. historian. Wr. a well documented history of France, 1643-51, which he subsequently abridged. M. received a pension from Richelieu (q.v.), but later attacked Mazarin (see s.v. *Mazarinades*), and was deprived of part of his pension by chancellor Colbert.

Michaelis, Johann Benjamin (1746-72) : Germ. poet ; a late adherent to the Prussian or Ana-creontic school (s.v. Anakreontiker). Attracted by Gleim (q.v.) to Halberstadt, where he died too young to do full justice to his vein of lyrical irony.

Michaelis, Johann David (1717-91) : Germ. Orientalist ; prof. at Göttingen ; writer of important works on Hebr. language and lit., father of Caroline, wife of A. W. v. Schlegel (q.v.).

Michelangelo Buonarotti (1475-1564) : It. painter, sculptor, architect, poet ; the ' nearest approach to a universal master of the Higher Fine Arts, for even Rossetti (q.v.) did not add sculpture or architecture to painting or poetry ' (Saints-bury, *P.E.L.*, v, 143) ; ' in him the quest for beauty was the uplifting of the soul towards God. Michelangelo felt with instinctive insight the tragedy of his own age and of the age to come ; that is why he towers above his contemporaries as a great man and points the way to further developments ' (C. Foligno, *Epochs of Ital. Lit.*, 31) ; and cf. R. Bridges, poet-laureate, *The Growth of Love*, 18 :

And three who all the rest had far outdone,
Mild Giotto first, who stole the morning hours,
I saw, and godlike Buonarotti's powers,
And Dante, gravest poet.

We are concerned here solely with M.'s poetry, to which he turned out of love for Vittoria (q.v.) Colonna, the great lady of the Ital. Renaissance. He wr. various lyrical verse, under the inspiration of that passion, but is chiefly memorable for his *Sonnets*, which, particularly for the feature of their striking opening verse, afforded a model to love-sonneteers in the more conventional vogue of that kind.

Michelet, Jules (1798-1874) : Fr. historian ; ' the most original and remarkable historian in point of style that France has ever produced ' (Saintsbury, *Hist. Fr. Lit.*, 596) ; as an admirer and a disciple of Vico (q.v.), whose neglected work M. helped to restore to fame, he made the ' noble attempt to reflect a nation's life by the aid of science ' (*C.M.H.*, x, 516) ;

and he would have been the first to acknow-ledge his debt to the inspiration of the Bible, Virgil, a-Kempis, and mystics of the Guyon type (see s.vv.). The combination was striking and effective ; it was a poet's temper-ament grafted on a philosopher's ; and to talk of realism or romanticism in such a con-text is to be considerably below the level of the immensities of M.'s thought. His mind ranged freely among bold generalizations, based on race, heredity, environment, and the physical causes behind political history ; and, though some of his writings are being super-seded and are falling into oblivion, Lanson (*Lit. fr.*, 1027) is probably right when he says that M. ' is one of those writers who seem to me destined to grow greater as time goes on '. M.'s works include monographs on topics obviously allied to the larger view of history as a science (but much less obviously then than now), such as *du Prêtre, de la Famille et de la Femme*, 1845, *du Peuple* (with an auto-biographical pref.), *de l'Oiseau, de l'Insecte, de la Mer, de l'Amour, de la Sorcière*, etc. A *Précis* of modern history, 1828, and an *Intro-duction* to universal history, 1831, showed the bent of M.'s studies, which he continued in a history of the Roman Republic, 2 vols., 1831. All these were preparatory to the *opus magnum*, known, briefly, as *Histoire de France*, the successive vols. of which occupied him through most of his hard-working life. ' Cleverer books we have in abundance ', says one critic, ' but a more luminous and more eloquent book does not exist ' ; and the epithets may stand as characterization. M.'s habit of tracing big events to small causes, and his constant Virgilian felicity in the art of ' rerum cognoscere causas ', may be illustrated by some of his chapter-headings : e.g., *le Café, Manon Lescaut*, etc., and it is always pointed out that he divides the long reign of Louis xiv by the ' fistula ', for which the king was operated upon. This personal and social conception of history, inherited from Montes-quieu (q.v.) and his forerunners, was extended and vitalized by M., who was consumed by a passion for humanity, and was moved in all his writings by a rare and scrupulous origin-ality in what may be called hist. evaluation. M. held several notable professorships, but was addicted to no school ; he shared with Quinet (q.v.), his friend, a distrust of Jesuit influences, and his poetic and mystical temper-ament brought him far closer in spirit to the Germ. than to the Engl. genius : indeed, he was openly opposed to the philo-Angloism of the Fr. romanticists. M. left a large quantity of MSS., some of which were publd. posth.

Mickiewiez, Adam (1798-1855) : Polish poet ; by common consent the national poet of Poland ; Lithuanian by birth, thus bearing much the same relation to Poland as a Scots-man to Engld., bringing to her, that is to say, an additional store of intensive patriotism, tradition and folklore. M.'s fantastic dramatic poem, *Dziady* (Ancestors), which he publd. in sections from time to time, and which, like the *Faust* of Goethe (q.v.) reflected his chang-ing experiences, is based on Lithuanian legend —the half-pagan rite of a feast for the dead,

—the past and present associations of which gave M. the opportunity of weaving into the old folk-tale all kinds of personal reflections on the history and future of his nation. For M. took, almost perforce, an active part in the political activities of his busy life-time. Almost inevitably, therefore, in that epoch, he was imprisoned as a member of a students' society, banished to Russia, and finally exiled, thus adding in the 19th cent. one more name to the martyrology of lit., which includes Tasso (q.v.) and many others. Among the external influences which reinforced this heritage of birth and manhood were the prevailing Byronism of M.'s times, so much stronger on the Continent than in Engld. (see s.v. Byron: M.'s transln. of the *Giaour* is exceptionally good), his meeting with Goethe (q.v.) in Weimar, and his residence in Italy and France. In Rome, 1848, he organized the Polish Legion, which brought him into contact with Mazzini, and in 1855, at the time of the Crimean War, he went to Constantinople, with a view to raising a similar Legion on the side of the Allies. There he died suddenly of cholera. His remains, interred in Paris, were removed in 1890 to Cracow, and a fine memorial was erected to him in Warsaw.

Miss Ashurst-Biggs, who transld. M.'s chief works into Engl., said in a lecture delivered, 1915, to the Royal Society of Lit., that M., 'in adopting the songs and legends of his native land, did precisely what was done by the Anglo-Norman minstrels and Provençal *trouvères* of the eleventh and twelfth centuries in relating anew the old Gallic and British traditions of king Arthur and his warriors': in other words, though these words are quite true and simple, he brought Romance into Polish lit., 700 years later than it was brought into the lit. of France. His 'Ancestors' and 'Pilgrims' Books', which 'no Pole, in the Babylonian century of the nation, could read in exile without becoming strengthened and ennobled' (Dyboski, *Polish Lit.*, Oxford, 1923; p. 94), were followed by an epical poem, *Pan Tadeusz* ('Master Thaddeus'), 1834, in 12 bks. of alexandrine couplets. He called it a story from the life of country gentlemen, but the Lithuanian country gentlemen whose life it narrated were the class, as prof. Dyboski reminds us, who produced Kosciuszko (1746-1817), the patriot-general, hero of Polish democracy; Moni-uszko (1820-72), the musician, second only to Chopin (1810-49), another Pole who owed much of his inspiration to M.; Siemirávski, Poland's Alma Tadema, and others; 'in the light of these facts', he adds, 'we admire in *Master Thaddeus* (which has been transld. into 10 foreign languages, including Engl.) not a creation of stupendous imaginative genius only, but the masterly representation of that particular element in Polish national life which concentrates in it the very life-force of Polish history during the age of captivity'. We may add that the thunder of Napoleon (how far the echoes of that thunder spread in the lit. of Europe!) echoes at intervals through the tale, which closed with the march of the Corsican's army to Lithuania on its road to Moscow, 1812.

We have omitted many of the writings —poetical, professional, journalistic—, which M. produced in Paris and elsewhere. He was, above all, a great Pole, in whose life, and experience, and works, we see the unconquerable strength of that much-tried and much-partitioned nation. A nation cannot be permanently destroyed which produces a poet like M.: 'We are all of his making', said Krasinski (q.v.) of him; and he made a national spirit as well as national poetry. Let who will make the laws of a nation, it is written, let me make its poems; and the more durable glory of the maker is M.'s.

Middleton, Thomas (1570-1627): Engl. playwright; collaborated, after the fashion of the day, with other dramatic writers, in the *Spanish Gipsy*, and about 20 comedies and masques, which enjoyed contemporary esteem.

Mil-Huit-Cent-Trente (Fr.): '1830'; catchword in Fr. literary history for the period of the Romantic revival, esp. associated with the dramatic surprises of that central year. See s.vv. Fr. Lit., Lyrisme.

Mill, -i. James (1773-1836): Engl. utilitarian philosopher; met Bentham (q.v.), 1808, and promulgated his system of thought; started, 1824, *Westminster Review* as Benthamite organ; contributor to *Edinburgh Review*; educational reformer, and part founder of univ. of London; wr. important *History of India*, 1818; encouraged Ricardo, the economist, and helped to found the Political Economy Club, 1820.

-ii. John Stuart (1806-73): Engl. philosopher; philosophical radical; son of above, and edu. solely by his father, on an intensive system, described objectively in J.S.M.'s intensely interesting *Autobiography*, 1873; founded, or helped to found, the Utilitarian and Speculative societies, and the *London Review*, 1835, which became his property 2 years later; author of a *System of Logic*, 1843, the result of many years' work; *Principles of Political Economy*, 1848; *On Liberty*, 1859, (with his wife: 'more directly and literally our joint production than anything else which bears my name'; *Autobiog.*); *Utilitarianism*, 1863; *The Subjection of Women*, 1869 ('all that is most striking and profound belongs to my wife'; *ibid.*); and other works; M.P., Westminster, 1865-68. M. touches lit. most directly in some of the essays collected in his *Dissertations and Discussions*. 'Eloquence is heard; poetry is overheard', is one of his most notable aphorisms; and we may recall from his *Autobiography*—from the man in his milieu —a remarkable tribute to the poems of Wordsworth (q.v.): 'From them I seemed to learn what would be the perennial sources of happiness, when all the greater evils of life shall have been removed. And I felt myself at once better and happier as I came under their influence'. And as to the influence of M. on others, we may quote the testimony of J. (vicst.) Morley (q.v.) in the *Fortnightly Review*, after M.'s sudden death at Avignon: 'We have lost a great teacher and exemplar of knowledge and virtue, but men will long feel the presence of his character, making them ashamed of what is indolent or selfish, and encouraging them to all disinterested labour, both in trying to do good and in trying to find out what good is—which is harder'.

Miller, Johann Martin (1750-1814): Germ. poet; an adherent to the Göttingen (q.v.) brotherhood, and an original member of the Hain (q.v.), devoted to the spread of the gospel of Germ. poetry according to Klopstock (q.v.). M.'s genuine lyrical gift found expression in songs, some of which passed into national possession; and he wr., 1776, a tale of tears and moonlight and didacticism, *Siegwart, a Cloister-tale*, which roused almost more enthusiasm than the *Werther* of Goethe, which had preceded it.

Milman, Henry Hart (1791-1868): Engl. historian; poet; divine; dean of St. Paul's, 1849. M. won the Newdigate prize at Oxford, 1812, with a set of verses on the *Belvidere Apollo*, still accounted by many the best prize-poem in a long series; prof. of poetry, 1821-31; edited Gibbon's (q.v.) masterwork, 1838, and was himself the author of 3 distinguished pieces of hist. writing: (1) *History of the Jews*, 1830, characterized by dean Stanley (q.v.) as 'the first decisive inroad of German theology into England', and by the *Jew. Encycl.*, viii, 594, as 'decisively rationalistic; it treats the Jews as an Oriental tribe, and all miracles are either eliminated or evaded. He was nevertheless presented with a piece of plate by some representative Jews in recognition of his sympathetic attitude'; (2) *History of Christianity under the Empire*, 1840, and (3) *History of Latin Christianity to the Pontificate of Nicholas v*, 1855, an important, if controversial, work. M.'s earlier *Poems and Dramatic Works* were collected in 3 vols., 1839; they included the *Fall of Jerusalem*, *Fazio* (a drama acted at Covent Garden, 1818), *Anne Boleyn*, etc., and shorter pieces, some of which are still in use as hymns; his *Annals of St. Paul's Cathedral* were publd., posth., 1868.

Milner, Alfred (1854-1925): Engl. statesman; historian; visct., 1902; K.G., 1921. Wr. *Engld. in Egypt*, 1892, *Questions of the Hour*, 1923, and other works, conveying the reflections and experience of his distinguished career in the public service; assistant-editor, 1882-5, of the *Pall Mall Gazette* (q.v.); chancellor-elect, 1925, of the univ. of Oxford, in succession to marquess Curzon (q.v.).

Milnes, Richard Monckton (1809-85): Engl. poet; statesman; created baron Houghton, 1863; his 'portrait has been etched skilfully, though not without acid' (Walker, *Lit. Victorian Era*, 334) in the Vavasour of *Tancred* by B. Disraeli (q.v.). There is truth without acid in the remark of W. E. Forster (1818-86; statesman), quoted *ibid.*: 'I have many friends who would be kind to me in distress, but only one who would be equally kind to me in disgrace'. Wr. verse-memorials of travels in Greece, 1834, and in Egypt, *Palm Leaves*, 1844; wr., too, legendary and hist. poems, and pleasant, light verse of various kinds, as to which prof. Saintsbury says: 'he was not a poet of the "big bow-wow" tone, but he was neither a twitterer nor a yelper' (*C.H.E.L.*, xiii, 185). Lord H. was the author, too, of a valuable *Life, Letters and Lit. Remains of John Keats*, 2 vols. 1848, extremely servicable in its time

and still authoritative. The second baron is the eminent statesman who was created first marquess of Crewe, 1911.

Milton, John (1608-74): Engl. poet; a Londoner by birth; son of John M., a scrivener (pettifogging lawyer) by trade, but a musician and scholar by taste; brother of Christopher M. (1615-93), a judge and knt., 1686, and of Ann, wife of Edward Phillips, whose sons (Edward, 1630-96, and John, 1631-1706), minor writers of no particular merit, their uncle consistently befriended; m. (1) Mary Powell, 1643, who left him in the same year, but returned, 1645, after her husband had publd. 2 much-discussed pamphlets on divorce, and bore him 3 daughters; died, 1653; (2) Catherine Woodcock, 1656; died, 1658, the 'late espoused saint' of her husband's sonnet; (3) Elizabeth Minshull, 1663, who survived him many years.

M.'s life falls naturally into 3 parts; 3 plays of a trilogy, as prof. Saintsbury describes them, 'the second of which had hardly anything to do with the first, though the third was to resume and complete it' (*C.H.E.L.*, vii, 100). After his education at St. Paul's School, he went up, 1625, to Christ's Coll., Cambridge, where he was known as 'the lady of Christ's', much as Virgil (q.v.) in his day had been called 'the maid of Naples'. From 1632-8, he resided at Horton, Bucks., with his father, who had retired from active business, and a year after his mother's death, 1637, he spent 15 months in foreign travel, meeting Grotius (q.v.) in Paris, and Galileo (q.v.) in Florence, and extending his journey to Rome, Naples and home by Venice. This ended part i,—the first act, or play, of M.'s life: 1625-39.

Part ii opened in London, where M. settled down to tutorial work, abandoning his earlier plan of entering the Church, and where he was quickly submerged by the political happenings of the time. Roughly, it extended from 1640-60, the date of the Stuart Restoration. It covered the period of his first and second marriages, with the painful domestic experiences, which he turned so promptly to general views on the law of marriage. It covered his increasing eye-trouble, which led to his total blindness in 1652. It covered the stirring event of 1649, towards which M. contributed a pamphlet—one of many which he composed,—with the terrible title: 'Tenure of Kings and Magistrates, proving that it is lawful, and hath been held so through all ages, for any who have the power, to call to account a Tyrant, or Wicked King, and, after due conviction, to depose, and put him to death, if the ordinary Magistrate have neglected to do it'; it included his reply, *Eikonoklastes*, to the 'King's (Charles i) Book', *Eikon Basilike*; his reply, 1651, to Saumaise (q.v.), the Dutch thinker, who had written in defence of the king; and his term of service, 1649-60, as Lat. secretary to the council of State, which brought him into intimate relations with Cromwell. How M. escaped a rebel's fate after the Restoration is even now not quite clear. He had good friends, A. Marvell among them; he was blind, elderly, and a poet; and the merry monarch was merciful. M. was fined and in prison for a while; and thus ended the second act of his life.

Part iii, 1663-74, commencing with his third marriage, lasted till his death. Its scene is laid in Artillery Walk, leading to Bunhill Fields, where the last of his London houses was located, and which he only left, 1665-6, at the time of the Great Plague, when he spent a few months in a cottage (now a Milton Museum) at Chalfont St. Giles. This period included the completion and publication of *Paradise Lost* (10 bks., 1667 ; 12 bks., by subdivision, 1674 ; M. sold the copyright for £20, of which he received one-half in his life-time, his widow afterwards compounding the second moiety for £8), and of *Paradise Regain'd*, in 4 bks., 'to which is added *Samson Agonistes*', 1671.

There was good poetry in part i ; there was better (the best) poetry in part iii ; there was nothing but prose in part ii. There were vision and contemplation in parts i and iii ; there was nothing but action in part ii ; and this brief summary illustrates effectively what Sainstbury meant by his dictum, that the second play of the trilogy had nothing to do with the first, though the third resumed and completed it. Quite literally, M. took up again, after the failure of his political career, the poetic task, or mission, which he had consciously laid down after his Ital. journey, 1638-9, and to which, deliberately, he had dedicated himself. Quite truly, and very remarkably, he refrained almost entirely from poetic composition during that middle period of his life. He collected and publd., 1645, his youthful Engl. and Lat. poems, the latest of which, *Lycidas*, had been written as early as 1637, for a collection of elegies in memory of Edward King, who was drowned in that year in the Irish channel ; and, though M. is said to have begun the composition of *Paradise Lost* in 1650, it is correct to say, that, between 1637 (*Lycidas*) and 1667 (*Paradise Lost*), with very insignificant exceptions, the great poet publd. no poetry. There was a complete break in his life, filled with controversy and polemics, consonant with the storms of the age, from which he came back late in middle life (and actually nearer to its close than he might have expected), with his resolve unchanged, and his capacity unimpaired, ' to leave ', as he had declared long since, ' something so written to after-times that they should not willingly let it die '. And this set purpose he fulfilled, comparably with Dante (q.v.) in imagination, and with Napoleon in his ' influence on the destinies and history of our literature ' (sir W. Raleigh, *Milton*, 264),

—though fallen on evil days,
On evil days though fallen, and evil tongues,
In darkness, and with dangers compass'd
    round,
And solitude.

Paradise Lost, vii, 25-8.

The record, thus summarized, is unique ; and, though, of course, there was only one Milton through all the changes of his experience and activities, though Cambridge and Horton and foreign acquaintance turned his thoughts to the *moral* needs of his times, and though such moralized reflection, concentrated on the high politics of a revolutionary age, was

turned to sublime poetic use in the councils of heaven and hell, and, again, in the drama of the fall of Samson, yet the historian of letters, foreshortening the perspective for his special studies, may observe this division into 3 parts, and, passing over the prose-works of the middle period—even the *Areopagitica*, 1644, with its purple passages on the liberty of printing,—is concerned chiefly with the youthful M., who had written the *Poems* collected in 1645, and with the old, blind poet of 1667 and 1671.

We come, then, first, to the first of these 3 vols., and to the poetry of 1626-37, which was resumed by the author of *Paradise Lost*, This collection included M.'s earliest poem, *On the Death of a Fair Infant*, the child of his sister Ann and E. Phillips (*supra*) ; the fine ode *On the Morning of Christ's Nativity*, 1629 ; *At a Solemn Music*, and others ; his sonnets, *To a Nightingale* (his only love-poem), *On Shakespeare* (' What needs my Shakespeare for his honour'd bones '), *On his having arrived at the Age of Twenty-three* (' How soon hath Time, the subtle Thief of Youth '), and others, 1630-1. It included, too, his Biblical paraphrases, some Ital. verse, and his Lat. poems, one of which celebrated his 21st birthday, and others of which display him more gay, more amorous, and more sociable than fate moulded him in later life. A sense of form and metre is evident in all these pieces ; the sonnets show his study of Ital. models, and sir Henry Newbolt, dismissing the diction of the *Nativity* stanzas, remarks on M.'s gift of ' natural magic, which takes common words, and suddenly in some way beyond explanation makes of them a strange and memorable picture, a strange and haunting melody, an irradiation, an enchantment '. But there was more than these *juvenilia* in the 1645 vol. It included *L'Allegro* and *Il Penseroso*, 1632, the twin praises of mirth and melancholy ; *Arcades*, 1633, with its sequent masque of *Comus*, 1634, for which Henry Lawes (1596-1662) wr. the music ; and *Lycidas*, 1637. These pastoral and elegiac exercises, fully steeped in the classical tradition reflected through the poetry and scholarship of the Renaissance (q.v.), yet radiantly Engl. in their circumstances and setting, mark M. as an authentic poet, who by study, travel, and self-dedication, was finding his vocation in life. He was true heir to ' sweetest Shakespeare, Fancy's child ', as M. called him in *Il Penseroso*, to Spenser, Phineas Fletcher (qq.v.), and the rest of the melodious Elizabethans, who married the open-air, candid Englishness of Chaucer (q.v.) with the art descended through Ronsard from Petrarch (qq.v.). We must not pause at these fruits of the Renaissance, save to note (1) that M. displayed his sense of the value of blank verse, which Marlowe (q.v.) had extended to drama from the first experiment of Sackville (q.v.) in *Gorboduc*, and which M. was to extend to epic poetry from the first experiment of Surrey (q.v.) in his *Æneid* ; (2) that M.'s subjects, though conventional in the sense that Mirth (*L'Allegro*), Melancholy (*Il Penseroso*), and Temperance or Chastity (*Comus*) had a long ancestry in European lit. (see s.vv. Folly, Death, Roman de la Rose, Richard Burton, for example), and that the pastoral treatment was similarly consecrated by use, were yet typical of the studious young poet, whose father hoped that he would enter the Church ; and (3) that *Lycidas*, the last of these early poems, and perhaps the greatest, 'a tissue of splendid passages, not unconnected, but sown cunningly together rather than woven in one piece ' (G. Saintsbury, *C.H.E.L.*, vii, 114), contained, in one famous passage, a forecast of the later and sterner M., and struck that polemical note which was to be the chief motive of his being in the middle period. Verses 113-31 of that poem, the episode of ' the Pilot of the Galilean Lake ', with his denunciation of the ' blind mouths ' (the *bishops* who would not *see*, and the *pastors* who ate instead of *feeding* ; cp. the splendid commentary on this passage in Ruskin, q.v., *Sesame and Lilies*), are clearly in anticipation of the prose-writings of the poet turned pamphleteer : *Of Reformation touching Church-Discipline in Engld.* (1641 ; about bishops troublesome to rulers) ; *The Reason of Church-Government urg'd against Prelatry* (1641 ; more personal in tone, ' with invective against some of his poetic contemporaries and exaltation of his own studies and purposes '), etc.

We pass over the intervenient prose, and the years of action in which it was composed. We pass direct from the young poet who laid aside his poetic mission in 1637 to the elderly poet who resumed it, when disappointed of his public hopes, embittered in his private life, totally blind since 1652, poor, unloved, and neglected. His enemies, the exulting royalists, whose ' savage clamour drowned both harp and voice ' (*Paradise Lost*, vii, 36), had, in sir W. Raleigh's words (*Milton*, 1900 ; p. 36), ' crippled only his left hand in silencing the politician, but his right hand, which had hung useless by his side for so many years while he served the State, was his own still, and wielded a more Olympian weapon ', Or, as M. himself wr., meditating the same monungonoo :

All is not lost—the unconquerable will,
And study of revenge, immortal hate,
And courage never to submit or yield,
And what is else not to be overcome.
Paradise Lost, i, 106-9.

But he, though blind of sight,
Despised, and thought extinguished quite,
With inward eyes illuminated,
His fiery virtue roused
From under ashes into sudden flame.
Samson Agonistes, 1687-91.

' His fiery virtue ' ; *Virtù*. We recall inevitably the noble lines, quoted s.v. Petrarch in this dict., and occurring in his ode to Italy : ' *Virtù* contro al Furore prenderà l'arme ' ; Courage shall take up arms against fury. We recall, too, that these lines were cited at the close of Machiavelli's (q.v.) *Prince*, and that Marlowe (q.v.), whose dramatic blank-verse was extended by M. to epos, had transported Machiavellism to the Engl. stage. This exaltation of *Virtù*, courage (' fiery virtue ' and the ' unconquerable will '), was very thoroughly in the tradition of the Renaissance, of which Satan and Samson, the heroes of

M.'s poems of 1667 and 1671, were thoroughly typical exemplars. Marlowe's Tamburlaine, Barabas and Guise are in the direct line of ascent to M.'s Satan,—of the same type, if not of the same stature as that ' apostate Angel ', whose fixed resolve it was ' to wage by force or guile eternal war ', and whose firm faith it was, that ' to be weak is miserable, doing or suffering '. Thus, it is an imperfect criticism which deems the Engl. puritan spirit the chief factor in M.'s poetic being. He was a puritan, and he toiled for 20 years in the van or the wake of Cromwell and his Round-heads ; his deity was the God of the Old Testament rather than of the New. But behind the puritan was the son of the Ital. Renaissance, equal to, if not surpassing, in scholarship the finest minds of that movement, and searching experience from pole to pole for conclusions adequate to his imagination. Continental opinion, which is so often in advance of (perhaps because it is detached from) native criticism of Engl. poets, has been reaching these conclusions in recent years, and special reference may be made in this context to the monograph, *Milton*, by prof. Denis Saurat, of Bordeaux (J. Cape, 1925).

The story of M.'s planning of *Paradise Lost* is probably familiar. The dream haunted him at Cambridge and at Horton ; he took it with him, when, like Chaucer (q.v.) before him, whom he studied so well, he visited the cities of Italy, and he cherished it, like the hope of immortality, in the long purgatory of his political activities. At first, the scheme took shape as an allegorical drama or mystery-play, with Gabriel, Eve, Conscience, Lucifer and Mercy among the persons. Then he seems to have abandoned this design in favour of an Engl. epic poem, dealing with the national hero, king Arthur (q.v.) and his Round Table. This was the subject, as we know, though overlaid with allegory and ornament, of Spenser's (q.v.) *Faerie Queen* ; and later it became the subject of Tennyson's (q.v.) *Idylls of the King*. But when, as Dr. Johnson (q.v.) writes, in his *Lives of the English Poets* ' after much deliberation, long choosing, and beginning late ', M. at last fixed on a subject for his masterwork, he returned to his youthful idea, recast in the form of an epic :

Of Man's first disobedience, and the fruit
Of that forbidden tree whose mortal taste
Brought death into the World, and all our woe,
With loss of Eden, till one greater Man
Restore us, and regain the blissful seat.
Paradise Lost, i, 1-5.

There, too, he had models and predecessors. Vondel (q.v.) had dramatized *Lucifer*, 1654, and Du Bartas (q.v.) had narrated the creation (*la Semaine*, 1578) ; and there are passages in M.'s epic, as in the choric songs of Vondel's play, where we may mark the effort, not always quite successful, to transpose the key of the Biblical narrative, and to attune it to that of a Carlovingian or an Arthurian epic poem as rendered by Ital. Virgil-votaries. The hero-ines of Boiardo and Ariosto (qq.v.) had enthralled the senses of man ; M.'s Eve should enthral super-sensibly. Romantic heroes (not excluding Gargantua) had proved themselves excellent trenchermen ; angels, too, should feast in the public eye, not 'in mist, the common gloss of theologians' (*Paradise Lost*, v, 435). Poets of chivalry had filled their pages with gorgeous processional descriptions; the poet of celestial knights would invent a retinue of one, to outshine all the rest. Reference should be made in this connection to *Paradise Lost*, v, 350-7, 377-85, and 433-50, whence it will be seen, further, that, in order to visualize Eve's succession to the love-sick maidens of medieval legend, M., too, had recourse to pagan myth, and called her lovelier than the goddesses whom Paris judged on Mt. Ida. So true is it that M., a second Dante in his mastery of the sublime (q.v.), celebrated, like a greater Tasso (q.v.), the exploits of the chivalry of heaven. He was the poet of Luther's Renaissance, in its double aspect as Renaissance and Reformation (see s.vv.). *Paradise Lost* is the greatest single draft of poetry which the tide of the Renaissance brought to Europe. And to his sacred epics (*Paradise Regain'd*, 4 bks., was publd., 1671), M. added the sacred play, *Samson Agonistes*, 1671, in which we hear the authentic accents of the blind poet's despair and recovery, and of the victory of will and mind over fate and matter. And, lastly, in connection with M.'s close contact with the classical Renaissance, moulding and modifying the Hebraism derived from his puritan associations and his selection of a Biblical theme, we may quote his own statement as to the metre of his epic poems : ' The measure is heroic English verse without rhyme, as that of Homer in Greek and of Virgil in Latin,—rhyme being no necessary adjunct or true ornament of poetry or good verse, in longer works especially, but the invention of a barbarous age '. This dictum should be compared with the distinctions drawn by the lawgivers of the Pleiad (q.v.) between the necessary requirements of ' longer ' and shorter works.

Paradise Lost is greater than its parts. It is the poem, as a whole, which conquers time. M.'s systems of theology and astronomy are not acceptable to-day (nor are the Æschylean, for that matter). But the further our knowledge recedes from the Ptolemaic universe and the Calvinist hell, the more freely we travel in imagination through the spaces of M.'s infinitude, and consort with the supermen of his creation. So, when his long day's work was done, and night had descended prematurely, M.'s second style surpassed his first. The elegiac note of *Lycidas* is not unmatched in Ital. poetry ; the masque of *Comus* is not beyond compare ; but the poems of M.'s second period (the third act, or play, in his life) resemble, in sir W. Raleigh's words, ' the achievement of Napoleon when he was winning the victories that changed the map of Europe '. So might his countrymen say of him, as Manoa said of Samson dead—

Samson hath quit himself
Like Samson, and heroicly hath finished
A life heroic.

Mingo Revulgo (1472): Span. anon. satire in 32 octosyllabic nine-line stanzas (*coplas*), formerly attributed to Mena (q.v.), who died 8 years before the date of its composition, and now generally ascribed by the weight of evidence to R. Cota (q.v.). The poem is dramatic in form, and even takes rank among the predecessors of Span. drama. The interlocutors are 2 shepherds, Mingo Revulgo (Domingo vulgus), representing the lower, and Gil Arribato (the elevated), representing the upper classes. Mingo blames the king (Henry iv of Castile) and his Portuguese mistress for causing the ruin of Spain, and Arribato exalts the middle-classes. The poem is an interesting and effective art-satire in the popular cause.

Minnesinger (Germ.): Lit., love-lyrists; Germ. poets of love-lyric (' Minnegesang '), founded at the courts of princes at the zenith of the age of chivalry, and dated conveniently from 1184 (though the class existed previously) when emperor Frederick Barbarossa held a great Whitsuntide festival at Mayence to celebrate with all the pomp of western chivalry the ceremony of the knighthood of his sons. ' Minne ' is correctly rendered ' love '; but the philologers point out, no doubt correctly, that the word is connected with the Sanscrit root *man*=thought ; and ' Minne ' at any rate conveyed a sense of thoughtful, or mindful, love, and was in fact the symbol of service to the Virgin Mary of the Roman Church. Thus, though Uhland (q.v.) declared that ' Minnesong sprang in the valleys of Provence, the child of love and spring ', his generous acknowledgment of its orig. should not disguise the fact that the Minnesinger surpassed the Troubadours. They overwent them precisely in the sense in which Spenser (q.v.) sought to ' overgo ' Ariosto (q.v.): the Minnesinger introduced a spiritual note into the sensuous lyric of Provence. There is less jealousy in Minnesong ; more longing, more faith, more steadfastness ; less brave colours, perhaps, but a more direct appeal to the heart. The Minnesinger have been called the masculine, the Troubadours the feminine voice of love-song. It is chiefly to the Germ. M. that we look for the passion of lyric verse in the 12th-13th cent. in Europe. Their practitioners numbered several hundreds, drawn chiefly from the knightly order, or from classes directly connected with it. They sang (like Herrick, q.v.) 2 kinds of love, sacred and profane, for God and women, ' Gottesminne ' and ' Frauenminne ', and they made noble numbers in each kind. Several of the great romantic epicists were Minnesinger too: Veldeke, Hartmann, Wolfram (qq.v.). The greatest of all was Walther (q.v.) von der Vogelweide, whose dream of love in the May-time of poetry has hardly, if ever, been surpassed. Particularly characteristic of Minnesong was the elemental, universal, ' I and thou ', the essential ' ich minne dich ' idea. Gottfried (q.v.) of Strassburg, though he stands at the head of the transition to a less courtly poetic inspiration, makes this lyrical cry effective in the prelude to his *Tristan* :

'Twas love alone that set the theme :
A lover and a lover's dream ;
A man, a woman ; woman, man ;
Tristan—Isold ; Isold—Tristan !

Minnesong, and its inspiration ' Minnedienst ', or the faithful service of this sublimated love, decayed and died with extraordinary rapidity. It descended (or, should we say, ascended ?)

from the court to the cottage, from the knight-hood to the peasantry. The courtly measures were employed for homely themes; Neidhart, Steinmar (qq.v.), and others poured the new wine into the old vessels, or grafted the fresh shoots of village-passion on the dying trunk of chivalric amours. The Germ. towns founded their guilds of minstrelsy, and the Meistersinger (q.v.) displaced the Minne-singer; the true descendant of the court-lyric, so vocal with springtide and young love, was the ' Volkslied ', or folksong, of the Germ. people, as perfect in sentiment as in form.

Minturno, Antonio Sebastiano (fl. 1560): It. critic. Wr. treatises (1558, 1564) on the art of poetry, in the course of the series of critical elucidations and expansions of Aristotle's (q.v.) text which occupied the scholarship of the 16th cent. M. was still bound by the literal Virgil-worship of Vida (q.v.), but the publica-tion of Aristotle's *Poetics* (1536, 1548, and in an Ital. version 1510; see s.vv. Robortello and Segni) modified in the direction of æsthetic principles the balder system of rules which had prevailed. M. was aware of the Unity of Time, but it was Castelvetro (q.v.) who gave the Unities (q.v.) their importance in classic drama.

Mirabaud, de, Jean Baptiste (1675-1760): Fr. *philosophe* (q.v.); secretary to the Fr. Academy (q.v.). The *Système de la Nature* (q.v.), 1770, was published under his name, though its authorship is now commonly ascribed to Hol-bach (q.v.).

Mirabeau, de, -i. Victor de Riquetti (1715-89): Fr. writer on economics; *marquis* by rank. (The illustrious and virile family of Riquetti migrated from Florence to France in the 13th cent.). M. wr., 1756, *l'Ami des Hommes*, which attracted considerable attention in the epoch of Montesquieu (q.v.). Its subsidiary title was *Traité de la Population*, and it became a serviceable weapon in the campaign of the economists, or physiocrats (q.v.), to whose leader, Quesnay (q.v.), M. was enthusiastically devoted. Indeed, with his lordly contempt for philosophizing and ratiocination, M. professed to owe all that he knew to Quesnay, the Socratic little physician of the king's mistress, and to derive the rest from his hereditary (and transmitted) genius for oratory and action. From M.'s meeting with Quesnay in July, 1757, the foundation of the physio-crats (Utopian economists) is properly dated; and their significance in the generation prior to the Fr. Revolution is obvious. M. was a curious type, not unknown in more recent times, of a reactionary in politics and a reformer in social legislation; if he had lived in Engld. towards the close of the 19th cent., he might have been classed as a Tory Democrat, or, later, as a Socialist member of the House of Lords. He was penalized for a work on *The Theory of Taxation*, 1760; ideas of progress and betterment filled his waking dreams, but he was by instinct a feudal monarchist and a ferocious tribal patriarch. To the Fr. Revolution, M. made a further notable con-tribution in the person of

-ii. Honoré Gabriel de Riquetti (1749-91): Fr. orator, statesman, man of letters; son of above; *comte* by rank. M.'s sudden death (2 April, 1791), when he was president of the Constituent Assembly, while Louis xvi was still nominally king of France, was a great loss to his country in the early stages of the Revolution. Here, however, we are not concerned with M.'s political career, nor with the despotism which his father exercised over him (despite his humanitarian views on political economy), nor with the record of his debts, vices, or scandals. It is for his speeches and letters, fiery, eloquent, and brilliant, that M. has a place in literary history; and esp. for his *Lettres à Sophie*, in which every aspect of his great talents dis-played itself, and which combine the frank self-revelation of Rousseau (q.v.) with the moral fervour of a social and political reformer.

Miranda, de, Francisco de Saa (c. 1485-1558): Port. poet; Italianate. Contributed poetry in the older courtly fashion to the *Cancioneiro* of Resende (q.v.), but returned from a visit to Italy (1521-26) as a convert to the measures and forms of the Ital. Renaissance, and composed epistles, eclogues, etc., in good Castilian verse, anticipating and afterwards emulating the reforms introduced by Boscan and Garcilasso (qq.v.), whose death he deplored in an elegy, *Nemoroso*. It is due to this elegy that a slight confusion arose as to the refer-ence of the pastoral name, Nemoroso. M. used it here to indicate Garcilasso; but Garcilasso himself, in his first eclogue, indicated Boscan by Nemoroso, and was so understood by Cervantes, *Don Quixote*, ii, 67. The name Boscan (cf. ' bosky ') obviously suggests Lat. *nemus*, a wood.

Mirandola, della, Giovanni Pico (1463-94): It. humanist and neo-Platonist. Born at Miran-dola, where his family were feudal lords; visited universities at Bologna and Paris; came to Florence in 1482; visited Rome, 1486, where he publd. ' 900 theses ', or philo-sophical propositions, which he was prepared to defend against ecclesiastical authority; 13 of these were condemned by pope Innocent viii, and M. had to retire to Spain; the ban was removed by pope Alexander vi in 1493, and M. died at Florence on the day (17 Nov., 1494) of the invasion of France by king Charles viii. M. was a remarkable figure in his own day, and deeply impressed later humanists, such as sir Thomas More in the 16th and W. Pater (qq.v.) in the 19th cent. Ficino (q.v.), head of the Platonic Academy in Florence, greeted the arrival of M., with the stamp of beauty, the reputation of scholar-ship, and the glamour of rank and youth upon him, as a kind of advent; the record is con-tained in the dedication to Lorenzo de'Medici (q.v.) of F.'s translation of Plotinus; and Reuchlin (q.v.) was influenced by M. in the direction of the study of Hebrew and of the Cabbala, in which labours M. is memorable as a pioneer. Apart from his personal fascina-tion, which, by all accounts, was exceptional, M.'s position in temperament and mind was of particular interest by its equipoise between the contrary tendencies of Medici and Savon-arola. He abandoned the lure of pleasure which had drawn him in youth, even destroy-ing his Ital. love-poems, and devoted himself to a mystical philosophy, as learned as it was uncritical, the object of which was to attain the underlying truth of all systems of knowledge, and to reconcile Christianity with Platonism. Though deeply spiritual and really scientific, according to the confused standards of the period, and though founded on close study of Gk. and Hebr. in the originals, when such recourse to sources was rare, M.'s works, scholastic in their tendency, are of far less moment than the part which he bore in forwarding the aims of the Florentine Academy, where he reigned, during his few years of ascendency, by the brightness of his spirit and his social charm.

Mirror for Magistrates, A (16th cent.): Engl. collection of tragical tales in verse, dealing with the fate of fabled and true British and Engl. princes, complementary to Lydgate's (q.v.) transln. (*Fall of Princes*) of Boccaccio's (q.v.) *de Casibus Virorum Illustrium*; issued in gradually enlarged edns., 1554-59, -63, -71, -74, -78, -87, 1610. The first editor was Wm. Baldwin, but the *Mirror* owed much of its interest to the advice and contributions of T. Sackville (q.v.), first earl of Dorset, who wr. the *Buckingham* poem for the edn. of 1563, and the *Induction* to that edn.; the chief value of the *M.* resides in those pieces. Its popularity was well maintained through the 17th cent.; and its hist. importance is still recognized. Itself an imitation and continuation, it gave rise to imitations in its turn, and, apart from such imitative collections, it supplied material to Daniel, Drayton, Fletcher (qq.v.) and other playwrights, including Shakespeare (q.v.), *Rape of Lucrece*.

Mistral, Frederic (1830-1914): Fr. poet; the son of a peasant at Maillaume, he learnt Provençal songs at his mother's knee, and, choosing the career of a poet, lived to revive in Southern France the departed glory of her Provençal lit. (see s.v.). He had to revive it out of a dialect into a living literary language, and he owed much in this respect, as he always dutifully acknowledged, to his schoolmaster, Roumanille. M.'s first considerable work was his epic, *Miréio*, 1859, which inspired Gounod's opera, *Mireille*; its freshness was noted by Lamartine, q.v., who called it 'a breath of the morning'. *Calendau* followed, 1866; *Lis Iselo d'Or*, 1876; and *Nerto*, 1886, compared by some admirers with the epic-romance of Ariosto (q.v.). M. founded, with Roumanille and others, the Society of the Félibrige, for the encouragement of Provençal studies and spent many years in compiling a Provençal dict., a veritable labour of love. On M.'s 83rd birthday, M. Poincaré delivered an illuminating address in his honour, referring to him as 'cher et illustre maître' and as having 'earned the gratitude of the Republic and of France'.

Mitford, Mary Russell (1785-1855): Engl. novelist; playwright; highly praised by Ruskin (q.v.); invented a new genre of lit. by her sketches of country life in the *Lady's Magazine*, 1812; expanded into *Our Village*, 5 vols. Wr. tragedies: *Julian*, *Rienzi*, and others; *Recollections of a Literary Life*, 1852.

Moe, Jörgen (1815-82): Norse poet; folklorist; bp. of Christianssand. Collaborated with Asbjörnsen (q.v.) in the collection of native

tales, familiar in Dasent's (q.v.) version as *Popular Tales from the Norse*. Wr., too, lyrical verse, finally publd. in 2 vols., 1877, 'as small, as unassuming, as exquisite as violets' (Gosse, *Lit. of Northern Europe*, 26).

Möller, Paul Martin (1794-1838): Dan. poet. Wr. *A Danish Student's Tale*, which is full of merriment and sentiment, and students' songs which abound in the same qualities. As prof. of philosophy in Oslo, and, later, in Copenhagen, M. lived the life which he described, and was eager to train the young in the virtues of patriotism, sanity, and love of beauty. These virtues shine in his sheaf of verses; and M. is also remembered for his verse-transln. of the *Odyssey*, the first in the Dan. tongue.

Möser, Justus (1720-94): Germ. publicist. M. held high offices of State in his native city of Osnabrück, and wr. its history in a work which is a model of prose-style and hist. skill and judgment. His contributions to the local press were collected under the title of *Patriotic Fantasies*, and a certain stateliness of patriotism, opposed to the more cosmopolitan tendencies of Romance (q.v.), was a mark of the man and of his writings.

Moi, dis-je, et c'est assez: 'I, I say, and that's enough'. Said by Medea, in the *Médée* of Corneille (q.v.), and since famous as the most telling statement of the individualist attitude, characteristic of the Cornelian stage and of the Cartesian philosophy. (See s.vv. Descartes, Cogito).

Molbech, Christian Knud Frederik (1821-88): Dan. poet. Wr. *Collected Poems* (second edn.), 1879, which evinced a rare mastery of lyrical expression, and wr., too, some well-known plays, including *Ambrosius*, 1878. M.'s most notable contribution to Dan. letters was a transln. of the *Divine Comedy* of Dante.

Molière (1622-73): stage-name of Jean Baptiste Poquelin, Fr. comic dramatist, actor, and actor-manager; by common consent, the Terence of France; 'the most exactly, fully, and completely French of all the writers in our seventeenth century. . . . Hardly was he dead, when all attacks, all jealousies, all reservations ceased; he was ranked as a genius, inimitable and without equal, and never perhaps has a reputation been sustained as consistently as his' (Lanson, *Hist. de la Lit. Fr.*, 530); 'If we leave purely poetic merit out of the question, and restrict the definition of comedy to the dramatic present-ment of the characters and incidents of actual life, in such a manner as at once to hold the mirror up to nature and to convey lessons of morality and conduct, we must allow Molière the rank of the greatest comic writer of all the world' (Saintsbury, *Hist. Fr. Lit.*, 286). There are 3 threads to follow in these eulogies: i, M.'s place in Fr. lit.; ii, his place in world-literature; and iii, the point of the 'attacks' and 'jealousies', which pursued him till the day of his death, or, more precisely, of his burial, which took place secretly at night-time. We may take the third, and least important, first. M.'s life was neither happy nor easy. He had the advantage of a good education, and the benefit of a small com-petency, and with these endowments he threw in his lot, 1643, with a theatrical company, *L'illustre Théâtre*, in which the Béjart family was prominent. He lost his money, but not his zest, and in 1646 his company went on tour to Nantes, Limoges, Bordeaux, Toulouse, Narbonne, Paris (1651), Lyons, Rouen, and elsewhere. Several pieces of his own, including *l'Etourdi* and *le Dépit Amoureux*, date from this period; besides these, the repertory contained mainly farces, patched and adapted by M., who, like Shakespeare, was trained to play-writing behind the footlights. On 24 Oct., 1658, M. played at the Louvre before the court, and in the following year, 18 Nov., 1659, he followed up his *début* with his first great comedy *les Précieuses ridicules*. Richelieu's theatre at the Palais Royal was leased to him in 1661, and from that date his fortune was made, and his misfortunes began. In 1662, he m. Armande Béjart, a member of the family of his fellow-actors, and the marriage proved unhappy. In the following year, he was accused at court of having m. his natural daughter, and king Louis xiv replied in 1664 by standing sponsor to M.'s son, and by installing M. at the head of the future Comédie Française, or the national Théâtre Français of Paris (united in 1680). But neither royal favour nor the powerful support of Boileau (q.v.) could save M. from the miserable experience of spite, jealousy, and detractation. He was an actor, and his profession was looked down upon. He could neither become a member of the French Academy, nor sit as an equal at the king's table; and to these social slights were added his own domestic troubles, and the accusations of plagiary and worse on the part of literary rivals. His *Tartufe*, 1664 (M. spelt it 'Tartuffe'; the Academy preferred *Tartufe*), was the occasion of a 5 years' interdict, on account of its alleged irreligious tendency, and, despite the good will of the king and the more solid favours of his brother, 'Monsieur', M. was often hard-pressed to maintain his serene outlook on the human comedy. He died, 17 Feb., 1673, during the performance of his *Malade Imaginaire*.

We come, next, to M.'s place in Fr. lit.; and, first, it is necessary to deal with an outpost of that position: was he, or was he not, 'mauvais écrivain' (a bad writer), as has been maintained from La Bruyère and Fénelon (qq.v.) downwards? The answer is, certainly not. The accusation rested to some extent on a narrow interpretation of M.'s indifference to the standard of diction laid down for polite society by the precious (q.v.) writers, and on an imperfect appreciation of M.'s dramatic verisimilitude. His characters talked their own language, and were true to the class from which they sprang; and to critics trained to the fastidious choice of words by the heroes of current romantic fiction, this popular, or natural, speech might well seem less than literate. We have also to take account of the fact that the guardians of public morals, which were confused with standards of art and letters, objected to the spirit of curiosity and exploration which distinguished the writings of M., and of other leaders of the naturalistic revival in his age. To such

keepers of royal and other consciences as Bossuet (q.v.), for example, M.'s human comedy, and its analogues in the maxims and memoirs of his contemporaries, were types of free-thought, or libertinism, and M. himself was a chief of the *libertins* (q.v.). And a word here may be added about the plagiary M. frankly acknowledged, 'je prends mon bien où je le trouve', and in this happy disposition towards the treasures laid up in Plautus, Terence, Boccaccio, and the tales of Italy and France, he agreed with Shakespeare and others. He was deeply in debt to the Span. school of comedy recently founded by Lope de Vega (q.v.); and it is true that he purloined in places whole scenes from Bergerac and Boisrobert (qq.v.), who might themselves have borrowed them from Spain. Such practices would now be indefensible; but the justification is more obvious to-day than it was to his contemporaries: M. survives; his tributaries are chiefly remembered in that connection. Moreover, invention in the 17th cent. meant new treatment and not new plot. These preliminaries stated, the grand and simple fact remains that M. created Fr. comedy, and that, as he made it, it has since been developed. There had been farce in France, and there had been stiff comedies (s.v. Larivey), and there had been the burlesque interludes imported from Spain (s.v. Scarron); but the discovery of comedy in real life, the invention of the comic spirit, as analysed by Meredith (q.v.), and its representation in stage-plays, was distinctively the contribution of M. to the lit. of his own country and generation. We may note, for what it is worth, the method of representation by types, opposed to that of representation by individuals, as distinguishing the Fr. dramatic genius from the Engl.; we may note that M.'s miser was avaricious, and his hypocrite hypocritical, and that their speech and action were directed to the single end of delineating these qualities, with some loss to complexity of character; and in this connection we may refer to the universal comparison of M.'s Tartufe with Shakespeare's Falstaff. M.'s method excluded the surprises which life's infinite humours supply. His characters were true to type, and were so far untrue to life. So far, too, by this deliberate simplification, M. was enabled almost without effort to preserve the dramatic Unities (q.v.), which loomed so large on the critics' horizon in his day. He did not bother about these rules; 'the rule of rules', he declared, 'is to please;' but he found that they observed themselves, and that, for the simple truths he sought to convey, there was little or no necessity to extend the time beyond a day, or the place beyond probability, or to multiply the action. His aim was to show up the follies, pedantries, affectations, hypocrisies, and delusions of ordinary men and women, in their habits as they lived: to strip vice of its cloak, to make pretence ridiculous, and exalt honour, sincerity, resolution, and grace. This aim, consistently followed, gives M. his place in world-literature. He filled his stage with universal types; he appealed to humanity at large: the 'Précieuses' of his play were the frequenters of the Hôtel de

Rambouillet (q.v.), but the preciosity which he laughed at is common to all times and climes, and has its seat in the vanity of every other man and woman. Hence it is that M., like Shakespeare, in the stock phrase, is 'full of quotations'. The caps which he fashioned always fit : 'nous avons changé tout cela ' ; ' que diable allait-il faire dans cette galère ? ' ; ' tu l'as voulu, Georges Dandin ' ; again and again, we use these counters, because once for all M. coined them for currency, in typical, recurring situations, which he arrested in the comedy of human life. M. is authentically Fr., in his directness, his insight, his incisiveness, his clear-cut, crystal-pure expression ; in all the qualities, by which, without conscious effort, he recommended himself to the critical favour of Boileau ; he is humanity's, in his reflection of the human spectacle ; in his employment of the stage, not for ribaldry, revel, or burlesque, not for pompous declamation or high tragedy ; but just for the common play of common characters, for the common conflict of common rights and wrongs ; like a plain, sympathetic country clergyman, teaching moral lessons by examples drawn from the experience of his parish, and aware that ' a verse may find him who a sermon flies '. The list of M.'s plays includes : l'Étourdi ; le Dépit Amoureux, 1656 ; le Docteur Amoureux, 1657 ; les Précieuses Ridicules, 1659 ; Sganarelle, 1660 ; l'École des Maris and les Facheux, 1661 ; l'École des Femmes, 1662 ; le Mariage Forcé, 1664 ; Tartufe, 1664, and again 1669 ; Don Juan, 1665 ; l'Amour Médecin (a ballet-comedy), 1665 ; le Misanthrope, 1666 ; le Médecin malgré lui, 1666 ; Georges Dandin, 1668 ; l'Avare, 1668 ; le Bourgeois Gentilhomme, 1670 (who can forget Jourdain's lessons in ' prose ', or his father's patent of nobility ?) ; Psyche, a ballet-tragedy, in collaboration with Corneille, Quinault, and Lulli (qq.v.) : one of the most remarkable instances of collaboration in literary history, 1671 ; les Femmes Savantes, 1672, and le Malade Imaginaire, 1673. Versailles and the Théâtre Français were the chief scenes of his triumphant first-nights ; at the former, mainly the ballets and masques, at the latter the dramas proper. It will be observed that M.'s titles deal largely with the institution of marriage and the physician's profession. It was from these 2 sources that ' the contemplator ', as M. was called, derived his most timely and telling effects.

Molina, de, Tirso (c. 1570-1648): Span. dramatist; nom-de-guerre of Gabriel Tellez, who habitually used it in lieu of his patronymic. M. followed the common course of education at Alcalá (q.v.) and preferment in the church ; and it is probable that his dramatic work was publd. (in 5 vols. ; 1627, -34, -35 bis, -36) out of his true name in deference to the Inquisition, which found cause to prohibit many of his plays. Of these the most famous outside Spain has been el Burlador de Sevilla (' The Deceiver of Seville ') ; its fame being due to the character of the typical libertine and fearless trifler, since immortalized as ' Don Juan '. Traces of this character are found in Cueva's (q.v.) Infamador and in Vega's (q.v.) ' Money makes the Man ' ; but the full delineation is first found

in the gay ' Deceiver of Seville ', and passed thence into the possession of Europe. Shadwell's (q.v.) Libertine, 1676, Molière's (q.v.) Festin de Pierre, 1665, Mozart's opera and Bryon's (q.v.) poem are all created in the likeness of this Burlador, though none of them quite attains to what Kelly (Lit. espagn., 353) calls ' the patrician intrepidity ' of the original. It is a great achievement to have begotten a dramatic type of such long and distinguished descent ; and it is a matter of regret to have to add that M.'s title to the honour of this achievement is not fully established by recent critics. They point out that the Burlador was publd. in none of M.'s 5 vols., but in a collection of ' twelve new plays by Lope de Vega, Carpio and other writers ', 1630. There it bears M.'s name ; but a new version discovered in 1878 bears the greater name of Calderon (q.v.), and the correct ascription must be left in doubt. Even without the authorship of Don Juan, M.'s claims to renown are considerable. His comedy ' Don Gil of the Green Pantaloons ' (de las Calzas verdes) is a diverting and ingenious piece of intrigue, and his |' Bashful Man at Court ' (Vergonzoso en Palacio) runs it close. Fr. playwrights, such as Scarron and Montfleury (qq.v.) found ample founts of inspiration in M., whose reputation has increased rather than diminished in course of years. Against ' the needless and shameless indelicacy of some of his stories ' Ticknor (ii, 328) sets M.'s more uniform merits of ' an invention which seems never to tire ; a most happy power of gay narration ; an extraordinary command of his native Castilian ; and a rich and flowing versification in all the varieties of metre demanded by the audiences of the capital '.

Molinet, Jean (died 1507): Fr. rhetoriqueur (q.v.); librarian to archduchess of Austria. Wr. verses in complicated measures, characterized by the affectation and artificiality of the school, and an Art and Science of Rhetoric, 1493.

Molinos, de, Miguel (1640-97): Span. divine ; Jesuit ; founder of the ecclesiastical heresy of Quietism (q.v.) ; went to Rome, 1665, where he wr. the ' Spiritual Guide ' (Guia espiritual), 1675, which became a powerful weapon to divide Fr. church opinion under Fénelon and Bossuet (qq.v.) in the hands of mme. de Guyon (q.v.). M. ' was always bidding the soul rise above sacraments and attributes and dogmas, beyond the Trinity and the Incarnation to " a view, wholly obscure and indistinct and general, of the Divine Essence as it was ". . . . All hope and fear, all thought and action, all life and feeling, must be laid aside ; the soul must enwrap itself in the " soft and savoury sleep of nothingness, wherein it receives in silence, and enjoys it knows not what " ' (C.M.H., v, 88 ; by visct. St. Cyres). Plainly, this quietist doctrine was derived from the thought of Span. mystics such as S. Teresa and Leon (qq.v.) ; plainly, too, it contained the seeds of what the Church would condemn as heresy, and M. was convicted in 1687 ; and plainly, it has affinities with Dutch and Engl. Pietism (q.v.), and with every manifestation of ' that form of Transcendental Feeling which manifests itself as solemn sense of Timeless Being—of "That which was, and is, and ever shall be ", overshadowing us with its presence ' (J. A. Stewart, *The Myths of Plato*, 22), in which the heart of all poetry resides, from Plato to Wordsworth. (See, too, the same learned writer, on ' Platonism in English Poetry ' ; *English Lit. and the Classics*, Oxford, 1912). This takes us a long way from M.'s ' Spiritual Guide ' ; but the chain is consecutive. (Shorthouse, q.v., author of *John Inglesant*, issued *Golden Thoughts from the ' Spiritual Guide* ', 1884).

Molza, Francesco Maria (1489-1544): It. poet. Wr. luscious verse of not edifying quality in Lat. and in the vernacular, including sonnets (q.v.), ' canzoni ', and courtesan-pieces, *Ninfe Tiberine*. Transld. *Æneid* of Virgil into Ital. blank verse (q.v.); his version was publd. at Venice, 1541, under the name of card. Ippolito de'Medici, and probably served as a model to Surrey (q.v.), thus linking M., for all his poverty of imagination and excess of ornament, to the great chain of poetry which is adorned by the names of Marlowe, Shakespeare, Milton, and Wordsworth.

Mommsen, Theodor (1817-1903). Germ. historian and antiquary ; member of the Prussian school of Treitschke (q.v.) ; wr. *History of Rome*, transld. into Engl. by W. P. Dickson.

Moncada, de, Francisco (1585-1635): Span. historian ; count d'Osona by rank ; sometime governor of the Span. Netherlands. Wr., 1623, *The Expedition of the Catalans and Aragonese against the Turks and Greeks*, a campaign of the 14th cent., admirably suited by its spirit of wild adventure to M.'s bold and picturesque style. Gibbon (q.v.) complains that M. never cites his authorities ; but it is clear that he had read Mendoza in MS., and relied on the contemporary chronicle of Ramon Montaner (q.v.).

Monluc, de, Blaise (1502-77): Fr. memoirist ; soldier of fortune ; supported the royal cause as page, archer, captain, governor of Sienna, infantry general, marshal of France successively ; sustained terribly disfiguring wound after nearly 50 years of fighting, and dictated his *Commentaires* (reprinted, 5 vols., 4 and 5 containing M.'s correspondence, 1864). M. was an ideal captain, rather than a general, and king Henry iv of France called his *Commentaires* a ' soldier's Bible '. It was at the same time a vivid account of the men and events of his active life, and has not unjustly been compared with the military ' commentaries ' of Cæsar.

Monroy y Silva, de, Cristobal (1612-49): Span. dramatist ; displayed the promise of great talent in the school of Vega (q.v.).

Montagu, Mary Wortley- (1689-1762): Engl. letter-writer ; wit ; daughter of first duke of Kingston, and bore courtesy-title of lady ; her mother's family was Feilding, ancestors of H. Fielding (q.v.) ; m., 1712, Edward W.-M., who was appointed, 1716, ambassador to the Porte. Lady Mary's *Turkish Letters*, 1716-8, are the best of the vast collection of MSS., which she bequeathed to her daughter, lady Bute, to whom, 1739-61, the bulk of her correspondence was addressed from abroad. Like mme. de Sévigné, q.v., not only in the fact that she wr. her letters to a daughter, but also to some extent in the topics which she adorned, ' her letters came more and more to resemble the epistles of that incomparable model ' (*C.H.E.L.*, viii, 245). Lady Mary, who lived in Twickenham for many years between the Turkish embassy period and her retirement abroad, quarrelled with Pope (q.v.), her former friend, and was busy with controversy against him, in which Swift (q.v.) also took part. Her *Town Eclogues* (or *Court Poems*, 1716) in heroic verse were of no great value.

Montaigne, de, Michel Eyquem (1533-92): Fr. essayist. M., whose name was derived from the *château* in Perigord where he was born, and of which he was *sieur* by title, was the son of a municipal dignitary at Bordeaux, and as parliamentary counsel in that city was colleague to E. de La Boétie (q.v.), whose friend he became. He m., 1565, Françoise de la Chassage, who bore him 6 daughters, of whom only one survived. M. retired from the bar, 1570 ; received order of St. Michael, 1571 ; travelled in Germany and Italy ; was elected mayor of Bordeaux ; received the king of Navarre at his *château*, 1584, and though loyal to Henry iii, recognized that the king of Navarre would succeed him. Was in Paris, 1588, where he met mlle. de Gournay, who became his adoptive daughter, and the first editor of his works ; met, too, Charron (q.v.) on the same visit. It was, thus, from 1570 onwards that M. set himself free for the congenial labour of reflection, comparison, and judgment, which solidified, 1580, in his *Essais*, books i and ii (Bordeaux). A fifth edn., augmented by bk. iii and by 600 additions to the former bks., appeared in Paris, 1588 ; and, in 1595, mlle. de Gournay issued a definitive edn., with the author's MS. and marginal notes, enlarged by one-third. This was the source of the Didot edn. of Naigeon, Paris, 4 vols., 1802. The process of recension suggests a more careful design and plan than the work actually reveals. Bk. i contains 57 essays in a little more than 500 pp. ; bk. ii 36 essays in a little less than 500 pp., and one essay, transld. from a Lat. treatise on natural theology by a Spaniard (*Apologie de Raimond Sebond*), of about 300 pp. ; bk. iii, 13 essays in about 550 pp. It may be stated with fair certainty that M.'s first method was to write annotations on selected texts ; these were the brief contents of bk. i. Presently, his own thought expanded into the lengthier contents of bk. ii ; and, finally, abandoning the method of doctrine, he wove his own philosophy as he went along, and composed the essays of bk. iii. Thus, M. founded the essay, as a definite literary form, even if the invention of the name is not to be ascribed to him. And the essay in this sense represented a step backwards in Fr. prose-composition. Calvin and even Rabelais (qq.v.) had developed prose style by sentence-building ; Calvin especially, in his Fr. transln. of his Lat. treatise on Christianity, had been careful to adjust the weight and study the structure of his sentences. M. went backward in order to go forward. Though he could be stately in places, he aimed, not at classical phrase-making, but at reproducing life in letters ; the essay-style is Montaigne ; we may call it colloquial, easy, vivid, expressive

—any epithet that suits: the fact is, M. created it, and imposed it by its suitability on his successors. It is the talk of a well-informed man on topics which he made his own by wide reading and deep reflection; too wide and too deep for dogmatism. His praise of Amyot (q.v.) is a happy illustration of his taste in style, which he has himself defined as a preference for simple talking, the same on paper as by word of mouth; more brusque and vehement than delicate and painted; difficult rather than monotonous; without affectation; bold and in undress; rather soldierly than forensic or pedagogic. Lastly, as to the contents, or, rather, since they are so multifarious, as to the general tone and effect of M.'s essays. 'It is an absolute and quasi-divine perfection, to know how to enjoy one's being loyally': this is M.'s conclusion of the whole matter, and to-day, as, even more, in the harassed France of the 16th cent. in which he wr., it is far from the faith of a mere sceptic, though M. is sometimes characterized by this epithet. Scepticism he displayed in plenty; it was inevitable to a contemporary of Calvinism and Rabelaisianism, to the genial spectator of views so much opposed, to the disciple of the new learning which Erasmus had imposed upon the institutions of the Middle Ages. Everything was in solution, including opinions on life, and conduct, or how to live. Thus it happened that M. became the accredited leader of the incredulous, and that the so-called *Libertins* (q.v.), or freethinkers, count their descent from him through St. Evremond and Bayle to Voltaire (qq.v.), and that his name is therefore linked with the ideas of emancipation and questionings which prepared the soil of thought for the furrowing ploughshare of the Fr. Revolution (q.v.). It has been well said that the work of the *Libertins* and the *Philosophes* (q.v.) was to ask questions, not to supply answers; and in this task M. was pioneer. But the philosophy, or the way of life, which M. constructed as a reasonable plan which every man might apply to his own fortunes, was by no means a sceptic's way of life. Scepticism was to teach independence, hedonism, cheerfulness; its positive side was to be cultivated more strenuously than its negative conclusions; there was a 'loyal enjoyment of being', the knowledge of which was the art of life. When plague visited Bordeaux, in the last year of M.'s mayoralty, M., like Boccaccio (q.v.) at Florence, found it due to himself to shun the contagion. He was right. It was due, as he believed; but the creed excluded that other creed of renunciation, altruism, abnegation, which leads to a higher way of life. Egotism—M.'s characteristic—is, after all, only the philosophy of selfishness; and the extraordinary attraction of the prince of essayists who never pretended or posed, and who was, accordingly, better than he seemed, does not blind us to the limitations of his genius. Voltaire unfolds from M., as the flower from the bud. 'Que sais-je'? was the motto of M., and the constant note of 'honest doubt' in lit. (say, from Shakespeare's *Hamlet* to Tennyson's *In Memoriam*), is directly to be traced to the

Gascon squire. Florio (q.v.) transld. M. into Engl.; Bacon (q.v.) followed M.'s lead of writing essays and comments, designed to bring wisdom 'home to men's business and bosoms', and was associated with him through his elder brother, Anthony Bacon, who was at Bordeaux, 1583-91 (see Lee, *Fr. Renaissance in Engld.*, 172); and Shakespeare's knowledge of and debt to the *Essais* is examined by J. M. Robertson, *Montaigne and Shakspere*.

Montalembert, de, Charles Forbes René (1810-70): Fr. writer on politics and religion; orator; *comte* by rank, and a peer of France. M. was born in exile, in London, of an Engl. mother, and visited Ireland in 1830; the experience may have contributed to form his character as a passionate champion of oppressed nationalities: Ireland, Poland, Greece. He founded *l'Avenir* (q.v.) with Lamennais (q.v.), whom he accompanied on the abortive visit to Rome. Thence he went to Germany, where he wr. a *History of St. Elizabeth of Hungary*, 1836; and *Vandalism and Catholicism in Art*, 1839. M. supported Louis Buonaparte in 1848, but retired from public life shortly after, and wr. in retirement his great work, *The Monks of the West from St. Benedict to St. Bernard*, transld. into Engl. by Mrs. Oliphant (q.v.). *The Pope and Poland, A Nation in Mourning* (i.q. Poland again), and *The Political Future of Engl.* were among other works from his pen, always ready to defend with religious fervour the sacred cause of religious liberty.

Montalvan, de, Juan Perez (1602-38): Span. dramatist; friend, eulogist, and biographer of Lope de Vega (q.v.), and, in a sense, his spiritual child. Wr., 1624, *Orfeo*, a poem, composed in rivalry to that of Jauregui (q.v.), and said on insufficient evidence to have been the work of Vega himself. M.'s rivalry with Jauregui was a far less serious matter than his literary quarrel with Quevedo (q.v.; M.'s father, Alonso Perez, the king's bookseller at Madrid, not the pastoral poet of that name, had issued without permission Quevedo's picaresque novel *Buscon*); in the course of that dispute Quevedo pleasantly prophesied that M. would die insane, a prophecy which was literally fulfilled. Overwork is alleged as the cause of the disease. Of the many plays, *autos*, etc., which M. composed in the course of his short life, the best remembered is his drama, *The Lovers of Teruel*, founded on a tradition of tragic love, utilized also by Molina (q.v.) and others.

Montalvo, de, Garci Rodriguez (fl. 1500; Ordoñez and Gutierrez occur as variants of Rodriguez early in the 16th cent.): Span. chivalric romancer; governor of Medina del Campo. M. issued at Saragossa, 1508, a Castilian version of *The Four Bks. of the Virtuous Knight Amadis de Gaula* (see s.v. Amadis), of which bks. i-iii were said to have been 'corrected' by M. and bk. iv to be original. The bibliography of this famous Welsh romance, naturalized in the Peninsula, and grafted on the stock of modern fiction by its Fr. descent through Herberay (q.v.) in the 16th cent. is still obscure; but M.'s part in it is notable, though his addition of the *Exploits of Esplandian* (the son of Amadis and Oriana) is far inferior to the bks. to which he added it : a point of criticism which was seized long ago by Cervantes (q.v. ; see *Don Quixote*, i, 6) who consigned M.'s bk. to the bonfire from which he let the barber rescue the true *Amadis*.

Montalvo, de, Luis Galvez (*c.* 1550-1590) : Span. pastoralist ; Italianate ; a friend and fellow-townsman of Cervantes (q.v.), who yet could find (*Don Quixote*, i, 6 ; in the famous chapter on bks. worth keeping) no more distinguished eulogy for M.'s *Pastor de Filida*, 1582, than ' this is not a shepherd, but a very complete courtier '. Its author, too, was a very complete courtier at the minor ducal court of Santillana. Later, he transld. the *Tears of St. Peter*, by Tansillo (q.v.), and left unfind. a transln. of the *Jerusalem* of Tasso (q.v.).

Montausier, de, Julie (1607-71) : Fr. literary hostess ; *née* d'Angennes de Rambouillet (see s.v. ; her mother was the famous leader of the precious, q.v., circle of letters in the reigns of kings Louis xiii and xiv) ; *marquise* by her marriage to Charles de Ste.-Maure, duc de Montausier* (1610-90 ; governor to the dauphin, 1668, and founder of the series of classics *in usum Delphini* ; his funeral oration was pronounced by Fléchier, q.v.). Julie d'Angennes was the heroine of the famous *Guirlande de Julie* (see s.v.), or anthology of verse presented to her on 1 Jan., 1641, by her future husband, who had wooed her for 14 years ; and she is prominent in the memoirs of the time.

Montchrétien, de, Antoine (*c.* 1575-1621) : Fr. dramatist ; political economist. A duel drove him from Fr. soil, 1605-11, when he visited Holland and Engld. ; took part in the religious wars of his generation, and was shot as a rebel in the Huguenot cause, 7 Oct., 1621. It was during his enforced residence in Engld. that M., whose adventurous and unsettled life seemed so far removed from economic speculations, made the observations on the relations of trade and industry to national policy which he turned to excellent account in his *Traité de l'économie politique*, 1615 (re-issued, 1889). M. is properly credited with the invention of this term, for the adjective and noun had never previously been combined in this signification ; and nearly 100 years elapsed before the science, invented by a Frenchman from his studies on Engl. soil, was resumed and amplified by Engl. writers. M.'s programme was protection and colonization, and the merit of his pioneer work lay partly in his sturdy recognition of the rights of the wealth-producing classes. M.'s liberal treatise is still one of the most readable bks. on the subject which he introduced. But it is as the successor to Jodelle (q.v.) and as the fellow-poet to Garnier (q.v.) in the development of Fr. tragedy on classic lines, that M., the fighting Huguenot and thinking economist, made his chief contribution to lit. ' If Garnier may be regarded as the Corneille of the drama of the French Renaissance, Montchrétien deserves to be regarded as its Racine ' (Lee, *Fr. Renaissance in Engld.*, 405) ; and Lanson (*Hist. de la Lit. Fr.*, 413), similarly looking at the elegiac note of M., in contrast to the more sententious rhetoric of Garnier, says that his ' six tragedies make him our last lyric poet, and verily an

admirable lyrist '. The 6 are : *Sophonisbe* (a common selection of the Senecan school ; the *Sophonisba* of Trissino, q.v., was the first vernacular tragedy), *David, Aman, Hector, Les Lacènes* (the Spartan women, out of Plutarch), and *l'Ecossaise*, the last and best, in which queen Mary of Scots was the heroine and queen Elizabeth was a protagonist. These nearly contemporary *dramatis personœ* mark a distinct advance on the Fr. stage from the classical and Biblical plots of the Ital. Renaissance in France ; and M. anticipated Vondel, Schiller and Swinburne (qq.v.), among others, in his choice of heroine.

Montégut, Jean Baptiste Joseph Emile (1825-95) : Fr. critic. Wr. *Nos Morts Contemporains*, *Poétes et Artistes de l'Italie, Écrivains Modernes de l'Angleterre*, etc., and effected translns. from Shakespeare, Macaulay, Emerson, and others. M.'s width of learning and breadth of judgment entitled him to a greater international reputation than he enjoys, and Saintsbury (*Hist. Crit.*, iii, 444) adds that M.'s method is ' extraordinarily enveloping, penetrating, intimate '.

Montemayor, de, Jorge (*c.* 1521-1561) : Port. pastoralist and poet ; wr. in Span. ; born at Montemâ-o-Velho, and adopted the Castilian form of that place-name (Montemayor) in lieu of his (now unknown) patronymic ; his paternal grandmother was a Jew, professional singer, and M. migrated to Spain at an early age as chorister in the chapel of the infanta (princess) Marie, elder sister to the future king Philip ii. Later, he returned to Lisbon in a similar capacity, on the occasion of the marriage of the infanta Jeanne to the elder son of king John iii of Portugal ; to this prince and princess M. dedicated his works (*Obras*), 1554. There is ground for the statement that he accompanied king Philip ii to Engld. on his marriage with queen Mary ; and M.'s early death by violence seems to have been connected with a love-episode. Wr. various verse, collected in the *Cancionero* (q.v.), dedicated as mentioned above, 1554 (placed on the Index Expurgatorius , reprinted, in 2 vols., Antwerp, 1558) ; transld. March (q.v.) into Castilian verse, and is to be reckoned low among the major or high among the minor Span. poets for his metrical skill and pleasant sentiment. But M.'s chief work was his prose-pastoral, intersected with admirable verses, the 6 bks. of the *Diana Enamorada*, 1542-59. In the comparative history of lit., this work transported the fiction of Arcadia (q.v.) from Italy to Spain, France and Engld. ; for M.'s *Diana* forms the link (first forged imperfectly by Ribeiro, q.v.) between Sannazaro (q.v.) and Sidney, Cervantes, Sarrasin (qq.v.), and the rest. Its importance in the development of pastoral fiction (see, too, s.v. Novel) depended, of course, on its popularity ; 16 edns. appeared in Spain in about 80 years, and it was transld. into Fr. (6 times), Germ., and Engl. ; the last by Bartholomew Young (or Yong ; fl. 1577-98), whose version is said to have been used by Shakespeare (q.v.) in his *Two Gentlemen of Verona*. Another test of its popularity is the transln. of *Diana* into the region of spiritual edification : the ' divine Diana ' of a certain brother Bartolomé Ponce was publd. in 1582 ;

and yet another test is to be found in the continuations of M.'s work by other hands (see s.vv. A. Perez, G. G. Polo, Texeda). These are distinct from the imitations of the kind by the greater writers who handed on the type in the Arcadian succession ; and it may be noted that, in the famous chapter of *Don Quixote* (s.v. Cervantes), i, 6, where the curate deals with his library, M.'s *Diana* is saved from the bonfire, for it does ' not and will not do the harm that books of chivalry have done '. Quixote's niece urges more drastic measures, ' or no sooner will mine uncle be cured of his chivalry-ailment than like enough, after reading all these verses, he'll want to turn shepherd and wander through field and forest with pipe and song. And 'twould be worse if he became a poet, a disease both contagious and incurable they say '. To save the worthy knight from this worse peril, the curate decided to deprive the *Diana* only of that part ' dealing with the sage Felicia and with the magic water, and of most of the longer verse. The prose, and the honour of being the first book of its kind, should be left it '. Cervantes's criticism holds good to this day, when it is recognized that the sorceress and her philtres were lifted by M. from Sannazzaro, and disturbed rather than improve the level excellence of M.'s prose narrative. An addition not due to M., which also disturbs the flow of *Diana's* story, is the episode introduced by subsequent editors, and entitled ' The Story of Abencerraje and the Beautiful Xarifa '. This tale is now acknowledged as anon., though it was formerly ascribed to A. de Villegas (q.v.). How far M. drew on facts of his life and surroundings for some of the adventures of Diana and Sereno in his tale cannot be established at this date ; in doing so, he would have been following Sannazzaro's lead. The *Diana*, though tedious to later readers, who fail to share the illusion of an Arcady at the busy heart of Spain, and though less authentic than the original *Arcadia* of Sannazzaro, is one of the important works in modern literary history.

Monteser, de, Francisco Antonio (17th cent.): Span. dramatist. Wr. a burlesque play, *el Cavallero de Olmedo*, and collaborated with other writers in the dramatic group inspired by L. de Vega (q.v.).

Montesino, Ambrosio (fl. 1500): Span. divine and poet ; Franciscan friar ; patronized by queen Isabella of Castile, and was nominated to a bishopric in Sardinia. Transld., 1502-03, a *Life of Christ* into dignified Castilian prose (4 vols., fo.) from the Lat. *Vita Christi* of Ludolphus of Saxony, a Carthusian monk (d. *c.* 1370) ; M.'s version was accordingly described as *Cartuxano* (Carthusian). Wr., too, some notable *romances* (q.v. ; Span. ballads) on sacred subjects (the Saviour, John the Baptist, Francis of Assissi, and others), thus contributing to the extension of the ballad-form ; and, besides his *Cancionero* (q.v.) ' of various works of new poetry ', 1508, which owed something to the Italianate influence of plebeian inspiration (see s.v. Todi), M. is credited with an anon. ballad (*romance*) on the death, 1491, of prince Alfonso of Portugal, son-in-law to Ferdinand and Isabella.

Montesquieu, de, Charles Louis de Secondat (1689-1755): Fr. jurist and political philosopher ; adopted, 1716, additional surname of de Montesquieu under the will of an uncle, whom he succeeded as president of a provincial court-of-law (*parlement*) ; came to Paris, 1722 ; member of the Academy (q.v.), 1728 ; travelled in Germany, Austria, Italy, Switzerland, Holland, and Engld. (resided, 1729-31), in the pursuit of his inquiries into politics and institutions. Wr. *Lettres Persanes* (' Persian Letters '), 1721 ; *Considérations sur les causes de la Grandeur et de la Décadence des Romains* (anon., 1734) ; *de l'Esprit des Lois* (anon., 1748, Geneva ; 3 vols., Paris, 1750). Minor works have been issued by a descendant of M., 1891-99, in several vols., useful in illustration of his main writings. It is interesting to review these in the development of M.'s genius, which exercised a profound effect on the political history of his country in later years. The form of the ' Persian letters ' was due to a prevailing mode of the age, traceable to the interest aroused by Galland's (q.v.) transln. of the *Arabian Nights*, 1708, and analogous to the *roman-à-clef* (q.v.) by which the novelists of a previous generation had disguised their references to living personages. Siam, Arabia, Persia—the precise locality was indifferent, and the local colour was of no urgent importance ; the point was to draw a discreet Oriental veil between the critic and his quarry, and to escape the rigour of the censorship by placing the reflections on home institutions in the mouth of a foreigner in Paris. The method became familiar in Engld. (cf. Goldsmith's *Citizen of the World*, originally *Chinese Letters*, 1762), and had obvious affinities with *The Spectator* (q.v.) ; and it possessed the further advantage of admitting a tone of voluptuousness, even of salaciousness, as a part of the local colour. The intimacies of Eastern domestic life were utilized in these ' Letters ' (and elsewhere) as a kind of decoy-duck for philosophic reflection. The women of the *salons* (q.v.) and other amateurs of study were attracted by the meretriciousness of Persian colour to plunge into the deeper speculation which M. wished to unfold. And this lighter ⎸note prevailed throughout his writings ; indeed, throughout the serious lit. of the 18th cent. from Fontenelle to Voltaire (qq.v.), the audience of the *salon* was always kept in view. The graver purpose of the *Lettres Persanes* was to illumine the wrongs and follies of Fr. law and institutions by the light of a visitor from Mars, as, in these times of geographical contraction, we should call the imagined Persian in Paris. From this more superficial inquiry M. went on to examine the causes of political change in the history of the most powerful nation of antiquity, the Romans. His ' decline and fall ' of Rome enlarged the boundaries of the republic of pure letters, and admitted history within its confines. As the wonders of the starry heavens had recently been popularized (some said, vulgarized) by Fontenelle (q.v.), so the hidden forces of hist. causation were made accessible to *les honnêtes gens* (ordinary folk) by M. He reduced the part of providence in human affairs, and substituted a working hypothesis of physical causes and effects; thus effecting for history a breach with the ecclesiastical tradition, which, in the province of lit., had prevailed from Dante to Bossuet (qq.v.). In this respect, M. may be entitled the Hippocrates of modern times; like the ancient Gk. physician, he made war against all supernaturalism, and ranks as 'the founder of national psychology' (Gomperz, *Greek Thinkers*, E.T., i, 311). Like Hippocrates again, M. depended for his facts not on bks. only but on travel; and it is interesting to learn from his brief 'notes on England' (he crossed from the Hague with lord Chesterfield, q.v., in Oct., 1729) that he found London the city of *liberté et égalité*; names, which, with *fraternité* added, acquired immense import in France of the Revolution. M.'s special study of Roman history, his observation of governments in other lands, and his experience of the practical working of social legislation in his magistracy, were combined to inspire his greatest work, *On the Spirit of Laws*. He poured into it all the learning which he had acquired, and his note-books prove that it was composed over a long term of years and out of multiform material. Two Fr. scholars, Barckhausen and Lanson, have recently laboured at these remains in order to construct a *vade-mecum* through the confused contents of the *Esprit des Lois*, and it has yielded a semblance of order to their untiring efforts. Briefly, it proceeds from particular examples of working constitutions to generalization on the 3 types of government, republic, monarchy, despotism, to which M. finds that they can be reduced; and it is a fault of his genius that he generalized too freely and too boldly. 'He draws the Monarchy and Republic as Molière drew the Miser and the Misanthrope'; as ideal types, that is to say, without respect to the unknown quantity of the peoples who composed them. This fallacy vitiated in part his otherwise admirable account of the Engl. constitution (bk. xi); and his uncritical attitude towards evidences, his lack of what we call to-day the historian's documentary sense—must detract from the present value of his logical deductions and compartmental theories. This said, we have said almost too much in detractation of one of the most significant, as it is one of the most brilliant bks. of any age. We recall mme. du Deffand's (q.v.) *bon mot*: it should have been entitled, she said, *de l'esprit sur les lois*, an essay in wit applied to laws; and in happy phrasing, keen observation, and profound insight and wisdom, the treatise takes its place among the classics. 'It was a work of reason and of humanity. A grave voice, moderate and powerful, denounced the abuses of the Fr. monarchy, and indicated an ideal of beneficent and liberal government, which appeared absolutely practical' (Lanson, *Hist. Lit. Fr.*, 724). This 'grave voice' of M. was the ruling voice in 1789, when the republicans attempted to translate his ideal into practice; and, again, in the monarchical epoch, 1815-48, Fr. constitutionalists returned to M. for the theory of their State. That no permanent and enduring form of government has ever been founded upon the principles of the *Esprit*

des Lois does not affect, M. might urge, the validity of his conclusions or the purity of his argumentation; and there we may leave the practical aspect. In lit. and in philosophy, to which ultimately his bk. belongs, it is a masterpiece of its kind, and its fairness may be judged by the fact that Jansenists and Jesuits were united in denouncing it.

Montfaucon, de, Bernard (1655-1741): Fr. scholar; Benedictine; visited Italy, 1698-1701, and wr. an *Italian Diary*, transld. from Lat. into Engl. M.'s *Palæographia græca*, 1708, effected for the study of Gk. MSS. and hagiography what Mabillon's (q.v.) *de re diplomatica* had effected for Lat. In 1719, he publd. by subscription his monumental guide to classical antiquities, *l'Antiquité expliquée*, 10 vols., with supplement, 5 vols.; in 1729-33, he publd. his *Monuments de la monarchie française*, 5 vols. (unfind.), and to these great folios he added learned edns. of St. Chrysostom and other writers. M.'s circle of pupils was known as the Academy of the Bernardins, and he enjoyed throughout his long life the respect and friendship of scholars in all countries, including M. Prior (q.v.).

Montfleury (1640-85): Stage-name of Antoine Jacob, Fr. actor and comic dramatist; member of the company at the Hôtel de Bourgogne (see s.vv. Confrérie, Hardy), afterwards absorbed in the Comédie Française. Wr. comedies founded on Span. comedies of manners, cruder and less pointed in wit than Molière's (q.v.); *la Fille Capitaine* and *la Femme juge et partie* (see s.v. S. de Villaviciosa), are the best known.

Montgomery, James (1771-1854): Engl. (Scot.) journalist, poet, hymn-writer, in ascending scale of merit. Born in Ayr, but edu. at a Moravian school in Yorks., and became clerk, contributor to, and finally editor and proprietor of the *Sheffield Register* (re-named *Iris*), 1795. Was twice imprisoned for political libel, and sold his paper, 1828. Publd. vols. of poetry—*The Wanderer of Switzerland*, 1806; *The West Indies*, 1809, and several others,—and lectured on poetry at the Royal Institution, 1830-1; is chiefly remembered to-day as the author of such well-known hymns as 'Prayer is the soul's sincere desire', 'For ever with the Lord', 'Go to dark Gethsemane', 'Songs of praise the Angels sang', etc.

Montgomery, Robert (1807-55): Scot. poetaster; divine. Wr. *The Omnipresence of the Deity* (eleventh edn., 1830), and *Satan* (second edn., 1830), solely memorable now, despite the excessive laudation of contemporaries, for the sake of Macaulay's (q.v.) 'purifying' blast of criticism in *Edinburgh Review*, April, 1830, included in all edns. of his *Essays*. Alas, Macaulay was not there to carry out, in the instance of sir L. Morris (q.v.) his promise: 'We hereby give notice that, as soon as any book shall, by means of puffing, reach a second edition, our intention is to do unto the writer of it as we have done unto Mr. Robert Montgomery'.

Monti, Vincenzo (1754-1828): It. poet; satirist and dramatist. By his command of language and metre, and his exceptional suppleness (it amounted to more than a susceptibility) to the movements of a great time (Revolution and Napoleon), M. imposed the impression of a great personality on his fellow-countrymen ; but it must be acknowledged that he ranks as a much smaller person to-day. A hundred years after his death, he is seen as a versatile writer, inspired with literary emotions derived at secondhand from Germany and Engld., and from Dante and Ariosto in his own country, but without moral judgment or more than transient enthusiasms. (The fact that he transld. Homer, though he hardly knew any Gk., is, perhaps, typical of his sincerity as a scholar). M.'s *magnum opus* was his epic *Bassvilliana*, 1793, written in Dante's *terza rima*, and with almost ultra-Dantesque invective, round the brutal murder in Rome of a Fr. envoy Hugo de Basseville. Like a new Klopstock (q.v.), M. conducts Basseville's soul back to Paris, in order to assist at the ' martyrdom ' of king Louis xvi, amid the lurid horrors of the Revolution, in which Voltaire, Rousseau and others are included among the hosts of darkness, and pope Pius vi is a kind of Moses. The epic machinery is so entirely disproportionate to the Basseville episode, that the poem fails to win assent, despite its technical excellence. Moreover, it proved a millstone round its author's neck, when times changed and he changed with them. His next epic (by ' citoyen Monti ', now resident, 1800, in Paris, as the stern ex-monarchist was satirically entitled), *Mascheroniana* (Lorenzo Mascheroni, 1750-1800, was an Ital. mathematician), was a palinode of the earlier epic. M. tried to prove his consistency ; but, though the instance of Wordsworth (q.v.) might be adduced as a parallel, the difference is painful and obvious. The Engl. poet subordinated events to the eternal ideas which they symbolized ; the Ital. poet subordinated ideas to the temporary symbols which they wore. His *Bardo della Selva nera* (' Bard of the Black Forest') 1806, was a blank verse epic in honour of Napoleon, reminiscent of *Ossian*, Gray, and, again, Klopstock, and even after 1814, when he retired to a professorate at Milan, M. continued to write imperial eulogies. As a dramatist, M. is more memorable. His *Aristodemo*, produced at Rome, 1797, in the presence of Goethe, is a romantic tragedy of real merit, and it was followed by *Caio Gracco*, 1800 (see s.v. J. Chenier), and other plays ; and he wr., too, excellent literary dialogues. Manzoni (q.v.), when M. died, said that he had the heart of a Dante and the tongue of a Virgil ; it has been added, that, with his great literary gifts, he lacked the conscience of a common man. He was a brilliant academic poet, but his character repels the admiration which is due to his undoubted talents.

Montiano y Luyando, Agustin (1699-1764) : Span. dramatic critic and dramatist ; secretary of the short-lived Academy of Good Taste, founded on the model of the Rambouillet (q.v.) at Paris ; joined Nasarre (q.v.) in his attempts to depreciate Cervantes (q.v.) : wr. *Virginia*, 1750, and *Ataulfo*, 1753, cold and correct neo-classic tragedies, with justificatory prefaces.

Montoro, de, Anton (*c.* 1404-1480) : Span. poet ; a converted Jew of Cordova ; commonly described as ' el Ropero ', from his business of old-clothesman ; a near relative to Baena (q.v.). M., despite his baptism, was always a warm defender of his race against their cruel persecution, but his talent was not equal to the cause, hopeless in any case, which he pleaded ; and his verse (edited, Madrid, 1900) is nearer akin in parts to the indecent *cancionero* (q.v.) of ' jests provoking laughter ' of 1519 than to the nobler court-poetry represented in Castillo's (q.v.) collection.

Montpensier, de, Anne Marie Louise (1627-93) : Fr. memoirist and letter-writer ; commonly known as *la Grande Mademoiselle* ; daughter of a duke of Orleans and cousin of king Louis xiv ; made considerable sacrifices for an unworthy and ungrateful lover, Lauzun, and wr. voluminous and sprightly *Mémoires* of her full life and experiences.

Montreuil, de, Jean (1354-1418) : Fr. humanist ; chancellor to king Charles vi, who sent him (1412) on an embassy to Rome, where he met Bruni, Niccoli (qq.v.), and other scholars of the day. M., who was an ardent admirer of Petrarch and Salutati, ranks as the earliest Fr. Italianate.

Montreux, de, Nicholas (16th cent.) : Fr. pastoralist. Wr., 1585-98, *les Bergeries de Juliette*, 5 vols., slavishly based on Ital. pastoral models, as reflected in Montemayor (q.v.), and his translrs. The romance had a notable success, till it was surpassed and its reputation submerged by the *Astrée* of Urfé (q.v.).

Moore, Edward (1712-57) : Engl. playwright ; writer of fables. Wr. *The Gamester*, 1753, a domestic prose tragedy, which, like the plays of Lillo (q.v.) exercised considerable influence on the European stage (see s.vv. Fate-drama, Saurin, and Diderot) ; this play was directed against the vice of gambling. Wr., too, *Fables for the Female Sex*, 1744, which are compared favourably with the *Fables* (q.v.) of Gay (q.v.).

Moore, John (1729-1802) : Scot. novelist ; memoir-writer. Wr. 3 novels, which enjoyed some esteem : *Zeluco*, 1786 ; *Edward*, 1796 ; *Mordaunt*, 1800 ; edited, with a memoir, the works of Smollett (q.v.), 1797, and was also a friend of Burns (q.v.). Wr. interesting *Journal during a Residence in France*, 1792, and *Causes and Progress of the Fr. Revolution*, 1795, which were extensively consulted, and earlier travel-books from France, Switzerland and Germany, 1779, and Italy, 1781. M. was the father of sir John Moore (1761-1809 ; lieut.-general ; of Corunna).

Moore, Thomas (1779-1852) : Irish poet ; born and edu. Dublin ; appointed, 1803, Admiralty registrar at Bermuda, important for the misfortune of 1818, when the dishonesty of M.'s deputy involved him in a loss of £6,000, and necessitated his going abroad. We may pass over M., the jester, who belongs to a generation that is dead : ' The sparkle, the sputter, the disconcerting jump and vapour of Thomas Moore's squibs, which served for the entertainment and gratification of this lively crowd, are not yet wholly damp to us as we read *The Twopenny Post-bag*, 1813, and *The Fudge Family in Paris*, 1818 ' (Elton, *Survey Engl. Lit.*, 1780-1830 ; ii, 272) ; but they are becoming damper as time goes on ; and even the Byronic Oriental love-idylls of M.'s *Lalla*

Rookh, 1817, for which Longmans paid him 3,000 guineas, are chiefly rememberable for F. Clay's (1839-89) brilliant musical setting of at least one of their lyric poems, ' I'll sing thee songs of Araby ', and have less interest to-day than his *Life of Byron*, 1830, and his destruction by fire, May, 1824, in the presence of John Murray (q.v.), of the autobiographical remains of Byron, which had been entrusted to his discretion. It is as the brilliant author of *Irish Melodies*, however, publd. at various dates between 1807-34, and supplied with musical accompaniments by sir John A. Stevenson (Mus. Doc., Dublin ; knt., 1803 ; died 1833), that M. lives, and will live, in the memory of his fellow countrymen and of all lovers of song. M. used at various times the *noms-de-guerre* of ' tho late Thomas Little ' and ' Thomas Brown the younger '.

Moraes, de, Francisco (*c.* 1500-1579): Port. romancer ; surnamed ' the Palmerin ', after the hero of his *Palmerin de Inglaterra*, 1544, which now comprises bk. iv of the Palmerin romance-cycle, rivalling that of Amadis (q.v.). Formerly, the Port. version, which was not publd., apparently, till 1567, was supposed to be later than the Span. version by Hurtado (q.v.) ; but the true order is now established as (i) Port., by M., (ii) Span., by Hurtado. (Hannay, *P.E.L.*, vi, 130, still supported the contrary view, and gave the date of M.'s death as 1572).

Morales, de, Ambrosio (1513-91): Span. historian ; held a professorship at Alcalá, and was appointed, 1570, historiographer to the court of Castile. Wr., 1574-77, a continuation of the Span. annals by Ocampo (q.v.), bringing the narrative down to 1037. A further continuation from the pen of Sandoval (q.v.) brought it down to 1097, where the work of triple authorship stops. The whole work (in 12 vols.) is entitled *La Cronica general de España*. M. was nephew to Oliva (q.v.), and edited his uncle's writings.

Morality (Engl.): Dramatic kind ; a secular variety of the **Mystery** (q.v.), combining amusement with instruction. The secularization of drama in Engld. proceeded more slowly than on the Continent ; and *Everyman* (*c.* 1475-1500), frequently revived in recent years, is the best type of M., being ' concerned, not with an episode or an example, but with the more general interests of humanity in its conflict with the True and False ' (*P.E.L.*, iv, 286).

Moratin, de, -i. Nicholas Fernandez (1737-80): Span. poet ; commonly known as ' the elder ' ; founded a little literary club, known by the name of its meeting-place at the (hotel) Fonda de San Sebastian at Madrid. M.'s plays were not successful, and one only, *Hormesinda*, 1770, is at all remembered to-day ; his verse is better ; esp. a poem on bull-fighting, and another on the story of the ships burnt by Cortez (*les Naves de Cortés destruidas*), 1777, which was submitted in competition for the first prize of the kind offered by the Spanish Academy (q.v.), and, missing the prize, was publd. by his son (see below), 1785.

-ii. Leandro Fernandez (1760-1828): Span. dramatist ; son of above ; secretary to the Span. embassy in Paris, 1787, by the patronage of Jovellanos (q.v.) ; entered and quitted the church, and devoted himself to lit. ; became librarian, 1811, to the Bonaparte king Joseph of Spain ; and afterwards settled in France under a delusion that his life was in danger. Wr. admirable prose comedies after the model of Molière (q.v.), whose *Médecin malgré lui* he adapted, 1814 ; perhaps the best of his own plays is the *Comedia nueva* (new), 1792, in which Comella (q.v.) appeared as one of the characters (Andorra).

More, Hannah (1745-1833): Engl. religious writer ; born at Stapleton, near Bristol, where her sisters conducted a boarding-house. Wr., after a brief period of experimentation in plays, novels and poems, now mostly forgotten, a series of moral and educational tracts, which led, 1799, to the foundation of the Religious Tract Society. Her *Cœlebs in Search of a Wife*, 1809, which enjoyed immense vogue, is described by prof. Elton (*Survey Engl. Lit.*, 1780-1830 ; i, 190) as ' a novel without a story, or rather a series of social sketches and aphorisms in the guise of a novel. The hero, a prig not without brains, reviews a whole regiment of damsels, in search of one who will rise to the ideal commended to him by his departed parents. There is a piquant mixture of observation and satire with mere droning and disquisition '. M., who was a friend of the leading men of the day, Johnson, Garrick (qq.v.), and others, ' found her bourne in an old age of charitable and admirable deeds, labouring to better the estate of the children in the Mendips ' (*ibid.*).

More, Henry (1614-87): Engl. divine ; philosopher ; Cambridge Platonist (see s.v. Plato) ; was known as the ' angel of Christ's College ', Cambridge, where he lived a secluded life, refusing all preferment, including 2 bishoprics. Wr. *Psychozoia Platonica*, in verse, 1642 ; *Philosophical Poems*, 1647, and some prose dialogues, steeped in the mystic lore of what may be called super-Platonism.

More, Thomas (1478-1535): Engl. statesman ; humanist. Son of a judge of the King's bench ; studied under Linacre and Grocyn, both recently home from Italy ; followed law with eminent success ; entered Parliament ; recommended to favour of king Henry viii ; privy councillor, 1518 ; attended court-functions, entertained foreign envoys, and was present at the Field of Cloth of Gold ; knt., 1521 ; speaker of House of Commons ; lord chancellor, in succession to Wolsey, 1529, and the first in the line of laymen to fill that office. M.'s rapid promotion had a more rapid fall, and he retired, 1532. The king's disfavour continued to pursue him. In 1534, when queen Catherine was set aside for Anne Boleyn, M. refused to take an oath involving recognition of the divorce and impugning the pope's authority. He was committed to the Tower, sentenced to be hanged, and was actually beheaded, 6 July, 1535. It is observed that the *Consolation of Philosophy*, composed by Boethius, q.v., in the Tower of Pavia in 524, brought solace to sir Thomas More in the Tower of London, 1535 (Sandys, *Hist. Class. Schol.*, i, 287). ' Has Nature ever moulded anything gentler, pleasanter, or happier than the mind of Thomas More ? ' wr. Erasmus (q.v.) in one of his letters ; and the mind of M., thus encouraged by his intimate friendship with the best representatives of Renaissance scholarship—Erasmus himself, Budé, Colet, Holbein—found expression in a work exactly suited to its ideals. He had already written verse and prose, had transld. Augustine's *Civitas Dei* and the *Life of Pico della Mirandola*, when, in 1515, on an embassy to Flanders in connection with a commercial treaty, the idea of *Utopia* occurred to him. A chance meeting with a Port. sailor—' a man well-stricken in age, with a black sun-burned face, a long beard, and a cloak cast homely about his shoulders '—on the brightly-dight quay at Antwerp quickened M.'s creative faculty to imagine an island beyond the ocean, unspoilt by the abuses exposed in *Utopia*, bk. i, and supplying patterns in bk. ii of social and political institutions. M. wr. in scholars' Lat., not in Engl. for the laity ; and, stainless though his personal record was, there is no sign that he attempted as an administrator to transplant the Utopian code into the legal system of his own country. But neither Lat. language nor imaginary scene deprives M. of the credit of using real records of ocean-traffic for the geography of an ideal republic. He placed his account of the wonders of *Utopia* (' Nowhere ') in the mouth of a companion (Raphael Hythloday, a fictitious character) of Amerigo Vespucci (1451-1512), thus representing them as things actually seen, and therefore not wholly remote from practice : a touch of realism significant to the purpose and influence of the bk. This mariner, ' for the desire that he had to see and know the far countries of the world ' joined Amerigo on his 4 voyages, ' saving that in the last voyage he came not home again with him ', but stayed behind ' for his mind's sake '. These touches of actuality blew a breath of the New World through *Utopia*, which, however faint, is yet salt to the taste. It was transld. into Fr., 1550 ; Engl., 1551 ; and later, Germ., Ital., and Span. Rabelais (q.v.) was the first great writer to treat *Utopia* as a European classic, and its latest editor (Mr. H. Goitein, in Broadway Translns., Routledge, N.D. [1924] ; reference should also be made, generally for M., to sir S. Lee, *Great Englishmen of the 16th Cent.*, ii), writes that the *Utopia* of M. was ' an original contribution to the Platonic tradition ' (see s.v. Plato). ' It struck a responsive chord in the hearts of thoughtful men and women everywhere in Europe, and Utopia became the day-dream of the Renaissance. The history of modern Europe is the story of the development of the Renaissance forces, and as each in turn has helped to mould the frame of its social life, it has realized one or other aspect of that wonderful dream. Slowly, but inevitably, the stuff of Utopia has replaced the outworn fabric of European Society. So thoroughly has this process worked itself out that at the beginning of the last century there were only two of its cardinal ideas still unrealized, and of these the abolition of chattel slavery was fast becoming the most urgent public question of the day. It was this that kindled for the

last time the embers of the Renaissance fires. A ghastly comedy had been enacting in Europe. The Congress of Vienna had staged a masque of the chief political vices with the crowning of virtue for an interlude. With stately phrase and solemn gesture the world was declared rid of chattel slavery. But the humour of Utopia was not to be baulked. The spirit of More walked the earth once more. It touched the minds of a small band of Englishmen, who learnt that true religion is not to retire from the world when evil triumphs, but to make the world its home and mould social life after the pattern it divines. It touched them with its pristine courage, its undaunted patience, its sacramental handling of all common things. Theirs was the fire of his imagination, theirs, too, his passionate humanism. And they set themselves to do what the Treaty had pretended to do, nowise daunted by its gigantic cheat. And thus it comes about that, with chattel slavery banished, there is but one thing left to realize of the day-dream of the Renaissance—to rid the world of organised war '.

Morelli, Giovanni (1371-1444) : Florentine historian.

Moréri, Louis (1643-80) : Fr. lexicographer. Wr., 1674, *Grand Dictionnaire Historique* (Engl. transln., 1694) of history, geography and biography, the errors and omissions of which formed the chief motive of the dict. of Bayle (q.v.).

Moreto y Cavana, Agustin (1618-69) : Span. dramatist ; entered the church, 1642, and resided at Toledo in the household of the card. archbp. Baltasar de Moscoso y Sandoval. M. issued one vol. of plays in 1654, and others were publd. posth. ; but he seems to have regarded his dramatic work as vanity after his pre-occupation with his religious duties. Possibly a sense of his too great debt to his predecessors may have caused (or increased) this attitude ; for M. pushed to its extreme the loose license of plagiary in his age. Lope de Vega (q.v.), particularly, served him as an exhaustless quarry ; and M.'s best play, *el Desden con el Desden* (' Disdain encounters Disdain ') is selected and recombined, with an extraordinary deftness, from at least 3 plays of Vega besides his *Milagros del Desprecio* (' Miracles of Contempt '), to which it is most commonly referred. The loan was carried on by Molière (q.v.) in his *Princesse d'Elide*, 1664, performed before king Louis xiv ; and Gozzi (q.v.) went to the same source (*los Milagros*) for his *Principessa filosofa*. But of all the originals and derivatives, M.'s *Desden* has had the most success. Another of M.'s plays, *el lindo* (elegant, handsome) *Don Diego*, was based on ' The Narcissus in his own Estimation ' of Castro (q.v.) ; it is the comedy of a lady-killer who ends by marrying the lady's-maid, and the title-phrase became proverbial in Spain. Amescua, Molina and V. de Guevara (qq.v.) were all laid under contribution by M., who nearly always surpassed his models : a record which adds to the literary, though not to the moral, success of his dramatic procedure. It may be noted that M. developed the part of the buffoon, or *gracioso* (q.v.).

Morgan, Sydney (?1783-1859) : Engl. (Irish) novelist ; daughter of Robert Owenson

(1744-1812), actor, whom Goldsmith introduced to Garrick (qq.v.); m., 1812, sir Thos. Chas. M. (1783-1843; knighted in Ireland, 1811), physician and philosopher. Lady M., whose novels include *The Heiress of Desmond*, 1804, *The Wild Irish Girl*, 1806, *Ida of Athens*, 4 vols., 1809, *Absenteeism*, 1825, and others, and who also wr. bks. on *France*, 1817, *Italy*, 1821, etc., is notable as a precursor in style and to some extent in outlook of G. Meredith, q.v. She is notable, too, as the object of bitter attacks in the *Quarterly Review*, the earliest of which appeared in its first number, Feb., 1809, when the printer of *Ida of Athens* was said to have produced 'four volumes from a manuscript, of which he could not read a word', and to have 'fabricated the requisite number of lines by shaking the types out of the boxes at a venture'. The attack was repeated at greater length, April, 1817, on lady M.'s *France*. Meredith had to pass through the same kind of experience.

Morier, James Justinian (? 1780-1849): Engl. travel-novelist; born at Smyrna, son of Isaac M., consul-general of the Levant Company; edu. at Harrow; entered diplomatic service in Persia, and wr. brilliant accounts of his travels. M.'s fame rests upon his novels of Oriental life: *The Adventures of Hajji Baba of Ispahan*, 1824; *Zohrab the Hostage*, 1832; *Ayesha, the Maid of Kars*, 1834; and *Hajji Baba in England*, 1828, a double-edged satire of the type familiar in the Persian and Chinese letters of Montesquieu and Goldsmith (qq.v.). M. 'wrought into his book' (that of 1824; the first and best) 'many actual persons and episodes; but, without being told, we should trace no seam between history and invention. His Engl., while easy and familiar, is noticeably pure; and his natural way of interweaving Eastern hyperbole, proverb, and poetic allusion with the dialogue is the admiration of those able to judge' (Elton, *Survey Engl. Lit.*, 1780-1830; i, 377).

Moritz, Karl Philip (1757-93): Germ. miscellanist. Met Goethe (q.v.) in Rome, and wr. psychological romance, *Anton Reiser*, 1785-90, which universalized his personal experience, moral and external, in the manner of *Wilhelm Meister*. The importance of seemingly insignificant things and the interest of a microscopic character-delineation are marks of fiction, popularized by M., which proved of real value in the development of the novelist's art. His travel-books (*in England*, 1782, and *in Italy*, 1792-93) are full of shrewd observation and topical interest; and his transln. of *The Fatal Curiosity* of Lillo (q.v.) helped to introduce the fate-drama (q.v.) into Germany. The Engl. *Reise* were transld. (anon.), 1795, and reprinted in Cassell's 'National Library', and, again, edited by P. E. Matheson, London, Milford, 1924.

Morley, Henry (1822-94): Engl. critic; editor; prof. of Engl. lit. at Univ. Coll., London, and Queen's Coll., London, successively; did very useful work in promoting lit. studies in the 19th cent. by editing 2 series of popular reprints: Morley's 'Universal Library' (Routledge) and 'National Library' (Cassell).

Morley, John (1839-1923): Engl. statesman, biographer, critic; visct., 1908; O.M. Wr. the authoritative life of his political leader, W. E. Gladstone, 3 vols., 1903; *a Life of Cobden*, 2 vols., 1881, and important monographs on Burke, 1879, Voltaire, 1872, Walpole, 1879, and Machiavelli (Romanes lecture), 1897. M.'s most enduring work, apart from the *Life of Gladstone*, is his *Diderot and the Encyclopedists*, 2 vols., 1878, which followed his *Rousseau*, 2 vols., 1873. A little vol. *On Compromise*, 1874, has enjoyed a considerable vogue. M. was a busy writer in the Victorian age of dignified daily and periodical journalism, and filled, in later life, high offices of State in Liberal administrations.

Morris, Lewis (1833-1907): Engl. (Welsh) poetaster; knt. Wr. *Songs of Two Worlds*, 1871; *The Epic of Hades*, 1876-7, and other vols. of verse, betraying the influence of Tennyson (q.v.) on his facile power of versification, but a disrepect (arising out of ignorance) for the dignity and seriousness of the material of poetry, which has submerged his contemporary fame.

Morris, William (1834-96): Engl. poet; combined with that high calling the rôles of a decorative artist, whose wall-papers, stained glass, fabrics, etc., rapidly became and remain a vogue, and of socialist politician. The combination needs a few words of explanation, which may be adequately conveyed by a brief consideration of the times in which M. lived. He grew to manhood in the resolutely industrial epoch, typified by the Great Exhibition opened by queen Victoria in Hyde Park, 1851. The object sought by the prince Consort, the founder of that show, was, as Mr. Lytton Strachey remarks (*Queen Victoria*, 142), that it 'should not merely be useful and ornamental; it should teach a high moral lesson. It should be an international monument to those supreme blessings of civilization —peace, progress, and prosperity'; and sir S. Lee (*Queen Victoria*, 223; his bk. is dated, 1904; Mr. Strachey's, 1922) notes that 'Tennyson, who had been appointed poet laureate in November, 1850, in succession to Wordsworth, in the noble address, "To the Queen", which he prefixed to the seventh edition of his *Poems* (March, 1851), wr. of the Great Exhibition:

She brought a vast design to pass
When Europe and the scatter'd ends
Of our fierce world did meet as friends
And brethren in her halls of glass.

The stanza', adds sir Sidney, 'was not reprinted'. Perhaps the glass was too transparent for Tennyson's social conscience; certainly, 'peace, progress, and prosperity' were not common in the world outside; and, quite as certainly, there were minds which were moving in a direction contrary to that pursued so persistently (and so nobly withal) by prince Albert, and which did not demand that art should subserve a high moral purpose. It was remarked of Ruskin (q.v.) for instance, that his *Seven Lamps of Architecture*, 1849, 'left one lamp out of account, and that was the Lamp of Industry'; and, while there were plenty of industrious apprentices to profit by the maxims for *Self-Help* laid down, 1859, by Samuel Smiles (q.v.), and to watch them teaching by example in the person of *John*

Halifax, Gentleman, 1857 (see. s.v. Craik), it is yet true to say, as was said by the authors of *Social England* (vi, 531 ; 1897), that ' we see in all the excitement and wonder over the " Palace of Glass " that curious idealization of the commonplace in which people indulge to whom the æsthetic side of life is unstudied and unknown '. But some of the young men were studying it, and proposed to remove the reproach noted by the same writers : ' if a woman with educated taste went (at that date) into one of the big London silk-mercers, it would have been impossible for her to make a satisfactory choice from among the colours and patterns shown her ' (*ibid.*, 537). Among them was M.'s friend at Oxford, (sir) Edward Burne-Jones, from whom he first learned to appreciate the picturesque language of Chaucer and Malory (qq.v.). Thus, it was as a reactionary against prevailing standards of taste that M. expressed his love of true beauty, in colour and line, not only by making poetry, but also by making furniture, and that he joined, in politics, the camp of social reformers. ' It is not too much to say that, by thirty-five years of ceaseless activity, from 1861 '—in that year, under the direct influence of Rossetti (q.v.), M. supplied most of the capital and a large part of the brains for the firm of artistic decorators known as Morris, Marshall, Faulkner & Co. ; in 1890, M. started the Kelmscott Press—' to his death in 1896, he effected an entire revolution in public taste. His love of medieval art and literature and his instinct for all that was beautiful in them were carried into practice in his workshops, and the contrast between the conditions under which the masterpieces of medieval art were produced and the commercialism of the nineteenth century ' (which stared out of the windows of the Crystal Palace) ' impelled him to his renunciation of distinctions of class and his fervent advocacy of the socialist cause ' (*C.H.E.L.*, xiii, 119). M.'s socialism, differing from some more recent varieties, has been well described by Mr. Alfred Noyes, a poet *de nos jours,* as ' the gospel of the joy of life ', and, so far as it found direct literary expression, this should be sought in M.'s *A Dream of John Ball,* and *A King's Lesson,* 1888, reprinted from the *Commonweal,* which he edited for some time, and in his *News from Nowhere, . . . Chapters from a Utopian Romance,* 1891. Romance (q.v.) is the right epithet for M.'s writings. He went back to old romance and its early home in Scandinavia (see s.v. Scand. lit.), in his translns. of the *Grettis Saga,* 1869 ; the *Volsunga Saga,* with E. Magnússon, 1870, and similar studies, which immensely enlarged the area of poetic invention. M.'s *Defence of Guenevere and Other Poems* was publd., 1858, and at once established his repute ; it was followed, 1867, by *The Life and Death of Jason* ; in 1868-70, by the 3 vols. (in 4 parts) of *The Earthly Paradise* ; and in 1877 by *The Story of Sigurd the Volsung and the Fall of the Niblungs.* He rendered Virgil's *Æneids* into Engl., 1875, and Homer's *Odyssey,* 1887, and he left a large body of misc. writings in verse and prose. Of all he *wrote,* the tales of *The Earthly Paradise* are his most permanent poetic monument, the *Lovers of Gudrun,* in Swin-

burne's (q.v.) opinion and others ', being the best of those melodious tales ; of all he *made,* the types of his Kelmscott Press are his finest contribution to the crafts which he practised and adorned. It has been well said that M. did what others dreamed : Kingsley, Ruskin himself, M. Arnold, Carlyle, the Tractarians, —they all reformed by precept, while M. reformed by example. (See a striking passage in prof. H. Walker's *Lit. Victorian Era,* 534 f.) A poetic disciple of Keats, even of Coleridge, and the Pre-Raphaelites (see s.vv.), ' no romancer was ever less allured by the common elements of medieval romance. He is not the fashionable novelist of the Middle Ages, interested merely in knights on horseback caracoling in search of adventure. Rather he loved the Middle Ages because they were so expressive both of good and of evil, because both were plain to see in them, like the saints and devils of a Gothic church. What troubled him about our own time was its inexpressive complexity, its evil that seemed to be causeless, its good that produced evil results. Looking back on the Middle Ages, from a distance, but with vast knowledge and still greater power of divination, he saw good and evil clearly opposed in them ; and in his romances he could bring them to an issue, and so for a little while escape from his unsatisfied longing to bring them to an issue here and now ' (*Times Lit. Supp.,* 8 Jan., 1914). M.'s *Life* by J. W. Mackail (2 vols., 1899) is an essential contribution to the history of Engl. art and letters in the 19th cent.

Moscherosch, Hans Michael (1601-69) : Germ. satiric novelist, after the pattern of Span. models. Wr. ' The wonderful and veritable visions of Philander von Sittewald ' (*Gesichte des Philander,* etc.), which owed its form to a Fr. version of the ' dreams ' of Quevedo (q.v.), though M. had patriotism and art enough to pour good Germ. wine into the Span. bottle. Esp. he exposed the demoralization caused by the Thirty Years' War (q.v.), and he joined other satirists of his age in ridiculing Germ. à-la-modishness, or obsequiousness to Fr. fashions and manners. M.'s style is far from exalted, but he wielded a vigorous pen and was moved by vivid imagination.

Moser, -i. Johann Jakob (1701-85) : Germ. poet and jurist. Wr. sacred verse of some merit, and suffered 5 years' incarceration by the reigning duke of Wurtemberg for his defence of popular rights.

-ii. Karl Friedrich (1723-98) : Germ. poetaster ; son of above ; minister of State in the duchy of Hesse. Was inspired by the prevailing mode of Klopstock (q.v.) to write sacred verse, which showed the worst faults of the master.

Moser, Moses (1796-1838) : Germ. critic ; friend and intimate correspondent of Heine (q.v.), who called him ' a living appendix to *Nathan der Weise* ' (see s.v. Lessing). M., who was a Jew, helped to found the Berlin Union for Jew. culture and learning.

Motet (Fr.) : Descriptive epithet of a class of medieval Fr. poetry, consisting of Lat. glee-songs for several voices.

Motteville, de, Françoise (1612-89) : Fr. memoirist ; *née* Bertaut. Her *Mémoires* have an added interest owing to her position at the court, in close intimacy with Anne of Austria, queen-mother, and regent during the minority of king Louis xiv.

Muddiman, Henry (17th cent.) : Engl. pioneer-journalist ; founded *The London Gazette*, Nov., 1665 ; sent out news-letters on f'cap sheets, ' headed " Whitehall " to show their privilege, beginning " Sir ", and without any signature, mis-spelt, the writing cramped and crabbed to a degree, but literally crammed with parliamentary and court news ' (*C.H.E.L.*, vii, 364). M.'s *Gazette*, adds the writer, may be said to have been the first printed newspaper, though other authorities refer to the issue of *Speciall Passages* in Aug., 1642. It was shortly after the appearance of the *Gazette* that the name ' newspaper ' began to find its way into common use, an early instance being found in a letter of sir W. Temple (q.v.) from the Hague, 23 Jan., 1679 : ' the last newspapers and journalls from England '.

Müller, Adam Heinrich (1779-1829) : Germ. critic ; associated with H. von Kleist (q.v.) in the editorship of *Phœbus*, 1808, and wr. on ' German Learning and Letters ', 1806, from the Romanticists' angle of vision. M., like Gentz (q.v.), tended gradually to Metternich's (q.v.) policy in Austria.

Müller, Friedrich (1749-1825) : Germ. poet and artist. His activity as artist earned him the name of *Maler* (painter) Müller, by which he is commonly known. Wr. idyls (in Gessner's vein ; see s.v.), and dramas, the latter including a *Faust*, eclipsed by Goethe, and a *Golo und Genoveva*, eclipsed by Tieck (q.v.).

Müller, Johann (1436-76) : Germ. astronomer and humanist. Adopted, according to learned convention, scholar's-name of Regiomontanus from his birthplace, Königsberg (king's mount). Studied Gk. in Italy ; worked under king Matthias Corvinus of Hungary (q.v.) ; founded observatory at Nuremberg ; wr. *Ephemerides*, an early navigators' almanack. M. illustrates the brief period before the Renaissance and the Reformation parted company. He applied to science the methods of humanism, without seeking to extend his practical studies in the direction of a new conduct of life. Hallam (i, 190) esteems him, on evidence beyond the range of this dict., ' the greatest mathematician of the fifteenth century '.

Müller, Johann Gottwerth (1743-1828) : Germ. novelist ; succeeded Musäus (q.v.) as editor of the *Straussfedern* (q.v.). M. was a sworn foe of the fanciful and romantic tendencies of his age, and ably backed Nicolai (q.v.) at Berlin in his championship of the Aufklärung (q.v.).

Müller, -i. Wilhelm (1794-1827) : Germ. poet ; of the so-called ' Greek Revolt ',—a group of lyric poets who formed (or are classified historically as forming) a bridge of transition between the Germ. Romantics and the Young Germ. (q.v.) movement. Byron (q.v.) was behind them ; the Gk. War of Independence was at their side, and the Revolution of 1848 was in front. Schubert, the composer, set to music M.'s love-songs, *die schöne Müllerin*, and M. is not unworthily said to be Heine's (q.v.) forerunner in the poetic art of evoking true beauty out of the simplest lyric metres. M.'s son (*infra*), whose descendants are Engl.,

piously collected his father's writings, 1868, out of the various vols. in which they were originally publd.

-ii. Friedrich Max (1823-1900) : Germ.-Engl. scholar ; son of above ; born and edu. in Germany ; came to Engld., 1846, and resided at Oxford from 1848, becoming Taylorian prof., 1854-68 ; curator of Bodley's (q.v.) library, 1856-63 and 1881-94 ; first incumbent of the univ. chair of Comparative Philology, 1868. Edited, among other famous oriental classics, the *Rigveda* and ' Sacred Books of the East ' ; collected his misc. essays as *Chips from a Germ. Workshop*, 1867-75, and immensely enhanced the scientific study of comparative philology and mythology. F.M.M. was appointed to the Privy Council, and his son, sir W. G. Max-Muller, is (1925) a distinguished member of the British Diplomatic service.

Müllner, Adolf (1774-1829) : Germ. dramatist. Wr. fate dramas (q.v.) of a gloomily tragic kind with a leaning to the romantic style. The best-known are his *February 29th*, 1812, which was prompted by the success of *February 24th*, a play of the same fateful-date type by Z. Werner (q.v.), 1810, and his *die Schuld* (' The Crime '), 1813, the scene of which is laid in Spain. The *Schuld*, which has been said to suggest the work of a criminal jurist, is written in the trochaic measure adopted by Grillparzer (q.v.) in his much greater fate-drama, *die Ahnfrau*, 1817. M. wr., too, comedies after Fr. models ; a prose-romance, *Incest* ; and, later, devoted himself to critical journalism, which included a miss-fire attack on Goethe.

Muiderkring (Dutch) : Circle (' kring ') of letters and learning, with its centre at the castle of Muiden, the official residence from 1609 to 1648 of P. C. Hooft (q.v.), the ' Tacitus of the Netherlands ', who was also its Edmund Spenser. The chief source of information on the Muiden Circle is in the correspondence of Hooft himself ; the *kring* included Coster, G. Vossius, Visscher and his gifted daughters, C. Huyghens (qq.v.), among men of letters, and many statesmen, diplomatists, and travellers. The wide hospitality of Hooft and his eminence in lit. and scholarship rendered the ' Muiderkring ' one of the chief splendours of the Dutch golden age.

Muloch, Dinah. See Craik.

Munch, -i. Andreas (1811-84) : Norse poet ; dramatist ; son of bp. of Christianssand. Sir E. Gosse (*Lit. of Northern Europe*, 22), calls M. a Niobe, and remarks that, ' after the rage of the great critical controversy ' (i.e. between Wergeland and Welhaven, qq.v., and their followers), ' it was rather refreshing to meet with a poet who was never startling or exciting, whose song-life was pitched in a minor key, and whose personality seemed moist with dramatic tears '. On this level, M. wr. *The Solitary* (a prose-romance), *Pictures from North and South* (also in prose), *New Poems*, 1850, *Solomon de Cans*, 1855, and *Lord William Russell*, 1857 (dramas). He belongs to ' the class of graceful sentimentalists ', which every age produces to its own measure.

-ii. Peter Andreas (1810-63) : Norse historian ; antiquary ; cousin to above.

Munchausen : Anglo-Germ. type of long-bow puller ; immortalized by Bürger (q.v.), in the *Marvellous Journeys by Water and Land of Baron von Münchhausen*, 1786, after an earlier Engl. version by R. E. Raspe (q.v.). The original M. is said to have been Karl Friedrich, baron v. M., 1720-81, who went through 2 Turkish campaigns .in the military service of Russia and embroidered those experiences into an increasing tapestry of very far-sought travellers' tales. The type of the braggart and liar was satirized by Immermann (q.v.) in the satiric portion of his novel, *Münchhausen*, 1838 ; and perhaps there were touches of M. in Jos. Sedley's reminiscences in Russell Square of his quite blameless career in India (*Vanity Fair*, 1847). De Rougemont, of course, was the M. of a later generation.

Munday, Anthony (1553-1633): Engl. poet ; dramatist ; translr. ; a strong anti-Catholic, wr., after a visit to Rome, *The Engl. Romayne Lyfe*, and a work giving the Protestant view of Campion's capture, 1581-2. M. became an actor for a while, went abroad with ' Pembroke's players ', and excited Ben Jonson's (q.v.) ridicule by his acting in *The Case is Altered*. Of 18 plays written by M. between 1584 and 1602, only 4 survive, viz.: *The Downfall of Robert Earle of Huntingdon* (with a certain Henry Chettle), *John à Kent and John à Cumber, The Death of Robert Earle of Huntingdon*, and *The Life of Sir John Oldcastle the good Lord Cobham*. He transld. *Amadis de Gaul* (q.v.) and other romances, and acted as Stow's (q.v.) literary executor in issuing his *Survey of London*, 1618. M. wr. and produced the greater number of the City pageants from 1592 to 1623.

Muñoz, Juan Bautista (1745-99): Span. scholar. Wr., 1793, a *History of the New World* (to 1500), which he left incomplete.

Muntaner, Ramon (born 1267): Span. (Catalan) chronicler. Wr., 1325-28, a chronicle of the deeds and exploits of king James i of Aragon (1208-1276), in 298 chapters, with a poem of 240 verses. It is a fine piece of work, executed in the knightly spirit and loyal style of Froissart (q.v.), and it is a valuable document of medieval history.

Muratori, Lodovico Antonio (1672-1750): It. archæologist, historian. 'The modest figure of this honest and conscientious parish priest ', writes a Fr. critic, ' seems almost an anachronism in an age *où pullulèrent les abbés galants* '. From 1700 till his death, M. was librarian at Modena, where Tiraboschi (q.v.) succeeded him, and Sandys (*Hist. Class. Schol.*, ii, 381) calls him ' the most industrious and the most widely learned Italian scholar of his time '. He devoted himself to the annals of Italy from the 6th to the 16th cent., and was fortunate in obtaining the subvention and support of the wealthy and learned Palatine Society. M.'s works, which extended to 46 vols., fo., and 34 vols. 4to, included, mostly notably, 6 vols. of *Antiquitates Italicæ Medii Aevi*. His treatise on poetics, *della Perfetta Poesia*, 1706, is characterized by Saintsbury (*Hist. Crit.*, ii, 541) as, ' given its lights and its time, a very good book '.

Muret, Marc Antoine (1526-85): Fr. scholar ; known as Muretus. Wr. Lat. play, *Julius*

Cæsar, produced as a college piece, in which Montaigne (q.v.) took part, and is praised by that authority as ' le meilleur orateur (stylist) du temps '. M. was a friend of Du Bellay (q.v.), and was thus admitted to the select circle of the Pleiad (q.v.), and wr. a Fr. commentary on the *Amours* of Ronsard (q.v.). The religious troubles of the age did not pass him by, and he is even said to have escaped a death-sentence for heresy by the complicity of a gaoler. He left France for Italy, and held chairs of humane languages at Venice and Rome, 1563-84. His chief work, apart from edns. of classical authors, was *Variæ Lectiones* (8 vols., 1559 ; 7 vols., 1580 ; 4 vols., 1585).

Murger, Henri (1822-61): Fr. novelist. Wr. *la Vie de Bohême*, 1851, brilliant sketches of Bohemian life and manners in Paris.

Murner, Thomas (1475-1537): Germ. satirist ; sturdy anti-Lutheran. Franciscan monk at Strassburg ; wr. *Gauchmatte* (' Fools'-mead '), and other folly-literature (see s.v. Brandt), directed against the excesses of his times, whether in Reformation-pamphlets, or the sciolism of divines, or the cocksureness of lawyers, or the anti-social spirit, or the vanity of princes. His *Great Lutheran Fool*, 1522, was the most notable satire which the work of the reformers encountered, and marked an advance in the literary use of personification, inasmuch as the ' Narr ' (fool) was not Luther, but his party.

Murray, John (1778-1843): Engl. publisher ; originally London agent to A. Constable (1774-1827), of Edinburgh ; founder, 1812, of the famous publishing house, established in Albemarle Street, London; memorable particularly for his association with Byron (q.v.) ; original publisher, 1809, of the *Quarterly Review* (see s.v. Wm. Gifford), and started, 1826, a daily newspaper, the *Representative*, in which B. Disraeli (q.v.) was interested, but which did not succeed.

Musäus, Karl August (1735-87): Germ. storyteller. Wr. *Grandison the Second*, 1760, modelled, like Wieland's (q.v.) *Don Sylvio*, on Cervantes mixed with Richardson (qq.v.) ; and, more memorably, a recension of Germ. fairy-tales (*Volksmärchen der Deutschen*), 1782-86. Started the story-books, in the nature of albums or keepsakes, publd. by Nicolai (q.v.) at Berlin, by the title of *Straussfedern* (q.v.).

Muse Française, la (Fr.): Title of a Paris literary organ, founded, 1823, as a mouthpiece of the young Romanticists (s.v. Romance) who gathered at the Arsenal (q.v.) at that date. The *M.F.* may be compared in tendency and scope with the *Germ* (q.v.) of the Engl. Pre-Raphaelite Brotherhood (q.v.). Among its most notable contributors were the Deschamps (q.v.) brothers ; and it was backed by a more or less closely associated annual, *les Annales Romantiques*, 1823 and foll., which counted all the leaders of *le lyrisme* (q.v.) among its supporters.

Musset, de, Alfred (1810-57): Fr. poet ; an early (1828) member of the *Cénacle* (q.v.), but, though the spoiled child of Nodier's (q.v.) *salon* at the Arsenal (q.v.), a deserter from the Romantic brotherhood, which was ' well quit of him ' (Omond, *P.E.L.*, xi, 226); by spontaneous genius, one of the greatest of the men of 1830. M.'s first bk. was *Contes d'Espagne et d'Italie*, 1830, written before he was 20. It was romantic, Byronic, Hugoese. Spain and Italy stood in his tales for the vague, ineffable South and East, with their deeper passions and brighter 'local' colours to excite staid readers in quieter climes. But M.'s misfortune was, that he never grew up. He always remained the passionate lyrist, impatient of all ideals, 'too late in a world too old'. This attitude was scarcely a pose, though M. employed it effectively; it was almost genuine in its indifference to the realities of hope and faith. In 1833 M. met George Sand (q.v.), and the result was a journey to Italy (1833-34), and a rupture, 1835, all of which, however interesting in the annals and scandals of biography, had little influence on M.'s poetry. His chief work is found in his *Nuits*, meditations of the poet with his muse on nights of May and December (1835; the best), August (1836) and Oct. (1837); he wr., too, dramas, *On ne badine pas avec l'Amour*, etc. (in *Comédies et Proverbes*); *Lorenzaccio*, an hist. play; prose-tales; a prose-romance, *Confessions d'un Enfant du Siècle*, 1836; and in verse again, *Rolla* and *Lettre à Lamartine*. Much of M.'s work appeared in the Paris *Révue des Deux Mondes*, in which Sainte-Beuve (q.v.) had early praised him, and which entertained him at a banquet (attended by G. Sand) after the publication of *Rolla*, 1833. This verse-tale particularly and M.'s writings in general exercised no little influence on the development of Russ. lit. (q.v.) in the eager 'forties. We need not refer at this date to M.'s *succès de scandale* in his poems of 1830, achieved by his description of the moon over a spire as 'a dot over an *i*'. It was too daring a departure from the conventions of poetic expression, and is characteristic of M.'s constant disregard for the literary controversies which rent his age. M.'s dramatic instinct was strong and correct, and he was particularly happy in his light plays written to illustrate the truths conveyed by proverbial phrases (*Proverbes*); but it is as lyric poet that M.'s fame is imperishable, against all the assaults of moral and æsthetic standard-bearers: the type of romantic sensibility.

Musurus (*c.* 1470-1517): Cretan teacher of Gk. in Italy. Pupil of Janus Lascaris (q.v.) at Florence; lectured at Padua and Venice, where he assisted Aldo Manuzio (q.v.).

Muth, Conrad (*c.* 1471-1526): Germ. humanist; known, according to the fashion of the times, by his scholar's-name of Mutianus Rufus. M. was a leader of the 'poets', or inner circle of young students at Erfurt univ., who produced the *Epistolæ Obscurorum Virorum* (q.v.). Was at school at Deventer with Erasmus (see s.vv.); visited Italy; settled at Gotha; his distinguished services to the cause of progress did not save him from attack and personal violence at the hands of the mob (1524) when the Reformation (q.v.) had overwhelmed the academic humanists.

Myers, Frederic William Henry (1843-1901); Engl. critic; poet. Wr. some vols. of poetry: *St. Paul's*, 1867, and others, and is chiefly memorable for his wholly admirable monograph on Wordsworth (q.v.; 1881, and frequently reprinted), in the 'English Men of Letters' series. The subject exactly suited M.'s powers. Three excellent papers (one of which is on Virgil) are included in his *Essays: Classical*, 1883. M. was a founder of the Society for Psychical Research, and contributed to its publications.

Mylius, Christlob (1722-54): Germ. journalist; cousin and friend of Lessing (q.v.).

Mystery (Engl.): Dramatic kind, equivalent to the **Sacra Rappresentazione** (q.v.) of Italy. The older name is Miracle or Miracle-play, the now common term, Mystery, being 'an academic refinement as modern as Dodsley's (q.v.) time' (*P.E.L.*, iv, 276).

Mysticism: 'der Mysticismus ist die Scholastik des Herzens, die Dialektik des Gefühls'; mysticism is the logic of the heart, the dialectics of the emotions. It is thus that Goethe (q.v.), a competent authority, defines this difficult term, and it will not be at variance with his masterly words to add that M., in its appearances in European lit., was the expression in a rule of life of a constant desire for immediate communion with God. It is not necessary for the purposes of lit. to pursue into philosophy, theology, and theosophy the narrower uses of the term, which originated in the idea of mystery or seclusion, and was derived from Plotinus and the Neo-Platonists by Dominican and Franciscan monks to denote the initiation by contemplation into a spiritual Being. All kinds of secondary or consequent -isms look back to M. as their parent, or as contributory to their import; quietism, pietism, asceticism, nihilism, pantheism, symbolism, Platonism, Rosicrucianism, spiritualism, Freemasonry—all have an element derived from or akin to Mysticism in their composition. But these aspects must engage special students of the sciences enumerated above. Here we may note with Vaughan (*Hours with the Mystics*, third edn., xvii) that, in medieval Europe, 'in an age when Scholasticism was submitting religion to cold and exact logic it was like turning from some dusty road into a quiet grass-grown lane, to hear of devout contemplation leading up to perfect holiness and spiritual knowledge'; and we may remark that Biese (*Deutsche Litteraturgesch.*, i, 233) employs almost the same language in his characterization of the earliest mystics in the land of their first significant manifestation (for 'Germany has been the native soil of mysticism in Europe'; Hallam, ii, 380): 'The main endeavour', says Biese, 'of these introverted natures, which could not acquiesce in the scholastic exactitudes of the theologians, was directed to classifying the relationship of men to God and the world, and to reconciling the contradictions between the inner and the outer life'.

We trace the beginnings of this inquiry, which was also a species of reform, in Germ. and Dutch religious thinkers before the Reformation (q.v.): in preachers such as Eckhart, Suso, and Tauler (qq.v.); in laymen who applied the contemplative rule to practical ends, such as Merswin, Ruysbroek, and Groot (qq.v.), founders of brotherhoods and societies; in the pure flower of mystic aspiration plucked by Thomas Kempis (q.v.) in his *Imitation of Christ*; in visionaries such as Paracelsus and Boehm (Behmen) (qq.v.); in Span. mystics, such as Ponce de Leon, Santa Teresa, Juan de Yepes de la Cruz (qq.v.); in the Fr. quietists, mme. Guyon and Fénelon (qq.v.; see also s.v. Bossuet); in the Cambridge Platonists, and so forth. We note the impulse to M. derived from the printing of the Bible (q.v.) in the 15th and 16th centuries, and we mark the revival of mystic thought, tending to 'theoretical voluptuousness', in Germ. philosophers of the 18th cent. (see s.vv. Hardenberg, Fichte, Schelling, and others), in some of whom the religious fervour of their fellow-countrymen seemed re-animate after 400 years.

Into the diverse tenets of modern sects of theology we cannot enter in this place, nor can we discuss the dictum 'which gives us Schelling as the Plotinus of Berlin, and Coleridge as the Schelling of Highgate' (Vaughan, *op. cit.*, 87). It is more germane to our business to note that there is M. in all imaginative lit. which employs transcendental feeling, from Dante (q.v.) downwards, 'especially that form of Transcendental Feeling which manifests itself as solemn sense of Timeless Being, of " That which was, and is, and ever shall be ", overshadowing us with its presence' (J. A. Stewart, *The Myths of Plato*, 22).

Examples might be sought from all countries in all ages; perhaps the latest of all may be appropriately mentioned here. It is in modern Russia especially (and Russ. lit.—see s.v.— did not start till the middle of the 18th cent.) that M. found its most congenial soil, prepared for it, as history shows us, by the affinity of the Slav to the Hindoo. The Nihilism of the one is alien to the Nirvâna of the other. Theosophical teachings, immigrant from Germany and Sweden (see s.v. Swedenborg) found their way into Russia in the reign of the empress Catherine ii (q.v.), and gave rise to that zest for Freemasonry, which the versatile empress satirized in her own comedies and penalized in her own laws. Novikov in 1792 (q.v.) was a victim of the imperial wrath, or, more exactly of the imperial fear, fulfilled to overflowing in the 20th cent., of a repetition in Russia of the events of the Fr. Revolution, though

he resumed his activities later on, this time under the new sovereign's ægis. Tolstoi's (q.v.) *War and Peace*, esp. the chapter describing Peter's initiation as a mason, should be consulted for the hist. conditions of this period. The movement of response to M. was not peculiar to Russia, but circumstances there were favourable to its manifestation, 'as a confused protest of the soul against the negative philosophy of the Encyclopedists (q.v.) and the invasion of rationalism'. And the same protest was repeated a little later by Russ. novelists such as Tolstoi and Dostoievsky, ' against the harshness of the positive sciences '. M. is Germ. by orig. and descent; but it found a congenial soil in Russia, where it preserved the native realism (q.v.) of the Russ. genius from the worse temptations of scientific materialism and of philosophic naturalism. The difference, e.g., between Fr. Zola and Russ. Dostoievsky is, at bottom, precisely the difference between a realist nakedly naturalistic and a realist veiled by mysticism. The vision of the one is limited by his senses, and of the other by a sense of something hidden from them. For the mystic looks at Nature as G. Meredith (q.v.) looked at Earth :

A wonder edges the familiar face ;
She wears no more that robe of printed hours ;
Half strange seems Earth, and sweeter than
    her flowers.

The naturalist succumbs to the illusion of Time, and is deceived by the robe of printed hours ; the mystic's mood is one of Timeless Being.

Seen in the perspective of European lit., the milder manifestations of M. in Engl. poetry pale into comparative insignificance. Our metaphysical (q.v.) poets, as Johnson (q.v.) called them, starting with Crashaw and Donne (qq.v.), and closing perhaps in our own time with J. Thompson and Alice Meynell (qq.v.), may be said rather to reflect the deeper ecstasies of Span. mystics, tried in the fiercer flames of the Inquisition, than to constitute a class apart. M., in fact, though it reached Engl. soil, did not effect a permanent station there. It is native to Germany, Spain, and Russia ; it is finely seamed with Platonic doctrine ; and it is an expression of the rapt religious mood, to which language is hardly adequate.

N

Nasarre, Blas Antonio (1689-1751): Span. critic ; of nugatory importance ; member of the short-lived Academy of Good Taste (a kind of analogue to the Rambouillet, q.v., at Paris). Wr. a pref. to the *Don Quixote* of Avellaneda (q.v.) to prove its superiority to the true Part ii, and otherwise sought to depreciate Cervantes (q.v.).

Nash, Thomas (1567-1601): Engl. misc. writer; satirist ; engaged in long controversy with G. Harvey (q.v.; in his *Have with you to Saffron Walden*, Harvey's birthplace, for example) and the Puritans, with whose principles, indeed, he had nothing in common. Wr. songs, like the rest of them ; ' Spring, the

sweet Spring, is the year's pleasant king ', being still popular. N.'s *Unfortunate Traveller, or The Life of John Wilton*, 1594, a tale of wild adventure, which, owing doubtless to non-success, is isolated among his writings, is in the line of the growth of the picaresque novel (q.v.).

Nature, Natural, Naturalism (Engl. ; Fr., *Nature*, etc.; It., *Natura*, etc.; Germ., *Natur*, etc.): There are no words more complex in meaning, more indefinite in scope, or more confusing in use, than the modern equivalents and derivatives of Lat. *natura* and Gk. *physis*. Each has its root in birth or being, thus assailing the infinite at the start.

Each is the All, the Pan, of Pan-worshippers and Pantheists ; each, and the Lat. term especially, has given rise to more creeds and heresies than any other single word in any language.

Lit. and literary history are little or not at all concerned with *physis*. Physics and the physicians belong to science by as clear a title as metaphysics and the metaphysicians to philosophy ; and, though science means knowledge, and philosophy means the search for it, and though both are parts of the investigation of Nature, as sung by Lucretius in the first cent. B.C., in his great poem *de rerum Natura*, yet it is legitimate in this place to accept the stricter specialization and departmentalization of inquirers, and to recognize that men of letters in Western Europe have tacitly, but commonly, agreed to take Nature (and its derivatives) as their province, and leave Physics (and its derivatives) untilled.[*] So much so, indeed, that the technical Nature of literary convention loses at times the recollection and the associations of its vaster meaning. Man, a part of Nature, stepped out of Nature to make his observations. He narrowed its immensity down to a doctrine of natural rights, or a principle of natural design, or a mode of nature-description. So, it passed into the possession of schools and partizans, and acquired the prejudices, the limitations, and and the more or less complete mechanical apparatus, inseparable from such appropriation.

It is not possible in this art. to discuss all branches and every aspect of the approaches to Nature by men of letters from the 12th cent. to the 20th. An encyclopedia would not suffice. The most we can do is to try to explain some of the uses of the term in bks. And, first, we shall bring together one or two of those uses, not, as yet, with a view to reconciling them, but in order to ascertain their differences, and as a first step to comprehension. The relation of Nature to Art is of the essence of the matter. Thus, Pope (q.v.), in his *Essay on Man*, said

All Nature is but Art, unknown to thee.

Landor (q.v.), implicitly rejecting the identity, declared his profession of faith,

Nature I loved, and, next to Nature, Art.

Young (q.v.), whose influence was considerable, declared in his *Night Thoughts*,

The course of Nature is the Art of God.[†]

Tennyson (q.v.), in *In Memoriam*, finding the Art of God cruel and crude, wr. of

Nature, red in tooth and claw.

[*] But note (and see, further, below) that the Romantic movement in lit. was 'all traversed with metaphysical tremors' (Lanson, *Lit. fr.*, 931). 'In proportion as orthodoxy waned and romanticism gathered force, a worship of Nature supplanted the more definite and metaphysical belief. A kind of humility, which once had flowered in fixed, Hebraic channels, found outlet in self-abasement before the majesty, the wildness and the infinite complexity of the physical creation.' (Scott, *The Architecture of Humanism*, 75). Reverence, we may say, was transferred from the supernatural to the natural sphere. Sermons were found in stones. (See, too, s.vv. Romance, Hain, etc.).

[†] Sir T. Browne (q.v.) in *Religio Medici*, has the quaint and logical corollary ; 'In brief, all things are artificial ; for Nature is the Art of God.' The natural is the artificial, accordingly !

Wordsworth, on the contrary, found it exemplary :

If such be Nature's holy plan
  Have I not reason to lament
What man has made of man ?

(Again, it will be observed, excepting ' man ' from ' nature '). So, long since, Lorenzo Valla (q.v.) had written : 'What Nature has formed and created cannot be otherwise than holy and admirable' (*de Voluptate* ; 1431). No wonder (or, presently, perhaps, we shall see less cause to wonder) that Valla is accounted a reformer before the Reformation.

The contradiction is obvious. Nature is Order, Nature is Chaos. Nature is Art, Nature is Destruction. Nature is God, Nature is Devil. Plainly, we are confronted with a contrast which admits of no compromise, and which will repay investigation. But how investigate it ? Only with courage, declares Nature's last high priest in the temple of Engl. poetry :

Toss your heart up with the lark,
Foot at peace with mouse and worm,
  Fair you fare.
Only at a dread of dark
Quaver, and they quit their form :
Thousand eyeballs under hoods
  Have you by the hair.
Enter these enchanted woods,
  You who dare.   George Meredith (q.v.),
                       The Woods of Westermain.

Courage, at any rate, has not been wanting. Natural philosophers in all ages—and these include geographers, discoverers, explorers, as well as astronomers, chemists, physicians—often worked with their lives in their hands ; ignorance, jealousy, superstition : all the forces of darkness were opposed to them ; and still knowledge made progress. But the progress was tidal. It had its ebb and its flow. There were times of attraction followed by times of repulsion ; a movement towards Nature, and a reaction against her. What is the key to medieval thought, for example ? The repression of natural appetites, the sophistication of natural emotions, and an ascetic habit of life ; carnal desire absorbed in spiritual love, earthly yearnings in divine energies ; *psyche* dominating *physis* :

For there where God immediately doth govern,
The Natural law in naught is relevant.
                      Dante, *Paradiso*, xxx, 122.

And what is the key to Renaissance speculation ? A return to Nature and to natural law ; *physis* regulating *psyche* ; a reversion from authority and monasticism ; Boccaccio's Garden of Delights ; Chaucer's loose tongues and quick hearts ; the torrential laughter of Rabelais. For 'a transformation in our attitude towards life, and in our general view of the world, always shows itself first in the æsthetic field' (Paulsen, *Immanuel Kant*, E.T., 17). Note, again, the re-invention of Arcadia (q.v.) at this epoch, as the garnished haunt of weary Nature-seekers, affecting the primitive virtues. Note, too, and more importantly, the main road by which men travelled back to Nature. Why was Petrarch 'the first modern man' (Renan) ? Not because he loved the birds and flowers and the rural retreat of Vaucluse ; Saint Francis (q.v.)

of Assisi would rather have earned that title : but because he first, in the dawn of the Renaissance, showed the way back to Nature (i.q., worldliness, Humanism) through Pagan spectacles and the outlook of the Pagan classics.

This point of view becomes significant at a later time. When the reformers went 'back to Nature', in the scholarly sense of studying texts at first-hand, they invented a tyranny of freedom as harsh as the tyranny of authority, and lost sight of their end in the means. Nature was smothered by puritans of all schools in a false, stiff robe of convention. It was even more fatally repressed by the canons of the *grand siècle* in France (see s.v. Fr. Lit.), when it suited the temper of fashionable *literati* to approach Nature at second-hand, and to accept a reflection in polished mirrors as the one and only ' Art of God '. The Gks. and Romans, according to this creed, had said all that could be said as well as it could be said. There was Nature, so to speak, and no need to go behind it to any more primitive prototypes. This doctrine of the finality of the classics rings falsely to-day, but its accuracy was not disputed by students of Horace and Virgil, of Aristotle and Homer. And a constant refinement of style kept pace with a fastidiousness in the selection of material. They never made bricks at all, these builders of neo-classic literatures ; they did not touch straw or mud ; they merely polished the finished bricks of ancient master-builders. They took the Renaissance road, ' the way of the ancients ', as Boileau (q.v.) called it, and they found in the models of antiquity the sole necessary guides to ' reason ', ' nature ' and ' good sense '. ' La Nature est admirable partout ', said St. Evremond (q.v.) ; ' Maintenant il ne faut pas Quitter la Nature d'un pas ', said La Fontaine (q.v.) ; ' First follow Nature ', echoed Pope :

First follow Nature and your judgment frame
By her just standard, which is still the same ;
Unerring Nature, still divinely bright,
One clear, unchanged and universal light,
Life, force, and beauty must to all impart,
At once the source, and end, and test of Art.

How to do it ? Pope's prescription was very simple :

Be Homer's works your study and delight,
Read them by day and meditate by night ;
Thence form your judgment, thence your
    maxims bring,
And trace the Muses upward to their spring.
Still with itself compared, his text peruse ;
And let your comment be the Mantuan muse.*

And the result ? An apostrophe to Vida (q.v.), at the head of the neo-classic critics :

Immortal Vida ! on whose honoured brow
The poet's bays, and critic's ivy grow :
Cremona now shall ever boast thy name,
As next in place to Mantua,* next in fame !

For, as Pope quoted from an *Essay on Poetry* by the first duke of Buckingham :

Nature's chief masterpiece is writing well.

So much in this place for the neo-classic faith, derived from Renaissance neo-paganism. We need not dwell on its obvious conclusion to

* Virgil was born at Mantua.

the want of order and decency in Shakespeare ; on its own decent and ordered architecture and landscape-gardening, whether illustrated at Versailles, or at Twickenham, where Pope cultivated 5 acres, 'inclosed with three lanes and seeing nothing' (sir Horace Walpole's *Letters*, iii, 318) ; on its narrow alleys for intrigue ; on its door closed to outer sympathies ; on its preference of symmetry over space ; on its false pretensions to completeness, since what it did not see, it could not know :

All Nature is but Art, unknown to thee ;
All chance, direction, which thou canst not see ;
All discord, harmony not understood :
All partial evil, universal good :
And, spite of pride, in erring reason's spite,
One truth is clear, whatever is, is right.

We shall not follow the revolt of Nature herself (*tamen usque recurrit*) against these drugged naturalists of a copybook optimism, who restricted the study of Nature to the study of man, considered as a social animal. This tendency may be dated back to Descartes (q.v.), whose philosophic theory 'tallies with the inclination of classicism to thrust the whole natural, non-human world out of art ' (Elton, *P.E.L.*, viii, 11), and left this ' proper study ' as the ' bequest of classicism ' to Voltaire and the *philosophes* (qq.v. ; *ibid.*, 12). The revolt came in little hints and runlets, partly as the result of industrial evolution reacting on the psychology of thought ; and, in Engld., at any rate, we may date its consummation in Wordsworth (q.v.), who re-admitted to the franchise of lit., and to the liberties of Nature and feeling, the countless victims of the Cartesian proscription. (See esp., Legouis, *La Jeunesse de Wordsworth*, 412 ; E.T., Dent, 402). ' As the social changes in the eighteenth century gave new influence to the middle classes and then to the democracy, the aristocratic class, which represented the culture at the opening stage, is gradually pushed aside ' (the push was more violent after 1789, when the heads of aristocrats began to tumble into baskets) ; ' its methods become antiquated, and its conventions cease to represent the ideals of the most vigorous part of the population ' (sir L. Stephen, q.v., *Engl. Lit. and Society in the 18th cent.*, 218). This temperate statement will suffice to indicate the method of the writers, who, before the 18th cent. had run its course, left the looking-glass land of Antiquity, and went to the common facts of actual experience for their equipment on their ' return to Nature '. This actual phrase was invented by Rousseau (q.v.) ; but, before Rousseau, the shy voices of Engl. poets had been raised in Nature's praise, and Fielding (q.v.) had said, ' The provision which we have here made is no other than Human Nature ' (Pref. to *Tom Jones*, 1749). Before Fielding, Thomson (q.v.), had found in springtide the sanction to ' feel the present Deity, and taste The joy of God to see a happy world ' (*Seasons*, i, 902 ; 1730) ; and a similar motive is to be traced in Haller (q.v.) in Germ.-Switzerland, and, however dimly, in other writers in other lands. It was this *natural* right to (human) happiness to which the Fr. Revolution was to give grave social and political expression, thus expanding the discovery of the Humanists.

The new Nature-note made its way slowly. As late as the 19th cent., Ste.-Beuve (q.v.) wr. of George Sand (q.v.), as an idyllist, ' elle s'est fait bergère '; and the swept and garnished countryside of Gray's (q.v.) *Elegy*, for example, was for many years more 'natural' to poets than the seamy side displayed, e.g., by Crabbe (q.v.). In other words, the Arcadian treatment survived into a generation, which still shrank from reality and clung to the picturesque illusion. As late as 1783, within a decade of the Fr. Revolution, Crabbe protested in his *Village* (i, 17):

Must sleepy bards the flattering dream prolong,
Mechanic echoes of the Mantuan* song ? . . .
But when amid such pleasing scenes I trace
The poor laborious natives to the place,
And see the midday sun, with fervid ray,
On their bare heads and dewy temples play, . .
Then shall I dare these real ills to hide
In tinsel trappings of poetic pride ?

These peasants, sweating in public in the heat of the noon-day sun, were the first of a long train of witnesses summoned by lit. from the fields (and, presently, from the factories and workshops), to correct the false idea of Nature, and to rebuke the deceptive images of rural plenty and rustic innocence which it had been the aim of the Mantuans to perpetuate. Of the consequences in Poor Law and Pension Law, in Education Acts and Land Acts, this is not the place to tell ; but readers of Wordsworth, *Excursion*, bk. ix, will not require to be reminded how closely the quickened Nature-sympathy of poets touched the sympathy of legislators and reformers. And students of schools of lit. will be reminded how the ' return to Nature ' announced by Rousseau led to the naturalism of the Zola type and the realism (q.v.) of later novelists.

Meanwhile, the older language died hard. The set Nature-description which Thomson used in his *Seasons*, worked its way into the poetry-books of Europe ; and, though Lessing (q.v.) objected to it in *Laocoon*, ch. xvii, it became a part of the baggage which all writers on Nature carried with them. Wordsworth used it in his youthful writings, and R. Burns (q.v.) was the first to break away from it, in such poems as *The Daisy*, for example. The re-discovery of Shakespeare ; the heady romantic adventures ; the unfolded mountains of Rousseau ; the colours and common names observed and dignified by Bernardin de St. Pierre, one of the most significant of the reactionaries from the followers of Cartesianism ; the peace on the heights of Goethe ; the 'natural magic ' of the later Wordsworth ; the calm afternoons and tenderness of Cowper ; the Ruskinian leaves and crystals ; the ' natural ' arts and crafts of W. Morris (see s.vv.) : a change was gradually made to a method of dealing with Nature, which would have been almost irrecognizable by disciples of Boileau and Pope.

If we may try to summarize the modern creed, fashioned after the second renaissance dated by the reign of science in the 19th cent., and to be subjected in the 20th to the searching tests of the new physics and the new psychology, we should define it somewhat as follows : First, investigate Nature, search out its secrets, wrestle with it on land, on sea, in the microcosm of the cell and in the macrocosm of the universe, conquer it, understand it, subdue it. Next, accept Nature ; recognize that man is a part of it, and so order man's life in Nature as to harmonize with it, not to oppose it. This involves an acceptation of the facts of nature, and at this stage the Naturalists stop, and give their special meaning to the name attached to them. Zola, e.g., sometimes stopped short at the natural facts of sex-relation, and, though a Naturalist in the special sense, never studied Nature as a whole. Thirdly, transform Nature. This is, so far, the final step, and we are still only at the beginning. The human spirit has the power to weld together all the parts of Nature, and to turn the lowest to the purpose of the highest. There is a new mysticism (q.v.) here, natural instead of theological, but spiritual as well as material, which seeks to use every phenomenon *in majorem gloriam humani generis*, and so, in religious language, to the greater glory of God. It is too soon, and too near to our time, to attempt to exhibit this creed in a synthesis. We must be content at present to hear the hints of it in Henley's (q.v.) :

Out of the night that covers me,
Black as the Pit from pole to pole,
I thank whatever gods may be
For my unconquerable soul.

Or in R. Jefferies (q.v.), *The Story of my Heart* : ' One of the greatest difficulties I have encountered is the lack of words to express ideas. By the word soul, or Psyche, I mean that inner consciousness which aspires. By prayer, I do not mean a request for anything preferred to a deity ; I mean intense soul-emotion, intense aspiration. The word immortal is very inconvenient, and yet there is no other to express the idea of soul-life. . . . Sometimes I stay on the wet sands as the tide rises, listening to the rush of the lines of foam in layer upon layer ; the wash swells and circles about my feet, I lave my hands in it, I lift a little in my hollowed palm, I take the life of the sea to me. My soul rising to the immensity utters its desire-prayer with all the strength of the sea. Or, again, the full stream of ocean beats upon the shore, and the rich wind feeds the heart, the sun burns brightly ; the sense of soul-life burns in me like a torch '.

Or in Joubert (q.v.), who, like Jefferies, ' could not build a house for his ideas '; or, partly, in Walt Whitman, and, abundantly, in Meredith (q.v.), who called-in old words as trite, and coined new words to express himself, and whose genius set in the old tracks the new lines of modern Nature-science :

For love we Earth, then serve we all ;
Her mystic secret then is ours.

Or, summarily, in the realism (q.v.) of modern Russian novelists.

The history of the growth or ' Development of the Feeling for Nature ' (*Entwickelung des Naturgefühls*) in medieval and modern times has been related with a wealth of illustration by A. Biese, the historian of Germ. lit. (second

---

* Virgilian as *supra*.

edn., 1892). Whether it is a growth, an increase, or more precisely an up-and-down movement, varying in intensity with social and local conditions, is a question too big to be raised here. The late sir A. Geikie, in his *Love of Nature among the Romans* (Murray, 1912), counted their devotion 'less comprehensive and intense than its representative has grown to be in the modern world'; but it was a Roman who wr. the immortal line,

Sunt lacrimæ rerum et mentem mortalia tangunt.

If *res*=nature, the *lacrimæ rerum* flowed before the age of sensibility. In Gk. lit., too, we find many anticipations 'of a mode of feeling that is often regarded as distinctively modern—the taste for picturesque beauty in landscape and for subtle effects of air and light; the attitude of mind that hears in the outer world the echo, the response, to human emotion' (Ruskin's 'pathetic fallacy', in a famous phrase); 'a peculiar vein of love and melancholy, often fostered by solitude' (Rousseau's discovery, as the direct follower of Petrarch), 'or by congenial influences from without, but growing into an independent kingdom of feeling, and absorbing in itself well-nigh every other sentiment; a pity and sense of tenderness' (Cowper's characteristic) 'towards the animal creation that reacts upon man, deepening his natural sympathies' (S. H. Butcher, *Some Aspects of the Gk. Genius*, 322; Macmillan, 1904). With these authorities to guide us, we shall be rash if we aver that the 'thoughts that do often lie too deep for tears' spring from natural sensibilities developed in modern times only. Our purpose in this place (and to write on Nature is to write on the sole topic of all art) has been put to show, as plainly as is consistent with brevity, the influence of the Greeks and Romans on modern lit., through the first impulse communicated by Petrarch, through the excesses of the 'follow the ancients' craftsmen, to the 'return to Nature' at the end of the 18th cent., with all the likeness that underlay these changes. It is but the fringe of a great subject; and the utmost we can hope to have proved is the gradual change in the literary rescript from imitation to direct observation with a view to re-interpretation.

Naudé, Gabriel (1600-53): Fr. physician and bibliophil. Librarian successively to president de Mesmes, cardinals Bagin, Barberini, Richelieu, and Mazarin. N.'s exertions greatly enriched the Mazarine Library by purchases in Engld., Germany, and Italy, so that it became, in his words, 'the eighth wonder of the world', and the resort of scholars from all parts. It was sold after Mazarin's fall in 1651, when N. went to Stockholm under queen Christina; but he did not long survive the wreck of his life's work. Mazarin reclaimed and restored the library on his return to power, and it is now an important collection.

Navagero, Andrea (1483-1529): It. Latinist. Resided at Venice, where he edited Lat. classics for Manuzio (q.v.); wr. Lat. verse in imitation of Catullus and Virgil (q.v.), among whose worshippers he was counted; librarian of St. Mark's, Venice, and was appointed to write a history of the republic, subsequently effected by Bembo (q.v.). N. is the chief dialoguer in a Lat. treatise on poetics, *Naugerius*, to which his name is given, by Fracastoro (q.v.). During his service as Venetian ambassador to Spain, N. met Boscan (q.v.) at Granada, and persuaded him to try the novel experiment of Italianate metres and measures in Castilian poetry. The story of this conversion is told s.v. Boscan, and is unique in its completeness and definiteness in literary history.

Navarrete y Ribera, de, Francisco (17th cent.): Span. novelist; of nugatory importance. His tale, 'The Three Brothers', 1641 (printed, Madrid, 1733, with Guevara's, q.v., *Diablo cojuelo*), displayed the feature of the omission of a vowel (*a*), which touched the bottom of the affectation of *cultismo* (q.v.; and see s.v. Alcala y Herrera).

Neander, Joachim (1650-80): Germ. hymn-writer; Lutheran.

Neander, Johann August Wilhelm (1789-1850): Germ. historian; of Jew. orig., and related to M. Mendelssohn (q.v.). N.'s most important work was a *Universal History of the Christian Religion and Church* (11 vols., 1825-52, and a *Life of Jesus*, in reply to that by D. F. Strauss (q.v.).

Necker, -i. Jacques (1732-1804): Fr. statesman. born at Geneva; acted as Genevan minister in Paris; banker; finance-minister, 1776. N. took a prominent place in the politics of the Revolution, and was dismissed and recalled more than once before his definitive resignation, 1790. As a man of letters, he won the Academy (q.v.) prize for a panegyric on Colbert, and publd. an essay on the grain-trade, 1775. He was a subscriber to Letourneur's (q.v.) transln. of Shakespeare, 1776.

　　-ii. Suzanne (1739-94): Fr. literary hostess; wife of above; *née* Curchod de Nasse; m. N., 1764, after love-passages with the Engl. historian, Gibbon (q.v.). Mme. N. held a much-frequented *salon* during the era of the Encyclopedia (q.v.), and it was at her house that St. Pierre (q.v.) read the MS. of his *Paul et Virginie*, 1787. The daughter of J. and S.N. was mme. de Staël (q.v.).

Neidhart von Reuental (*c*. 1180-1250): Germ. Minnesinger (q.v.); accomplished in song what Wernher (q.v.) accomplished in story, viz., to graft the fresh interest of village-life on the decaying chivalric convention. The so-called 'court-lyric of the village', i.e. realistic poetry in ideal form, was N.'s very valuable contribution to the development of Germ. lit.; and though he introduced a coarser note than that of the master-Minnesinger Walther (q.v.) von der Vogelweide, and dared to be outspoken when he sang of rustic love in knightly measures, yet his extension of the legitimate scope of 'Minnegesang', and his anticipation of the 'Volkslied' (or, folksong) mark a significant stage of advance.

Němcová, Božena (1820-62): Czech novelist; born in Vienna, but brought up by her grandmother, a simple countrywoman in Bohemia, where she made acquaintance with the peasants and their folklore. Wr. an idyl in prose called *The Grandmother*, based largely on recollections of childhood, during the stress of her married life as the wife of a customs-house official in Prague ; a novel, *Mountain Village*, similarly sentimental ; fairy-tales, etc. ' She lived in misery ', says Chudoba (*Czech Lit.*, 111), writing of the latter period of N.'s short life, ' surrounded often by selfishness and narrowness of mind. But in her dreams she saw a better world, and reproduced it with such warmth and directness that it acquired an enduring existence '.

Nemoroso (Span.) : Pastoral name for Boscan (q.v.) in first eclogue of Garcilasso (q.v.), and for Garcilasso in an elegy for Miranda (q.v.). Lat. *nemus* means a grove of trees, and its boskiness suggests the name of Boscan.

Neogeorg, Thomas. See **Kirchmayer.**

Neruda, Jan (1834-91) : Czech poet and novelist ; leading member of the Generation of May (q.v.), and a man of wide reading and extensive travel.

Nerval, de, Gérard (1808-55) : Fr. poet. Transld. *Faust* from the Germ. of Goethe (q.v.), 1828, the year of Nodier's (q.v.) drama on that theme, thus contributing to the romantic beginnings (see s.v. *Lyrisme*) ; wr., too, travel-books (*Voyage en Orient*, 1848-50) and tales : *Sylvie*, 1854, *Filles du Feu*, *la Bohême Galante*, etc. ; G. Du Maurier, q.v., in his novels, was conspicuously indebted to N., and his rare and exquisite texture of prose composition. These epithets characterize N.'s mind, which was always delicately poised on the edge of the excess of sensibility, and which gave way before the end. ' No religion ! I have eighteen ', he declared one night at Hugo's (q.v.) house ; and the claim was not without justice.

Nestor (12th cent.) : Russ. chronicler. The so-called ' Chronicle of Nestor ' is of clerical authorship and cloistral orig., and belongs to the cycle of Kiev (q.v.), the oldest home of epic tradition on Russ. soil. Its composition is a little earlier than the 12th-cent. epic-idyl of *Igor* (q.v.), and it is the source of our knowledge of the warfare and ambitions of the Scand. invaders of W. Russia in the 9th cent., and their descendants. By its fresh, plastic style and its popular, or democratic, note, characteristic of Russ. lit. in all ages, the N. chronicle is unique in the comparative story of early national epic narratives.

Neukirch, Benjamin (1665-1729) : Germ. critic. Transld. the *Télémaque* of Fénélon (q.v.), and publd. anthology of verse by Hoffmannswaldau (q.v.) and others, with a good critical introduction.

Neumark, David (1866-1924) : Germ. scholar; of Jew. orig. Wr. vols. i and ii of a *History of Jewish Philosophy*, planned in 10 vols. ; *History of Dogmas in Judaism*, 2 vols., 1913, 1919 ; *The Philosophy of the Bible*, 1919, and other learned works, including a brilliant study of Crescas and Spinoza (q.v.).

Neumark, Georg (1621-81) : Germ. hymn-writer ; Lutheran ; a disciple of Opitz (q.v.).

Newman, -i. John Henry (1801-90) : Engl. divine ; edu. Oxford, where he became vicar of St. Mary's ; travelled, 1832, with H. Froude, q.v., and prepared his *Lyra Apostolica*, 1834, which included the famous ' Lead, kindly Light ' ; joined Keble (q.v.) and his group in the Tractarian movement, and wr. tract 90,

which proved its crucial manifesto. With the theological aspects of this movement, as with N.'s retirement, 1842, to Littlemore, his reception, 1845, into the Church of Rome, and his subsequent election, 1879, as card., we are, of course, not concerned. Lit. is more directly concerned with his *Apologia pro Vita sua*, 1864, written in reply to C. Kingsley (q.v.), and, unquestionably, a *tour-de-force* of religious autobiography ; with his religious poems, *The Dream of Gerontius* ; with his essay on *The Idea of a University* ; with his sermons and hist. works. His subtle and brilliant mind was matched by a power of expression almost unique even among the princes of the Roman Catholic Church, and recalls the great Frenchman of the past (see s.v. Bossuet, e.g.).

-ii. Francis William (1805-97) : Engl. scholar ; theologian ; brother of above. Wr. *History of the Hebrew Monarchy*, 1847 ; *Phases of Faith*, 1850, analogous to the *Apologia* (*supra*), but in a contrary direction ; a dict. of modern Arabic, and misc. essays.

Newton, John (1725-1807) : Engl. divine ; hymn-writer ; after an adventurous life at sea felt a call to the church, and became curate of Olney, 1764, and rector of St. Mary, Woolnoth, 1779. At Olney, N. proved a very sympathetic friend and host to Cowper (q.v.), with whom he collaborated in the *Olney Hymns* ; some of those in most common use are of N.'s composition.

Nibelungenlied : Germ. national epic poem ; lit., lay of the Nibelungs, or mist-dwellers (in modern Germ., Nebel=fog) ; composed by an Austrian poet, unknown by name, probably about 1190-1220. There are, properly, two parts to the poem, of which the older is the *Nibelungennot* (Not=fate), written in 4-line strophes of octosyllabic verses, rhymed in pairs, with a cæsura in each verse, and the later is the *Klage* (=lament), comprising 2,000 verses in more rapid measure, in which the survivors deplore the tragedy which overtook the heroic race. Briefly, the main portion of the N. is the romantic 12th-cent. redaction of Northern saga and legend, combined with half-historical traditions of Barbarian heroes, and overlaid with the manners of Frankish chivalry. Charlemagne (q.v.) collected the songs on which this epopee was based ; but his invaluable trove was destroyed. The romance of wood and river has ever stimulated Teuton imagination, and the N. contains elements of ancient Teuton paganism, derived, through the legendary tales of an 8th-cent. *Lay of Hildebrand*, from even remoter sources of myth clinging to the Danube and the Rhine. (Hildebrand was armourer to Theoderic, king of the East Goths, and his lay is akin to an Oriental tale, retold, from the Persian, in *Sohrab and Rustum* by M. Arnold, q.v.). All Germany is in the N.: her passionate faith in faith (*Treue*), her sense of destiny and justice, her romantic love, her domestic piety, her ruthless purposefulness ; and the Austrian furbisher, whoever he was, succeeded in a unique degree in preserving for 700 years, as Wagner and W. Morris, e.g. (qq.v.), stand to witness, the fascination and abiding interest of the old themes of the love, and hate, and jealousy, and wrong-doing, and brave exploits, and tragic fate of the Huns, Burgundians, and Franks of ancient Germ. story. The epic falls into 2 divisions, both dominated by the personality of Kriemhild, the Burgundian princess of Worms. Her first husband is Siegfried, son of a Netherlandish king, and the resources of mythology are selected and re-combined with the resources of chivalry to exalt the wooing and to idealize the marriage of this heroic and ill-fated pair. The Siegfried-tragedy is accomplished, and leads to the Nibelungen-tragedy. Thirteen years after Siegfried's death, Kriemhild, changed from the romantic maiden and the loving wife of the earlier 'adventures' to the brooding queen of vengeful purpose, marries Etzel (Attila), king of the Huns ; and the epic rises to Homeric heights in the terrible slaughter that ensues, and the terror and pathos of the scene, when Kriemhild's grim vengeance is fulfilled. Discrepancies, contradictions, and obscurities there are in plenty in this poem ; it is more primitive in form than the *Iliad*, to which it is frequently compared, and belongs to an earlier period of national craftsmanship ; but the singleness of design raises it far above the lays and songs of the epic-cycle out of which it sprang ; it passed into the very life-blood of the nation to which it belongs, and it forms an essential part of the sources of the lit. of modern Europe. In the time of the medieval revival, associated with the heyday of Romance (q.v.), Bodmer (q.v.) edited, 1757, the latter part of the *N.* and the *Klage*. Later, 1782, the first critical edn., the *editio princeps* of the heroic poem, was publd. by the scholar, Myller ; and later still, K. K. Lachmann applied to the *N.* the canons of criticism which F. A. Wolf (q.v.) had first applied to the epics of Homer.

Niccoli, Niccolò de' (1363-1437): It. humanist ; revived the study of Gk. and Lat. in Florence. Member of the circle of scholars gathered round the convent of Santo Spirito ; diligent copyist of MSS., of which he bequeathed about 800 to executors, including Cosimo de' Medici, who kept some for Medicean library, and gave 400, *ex hereditate doctissimi viri Nicolai de Nicolis de Florentia*, to library of S. Marco, catalogued by Parentucelli, afterwards pope Nicholas v. Niccoli ran into debt as a bibliophil and *virtuoso*, and was generously helped by Cosimo, but deserved every consideration which wealth and patronage could bestow for his life of self-sacrifice and devotion to the cause of scholarship and humane letters. He worked by influence rather than by 'output', and became the 'censor of the Latin tongue' (Bruni) and a dictator of literary taste at Florence. A type of 'Christian' humanism.

Niccolini, Giovanni Battista (1782-1861): It. dramatist, poet ; secretary to Academy of Fine Arts, Florence ; and displays in his writings the transition of style in Tuscany from the classical to the romantic, under the influence jointly of hist. events and of Scott, Goethe and Byron (qq.v.), of whom the last added by his visits to the impression which his ideas were communicating. In this sense, N. was a disciple of his own fellow-countryman, Manzoni (q.v.). Wr. plays of no great distinction, including

Arnold of Brescia, 1845, which was much admired ; and *National Poems*, 1859. In 1860, the Cocomero theatre at Florence was renamed Teatro Niccolini.

Nicholas, v, Pope ; Tommaso Parentucelli (1398-1455): It. scholar and statesman. Succeeded Eugenius iv as pope, under style of Nicholas v, 1447. A man of plain appearance and humble orig., who attained the supreme position by his merits, he modified the influence of the Holy See in the direction of the revival of classical learning, and left, after a brief reign, a name unsurpassed till Leo x (q.v.). His papal policy does not concern us here, except to note 2 signs of the relaxed religious zeal which marked the diffusion of humanism : (1) N. commissioned Giannozzo Manetti (q.v.) to make a new Lat. transln. of the Bible (q.v.) from the Hebr. and the Gk., despite the authority attaching to the Vulgate ; and (2), his chief interest in the fall of Constantinople (1453) was to ensure by secret agents the rescue of MSS. from destruction, rather than to take vigorous steps, as he was urged by emperor Fredk. iii and Æneas Sylvius (q.v.), then bp. of Siena, towards organizing a crusade against the infidel. 'The character of the man prevailed over the interest of the pope, and he sharpened those weapons which were soon pointed against the Roman church' (Gibbon). Catholic historians are disposed to minimize, or excuse, his genuine humanistic sympathies. Before ascending the throne, he had catalogued the library of San Marco at Florence for Cosimo de' Medici, and was discoverer of the works of Tertullian at Basel. The transition to a patron of scholarship was easy. He attracted Lorenzo Valla to his court, thus housing in the shrine of tradition and superstition the stormy petrel of lay criticism. By munificent but tactful generosity he gathered round him a select *corps* of translrs. and copyists, with a nucleus of 3 learned Greeks, George of Trebizond, Bessarion, and Theodorus Gaza, to give effect to his ambition of providing Lat. versions of the chief writings in Gk. prose. Poggio transld. Xenophon's *Cyropædia* ; Valla himself Thucydides and Herodotus ; while Polybius, Appian, Theophrastus, Strabo, parts of Plato, Aristotle, Eusebius, and the fathers of the Gk. church, were among the authors whom N. opened to the Latin-reading world. His agents collected MSS. (or copies of them) from all parts, and brought them to the library of the Vatican, of which he justly ranks as the founder. He enriched it with 824 Lat. and 352 Gk. MSS., and left it with 5,000 vols. As a proof of his broadmindedness, it may be added that he first permitted Aristotle to be read without restriction in the universities. (See s.vv., and s.v. Libraries).

Nicolai, Christoph Friedrich (1733-1811): Germ. bookseller and publicist ; prominent patron at Berlin of writers, including Musäus and the youthful Tieck (qq.v.), who were willing to lend their talents to the cause of rationalism and commonsense. Wr., 1773, a *roman à clef* entitled *Sebaldus Nothanker*, which has been called the *Robert Elsmere* of the 18th cent. It was a document of the Enlightenment (s.v. Aukflärung), and satirized the follies of excessive orthodoxy in N.'s day. Lessing's adversary, Goeze, the chief pastor of Hamburg, was depicted in it, as were Lessing and N. themselves. N. was a contributor to the 'Letters on Literature' (1759-65; see s.vv. Lessing, Mendelssohn), and enjoyed the friendship and confidence of Lessing during his residence in Berlin. He continued the 'Letters' independently, 1765-1806, as a journal, the *Allgemeine deutsche Bibliothek*, and expressed in a *Werther*-parody his adhesion to the more classical tradition in Germ. literary tendencies, and a Voltairian suspicion of the nascent forces of Hellenism and Romanticism.

Nicole, Pierre (1625-95): Fr. moralist; follower of Jansen (q.v.), and one of the most eminent teachers in the schools of Port Royal (q.v.). N. owes no little of his fame to the praise and admiration of mme. de Sévigné (q.v.); he was joint-author with Arnauld (q.v.) of the 'Port Royal Logic', and his *Essais de morale* ('Moral Essays', first series, 1671) reached a high level of thought and were greatly esteemed by Voltaire (q.v.); his *Lettres sur les Visionnaires* and *Pensées* have even been compared with Pascal (q.v.). N. followed Arnauld into exile, 1678, but obtained an ecclesiastical permit to return to Paris.

Niebuhr, Berthold Georg (1776-1831): Danish-Germ. historian; lectured on Roman history at Berlin, 1810-12, and wr. his celebrated *Römische Geschichte*, transld. into Engl. by bp. Thirlwall, Julius Hare (1795-1855), who publd., 1829, his own *Vindication of Niebuhr's History*, and others. Why did this pioneer bk. and the subsequent hist. writings by N. require 'vindication'? His hist. method was revolutionary, even iconoclastic, in his day. It was a part of the Romantic movement as a whole, which led to Young Germany (q.v.) and political upheaval, to Grimm's (q.v.) laws of philology as well as to his fairy-tales of folklore. *Quellenkunde* (the study of origins) is the Germ. name for what we honour as a Germ. science, which flourished through the greater part of the 19th century, and in the science of history N. was a leader.

Nieremberg, Juan Eusebio (1595-1658): Span. divine; his parents migrated to Spain from Germany, and N.'s works display traces of Germ. pietism (q.v.). Wr. 'Difference between the Temporal and the Eternal', 1654, transld. into Engl., 1672, and re-appearing, 1684, as *Contemplations on the State of Man*, ascribed posth. to bp. J. Taylor (q.v.). Wr., too, 'On the Beauty of God and his Loveableness', 1641, and a 'Manual for Gentlemen and Princes', 1629.

Nietzsche, Friedrich Wilhelm (1844-1900): Germ. paradoxist and poet; a writer difficult to classify, since his genius chiefly consisted in being different,—'different from the teachings of Christianity; different from those of accepted ethics, Christian or not; different from his first two masters (Schopenhauer and Wagner, qq.v.); different from himself' (Saintsbury, *P.E.L.*, xii, 24). The whole of the brilliant characterization of Nietzsche in this chapter should be read, together with Saintsbury, *Hist. Crit.*, iii, 581-86). N. started with the advantage that Schopenhauer had lifted from the mind of Europe the pall of the all-embracing Hegelian system, as expanded by Hegel's disciples; he started, too, in the lit way of Wagner's hero-worship, and both roads led him back to a form of romantic individualism. But the end was not consistent with the beginning, and after 1889 N. was insane. What degree of mental equilibrium was maintained in his working years cannot now be accurately determined. But the Superman (q.v.; *Uebermensch*) of N.'s philosophy was not a wholesome conception, linked though it be with the heroism enucleated by Carlyle from Fichte (see s.vv.); and even if its application in Prussia to the theory of the Super-State be forgotten, or forgiven, by the generation which saw the war, 1914-18, N., says Saintsbury, 'developed what can hardly be called a system, but a concatenation of elaborate parody-reversals' (the reversed platitude, which became a trick of polite letters) 'of *all* belief and morality as entertained and championed by negative as well as positive thinkers from Socrates to Schopenhauer. There is no God, *He* is dead long ago; actual Humanity is effeminate silliness; what we must strive to produce and develop into is the *Uebermensch*, a being with no virtues in the present sense of that word except an infinitely strong will, endurance, and determination to enjoy. Cæsar Borgia and a "fallow wild beast" are the moderate examples tendered; but they are to be much improved upon'. Why read N., is the obvious question. The answer is twofold: (1) he writes so well, and (2) 'the temper which is shown in Nietszche —variant as it is of the temper which is shown in Ibsen, in Tolstoi, and to no small extent in Zola (see s.vv.)—has had a very large influence not merely on the matter but on the form of every literature in Europe during this generation'. It has corresponded to some element in experience, even a floating element it might be, which has caused it to germinate and make wood. We may deal with (1), the style, first, and we cannot deal with it better than Saintsbury, who says straight out: 'He has the most astonishing force of wit, the most enchanting grace of melody, and the strangest power of suggestion. The irony of the fact that it took a madman to make German prose thoroughly beautiful may be rather terrible; but the fact of the beauty does not admit of question', and any other questions that may be asked must be answered in Germany. As to (2), the matter, we may cite the same authority: 'a mere variety of negation of the parasitic kind'. It is useful to have it dealt with so fearlessly, and with so sane a disregard of what we may call intellectual snobbishness. But, in regard to that matter, N. looked back as well as forward. He had sources as well as derivatives; and, if the *Kultur* of the Prussian super-State is a derivative from N., the *virtu* of the Ital. super-prince is a source. Briefly, and remembering the chain of thought which links Cicero to Petrarch, and Petrarch to Machiavelli (see s.vv.), we may say that the doctrine of N. rose out of Cicero's reflection on his consulate: 'O fortunatum natam me consule Romam'.

N.'s writings included a vol. of essays, *Unzeitgemässe Betrachtungen*, 1876, [2 of which discussed his masters, Schopenhauer and Wagner, respectively, as the 'great educator' and the 'Alexander Magnus' of art. This was followed by *Morgenrothe* (Dawn), 1881; *die fröhliche Wissenschaft*, 1882, and others, culminating, in effects of matter and form, in the aphoristic, *Also sprach Zarathustra* (Thus spake Zoroaster), 4 parts, 1883-91.

One last word, perhaps, is required. N. was strongly anti-Prussian. He held that military discipline could never lead to a culture-State. He denounced Prussia for every crime against Humanism, including the Reformation itself, which, in his view, had wrecked the Renaissance. But professors of the Prussian school of history, seeking a moral sanction for their creed, took recourse to the *Uebermensch* doctrine of the 'will to power' implementing the 'will to live'. The higher species of humanity, which demanded for its survival a sloughing of the mistaken virtues of pity, sympathy and the rest, fitted the Prussian historians like a glove. Treitschkean history (see s.v. Treitschke) became Nietzschean philosophy teaching by examples. The whole subject had no importance till 1914, when civilization was startled into the study of the 'moral' teaching of this eloquent madman. The pity was, that his unsurpassed style had made him a European classic.

Nieuwland, Pieter (1764-94): Dutch poet; was nominated to the chair of natural philosophy at Leyden just prior to his early death. One vol. of his poems was issued, 1788, and a second posth., 1797. An ode, *Orion*, is described as best-known, and the lines to his wife as 'one of the best poems of the eighteenth century'.

Nihilism: Engl. term denoting a system of Russ. thought, half political, half religious in orig., and mainly academic-literary in expression. Wholly political N. was expressed in acts of violence and revolution, which were expressly repudiated by the contemplative Nihilists, whose not unjust fate it was, however, to be credited, partially, at least, with the responsibility of causing the acts which their principles were deemed to justify. N. is a product of Russ. thought and of the conditions of the life of Russ. thinkers in the first half of the 19th cent. Vogüé (*Roman Russe*, 2) writes of an 'hereditary evil' in the Russ. people, 'preserved from a most distant beginning, and consisting in a tendency of the Slav temperament towards that negative doctrine, which to-day is called Nihilism, and which was called by the same name by the Hindoo fathers, Nirvâna'; the word Nihilism being invented by E. L. Burnouf (1821-1907), a Fr. antiquary, in order to translate the term Nirvâna. Max Müller (q.v.) defines the latter as 'the act of extinguishing a light by blowing it out', and the light extinguished by the Russ. Nihilists was that of civilization itself (Vogüé, *ibid.*). However remote the origins of N., and to whatever atavistic springs it may be traced, its actual rise as a philosophy of life occurred, as has been said, in the 19th cent., in a circle of journalists and students, who 'followed no definite revolutionary, political or social programme, but were active in the field of religious philosophy. Atheists and materialists, bitterest critics, repudiators of the existing state of

things, they urged the equal emancipation of the sexes, they affected republican principles, they aimed at the expression of individuality, and they employed the catchwords of association and popular enlightenment as universal panaceas' (Brückner, *Gesch. d. Russ. Lit.*, 298). The names of Nekrassov, Dobrolubov and Pisarev (qq.v.) are familiar as leaders of the circle; and Michael Bakunin (1814-76), the active anarchist, who escaped from Siberia in 1864, 'marked a new era in the development of militant Nihilism', with which we are not here concerned, but which 'preached the destruction of all existing political institutions' (*C.M.H.*, xi, 630). The attempted assassination of the emperor in 1866 added force to the reaction of Katkov (q.v.) and others. Russ. fiction reflects this movement of thought; indeed, Turgenev (q.v.) in his 'Fathers and Sons' (1862), may be credited with the invention of the term, or, at least, with the definition of the type. There, the hero, Bazarov, is described for the first time as a 'Nihilist; from the Latin *nihil*, signifying a man who admits nothing, who respects nothing, who considers all things from the point of view of criticism . . . who bows to no authority and admits no principle as an article of faith, whatever degree of respect may attach to such principle'. The career of this 'bourgeois Hamlet' in the Russ. novel, descended from Gogol through Turgenev to Tolstoi and Dostoievsky (qq.v.), forms a distinct chapter in the history of modern fiction, though the story of journalistic N. is but a passing phrase in Russ. literary annals; and, while it is correct to call Turgenev the father of N. in this sense, Tolstoi, who frankly proclaimed himself 'neither Socialist nor Revolutionary, but Nihilist; that is, void of all faith', is properly accounted the interpreter and true propagator of the doctrine.

Nikolai, Philip (1556-1608): Germ. hymn-writer; Lutheran.

Nil Volentibus Arduum (nought arduous to the willing): Lat. name and motto of Dutch poets' society, founded at Amsterdam, 1669, after the split of the dramatists' section of the Academy from the older Eglantine (q.v.). Among the leaders was van der Goes (q.v.), who seceded, however, at an early date, and became an antagonist of the new movement. The object of the brotherhood, which included some bearers of notable names, was to replace the easy and familiar forms of Dutch drama by regular plays on strict classical models. But the members interpreted their motto too literally; and, though they procured the foundation of similar societies in the late 18th and early 19th centuries, their independent activity ceased in 1679. Their chief light was Pels (q.v.); but their principles led to frigid and lifeless plays, such as those of Vos (q.v.), and hastened the invasion of Holland by Fr. taste.

Niño, Pero (fl. 1375-1446): Span. commander; created count of Buelna, 1431; the subject of a biographical chronicle by de Gamez (q.v.), entitled *el Victorial*, and first publd., with omissions, under the simpler name of *Cronica de don Pero Niño*, Madrid, 1782. It is a wonderfully loyal account of invincibility in love and arms, and is more creditable to de Gamez, the hero-worshipper, than it is credible of Niño, the hero. N. was fortunate, too, in obtaining the professional services of Villasandino (q.v.) in order to write the poems which he addressed to the royal lady Beatrice, who afterwards became his second wife.

Ninon (1620-1705): Anne de l'Enclos; Fr. *courtisan libertin*; the Fr. phrase is more adequate and appropriate than any coarser Engl. rendering could be, to a woman, not unique in class, but unique in her influence and charm on a generation, or more than one generation, of Fr. men of lit. and letters. (H. Walpole, q.v., called her 'Notre Dame des Amours'). Of men of letters, especially; for, in an epistolary age, N. was a writer of letters of a high order of merit. She was frankly and thoroughly an epicurean, and attracted the admiration and gallantry of men as different from one another as Richelieu, Huyghens, Molière, St. Evremond, Fontenelle (qq.v.), while, late in her life and early in his, the boy Voltaire (q.v.) won her affection and a legacy. Queen Christina (q.v.) of Sweden insisted on paying N. a visit in 1654, when she was at the height of her pleasure-loving and brilliant life; and her career is a thread of colour in the splendid history of the *grand siècle*. St. Simon (q.v.) records that, in her house in the rue des Tournelles, N. 'was surrounded with all the respect and outward decency, which the most virtuous princesses cannot always command'. Boileau, La Fontaine and Racine (qq.v.) were among her friends, and Molière owed her the idea for his character of Tartufe. N.'s own little vol. of sketches, la *Coquette Vengée*, 1659, is now a great rarity.

Nisard, Désiré (1806-84): Fr. critic; represented the classical tradition against the conquering romanticists. Held professorships and other teaching appointments, and wr., 1844-49 (vol. iv, 1861) a *History of Fr. Lit.*, which was almost as polemical in tendency as his earlier manifesto *contre la littérature facile*, 1833. But the battle of 1830 had been fought and lost when N. composed his history.

Nodier, Charles (1783-1844): Fr. librarian; misc. writer; 'one of the most remarkable failures of a great genius in French literary history' (Saintsbury, *Fr. Lit.*, 492): a harsh saying, due mainly to the variety of N.'s literary experimentation; he is said to have forgotten the names of some of his own writings. These included, mainly, short tales of a weird or fantastic character, such as *Jean Sbogar*, 1818, a kind of Fr. *Karl Moor* (see s.v. Schiller); *The Painter of Salzburg* in the vein of Goethe's (q.v.) *Werther*; *Histoire d'un roi de Bohême et de sept châteaux*, reminiscent of Sterne (q.v.); *les Quatre Talismans*; and *Trilby*, an earlier love-tale from which Du Maurier (q.v.) borrowed only the title. Among N.'s other admitted works were a *History of Secret Societies in the Army*, dictionaries, poems, etc., not any of which is in vogue to-day. It was by his influence rather than by his writings that N. acquired among his contemporaries and has preserved since his own day the fame of a founder of the new Romance (q.v.) in France. His taste naturally inclined

(in lexicography no less than in fiction) to the exotic and the bizarre, which had so strong an attraction for the young romanticists; and N.'s appointment, 1824, as director of the Arsenal Library in Paris (Mazarin library) gave him the welcome opportunity of making his house and office the centre of the early Romantic circle, to whom his bibliographical knowledge and philological studies formed a valuable source of inspiration. The first *Cénacle* (q.v.) met in the *salon* of the Arsenal, where N. was the genial host of Hugo, Vigny, Sainte-Beuve, and others; of the romantic artist, David d'Angers ('David'); and of their still younger contemporary, de Musset. (See s.vv.). It is to the last that we owe a poetic tribute to these Romantic beginnings. (See s.v. Arsenal).

Nordau, Max (1849-1923): Hungarian physician; sociologist; *né* Suedfeld, of Jew. parentage; lived in Paris, 1880-1914, when he became technically an alien at the outbreak of the Great War. N., cosmopolitan by residence, was thoroughly master of several languages, and wr. with almost equal facility in various fields of lit. Special mention is due to his play, *das Recht zu Leben* ('The Right to Live), which has been played in several countries; to his attack (in Engl.) on *Conventional Lies*, 1883, of religion and politics; and to his *Degeneration* (*Entartung*), 1893, analysing the causes and signs of morbidity in art and thought. The permanent value of N.'s writings is very doubtful.

Nordenflycht, von, Helwig Carlotta (1718-63): Swed. poet; m., 1743, a young pastor named Fabricius, who died in the same year. Fru v. N., who resumed her maiden surname, sought consolation amid natural surroundings, and wr. a vol. of verse *The Mourning Turtledove*. This was followed by an annual poetic miscellany, by heroic poems, and other writings, less notable 'for any real native power than for her romantic, somewhat *schwärmerisch* life, and for her sensitive subjection, first to the devout school of native hymnodists, and gradually to French verse of the sentimental type' (*P.M.L.*, viii, 363).

Normann, Lars (1651-1703): Swed. scholar; held chairs of Gk. at Lund and Upsala; archbp. of Upsala; collected bks. and MSS., which passed at his death to the Upsala library. N.'s chief writings were in the Lat. language, and were collected, 1738.

Norris, John (1657-1711): Engl. divine; rector of Bemerton. N.'s reputation as writer and logician rests mainly upon *An Essay towards the Theory of the Ideal or Intelligible World*, 1701-4. Therein, N. argued that the nature and essence of things are divine, as well as our perception of them—in short, that we 'see all things in God'. In this he was a follower of Malebranche (q.v.), whose *Récherche de la Vérité* influenced him a great deal. N. was strongly idealistic and mystical, and Southey (q.v.) declared that the Metaphysical (q.v.) school expired in N.

North, Christopher. See s.v. **Wilson, J.**

North, Thomas (c. 1535-c. 1601): Engl. scholar; knt., 1591; son of first baron N.; transld. *Parallel Lives* (Gk. and Rom., in pairs) of Plutarch (*fl.* 60-100 A.D.), from Amyot's (q.v.) Fr. version of the original crabbed Gk., into

24

fine, idiomatic Tudor Engl., 1579. N.'s Plutarch was a rich source-book for Shakespeare (q.v.) in *Julius Cæsar, Coriolanus*, and other plays. Transld., too, Guevara's (q.v.) *Dial of Princes* partly from a Fr. version and partly from the orig. Span. (see, too, s.v. Berners), 1557, and thus assisted to introduce into Engl. the technical elements of prose style which, later, were partly identified with Euphuism (q.v., and see s.v. Lyly). The *Moral Philosophie of Doni* from the Ital. was another of N.'s invaluable contributions to the knowledge of European letters in his age.

Norton, Caroline. See s.v. **Sheridan.**

Norwegian Society (Norske Selskab): Literary society founded, 1772, at Copenhagen by men of letters, Danes by political circumstances, Norse by birth and sympathy. Its most eminent member was Wessel (q.v.), whose play *Love without Stockings*, which drove the Fr. pseudo-classical conventions off the Dan. stage, was produced in the same year, 1772. Sir E. Gosse (*Lit. Northern Europe*, 3), speaks of the society as the ' evil genius and yet, in a measure, protector of the literature it presumed to govern '. When Norway gained independence from Denmark, 1814, ' this singular association ', he continues, ' that had nourished Wessel, snubbed Edward Storm, and hunted Ewald to death, no longer possessed its ancient force. The glory was departing, and when the rupture with Denmark came about, the Norske Selskab began to feel that Copenhagen was no longer a fit field of action, and, gathering its robes about it, it fled across the sea to Christiania, where it dwindled to a mere club, a shadow of its former self '. Schweitzer (*Skand. Lit.*, ii, 193), with, nationally, more deference towards academies and rules, takes a less cheerless view of the Selskab and its activities : ' It soon acquired ', he writes, ' a wide literary significance. It embraced, with but few exceptions, the most eminent poets and thinkers of Copenhagen. . . . It kept a keen eye open for opposition tendencies, and persecuted them with brilliant satire, epigram, and pun. . . . Its activity was not merely negative, but it offered prizes for competition, and its first poetic publication, 1775, was warmly received in its own day '. The N.S. was a fair specimen of its kind in an age of academies ; but plainly there was bound to be friction between Norw. national strivings and a Dan. political centre. See, too, s.v. Scand. Lit.

Novel : Engl. form of Ital. *novella*, a tale which, by its brevity, realism, and direct reflection of life, was sharply distinguished from the Fr. *roman*, or narrative of chivalry and adventure, derived from one of the stock matters of Romance (q.v.). This distinction governs the N., throughout its separate history in European lit. It might be romantic in the colloquial sense of treating an aspect of real life which happens to have strange, even weird (romantic) qualities. But that is an accident of circumstance. Life contains romantic elements for reflective treatment, but the romantic *novel* differs from the romance (*roman*) proper by the same marks as the unromantic novel,—that is, the novel is founded on observation of real, the *roman*

on imagination of unreal conditions. The world of chivalry, of faery, of Arcadia, of Utopia, is not the real world, but a realm of voluntary withdrawal from the real, and it is in that realm that romance finds its subjects. The N. finds its subjects in the real world of actual living men and women. It dresses them in a guise of fiction, only because to leave them undisguised (*a*) would be to write history or biography, not a story, and (*b*) would sacrifice the novelist's art of selecting and recombining the real elements into a fictitious whole. For life leaves loose ends and unrevealed solutions ; it is the proper business of the novelist to employ the key of human character to interpret life to mankind. Two common phrases may be cited in illustration of what is stated above : (1) the fallacy of the happy ending. A novelist seeking this reconciliation between character and fate departs sometimes too far from probability, which means from the illusion of reality. He uses his prerogative over-arbitrarily, and an ending that would have raised no demur in a romance proper is found unlikely (i.e. unreal) in a novel. A striking example is in *The Light that Failed* by R. Kipling, to which the author actually wr. 2 endings : one *real*, arising out of character and incident ; the other *false*, arising out of the spoilt taste of merely sentimental romanticizers, for whose pleasure Kipling forced fate to defy character. The *real* version was proper to the novel, because it was proper to life. (2) The second illustrative phrase is, that truth is stranger than fiction. This means that the novelist, in his anxiety to display what is real in fictitious guise, and hampered, as he must be, by the physical limitations of a bk., does not trust himself to carry the illusion of reality beyond a restricted (however wide) range of circumstances. His art cannot be stretched to the demands upon it. There are real things in life so strange, and so remote from the limits set to a novel, as to lie outside a novelist's compass. If he tried to represent them, his novel would seem to be a romance.*

The N. may be defined, accordingly, relying partly on the assistance of Dr. E. A. Baker (*Hist. Eng. Novel*, i, Witherby, 1924), as a selection and recombination of episodes or aspects of human life, possessing spectacular or dramatic interest, and their interpretation by means of a fictitious narrative of unfixed but readable length, almost invariably in prose. The qualification, ' almost invariably ', is necessary in order to admit such novels in verse as Chaucer's (q.v.) *Troilus and Criseyde*, Pushkin's (q.v.) *Oniégin*, E. B. Browning's (q.v.) *Aurora Leigh*, and others.

In this sense, the earliest novels in Europe were the *sagas* (q.v.) of Iceland, which differed, e.g., from the *Cid* (q.v.) of Spain, inasmuch as, though founded similarly on the real, they did not romanticize the real out of the semblance of reality. The Icelandic *sagas* made no propaganda : they rose and fell, without

---

* The law-courts often illustrate this proverb. A striking instance was supplied by the Midland Bank Case, November, 1924, the true ' plot ' of which was stranger than any novelist would have ventured to invent for the illusion of his readers.

posterity or imitators ; and the N. in European lit. is traced directly to the first stories founded on experience, dressed in fiction, and interpreted by psychology (or, the automatic laws of character in action), which were written by Boccaccio (q.v.) in Italy in the 14th cent. Chaucer's (q.v.) *Canterbury Tales* may be described as novels in solution ; they display certain essentials of the art—character-study, narrative power, selection of milieu (amounting to plot), etc.,—but they lack construction, or the interaction of characters, with the resultant development of a single action from its beginning to its inevitable close. This special quality of the novelist's art is at the same time the most difficult. Not only does it require that character and its motives should be understood, but also that they should be interpreted intelligibly to readers, within a limited space for description and display, and without the aid of visible scenes and spoken words. In this sense the N. moves in a dimension less than an acted play. These difficulties, including the fact that a novel, unlike life, is discontinuous, and that the illusion of reality must yet be maintained, caused practitioners of the art in Europe to postpone (unconsciously, of course, and by the instinctive choice of the line of least resistance) the N. of the interplay of characters worked out to a probable conclusion of the action thus caused and coloured, and rather to concentrate their skill on depicting the progress of one character through a series of linked happenings. Bunyan's (q.v.) *Pilgrim's Progress* is a novel of this kind—the greatest novel in the world—and its success is permanent and enduring. Far more commonly, however, the hero of such a novel was selected for his habit of yielding to, not of resisting and conquering, temptation. The vagabond- or rogue-hero was a favourite choice of novelists, and his vagabondage was along the down-hill path. The Picaresque Novel, as it is called, from Span. *pícaro*, a rogue, took its rise in the country whence it took its name, and where the humours of the road enjoyed the encouragement of the southern sun and of the easy temperament of those on whom it shone. *Celestina* (q.v.), 1499, and *Lazarillo* (q.v.), a few years later, were the first of a long line of picaresque fiction, in which Aleman's (q.v.) *Guzman* (we are still in Spain) marked a milestone on the road which Sorel, Lesage, Defoe, Fielding and Smollett (see s.vv.) were to travel. The *Pickwick Papers* (s.v. Dickens) was the last of this kind : ' with the extinction of the highway and the slow death of our country inns, the picaresque novel ceased to be ' (*Times Lit. Supp.*, 30 Oct., 1913) ; and probably the pace is too swift for the motor car to revive it. (A learned essay on the Picaresque N. forms the introduction by Mr. H. Warner Allen to his edn. (Routledge, N.D.) of Mabbe's transln. of *Celestina*).

To the major names mentioned above of the writers of the 18th and 19th centuries, to whom we owe the N. in its present form, are to be added those of Prévost (q.v.) for *Manon Lescaut*, and of Sterne (q.v.), for the sake of *Tristram Shandy*, 1760. Sterne 'was nothing if not an innovator. And in no

innovation was he more daring than in that which widened the scope and loosened the structure of the novel ' (*C.H.E.L.*, x, 48). Prior to 1749, it may be said, when Fielding publd. *Tom Jones*, the N. did not exist, or hardly existed, in its modern guise ; and between 1749 and 1849, when Dickens publd. his *David Copperfield*, we may date its golden age. 'The provision which we have here made ', declared Fielding in his ' bill of fare ' to *Tom Jones* (bk. i, ch. 1), ' is no other than Human Nature ', and naturalism in fiction, as a critical category, may be deemed to have started with that dictum. (Note that Fielding's ' human nature ' was internal—the operation of character and psychology ; Pope's ' nature ' was external,—the laws deduced from phenomena ; and see s.v. Nature).

Novels with a purpose, political novels, hist. novels, novels of adventure, domestic novels, and so forth, with all the resources of love, crime, war, etc., as the milieu in which to exhibit the ordeal of character in action, have flowed in full spate since the middle of the 18th cent. The *genre* acquired in the clear air of France a fine quality of realistic transcription which crossed to the fogs of Engld. with some of its sharpness blurred. In Russia, the vastness of the country, and a certain nervousness produced by political conditions, introduced into the criticism of life, which is the philosophy of the novel, a bigger sense of contrast between spiritual values and material possessions than is found in fiction further West. Something is said s.vv. Russ. lit., and the names of individual Russ. novelists, of this peculiar temper of resignation.

It will have been gathered that the N. in Europe is really a plant of indigenous growth ; and that, whereas tales or stories have been narrated in every clime and age (e.g. the *Arabian Nights' Entertainments*, fairy-tales, fables, and so forth), the true N. of psychology, which has grown to such immense vogue, is a product of modern, as distinct from ancient conditions. But this must not exclude the influence, comparatively small, of Gk. fiction (see s.v.) on European letters. The Gk. novelists were not available till a late date : Heliodorus, for instance, was first known by a Lat. transln. of his *Theagenes and Chariclea*, publd., 1551 ; Amyot (q.v.) transld. it into Fr., and Thos. Underdowne into Engl., 1569. He wr., says lord Ernle (*Quarterly Review*, July, 1913), ' like a learned recluse, a Mr. Barlow of the fourth century ' (see s.v. T. Day), and, though he became a true father of the romance of adventure in the 16th and 17th centuries, yet the N. in Europe traces its direct descent from other fathers. (Reference may be made to the monograph of Dr. E. A. Baker, *supra*. ; to the *Hist. of the Fr. Novel*, by prof. G. Saintsbury, 2 vols., Macmillan, 1917-9 ; to *The Historical Novel*, by Dr. M. E. Speare, Oxford Univ. Press, N.Y., 1924 ; and s.vv. Woman, Troilus, Roman-à-clef, Femme incomprise).

Novikov, Nicolai Ivanovich (1744-1818) : Russ. publicist ; illustrated in his unhappy experience the intellectual *volte-face* executed by the empress Catherine ii (q.v.) between 1768 and 1790 ; in this respect, N.'s experience was similar to that of Radishchev (q.v.). N. was first recommended to the favour of the empress as a soldier of the time of the so-called Palace revolution, and became secretary to her constitutional commission of 1768. His literary gifts were a further recommendation to the imperial bellelettrist, and he publd. successively 2 social weekly newspapers, 'The Drone', 1769, and 'The Pourtrayer', 1773. In the latter was issued a travel-narrative, which really anticipated Radish-chev's. N. was also editor and publisher of an hist. 'library', and varied these vols. with social studies, leading to his next journalistic venture, the weekly 'Morning Light', filled chiefly with translns. from Germ. pietists. The profits of this venture are said to have covered the costs of founding 2 schools for orphans. Gradually, N.'s philanthropic and public-spirited interests deepened ; he made acquaintance with leaders of thought in Rosi-crucian and Freemason circles ; both obnox-ious to the hardening autocracy of the empress. He helped to found a ' society of the friends of the sciences ', which was converted, 1784, into a publication society ; and N. is said to have increased the circulation of bks. in Russia, reaching untapped channels of popular dis-tribution. Among the many works of his press was a life of Washington, which closed with the remark, that liberty, exiled from Europe, would seek refuge in America. N. at the same time, from funds placed at his disposal, undertook large works of social welfare ; and the whole tendency of his activi-ties became more perilous and obnoxious to authority in this epoch of the Fr. Revolution. The Church was invited to examine his publications, now numbering several hundreds ; and though N. was pronounced an exemplary Christian, he was found to have issued vols. (chiefly dealing with the Fr. encyclopedists) of a harmful and dangerous character. In 1792 he had to close down his press ; he was incarcerated as a revolutionary, tainted with the infection of the Fr. plague ; and it was not till after Catherine's death, 1796, that her

successor, the emperor Paul, released N. ; then too much shaken by his losses and sufferings to enjoy the remnant of his life. N.'s mysticism (q.v.), writes Vogüé (*Roman Russe*, 31) ' was the confused spiritual protest against the negative teaching of the encyclo-pedists and the invasion of rationalism ; we re-discover in a Tolstoi and a Dostoievsky the same protest renewed against the harshness of the positive sciences '.

Noydens, Benito Remigio (17th cent.): Span. moralist. Wr., 1666, *Moral History of the God Momus*, and his mischief on earth in various incarnations ; and other bks. of a similarly edifying tendency. N. edited, 1674, the *Tesoro* of the Castilian language by Cobarrubias (q.v.), much to the benefit of the labours of the Spanish Academy (q.v.), when they undertook their definitive *Diccionario* (q.v.).

Nuñez, Hernan (*c.* 1475-1552): Span. humanist ; described as de Guzman and de Toledo alter-natively, and known by the scholar's-name of Nonius Pincianus. N. was associated with the Gk. text of the polyglott Bible of card. Ximenes (q.v.), and taught at Alcalá and Salamanca univs.; he edited Seneca, 1536, and ' was the most learned man whom Spain had possessed ' (Hallam, i, 343).

Nutzhorn, H. F. F. (1834-66): Dan. scholar ; Homeric critic. Wr. Dan. treatise on the subject, 1863, transld. into Germ. and publd. (*The Method of the Origin of the Homeric Poems*) with a pref. by Madvig (q.v.), 1869. ' The author is perhaps unduly violent in his invective against the views then prevalent in Northern Germany, and political differences between Denmark and Prussia appear to give a keener edge to his controversial temper' (Sandys, iii, 328). But the work has permanent value in Homer (q.v.) -lit.

Nyerup, Rasmus (1759-1829): Dan. literary critic. Wr., jointly with Rahbeck (q.v.), a *Contribution to the History of Dan. Poetry*, 1800-08 ; and, jointly with Kraft, a native of Norway, a *Dict. of Dan. and Norse Writers*, 1818-20. N. was busied, too, with Rahbeck, again, and a like-minded antiquary named Abrahamson, with the study of Dan. folklore and antiquities.

O

Oberon : See s.vv. **Huon of Bordeaux,** and **Wieland.**

Ocampo, de, Florian (*c.* 1499-*c.* 1555): Span. historian ; of mean parts ; wr. 4 bks. of a general history of Spain, which began at the Flood, and left off before it became interesting. The work was continued, but still not com-pleted, by Morales (q.v.).

Occleve, Thomas (*c.* 1370-*c.* 1450): Engl. Chaucerian poet ; variously written Hoccleve. Wr. chiefly religious verse, in Chaucer's metres.

Ockley, Simon (1678-1720) : Engl. Orientalist ; prof. of Arabic at Cambridge, 1711 ; wr. *Conquest of Syria, Persia, and Egypt by the Saracens*, vol. i, 1708 ; vol. ii, 1718 ; transld. into Fr., 1748 ; for many years, the leading authority on Mohammedan history ; much

utilized by Gibbon (q.v.) in his *Decline and Fall*, esp., ch. 51, where Gibbon deplores in a foot-note the harsh fate of O., whose ' labours were consummated in a jail ' for debt ; O. was a poor clergyman with a large family.

Oehlenschläger, Adam Gottlob (1779-1850) : Dan. national poet ; by common consent, the most eminent poet of Denmark. O. was inspired by Steffens (q.v.), the Scand. missionary of culture, who brought romance (q.v.) home from Ger-many ; and, in addition to this foreign romantic influence, by which he was ' converted at one sitting ', O. succumbed at another sitting to the genius of his own forefathers, discovered in an Icelandic copy of the *Heimskringla* (q.v.) of Snorri (q.v.). ' The event was as full of import to Scandinavian literature as Luther's famous discovery of the Bible was to German liberty ' (E. Gosse, *Lit. Northern Europe*, 148). From *Hakon Jarl's Saga* in Snorri's bk., O. constructed his tragedy of *Hakon Jarl*, the first of a series of national dramas, at once reviving the national memory of the past glory of the North and liberating the Dan. stage from the thrall of Fr. classical drama : the first being the fruits of Snorri's Norse histories, and the second of Steffen's romanticism. ' The strings that Oehlenschläger touched had never before been heard in Denmark ; he led his audience into a world of thought and vision where its feet had never stood before, and he spoke in a language that had never yet been declaimed from behind the footlights ' (Gosse, *ib.*, 151). O.'s good fortune in obtaining the services of Fru Nielsen (' the Mrs. Siddons of the Danish stage ') to act the parts of his national heroines, is also worthy of mention. In 1829, he was crowned by Tegnér (q.v.) in Lund cathedral as the Scand. laureate ; and, though his genius was adversely affected for some years on account of the very excess of popular adulation, he maintained his supremacy unchallenged. Baggesen (q.v.) was opposed to the assault on the classical tradition, and selected O.'s dramatic poem, *Aladdin*, 1805, for his main attack ; but O.'s fame rose above controversy, and soared securely on the wings of such masterpieces of drama as *Helge*, 1814, and *Dina*, 1842. There was a long series of plays between these 2, as well as several vols. of poetry, some tales, and satires (directed by Baggesen), and a monthly review, *Prometheus*, which O. edited, 1832-34. Danes, declares the critic whom we have quoted, measure other poets by the standard of O., but there is no one by whom they dream of measuring *him* ; and native and foreign readers concur in reverent appreciation.

Oersted, Anders Sandoë (1778-1860) : Dan. jurist. Wr. a special treatise on the theory and history of law, which aimed at elucidating the principles of society. O.'s *History of my Life and Times*, 1851-57, is a valuable document of the age. O.'s brother, Hans Christian Oersted (1777-1851) won repute as a natural philosopher, and his name, though inappropriate here, is for ever associated with the discovery of electro-magnetism.

Ogilby, John (1600-76) : Engl. printer ; translr. O.'s verse transln. of Homer's *Iliad* was utilized by Pope (q.v.).

Ohnet, Georges (born, 1848) : Fr. novelist ; popular and prolific. His best-known tale, *le Maître des Forges*, had an extraordinarily large sale ; and O. may, perhaps, be called the Mrs. Henry Wood (q.v.) of France.

Oldmixon, John (1673-1742) : Engl. poet ; historian ; pamphleteer. Wr. *The Secret History of Europe*, 1712-15, an attack on the Tory Government ; *The Critical History of Engld. Ecclesiastical and Civil*, 2 vols., 1724-6, to which he added *An Essay on Criticism ; as it regards Design, Thought and Expression, in Prose and Verse*, ' an avowedly and, perhaps, intentionally, rambling discourse, supposed to be in the manner of Montaigne ', q.v., and containing ' some fair hits at Dryden, Addison, Pope, and others ' (qq.v. ; *C.H.E.L.*, ix, 237). Pope replied by

putting O. in his poets' inferno of the *Dunciad*. O.'s *History of Engld. during the Reigns of the Royal House of Stuart*, 1730 (continued forwards, 1735, and backwards, 1739) was controversial in purpose. Wr., too, a tragedy *The Governor of Cyprus*, 1703, and an opera, *The Grove*, 1700.

Oldys, William (1696-1761) : Engl. antiquary : Norroy king-at-arms ; edited, with a biography, sir W. Ralegh's (q.v.) *History of the World*, 1736 ; literary secretary to Robert Harley, earl of Oxford and Mortimer, and was associated with Dr. Johnson (q.v.) in editing the *Harleian Miscellany*, 1744-6 ; an industrious delver, before I. D'Israeli (q.v.), into the curiosities of lit.

Olearius, Adam (1603-71) : Germ. Orientalist. Travelled 6 years in the East with P. Fleming (q.v.), and wr., 1647, a prose description of the journey, which had extended as far as Ispahan ; made translns. from Oriental lit.

Oliphant, Laurence (1829-88) : Engl. novelist ; mystic ; traveller. ' As a man of letters, Oliphant will rank neither as a religious philosopher, nor as a novelist, but as a satirist of society. His bks. of travel, *The Russ. Shores of the Black Sea* (1853), *Episodes in a Life of Adventure*, etc., interesting as they are, are not unique like (sir R.) Burton's (q.v.). His *Piccadilly* (1870) and *Altiora Peto* (1883) have the form of novels, but not the reality. Their vitality lies in the satire which runs through them ' (H. Walker, *Lit. Victorian Era*, 1046). The most remarkable episode in O.'s adventurous career was his resignation of his seat in the House of Commons, in order to join the religious community of the ' prophet ', Thos. Lake Harris (1823-1906), the mystic and medium, in America. O. was correspondent to *The Times* in the Franco-Prussian War, and, generally, a brilliant, if erratic, writer, of a type as rare as it is undefinable.

Oliphant, Margaret (1829-97) : Engl. novelist ; biographer ; *née* Wilson ; a distant relative to her husband and to L.O. above, of whom she wr. a *Memoir*, 1892. Wr., too, *William Blackwood and his Sons*, 1897, a vivid sketch of the founder and members of the great publishing-house in Edinburgh, which fathered Mrs. O.'s writings ; and a *Life of Edward Irving*, 1862 (Irving was the founder of the Irvingite or Catholic Apostolic Church). These are 3 excellent biographies, and Mrs. O. did good work, too, as editor of the ' Foreign Classics for English Readers ' (Blackwood), for which she wr. the vols. on Dante and Cervantes and collaborated in the vol. on Molière (qq.v.). Her novels, contributed to *Blackwood's Magazine* from 1853 onwards, included *Mrs. Margaret Maitland*, 1849 ; *Salem Chapel*, *The Perpetual Curate*, and *Miss Marjoribanks*, comprising *The Chronicles of Carlingford*, 1861-5 ; *A Beleaguered City*, etc. The self-imposed necessity of supporting a family of nephews and nieces as well as her own children undoubtedly caused her to overproduce, but she is memorable for several good bks., and for her zest in popularizing knowledge.

Oliva, de, Hernan Perez (c. 1494-1533) : Span. moralist ; edu. at Salamanca, Alcalá, Paris and Rome, and became prof. of theology and of 8 hendecasyllabic (11-syllabled) verses, rhyming *ab ab ab cc*. Its origins are traced to the popular poetry of Sicily and the mainland ; Schiller (q.v.) is correct in calling love its creator :

Stanze, dich schuf die Liebe, die zärtlich schmachtende. Dreimal
Fliehest du schamhaft und kehrst dreimal verlangend zurück.

Its more formal adoption for serious purposes was due to Boccaccio (q.v.), and Lorenzo de Medici (q.v.) used it as a vernacular model, in his programme for raising the dignity of the Tuscan tongue. Its true founder in Ital. poetry was Politian (q.v.), who ' applies the experience of his age towards the fuller development of the innate powers of the national measure, and hands it on perfected to Ariosto ' (*P.E.L.*, iv, 134) ; he ' gave to Ariosto the Italian epical metre perfected, and established a standard of style amid the anarchy which threatened the literature of Italy with ruin ' (Symonds, *Ital. Renaissance* iv, 351). The successive practitioners of the metre in Italy were Boiardo, Ariosto and Tasso (qq.v.). The octave stanza is difficult to manipulate, and calls into action the highest qualities of a poet in his command of rhythm, harmony, and versification. The rhyme-scheme, it will be seen, is exacting, and the up-and-down movement, noted by Schiller (*supra*), had to be fitted in epic poetry to military as well as erotic topics : when we recall what Hallam (q.v. ; *Lit. of Europe*, ii, 98) said of Tasso, we realize the value of the service rendered by Politian to Ital. poetry by his choice and use of this measure. ' The *ottava rima* ', says Hallam, ' has its inconveniences ; even its intricacy, when once mastered, renders it more monotonous, and the recurrence of marked rhymes, the breaking of the sense into equal divisions, while they communicate to it a regularity that secures the humblest verse from sinking to the level of prose, deprive it of that variety which the hexameter most eminently possesses. Ariosto lessened this effect by the rapid flow of his language, and perhaps by its negligence and inequality ; in Tasso, who is more sustained at a high pitch of elaborate expression than any great poet except Virgil, and in whom a prosaic or feeble stanza will rarely be found, the uniformity of cadence may conspire with the lusciousness of style to produce a sense of satiety in the reader. This is said rather to account for the injustice, as it seems to me, with which some speak of Tasso, than to express my own sentiments ; for there are few poems of great length which I so little wish to lay aside as the *Jerusalem* '. Chaucer (q.v.) nowhere uses the *ottava rima*, though it became naturalized in Fr., Germ., Engl. and other verse : it was an 8-line stanza of Machault (q.v.), which, with the addition of an alexandrine (s.v. Alexander) verse at the end, became the famous and favourite stanza of Spenser (q.v.) in the *Faerie Queen*, and of many succeeding poets ; and to Machault, again, Chaucer went for his 7-line stanza, and, probably, for his heroic couplet. This last measure became the national measure in Engl. poetry, and was adopted by Pope (q.v.) for his transln. of the *Iliad*. But blank verse (q.v.) was rapidly overtaking the heroic couplet ; and, if a parallel be sought to Politian's achievement with the Ital. measure of *ottava rima*, it will be found in Marlowe's (q.v.) similar achievement in Engld. with blank verse.

Otway, Thomas (1652-85) : Engl. dramatist ; Wr. *Don Carlos*, 1676 ; *The Orphan*, 1680 ; *Venice Preserved*, 1682 ; these 2 comedies have been frequently revived, and have been transld. into Fr. and other languages. Taine (q.v.) praises O. highly, but thinks he was born 100 years too late to repeat the triumphs of Shakespeare and Webster (qq.v.) : ' for the most part, Otway is a poet of his time, dull and forced in colour ; buried, like the rest, in the heavy, grey, clouded atmosphere, half English and half French, in which the bright lights brought over from France are snuffed out by the insular fogs '. O. died in great poverty.

Oudaen, Joachim (1628-92) : Dutch poet ; imitator of Vondel (q.v.), but failed to attain the vigour and nobility of his master.

Ouida, pen-name of Louise de la Ramée (1840-1908) : Engl. novelist ; of Fr. orig. on her mother's side ; lived mostly in Italy. Wr. *Under Two Flags* and other novels, which enjoyed considerable vogue, but were characterized by an exuberant zeal for reproving social vices and by an exaggerated enthusiasm for military and sportsmen heroes. Lang (q.v., *Hist. Eng. Lit.*, 634) derives her from G. A. Lawrence (1827-76; author of *Guy Livingstone, or Thorough*, 1857) ; prof. H. Walker (*Lit. Victorian Era*) does not mention her at all ; an interesting biography of her was written by Elizabeth Lee ; and it may be suggested that O.'s inspiration came more directly from George Sand (q.v.) than from any Engl. predecessor. Her luxurious, even sumptuous, milieu has not survived the disintegration of a mixed society.

Overbury, Thomas (1581-1613) : Engl. poet. ; knt., 1608 ; implicated in a court intrigue, and was poisoned in the Tower of London. Wr. *A Wife : now the Widow of sir Thomas Overbury. Being a most exquisite and singular Poem of the choice of a wife. Whereunto are added many witty Characters, and conceited Newes, written by himself and other learned Gentlemen his friends*, posth., 1614. The *characters* were devised as a compliment to O.'s memory, and kept fairly closely to the class of society which the ill-fated young poet had adorned.

Ovid ; Publius Ovidius Naso (43 B.C.-17 A.D.): Roman poet ; a favourite author in medieval schools ; familiar at the court of Charlemagne. His *Ars Amatoria* (Art of Love) had immense influence on the code of chivalric courtesy (see s.v. Love) ; it was transld. by Chrétien de Troyes (q.v.), whose version has been lost ; and it directly inspired the Lat. work *de arte amandi* by André (q.v.), chaplain to the Fr. court, in the early 13th cent. This work was shortly afterwards rendered into the vernacular by Drouart la Vache, and expounded elaborate rules for governing the approach of the sexes and the service and psychology of love, as binding on aspirants to chivalry, and as exemplified in the manners of the Round Table (q.v.). Part i of the *Romance of the Rose* (q.v.) is the most exhaustive exposition of the whole matter in medieval poetry, and transmitted the Ovidian love-lore to generations of chivalric romancers. O.'s *Metamorphoses* and *Heroides* were only second in popularity to his *Art of Love* at this time, and, later, surpassed it. Chrétien, again, transld. portions; and separate tales, such as Pyramus and Thisbe, Dido, Medea, Orpheus, Ariadne, Philomela, Narcissus, and many others, became part of the common stock of romance (q.v.), and found countless imitators. Paris is bracketed with Tristan as a type of true lover by Dante (*Inf.* v, 67), who spoke of the *Metamorphoses* as supplying a model of style, requiring allegorical interpretation (*Vulg. Eloq.*, ii, 6); the interpreter was found in Virgilio (q.v.). A later remarkable production in the interpreter's vein was a Fr. anon. poem, dating from 14th cent., in about 70,000 8-syllable lines, containing a transln. of each of O.'s fables, and an allegorico theological disquisition on each; a similar 'moral Ovid' in Lat. was written by Pierre Bersuire (d. 1362). Chaucer (q.v.) was an avid reader of O., and frequently quotes from his stories, which, since Chrétien's time, have found their way into all literatures, though his authority as arbiter of manners has naturally declined since the decay of courtesy. 'Trans ego tellurem, trans altas audiar undas' (over the earth and o'er the mighty seas, my voice shall ring), he wr. of himself, in one of those appeals to personal fame (q.v.) which lifted up medieval intellects; and the prophecy is just. The *ed. pr.* of his works was issued at Rome, 1471, under the supervision of bp. Andrea de Bussi (q.v.); Marot (q.v.) was among the translrs. (1552) of the *Metamorphoses*; Arthur Golding (q.v.) rendered it in Engl. alexandrines (1565-67), and Tuberville rendered the *Heroides* (1567). Both these versions, esp. the former, were familiar to Shakespeare, who was at the same time a student of O. in the original Lat. [The main evidence is *Rape of Lucrece* from O., *Fasti*, ii, which was not transld. at that date; Meres (q.v.) wr., 1598: 'the sweet, witty soul of Ovid lives in mellifluous and honey-tongued Shakespeare']. Dryden, Swinburne, and W. Morris are among later Engl. Ovidians.

Oviedo y Valdés, Gonzalo Hernandez (1478-1557): Span. conqueror and historian. O. was edu. with prince Jean, son of king Ferdinand and queen Isabella; assisted at the siege of Granada; fought in the Ital. campaign, and was a friend of Columbus (q.v.). In 1514, he set sail for the New World, in which the greater part of his life was spent in various administrative posts. Wr., 1555, a poem of 7,500 lines on eminent men of Spain in all ages, a part of which was first issued in 1880 under the title of *las Quinquagenas de la Nobleza de España*, and which is sometimes confused with his bk. of prose-dialogues, *Batallas y Quinquagenas*, 1550, which is not accessible. His best-known work is a 'Summary of the Natural and General History of the Indies', 1525, which he amplified in a longer and independent work on the same subject, 1535-57.

Owen, John (1560-1622): Welsh Lat. poet. Born in Carnarvonshire; headmaster of Warwick school; buried in St. Paul's Cathedral. Wr. Lat. *Epigrams* (1606; re-issued, 1624),

less famous in Engld. than on the continent, where they found ready appreciation by cosmopolitan scholars. O. possessed genuine wit, and a happy faculty of neat expression, which served him in good stead in the age when Buchanan (q.v.) was at the head of literate Latinists.

Oxenstjerna, Johan Gabriel (1750-1818): Swed. poet; a member of the great family of diplomatists, though hardly their compeer in the literary field; count by rank. O.'s light verse, which recommended him to the favour of the literate and Francophil king Gustavus iii (q.v.), is in curious contrast with his choice of Milton's (q.v.) *Paradise Lost* for the exercise of his talents as translr.; even more surprising are the merits of the transln., which Tegnér (q.v.), no mean judge, greeted as 'not a foreign Milton, but Milton rejuvenated.'

Oxford Movement (Engl.): Descriptive epithet of the religious revival, directed partly against the rise of rationalism in Germ. theology, and partly against the perfunctory manner in which the clergy performed their appointed duties. Strauss (q.v.) in Germany, and Comte (q.v.) in France may be taken to represent the rationalistic doctrine to which the Catholic reaction was a reply. The movement, as such, took 2 lines: (1) intellectual, and (2) æsthetic. With the former, or Tractarian movement, so called from the *Tracts for the Times*, no. 90 of which was Newman's (q.v.) *Remarks on certain Passages in the xxxix Articles*, and with the ensuing clerical and lay controversies, we are not here directly concerned. With the latter, the æsthetic movement, lit. is directly concerned, both in its action and reaction. Noting, first, that there was an Oxford Movement before it moved, in the sense that the 'Noetics' of Oriel Coll. had preceded Keble's Assize sermon (see esp. *Pre-Tractarian Oxford*, by Rev. W. Tuckwell; London, 1909), and, next, that the Movement proper started in 1833, and is dated by Newman, its leader, from 14 Jan. in that year, when Keble preached on *National Apostasy* at St. Mary's, Oxford ('I have ever considered and kept the day as the start of the religious movement of 1833'), we have to observe that, with 2 exceptions, to which we refer immediately, the intellectual leaders were not the æsthetic leaders. The intellectual attraction of the Church of Rome, which Newman entered, 1845, when the Movement proper may be said to have closed, corresponded to an æsthetic attraction to romanticism (see s.v. Romance), which was, in most of its exemplars, wholly independent of religion. They even used, with complete appreciation, the romantic cadences of the Engl. Bible (q.v.), without in the least succumbing to the spiritual content of the words used; and it was this secondary, æsthetic, non-religious reaction from rationalism which found abundant expression in Engl. lit., and which reinforced (and was in turn reinforced by) the ritualistic and intellectual movement. The sensuous beauty of medieval art made its powerful appeal to D. G. Rossetti (q.v.) and his Pre-Raphaelite (q.v.) brethren, at the same time as the Tractarians were moved by the religious ideas which that art expressed: the form superior to the poetic expression with which it is united' (*C.H.E.L.*, xiii, 193). Sir F.P.'s (*supra*) other sons were (iii) Wm. Gifford P. (1846-88), traveller and diplomatist ; author of *A Year's Journey through Central and Eastern Arabia*, 1865 ; (iv.) Robert H.I.P. (born, 1827), editor of the *Dict. of Political Economy* ; and (v) sir Reginald F.D.P. (1829-1903), an official in the House of Commons.

Palimpsests : See **Copyists**.

Palissot de Mantenoy, Charles (1730-1814) : Fr. dramatist and critic. Wr., 1757, *Petites lettres contre les grands philosophes*, aimed at Rousseau, Diderot, and others (qq.v., and s.v. Philosophes), and dramatized the letters in his play, *les Philosophes*, 1760. To this comedy the *Écossaise* of Voltaire (q.v.) was the immediate reply. Wr., too, satiric comedy, *les Courtisanes*, 1782, in the manner of Molière's *Tartufe*, but can hardly be said to have succeeded in rehabilitating Aristophanes on the Fr. stage, though his plays and critical writings no doubt considerably exasperated his adversaries.

Palissy, Bernard (1510-89) : Fr. man of science and letters ; he died in the Bastille, where he was imprisoned for his Protestant convictions, which had very nearly involved him in the massacre of St. Bartholomew. P. was a potter by trade, and after 20 years' experiments discovered the secret of his enamel, by which he has become renowned. The famous passage is to be found in his treatise *Art de la Terre*. His works, which combined technical knowledge and scientific research with considerable literary skill of exposition, treated of natural and artificial waters, of metals, salts, stones, pottery, etc. The short Fr. titles of his treatises are *Recette Véritable* (for art-collectors) and *Discours Admirables*.

Pall Mall Gazette (7 Feb., 1865-27 Oct., 1923) : Engl. evening newspaper, founded by George Smith (q.v.), and edited successively by Frederick Greenwood (1830-1909), John Morley (q.v.), W. T. Stead (1849-1912), E. T. Cook (q.v.), on the model, rough but recognizable, of the *Anti-Jacobin* (q.v.) in the 18th cent. ; Alfred, visct. Milner (1854-1925) was an assistant editor under Stead. Another literary association was the extraction of its title from *Pendennis* by Thackeray (q.v. ; died, 1863), formerly an intimate friend of the founder.

Palmenorden (Germ.) : Order of the Palm ; title of a literary society, founded, 1617, under the patronage of prince Louis of Anhalt. Its original name was the Fructifying (*fruchtbringende*) Society, reminiscent of the Florentine Academy *della Crusca* (q.v.) : each member assuming a name and coat-of-arms fancifully appropriate to methods of fructification. Thus Schottelius (q.v.) was the 'sifting' (*der Suchende*) member. The society was one of many formed in the 17th cent., mainly with the object of disseminating the seeds of linguistic, metrical, and stylistic reform sown by Opitz (q.v.).

Palmieri, Matteo (*c*. 1405-*c*. 1478) : It. theological poet ; judiciary office-holder in Florence. Wr. lives and histories in Lat., and (1451-65) *La Città di Vita* in the vernacular, in 100 cantos and 3 bks., on the model of the *Divina Commedia* ; a long allegory of the soul, circling

through planetary regions, under the doctrine of free-will ; interesting in its own times on account of P.'s consciousness of heresy in his theological views, and, historically, as the latest example of *terza rima* (q.v.) employed on a worthy theme. Sir John Davies' (q.v.) poem on the soul in 4-line stanzas, 1599, was an enterprise in the same class.

Palsgrave, John (died, 1554) : Engl. grammarian. Tutor to princess, later queen, Mary, and chaplain to king Henry viii. Wr., 1530, *l'Eclaircissement de la langue française*, earliest considerable Fr. grammar for Engl. students ; and displayed his equal readiness to introduce other resources of continental scholarship to his countrymen by his transln. of Volder's (q.v.) Lat. play *Acolastus*, 1540, which he eulogized as a choice nosegay gathered out of the sweet-smelling gardens of pure Latinity : an estimable and useful pedant.

Paludan-Müller, Frederik (1809-76) : Dan. poet ; son of bp. of Aarhuus ; a contemporary, it will be noted, of Tennyson (q.v.), and not unlike the English laureate in his cultivation of delicate beauty in expression. P.-M. has been compared, too, with Swinburne (q.v.) for his union of classic themes with dramatic passion. The date of his début was the same as Tennyson's : *Love at Court*, a romantic play, appeared in 1832, and *The Dancing Girl* in 1833 ; 2 lyrical dramas, *Amor and Psyche* and *Venus*, 1834 and 1841, led up to P.-M.'s most striking poem, the epic *Adam Homo* (part i, 1841 ; part ii, 1848). Composed in the Ital. measure of the 8-line stanza (see s.v. Ottava rima), *Adam Homo* ' is the history of a single man, a Dane in the Denmark of the poet's day, from his cradle to his grave. The hero is a Philistine of the Philistines, but his character is worked out with an irony so subtle, that we begin by sympathizing with the man whom we end in ridiculing and despising. The poem is full of great and original qualities ' (sir E. Gosse, *Lit. of Northern Europe*, 188 ; sir Edmund cites the remark of G. Brandes, q.v., that ' *Adam Homo* is a piece of Denmark, a piece of our history, a piece of living cloth cut out of the web of time '). P.-M.'s other works include *Kalanus*, a lyrical drama, 1857 ; *Tithonus* (another Tennysonian parallel), 1844 ; and *Adonis*, 1874, the last-named being in many respects the most moving and highly-finished poem which this eminent writer produced.

Panckoucke : Fr. family of booksellers and publishers, settled, first, at Lille, later, 1798, in Paris ; a mlle P. married Suard (q.v.), the journalist.

Pandolfini, Agnolo (1360-1446) : It. moralist. Reputed author of treatise on domestic economy (*del Governo della Famiglia*), which is of exceptional interest, and ranks with Castiglione's *Courtier* of the next century as a picture of private life in the Renaissance. P. belonged to an influential family, and it is probable that this bk. was adapted from Alberti's third bk. *della Famiglia* and was ascribed by its adapter to P.

Pantagruelion : Sacred herb of Pantagruel (see s.v. Rabelais ; bk. iii, ch. 49 to end of bk.). By P. Rabelais intended hemp, which was first used in the time of Francis i to make ropes by which to suspend the victims of religious bigotry while the fire was kindled at their feet. Rabelais, not venturing an open protest against this misuse of the herb, discusses its virtues and wonders, and hints at his deeper meaning in his usual style of oblique and profuse narrative.

Panurge : Companion of Pantagruel (see s.v. Rabelais) on his expedition to the Oracle. S. T. Coleridge (q.v.) calls him (*Table Talk*, 15 June, 1830), ' the pollarded man, the man with every faculty except the reason ' ; sir W. Besant (q.v.; *Rabelais*, Blackwood) writes, ' Panurge is, I believe, the careful portrait of a man without a soul ' ; and prof. Saintsbury (*Short History Fr. Lit.*, 159) declares that, ' the main idea of Panurge is the absence of all morality in the wide Aristotelian sense with the presence of almost all other good qualities '.

Papebroch, Daniel (17th cent.) : Dutch scholar ; Jesuit. Edited ecclesiastical texts ; and incurred the resentment of the learned Order of the Benedictines, whose chief scholar, Mabillon (q.v.), took up the challenge in a vol. which founded textual criticism on true principles of the science of palæography (q.v.).

Paradol, Prévost (1829-70) : Fr. journalist ; disputes with Veuillot (q.v.) the title of the first journalist of his age ; Fr. minister at Washington ; died by suicide. Wr. for *Journal des Débats* and *Courier du Dimanche* (one number of which was suppressed in consequence of his article, 1866). P.'s works include *la France Nouvelle*, 1868, in which he clearly foretold the coming conflict of the Franco-Prussian War ; and *Studies of Fr. Moralists*, 1864, which is still widely read.

Paré, Amboise (c. 1510-89) : Fr. man of science and letters ; court-surgeon. Wr. medical treatises, and a vol. of memoirs, *Apologie et Voyages*.

Parentucelli, Tommaso. See **Nicholas v, pope.**

Parini, Guiseppe (1729-99) : It. poet ; wr. *il Giorno* (the Day, i.e. the day of a young Italian of fashion in Milan), a poem of manners, or a satire, in 4 bks., of which bk. i, *il Matino*, was publd., 1763, and created an immediate sensation; bks. ii, *il Mezzogiorno*, 1765, and iii and iv were publd. posth. ; iv, *la Notte*, being left unfind. P.'s place is amongst satirists of the type of Horace (q.v.), and his blank verse and style in general revert to the better classical tradition. It was derived, however, through the Engl. Augustan imitators ; and ' what is an unlucky poet to do ', asks Vaughan (*P.E.L.*, x, 444), ' when he has chosen to write of hair-powder and lace-ruffles and strawberry-ices ? ' P. had evidently read Thomson and Pope (qq.v.), and he solved this problem with conspicuous success.

Paris : Capital city of France, and the undisputed centre of European culture since the dawn of modern history ; the Athens of the European States. A history of Paris under this aspect is outside the scope of the present vol., but reference may be made to the evidence of Alexander Neckham, a native of St. Albans', who was in Paris, 1180, and called its univ. a ' paradise of delights ' (*paradisus deliciarum*) ; of Richard de Bury (q.v.), who visited Paris in the 14th cent., and called it

' the paradise of the world ', where ' the Latin muse reproduces the lore of Greece ' ; and the remark by sir S. Lee (*Fr. Renaissance in Engld.*, 111) : ' At every turn in our story, Paris presents itself as the chief mission-station of Renaissance culture ' ; and cf. *ibid.*, 13 : ' Her (i.e. Paris') expository power has constituted her for fully three centuries a universal court of taste, an apostolate of humanism *urbi et orbi*, the world's *arbiter elegantiarum* '.

Paris, de, Juan (16th cent.) : Span. dramatic poet ; wr., 1536, dialogue-eclogue of the type described by Cervantes (q.v.) in a prologue, from which a citation is given s.v. Rueda.

Paris, Matthew (c. 1195-1259) : Engl. chronicler ; monk, at St. Alban's, 1217 ; continued the *Chronica majora* of the monastery, and expanded its scope ; visited Norway and other countries, and acquired from travel and acquaintance with great personages a faculty of observation and narration, which turned the monkish chronicler into an early historian.

Parker, Matthew (1504-75) : Engl. divine ; archbp. of Canterbury under queen Elizabeth, 1559, after a period of retirement enforced in the reign of queen Mary by his espousal of the cause of lady Jane Grey ; formerly, dean of Lincoln, 1552, and master of C.C.C., Cambridge, 1544; his vicissitudes did not cease at his death, for his remains were disinterred, 1648, and burried under a dunghill, though reverently replaced in his private chapel at Lambeth after the Restoration. P.'s great service consisted in his preparation of the Bishops' Bible (see s.v. Bible), on which he was engaged, 1563-8 ; as many as 12 bps. (Chichester, Coventry, Ely, Exeter, Lincoln, Llandaff, London, Norwich, Peterborough, St. David's, Winchester and Worcester) were associated with him in this work ; ' but, because it was issued under, and possessed the hall mark, as it were, of, ecclesiastical and every royal patronage, we must not conclude that it was the Bible in general use at the time. Such was far from being the case. The popular Bible—the Bible of the people—was that of Geneva ' (Jannaway, *The Bible*, 19). Still, P.'s services to theological studies were very considerable ; he founded the Antiquarian Society, and enriched several univ. libraries with records rescued by him from the ruins of the monasteries, and he edited, the *Chronicles* of M. Paris (q.v.) and others.

Parnasse Contemporain, le (Fr.) : ' The Contemporary Parnassus ' : Title of a collection of verse, issued in 3 series : i, 1866 ; ii, 1869-70, and iii, 1876 ; representative of the poetry of the period (rather than of any definite school) which succeeded the revolt of 1830, and associated chiefly with Hugo (q.v.). The *Parnassiens*, as the contributors to these vols. came to be called, are not to be classified by any single epithet. They were a heterogeneous collection of contemporary talent, united in time rather than in inspiration ; and they included writers as diverse as A. France ; Laprade ; Menard ; Prudhomme ; Herédia (qq.v.) ; A. Vacquerie (1819-95), the shadow-Hugo, not otherwise notable, and others. The moving spirits among the Parnassians of 1866, though they publd. no manifesto, were 2 young poet-critics, Catulle Mendès and Xavier de Ricard. Mendès became son-in-law to Gautier (q.v.), to whose example as leader, if the epithet is applicable, was due the association of the group with a certain distinct mental quality. They were known by the name of *les impassibles*, due to an alleged impassivity, or insensibility, of temperament, and to their single devotion to *l'Art pour l'Art* (q.v.). Gautier's bk. on *Rapports sur le Progrès de la Poésie depuis 1830* is a kind of handbook to the movement, which was less a movement in lit. than an expression of simultaneous and sometimes contrary tendencies in a time of political and social change.

Parny, de, Evariste Désiré des Forges (1753-1814): Fr. poet; *comte* by rank. Wr. *Poésies erotiques*, which earned him the title of Tibullus, at a time when similar ascriptions were commoner than the veritable muse (see s.v. Le Brun, e.g.); and, in later life, composed a mock-epos, *La Guerre des Dieux*, on the model of Voltaire's (q.v.) *Pucelle*, which was unredeemed in dulness and grossness.

Paruta, Paolo (1540-98): It. historian; successor to Bembo (q.v.), whose *History of Venice* he continued to 1551. Unlike Guicciardini, Boccialini (qq.v.) and other more scientific writers in this age, P. was still content to found his history on certain preconceived axioms of morality and religion.

Pascal, Blaise (1623-62): Fr. moralist; superlatively praised in terms which are worth quoting in chorus. 'The shining clearness, the unerring dialectic, the humour, the irony, the grave expostulation of the *Lettres Provinciales*, are unequalled in literature since the Platonic dialogues' (Grierson, *P.E.L.*, vii, 279); Perrault (q.v.), had said much the same; and Gibbon, q.v., attributed to his perusal of Pascal his own 'grave and temperate irony'; 'In sheer genius Pascal ranks among the very greatest writers who have lived upon the earth' (Strachey, *Landmarks in Fr. Lit.*, 58); 'To this day Pascal, with Swift and Courier, is the greatest example in modern literature of controversial irony' (Saintsbury, *Short Hist. Fr. Lit.*, 330); 'Demosthenes is comparable, by no means superior, to Pascal. The *Provinciales* are the first masterpiece of classic taste in our prose literature. . . . There is not a page in his book of which the force is dissipated, or the colour has faded' (Lanson, *Hist. Lit. Fr.*, 463). We have brought together these 4 extracts from one Fr. and 3 Engl. writers, in order more effectively to illustrate the common agreement as to P.'s supremacy. He is compared, with no sense of extravagance, to Demosthenes for the vigour of his invective and to Plato for his keen edge of irony (q.v.), —the irony of Socrates, not of Sophocles; and, apart from comparative qualities, P.'s supremacy rests securely on the merits of his own Fr. style. It is a matter of common knowledge that the Fr. genius presents the nearest analogue to the Gk., which post-Renaissance peoples have supplied from the models on which they built. The curiosity, the audacity, the grace, the dexterity, the suppleness, the sense of proportion: these Attic qualities of a Phidias and a Plato are

remarkably reproduced in France, where Paris has justly been termed the modern Athens; and if Petrarch's (q.v.) humanism earns him the title of 'the first modern man' (and the perception is a Frenchman's, Renan's, q.v.), P. may fairly be described as the first modern Attic, which is equivalent to Lanson's statement that his *Lettres Provinciales* are 'le premier chef-d'œuvre du goût classique'. This 'classic taste' grew by rapid degrees. The Pleiad (q.v.) discovered the classics when they discovered Italy. Rabelais (q.v.) made infinitely supple the resources of the Fr. tongue; like Lewis Carroll's (q.v.) Humpty-Dumpty, he compelled words to act as he wished. The alien immigrants into the language, having enlarged, amplified, and adorned it, were next subjected to a rigid scrutiny by precursors of the 'lawgiver of Parnassus' (Boileau, q.v.): by the grammarians and pedants who attended the *salons* of the Precious (q.v.) writers, such as Malherbe (q.v.) in verse and J. L. de Balzac (q.v.) in prose. To these eclectic and fastidious scholars, from whose ranks the new Fr. Academy (q.v.) was recruited, there succeeded Montaigne (q.v.), with his personal essays, Corneille (q.v.), with his intense *Moi*-motive, and Descartes (q.v.) with his *cogito, ergo sum*. Cumulatively, they made the Fr. language self-reliant, and extended its independent resources. But it still awaited the magician of style, the modern hand attendant on the modern eye; and this transformation, which was just a consolidation, or re-combination, as it were, of the tentative experiments at truth by Calvinists, rationalists sceptics, pioneers along every road of reform, was first and principally the triumph of bp. Jansen (q.v.) and Port Royal (q.v.), by whose influences P.'s genius was moulded.

Thus, the record of P.'s opinions, which were his life, are essential to a study of his writings. When he was 8 years old, his father moved from Clermont to Paris, 1631, and encouraged in every way his son's marked aptitude for mathematics. Young Blaise wr. a treatise on conic sections, when he was only 16, which 'astonished' Descartes, and at 19 he invented a calculating-machine. His reasoning mind fell at a touch, when the doctrine of Jansen, St.-Cyran and Arnauld (qq.v.) was brought almost by accident to his ken. Its reasonableness appealed to him irresistibly, and fired the spark of mystical asceticism which lay hid in his deeply poetic nature. His scientific studies became thereby related to infinite ends and ardent desires. The same apparent paradox which made the Petites Écoles de Port Royal the homes of the most liberal system of education ever dreamed of by Erasmus, although Port Royalist orthodoxy counted a love of science among the temptations of the flesh, was reproduced in the mentality of P. He, too, sought science, not for its own sake, but for the sake of strengthening his will, of confirming his devotion, and of increasing his power for good. P.'s conversion to Jansenism was complete, and he carried his family with him. Especially his sister Jacqueline (1625-1661), who entered Port Royal in 1652, became an ardent disciple, a keen champion, and an inspiring teacher under the name of sister (and saint) Euphemia. P. continued his former pursuits with a new heart; in 1648 he demonstrated his famous barometrical experiments on atmospheric pressure; he wr. treatises, *de la Pésanteur de l'Air* and *de l'Equilibre des Liqueurs*, which, according to sir David Brewster 'form the basis of the modern science of Pneumatics'. Always he sought unity in diversity; and this idea of satisfaction by function made happiness, in Montaigne's sense of 'enjoyment of being', the common object of his quest, in science, in philosophy, and in the world of men. A carriage-accident on the bridge of Neuilly (23 Nov., 1654) had brought P. face to face with death and God: the mortal mystery was nearly solved; theology and science had nearly rendered up their secrets; the 'abyss of Pascal' had opened its depths, and P. gave up the rest of his short life to a defence of the truth which had convinced him. He was a man of science, whose zeal for knowledge was touched to deeper issues by this experience of impending death. Science and theology joined hands, and it was a part of the secret of P.'s power and influence that he discoursed to laymen with the passion of a believer and to the devout with the method of a *savant*. Precisely the right man was endowed with precisely the right preparation for the bk., which issued in the moral letters of a layman, entitled *Lettres Provinciales*, serialized as *Lettres écrites par Louis de Martalte* (a pseudonym) *à un Provincial de ses Amis et aux Révérends Pères Jesuites sur le Sujet de la Morale et de la Politique de ses Pères*; 23 Jan., 1656, to 24 March, 1657; collected, Cologne, 1657.

The *Provinciales* were polemical pamphlets, and were treated as such. They were condemned by parliament and the pope, and the Lat. transln. by Nicole (q.v.), under the pseudonym of Wendroche (Cologne, 1658), was publicly burned. But, whatever their polemical excesses, they struck a blow at the Society of Jesus from which, as Saintsbury writes (and it is not within our province to go outside literary evidence), 'it has never wholly recovered, and it can never wholly recover'. In the new conflict between Jansenists and Jesuits, the shattering victory lay with Port Royal. Most pertinent to lit. it is to observe that the *Lettres Provinciales*, which grew in vigour and width of view as the front of the defence of Arnauld was enlarged after Letter v to an attack on the 'Reverend Fathers' themselves, form a permanent monument of literary skill, apart altogether from their subject. Compare them for a moment with another and an earlier famous series of controversial letters, similarly directed against the obscurantists of Rome, the *Epistolæ Obscurorum Virorum* (q.v.), and the refined irony of the Port Royalist philosopher shines immeasureably more illustrious than the horse-play satire of the Erfurt 'poets'. P. also meditated an *Apologie de la Religion chrétienne*, and his note-book *Pensées* towards this work were issued posth. by his Port Royal friends in a fragmentary condition, 1670; they were edited by Condorcet (q.v.), 1776, and definitively by Faugère, after Victor Cousin (q.v.), 1843. This work is a prose-poem of the highest

spiritual value; supremely and intimately eloquent of that contrast between the infinite conceptivity and the finite capacity of man, which, immanent in medieval thought, ever submissive to the rule of authority, rose to the sublime protest of conscious humanity in great passages in a Shakespeare or a Pascal. We have no space for quotations, but must find room to compare, from Shakespeare, *Hamlet*, ii, 2, the speech containing 'What a piece of work is a man', with Pascal, *Pensées*, 'Quelle chimère est-ce donc que l'homme ! quelle nouveauté, quelle monstre, quel chaos, quel sujet de contradiction, quel prodige ! ' We must find room, too, for the cry of the soul, ' Le silence éternel de ces espaces infinis m'effraie '. The multifarious movement of Fr. lit., culminating in 1660, when king Louis xiv became master of France, had no greater glory than Pascal, whose bk. was burned two years before. In his supreme work in Fr. prose, all that went before him was resumed and completed.

Pasqualigo, Luigi (16th cent.): It. dramatist. Wr. prose comedy, *il Fidele*, 1575, presenting the familiar plot of rival candidates for the favours of a married lady, with consequent transpersonation and disguises. The play was transld. into Fr. by Larivey (q.v.), into Lat. verse by Fraunce (q.v.), and into Engl. by Munday (q.v.), as *Le Fidelle, Victoria*, and *The Comedy of Two Italian Gentlemen* respectively, the last in 1584; and Shakespeare's (q.v.) *Two Gentlemen of Verona*, though much indebted to the *Diana* of Montemayor (q.v.), reproduces the title and intrigue of P.'s play in its later versions.

Pasquier, Etienne (1529-1615): Fr. jurist and miscellanist. Born at Paris; defended univ. of Paris against the Jesuits, 1565. P.'s most interesting contribution to lit. was his *Recherches de la France*, an early example of the art of learned gossip on the spectacle of society and politics; it included an account of the literary movement known as the Pleiad (q.v.).

Passerat, Jean (1534-1602): Fr. poet and scholar, satellite of the Pleiad (q.v.); succeeded Ramée (q.v.) as Royal Reader (see s.v. Corporation) in eloquence at Paris, 1572; was eminent Latinist, and surpassed most poets of his time in Fr. verse-composition, esp. in lighter and comic veins. P. was the leading poet who contributed, 1594, to the successful *Satyre Ménippée* (q.v.).

Passion-Play: Sacred amateur dramatic entertainment, contemporary with and akin to the Ital. ' sacra rappresentazione ' (q.v.); flourished in France, Spain, and Germany in the 15th cent. The *Confrérie de la Passion* (q.v.) in Paris was licensed for its performance as early as 1402. Its popularity spread from the villages to towns, where the authorities would combine to furnish the players with suitable stage and scenery; and, gradually, the sacred topics were interspersed with selections from the repertory of profane lit., and even descended to folly and farce. Thus, the boundary-line between passion-play and shrovetide-play (q.v.) in Germany became obliterated. In more recent times the passion-play has been revived with every accessory designed to promote its emotional appeal.

Passo Honroso (Span.) : Short title of a chivalric chronicle compiled in the 15th cent. by de Lena (q.v.), an official scribe to king John ii (q.v.) of Castile. The full title was 'The book of the Pass of Honour (*Passo Honroso*) defended by the excellent knight Suero de Quiñones', and an abridgement, edited by Juan de Pineda, was publd. at Salamanca, 1588. A new edn., Madrid, 1783, was issued by the Academy of History. The work is the formal chronicle of a tournament which lasted from 10 July to 9 Aug., 1434, when Quiñones and 9 companion knights held St. Mark's Bridge, at Orbigo, near Leon, against all the champions of Europe ; the object of the challenge was to win release for Quiñones from his vow to wear an iron chain round his neck every Thursday, as a symbol of his captivity to a lady-love. 627 encounters took place, with considerable loss of life, and Lena, writes Kelly (*Lit. espagn.*, 109), continues his account ' with the imperturbable gravity of a *croupier* at a gaming-table '. This even level of narration is precisely the interest of the bk., for the sake of its evidence to the manners of the age of chivalry. Froissart (q.v.) becomes more intelligible, in the sense of finding his way more easily to the sympathy of modern readers, when we remember that the episode of the ' Pass of Honour ' was a common fact of chivalric institutions. It is referred to in the famous chapter (bk. iv, xxii) of Cervantes (q.v.), *Don Quixote*, where the hero discourses of truth and fiction with the canon.

Paston Letters, The (1422-1509): Engl.; upwards of 1,000 valuable letters written by members of the Paston family of Paston in Norfolk— and notably by John, William, Margaret, and Clement Paston, who overlapped the reigns of kings Henry vi to Henry viii. ' The *Paston Letters* are full of litigation ', says a modern authority, ' but John Paston's troubles came largely from his inheritance of the great Fastolf estate by methods which at the time were condemned as flagitious by his foes and have never been fully justified '. (John P. was executor to sir J. Fastolf). The *Letters*, which are a storehouse of information on Engl. domestic life, afterwards passed from hand to hand. In George iii's reign (sir) John Fenn selected some of them for publication, and gave the original copies to the king; but these were mysteriously ' lost '. Others were edited by sergeant Frere, 1823, and about 300 of them were put up for sale in London, 1888, and withdrawn at 500 guineas. J. R. Gairdner, who successfully vindicated the genuineness of the *Letters*, edited the whole series, in Arber's (q.v.) *Annotated Reprints*, 1872-5. See, too, C. L. Kingsford's *Prejudice and Promise in Fifteenth-century England*, 1925.

Pastoral : Descriptive epithet of a class of writings in prose or verse, which took its orig. in Europe chiefly from Theocritus and Virgil (' cecini pascua '), and the common mark of which is a rustic setting and scenery. The earliest native form was the medieval Fr. *pastourelle* (q.v.), where the poet made love to a shepherdess, with more or less success, according to the shepherd's proximity and to the knightly lover's adherence to the rules of the game. At the period of the Revival of Learning, the classical forms were re-invented, and Damon and Pythias, Mopsus, Gallus, Lycidas, Thyrsis and Corydon, Admetus and the rest of the company from the hills and vales of Sicily and Arcadia (q.v.) brought back the rural illusion of peace, innocence and fleeciness to the weary townsman of 15th cent. Italy, and, through his poets, to their imitators and expanders in France, the Peninsula, and Engld. The *Ameto* of Boccaccio (q.v.), the *Arcadia* of Sannazzaro (q.v.), which was really a pioneer-piece—' the Columbus of a visionary hemisphere ', Symonds (q.v.) called its author,—the *Diana* of Montemayor (q.v.), the *Galatea* of Cervantes (q.v.), the *Eclogues* of Mantuan (q.v.), imitated by Barclay (q.v.), the *Arcadia* of Sidney (q.v.), the *Shepherd's Calendar* of Spenser (q.v.) : these are a few examples, duly noted under their writers' names, of the vogue of the pastoral convention. Country tastes are less a mark of true pastoral lit. than an imaginary bliss, which passed in the hands of great masters into a sentimental atmosphere attached to character and landscape, as, e.g., in the melancholy Jacques and in Prospero's island ; both Shakespearean. The poem of pastoral life, of which Wordsworth's *Michael*, Meredith's *Love in a Valley*, and even Tennyson's *Enoch Arden* (see s.vv.) are examples in recent lit. without the definite Theocritean setting, are the modern representative of the old type ; and the change from the Renaissance pastoral to the epic-idyl of the countryside is nowhere more clearly seen than in the contrast between S. Gessner and J. H. Voss (qq.v.) in 18th-cent. Germany. The epic type was perfected by Goethe (q.v.) in his *Hermann und Dorothea*. The *Alcon* of Castiglione (q.v.) and the *Lycidas* of Milton (q.v.) are fine instances of classical pastoral elegy ; Gray's *Elegy in a Country Churchyard* (see s.v.), in which Sannazzaro's ' Lontano della moltitudine ' reappears, no doubt unconsciously, as ' far from the madding crowd ', is a pastoral elegy without the classical imagery. This imagery was applied to allegory, elegy, romance, idyl, masque, eclogue, lyric, etc.; and though it was degraded during the 18th cent. into stock images of rustic life—ribboned crooks and rural pipes,—and has passed at last out of lit. altogether from very tenuity and vacuity of appeal, yet it succeeded in creating an illusion during the years, or centuries, of its prosperity, which undoubtedly affected thought outside of the sphere in which it flourished. The theories of Rousseau (q.v.), Thoreau, and even of Emerson to some extent, are theories of nature, and of man in nature, which derived no little of their validity from the sanction which the pastoral conventions had established ; and, if we let these go to-day, and greet Lycidas and Corydon as old-fashioned, we should recognize that the ideas for which they stood have penetrated to our deepest consciousness, and that pastoral lit., in its various forms, despite an obvious unreality, or a discrepancy between the characters and the scene, has conserved in hyper-civilized mankind that eternal wellspring of mental refreshment without which civilization decays. The ' return to Nature ' has meant from time to time an exchange of one burden for another ; the Nature of the pastoralists has always been ' for ever panting, and for ever young '. (See, also, s.v. Nature). Two points may briefly be added. First, the obvious contrast between the literary Arcadian (see s.v. Arcadia) illusion and the realities of rural experience was marked as early as Lope de Vega (q.v.), himself a pastoralist, in his comedy, *el Cuerdo en su Casa*, where a shepherd says in a storm :—

'And I should like just now to see those men
Who write such books about a shepherd's life,
When all is spring, and flowers, and trees, and
    brooks'

(quoted by Ticknor, iii, 93). A similar sense of contrast was expressed by Crabbe (*The Village*, i, 15ff.), in a passage quoted s.v. ; and the pastoralist's fair-weather shepherd and the realist's shepherd in a storm are both represented in lit. Secondly, it is to be observed that the vogue of pastoral fiction was preserved, and its inevitable decadence postponed, not merely by its intrinsic attractiveness, and by the townsman's delight in a countryside, garnished and swept to his liking, but also by the opportunity which it afforded of writing of personages in real life under the guise of shepherds and shepherdesses D'Urfé's (q.v.) *Astrée* and its Fr. successors were to some extent *romans-à-clef* (q.v.) ; and Montemayor's ' *Diana* ' has been identified, as have the fictitious heroines of the pastoral romances of Montalvo, Cervantes, and others. This device helps to account for the permanence of the type, which added considerably to the machinery out of which the modern novel (q.v.) has been fashioned.

Pastourelle (Fr.) : Descriptive name of a class of medieval (Northern) Fr. verse-compositions, treating of the encounter of a knight (or of the poet) with a rustic beauty, and of his success or otherwise in making love to her. There were dramatic elements in the kind, for the shepherdess commonly had a husband, and the rustic setting admitted the ' sunburnt mirth ' of village-life. Provençal influence is frequently marked in this early type of native Fr. pastoral, which flourished in the 13th cent., and was *bourgeois*, or middle-class, in its scope.

Pater, Walter (1839-94) : Engl. critic ; impressionist, æsthete, hedonist ; type and virtual leader of a reaction from the moralized beauty sought insistently by Ruskin (q.v.). P.'s beauty, as a cult, not unlike Swinburne's (q.v.), was learned partly from France (see s.v. Fr. lit.), and consisted in a constantly renewed pleasure of sensation : ' not the fruit of experience, but experience itself, is the end. A counted number of pulses only is given to us of a variegated and dramatic life. How may we see in them all that is to be seen in them by the finest senses ? How shall we pass most swiftly from point to point, and be present always at the focus where the greatest number of vital forces unite in their purest energy ? To burn always with this hard, gem-like flame, to maintain this ecstasy, is success in life. . . We are all under sentence of death, but with a sort of indefinite reprieve. . .

Our one chance lies in expanding that interval, in getting as many pulsations as possible into the given time ' (from Conclusion to P.'s *Renaissance*, 1873; omitted from second and third edns., ' as I conceived that it might possibly mislead some of those young men into whose hands it might fall '—like Socrates, corrupting the young,—but restored by P., 1888 and onwards). It is obvious that ebullient and revolting youth, seeking a philosophy which would sanctify the pursuit of pleasure, would seize on the doctrine of *pater* Pater, which he taught through a series of works : *Imaginary Portraits*, 1887 ; *Appreciations*, 1889 ; *Plato and Platonism*, 1893 ; *Gk. Studies*, 1895 ; and 2 romances, *Marius the Epicurean*, 1885, and *Gaston de Latour* (unfind.), 1896. Remember that it *was* a philosophy : a system of learning ; an apprenticeship to hard thinking ; a difficult way to ease in Zion. P., who was a fellow of B.N.C., Oxford, and spent a reclusive life at the univ., emanating influence and magnetism, was a scholar of rare perceptive powers. Particularly, his skill consisted in threading his way through half-lights of history and thought. The border countries of thought attracted him irresistibly,—Christianity trembling at the portals of Paganism ; Humanism knocking at the gate of Ecclesiasticism. And his skill corresponded to these affections. No one has succeeded so finely as he in expressing the shades and delicate nuances of meaning. Out of his donnish celibacy, he exalted the joy-search to a science, insulated from distracting influences, in which Kingsley's (q.v.) idealism, and Arnold's (q.v.) moralism, and altruism itself, were as naught,—a splendid selfishness, which must not, however, induce his readers to depreciate, or, still less, to ignore, the exceptional, rarefied excellence of P. as a critic, and the perfect, almost super-perfect, skill of his interpretation of motives in art and character.

Pathelin (Fr.) : Famous comedy ; of the indigenous farcical variety ; a masterpiece of 15th-cent. lit. ; first printed at Lyons, 1485, under its full title of *Maître Pierre Pathelin*, and frequently reprinted ; the authorship has been ascribed to Antoine de la Salle (q.v.), but the evidence is doubtful. Written in Fr., in 8-syllable verses, it enjoyed a considerable vogue in its own day, and it effectively paved the way for the transition from morality-play to drama. The plot, which satisfied the primitive sense of satire, based on a successful practical joke, turns on the device of a rustic lawyer who advises one of his clients to practice bleating like a sheep when he is at a loss for words ; the device is turned against the lawyer when he seeks his fees, and a pretty little comedy of manners is constructed round this old tale. The judge's ' revenons à ses moutons ' is a proverb which dates from P. The play was greatly extolled by Pasquier (q.v.), the critic and historian of the Fr. Renaissance ; its legal atmosphere, which is more of a full-grown comedy than a farce, suggests its origin among the clerks of the Basoche (q.v.), and internal evidence proves it true Parisian. A modern version, *l'Avocat Pathelin*, was written by the Beaumont and

tragedy on Dido, 1668; adapted Horace's *Ars Poetica*, 1677; publd. a vol. of poems (*Minne-Liederen*), 1684; and regarded himself as the Boileau of (q.v.) the Netherlands.

Penn, William (1644-1718): Engl. religious reformer; son of sir Wm. P. (1621-70; admiral; superior officer to Pepys, q.v., who frequently refers to him in the *Diary*); Quaker; founder of Pennsylvania; enters lit. as the author of several works in defence of religious liberty: among them, i, *The Sandy Foundation Shaken*, 1668, for which he was committed to the Tower; the foundations of sand being the doctrines of the Trinity, Atonement, and Justification by faith; ii, *No Cross, No Crown*, 1669, an eloquent treatise on the Christian virtue of self-sacrifice.

Pepys, Samuel (1632-1703): Engl. diarist; son of a London tailor; edu. St. Paul's School and Trinity Hall and Magdalene Coll., Cambridge; owed much to his cousin, sir E. Montagu, afterwards first earl of Sandwich, who obtained for him, 1660, the clerkship which led to his appointment, 1665, as surveyor-general of the victualling-office; deprived of his office, 1679, and sent to the Tower on a charge of complicity in the popish plot; released, 1680; secretary to the Admiralty, 1686; retired after the Revolution. Some light, not very flattering, has been cast on P., as a man in undress, by a little bk. by M. Lucas-Dubreton, transld. from the Fr. by Mr. H. J. Stenning (Philpot, 1925); but no amount of personal detractation—much of which is supplied by P. himself—can destroy, or even diminish, the interest and perennial charm of the unique *Diary* kept by P., 1659-69, which was written in a cipher of his own device, and was deposited by him in the coll. library at Magdalene. Part of it was deciphered by John Smith and edited by the third baron Braybrooke, and publd., 1825, more than a century after P.'s death; an enlarged edn. by Mynors Bright (1818-83; president of the coll.) was issued, 1875-9, and the whole *Diary*, except for a few passages, too intimate for publication, was edited by H. B. Wheatley, 1893. It is a human document of singular importance, and has no parallel in lit. history.

Perceval: Welsh hero of the cycle of Arthur (q.v.); known as Peredur in the *Mabinogion*, or Welsh tales for the young; is brought up by his widowed mother in ignorance of his chivalrous birth, learns it by accident, and thoroughly lives up to it through a series of knightly adventures. So far, there is a family likeness to many of the Breton romances, founded on older lays; but P. is also associated with the grail (q.v.), in its form of a magical dish in an enchanted castle. In the Fr. *Perceval* of Chrétien de Troyes (q.v.) and in the more deeply-studied Germ. *Parzival* of Wolfram von Eschenbach (q.v.), the grail-quest is fairly started, though it does not appear in the Engl. *Sir Perceval of Galles*. The transition to the Holy Grail idea was the great contribution of Robert de Boron (q.v.); and later redactions transferred the quest from P. to Galahad (q.v.).

Percy, Thomas (1729-1811): Engl. medievalist; bp. of Dromore, 1782. P.'s name is permanently associated with the *Reliques of Ancient Engl. Poetry*, edited by him in 3 vols., 1765 (second edn., 1767) from a folio MS., in early 17th cent. hand-writing, rescued from Humphrey Pitt of Shifnal. 'The book when Percy found it was being treated as waste paper and used for fire-lighting. When it was saved from total destruction, it was still treated with small respect; Percy, instead of copying, tore out the ballad of *King Estmere* as copy for the printers, without saving the original pages' (*C.H.E.L.*, x, 233; by prof. Ker). Instead of copying, too, P. mended and restored what he took: 'his processes are not those of scrupulous philology, but neither are they such as Macpherson (q.v.) favoured' (*ibid.*); he was an editor, not an inventor, and still less a forger. The difference was early felt, and evidence may be sought from Wordsworth's (q.v.) *Essay*, 1815, *on Poetry as a Study*. There he wr., with acute perception: 'Next in importance to the *Seasons* of Thomson (q.v.), though at considerable distance from that work in order of time, come the *Reliques of Ancient Engl. Poetry*; collected, new-modelled, and in many instances (if such a contradiction in terms may be used) composed by the editor, Dr. Percy. The compilation was ill suited to the then existing taste of city society; and Dr. Johnson (q.v.), 'mid the little senate to which he gave laws, was not sparing in his exertions to make it an object of contempt. The critic triumphed, the legendary imitators were deservedly disregarded, and, as undeservedly, their ill-imitated models sank, in this country, into temporary neglect; while Bürger (q.v.), and other able writers of Germany, were translating, or imitating these *Reliques*, and composing, with the aid of inspiration thence derived, poems which are the delight of the German nation. . . . But from humble ballads we must ascend to heroics. All hail, Macpherson! hail to thee, sire of Ossian! The phantom was begotten by the smug embrace of an impudent Highlander upon a cloud of tradition. . . . Contrast', continued Wordsworth, 'the effect of Macpherson's publication with the *Reliques* of Percy, so unassuming, so modest in their pretensions! I have already stated how much Germany is indebted to this latter; and for our own country, its poetry has been absolutely redeemed by it. I do not think that there is an able writer in verse at the present day who would not be proud to acknowledge his obligations to the *Reliques*; I know that it is so with my friends; and, for myself, I am happy in this occasion to make a public avowal of my own'.

It is not possible to add to these praises, which come from so high an authority, so soon after P.'s death, and which were so discriminating in judgment. The MS. used to light fires (see *supra*) lit a fire in Europe, which, since Bürger's *Lenore* and Coleridge's *Ancient Mariner*, has never been put out; 'it was through Percy's *Reliques* that the Middle Ages really came to have an influence on modern poetry' (*C.H.E.L.*, *loc. cit.*); 'it would be difficult to name a book which had more to do with the Romantic Revival' (Saintsbury, *First Bk. of Engl. Lit.*, 159; and see s.v. Romance); 'in Germany the

Reliques were a fruitful source of poetic inspiration. . . As Bürger himself tells us, they were " the matins and the evensong " which inspired *Lenore* und *der wilde Jäger*. To them also, in the last resort, we owe *der Taucher* of Schiller, and *Erlkönig* and *der König im Thule* of Goethe. A distant echo of them is to be heard even in . . . the *Lorelei* of Heine ' (see s.vv. ; Vaughan, British Academy Warton Lecture, 1913). It was an immense achievement, and it was a genuine sense of the poetic value of the old poems which enabled P., to accomplish it. His other works included *Five Pieces of Runic poetry transld. from the Islandic language*, 1763 (a rune was an old Norse symbol ; Islandic = Icelandic) ; *Key to the New Testament*, 1769 ; *Northern Antiquities*, 2 vols., 1770 ; *The Hermit of Warkworth*, 1772. P.'s fo. MS. was edited, 1868, by Hales and Furnivall.

Pereda, de, José Maria (1833-1906) . Span. novelist ; excels in country scenes.

Perez, Alonso (16th cent.) : Span. pastoral poet ; physician at Salamanca. Wr., 1564, a continuation, *Segunda Parte*, of *la Diana* by Montemayor (q.v.), in whose confidence he claimed to have been. Wr., too, a pastoral *Thisbe* (see, too, s.v. Silvestre), which was transld. into Engl. by B. Young (q.v.), Montemayor's translr. Cervantes committed P.'s *Diana* to the bonfire (*Don Quixote*, 1, 6) from which the chief portions of Montemayor's *Diana* were to be saved.

Perez, Andreas (fl. 1615) : Span. divine ; Dominican monk of Leon. Wr. a life of St. Raymond of Peñaforte, 1601, and 2 vols. of sermons at a later date. P. was commonly reputed to be the author of a picaresque novel publd. under the name of Ubeda (q.v.), and now ascribed to a genuine bearer of that name.

Perez, Antonio (1540-1611) : Span. letter-writer. P. was at one time secretary to king Philip ii of Spain, and had a disastrous experience of the vanity of princes' favours. With his life we are not further concerned, save to note a period of his residence in Engld., where he became more intimate with F. Bacon (q.v.) than the prudent mother of the future chancellor thought desirable. P. wr., 1598, *Relaciones*, or narratives of events, which have considerable interest in diplomacy, and his correspondence, which was extensive, is exceptionally interesting, and may have influenced the epistolary vogue of the 17th cent. in France.

Perotti, Niccolo (1430-80) : It. humanist. Pupil of Vittorino (q.v.) at Mantua ; learned Gk. from card. Bessarion (q.v.) ; wr. Lat. grammar, 1468 ; took Bessarion's side of Plato (q.v.) in the dreary Plato v. Aristotle controversy of the times ; transld. Polybius for pope Nicholas v (q.v.).

Perrault, Charles (1628-1703) : Fr. writer of fairy-tales ; poet and critic. P. was the eldest of 4 sons (Claude, a well-known architect and physician, translr. of Vitruvius, died 1688 ; Pierre, died 1680 ; Nicholas, theologian, died 1661) of Pierre P., a notary, and served Colbert, the great finance-minister of king Louis xiv, as confidential adviser in matters of art and learning. He was elected to the Academy (q.v.), 1671, and took up the quarrel, bequeathed by St. Sorlin (q.v.), and known as that of the

Ancients (q.v.) and Moderns. P. sustained the cause of the Moderns in his poems *le Siècle de Louis le Grand* and his dialogues, *Parallèles des anciens et des modernes*, 1688-97, against La Fontaine, La Bruyère, and, chiefly Boileau (qq.v.) ; Fontenelle (q.v.) was ranged on his side. The contest was active till 1700, when Boileau and P. were reconciled. More permanent fame attaches to P.'s fairy-tales, 1696-97.

Personification : Literary device, almost exclusively poetic, for heightening imaginatively the illusion of presence and vitality in abstract qualities or intangible ideas. The use of this device is traced from Prudentius (Span.-Christian Lat. poet and allegorist, A.D. 348-c. 405 ; see s.v. Allegory) to the Debate (q.v.) of early Fr. medieval poetry, especially in its didactic-religious kind, such as the *Dream of Hell* and *Road to Paradise* (see s.v. Dream). It was adopted by Guillaume de Lorris in his *Romance of the Rose* (q.v.), and was extended by him to important dramatic purposes by the isolation of qualities of character and temperament, such as feminine accessibility or repulse ; thus developing the study of psychology. This method led to frigidities and insipidities in later uses of the device ; but it was utilized and given fresh life by Erasmus and Hutten (qq.v.) and by the Lat. Reformation pamphleteers.

Pestalozzi, Johann Heinrich (1746-1827) : Germ. (Swiss) educationist. Studied at Zurich, where he was born, and was engaged throughout his life in active efforts towards educational reform. The value and significance of his work must be sought in specialist histories ; as a lover of children and a founder of method, his reputation is secure. P.'s place in lit. rests on his popular-romance (*Volksbuch*) ' Leonard and Gertrude ' (*Lienhard und Gertrud*), first issued in 1781, and completed in 4 parts, 1783-87. Therein P. depicted the life of the Swiss peasantry whom he knew and loved (like Wordsworth, he might have said, ' My heart was all given to the people, and my love was theirs '), and revealed the causes and the remedies of their social degradation. ' The delineation is evidently true to nature, and, at the same time, shows nature as she reveals herself to genius ' (Quick, *Educational Reformers*, 305). The bk. had an instant success, and made its author famous ; and, though the sequels which P. added were less spontaneous than the original vol., ' the book is and must remain a classic ' (*ibid.*). Its supreme merit resides in its faithfulness to facts, and in its hopeful picture of the fruitful use to which those facts can be applied. P. drew educational reform out of the seemingly barren soil of ignorance and neglect ; he did not plant a Utopia in rustic Switzerland, but founded a conduct of life on the actual conditions of peasant-life. His more definitely pedagogical writings, *Christopher and Eliza*, 1782 ; *Development of the Human Race*, 1797, and his weekly *Swiss Journal*, started for the propagation of his views, did not prove financial or popular successes ; but his *Leonard and Gertrude* set a fashion in educational writings which has been freely followed.

Peter i (1672-1725) : Russ. emperor, 1689 ; surnamed ' The Great ' ; maker of modern

Russia in the sense that he expedited forcibly the works and tendencies of reform in every department of public life. The history of Russ. lit., at least till the beginning of the 19th cent., is a part of the history of Russia ; and P. forced the pace of that history. He broke down big sections of the wall which divided Russia from the civilization of Europe ; his linguistic and literary reforms were a part of the imperial policy for the Europeanizing of Russia, and had no title at all to any æsthetic sense or taste. P. built his ships, and drilled his army, and clothed his populace in modern dress, by the same token of reform as he employed typefounders in Holland to simplify the print of Russ. bks., and had translns. effected of practical manuals in economy, geography, and law. His object was to impose on a backward people the conditions essential to national prosperity ; and he hesitated neither at the removal of his son and heir, who seemed to him unfitted for the succession, nor at the closure of the patriarchate of Moscow, when Adrian, its last incumbent, died in 1700, and left the emperor free to found his own schools and rules—and to cut the beards of his subjects. P. is not to be called a patron of lit., in the sense that this claim appertains to the empress Catherine ii (q.v.), for example : but he energetically crushed the barriers which the long Middle Ages of Russ. history had interposed between art and the people. He created the utterance of Russ. lips by sifting a lay language out of the ecclesiastical overgrowth. 'Since Peter and by his means ', says Brückner (*Gesch. der Russ. Lit.*, 67), 'the erstwhile unbroken union between religion and literature was sundered for ever '.

Petersen, Niels Mattias (1791-1862) : Dan. literary historian. P.'s *History of Dan. Lit.*, 1853-64, is still valuable and authoritative.

Petrarca, Francesco ; Petrarch (1304-74) : It. poet ; leader of the Humanists. Born at Arezzo, his father having been exiled from Florence in the same year and by the same party as Dante (q.v.) ; used the name of Petrarca in place of his patronymic, Petracca, and is commonly known by the anglicized form. P.'s boyhood and youth were spent in or near Avignon, then the seat of what Luther (q.v.) later called the ' Babylonish captivity ' of the pope ; first, in the valley of Vaucluse, and, afterwards, at Arqua, near Padua, in the Euganean hills. P. wr. of both retreats in separate letters as ' lonely and delightful ', epithets which express his tastes ; for P. was a scholar by temperament and training, and a man of letters by every fibre of his being. Like Dante, an ardent patriot, P. devoted much time and thought to diplomatic missions and political activities ; but his methods differed from Dante's by the least touch of opportunism, which made him a welcome guest at the houses of the great, and his aim differed from Dante's by its departure from the medieval idea of a just and beneficent autocracy, reconciling Church and State, and admitted considerable latitude to personal ambition and individual hopes of fame. But, opportunism and modernism apart, P.'s *Ode to Italy*, with its magnificent appeal :

Virtù contro al 'Furore
Prenderà l'arme, et fia il combatter corto ;
Che l'antico valore
Negli italici cuor non è ancor morto,

quoted by Machiavelli (q.v.) at the close of *il Principe*, is a perpetual glory of Ital. national song.

Like Dante, again, P. was a lover ; Sismondi (q.v.) even classed him as a Troubadour (q.v.) ; at any rate, his Laura differed from Dante's Beatrice by ever so little a defect in P.'s power of self-forgetfulness. According to the best tradition, P.'s first meeting with his lady occurred on Easter Monday (regarded in the Middle Ages as the date of the Crucifixion ; whence otherwise mentioned as Good Friday), 6 April, 1327. Laura, de Noves by birth, was then 20 years of age, and had been married for 2 years to count Hugh de ¦Sade, to whom she bore 11 children ; she died of the plague in 1348. Little else is definitely established, and even the relation of these facts to the Laura of P.'s poems has been questioned in parts of the vast lit. on the subject. What seems to be certain is this : first, Laura was a real person ; secondly, the Troubadour fashion of amatory verse appealed irresistibly to her lover. Avignon was in the country of the Troubadours, and P.'s temperament predisposed him to brood over ' lonely delights '. This double temptation to idealizing sentiment and idealized expression produced the love-in-Laura poetry, which, (1) is directly filiated with the lyric of Provence (q.v.) and of Cino da Pistoja (q.v.) and his successors, and, (2) directly inspired the Petrarchist schools of Italy in the 16th cent., and the sonneteers and singers of France, Engld. and Spain. (See s.v. sonnet, especially). We must add that it is gravely probable that this vogue of sonneteering and love-ditties, which has made P.'s name famous in European lit., was determined, partly, at least, by the virtue of de Sade's wife ; for there are hints, querulous or plaintive, that P., as idealist and lover, would not have been averse from writing less and enjoying more. It was not till after Laura's death estopped his natural desire that the more Dantesque note of distant worship occurred more dominantly in his poems ; and it is that note which took the fancy of later writers of sonnet-sequences and ideal love-verse. This change is particularly marked in his *Triumph of Death*, one of a series of ' trionfi ', written in *terza rima* (q.v.), and depicting the successive victories of love, charity, death, fame, time and God, in which each victor brought his train of witnesses.

But though it is Laura's lover, the ingenious Ital. metrist, and the melodious writer of songs in native measures, whom the modern world honours in P., his fame throughout the Renaissance was founded on quite other grounds ; and he himself affected to despise this trifling with native measures. ' The first modern man ', Renan (q.v.) called him ; ' the Columbus of a new spiritual hemisphere ', is the title given to him by Addington Symonds (q.v.) ; and sir John Sandys (d., 1922) justly writes : ' his efforts to return to the Old World of the Latin classics led to his discovery of the New World of the Italian Renaissance '

(*Harvard Lectures*, 19). ' I devoted myself singly, amid a multitude of subjects, to the knowledge of antiquity ', wr. P. himself in his Lat. *Epistle to Posterity* ; ' as I could not live without your Cicero, and could get no one to copy the book, I turned from outward to inward resources, and set my own tired fingers and used-up pen upon the work ', he wr. to a citizen of Florence. The ' two eyes ' of learning he called Cicero and Virgil (qq.v.) ; and to the recovery of the Ciceronian outlook in the criticism of life, including politics, P. was consistently devoted. ' Father supreme of Roman eloquence ! Yours are the springs from which we water our meadows ; yours the light that shines upon our path ', he apostrophized ' my Cicero ' in another letter. Not without pains and devotion, long nights and arduous days, did P. became a Ciceronian, and, by his Latinity, the founder of the New Learning, which was to lead men out of medieval submission into the new life of free-will and free-thought. P. discovered, 1329, Cicero's speech *pro Archia*, and, again, 1345, at Verona, the letters *ad Atticum*, which brought the Roman statesman, philosopher, and orator down to homely, daily things, and, after a momentary disillusion, raised him yet higher as a model of familiar, personal style, so different from the uncritical divagations of medieval prose. In this spirit, P. expressed himself, by a novel literary departure, in the manner, not the letter, of his idol. He composed Lat. letters, 559 in all, familiar, senile (of old age), and miscellaneous ; letters to dead authors ; lives, some of scriptural characters ; a *Secretum* (or, *Contempt of the World*), 1342 ; a *Solitary Life*, 1346, and a *Monastic Leisure*, 1347, 2 treatises appropriate to his homes at Vaucluse and Arqua ; and, among others, an *Epistle to Posterity*, 1370, which, as a human document, is at least as sincere as such a testament ever can be. In this spirit, too, P. ruled the friendship proffered him by Boccaccio (q.v.). For living Florence, its sun and sins, which was Boccaccio's quarry for the *Decameron* P. cared less than for Boccaccio's example as the earliest Homerist in Italy (see s.v. Homer) ; he treasured a MS. of Homer, and eagerly studied the bad Lat. version prepared by Pilatus (q.v.), and he was influential in forming the Hellenic circle at the Florentine convent of San Spirito (q.v.). Again, all his life through, P. nursed and cherished a Lat. epic, never publd. in his life-time, called, classically, *Africa*, and loved the renown which it brought him from occasional glimpses by his friends.

Moreover, P., the ardent Lat. student and disciple of Cicero, practised what he taught, even at the expense of political consistency, or at the worse risk of personal ridicule. Two events stand out in his biography of honourable toil and industrious leisure. In 1341, he was crowned poet-laureate at Rome. The coronation took place on the Capitol, disinterring old sentiment from the dust, and was accompanied by all the ceremonies which had been in abeyance for 13 centuries. A few years later, in 1348, Rienzi's brief spell of glory as ' last of the tribunes ' of Rome, gave P. another opportunity of attesting his faithful love of the past, on which he built his hopes of future Italy. For Rienzi's sake he disowned his friends and patrons of former years, even the powerful family of the Colonni, to whom he owed so much. As readily, when the adventurer-tribune became the senator and tyrant, P. retransferred his allegiance. But those who smile at the coronation and who condemn the political vagaries miss the ardour of patriotism which moved the great Italian scholar-poet. Clement v was in retreat at Avignon, and, in the absence of the pope, P. had dreamed that the old times, which seemed to him such recent times, might be renewed. As Rome had been, so Rome should be ; not in vain should Italia have nurtured Cicero, for the filial instruction of her sons. Ital. liberationists after Dante did not build a medieval state, as in that great visionary's *de Monarchia*, on the abstract necessities of creatures midway between corruption and incorruptibility. They sought their polity, where they found their joy, on a proved human foundation. The past greatness of Rome was to be revived by a recovery of the old fearlessness of Roman government, art, and letters. This is the key to P.'s activities as antiquary, stylist, republican, copyist, laureate, and diplomatist. He ranks as the herald of Humanism, as the true morning-star of the Renaissance, because his zeal for a Revival of Learning was equivalent to a patriotic attempt to renew the ever-living past of Italy in the land which had temporarily forgotten it. Like the Jews by the waters of Babylon, his right hand could not forget Rome. It is difficult to realize to-day the intense passion for Gk. and Lat. culture by which the first Ital. Humanists were moved. P.'s coronation in the Capitol and his support of Rienzi at Rome were no chance manifestations of the spirit which led him to lead others out of the cloister into the world ; they were but the bubbles on the surface of an energy which burned below. Hitherto, and not excluding Dante (but excepting popular protest and reaction ; wine-songs, women-songs and satire), the ' other-worldly ' point of view had prevailed ; now the worldliness of Humanism was to succeed to it, and its succession was a renewal, not a new thing : ' the pagan view was now once more proclaimed that man was made, not only to toil and suffer, but to enjoy. . . It was thus that Humanism first appeared, bringing a claim for the mental freedom of man, and for the full development of his being ' (*C.M.H.*, i, 533 ; the writer was sir R. Jebb, himself a Hellenist and Humanist). In this movement, magnificently inspiring, and happily not yet exhausted, P., Laura's lover, was the immortal pioneer.

Petrashevsky, Michael Vasilevich (1819-67) : Russ. civil servant ; employed in the Foreign Office ; wr. a *Dict. of Foreign Terms* (in use in Russia), which, like the Fr. dictionaries of the 18th cent. (see s.vv. Bayle, Encyclopedia) served a semi-political purpose : certain terms of statecraft and sociology, for instance, acquired Russ. equivalents. P.'s house became a centre for Friday evening talks on topics of public interest, for reading Fr. social lit., and even for discussing the installation of a private printing-press : all very harmless and youthful, and never straying beyond the region of talk. The consequences (instigated, ironically enough, by an official whose family was to produce Sophia Perovskaja, of later nihilistic activity) were serious and vindictive. The so-called Petrashevtsy (as the frequenters of P.'s house came to be named) were raided for ideas, as Herzen (q.v.) said, and not for acts, on 23 April, 1849. Eight months later, sentence was pronounced. Twenty-one of the 'criminals' were condemned to be shot, and were actually subjected for half an hour to the ordeal of awaiting execution. Among these, Dostoievsky (q.v.) was number 4, in the projected order of shooting. At the last moment they were reprieved, and sent to Siberia for various terms of exile.

Petri -i. Olaus (1497-1552): Swed. reformer; theological writer; studied in Wittenberg under Melanchthon (q.v.) and became chancellor to king Gustavus i, 1531. P.'s fiery, energetic nature moved too quickly for his royal patron, and in 1540, he was actually condemned to death. The king's clemency was successfully invoked, and P. returned to Stockholm and to his Reformation campaign by word and pen. He replied to the remonstrance of Helgesen (q.v.), the Dane, and publd. a large number of liturgical and theological writings. He was also favourably known as a hymn-writer, and a compiler of Swed. chronicles.

-ii. Laurentius (1499-1573): Swed. theologian; reformer; brother to above; archbp. of Upsala from 1531. L.P.'s name is bound up with the Swed. version of the Bible (q.v.), 1540-41, corresponding with the archetypal vernacular Bible of Luther in Germany, and with Christian iii's Bible in Denmark (s.v. Pedersen). In effecting this rendering, the learned archbp. had the advantage of consulting Andreæ's (q.v.) version of the New Testament, 1526; and doubtless he was assisted by his more impetuous but like-minded brother. The brothers, who were of peasant orig., are also known as Olaf and Lars Peterssen.

Peutinger, Conrad (1465-1547): Germ. humanist; resided at Augsburg; numismatist and antiquary.

Pfeffel, Gottlieb Konrad (1736-1809): Germ. writer of fables (q.v.); of the school of Gellert (q.v.), but in its decline.

Pfeiffer, Emily Jane (1827-90): Engl. (Germ.) poet; née Davis; m., J.E.P. (Germ.), 1853. Wr. *Margaret*, 1861; *Poems*, 1876; etc.; belongs to the school of E. B. Browning (q.v.), but, though 'the compassionate sonnet, which will tolerate and, to some extent, ennoble all faults except triviality and carelessness, enabled her to do her most tolerable work, the rest was mostly negligible' (*C.H.E.L.*, xiii, 180).

Phébus (Fr.): Colloquial term in France for the fashionable diction of the heroes and heroines of the Precious (q.v.) novels of the 17th cent.; the Euphuism (q.v.) of Paris. (see s.vv. Scudéry, La Calprenède, Gomberville). Tallemant (q.v.) says, in his *Historiettes*: 'The heroes are all as alike as two drops of water, they all talk *Phébus*, and they are all a hundred thousand leagues above the rest of mankind'.

Philip iv (1605-65): King of Spain, 1621. With the policy of his reign, and with the War of Devolution started at his death by king Louis xiv of France, we are not here concerned. But P. was a patron and a lover of lit.; he transld. works of Guicciardini (q.v.), and is reputed to have composed sundry dramas, among them 'The Earl of Essex' (*le Conde de Sex*), which must almost certainly, however, be ascribed to Coello (q.v.).

Philips, Ambrose (c. 1675-1709): Engl. poet; dramatist. Wr. 6 pastorals (q.v.) for a *Miscellany*, 1709, and earned thereby the vindictive jealousy of Pope (q.v.), who considered himself affronted by the praises bestowed on P. Henry Carey (d., 1743; author of *Sally in our Alley*) affixed the nickname of 'Namby-Pamby' on Ambrose, on account of certain of his odes written to suit the taste of children. P.'s *Briton* and *Humphry, Duke of Gloucester* were indifferent plays quickly forgotten; but for his tragedy, *The Distress'd Mother*, 1712, adapted from Racine's (q.v.) *Andromache*, P. received more consideration. For some time he edited an Addisonian journal called the *Free Thinker*, and was successively secretary to archbp. Boulter and to the lord chancellor, and M.P. for Armagh. He is the subject of one of Johnson's (q.v.) *Lives of the Poets*.

Philips, John (1676-1709): Engl. poet; wr. *The Splendid Shilling*, 1705; *Cyder*, 1708, and others: the former was a Miltonian mock-heroic poem: the latter, a Virgilian *Georgic* of Devon. P.'s historic interest resides in the fact, that, many years before J. Thomson (q.v.), he 're-introduced blank verse, the very Trojan horse of the citadel of the couplet' (Saintsbury, *C.H.E.L.*, ix, 181); Thomson himself apostrophized P. (*Autumn*, 645), as
Philips, Pomona's bard, the second thou
Who nobly durst, in rhyme-unfettered verse,
With British freedom sing the British song.
(The first was Wentworth Dillon, first earl of Roscommon, died 1685, who transld. in blank verse Horace's, q.v. *Ars Poetica*). P.'s poetic value, a very different thing, is somewhat overstated in the very interesting ch. x. of the *History of Modern Engl. Romanticism*, i, by Dr. H. G. de Maar (Oxford, 1924). He is the subject of one of Johnson's (q.v.) *Lives of the Poets*.

Philips, Katherine (1631-64): Engl. poet; née Fowler; m. James P., 1647; 'known as the matchless Orinda', from her choice of the name (not the epithet) as a *nom-de-guerre*. Transld. Corneille's (q.v.) *Pompée*, and wr. verses introductory to the poems of H. Vaughan (q.v.).

Philistinism: Descriptive epithet, borrowed from Germany, for a hard, material, common attitude towards the things of the imagination. 'We have not the expression in English. Perhaps we have not the word because we have so much of the thing. . . The French have adopted the term *épicier* (grocer) to designate the sort of being whom the Germans designate by the term Philistine. . . Efforts have been made to obtain in English some term equivalent to *Philister* or *épicier*; Mr. Carlyle has made several such efforts: "respectability with its thousand gigs" he says. . . . However, the word *respectable* is far too valuable a word to be thus perverted from its proper meaning ; if the English are ever to have a word for the thing we are speaking of . . . I think we had much better take the term *Philistine* itself ' (M. Arnold, q.v., *Essays in Criticism* : ' Heinrich Heine '. See too, Arnold, *Culture and Anarchy*, ch. iii, where he makes a ' humble attempt at a scientific nomenclature ' of Barbarians, Philistines, Populace, for the 3 classes—upper, middle, lower—of British society). The social philosophy of Carlyle and Arnold exercised considerable influence in Engld. during the 19th cent. ; and it formed at the time a salutary corrective to the smug attitude of plate-glass prosperity which stared from the windows of the Crystal Palace and from the shop-fronts of the industrious apprentices delineated by Smiles (q.v. ; and see s.v. W. Morris), in the era of British commercial peace and growth, when France was recovering from her war and Germany was consolidating her empire (1871-*c*. 1888). Arnold's principle of culture, which had an immense vogue, resembled to some extent the method of Alice (in Wonderland ; see s.v. Carroll), taking bites off alternate sides of the magic mushroom. Arnold's countrymen were similarly to be fed on Hellenism and Hebraism alternately, in order to strengthen respectively their consciousness and their conscience ; and Goethe's Germany and Hugo's France afforded models to us of the good results of a hellenized diet. But even Philistia has its pleasaunces, and its close neighbourhood to Palestine has literary as well as geographical significance.

Philosophes (Fr.) : Philosophers ; the special application of the term in Fr. literary history (comparable to the use of *sophist* in Greece) dates from the 17th cent., when *philosophie* meant simply free-thought in religion. (See s.v. *Libertins*, of whom Saint-Evremond, q.v., was the most distinguished). A further specialization of the word, elsewhere honourable and general in its connotation, occurred towards the middle of the 18th cent., when the *philosophes*, reinforced by Locke (q.v.), and by the example, eagerly sought in visits by Montesquieu, Voltaire (qq.v.) and others, of Engl. parliamentary institutions, became definitely and narrowly identified with the school of Fr. thinkers and reformers, associated by their labours on the *Encyclopédie ; ou Dictionnaire des Sciences, des Arts, et des Métiers*, Paris, 1750-76. (See s.v. Encyclopedia, where the history of this enterprise is related. Reference may be made to Morley's *Diderot*, Macmillan, 2 vols.). The *philosophes*, thus banded together for social and political purposes, were united by certain broad, common principles, however much they might differ, one from another, in their actual writings and opinions. The *écrasez l'infâme* of Voltaire (q.v.) was conceived in the veritable spirit of *philosophie*, as interpreted by the militants of the *Encyclopédie* : the *infâme* was religion, or, more strictly, credulity to authority in religious affairs ; and the summons to inquire and to investigate, and to found conclusions upon reasonable evidence, instead of upon acquiescence in tradition, was carried into every

department of human thought. Buffon (q.v.) applied it to natural history ; Montesquieu (q.v.) to Roman history ; Quesnay (q.v.) and the physiocrats (q.v.) to political arithmetic, as a branch of economics. It was carried into spheres seemingly remote from its interest : Voltaire's oriental tales concealed a social reformer's purpose under their lascivious eastern veil ; Dalembert's (q.v.) funeral eulogies on departed members of the Fr. Academy (q.v.) enabled him, as a *philosophe*, to insinuate the tenets of his creed. There was hardly a department of life or learning which was not captured by a propagandist of the school, and the 10 years, 1760-1770, were patricularly fertile in this respect. Quesnay's *Tableau économique* and Helvétius' (q.v.) *de l'Esprit* had both appeared in 1758 ; and the definitive *Système de la Nature* (q.v.), commonly ascribed to Holbach (q.v.), appeared in 1770. The ranks of the *philosophes* included, either temporarily or permanently, men as diverse on their eminences as Voltaire, Buffon, and J. J. Rousseau (q.v.), as well as a crowd of minor writers, united by a belief that it was essential to their scheme of the universe that its Maker should be repudiated at every stage. But the grand triumph of the school was the transformation of Chambers's modest *Cyclopædia*, 1728, into the *Encyclopédie* of the meliorists of France, under the resistless direction of Diderot (q.v.) ; and we cannot part from their company, nor from their influence for evil and good in the history of Europe, without referring to the sketch, *Esquisse d'un Tableau historique des Progrès de l'Esprit humain*, 1794, which, in its title, contents, and aim, and in the indomitable optimism which informed it, sums up the whole movement in one example. This was the work of Condorcet (q.v.), written in the shadow of the guillotine, which he escaped only by taking poison. And in these facts, as in the story of the draught of hemlock taken by Socrates, lies an allegory, which is a little outside our scope. The teachings of the Fr. encyclopædists led to the reign of Terror in France and to the reign of Napoleon in Europe. Though they helped to break down the barriers of the Middle Ages, yet the new age opened in bloodshed. And still the example of great souls, ' hot for certainties in this our life ', and struggling valiantly amid the ' dusty ' answers, lent serenity and confidence to the spectacle of old things in ruins. ' More light ' was their quest, however brokenly, as it was the quest of Luther, Rabelais and Goethe (qq.v.) ; and if the white radiance was stained by the many colours of experience, if the Voltairean note of levity and the Benthamite note of utilitarianism were evoked among the deeper music of the notes of liberty and justice, yet these were greater and more abiding than the errors which mocked them. And one reflection may be added in conclusion. History does not repeat itself, despite easy assertions to the contrary ; but the past illustrates the present, and throws light upon the future ; and the generation which has lived through the Great War, 1914-18, may see a likeness and some differences in the circumstances of the Fr. *philosophes* and of the

Germ. professors. In both instances, there was a period of learned preparation for the arbitrament of violent acts ; and any surprise which we may feel at the influence of men of science and of letters on politics and public affairs is cancelled by the experience of those later times. Germ. *Kultur* and Fr. *philosophie*, though the former had the sanction of Church and State, and the latter was bitterly opposed to them, were alike in their aim and methods. Both were missionaries of a new culture. Both compromised their teaching functions with social and economic aims ; each employed a great word—*Kultur, philosophie*—to convey a special meaning of material progress ; and both were moved by a conviction that mankind could be tabulated and inspected into happiness. The *philosophes* of Louis xvi, like the *Kultur*-professors of kaiser Wilhelm ii, attempted to harness learning to the cause of a militant social policy, and to *sabrer* (the word is Diderot's) theology, ethics, metaphysics, physical science, history, and æsthetics ; compelling at the sword's point, that is to |say, the assent of public opinion to their new interpretation of the universe. How far learning may safely be yoked with militancy, and philosophy and culture be made to serve political causes of reform, are questions which historians will answer according to their knowledge. Of the *philosophes* of the 18th cent., we may perhaps aver that their polemics were unavoidable ; and that, in their great zeal as popularizers of militant thought, at least they did not fall short of the civic ideal as defined by Plato : ' he who from cowardice or self-interest or over-refinement or indolence or irresolution fails in resisting the prejudice or injustice or falsehood of his age, is wanting in the fulfilment of the highest duty of a citizen and a man ' (Jowett, *Plato's Republic*, iii, 286 ; note on Plato, *Rep.*, vi, 497a).

Phosphorus (Swed.) : Title of a journal, founded, 1810, by Atterbom (q.v.), in order to promote the cause of literary neo-Romanticism in Sweden. (See s.v. Swed. lit.). The journal survived till 1815, and Atterbom and his school were commonly known by the name of Phosphorists. Their principles were sought in Germany, from the brothers Schlegel, Tieck (qq.v.), and the rest (see, too, s.v. Romance), in opposition to the older Fr. tendencies which had prevailed since the time of queen Christina (q.v.) ; and their themes were sought mainly from native sources, in conformity with the tenets of the contemporary Gothic League (q.v.). A healthier and more virile strain was introduced by Tegnér (q.v.), who had several bouts with the Phosphorists and their leader, esp. in their later journal, the *Svensk Litteratur-Tidnung*, and the movement, so far as it did not die of inanition, was absorbed in the national lit.

Physiocrats : Fr. school of economists in the 18th cent. The name was given by J. B. Say (q.v.) to a group of writers on political economy, whose corporate existence, so far as it was effective, dated from July, 1757, when the marquis de Mirabeau (q.v.) met Quesnay (q.v.), physician to mme. de Pompadour, in his lodgings at Versailles. Quesnay was the author of a *Tableau Économique*, printed at the royal press, 1758, and subsequently re-issued with a commentary by Mirabeau, author of *l'Ami des Hommes*, who affected to ascribe the foundations of society to writing, money, and the *Tableau* of his friend and master. The real orig. of the P. is doubtless to be sought in *L'Esprit des Lois* of Montesquieu (q.v.), 1748, and to that extent its orig. is Engl., inasmuch as Montesquieu, like Voltaire (q.v. ; Voltaire ridiculed Quesnay's Socratic manner, as he ridiculed most things in which he saw good), owed part of his curiosity about institutions to his observation of Engl. practice. But ' the Confucius of Europe ', as Quesnay was called by his disciples, and Mirabeau, the descendant of the Riquetti of Florence, and the father of the great Mirabeau of the Revolution, undoubtedly gave a lead to the concentration on economic problems, which was itself, in the middle of the 18th cent., a forerunner of the cataclysm at its close. The aim of physiocracy, as its name implies, was to promote the welfare of humanity under the laws of nature ; God intends man's good, and the physiocrats were convinced deists ; happiness would follow from obedience to natural laws, which require the practical abrogation of man-made laws (except a compulsory-education law), and esp. of the financial legislation of king Louis xv ! Accordingly, national wealth was to spring from the cultivation of the soil ; there was to be no artificial interference with the laws of production and exchange ; and *l'impôt unique*, or the ' single tax ' levied on land, an imposition which still finds adherents, was to be the sole source of public expenditure. The members of the P. included Mercier de la Rivière (1720-94), Dupont (1739-1817), and others. They worked at a little distance from the *Philosophes* (q.v.) of the Encyclopedia (q.v.), but their separate activity virtually ceased, when Turgot became minister.

Picard, Louis Benoit (1769-1828) : Fr. playwright; satirist, comedian. P. has no present interest to lit., but his plays enjoyed a vogue under the First Empire, and his name is commonly mentioned in the transition of Fr. comedy to Scribe (q.v.).

Pickelhering : Dutch name for the Fool in Engl. comic drama, as adapted to the Germ. stage in the 16th cent. (see s.v. Englische Comödianten), whence the comedies in the Germ. repertory were known as P. plays.

Pidal, Pedro José (1809-65) : Span. literary critic ; *marquis* by rank. P. was a brilliant student of early texts in his national lit., and edited for the first time various important works from MSS. Among these were the *Disputa del Alma y el Cuerpo* (debate between the soul and the body), a famous medieval theme, and undoubtedly the oldest surviving fragment (in 37 verses) of Span. romance (*ed. pr.*, 1856), and the *Vida* (life) *de Santa Maria Egipciaqua*, ed. pr., 1841.

Pietism : Mode of thought in the sphere of religion, which spread from the Calvinist communities in the Netherlands to Germany, north and south, where it found a congenial soil already prepared by the mystics. The time of its appearance was towards the close of the 17th cent., when men of deep thought and feeling sought to turn the stream of Protestantism, caught up in the turbid waters of religious warfare, into the quieter channel of individual practice of the Christian life. Pietism, unlike Puritanism in Engld., operated by meekness, not by militancy ; by dulcet hymn and eloquent sermon, it softened the rigour and harshness of aspects of the Lutheran faith, and strove to rekindle the sense of intimate union with God from which the Reformation itself had derived so much of its strength ; ' Luther rebels against Lutheranism ' (Paulsen, *Kant*, E.T., 13). Thus, on its constructive side, P. was a part of that intellectual movement towards liberalism and an awakening of the national consciousness, paralysed by the Thirty Years' War (q.v.) of which Leibniz's (q.v.) rational philosophy and personal optimism were another part ; and each contributed to the Aufklärung (q.v.), or enlightenment, which characterized the age. Not the least merit of P. was its influence on the music of Bach, nor was its literary influence exhausted when Goethe (q.v.) was meditating his *Wilhelm Meister*, and writing of the ' beautiful soul '. P. is derived ultimately from Spinoza (q.v.) : ' the common ground of Spinozism and Pietism is their cheerful quietism in the imperturbable tranquillity of the mind in its complete union with God ' (*C.M.H.*, v, 754) ; and thus it had a close likeness to the specific Quietism of the Span. mystics, derived from S. Theresa and Molinos (qq.v.), and introduced by mme. Guyon (q.v.) into France. The kinship of P. to Quakerism in Engld. is obvious. Its foremost representative in Germany was Spener (q.v.), and the duchy of Würtemberg was regarded by some of its adherents as ' God's apple of the eye ', on account of its partial exemption from the storms which followed the Thirty Years' War. As a literary force, the movement was short-lived ; as a social force, it was gradually absorbed in associations of secular endeavour.

Pietsch, von, Johann (1690-1733) : Germ. poet and critic ; an opponent of the Second Silesian School (q.v.), and, despite his contemporary fame, as uninspired and tedious as Canitz (q.v.).

Pilatus, Leontius (14th cent.) : Gk. (Calabrian) scholar-exile. P. was almost the first of the line of grammarians, librarians, and teachers, who so ably and unselfishly backed the Humanist zeal of their patrons in Italy ; but he was of a vastly inferior type to the majority of his successors. He came (1360) to reside with Boccaccio (q.v.) at Florence, where it was his task to effect a Lat. version of Homer (q.v.) for Boccaccio and Petrarch. Reports of his unmannerly behaviour suggest a kind of Silas Wegg, domiciled with the first Homerist of modern Europe.

Pinciano, El. See **Lopez, Alonso.**

Pindar, Peter. See **Wolcot, S.**

Pindemonte, -i. Giovanni (1751-1812) : Ital. dramatist ; wr. tragedies of no great intrinsic merit, the main hist. interest of which is that they helped to break up the classical tradition of the Ital. stage. *Orso Ipato*, e.g., 1797, is said (*P.E.L.*, x, 449) to be remarkable for

the elaboration of its scenery and the violence of its action : ' the last act positively reeks with corpses ', at the time when Verri (q.v.) was translg. *Hamlet*.

-ii. Ippolito (1753-1828) : also recorded as 1754-1825) : Ital. poet ; brother of above ; described as a kind of Ital. Cowper (q.v.), whom he resembled not merely in the fact that he transld. the *Odyssey* of Homer (he also transld. Virgil's *Georgics*), but likewise in a certain romantic sensibility which corresponded to his brother's anti-classical taste in drama. I.P., whose native melancholy, acquired partly from a study of Gray and Young (qq.v.), was deepened by ill-health, commenced a poem, ' The Cemetery ', which he broke off when Foscolo (q.v.) wr. his *Sepolcri*. I.L. wr. *le Poesie Campestri*, 1785, and a moving tale in verse, *Antonio Foscarini*.

Pinkerton, John (1758-1826) : Scot. scholar. Wr. *Essay on Medals*, 1784, which procured him an introduction to sir H. Walpole (q.v.), and publd. *Ancient Scottish Poems*, 1786, in the pref. to which he acknowledged the forged orig. of some of the contents of his earlier vol., *Select Scottish Ballads*, 1783.

Pinnock, William (1782-1843) : Engl. educational writer ; joined **Samuel Maunder** (1785-1849) in London, 1817, in the preparation of a series of works for popular instruction, including the famous *Juvenile Cyclopædia, Treasury of Knowledge*, etc. ; abridged Goldsmith's (q.v.) histories.

Piozzi, Hester Lynch (1741-1821) : Scot. biographer ; *née* Salusbury ; m., i. Harry Thrale, 1763, and opened her house at Streatham to Dr. Johnson (q.v.), whose intimacy with the Thrales constitutes their title to fame ; ii, 1784, 3 years after Thrale's death, Gabriel P., an Ital. musician. Her second marriage was distasteful to her friends, and most deeply so to Johnson. Wr. *Anecdotes of the late Samuel Johnson*, 1786 (see s.v. Boswell), *Correspondence*, 1788, etc.

Pirkheimer, Willibald (1470-1530) : Germ. humanist ; associated with Celtes (q.v.) at Nuremberg ; scholar, statesman, and collector ; wr. Lat. *Historia belli suitensis* (history of the Swiss War).

Piron, Alexis (1690-1773) : Fr. poet ; a writer of genuine wit and originality, but too indolent to do his gifts thorough justice. Wr., 1722, *Arlequin-Deucalion*, a comic-opera in monologue, and other works in irregular dramatic form of a high order of satire and brilliance ; 1738, *Métromanie*, a comedy in the vein of Molière (q.v.), directed against the pretensions of second-rate culture. P. was a fertile maker of epigrams, a branch of lit. cultivated by Voltaire and Le Brun (qq.v.), and practised by P. with conspicuous success. Many of his best and most bitter epigrams were launched against La Chaussée (q.v.), and P. is reasonably esteemed as one of the major names in the first half of the 18th cent. He founded a social and literary club, the Caveau moderne, in Paris.

Pisan, de, Christine (1363-*c.* 1429) : Fr. lyric poet. Born at Venice, but is counted Fr. by her marriage in Picardy to one Castel, and by her industrious apprenticeship to the muse of Deschamps (q.v.). She wr. *ballades, rondeaux*, etc., and is somewhat unkindly dismissed

by Lanson (*Hist. Lit. Fr.*, 167) as ' the first of
the intolerable line of blue-stockings, who
make it the business of a long and useless life
to multiply the evidences of their indefatigable facility, equalled by their universal
mediocrity '. C. defended her sex against
the attacks of Jean de Meung in the *Romance
of the Rose* (q.v.), and her moral and patriotic
tales (*dits*), which included one of Joan of Arc,
were issued by Caxton (q.v.) in an Engl.
transln., which gave C. a great vogue in early
Tudor times.

Pisarev, Dimitri Ivanovich (1840-68): Russ.
critic ; follower of Chernyshevsky (q.v.),
and even more resolute materialist and anti-
æsthetist than his leader. ' His critical essays ',
says Brückner (*Gesch. d. Russ. Lit.*, 307),
' were all devoted to the aim of setting the way
free for the type of the contemplative, or
doctrinaire, realist. This type he deemed to
be incorporated in Turgenev's Bazarov ',
a character supposed to be drawn from
himself ; and he aimed at the multiplication
of this type in the youth of his times and in the
readers of the newspapers which he edited.
P.'s early death, adds the historian a little
grimly, saved him from many disappointments.
Of a truth, this journalistic nihilism (q.v.)
was but a passing phase in Russ. lit.

Pisemsky, Alexi Theophilaktovich (1820-81):
Russ. novelist and dramatist ; formerly
ranked as one of a trinity of social novelists with
Goncharov and Turgenev (qq.v.),' but now
recognized as inferior to these 2 in style.
Mirsky (*Modern Russ. Lit.*, Oxford, 1925 ;
p. 35) compares P. to Balzac (q.v.) as a writer of
stories, among which *The Muff*, 1850, and *A
Thousand Souls*, 1858, are mentioned as the
best. P.'s drama, *A Bitter Fate* is characterized as ' the only realistic drama in Russian
that deserves the name of tragedy ' (*ib.*, 68).

Pithou, Pierre (1539-96): Fr. poet ; converted
Huguenot, and prominent in counsels of
moderate party. As such, became chief
contributor to the famous *Satyre Ménippée*
(q.v.).

Pitt, Christopher (1699-1748): Engl. translr.
Friend of Pope (q.v.), and transld. the *Æneid*
of Virgil (q.v.), 1740.

Pius ii : Æneas Sylvius Piccolomini (1405-64):
It. statesman ; patron of learning ; pope,
1458, till his death ; resided at Naples under
the patronage of king Alfonso v (q.v.) of Aragon
after his victory in 1443. Wr., 1444, Lat.
romance, *History of Two Lovers*, which was
transld. into Span., *ed. pr.*, 1496. Wr., too,
1443, Lat. epistle to archduke Sigismund of
Tyrol *on the Right Education of a Prince*, and
1450, Lat. epistle to king Ladislas of Bohemia
and Hungary *on the Education of Children*
(Engl. transl. by W. H. Woodward, *Vittorino
de Feltre*, Cambridge, 1905). It is a notable
educational treatise, which urges the methods
of Quintilian and Plutarch, without recourse
to the rod, and defends (against ' the opposition of the shallow churchman ') a devotion to
the language and lit. of ancient Rome.
' Happily ', wr. the future pope, ' there are in
Hungary not a few to whom the poets of antiquity are a precious possession ', a dictum
which was justified by the record of king
Matthias Corvinus (q.v.). P.'s devotion to

learning did not lead him, as it led Nicholas v
(q.v.) to neglect the church militant, and
he died at Ancona at the head of his own
crusade against the Turk ; a forlorn but
heroic venture. In 1462, he issued a Bull
for the protection of the remains of ancient
Rome, and his attitude towards lit. is well given
in one of his letters : ' neither the morning-
star nor the evening-star is fairer than the
wisdom that is won by the study of letters '.

Planché, James Robinson (1796-1880): Engl.
playwright ; antiquary ; Somerset herald.
Wr. farces and burlesques, beginning with
Amoroso (Drury Lane, 1818), frequently
introducing mythology and fairy lore, at a time
when ' the gods and goddesses of Greece and
Rome were more familiar to the public than
they are now ' (*C.H.E.L.*, xiii, 271 ; and see
s.v. Gozzi C.). Wr., too, *History of British
Costumes*, 1834, of permanent value.

Plantin, Christopher (1514-89): Fr. printer,
resident in Holland. Born at Tours ; apprenticed in Caen and Paris ; settled at Antwerp,
1550, and appointed, 1570, printer of sacred
lit. by royal patent of Spain ; issued, at
serious financial loss, famous Antwerp Polyglot
Bible (q.v.) in 8 folio vols. The Dutch revolt
against Spain drove P. from Antwerp to Leyden
from 1583-85, when he returned to his business,
leaving the Leyden press to a son-in-law. P.
was honoured with burial in Antwerp Cathedral,
and the Plantin press was carried on in the
same premises by his descendants through
another son-in-law, Moretus, till 1876, when
it was purchased by the city of Antwerp to be
preserved as a museum.

Platen (-Hallermünde), von, August (1796-1835):
Germ. poet ; count by rank. Max Müller
(q.v., *German Classics*, Oxford, ii, 614) selects
for special mention P.'s lyric poems, esp. the
sonnets and the (Persian) *ghazels*, first publd.
in 1821 ; likewise, his satiric comedies, written
with Aristophanic spirit, *The Fateful Fork*,
1826, *The Romantic Oedipus*, 1829, etc. We
may also mention his fanciful dramatic poem,
The Glass Slipper, 1824, from the Cinderella-
tale, and his epic romance, *The Abbasids*, 1834,
from the Arabian Nights. These themes,
and his metrical schemes, and his love of Italy,
constitute his claim to be included in the
Germ. Romantic movement, and he displayed
the individualism which descended to it from
the Renaissance (q.v.), and to the Renaissance
from Ovid (q.v.), in such lines as the following
from his epitaph-sonnet :

Ich was ein Dichter, und empfang die Schläge
  Der bösen Zeit, in welcher ich entsprossen ;
  Doch schon als Jüngling hab' ich Ruhm
    genossen,
Und auf die Sprache drückt' ich mein Gepräge.
But at the same time P. stood aloof from the
more sentimental romanticism of his contemporaries, and helped to kill the so-called fate-
drama (q.v., and see, e.g., s.v. Grillparzer),
by his fork-drama, which substituted a fork
for the regulation dagger. He laughed, too,
at Immermann (q.v. ; ' Nimmermann ') in his
Romantic Oedipus, which drew upon him a
bitter attack from Heine (q.v.), and, as
literary satirist, a comparison of P. with
Aristophanes is defensible.

Platina. See **Sachi, Bartolommeo.**

Plato (427-347 B.C.) : Gk. philosopher ; of noble birth, his father claiming descent from Codrus, the last king of Athens, and his mother coming from a distinguished family, to which Solon also belonged. P.'s proper name was Aristocles, and he is said to have acquired the name of *Platon* from the breadth of his shoulders, displayed in gymnastic feats. Socrates, whose death occurred in 399 B.C., brought his magnetic, even mesmeric, influence to bear on the young, ardent and sensitive spirit of P. during the impressionable early twenties, and dominated by his personality the greater part of P.'s writings. It may almost be said, that, until P. wr. the *Laws* in old age, the central, animating figure of his composition was always Socrates : 4 of these writings, particularly, *Euthyphro*, *Apology*, *Crito* and *Phœdo*, deal with the master's trial and death ; and 'there is nothing in any tragedy, ancient or modern, nothing in poetry or history (with one exception) like the last hours of Socrates in Plato' (Jowett, q.v.) ; or, as prof. J. P. Mahaffy writes (*Hist. Gk. Lit.*, ii, 186) : 'The *Phœdo*, or last conversation and death of Socrates, is certainly the most famous of all Plato's writings, and owes this renown not only to the infinite importance of the subject— the immortality of the soul—but to the touching scenery and pathetic situation in which the dialogue is laid. . . These pictures are only paralleled in literature by the one sacrifice which was greater and more enduring than that of the noblest and purest pagan teacher'. Jowett and Mahaffy, each a competent Hellenist, make, it will be observed, the same exception, and it is important to note that, in a later epoch of Platonic study, P.'s disciples sought to combine in one system of revelation the truths of Socratianity and Christianity.

This, then, first : the dominance of Socrates, the inspired, irresistible Gk. sophist, with his ugly face and searching tongue, and the fascination of his truth-compelling genius. But Socrates left nothing written, 'and the vast and varied influence which proceeded from Plato and affected the history of the world may perhaps be best summed up in the remark that without Plato we should have had no Aristotle, no Carneades, no Augustine' (Gomperz, *Gk. Thinkers*, E.T., iii, 266). As to Aristotle, see s.v. ; as to Carneades of Cyrene, who died 129 B.C., Gomperz (*ib.*) says that he 'has been rightly named the David Hume (q.v.) of antiquity. But he also reminds us of Montaigne (q.v.), the great questioning spirit of the Renaissance'; and as to St. Augustine (354-430 A.D.), whose *Confessions* moved Petrarch (q.v.) so forcibly, 'his influence upon later ages has been of incalculable depth. The Catholic Church numbers him among the foremost of those who have shaped her destinies. Yet also that form of Protestantism which has ploughed most deeply into the souls of men—the faith of Calvin (q.v.)—has been most powerfully influenced by Augustine and his doctrine of predestination. In taking his stand upon self-consciousness as the foundation of all knowledge, wherein he shows himself pre-eminently a powerful thinker partly inspired by Platonism, he became the predecessor of Descartes (q.v.), the creator of

modern philosophy' (Gomperz, *ib.*, 269). And these, too, are parts of P.

Let us turn to another part of P. His treatise, the *Timæus*, we read, 'is a Myth, not a scientific treatise, although it was its fortune from the very first to be treated as if it were the latter. No other work of Plato's was so much read and commented on in antiquity, and throughout the Middle Age, as the *Timæus* ; and that chiefly because it was regarded as a compendium of natural science, all the more valuable because its "natural science" was not presented as something apart by itself, but "framed in a theological setting." Aristotle, of course, treats it *au pied de la lettre*. With the Christian Platonists it took rank as a scientific and theological authority along with the Book of Genesis' (J. A. Stewart, *The Myths of Plato* ; 210). 'Moses Atticus', the Athenian Moses, was a name given to P. by Numenius (fl. 160 A.D.) in this connection ; and thus Gomperz (*ib.*) succinctly writes : 'The Sufism of Islam, German mysticism, the Jewish Kabbalas, are one and all saturated with Platonic thoughts'. More particularly, too, to Jew. thought, to the *Timæus* as parallel to the Book of Genesis, and to P. as the Gk. Moses, we note the work of Philo (20 B.C.—after 40 A.D.), the Alexandrian Jew, whose life of study was 'mainly spent on Plato and on the allegorical interpretation of the Book of Genesis and the exposition of the Law of Moses' (Sandys, *Hist. Class. Schol.*, i, 296). Either Philo platonizes or Plato philonizes, was a saying current in the first cent., A.D., and 'Philo gave a new vent to the Greek philosophy which he assimilated' (N. Bentwich, *Hellenism*, 174). We cannot follow here—it belongs to the history of philosophy, not of lit.—the descent of Plato through 'Moses Atticus' to Malebranche (q.v.) and the Cambridge Platonists of the 17th cent. The recital would include the Neo-Platonists, whose doctrine, founded at Alexandria in the 3rd cent., A.D., was reduced to writing by Plotinus (204-70) and Porphyry (233-c. 300), and was revived, again at Alexandria, by Hypatia, early in the 5th cent. The emperor Justinian i broke the 'golden chain' of the Platonic succession, when he closed the school at Athens, 529 A.D. Very briefly, perhaps, we may say that the long night of Scholasticism (q.v.), which now descended on learning, left the study of P., latent in Abelard, Roger Bacon (qq.v.), and other teachers, to await the light of Humanism in the 14th cent., kindled by Petrarch (1304-74). A century later, 'Niccoli, Traversari, Maretti, Bruni and Marsuppini were the foremost of the humanists of Florence in the age of Cosimo de' Medici. All of them, in their various ways, were actively engaged in promoting the Revival of learning, when the study of Gk., and of Plato in particular, incidentally received a new impulse during the conference between the Greek and Latin Churches at the Council of Florence, 1439 ' (Sandys, *op. cit.*, ii, 48 ; and see s.vv.). So we come to Gemistos Pletho (q.v.) 'the second Plato', and the Platonic Academy at Florence, and Bessarion (q.v.), and Ficino (q.v.), who 'received holy orders at the age of forty, and spent the rest of his days in the honest and reverent endeavour to reconcile Platonism and Christianity' (Sandys, *ibid.*, 82), and Pico della Mirandola (q.v.), who died in 1494, while meditating a harmony of Platonic, Christian and Cabbalistic lore, and who left a name which the world of letters does not let fade. By this road we reach the Cambridge Platonists, who join us to P. across the centuries. They include Henry More, Cudworth, and Theophilus Gale (qq.v.), who shared Philo's belief that Plato derived his wisdom from Moses : 'Philo was their master in Scriptural exegesis, but Plotinus was especially their master in what concerned devotional religion' (J. A. Stewart, *op. cit.*, 479), and Plato was the master of both. Moreover, from the Cambridge Platonists may be traced relationships to the ethical doctrine of Kant (q.v.) and later idealists. For 'Platonism is a temper as well as a doctrine' (Stewart, *ib.*), and the philosophic temper of the pupil of Socrates has passed into the intellectual and spiritual heritage of adherents to every system of religious thought. And these, too, are parts of P.

Let us turn to yet another part. P.'s *Polity*, or *State*, or *Republic*, as it most commonly and least correctly called, is his principal and still his most famous work. Its preoccupation is justice, and the happiness which crowns just action, and the inquiry leads inevitably from the study of the individual to that of society. Again, we must forgo analysis of the contents of this masterpiece. It discusses under the aspects of the State education, marriage, the fine arts, and the prizes and rewards of virtue. 'Modern associations lead us to expect that the book should be either distinctly ethical or distinctly political, that it should either consider man in his relations as a citizen or consider him simply as a moral agent. Because the Greek philosophers did not separate these two questions it is frequently said that they confused them ; whereas it would be truer to say that they looked at human life more simply and more completely than we are apt to do. Law, custom and religion were not in practice the distinct things that they are now' (R. L. Nettleship, *Lectures on the Republic of Plato*, 5) ; or, in Jowett's words : 'The idea of the individual as distinct from the State or family is not one of the earliest but one of the latest of human conceptions, not having yet emerged in ancient times from the unity of the family which expanded into the State' (*Republic*, ii, 33). So, to P. we look back as the founder of the ideal commonwealth, sought by Augustine in the *Civitas Dei*, by More in the *Utopia*, by Machiavelli, Harrington, Francis Bacon, Coleridge (qq.v.) and Mr. H. G. Wells. And these, too, are parts of P.

We may turn to yet another part. It is obvious that a writer whose influence is to be discerned in the Sufism of Islam, Germ. mysticism and the Jewish Kabbalas, and whose Myths, or art-tales, illustrating his arguments, 'regulate Transcendental Feeling for the service of conduct and science' (J. A. Stewart, *op. cit.*, 43), must have produced a profound effect upon that class of writers—the

poets,—whose special function it is to interpret experience imaginatively. This effect is marked already in the *Divina Commedia*, where Dante (q.v.) shows acquaintance with a Lat. transln. of P.'s *Timæus*. The sublimation of human love is a Platonic concept ; the heavenly patterns of earthly objects are another ; and the so-called Metaphysical (q.v.) poets, who trace their descent from the Troubadours of Provence and Sicily, are Platonists to a man. The transcendental quality of the *Phædrus*, the *Symposium* and the *Timæus* is the very basis of the thought, and enters into the very texture of the language, in the poetry of Spenser, Coleridge, Shelley and Wordsworth (qq.v.), to select 4 Engl. poets only ; and of these Wordsworth is the chief. 'In *The Prelude* ', writes prof. J. A. Stewart (*Engl. Lit. and the Classics* ; 'Platonism in Engl. Poetry' ; 35), 'Wordsworth produced a work which must be regarded as the classic authority on Platonism in Poetry. The essential nature and the necessary conditions of the platonist mood, as experienced by one who is a poet, are set out by Wordsworth in the *Prelude*, with so much first-hand knowledge, and with such subtlety of analysis and completeness of circumstance, that I would say that the study of this poem ought to precede the study of Platonism in other English poets—especially where the Platonism is much influenced by tradition, as it is in Spenser and his successors '. And, very similarly, we read, in an essay by Mr. Lascelles Abercrombie : 'Is there, outside Milton and Dante, anything really comparable with the *Ode on the Intimations of Immortality* ? The theme is a peculiarly specialized version of Wordsworth's dominant idea : but the form it gives to the process of the idea's continually widening power, and to the growth of its harmony over the whole discord of personal life in an impersonal world, makes it, at any rate, the height of modern poetic art in English. Who else has found such security of harmony in such a range of experience ? ' (*The Idea of Great Poetry*, 115).* And this, too, was a part of P.

We should like to pause on P.'s form and style, and his notable contributions to the technique of lit. The dramatic dialogue, so closely connected with the Gk. triumphs on the stage, though not invented in prose by P., was brought by him to a degree of perfection, at which it descended as a finished model to Bunyan, Berkeley, Landor (qq.v.); and others. We might write, too, of P. in European lit., in the more specialized sense of enumerating the scholars and translrs., whose renown rests on their contributions to Platonic studies. But the essential, the vital P., belongs not to scholarship but to letters. Platonism, says prof. Stewart, whose eloquent praises of

---

* It is just worth noting, as marking the continuity of the Platonic *temper*, that the late prof. sir W. Raleigh, in his *Wordsworth* (1903; p. 148), remarked that, in the *Life* of Henry More (q.v.; the Cambridge Platonist; see *supra*), written by Richard Ward, 1710 'there are passages descriptive of ecstasies of joy, which might truly be applied to Wordsworth'; and he quotes : 'a good man would be ready some times to kiss the very stones of the street'. This *ecstasy* goes back to Plato through Plotinus (*supra*).

his Master we have quoted freely in this inadequate conspectus, ' is love of the unseen and eternal cherished by one who rejoices in the seen and temporal '. So, Plato the Prophet lived on, when Plato the philosopher was absorbed by Aristotle and his successors : ' Plato the prophet lived on in the speculation of theologians, the inspiration of poets, and the lives of religious men, Pagan, Jewish, Christian and Moslem, through the Alexandrine period and the early centuries of our era, through the dark ages so-called, through the two centuries of the dawning Renaissance, till in the latter half of the fifteenth century, with the foundation of the Platonic Academy at Florence, his personality became the object of a cult, to which zeal for the new learning, love of earthly beauty, and love of heavenly beauty, all gave fervour. Plato's *Dialogues*, as translated and commented on by the chief devotee of this cult, Marsilio, Ficino, and the *Enneads* of Plotinus, as translated by the same hand, now began to be read in the West, and while they influenced philosophy and theology chiefly, also influenced poetry by adding volume and weight to a stream of " Platonism ", which could be traced back beyond Dante, and in the sonnets of Petrarch, had already became a classic river, which was to flow on through Italian, French, and English love-poetry (see, too, s.v. Sonnet), till at last it was lost in the confluence of other waters '. It is an inexhaustible fount.

Pleiad : Astronomical term for a constellation of 7 stars ; transferred to denote a movement conspicuous by 7 eminent leaders. The earliest Pleiad in lit. history was a group of Gk. poets at Alexandria, and the most famous is the ' learned brigade ', founded, 1549, at the collège de Coqueret in Paris, which is the subject of the present article. The 5 original stars in this Pleiad were Ronsard, Du Bellay, Belleau, Baïf, and Jodelle (qq.v.) ; they added to their number Tyard (q.v.), and Dorat (q.v.), the Hellenist, to whose teaching they owed the direction given to their enthusiasm. Other names are sometimes included in, or substituted for, these 7 stars ; but the correct nominal roll is as above. If Dorat was the tutor of the P. (and his admission was the acknowledgment of his inspiration) Ronsard was the leader and the guiding-star, and Du Bellay, like another John the Baptist, was the prophet who went before, by however little, the coming poet. For Du Bellay's *Défense et Illustration de la langue française*—of the language as an instrument of the lit.—was publd. in 1549, and within a few months he had issued 2 vols. of poems exemplifying the principles which he had enunciated. His haste to be first in the field seems to have caused a temporary coolness between him and Ronsard, whose first 4 bks. of *Odes* appeared in 1550 ; but then and thenceforward Ronsard was the moving spirit in the brotherhood, which recalls in some of its features, as Ronsard recalls in his personal charm and magnetism, the Pre-Raphaelite Brotherhood (q.v.) 300 years later in Engld. Briefly, the aim of the P. was the reform of Fr. lit. and language; and its success is the measure of its aim. The young men (except Tyard and Dorat, none

was over 24) were moved by a common impulse, derived from their study of Gk. letters, to make, even to manufacture, a body of Fr. lit. equal to the highest models of antiquity. They agreed in regarding the existing lit. as jejune, insipid, graceless, and inadequate ; as unworthy of the greatness of France, and of the place which she was destined to fill in the culture of Europe. There were defects in the Fr. vocabulary, to be repaired out of Gk. and Lat. words ; there were forms of verse not yet acclimatized in France—the ode, the sonnet, the epic, the drama, the satire,—which the restored dignity of the Fr. tongue should use for the expression of ideas unsuited to the current forms of rondeau, virelay, chanson, and similar ' fripperies ' or confectionery (*épiceries*) of that kind. The recent discovery of the poems incorrectly attributed to Anacreon (q.v.), but plainly of his school, which H. Etienne (q.v.) publd. in 1554, but which must have been circulated in MS. a little earlier, gave a zest to the joyous attitude towards experience as well as to its artistic expression, which inspired and added grace to the lyric measures so ardently practised by the poets of the P., and including, it is interesting to note, the metre finally acclimatized in Engld. by Tennyson (q.v.) in *In Memoriam*. The actual contributions to Fr. lit. rendered by the leaders of this movement must be sought under the names given above, and under those of Bertaut, Desportes, Du Bartas, D'Aubigné, Garnier, Larivey, La Taille, Regnier (qq.v.), who, though not all of them Ronsardists in all things and some of them least of all in the leader's easy orthodoxy of faith, reflected the brilliance of the Pleiad in many aspects of their literary work. To re-write their achievements here would be to narrate the history of Fr. lit. from the middle of the 16th cent. for 60 years. What they sought to accomplish in the region of style was to introduce the modern meaning of that word ; to provide each class of writing with suitable and appropriate moulds ; to wean satire from its cradle of allegory (q.v.), drama from its cradle of mystery (q.v.), politics from its illusion of dream (q.v.), and to release language from its cramping servitude to authority. From this work Fr. lit. could never go back. Faults numberless were imputed to the Pleiad by the purists of another generation, Malherbe and Boileau (qq.v.) particularly ; and some at least of the criticism is merited : they turned their backs too fully on the past ; they ignored many good |features which they should have conserved ; they were too certain of their own immortality ; they imported more than they could carry ; and they did not always conceal a tendency to pedantic rules, such as Baïf (q.v.) adopted for his academy and handed on to Harvey's ' Areopagus ' (q.v.). But when all the blame is admitted and distributed, the solid achievement of the P. remains, comparable to nothing else in the history of lit., unless, perhaps, to that invasion by Greece, which the old Roman poet, Naevius, confessed his inability to stem : ' obliti sunt Romæ lingua loquier Latina '. They did not forget to speak the Fr. tongue in France ; but, by an analogy which Du Bellay and his disciples pressed for all that it was worth, Frenchmen were to assimilate other tongues, as Rome had assimilated the lit. of Greece ; and not Gk. and Lat. only, but the best, too, from Italy and Spain. There was no plagiary in the 16th cent., and the Pleiad's frank counsel to assimilate the best elements in ancient and modern poetry was obeyed by their contemporaries in Tudor Engld., who added France to their spoils, and, through France, possessed all the rest. Sir S. Lee, in his *Fr. Renaissance in Engld.* (Oxford, 1910), shows how our poets of the Tudor period were directly and indirectly indebted to the example and models of the Pleiad in France (see esp. s.v. Sonnet) : how they borrowed from that source metres, sentiments, word-forms, and themes ; and how it was through Ronsard and his circle that the Renaissance, which had started in Italy when Petrarch was worshipping Laura, culminated in the dramatic and lyric triumphs of Shakespeare himself. Simplicity in place of the ornateness with which the 'Rhetoriqueurs' (q.v.) had sought to disguise the tenuity of their inspiration, is, perhaps, the final gift of the Pleiad. Their most ambitious poems were not their most successful. They failed in drama ; they left prose aside ; and the spoils of Greece and Italy were not always more perfect than the lilting melodies of the native woodnotes of sunny France. There is something oppressive in the calculation (Lee, *op. cit.*, 202) that 1,686 out of 3,516 poems by Ronsard, Du Bellay and Baïf, were sonnets, often literally rendered from the Ital. But it is the music which they cultivated by this training, taught by Dorat in his classroom, sought by Du Bellay in his *Défense*, and caught by Ronsard in his verse, which makes the P. for all time deserving of the gratitude of lovers of great poetry The violence of their invasion of Fr. diction, their inability to bear the burden of their own conquests, and their indifference to the genius for order and reason inherent in the Fr. mind, were amply rebuked and avenged when Malherbe, by his poetics, and J. L. de Balzac (q.v.), by his prose, prepared the way for the classical correctness of the age of Racine, and the French Academy, and the rational philosophy of Descartes (see s.vv.). But, though lyrical inspiration failed when the appeal to oratory was made by the pioneers of Fr. lit. in the 17th cent., the P. added to Fr. poetry graces of sweetness and harmony, the recognition of which increases as the memory of their mistakes recedes.

The name Pleiad, it should be added, is often applied to the group of poets who clustered around Pushkin (q.v.), the first Russ. poet of European note ; in this group the chief star was Lermontov (q.v.).

Plethon. See **Gemistos Georgios.**

Plumptre, Anne (1760-1818) : Engl. scholar ; great grand-daughter of Henry P., president of the Royal Coll. of Physicians, 1740-5, and daughter of Robert P. (1723-88), president of Queen's Coll., Cambridge. A.P. did excellent work in promoting Germ. studies by her translns., 1798-9, of plays by Kotzebue (q.v.) ; wr., 1810, *Narrative of a Three Years'*

Residence in France ; novels, travel-books, etc.

Poet Laureate* (Engl.) : Court-poet (see too, s.v. Court). The ceremony of laureation, or coronation, began in Engld. at the univ. of Oxford, and early references to a laureate poet are reminiscent of that ceremony, and likewise of the famous episode in the life of Petrarch (q.v.) in Italy, who received the crown on the Capitol in Rome. Passing these academic bays, and noting that B. André (q.v.) was definitely appointed king's poet and historiographer royal at the court of Henry vii (the letters-patent granting an annuity of 10 marks to 'Bernard Andreas, Poet Laureate', were dated 21 Nov., 1486), we observe that the office lapsed until the beginning of the 17th cent., when it was revived in name, if not constitutionally, in favour of Ben Jonson (q.v.). He was granted, 1630, the pension and the butt of Canary wine, and a more formal nomination to the same office was made, after Jonson's death, to sir Wm. Davenant (q.v.), who enjoyed ' a popular, and perhaps also a quasi-official, recognition as laureate from 1637 to the downfall of the monarchy, and the idea that such an officer was a proper part of the official household took definite shape at this period '. This is proved by the action of king Charles ii, who, 6 days after Davenant's death, 1668, signed a warrant ' for a grant to John Dryden of the office of Poet Laureate, vacant by the death of sir Wm. Davenant '.

The official list of poets laureate is, accordingly, as follows :—

John Dryden, 1668.

Thos. Shadwell, 1689.

Nahum Tate, 1692.

Nicholas Rowe, 1715 (whose ' accession marks the beginning of the second period of the laureateship, the period during which the laureate was required to furnish, annually, a New Year's Ode and a Birthday Ode, to be sung before the king, . . . the custom lapsing under George iv, during Southey's tenure of the office ').

Laurence Eusden, 1718.

Colley Cibber, 1730.

Wm. Whitehead, 1757.

Thos. Warton, 1785.

Henry Jas. Pye, 1790.

Robert Southey, 1813 (whose ' laureateship marks the transition from the old order to the new ' ; the choice lay between sir W. Scott, q.v., and Southey).

Wm. Wordsworth, 1843 (when ' the laureateship had become not so much an office as an honour, not so much an obligation as a decoration ').

Alfred (lord) Tennyson, 1850 (S. Rogers, q.v., *ætat*, 87, declined it ; Tennyson accepting ' this laurel greener from the brow of him who utter'd nothing base ', did not, like Wordsworth, who was excused by age, avoid the duties of the office. He discharged them with unerring taste, finding them easier, no doubt, by the fact that a woman was on the throne, and that woman queen Victoria).

* The information in this art. is derived immediately from *The Laureateship : a Study of the Office of Poet Laureate in England. With some Account of the Poets.* By Edmund Kemper Broadus, prof. of Engl. at the univ. of Alberta. Oxford, 1921.

Alfred Austin, 1896 (Tennyson had died in Oct. 1892; Gladstone and the earl of Rosebery, as premiers, refrained from recommending an appointment; the claims of Swinburne, q.v., were paramount, and sir Lewis Morris, q.v., Mr. Rudyard Kipling, and others were freely spoken of in the long interval. The nomination of a good Tory journalist but a very mediocre poet was finally made by the third marquess of Salisbury).

Robert Bridges, 1913.

The office of historiographer royal, which Dryden and Shadwell had doubled with the laureateship, lapsed, 1860, at the death of G.P.R. James (q.v.).

Poggio (1380-1459): It. humanist; son of Guccio P., an apothecary in Terranuova; assumed late in life the name and arms of the family of Bracciolini, and is sometimes misdescribed by the name of one of his sons, Gianfrancesco and Jacopo. P. came to Florence at an early age, and was employed by Coluccio (q.v.) as a copyist at the chancery. There, his chief friends were Aretino and Niccolo (qq.v.); and there, after his travels, which included a visit to Engld. in the train of card. Beaufort, P. became chancellor to the Florentine republic, 1453; in this capacity, he completed the *History* of the republic (from 1350 to 1455) by Bruni (q.v.). P. devoted his leisure to the fashionable, fascinating hunt for classical MSS.; he refreshed himself by the composition of Lat. letters, and he compiled a vol. of *Facetiæ*, described by S. Gaselee (*Anthology of Medieval Latin*, 1925) as: 'some were inventions, some actual occurrences, some were the floating stories of the ages, such as are now told by commercial travellers to one another in the bars of hotels'. P.'s stories, most of which took the church as their butt, are said to have relieved the tedium of meetings of apostolic secretaries; his bk. was condemned at the Council of Trent, but it was read by pope Nicholas v, without prejudice to P.'s position in the curia. P., who was a brilliant scholar, engaged in the noisy and dreary lit. of epistolary (Lat.) controversy, which degraded the learning of the age by its ferocious and jealous invective. Aurispa (q.v.) was attacked in his grave, and George of Trebizond (q.v.) in his person, and P., whom the pope employed to bludgeon the anti-pope Felix, surpassed even his own record in that commission in his combats with Fifelfo and Valla (qq.v.). With the former he was ultimately reconciled; but, since Valla was accounted a forerunner of the Reformation (q.v.), reformers in the 16th cent. took P. at Valla's valuation, which was far from fair to his true merits. Thus, he has been called 'the most formidable gladiator in that age of literary duellists' (Symonds, *Ital. Renaissance*, ii, 171, quoting Vespasiano, q.v.: 'he displayed such vehemence that the whole world was afraid of him'). But P. is more justly celebrated as letter-writer, translr., collector and copyist of MSS.,—the fourfold humanism of the epoch. His opportunity came at the Council of Constance, 1414, when he explored the Swiss libraries, and raided neighbouring treasuries. Thus, at St. Gall, he tells us, in the library of the convent, 'we discovered Quintilian,

safe and sound, though covered with dust and filthy with neglect' (Lat. letter from P. to a friend). This *Institutio oratoria*, which he set himself to copy at once, was his most important find; but several of Cicero's speeches depend on MSS. first transcribed by P., and Lucretius, Statius, Silius, Italicus, and others were included in his net. Gibbon (q.v.; *Decline and Fall*, chs. 65 and 71) refers to and quotes P.'s 'elegant dialogue' *de varietate Fortunæ*, a documentary study of the antiquities of Rome, and none of his detractors, who fasten on the 'heathen' aspect of P.'s humanism, denies his eminent merits as commentator and scholar.

Poinsinet, Antoine (1735-69): Fr. dramatist; wr. *le Cercle*, 1761, a typical example of the moral comedy, aimed at exposing the emptiness of the exteriorly brilliant life of the Paris *salons*. Written in prose in one act, this piece enjoyed great success at the Théâtre français.

Polevoy, Nicholas Alexeyevich (1796-1846): Russ. publicist. P. was a born journalist, defrauded of his inheritance by the inhibitive conditions of his day, and it was his fate, as a poor man, always on the edge of bankruptcy, to be driven to pot-boiling for a living. In this secondary work, his best piece was an hist. novel of Russia in the 15th cent., far and away better than anything attempted by his popular contemporary, Bulgarin (q.v.). A novel of artistic life, *Abbadonna*, 1835, was received with more favour, but did not survive its second edn. P. edited the *Moscow Telegraph*, 1825-34.

Politian (1454-94): It. humanist; Angelo Ambrogini, commonly known as Poliziano, after his birthplace, Monte Pulciano; one of the most brilliant, if not actually *primus inter pares*, of the bilingual scholars of his age. P. came to Florence, 1464, and won the patronage and friendship of Lorenzo de' Medici (q.v.), to whose children he was tutor for a time, and whose humanizing aims he helped splendidly to advance. In accordance with the prevailing custom, P. wr. works which fell into 2 groups, i, classical, and ii, vernacular. In i, as Hellenist, he composed Gk. poems; he transld. parts of the Gk. anthology into Lat., and rendered similar service to parts of Plato, Epictetus and Herodian. Scholars record with admiration his introduction to the *Prior Analytics* of Aristotle; and, most notably, before he was 18, he had transld. the first 5 bks. of the *Iliad*, in a style which won him from Ficino (q.v.) the appellation of 'Homericus juvenis'; in i, again, as Latinist, he composed original Lat. verse-declamations to accompany his lectures, which were attended by Reuchlin, Linacre and Grocyn, among others. Four such pieces are still extant in hexameter verse, described by Symonds as 'leaping' and by Saintsbury as 'exultant': viz. *Manto* on Virgil's *Eclogues*, *Rusticus* on his *Georgics* and Hesiod, *Ambra* on Homer, and *Nutricia* on the poetry that had nurtured him, leading through Homer, Virgil, the Gk. dramatists and the Tuscan triumvirate (Dante, Petrarch, Boccaccio) to a glowing pæan to his patron, Lorenzo; further, *Miscellanea*, 1489, a notebook on grammar and rhetoric. P. was famous, too, for his pioneer 'we must place ourselves in Twickenham on some fine day, when the long disease has relaxed its grasp for a moment; when he has taken a turn through his garden, and comforted his poor frame with potted lampreys and a glass or two from his frugal pint. Suppose two or three friends to be sitting with him. . . . Let the conversation kindle into vivacity, and host and guests fall into a friendly rivalry, whetting each other's wits by lively repartee, and airing the little fragments of worldly wisdom which pass muster for profound observation at Court; for a time they talk platitudes, though striking out now and then brilliant flashes, as from the collision of polished rapiers; they diverge, perhaps, into literature, and Pope shines in discussing the secrets of the art to which his whole life has been devoted with untiring fidelity. Suddenly the mention of some noted name provokes a startling outburst of personal invective from Pope; his friends judiciously divert the current of wrath into a new channel, and he becomes for the moment a generous patriot declaiming against the growth of luxury; the mention of some sympathizing friend brings out a compliment, so exquisitely turned, as to be a permanent title of honour, conferred by genius instead of power; or the thought of his parents makes his voice tremble, and his eyes shine with pathetic softness; and you forgive the occasional affectation which you can never quite forget, or even the occasional grossness or harshness of sentiment which contrasts so strongly with the superficial polish'. Such, briefly, was P., the man. We come next to the consideration of P., the poet, who so exactly expressed the man.

He wr. *Pastorals*, circulated by hand, and publd., 1709, in vol. vi of Tonson's *Poetical Miscellanies*, *An Essay on Criticism*, 1711; *The Messiah*, publd. by Addison in the *Spectator*, 14 May, 1712, and *Windsor Forest*, 1713. Each of these was, in its own kind, a product characteristic of the times. *Windsor Forest* and the *Pastorals* were continuations of the muse of Waller and Denham (qq.v.): not worse for this, of course, but not better, though Wordsworth (q.v.) generously discovered one or two new images of natural scenery in the later and local poem. The *Messiah* was cited by the same authority to illustrate the vice of 'poetic diction'; and prof. Courthope (*Hist. Engl. Poetry*, v, 117), writing of Prior (q.v.), says that 'his *Harry and Emma* makes a futile attempt to apply the external classical style to what is in its essence romantic, just as Pope's *Messiah* seeks to Hellenize ideas that are in spirit Hebraic'. The *Essay in Criticism* is likewise of its own time; and prof. Saintsbury (*Hist. Crit.*, ii, 455) succinctly says of it: 'All Pope seems to have done is to take the *Arts* of Horace, Vida, and Boileau (qq.v.), to adopt as many of their principles as he understood, and as would go into his sharp antithetic couplet, to drag their historical illustrations head and shoulders into his scheme without caring for the facts, and to fill in and embroider with criticisms, observations, and precepts, sometimes very shrewd, almost always perfectly expressed, but far too often arbitrary, conventional, and limited'. Two remarks may

be made at this point: (1) The 'sharp antithetic couplet' reminds us to remind readers that P.'s metre was the heroic couplet, which he inherited from Dryden and Waller, and which he brought to its highest degree of perfectness. P.'s 'poetic criticism of life', says Mr. Lytton Strachey (*Pope*; Leslie Stephen Lecture, 1925), in reply to M. Arnold (see *infra*), 'was, simply and solely, the heroic couplet'. (2) It is really fairer to judge this *Essay* by the *need* of it in 1711, than by its *superfluousness* in 1744 (when Pope died), or in 1902, when Saintsbury wr. his *History*. Addison did not hesitate to compare some sustained passages of finished eloquence in the *Essay* with Longinus (q.v.); and the triumph of the gospel to get 'order', and to follow that nature (q.v.), which was identified with Homer, Virgil, good sense, and the Ancients generally, had never been promulgated for Engl. practice till this lad of 21 expressed it in crystal. He brought to our shores, and completely naturalized upon them, the theory current in France in the *grand siècle*: a great feat, and a necessary one, if we come to think of it. For closely connected with this aspect is the uncanny cleverness of P. in fitting the gospel to his audience. J. R. Green, in his *Hist. of the Engl. People* (bk. viii, ch. iv), reminds us that Walpole's 'prosaic good sense turned sceptically away from the poetic and passionate sides of human feeling'; and, if we postpone acceptance of the challenge conveyed by the word 'poetic', we may conclude that P. was the very poet of that policy of good sense.

Returning to the list of P.'s writings: *The Rape of the Lock*, 1712—very brilliantly expanded, 1714,—was an adaptation of Boileau's *Lutrin* and Tassoni's *Secchia Rapita* (see s.vv.) to a social tragi-comedy of the day. Lord Petre had snipped off a lock of Miss Fermor's hair, and P. was invited to dissolve the tablets in laughter. He admirably succeeded by this exquisite specimen of filigree-work, as Hazlitt (q.v.) called it, and *The Rape* in Germany and elsewhere was endlessly imitated. More permanent interest attaches to P.'s heroic-verse *Iliad*, vol. i, 1715; ii, 1716; iii, 1717; iv, 1718; v, and vi, 1720. The public and the critics supported him, and the villa at Twickenham and other amenities were bought out of the proceeds of this venture and of P.'s *Odyssey* (1725-6; not so brilliant in its reception), for which he employed the services of 2 assistants, rev. Wm. Broome (1689-1745) and Elijah Fenton (1683-1730), who may be more appropriately commemorated here, since P. mentioned them—and remunerated them—inadequately. P.'s knowledge of Gk., as we saw, was small, and he depended very much on the prior labours of Chapman (q.v.) and other translrs. But he did not aim at a literal transln. He aimed at popularizing the *Iliad* for Engl. readers in the age of queen Anne,—a very different, a fully reasonable, and really a much more complex aim. Bentley (q.v.) might rightly say: 'A pretty poem, Mr. Pope, but you must not call it Homer', though P. was not the kind of man to whom to address such a remark with impunity. Johnson characterized it, on the contrary, as 'the noblest version of poetry the world has even seen '; Byron thought much the same, and Coleridge testifies to its influence and long popularity. We cannot fight this battle over again, but we may remark with sir L. Stephen (*op. cit.*, 75) : ' After all, a wit was still a human being, and much more nearly related to us than an ancient Greek '. We propose to omit P.'s *Dunciad*, which he nursed, like a savage with an idol, through the greater part of his life, and which ' is beyond all question full of coarse abuse ' (*ibid.*, 118), not less distasteful to-day because P. leaned on the example of Boileau (q.v.), and of Dryden's *MacFlecknoe*. Swift (q.v.) was privy to its publication, or, at least, to the earlier stages of its leisurely and, in places, subterranean appearances. Theobald and, later, Bentley and Colley Cibber (qq.v.) were the chief butts of the satire on dulness, and the *Dunciad* formed, like Dante's *Inferno*, at how-ever long a remove, a convenient limbo to which to commit, in various degrees of obloquy, P.'s enemies and detractors. Of course, it is extraordinarily clever, and, equally of course, it gave rise to endless controversy and replies, which delighted P.'s ingenious malice. But, on the whole, this poem, which accompanied P. through 30 years, 1712-42, is more interesting to antiquaries than to the ordinary reader. We must pass over, too, P.'s Horatian and other epistles in verse, his *Universal Prayer*, 1738, and the competitive version of the emperor Hadrian's *Animula vagula, blandula*, leading to his *The Dying Christian to his Soul*, 1730, etc., and come to his *Essay on Man*, parts i, ii, iii, 1733 ; part iv, 1734. This is P.'s most ambitious work, designed to develop into a theodicy (the verse-epistles called *Moral Essays* are connected with it), and ' to vindicate the ways of God to Man '. It was dedicated appropriately to H. St. John (q.v.), lord Bolingbroke, to whom its inception was wholly due, and for whom, as P. said, he held the pen. Its success, again, was immense : in France and Germany, where translns. were publd., as well as at home ; and, though P. was as little qualified to specialize in philosophy as in the Gk. text of Homer, he did produce a poem, or, rather, an inter-mittent series of states of mind in verse, the effect of which had profound repercussions in philosophic circles,—not least on Voltaire and Rousseau (qq.v.), on the eve of the shattering reconstruction of thought, of which the Fr. Revolution was the political expression.

Such, then, briefly, were the man and his work. It may be suggested, in conclusion, that too much has been written about P. Two moments of this excess stand out particu-larly in retrospect : (1) in the first quarter of the 19th cent., when W. L. Bowles (1762-1850), whose edn. of P.'s works, with a memoir, appeared in 1806, T. Campbell (q.v.), lord Byron (q.v.) and Wm. Roscoe (1753-1831) engaged, 1819-26, in a long, acrid, and inconclusive controversy on the poetical and personal character of P. ; and (2), much later in the century, when M. Arnold (q.v.), in an essay on ' The Study of Poetry ' (Introduction to T. H. Ward's *Engl. Poets*, 1880 ; now one of the *Essays in Criticism*, second series), expressed

the opinion, that, ' Though they may write in verse, though they may in a certain sense be masters of the art of versification, Dryden and Pope are not classics of our poetry, they are classics of our prose '. Poetry, it seems to us, is bigger than any critical theory invented to contain it, and P. is a poet because he wr. poetry which gives pleasure. Elsewhere the present writer has suggested that the criticism of P.'s poetry should be connected with a con-sideration of his garden. ' Il faut cultiver notre jardin ', wr. Voltaire at the close of *Candide*, and the saying possesses profound truth. P.'s 5 acres of garden land at Twicken-ham, according to a letter (20 June, 1760) from Walpole (q.v.), to sir H. Mann, were ' inclosed with three lanes, and seeing nothing. Pope had twisted and twirled, and rhymed and harmonized this, till it appeared two or three sweet little lawns opening and opening beyond one another '. As his garden, so his life ; so his habit of twisting facts, and so his method of constant revision. P. lived, it is not unfair to say, in a *hortus inclusus* all his life, ' inclosed with three lanes, and seeing nothing '. Deliberately, or, rather, inevitably, according to the conditions of his age, he set limits and bounds to the possible vagaries of the lanes. He felt no desire to escape, no caged bird's longing to try his wings, and to seek adventures in the unknown which lay outside of the enclosure. It was enough for him to ' twist and twirl and rhyme ' the subject-matter which was before him. All his words have boundaries, all his sentences are self-contained. It is a natural method applied to gardening, but it has its inherent weakness in an incurious acceptance of limitations ; and Pope's *Essay on Man*, illustrates in a special degree the ' rhyming and harmonizing ' method applied to an enclosure ' seeing nothing '. What he shut out returned with a rush towards the end of the 18th cent., and in the force of the reaction lies the valid measure of P.'s strength, his courage, and his defects. (See, too ; s.v. Engl. Lit.)

Popularphilosoph (Germ.) : Popular philosopher ; a class of writers who began to claim attention in Germany towards the end of the 18th cent., when neither fiction nor journalism was adapted to the popular presentation of the new ideas with which the mind of the age was teeming. It would be unjust to call such writers either sciolists or sophists. Their function was definite, and it was well performed. They filled the place in their own day which con-tributors to *The Nineteenth Century Review* filled in the earlier years of its publication ; they provided a forum for the discussion of great subjects, not as specialists, but rather as ventilators ; they assisted the transference of the new thought from the study to poetry and the stage. Somewhat similarly, Huxley may be said to have mediated between Darwin and Tennyson. (See s.vv. Abbt, Engel, Zimmermann, e.g.).

Pordage, Samuel (1633-91) :   Engl. poet ; translr. ; described in *C.H.E.L.*, viii, 91, as ' a byword for Grub-street poverty '; wr., 1682, *Azaria and Hushai*, in reply to Dryden (q.v.), *Absalom and Achitophel* ; transld. Seneca, q.v., and wr. some original plays.

the succour of instructors more polished than themselves : the Italy of conceits and of hyperbole, of far-fetched metaphors and strained antitheses, the Italy of Guarini and esp. of Marino (qq.v.), proved a fruitful mistress of preciosity ; and Italy's apt pupil, Spain, became a mistress in her turn, through Montemayor, Guevara, and Gongora (qq.v.). Preciosity, like Euphuism (q.v.) in Engld., began as a reform of style, though it ended as a style needing reform. The Fr. equivalent of *concetti* (conceits) is *pointes*, and the cultivation of ' points ' encouraged the composition of epigrams and of odes (which Malherbe had employed against his own principles), and thus postponed till the time of Boileau (q.v.), who was not even a disciple of Malherbe, the full effect of Malherbe's doctrine. Of course, there was much exaggeration in the Hôtel de Rambouillet and its congeners. There was bound to be preciosity among the precious, and Molière did not write his comedy in the air. But it is to be noted that the first 40 Academicians (s.v. French Academy), and the authors of the *Dictionary* which they undertook, included many of the foremost *précieux*, and that, though they withdrew from the polite society of the *salons* the nominal control of lit. and language, they preserved throughout the 17th cent. the polite atmosphere which the *salons* had created. It was a large part of the aim fostered by the P. stylists to pare down the content of words till they became the bare symbols of ideas ; to deprive them, that is to say, of their edging of mystery and association, and to reduce them to abstract signs, as few as possible in number, but sharp of outline, clear and precise, and capable of infinite combination. Many phrases in the *Dictionnaire des Précieuses*, compiled, 1660, are happy idioms of literary French. In orthography, among other reforms, they dropped the parasitic letters, writing, e.g., *tête* for *teste*, and they sought more doubtfully to exclude terms ' soiled by ignoble use ', however noble in orig. These grave matters and the like were the topics of talk among the precious, varied by discussions of bks. and authors, and such talk was conducted in the style sanctioned by the rules of the *côterie*. For that precious lit. was the cult of a *côterie* rather than the free expression of a people was true in 17th cent. France, as it has been true in every age and every clime. But this truism does not detract from the debt which every free people owes to its cultivators of preciosity, at times when, as in France in the 17th cent., the rights of the intellect have been shoved aside by the usurpers of rude passion and brute force.

Pregunta (Span.): Question and Answer ; a form of verse-composition, employed in early Span. lit. for riddles and jests, and, later, for more didactic purposes of amusement and instruction. (See s.vv. Mena, Lopez de Corella, Villalobos). The posing of *preguntas* became a feature of less serious academies of wit.

Pre-Raphaelite Brotherhood (1848): Engl. group of painters and men of letters ' united in opposition to conventional systems of artistic teaching ' (*C.H.E.L.*, xiii, 110), and, ' moved by the " contemptible and even scandalous " condition of British art ' (H. Walker, *Lit. Victorian Era*, 493 ; prof. Walker adds that ' the year of political revolution was not inappropriately, though doubtless by pure accident, selected by these youths for the initiation of a revolution in art '). The revolt was started at the initiative of the painters, Wm. Holman Hunt (1827-1910 ; afterwards O.M.) and John Everett Millais (1829-96 ; afterwards P.R.A. and a bt.,) who were joined directly by Thos. Woolner (1825-92 ; R.A.), sculptor and poet, James Collinson, painter, Fredk. George Stephens, art-critic, Wm. Michael Rossetti, secretary and, later, historian of the group, and, above all, by his elder brother, Dante Gabriel Rossetti (q.v., 1828-82), who, though only 20 years old at the time, became its dominating personality. These 7 constituted the Brethren. Others near them and dear to them included Ford Madox Brown (1821-93), the painter, whose wonderful son, Oliver (1855-74), was an heir of unfulfilled renown ; Christina Rossetti, Wm. Bell Scott, Coventry Patmore, Ruskin (qq.v.), with Wm. Morris (q.v.) a little later. Swinburne and Tennyson (qq.v.), in certain aspects, and, in certain others, T. Watts-Dunton and sir Hall Caine, were in intellectual or personal relationship to the movement. But the real and vital P.R.B. was founded in 1848, and was composed of the 7 painters and poets, or poet-painters, mentioned above, with young Rossetti as their guide and moving spirit,—the chief star of the new Pleiad (q.v.). The orig. of the Brotherhood may be fixed with comparative certainty. In a letter written by Keats (q.v.), which Rossetti was reading in 1848, we read : ' When I was last at Haydon's, I looked over a book of prints, taken from the fresco of a church at Milan, the name of which I forget. In it were comprised specimens of the first and second age of Art in Italy. I do not think I ever had a greater treat out of Shakespeare ; full of romance and of the most tender feeling ; magnificence of drapery beyond] everything I ever saw, not excepting Raphael's—but grotesque to a curious pitch '. Rossetti refers to this passage in a letter to his brother, and in this ambition in painting to go beyond and behind Raphael is doubtless the source of the P.R.B. There are those who will cite the same passage as the source of its decline ; who will trace that decline to an excess of ' tender feeling ' and to a too ' curious pitch ' of grotesqueness. And this criticism might be justified out of the records of the Brethren. But the high enthusiasm at the start, and the fresh delight of Rossetti in his sense of beauty, are at once more inspiring and more important than any signs or causes of decline,—intimately allied as these are with the biography of Rossetti himself (see s.v.). Like Tennyson's (q.v.) rendering of the oath of the Round Table, the parage of the P.R.B. were sworn to oppose unworthy aims, in art, letters, and conduct. Ruskin set the standard in ethics and economics, and W. Morris in decorative and domestic crafts ; and, if the ideal of the Brotherhood bred its own conventions ; if Rossetti's natural taste for old china fostered in lesser men an acquisitiveness for *bric-a-brac*; if Morris's natural taste for harmonious colours fostered in lesser men the 'greenery-yallery' vogue; if some of the knights proved false and others fickle to their vows; if some turned aside to other gods, 'lest one good custom should corrupt the world', yet the essential thing is (1) to define the custom at the height of its good intent, and (2) to note that sir W. Gilbert and sir A. Sullivan lay in waiting to ridicule in opera (q.v.) the excesses of a cult; and that before them went R. Buchanan (q.v.), with his anon. attack in 1870 on the 'fleshly' school, which marked the decadence of the Brethren's serious sensuousness.

Returning, then, to the heights of 1848, when the esoteric sign, P.R.B., was first affixed to the Brothers' pictures in the Royal Academy, and keeping strictly to our proper field of the literary aspect of the movement (only noting that Millais' *Ophelia*, 1852, preserves in the Tate Gallery the lineaments of Elizabeth Siddal, who became Rossetti's wife, and that other pictures by Brethren in that gallery possess a similar secondary interest), we have to remark: (1) the publication, 1850, of *The Germ* (2 numbers under that name; 2 more as *Art and Poetry*; and then silence), which served the group as its lit. organ, and, later, 1856, the *Oxford and Cambridge Magazine* which Rossetti used for the same purpose; and (2) the powerful influence on the poetic practice of the group of *The Lady of Shalott*, 1832, by Tennyson. This poem was founded on an Ital. story; it repaired to the wonderland of king Arthur (q.v.); it revived the device of a refrain; it affected an archaic diction, and it sought effects by a soft and liquid vocabulary ('lilies', 'willows', 'carols', etc.), all of which were authentic signs of the P.R.B. note in poetry. The note was derived by Keats from Spenser and the medievalists, and descended through Tennyson and Rossetti. But it did not retain its distinctive qualities unalloyed. Patmore and G. Meredith (q.v.) were pre-Raphaelite, but not exclusively pre-Raphaelite. Meredith's sonnet-sequence, *Modern Love*, has affinities with Rossetti's *House of Life*; but the extra-precious note of the P.R.B., their unique, particular, momentary blend of *pictorial* detail with *poetic* expression, so that the thing seen became the thing felt, the fusion in one mould of the two arts of poetry and painting,—this note disappeared in a fuller and wider stream. Browning and Tennyson, who preceded the P.R.B., survived it and absorbed it, while they transmitted it. The evidence is too fine to permit us to follow it here; but the student may be recommended to start it by comparing the sonnet 'Vain Virtues' in Rossetti's *House of Life* with the 'frustrate ghosts' in R. Brownings' *Statue and the Bust*. He may be led to the conclusion that the P.R. brothers tend to miss, in their poetry, men's response, never perhaps, to the beauties of their style, but, ultimately, to the images of their thought; that, by their return to what they deemed a purer medium of art-expression, they tended to lose contact with humanity; that they sacrificed a universal to a particular appeal, and concentric to eccentric art. Leaving these

considerations, however, it is more pertinent to state that the P.R. movement, when it came, arrived wholesomely and desirably. It created, largely by the temperament of its prime mover, with southern springs in his blood, a respect for beautiful writing, re-animate, through Keats, from the Elizabethans, and their Fr. and Ital. teachers, and for simple writing, taught to Morris by Chaucer. It supplied an antidote and an alternative to the smug, prosperous, plate-glass window point of view, which was staring out of the walls of the Crystal Palace in Hyde-Park, 1851. It strengthened utility to beautiful aims, whereas M. Arnold (q.v.) tended to stiffen it to resistance to them. This is the larger outcome of that search for 'romance and tender feeling' in the expression of the details of composition, which was the first principle, or point of departure, of the P.R.B.

Prévost D'Exiles, Antoine François (1697-1763): Fr. novelist, commonly known as l'abbé Prévost; Jesuit; soldier; returned to the cloister of the Benedictines of St.-Maur; broke his cloister (like Rabelais, q.v.), 1727, and was in exile from France in Holland and Engld. till 1733; returned under the patronage of the prince de Conti, when he started a newspaper, *le Pour et le Contre* ('Pro and Con'), 1733-40, more philosophical in tendency than some similar imitations of Addison's (q.v.) *Spectator*, one of which was then being edited by Marivaux (q.v.). Wr. industriously for 30 years (he was said to have died under a *post-mortem—sic*—examination after an apoplectic trance) at fiction, memoirs, etc., but is remembered now as the creator of Manon Lescaut: *l'Histoire du chevalier des Grieux et de Manon Lescaut*, 1731. The praises of Manon have been sung by eminent writers of later days, including Guy de Maupassant and R. L. Stevenson (qq.v.), and her sad, grim story of love and poverty is so well-known on both sides of the channel which unites Great Britain to France that it is superfluous to rehearse it here. P. created in his heroine a true and a permanent picture. Doubtless, he owed something to the memories of the great courtesans of the age of Louis xiv (see s.v. Ninon, e.g.), and doubtless, he contributed something to that lit. of sensibility and love-in-the-world, which Richardson (q.v.) was handing on to his successors. Moreover, P., as the translr. of *Clarissa* and other novels of Richardson, increased the great debt which Fr. fiction owes to his genius. For *Manon* is distinctly a work of genius. Brunetière (q.v.) compares P. with Racine (q.v.), for his exaltation of the divine right of the passion of love; and 'racinien', again, is P.'s 'sparseness of descriptive detail' and his 'astonishing rapidity' of narrative.

Priamel (Germ.): Descriptive name of a class of short poems, which flourished in Germany in the 14th and 15th cents., and which, while nearly always anon., is doubtless to be referred to the activity of the Meistersinger (q.v.). The P. started with a 'preamble' (*priamel*), or, prelude, consisting commonly of one verse, and illustrated its theme by adducing similar propositions in the succeeding verses, which led to an epigrammatic conclusion, summarizing

-ii. Adelaide Ann (1825-64): Engl. poet; daughter of above; a contributor to *Household Words* and *All the Year Round*, under the editorship of Dickens (q.v.), where she used the *nom-de-guerre*, of Mary Berwick, and to the fashionable albums of the day; her poems, which include *The Lost Chord*, were collected, 1858, as *Legends and Lyrics*, and enjoyed considerable esteem; some of her hymns (' I do not ask, O Lord, that life may be ', e.g.) are still in use, and Miss P. took a prominent interest in matters affecting the social work of women.

Prodigal Son: Dramatic motive derived from the parable in the New Testament, and employed effectively in Germ. lit. in the 16th cent. Its sudden appeal to the dramatic instinct of that age has been plausibly ascribed to its dual character; the plot lent itself to the search of the Lat. humanists for a domestic intrigue of the type of Terentian comedy, while its moral satisfied the requirements of the Lutheran reformers. The vogue was not long-lived (see s.vv. Gnapheus, Macropedius), but it found its imitators in Engld., notably in the *Glasse of Government* of Gascoigne (q.v.).

Prokopovich, Theophan (1681-1736): Russ. divine; summoned from Kiev (q.v.) by emperor Peter (q.v.) the Great to give effect to the imperial policy of reform. P. was a man of vast learning, and played Wolsey to Peter's Henry viii with unscrupulous vigour and self-reliance. With P.'s politico-ecclesiastical policy (in relation to the Patriarchate, the dissolution of monasteries, the succession to the throne, etc.) we are not here concerned; as the last prince of the church who was likewise a man of letters, his activity was untiring and many-sided. He wr. a univ.-drama *Vladimir*, 1705; text-books on poetics and rhetoric, works on history and theology, and experiments in Russ. verse. He energetically backed the emperor's efforts to provide the populace of Moscow and Petrograd with suitable versions of classic works on practical topics—economics, navigation, etc.; etc; and he ranks as one of the chief makers of Imperial Russia after its long Middle Ages.

Proudhon, Pierre Joseph (1809-65): Fr. economist, socialist; revolutionary journalist. P., who was born of poor parents, was self-nurtured on the writings of Rousseau (q.v.), and made his *début* in lit. as a contributor to the *Encyclopédie catholique*. His birthplace was Besançon, and P. was a prizeman at its local academy, in connection with which he wr. in 1840 a treatise on *Qu'est-ce que la Propriété*? In P.'s reply to this question occurred the famous apophthegm, ' La propriété, c'est le vol ', i.e., that landowners and capitalists do not return an equivalent for the labour they exact. The doctrine made a noise in its own day, and has been quoted out of its context ever since; but socialism has moved far away from the timid ratiocinations of P. His next work was the *Système des contradictions économiques*, 1846. He was elected deputy for the Seine department in 1848; but he was not sufficiently clear-thinking or clear-spoken to take advantage of the opportunities afforded by that revolutionary epoch. He founded a bank (*du Peuple*), 1849, and several

newspapers with variations on the same name; but all alike proved failures, and P. was twice sentenced to terms of imprisonment, receiving a final amnesty in 1860. His doctrine (or paradox) of anarchy belongs to politics rather than to lit.; its argument was based on the theory, obviously extreme, that as society grows more civilized, it requires fewer laws for its government, and that the highest social system would need no laws.

Provençal Literature: Generic name of the lit., dating mainly from the 12th and 13th cents., of the South of France, including the old provinces of Perigord, Limousin, Auvergne and Dauphiné, and over-lapping Savoy and Catalonia on the north-east and south-west respectively. The Pyrenees and gulf of Lyons formed the southern frontier; and the river Loire is commonly selected as the boundary-line between the two Frances, North and South. For France was bi-lingual in that age. North of the Loire flourished the lit. and language, or, rather, the literatures and dialects of the so-called *langue d'oïl* (see s.v. French Lit.): the Picard, the Norman, the Champenois, the Angevin, etc., and *français* proper, which gradually absorbed the rest. South of the Loire were the regions of the *langue d'oc*, which, in the chief period of its flowering-time, was entirely distinct from French, the term *français* being limited to the main dialect of the North, and the language of the South being designated Limousin, or, more generally, Provençal. (The names *d'oïl* and *d'oc*, from Lat. *illud* and *hoc*, were derived from the respective particles of affirmation, and were employed at an early date as a convention of philologers; Dante, in his treatise *On Vulgar Eloquence*, compares the claims to precedence of the *langues d'oïl*, *d'oc* and *de si*, i.e., Ital.). The difference in the languages South and North of the dividing-line are a matter of philological interest: briefly, the *langue d'oc* of Provence is more akin to Span. and Ital.; its Lat. vowels are more clearly marked, and its inflections and vocabulary are less changed and less fully assimilated; the most characteristic word by which to test the difference is the ' Troubadour ' of the South as compared with the ' Trouvère ' of the North; the former is quite close to its Lat. orig., *trovator*, the latter has been inflected and assimilated. Passing from the languages to the literatures, the contrast is even more striking. Arguably, Prov. lit. is the oldest and longest-lived in Europe; there was a sense of poetic form in the *langue d'oc* almost before the dialect had unfolded from the Lat., and the name and dates of Mistral (q.v.; he died in 1914) are evidence of the permanence of its vogue and inspiration. But the hist. view must neglect the sentiment of revivalists. Properly speaking, Prov. lit. had flourished and decayed before the period of the Renaissance (q.v.), which blew its creative spirit into the other literatures of Europe. Of the 3 stages into which it has been divided, we are concerned only with the second, namely, the florescence of Prov. lit. in the 12th and 13th cents. The crusade, 1208, preached by pope Innocent iii against the Albigenses (from Albi, in Provence, where independent thought, driven from the Northern schools, had founded a centre of so-called heresy), and followed by a bloody war of extermination, scattered the seeds of Prov. culture through Spain, Portugal, Sicily, and Italy, but was cruelly successful at the same time in uprooting the flowers, which withered on their native soil. Thus, we mean by the lit. of Provence the expression during little more than a hundred years of the genius of a separate people, inhabiting the provinces of Southern France, and speaking and writing a language which was afterwards absorbed in Fr. The people and the language passed ; but, though the vessel split, the wonderful thought survives, and our Engl. Keats (q.v.) seized its essential spirit in his phrase, ' dance, and Provençal song, and sunburnt mirth '. Seven centuries have gone by since Innocent's decree drenched fair Provence in blood, and still the dance and the song are filled with her own warm sun, as a shell with the sea. It is difficult not to rhapsodize on this subject, for Prov. lit. is all a rhapsody. Many factors conspired to produce it : the sunshine, the scenery, the Moors, chivalry, Ovid, light-heartedness, wandering scholars from the North, and the buoyant freedom which was punished so severely ; and to these was added the grace of a native instinct for music and form. The outcome was a burst of lyric love, which still makes the troubadour of Provence a synonym for the passion of romance. Passion, indeed, is the keyword. As sober an historian as prof. Saintsbury (*Short Hist. Fr. Lit.*, 25) declares, that ' passion is not the only motive of the Troubadours, but it is their favourite motive, and their most successful '. ' In that land ', writes Annie L. Konta more ecstatically (*Hist. Fr. Lit.*, 78), ' all women were loved, all knights were poets ', and in her ecstasy she transfers without acknowledgement an eloquent paragraph from Lanson (*Hist. Lit. franç.*, 86), in which he points out that social conditions in southern France ' gave women a dominion, and made their taste a law '. William ix (q.v.), count of Poitiers, was the first of the princes and barons who responded to the Troubadour infection ; as many as 460 (Saintsbury) names have come down to us from this second period of Prov. lit., and they include writers in all ranks of life, some of whom are noted s.vv. Here, a few words must be added, i, as to the forms of Prov. lyric, and, ii, as to the spread of its inspiration. In i, we have the *canso*, love-song, the *planh*, lament, the *alba*, morning-farewell, the *serena*, evening farewell, the *tenson* (*tençon*), debate, or lovers' dispute, the *balada*, or narrative lyric, the *pastorela*, pastoral, the *sirvente*, satire, the *retroencha* (*retroensa*), stanzas with refrain, the *sestine*, six-stanza ode, and others. Within these lyrical variations, the art of the Provençal Troubadours invented more and more elaborate systems of versification, and more and more deftly complicated schemes of rhyme. Herein lay their excellence, and it was displayed in the passionate celebration of 2 themes, love and arms—themselves but several aspects of one theme, gallantry or chivalry. There was little power of or appeal to imagination ; the competition of wit was directed mainly to points of technique, and sunshine and flowers and bird-song sufficed to support the muse. As to ii, the influence of Prov. lit., we note, first, its spread to Northern France. The northern *romance* and *pastourelle* were probably indigenous kinds, but the trouvères, who succeeded the troubadours, founded the *serventois* on the *sirvente*, the *jeu parti* on the *tenson*, the *aubade* on the *alba*, and so forth. More ingenious variations were added in *ballade*, *rondeau*, *chant-royal*, and others, with no Provençal prototypes, but the influence of the South on the North in the 13th cent., when Thibaut (q.v.) of Champagne was king of Navarre, is at once obvious and considerable. The decline of Prov. lit. into the *gai saber* (s.v.), the gay science, of the courts of love of the 14th cent., and the formal revival of the cult at the Floral Games (q.v.) of Toulouse—a decline which had its analogue in the 15th cent. in the artifices of the Rhétoriqueurs (q.v.),—is not immediately to the point. Formally, as stated above, Prov. lit. was destroyed by sword and fire at the time of the Albigensian heresy. Its influence was communicated, however, not by its formal practitioners and revivalists, but by those who brought the scattered seeds to fruit. They crossed the Pyrenees into Spain (see s.v. Barcelona, e.g.). They were sown in Sicily and Tuscany. They took root in the soil of mysticism, and flowered into expressions of love and worship, which owed a large part of their inspiration to Platonic love (see s.v. Plato). Dante, as Beatrice's lover, was at once a Platonic lover, a scholastic reasoner, and a sublimated Troubadour ; Petrarch continued the tradition, and Chaucer brought it to Engld., where it made its entry again through queen Elizabeth's Petrarchist sonneteers. The brief and happy spring-tide of Provence, though none speaks its language to-day, is an eternal spring of passion in the poetry of every European people ; every lover in every May has the tunes of a Provençal Troubadour in his heart or on his lips.

Providence : The theory of a providential order in human affairs is of the essence of the cosmogony of Dante (q.v.), and of the ecclesiastical doctrine of the Middle Ages. It was maintained unimpaired through succeeding centuries, though it was attacked or ridiculed by critics and scoffers. The first hist. work which left out Providence from its scheme of causation, and sought the causes of things in the evidence of the effects ; in other words, which treated history logically, and applied to it the methods of the physical sciences, was the *Considérations sur les causes de la Grandeur et de la Décadence des Romains*, by Montesquieu (q.v.), publd. at Amsterdam, anon., 1734.

Prudhomme, Sully (1839-1908) : Fr. poet ; transld. Lucretius, *de rerum natura*, bk. i, and proceeded, after this difficult apprenticeship, to compose philosophical poems, tinged by the prevailing pessimism of the period, and combining a large amalgam of science and metaphysics with the poetry. It is too early to determine the ultimate literary value of this mixed class of verse, inevitable, perhaps, at the time of the rapid development of scientific thought in the 19th cent.; Tennyson (q.v. was a skilful practitioner, and Meredith (q.v.) practised it with less limpidness. Future criticism may label it a bastard. P.'s works include: *Stances et Poèmes*, 1865; *Solitudes*, 1869; *Vaines Tendresses*, 1875; *Justice*, 1878; *Bonheur*, 1888; *Testament poétique*, 1901.

Prussian Poets. See. s.v. **Anakreontiker**.

Prynne, William (1600-69): Engl. pamphleteer; native of Bath. P. enters lit. only by his *Histrio-mastix* (or, Scourge for Stage-players), 1633, which, as the title implies, attacked the chief amusement of the day; but, having thus entered lit., it is proper to observe that he was brutally served by pillory, fine, imprisonment and the cutting off of his ears on the ground that a thong of the *Mastix* has touched the honour of king Charles i. P. went on writing in the Tower of London, with no better fortunes from his muse, and was again, 1637, fined, pilloried and mutilated by branding on both cheeks. Released by the Long Parliament, 1641, P. pursued his campaigns from inside the House of Commons, and was again imprisoned. His biography is political till 1661, when king Charles ii appointed him keeper of the Records in the Tower of London, to which, accordingly, he returned with his sheaves. He publd. about 200 bks. and pamphlets in the stormy course of his life.

Pucci, Antonio (14th cent.): It. 'cantore di piazza' (q.v.); street-minstrel, or singer of ditties on patriotic or political themes (see s.v. 'serventes'). P.'s activity fell at a time when the calling of 'cantore', or 'cantatore', was held in high esteem in republican Florence, and his songs, or ballads, took a place not unlike that which was taken by the printed 'broadsheet' in Engld. at a later date. The cities of Italy, distracted by civil war, suppressed this class of minstrel not long afterwards, but P.'s licence in censure and exhortation entitled his poems to respect, and they may still be read with interest and pleasure.

Pufendorf, Samuel (1632-94): Germ. political philosopher; prof. of natural and international law at univ. of Leipsic, the first chair in that faculty in Germany. Wr. Lat. treatises in the subjects of his professorate, in which he expounded and amplified for Germ. conditions the ideas of Grotius (q.v.) assisted by the theories of Hobbes (q.v.). Wr., too, anon. Lat. letter, ' on the status of the German Empire', which started from the proposition that 'Germany is some irregular body and like unto a monster' (*monstro simile*), and sketched a new order of government, founded on the principles of liberal law. P.'s writings, which included histories, were of the utmost value to the reconstruction of Germ. thought after the Thirty Years' War (q.v., and see s.v. Aufklärung).

Pulci, Bernardo (1438-88): Florentine minor poet. Elegist and translr. Wr. *Barlaam*, a passion-play, and was assisted by his wife, Antonia, in the composition of similar *rappresentazioni*.

Pulci, -i. Luca (1431-70): Florentine minor poet. Wr. on Lorenzo de' Medici's tournament

(*giostra*; see, too, s.v. Politian); and collaborated at least once with his more famous brother.

-**ii. Luigi** (1432-84): Florentine poet and humanist; brother of above; first composer of a romance-epic poem as a separate kind of Ital. verse. P. was a member of a cultured family, which kept in close touch with Lorenzo de' Medici (q.v.) and his circle. Like Lorenzo, Boiardo, and Politian (qq.v.), he was faced with the dual problem of the creators of national poetry at the dawn of the 'golden age '—how to find adequate material, and to endue it, when found, with suitable forms in the vernacular. Happily, P. was less subject than scholars nearer the court to the retarding Latinism of his times. He sought his subject from the romantic 'matière de France' (see s.v. *Bodel*), never disused in the plebeian verse of Italy (at Bologna, in 1288, the itinerant minstrels of the Charlemagne-romances had to be forbidden by public decree to obstruct the traffic), and available, too, through the *Reali di Francia* (q.v.), a dull compilation in prose. This choice of the Charlemagne-cycle in preference to the Arthuriad is explicable on several grounds: first, it was already familiar; secondly, it appealed to such national sentiment as existed in Italy at that date, in memory of the long feud between the empire and the papacy; thirdly, the chivalric note of the Arthuriad was opposed to the sentiment of Ital. city states, and of Florence in particular. Thus, as between rival epic matters, P.'s choice was instinctive as well as deliberate; but his adoption, whether a discovery or a recovery, of Charlemagne and his paladins for Ital. poetry at this epoch was a veritable naturalization, and, by treating the theme in octave stanzas (*ottava rima*), P. divides with Politian (q.v.) the use of a measure which was to prove national and lasting, and to be continued through Ariosto and Tasso (qq.v.). He selected as his hero Roland (q.v.) who, in his Ital. form of Orlando, was almost immemorially popular in marketplace shows in Sicily and Italy; and he called his poem *Morgante Maggiore*,—' Morgante ' from the name of the giant whom Orlando captured and tamed, and ' maggiore ' (longer) because the Morgante portion of the 23+5 cantos of the romance had previously been issued independently. But Orlando was something more than Roland transferred to Italy. Lorenzo and his brilliant circle were present at the cradle of P.'s poem, and the gifts these god-parents brought were genial to the time and place. They introduced that mocking note, that note of irony and speculation, which Byron (q.v.), the P. of a later day, was perhaps the first alien fully to understand. It could be boisterous, dare-devil, insolent, hearty, swaggering, profane. It would even insert solemn passages, so that, as Hallam remarks, ' it has been a question among Italian critics whether the poem is to be reckoned burlesque '. But, whatever the native critics' decision, this, at least, foreign readers may say: P. naturalized in humanistic garb the old themes of romance for his modern Italy. It was difficult, in the Florence of his day, to take the old themes too seriously. Charlemagne was credulous and senile. Gano was traitorous and wily. Morgante met Margutte, a bigger giant than himself. The temptation to tweak the strings and to adopt the showman's attitude proved in places irresistible. But a love of beauty kept the buffoonery in bounds, and P., who was also occupied with invective sonnets and minor versatilities, is famous in the history of Ital. lit. as the creator of the romantic-epic, which Spenser (q.v.) learned from P.'s successors.

Pulgar, del, Hernando (*c.* 1436-*c.* 1493): Span. chronicler and biographer; councillor and secretary of State to the Catholic sovereigns, Ferdinand and Isabella, whose official *cronica* he wr.; *ed. pr.*, Valladolid, 1565, when it appeared under the name of Lebrixa (q.v.), who had effected a Lat. transln. of it. The error was soon set right; but P.'s far more memorable monument is in his letters, 1473-85 (32 in all), and, chiefly, in his *Book of the Illustrious Men of Castile*, 1486. This is a portrait-gallery of contemporaries, conceived in the spirit of Guzman's (q.v.) *Genealogies and Portraits*, and therefore of Plutarch himself, the Lat. prototype of all later biographers. Apart from its charm and interest, P.'s *Claros Varones de Castilla* has real hist. value.

Pulgar, del, Hernando Perez (1455-1531): Span. knt.; chronicler; hero of an exploit in Granada, while it was beleagured by Ferdinand and Isabella, and carefully to be distinguished from his peaceful namesake and contemporary at the court of those sovereigns. Wr., 1527, at the desire of emperor Charles v, *Breve parte delas Hazañas del excelente nombrado Gran Capitan*, 'A brief part of the exploits of the excellent man called the "Great Captain"', i.e., Gonzalvo (1453-1515); whence P. was often known as *el de las Hazañas*, 'he of the exploits'. The bk. was reprinted at Madrid, 1834, and is a stirring and vigorous narrative.

Pullen, Henry William (1831-1903): Engl. satirist; wr., 1870, *The Fight at Dame Europa's School: showing how the German boy thrashed the French boy; and how the English boy looked on*, which was a plea for Engl. intervention on the side of the Fr. in the Franco-Prussian war. The satire had an immense vogue, and was transld. into 14 languages; but P.'s further writings possess no further interest.

Purchas, Samuel. See s.v. Hakluyt.

Pusey, Edward Bouverie (1800-82): Engl. divine; leader of the Oxford Movement (q.v.), to which his exemplary career properly belongs, after 1841; regius prof. of Hebr. at Oxford univ., 1828, and joint founder, with his brother, Philip P. (1799-1855) and Edward Ellerton (1770-1851) of the scholarships bearing their names. As fellow of Oriel Coll., 1822, P. met Keble and Newman (qq.v.), and, as a strong opponent of Rationalism, contributed nos. 18 and 67-9 to the *Tracts for the Times*; was inhibited from preaching at Oxford, 1843-5. P. made important contributions to the theological lit. of the day, including a *Letter to the bp. of London*, 1851; his *Councils of the Church* was publd., 1857; his *Lectures on Daniel*, 1864; his *Minor Prophets*, 1877; and his *Life* was written by canon H. P. Liddon.

Pushkin, Alexander Sergivich (1799-1837): Russ. poet; P.'s 'place in Modern Russian literature is very similar to Chaucer's place in Medieval English literature' (prince Mirsky, *Modern Russ. Lit.*, 8); P. has been designated, too, the Russ. Byron (q.v.) and the Peter the Great (q.v.) of Russ. lit.: the former in virtue of his period of voluntary apprentice-ship to the style and even the subjects of Byron; and the latter, in virtue of his unique con-tribution to what may best be described as the technique of Russ. poetry. Peter had been the emperor-technician, extracting from an un-practised populace the utmost powers of civil craftsmanship of which it was capable; P. was similarly the refiner of the language, extracting the utmost results from the factors which he found in solution. P. is called a national poet. This epithet too, is just, if it be understood to refer not so much to his themes or his sympathies as to his unique services to Russ. lit. by drawing it into the circle of world-literatures. He was the first national poet of Russia because he was Russia's first world-poet; the first who challenges comparison with the major names in other countries, and the first who founded a school in his own. Former Russ. writers had come and gone, in the splendour and security of their own orbit; P. was followed by a Pleiad (q.v.); for the Fr. name and metaphor are extended to his own satellites; and, though P.'s star sank for a while, during the worse political troubles of his country, when ardent youth sought his oracle in vain, it rose to its height before the century's end. A national memorial was unveiled to P. at Moscow in 1881, when Dostoievsky's (q.v.) noble tribute, almost extravagant in its eulogy, found response throughout all Russia. Thus, as a Fr. critic has said, it is no diminishment of P.'s fame 'de l'enlever à sa race pour le rendre à l'humanité' (Vogüé), and the epithet *pan-humanity* was applied to him by Dostoi-evsky.

It is pertinent to the writings of P. to mention some personal details. He sprang of a long-descended family, and, like Byron, was conscious of the fact. His blood was crossed with an African strain, through his maternal great-grandfather, Hannibal (the negro of Peter the Great), and this strain was manifest in his appearance, in the voluptuous, even lascivious, imagery in which his poems abounded, and likewise in the jealous disposi-tion which brought him to his early death. This occurred as the result of a duel with a Fr. officer named d'Anthès, whom P. suspected on evidence not clear to-day of making love to his wife. (The wife was a simple soul, who chose a more commonplace second husband, and survived till 1863). P.'s upbringing has also some interest. He was turned loose in his father's library, where the selection of Fr. lit. was not suited to the young, and where he acquired a passion for Voltaire (q.v.) and a facility in Fr. composition. P.'s Fr. period preceded his Byronic, which was succeeded in turn by a Shakespearean; and to the early influence of a large library is to be added the folklore of P.'s nurse, Anna Rodionovna, who has the distinction of having related the tales which he later enshrined in immortal verse. In 1812, P. was sent to the new *lycée*, just founded on the model of the Fr., at Tsarköe Selo, a suburb of Petrograd, and in 1815 he recited his ' Recollections ' of the school, the most fashionable and exclusive of its day, at a prize-giving attended by Derzhavin (q.v.), the laureate, who was enthusiastic in appreciation. Indeed, P.'s youth, like Byron's again, or Lamartine's (q.v.), was one of homage and honour from the start. The older men recognized him as their successor—their rightful supplanter,—and the younger men (and women, it is to be added) crowned him with wreaths. Whether or not the incense went to his head is immaterial to-day. We are concerned now with his works ; but one more fact of P.'s biography is important to his literary career. He held himself aloof from the semi-political societies which the past students of Tsarköe Selo thronged. The Arzamas (q.v.), for instance, a happy breeding-ground of poetry and revolt, received P. as patron rather than participant ; and it was his good fortune to be removed in 1820 from his clerk-ship in the Foreign Office at Petrograd to the administrative staff in the south : his good fortune, since, first, it removed him from the dangerous and heady life of society and politics in the capital, and, secondly, it opened to him, and, through him, to European lit., the scenery and associations of the Caucasus and the Crimea. P.'s first important poem had been publd., 1820, under the title of *Ruslan and Ludmila*. The names were taken from Russ. folklore ; the material, therefore, was national ; but the treatment was thoroughly in the style of the Fr. masters who held his allegiance. He wr. an epilogue to it in the Caucasus, and added in 1878 a prologue on Russ. faëry which burns with patriotic fervour.

P.'s first southern sojourn, 1820-26, was extraordinarily prolific. He wr. there the greater part of his verse-romance of contemporary life, *Eugène Oniégin* ; completed 1831, in 9 cantos (or chapters, as P. called them), of which he suppressed the 9th, dealing with the hero's travels, as irrelevant. The poem is Byronic in conception, reminiscent chiefly of *Beppo*, and partly of *Don Juan*, and is the best-known and the best of P.'s works. ' It is, moreover, the first Russian novel, and as a novel it has never been surpassed. . . It is a realistic novel,—not realistic in the sense that Zola's work was miscalled realistic, but realistic in the sense that Miss Austen is realistic '. (See s.vv., Realism, Zola, Austen). ' The hero is the average man about St. Petersburg . . . Tatiana is as real as one of Miss Austen's heroines ; as alive as Fielding's Sophia Western, and as charming as any of George Meredith's women ; as sensible as Portia, as resolute as Juliet. . . . She is the type of all that is best in the Russian woman ; that is to say, of all that is best in Russia ; and it is a type taken straight from life ' (Baring, *Russ. Lit.*, 74-6). These considerations are important, not merely to the appreciation of P.'s *Oniégin*, but to the history of fiction in Russia. Mr. Baring agrees with Vogüé and Brückner and other critics of all countries, in dating from the creation of Tatia, or Tatiana,— the loveable, charming, natural heroine of this verse-novel—the new line of ' Russian women which Turgenev, Tolstoy and Dostoyevsky have given us, and which are the most precious jewels of Russian literature, because they reflect the crowning glory of Russian life '. Attention is called to the naturalness of Tatia, as distinct from all academic theories of naturalism (q.v.), and a special note of direction should be given to her love-letter to Oniégin, which is one of the famous passages in the world's lit. And here, perhaps, should be mentioned the fact, more important to classification than to appreciation, that P., though romantic in his choice of subjects, was essentially a realist in his treatment of them, and aimed always (certainly after his first few experiments) at a classical propriety of form.

To go back now to his first sojourn in the Caucasus and the Crimea : To the same period belongs his great experiment in chronicle-playwriting, after the Shakespearean model of hist. drama, entitled *Boris Godunov*. The matter was found in Karamsin (q.v.), and the time was that of the false Demetrius, the pretended son of tsar Ivan the Terrible, who for one brief year of sordid glory tried to force the pace of Russ. patience. Schiller (q.v.) wr. a play on the same subject, but with less success, though P.'s mode of exposition was successive rather than accumulative, episodic rather than dramatic, and has been finely rendered into opera. More close to the Byronic vein are P.'s narrative poems in this period : *The Prisoner of the Caucasus*, publd. 1821 ; *The Fountain of Baghchi-Sarai*, 1824 ; *The Gipsies*, 1827 ; *Poltava* (originally called *Mazepa*, and changed on Byron's account), 1829, etc. ; but P.'s debt to Byron, though considerable, must not be overstated. Like so many debts by genius in literary history, it was liquidated by the use of what was borrowed.

The *Oniégin* poem was on the stocks from 1823-31 ; and P.'s second visit to the south in 1829 inspired him with a plan of a new epic-idyl, *Galub*, which was left unfind., and with a rich store of lyric verse. To this important branch of P.'s writing, and to his prose-works, mainly hist., the aftermath of *Boris Godunov*, and to his delightful fairy-tales and ballads, we can but direct passing attention : *The Story of the Fisherman and the Fish* and *The Brazen Horseman* may be selected for special mention. Young, ardent, fortunate, intense, brilliant, universal ; of level judgment in the great affairs of life ; a finished artist to his finger-tips ; human, spontaneous, noble ; ' like Peter the Great, he spent his whole life in apprenticeship, and his whole energies in craftsmanship ' (Baring, *ib.*, 97) ; and his country looks back to him as the great beginner of the craft of letters. The warning must be added, however—it is taken here from prince Mirsky and Mr. Baring,— that ' only Russians can fully appreciate him ', and that ' to appreciate him it is necessary to learn Russian '. One who is neither a Russ. nor a Russ. scholar must be content to quote the Russ. critic, who knows our own language so well : ' It is indeed difficult for the foreigner, perhaps impossible if he is ignorant of the language, to believe in the supreme greatness of Pushkin among Russian writers. Yet it is necessary for him to accept the belief, even if he disagrees with it. Otherwise every idea he may form of Russian literature and Russian civilization will be inadequate and out of proportion with reality ' (Mirsky, *Modern Russ. Lit.*, 8).

Puttenham, Richard (c. 1520-c. 1601): Engl. critic; probable author of *The Art of English Poesy: contrived into 3 Books: the first of Poets and Poesy, the second of Proportion, the third of Ornament*, 1589. The earliest mention of P.'s name occurs in a MS. by one Edmund Bolton, entitled *Hypercritica*, which, though written in the reign of king James i, was not publd. till 1722. There, this *Art of Engl. Poesy* is ascribed to one of ' queen Elizabeth's gentlemen-pensioners, Puttenham ', and it is disputed between the 2 sons of Robert P., a country gentleman, namely Richard and George (d., 1590), his younger brother. Arber (q.v.) favours George, but the *Dict. Nat. Biog.*, favours Richard. A passage in the treatise suggests that P. wr. it with an eye to patronage at court.

Pye, Henry James (1745-1813): Engl. poetaster; transld. the *Poetics* of Aristotle (q.v.), 1788; wr. an epical *Alfred*, 1801; poet-laureate (q.v.), 1790.

Pyra, Jakob Immanuel (1715-44): Germ. poet; studied at Halle (q.v.). Wr., with Lange (q.v.), *Songs of Friendship*, in unrhymed verses and classical metres, thus ranging with the Anakreontiker (q.v.).

Q

Quarles, Francis (1592-1644): Engl. sacred poet; chronologer to the City of London, 1639; his valuable collection of MSS. was destroyed in the Civil War, when he wr. on the side of king Charles i. Q., like his contemporary, P. Fletcher (q.v.), affected the artifices of the school of Spenser (q.v.), and cultivated in his *Emblems*, 1635, the art of the emblem-books (q.v.), of which Alciati (q.v.) was the leading exemplar. Wr., too, a paraphrase of the Book of Jonah, called *A Feast for Worms*, 1620, and *Divine Fancies*, 1632. His style is full of the fashion of verbal conceits (q.v.), but ' sometimes he reveals an unexpectedly musical quality, and . . . his liveliness and good sense, his free use of homely words and notions and his rough humour are enough to account for, and to justify, his popularity ' (*C.H.E.L.*, vii, 47).

Quarrel (Querelle) of the Ancients and Moderns. See s.v. **Ancients.**

Quesnay, Francois (1694-1774): Fr. economist; surgeon; physician to mme. de Pompadour, mistress of king Louis xv, and called by his followers ' the Confucius of Europe '. Q. was a contributor to the *Encyclopédie* (q.v.), in which he wr. the art. on *Fermier*, *Grains*, etc.; and in 1758 his *Tableau Economique* achieved the honour of publication at the royal press at Versailles, where Q.'s professional duties gave him access to the king. The treatise was reprinted two years later by the marquis de Mirabeau (q.v.), a devoted disciple of Q., and founder of the society of economists, or physiocrats (q.v.), whose effective existence dates from the publication of Q.'s *Tableau*. The lively interest in economic problems at this date (c. 1750) will be recognized as a forerunner of the Fr. Revolution.

Quesnes (or, Conon) de Béthune (d. c. 1224): Fr. song-writer. Took part in the crusades of 1189 and 1199, and was a notable statesman in his day. His early lyric verse treated of satire, politics, and love.

Question de Amor de dos Enamorados (Span.): ' Question of Love of two lovers '; Span. *roman-à-clef* (q.v.); half-social, half-historical; issued anon., c. 1513. The present interest of this prose-dialogue is small; but it enjoyed some vogue in its own time, owing partly to the disguised personalities of Hispano-Neapolitan society, and it is still valuable as an early example of the hist. romance.

Quevedo y Villegas, de, Francisco Gomez (1580-1645): Span. satirist; poet; picaresque novelist (see s.v. Novel). Q. was a writer of rare talent, even of genius, and commanded a mordant and bitter humour. His life and health were broken by misfortune; he was a brilliant student at Alcalá (q.v.), but was driven to Sicily, 1611, in consequence of a duel; he attained high office at the courts of Naples and Madrid; was twice exiled for political causes, and spent 4 years in prison, 1639-43, on the probably unfounded charge of writing an anon. poem to the king of Spain. These vicissitudes may have embittered a mind, never remarkable for self-restraint, and there was a distinct personal note in his somewhat savage cynicism; his direct influence is more apparent in the Germ. satires of Moscherosch (q.v.) and Grimmelshausen (q.v.; author of *Simplicissimus*) than in the traditional line of *Lazarillo* (q.v.) or *Don Quixote* (s.v. Cervantes) in Q.'s own country. Even his style departed from tradition, and he cultivated an excessive *conceptismo* (see s.v. Conceits), or practice of rhetorical points, which is at once deterrent and fatiguing. It was not the *cultismo* (q.v.) of Gongora, though that was harmful enough; Q.'s special affectation of learning went beyond mere verbal ornaments and vocal appeal to an involution and a confusion of thought. Still, Q., with all his faults and despite his misfortunes, is a very considerable personage in Span. lit. It is no longer legitimate to identify him with La Torre (q.v.), whose verses he publd.; but in this instance and in others he displayed his appreciation of an art in which he was competent to excel, and he was represented in the *Florilegium* of Espinosa (q.v.). The best known among his prose-writings are the ' History of the Life of Buscon ', 1626, commonly called ' The Great Sharper ' (*el gran Tacaño*), a title which reveals its picaresque character; and the ' Dreams ', or visions

(*Sueños*), 1627-35 in which Q. gave full scope to his power of satiric observation and almost vitriolic expression. These were transld. and adapted in Engl. by sir R. L'Estrange (q.v.).

Quietism: A heresy of the Catholic Church, initiated in Spain by Molinos (q.v.), who partly derived it from the mysticism (q.v.) of S. Teresa and Leon (qq.v.); and spread from Spain to France by mme. de Guyon (q.v.), whose doctrines started the controversy between Fénelon and Bossuet (qq.v.). The substance of quietist thought will be found by reference to these articles; and see, too, s.v. Pietism.

Quillinan, Edward (1791-1851): Engl. poet; transld. the *Lusiads* of Camoens (q.v.); m. Dora, daughter of Wm. Wordsworth (q.v.).

Quinault, Philippe (1635-88): Fr. dramatist; modestly and efficiently filled the brief interregnum in tragedy between Corneille and Racine (qq.v.). Wr. *The Death of Cyrus*, 1656; *Amalasontes*, 1657; *Astrate*, 1664. Poor as these plays were, they struck a note which corresponded to an emotion latent in the audiences formerly rapt and bemused by the grandeur of the tragic theatre of Corneille (q.v.). This note was tenderness, and the emotion was love: not love as duty, as in Vondel (q.v.), nor love as self-respect, as in Corneille himself; but love as human passion, even as human weakness. The step from Q. to Racine is thus a short one, and Corneille, on his return to the stage in 1659, found a successor, however inferior, in occupation. Q. retired in turn shortly after Racine's emergence (*c.* 1670), and devoted his last years to opera (q.v.) and comedy. In the former, he was appointed, 1672, poet to Lulli, manager of the new (1668) academy of operas in the Fr. language; he had already worked at a *Psyche* (with Molière and Corneille), and his new operas included *Alcestes*, 1674, *Atys*, 1676, *Roland*, 1685, *Armida* (perhaps the best), etc. Though Q. had predecessors in this kind,

his excellent work almost constituted a new departure. His comedies (e.g. *L'Amant indiscret*) are better than his tragedies, but not comparable to Molière's.

Quinet, Edgar (1803-75): Fr. (-Swiss) philosopher; historian. Critics argue (see Lanson, *Hist. Lit. fr.*, 927, and Omond, *P.E.L.*, xi, 271) that Q.'s correspondence (with Michelet, q.v., and others) is the best of his works, and that his life was more interesting than his writings. These extend in the collected edn. to 30 vols., and include a transln. of Herder (q.v.) on the philosophy of history, 'Germany and Italy', 'French epopees', etc.; the Michelet letters are contained in *Cinquante ans d'Amitié*. Q., whose career included political adventures which displayed the pure fire of his character, was prominent in the siege of Paris by the Prussians, 1870.

Quintana, Manuel Josef (1772-1857): Span. poet; patriot; supported the revolution of 1808, and took a leading and an enlightened part in the proclamations and manifestoes of that epoch; was imprisoned, 1814, at the restoration of king Ferdinand vii, but enjoyed another brief period of well-earned distinction after 1820; was publicly crowned, 1855: a fitting testimony to the undiminished idealism of the laureate of national independence. Q.'s first work was a tragedy, *The Duke of Visco*, 1801, a poor copy of a feeble model, *The Castle Spectre*, 1798, of M. G. Lewis (q.v.); a patriotic play, *Pelayo*, followed in 1805; an anthology of Castilian poetry, in 1807; prose lives of celebrated Spaniards; and patriotic odes and other poems, including the odes of liberation, 1808, the ode to the Span. expedition carrying the boon of vaccination to America, the Trafalgar ode, 1805, and several more. These fired the imagination of Q.'s countrymen, and roused them in much the same way as Fichte (q.v.) was rousing the Germ. people at the same time. The honours paid to Q. in his old age were a worthy reward after the buffets of middle life.

R

Rabelais, François (1495-1553): Fr. humanist-satirist. Born of humble orig. at Chinon, Touraine; trained at convent-schools for vocation of monk; left the Franciscans for the milder rule of the Benedictines; finally broke his cloister altogether; practised as a physician at Lyons (q.v.) and elsewhere; read widely in the learning of the day, with special interest in travel and scientific speculation; appointed *curé* of Meudon, 1551, and is often called by that title, though he held the post only a brief while; enjoyed the powerful protection of king Francis i, his sister, queen Margaret of Navarre, card. du Bellay (qq.v.), and others, but was never completely released from the vigilance of Rome, nor from occasional persecution by the Franciscans for his free opinions and still freer expression of them. Wr., 1531, a story-book based on the local legend of a Touraine giant, *The Great and Inestimable Chronicles of Gargantua*; added,

1532, an original continuation to the tale, *The Horrible and Terrible Deeds and Prowesses of the well-renowned Pantagruel, King of the Dipsodes, Son of the Great Giant Gargantua*; next, replaced the *Chronicles* by an original *Life of Gargantua, Father of Pantagruel*, which became bk. i, preceding and harmonized with the *Pantagruel* as bk. ii; bk. iii, *The Heroic Life and Sayings of the Good Pantagruel* appeared, 1546; bk. iv, the same, with *His Wonders and Voyages*, 1552; and bk. v, the same, with *His Visit to the Oracle*, posth., 1564, in the year of Shakespeare's birth. Thus, briefly, there are 2 romances in the complete work: *Gargantua*, the father, in 1 vol., and *Pantagruel*, his son, in 4 vols. The standard Engl. transln. is by sir Thomas Urquhart, or Urchard (1611-60), and Peter Motteaux (1660-1718). The work itself may best be understood by remembering its author's place between the cloister and the world; never wholly of one or of the other.

He stood at the forest's edge, shaking off the last shadows of the Middle Ages, and rending the morning sky of the Renaissance with the laughter of the wine of life. Yet he might never pass out into the full light. The death-writ ran up and down the land, summoning great men and small to the silence of the stake or axe; and R., who had been a monk, would have had short shrift as an open rebel. Accordingly, he had recourse to subterfuge, and, even so, did not escape obloquy. He disguised his opinions. He was serious about things ludicrous, and derisive about serious things. As reformer, scientist, humanist, he masqueraded in the cloak of a buffoon. He sowed his thoughts with whimsey and mixed his wheat with tares, till the jealous eye slept again and the lithe prey slipped the shears. He drew largely on Lucian, the Gk. travel-satirist of the 2nd cent., A.D., for the wonderful voyages of Pantagruel, which were at the same time a burlesque of the old romances of chivalric adventure, and thus owed a debt to Folengo (q.v.). The message of the far-sought ' oracle ' (bk. v) was ' Trinq ' (Drink); and R. could quote scriptural authority for using, as the symbols of his creed, ' herb for the service of man, and wine that maketh glad the heart of man ' (Psalm civ, 14-5). But the bk. which opened with a drinking-bout ended with a gospel for the conduct of life. Clowns would apply it literally; they suggested, after R.'s death, that ' hams and sausages ' should be strewn on his tomb instead of lilies; but philosophers would interpret it symbolically. To be ' yourself the expounder of your undertaking ' and to add ' man's assistance ' to the formulas by which the Church directed its disciples, were the recipes for complete living derived by R. from the signs of the Renaissance; like F. Bacon (q.v.), exalting science and its application to industry. The ' herb ' (see s.v. Pantagruelion) and the wine were there in plenty; if they typified the joys of the flesh, they led to the conquest of the physical universe, and the repulse of the thin and pallid ghosts of the cloister from which R. sought escape. Likely enough, he might forget the hidden symbols in the tangible reality. The gladness of the heart over-flowed, and all kinds of topics and ou-topics (utopics) were swept into the full and vocal stream. R.'s teeming invention and inexhaustible rush of words, in the new Fr. moulded to lay uses, which he suppled and tamed like a living thing, may well have distracted his plan and led him from digression to digression, apart altogether from his prudent habit of bemusing the adversary whom he belaboured. But through all the medley of the material, and the indecent foolery of the treatment, it is possible to trace an idea, and, moreover, an idea which grew. There is an increasing purpose in this epic-romance of earth-laughter, ' broad as ten thousand beeves at pasture ', as Meredith (q.v.) wr. of Shakespeare's. Rely on yourself. Seek truly. Trust experience. Meet life with both hands open. Play the man; oust the ascetic. Eat, drink, and be merry, for to-morrow we—*live*; such was R.'s invincible belief in the life of the morrow of the Renaissance,

which he was not to see with his own eyes. His buffoonery, his profusion, his obscenity : these, we admit, deter; and we may deplore, with sir W. Besant (q.v., *Rabelais*, Blackwood, 193) that his genius and learning were not put at the disposal of the Reformation in France. But we are dealing with things as they are; with R. as he was, not as he might have been. Comedy, or the comic element, was his. In Shakespeare himself, in Swift and Sterne (qq.v.), and, less directly, in every great writer who has seized the comedy of life—not Dante's *Commedia*, but humanity's—the influence of R. is present. He laughed many evils out of life and language, and much good in; and his bk., however free—in one sense because so free,—is a true criticism of life, as realized by a great man in a great time. The pale scholars who spoke with the tongue of ghosts, and elucidated Gk. texts for Lat. pedants : R.'s blood was transferred to their veins as their learning mounted to his brain.

Rabener, Gottlieb Wilhelm (1714-71): Germ. satirist; Saxon revenue-officer. Contributor to the *Bremer Beiträge* (q.v.). Wr. pleasant, non-personal, ironical reflections on the humours and habits of the day; frequently reprinted.

Racan, de, Honorat (1589-1670): Fr. poet; orig. member of the Fr. Academy (q.v.); disciple of Malherbe (q.v.); *marquis* by rank. R.'s reputation is sustained in a diminishing scale of affirmation; he ' owed his immortality as much to his *bizarreries* as to his genius ' (Lanson, *Hist. Lit. fr.*, 383), and ' the compliance of his principal work with a fashionable folly of the time has caused him to be somewhat overestimated traditionally ' (Saintsbury, *Short Hist. Fr. Lit.*, 248). Wr. *Les Bergeries*, a pastoral-drama, originally called *Arthénice* (see s.v. Rambouillet), and modelled on Tasso, which would have benefited by the labour of the file, which R., despite his correct ear for rhythm and sound, was too lazy to employ on his own writings.

Rachel · Elisa Rachel Félix (1820-58): Fr. actress at the Comédie Française; Jewess. R.'s art and fame belong to the history of the theatre, not of letters; but lit. is interested in her triumphs, because her brilliant representation of the heroines of the classical Fr. drama of Racine and Corneille (qq.v.) assisted, from 1838 onwards, the retirement of romanticism (s.v. Lyrisme) from its brief usurpation of the stage. Hugo, Vigny and Dumas *père* (qq.v.) reigned at the theatre, 1829-43, and ' made hay '—the colloquialism is appropriate—of the older conventions of drama. But their plays, having discharged their function, were not of the stuff that endures, and the comedies of Augier and Dumas *fils* (qq.v.) replaced the tragedies of the romanticists, in much the same way as classical tragedy merged into domestic drama in the 18th cent. The return of the character-play was the occasion and the opportunity of R.

Rachel, Joachim (1608-69): Germ. satirist. Commenced in the popular vein and Low Germ. dialect chosen by Lauremberg (q.v.); but composed his eight satires after the more expedient model of Opitz (q.v.), and earned for himself the title of the Juvenal of that school.

Racine, -i. Jean (1639-99) : Fr. tragic dramatist. R.'s life falls into 3 divisions : Port Royal (q.v.), Paris under king Louis xiv, and Port Royal again. But before speaking either of his life or of his plays, a few words may be said in explanation of his fame, as incomparably the greatest representative of the classical style in Fr. lit. He moved with delicate liberty within the area delimited by Boileau (q.v.) for the ambition of men of letters, and he enjoyed throughout the period of his active career the patronage, help, and approval of that strict ' lawgiver of Parnassus.' Outside the area were Shakespeare (q.v.), and the irregular stage of the Elizabethans, and the infinite variety of nature, her frequent paradoxes and surprises, the multiplication of incidents, the diversity of circumstance, the changes wrought by passing years—in a word, the stage which was indifferent to the Unities (q.v.) of time, place, and action. Fr. logic or pedantry (the choice of epithet is a matter of temperament) had elaborated the stage-law of the Unities from Ital. interpreters of Horatian renderings of Aristotle's precepts. But still outside that guarded compound was the wide region of Romance (q.v.) ; within it was the ' nature ' of Boileau, widely removed from Nature (q.v.) herself, according to his critical theory, by the labour-saving machinery of the ancients. These had observed men and things at first-hand, and had imitated them with consummate art ; therefore, art thenceforward was to be spared the labour of the Gks., and of the grecizing Romans. The imitation of nature by modern classicists meant the construction of works of art according to set rules to be derived from the practice of the classical writers ; any departure from these rules, any breach of their inhibitions, was a departure from nature and a breach with truth : it was against reason, and therefore against beauty.

The perils of this doctrine are obvious, and are encountered in every age ; not least in the age of R. We may agree or not with prof. Saintsbury that Shakespeare could have satisfied Boileau by writing a *Phèdre*, but that Racine could not have satisfied Elizabethan London by writing an *Othello*. Every writer has commonly an ideal audience ; one man, or one type, to whose taste he writes ; and, if so, Boileau was Racine's. But this is not the right spirit in which to approach R.'s genius. ' Englishmen have always loved Molière. It is hardly an exaggeration to say that they have always detested Racine ', declares Mr. Lytton Strachey (*Landmarks of Fr. Lit.*, 89). But this, too, as the writer shows, is not the right spirit of approach. The point is, that R.'s expatiation within the limits of the theory of classic art was as free, as untrammelled, and as complete, as that of the greatest Romantic playwright within the boundless frontiers of the Elizabethan stage ; and that, if each is to be judged by his failures as well as by his successes, the triumph of R.'s method had no such feebleness to condone as *Timon of Athens* or *Pericles*, or some other Elizabethan dramas, in which the method missed the genius of its chief manipulator. To like or to dislike R. is not simply a question of taste.

It is, first, a question of knowledge ; and knowledge brings power. It is as ignorant and futile to dislike R. on an Englishman's part, as it would be for a Frenchman to dislike Shakespeare ; our first duty is to understand him ; thereafter, we may indulge the luxury of taste.

The common comparison of R. with Corneille (q.v.), his elder contemporary playwright, is interesting, if it is not pushed too far ; like the Victorian comparison between Dickens and Thackeray (qq.v.), or the Weimar comparison between Goethe and Schiller (qq.v.), it should not be carried to the extreme of excluding one for the sake of the other. In the age and at the court of Louis xiv, it was merely human to encourage the rivalry ; and R. is not to be acquitted of a somewhat acrid attitude towards it, for which he suffered in turn when the worthless Pradon (q.v.) was run against him. But in a literary sense, the 2 dramatists were complementary rather than competitive. They approached the problem of tragic character from opposite points of view. Corneille was the poet of the mind, and R. of the heart. In Corneille's plays, the will won the battle ; in R.'s, the affections ; and, if there is sex in style, as Marivaux (q.v.) affirmed, Corneille's style was masculine, and R.'s feminine. This brings us directly to a characteristic of the drama of R., which possesses wide interest : ' the empire of woman in literature dates from Racine ', declares Lanson (*Hist. Lit. Fr.*, 546) ; and if this claim strikes strangely on the countrymen of Sidney (q.v.) and on admirers of Desdemona, Cleopatra, Dame Quickly, and other female figures in the Shakespearean gallery (see s.v. Woman), we shall find justification for it in the fact that R. penetrated very deeply into women's heart and passions. He gave his characters well-known names : Andromache, Hermione, Phædra, Roxana, Berenice, and the rest ; but 'beneath the heroic names, and transcending their extraordinary misfortunes or crimes, it was the simple, general, human truth which Racine wished to illustrate ' (Lanson, *ibid.*, 544) ; and herein lies R.'s affinity with the master of comedy, Molière, his friend, contemporary, and the producer of his first play, *la Thébaïde*, 20 June, 1664. Both playwrights generalized from the particular instance ; both drew types in the dress of individuals ; and both, accordingly, supply for reference simple phrases for recurring situations, in which, as, again, in Dickens, the actual place and character are forgotten in the universal applicability of the sentence. R. is rich in saving commonplace. Having stripped his heroic theme, and reduced its content to its bare human essentials, he gives it practical expression, without straining after sublimity or effect. *Tendresse* is the accepted term employed by Fr. critics of R. to mark the note of his psychology (see, too, s.v. Quinault, who wr. a few good tragedies in the interregnum between Corneille and R.). It was a note described by Corneille as derived from the commerce ' of sighs and flames ' ; and the sighs of longing and flames of love mastered the hearts of R.'s heroines and conquered the will of his heroes. But the crises of passion which he staged at the tragic moments of their greatest activity differed minutely one from another; he admitted no element which would distract him from his study of naked emotion, and each character stands unique in the circumstances of its tragic ordeal. Thus, R. advanced the dramatic method, and enhanced its skill. He proved that his would-be Gk. drama was competent to express the psychology of the age which had studied Descartes (q.v.); he proved, too, that princes and potentates, queens, empresses, and the distant figures of a mythological past, were men and women moved by the master-passion, analysable by the playwright's insight within the limits of his classic art.

Thore are 2 marks by which to characterize R.'s genius: his Jansenism (s.vv. Jansen and Port Royal) and his Hellenism (q.v.). As an orphan in his paternal grandparents' charge, he was sent for 6 years (1649-55) to a school at Beauvais, where 'the beautiful, delicate, imaginative boy' acquired 'a certain love of reserve, of seclusion; a restive independence; a certain selfishness too; an Ishmael-like resolve to fight for his own land' (*Times Lit. Supp.*, 7 May, 1925). At 16 years of age, when his character was to some extent formed, came the welcome change to Port Royal, where he felt himself—happy and at home, and where 'il aimait se promener dans les jardins et converser avec les arbres'. Nicole (q.v.) was among his teachers. To them he dedicated his first literary efforts, and to them he returned, or retired, in middle life (1677), when court-cabals and wounded self-esteem conspired with his sensitiveness and pietism to bring to a sudden close his series of masterpieces of tragic drama. R.'s *Nymphe de la Seine*, a royal marriage-ode for Louis xiv and Maria Theresa, introduced him to fashionable Paris and to the useful friendship of Chapelain and Perrault (qq.v.). His odes, *Convalescence du Roi* and *Renommée aux Muses*, 1663, brought him acquaintance with La Fontaine, Molière and Boileau, who taught him to laugh at Chapelain; it was like a little boy's progress through a school, and veritably Boileau became his fagmaster. He steeped himself more deeply in Parisian social life, including the life of the taverns (*cabarets*—the *Mouton Blanc*, for example); and his *Thébaïde*, produced, as we saw, by Molière, caused a breach with his old teachers of Port Royal. He deemed himself counted among the 'public poisoners, not of the body but of the souls of the faithful', and wr. bitterly in defence of his profession. His second play, *le Grand Alexandre*, was produced simultaneously at 2 theatres—Molière's and the Hôtel de Bourgogne—on 18 Dec., 1665; and this procedure caused a breach of R.'s friendship with Molière (see, too, s.v. Confrérie). Then came *Andromache*, 1667, which recalled the triumph of the *Cid* (q.v.), and which is the *Romeo and Juliet* of R.'s stage. It was written for mlle. Marquise du Parc, whom R. perhaps secretly married, and with whom he lived till her death, 1668. His subsequent tragedies included: *Britannicus*, 1669; *Bérénice*, 1670; *Bajazet*, 1672; *Mithridate*, 1673; *Iphigénie*, 1674; *Phèdre*, 1677. The

Fr. Academy (q.v.) had elected him in 1673; and, except for the jealousies to which we have referred, a long career of success seemed to open out. But R.'s decision, dictated by temperament, was taken and maintained. He accepted, 1667, the post, with Boileau, of historiographer, which meant war-correspondent, to the king, and was surely a strange figure in the camp; he married, and brought up a large family; but he would no longer face the ignominy of competition with a Pradon or the accusation of poisoning men's souls. Not till 1689, when, at the request of mme. de Maintenon (q.v.), he wr. *Esther* for her pupils at St. Cyr, followed by *Athalie*, 1691, for the same audience, did R. resume his work as a dramatist. But then it was for a very different stage. If *Andromache* is R.'s *Romeo and Juliet*, *Esther*, it has been well said, was his *Comus*. He had found again the 'grace' of the Port Royalists, whose history he wr., and within whose precincts, by his own desire, he was buried. R. ranks with V. Hugo (q.v.) as one of the 2 greatest writers in Fr. lit., and the Racinian verse, at its height, is incomparable for its passion, restraint, majesty and music.

-ii. Louis (1692-1763): Fr. poet; son of above. Wr. didactic verse of no merit, and was properly discouraged by Boileau (q.v.).

Radcliffe, Ann (1704-1823): Engl. novelist; née Ward; m. Wm. R., 1787. Wr. *The Sicilian Romance*, 1790; *The Romance of the Forest*, 1791; *The Mysteries of Udolpho*, 1794, and *The Italian*, 1797. There was one early (1789) and one posth. (1826) novel, and a vol. of *Poems*, 1816; in 1824, the *Novels* were issued with a *Memoir of the Life of the Author*, by sir Walter Scott (q.v.). It is difficult and perhaps ungallant to write judicially about Mrs. R., more than 100 years after this signal compliment was paid to her by Scott: indeed, as prof. Saintsbury remarks (*C.H.E.L.*, xi, 300): 'It has not happened to any other. To give a novelist like Scott something of his method, and a poet like Byron nearly the whole of his single hero'; and if we add the indirect influence which she exerted *through* Scott and Byron (who 'boldly mentioned her in the same breath with Shakespeare'; *P.E.L.*, x, 100), it would seem incompetent as well as ungallant to refuse her incense and laurel. Yet the 20th cent. has its rights, equally with the 19th; and modern readers will not taste those particular cates that diverted Eve so raptly a century ago. Why not? Because her romances and mysteries have lost their flavour to-day. She may have given hints to Scott and Byron about hist. setting, local colour, and the enchantment of distance, just as she accepted hints about horror and suspense from sir H. Walpole and Clara Reeve (qq.v.). The rich furnishings of *Udolpho* may even have given hints to Coleridge (q.v.) in *Christabel* and Keats (q.v.) in *The Eve of St. Agnes*. But since, with ultra-feminine conscientiousness, she always explained away everything supernatural by mechanical pulleys, and since her local colour was mostly wrong, and since, finally, the greater masters improved on the hints which they received, the name of Mrs. R.

May he then but gie then
   Those blessings for my *skair* (share),
I'll fairly and squairly
   Quite a' and seek nae mair.

Ramsay, Edward Bannerman (1793-1872): Scot. anecdotal historian; dean of Edinburgh, 1841. Wr., 1858, *Reminiscences of Scottish Life and Character*, a valuable and popular repository of fact and fable.

Ranke, von Leopold (1795-1886): Germ. historian; prof. of history in Berlin from 1825 till his death. The Prussian government sent him on a learned mission to Vienna, Venice, Rome, and Florence (1827), and his series of important works on periods and aspects of history benefited immensely by his researches. These works included, *Princes and Peoples of Southern Europe in the 16th and 17th Centuries; The Servian Revolution; The Popes of Rome: Their Church and State in the 16th and 17th Centuries*, 1834-36; *German History in the Age of the Reformation*, 1839-41, and weighty tomes on Fr., Engl., Germ., and universal history. R.'s greatest works have long been familiar in foreign versions, including Engl.; Macaulay's (q.v.) review of Sarah Austin's (q.v.) transln. of the 'Popes' (*Edinburgh Review*, Oct., 1840) is well known.

Rapin, Nicholas (1535-1608): Fr. satirist; follower of Ronsard (q.v.). Contributor to the famous *Satyre Ménippée* (q.v.).

Rapin, de, Paul de Thoyras (1661-1725): Fr. historian; Huguenot; retired to Holland after the revocation of the edict of Nantes, 1685, and followed prince of Orange to Engld., 1688; fought at the battle of the Boyne. Settled at Wesel, and wr. *Histoire d'Angleterre*, 1724, 'the first bk. deserving the title of a History of England' (Saintsbury, *Fr. Lit.*, 306). It was transld. into Engl. by M. Tindal (q.v.).

Raspe, Rudolf Eric (1737-94): Anglo-Germ. satiric writer; adventurer; born in Hanover, studied in Göttingen, and held appointment as numismatist at Cassel; fled to Engld., 1775, to escape punishment for theft of gems in his charge, and obtained post as mining expert, adding to his income by writing. His chief work is *Baron Munchausen's Narrative of his Marvellous Travels and Campaigns in Russia*, 1785; second edn. (enlarged by another writer), 1786; seventh edn. and sequel (parody of *Travels* by James Bruce, 1730-94; African traveller), 1793. See also s.vv. Munchausen and Bürger. R. entered lit. by another door in 1815, when sir W. Scott, q.v., introduced into the *Antiquary* the incident of his obtaining money by the false pretence of discovering gold and silver on his estate. But R.'s adventures were over before then.

Rastell, John (d., 1536): Engl. printer; lawyer; died in prison, in consequence of a dispute about tithes; m. Elizabeth, sister to sir Thomas More (q.v.); became father of Elizabeth, wife of John Heywood (q.v.), whose third daughter, Elizabeth, m. John Donne (q.v.). These relationships are of interest in connection with R.'s work in the early history of romantic drama in Engld. Thus, *c.* 1530, he imprinted (we modernize the spelling): 'A new comedy in English, in manner of an Interlude, right elegant and full of craft of rhetoric, wherein is showed and described as well the beauty and good properties of women as their vices and evil conditions; with a moral conclusion and an exhortation to virtue'. With the exception of the 'moral conclusion' and the 'exhortation to virtue', which are deplored in *C.H.E.L.*, v., 100: 'There is no Tudor play in which the romantic and the didactic tendencies meet in such violent collision', this verse-drama of 1,088 lines is adapted from the first 4 acts of the famous Span. tragi-comedy of *Celestina* (q.v.), 1499, and is entitled by Hazlitt (q.v.) *The Tragicomedy of Calisto and Melibœa*, and by its latest editor, Mr. Warner Allen (*Celestina*, Routledge, 1908) *An Interlude of Calisto and Melebea*. On all hands, the publication is recognized as a significant step in advance towards the romantic drama of the Elizabethan stage; and Shakespeare had doubtless read it in connection with his *Romeo and Juliet*. 'Its very title is suggestive; for it is the first time that a play in English, not derived from classical sources, had been called a comedy' (Allen, *op. cit.*, 335); and the Cambridge historian writes that the author's 'power of turning the prose of Rojas (q.v.) into verse, with the minimum of verbal change, anticipates, in humbler fashion, Shakespeare's marvellous transmutation of the prose of Holinshed and North'. How did R. get hold of *Celestina*, and who effected this Engl. Interlude (q.v.)? It has been conjectured that the association of R.'s brother-in-law, More, with Vives (q.v.), who was on a visit to Engld. about that time, is the reply to the first question; for Vives, in his *Institution of the Christian Woman*, had expressed himself strongly on the subject of Celestina's immorality; and if an Oxford pupil of Vives had been directed to the bk. by this means, he certainly purged the Engl. version, and substituted the 'moral conclusion', to which the dramatic sense takes exception. Further, Heywood himself has been suggested, but is not accepted, as the author. Apart from this important publication, R. wr. an *Interlude of the Nature of the Four Elements*, which was a kind of forward-striving Morality (q.v.), and he plainly conducted his business with an enlightened appreciation of progressive thought.

Rawlinson, -i. Thomas (1681-1725), **-ii. Richard** (1690-1755): antiquaries; sons of sir Thomas R. (1647-1708; lord mayor of London, 1705). The valuable bks. and MSS. of both brothers are now in Bodley's (q.v.) library at Oxford. The elder brother was the 'Tom Folio' of Addison's (q.v.) *Tatler*, whose scholarship did not extend beyond the title-pages of his bks.; the younger wr. on topographical subjects, and was a non-juring bp., 1728.

Raynal, Guillaume Thomas François (1713-96): Fr. historian; *abbé*. Wr., 1780, a 'philosophical and political history of the Settlements and Commerce of Europeans in the Two Indies'; a work of no importance, save for its indication of the new critical tendencies in hist. writing.

Razon de Amor (Span.): 'The Reason of Love', lyrical poem, dating from early in the 13th cent., and preserved in only one MS. 'with the Disputes of Water and Wine' (*con los*

Denuestos del Ague y del Vino), ed. pr., 1887. The two poems, as their titles signify, are quite distinct in subject and character, and no explanation is found of their common descent. Formerly, they were attributed to a common author, Lope (q.v.) de Moros, whose name occurs in the last line of the MS. (*Lupus me fecit de Moros*), but is now regarded as that of the copyist. However this may be, the lovers' *Razon* is unique in the time of its appearance, as an early and premature bud of the future springtide of Span. lyric poetry.

Reade, Charles (1814-84): Engl. dramatist, novelist, journalist, to adopt the order of epithets chosen by R. himself for his tombstone; posterity remembers him in the second capacity chiefly or alone. R.'s most justly celebrated novel is *The Cloister and the Hearth*, 1861, a romance of the life and times of Erasmus (q.v.), and as extraordinarily exact in its documentation as it is moving and absorbing as a tale. Swinburne (q.v.) described it as ' among the greatest masterpieces of narrative ', and sir W. Besant (q.v.), himself a novelist, believed it to be ' the greatest historical novel in the language '. Great it certainly is, in whatever degree: it is ' great, because of its broad and deep humanity and its splendid subject ; . . . great, again, because of its immense scope and variety. This bk., if anything, is Reade's passport to immortality ' (Walker, *Lit. Victorian Era*, 764). It is available as a passport in another sense. Students of the Middle Ages, who are anxious to travel with Erasmus, the educator of Europe, and actually to meet Froissart, Villon, Luther (qq.v.), and others, whose shadows flit through this dictionary, may use the passport of R.'s great ' tale of the Middle Ages ' as a secure and trustworthy guide. R. wr. nothing else as good, but *Peg Woffington*, 1852 (first produced as a play, *Masks and Faces*, written by R. in collaboration with Tom Taylor, q.v.), is an excellent novel of the theatre ; *It is Never too late to Mend*, 1856, was a pioneer of the novels written for social reform purposes, and was devoted to the reform of prisons ; *Hard Cash*, 1863, applied to same method to lunatic asylums ; and there were others, between *Christie Johnstone*, 1853, and the autobiographic *Terrible Temptations*, 1871. R. was a scholar of distinguished parts, who held a fellowship at Magdalen Coll., Oxford ; but he resided mostly in London, where his theatrical ventures, in which he sometimes dealt a little impulsively with other people's rights, involved him in constant law-suits. Among other plays, he adapted Zola's (q.v.) *L'Assommoir* as *Drink*, with great success, 1879. He described his own best novels as ' matter-of-fact Romance—that is, a fiction built on truths ; and these truths ', he added in the pref. to *Hard Cash*, ' have been gathered by long severe, systematic labour, from a multitude of volumes, pamphlets, journals, reports, blue-books, manuscript narratives, letters, and living people, whom I have sought out, examined, and cross-examined, to get at the truth on each main topic I have striven to handle '. At the same time, he objected to the title of a ' sensation novelist ' ; ' this slang term ', he wr., ' is not quite accurate as applied to me. Without sensation there can be no interest ; but my plan is to mix a little character and a little philosophy with the sensational element '.

Reali di Francia (*c.* 1400): ' Tales of the Fr. Court ' ; It. anon. prose compilation on the topics of the ' matière de France ' from Constantine to Roland ; ed. pr., Modena, 1491. The authorship is ascribed to Andrea de Barberino, translr. and romancer, who may be proud of having supplied a vernacular version of the Carolingian tales for the use of Boiardo (q.v.) and his successors, but who is otherwise a dull fellow employing the style which we should now call journalese. His date is uncertain, but he was born later than 1370.

Realism : After Naturalism (q.v.) Realism. The consecution is simple to follow, and a clear review of it will help to sort the -isms and to rob them of a large part of the illusion of their technical apparatus. For it should always be remembered that the critics come after the writers, and that no -ist or -ism is so definite as the inventors of the terminology would have us believe.

In the first place (for the literatures of modern Europe) were the pagan writers of Greece and Rome. The re-discovery of these, and of the pagan philosophy of life, was the boon of the Humanists of Italy, starting with Petrarch (q.v.) in the 14th cent. It was the aim of Renaissance (q.v.) writers in Italy, Spain and France, and in the Northern Renaissance of the Reformation, to supple the European languages till they became adequate to the Gk. and Lat. powers of expression ; to reform the medieval moulds, so top-heavy, cumbrous and unsymmetrical, and so grievously burdened withal by the weight of ecclesiastical authority, and to remodel them after Gk. and Lat. patterns ; and thus, alike in manner and in matter, to renew the mind of antiquity.

In the second place, omitting much besides, the pagan writers of Greece and Rome were strained beyond their capacity. The classicism of the legislator of Parnassus, as Boileau (q.v.) was called in the Fr. *grand siècle*, outwent the merits of its objects, and when Boileau was reproduced by imitators who outwent the dogmatism of their master, his classicsworship was turned into an idolatry, mildly described as neo- or pseudo-classicism. Boileau's most devout Engl. follower was Pope (q.v.), who built on the foundations of H. St. John, lord Bolingbroke (q.v.) ; for Pope's friend, lady Mary Wortley Montagu ' was perfectly right as to fact when she told how her original admiration of the *Essay on Criticism* ceased when she found it was all stolen from the ancients ; except that, if she had herself known a little more, she might have perceived that most of it was stolen or borrowed at second-hand ' (Saintsbury, *The Peace of the Augustans*, 47). Still, Pope's evidence is the more valuable, since he crystallized in unfading forms of verse the neo-classic doctrine of ' Follow the Ancients ', as it appeared to a would-be truthful witness. He rendered its reflection at its best, and revealed its full effect on European letters. To those who were thus bent on obeying the Fr. law according to

Boileau, the rules of ' the ancients ' did duty as Nature's own :

Those Rules of old discovered, not devis'd,
Are Nature still, but Nature methodiz'd.

Those rules, that is to say, were not invented, but natural ; man's business in the matter had been merely to collect them for methodical practice :

Learn hence for ancient rules a just esteem,—
To copy Nature is to copy them.

Where are we ? Plainly, thrice removed by a dense wall of classical superstition, as obstructive (if not more so) as the obscurantism of authority in the Middle Ages, from the right of direct and spontaneous approach to the fountain of Nature undefiled. Horace's way, Virgil's way, Homer's way, were open to all who would tread therein ; but the ways of investigation and research, of laborious building-up of inductions from minute and particular study, were shut out from vulgar curiosity. Pope's garden at Twickenham, ' inclosed with three lanes, and seeing nothing ', was typical of the garden of criticism which he cultivated, inclosed by the triple fences of Horace, Vida (q.v.) and Boileau. Thus, Nature was viewed through blinkers, though these were labelled with the reputation of great ancients. How long was this blindness to last ? Once more, we skip an interval, and come thirdly and successively to the re-action from this neo-classicism by the Romanticists, Naturalists, Realists.

Why has not man a microscopic eye ? Pope had asked in his *Essay on Man* ; and he found his own answer sufficient :

For this plain reason, Man is not a fly.

We are not intended, he held, ' to inspect a mite, not comprehend the heaven ' ; and he would straightly have opposed the aim stated by Blake (q.v.) not a hundred years after :

To see the world in a grain of sand,
And a heaven in a wild flower.

For it was the *limits*, not the breadth, of Pope's philosophy which evoked his false and famous creed :

The proper study of Mankind is Man.
           Essay on Man, ii, 2,

i.e., should be confined to Man.

The reaction was obvious and overdue. Obedient mankind refused to acquiesce ; refused to seek Nature in the mirror of pagan classical interpreters ; refused to believe that their records had exhausted the message of *rerum natura*, the real ; refused to believe with the elect that ' Nature and Homer were the same ' ; refused to confine its study to man. The so called Romantic revolt (s.v. Romance) is implicitly a revolt against this paralysis. Romantic excesses, grievous, ludicrous, often repellent (as when Germ. burghers danced in an oak-grove ; see s.v. Hain), are merely so many signs of the ecstasy of rediscovering Nature in field and hill and wood, in humble homes and lowly lives, in the song of a bird and the scent of a flower. The moon shone again in Germ. skies (see s.v. Tieck). The mountains were unrolled by Brockes and Rousseau (qq.v.). St. Pierre (q.v.) saw colours undetected by the ancients. The sea was spread before its worshippers. Nature—this was the great discovery—might be copied afresh without

copying ' them '. The pall of the ancients was lifted from European letters.

But there was one more stage of this journey ' back to Nature ', as it came to be called after Rousseau. Nature-lore had still to be purged of the inherited stock epithets, the lumber and furniture of secondhand observation, which persisted even in Wordsworth's (q.v.) early poems. Nor was phraseology the sum of the inheritance. Beyond this, and inevitably almost, the rebels had acquired from the objects of their revolt a more fatal and insidious temptation. Their Romantic heroes were fashioned on Classical lines. Lit. was unable to get away from the old, persistent conviction, so ably expressed by Puttenham (q.v.) in an *Art of English Poetry*, dated 1589, that ' Because the actions of mean and base personages tend in very few cases to any great good example— for who pauseth to follow the steps and manner of life of a craftsman, shepherd or sailor, though he were his father or dearest friend ?— therefore was nothing committed to history but matters of great and excellent persons and things '. Have we not here the *causa causans* of the dignified and exalted language of Gray's (q.v.) *Elegy in a Country Churchyard*, so different in its sanctions and licences from the country-idyls of Mr. John Masefield, for example ; so significant in its postponement of the hero-worship till the humble heroes had been consecrated by thick layers of dust ? It wanted more than a romantic revolt from the conventional apparatus of the classicists to break down the literary tradition excluding the ' mean and base personages '. Gray might moralize at their graves ; Crabbe (q.v.) might wipe the sweat from their brows ; but a social and an industrial revolution had to take place before the subjects of humble life were admitted to the republic of letters, unless they walked in on stilts. And out of that social revolution, accomplished in France at the end of the 18th cent., came, very gradually and tentatively, the spiritual and moral changes which, in the literary sphere, made the methods of Naturalism and Realism as trustworthy in interpretation as the methods from which they had proceeded by reaction.

We are dealing with broad effects and with long spaces of time. But the development of modern lit. through Bryon, Rousseau and Wordsworth to Zola, Meredith and Dostoievsky (see s.vv.) should now be clearer than it was. Science aided the transition. Modern writers aimed at reproducing, not the ideal conditions of an artificial society, but the infinite disarray of nature ; not nature ' methodized ' but dishevelled. Politics, aided, too, by the overlaying of democracy on aristocracy. History aided, too, by discovering the causes of the movements represented by captains and kings, so that these sank to secondary places, as the puppets of forces greater than they wielded. And the new broom of psychology was gathered out of remnants of the older sciences, and swept away many delusions.

From all these, Realism sprang, out of Naturalism, the offspring of Romanticism. We may trace its new beginnings back to Stendhal or Balzac (qq.v.) ; or we may find it full-grown in Flaubert (q.v.) : names matter little in such a context, for Realism is not a religion or a policy by which a man is ticketed and labelled ; it is a mode of approach to the problems which fate proposes to experience. Taine (q.v.), with his genius for generalization, hit on one mark of the realist in his comparison (*Hist. Engl. Lit.*, E.T., v, i) between Stendhal, Balzac and Dickens. The Fr. writers, he says, 'love art better than men ', and this preference is fatal to the realistic method. 'They do not write from sympathy with suffering, but from love of beauty ' ; and the *amour du beau*, which idealizes the spectacle, tends to falsify the real, and to adulterate the substance. For the beauty of the real is in its truth, not in its make-up ; it is the simple, limpid beauty of actuality, such as is rendered so frequently in the Biblical narrative (of *Ruth*, for example), unaffected by schools of style or artifices of the muses. In the clear vision of a recent Fr. critic, the palm of Realism in fiction is divided between 'G. Eliot (q.v.) in Engld. and the modern novelists of Russia. Turgenev, Tolstoy and George Eliot, he declares, will be the chosen novelists of 100 years hence ; and ' the English and Russians have succeeded, where we have failed ', he adds, ' because they apply in its entirety the principle of creation : they took man from the dust, but they inspired him with the breath of life, and they formed " living souls " ' (Voguë, *Roman Russe*, xlvii). It is a generous award by a critic who springs himself from the nation which holds the primacy in creative art. And if this tribute to Engl. Realism be accepted by the countrymen of Richardson and Jane Austen, of Emily Brontë, George Eliot and Dickens, not to mention more recent writers, let us remember the conclusion of the whole matter. Realism and mysticism (q.v.) join hands in modern Russ. fiction, because the real, faithfully sought, always leads to mystery. Again and again this truth confronts us from the pages of realistic writers. Ptolemy, the astronomer of the 2nd cent., A.D., tells us, ' Mortal though I be, yea ephemeral, if for a moment I gaze up to the night's starry domain of heaven, then no longer on earth I stand ; I touch the Creator '. Pascal says in the 17th cent. : ' Le silence éternal de ces espaces infinis m'effraie ' ; yet he but takes us back to the realistic utterance of Marcus Aurelius, the emperor-philosopher of the 2nd cent., A.D. : ' I am at one with everything, O Universe, which is well-fitting in thee. O Nature, from thee are all things, in thee are all things, to thee all things return. The poet saith, Dear City of Cecrops ; shall I not say, Dear City of God '. For truly, Nature being universal, no naturalistic or realistic scheme of any reader or interpreter can operate otherwise than by selection ; and the most convinced of the realists is an idealist in his own despite. So that the highest realism, like so much else that is highest in the art of letters, is, after all, Shakespeare's ; and when we render it in the words of S. T. Coleridge (q.v.), it will be found to refute many pretentious claimants to realistic art : 'Keeping at all times in the high road of life, Shakespeare has no innocent adulteries, no interesting incests, no virtuous vice :—he never renders that amiable which

religion and reason alike teach us to detest, or clothes impurity in the garb of virtue '. (' Oh ! I know well ', says the author of *le Roman Russe*, who bade us, as we saw, seek true realism in Engl. and Russ. fiction, and his interjection is appropriate at this place, ' I know well that in assigning a moral purpose to the art of writing, I shall cause a smile in the devotees of the doctrine now in honour of *l'Art pour l'Art* [q.v.]. I confess that I do not understand that doctrine, at least in the sense in which it is used to-day. Certainly, morality and beauty are synonymous in art. . . . Happily, the very people who support the heresy are themselves the first to betray it, when they possess the heart and the talent.') And now, to continue Coleridge on Shakespeare, who plainly had heart and talent, courage and genius enough : ' He does not use the faulty thing for a faulty purpose, nor carries on warfare against virtue, by causing wickedness to appear as no wickedness, through the medium of a morbid sympathy with the unfortunate. In Shakespeare vice never walks as in twilight : nothing is purposely out of its place ; he inverts not the order of nature and propriety,—does not make every magistrate a drunkard or glutton, nor every poor man meek, humane, and temperate ; he has no benevolent butchers, nor any sentimental rat-catchers '. Let demi-realists beware ; for selection, even of nastiness, is a process of idealization.

Rebhun, Paul (*c.* 1500-46) : Germ. playwright ; of the generation of the Lat. dramatists, but successful beyond his contemporaries in overcoming the difficulties of subjects and technique in adapting Biblical plays to Saxon burghers' taste. Wr. *Susanna*, 1535, *The Marriage at Cana*, 1538.

Rebolledo, de, Bernardino (1597-1676) : Span. poet ; count by rank ; served as ambassador to Denmark and in other high offices of state ; was received by queen Christina (q.v.) of Sweden, and played a part in the change of thought which caused her abdication. R. publd. several vols. of verse at Cologne, 1660 ; Copenhagen, 1655, etc. ; of some interest and value, though marred in places by the *estilo culto* of Gongora (q.v.).

Rederijkers : Dutch school of formal poetry, which started at the end of the 14th cent. and continued right down to the 17th. These practitioners of the art of rhetoric (didactic and moral poetry) were banded together in ' kamers ', or chambers, of *rhetorica*, in accordance with the guild-instinct which flourished so well in the towns of Flanders, Holland, and Brabant. The dominant style of the ' rederijkers-kamers ' was determined mainly by the influence of the writings of Maerlant (q.v.) ; and there was a distinct affinity between these medieval Dutch literary brotherhoods and the Fr. courts-of-love. They combined convivial with professorial functions, and were largely reinforced by members connected with the church-choirs. Though the forces of the Renaissance (see s.v. Latin) and Reformation interrupted the tradition, there were as many as 250 such chambers in the first half of the 16th cent. Some of those in South Netherlands were the oldest, and their social influence was more considerable, but the most famous of any was in the North, and was known as the Eglantine (q.v.) at Amsterdam, where it was also called the old, or ' Oude Kamer '. A central chamber was founded, 1503, at Ghent, and the poetic and dramatic activity of the guilds was a powerful feature in the history of Dutch letters. On the social side, the chambers instituted processions, prize-givings, and other attractive functions ; and, even despite the Renaissance influence, the ' Rederijkers ' remained ' Rederijkers ', and attempted rather to force the newly revived classics into their forms than to assimilate those forms to the new spirit breathed through art.

Redi, Francesco (1626-98): It. Bacchic poet, Hellenist ; physician to the grand-dukes of Florence, and, unexpectedly, the author of a fine specimen of dithyrambic verse, *Bacchus in Tuscany*, 1685. (The equal devotion to scholarship and wine may be seen again, *longo intervallo*, in the bibliography of prof. G. Saintsbury). R. took up the metrical reforms of Chiabrera (q.v.), and easily passed his master on this occasion : Bacchus sings the praises of the different vintages of Tuscany ' with a *verve*, a *brio*, and a variety of rhythm, which ingeniously express the growing intoxication of the deity ' (Hauvette, *Lit., Ital.*, 305). ' Dryden evidently had it in mind ', says R. Garnett (*Ital. Lit.*, 281), ' when he wrote *Alexander's Feast*, and the difficulties of translation have been surprisingly overcome by Leigh Hunt ' (see s.vv.). R. followed up this ode with a learned work on philology. It is a pity that no specimen of the *Bacco in Toscana* were included in Mr. W. G. Hutchison's *Songs of the Vine* (A. H. Bullen, 1904).

Reeve, Clara (1729-1807): Engl. novelist ; wr. *The Old English Baron*, 1777, at first entitled *The Champion of Virtue, a Gothic Tale;* ' undeniably what *The Castle of Otranto* (see s.v. Walpole) professes to be, " an attempt to unite the merits and graces of the ancient Romance and of the modern Novel " ' (*C.H.E.L.*, x, 61). The appeal to terror, and, still more, the appeal to history, as channels for enlarging the province of fiction, both led to the triumphs of Scott (q.v.).

Reeve, Henry (1813-95): Engl. journalist ; editor ; wr. 2482 leading-articles in *The Times*, 1840-55 (a period long anterior to the reforms of visct. Northcliffe), and edited the *Edinburgh Review*, 1855-95. R. was the editor of the famous and interesting *Greville Memoirs : a Journal of the Reign of King George iv and King William iv*, 3 vols., 1874 ; *A Journal of the Reign of Queen Victoria, from* 1837 *to* 1852, 3 vols., 1885 ; *A Journal of the Same, from* 1852 *to* 1860, 2 vols., 1887, by Charles Cavendish Fulke Greville (q.v.).

Reformation (Hist.): Descriptive name of a branch of the Renaissance (q.v.), which, starting in Germany early in the 16th cent., spread rapidly through northern Europe, and matured in new forms of Christianity known as Lutherism (after Luther, q.v.), Protestantism, etc. The progress of the R. was resisted by the ruling Church and its secular chiefs, and was accompanied by devastating wars of religion, which merged into dynastic and territorial wars, the last of which is now known as the Great War, 1914-18.

We may neglect in this survey, which looks primarily at the R. in its literary aspect, the earlier reformers before the R., who are the theme of a learned work by K. Ullmann (1796-1865 ; transld. by rev. R. Menzies), and whose ranks included Wiclif (q.v.), the Englishman (died 1384), and Hus (q.v.), the Bohemian (burned, 1416). For the purposes of lit. in Europe, the R. took its rise out of the critical spirit manifested as Humanism (q.v.) in Italy. Northern students who had visited Ital. cities in order to acquire Hellenistic learning from the Gk. scholar-exiles out of Constantinople, returned to Germany across the Alps with the new wine mounting to their heads. The harder and more positive temperament of the North, and its greater concentration on practical results, led these home-coming missionaries of culture to apply the new critical method to social and ecclesiastical accepted tenets, and esp., in the first instance, to the Hebr. and Gk. texts of the Bible (q.v., and see s.v. Valla). The method which was legitimate in connection with Gk. and Rom. classics, and which led to so much new light on old authors, should be not less legitimate, and might lead to not less illumination, if extended to the sacred texts, preserved in the Vulgate and by the Church. Thus, the R., as a literary movement, or as a branch of the literary Renaissance, began in Biblical criticism and Biblical transln. Its real beginning was Reuchlin's (q.v.) Hebr. grammar, 1506, without which Luther's Germ. version of the Old Testament could not have been effected ; and it belongs to a history of religion, not of lit., to recall the obscurantism, the suspicion, the opposition, and the persecution, with which the guardians of the ' mysteries ', which Erasmus (q.v.) sought to open, defended their assailed authority. ' The Reformation ', says a lucid and learned writer (Figgis, *Divine Right of Kings*, pp. 259-60), ' is the assertion of the claims of the human spirit to carry on independent work in all branches of inquiry and activity, under the consciousness that truth cannot contradict itself, and that the results of every sort of labour carried on with appropriate means and for worthy objects will tend to unity at the last '.

Thus, the R. is seen, in the perspective of history, as a part of the long and arduous movement, much vexed by false aims, wrong means, side-issues, and blind alleys, deeply dyed with martyrs' blood, and stained with the record of many cruelties, as well as of splendid heroism, by which men emerged from the Middle Ages. They took 3 roads to modern thought : the early Ital. road of Humanism, of which Petrarch (q.v.) was the pioneer ; the Port. road of exploration, of which Camoens (q.v.) was the poet and Vasco da Gama the leader ; and this Germ. (or North) road of dissent, associated with the names of Luther and Zwingli. None of the roads is fully explored : learning, discovery and dissent have still secrets to unfold, and will still claim sacrifices in their service. But the Germ. R., despite its sequel, chiefly disastrous to Germany herself (see s.v. Germ.

lit.), marked a big and a notable advance on that road where scholars, protestants and voyagers have all learned the truth of such sayings as More (q.v.) placed in the mouth of the companion of Amerigo Vespucci, who gave his name to America : ' He that hath no grave is covered by the sky ' ; ' the way to Heaven out of all places is of like length and distance '. ' The German Renaissance is the Reformation ' (*C.M.H.*, i, 575) ; and it is under this aspect that it has its place in the history of European letters. It may be dated, if revolutions have a date, for each start is the close of old beginnings, and Dante's (q.v.) *De Monarchia* was a kind of document of reform, from 18 April, 1521, when Luther, at the Diet of Worms, met the majesty of Rome incarnate in the person of the emperor Charles v (q.v.). It was caused, so far as it had an immediate cause, by Luther's quarrel with Tetzel, the Dominican, who was touring Saxony in 1517 with a Bull for the sale of Indulgences. So clashing with authority from the start, the R. did not end as it had begun, in the modest aim of humanistic scholars to apply lay learning to sacred texts. Not even the genial influence of Erasmus (q.v.), which was abroad in Europe at that date, softening the furrows for the ploughshare and breaking the green upon the trees, availed to save Luther from Lutheranism, or religious reform from the politics into which it unfolded. ' Theology ', says Figgis (*loc. cit.*), ' had attempted unreasonably to dominate politics, and had committed men to an unphilosophical basis and an uncritical method. The only way to escape from the fetters imposed by traditional methods was to assert from the old standpoint of a Scriptural basis and to argue by the accustomed fashion of Biblical quotations that politics must be freed from theology, and that the Church must give up all attempts to control the State '. So, the reformer quoted Scripture for his own purposes ; and thus the R. produced a lit. of politics as well as of religion, and political wars arising out of religious wars. But this, at least, we may say : the gain was greater than the loss. The light of the lt. was indispensable to Europe's full awakening from the long night of the Middle Ages. We need but mention the names, chosen almost at random, of Rabelais, Montaigne, Calvin (see s.vv.) and the Hugenots as a class, to prove that Europe, north and west, would have sunk into Italy's long decline if the revival of learning at the univs. (see, e.g., s.v. *Epistolæ Obscurorum Virorum*) had not led to religious reform, and the reconstruction of the foundations of belief, with the men of learning enlightening the men of letters, down to Darwin (q.v.) in the morning of our own age. Politics, released from theology, may have invented, in the doctrine of the Divine right of kings, a worse evil than it exorcised, but this evil, too, has been overcome. Never again can Europe slip back into the ring-fenced, sheltered days before Reuchlin and his fellow-students began to learn Hebr. and Gk. Without the R. and the vernacular Bibles, which owed their origin to its inspiration, the Old World and the New alike would be irrecognizably deformed. Mind would lack the purest of its images, speech the brightest of its idioms, and the courageous spirit of man its noblest incentive to persevere. And, confining ourselves to lit., which, after all, is but one expression of experience, we may dispute the dictum of Warton (q.v.), in his *History of Engl. Poetry*, 1778, that ' ignorance and superstition, so opposed to the real interests of human society, are the parents of imagination ', and may concur respectfully with the dictum of a later prof. of Poetry at Oxford, M. Arnold (q.v.), when he says (*Essays in Criticism* : ' Pagan and Medieval Religious Sentiment ') : ' The poetry of later Paganism lived by the senses and understanding ; the poetry of medieval Christianity lived by the heart and imagination. But the main elements of the modern spirit's life is neither the senses and understanding nor the heart and imagination, it is the imaginative reason '.

Regnard, Jean François (1655-1709) ; Fr. comic dramatist. Travelled extensively in Italy, Poland, etc., and was captured in Algeria and ransomed from slavery. Wr. for Molière's (q.v.) company and afterwards for the Comédie Française : *le Joueur*, 1696 ; *les Folies Amoureuses*, 1704 ; *les Ménechmes*, 1705 ; *le Légataire*, 1708, and others. It was all very light comedy, of the ' vaudeville ' kind, without deference to probability, or psychology. Boileau (q.v.), when asked if he did not think R.'s talent mediocre, replied : ' Il n'est pas mediocrement gai ', and an extravagant gaiety is, perhaps, the best merit and worst fault of this would-be successor to Molière.

Regnier, Mathurin (1573-1613) : Fr. satirist ; nephew to Desportes (q.v.), through whom he obtained ecclesiastical preferment, though his tastes were always dominantly bohemian, and his early death is said to have been caused by excesses. R. was more fortunate in his literary destiny than in his mortal life ; De Musset (q.v.) has acclaimed him as ' immortal Molière's immortal forerunner ', and, though a follower of Ronsard (q.v.) and of the light of the Pleiad (q.v.), R. escaped the condemnation of Malherbe (q.v.) and conciliated the praise of Boileau (q.v.), who thus kept him afloat in the 18th cent. Having weathered these contrary winds of outblown critical controversy, R.'s fame as a satirist of manners has grown steadily in appreciation. His style was cultivated and vigorous ; his observation keen and shrewd ; and his outlook bold and elevated. His 16 satires are written in Alexandrines (q.v.), and reach a very high level in a kind which has since declined (see s.v. Satire).

Reid, Thomas (1710-96) : Scot. philosopher ; leader of the so-called Scot. school, which was opposed to Hume (q.v.), and appealed to common sense against the results of analytical philosophy. Wr., 1764, *Inquiry into the Human Mind on the Principles of Common Sense*.

Reinhold, Karl Leonhard (1756-1823) : Germ. (Austrian) popular philosopher. Born in Vienna ; converted in Weimar to the Protestant faith ; m. a daughter of Wieland (q.v.) ; was successively prof. of philosophy at Jena, 1787, and Kiel, 1794, where he died ; was succeeded at Jena by Fichte (q.v.). R.'s pupils included Novalis (q.v.) and others, whom he infused with his own enthusiasm for the teachings of the sage of Königsberg (q.v.), and his *Letters on Kantian Philosophy* and other works, together with his letters to and from the greater men of his day, give R. a considerable standing in the formation of the thought of the age.

Reinmar von Hagenau (*c.* 1160-1210): Germ. Minnesinger (q.v.); taught his art to Walther (q.v.) von der Vogelweide, and has been eulogized, from Walther to Uhland (q.v.), who called him ' the doctor of unhappy love ', by those best able to appreciate the charm of courtly lyric.

Renaissance (Hist.): Descriptive name of the period of Europe's transition from medieval to modern thought, especially regarded from the aspects of art, architecture, literature, education, philosophy, etc. Summarily, the R. (which means re-birth) started in Italy (Florence, q.v.) in the 14th cent., and passed through France (Paris, q.v.) into Spain, Holland and Engld., gathering force from religious interests on the northern side of the Alps. The R. took its rise in a study of the ancient classics, in that Humanism (q.v.), or revival of learning, which was ' born in Italy of a new feeling for the past greatness of Rome. The pagan view was now once more proclaimed, that man was made, not only to suffer and toil, but to enjoy ' (*C.M.H.*, i, 532-33). ' Europe, after having lived in the shadow of Antiquity, lived in its sunshine once more ' (J. Huizinga, *Waning of the Middle Ages*, 308). Thus, difficult though it plainly must be to distil the R. into a paragraph*— Addington Symonds wr. 7 vols. on *The Renaissance in Italy*, and this was but the beginning of a movement, which overspread every country in Europe and found expression in many diverse manifestations,—it is yet possible to suggest in a sentence its essential and recognizable features. The name itself is of recent invention, and M. Arnold (q.v.) even more recently would have changed its spelling to Renascence (*Culture and Anarchy*): a change with little to recommend it. But behind the name, however written, lie the facts to which the name bears witness, and the 3 main symbols of those facts are a Lat. grammar, a sailing-ship, and an open Bible. It was the fearless employment of these tools by pioneers on the roads out of the Middle Ages which prised open the treasuries of the modern world. Petrarch (q.v.), ' the first modern man ', as Renan (q.v.) called him, first used a Lat. grammar in this way. He inaugurated the study of the classical writers as living masters and models of thought and style (see s.vv. Cicero, Lat., and other articles), and no praise can be too high for the service which he and Boccaccio (q.v.) rendered to the development of modern Europe. If they did not succeed in reading Homer (q.v.) in his original Gk., while they reclined in armchairs with their feet on the mantelshelf, at least they worked in the spirit of this ambition; the ' Greats' school at Oxford could teach

* ' It would not have been the process of world-wide significance which it is, if its elements could be so easily separated from one another.' Burckhardt, *The Renaissance*, 1878 ; 2 vols. E.T., i, 239.

them nothing except envy of the good fortune of modern undergraduates. And while the old world was explored, *duce* Petrarch, under the symbol of the Lat. grammar, the new world was explored by the sailing-ship under the leadership of Vasco da Gama, the Portuguese, to whom Camoens (q.v.) acted as laureate. The changes wrought by the R. on the fabric of medieval thought included the immense exhilaration brought by knowledge of new lands beyond the seas. Ports of debarkation became gateways instead of barriers ; and geography, astronomy, and other sciences were transformed by these agents of the R. as completely as trade and commerce throughout all their relationships and consequences. Lastly, Luther's (q.v.) Germ. Bible, which the early mystics (see s.v. Mysticism) had first sought to open, was the third instrument of the passage from the medieval to the modern world, and powerfully moulded the influence of such leaders of the R. as Reuchlin, Erasmus, More (qq.v.), and others. Under one or more than one of these symbols may be ranged all the men, women, and movements included in the literary R. of the 14th to the 16th cent. : Politian, Ariosto, Margaret, Ronsard, Rabelais, Spenser (qq.v.), and the rest. A catalogue of names is less instructive than this central idea of an escape from the bonds of ignorance and superstition along 3 roads of progress : the Ital. road of humanism, the Port. road of navigation, and the Germ. road of dissent. Each road had its full toll of martyrs ; but, though the work of the R. is not yet complete, they led at last to the edge of Dante's ' forest ' (*Inf.*, i) and to the recovery of the path which had been lost. Thus, ' it was not the revival of Antiquity alone, but its union with the genius of the Italian people ' (and, through Italy, we may add, with the genius of France, the Peninsula, Holland, Germany and Engld.), ' which, under the name of the Renaissance, achieved the conquest of the Western World ' (Burckhardt, *op. cit.*).

Renan, Ernest (1823-92): Fr. humanist, if a term commonly reserved for an earlier class of scholars who combined lit. with learning (s.v. Humanism) may be applied, where it is most appropriate, to the most bellelettristic of philosophers and the most philosophic of bellelettrists of the 19th cent. ; a Breton by birth, and filled with the glamour of his Celtic origin. Saintsbury (*P.E.L.*, xii, 186ff.), in a less than fully adequate account of R., admits the beauty of his style, but says that ' everything about him—his gifts and his graces, his failings and his faults alike—is feminine '. The epithet is not unjust ; perhaps it was reminiscent, even unconsciously, of M. Arnold's verdict on Celtic writers ; but its application is too wide. There is far more in R. than its depreciatory use suggests : force, vigour, imagination, and a keen appetite for truth ; and Saintsbury's contrast of R. with Nietzsche (q.v.), as the feminine and the masculine notes in social philosophy, though it hints at R.'s hate of mediocrity, at his faith in the future *intelligence supérieure*, and even at his partial responsibility, accordingly, for the perversion of the conception of perfectibility into the later Superman (q.v.) -creed, is corrected, in its ultimate implication, by the verdict of time itself. The fact is, that R.'s rare gifts of style make him suspect in the jealous compound of expert scientific writers ; he could not touch the most dryasdust topic without irradiating it with the beams of his gentle irony and leisurely love of beauty. He was filled with the spirit of Germ. philosophy (the Germany of Herder and Kant, qq.v.), and with the brilliance of Ital. skies ; he led a life of extraordinary industry, rounded by a kind of patriarchal fame. Apart from his professorial activity, and from his work on the *Journal des Débats* and the *Révue des deux Mondes*, R. wr. a large number of bks., the interest of which is situate in that borderland of history, religion and philosophy, which was so frequently explored in the 19th cent. M. Arnold (q.v.), who owed nearly as much to R. as to Ste-Beuve (q.v.), was an obvious pilgrim to that resort. R.'s chief science was philology, which he was the first in his generation to apply in a liberal spirit to the problems of thought ; and, like so many of his generation, he broke, on strictly ' scientific ' grounds, with formal Christianity, and compelled that choice between determinism and revelation, which exercised so powerful an effect on the intellect of many contemporaries. With these matters of creed and doctrine we are not here concerned ; Comte (q.v.), as we know, went so far as to found a new religion ; and the era of Darwin and Huxley (qq.v.) was likely to prick the acquiescence of so diligent a philosopher as R. ' Faith,' we were reminded, in a centenary art. in the *Hibbert Journal* (July, 1923), ' was his favourite word ', and always ' in his own fashion he worshipped Jesus ', despite the flood of vituperation which greeted his fashion in his own generation. His first bk. was *The Future of Science : Thoughts of* 1848 ; next came *Averroes and Averroism* (see s.v. Averroes), 1852 ; next—the consecution is important, as illustrating R.'s conscientious scholarship,—*General History and Comparative System of Semitic Languages*, 1855 ; next, 2 vols. of religious and ethical studies ; then the famous *Origines du Christianisme*, which comprise : *Vie de Jésus*, 1863, in which he followed the lines set by Germ. hist. research, and applied to the same subject by D. F. Strauss (q.v.) nearly 30 years before ; *les Apôtres*, 1866 ; *St. Paul*, 1869 ; *l'Antéchrist* (Nero), 1873 ; *les Evangiles*, 1877 ; *l'Église chrétienne*, 1879 ; and *Marc Aurèle*, 1881, which has been described as the crown of his hist. writings. Another great work followed, 1888-94, in his *Histoire du Peuple d'Israel* ; and, apart from vols. of essays, chiefly republd. from the reviews, R. found time for a remarkable series of *Drames philosophiques*, 1878-86, of *Souvenirs d'Enfance et de Jeunesse*, 1883, etc. R.'s letters were posth. publd. ; and, though the conclusions of science have moved away from R. to some extent, and though the reign of specialists has succeeded to the reign of generalizers, R.'s writings, however typical his age, are not therefore less estimable and valuable. As a fellow-countryman writes in the hospitable pages of the *C.M.H.* (xi. 527) : ' In Renan there were two personalities, representing the dual tendencies of the time—

a delicate and exquisite artist, a weighty historian and man of learning. For France he will ever stand as the founder of religious history. It was he who first brought the method of comparative philology to the study of History. As a writer he is especially remarkable for a simplicity, a subtlety, a harmony, which do not exclude the gifts of a painter or of a colourist; and, because of his very delicacy, he has influenced only a few choice spirits ' (prof. R. Bourgeois). We may cite, too, an Englishman's tribute, that of the rt. hon. H. A. L. Fisher, of Oxford, recalling in this connection that R. was once Hibbert lecturer under a foundation of that univ. : ' In an historical age Renan was a prince among historians. What serious writer in the nineteenth century, Darwin excepted, has put into general circulation so vast a body of important knowledge or so many original and formative ideas ? What historian has been at once so sure a master of the most delicate critical implements and yet so rich in the imaginative gifts which recreate the distant past '.

R. died in the Collège de France, of which he had been principal for some years, and which was the scene of his earlier theological struggles. In 1862, he had been appointed to the chair of Hebrew in the coll., but he was dismissed after his inaugural lecture, which was taken as a test case by the clerically minded governing body. He returned to it after 1870, and, though the Franco-Prussian war shook his faith almost to its foundations, he lived to recover the intellectual equipoise which his style so perfectly reflects.

Resende, de, Garcia (1470-1540) : Port. anthologist. Publd., 1516, a *Cancioneiro general* (see s.v. *cancionero*, the Span. equivalent of this song-book), containing specimens of more than 40 Port. poets who employed the Castilian tongue. This collection is one of many pieces of evidence which show the dominance of the conquering Castilian in the lit. of the whole peninsula.

Resende, de, Luis Andrea (1498-1573) : Port. humanist. Wr. Lat. grammar, 1540.

Restif de la Bretonne, Nicolas Edmé (1734-1806) : Fr. novelist and miscellanist. R. has been called the Fr. Defoe (q.v.) and the gutter-Rousseau (q.v. ; ' Rousseau du ruisseau '). Certainly, he owed the motives of his novels to Rousseau, and in his breadth of observation and a certain vagabondage of mind he had affinities with Defoe. But he was a vulgar and voluminous writer ; and nothing which he wr. is worth recalling by name, except, perhaps, his *Paysan perverti*, 1766, founded on Marivaux (q.v.), *le Paysan parvenu*, and supplying a model for Tieck (q.v.), *William Lovell*; and his *Monsieur Nicolas, ou le Coeur humain dévoilé*, 1796-97. There was too much ' unveiled ' humanitarianism in R., and his Rousseauan works remind us of Nietzsche's (q.v.) epigram about Rousseau, that his ' return to nature ' was a return to nature *in impuris naturalibus*.

Restoration Comedy (1660-1720) : Generic name for a class of Engl. drama, which flourished, as the dates indicate, for a period of about 60 years after the termination of the Commonwealth. ' The nearest approaches to Molière ' (q.v.), says prof. Saintsbury (*First Bk. of*

Engl. Lit., 142), briefly, ' were made by two gentlemen of the Court, sir George Etherege (1655 ?-1691, *Sir Fopling Flutter*) and William Wycherley (1640 ?-1716), especially the latter (*The Country Wife, The Plain Dealer*). They introduced a kind of comedy which, not very regular in plot and very irregular in morality, presented sharply if rather artificially drawn characters, more than abundantly provided with witty dialogue. Years later, chiefly in the reign of William iii, three other writers, William Congreve (1670-1729, the best of all), sir John Vanburgh (1664-1726), and George Farquhar (1678-1707), took this up and improved it into really brilliant stuff. But their neglect of decorum brought upon them, upon Dryden, and upon others, a violent attack by Jeremy Collier (1650-1726), a famous nonjuring clergyman, to which Dryden practically pleaded guilty, and against which 'Congreve and one or two more made very lame defences '. With the exception of Dryden (q.v.), the dramatists of the Restoration Comedy do not require separate consideration in this vol. Their indecorum is obvious, and, despite some external debts to Molière as well to as other Fr. and Span. playwrights, they are mainly of Engl. descent, with direct filiation to the Elizabethans, and have no real influence on or relation to European letters. In a special monograph on Restoration Comedy by Mr. Bonamy Dobrée (Oxford, 1924), we are asked, reasonably enough, to get away from this charge of indecorum : ' We must not confuse moral and æsthetic values. . . . It is admittedly tiresome, but it seems unavoidable, to have to approach this work through Collier and Swift, Johnson, Macaulay, and Taine, and excuse its "impurity". For " impurity " was its most important subject. How could it avoid dealing with sex when the distinguishing characteristic of Restoration Comedy down to Congreve is that it is concerned with the attempt to rationalize sexual relationships ? ' (Perhaps *The Second Mrs. Tanqueray* type of play in the 19th cent. may be cited as a modern analogue). We need not discuss this defence, save to note, with Mr. Dobrée, that this 'important question of sex-antagonism, revealing itself in a dislike for marriage, the defence of young women against ardent besiegers, and the desire of married women and widows to take their freedom and preserve their " honour " or " independence " ', was indigenous to the Engl. stage (e.g. in Richard Brome, d. *c.* 1652 ; servant and friend of Ben Jonson, q.v. ; wr., among other plays, *The Mad Couple*, with which Wycherley, Congreve, and perhaps Etherege were acquainted), and ' is almost completely absent from French comedy '. Thus, its expression in an intensive form in the Engl. Restoration Comedy is almost exclusively insular. Apart from the names mentioned above, other playwrights in the group included—sir Charles Sedley (1639 ?-1701), Thomas Shadwell (1642-92), and Mrs. Aphra Behn (q.v.). Dryden's chief play in this class, referred to by Saintsbury above was *Marriage à-la-Mode*, 1672. The finest plays in the school, which has been well said to lack spiritual nourishment, were Wycherley's *Country Wife*, 1675, and Congreve's

Way of the World, 1700, revived in London, 1924. (The reference to Taine, above, is *Hist. Engl. Lit.*, E.T., Bk. iii, ch. 1).

Retroencha (Provençal) ; **Rotrouenge** (Fr.) : Descriptive name of a class of medieval Fr. songs with refrain ; Richard Coeur de Lion sung such a R. to his followers out of his Germ. prison.

Retz, cardinal de ; **Paul de Gondi** (1613-79) : Fr. memoirist ; nephew, coadjutor, 1643, and successor, 1653, to the archbp. of Paris ; card. of Retz, 1651. A born conspirator, de R. was early implicated in the anti-ministerial Fronde (i.e., anti-Richelieu and -Mazarin, successively), and took a leading part in its machinations, and shared in its failure. He was imprisoned, 1652, but contrived to return to Paris, and to some extent to power, 10 years later, and was sent to conclaves at Rome for 3 papal elections. R.'s debts accumulated in his years of adverse fortune, and he provides an honourable example of the rare class of conscientious debtors in high places, among whom Scott (q.v.) is conspicuous. R. wr., 1630, an hist. sketch, the *Conjuration* (Conspiracy) *de Fiesque*, which displayed considerable talent ; but his fame rests on his *Mémoires*, written, 1671, first publd., 1717, but dealing with the years anterior to 1660, the dividing-line of Fr. lit. in the 17th cent. The literary interest of these memoirs lies in their revelation of the struggle of a hero out of Corneille (q.v.), almost of Marlowe (q.v.), in real life. Through all the vicissitudes of his career, as a politician drafted into the church, in order to keep the archbishopric in his family, as an archbp. in prison and in exile, as a fighter against desperate odds for position, power, prestige, de R. contrived to preserve his self-respect, to turn an unperturbed countenance to a world of opponents, creditors, and detractors, and to display on the stage of his *Mémoires* the indomitable ' Moi ' of the Cornelian drama. The other personages fall into their places in his memoirs ; and without travesty or caricature, de R. represented the great men of his day—the princes, the cardinals, the leaders of the Fronde—in their habit as they were, or, at least, as they were to him ; and his work ranks as one of the most important in an age which was rich in the kind.

Reuchlin, Johann (1455-1522) : Germ. humanist and Orientalist. Studied Gk. at Paris, and afterwards at Rome, under Argyropoulos (q.v.), who, according to tradition, was so much struck by his pupil's knowledge of Thucydides that he exclaimed, ' Ecce, Græcia nostro exsilio transvolavit Alpes ' (lo, Greece by our exile hath flown across the Alps). The exclamation, whether genuine or not, carries more than its literal meaning. These early missionaries of culture, More, R., and others, who were sowing the Renaissance beyond the Alps, wore their learning with difference. In Italy, to state it quite neutrally, there had been a *modus vivendi* between Humanism and the Church. The new learning had seldom been aggressive ; the pope, even when reactionary, had seldom been actively hostile. Valla (q.v.), in conflict with pope Eugenius iv, had made terms with Nicholas v (q.v.) ; Pico della Mirandola (q.v.), exiled by Innocent viii, was restored by Alexander vi ; Savonarola (q.v.), the one great Ital. reformer, attacked the manifestations of impiety rather than the causes why the pious life had failed. Despite the spread of scepticism and irreligion, there had been little open warfare against dogma. Even the Christian humanists, such as Ficino (q.v.) and Mirandola, were philosophers rather than reformers. But Humanism outside Italy seemed to change character with climate. ' Greece ', in the exile-scholar's meaning, came in contact with the Northern temperament, more positive, less sensuous and æsthetic ; applying men's recovered self-dependence to matters of conscience and belief ; employing Gk. criticism and reasoning as well as Gk. art and love of beauty ; editing texts, founding schools, sifting opinions ; always proving something, building something, even destroying something. There had been positive thinkers in Italy, e.g. Machiavelli, Guicciardini, Pomponazzi (qq.v.), but their thought fell on more barren soil ; it missed the responsive air in which Budé flourished in Paris, Erasmus in London and N. Europe, and Luther in Saxony. Thus R., home from Italy, employed his humanism to quicken the forces which were soon to take shape as the Reformation. There were liberal thinkers in high places: Maximilian, the Roman emperor ; elector Frederic of Saxony ; elector Joachim of Brandenburg ; Albert, archbp. of Mayence ; there were liberal univ. centres, such as Erfurt and Heidelberg ; and all these patrons and homes of the new learning were opposed to the scholastic philosophy and the rest of the buttresses of Roman theological orthodoxy, as represented particularly by the stronghold of the Dominicans at Cologne. R. was drawn into the vortex. During his sojourn in Italy he had come under the spell of Pico della Mirandola's forward-straining vision. The imagined house of revelation, in which the separate mansions of Christian, Cabbalistic and Pagan (Platonic) lore should be united in one system of knowledge, appealed to R., the Christian mystic. He set himself the practical task of learning Hebrew from a Jew (1492), thus taking with Germ. thoroughness the first necessary steps towards the triple reconciliation of theosophy, philosophy, and doctrine. ' The language of the Hebrews ', he wr. (1494, in *De Verbo Mirifico*, quoted by Graetz, *History of the Jews*, E.T., iv., 463), ' is simple, uncorrupted, holy, terse, and vigorous. God confers in it direct with men, and men with angels, without interpreters, face to face, as one friend converses with another '. His *Rudimenta Hebraica* appeared in 1506, and was driven like a pier into the sands of fanciful, fashionable mysticism. The Old Testament was to be read in its own language, and the tests of criticism applied to the consecrated canon of authority. Germ. scholarship, naturally inclined to approach Humanism through religion, was thus armed with a powerful weapon of doctrinal attack and reform. Luther was still to translate the Bible (1522-24) ; but ' the event which took the Old Testament out of the hand of phantasy and turned it into an instrument of reform ' (*C.M.H.*, ii, 696) necessarily preceded the translation. This event was the Prometheus-gift of R., his live coal from Mirandola's altar. The spark was to spread conflagration. R.'s emergence as a Hebraist, and his accessibility to the Jews, aroused the resentment of a Jew. pervert, Johann Pfefferkorn, who regretted his apostasy, perhaps, now that Hebrew promised to be lucrative. In 1509 he got the ear of Maximilian, and sought an imperial decree for the suppression of all Hebrew bks. except only the Old Testament. R. defended the Jews from this threatened attack on their lit., which was at the same time an attack, as the humanists quickly recognized, on the liberty of the new learning. A brisk polemic ensued, enlivened by the brilliant squib of the *Epistolæ Obscurorum Virorum* (q.v.), let off in 1516-17 by the young ' poets ' of Erfurt univ. R. was haled by Hochstraten, the inquisitor, dean of the Dominicans at Cologne, before the ecclesiastical court at Mayence, which acquitted him (1514 ; confirmed at Rome, 1516). The acquittal was reversed (1520), when R. was mulcted in costs, but the conviction weighed lightly on the last years of a man inured to scholars' poverty, and inspired throughout his life by a devotion to learning for its own sake. R.'s victory over the obscurantists in the dawn of the Germ. Reformation is a prominent landmark in the history of learning and lit. in Europe. R. was prof. of Gk. and Hebr. at Tübingen, 1521.

Reuter, Christian (17th cent.): Germ. satiric novelist. Wr., 1696, *Schelmuffsky*, ' a veritable, curious, and very dangerous account of adventures by land and sea ' ; to some extent a reaction from the exaggerated cult of the romance of gallantry and adventure called forth by the success of Grimmelshausen's (q.v.) *Simplicissimus*.

Reuter, Fritz (1810-74): Germ. dialect-novelist, a founder of the ' Plattdeutsch ' (cf. Kailyard) school, which depended partly for its effects on the realism of the language spoken by the provincial or rustic characters. Auerbach (q.v.) had started the vogue with his tales from the Black Forest, and R. enlarged on his master's lead, and added a touch of the humour of Dickens to his character-types. Mecklenburg was the scene of his *Ut mine Stromtid*, 1862-64 ; and more recent students of the ' Plattdeutsch ' school will recall the Silesian plays of Gerhart Hauptmann, which took Berlin and other capitals by storm at the end of last century. (See *Quarterly Review*, no. 382, April, 1900).

Reyna, de, Cassiodoro (16th cent.): Span. Biblical scholar ; Protestant. Associated with Valera (q.v.) in the Amsterdam transln. of the Bible, 1602.

Reynard (see also s.vv. Bestiary and Fable): Fox-hero of the popular (*bourgeois*) tales and fables, collected in medieval France into the romantic beast-epic, known as the *Roman de Renart*, and extending to considerably more than 100,000 lines in all its branches. The fabric was derived from ancient sources ; the beast-man is older than Æsop ; its modern birthplace is obscure, and may be sought in the debateable Rhineland between what are now Germany and France. In the Teutonic dialect there are fragments of a *Reinhart Fuchs* (originally, *Isengrims Nôt*, or the fate of Isengrim), dating from *c.* 1170 ; and a little later, *c.* 1180, it had become a kind of *Volksepos* in Germany. Pursuing its adventures in that country, we may note that the primitive version, ascribed with some plausibility to an Alsatian, Heinrich the Pseudonymous (*der Glichesäre*), was followed, *c.* 1250, by a version based on the Fr., and compiled by a Fleming, named Willem. A 14th-cent. redaction, effected by Heinrich von Alkmar, and known as *Reinke de Vos*, became classic in a definitive poem, printed at Lübeck in 1498. (The equivalent classical Engl. rendering had been printed by Caxton in 1481; republd. by Routledge, 1924). The fable maintained its vogue down to the 19th cent., and enlisted as distinguished an exponent as Goethe (q.v., *Reineke Fuchs,* 1794,) while the name of Simrock (q.v.), its later Germ. modernizer, should not be forgotten. But, whatever credit of priority attaches to the versions in Lat., Germ. or Flemish, the true home of the romance is France. The names of the animals are Fr.; there are indications pointing to Picardy as the original source of the oldest rendering; and there is the Fr. *esprit gaulois*—the native spice of malicious wit—to fasten the authorship on the *bourgeoisie,* or middle-classes, of France. The *roman* is composed of several parts: the first, known as *Ancien Renart,* was the work of a certain Pierre of St. Cloud, and was written in Fr. octosyllabic verses *c.* 1200; another, *Renart le Couronné,* dates from the middle of the 13th cent.; a third, *Renart le Nouvel,* was completed by Jacquemart Giélée in 1288, and a *Renart le Contrefait* was added early in the next century. The *Ysopet* of Marie de France (q.v.) is a kind of link between the epic and the fable (q.v.), and Chaucer's *Nun's Priest's Tale* makes us regret that the greatest Engl. fabulist did not apply his genius to the whole of the animal-epopee, of which the editors have counted as many as 27 branches. What is the secret of its popularity? Some clues to this problem are suggested in the art. on Bestiary and Fable (qq.v.). Here we further point out that the basis of the *roman* is as simple as its popularity proved to be extensive. The fox is haled to judgment for his many social crimes and depredations, but deludes the court by his cunning, and outwits his accusers by playing upon their vanity, cupidity, and other weaknesses. The human analogy is obvious, and the fable lent itself to endless moralizing, in a society where monarchy, represented by Noble (the lion), was declining, and the victims of feudalism might fail again and again to carry to the king's ear the true story of their wrongs. Reynard (Reinhardt, 'strong in counsel ') became a synonym of fox, and Chanticleer, Bruin, and other beasts, were hardly less well known. Bitterness was added to satiric humour, especially in the attacks on the clergy, and the comparative simplicity of *Ancien Renart* was soon abandoned by the later romantic-epicists in N. France. The moral became greater than the tale; the sophisticated Reynard of later versions reconciled the disputes of theologians; made a pilgrimage to Palestine; became a monk, and confessor to the king; related the story of Alexander; and, in a word, was

expanded into a kind of cyclopedia of popular thought in the Middle Ages. It should be noted that the outspoken satire and clear anti-clerical bias of the *Roman de Renart,* so characteristic of Fr. popular poetry (as distinct from court-lyric and romance) in the 13th and 14th cents., was reformatory as well as rebellious : ' the spirit of the age is changing from the medieval to the modern. . . Never before have we had so many poets to satirize the stains upon the garments of humanity, which does not necessarily prove that the stains are deeper, but certainly suggests that the poets are more moral' (E. Dale, *National Life and Character in the Mirror of Early English Literature,* 278); and, as to the out-spokenness in general, while there was acute dissatisfaction, as the life of Arnold of Brescia reminds us, and as the crusade against the Albigenses proves, at the discharge of their duties by the clergy, it should be remembered that frank criticism was the very life of early Fr. lit. on its popular side. Even the Lat. so-called ' Goliardic ' poetry (after a tradi-tional Golias or Goliardi) of the 11th and 12th cents., with its quaint mixture of Christian theology and heathen deities, and its un-blushing Bacchus-worship, was satirical in the same social sense as these poems of the Rey-nard-cycle, ' which contemplate the fabric of medieval thought from a Goliardic stand-point ' (Owen, *Skeptics of the Ital. Renaissance,* 44; he adds that ' Rabelais may, in tone and method, claim to be the last of the Goliards ', nor should Voltaire's Gallic spirit be forgotten). Thus, Ste-Beuve calls the *Roman de Renart* ' the satirical masterpiece of the thirteenth century. It echoes the rancour of the small against the great, and expresses the political or religious audacity of statesmen, *jongleurs,* monks, scholars. It is also animated with that imperious spirit against women which is so strongly and so repugnantly emphasized in many of the *fabliaux* '. As such, it ranks as the chief expression of the voice of the middle-classes in N. France, rising to take their place in the 13th cent. as the equals in literary rank of the feudal aristocracy, endowed with the romantic inventions of their own *trouvères* (see s.v. Fr. Lit.).

Reynolds, Joshua (1723-92): Engl. painter; critic; first president of Royal Academy, 1768; knt., 1769; enters lit. hist. as friend of Johnson (q.v.), for whose sake he is said to have founded the Literary Club, 1794. Delivered, 1769-90, 15 *Discourses on Art* to the students of the R.A., which were printed by order of its members. G. Clausen, R.A., prof. of Painting, said of them, 1904: ' There is no book that an artist can read so illuminating and helpful as the *Discourses* '; prof. Walker (*Lit. Victorian Era,* 983) writes : ' None but an extravagant panegyrist could pretend that the literature of that time would be seriously impoverisbed if they were lost '.

Rhenanus, Beatus (1485-1547): Germ. humanist. Issued *ed. pr.* of Velleius, 1520, and other classical texts, including Curtius, with notes by Erasmus, whose biographer he became. Was a member of the Basel (q.v.) group of scholars.

Rhétoriqueurs: Fr. school of formal poetry, which flourished in the 15th cent., and over-lapped into the Renaissance (q.v.). Its beginnings may be dated back to Machault (q.v.), who, as an ingenious manipulator of complicated schemes of rhyme and metre, has been designated the founder of rhetoric, as a synonym of poetry. However that may be, there were at least 4 considerable works on the Art of Rhetoric (*ars poetica*, new style) at the turn of the 15th and 16th cents.; and practitioners of the art infested the courts of kings Charles viii and Louis xii, and sprang up in every provincial duchy. The name, which criticism had supplied from its confusion of poetry with rhetoric, was derived immediately from a chance reference in a satire of Coquillart (q.v.) to his contemporaries, the 'grands rhétoriqueurs'. They were by no means all 'grands'; many little ones made their rhetoric more complicated; but the term is a fair description of the style which they affected. An admirable general impression of the manner of the school is given by the modern Fr. critic, Jusserand (*Ronsard*, Hachette, 31): 'Rhétorique: art de bien dire. Pour eux, bien dire c'est dire autrement que le vulgaire; plus on sera ingénieux et compliqué, plus on sera loin de vulgaire et mieux on aura dit. Les sons et les mots avant tout, la pensée ensuite; leur art de bien dire devient ainsi, la plupart du temps, un art de ne rien dire': and he points out that this elegant art of saying nothing in the most complicated measures was a matter of tormented rhyme-systems, of recurring irregularities of alliteration, of verbal *tours de force* so ingenious that a poem might be construed in twenty ways of various sounds and sights to ear and eye, without carrying any meaning to the brain. Another Fr. critic (Lanson, *Hist. Lit. Fr.*, 186) adds that, 'the least insupportable are those with least genius; their platitude condemns them to be intelligible, or nearly so'. This garden of artificial blossoms was the last, bad phase of the medieval garden of the rose (see s.v. Romance of the Rose); it was full time for the Pleiad and Rabelais (qq.v.) to breathe new life into this decay, and to supple the resources of the Fr. vernacular. The principal leaders of the *rhétoriqueurs*, against whom C. Marot (q.v.) and the school of Lyons (q.v.) led the reaction, were Chastellain, Robertet, Molinet, and St. Gelais and Marot *seniores* (to be distinguished from their more famous sons), and, chiefly, Crétin, who gave his name to the vogue of Cretinism (see s.vv.). Their rhetoric was founded on *ex-post-*Aristotelian poetics tortured by Lat. interpreters; it comprised in its system an all-devouring Latinism of diction and an excess of allegory and allusiveness, conceived in the letter (though not the spirit) of the Romance of the Rose tradition. It was the swept dust of the dead letter of the Middle Ages.

Rhua (Rua), **Pedro** (16th cent.): Span. scholar; lecturer at the coll. of Soria; wr., 1540, letters to Guevara (q.v.), pointing out the hist. shortcomings in his 'Marcus Aurelius'. Guevara was not very grateful for the attention.

Ribadeneyra, de, Pedro (1527-1611): Span. theologian. Wr., 1595, a polemical treatise on 'the religion and virtues of a Christian prince.'

Ribeiro, Bernardim (*c.* 1482-1554): Port. pastoral romancer. Wr. a romance inspired by the *Arcadia* of Sannazarro (q.v.), which served in turn as a model for Montemayor (q.v.).

Ribera, de, Ruy Paez (fl. 1397-1424): Span. poet; native of Seville; disciple of Imperial (q.v.). R.'s personal experience of poverty and suffering found lyrical expression in poems which rise in places to the poignancy of Villon (q.v.).

Ricardo, David (1772-1823): Engl. economist. Wr., 1817, *Principles of Political Economy and Taxation*, which is recognized as a standard textbook. R., like Jas. Mill (q.v.), belonged to the generation between Adam Smith and J. S. Mill (qq.v.), and contributed as much to the latter as he owed to the former. His experience on the Stock Exchange gave him knowledge of business, and his experience in the House of Commons, 1819-23, added knowledge of men. It is worth noting that R. was the son of a Dutch Jew, and, having embraced Christianity, sat in Parliament, like B. Disraeli (q.v.), many years before the disabilities on Jews were removed, 1858.

Riccoboni, Marie Jeanne (1713-92): Fr. novelist; *née* Laboras de Mézières. Wr. *le Marquis de Cressy*, *My Lady Catesby*, and other sentimental novels, and 'an exceedingly clever' continuation of the *Marianne* of Marivaux (q.v.), to whose school of fiction mme. R. belonged by taste and practice.

Rice, James (1844-82): Engl. novelist. See s.v. **Besant.**

Rich, Penelope (*c.* 1562-1607): Engl. author's model, if a term analogous to artist's model may be invented to describe the career of the lady Penelope, daughter of first earl of Essex, who m. Robert, third baron Rich (later, earl of Warwick), 1581, and was divorced by him, 1605, when she m. eighth baron Mountjoy (first earl of Devonshire). For, during her first unhappy marriage, she was the lover and beloved of sir Philip Sidney (q.v.), and she enters lit. by the fact that she became the 'Stella' to his 'Astrophel', in that sonnet (q.v.)-sequence of the soldier-poet, which, however conventional and however much bound by Ital. and Fr. example, did reflect, in at least a few of its specimens, 'the heat of passion which the genuine intrigue developed' (see sir S. Lee, *William Shakespeare*, 708).

Richardson, Samuel (1689-1761): Engl. novelist; printer by trade; eldest of the delineators of middle-class sentiment in fiction, who, availing themselves of the realism of Defoe (q.v.), and interpreting contemporary signs of social evolution, enucleated the modern novel (q.v.) of character and manners out of the tale of adventure and incident. Fielding, Smollett, Sterne, F. Burney (qq.v.), and the novelists of the 19th cent. were R.'s successors in Engld.; to some of his successors, imitators and adapters in other countries we refer below; here we note at the outset that R. supplied a real and a new want, probably merely by feeling it and by making the experiment of supply; he was over 50 years of age when he began novel-writing, and the late beginning seems to show that opportunity was the midwife of his genius. He swam slowly on a rising tide.

The middle-class, for and of whom R. wr., wanted reassurance as to their position; wanted their lives made interesting to them, and wanted to prove their moral value. The backbone of Engld., they came to be called by politicians seeking their suffrages in a later generation, and the epithet 'solid' was commonly applied to what may perhaps be termed their material-moral complex. In R.'s long-winded novels we mark the solidification and vertebration in process: he invests them with, and expresses, their bourgeois virtues; he sentimentalizes their ordinary happenings, and he shares their prejudices, even their snobbishness, as to the classes immediately above and below them. This, if we try to analyse it, is a part of the secret of the elderly printer's extraordinary success. As he went on writing the vols. of letters, in which his domestic stories were unfolded, he received genuine letters from scores of unknown correspondents, begging him to do this or not to do that in the further stages of the narrative. Thus, he wr. 'best-sellers', in the current phrase, which were publd. in serial form, and which their eager readers regarded as real and near. It is said that, when 'Clarissa' died, despite appeals from her doom, and after most ample preparation, 'England burst into a wail of lament, nor was it long before the contagion of sorrow spread to the Continent'. Chronologically, R.'s novels were: (1) *Pamela, or Virtue Rewarded. In a Series of Familiar Letters from a beautiful young Damsel to her Parents*, 2 vols., 1740; 4 vols., 1741-2; (2) *Clarissa: or the History of a young Lady, comprehending the most important concerns of private life, and particularly shewing the distresses that may attend the misconduct both of Parents and Children in relation to Marriage.* 7 vols., 1747-8 (Clarissa had to die, because Pamela made a happy end); (3) *The History of Sir Charles Grandison*, 7 vols. All 3 were in the epistolary style. The last was the good man as the complement to Clarissa, the good woman; and probably *Grandison* was a kind of reply to *Tom Jones* (1749, by Fielding, q.v.), as Fielding's *Joseph Andrews*, 1742, had been a kind of counterweight to *Pamela*.

It remains, briefly, to refer to the positive rage for R. on the Continent. He exactly touched Germany on her tenderest spot,— in that mood of mild sentiment and religiousness, with certain wilder impulses to revolt, which was met universally in the Fatherland. Gellert, Wieland, Klopstock (qq.v.), and their circles, were Richardsonians to a man, and the floods of tears which R. set flowing in Engld. were turned to torrents in the Germ. bks. In France, R. was fortunate in his translr., no other than the abbé Prevost (q.v.); Diderot (q.v.) wr. an *Eloge de Richardson*, 1761, and Rousseau's (q.v.) *Nouvelle Héloïse*, 1756-60, is recognizably Clarissa gallicized. There were Span., Dutch and Ital. translns. (Goldoni, q.v., adapted *Pamela* for the stage); and thus, directly or indirectly (for much of R. was absorbed in Rousseau), this typically Engl. writer of domestic-sentimental fiction, unwinding itself in a maze of letters, 'inspired men of larger scope, of greater genius, than his own'

(prof. Vaughan, British Academy Warton lecture, 1913). It was a very notable achievement.

Riche, Barnabe (*c.* 1540-*c.* 1620): Engl. storywriter; soldier; a busy and voluminous delver in the stores of Ital. and Span. romance, which he treated somewhat after the manner of Lyly (q.v.) in *Euphues*. A collection of R.'s tales is contained in his *Farewell to Militarie Profession, conteining verie pleasannt discourses fit for a peaceable tyme*, 1581. The second of these tales, *Apolonius and Silla* was based on Cinthio (q.v.), *Hecatommithi* (1565), part i, 15th day, *novella* 8, and told the story of a girl in male attire, which may have been utilized by Shakespeare (q.v.) for Julia, in *Two Gentlemen of Verona*. The same tale, or another version of it in Bandello (q.v.), *Novelle* (1554), ii, 36, supplied Shakespeare with material for *Twelfth Night*. R.'s industrious talents have little more actual significance to-day.

Richelieu, de, Alphonse Louis du Plessis (1585-1642): Fr. patron of letters; card. R.'s influence on the lit. of his age, which was nearly as much his age as that of king Louis xiv, and far more Corneille's than either, was very considerable. His advice, which was virtually a command, caused the French Academy (q.v.) to be reared on the less substantial foundation of the pleasant gatherings in Conrart's (q.v.) drawing-room. His jealousy of Corneille (q.v.) was partly (but more nominally than actually) responsible for the formal adoption in 1640 of the principle of the Unities (q.v.) in classic drama. Corneille's *Cid* (q.v.) was the *casus belli*, and, in the event, after Chapelain's (q.v.) pamphlet expressing the sentiments of the Academy, inspired, as is admitted, by R., Corneille discreetly capitulated, and dedicated his next play to R. The tastes which the card. displayed were derived in large measure from Marino (q.v., and see s.v. Precious), and fitted in with several tendencies of the age. That his patronage was always wise or welcome cannot justly be affirmed; but he used his power and opportunities with moderation, and was a great man in a great time. He collected round him a band of 5 poets, who discharged the somewhat derogatory task of writing up to R.'s instruction; they were Richelieu's shadows, in a word; these were Colletet, Boisrobert, L'Etoile, Rotrou (qq.v.), and Corneille himself, who chagrined R. by withdrawing at an early date. Their chief production was R.'s play, *Mirame*, produced at his Palais Cardinal (now the Palais Royal) at an extravagant cost.

Richter, Johann Paul Friedrich (1763-1825): Germ. Romantic novelist; wr. under the name of Jean Paul; 'the giant Jean Paul, who has power to escape out of hearsays' (Carlyle, *Lectures on Heroes*, i); 'that vast World-Mahlstrom of Humour' (*id.*, *Sartor Resartus*). R. was bred in rural poverty, the pinch of which was increased by the death of his father, 1779; his fanciful and dreamy nature, says one biographer, was nurtured by the village surroundings of his boyhood. In 1780, he was attending lectures in theology at Leipsic univ., and for the next 10 or 12 years his life was a continuous struggle. His first bks. were satires which missed fire ; he had a turn at tutoring and teaching ; and his personal sufferings were enhanced by the suicide of one brother and the failure of another. But the call to letters was insistent, and 2 works in educational fiction, issued in 1793, and conceived in the spirit of Rousseau's *Emile*, broke the spell of ill-fortune, and inaugurated the 30 years' successes. *Hesperus*, 1795, was the first of a series of romances which more and more seized the fancy of a public eager for sentiment ; its hero, Victor, is foster-son to a certain lord Horion, and is tried by various emotional experiences, in accordance with the prevailing taste for the conflict of idealism with reality. *Quintus Fixlein*, 1796, marked an advance in R.'s idyllic representation of the life which he knew best : that of a teacher in humble circumstances. The characteristic note of an age of moral reflection, strictly romantic in its point of view, is caught in the author's expression of his creed : ' small joys of the senses are to be valued higher than great joys ; man is rendered happy, not by great but by little strokes of luck '. Fixlein was followed by the tale, mixed idyl and novel, of *Siebenkäs* ; the matrimony, death, and wedding of a poor advocate, or *Flowers, Fruit and Thorns*, as it was variously entitled, 1796-97. Siebenkäs is married uncongenially, and both partners find release by his fictitious death. The theme is romantic, in the worse acceptation of the term, which admitted freedom-at-any-price as more desirable than no-freedom-at-all ; but the graceful background of rusticity and the sentimental atmosphere atone for the loose moral structure ; the times, moreover, were hospitable to both aspects of the ' natural ' man. R. was now an author of some repute, with an enthusiastic following mainly among the younger men ; and he found his way to the literary Mecca of Weimar, where, though Goethe (q.v.) stood aloof, the duchess-mother Amalia received him, Wieland and Herder (qq.v.) were friendly, and the literate ladies, led by Charlotte von Kalb,—Schiller's (q.v.) Charlotte,—were ready to welcome him with open arms. He finally settled at Bayreuth. R.'s chief work was his *Titan*, 1800-03, in 4 vols., of which the real hero is Roquairol, the Mephistopheles to its Albano's Faust. These parallels from Goethe, though accurate in kind, are inaccurate in time ; for R.'s *Titan*, like Tieck's *Sternbald*, F. Schlegel's *Lucinde* (qq.v.), and other novels, was directly fathered, not by *Faust*, but by *Wilhelm Meister* : the theme was the apprenticeship of youth to life ; the treatment which R. brought to it was that of the ' Storm and Stress ' (q.v.). Even more in the manner of *Wilhelm Meister* was R.'s romance entitled *Flegeljahre*, 1804-5 (left unfind.), which stands out among his later fiction and essays for its ideal aim and idyllic treatment. It is difficult to reconstruct to-day the reputation of ' Jean Paul ', or his appeal to his near contemporaries, with Carlyle (q.v.), perhaps, at their head. They admired him for his humour. He began to write as a satirist, and the vein persisted through his work. It was not the easier

satire of the 17th cent., but the deeper note which was struck by a keen perception of the tragi-comedy of life ; of the contrast between aim and achievement, between the eternity of desire and the temporal conditions set to fulfilment. This perception coloured R.'s view of life, and his characterization of the earth-bound heaven-stormers whom he chiefly cared to depict ; and it illustrates his kindship with the genius that burned in Carlyle. They admired him, too, mistakenly, as we should now say, for the neglect of form which was habitual to him. His romantic thought outran his vocabulary ; ' in the milky ways of the wastes of the firmament ', where ' eternity lay upon chaos ', a logical language had still to be fashioned ; and this, again, found its analogue in Carlyle. R. enlarged the resources of Germ. prose by his boldness, his imagination, and his sense of beauty ; and he is, perhaps, chiefly admirable for a feature which characterized his writings from first to last, and which was deeply founded in the memoirs of his village-childhood. His bks. are full of vignetted pictures of common life, idyllic rather than idealized, and attractive for their simple charm. Thus, he looks before and after ; and, for the rest, as there are ' poets' poets ', among whom is commonly counted Edmund Spenser, so, we may take it, there are romanticists' romanticists. Among these ' Jean Paul ' is leader, though he goes unread to-day, for the love that men and women once bore him, and for his influence chiefly on Börne, De Quincey, and Carlyle.

Rickhart, Martin (1586-1649): Germ. hymn-writer ; author of the famous Lutheran thanksgiving ' Nun danket alle Gott '.

Ringwaldt, Bartholomeus (*c.* 1530-99): Germ. satirist. Wr. long didactic-satiric poems, which proved popular in their age, and a dramatic piece, *Speculum Mundi*, 1590, in which his ' mirror ' reflected the usual vices of his ' world ', viz. the world of the rich through the eyes of a reforming pastor.

Rioja, de, Francisco (*c*, 1590-1659): Span. poet ; divine. The *ed. pr.* of his poetical works was as late as 1797, and includes some admirable sonnets, and odes in imitation of Horace. (See too, s.v. Caro).

Rist, Johann (1607-67): Germ. poet ; founded a literary society at Hamburg—the Elbschwanenorden, the Order of the Swans of the Elbe —in order to promote the reforms initiated by Opitz (q.v.). Wr. dramas, no longer extant, conjecturally more nearly akin to the old Shrovetide-play (q.v.) than to the nascent Reformation-drama of the Lat. school-play type. R.'s lyric verse marked an advance in spontaneity on the frigid mechanism of Opitz and the literary cliques.

Ritterdrama (Germ.): Chivalric drama ; descriptive name of a type of play freely produced in Germany about the end of the 18th cent., and characterized by features of blood and arms, inherited (or, degenerated) from the hist. drama of the *Götz von Berlichingen* (s.v. Goethe) type. The R. was as far removed from the hist. play as the hist. novels of G. P. R. James are from those of sir W. Scott (see   s.vv.) ;   the   stage-properties

Rôling, Johann (1634-79): Germ. minor poet; prof. of poetry in succession to Dach (q.v.) at Königsberg. Wr. lyric verse on metrical models as reformed by Opitz (q.v.).

Rogers, Samuel (1763-1855): Engl. poet; Londoner; banker, but retired early from the family business on a large income; one of the most generous of men, though sometimes satirical; T. Campbell (q.v.) gave good advice to a wounded friend when he said: 'Borrow money of Rogers, and he will never say a word against you again'. R. is better remembered to-day for his hospitality, esp. at the break-fast-table at 22, St. James's Place, than for his poems, which included *The Pleasures of Memory*, 1792, and *Italy*, 1822, which he pro-duced in a sumptuous edn., reputed to have cost him £15,000. Byron (q.v.) thought highly of R.'s poetry, which certainly displayed good taste, though that taste was better employed in collecting the pictures, which realized £50,000 after his death. R.'s long life, like that of H. C. Robinson (q.v.), his contempor-ary, covered many literary memories: 'he read Goldsmith's *Traveller* on its first appear-ance, and he died in the year in which Browning showed the full flower of his genius in *Men and Women*' (sir E. Boyle, *National Review*, Aug., 1925). Another proof of longevity (*ibid.*) is, that 'he knew Boswell, and he lent Tennyson his suit in which to go to Court'. He might have gone in Tennyson's shoes, for the prince consort offered R. the poet-laureateship (q.v.), 1850, before it was offered to Tennyson.

Rohan, de, Henri (1579-1638): Fr. memoirist; *duc* by rank; member of an illustrious Fr. family; soldier; Huguenot leader; died from wound in battle. Wr. *le parfait Capitaine*, and *Mémoires* of considerable interest for the stirring times in which he took an active and a gallant part.

Roig, Jaume (died 1478): Span. poet; native of Valencia. Wr. poetic *Libre de Consells*, a spirited satire, mainly on women's foibles, frequently reprinted down to the 18th cent.

Rojas, de, Fernando (15th cent.): Span. reputed author of the tragi-comedy of Calisto and Melibea, commonly entitled *Celestina* (q.v.), written shortly (within 10 years) before 1499. The facts are as follows: An edn. of this famous prose-dialogue, of prime importance in the history of the novel (q.v.) and the stage, was publd. at Seville in 1501. It contained an unsigned dedicatory letter 'from the author to a friend', which states that the writer, when away from home, found an uncompleted MS., 'the authorship of which some ascribed to Juan de Mena and others to Rodrigo Cota'. He set himself to complete the work, and finished it in 15 days, 'and that you may know', he said, 'where my unpolished work begins, I arranged that all that was due to the old author should be included without a division in a single act or scene, down to the first words of act ii'. So far the statement gives us *obscurum per obscurius*, for everyone to-day rejects the identification of 'the old author' with either Mena or Cota (qq.v.), and the new author did not give his own name. His reluctance was probably due to his professional reputation as a lawyer, which might have been prejudiced by association with this holiday-task.

But the letter is followed by stanzas in *ottava rima* (q.v.), the significance of which was revealed by a certain Alonso de Proaza, who saw the bk. through the press: the initial letters of the 88 lines of the poem com-pose a Span. sentence, the Engl. transln. of which is, 'The bachelor Fernando de Rojas completed the comedy of Calisto and Melibea, and he was born in the town of Montalvan'. Thus, the acrostic disclosed the secret which the letter guarded; and, if the statements are trustworthy, act i of *Celestina* was due to an 'old author' unknown, and acts ii-xvi to R. Subsequently to the 1501 edn., there were 21 acts in all; and even if these facts may stand, the question arises, who wr. acts xvii-xxi ? (There are sundry minor dovetailings between the acts which may be ignored for this purpose). Meanwhile, at the beginning of the present cent. the whole fabric of these statements was severely shaken, if not demolished, by the critical investigations of M. Foulché-Delbosc. In an exhaustive examination of the evidence (*Revue hispanique*, vi, 1900; resumed, 1902) this formidable and brilliant scholar arrived at the threefold conclusion, that (*a*) the 16 original acts were all by one author, (*b*) that author was unidentifiable, (*c*) he did not write the later additions. Still, R.'s name stood unchallenged as author from 1501 to 1900; and Mr. H. Warner Allen, in his edn. of *Celestina*, Routledge, *n.d.* (but fixed at 1908), inclines (Appendix ii) to its retention, and his view is adopted here: 'I hope', he writes, 'that the foregoing considerations show that Fernandez de Rojas has not yet been proved to be a fraudulent claimant, and that, consequently, pending further evidence, we may regard him as the original author of the *Comedia de Calisto y Melibea*'. Mr. Allen's view includes acts xvii-xxi as well as acts ii-xvi; in this respect, agreeing with Mr. Fitz-maurice-Kelly (*Lit. espagn.*, 166) that, though the 5 last acts are in some ways inferior to the rest, yet 'les retouches d'un auteur sont souvent malheureuses'. Thus, act i only is of unknown authorship, and even this may have been re-touched in that brief vacation from the law spent by R. at Salamanca, when he added 15 acts to the MS. which he was so fortunate as to discover. The ascertained facts as to R.'s biography are very few. He was a converted Jew, whose wife was 35 years old in 1525, and who held a municipal office in 1538. From these dates Delbosc argued that, if his authorship were admitted, he must have written *Celestina* at the early age of 20, but 'our chronological data are too vague at present to form a valid objection' (Warner, *ibid.*); and the scale inclines in R.'s favour; in which case 'we should be presented with a striking triumph of the Jewish genius' (Kelly, *Lit. espagn.*, 170).

Roland (died 778): historically, Hruotland, warden (or wargrave) of the Breton marches; killed, in command of Frankish rearguard under Charles the Great (Charlemagne, q.v.), by Basque hillsmen in the defile of Roncesvalles, N. Spain. The disaster appealed to popular imagination, and passed through song into legend, forming eventually a prom-inent episode in the 'matière de France' (see s.v. Bodel), celebrated in the *chansons de geste* (q.v.) of 11th to 14th cent. Fact. and fiction were combined to exalt the legendary R. beyond the measure of his hist. significance. The Basques were changed to Saracens, the traditional foemen of the Cross; their legitimate surprise of the baggage-waggons was represented as a breach of truce; and, in order to make it plausible, a Frankish accomplice of the Saracens was invented in the person of Ganilo (Ganelon, Gano, Wenilo), who in one version was the stepfather of R. Further sophistication was introduced in a fictitious rout of the Saracens, and the avengement of R.'s betrayal. Charlemagne, majestically transformed into a veteran with a flowing beard, destroys the whole pagan force and slays its leader in single combat; and Ganilo pays the price of his treachery. Another romantic accretion is R.'s brother-in-arms and the brother of his wife to-be, the heroic Oliver. This epic tale thus embellished has been preserved in 2 Lat. versions (one was ascribed to Turpin, Fr., archbp. of Rheims, who d. 800), and also in the assonant ' laisses ' (q.v.) of the *Chanson de Roland*, the best and oldest *chanson de geste* now extant. Tailleter, the fighting herald, chanted a Roland poem at the battle of Hastings, 1066. The naturalization of Roland (Orlando) in Italy made a European possession of the romance into which the old legend grew (see s.vv. Pulci, Boiardo, Ariosto).

Roland, Marie Jeanne (1754-93): Fr. woman of letters; *née* Phlipon; m., 1780, J. M. Roland de la Platière, Fr. statesman and orator; perished on the guillotine. Mme. R., who owed inspiration to the writings of Rousseau (q.v.), wr. letters and memoirs, the last composed while she was awaiting execution, and entitled *Appel à l'impartiale postérité, par la citoyenne Roland*. Posterity remembers, too, her last words : ' O Liberty, what crimes are committed in thy name '.

Rolle, Richard (*c.* 1300-49): Northern Engl. theologian; ' as significant in the history of popular medieval religion as in that of medieval letters ' (*C.H.E.L.*, ii, 48). R. was born and edu. in Yorks., and, though he neither took orders nor was canonized, lived as a hermit, and was honoured as a saint. He wr. in Lat. and Engl., and some works ascribed to his authorship may not be from his pen. They include the *Pricke of Conscience*, a long Engl. didactic poem based on Grosseteste; a Lat. *Commentary on the Psalms*, composed at the request of Margaret Kirkby, the recluse; *Ego dormio et cor meum vigilat*, written for a nun at Yedingham, etc. R. was a mystic by temperament, and ' brings to his teaching more heart than mind. His ideas are diametrically opposed to those of the other great figures in the religious life of fourteenth century England,—Wiclif ' (q.v.; Sisam, *Fourteenth Century Verse and Prose*, 37).

Rollenhagen, Georg (1542-1609): Germ. satirist. Wr. Biblical school-plays according to the fashion of his age and of his class, which was that of a teacher-preacher, but achieved permanent fame by his Germ. redaction of the Gk. *Batrachomyomachia* (battle of frogs and mice), orig. a Homeric parody. R.'s *Froschmeuseler* owed some attractive features to the most popular bestiary (q.v.) of his day, the *Reineke Fuchs* (s.v. Reynard), and took shape as a pro-Reformation satire.

Rolliad, The (1784 and following) : Engl. satire, deriving its title from an *ad hoc* imagined epic poem of that name, the ' hero ' of which was ' an unlucky, jolter-headed Devon squire ', colonel (afterwards, lord) Rolle (Elton, *Survey Engl. Lit.*, 1780-1830, i, 32), M.P., who acquired his unsought and undeserved notoriety from a speech in the House of Commons, just prior to the triumph of Pitt, 1784. Col. Rolle was selected as the peg for the wit and humour of the beaten politicians, who kept the ball rolling with extraordinary velocity for several years. Col. Rolle claimed descent from duke Rollo,—a convenient item for the mock epicists, who pretended to quote fragments of the illusory poem in their *Criticisms on ' The Rolliad '*, which formed part i of this series of Whig pasquinade. Part ii took shape as *Probationary Odes for the Laureateship*, vacated by the death of W. Whitehead (q.v.), and part iii as *Political Miscellanies*. Among the group of authors were G. Ellis (q.v.), and R. Tickell, grandson of Addison's (q.v.) friend.

Rollin, Charles (1661-1741): Fr. historian; rector of the univ. of Paris. Wr., *Histoire Ancienne*, 1730, transld. into many languages, and figuring in Engl. as *Ancient History of the Egyptians, Carthaginians, Assyrians, Babylonians, Medes and Persians, Macedonians and Grecians* (fifth edn., 7 vols., 1768; the date shows the rapidity of the reputation which it established). R. followed this work with an *Historie Romaine*, 1738, and was also the author of a valuable *Traité des Etudes*, 1726. His *Ancient History* maintained its place for several generations. But it belongs to the old, incurious tradition of historians; and M., though he was contemporary with Montesquieu (q.v.), took no part in the speculations which inspired the *Considerations on the Greatness and Decadence of Rome* by that eminent philosopher.

Roman à Clef (Fr.) : ' novel with a key '; descriptive epithet of a novel depicting real characters under a more or less thin disguise. The term which originated in France in the 17th cent., is usually confined to novels which delineate characters of the actual period at which the novel is issued ; thus, the work of fiction acquires a kind of meretricious interest by the support which it lends to one side of a current controversy.

Romance : Engl. generic term, employed, with reference to the art of lit., chiefly in one of four senses, as follows :—i, In philology ; the modern name of the old *lingua Romana* (Roman tongue), i.e., the colloquial Lat. language, spoken in Gallia (France), and distinguished from the *lingua Latina* (Lat. tongue), i.e., the pure Lat. language of the Church. Clerks (that is, clerics as distinct from laity) added the epithet *rustica* to *lingua Romana*, in order to show their contempt for the uneducated countrymen who talked *romane, romanice*, or *romance*. From this early lay variant of the Lat. speech foliated the Romance-languages of modern Europe: Ital., Fr., Span., Port., and the Norman element in Engl. ii, In medieval lit.; compositions in a Romance-language, to which the name *roman* was attached. The characteristics of this class of compositions lent significance to the name which they adopted. Romance is not romantic because of its meaning in philology; it was the contents of the earliest *romans*, or compositions in a Romance-language, which gave its romantic flavour to the old philological name. The elements of love and adventure, now inseparable from the meaning of Romance, were derived from the subject and treatment of these first *romans*, or romances.* iii, In modern lit.; the use of personal, subjective and natural tones and colours, derived directly from feeling and observation, in distinction to those deduced from the set and formal rules of the classical tradition. This sense of the term (and the distinction) is comparatively recent. It reached Engld. from the continent at the beginning of the 19th cent., when it replaced the older term Gothic, which had been transferred to lit. from architecture. It fitted the tastes of medievalists, such as Scott. The sensuous elements of adventure and love, characteristic of the old *romans*, vividly struck the imagination of those who sought Romance in the early 19th cent., as a corrective to and a protest against the precision, symmetry, and regularity of the Augustan (or Latin-classical) schools; and this renewed Romance was consummated in its derivative Romanticism (Germ. *Romantik*; the commoner Fr. name is *le lyrisme*, after its main channel of expression).—iv, Colloquial; the vulgar use of 'romance' and 'romantic' for scenes and incidents of daily life, removed however slightly from common experience, need not detain us here. Our main business is with ii and iii: the exercises of the Romance languages in the medieval *roman*, or tale; and the Romantic revival of the 18th and 19th cents. But before definitely leaving i, the Romance of philology, i.e. the *lingua Romana*, one or two points of general interest may be noted. First, Romance, which, later, came into so violent conflict with the classical (or Lat.) tradition, was equally descended from ancient Rome. Even more conspicuously than with the Classicists, the origin of the Romanticists is in Rome. But Romance, despite its derivation, is one of few words, which, intensively viewed, belong wholly to post-Pagan Europe. It is possible, as Butcher (*Some Aspects of Greek Genius*, last ch.) and others show us, to attach the label of romantic to lines and episodes in Homer; it is possible to thrill to Romance in the undernotes of Virgil's epic; but it would not have been possible to say to Homer or Virgil, ' how romantic this is '. Rome herself had no word for Romance. Though Rome herself is at its root, it flowered in the sunshine of France, it was fed by moisture from Welsh hills, and

* This art. was in type some time before the publication of *Words and Idioms*, by Logan Pearsall Smith (Constable 1925) which contains an illuminating ch. (iii, pp. 66-134) on ' Four Romantic Words'. Mr. Smith reminds us that, according to the *Oxford Engl. Dict.*, the first use of the Engl. word *romantic* is found in H. More (q.v.), *The Immortality of the Soul*, 1659. He emphasizes the fact that ' *romantic* means Nature seen through a literary medium '.

its spread its leaves by the waters of the Rhine. A second paradox of Romance, under its philological aspect, may be noted in the fact that, though the early medieval clerks attached a derogatory *rustica* to the lay-Latin *lingua Romana*, the mother of the literate tongues of Europe, this contempt was, later, reversed. At the time of the eve of the Reformation, it was the proud *lingua Latina* of the Church which was incontrovertibly convicted of rusticity and boorishness in the famous satire on clerical dog-Latin penned by the indignant champions of the rights of vernacular lit. The *Epistolæ Obscurorum Virorum* (q.v.), in which the defenders of Reuchlin exposed the obscurantism of the monks, transferred, in effect, the derogatory epithet from the *Romana* to the *Latina lingua*. One more point may be noted in connection with the Romance of philology. We have seen that the first *romans* —the earliest compositions in a Romance-language—derived their features recognized as romantic, not from ancient Rome, which gave her name to the family of languages, but from their topics of European origin. This statement will be partially modified, when we examine the sources and the treatment of (ii) medieval Romance; but, generally, it is correct. We have seen, too, that the lay Romance became ultimately more polished than the clerkly Lat., and retorted (in 16th-cent. satire) the charge of rusticity upon its early detractors. Now, it is interesting to remark that the Romantic triumph over Classicism in the 18th cent. was partly, at least, assisted by Classicism itself. Romanticism was many things at once; and, among others, it was a return to ancient Greece, by a direct approach to Gk. antiquity as distinct from its Lat. interpreters. To this aspect we shall revert, when we discuss the factors of (iii) the revival of Romance, or Romanticism in modern lit. Here, we would only suggest that ' romantic ' and ' classic ', though commonly set in such clear opposition, have often crossed and interacted, and even come very close together, since the *lingua Romana* of the countryfolk was first unfolded from the *lingua Latina* of the clerks.

We turn now more particularly to (ii) the Romance of medieval lit.; the compositions in Romance-languages, by the diffusion and popularity of which the name *roman*, or romance, was transferred from the language employed to the type with which it became identified. This *roman* was a chivalric tale. It was governed from first to last by the conventions and rules of chivalry; and, though it owed much to Lat. models for its manner, and to ancient sources for its material, its romantic quality was firmly rooted in its zest for chivalric adventure. It was adventurous in deed and word, right down to Shakespeare and beyond. Such a passage, for example, as Shakespeare, *Winter's Tale*, iv, 3,

Daffodils,
That come before the swallow dares, and take
The winds of March with beauty; violets dim,
But sweeter than the lids of Juno's eyes
Or Cytherea's breath,

is instinct with the romantic method, and drenched in the hues of Romance. The observation of nature (q.v., ' Nature I loved, and, next to Nature, Art ', said Landor, at the noon of the Romantic revival) ; the appeal to the senses (' Shakespeare, Fancy's child, warble his native woodnotes wild ', wr. Milton, *L'Allegro*, 131) ; the connotative words, ' before the swallow *dares* ', ' *take* the winds with beauty ', ' violets *dim* ' ; all this is of the essence of the romantic point of view. But Rome is confessed as plainly as Romance. Juno's eyelids and Cytherea's breath are the matter of the *lingua Latina* in the manner of the *lingua Romana* ; the matter of Classicism, the manner of Romance ; the voice of Jacob, the shape of Esau. And this identity in diversity makes frequent confusion of the contrast between classic and romantic. Take More's *Utopia*, for example. It was written in Lat. for Latinists ; it was a product of the classical Renaissance ; yet the *lingua Latina* of its speech was broken by rays of the *lingua Romana* of its content. The form was classical, but the matter was romantic. No scholar's Latinity could cloak the chivalric origin of the sentiments which More's hero had ' customably in his mouth ' : ' He that hath no grave, is covered with the sky ', and ' the way to heaven out of all places is of like length and distance.' These sayings were penned by Thomas More in the elegant Lat. of 1516, but they echoed the chivalric *roman* of the 12th cent. in Norman France, and they have been attested by modern knights of Romance as recent as captains Scott and Oates in the Antarctic expedition of 1912 ; 800 years of chivalric adventure.

This *roman* of chivalric invention started about 1100, and its birthplace was in Norman France. Its method was to concentrate on love, or ambition, or another compelling motive ; to adopt from Roman Ovid (q.v.), or elsewhere, the code of right diction under such motivation, and, thus equipped with material and style, to refashion at will the tales of bygone times, without further respect to the proprieties of persons, places, or dates. The Fr. romancer has been described as the sophist of medieval lit., and the same writer (Ker, *Epic and Romance*) compares the succession of chivalry to heroism, and of the artistic tale to the heroic *chanson*, with ' the victory of the Norman knights over the English axemen ' in 1066 (See art. Chansons de Geste, for the researches of Bédier). However this may be, the romancer acquired from reputable masters and elaborated for punctilious audiences a machinery and an apparatus of Romance, with set rules for recurring situations, and stock sentiments and ornaments as required. Given the necessary material of adventure, it was his well-understood business to supply the forms of attractive exposition. Where was the material found ? Briefly, the method was applied to 3 main storehouses, or quarries, summarized by an old romancer (Bodel), as France, Bretagne, and Rome (the Rome of the *romans* meant all Antiquity). From these quarries the romance-writer would select the material which suited him, and, so furnished, he would set at work to shape it in verse or prose by the tools of his romantic craft. Within the limits of his material, he was free. He would add, reduce, expand, contaminate (in the rhetorical sense of recombining parts ; thus, he would send Alexander of Macedon crusading against the heathens, or make Brindisi a port for fairyland), with no other conscious aim than to please an exacting and a sophisticated audience in castle and hall, or later, in square and market place. The quarries were infinitely fertile. ' Rome ' (i.e., Antiquity) supplied, e.g., the Alexander-cycle, elaborated, *c.* 1180, into the *roman d'Alixandre*, which transformed the pagan conqueror into a paladin of chivalry. It supplied Helen of Troy to an unending troop of worshippers, and the tales of the Trojan War, elaborated, *c.* 1160, in a *roman de Troie*, which passed through Chaucer's *Troilus* into the line of the modern novel. It supplied the tales of Thebes, and the plots of Byzantine fiction. It ransacked Statius (Stace) and Ovid, and the Dido episodes in Virgil, to provide Chrétien (q.v.) and his successors with the substance of their various romances. ' Bretagne ' yielded the Arthuriad of Perceval, Tristan, and the Grail ; and ' France ' (which was Germany too) was the source of the Charlemagne-cycle of Roland and the paladins and pagans, which Ital. romance-epicists wrought to poems of a perfect art. This catalogue is far from exhaustive, though even within its limits there was endless scope for variety and combination. Miscellaneous sources of Romance were found in outlying tales ; thus the romance of *Amadis of Gaul*, originally a branch of the Breton cycle, was expanded and naturalized in the Peninsula, the home of another heroic *chanson*, the *Poema del Cid*, and became the most fashionable bk. of manners at the Fr. court of the 16th cent., and the fruitful mother of heroic fiction and tales of hist. gallantry. The *Romance of the Rose* (1237-77) formed a kind of comprehensive *ars amoris*, drawing subventions from all corners of romantic lore, and handing on fresh storehouses to later ages ; thus, it was studied by Chaucer, and partly edited by Marot. Where courtly inspiration failed, the inventions of the commonalty had their turn. The fables of Æsop were romanced into the *roman de Renart* and its variants, from Dutch Willem to Germ. Goethe.—The romantic ballads of Denmark and Castile, the romantic lyric of Provence and the Minnesinger, the romantic verse of Fr. and Germ. narrative, the romantic prose of Froissart and Malory, the romantic epos of Ariosto, the romantic discipline of Castiglione, all these influences and others went to form the romantic point of view. ' The true romantic interest ', writes prof. Ker (*op. cit.*, 326), ' is very unequally distributed over the works of the Middle Ages ' ; the magical touch and the sense of mystery, that is to say. There is least of it, he warns us, ' in the authors who are most representative of the Age of Chivalry ' ; more of it in the Northern poems than in the French ; more, again, in the French prose redactions, such as the *Queste del S. Graal*, or in such a tale as *Aucassin et Nicolete*. But, though it is impossible to generalize into a paragraph a mode of life which found literary expression in divers forms and different countries through several centuries, Romance, we may say, reached its height in the age of queen Elizabeth in Engld., when her seamen sailed the Span. Main, when sir Philip Sidney lived the knightly life, which Edmund Spenser delineated in the *Faerie Queen*, and when Shakespeare filled his stage with types of Romance in action. And contemporary with Elizabethan Romance, to which all later Romanticists recurred, was the romantic anti-Romance of Cervantes, whose mock-hero, Don Quixote of la Mancha, with his Rozinante (signifying, ex-carriage jade), had read so deeply of ' enchantments, quarrels, battles, challenges, wounds, wooings, loves, tempests, and other impossible follies ' (cf. Ariosto, *Orlando Furioso*, init. : ' Ladies, and cavaliers, and arms, and loves, and courtesies, and daring deeds, I sing '), that ' it seemed unto him very requisite and behooveful, as well for the augmentation of his honour as for the benefit of the common-wealth, that he himself should become a knight-errant, and go throughout the world with his horse and armour, to seek adventures, and practise in person all that he had read was used by knights of yore '. Thus, the 16th cent. was filled with Romance, as adventure, love, and courtesy, of 12th-cent. invention in Europe, and its overflow was gathered into the channel of the great Span. romance-parodist. The true antidote to Cervantes in Europe— Romance, revived, vanquishing anti-Romance— was sir Walter Scott, ' the Ariosto of the North '.

The romantic manner was now established in lit. ; and in (iii), Romance in modern lit., we reach the contrast between the classical and romantic schools which plays so prominent a part in many text-books of literary history. Remember that, despite the text-books, there are no revolutions in literary history ; and it is well to recall from Hugo in 1819 that the distinctions between the classicists and romanticists are at bottom, ' assez insignifiantes '. But insignificant though they were, and fully as we may agree with Kuno Francke (*Hist. Germ. Lit.*, E.T., 401*n*.), that ' the formation of an international league for the suppression of the terms both Romanticism and Classicism would seem to me a truly philanthropic undertaking ', it is not possible, as yet, to ignore the existence of these terms, which came most sharply into contrast in 19th-cent. criticism of the lit. of the previous half-century.[*] Briefly, the contrast lies between the classical atmosphere of form and the romantic atmosphere of matter ; between duty, or legality, on the one part, and love, or sympathy, on the other. (See R. M. Wernaer, *Romanticism and the Romantic School in Germany*, 5 ; reference is also suggested to R. Haym, *die romantische Schule* ; G. Brandes, *The Romantic School in Germany*, E.T., Heinemann ; H. A. Beers, *A History of English Romanticism*, 2 vols., Holt ; D. Mornet, *le Romantisme en France au xviii*[e] *siècle* ; and De Maar quoted in footnote. But the bibliography is really enormous : many of the most interesting

[*] ' It was the mistake of the nineteenth century to force that contrast too strongly upon the eighteenth.'. H. G. de Maar, *Hist. of Mod. Engl. Romanticism* (Oxford, 1924), I, 9.

works are studies of foreign—not native— manifestations of the romantic spirit). This contrast is met in architecture, where the Classical was contrasted with the Gothic style, and whence the name Gothic was transferred as a synonym for Romantic in other arts. It is met in painting, and not least in landscape-gardening, in which the romantic reactionaries against the formalists at Versailles and elsewhere had a ready opportunity of making experiments in the style associated with the interpretation of romantic as picturesque-tending-to-wild. The name Romantic gradually acquired its special meaning, as distinct from wild, barbarous, medieval, Gothic, picturesque and romanesque, during the 18th cent. In France, Diderot did not know it ; Rousseau used it doubtfully, and it was definitely acclimatized by Letourneur, 1776. It crossed into Engld. long after it had been adopted in Germany, and its definite introduction may be dated about 1813 at the instance of mme. de Staël.

Thus, the revival of Romance in lit. was partly the expression and expansion of sensibility to external nature. The open eye was turned to scenery. James Thomson (1700-1748), of *The Seasons*, Edward Young (1683-1765) of *Night Thoughts*, and William Shenstone (1714-63) of *The Schoolmistress*, not without influence by Pope in *Windsor Forest* (1713) and his pastorals, are duly credited with the early signs of such feeling in Engld. Wm. Collins (1721-59) and Thomas Gray (1716-71) are commonly joined as its harbingers in true poetry,—the one with his ' lonely vesper-chime ', and the other with the ' frugal note '. Mention, too, is due to Samuel Croxall (died, 1752), whom de Maar (*op. cit.*) calls ' an abandoned Romantic ', and ' essentially one of the romantics of an unromantic time '. But, keeping to the heights, Thomson's muse saw ' Caledonia in romantic view ', and he wr. in a letter to a friend that ' Retirement and Nature are more and more my passion every day '. We cannot follow the development of this sensibility through Brockes and Gessner, and Haller in his native Alps, to the definite ' return to nature ', identified, as a synonym for Romance, with Rousseau and the literary movement which acknowledged his romantic spell. Romance was further associated with a sensibility to human nature ; so, the ' romanesque ' became the ' romantique ', and the appeal was extended from the eye to the soul. Here, too, an Engl. writer showed the way. It was Samuel Richardson (1689-1761), whose emotional fiction first opened the floodgates which poured a torrent of tears through the novels of the 18th cent., and Defoe's nearly contemporaneous *Robinson Crusoe*, 1719, was also of immense influence on the Continent in stimulating the fiction of self-resource and adventurous quest. And this revived lit. of feeling took a fresh departure in Engld., again, in the ' return to the Middle Ages ', which is Heine's description of Romance. Once more, it was an expression of emotions, of a sensibility to the past, the distant, and the supernatural, which inspired bp. Percy in his *Reliques of Ancient Poetry*, 1765, and James Macpherson in his Ossianic poems, 1761-63, to appeal to the sense of wonder, and to evoke the colours of the early world, for the refreshment of a literary tradition too closely cramped by later rules. Macpherson was transld. into Fr. by Turgot, into Ital. by Cesarotti, and Goethe was captivated by him in his *Sorrows of Werther*. Percy's *Reliques* is known as 'the Bible of the Romantic Reformation', and the cumulative influence of his collection was immense. Klopstock, Herder Bürger, and others, including the Goethe of *Götz von Berlichingen* and *Erlkönig*, raised flowers from the seeds which they borrowed. To translate Bürger's *Lenore* became a kind of Romantic matriculation from Scott to Rossetti, and it need hardly be added that the Middle Ages, thus revived, were transformed out of all likeness to their original features. Certain aspects were selected, and were used as stage-properties : moonlight, for instance, flooded the romantic pages of Tieck ; Mrs. Radcliffe's heroes clanked in chains ; Hardenberg (Novalis) specialized in mysticism ; and *The Medieval Mind*, even as delineated by a learned American in our day (2 vols., Macmillan), could not have recognized the patterns ascribed to it by these medievalists. Romanticism, says a modern writer (G. Scott, *The Architecture of Humanism*, Constable, p. 39), 'is always idealistic, casting on the screen of an imaginary past the projection of its unfulfilled desires'. The Romantics proceeded by selection and combination, and on these lines and others, accordingly, the 'emancipation of the ego', in Brunetière's phrase for Romance (Mr. Watts-Dunton called it a 'renascence of wonder'), was effected in all departments of thought. Through movements which we cannot pause to trace, Western Europe and Germany particularly became conscious in many places at once of a national and of an individual *ego*, which expressed itself not merely in pure art and lit., but also in criticism and in philosophy, and in hist. and political theory. It was marked in all its variants by passion, personality, speculation, and a deep, imaginative sensibility. It survived the Storm and Stress of Germany's youthful ebullition ; it survived Rousseau and the Fr. Revolution ; and it passed through the calm which Goethe won on the heights into the Romance of the 19th cent., from Chateaubriand and Scott downwards.

We remarked above that Romance, in its revival, was partly assisted by Classicism, with which it is so insistently contrasted. This contrast, as we suggested, is fallacious, if it be taken to mean that Romance and Classicism are mutually exclusive contraries. Nothing is further from the truth. The actual frontage of contrast is much less extensive than the common opposition of the terms might lead students to suppose. It was much more a critics' quarrel than a conscious departure of literary aims. From the 16th cent. onwards, the critical taste of Europe, starting with Vida (*c.* 1480-1566) in Italy, had tended to fasten on Lat. models without sufficient reference to the Gk. sources from which they drew. Vida's heirs in France and Engld., the schools of Boileau

and Pope ('Immortal Vida! on whose honour'd brow The poet's bays and critic's ivy grow'; Pope, *Essay on Criticism*, 708), perpetuated his canons, so that literary taste in Europe, when it obeyed rules at all, was governed for more than two centuries by modern versions of Horace's *Art of Poetry*, with illustrations from Virgil's poetic practice. The apogee of this school was reached by Gottsched (1700-1766) in Leipsic. Such excessive (or predominantly Lat.) Classicism is described by Saintsbury as 'prosaism', and is more commonly termed pseudo- or neo-classic ; and it was a part of the Romantic revival of the 18th cent. to overthrow the neo-classic yoke. Humanism, as a branch of the Renaissance, retraced its own steps to some extent, and Herder, for instance, inveighed against the excessive deference to Latinity which had deprived the classical tradition of the ripest fruits of Hellenism (See also s.vv. Lat., Hellenism). It was Winckelmann, in his studies of Gk. sculpture, who led Europe back to Hellas, across the superstructure of Lat. interpretation, which the Ciceronian ages of Europe, and the use of the Lat. tongue by scholars and statesmen, had gradually erected as a barrier ; and the new Hellas, thus revealed by the science of the footrule and the compass, proved a far more inspiring mistress than the Hellas of the neo-classic tradition, studded with Horatio-Aristotelian rules, 'like quills upon the fretful porcupine'. The new Hellas gave Europe Goethe's *Iphigenie*, Schiller's *Wallenstein*, Wordsworth's *Laodamia* ; and André Chénier and John Keats show signal examples, more illuminative than a column of analysis, of the union of Romanticism (that is, Romance revived) with Hellenism (that is, Classicism restored from its neo-classic usurpers to its sources in Gk. art) ; of 'that marriage of Faust and Helena', as Walter Pater admirably calls it (*Renaissance*, 240).

A by-product of the Romantic revolt against the tyranny of reason and commonsense, of the victory of feeling over intellect, sympathy over law, love over duty, colour over symmetry, which were all aspects of the same movement, was the enhanced appreciation of words. The Horatian legislators had insisted on the subordination of words to sense. Vida's own counsel ran,

Let things submit to words on no pretence,
But make your words subservient to your sense ;
and, though poets in every age had chafed under this regulation, formal critics of Shakespeare and Milton, for example, were disposed to re-write the masters' works in language more appropriate to its requirements. But the Romantic opponents of neo-Classicism cultivated words again for their own sake ; for the sake of the sudden brilliance which an unfamiliar word might strike, or for the edging of mystery which an associative word might wear. Thus, in Fr. criticism of the early 19th cent., we meet the expression *mot propre*, signifying the choice of exactly the right word, however lacking it might be in the dignity valued by the classicists. With the *mot propre* went the *vers libre*, such as the *enjambement* of Victor Hugo's alexandrines, or the similarly over-running lines of Keats's heroic

couplets. In fact, Hugo defined Romanticism as 'nothing else than liberalism in literature'; and the same 'wild' or 'savage' taste which let the hedgerows grow untrimmed and the waters flow unrefrained in the gardens of the landscape-poets and -painters released the confines of lit. from the rules of the classical school. Everyone will select his own examples: the point is, that the revival of Romance had its philological and hist. aspects, which tended to bring back into literary repute not merely the 'old, unhappy, far-off things, and battles long ago', and many happy things among them, but also the rejected, the disinherited, and the despised, in language as well as in life. This exaltation of the substance and its effect over the form and its style, of vagueness over outline, suggestion over precision, adumbration over clarity, energy over method, is the key to a difference which can be felt, not merely in opposed schools of lit., such as the dramas of Racine and Shakespeare, or the pastorals of Pope and Wordsworth, but sometimes in separate works of one writer, and lies at the root of the distinction between Classicism and Romance. But always, in observing this distinction, which claims, as has been shown, a true patent of origin, Pater's warning (*Appreciations, fin.*) should be remembered: 'To discriminate schools of art, of literature, is, of course, part of the obvious business of literary criticism: but, in the work of literary production, it is easy to be overmuch occupied concerning them. For, in truth, the legitimate contention is, not of one age or school of literary art against another, but of all successive schools alike, against the stupidity which is dead to the substance, and the vulgarity which is dead to form'. And here we may leave this contrast. We must further be content to leave Romance finally undefined (' La magic du *je ne sais quoi* était le romantisme tout entier ', says one Fr. critic; and another reminds us that romanticism was seamed with metaphysical streaks); even to leave unrefuted the burden with which it is charged of occasional triviality, laxity, and morbidity. It remains the greatest indigenous force which the composite lit. of Europe has created and increased from age to age out of the resources of its own life. Greeks, Romans, and Hebrews have gone to the making of our civilization, the common heir of theirs. But into these elements that inform us, we ourselves, out of our own experience, have infused the element of Romance. The need might lie dormant at times and in places; but again and again it asserted itself; in the 13th cent., in the 16th, in the 19th; the urgent, unappeasable invocation to strangeness, and beauty, and the quest; the ' roots of relish sweet ', of Keats, ' And honey wild, and manna dew '; the ' vision of the blue flower ' of Novalis; the desire of Meredith for Love or Colour, identified, ' because his touch is infinite, and lends a yonder to all ends '.

It remains, briefly, to characterize the last phase of Romanticism, in the course of the 19th cent.

Noch einmal sattelt mir den Hippogriffen,
  ihr Musen,
Zum Ritt ins alte romantische Land!

(' Now once more saddle me the hippogriff, o ye Muses, And off to the old romantical land! ') So Wieland in 1780 renewed the forgotten spell of Oberon from Huon of Bordeaux and Shakespeare (*Midsummer Night's Dream*). It is not possible in a paragraph to recount the response to this appeal, or to trace in detail the exploration of ' the old land of Romance ' from 1780 to this day. The expression was as multiform as the invocation. Note, first, that in Germany and France Romance had a school and leaders, disciples, polemic, propaganda. In Engld., it merely had practitioners. Germany esp. was distinguished by her organization of Romance, and by her application of romantic principles to all departments of thought. Kant's philosophy deeply influenced the movement. In metaphysics, in ethics, in anthropology, Romance, first expounded in criticism, had effects as profound as in pure lit. The nearest single example to the diffusion of Germ. Romance is to be found in Samuel Taylor Coleridge, who taught, as critic and thinker, what he wrought as poet; and his debt to the Schlegels was enormous. The Schlegel brothers, Tieck, Hardenberg (Novalis), and, a few years later, Brentano, Arnim, Uhland, and the brothers Grimm, may be selected as the central figures of literary Romanticism in Germany, in which the ' discovery ' of Shakespeare and the emancipation of lit. and life from the conscious bondage of rules were salient features. In Paris (France was Paris) the leader was Victor Hugo, though its beginning is properly dated from the *Génie du Christianisme*, 1802, of Chateaubriand. Both in Germany and Engld., if definite dates are of interest, the year 1798 may be taken as significant. It was the year of the foundation in Berlin of the Schlegels' review, *The Athenæum*, and of the publication at Bristol of the anon. *Lyrical Ballads*. To these archives of the movement may be added, in France, Victor Hugo's pref. to *Cromwell*, 1828, and the production of his tragedy, *Hernani*, at the Théâtre Français, 25 Feb., 1830. Keats in *Sleep and Poetry*, 1817, likewise flung down a gage which Byron and others took up. But Byron, despite his reverence for Pope, was romantic by temperament, and Byronism in France and Germany, with the Byronic collar and all, was a kind of synonym for the cult. For dress, too, had its part in Romance. A full beard and an open neck marked, in France especially, the protest against the classicist and academician, with his *perruque* and shaven chin.

Passing from the manifestoes of the Romantic movement to the earliest histories of the school, mention is due to mme. de Staël's *l'Allemagne*, which she composed for the information of Parisians after an expedition of reconnaissance to Germany, and which was publd., not without opposition from high quarters, in 1813; to the *Racine and Shakspere*, 1822, of Henri Beyle (Stendhal), who, though not a Romanticist, was a champion of the cause; and to Heine's *Romantische Schule*, 1833, a brilliant and mordant essay supplementary to mme. de Staël. But the signs and the documents were ubiquitous. ' All Europe ', says one writer, 'from Greece to Scotland, and all modern works, from the Troubadours to Byron, invested the classical ideal and dispossessed it'. The Bible, as language and style, was one of the romantic founders. Painting, released by Diderot from its exclusive barriers, joined the revolt of letters, and produced its David (d'Angers) in Paris, and its exotic subjects from the Napoleonic campaigns. The universities contributed rebellious professors (see s.vv. Cousin, Guizot, Villemain), anticipating the *ex-cathedra* activities of the Berlin hist. school of a later date ; and, similarly, the côterie of the *Cénacle*, which gathered round Nodier at the Arsenal Library in Paris in 1823, anticipated the activity of the Pre-Raphaelite Brotherhood in London 25 years afterwards. The men and movement of 1830, famous in the history of *le lyrisme* in France, were founded in the preceding decade.

In the almost infinite diversity of Romance in this period, there were always certain features in common. Thus, the nearly simultaneous publication of Chateaubriand's 'Genius of Christianity' and Coleridge's lyrical ballad, *The Ancient Mariner*, differently inspired though they were, suggests another aspect of the romantic movement. On the religious side it tended to Roman Catholicism, through its attempt, exemplified in Chateaubriand, to reintroduce into Christianity the colours and the confessional of which the deists and rationalists had deprived it. Stolberg, F. Schlegel, his wife, and others definitely entered the Roman Church, and Heine makes merry at the 'pilgrimage to Rome for the reinvigoration of consumptive German art'. The same tendency is to be observed in the moral penance or expiation of sins which is the motive of the *Ancient Mariner* (and, save for the symbolic imagery, of Wordsworth's *Peter Bell*) ; and, generally, the tone of the poem (as of much of the later pre-Raphaelite poetry and painting, of which Coleridge and Keats were part-begetters) is seamed with threads of the same dogma and diction. This conclusion is not impaired by the fact that the earliest version of the *Ancient Mariner* showed more indications of a parody of medieval verse-forms than its later recensions. With this aspect of the medieval revival we may associate the new cult of Dante, led by A. Deschamps, Cary and Flaxman, and leading to endless imitators. The speculative, or metaphysical, elements with which Romance in Europe was thus filled enable the historian of Romanticism to cast a fairly wide net, and to include the transcendental platonism of Wordsworth as well as the ornamental symbolism of Rossetti, and touches of Newman's piety as well as of Stevenson's style. He is enabled, happily, too, to commit to well-merited oblivion the pygmy quarrels of the critics in all countries, among which the controversy over the poetic body of Pope between Bowles and Campbell and others (1819-26) was the most notorious in Engld. At bottom, it attacked the problem of nature *versus* art, and Shakespeare's 'art itself is nature' is its ultimate and final solution. Romance, as a force in lit. from 1100 to 1900

(and probably throughout the present century) is far too significant an expression of an inalienable part of the mind of man to be allowed to lose itself in the bogs and quick-sands of controversial criticism. The most helpful lamp in such twilight is the couplet which opens Ariosto's *Orlando Furioso* :

Le donne, i cavalier, l'arme, gli amori,
Le cortesie, le audaci imprese, io canto.

'Dames and knights, and arms, and loves, courtesies, and daring deeds, I sing'. It happened, in the romantic revival, known in the 19th cent. as Romanticism in Engld., *Romantik* in Germany, and *lyrisme*, or *romantisme*, in France, that one romanticist was seized with one aspect, another with another, of this programme. Scott fastened on the arms and deeds, Keats on the dames and loves, Fouqué on the knights and courtesies ; and an endless range from history to mystery was offered to practitioners of the Romantic method. Romance sprang, declared mme. de Staël, from the union of Chivalry with Christianity ; 'it expresses our religion, it recalls our history' ; Victor Hugo called it 'liberalism in art', and in that aspect particularly it appealed to the radical duke de Rivas in Spain, whose *Don Alvaro*, 1834, was the *Hernani* of the Span. stage. Within such spacious limits there was infinite scope for variety of treatment. Eight centuries have not dulled the appeal nor set bounds to the inspiration of Romance. 'Romantic poetry', wr. F. Schlegel, its prophet, 'is a progressive World-poetry. . . . In a certain sense, all poetry is or tries to be romantic' ; and in this sense Romance has permeated European lit. from Chrétien de Troyes to Tennyson's *Idylls of the King*.

Nor is it unfitting that we should mention a Frenchman at the beginning and an Englishman at the close of this record. Romance began in sunny France ; but the revival of romance in the 18th cent., though splendidly reinforced in France, was due to England's initiative. The Fr. fortress of classicism in tragic drama was overthrown between 1778 and 1828—between Mercier and Hugo—by the examples of Lillo (*George Barnwell*, 1735), Moore (*The Gamester*, 1753), and, above all, Shakespeare. The novel was reformed by the contagion of the sentiment and sensibility of Richardson and Sterne ; poetry by Macpherson and Percy, with something of Gray and his congeners. 'In all other periods, England has been content to receive. It was so in the Middle Ages ; it was so in the Elizabethan age ; it was so in the Restoration period ; it was so, though to a less extent, even in the Augustan age. . . . In this period, and in this alone, England did not receive, but give. It was in England that the movements started, which, under different forms in each country, gave fresh life to the literature of Europe. It was in England that the seed was sown, the harvest of which was reaped during the next half-century by all the nations of Europe' (C. Vaughan, *The British Academy : Warton Lecture on English Poetry, iv—The Influence of English Poetry upon the Romantic Revival on the Continent* ; 1913). This claim, which is a big one, suggests responsibility to the future as well as pride in the past.

[N.B.—The separate artt. on the various *nomina* and *res* above should be consulted, though the indicative *q.v.* has been omitted throughout].

Romance (Span.) : Ballad, and

Romancero (Span.) : Ballad-book, collection of ballads, which have a place in the history of lit. separate from and independent of the allied topic of Romance (q.v. above, and see, too, s.v. Ballad). The restriction of the great name of *romance* to a comparatively small class of romantic writings of the ballad-variety is peculiar to the Span. language, and may be dated, according to the most recent authorities, from about the year 1400. The history and chronology of the Span. ballads (*romances*) have been the subjects of long and difficult discussion ; if we may borrow a term from the *chansons de geste* (q.v.), from which in their Span. form of *cantare de gesta*, the *romances* were alleged to be derived by a process of oral transmission, we should say that the *enfances*, or early exploits, of this famous branch of letters are wrapped in exceptional obscurity. Thus, prof. W. P. Ker asked, in a paper *On the history of the Ballads*, 1100-1500, read before the British Academy, 15 Dec., 1909 : ' Are we to accept the theory that the ballads are derived from older narrative poems, or (it may be) from narrative prose ? This theory has been proved for the Castilian romances or the chief of them. The best of the Castilian *romances* came from older epic poetry ; they are fragments of *cantares de gesta* ; . . . They have something of the nature of epic, and even if evidence were wanting it would be plausible to suppose them fragments of an earlier epic world '. But Mr. J. Fitzmaurice-Kelly, in the second edn. (1913) of his Fr. *Littérature espagnole* (Paris, Colin), in reliance on the researches of M. R. Foulché-Delbosc, sometime editor of the *Révue hispanique*, writes (p. 134), in partial opposition to M. Ramon Menéndez Pidal, on whom prof. Ker was to some extent relying : ' It seems clear that the *romances* appeared not at the beginning of the fourteenth century [nor, à fortiori, at any earlier date], but about the year 1400, and there is no authority for believing that the form in which they have reached us differs sensibly from the primitive form. Several *romances* were obviously inspired by epic poems of the decadence, but it is by no means proved that these ballads are the oldest, and it is wholly improbable [*invraisemblable*] that a *cantar de gesta* became a *romance* by oral transmission '. In other words, this study of *enfances* has tended steadily to diminish the probable antiquity of the Castilian romance-ballad ; and if we abandon the cut-and-dried theory of epopee descending into the market-place and more or less spontaneously dissolving itself into fragments of popular song, afterwards to be re-composed into ballad-form, we shall probably be correct in affirming that the *romances* were first written in the 15th cent., and that their authors, who are mostly anon., drew their material from the epical lit., and were perhaps directed in their choice by the popularity of certain portions as evidenced by story and song. Certainly, we shall be right in affirming with Ticknor (i, 141 ; 1863),

that ' the ancient Spanish ballads are so truly national in their spirit, that they became at once identified with the popular character that had produced them ; and with that same character will go onward, we doubt not, till the Spanish people shall cease to have a separate and independent existence '. Kelly (*op. cit.*) defines *romance* as ' a poem half-lyrical half-narrative in 16-syllable verse with a uniform assonance from the beginning to the end ' ; and collections of such poems were made at an early date after their composition came in vogue. The chief of these ballad-books was the famous *Romancero General*, ed. *pr.* Madrid, 1600 (incorporating 9 sections, or divisions, compiled during the previous half-century) ; fourth edn., 1614 (with 4 new sections). Various smaller compilations were selected or made during the 17th cent., and admirable work in classification, elucidation, and popularization was done by Hegel, J. Grimm, Southey, Lockhart, F. Wolf (qq.v.), and others in the 18th and 19th cents., including the *Romancero General* of A. Duran (q.v.), *c.* 1850, and the critical labours of Menéndez y Pelayo (d. 1912) and contemp. scholars mentioned above. It remains briefly to characterize the main subjects of this special branch of romantic lit. They comprise Don Roderick of the 8th cent. (see s.v. Corral) ; Bernardo del Carpio of the 9th, a Carlovingian hero ; Fernan Gonzalez of the 10th, first sovereign count of Castile ; the Infantes (children) de Lara, in the age of Garcia Fernandez, son of the first count ; the Cid (q.v.), who achieved in 1612 a *Romancero* of his own, frequently re-issued ; Castilian annals ; border-warfare (*romances fronterizos*, border-ballads), in connection with the Moorish campaigns : many of them the compositions of G. P. de Hita (q.v.) ; and other groups of less national significance. Plainly, the chronicles and song-books (see s.vv. *Cronica*, *Cancionero*) afforded rich material for the balladists, who created in the 15th cent. a class of poetry which was peculiarly characteristic of Spain, and which has proved the study and delight of all admirers of Span. lit. till this day.

Romance of the Rose ; Roman de la Rose (1237, 1277) : Fr. verse romance ; the most popular poem of the Middle Ages, in many respects the best mirror of their life, and an indispensable source-book for later European lit. It was written in 2 instalments at an interval of 40 years, part i by Guillaume de Lorris (q.v., *c.* 1237) and part ii by Jean Clopinel de Méun (q.v., *c.* 1277). Fr. romance in the 13th cent. followed 2 main lines, one of which reached its height in the *Roman de Renart* (see s.v. Reynard), and the other in the *Rose*. Assuming the background to each, and their various sources in ancient and early lit., we may say that the key to the former is human nature illustrated by analogy, and that the key to the latter is human nature revealed in allegory (q.v.). The one typified qualities by examples from the brute creation ; the other abstracted the qualities, and treated them as independent personages. The difference is between symbolism and personification (q.v.) ; and each method was elaborated in a manner characteristic, first of the 13th cent., when curiosity, unchecked by criticism, invaded the valley of knowledge and the adjacent plains of belief, and submerged the frontier which divided them ; and, secondly, of the Gallic genius of the romancers of that age, with their popular tradition of free speech, their growing suspicion of the clergy, their ready laugh at their womankind, and their vital necessity to please. The allegorists, starting from Love as the prime mover in the complex of experience, a starting-point set by Ovid (q.v.), the classical fountain of romance, provided the entertainment which was their aim by inventing a variety of situations in which Love had to struggle for his own. So, the dream (q.v.) of Guillaume in the 13th cent. was to be an allegory of the art of love, in which the lover, *Amant*, who desired to pluck the Rose growing in the magic garden, was helped or hindered in his quest by various symbolic personifications, Bialocoil (*Bel-Accueil*, Fair-Welcome), sir Mirth, the lady Gladness, Wanhope (Despair), Beauty, Fraunchyse (frankness), Courtesy, Shame, Jealousy, Fear, *Dangier* (dangerous-power), Sweet-Seeming, and many others :

It is the Romance of the Rose,
In which al the art of love I close. . . .
That it was May, thus dremed me,
In time of love and Jolitee. . . .
Hard is his herte that loveth nought
In May, whan al this mirth is wrought.

Or, to give Guillaume's old Fr. verses :

Ce est li Rommanz de la Rose,
Où l'art d'Amors est tote enclose. . .
En Maie estoie, ce songoie,
El tems amoreus plein de joie . . .
Moult a dur cuer qui en Mai n'aime. . . .

Guillaume probably died young, for he left his *Rose* unfind. at line 4,070 of the Fr. text, corresponding to line 4,432 of the Chaucerian transln. This line reads,

Than shulde I fallen in wanhope.

The next line (4,071 ; 4,433) reads,

Allas, in wanhope ?—nay, pardee,

But Guillaume had been in his grave for 40 years before this relief was brought to Amant's despair. Why Jean of Meung took it over is not certain ; but the romance had been growing in popularity, and it suited the message he had to tell. To Guillaume's 4,070 lines Jean added 18,004, thus bringing the romance to the somewhat unwieldly bulk of 22,074 verses. (Another computation yields : Guillaume, 4,669 vv., Jean, 18,148 vv., total vv., 22,817). But though there was no break in the sense, there was a distinct break in the sentiment. The 2 writers were different by temperament, as well as by the span of half a century. Guillaume had the sweeter fancy, Jean the more vigorous imagination, and the original scheme was merged in a more ambitious and more captivating design. The fanciful allegory of the metaphysics of love is extended to what may be compared with a politico-social diatribe against the things that are. Jean, who was a considerable scholar, and plainly a free-thinker, enlarged the part of Reason and introduced Nature and False-seeming (Faux-Semblant), as well as other characters. The familiar stories of the romantic cycles are placed in the mouth of Reason, and their moral pointed satirically against the idealism of love. Nature discourses on the systems which ranked as philosophy in the 13th cent. ; and False-seeming is a kind of Reynard (or is conceived in the spirit of the fabulists) so that the exposure of his hypocrisy is the occasion for long harangues on religion and other topics. Thus, the *Romance of the Rose* drew together, by the genius of its 2 authors towards the beginning and the close of the 13th cent., all the threads of medieval inspiration. The Ovidian psychology of love was the chief contribution of Guillaume ; Jean incorporated the repertory of the *chansons de geste*, and added the attacks of the Reynardists on conventional morality and on women. Herein, as in respect to Reynard, we may urge that the protests against hypocrisy are signs that the poets were becoming more moral, as keepers of the public conscience. The poem has great beauties in both kinds, and its influence was immediate and permanent. It was multiplied in MSS. ; preachers quoted from it, as from the Bible ; critics assailed its morality, and admirers extolled its art. After the invention of printing (q.v.), it was issued in many edns. in 15th and 16th cents. It had already been transld. into Flemish and Engl., and was well-known to Petrarch (q.v.) and the Ital. romancers. (The Engl. version was formerly ascribed to Chaucer, and Skeat concludes that the first 1,705 lines were by him, and the rest by 2 unknown translrs.). Marot (q.v.) 'edited' the romance, in the sense of modernizing it for his own generation, and at a later date it was 'moralized' by Molinet (q.v.) in the sense of a mystical interpretation. To many its music must still appeal, with more force than its allegory or its satire, as a faint clear prelude to the orchestra, which, to vary a well-worn phrase, has made poetic Europe what it is.

Romans Bretons : Tales of the 'matière de Bretagne' (see s.vv. Bodel and Romance), being the collection and redaction by the hands of Fr. troubadours and romancers of the tales derived from Celtic legend, and especially from the Welsh hills of king Arthur (q.v.). 'The Breton romances', writes Lanson (*Hist. Lit. Fr.*, 49), 'are the re-entry on the scene and virtually the revenge of the Celtic race : in appearance, at least, it is the capture of the Romanized, Germanized, Christianized, feudal Occident by the imagination of the Celts of Bretagne, who contrived to evade, if not altogether the domination, at any rate the civilization of Rome'. By 1250, or thereabouts, a huge mass of romantic lit. had been reared on the Celtic foundation : lays, or love-poems, mostly about Tristan (q.v.) ; tales of adventure, about the knights of the Round Table (q.v.) ; and the Grail (q.v.) tales of quest and mysticism.

Rondeau : Descriptive name of a class of medieval Fr. songs, developed in the 14th cent. in Northern France out of models imitated from the Troubadours of Provence. The R. contained 13 lines, of which the first 8 were in the triolet form,—verse 4 repeating verse 1, and verses 7 and 8 repeating verses 1 (4) and 2. The concluding 5 lines contain similar refrains and repetitions. The metrical scheme was subject to ingenious variations, alike in rhymes and in the number of verses, which ranged from 10 to 19. The revival of the R. in later centuries always creates an artificial and fanciful impression.

Rondel : Descriptive name of a class of medieval Fr. songs, developed in the 14th cent. in Northern France from a model supplied by the Troubadours of Provence. The chief variety of the R. consisted of 13 lines, containing two sets of 4, equivalent to a triolet, *plus* a stanza of 5 lines. Lines 1 and 2 were repeated at 7 and 8.

Ronsard, de, Pierre (1524-85): Fr. lyric poet; known to his contemporaries as prince of poets; moving spirit of the Pleiad (q.v.) or 7 stars risen in the firmament of Fr. poetry. R.'s family had been associated with Vendôme for more than 500 years, and the poet was born in the ancient castle of la Poissonière; his father was a soldier-scholar, and obtained for him, 1536, the post of page, first, to the dauphin of France, and, after his untimely death (' Six jours devant sa fin je vins à son service ') to the duke of Orleans, youngest son of king Francis i. At the marriage of king James v of Scotland with princess Madeleine, sister of the duke, R. was transferred to her service ; she also died untimely (' au lieu de royaume elle y trouva la mort '), and R. remained at the Scottish court till king James m. Marie de Guise ; they became the parents of queen Mary Stuart, to whom R. in later life paid brilliant tributes of poetic adoration. Meanwhile, R.'s travels in the suites of princes and ambassadors ended about 1540, when his public life was merged in his poetic. He studied under Dorat (q.v.), the Hellenist, and his fellow-pupils included his most ardent colleague in the Pleiad, J. Du Bellay (q.v.), and likewise Belleau and Baïf (qq.v.) ; and master and pupils were united in a common enthusiasm for learning, a common departure from the Middle Ages, a common conscious glorification of France, and a common veneration for antiquity, the ' science hautaine ' of Dorat and Turnebus (q.v.), and for the nations which practised its tongues. R. was the leader of this circle, the head of the buoyant young brigade, by much the same right of high spirits and personal charm as distinguished Rossetti (q.v.) just 300 years afterwards in the Pre-Raphaelite Brotherhood ; and the *pièce justificative* of the earlier brotherhood appeared in 1549 in Du Bellay's eloquent plea, *Défense et Illustration de la Langue française*. It was the lit. rather than the ' language ' which the prophet of this movement was concerned to ' defend ' from the limitations which Fr. diffidence set to it, and from a merely servile imitation of classic models : the ' épiceries ' (sugarplums) of medieval tradition—the virelai, the rondeau (qq.v.), etc.—were included in the same attack as the ornate, aureate affectations of the Italianate ' Rhétoriqueurs ' (q.v.). A bolder conception of Fr. capacity, a more patriotic resolve and aim, and an assimilation, not a transln., of good examples, were the principles which R. was to practise. The illustrations quickly followed the defence. Du Bellay's sonnet-sequences,

Olive and *Recueil de Poésie*, appeared in 1549-50, and a memorable hour in Fr. lit. was struck by the publication in 1550 of *Les Quatre premiers livres des Odes de Pierre de Ronsard, Vendômois, ensemble son Bocage*; ' the four first books of (94) Odes ' were followed by a fifth bk. 2 years later ; the ' Bocage ', additional to them, consisted of 14 poems named after the *Sylvæ* of Statius (Rom. epicist of the 1st cent., A.D. ; the Stace of his Renaissance imitators and admirers). There were 3 poetic experiments reserved by the prophet of the Pleiad for the Fr. master-poet to-be : the ode, aloof from the vulgar ; the sonnet, at once learned and pleasant ; and the long Fr. poem. To these 3 R. devoted himself, following his first brilliant success, ably ' boomed ', as we should say to-day, by Dorat and the brotherhood, with his *Les Amours de Cassandre*, 1552 ; *Hymnes*, 1553 ; *Le Bocage Royal* and other vols. collected, by request of queen Mary, in 1560 ; the epic *Franciade*, written by royal command, and issued, unfortunately, on the eve of the massacre of St. Bartholomew, 1572 ; and more odes, *Amours*, and sonnets. It was objected to R. in his lifetime that Saint-Gelais (q.v.) had written sonnets before him and that the ode was the old ' chanson ' under another name ; it was objected to R. after his death by Malherbe and Boileau (qq.v.) that his poetry was too natural and did not ' tend towards Good Sense ' ; and R.'s fame has suffered restoration and eclipse more than once during the changes of taste in succeeding centuries. To no generation, perhaps, will he ever be again, as he was to his own, the ' French Pindar ' and the ' prince of poets '; but the vain quarrels of the ' romantics ' and ' classics ' are, one hopes, so far left behind in the Middle Ages from which criticism is at last emerging—the rearguard of the army of letters—that R. can never again forfeit his high and unique place in Fr. lit. as the true refounder of her poetic genius, by virtue of his careful, loving study of the words that compose the line and of the rhythm of the line which they compose. The measured stateliness of Gk. Pindar was not less his than the tenderness of Rom. Catullus's diminutives ; the curious felicity of Horace and the plenary grace of Petrarch and Bembo ; he took the best where he found it, and assimilated it to the requirements of his native tongue ; abolishing the languor, and the artifice, and the ineffective experiments of his predecessors. The constellation of the Pleiad rose and set ; but R., its brightest star, shines in undiminished splendour ; he enhanced the glory of his country, and communicated to other countries the revelation of a vernacular language as a potent vehicle of high and serious poetry.

Roper, William (1496-1578): Engl. biographer; m. Margaret, daughter of sir Thomas More (q.v.), whose *Life* he wr. ; *ed. pr.*, 1626.

Rosa, de la, Francisco Martinez (*c.* 1787-1862): Span. dramatist. R.'s early plays were in the manner of his Span. predecessors ; the best known is the patriotic piece on the *Viuda* (widow) *de Padilla*, 1814. But his residence in Paris as a political *émigré* introduced R. to the romantic movement on the Fr. stage ;

and he composed some plays in Fr. and others in Span., notably *la Conjuracion de Venetia*, 1834, which struck out a more modern line. R. also attempted to exploit sir W. Scott's (q.v.) vein of hist. romance in an *Isabel de Solis, queen of Granada*, 1837-46.

Rosa, Salvator (1615-73): It. painter; wr. satires in verse on painting, music and poetry, somewhat languid and diffuse.

Roscoe, William (1753-1831): Engl. historian; member of a well-known family in Liverpool, which he represented in the House of Commons, 1806-7; bankrupt, 1820, owing to suspension of payment by his bank, a type of misfortune frequently utilized by novelists in the 19th cent., when his library and pictures were acquired by the Liverpool Athenæum. R. had 3 sons: **Wm. Stanley R.** (1782-1843), a writer of minor verse; **Thomas R.** (1791-1871), a translr. and misc. writer; and **Henry R.** (1800-36), who wr., 1833, his father's life; **Wm. Caldwell R.** (1823-59), a poet and essay-writer, was a son of Wm. Stanley R. (*supra*), and another kinsman was the rt. hon. sir Henry E. Roscoe (1832-1915), M.P., and an authority on education. W.R., to return to him, was keenly interested in Renaissance lit., and his *Life of Lorenzo de' Medici*, 1795, the tenth edn. of which, with valuable appendices, was revised by his son, T.R., 1862, is still a classic authority. Wr., too, *Life and Pontificate of Leo x*, and other works.

Rossetti, i. Gabriele (1783-1854): It. poet; born at Vasto, where the central piazza was renamed in his honour, 1883; was at one time librettist to the theatre of S. Carlo, Naples; escaped from Italy as a proscribed liberal, 1821, reaching Engld. via Malta, 1824; m., 1826, Frances Mary Lavinia, daughter of Gaetano Polidori, sometime secretary to Alfieri (q.v.), and his wife, *née* Pierce, formerly an Engl. governess; appointed, 1831, prof. of Ital. at King's Coll., London.

ii. Maria Francesca (1827-76): Engl. 'religious'; daughter of above; wr. *A Shadow of Dante*, 1871; entered an Anglican sister-hood, 1874.

-iii. Gabriel Charles Dante (1828-82): painter and poet; brother of above; founder of the Pre-Raphaelite Brotherhood (q.v.); named Charles after his godfather, Charles Lyell (father of the great geologist), but is always known by his 2 other baptismal names in the order in which he invariably used them, as **Dante Gabriel Rossetti**. The name represents a big debt, comparable with those represented by the name Disraeli, due by Engld. to immigrants from Italy, in the days when our gates were open to religious and political refugees. D.G.R.'s services to British art, in conjunction with Ford Madox Brown (1821-93), Holman Hunt, and others, and with the critical support of Ruskin (q.v.), lie outside the purview of lit.; the object of the allied painters, we are told, 'was to break with the empty conventionality which had gradually dominated English art, substituting for it real, even if primitive ideas, and the sincere study of nature down to her most intimate details' (sir Walter Armstrong, *Art in Great Britain*, 230). Similar principles governed R.'s poetry, in which he was not less

proficient than in painting. The organ of the P.R.B., *The Germ*, no. 1 of which appeared on 1 Jan., 1850, had as sub-title, *Thoughts towards Nature in Poetry, Literature and Art*; and, since poetry is a branch of lit., it is obvious that the thoughts towards nature were directed at once along 2 channels. The influence of Keats (q.v.) on R. is discussed s.v. Pre-Raphaelite Brotherhood, and the influence of R. on W. Morris is discussed s.v. R.'s biographers tell the moving story of his engagement, c.1850, to Elizabeth Siddal, whose beautiful features are preserved by his brush, of its protraction till 1860 owing to lack of money and her ill-health, and of the death of Mrs. R., 1862, from the effects of an overdose of laudanum. They tell, too—the late A. C. Benson (q.v.), in his ' English Men of Letters ' monograph, most sympathetic-ally—of the *impar congressus* : ' it is enough to say that Rossetti's conscience-stricken condi-tion at his wife's death was based on the knowledge that he had not failed to wound a faithful heart'. The moving personalia enter lit. history by the fact that R. buried in his wife's grave the only copy of a manu-script bk. of poems, on which he had often worked when she was suffering, ' and it may be doubted whether in the annals of literature there is any sorrow which strikes so vehement a note of sorrow and self-reproach ' (Benson, *op. cit.*, 50). Lit. history has further to record that, in 1869, by permission of the Home Office, when the first lord Aberdare was Home Secretary, the vol. was exhumed. So, in 1870, R. publd. his *Poems*, nearly all of them written years before; and Swinburne (q.v.), among others, accorded them a brilliant reception; a new edn., altered and enlarged, was publd., 1881, in the same year as *Ballads and Sonnets*. Meanwhile, in Oct., 1871, R. Buchanan (q.v.) had publd. in the *Contemporary Review*, under the name of Thomas Maitland, his fierce art. on 'The Fleshly School of Poetry', to which R. replied in *The Athenæum*, 16 Dec., 1871, with ' The Stealthy School of Criticism '. Let us say at once, that, though the stealthi-ness was indefensible, the fleshliness was open to attack. Going back to sir W. Armstrong's words (*supra*) about ' the sincere study of nature down to her most intimate details ', and assuming the value of the sincerity, it is obvious that there are intimate details not suited for art or poetry. Certain passages to which Buchanan took exception have been removed from the poems; but we have to note that the poet's very sincerity led him to omit no evid-ence which was revealed to his sensuous perception. With this brief reference to an aspect, to which too much attention has been given, R.'s brilliant and glowing muse, esp. in his earlier poems, may be unreservedly admired. As the glow faded, a second manner supervened, which was rather that of a collector than of a creator, of a connoisseur than of a lover inspired. There was the same sensibility to beauty, the same delight in touching it and handling it, but less spontaneity in its enjoy-ment. Handling is of the essence of his style. His vivid decorative instinct seized on the visible shapes of imagined emblems of beauty, and his poems, early and late, are full of such articulated images, sometimes directly transposed from the canvases of the Ital. masters whom he loved. 'She had three lilies in her hand, And the stars in her hair were seven'; 'As low as where this earth, Spins like a fretful midge'; 'And the souls mounting up to God, Went by her like thin flames'; 'The curled moon was like a little feather Fluttering far down the gulf', are clear examples of this imaginative realism selected from *The Blessed Damozel*, in the final stanza of which the 2 sentences in brackets—('I saw her smile') and ('I heard her tears')—exemplify a like vividness in symbolism.

We must not dwell on this prince of poets, the Ronsard of a new Pleiad (see s.vv.); who, young, and ardent, and beautiful, swept along in the stream of his beauty-worship lover and friends and critics, and the very implements of his double art. Nor need we pause to contrast —fascinating though the study is—the attitude towards experience of R. and his contemporary, M. Arnold (q.v.); a fair beginning of the study might be made by reading in rapid succession R.'s poem, *Jenny*, and Arnold's reference to *Wragg* in *Essays in Criticism*, i ('The Function of Criticism'). We must be content, with prof. Walker (*Lit. Victorian Era*, 494) to concur with Ruskin's dictum, that R. was 'the chief intellectual force in the establishment of the Modern Romantic School in England'. It is high enough, but not too high, praise. Two points have still to be mentioned: first, the issue, 1861, of *The Early Ital. Poets from Ciullo d'Alcamo to Dante Alighieri*, 1100-1200-1300, *in the original metres, together with Dante's 'Vita Nuova'*, transld. by D.G.R.; re-arranged, 1874, as *Dante and his Circle*: a very valuable and original piece of work, with which should be joined R.'s sequence of poems (sonnets) *The House of Life*, which, wrought out of his personal experience, is moulded into the forms of his early Ital. masters; and, secondly, that experience itself. No man, least of all a sensitive poet, can bury and exhume a passion without leaving a mark on his soul. R.'s act of renunciation at his wife's grave, and his repudiation of that act 8 years afterwards, when he slew his own fancy, and reclaimed it from hell, rendered him a victim to insomnia and delusions, from which chloral alone could give relief. His disease was at times so severe, that he suspected even the birds in the garden of complicity in a plot to insult him and drive him out of society. His friends did all they could to help: 'perhaps something of a tragic pity for the doom under which their hero lay imparted a deeper quality to this devotion'. But 'even when broken with illness and enslaved by the sad bondage of habit, this personality still dazzled and almost hypnotized all who were brought into contact with him, up to the very end' (Benson, *op. cit.*, 207, 226). And, beyond the mortal end, the dazzling personality prevails, and the great artist and poet imposes his will for beauty on wider circles of friends and admirers.

-iv. **William Michael** (1829-1919): Engl. critic; original member of the P.R.B., and a busy editor of the works of his elder brother (*supra*), whose *Family Papers, with Memoirs*, 2 vols., he publd., 1895; adding a *Bibliography of the Works of D. G. Rossetti*, 1905; m., 1874, Lucy (1843-94), daughter of Ford Madox Brown, the painter.

-v. **Christina Georgina** (1830-94): Engl. poet; sister to above. Wr. *Verses*, privately printed, 1847; contributed to *The Germ*; publd. *Goblin Market, and other Poems*, 1862; and lesser works in prose and verse; her *Works* were edited, with memoirs, notes, etc., by W. M. Rossetti, 1904, who also made a selection from them for the Golden Treasury series. In the excellent ch. (v. of vol. xiii) devoted in *C.H.E.L.*, to this extraordinarily gifted family, we read, that: 'unlike her brother, whose sympathy with religion was purely artistic, and still more unlike Swinburne, whose attitude to the orthodox conceptions of Christianity was openly hostile, Christina Rossetti was, to the end of her life, a devout Christian, finding the highest inspiration for her song in her faith and investing Anglican ideals of worship with a mystical beauty. Her vols. of collected verse are permeated, even when they deal with subjects not primarily religious, with this devotional feeling. If she had less intellectual force and a more confined range of subject than Elizabeth Barrett Browning, who certainly, by virtue of her more liberal sympathies, makes an appeal to a wider audience, C. R. unquestionably had the advantage in melodiousness'. Her 'verse has a natural kinship with the religious poetry of the seventeenth century', and 'no religious poet of the nineteenth century, even if we take into account the brilliant but more turbid genius of Francis Thompson, can be said to challenge comparison with her whose "shrine of holiest-hearted song" Swinburne approached with reverent admiration'. When we recall the accident of Ital. politics which brought old Gabriele R. to our shores in 1824, and the immense return which he made for their hospitality through the Engl. children whom he brought up, we may reasonably agree with M. Arnold, in the essay mentioned above, that, though epochs of concentration have their uses in a nation's political affairs, its intellectual progress is better served in the alternating epochs of expansion.

Rossi, de, Roberto (14th-15th cent.): It. humanist. Florentine pupil of Chrysoloras (q.v.); eminent Gk. scholar.

Rotgans, Lucas (1654-1710): Dutch poet; he used to recite his poems at social gatherings with a shattering effect on the ears of his friends. Wr., epic poem on king William iii of Engld., which included a description of the battle of the Boyne.

Rotrou, de, Jean (1609-50): Fr. dramatist; one of the 5 tragic playwrights whom Richelieu (q.v.) employed as his shadows; succeeded Hardy (q.v.) as dramatic author to the Hotel de Bourgogne (q.v.); he died courageously at a municipal post at Dreux in consequence of a local epidemic. R. composed rapidly, and wr. about 35 plays in about 20 years of active life. He was always intimate with Corneille (q.v.), and, though surpassed by him, like other contemporaries, R. was able to benefit by his example as well as, possibly, to repay his friend a little in kind. He 'is readable, even after Corneille', says one critic, and his best pieces, by common consent, are his *Saint-Genest* (with a play within the play), 1646, and his *Venceslas*, 1647; both from Span. prototypes. His relation to Corneille has been compared with that of Marlowe to Shakespeare (qq.v.), and the comparison is just in the sense that R., with less mastery than Corneille, assisted the transition of Fr. drama from romantic extravagance to classic art.

Roucher, Jean François (1745-94): Fr. poet; Wr. didactic *les Mois*, after the model of Thomson's (q.v.) *Seasons*, but marred by the fatal periphrastic style of second-hand observation, which characterized the philosophic era in 18th-cent. France. R. perished by the guillotine.

Rouget-de-L'isle, Claude Joseph (1760-1836): Fr. poet; composer of the Fr. national melody, the *Marseillaise*, which was sung by the men of Marseilles at the time of the Fr. Revolution. He publd. other verse of less merit.

Round Table: The knights at the court of king Arthur (q.v.); traditionally represented as possessing a Table, round which they sat in conclave, devising deeds of heroism and arms; the Table-idea may have been due to a confusion with the alleged Sacred Table on which Joseph of Arimathea, in his missionary wanderings, was supposed to enhearten his followers by exhibiting the vessel containing the drops of the Saviour's blood. (See s.v. Grail). The common form of a Round-Table tale in the first period of Fr. romance (q.v.) was the arrival of a young knight, often of unknown birth, at Arthur's court; he would be entrusted with a chivalrous mission of danger and difficulty; and, having accomplished his adventures, would marry the lady whom he had rescued.

Rous, Francis (1579-1659): Engl. theologian; 'in 1650 the General Assembly (of Scotld.) adopted, with many variations, the (metrical) version (of the Psalter) of Francis Rous, an English puritan, M.P. for Truro, ultimately speaker of the Barebones Parliament and provost of Eton College' (lord Ernle, *The Psalms in Human Life*, 150). 'In no other country', he adds, 'except France, have metrical paraphrases of the Psalms exercised a greater influence than in Scotland.'

Rousseau, Jean Baptiste (1669-1741): Fr. poet; of the school of Boileau (q.v.) in his odes and epistles. Wr., too, sacred verse, which obtained a certain vogue in the latter part of the reign of king Louis xiv, when piety was fashionable, and was, first, admired, and, later, attacked by Voltaire (q.v.). R. was unfortunate, too, in being exiled from France on account of a satire on the fiancée of prince Eugène of Savoy, of which he was probably not the author.

Rousseau, Jean Jacques (1712-78): Fr. (-Swiss) philosopher, if a common term must be found for the manifestations of the most irregular genius which adorned Fr. lit. in the 18th cent. Yet a genius unmistakably; and, if greatness is measurable by influence, the greatest single name since Rabelais (q.v.) in the illustrious literary history of his country. R. was contemporary with Diderot (d. 1784) and Voltaire

(d. 1778), of whom the one had learned from lord Bacon (q.v.) more penetrating methods of thought, and the other had evolved from experience a more direct approach to reality. R. possessed little learning and less wit; his originality was audacious, but unconscious; and, if he is sometimes suspect of posing, this attitude, when it is assumed, is plainly the result of his second thoughts, and not of the primary convictions which he expressed with the fervour of a white-hot sincerity. We may submit some cumulative evidence in proof of the immensity of R.'s influence. High authorities on both sides of the channel (Morley's *Rousseau*, 2 vols., 1873; *C.M.H.*, vi, ch. xxiv; D. Mornet, *le Romantisme en France au xviii° Siècle*; Lanson, *Hist. Lit. Fr.*, 798ff.) agree in ascribing to R.'s writings an influence which permanently impressed itself on religious, moral, and political thought; which opened out new avenues of approach to romance, sentiment, psychology; which profoundly modified men's views on social justice, national beauty, individuality; and which found expression in speculation and action, proceeding from men as diverse as Robespierre, Kant, Schiller, Chateaubriand, Paine, Byron, Wordsworth. More and more, as historians of the 19th cent. trace to the fountainhead the springs of social and literary emancipation, and of release from the restrictive bondage of 18th cent. rationalism, they find R. at the source, and greet him as the author who changed the values of things. We may cite one authority only. Prof. C. E. Vaughan, in his edn. of *The Political Writings of Rousseau* (Cambridge, 2 vols., 1915), says that R. 'gave men faith in their power to redress the wrongs of ages. And he held forth an ideal of civic life which has changed the face of Europe. . . . This is the glory which nothing can take from him'. And the claim, high though it be, is conceded by the first earl of Cromer (*Nineteenth Century and After*, May, 1916): 'Rousseau made the world think. He introduced new ideas, which were often wrong, but almost always fruitful.'[*]

This testimony becomes more striking from the contrast presented between R.'s work and his life. The nearest analogue in this respect is the Scot. poet, R. Burns (q.v.), of whom Wordsworth (q.v.) finely wr., 'on the basis of his human character he has reared a poetic one'; and even more requisite is this insight in discussing the contrast between R., in his human character, and R., as pioneer of the new humanism. 'Rousseau, sir, is a very bad man', declared Dr. Johnson (q.v.) to Boswell, freshly back from a visit to Paris, and Brunetière (q.v.) called him 'un plébéien et un fou'. If ordinary standards of conduct are applied, it is difficult to dispute these judgments. But we have to suspend the common standards. This descendant of Swiss Calvinists, the son of a watchmaker at Geneva, whose mother died in giving birth to him, and whose irresponsible and feckless father left him at 10 years old, was an

[*] A very fair estimate of the debt which posterity owes to R. will be found in the excellent Introduction to the *Age of Wordsworth*, by prof. C. H. Herford; Bell, 1897.

untamed savage of the fields, whom God charged with a new gospel. Baptist crossed with Caliban, is the best description we can formulate. He lied, he thieved, he hit out ; he ran away, 1728 ; he attracted the interest of a mme. de Warens at Annecy ; he took and lost situations as footman ; he gave music-lessons ; he returned to Annecy, where his ' maman ' gave him pens, and bks., and three lovely summers of solitude ; he taught the children of a de Mably (brother to G. de Mably and to Condillac, qq.v.) ; and, at last, 1741, he reached Paris ' with fifteen louis, a comedy on *Narcissus*, and a new system of musical notation which was to bring him fame and fortune '. It brought nothing better than employment at copying music in a garret ; and R.'s next situation was as secretary to de Montaigu, Fr. ambassador in Venice, whom he neither suited nor found suitable. He was back in Paris in 1743. This time he took a lodging in the squalid rue des Cordiers (between the rue St. Jacques and the rue Victor Cousin) at a low hostelry now known as the Hôtel J. J. Rousseau ; and this particularity is important, since it was there that R., the ex-footman, deliberately gave his protection to the kitchen-maid, Theresa Le Vasseur. She lived with him till about 1770, and he m. her (by a ceremony of his own devising), after 25 years' attachment, in 1768. It is not possible to idealize Theresa. She was a common lodging-house slut, even more illiterate and unteachable than the majority of her kind ; her mother and relatives preyed on R., whose true life she never tried to share ; she had recourse to brandy-bibbing and other vices ; and she left R. to follow a stable-boy. On the other hand, the 5 babies that she bore him were calmly deposited by R. at the Foundling Hospital ; there is evidence to show that this treatment was repugnant to the mother's feelings. The whole episode, which lasted nearly a lifetime, or, at any rate, through the best years of a man's life, is one of the most curious in all the annals of human partnership. Probably, the only explanation is, that the living man who was Rousseau, and who was always imagining slights directed to him from the tables of the great, found contentment in mating with his kind ; while the poet-prophet, who was also Rousseau, was inspired to write his immortal bks. independently of his domestic circumstances. After all, the fame of Socrates does not rest on his relations with Xantippe. But the contrast was extraordinary enough. The ' father of Romanticism ' in Europe, as R. has been aptly called, carried his babies to the Foundling hospital ; the restorer of religion, the worshipper of nature, the champion of the oppressed, the rebel against convention, the social reformer, the prophet of individualism, the fountain-head of Byronism, the well-spring of sentiment, was by his free choice ' mated with a clown ', to whom he refused the elementary rights of motherhood. We must leave the mystery as we find it ; remembering only that, as years went on, and as the persecution of his enemies and detractors grew more bitter, R.'s taste for seclusion, and his restless, morbid shrinking from the company and

commonplaces of his fellowmen, developed into a monomania ; that, like Rossetti (q.v.), in his last years, R. was tormented by terrors of his imagination ; and that he died, possibly by suicide, certainly in misery and destitution.

It is time to return from Theresa to Jean Jacques. His first opportunity came when Diderot offered him employment as musical contributor to the Encyclopedia (q.v.), 1749. In the same year, the Dijon academy offered a prize for an essay on the subject : ' Has the progress of the sciences and arts tended to corrupt or to purify manners ? ' R., instigated possibly by Diderot, entered for the competition with a discourse, which maintained the paradoxical view that *les moeurs* had corrupted *les arts*, and that natural man was worse for civilization ; and a further discourse, publd. at Amsterdam, 1755, ' on the origin and foundations of inequality ', pushed the same argument nearer home, and made R. a personage among the *philosophes* (q.v.). He signalized his success, characteristically, by escaping from Paris, with all his household and chattels, to a charming asylum provided by mme. d'Epinay (q.v.) on her estate in Montmorency. The date was April, 1756, and the promise of springtide in the forest seemed at last to be shining on the ex-footman and music-teacher, who had the heart of a child and the soul of a prophet. But fate had a grudge against R. ; the gods gave him every gift except peace. He came to loggerheads with Diderot and baron Grimm, and with his benefactress, mme. d'Epinay ; and, through the middle-class pride which always distinguished him, and which prevented him from accepting various proffered pensions, R. quitted his hostess for a little house, Montlouis, situated in the forest (Dec., 1757). There he spent some tranquil years, interrupted, alas, by the obscurantism and persecution of the Sorbonne, occasioned by the publication of his bks., till, in 1762, he had to flee from the danger of arrest. Even Geneva was closed to him, and R. took refuge at Neufchâtel, then under the suzerainty of the king of Prussia (Fredk. ii, q.v.), to whom R. wr. some delightfully frank letters. He was again driven away ; and the phantoms of his imagination were even worse than the terrors of the Church. In 1765 he reached Engld., where Hume (q.v.) befriended him ; with the same inevitable results : quarrels, jealousy, flight. The hounds of heaven pursued him from one miserable foothold to another, till ' at last he returned to France, to end his life, after years of lingering misery, in obscurity and despair ' (Strachey, *Landmarks of Fr. Lit.*, 196).—On the basis of his human life, he reared a creative one ; and it is good to get away from the garrets, the ghosts, and the dirt, to the immortal works of genius by which R. impressed his personality on the mind of his age and of succeeding ages. Briefly, the central principle of R.'s revelation may be stated as a mathematical formula, thus :

Society : Nature : : evil : good.

This principle having been stated in the 2 *Discours* of 1750 and 1755, and having been driven home in a letter to Dalembert on art, and in another *Lettre sur les Spectacles*, opposing a theatre at Geneva, R. sought to draw its consequences in a series of works, which surveyed the problems from different angles. These were written chiefly in the forest of Montmorency, under the gentle influences of flowers, and shade, and country peace. The first was *la Nouvelle Heloïse, ou Lettres de deux Amants*, 1761, in which the problem of a return to nature was examined from the point of view of sex-love and family-life. Richardson (q.v.) imposed the form of letters, and Richardson and Prévost (q.v.) together inspired the tenderness and sentiment which took female Paris by storm. But what was wholly R.'s, was the doctrine of individual right defeated by social wrong, and the exaltation of the family as the nucleus of true human society. This doctrine placed rebellion against philosophy (against the *philosophes* of the Encyclopedia) on a philosophic basis. Next came *Emile, ou de l'Éducation*, Amsterdam, 1762 ; a necessary sequel to the *Heloïse*, and, with all deductions, a very valuable pioneer-work in modern educational lit. In this work, R. laid down the principle that the psychology of the child corresponds to the psychology of the race, with sensation preceding reflection, and reflection preceding religious faith. So, even through the trammels of civilization which it is impracticable to lay aside, the dues of nature may be consulted, and natural virtues inculcated in the child. The *Profession de foi du Vicaire Savoyard* ('the Savoyard vicar's profession of faith') is really a part of *Emile* ; and it is interesting to note how the Huguenot strain in R.'s blood, and his self-adaptation to his own theories and method, brought about a simplification of his own faith, and restored the idea of God from the harsh judgment of philosophic doubt. R.'s next great work was *du Contrat Social*, Amsterdam, 1762, in which, whatever its faults, and whatever deduction must be made from its paradoxes, R. enunciated a simple principle of assent to government, which had immense influence on future practice in his own country and beyond it. It went back, with special reference to the hist. method of Montesquieu (q.v.), from the theorizing of Locke (q.v.) and his school to the simplicities of political thought, discoverable in the masters, Plato and Aristotle. Thus founded on an attempt to make an individualist happy in a social state, it was bound, as R. knew well, to supply arguments to all parties ; 'they who boast that they understand the whole of it', he wr., 'are cleverer than I am'. It is, indeed, in the reduction of bookish philosophy to the test of common human conditions of the heart as well as of the head, that the magic of R.'s work lies ; and the naked sincerity of it all is displayed in the vols. of *Confessions*, issued posth., Geneva, 1781-88, in which R. subjected his very soul to a scrupulous and faithful analysis. Love, education, government, religion ; and, finally, the bared soul of the sinning reformer : that is the order of R.'s works, launched by stealth on a world of persecutors. His doctrine has prevailed ; and for the sake of the fresh ideas which he restored to mankind, wearied by its own too much learning, the acrimonious

philosopher of Geneva, with all the sordidness of his private life, and with all the immodesty of his public confessions, is counted as an apostle of humanity, and as a source of inspiration to the makers of modern thought. A 'return to nature' is the common postulate of the essence of the Rousseauan philosophy. It may have been in certain aspects a return to nature *in impuris naturalibus*, as Nietzsche (q.v.) epigrammatically said. The natural life, that is to say, may be less pure than R. represented it, and may lack many of the virtues which the civilization which he attacked has introduced. R.'s more natural man may have trailed quite other qualities from his arboreal, four-handed ancestors than the 'clouds of glory' sung by Wordsworth *in verba magistri*. All this, and more, may be urged against Rousseauism as a system of thought. But no one takes it systematically to-day, and the new ethnology is less harsh to primitive man than the 'noble savage' theorists of a previous epoch. It is to Rousseauism as thought-provoker and path-finder that the secure judgment of the world has turned ; not in vain : to R. in Kant, R. in Byron, R. in Wordsworth ; R. in France, R. in America, R. in Switzerld., where he unfolded the valleys of the Alps, and laid us in nature's lap. R. taught men to aspire ; he 'first in our modern time sounded a new trumpet note for one more of the great battles of humanity' (Morley, *op. cit., init.*) ; and beyond the sound of the battles are the gentler sounds of R.'s influence, derived from his discovery of natural scenery as an inalienable portion of human consolation. For R. did not discover Nature (q.v.), but he first 'gave her an everlasting soul. He sought her inspiration, and gave her his confidence. He invested our life with hers, making her not a dwelling nor an embellishment, but as it were a speaking conscience, docile or imperious in turns.' (Mornet, *op. cit.*, 269).

Rowe, Nicholas (1674-1718) : Engl. poet ; dramatist ; poet-laureate (q.v.), 1715 ; clerk to the council of George, prince of Wales ; friend of Addison and Pope (qq.v.), who wr. an epitaph on R.'s burial in Westminster Abbey, 'by Dryden's awful dust', and succeeded R. as the second editor of the works of Shakespeare (q.v.). R.'s pioneer work in this field comprised an edn. of the plays in 6 vols., 1709, in which 'he made a few happy emendations, some of which coincide accidentally with the readings of the First Folio'. He was the first to supply 'a list of *dramatis personœ* to each play, to divide and number acts and scenes on rational principles, and to mark the exits and entrances of the characters'; and he prefixed to his edn. of the plays, according to his latest successor as biographer, sir Sidney Lee (*William Shakespeare*, 574), from whom we have been quoting, 'a valuable life of the poet, embodying traditions which were in danger of perishing without a record'. R.'s own plays include *The Ambitious Stepmother*, 1700 ; *The Fair Penitent*, 1703 ; *Jane Shore*, 1714 ; *Lady Jane Grey*, 1715 ; the two last produced at Drury Lane Theatre.

Rowley, William (*c.* 1585-*c.* 1642) : Engl. playwright ; collaborated with others—Middleton,

Webster, Massinger, Ford, Heywood (qq.v.), and the rest,—in accordance with the stage fashion of the times, and possibly with Shakespeare (q.v.) in *Pericles*. *The Birth of Merlin*, 1662, which was described on its title-page as 'written by William Shakespeare and William Rowley', is R.'s unaided work, and 'cannot be safely dated earlier than 1622, six years after Shakespeare's death' (sir S. Lee, *Wm. Shakespeare*, 265). Wr., too, *A Shoemaker a Gentleman*, 1638, and several other dramas all his own.

Roxas Zorilla, de, Francisco (1607-48): Span. dramatist; knt. of the order of Santiago, 1641; publd. 2 vols. of plays, 1640, 1645, and promised a third which did not appear. R.'s best-known drama is not in either of these vols. (which contain 24 plays), but is one of his *Comedias sueltas* ('detached') otherwise preserved. It is commonly called *Del rey abajo, ningano* ('no one, lower than the king', —*impune me lacessit*); the crucial words of the hero, Garcia, when he discovers that he is free to avenge his wife's honour, since it was threatened, not by the king (Alfonso xi), as he had thought, but by a courtier, Mendo. The play has been reprinted under other names: *el Labrador mas Honrado* ('A Peasant but a Man of Honour'); *Garcia del Castañar*; and *el Conde* (the Count) *de Orgaz*; and it has been erroneously ascribed to Calderon (q.v.). It is a fine example of Calderon's convention of the punctilio, or Span. point of honour. R.'s other plays are mostly known to-day by the use which was freely made of them in Fr. drama. Scarron, T. Corneille, Boisrobert and Rotrou (qq.v.) were the chief playwrights who put R. under levy; most notably, perhaps, in Scarron's *Jodelet* (from R.'s *Donde ay agravios no ay zelos*, 'where there are real grievances, there are no jealousies').

Rubens, Philip (1574-1611): Dutch scholar; brother of the artist. Pupil of Lipsius at Leyden, with whom he figures in a picture by his brother, now in the Pitti palace, together with his friend and contemporary, Wouwer (q.v.).

Rucellai, -i. Bernardo (15th cent.): It. antiquary; a pioneer in that branch of humane studies; wr. *de urbe Roma*, on the antiquities of Rome, which was not publd. till 18th cent.; also hist. works in Lat.; dedicated his fine garden in Florence to the use of the Medicean Platonic Academy (see s.v. Academy).

-ii. Giovanni (1475-1525): It. poet; son of above. Wr. *Rosmunda*, Ital. tragic drama in 5 acts with chorus; produced at Florence, 1515, in presence of pope Leo x (q.v.), and 'led the way to those accumulations of horrible and disgusting circumstances which deformed the European stage for a century afterwards' (Hallam). R. was among first to employ blank verse (q.v.; *versi sciolti*, loose or released verse) for Ital. drama, and, again, for Ital. narrative poetry, as in his posth. (1539) didactic poem on apiculture, one of the many imitations of Virgil (q.v.).

Rückert, Friedrich (1788-1866): Germ. poet and translr.; Romanticist; visited Italy, 1817; studied Oriental languages and lit. in Vienna; appointed to professorships in Erlangen and Berlin successively, retired to his country-house near Coburg, where he died. R.'s original lyric gifts and his taste for Oriental learning associate him intimately with the infinitely greater Goethe (q.v.), who recognized the kinship, and it is further to R.'s credit, that, if he did not found a school of Germ. poets of the Orient, he had eminent successors in the exploration of these sources of poetry, at the head of which is Goethe's *West-Ostliches Divan*: among those successors may be named Platen, Schefer, Daumer and Bodenstedt (qq.v.); perhaps we may add M. Arnold in Engld., since R. preceded Arnold in quarrying a *Rostem und Suhrab*, 1838, ('Sohrab and Rustum') out of the Persian of Firdusi. Thus, Rückert has a normal place in Germ. literary history, and it is not necessary to represent him as fleeing to Oriental topics from his disappointment at Germ. conditions. His flight to the ancient East was in the normal course of his poetic progress, and was probably not particularly affected by the politics of the Liberation epoch. Still it is true that R.'s first bk. of verse was the 'German Poems' (by 'Freimund Reimar') of 1814, containing *die geharnischten* (passionate) *Sonnette*, afire with patriotic ardour, aroused by the struggle against Napoleon (the one on the Battle of Leipsic, 1813, is still regarded as the best in this series) and the era of disillusionment which succeeded 1813. See s.vv. Young Germany and Metternich; it should be remembered, however, that Wordsworth, q.v., likewise wr. glowing patriotic sonnets in his youth, and that R.'s later studies probably contented him as fully. R.'s translns. and adaptations include: *Ostliche Rosen*, 1822, from Hafiz; the *Makámen*, 1826, of Hari' ri'; *Nal und Damajanti*, 1828, from the Sanscrit; the *Shi-King*, 1833, from the Chinese; Arabian folksongs, 1846, and, among several others, an ambitious collection of verse and aphorisms, representing the *Weisheit der Brahmanen* (6 vols.), 1836-39. R. also wr. plays, and one or 2 more vols. of lyric poetry.

Rudolf von Ems (1220-54): Germ. poet and chronicler. His verse-chronicles, which show acquaintance with the monastic authorities of the day, included a *World-chronicle*, of the common encyclopedic scope, which R. brought only down to Solomon, but which found ready continuators; an *Alexander* epos, now very fragmentary; and a *William of Orleans* (king William the Conqueror) and his love for queen Amelia of Engld., after the best models of chivalric convention. Far more notable were the poems of R. where he departed from medieval tradition. His verse-tales from monkish source-books open a new chapter in Germ. lit., rather in the vein of Boccaccio than of Froissart (qq.v); the novellistic rather than the chronicler's vein. The best of these are *der gute Gerhard* (the moral tale of 'the good' merchant of Cologne) and *Barlaam and Josaphat*, a Christian version of an old Buddhist legend, relating the influence of the hermit Barlaam on the wealthy and worldly prince Josaphat. The poem, with its valuable and convenient application, achieved wide popularity, esp. in the nascent age of drama.

Rueda, de, Lope (*c.* 1510-*c.* 1565) : Span. dramatic writer ; much praised, 1615, in a prologue by Cervantes (q.v.), who speaks of him as ' the great Rueda ', from whom Span. comedy took its start. Cervantes was 18 years old in 1565, and may well have seen R. as an actor on his rude stage ; indeed, he writes in the same context : ' In the time of this celebrated Spaniard, the whole apparatus of a manager was contained in a large sack, and consisted of four white shepherd's jackets, . . . four beards and wigs, and four shepherd's crooks more or less. The plays were dialogues, like eclogues, between two or three shepherds and a shepherdess, fitted up and extended with two or three interludes, whose personages were sometimes a negress, sometimes a bully, sometimes a fool, and sometimes a Biscayan. In all these four parts and others, Rueda himself acted with the greatest possible skill ' (Ticknor, ii, 55) ; and the primitiveness of the proceedings may be judged from the address to the audience in R.'s comedy, *Eufemia* : ' Ye who listen, go and dine ; and then return to the market-place, if you wish to see a traitor's head cut off, and a just man set at liberty '. It is well thus to reconstruct the atmosphere and surroundings of R.'s stage before discussing, as ' comedies ' and ' interludes ', the early compositions in those classes to which those names, afterwards so technical, were already attached. The realization helps to emphasize the significant departure made by R. in appealing for the first time in Span. drama, not to the associations of religious sentiment or to any ready-made audience, but to a chance collection of the judges by which all drama ultimately stands or falls—public opinion. R. was actor-manager and playwright too, in the line of Hardy, Molière, and Shakespeare (qq.v.) ; and within the humble limits of his opportunities and powers, he belongs to their class and kind. He took his theatre round the towns ; Segovia, Toledo, Seville, Madrid ; and, behind the ' old blanket drawn aside by two cords ' (Cervantes, *ibid.*), he prepared the dramatic effects which were to attract and amuse his audiences. Timoneda (q.v.) publd. R.'s works in 1567 under the title of ' The Four Comedies and Two Pastoral Colloquies of the Excellent Poet and Graceful Actor Lope de Rueda ' ; we also have some examples of his *pasos* (passages ; interludes in prose ; later known as *entremeses* in Timoneda's own works), and Cervantes mentions his ' pastoral verses '. It is by what he inaugurated rather than by what he wr. that R.'s fame abides in literary history ; but it is clear that he read widely and wisely in the preparation of his pieces ; Shakespeare's *Cymbeline*, e.g., recalls R.'s *Eufemia*, which is referred to Boccaccio (q.v.), *Decameron*, ii, 9 ; his *Twelfth Night* is derived from the same Ital. source (in Piccolomini, q.v.) as R.'s *Engaños* or *Engañados* (' Cheats ' or ' Cheaters ') ; and R.'s 2 remaining comedies, *Armelina* and *Medora*, have likewise been traced to the all-mother Italy. His *pasos* exhibit more horseplay, intended to appeal to the gallery, which, in R.'s theatre, comprised the whole audience, uncomfortably accommodated on a few rough benches ; and they mark a milestone in the progress from *Celestina* (q.v.), by which R. had obviously profited, to the plays of Cervantes and Vega (q.v.). ' The true founder of the popular national theatre ' (Ticknor, ii, 56), and ' Rueda's greatest title is to have inaugurated a true national theatre ' (Kelly, *Lit. espagn.*, 231), are estimates based by modern historians on the indirect evidence and personal testimony of R.'s most notable successors in Span. drama.

Ruiz, Juan (*c.* 1280-*c.* 1350) : Span. poet ; archpriest of Hita, by which description he is commonly known ; is said to have been imprisoned by the archbishop of Toledo, but the facts of his biography are quite obscure. R. lives and is revealed by his poems, consisting now of about 7,000 lines, collected in ' The book of true love ' (*Libro de buen amor*). The excellent humanity, keen shrewdness, happy vivacity, metrical variety, and licentiousness of this work recommend it to many tastes ; and the archpriest, at the dayspring of Span. lit., is not unjustly compared by Ticknor (i, 77) with Chaucer (q.v.), his Engl. contemporary : ' he has not, indeed, the tenderness, the elevation, or the general power of Chaucer ; but his genius has a compass, and his verse a skill and success, that show him to be more nearly akin to the great English master than will be believed, except by those who have carefully read the works of both '. Kelly (*Lit. espagn.*, 50ff.) concurs with this opinion, adding that, ' as a master of realism, Ruiz perhaps surpasses Chaucer ', but pointing out that, ' To say that the archpriest is the most significant figure in the origins of Castilian literature, is to state a truism ; to try to present him as a respectable person, is to commit a manifest absurdity '. Neither in his life nor in his writings was R. a model of moral propriety, and in his ample borrowings from the repertories of early romance (q.v.) he reproduced many features and tales which a more delicate taste lets go ; but not even the most fastidious reader fails to appreciate the artistic and dramatic instinct which raised R. from the ranks of romantic adapters and endowed him with true creative genius. An individual touch was given to all that he attempted ; and it passed sometimes into the national possession. Thus, he invented, by re-shaping what he found, and is fully as original a writer as any poet of his own or another age. The example commonly selected is his invention of the female messenger, or go-between (the ' nurse ' in Shakespeare's *Romeo and Juliet*), who, though derived from Ovid (q.v.), and not unknown to the authors of the *Romance of the Rose* (q.v.), was first acclimatized by our archpriest in Span. fiction, to re-appear, later, most typically, in the character of Celestina (q.v.), in the tragi-comedy of *Calisto y Melibea*, 1499. R. calls his messenger *Trota-conventos* (' convent-runner '), since she had so often to go between lovers in monasteries or nunneries. Standing at the head of the line of the picaresque novel (q.v.), even before the arrival of the *pícaro*, widely-read, with broad sympathies, and with a flexile style, the archpriest of Hita is the first individualized poet in Span. lit.

Rulhière, de, Claude Carloman (*c.* 1735-91) : Fr. historian. Wr. from personal observation in a diplomatic post at what was then St. Petersburg, an account of the events by which the empress Catherine ii (q.v.) had acceded to the Russ. throne. R.'s other works, some of which were publd. posthly., included a history of Poland ; ' historical considerations on the causes of the revocation of the Edict of Nantes ', and others. He was elected to the Fr. Academy (q.v.), 1787, and was a writer of verse-tales and epigrams. R.'s hist. works are still of value for their vivid narration of contemporary events.

Runeberg, Johan Ludvig (1804-77): Swed. (-Finnish) poet ; he just remembered the annexation of Finland to Russia, 17 Sept., 1809 ; was appointed registrar of the univ. of Helsingfors, 1830, in which year he publd. a vol. of lyrics and idyls (transld. into Engl., 1878, by Magnusson and Palmer) ; and was early subjected to the inspiring influence of the Finn. poet Franzén (q.v.), bp. of Hernösand, to whom he addressed a set of verses printed in the forefront of his works. R.'s *Grafven i Perrho* (' The Grave in Perrho ') was awarded a gold medal by the Swedish Academy, 1831, and would probably then have received the highest prize at the disposal of the nation (this was voted to him in 1859) if the young poet had been content to follow more closely in the artificial manner of Tegnér (q.v.), then at the zenith of his great career. But R. had his own *ars poetica*, his own sense of what was fitting in national verse, his own swing and rhythm in the national hexameter, and his own clear outlook on life. His realism found expression, 1832, in his dramatic-idyl of Finnish rural life, *The Elk-hunters*, which marks a point of departure and a fresh start in Swed. literary history. Mean-while R. had founded, and edited till 1837, a critical journal, the *Helsingfors Morgonblad*, which he made the channel of the new criticism, illustrated by examples in his works. His *Hanna*, 1836, was another idyl of the *Elk-hunters* type, somewhat akin to the *Michael* type of Wordsworth (q.v.). In the next year he moved to Borga, where he occupied suc-cessively the chairs of Lat. and Gk., and the rectorate, and which he made his headquarters till he died. His *Nadeschda*, an idyl of Russ. manners, appeared in 1841 ; *Kung Fjalar*, a vol. of romances, in 1844 ; and the first series of ' Ensign Stol's Stories ' in 1848 (second series, 1860). It is by this work, more than any other, that R. takes rank as the leading national poet of Sweden in the 19th cent. The hero and supposed narrator of these poetic recitals is a veteran of the Russo-Finnish war, which R., as we have seen, could just recall. The patriotic, stirring, simple, realistic ballads, hymns and tales in this collection are masterly in their kind, and, as a master should, R. has found many admirers and a band of ardent disciples in yet more recent singers of Swed. and Finn. story.

Ruskin, John (1819-1900): Engl. critic, poet, social philosopher. ' For fifty years con-tinuously ', says Frederic Harrison (q.v.), in the ' English Men of Letters ' monograph, R. ' wrote, lectured, and talked about Mountains, Rivers, and Lakes ; about Cathedrals and Landscapes ; about Geology ; about Minerals, Architecture, Painting, Sculpture, Music, Drawing, Political Economy, Education, Poetry, Literature, History, Mythology, Socialism, Theology, Morals '. He was born of wealthy if somewhat severe parentage, and his childhood was comparatively lonely. At the same time he was a child-prodigy ; he taught himself to read and write at the age of 4 or 5, while at 7 he began to compose and illustrate ' original pieces '. He saw the field of Waterloo when 6, and at 10 wr. and gave to his father *Battle of Waterloo : a Play in two acts*. Edu. first at Peckham, he went to Christ Church, Oxford, at 18. In the same year, 1837, he wr. a series of essays on architecture in the *Architectural Magazine*, and its editor wr. to R.'s father : ' Your son is certainly the greatest natural genius that ever it has been my fortune to become acquainted with '. At Oxford he met Darwin (q.v.), and took his B.A. in 1842. But his meeting with J. M. W. Turner, the artist, influenced him more than aught else : Turner, he said, inspired *Modern Painters*, and ' is beyond all doubt the greatest of the age '.

At home, 1842-3, R. wr. and publd. the first vol. of *Modern Painters*. It made a sensation, and was acclaimed by such men as Tennyson, S. Rogers, sir H. Taylor, and Sydney Smith, the latter describing it in the *Edinburgh Review* as ' a work of transcendent talent, presenting the most original views and most elegant and powerful language, and will work a complete revolution in the world of taste '. And the author was only 23 ! He and his parents made repeated visits to Switzerld. and Italy, and R.'s love for the Alps was firmly implanted. The second vol. of *Modern Painters* appeared, 1846, and inter alia, provoked from *Punch* the witty reference containing the lines :

     ' Till savage Ruskin
     Sticks his tusk in '.

In 1848, R. made his unhappy marriage with Euphemia Chalmers Gray which was dissolved a few years later, the lady marrying Millais the artist. R. rejoined his parents at Denmark Hill, after a very severe illness. Wr. *Seven Lamps of Architecture*, 1849, in some sense a companion work to *Modern Painters* : it had the same fearlessness of outlook and graces of eloquence, and appreciably enhanced R.'s fame. So also did *The Stones of Venice*, of which vol. i appeared, 1851, in the year of Turner's death. R. had long loved Venice, and knew it intimately ; and his bk. was illustrated by some of the most famous engravers. Charlotte Brontë (q.v.) wr. of it that ' Mr. R. seemed to her one of the few genuine writers, as distinguished from book-makers, of this age ' ; while Carlyle (q.v.) characterized it as ' a strange, unexpected, and, I believe, most true and excellent " sermon in stones " '. Further, in 1851, R. identified himself with the Pre-Raphaelite (q.v.) movement, inspired by Rossetti, Holman Hunt, Burne-Jones, Millais, and others. In 1853 he wr. for the Arundel Society his valuable reflections on Giotto's frescoes, and began work as public lecturer. He helped Kingsley, F. D. Maurice (qq.v.) and others to found the

Working Men's coll. in Ormond Street, London, and assisted it generously with time and money, teaching drawing, etc., with his friend, W. Morris (q.v.), and others. Wr., 1855, the first of his Notes on the *Pictures of the Year*, which constituted him a recognized authority : *The Harbours of England*, 1856 ; *Elements of Drawing*, 1857. The *Harbours* must ever live as a glorious prose-poem. Vol. v of *Modern Painters* was publd., 1860, and, in 1862, *Unto this Last*—actually, his own definition of wealth—which had appeared serially in the *Cornhill Mag.* It preached that 'riches is essentially power over men '; and its doctrine caused these essays to be suspended by Thackeray (q.v.), then editor of the *Cornhill*, at the request of its publishers. A similar fate attended some papers by R. on political economy in *Fraser's* : they were issued as *Munera Pulveris*, 1872, dedicated to Carlyle.

R.'s father died in 1864, leaving him in money alone nearly £160,000. It is estimated that, before he died, he gave away the whole of this fortune. At this time he was busy as a lecturer, and publd., 1871, a vol. of lectures with the odd title, *Sesame and Lilies*. It has been called 'a sermon for women ', and contains some very beautiful theorizing on women's capacities and duties, couched in exquisite language. *The Crown of Wild Olive*, 1865-6, consisted of lectures on Work, Traffic, War, and England's Future. In 1869, R. accepted the Slade professorate of Art at Oxford, and, being re-elected, held it for about 10 years. His lectures were always crowded, and were issued as follows : *Lectures on Art, Michael Angelo and Tintoret, Aratra Pentelici*, 1870 ; *The Eagle's Nest, Ariadne Florentina*, 1872 ; *Val d'Arno, The Art of England, Love's Meinie*, 1873 ; and *The Pleasures of England*, 1884. He ultimately quitted Oxford because it had been decided to establish a laboratory in the Museum, and R. was opposed to vivisection. R.'s later years were clouded by ill-health and depression. He tried more continental travel, but had a serious breakdown in 1878. Giacomo Boni (1859-1925), later celebrated as an archæologist, met R. in Italy, 1882 ; and always expressed his obligation to the older man's teachings. In 1879, R. had retired to his quiet home at Coniston, in the Lake country, where he was lovingly tended by his cousin, Mrs. Arthur Severn. As for the good that he did, 'his pensioners were numbered by hundreds ; his charities were as delicate as they were generous. He educated promising artists and gave commissions for semi-public enterprises. He presented valuable collections of Turners to Oxford and Cambridge. He established a model tea-shop. He gave a relative £15,000 to set him up in business '. Between 1871-84 he also spent much money on his fanciful idea of a guild of St. George, ' to slay the Dragon of Industrialism '. With his publisher, Mr. G. Allen, he issued about 100 numbers, or ' letters ' of *Fors Clavigera* between 1871-84. *Fors* was ' R.'s *Hamlet* '. The whole series formed a satire of modern life, but contained wonderful, almost terrible, truths reflected from that life ; on the other hand, parts of it gave evidence of a sensibly disordered mental

balance. Lastly, his *Præterita* was largely biographical—a striking document of genuine human interest. The prince of Wales (king Edward vii) headed the band of admirers who presented R. with an illuminated address on his 80th birthday at Coniston, where, a few months later, he died. The offer of an Abbey funeral was declined, but in 1902 a medallion, by Onslow Ford, R.A., was unveiled in Poet's Corner by Mrs. Severn. Sir Edward Cook (q.v.), R.'s pupil and friend, wr. *Studies in Ruskin*, 1890, the *Life of Ruskin*, 2 vols., 1911, and prepared the standard edn. of his works.

Russian Literature : The youngest, the most self-contained, and in some respects the most interesting of the major literatures of modern Europe.* Russ. lit. is Russ. history ; ' the history of Russian literature ', writes the hon. Maurice Baring, ' up to the nineteenth century is not a history of literature, it is the history of Russia '. Another writer tells us that the Russ. Middle Ages extended to the reign of Peter the Great (*regn.*, 1689-1725), and speaks of ' the historical pain, the travail and profound discouragement of the people to whom God never said clearly " Go there ! " ' (Vogüé). The native Russ. critic, Biélinsky, declares : ' Our literature starts in 1739, at the appearance of the first ode of Lomonosov ' (q.v.) ; and the Germ. historian, Brückner, writing before the Russ. Revolution, truly said : ' A knowledge of the conditions which have made modern Russia what she is, is the indispensable preliminary to a right appreciation of her literature, which is the fullest and most spontaneous expression of her self '. Of no other country in Europe are similar propositions to be stated.†

On what grounds are they stated ? On the successive invasions of Russia : by merchant-buccaneers from Scand. in the 9th cent., by Mongolian Tatars in the 13th. The Asiatic yoke of the Tatars was heavy and enduring ; it was not till the middle of the 16th cent., when happier countries were in the flood of the Renaissance, that the sign of the Crescent began to fade. The habits of the East remained, and to these was added the grave fact of the separation of Byzantium from Rome : of the Gk. church from the Western Papal court. There was no literary language ; no printing-press in Russia till 1553, in the reign of

* The writer wishes to state that, unlike his late brother, Leonard Arthur Magnus (1879-1924), he is ignorant of the Slav. languages, and has had to rely on translns., histories and criticism, in Engl., Fr. and Germ. The chief Engl. authority is the hon. Maurice Baring, in *Landmarks of Russ. Lit.* (Methuen, 1910), *Outline of Russ. Lit.* (H.U.L., 1914-5), and *Oxford Book of Russ. Verse* (1924). Vogüé's *Roman Russe* is an invaluable little work in Fr. criticism, and Brückner has written a very serviceable *Geschichte d. Russ. Litt.* Other brief histories are by Friedrichs (Perthes, 1921), Shakhnovski (*E.T.*, Kegan Paul, 1921) and prince Mirsky (Oxford, 1925). The Russ. capital, formerly St. Petersburg, is now known as Leningrad, but the intermediate name, Petrograd, is employed, as more familiar, in this bk.

† Modern Norse lit. similarly made a start after 1814 ; but the conditions were different : Norway's independence from Denmark was not complete till that date. (See s.v. Scandinavian Lit.). Modern Czech lit. (see s.v.) may be redated from the establishment of the Czecho-Slovak Republic, 1918, but its foundations are old.

Ivan the Terrible, and even then its service was confined to ecclesiastical uses. Only very slowly and gradually was the heavy curtain withdrawn, and the light of the West let in. Very slowly and gradually did the national policy of Peter the Great and the European policy of Catherine ii (see s.vv.) succeed in imposing on a reluctant, acquiescent, fatalistic, Oriental, unsecularized population the external signs of dress, language, customs, etc., which were intended to transform the inner mind to Western ideas. And even then, assuming with Biélinsky, that the first ode of Lomonosov in 1739 struck the first note of modern Russ. lit., and that Russia accomplished in the 18th cent. the changes which more fortunate countries had left behind them in the 16th, we have to reckon with the reaction in high places which set in about 1790, when the example of revolution in France turned the current of the empress Catherine's reform backwards.

Such, very briefly and with big omissions, is the hist. background of the lit. which first began to have a history in the 19th cent., and which was so fatally interrupted in the 20th. Its earlier annals need not detain us long. 'Modern Russian literature', says prince Mirsky, 'owes next to nothing to Old Russian literature'. There was always a popular lit., transmuting old tales of gods and heroes into narrative tales of verse and prose : epopee, ballad, folk-tale, chronicle. The cycles of the *byliny* (q.v.), as they are called, or the oldtime *sagas* or *chansons* (see s.vv.) of Russia, include one prose-poem at least which takes rank with the *Cid* or the *Song of Roland*. This famous *bylina* dates from the epoch of the Scand. dynasty at Novgorod, founded by Rurik in 892, and celebrated in the chronicle of Nestor (q.v.). It narrates the foray of Igor (q.v.) against the pagan Polovtzy in the spring of 1186. It is one of innumerable struggles in the long and desultory warfare for the possession of the waterways of Kiev (q.v.) ; and, though Igor was rather less than more distinguished than other warriors of his race and time, his lay is in the Homeric tradition. Its profound sensibility to natural objects—sun, river, flowers and winds—is at once its greatest charm and evidence of the superficiality of the culture imposed on a world of pagan thought. This lay, which, as Vogüé tells us, 'contains *in petto* all the lyric poetry of the nineteenth century in Russia', was lost for 6 centuries. The MS. was discovered in 1795, and was printed just in time to preserve it before it was finally burned in the Moscow fire, 1812. Meanwhile, its authenticity had been fully established against the scepticism reinforced by the somewhat analogous instance of Macpherson's (q.v.) *Ossian*.

Taking the *Armament of Igor* as typical of the Russ. *byliny*, and adding an appreciative reference to the large *corpus* of Russ. folklore, we skip the intervening centuries till we reach 1518, in which year Maxim (q.v.), a Gk. monk of Mt. Athos, came from Florence (q.v.) to Moscow, bringing with him, as a missionary of culture, the breath of the spirit of Manuccio, Savonarola and Pico della

Mirandola (see s.vv.). He received hard shrift in the northern capital ; but something at least he contributed, at the cost of personal martyrdom, to the slow-moving cause of Western civilization in Russia ; and the iron hand of Peter the Great in the next cent. drove his subjects yet further in the new roads. Peter was the emperor-mechanician : his fleet, his army, his church, his language, had all to serve practical ends. He founded the Academy of Sciences at Petrograd, and commissioned endless translns. of foreign works useful to home culture, and, though no stanza of poetry nor any chapter of prose was written in his reign, he bequeathed to poets and prose-writers a malleable instrument of secular speech, released from the hampering confines of Latinity and ecclesiasticism.

The harvest was reaped by Catherine ii, the Semiramis of the North. She was iron to her subjects, and wax to her correspondents abroad. Her letters were honey, her laws were gall ; for, though her *Nakás*, or constitutional instructions (1768) were framed in so enlightened a mood that their circulation was forbidden in France, she was found in 1790 on the side of repression and despotism, however benevolent in its intention towards the rights of kings. The tragedy of the life of Radishchev (q.v.), who ventured to write an account of his journey through the rural districts between Petrograd and Moscow, is properly cited as the crucial illustration of the contrast between his sovereign's professions and her performance. Of the empress's own experiments in drama and journalism an account is given s.v. ; here we have only to remark her eager and intimate correspondence with such leaders of European thought as Voltaire, Grimm, Montesquieu, and Diderot (qq.v.). In her reign, for the first time, the Russ. court was Europeanized.

Lomonosov, whose name has been mentioned as the starting-point of modern lit. in Russia, was a man of varied accomplishments. His Russ. grammar, 1755, his orthographical and linguistic labours, and his efforts in the cause of the foundation of the univ. of Moscow (1755 ; the first in Russia) give him a higher title to fame as a loyal servant to the policy initiated by Peter the Great than his *Petriad* and other poems. Neither he nor his contemporary, Sumarokov, despite their good journeyman work, ranks as a creative artist. That claim is far more amply vouched by the verse of Derzhavin (q.v. ; 1743-1816), who was ode-writer imperial to Catherine, and by the prose of Karamsin (q.v. ; 1765-1826), the true fathers of modern Russ. letters. Karamsin's *Russian History*, indeed, was a work epoch-making in its generation and of permanent value and interest. To these names should be added, even in the briefest survey, those of Kheraskov, Visin, Krylov, Novikov, Griboyedov, and Zhukovsky ; the last, a great translr. (' the first and best in European literature ', says Mr. Baring), and predecessor of Pushkin ; before reaching that very major name. (See s.vv.).

A great translr. we called Zhukovsky. So were they all, more or less. Transln. and assimilation into Russ. letters was by far the best service that her writers were able to render at the close of the 18th and the opening of the 19th cent. Ideas sprung in France, Engld., and Germany were transplanted to Russ. soil : the fable by Krylov, elegy and ballad by Zhukovsky, etc. ; and on the new soil they took root again and put out new forms of the old flowers. Especially Germ. Romanticism (q.v.), and Mysticism (q.v.) immigrant from Germany and Sweden (s.v. Swedenborg), found ready discipleship in Russia. Freemasonry and the Rosicrucian movement and other semi-religious, semi-political fraternities were founded and persecuted and revived, and led at last to the ' Society of Welfare ' (imitative of the Germ. *Tugendbund*), established in 1815 by idealists home from the Vienna Congress, and crushed in 1825 under the guise of the ' Decembrist ' rising, in which one victim was Ryleev, the poet. ' Modern Russian literature ', says prince Mirsky, ' began in the seventeenth century as an imitation of Polish models ', and Karamsin and Lomonosov, ' two great pedagogues, familiarized Russia with Rousseau and Ossian and Herder and all the pre-Romantic literature of England and Germany '. We refer to these cross lights on Russ. lit., since they illustrate effectively the course which it took from romanticism to realism (q.v.). To this development we shall come when we reach the novelists of yesterday. Here and now our business is with Pushkin, ' le prédestiné, lumineux, et insolent de bon-heur ' (Vogüé) ; the revealed leader of all who had preceded him.

' At the appointed hour the man came '. Pushkin (1799-1837) was the Dante, Chaucer and Goethe of Russia. Well-born, fortunate, brilliant, with the romance of the south and the realism of the north in his blood, he is the first writer of Russ. lit. who is at the same time one of the major company famous in the lit. of the world. For his technical skill and craftsmanship they call him the Peter the Great of Russ. letters ; and the title is only unjust to his great push forward in his craft inasmuch as it seems to overlook his consummate art of style. His chief works are the Byronic verse-novel, *Eugène Oniégin* (in 8 cantos) and the Shakespearean chronicle-play, *Boris Godunov* ; but in his too short life, which had a tragic ending, Pushkin wr. fairy-tales, little epics, histories, novels, and a quantity of fine lyrical poetry, drenched in the warm colours of the Caucasus and the Crimea, where he spent the best years of his life, and filled with rich images and luscious word-painting. Pushkin founded a school ; or, rather, it is correct to say (and here the analogy with Peter the Great is obvious) that Russ. lit. never went back from the conclusions and results which he registered. The modern outlook on life and affairs, the marriage of high poetry with common life, the natural and unforced art, these were Pushkin's largess to his country's life in letters, so long shut-in and shut-out ; and henceforward its development is a true progress.

Of Pushkin's Pleiad (q.v.), as the Arzamas (q.v.) circle was called, after a famous analogy, the most conspicuous member was Lermontov (q.v.), 15 years younger than Pushkin, his

survivor by few years, and like him in the surroundings of his life and the tragedy of his death. And, even more pregnantly than Pushkin's, Lermontov's work looked forward as well as back. He tamed the wilder and more exotic style of Pushkin by a contact with the actualities and realities of life. He wr. what is virtually the first Russ. novel, *A Hero of our Days*, 1839 ; and it is not without significance that the last poems of Lermontov were simultaneous in appearance with the earliest writings of Gogol. For it was not on the lines, romanticist and gorgeous, of Oriental sketches of Circassian maids' amours, nor in the scenery of the Caucasus and with the colours of Southern blooms and complexions, that the panoramic mass of deep and repressed feeling was to roll into expression in Russ. lit. Biélinsky, the one great Russ. critic of this epoch, sets the facts in their right perspective. Writing in 1843 (Lermontov had died in 1841, Gogol's *Dead Souls* was publd. in 1842), he said : ' The melancholy, the disillusion, the ideal, heavenly virgins, the moon, the hate of our kind, vanished youth, treason, daggers, and poisons—the time for these has been, whether in the beautiful works of Pushkin, or in those of his crowd of imitators. . . The hour of juvenile enthusiasm has passed : the hour of thought has arrived '.[*] And at this hour the ' fausse route ' of Pushkin was diverted by the genius and reason of Gogol into the progressive way of realistic prose fiction. The mirror was held up to Russian life, and it was not the mirror which was cracked because the mouth looked awry.

But criticism in Russia, however valuable, was neither free nor unbiased. The iron hand of the censor was over all, and the immense influence which he exercised had some curious results. It divided the critics into 2 parties : those who supported and those who opposed the censor's views. The first came to be called Slavophils, and the latter Westernizers : names which explain themselves as the friends of orthodoxy and constitutionalism and the champions of reform and new ideas : conservatives and radicals, in a word. Neither side escaped the shears. But the distinction, while it was effective, tended to sort men of letters into the categories of the critics, thus adding politics to lit. To what party a man belonged was a question of even more importance than that of his aim in his own faculty. We cannot follow these dubieties, essentially temporary and local, through the reviews and newspapers of the period, 1835-48. It must suffice to refer to the letter on ' The Philosophy of History ', which Chaadaev (q.v.) dropped like a bombshell into the *Moscow Telescope* (1836), and to the rapid impetus which he gave to the Westernizers ; to Herzen on Chaadaev's side, and to Serge Aksakov on the other (see s.vv.), both of whom were noted memoir-writers ; above all to Biélinsky himself, who, though never the Russ. Lessing (q.v.) of his friends' flattery and claim, helped very considerably the forward movement of the 'forties. This movement was estopped by his own death, 1848, and by the events of

[*] Quoted in Vogüé, *Roman Russe*, 65.

Western politics in that year. *Tout finit par des chansons* (see s.v. Banville), ran the popular comment on politics in France. *Tout finit par la Sibérie*, might have been said in Russia ; for Slavophil and Westernizer alike were exposed to the terrors of the censorship. Biélinsky, the critic, had westernized ; Dostoievsky (q.v.), the prince of Russ. novelists, whose faith was as wise and pure as his knowledge was terrible and deep, was led out to be shot on 21 Dec., 1849, and was reprieved only in the twelfth hour. *Tout finit par la Sibérie*, and a Siberian silence ensued after 1848.

When the curtain rose again, the literary stage was occupied by Turgenev (q.v.). His *Sportsman's Sketches*, in the same class as Gogol's first book of *Farmhouse Evenings*, appeared in 1847, the year of Biélinsky's death and 5 years before Gogol's. It was followed by a series of novels, including *The Nest of Gentlefolk* and *Fathers and Sons*, which achieved European reputation, and fulfilled the ambition of old Peter the Great by bringing Russia into the orbit of Western Europe. Its hero, we read (Mirsky, 27) ' is the " nihilist " (the word is of Turgenev's coinage), materialist, and atheist Bazarov, a " strong, silent man ". Turgenev most obviously drew him with love and sympathy. The Radicals, however, took exception to Bazarov and proclaimed him an impertinent caricature. But soon there came up a new set of younger and extremer Radicals who gloried in their atheism and materialism and in their contempt for art and beauty. They accepted Bazarov as a portrait of themselves, recognized him as their ideal, and took up the name of Nihilists '. When that happened— it was all a matter of a year or two,—Turgenev, who had anticipated Nihilism, was not Nihilist enough for its exploiters. The Virgil of Russ. prose, as he has been admirably called, and, like Virgil, responsive to the charm of *latis otia fundis*, the ' haunt of ancient peace ' of Tennyson's line, was, on the whole, too gentle an artist to satisfy the spirit of young Russia :

And all these maiméd wants and thwarted thoughts,
Eternal yearning, answered by the wind,
Have dried in me belief and love and fear.

In these words, or in words like these, Turgenev's successors might have stated their negative creed. One after another, they delineated the type of philosophic fatalism : the national quality of *ochaïania*, which means no-belief, no-love, no-fear. It is a Hamlet type, yet it out-Hamlets Hamlet. We meet it in Goncharov's (q.v.) Oblomov, 1858, the hero of a novel of that name, after whom the quality was called : the quality of lying on a sofa, not from physical laziness, but from intellectual fastidiousness and spiritual (shadowy-spiritual) idleness ; and in this context it is relevant to observe that, in Russia, where Shakespeare ' has been transfused into Russian literature and the Russian spirit ' (prof. K. Arabazhin, *Times Lit. Supp.*, 25 May, 1916), of all Shakespeare's works, *Hamlet* has been by far the most frequently transld. The latest of such translns., it may be added, was effected by the late grand-duke Constantine (1858-1915), president of the Russ. Imperial

Academy of Sciences, who himself played the title-rôle at the Théâtre de l'Ermitage.

Leskov, Dostoievsky, the giant Tolstoy himself, Tchekhov, Gogol, and the rest, will be found s.vv. in these pages. They are extraordinarily recent in date, yet with the deposit of centuries upon them. What strikes us about Russ. lit., says Mr. Baring, ' is that, in spite of its being the youngest of all the literatures, it seems to be spiritually the oldest '. Historians employing psychoanalysis may discover a clue to this paradox, and may seek it, perhaps, since it is a literary clue, from a famous passage in lit. ' Like the vampire, she has been dead many times, and learned the secrets of the grave ; and has been a diver in deep seas, and keeps their fallen day about her ; and trafficked for strange webs with Eastern merchants '—Pater's (q.v.) exquisite words are well known, and may be transferred to our present conclusion. For Russia, too, has died many times, and brought back her argosies from the grave. She, too, has the sunset over the sea and traffic with the East in her experience ; and the smaller and greater revolution of 1905 and 1917 may prove to be stages in a new beginning of a nation which, Hellenic in its art but anarchic in its experience, has still to reconcile the two. Maxim Gorky, one of the greatest of recent writers in Russia, expressed her spirit in 1916, in an open letter to his colleagues abroad : ' We look forward to an atonement of the evil dispositions in men's hearts, and to the reconciliation of their exacerbated differences. The wheat will spring again in the fields drenched with human blood, and flowers will deck the graves of the fallen. Then the divided peoples will once more walk together on the broad, great, common path of progress. We believe and hope ! ' It would ill become a foreign student of Russ. lit. to let events since 1916 make him unfriendly to this hope or indifferent to this belief.

Rusticiano (13th cent.) : It. writer of epitomes. Native of Pisa. Compiled, *c.* 1270, abstract of cycle of Arthur (q.v.) legends, which became valuable source-book ; and, later, *c.* 1299, Fr. version of travels of Marco Polo (q.v.), which R. probably received direct from the voyager's lips in Venetian dialect.

Rutebœuf (13th cent.) : Fr. lyric poet. R.'s name was probably a pseudonym, and of his life little is known, except that most of it was spent in Paris, that he was alive in 1230 and in 1285, and that he married in 1260. The rest we infer from his writings, which included practically all kinds of the *bourgeois* poetry of his age : satire, fable, lament, lives of saints, a miracle-play, political and didactic dialogues. These reveal a striking personality ; ' for the first time ', says a Fr. writer (Lanson, *Hist. de la Lit. Fr.*, 113), ' we meet in the history of our own literature an individual with strongly marked characteristics ' ; R., though but the shadow of a name, becomes as familiar to us, for instance, as Robert Burns (q.v.). R., too, was a son of the people ; he is the first Parisian of pure blood, and the variegated life of that city in its early medieval colours is reflected in R.'s verses. It is further to be observed, that, chronologically, the muse of

R. appears between the 2 parts of the *Romance of the Rose* (q.v.): he was attracted by Guillaume's allegorizing; he influenced the harsher notes of Jean de Meung. He was acquainted with need and greed, and was 'a kind of premature journalist, not always independent, but always original. Anyone seeking to learn the views of the Paris *bourgeoisie* in the reign of Saint Louis has only to consult him' (Lanson, *ibid.*); he showed the seamy side of the garment woven by Joinville (q.v.). To this outspoken minstrel of the middle classes, 'Oliver and Charlemagne were dead'; the nobility were degenerate and the clergy corrupt; he held up to life itself the mirror of the *Roman de Renart* (s.v. Reynard). His poems of a more sacred character were, conjecturally, commissions, written for reward to the order of ecclesiastical corporations or noble clients: among these were *Théophile*, the miracle-play, lives of Sts. Mary and Elizabeth, a 'way to Paradise', and kindred themes. More direct of his own genius were the 'complaints' of his poverty and marriage, in which the tone was more satirical than esurient, and many poems of the Fable (q.v.)-type. Somewhat between the two was the famous dialogue entitled *Débat du Croisé et Decroisé*; whether to go crusading or not, was a question which R. would have decided by the test of *noblesse oblige*: it was not his business to follow king Louis, but those whose business it was were not therefore to be excused for shirking it. In the dawn of dramatic and lyric poetry, independent of the chivalric convention of the professional *trouvères*, R. stands as a significant maker of vigorous and forcible verse.

Rutherford, Mark. See White, Wm. Hale.

Ruysbroek, von, Johann (1293-1381): Dutch (or Germ.) mystic (see s.v. Mysticism) and priest. 'From his day, and by his means, the mystical tendency in the Netherlands and Germany underwent a revolution, and purified itself in higher and higher degrees, until it produced the noblest specimens of Christian character and life' (Ullmann, *Reformers before the Reformation*, E.T., ii, 31). R. exercised considerable influence on Tauler (q.v.) in Germany, and Groot (q.v.) in Holland, where the Brethren of the Common Lot were founded in the spirit of his teaching, and, later, on los Angeles (q.v.) in Spain.

Ryleev, Kondrati Fyodorovich (1795-1826): Russ. poet; hanged 14 July, 1826, with 4 other victims of the Decembrist rising (1825), the politico-revolutionary outcome of the 'Society of Welfare', which was itself the social and philanthropic outcome of the freemasons' lodges and mystic fraternities, imported into Russia from Germany and Sweden towards the close of the 18th cent. R. was a willing martyr to the cause of liberty and reform, as Russ. visionaries imagined it in the harsh reign of emperor Alexander i. 'I am not a poet, I am a citizen', he declared; and he anticipated Pushkin (q.v.), his friend, in seeking the foundations of those sentiments in the earlier history of his country. Employing a favourite Germ. epithet, Brückner (*Gesch. d. Russ. Lit.*, 148) describes R. as the first 'tendenziös' poet of the period, the first poet with a mission or purpose, that is to say; and his verses written in prison before his cruel execution were greeted as the lark-song of morning.

Rymer, Thomas (1641-1713): Engl. critic. Wr. *Tragedies of the Last Age Consider'd*, 1678; *A Short View of Tragedy*, 1693; poems, and a rhymed-verse play, *Edgar, or The English Monarch*; was appointed, 1693, to edit the public treaties of Great Britain, publd. as *Fœdera*, 20 vols., 1704-35. This little-read writer was described by Macaulay (q.v.; in his *Essay* on Boswell's *Life of Johnson*) as 'the worst critic that ever lived'; and prof. Saintsbury gives chapter and verse for his considered judgment: 'Though no Macaulayan, I venture to endorse my unimportant name on a dictum of Macaulay's. I have known several bad critics from Fulgentius to the abbé d'Aubignac, and from Zoilus to persons of our own day, whom it is unnecessary to mention. But I never came across a worse critic than Thomas Rymer' (*Hist. Crit.*, ii, 307). We may leave poor Tom in the cold.

S

Saavedra, de, Gonzalo (fl. 1620): Span. pastoralist. Wr. the *Pastores del Betis*, publd. posth., 1633, in the manner of Montemayor (q.v.).

Saavedra-Faxardo, de, Diego (1584-1648): Span. moralist; historian; diplomatist, in which capacity he lived away from Spain for 40 years, and so escaped the contemporary infection of *cultismo* (q.v.); *comte* by rank. Wr. a rather charming bk., *Empresas politicas*, 'Political Maxims: The Idea of a Christian Prince', 1640, consisting of 100 chapters of moral instruction tacked on to emblems with mottoes, and written for the benefit of prince Balthasar, who died young, son of king Philip iv of Spain. It is not equal in observation and originality to Bossuet's (q.v.) writings for the dauphin of France; but it was a pleasant piece of sententious prose, and was often reprinted and transld. Wr., too, a 'History of the Goths in Spain', and a *Republica literaria*, first issued, 1655, under the title of 'Judgment of Arts and Sciences', and ascribed (erroneously) to C. A. de Cabrera (q.v.).

Sacchetti, Franco (c. 1335-c. 1400): Florentine novelist and poet. His town-songs of rustic pleasures (mostly amorous) enjoyed considerable vogue in his own day, and rose in places to true poetry. S. was essentially a 'cit', as that term was understood in Engld. in the 18th cent., and he wr. in a racy vernacular, which made him even more popular than his model, Boccaccio, or than Politian (see s.vv.), whom he influenced to some extent. Wr. a collection of 300 *novelle*, mainly anecdotal, with a sting, which illustrate, though they do not illumine, the amusements of the *bourgeoisie* of Florence. He claimed veracity for his tales, which introduced at times well-known personages, and he exhibited in a marked degree the native Florentine quality of malice, 'the malice Dante took with him to the Inferno' (Symonds).

Sachi, Bartolommeo (15th cent). : It. bibliophil. Commonly known as Platina, Latinized from his birthplace, Piadena. S. was appointed by pope Sixtus iv librarian of the Vatican, 1475, and he held the post till his death, 1481, when the collection of books had been housed in its present quarters.

Sachs, Hans (1494-1576): Germ. Meistersinger (q.v.); poet; cobbler. Born at Nuremberg; son of a tailor; made a 5 years' tour through Germ. cities, visiting the craft-schools of shoe-making and Meistergesang; returned to Nuremberg, 1518, where he spent the rest of his long and happy life, bringing up his large family by 2 wives, and practising his trade and recreation; a homely, lovable, medieval, burgher-poet, made real to modern eyes through Wagner's (q.v.) opera. S. outlived Luther (q.v.) 30 years, and in a poem, 1523, had apostrophized him as 'the nightingale of Wittenberg, whom one now hears everywhere'; his sympathy was on the side of the reformers, but his life and tastes are an admirable illustration of the complacent indifference to rational criticism and social morality which it was Luther's mission to shake. S. was essentially conservative, and plied his last for 60 years with a contentment as shrewd as it was unquestioning. In this regard he typified the ideal extolled by Brant (q.v.) in 1494, the very year of S.'s birth; and his writings exemplified, like his life and character, his faithfulness to the old ideals. He composed 'master songs', to the number, by his own computation, of 4,275; tales and fables, over 1,700; Shrovetide-plays (s.v. Fastnachtspiel) and other comedies and interludes, with tragedies, as he described his plays with battles in them, to the number of 208; and miscellaneous pieces of all kinds; so that there is some justice in the unkind epigram of a Germ. critic who said that S. made a poem of everything, but made nothing poetic. He took his matter where he found it, from repertories of classical and fairy lore, from the chivalric source-books, and, chiefly, from the Bible; and an excellent example of his method and merit is the little Shrovetide-play, 'Eve's Dissimilar Children' (*Die ungleichen Kinder Evas*), derived through Birck (q.v.) from a Lat. rendering of the legend by Melanchthon (q.v.). Here Adam and Eve are shown, bringing up their numerous offspring, like a pair of jolly farmers on Germ. soil. Some of the children were good, others naughty. One day an angel intimates that God is coming to see them, and Eve gets her house in order, while Adam fussily supervises. The good children are brought down to meet the Lord, but the naughty ones are kept in the background. God gives the good ones all kinds of blessings—rank, riches, etc., and Eve, finding him so gracious, brings out the naughty

lot too. The Lord is heartily amused at their unwashen and rough appearance, but extends his blessing to them as well, and appoints them to menial callings in various trades and crafts. The parents show their disappointment; and God rebukes them in the vein of the old mystic demotism of Tauler (q.v.) reminding them that all service is equal in his eyes. The sentiment is admirable, and in accordance with the burgherly dignity of S. and his audience; but the familiarity with which the sacred theme is treated, in the easy jog-trot of the 8-syllabled verse couplets, shows how much the reformers had to accomplish in order to assert the holiness as well as the homeliness of the beauty of the vernacular in religious writings.

Sackville, -i. Thomas (1536-1608): Engl. dramatist; poet; statesman; first earl of Dorset and baron Buckhurst; wr., 1561, with T. Norton (1532-84), a Senecan tragedy, *Gorboduc*, in blank verse, which, with Udall's (q.v.) Plautine comedy, *Ralph Roister Doister*, 1540, 'are the starting-points of dramatic art in this country' (sir S. Lee, *William Shakespeare*, 91). Wr., too, the *Induction* and the *Complaint of Henry, duke of Buckingham* for the 1563 edn. of the *Mirror of Magistrates* (q.v.), thus adding considerably to the literary value of that monument of medieval industry. For 'only the small extent of Sackville's poetical works has prevented him from inclusion among the masters of the grand style' (*C.H.E.L.*, iii, 200).

-ii. Charles (1638-1706): Engl. poet; sixth earl of Dorset; descendant of above, and father of the first duke of Dorset; patron of Dryden (q.v.). Wr. poems, 1701, with sir Charles Sedley (d., 1701) a notable Caroline wit, and shared in the dissolute life of that time. S.'s best-known stanzas are the song beginning 'To all you ladies now on land', 1665.

Sacra Rappresentazione (It.): Sacred play, miracle, mystery (q.v.); Tuscan, specifically Florentine, type of dramatic composition, intermediate between the 'Divozione' (of Umbria) and drama proper. The species flourished, roughly, from 1450 to 1520, starting with Feo Belcari's *Abraham and Isaac* (1449). It never became as perfect a type as its Engl. or Fr. counterpart; and this failure may be ascribed to the subordination of the literary and dramatic elements to those of pageantry and music; the spectacular element being introduced in connection with the annual civic tableaux associated with St. John's day, 22 June, at Florence. Substituting Florence in midsummer for London in November, and the open-air instincts of the South for the home-keeping wit of the North, it is as if Engl. drama had been tied to the car of the lord mayor's show. However this may be, the *sacre rappresentazioni* were run by religious brotherhoods, who did not spare expense; they took the form of irregular scenic stagings of tales versified in the vernacular from the Bible, the Legends of the Saints, or, rarely, from secular stories covered with a thin coat of pietism, and were played in public squares or in conventual halls. The main metre was the octave stanza (*ottava-rima*, q.v.) with intervals of *terza-rima* and songs with music. According to the kind of performance, the 'representations' were sub-entitled Mystery, Passion, Miracle, etc. The tone in general was not high : ' We feel that we are reading what a set of feeble spiritual directors wrote with a touch of conscious but well-meaning insincerity for children. The glaring contrast between the professed asceticism of the fraternities and the future conduct of their youthful members in the world of the Renaissance leaves a suspicion of hypocrisy '. Thus, it is not surprising to learn that the type died out in painted pageants and translated comedies. But it gave hospitality to some notable talent, and some writers in this class and some of its productions by anon. authors will be found here under their own names.

Sadler, Michael Thomas (1780-1835): Engl. tory pamphleteer ; F.R.S., 1832. Wr. bk. on Ireland, 1828, and *The Law of Population*, 2 vols., 1830, which Macaulay (q.v.) attacked. A *Memoir* of S. was written by R. B. Seeley (1798-1886), publisher.

Sadler, Thomas (1822-91): Engl. divine ; edited *Diaries* of H. C. Robinson (q.v.), 1869.

Sadoleto, Jacopo (1477-1547): It. Latinist ; card. Was the constant friend of Bembo (q.v.), a better man and a deeper thinker, and his colleague as papal secretary ; wr. Lat. poems on the recovery of the Laocoon (q.v.) group of statuary and on Marcus Curtius ; Ciceronian treatises on fame and philosophy ; Lat. dialogue on the choice of bks., 1534 ; and Lat. letters to various correspondents, including Erasmus, very valuable for the history of his times.

Saga (Icelandic): Generic name of a form of lit. composed in Iceld., *c.* 1100-1300 ; 2 centuries, which may roughly be called the classical age. The name S. means story ; and the S., throughout its course, was a story, most commonly in prose, and mostly (invariably, many critics say) founded on the facts of hist. (or, alleged-hist, *i.q.*, mythic) happenings. ' Nothing Icelandic makes its appearance elsewhere ' (Saintsbury, *P.E.L.*, ii, 339), at least till a much later date, when it was introduced deliberately as an exotic (s.vv. Macpherson, Gray, W. Morris) ; and the Iceld. story-chronicles differ from the co-eval *chansons* (q.v.), to which the romancers went for their quarry (see, e.g., Chrestien, Benoît, and see also s.v. Bodel), in their remoteness from common knowledge, their unperturbed insularity of interest, and their national, even local, characteristics. Critics have divided extant Sagas into 2 main classes, known as the greater and the lesser, and they include in the former class 5 only, viz., *Njála*, the story of burnt Njal, *Laxdaela*, the dwellers in Laxdale, *Eyrbyggja*, *Egla* (Egil's Saga) and *Grettla*, the story of Grettir. Dasent (q.v.), of Norse folk-tale fame, transld. the first ; ' the Lovers of Gudrun ' in *The Earthly Paradise* (s.v. W. Morris) reproduced the second ; sir W. Scott (q.v.) handled the third and fourth, and the fifth was transld. by W. Morris and Dr. Magnusson. (Reference on the whole subject should be made to the *Corpus Poeticum Boreale* of Vigfusson and York Powell, Oxford, 1883, and to W. P. Ker, *Epic and Romance*, Macmillan,

1908). The lesser Sagas must not detain us ; the points to be noted are 3 : (1), the hard, positive genius which marks this class of writing ; (2), its dependence on the Teutonic stock of legends, which, later, inspired the Nibelungenlied (q.v.) ; and, (3), the admirable qualities of its writers' heroic prose. A fourth point is bibliographical, viz., the inestimable value of the MS. known as *Codex Regius* (q.v.) in the King's library at Copenhagen ; the chief source of all Saga-books. More fully within the scope of modern lit. are the family Sagas compiled by members of the Sturla dynasty. They wr. contemporary history, and a wild, adventurous history it was. There was a certain Hvamm Sturla in the 12th cent., who had 2 sons, Thord and Snorri. Snorri wr. the *Lives of the Kings of Norway*, which are preserved by the *Codex Regius* in an abridgement known as the *Heimskringla* (q.v.), and containing, *inter alia*, the great story of the last sea-fight of king Olaf. And Thord had a son called Sturla (q.v.) who wr. the *Sturlunga Saga* (edited by Vigfusson and York Powell, Oxford), which ' tells the story of the days of freedom ' in Old Iceland, and ' is the last word of the Teutonic heroic age ' (Ker, *op. cit.*, 61). After Sturla, the Sagas declined : partly, an inherent tendency to exaggeration and elaboration destroyed in later examples the balance between reality and romance, and helped to create the mock-heroic figure of the stock Viking of modern revival ; partly, foreign influences from France and Germany undermined the simple self-sufficiency of the domestic annalists of Iceld., and the great prose degenerated into feeble poetry. For ' the children of the *vates* of Grettir and Njal contented themselves, like others, with adapting French romances, and, unlike others, they did not make this adaptation the groundwork of new and original effort ' (Saintsbury, *op., cit.*, 418). But the S. in its classical age is a unique and a noble example of the genius of the people which made it, and which made it exclusively their own.

Sagon, François (16th cent.): Fr. poet ; rival to Marot (q.v.) ; founded a little school of ' Sagontiques ', but has no claim to rescue from oblivion.

Saint-Amant, sieur de ; Marc Antoine de Gérard (1594-1661): Fr. poet ; addicted to the style of the Precious (q.v.) poets of his age, but tended to a more convivial variety of light verse, as the boon-companion of the comte d'Harcourt on land and sea. Wr., heroicidyl, *Moïse Sauvé* (' the rescue of Moses ') and sonnets and other lyric poems. St. A., was an original member of the Fr. Academy (q.v.).

Saint-Cyran, de, Jean du Vergier de Hauranne (1581-1643): Fr. moralist ; *abbé* ; founded the community of the *solitaires* of Port Royal (q.v.), 1636, and associated the Port Royalists with the doctrine of Jansen (q.v.), to their immediate trouble and undying fame. The fame came through Pascal (q.v.) ; the trouble swiftly overtook St.-C., who was imprisoned at the instance of Richelieu (q.v.) and the Jesuits, 1638, and died in confinement. St.-C. left some *Spiritual Letters* and other theological writings.

Saint-Évremond, de, Charles de Marguetel de St. Denys (1613-1703): Fr. *libertin* (q.v.) and letter-writer; soldier; *seigneur*; was implicated by the papers discovered after the fall of Fouquet (q.v.), and was exiled, 1661, in consequence of an anti-Mazarin pamphlet on the subject of the Peace of the Pyrenees; spent his exile in London, where he took a prominent part on the sunny side of the Parnassian way, and where he was buried in Westminster Abbey. Wr. occasional pieces of hist. and philosophical reflection, not primarily intended for publication, and was, like so many men and women of his age, a voluminous and brilliant letter-writer. His *Conversation du Père Canaye* has been likened to Pascal's (q.v.) *Provincial Letters* for its qualities of irony and knowledge. St.-E. was frankly an epicurean, a seeker of pleasure, and a lover (see, too, s.v. Ninon), and deemed the existence of *l'estomac* more easily demonstrable than that of the soul. He forms an intellectual link between the 17th and 18th cents., and joined the rationalism of Pascal to the scepticism of Voltaire (q.v.), with Bayle (q.v.) as another intervener. St.-E., for all his cultivated dilettantism, had a nice taste in lit., and he amused his leisure more than once with flings at the new Fr. Academy (q.v.), and its tendency to meticulous dogmatism. Thus, he wr. a *Comédie des Académies*, and a dissertation on the word *vaste*. He was an able critic, too, of Ben Jonson, Corneille, Racine (qq.v.), and other dramatists, and enjoyed an extensive acquaintance with Engl. literary and aristocratic society. St.-E. supplies an interesting type of the rapid decay of the Precious (q.v.) style in Fr. lit., in which he was nurtured by taste and age.

Saint- Gelais, de. -i. Octavien (1466-1502): Fr. poet; a member of the school later known as the ' Rhétoriqueurs' (q.v.), in deference to their view of poetry as rhetoric, heavily aureated with the gilt of Latinism.

    -ii. Melin, or Mellin, or Melusin (c. 1490-1559): Fr. poet; Marotique (see s.v. Marot), son of above. Studied in Italy, and reproduced Ital. models in Fr. poetry far more directly than Marot; wr. a considerable quantity of the short poems practised by his school, and was the earliest Fr. sonneteer after the Ital. pattern. M. St. G. seems to have spent his life as a type of the gross ecclesiastic, and no little of the coarseness found its way into this verse. As a court-favourite, he opposed the rising sun of Ronsard (q.v.), but later warmed himself in its rays, and was honoured, 1553, by an ode of reconciliation.

St. John, -i. Henry (1678-1751): Engl. statesman; held various high offices, and was created visct. Bolingbroke, 1712. His political career does not concern us; he enters lit. as an exile in France, 1714-23, where he pursued philosophical studies (' he seems to have thought that a brilliant style would justify a man in laying down the law to metaphysicians as well as to diplomatists and politicians'; sir L. Stephen, *Pope*, 160), and, on his return to Engld., he settled at Dawley, nr. Uxbridge, when Pope (q.v.) was his neighbour and a frequent visitor. Pope, says sir L. Stephen (*loc. cit.*) ' spoke him with bated breath, as a

being almost superior to humanity ', and it was by the stimulus of St. J., that Pope sat down to compose a philosophical poem, of which his *Essay on Man*, designed to ' vindicate the ways of God to man' (1733-4), was ' only to be considered as a general map'. It was dedicated to St. J., whom the poet apostrophized,

> Awake, my St. John ! leave all meaner things
> To low ambition, and the pride of kings.
> Let us (since life can little more supply
> Than just to look about us and to die)
> Expatiate free o'er all this scene of Man.

D. Mallet (q.v.) was lord Bolingbroke's lit. executor, and publd. his collected works, 5 vols.,1754. St. J. is commonly mentioned as a predecessor of Disraeli (q.v.) in the history of tory democracy.

    -ii. John (1746-93): Engl. dramatist; nephew of above. Wr., *Mary, queen of Scots*, played by Mrs. Siddons at Drury Lane Theatre, 1759, and other works.

Saint-Lambert, de, Jean Francois (1717-1803): Fr. poet, wr. *les Saisons*, 1769, a didactic poem in imitation of J. Thomson (q.v.). St. L. went further than his master in susceptibility to romantic sentiment.

Saint-Pierre, de, Bernardin (1737-1814): Fr. nature-writer; naturalist; disciple of Rousseau (q.v.), and companion of his master's last years. St. P. had an adventurous, or, at least, a vagrant career in Poland, Siberia and Malta, before king Louis xvi appointed him curator of the Royal Botanic Gardens; he was deprived of his emoluments during the Fr. Revolution, but was restored by Napoleon. St. P. was twice married, and was the father of a Paul and a Virginie (see below); he was a man of difficult temper, and had some points of resemblance to the type caricatured by Dickens (q.v.) in Harold Skimpole : his love of the birds and flowers was unpractical to the point of excess; and he exceeded, too, the standard of sensibility which Rousseau laid down; at least, it would seem so at the centre of Virginie's tragedy in his best-known bk., *Paul et Virginie*, 1787, when the heroine is drowned within sight of her lover because her delicacy could not consent to be saved by a naked sailor. St. P. is ' a Rousseau affected by a superabundant secretion of the lachrymal glands ' (Lanson, *Hist. Lit. Fr.*, 829); and the historian adds with a touch of irony, that France owes to St. P. ' the trees on our boulevards and music in our lunatic asylums '. It is further to be noted, to his more considerable credit, that St. P. introduced a new vocabulary of nature (q.v.) into literary use : he discovered green in the sky as well as blue, and distinguished between shades of red ; and, besides this departure from the consecrated tradition of colours, he initiated the employment of the real names of natural objects, especially, e.g., the Lat., names of flowers, thus helping to familiarize in lit. the proscribed hosts of the vegetable and mineral worlds. When Wordsworth wr., 1798, ' 't is my faith that every flower enjoys the air it breathes ', he was writing in the spirit of St. P., which Rousseau had breathed into his nostrils. Further, St. P.'s influence is marked in the writings of Chateaubriand (q.v.), thus definitely ranging him among the most forward precursors of the romantic movement (s.v. Romance) in France, commonly dated at 1830; and, lastly, this feature was enhanced by the tropical scenery in which St. P. placed his romantic lovers. Rousseau's method of nature-description in Switzerld. and Savoy was extended by his disciple to the strange distances of deserts and palm-trees. St. P.'s chief work was *Études de la Nature*, 1784, of which the tale of *Paul et Virginie* properly formed a part (little appreciated, by the way, when the MS. was first read to mme. Necker, Buffon, qq.v., and their circle): it is a moving story of lyric love, not to be compared with the more robust love-tales of Shakespeare or even of Prévost (qq.v.), but graceful and elemental in its kind, and suffused with the natural sensibility which was to dominate the romantic creed. St. P. also wr. *Voyage à l'île de France*, 1773, and later stories, including *l'Arcadie*, which, though unfind., looks back and forward to Rousseau and Chateaubriand.

Saint-Pierre, de, Castel (1658-1743): Fr. economist; abbé; 'spent his life in propounding Utopian schemes of universal peace and general prosperity' (Saintsbury, *Short Hist. Fr. Lit.*, 461); was a member of the club of the Entresol (q.v.), which must have had 'a most vigorous interest in the subjects discussed, or it would not so long have survived the lucubrations of so pitiless a pedant, so indefatigable a reformer as the excellent Abbé' (*C.M.H.*, viii, 15). These epithets may sufficiently characterize St. P., whose views on human progress and possibilities were to some extent important in fertilizing the soil for the latter *Philosophes* (q.v.).

Saint-Réal, de, César Vichard (1631-1692): Fr. historian; abbé. Born at Chambéry; visited London and Paris, and returned to Chambéry, 1679, as historiographer to the duke of Savoy. Wr., 1672, a well-known history of the *Conjuration* ('Conspiracy') *que los Espagnols formèrent en 1618 contre Vénise.*

Saint-Simon, de, Claude Henri (1760-1825): Fr. philosopher, adventurer, socialist (before the invention of socialism); *comte* by rank; a descendant of the *duc* (see next entry), author of the *Mémoires*, which did not appear, as it happened, till 1829. S.S., who, like his greater namesake, was fully conscious of his traditional descent from Charlemagne, imagined that he was to be the philosopher of the family in which Charlemagne was the statesman; and his experience of hist. changes in the American and Fr. Revolutions (he served under Washington for 5 years) lent him admirable themes for reflection. His actual writings were not significant, though he was a busy pamphleteer in the first decade of the 19th cent., and collaborated with A. Thierry (q.v.). His *Nouveau Christianisme*, 1825, attracted considerable interest. S.S. founded a journal, *le Producteur*; and a busy army of disciples kept his memory green. Indeed, to a large extent, he figured as a Messiah to the Socialist leaders to-be, and Saint-Simonian became the epithet of a school, which included votaries of many shades of political thought. A recent biographer (Maxime Leroy, 1925) has collected many details of the ups and downs

of S.S.'s strange life. In 1790, he renounced his name and title and called himself *citoyen* Bonhomme. A year or two later, he was in prison, and, after his release, he became rich and then poor again. But keeping strictly to his work as a social reformer, it was an easy step from S.S. to Comte (q.v.).

Saint-Simon, de, Louis de Rouvroy (1675-1755): Fr. peer; *duc* by rank; memoir-writer. It would be an affront to the dust of S.-S. to describe his functions in the reverse order of precedence. For Louis de Rouvroy, duc de Saint-Simon, and a descendant of Charlemagne, was first of all and above all 'pair de France'; member of an order, that is to say, which looked back to a record of nobility and to the possession of lapsed privileges, beside which the pretensions of king Louis xiv seemed but an idle boast. Those in this country who remember the general election of December, 1910, may indulge the fancy of an 'imaginary conversation' between S.-S. and Mr. Lloyd George, then chancellor of the exchequer, and the leader of a campaign against dukes. To S.-S., *duc et pair*, his title and its rights and obligations were the only sacred things in a profane world, and his life and literary remains were the expression of his creed. His allegiance was reserved to king Louis xiii, his father's king, 'the king of gentlemen', and he resigned his commission in the army in 1702. He continued to live at court, in compliance with the social conditions of his times, though he did not enjoy the favour of the ageing monarch, but rather fastened his hopes on Fénelon's (q.v.) pupil, the duc de Bourgogne, who died, 1712. The duc d'Orléans summoned him to the council of the regency, established in 1715, and, in 1722, he was ambassador extraordinary to Spain to arrange the marriage of the infanta to the young king Louis xv. At the regent's death, S.-S. retired to his own estates, and devoted himself to reading and writing. A bk. which he read with most avidity was the lacquey's-memoirs of Dangeau (q.v.), who had kept a diary at Louis xiv's court. This work S.-S. annotated out of his capacious and retentive memory, and the voluminous material of observations, records, journals, etc., which he had been in the habit of collecting. From the annotation of Dangeau he went on to the compilation of his own *Mémoires*, or, rather, of vols. of recollections, out of which his memoirs were publd. in 21 vols., *ed. pr.*, 1829-30. Further ore of inferior quality has since been extracted from the same mine; but S.-S.'s literary remains mean for the vast majority of his readers the *Mémoires* originally issued 174 years after his death. They form a most fascinating and valuable bk. We have mentioned, or implied, S.-S.'s hatred of the *bourgeois* court (as he deemed it) of Louis xiv; and further evidence to his feudal aristocracy, and to his survival, as it were, from the epoch of Froissart (q.v.) into the 18th cent., is to be found in his casual reference to his great contemporary (though much junior), Voltaire (q.v.). At the time when this giant of Fr. thought was wooed by kings and empresses, and when his lightest word set Paris ablaze, the old duke and peer of France put him in his proper place, according to ducal notions, and without the faintest suspicion that there was anything ridiculous in his attitude. S.-S. referred to ' Arouet ' (Voltaire) as ' the son of a notary whom my father and I have employed ', such being his title to distinction ; and added that he would not have troubled to mention him ' if he had not become a sort of personage in the republic of letters, and even a man of some importance of a kind in a certain world '. That world—the world of letters—had no claim on the pen of this duke ; grammar was invented by schoolmasters for scribblers who had to earn a living, and S.-S. wr. as he chose. The glorious thing is that this amateur author was born to the trade to which he was not bred, and that his bk. is the work of an artist, and of an artist, defying chronology, of the period of Romance (q.v.) after the Fr. Revolution. Graphic, vivid, passionate, fluent ; in every attribute, save only its picture of the time and manners of the *grand siècle*, it might have been written at the date (1830) at which it was first publd. : the date of Hugo (q.v.) instead of Voltaire. Accurate in detail it is not ; but it has an accuracy higher than of detail ; an accuracy familiar to the romanticists, and dependent on atmosphere and impression. S.-S. was a painter who wr. memoirs. He had a remarkable faculty of deploying crowds through his pages, and certain descriptive passages in which this art is displayed are unapproached by any professional historian. In character-drawing, too, S.-S. is supreme. He belonged to the generation of La Bruyère (q.v.), and he worked with an even firmer touch. Moreover, he gave several sittings—in certain instances, even very many—to his more important characters : mme. de Maintenon and the king, for example ; and when, as was most frequently the case, he dipped his pen in gall, and described what he hated or despised, his words, which he selected as a master, not a craftsman, gave an immense and multiple result. S.-S. was well-meaning enough. When his point of view is once grasped, we see that the peers of France, restored to their ancient rights, would have governed France well and nobly ; it was not the will, but the power that was lacking to this representative of an *ancien régime*, who spent the last 30 years of his life in compiling from intimate knowledge and a profound store of memories a vivid and detailed picture of the great age and court of Louis xiv, surveyed (and this is the miracle) from above, as the writer believed, not from below. Court-gossip has been written by flunkeys, and court-scandals have been reviewed by moralists, but these *Mémoires* are the unique example of court-history reflected by a court-newsman who never condescended to court his prince. It re-opened Versailles in the 19th cent.

Saint-Sorlin, de, Jean Desmarets (1595-1676) : Fr. poet, critic and dramatist. S.-S. was closely allied with Richelieu (q.v.), as a kind of jackal to the lion in various literary offices. Wr. *Clovis*, heroic epopee, 1657, in 26 cantos (reduced to 20 in 1673), and a *Defence of the Heroic poem*, 1674, in opposition to Boileau (q.v.), whose neo-classicism was outraged by the choice of a modern hero for epic verse.

This quarrel has some historic interest, as S.S.-'s *Clovis* led Boileau (*Art poétique*, canto 3) to exceed his brief, and to require the exclusion of Satan from the region of poetry, at the very time when Milton (q.v.) had finished his *Paradise Lost*. S.-S. who was a busy pamphleteer, left the quarrel at his death to be taken up by C. Perrault (q.v. and s.v. Ancients and Moderns). Wr., too, *Les Visionnaires*, 1637, a comedy of manners, and among the earliest of its kind—the burlesque-polite kind, founded on Span. models. It is nearer akin to the art of Jonson than of Molière (qq.v.), and there is much good humour in the clash of temperaments. S.-S. was an original member of the Fr. Academy (q.v.).

Sainte-Beuve, Charles Augustin (1804-69) : Fr. critic, poet ; by common consent, the leading critic of the first half of the 19th cent. ; as such, justly lauded by Saintsbury in vol. iii of his *History of Criticism*, and blessed with the compliment of imitation by his Engl. contemporary, M. Arnold (q.v.). S.-B. began by studying medicine, but, turning at an early age to letters, became a valued contributor to the *Globe* (q.v.), and publd., 1828, his *Tableau de la Poésie au xvie Siècle* from his writings in that organ of the new Romanticism (s.v. *Lyrisme*). What did he prove by his researches in the 16th cent.? Chiefly, he wanted to justify his alliance with the romantic brotherhood by attaching it, historically, to Fr. lit. of an earlier age. ' Between Régnier and Chénier, he interred the age of classicism, which had interrupted the spontaneous development of French genius ' (Lanson, *Lit. fr.*, 940). The attempt was as timely as the perception of it is acute ; for, plainly, the experiments of Hugo (q.v.) and the rest of the literary enfranchisers derived force and advantage from this hist. and critical support. But S.-B., though elevated at once to the post of critic-in-ordinary to the Romantics, was not anxious to attach himself to any school. His study was lit., not schools thereof : he started from the bk. and the writer, not from the class or kind of composition and its rules ; and this direct comparative method, based on wide knowledge and deep sympathy, was at once new, and true, and interesting—the last characteristic being of importance to the editors who employed S.-B.'s pen, and through whom the literary *critique* became a regular feature (however much fallen) of modern journalism. Omitting his poems (*Poésies de Joseph Delorme*, 1829, and *Consolations*, 1830) and his novel (*Volupté*, 1834 ; a kind of stepping-stone from poetry to criticism), we come at once to S.-B.'s contributions to the *Constitutionnel*, from 1850, and, later to the *Moniteur* and the *Temps* : the ' Monday talks ', *Causeries du Lundi*, which were ' the chief recurring literary event of Europe '.

Some account, however inadequate, has been suggested of the *quality* of S.-B.'s criticism ; its *quantity* and range are exceptional, and his ' contemporary ' and ' literary Portraits ', his ' First Mondays ', ' New Mondays ', etc., cover an astonishing space of history and geography. ' He possessed in the supreme degree the qualities essential to the critic—profound erudition, vivacity, intelligence, above all, an insatiable curiosity, which caused him to seek in everything the spectacle of humanity engaged in the actual work of living. His criticism, by its pure realism, by its elucidation of individual character, possesses an immense artistic value' (*C.M.H.*, xi, 526). And it is never likely, we may add, to lose its appeal to the interest of cultured people, or its challenge to the standard of the higher journalism. It remains to mention the *History of Port-Royal* and the vol. on *Chateaubriand and his Circle*, which S.-B. wr. in connection with his lectures as prof. at various times at Lausanne and Liège. His career has a curious likeness to that of M. Arnold, his devoted admirer, who similarly entered the lists of poets, wr. serious bks. as a prof. at Oxford, and contributed his best critical essays to periodical publications. But none knew better than Arnold who was master and who was disciple.

Saintine, Joseph Xavier (1798-1865): Fr. novelist; author of *Picciola*, the story of a flower in a prisoner's cell, which was the wellspring of floods of romantic tears. S. collaborated with Scribe (q.v.) in many of his plays.

Sala, George Augustus Henry (1828-96): Engl. journalist; on the staff of *Household Words*, edited by Dickens (q.v.); founder and editor, 1860-6, of *Templebar Magazine*, since defunct, and a member of the staff of the *Daily Telegraph* from 1857. In that capacity, this versatile and accomplished writer helped to invent and encourage a style in journalism, which was known, from its place of orig., as *Telegraphese*, and which consisted chiefly in an earnest turgidity. 'My "vivacity"', wr. M. Arnold (q.v.), in reply to a critic's letter (Pref., 1865, to *Essays in Criticism*, i), 'my "vivacity" is but the last sparkle of flame before we are all in the dark, the last glimpse of colour before we all go into drab— the drab of the earnest, prosaic, practical, austerely liberal future. Yes, the world will soon be the Philistines'! and then, with every voice, not of thunder, silenced, and the whole earth filled and ennobled every morning by the magnificent roaring of the young lions of the *Daily Telegraph*, we shall all yawn in one another's faces with the dismallest, the most unimpeachable gravity'.

Salamanca: Span. city. The *Siete Partidas*, or Seven Divisions of learning, drafted by king Alfonso x (q.v.) of Castile, recognized the rudiments of a univ. in S., and endowed its *estudios generales*, as such schools of study were then called. This was in 1254; but by the end of the century the univ. had fallen into decay, and Spaniards went abroad for their education to Bologna. The revival of S. as a seat of learning was postponed till the era of card. Ximenes (q.v.) at the opening of the 16th cent.; and from that time forward it took an assured place. A distinctive school of poetry was associated with S. in the second half of the 18th cent., where Melendez Valdés and Jovellanos (qq.v.) tried to reconcile the extremes of taste which divided their poetic countrymen into Francophil and old-Castilian camps.

Salas Barbadillo, de, Alonso Geronimo (1581-1635): Span. novelist. Wr. about 20 different bks., some of them containing verse and drama

in the school of Vega (q.v.), others consisting of tales of the picaresque (or rogue) variety, others again purely amatory or chivalric. B.'s *Curioso y sabio* (sage) *Alexandro*, 1634, is a bright collection of satiric character-sketches, but perhaps his best-known work is the courtesan-tale of 'The Ingenious Helen, daughter of Celestina' (see s.v. *Celestina*), 1612, adapted in Fr. by Scarron (q.v.; in *les Hypocrites*), and not without use to Molière (q.v.; in *Tartufe*).

Salazar, de, Francisco Cervantes (c. 1514-75): Span. scholar; prof. of rhetoric at Osuna, and, later, in Mexico. Publd., 1546, Oliva's (q.v.) *Dialogue on the Dignity of Man*, with a sequel from his own pen.

Salazar Mardones, de, Cristobal (fl. 1636): Span. critic. Wr. an 'Illustration and Defence of the Fable of *Pyramus and Thisbe*', as a pro-Gongorist contribution to the polemical lit. evoked by the stylistic experiments of Gongora (q.v.).

Salazar y Torres, de, Agustin (1642-75): Span. poet. Wr. *Cythara de Apolo*, 1681, a vol. of verse of ample promise, though marred by affectations in the manner of Gongora (q.v.).

Salcedo Coronel, de, Garcia (d. 1651): Span. poet; Gongorist. Wr. an elaborate commentary on the works of his master (see s.v. Gongora), 1636-48, and *Crystals from Helicon*, Madrid, 1650, 'one of the worst productions of the school' (Ticknor, iii, 23, n. 44).

Sales, de, Francois (1567-1622): Fr. theologian. bp. of Geneva; preacher at Paris and Dijon; achieved the dignity of canonization, due to the mystic saintliness of his life and doctrine. His chief works were *Introduction to the Devout Life* and *Treatise on the Love of God*, and these opened the divine lit. of the 17th cent., while they continued the work of Calvin (q.v.), alike in their direct address to the Christian soul, and in their formal use of the vernacular for spiritual eloquence. St. Francis of Sales was a wide reader,and his discourses are filled with illustrations drawn from all kinds of sources, almost as indiscriminately as by Montaigne (q.v.); there is in his prose-style an indication of the precious note associated with d'Urfé (q.v.), whose didactic intention in his *Astrée* was warmly approved by S.

Salimbene (1221-80): Franciscan monk of Parma. Wr. *Cronica* (Chronicles) of worldly and other-worldly interest.

Salis, Johann Gaudenz (1762-1834): Germ. (-Swiss) poet; baron of Salis-Seewis; soldier and statesman. S.'s poems belonged to the sentimental school of nature-description, but his idyls, pastorals, and elegies reflected a more lively experience than the similarly-inspired writings of his friend and contemporary, Matthisson (q.v.).

Salutati, Coluccio (1330-1406): It. humanist and statesman; chancellor of Florence (1375); friend of Boccaccio. Was instrumental in bringing Chrysoloras to Florence, in publishing Petrarch's *Africa*, and in popularizing Dante in Lat. (See s.vv.) His erudition and unremitting industry, added to the patronage attaching to his position, invested S. with considerable influence as a stylist, at a time when the weapons of rhetoric were as much respected as the weapons of war. The Ciceronianism persecution of the Jews at that time, ha-Levi accepted the rite of baptism, and rose to eminence in the Span. Church, of which he became primate. As a pervert, his views were characterized by excessive zeal against his former brethren in faith. His brother, **Alvar Garcia de S.M.**, similarly an apostate from Judaism, was the author of the first sketch of the *Chronicle of king John ii* (see s.v. *Cronica*), which, with the *Portraits* of Perez de Guzman (q.v.) is our chief authority for the events of the time.

-ii. **Alonso** (died 1456): Span. scholar; son of Pablo de S.M., above; bp. of Cartagena for many years, whence he and his brothers (Gonzalo, Pedro; the latter was still living in 1480) are often described as de Cartagena, from the name of A. de S.M.'s see. His immediate connection with lit. is through the elegy written on the occasion of his death by Guzman; but A. de S.M. and his 2 brothers were alike scholars and poets, apart from the exalted position which their family took in the church; and a considerable number of poems in the anthologies of the age is ascribed, generically, to de Cartagena, and must be distributed among the members of old Solomon ha-Levi's clever family.

Santa Uliva (It.): A 'sacra rappresentazione' (q.v.; sacred play). The earliest extant edn. dates from Florence, 1568, but the play belongs to the age when the type flourished in Tuscany, about the end of the 15th cent., and the legend which it represents is much older. It is found in Gower, *Confessio Amantis*, bk. ii, in Chaucer, *The Man of Lawes Tale*, in Ser Giovanni, *Il Pecorone* (Day 10, Tale 1), in Straparola, (Night 1, Tale 4), etc. Uliva in the Ital. version is a daughter of the emperor Julian; she is princess Dénise of France in Ser Giovanni, and princess Constance in Chaucer, both of whom drew from the Anglo-Norman Chronicle of Nicholas Trivet, c. 1334. Thus, *S. Uliva* is a dramatic version of a chivalric 'novella', and her sainthood is the meed of the pity she inspires, and is not derived from the calendar.

Santillana, de (1398-1458): Span. poet, statesman; Iñigo Lopez de Mendoza, created marquis de Santillana, 1445, after the battle of Olmedo; the second Castilian marquisate, the first (of Villena, q.v.) having been reabsorbed in the Crown, 1412. As a descendant (and an ascendant) of the great house of Mendoza, the future marquis was naturally prominent in the wars and diplomacy of king John ii (q.v.) and his successor (Henry iv), and his conflict with the constable of Castile, Alvaro de Luna (q.v.) whose fall occurred in 1452, figures largely in the annals of the age. It was a part of S.'s transcendent powers that his contribution to and interest in lit. persisted throughout his career, despite his more active and public avocations; and, as a friend of don Enrique (s.v. Villena), his slightly older contemporary, who dedicated to S. his *Art of Poetry* and his translns. of the *Æneid* and the *Divine Comedy*, S. partook at an early age in the culture and letters of the Johnian court of Castile. Without Villena's wide erudition, S. was a diligent student of the old Provençal and Galician traditions in Castilian lit. and

had read and marked the *Romance of the Rose* (q.v.), and the works of Dante, Petrarch and Boccaccio (qq.v.); thus contributing to the growing Italianization of Span. literary types. He was the first to write sonnets (see s.v. sonnet)—*al italico modo*, as he said—in Span., and his example, however poor and wooden in achievement, was amply vindicated by later poets; and his other Italianate poems include a Petrarchan *Triumph of Love*, a Dantesque *Inferno of Lovers*, and a dialogue, *The Little Comedy of Ponza*, an island off the coast of Naples, where the Span. fleet had suffered in a sea-fight, 1435, under Alfonso v (q.v.) of Aragon, afterwards Alfonso i of Naples. This so-called, or Dantesque-called, comedy, in 120 octave stanzas (*ottava rima*), is in the nature of a vision, and Boccaccio takes part in the dialogue in his own language. More spontaneous in inspiration were the dramatic poem *Bias contra Fortuna*, 1448; the *Doctrinal de Privados* (favourites), 1454, a philippic against Alvaro de Luna (q.v.); and a *Serranilla* (little mountain-song), to be found among charming shorter pieces. There were also coronation-odes and other works; most notably, a collection of Proverbs, made at the request of king John ii for the advantage of his son, and consisting of 100 adages, which display the sententious genius of the maxim-making nation, in the dawn of whose greatness S. takes a high and a permanent place. It is to be noted that S. had no sympathy for the balladizing vogue of his generation (see s.v. *romancero*), which he described as irregular and inharmonious, and fit only for 'base and servile people'. His muse was essentially courtly and aristocratic.

Santo Spirito: Learned society at Florence, founded in 14th cent. mainly by the zeal of Boccaccio, stimulated by the example of Petrarch. Its first head was Marsigli (q.v.), and Salutati and Niccoli (qq.v.) were among its members.

Santob (13th-14th cent.): Span. poet; Jew. rabbi, also known as Don Santo (the words *San* (*Shem*) *tob* are Hebrew for good name). The facts of S.'s life are obscure, but he was born or resided at Carrion, and was described by that place-name, and lived in the reigns, and possibly in the service of kings Alfonso xi and his son Peter (the Cruel), 1350-69, to whom the 'white-haired' poet dedicated his *Moral Proverbs*, thus fixing their approximate date. These 686 (in another MS., 627) sets of gnomic verses, drawn from Biblical and Talmudic sources, from Avicebron (q.v.) and oriental lore, combine the native Span. genius for maxim-making with the Hebraic genius for moral didacticism; and are remarkable as the first composition of their kind in the vernacular, and as the first instance of Jew. authorship in the Span. tongue. Santillana (q.v.) entitled the rabbi a *grand trovador*.

Santos, Francisco (17th cent.): Span. novelist. Wr. several vols. of short tales, more or less in the manner of Quevedo (q.v.); among them, the one usually selected for honourable mention is *Day and Night in Madrid*, 1663, containing 18 so-called 'discourses', which give a faithful and entertaining picture of certain aspects of life in the Span. capital.

Lesage (q.v.) was obviously acquainted with this bk.

Sarcey, Francisque (1828-99): Fr. journalist; dramatic critic of the *Temps* from 1867. S. brought to a high pitch of excellence the method of 'conference', or 'imaginary conversation'.

Sardou, Victorien (1831-1908): Fr. playwright; composer of *vaudevilles*, relished in a diminishing scale of appreciation. His best piece, perhaps, was *Rabagas*, directed against demagogue-politicians; but, on the whole, it is flattery to describe S. as a Beaumarchais (q.v.) *manqué*.

Sarmiento, Martin (1695-1771): Span. scholar; botanist; Benedictine; his lay name was Garcia Balboa. Wr., 1732, a defence of the *Teatro critico* of Feyjoo (q.v.); and, 1745 (*ed. pr.*, 1775), 'Notes on the History of Poetry, and the Poets of Spain'; an important work.

Sarpi, Pietro (1552-1623): It. historian; wr. *History of the Council of Trent*, 1619, by virtue of which he has been accounted second only to Machiavelli (q.v.) in the line of Ital. historians. S., who is better known by his religious name of Fra Paolo, was the object of an official reply to his history of the Council, from the pen of card. Sforza Pallavicino (1607-67), and the studied elegance of the prince of the Church is noted as forming 'a characteristic contrast with the flame that colours the style of the Venetian monk, who poured all his soul and passion into his writing'. Both are subjected to the scrutiny of the 'equitable' Ranke (q.v.).

Sarrazin, Jean François (1605-54): Fr. poet and historian. Wr. an unfind. piece of hist. portraiture, *Conspiration de Walstein*, and burlesques and other poetry in contrast with the style of the precious (q.v.) set which congregated at the Hôtel de Rambouillet (q.v.), and which dubbed S. their 'Hamilcar'.

Satire: Descriptive name of a class of lit., originally of lyric descent, and directed to cause laughter by mimicry, mockery, taunts, or caricature. More immediately, the forms of satire are Roman by invention, and Quintilian has not been shaken in his Lat. contention, 'satira quidem tota nostra est' (satire, indeed, is wholly our own). The early 'satura', which means 'full', and which may be, derivatively, 'satura lanx', or a 'full dish', was a kind of folkshow mixture, a mixed grill, as we might say in a more recent culinary metaphor, comprising jest, story, fable, and song. The type was gradually formed by the Lat. poets Lucilius (born, 168 B.C.), Horace (65 B.C.), Persius (34 A.D.), Martial (40 A.D.), and Juvenal (62 A.D.); and it may be noted that, while the later Roman satirists introduced a more polished irony and a more pointed wit into their compositions, the tradition of rough humour was to some extent preserved in a certain harshness of versification, the more deliberate in contrast with the felicity of the Horatian lyric verse. Medieval satire was partly of indigenous origin, arising from attacks on the church (see s.v. Golias) and from the revolt of the *bourgeoisie* against the chivalric idealization of women (see s.v. Woman); in its development it rapidly assimilated itself to the models of antiquity. Its practitioners included the fabulists (see s.vv. Fable, Reynard), and examples may be sought in the works of Jean de Meung, Langland, Dunbar, and the street-urchin's muse of Villon (qq.v.), to name only few out of many. Presently, the objects of satire came to be more sharply distinguishable. The folly- (q.v.) lit. constituted a distinct class; the folk-book lit. constituted another (s.vv. Grobian, Kalenberg, for examples); the 'sotties' (q.v.) of the early theatre formed another; the conflict between Humanism (q.v.) and tradition produced another class, represented by the *Epistolæ Obscurorum Virorum* (q.v.), the works of Rabelais (q.v.), and others, in which the novellistic influence of Lucian (q.v.) and the ridicule suggested by his *Vera Historia* were applied to the waning taste for the quests of chivalric tradition; in this sense *Don Quixote* is satirical. Another class of satire arose on the model of the 'sermo' of the Romans: the descriptive so-called 'conversation', which passed into the sermons of the pulpit and into the reflective mono logues of satire-writers. Many of these took lit. as their subject; many others, more ephemeral, took politics; and others again, took social manners. In this category occur the names of Marston, Hall, D'Aubigné, Logau, Régnier, Butler, Donne, Boileau, Pope, Dryden, Voltaire (qq.v.); the Huguenot authors of the *Satyre Ménippée* (q.v.); the *Anti-Jacobin* (q.v.), and others enough. More universal in its appeal was the work of such writers as Béranger, Heine, and Burns (qq.v.), the last of whom may be said to have reverted to the simpler type of satire in Villon, and to have achieved exceptional success. Satirical verse is still written, as, e.g., by sir William Watson in our day, and the satirical vein is found in many literary formations. But since Byron (q.v.), the type has declined as a distinct class of lit., and it is mainly in magazines and newspapers, with the opportunities provided by their 'satura', or miscellany, that the gift of satirists continues to be displayed. The growth of courtesy in public life, the convention of religious tolerance, the discouragement of personalities, and the distribution of social criticism and moral reflection through the medium of the novel (q.v.), together with the rise of a cosmopolitan sentiment, tend to render satire, as such, an antiquated literary form.

Satyre Ménippée (1594): Fr. satiric pamphlet, of multiple authorship, and composed partly in prose and partly in verse. Menippos, a cynical philosopher of Syria, who figures in its title, and whose opinions found an echo in the Lucian, Gk. novelist, and in Varro, a contemporary of Cicero, had written *Saturæ Menippeæ*. But the title by which the 'S.M.' is known was a happy afterthought; the pamphlet was put together out of broadsheets, and at first bore the name, *La vertu du catholicon de l'Espagne, avec un abrégé de la tenue des Etats de Paris*—'The virtue of the catholicon (i.e., panacea, quack remedy) of Spain, with a review of the position of the Estates-general of Paris'. Lucianic though the point of view may have been, the more immediate models for the satire were Rabelais (q.v.), makers, quarried for their inexhaustible material. It is independent of the threefold material of romance (q.v., and s.v. Bodel)— Bretagne, France, and Antiquity,—though a period came, as we shall see, when it took the romantic infection ; and the best introduction to the study of this lit. is the *Corpus Poeticum Boreale*, or body of Northern poetry, edited at Oxford, 1883, by G. Vigfusson and F. York Powell. (Reference may also be made to the fascinating vol. on *Epic and Romance*, by W. P. Ker, Macmillan, 1908, from which some citations will be given in this article). Here we are chiefly concerned, not with the contents of the *Codex Regius* (q.v.), which has preserved (in the King's Library, Copenhagen) the so-called Elder Edda (q.v. ; MS. collection of Icel. heroic verse) from the perils of fire and flood ; nor yet with the *Njála* and *Laxdæla*, the two finest of the ' five greater '* prose-epics ; but rather with the close in the 13th cent. of the ' Saga Age ' in Iceld. It is a period which is covered by the life-time of Sturla (q.v.), *c.* 1214-1284. Sturla, as author of the *Sturlunga Saga* (edited by Vigfusson and Powell, 2 vols., Oxford), is the foremost representative of this class of writing ; and, as a contemporary of Joinville (q.v.), he enables us to compare and contrast the Fr. method in Joinville's history of the *Life of Saint Louis* with the Icel. method in Sturla's story of his own royal family : the one, subjection, even romantic ; the other, ' reso-lute, secure and impartial ' (Ker), as befitted the heir of the heroic *Saga*-makers. For the genius of Iceld. was positive. It lay beyond the ken of neighbours, and ' had no need of the great movements of European history '. The Icelanders, according to the same author-ity, possessed ' a humanism of their own, and a rationalism of their own ', gained without the labour of the Middle Ages.

At the close of the classical age, accordingly, and in a literary, not a legendary, time, as late as Villehardouin (q.v.) in France, we meet this great *Saga* of the Sturlungs, written by Sturla, son of Thord, and grandson of old Hvamm Sturla who founded the dynasty which it celebrated. Sturla's uncle, Thord's brother, was Snorri (q.v.), who himself had written Norse king's *Lives* (abridged in the *Heimskringla*, q.v.), and who, as the author of a little ' Art of poetry ', properly known as *Edda*, uncon-sciously caused a misleading name to be given to the MSS. in the *Codex Regius* (above). Late though Sturla's own-time chronicles are in the line of Icel. *Sagas*, and though they mark ' the end of the heroic age, both in politics and literature ', yet his *Sturlunga Saga* ' is not a decrepit or imitative or second-ary thing '. It is, on the contrary, a master-piece ; epoch-making, as masterpieces should be, but at the end, not the beginning, of an epoch. For, ' after the loss of Icelandic freedom, there is no more left of Germania ;

and the *Sturlunga Saga*, which tells the story of the last days of freedom, is the last word of the Teutonic heroic age. . . . With this true history, this adaptation of an heroic style to contemporary realities, the sequence of German heroic tradition comes to an end ' (Ker, *op. cit.*, 61). A noble and satisfactory end. There had always been history in the *Saga* ; it was Sturla's feat to apply the *Saga*-method to historical composition, to make the story of his own times, *quorum pars magna fuit*, vivid, imaginative, semi-epic, all-heroic. He had the gifts of narration and of vision, and his *Saga* ' contains one of the finest passages of narrative in the whole of Icelandic literature ' (*ibid.*, 252). ' Germania ' passed away in Iceland, but Gray and W. Morris (qq.v.) in Engld. and Tegnér and Ibsen (qq.v.) in Scand., are 4 of many modern writers who have revived Germania out of Iceld. ; while the influence of Macpherson's (q.v.) so-called *Ossian*, 1762, and of bp. Percy's (q.v.) *Five Pieces of Runic Poetry*, 1763, on the second coming of Romance (q.v.), is famous throughout Europe. The Viking of that romantic revival in the 18th cent. displayed attributes and qualities beyond the experience of his prototype in Iceland's classical age. The stern beauty and bold glamour of the North, the symbolic ' twilight of the gods ', and so forth, even Carlyle's (q.v.) masterly reconstruction of Icel. thought and belief, reveal some ideas of a later time than the 13th cent. of Sturla, or the earlier centuries of his heroic predecessors. But the new taste was always pressing on the old. The example of Fr. romancers, such as Chrétien (q.v.), was not the only cause of the sophistic-ation of the *Sagas*, or of the romantic strain which invaded their simple heroism. Foreign influences fall on ready soil, and the stock Viking of 19th-cent. convention may even have ' begun to be a bore, at a time when the historical " Viking Age " had scarcely come to its close ' (Ker, *op. cit.*, 218) : in other words, the seeds of change were inherent in the *Saga* itself ; and ballads and other rhyming measures (including the Icel. *Rímur*, q.v., or narrative poems) completed the transformation of the history-chronicles. Such a poem as Tegnér's (q.v.) *Frithiof*, for example, was taken from an intermediate ' super-romanced ' (Saintsbury's word) poem, and not from the pure wells of *Saga* undefiled.

It is a long way from the 13th to the 18th cent. Before traversing it, we may quote some general remarks on Icel. lit. in its flower, from Saintsbury, *P.E.L.*, ii, 340ff. Discussing the point which we illustrated from Ker, that Iceld. had no need of the great movements of European history, Saintsbury writes that *Saga*-literature ' was as indifferently and almost superciliously insular as the English country-house novel itself '. Charlemagne, Arthur, Alexander, and the tales of Troy and Thebes were everyman's property and no man's monopoly ; ' but the Sagas are from the first and to the (at least genuine) last nothing if not national, domestic, and personal. . . The Saga, the story, was so emphatically the natural mould into which Icelandic literary impulse threw itself, that it is

---

* ' There seems no reason to quarrel with the classification which divides the Sagas proper into two classes, greater and lesser, and assigns position in the first to five only—the Saga of Burnt Njal, that of the dwellers of Laxdale, the *Eyrbyggja*, Egil's Saga, and the Saga of Grettir the Strong.' (Saints-bury, *P.E.L.*, ii, 346 ; directions to Engl. versions of the 5 will be found *in loc. cit.*).

even more difficult here than elsewhere at the time to separate story and history, fiction and fact. Indeed, the stricter critics would, I believe, maintain that every Saga which deserves the name is actually founded on fact'. Iceld. submitted to Norway in 1262. The heroic age buried its dead; and, after the Saga of the Sturlungs there was no one who would sing the old songs in a new land. The splendid Saga-literature of Old Iceld., anon. for the most part and always reticent and objective, declined into the *Rímur* (q.v.) of rhyming, romantic court-poets; and 'the difference between new and old was still more marked by the Reformation, which cut the last link which bound Iceland to the past—the Old Church'. 'To the Icelander of the sixteenth century, even the fifteenth century was a mythical, semi-fabulous age' (Vigfusson and York Powell, *op. cit.*, i, Introduction xix). We need not dwell on the few Icel. scholars who sought to revive that past during the 17th and 18th cents. The best of their work was absorbed by the King's Library at Copenhagen; and the Dan. capital became the headquarters of Icel. scholarship and erudition, and the starting-point of an Icel. renaissance (see s.v. Jon Eiriksson). The literary darkness of Iceld. itself is hardly noticeably relieved till we reach the 19th cent., when a poet like J. Hallgrimsson (q.v.), a poet and novelist like J. P. Thorodssen (q.v.), remind us that this hardy northern people are the honoured possessors of the greatest prose-literature of medieval life. And one more reminder may be added, on the authority of Mr. G. Ainslie Hight, in the *Nineteenth Century and After*, June, 1924. There he writes that this 'Northern literature has a place among the very highest, and that, although almost unknown in this country, it is in a certain sense *our own*. Next to the peoples of Scandinavia, we Britons may fairly claim a share in their inheritance. What were the raiders who conquered or colonized our island in the fifth century but early Vikings? What else were the "Danes" of Ragnar, Hasting, Svegn and Knut? The Normans of the Conqueror, though no doubt somewhat Frenchified by residence and intermarriage, were of the same Scandinavian stock. In 879, at the Peace of Wedmore, half our country was given up to them, and not only does their blood flow in our veins, but our language, our social institutions, our habits of thought—everything except our religion—are rooted in those of the North Germanic or Scandinavian race. The sagas are throughout in close relation to the British Isles, where many of their episodes are laid. Moreover, it has been held by some high authorities that the bulk of the Eddic poems, and perhaps some of the sagas, originated in our country, a hypothesis which, although not capable of proof, has, in my opinion, much to be said in its favour'. A fascinating speculation.

-ii. **Denmark.** Dan. lit. has a more continuous history than Icelandic; and, except—a big exception—for the material of the Dan. ballads, it makes a later and a more modern start. The problem of ballad-origins is not to be lightly dismissed (see s.v. Ballad);

here we have only to remark that these poems may be taken to have been in course of composition or transmission from the 12th cent. to the close of the 15th; that Vedel (q.v.) collected 100 of them in the 16th cent., Syv (q.v.) about 100 more in the 17th; and that their main storehouse in Denmark is the *gamle Folkeviser* of S. Grundtvig (q.v.), 5 vols., 1853-83; thus completing 7 centuries of making.

For a consecutive survey of Dan. lit., the line of Dan. history must be followed; and an appropriate beginning will be found in the reign of queen Margaret (1375-1414), the Semiramis of the North, daughter of the excellent king Valdemar iv, and in her dream of a union between Denmark, Norway and Sweden, with her own country as predominant partner. This dream, visualized in the Union of Kolmar, 1397, became effective in the reign of Christian ii, who was elected king of Denmark and Norway, 1513 (the 2 countries had been united since 1448), and who brought Sweden to submission. There was a period, from 1544 to 1626, when Denmark led in Scandinavia; and if her power subsequently shrank before the growth of Sweden in her greater days, and before Germany's greed of territory, this was due partly to social and economic causes with which we are not immediately concerned. Our interest is to note that Norway was subject to Denmark from the 15th cent. to 1660, and remained united with her, though on more equal terms, from 1660 to 1814 (see s.v. *Syttendemai*). So that Dan. lit. for more than 300 years includes Norwegian too, though a distinctive Norse colour is to be marked in some foremost Dano-Norse writers. But till 1814, Danish is the literary language of Norway as well as of Denmark, and from Copenhagen the law went forth.

There is another point to be noted: the strength of Germ. influence in Denmark in her period of greatest prosperity. 'The Danish kings were of German origin and made German marriages; the language of their Court and Chancery was German; the nobles imitated the social and political pretensions of their German peers; Danish commerce was largely in German hands; and the Danish Reformation had been introduced and nourished from Germany' (*C.M.H.*, iv, 561). It is with the Reformation that Dan. lit. properly begins; not with Saxo (q.v.) or the balladists; but with Pedersen (q.v.), who transld. the Bible (Christian iii's Bible) in 1550; with Vedel (q.v.), who transld. Saxo, 1575; with Tausen (q.v.), the Danish Luther (q.v.), and so through a series of writers, some imitative, some original, none great, to the major name of Ludwig Holberg (q.v.), 1684-1754. From this date the pace is accelerated, and Dan. letters for 150 years wrought more enduring fame for the Dan. name than the dreams of her rulers or the battles of her seamen. The King's Theatre at Copenhagen was started in 1722; and the plays of the erudite historian who was Holberg, 'the Danish Molière', were the first glory of the new national stage. *Moles acquirit eundo*. Eminent name succeeded eminent name, and poets, scholars and Danes out of Norway made the roll of Dan. letters illustrious. Klopstock (q.v.), it is to be noted, made Copenhagen his headquarters for a while, and Tullin (q.v.) derived from him and from J. Thomson (q.v.) that call to the fresh lore of nature which was new in Dan. poetry in the 18th cent. Ewald and Wessel (qq.v.), Danes both of Norw. orig., continued the poetic tradition, which culminated in Baggesen (q.v.) and Oehlenschläger (q.v.), 1779-1850, the foremost name in a great time. Nor does the record cease with his name. ' The efflorescence of Danish poetry ', writes sir E. Gosse (*Lit. Northern Eur.*, 157) ; ' lasted about half a century, from 1800 to 1850, and in this short space of time the valuable part of the literature of Denmark was trebled in bulk '. We can but name some of its enhancers here ; the details must be sought s.vv. Steffens, poet and novelist ; Heiberg, poet and critic ; Grundtvig, poet and preacher ; Madvig, the humanist ; Kierkegaard, the philosopher ; Rask, the philologer ; Bödtcher, Hertz, Paludan-Müller, Hauch, Ingemann, Winther— these are some of the writers in various departments of pure lit. who adorned Denmark in the 19th cent. And the best of all we have kept to the last : Hans Christian Andersen (1805-1875), the universal delight of children's nurseries. Truly might sir E. Gosse say in 1879 ; ' Denmark is an extremely insignificant country ; but that exemplary insect, the ant, is also small, and yet the wisest of men deigned to recommend it to human attention ' (*op. cit.*, 156).

-iii. Norway. Norse kings were subjects of the Icel. sagas ; Norse soil was the foster-mother of Dan. poetry ; but, despite these accidents of political power and geographical distribution, despite, too, the distinctly Norse note in Holberg himself and Wessel, and, indeed, the greatest Dan. writers between Ewald and Baggesen, respect must be paid to the facts of history, and Norway must be treated as a part of Denmark. The Norske Selskab (see s.v. ; Norwegian Society) of 1772 was the visible centre in the Dan. capital of Norsemen of letters who were conscious of feeling like strangers in a strange land.

The birth of modern Norway is fixed at the date of the declaration of Independence, 17 May, 1814, and the literary relations of the 2 countries have been cleverly compared with those between America and Engld. ; the new country striving to sing herself free of the old. At first, it was all hallelujahs to liberty, and the *Syttendemai* (q.v.) *-poesi*, or 17th of May poetry, is represented by the so-called trefoil of patriots—Schwach, Bjerregard and Hansen (qq.v.). These ecstasies were presently exhausted : the key was too high to be sustained, and the shriller notes died into silence. Wergeland (q.v.), somewhat self-consciously, sought to revive an interest in Norw. life ; and Welhaven (q.v.), in *Norway's Twilight* and other writings, appealed more soberly for moderation, even against the fervour of Wergeland. The minor writers, Munch, Landstad, and the rest, need not detain us here ; for Norse letters passed into the ampler keeping of men of European fame : Ibsen, Björnson, Lie, and

Kielland ; true ornaments of the 19th cent. In their lifetime the independence of Norway, which had been transferred from Denmark to Sweden in 1814, was made real and effective in 1905 by the complete separation of the kingdoms, and the assumption of the Norse throne by a new Hakon, who was the husband of an Engl. princess. The social re-awakening of Norway in the second half of the 19th cent. is one of the most interesting phenomena ever reflected in literary history, and Björnson's name particularly is associated with it. We can see the dawn breaking on the North ; we watch the curtain being drawn back, and many strange lights fall alike on old things and on new. The death of these giants is so recent—Ibsen and Kielland, 1906 ; Lie, 1908 ; Björnson, 1910—that the record hardly falls within our survey ; the opportunities of the small nations are so new, and have been won by so stern a contest, that their future may hold more than their past ; and the history of Norse letters may still be waiting to be written. In the meanwhile, it may be conjectured that the movement, which was started about 1868, to expel Dan. words from the Norse language, and to invent, and impose on lit., a pure Norse-Norse (as distinct from Dano-Norse) tongue, is not set on the lines of true progress. Ibsen opposed it even more strongly than Björnson, and the patriotism of both was beyond question. (See s.vv. Landsmaal, Aasen).

-iv. Sweden. We said in a previous section that Sweden submitted to Denmark in the reign of king Christian ii, who was elected king of Denmark and Norway, 1513. Prior to this date, we have to note the foundation of the univ. of Upsala in 1477. ' Hitherto ', writes sir J. Sandys (*Hist. Class. Schol.*, iii, 334) ' the Swedes had studied mainly in Paris, Prague, Erfurt, Leipsic, Rostock or Griefswald ' (which did not belong to Sweden till 1648). And ' even after 1477 ', he continues, ' they resorted to the last three universities, and, early in the next century, to the Protestant university of Wittenberg or the Catholic university of Cologne '. These Swed. missionaries of culture, resorting to Wittenberg or Cologne, brought home more than the zeal for university reform, which found expression in the endowment of Upsala univ. by king Gustavus Adolphus (1611-32), in the foundation of the univ. of Dorpat by the same monarch, and of the univ. of Lund, 1688. They brought home, too, the seeds of the Reformation, for the reception of which the stubborn soil of Sweden had already been scored with deep furrows. Sweden's submission to the Dan. king is a true event in the history of Denmark ; in Swed. history, submission spelt rebellion. King Christian entered Stockholm for the ceremony of coronation on 4 Nov., 1520. Four days later, the chief Swed. magnates were executed in *Stockholms Blodbad* (' Stockholm's bath of blood '), in which the Vasa (=sheaf, the family badge) dynasty was baptised. For on 7 June, 1523, Gustav Eriksons (whose father had been a victim in the massacre of 1520) was elected king of Sweden, under the style of king Gustavus Vasa.

With his reign commenced the period of Sweden's greatness in the history of Europe, and, accordingly, of her effective place in the annals of art and lit. His House retained the throne till the beginning of the 19th cent., when the crowns of Sweden and Norway, released from her long allegiance to Denmark, were united on the head of the Bernadotte king, Charles xiv (1818-44), the ancestor of the reigning (1925) kings in Sweden and in Norway. Meanwhile, Gustavus i was succeeded by his two elder sons, by a nephew, and by his third son, Charles ix, father of Gustavus ii. This monarch, commonly known as Gustavus Adolphus, was succeeded by his daughter, queen Christina (q.v.), who reigned from 1633-1654, and who was the chief Humanist who ever occupied the Swed. throne. Her reign, and that of Gustavus iii, 1771-92, in the period of the benevolent despots, formed, with the reign of Gustavus i—the first of the Vasa dynasty—the 3 most important epochs in the history of the Swed. nation.

We are discussing lit., not history, but, more obviously than in the other Northern countries, the lit. of Sweden arose out of her history. There was the Reformation lit. of Gustavus i; the King's Bible, as it is called of 1540, effected in the Swed. vernacular by Laurentius Petri (q.v.), after the version of the New Testament by Andreæ (q.v.), both alike dependent on Luther (q.v.). There was the epoch of Lilje, or Stjernhjelm (q.v.), 1598-1672, for some time court-poet to queen Christina, and decisively the father of modern Swed. poetry. And, thirdly, not omitting the eminent name of the religious philosopher, Swedenborg (q.v.), 1689-1722, there was the reign of king Gustavus iii (q.v.), himself a practised man, of letters, who founded the Swedish Academy, 1786. This period, anticipated by such writers as Nordenflycht, von Dalin, Creutz, and Gyllenborg (qq.v.), was crowned by the greater names of Bellman, Kellgren, Thorild, and Franzen (qq.v.). From them it is but a step to the most eminent of Swed. men of letters, Esaias Tegnér, 1782-1846, and the romanticist movement in Sweden. (See s.vv. Atterbom, Phosphorus). Nor must the name be forgotten of the Finlander, J. L. Runeberg, 1804-77, ' the greatest poet that has ever used the Swedish tongue ' (E. Gosse, *Scand. Lit.*, 99). It has been used with good effect by many writers, poets, scholars, philosophers, historians, during the centuries of Sweden's rise and fall as a great power among the nations of Europe ; and, looking back on the literary record of these 4 peoples who form the Scandinavian North, recalling the story of their unions, their severances, and their transpositions, of their sufferings at the hands of bigger neighbours, especially Germany and Russia, it is a matter of astonishment as well as of congratulation that we owe to them, first, the Sagas, unique in kind and splendid in achievement ; next, a long line of worthy bks., ballads, dramas, novels and narrative poems, associated with the immortal names of Holberg, Oehlenschläger, Andersen, Björnson, Ibsen, Lie, Stjernhjehm, Tegnér, Runeberg ; and lastly, Linnæus, the botanist, Kierkegaard and Swedenborg, the philosophers ;

Madvig, the scholar, and Bergmann the chemist.

Scarron, Paul (1610-60) : Fr. novelist ; a prominent personage in the literary life of Paris, owing to his vigorous and remarkable spirit, his brilliant powers of burlesque, and the incidents of his life. At the age of 27 he was attacked by rheumatic fever, but, like Heine (q.v.), he defied deformity and pain. In 1652, he ' astonished Paris ' by his marriage with Françoise d'Aubigné, later mme. de Maintenon (q.v.), and granddaughter of T. A. d'Aubigné (q.v.). S.'s plays and poems are not of much value : the trend of his taste in poetry may be judged from the title, *Virgile travesti*, of his mock-epopee ; and his most notable comedy was *Jodelet*, which was ' desperately indebted ' (Ticknor, ii, 420 n.) to the Span. original of Roxas (q.v.), entitled *Donde ay Agravios, no ay Zelos* (' Real Wrongs make no Jealousies '). S., indeed, was the most shameless of the many Fr. pilferers from Span. fiction and dramas (see s.v. Castillo Solorzano, e.g.). His chief claim to renown rests on his *Roman comique*, 1651, the unfind. picaresque novel (q.v.) of a company of play-actors, in which he showed the way to Lesage (q.v.) and others to draw from Span. exemplars a corrective to the aristocratic lit. of mlle. de Scudéry (q.v.) and her compeers.

Sceaux : The *château de S.* was the residence and seat of the court of the duchesse de Maine (granddaughter of prince de Condé, 1621-86, of Chantilly, Fr. general and Bourbon prince). The duc de Maine was a natural son of king Louis xiv, and ' the court of the bastards ', as S. is termed in Fr. memoirs of the 18th cent., was a kind of miniature Versailles or a second Chantilly, where the duke and duchess held their similar revels, and extended their powerful patronage to Chaulieu, La Motte (qq.v.), and other men and women of the *salons*. The *grandes nuits de S.* figure in many memoirs of the age (see s.v. Staal).

Scève, Maurice (died, 1564) : Fr. metaphysical poet ; follower of Marot (q.v.), and leader of the ' Marotique ' school, or côterie, at Lyons (q.v.). Wr. long poem of 458 10-line stanzas in Platonizing vein of speculation on the theme of earthly delights as a mere reflection of heavenly beauty.

Schede, Paul (1539-1602) : Germ. Renaissance-writer ; known by Lat. name of Paulus Melissus ; librarian, 1586, at Heidelberg (q.v.). Wr. transln. of *Psalms* after the model of Marot (q.v.), thus paving the way for Fr. literary ideals in Germany. S.'s position was a focus for scholars and writers with similar tastes, whose pioneer work was so fatally interrupted by the Thirty Years' War (q.v.).

Schedel, Hartmann (1440-1514) : Germ. Humanist, in brief period before Renaissance and Reformation parted company. Collected inscriptions in the footsteps of Ciriaco (q.v.), and wr. *Nuremberg Chronicle* (a history of the world), 1493.

Scheffel, von, Joseph Victor (1826-86) : Germ. poet and novelist, whose final place in lit. is not yet fixed. His romantic epic, *Der Trompeter von Säkkingen*, 1854, was a ' best seller ' in its day, repeating and surpassing the success of Kinkel's (q.v.) not dissimilar *Otto* *der Schutz* eight years earlier. He followed it with an hist. romance, *Ekkehard*, 1857, a story of the 10th cent., of which the hero is a monk of St. Gall.

Scheffer, Johannes (1621-79) : Germ. scholar. Left Strassburg for Sweden at queen Christina's (q.v.) invitation, and made his home at the univ. of Upsala. S.'s valuable work in philology and criticism 'was in fact the principal permanent result of Christina's patronage of learning in the North' (Sandys, iii, 341). S.'s daughter married another prof. at Upsala, S. Columbus, who was a noted humanist in his day.

Scheidt, Kaspar (died, 1565) : Germ. satirist ; tutor and father-in-law of Fischart (q.v.), whose attention S. directed to the Eulenspiegel (q.v.) folk-tale. Similarly, S. effected a free rendering into the vernacular of the Lat. *Grobianus* of Dedekind (q.v.), and his jog-trot 8-syllable verses did much to popularize the theme of Dedekind's poem (1549 ; S.'s version appeared in 1551). The *Grobiana* which the author added in 1552 owed something to S.'s expansion.

Schélandre, de, Jean (1585-1635) : Fr. poet and dramatist ; eschewed Malherbe (q.v.) and all his works, and aimed at an imitation of Ronsard (q.v.). There is no record that his only play, *Tyr et Sidon*, 1628, was ever put on the stage ; it was accompanied by a pref. (penned by a certain François Ogier) in defence of the unregulated drama of the Engl. rather than the Span. type, and is an interesting but unique example of a Fr. tragicomedy free of the Unities (q.v.) in the very epoch of their tyranny.

Schelling, von, Friedrich Wilhelm Joseph (1775-1854) : Germ. philosopher ; a leading member of the circle of young Romanticists, including Hardenberg, Tieck, the brothers Schlegel and their wives (see s.vv.), at Jena, where he was appointed prof. of philosophy, 1798, the golden year of the Germ. Romantic movement (s.v. Romance). When S. left Jena for Würzburg in 1803, he took with him Caroline Schlegel (q.v.), formerly Böhmer, and *née* Michaelis, whom her second husband then divorced. Her marriage with S. was closed by her death in 1809. In the previous year S. had been appointed head of the Academy of Fine Arts at Munich, where he became prof. of philosophy at the new univ. in 1827. The king of Bavaria gave him his patent of nobility (' von '), and king Fredk. Wm. iv of Prussia invited him, 1840, to Berlin. As S.'s life was serenely spent between Jena, Munich, and Berlin, so his system of thought moved securely within the regions of idealism and mysticism mapped out by Fichte and Böhme (qq.v.). Thus, it lay wholly in the world of ideas which it was the aim of the Romanticists to explore in the sphere of pure lit. S. 'is the typical philosopher of Romanticism' (Höffding, *Modern Philosophy*, E.T., 177) ; representing its mystical, in distinction to its (Fichtëan) moral, aspect. His chief works were *Ideas towards a Philosophy of Nature, System of Transcendental Idealism*, 1800 ; *Investigations into the Essence of Human Freedom*, 1809, and his Berlin lectures in later life on mythology and revelation. An

essay on *Philosophy and Religion*, 1804, marks the change of centre in S.'s system from the philosophy of nature to that of religion ; and it is from the earlier and more vivid of his writings that the Romanticists derived the philosophic sanction of their æsthetic principles. Coleridge (q.v.) in Engld. mainly popularized S.'s teaching, which enjoyed a personal and brilliant, if brief, vogue of authority in his own country.

Schenkendorf, von, Friedrich Max (1784-1817) : Germ. poet. S. belonged, like Arndt (q.v.), to the little group of singers who celebrated the rising against Napoleon ; but his poems had less staying-power than Arndt's. They were collected, 1815, and reveal the reflective and sentimental talent of a writer, whose affinity to Romanticism in style was hardly disguised by the patriotic fervour of his message.

Scherenberg, Christian Friedrich (1798-1881) : Germ. poet. Wr. chiefly battle-pieces, *Waterloo, Aboukir*, etc., of a novel and even original type, which attracted the favourable notice and patronage of king Fredk. Wm. iv of Prussia.

Schérer, Edmond (1815-89) : Fr. critic ; of Swiss extraction ; prof. of Biblical exegesis in Geneva ; studied in Engld. and Germany. Wr. *Mélanges d'histoire réligieuse, Études sur la littérature contemporaine* (9 vols.) ; *Diderot, Grimm*, etc. Prof. Saintsbury, who selected for transln. a vol. of S.'s *Essays on Engl. Lit.* (Low, 1891), writes that, ' when his vision is not distorted by prejudice, he is the inferior of hardly any critic in argumentative power : there is a directness, solidity, simplicity about his methods and his conclusions, which, without being in itself better or worse than the accumulative but not always decisive method of Ste-Beuve and the suggestive approaches of Montégut, forms a very useful alternative and complement to both ' (*Hist. Crit.*, iii, 449). M. Arnold (q.v.) declared : ' What M. Edmond Schérer writes I do not easily resist reading ' ; and there is no doubt that S. exercised a considerable influence for good on opinion and taste in the 19th cent.

Schildbürger : Germ. folktale (Volksbuch, q.v.), comprising ' the wonderful exploits of the Schildbürger ', 1598 ; prof. C. H. Herford (*Literary Relations*, 248, note 2) calls the S. a ' veritable epic of the rustic Dogberry '.

Schiller, von, Johann Christoph Friedrich (1759-1805) : Germ. dramatist, lyric poet, critic, and philosopher ; one of the greatest names in Germ. lit., in the native histories of which he is commonly compared with his elder contemporary, Goethe (q.v.), whose lifetime (1749-1832) included his, whose friend he became, and whose statue stands with Schiller's on one pedestal at Weimar (q.v.). We shall forgo here the futile task of comparison. For one thing, there was room for both, and, for another, outside Germany, S.'s reputation and achievement take, decidedly, a lower place than Goethe's ; *Faust* is world-poetry ; *Wallenstein* is national drama. S.'s father was an army-surgeon, who settled, 1766, at Ludwigsburg, where duke Karl Eugen of Würtemberg appointed him curator of the gardens of the military school known as the ' Solitude '. The offer to receive the curator's son as a pupil in this institute was equivalent to a royal command, and S. was subjected to its discipline from 1773 to 1780 (the school was transferred, 1775, to Stuttgart). S. hated the training, which seems to have been eminently unsuited to his sensitive mind housed in a delicate body ; ill-health pursued him all his life through, and his death occurred in his 46th year. Klopstock's (q.v.) *Messias*, Goethe's *Götz*, and other poems and dramas of the period fired the genial spirit of the duke's rebellious protegé, and his friendship with Schubart served at once as a call to revolt and a warning against precipitancy. When at last S. was discharged from the military academy, he had his medical diploma in one pocket and his romantic diploma in the other, in the shape of his finished drama *die Räuber* (' the Robbers '). This he printed, 1781, at his own expense, and the success of its publication determined the young author's future. The play was produced at Mannheim by Dalberg (q.v.) in Jan., 1782, and, in the following Sept., S. resolved on flight from the disciplinary jurisdiction of the duke, who disapproved of these literary vagaries. Debts and disappointments accumulated, but S. found a friend in need in frau Henriette v. Wolzogen, who invited him to her rural retreat at Bauerbach, in Meiningen, in Thuringia. In July, 1783, the leisurely Dalberg came to the rescue, and appointed S. to the post of poet at the Mannheim theatre. What were the qualities of the *Räuber*, we must now ask, which captured the play-going public of the day, and encouraged a business-manager like Dalberg to abet a lad of 22 in his defiance of his princely patron ? In the first place, remember the day. The ' Sturm und Drang ' (q.v.) was at its height. Klinger's (q.v.) drama of that name had appeared in 1776, and young Germany's dream of freedom had been directed by *Götz von Berlichingen* to clutch at the untamed hope of wild and noble self-expression. The ' noble robber ', Karl v. Moor, was exactly fitted to this mood. S. chose the motto for his play from his medical readings in Hippocrates : ' What herbs cannot cure, iron cures, what iron cannot cure, fire cures ', and his hero of iron and fire sought to right ' the whole structure of the moral world '. It was in accordance with the teachings of Rousseau (q.v.), the father of the Germ. ' Sturm und Drang ', that Karl v. Moor ' returned to nature ', in the sense that he took refuge in the forests of Bohemia from the machinations at his father's court, and attempted to repair the evils of that court by the robber-morality of the open woods. It was in accordance with a stage-convention beloved by the dramatists of passion that the good brother of the wild life should be opposed to the wicked brother of the court ; that a concatenation of horrors should involve the chief characters in violent death ; that the motive of patriotism should be strongly emphasized (see Act iv, Sc. i, where the ' Lebt wohl, ihr Vaterlandsthäler ' anticipated the ' Lebt wohl ' song of the *Jungfrau von Orleans*, Prol., Sc. iv), and that the love-motive should be virile and intense ; thus, Karl Moor's murder of his Amalia—' only by Moor's

hand shall Moor's beloved die '—recalls another ' Moor's ' act of violence on Desdemona in Venice. The whole play was designed to communicate the spirit of revolt against oppression and of nature's remedies for man's iniquities which S. had conned from the lit. of the day in his solitary musings at the military school. Two more dramas were produced during the period of S.'s activity at Mannheim ; *The Conspiracy of Fiesco at Genoa*, sub-titled ' a republican tragedy ' of the doge Andreas Doria (see, too, s.v. Retz), and ' Intrigue and Love ' (*Kabale und Liebe*), at first called *Louise Millerin*, and sub-titled ' a family tragedy ', of the type of Lessing's (q.v.) *Emilia Galotti*, and traceable alike to Rousseau's influence. Both plays had, as background, a petty Germ. principality, but Louise and her Ferdinand, son of the political president, who favours an alliance with a charming lady Milford, a former court-mistress, are young lovers of tragic fate in the van of the social-problem play. Partly, no doubt, it was due to S.'s irregular entry that his literary career was never financially successful. He started several journals, of which the *Thalia* in several variants, 1785-93, was the first, and he formed some warm friendships, one of which, with frau v. Kalb, was a genuine affair of love ; another, with Chr. Gottfried Körner, father of Theodor Körner (q v.), the poet, by his marriage with Minna Stock, brought S. a welcome letter of admiration, 1784, from the affianced pair and from Minna's sister, Dora, and her fiancé, Ferdinand Huber, which was particularly timely, since the lapse of the Mannheim agreement found S. at a loose end. He visited the Körners at Dresden, 1785, and wr. their epithalamium, and other poems, notably *An die Freude* (' To Joy '). This, too, was the period of *Don Carlos*, S.'s first drama in blank verse, which Lessing's *Nathan der Weise* had naturalized after earlier experiments. *Don Carlos* may be taken as the close of S.'s apprentice-years. In 1787 he went to Weimar (q.v.), the Mecca of Germ. talent at that epoch, and was cordially, if not warmly, received. Goethe was in Italy, but the ducal court gave him an appreciative welcome, seconded by Wieland, Herder, and others. In 1789 he was appointed prof. of history at Jena, and his various hist. works on the United Netherlands, the Thirty Years' War, etc., were composed in preparation for or in discharge of the duties of his chair. They must not detain us here ; nor need we more than mention his marriage in 1790 with Charlotte (Lotte) v. Lengefeld, who was related to his old patroness, frau v. Wolzogen. Subsidies from princely benefactors facilitated the housekeeping of the happy couple. We come now to the important years of Kantian influence on S., the expression of which in prose and verse bridged the gulf of jealousy and misunderstanding between S. and Goethe, Germany's 2 greatest living men of letters. Philosophy ousted history from the foreground of S.'s interest, and the principles of Kant's (q.v.) æsthetics, and the application of those principles through literary criticism to conduct, evoked a rapid succession of thoughtful and valuable writings. ' Philosophic Letters ' in the *Thalia*, treatises on ' Grace and Dignity ' (*Anmut und Würde*), on ' The Æsthetic Education of Man ' (in 27 letters), and, even more importantly, on ' Naïve and Sentimental (almost equivalent to Realistic, or Objective, and Idealistic, or Subjective) Poetry ', 1795-96,—the last 2 series in his new journal, the *Horen*,—were matched in his lyrical verse by such poems as ' The Gods of Greece ', ' The Ideal and Life ' (originally, ' The Realm of Shadows '), ' The Might of Song ', and others, contributed to the *Musenalmanach*, which he issued annually from 1795 to 1800. The total effect of this multiform expression of the discipline of Kantian philosophy was to change, or, more precisely, to steady S.'s outlook on life. Thus, the ' naïve ' poets were, chiefly, Homer and Shakespeare, to an appreciation of whom S. had arrived not without misgiving ; and so he came full-circle to that distinction between ancient and modern art and poetry, between the Hellenic and the Romantic methods, which was to prune his youthful extravagances and to correct his youthful errors. Goethe ascribes to S. the early germination of the idea, developed by the brothers Schlegel (q.v.), and long since familiar *usque ad nauseam*, of Classicism *versus* Romance (q.v.). If the ascription is just, it is likewise just to refer to the influence of Kant the transformation, or, rather, the interpretation of the ideal towards which S. and other innovators had been feeling their way in the period of the ' Sturm und Drang ' ; and out of this exalted interlude of æsthetic prose and philosophical verse were spun the threads which drew together Goethe, refreshed in Italy, and Schiller, recreated by Kant. Who benefited more by the friendship is an idle inquiry to-day ; it added height to Goethe's thought and depth to Schiller's vision. If, as J. G. Robertson writes (*Hist. Germ. Lit.*, 366), it sums up the classical age of Germany, we may add that its factors were combined to realize the aspiration of the historian-philosopher of ancient Greece : ' we seek wisdom for noble ends and beauty without softness ' ; in other words, it availed to avoid the commonplace, which is the special danger of the ' naïve ', and the extravagant, which is the special danger of the ' sentimental '. Omitting the 2 poets' joint epigrams (*Xenien*, after Martial's *Xenia*) and others, S.'s chief works in the last decade of his life comprised ballads (' The Diver ', ' The Glove ', ' The Ring of Polycrates ', etc.), lyrics (' Expectation ', ' Happiness ', etc.), hymns (notably *der Spaziergang*, ' The Walk '), the magnificent ' Song of the Bell ', and the 3 plays combined as *Wallenstein*. This tragedy in 10 acts consists of *Wallenstein's Camp, The Piccolimini*, 1799, and *Wallenstein's Death*, 1799, and in it S. attained the summit of his dramatic power. The hero, historically Waldstein, who aims at the Bohemian crown and the primacy in Germany, and who believed so firmly in his destiny of greatness that ' he did not fall because he was a rebel, but rebelled because he fell ', is drawn on the grand lines of tragedy ; and the production of this play at Weimar was an event of first importance in the history of European drama. It was

followed, from S.'s pen, by *Maria Stuart*, 1800, *die Jungfrau von Orleans* (a ' romantic tragedy ' of Joan of Arc), 1801, *die Braut von Messina*, 1803, and *Wilhelm Tell*, 1804 ; and a *Demetrius* was on the stocks when he died ; a remarkable list of masterpieces, and the more remarkable in the circumstances of the poet's increasing ill-health. It is as a playwright that S. is famous, and that he would have wished to achieve fame ; and, in comparison with his plays, less attention is properly due to his professorial activities in history and criticism, or to his first-rate translns. from foreign dramatists for the Weimar theatre. But admiration for *Wallenstein* and its successors must not detract from the splendour of S.'s lyrical poems. The philosophic lyrics and the lyrical ballads, some of which have been enumerated in each class, and the kind of half-way poem between the 2 classes, the altogether charming *Lied der Glocke*, form a poetic possession of the highest intrinsic value ; and there are notes in S.'s lyrical philosophy which it would be hard to match in any lit. Like many men of sensitive disposition, S. had a genius for friendship, both with women and with men. Some of these have already been mentioned ; we may add a reference to Wilhelm v. Humboldt (q.v.), with whom, as he wr. to the constant Körner, he formed ' an infinitely agreeable and at the same time, useful acquaintance ' at Jena in 1794. His ideas flowered more richly in the sunshine of genial talk ; and in this connection the Schiller-Goethe friendship was an event fraught with real increase to the lit. of their country. His relations with the brothers Schlegel did not always run smoothly, and various difficulties connected with the journalistic activities of the circle led in 1797 to a definite breach. The Dec., 1797, issue of Schiller's *Horen* was belated till June, 1798, when its impending doom was manifest ; and shortly after Easter, 1798, the brothers Schlegel, who had deserted from its flag, issued their own new publication, the *Athenæum*. We quote s.v. Goethe the famous stanza from his epilogue to Schiller's *Glocke* (' Bell '), written, Aug., 1805, as the living friend's tribute to the dead : ' Behind him lay the bodiless phantom of *das Gemeine* '. To have won this tribute from Goethe is itself a title to immortal renown.

Schirmer, Michael (died, 1673) : Germ. hymn-writer ; Lutheran.

Schlegel, -i. Johann Elias (1718-1749) : Germ. critic and playwright. His critical and dramatic writings possess considerable value in the age before the golden age. He was a discriminating admirer of Shakespeare, and wr. a review of a recent transln. of *Julius Cæsar*. In a treatise on the Dan. theatre, S. proved himself a forerunner of Lessing (q.v.) in dramaturgic theory. His tragedies, *Hermann, Canute*, and others, were founded on Gk. models.

-ii. Johann Adolf (1721-1793) : Germ. publicist ; brother of above. Helped to found the *Bremer Beiträge* (q.v.), which played a conspicuous part in the Swiss-Saxon feud round Gottsched (q.v.). Transld., 1751, with copious original matter, Batteux (q.v.)

on ' the principle of art ' (1747). There was a third brother, **Johann Heinrich** (1724-1780), who had the credit of introducing the Engl. 10-syllable line into Germ. drama in place of the Fr. alexandrine.

-iii. **August Wilhelm** (1767-1845) : Germ. Romanticist ; Engl. scholar ; elder son of J.A.S., above ; more eminent, like his brother (*infra*), and like their father and elder uncle in the previous generation, for criticism than for creation : a unique instance of talent repeating itself in 2 successive pairs of brothers. Studied at Göttingen under Bürger (q.v.), who called him his ' poetic son ', and prophesied, in a sonnet addressed to the ' young eagle ', a better poet's wreath than his own. Another Göttingen teacher, Heyne (q.v.), trained A.W.S. in Hellenism and Latinity. It was under Bürger's influence, and partly in collaboration with him, though the study of Shakespeare was in his blood (see s.v. J.E.S., above), that A.W.S. began a transln. of the *Midsummer Night's Dream*. Schiller's (q.v.) influence supervened on Bürger's, and, after a year or two at Amsterdam, A.W.S. settled, 1796, at Jena, where he lived till 1801. He was a contributor in these years to Schiller's *Horen* and *Musenalmanach*, and laid the foundations of his fame as a transkr. and critic of Shakespeare, and as the constructive critic of the Germ. romantic movement. In this Jena-period he enjoyed the great help of his accomplished wife, Caroline (q.v. *infra*). The circumstances of her marriage, 1796, to A.W.S., and of her divorce from him, 1803, are not of immediate interest to literary history. Here, 2 facts may be noted : first, the Schlegel household at Jena, at which F. Schlegel (see *infra*) and his wife soon arrived, became a headquarters and rallying-place of the Romanticists and their friends ; secondly, Caroline took a large part in the Shakespearean labours of her husband. Indeed, for that reason, if for no other, he abandoned the task of transln. after she left him under the protection of Schelling (q.v.). By that time (between 1797 and 1801) A.W.S. had publd. 16 plays of Shakespeare in the Germ. language ; a 17th, *Richard iii*, followed from his pen in 1810. These included the greatest plays, such as *Romeo and Juliet*, *Julius Cæsar*, *Hamlet*, *Merchant of Venice*, etc., and all the Engl. history plays except *Henry viii*. The transln. of the dramas was completed eventually by Dorothea Tieck (q.v.) and Baudisson (q.v.), and is commonly known as the Schlegel-Tieck transln. As such, it is a masterpiece of the Germ. tongue. ' Schlegel's Shakespeare takes its place beside the works given to the world by Goethe and Schiller during the period when they worked in fellowship ' (Scherer, quoted by Brandes (q.v.), *Main Currents*, E.T., ii, 57). Brandes adds : ' Let us consider what this really means. It means not much less than that Shakespeare, as well as Schiller and Goethe, saw the light in Germany in the middle of the eighteenth century. He was born in England in 1564 ; he was born again, in his German translator, in 1767. *Romeo and Juliet* was published in London in 1597 ; it reappeared in Berlin as a new work in 1797 '. (*ibid.*). This work, so

necessary to do, so late in the doing, was the chief positive contribution of A.W.S. to the cause of the Romantic revival, which he and his brother, with Tieck, Wackenroder, and others, including the greater genius of Hardenberg (qq.v.) served by their critical writings ; in the *Athenœum* (q.v.), founded 1798, in its predecessors, contemporaries, and successors ; and in courses of professorial lectures. Saintsbury (*Hist. Crit.*, iii, 393 ff.), selects as the most important of the critical writings of A.W.S. his papers on Bürger, on Voss's *Homer*, his ' Lectures on Dramatic Art and Literature ' (delivered in Vienna, 1808), and his ' Lectures on Belles-Lettres and Art ' (delivered in Berlin, 1801-03). This last-named course brings us back to the year in which he quitted Jena. His 4 years' residence in Berlin was followed by a lengthy period of attendance on mme. de Stael (q.v.), who ' is mainly, if not merely, as much Schlegel as could go clothed in French petticoats, and remember itself there ' (Saintsbury, *ibid.*), a judgment more flattering to the master than the pupil, but not more than adequate to A.W.S.'s influence on his age. This influence was not exercised through mme. de Stael alone ; in Engld., too, to which the Germ. critic went for his best Romantic exemplars, he was venerated by thinkers like Carlyle and Coleridge (qq.v.) for the lights which he shed on the theory of poetics ; and, though the debt which Coleridge, e.g., owed to him is diminished by the recollection that *Lyrical Ballads* was publd. in the same year as the first number of the Schlegelian *Athenœum*, there is no doubt that, historically, the Romantic school of lit. in Europe was established in Berlin about 1797-98. ' The new poetry acquires a new criticism . . . and the Romantic teaching is added to Romantic criticism and poetry. To Romantic æsthetics Romantic ethics succeeded, and a Romantic theory of religion was soon developed therefrom. Briefly, as the circle of likeminded men and women was enlarged, the circle of tendencies and interests was likewise enlarged, and the conception of Romance broadened and defined itself ' (Haym, *Romantische Schule*, 269). This conception was dominated for many years by the work and thought of the brothers Schlegel. A.W.S.'s later life may be more rapidly reviewed. In 1818, he was appointed to the chair of letters in the new univ. of Bonn, where he lectured mainly on Indian lit. ; in 1827, he returned to Berlin ; and among his many works were vols. of poetry, which failed to win him the greener laurel modestly prophesied by Bürger ; a classical drama, *Ion*, with which Goethe made a failure at Weimar ; translns. from Calderon (q.v.), etc. A.W.S. was very widely read, and employed the critical faculty of comparison with excellent, novel, and illuminating effect : so much so, that the literary historian is glad to be able to forget some personal aspects of the Romantic movement in Germany, such as A.W.S.'s quarrel with Schiller ; for the critic was greater than the man.

-iv. **Caroline** (1763-1809) : Germ. Romanticist ; wife of above. C.S. was the daughter of J. D. Michaelis (q.v.) of Göttingen, and m., (1) 1784, a Dr. Böhmer, who died in 1788. In

Mayence, in 1792, when on a visit to J. G. Forster (q.v.) and his wife, daughter of Heyne (q.v.), and afterwards the wife of L. F. Huber (q.v.), C.S. became implicated in the politics of the Fr. Revolution, and suffered imprisonment and other evils. A.W.S. was an old acquaintance, and he and she had more in common than many friends ; and chivalry and admiration combined, at the time of Caroline's greatest trouble, to bring about (2) their marriage in 1796. ' It was a genuine literary marriage ', says Haym (*op. cit.*, 164), and he quotes her husband's testimony, that ' she possessed every talent to shine as an author '. She worked brilliantly at A.W.S.'s right-hand during the golden years of his Shakespearean labours, and helped him not merely in his reading, but in his writing, reviewing, and translating. She held a kind of *salon* at Jena, where her wit and fascination held the young Romantics enchanted. The death, 1800, of her daughter by her first marriage, with whom Schelling (q.v.) had begun to fall in love, brought the mourning lover and the mourning mother too near in sympathy, and the loose morality, which was, unfortunately, a feature of Romanticism in its narrower sense, found its expression in the consequent divorce, and in Caroline's (3) marriage, 1803, to Schelling.

-v. Friedrich (1772-1829) : Germ. Romanticist ; younger son of ii, Johann Adolf, and brother to iii, August Wilhelm. Married Dorothea (q.v., *infra*), daughter of M. Mendelssohn, herself an author, and even more than her sister-in-law, Caroline (*supra*), subject to the Romantic temperament. F.S., though associated with his elder brother in the foundation of the *Athenæum* (q.v.), and in the beginnings of the literary movement at Jena and Berlin in the last years of the 18th cent., was at once less considerable as a critic and more ambitious as a creator than he. But the defects which marred his criticism, and which curtailed his best work to ' fragments ' and aphorisms, affected, too, his original writings. His genius, as distinct from the elder's talents, was somewhat morbid and unbalanced ; and the irregularity of his marital relations was reflected in the Romantic novel, *Lucinde*, 1799 (itself a fragment, by the way), on which much controversy has turned. Lucinde *is* Dorothea : this, after all, is the most important point ; and if we recollect that the real heroine lived with the author of the fictitious heroine for some years before they were legally married, we shall see less of the Romanticists' theorems, less of Schleiermacher's (q.v.) generous praise (in his *Familiar Letters on Lucinde*), and more of Friedrich's and Dorothea's practice in this not very salutary romance of free-love masquerading as true-love. But F.S., and his noble-minded Dorothea were both better than the morality, to which, in their novels, they lent their names. (See also s.v. Woman). F.S.'s other works included a poor tragedy, *Alarkos*, a *History of Ancient and Modern Literature*, a *Language and Wisdom of the Indians*, and misc. writings, all of which were characterized by brilliance and vigour, and powerfully assisted the promulgation of the

gospel of Romance. His conversion, 1808, with Dorothea, to the Roman Catholic Church, belongs to personal rather than to literary history.

-vi. Dorothea (1763-1839) : Germ. Romanticist ; wife of above ; daughter of Moses Mendelssohn (q.v.) ; m. (1), 1781, Simon Veit, a Berlin banker. Frau Veit met F.S. in Berlin, 1797, and an affinity at once declared itself between the repressed intellect of the business man's brilliant wife and the manifest genius of the young man of letters. Her divorce ensued in the following year, but from 1798-1802, Friedrich and Dorothea were content to live together at Jena as lovers only. With this relationship lit. is not concerned, save to note that D.S.'s romance *Florentin* defended the same principles with the same devotion as were displayed in her husband's *Lucinde*. They were m. in 1802, and subsequently embraced Roman Catholicism. D.S., who, by common consent of her contemporaries and by the evidence of her own letters, was as strong in her spiritual idealism as she was physically frail and slight, was at once a scholar and a brilliant talker. Her correspondence with men of letters and others (including her sons by her first marriage) takes a high place even in the age of letter-writing, and her poems, her contributions to the literary journals, and her transln. of mme. de Stael's (q.v.) *Corinne*, were valuable additions to the lit. of the time.

It is inevitable, in writing of the brothers Schlegel, to discuss their lives and their wives in connection with their writings. Romanticism, as they taught it, included views on morality and feminism, as well as on metres and the tragic conflict ; and it so happened that they lived and loved in accordance with the viewy doctrines which they formulated. But no personal aspects can detract from the huge debt which Romance in Europe owes, and has lavishly acknowledged, to this brilliant pair of brothers. In formal treatises, in academic lectures, and in the pages of many reviews, these widely-read and deeply-thinking brothers completed the critical labours of Herder and Lessing (qq.v.), founding the sciences of comparative mythology and philology, and inspiring a movement in creative lit. which has grown stronger, purer, and more self-reliant in every generation since their day. ' The world must be romanticized ', declared Novalis (q.v.) ; and the establishment of the Romantic point of view, which may be defined, as well as otherwise, as a consecration of the commonplace, was the object and the task of these 2 brothers. ' Their Romanticism made the Schlegels cosmopolites '. They aimed at giving man a new inner world, balancing the new outer world revealed by science ; and they aimed, beyond that, at a reconciliation of the Inner and the Outer. They were idealists, emancipators, glorifiers, lovers, egoists, deconventionalists ; and, though they and their friends made mistakes, they were the mistakes of men and women who saw visions.

There is one word still to be added, in connection with the Schlegelian irony (q.v.). It was particularly the mark of F.S., who crystallized into a hundred hints and brilliant aperçus and epigrams his sense of the contrast between the unreality of experience and the reality of the mind which grasped it. Over this vast field of contrast, romantic Irony was king. Irony, said F.S. accordingly, is 'the form of paradoxes'. The creative faculty, he said again, may be employed *bis zur Ironie*, till the irony-point is reached, when the sense of world-possession is pricked, and self-restraint becomes self-destruction. At the root of F.S.'s irony, which he borrowed from Socrates and enhanced, is the idea—the saving idea—of proportion, of a reminder brought out of the reserve of creative consciousness (the more effectively as it was the more sudden) of the true relation between the Ego and the non-Ego, displayed in Fichte's (q.v.) philosophy of freedom, which mediated between Kant and the Romanticists. This perception was much needed in Germ. lit., in which feeling had overflowed form, as in Klopstock (q.v.) and his school, e.g.; and it opened the doors to many playful passages in Tieck, Grimm (qq.v.), and others. A simple example of the irony exalted by F.S. to the high place of 'logical beauty' in the philosophic scheme of Romanticism, will be found in Thackeray (q.v.), *Vanity Fair*, fin : 'Come, children, let us shut up the box and the puppets, for our play is played out'. The creator, as F.S. would have said, pursued his expression *bis zur Ironie*, and thus became the destroyer.

Schleiermacher, Friedrich Ernst Daniel (1768-1834) : Germ. philosopher. His 'position in the history of philosophy is characterized by the fact that he keeps the spirit of the critical philosophy alive within the ranks of Romanticism. His Socratic personality, in which the capacity for complete inner devotion was united with a remarkable degree of calm discretion, furnished the basis for the combination of Romanticism and criticism ' (Höffding, *Hist. Phil.*, E.T., 190). S. has been called the high priest of the Romantic movement, and the blind eye which he turned to the worse side of the *Lucinde* of Fr. Schlegel (q.v.) presumes the zeal of the hierarch ; still, the theological speculation of Romanticism was emancipated by Schelling (q.v.) and S. from the dryness and dreariness of dogma, and was renewed by the fine breath of feeling : in this aspect, the writings of S. exercised considerable influence on the religious revival at the beginning of the 19th cent. In 1804, S. was appointed preacher and prof. of theology at the univ. of Halle ; in 1806, he went to Berlin, and was associated with the foundation of its univ., where he held, 1810, a like post. He was incomparably the most literary theologian of modern times, and his best known works include *Monologues*, 1800 ; *Familiar Letters on Schlegel's ' Lucinde '*, 1801 ; a transln., with introductions, of Plato's dialogues, 1804-10, and his masterpiece, *der christiche Glaube*, 'The Christian Faith', 1821-22. Besides these, he revised for publication several series of lectures, on dialectics, æsthetics, education, etc., and he was a busy contributor to the many reviews of his day, including the *Athenæum* (q.v.).

Schmidt, Klamer Eberhard Karl (1746-1824) : Germ. poet ; Anakreontiker (q.v.). Attracted by Gleim (q.v.) to Halberstadt, a headquarters of the Prussian or Anacreontic school, and wr. several vols. of light imitative verse.

Schmied, Erasmus (1570-1637) : Germ. scholar. Edited works of Pindar (1616) with Lat. transln. and commentary, which held the field till the time of Boeckh (q.v.).

Schnabel, Johann Gottfried (1692-*c*. 1742) : romancer. Wr. ' Wonderful Adventures of some Mariners, particularly of Albert Julius, the Saxon, and the Colonies he planted on the Island of Felsenburg ', in 4 vols., 1731-43, commonly known by the short title of *Insel Felsenburg*. The hero of this romance was driven into exile by the exigencies of the Thirty Years' War, and S.'s version is the most notable product of the *Robinson Crusoe* (1719) harvest (see s.v. Robinsonaden). It was re-issued later with an introduction in 6 vols. by L. Tieck (q.v.).

Schönaich, von, Otto (1725-1807) : Germ. epic poet. The dreary heroic poems of this eposmaker *pour rire* are only remembered to-day as an incident in the tragic story of the downfall of Gottsched (q.v.), one of the last acts of whose long dictatorship of taste at Leipsic was to crown S. with the poetic bay for his *Hermann, or Liberated Germany*, 1750 ; and it was this obstinate tribute to the worst example of the faults of the neo-classic style which completed the victory of the Zurich school, who had just issued in their *Bremer Beiträge* (q.v.) the first 3 cantos of Klopstock's (q.v.) *Messias*, the very antithesis to S.'s *Hermann*.

Scholasticism, Schoolmen. See s.v. **Aristotle**.

Schonaeus, Cornelius (1540-1611) : Dutch Latinist ; rector of Haarlem ; known to his contemporaries as ' the Christian Terence ', and wr. Terentian dramas on sacred subjects, such as Judith, Susanna, Joseph. S. was at one time popular as a dramatist in Engld.

Schopenhauer, Arthur (1788-1860) : Germ. metaphysician. S.'s chief work was *die Welt als Wille u. Vorstellung* (The World as Will and Idea), which, though publd. in 1819, had to wait 40 years for full recognition. Briefly, its theory is that the visible world is merely 'idea', and that 'will' is the only entity. But will is stimulated to action by suffering, and the abandonment of the 'will to live' is, consequently, the elixir of life,—a suicidal conclusion. One aspect of S.'s philosophy was the release of thought from the word-drift of Hegel (q.v.) and the hist. school. When once the brooding spirit of Hegelianism had been lifted from thought, thinkers demanded something more positive and hopeful than the gracefully written pessimism of S., who stands, accordingly, in the direct line to Nietzsche (q.v.) and the new school.

Schott, Andreas (1552-1629) : Dutch scholar. Resided in Spain ; joined the Society of Jesus (q.v.) ; taught at Rome ; returned, 1597, to his native Antwerp, and publd. works in Latinity and Gk. learning, including *Proverbs* of Diogenianus (1612), an Alexandrian lexicographer.

Schottelius, Justus Georg (1612-76) : Germ. grammarian ; member of the Palmenorden (q.v.). Wr., 1663, a valuable work on Germ. language.

Schröder, Friedrich Ludwig (1744-1816): Germ. actor and playwright; chiefly associated with the stage at Hamburg. S. was an early adherent to the Shakespeare-worship which characterized the Sturm und Drang (q.v.), and adapted plays by Calderon, Lillo, Beaumont and Fletcher (qq.v.), and others to Germ. taste. His preference was for the domestic drama of the sentimental variety, equivalent in its kind to the type of Mrs. Henry Wood in the field of fiction.

Schubart, Christian Daniel (1739-91): Germ. poet and publicist. His unbridled pen, esp. in the conduct of his review, the *Deutsche Chronik* (started, 1774) brought him into conflict with duke Karl Egon of Würtemberg (Schiller's duke), who had him confined to a fortress for 10 years. Later, he became court-poet and director of the theatre at Stuttgart. He did not live long to enjoy his prosperity. S.'s early works were composed under the influence partly of Klopstock, partly of Wieland (qq.v.); his later writings were in the Sturm und Drang (q.v.) vein, and stormed, not unreasonably, and, at the same time, melodiously, against tyrants and kings.

Schulze, Ernst (1789-1817): Germ. poet; wr. epic romances, a little in the style and altogether in the metre (*ottava rima*) of Ariosto (q.v.), on themes of myth and legend. One was *Cecile*, 1817; another, *die bezauberte Rose* (the enchanted rose), 1818: the personal object of both being to create a memorial to the poet's dead love, Cecilia Tychsen, who typifies, in the epic, a Christian's longing for eternity. S. was, in technique at any rate, a throw-back to the Ital. romance-epicists, and even (Cecile= Beatrice) to Dante.

Schuppius, Johann Balthasar (1610-61): Germ. preacher and satirist; Protestant; prof. of history at Marburg for some years, and afterwards at Hamburg, where his habit of mixing satire with sermon earned him some ecclesiastical odium. S. was a geniune hater of all affectation and sham, and included the literary reforming zeal of Opitz (q.v.) in his net of ridicule.

Schuurman, Anna Maria (1607-84): Dutch poet and scholar; an admirable type of the Renaissance woman of learning.

Schwab, Gustav (1792-1850): Germ. poet. follower of Uhland (q.v.) and proud to be known as his pupil. As a member of the so-called Swabian school, S. is necessarily numbered among Germ. poets, but his place, if permanent at all, will be more probably won by his life of Schiller (q.v.), 1840, and his popular works on folklore (German, 1835; Classical Antiquity, 1838-40).

Schwabe, Johann Joachim (1714-84): Germ. publicist. Edited, 1741-44, a Leipsic *Spectator* entitled 'New Transactions for the Delight of Understanding and Wit', the official paper of the Gottsched (q.v.) literary circle. In the decline of Gottsched's star, the paper was transformed to the *Bremer Beiträge* (q.v.).

Schwartzerd, Philip. See **Melanchthon.**

Schwenkfeld, Kaspar (1490-1561): Germ. sacred poet; Catholic mystic.

Scot, Michael (*c.* 1175-1234): Medieval scholar, probably of Scot. birth; is said to have studied at Oxford and Bologna, and is known to have studied at Paris and to have been attached to the court at Palermo of king Fredk. ii of Sicily; went to Toledo, *c.* 1209, then the centre of the study of Aristotle (q.v.). S. effected various translns. of that master and of Averroes (q.v.) his commentator, into Lat. from Arab. and Hebr., but is said to have known no Gk.; in his Hebr. studies, he is reputed to have had the advantage of the aid of a learned Jew, Andreas. R. Bacon (q.v.) attacked S. for the gaps in his equipment as a complete Aristotelian, but he proved a valuable transmitter of the foreign learning. S.'s skill in the sciences earned him, as others, the repute of necromancy and magic: e.g., in Dante (q.v.), *Inf.*, 116-7, 'Michael Scot, who of a verity of magical illusions knew the game'; in Boccaccio (q.v.), *Decameron*, viii, 9, 1 'a great master in necromancy, Michael Scot'; and in sir Walter Scott (q.v.), *Lay of the Last Minstrel*, 13,

In these far climes it was my lot
To meet the wondrous Michael Scot,
A wizard of such dreaded fame. . .

Many of S.'s works still await publication.

Scott, Jonathan (1754-1829): Engl. scholar; Persian secretary to Warren Hastings; transld. and revised the Fr. version by Galland (q.v.) of the *Arabian Nights Entertainments*, 1811; prof. of oriental languages at Royal Military Coll., 1802-5. S.'s brother, John Scott-Waring (1747-1819), was agent to Warren Hastings, 'whose impeachment was probably due to his injudicious zeal in his behalf' (*D.N.B.*, s.v.).

Scott, Michael (1789-1835): Scot. novelist; in business in Jamaica; wr. a romance of his experiences, *Tom Cringle's Log*, issued in *Blackwood's Magazine*, 1829-33.

Scott, Robert (1811-87): Engl. scholar; master of Balliol Coll., Oxford, 1754-70; dean of Rochester; joint-author of Liddell and Scott's *Greek-English Lexicon*, 1843, and often reprinted; new edn., Oxford, part i, 1925.

Scott, Walter (1771-1832): Scot. poet, romancer and novelist; created baronet, 1820. We may put ourselves at once *en rapport* with the fame of S., after a century of criticism, by quoting 2 or 3 opinions from the latest and the leading critics. Thus, as to his poetry, we read that S. was 'the greatest of our lyric poets between, Blake, or Burns, and Shelley: Coleridge, who wr. less that is lyrically perfect, not being excluded' (prof. Elton, *Survey Engl. Lit.*, 1780-1830, i, 310). As to his romantic fiction, prof. Omond (*P.E.L.*, xi, ch. ii), after remarking that S. 'carried the historical novel to perfection at one bound', adds that 'he is himself the arch-romancer. Take any definition of the Romantic Movement, and it will be found embodied in his work. His novels are in prose what Shelley's poems are in verse, the triumph and consummation of the great progress which forms our subject', i.e. 'The Romantic Triumph' in European lit.'; and, as to his influence abroad, S. 'shared with Byron a vogue denied to all other writers except Shakespeare, and his influence was closely interwoven with the romantic movement on the continent, and more especially, with its progress in France' (*C.H.E.L.*, xii, 30). Prof. Omond, *loc. cit.*, computes this debt a little differently : ' His novels with Byron's poetry, carried the Romantic seed far and wide. France, Germany, and Italy value him as we do ; Germany, in particular, receives her own with interest, and hails a kinsman as well as a leader '. The reference in the words ' receives her own ' is to the early debt incurred by S. to Bürger, q.v., whose *Lenore*, in Taylor's transln., introduced him to Germ. studies, 1792 ; S. publd. original translns. of 2 of Bürger's ballads, 1796, and a transln. of Goethe's *Götz of Berlichingen*, 1799. In lyric poetry, in the romance-novel, and in influence on the Romantic movement, accordingly, S., by common consent, is a voice clamant in a populous city ; and the year 1832, S.'s death-year and Goethe's, is, as we remark s.v. Goethe, *a terminus a quo* in the one instance, a *terminus ad quem* in the other.

Our account of S. might stop at this point. The rest is a thrice-told tale. How he started from the Germ. example, from his own local patriotism and antiquarianism, and from a chance hearing, or news, in 1802, of Coleridge's *Christabel*, with border ballads and *Minstrelsy of the Scottish Border*, vols. i and ii, 1802, vol. iii, 1803 ; how he turned from the romance-ballad to the romance-lay, and poured out, in rapid succession, *The Lay of the Last Minstrel*, 1805 ; *Marmion*, 1808 ; *The Lady of the Lake*, 1810, *Don Roderick*, 1811, *Rokeby*, 1813, and others ; how he experimented, briefly, in drama ; how he recognized that the risen light of Bryon was too strong for his tales in verse, and how *The Lord of the Isles*, 1815, may be regarded as, in a sense, the earliest of the ' Waverley ' novels (*Elton, op. cit.*, i, 316) ; how those novels followed one another, visiting the Middle Ages, the 16th and the 18th cent., always with his hand on the pulse of his readers, —*Waverley*, 1814, *Guy Mannering*, *The Antiquary*, *The Black Dwarf*, *Old Mortality*, *The Heart of Midlothian*, *Rob Roy*, *The Bride of Lammermoor*, *The Legend of Montrose*, *Ivanhoe*, *The Monastery*, *The Abbot*, *Kenilworth*, *The Pirate*, *The Fortunes of Nigel*, *Peveril*, *Quentin Durward*, *St. Ronan's Well*, *Redgauntlet*, *The Betrothed*, *The Talisman*, *Woodstock* ; how all the above, after *Waverley*, which was anon., were ascribed to ' the Author of *Waverley* '; how, finally, *Chronicles of the Canongate*, 1827, contained S.'s acknowledgment of the author-ship ; how 3 more vols. were added to the *Chronicles*, 1828, with *Anne of Geierstein*, 1829, and *Count Robert of Paris* and *Castle Dangerous*, 1832 : these facts are matters of common knowledge, and the titles are as familiar as Shakespeare's plays. Familiar, too, is the cause of the anonymity, and the cause of its breach in 1827. ' The Author of *Waverley* ' did not ' sell ' worse on account of his mystery as ' the Great Unknown ', and sir Walter Scott, bart., of Abbotsford, the estate which he purchased in 1812, was a more personable and likely Scot. laird since his fingers were not stained with writer's ink nor his hands soiled with printers' profits. Yet, by his business relations with J. Ballantyne (q.v.), S. was

publisher-printer as well as author of his works, and was deeply involved, 1826 (to the amount of over £120,000), by the bankruptcy of the firm. So, we reach the romance which he lived, subsidiary to the romances which he wr. ; his retirement from the lavishness of Abbotsford to a lodging in Edinburgh ; his heroic efforts to satisfy his creditors, whom he identified with his honour ; the strain of the last years, the breakdown, the final journey in Italy (see, too, Wordsworth's, q.v., introductory note to his *Yarrow Revisited*, 1831), and the fact that the proceeds of his copyrights completed the liquidation of his debts, so that he sleeps in peace by his wife's side. One word more out of the record of those years. The great romancer wr. hardly anything more romantic than an entry in his diary, 8 June, 1826 : ' Bilious and headache this morning. A dog howled all night, and left me little sleep. Poor cur ! I daresay he had his distresses, as I have mine. . . . I finished four pages to-day, headache, laziness, and all '. The sympathy with the under-dog, the courage conquering circumstances, are of the essence of S., who seems to incorporate every shade of meaning of the epithet, brave ; and the diary entry might be collated with a passage from *The Fortunes of Nigel* (quoted in *C.H.E.L.*, xii, 19) : ' We can assure the reader that we never found ourselves in company with the stupidest of all possible companions in a post-chaise, or with the most arrant cumber-corner that ever occupied a place in the mail-coach, without finding that in the course of our conversation with him we had some idea suggested to us, either grave or gay, or some information communicated in the course of our journey, which we should have regretted not to have heard, and which we should be sorry immediately to have forgotten '.

We have mentioned S.'s cult of anonymity—partly from inverted but quite innocent vanity—during the first big spate of his novels. A writer in the *Cornhill Magazine*, Sept., 1864, related on ' very competent authority ' the way in which the secret was discovered. Premising that John Leycester Adolphus (1795-1862), a barrister by profession, had publd., 1821, *Letters to Richard Heber containing Critical Remarks on the Series of Novels beginning with ' Waverley '*, and an Attempt to ascertain their Author, and that he had identified, on internal evidence, the author of *Waverley* with the author of *Marmion*, we cite the extract from *Cornhill*, less for the value than for the interest of the story : ' Just before the mystery of the authorship of the Waverley Novels was discovered, great was the excitement of the public, and many were the random bolts shot and guesses made. The truth had been whispered more than once, and the right man spotted, but as sir Walter energetically disowned his offspring and recorded his plea of " not guilty ", like any other accused man, as, moreover, his friends had sustained cross-examinations with great staunchness and assurance, nothing certain was elicited. How it was eventually revealed was in this way :—An American clergyman calling at the shop of the eminent publishing firm of Messieurs Constable, and being

Scribe—Seeley 488

acquainted with Mr. Constable, who happened to be present, the conversation turned on the secret, which every one desired to know. Mr. Constable, partly perhaps to pique the stranger's curiosity, and partly, it is probable, to prove that he was himself honoured with the confidence of the author, pointed to two books lying on the table, and remarked, "I am sending those very books to-day to the real author of Waverley". The American naturally enough took them in his hand and cursorily examined them, and left immediately after to pay a visit to captain Hamilton of Chiefswood, who took him next day to see Abbotsford. There, on the library table, lay a newly opened parcel, labelled from Constable and Co., and containing the identical two volumes in question. From that date the secret was public property, and sir Walter was obliged to bear as he best might the brunt of the honours which were showered on him'.

We turn back from the writer to what he wr. This included a vast amount of misc. works—a *Life of Napoleon*, an edn. of Dryden (q.v.), etc.—testifying to S.'s extraordinary industry and quickness. But he lives by his lays, lyrics, and novels. The defective love-interest in his romances, and his preference for the happy ending, are the only points at which his novels have been successfully attacked, if any attack is successful against the secure verdict of time; and here the reply was given once for all by S.'s fellow-countryman, A. Lang (q.v.), in his introduction to *Waverley*, in the Border edn., 24 vols.: 'He does not deal in embraces and effusions, his taste is too manly; he does not dwell much on Love, because, like the shepherd in Theocritus, he has found him an inhabitant of the rocks. Moreover, when Scott began novel-writing, he was as old as Thackeray when Thackeray said that while at work on a love-scene he blushed so that you would think he was going into an apoplexy. . . *Waverley* ends like a fairy-tale, while real life ever ends like a Northern saga. But among the good things that make life bearable, such fairy-tales are not the least precious, and not the least enduring'. And if the wide range of S.'s power is still questioned by any doubting Thomas, we may commend him to a little poem by S., which is quite one of the greatest poems in the Engl. language:

Proud Maisie is in the wood,
  Walking so early;
Sweet Robin sits on the bush
  Singing so rarely.
'Tell me, thou bonny bird,
  When shall I marry me?'
'When six braw gentlemen
  Kirkward shall carry ye'.
'Who makes the bridal bed,
  Birdie, say truly?'
'The gray-headed sexton
  That delves the grave duly.
'The glow-worm o'er grave and stone
  Shall light thee steady;
The owl from the steeple sing—
  Welcome, proud lady'.

Scribe, Augustin Eugène (1791-1861): Fr. playwright; comedian; the A. Hardy (q.v.) of his day (between 1815-50), whose dramatic works fill nearly 50 vols., and who, like Dumas *père* (q.v.), employed lesser men to do his hackwork; 'one of the most prolific, one of the most successful, and one of the least literary of French dramatists' (Saintsbury, *Fr. Lit.*, 547). Yet 'the completeness of the oblivion, disrepute even', says another writer, 'into which he has fallen, cannot alter the fact that he was the most successful and most popular dramatist, not only in France, but in all Europe, for nearly fifty years'. There is nothing to add to these descriptions of an author whose sense of the theatre was almost miraculous, and who catered infallibly for the *bourgeoisie* of the Restoration, except the names of some of his 400 chief plays. These are: *Mariage de Raison*, 1826; *Camaraderie*, 1837; *le Verre d'Eau*, 1840; *Adrienne Lecouvreur*, 1849; *Bataille de Dames*, 1851— a perfect piece of stage-mechanism. S.'s more permanent achievement, though his initiative is too often forgotten, was to secure royalties for playwrights, calculated on a percentage of the nightly takings at the theatre, in lieu of the former system of a single payment for the play.

Scriver, Christian (1629-93): Germ. divine; a sweet singer of Pietism (q.v.).

Scudéry, de, -i. Georges (1601-67): Fr. novelist; served with distinction in the army; retired, 1630; set up house in Paris with his sister (*infra*), and to some extent exploited her talent till his marriage, 1654; was implicated in the politics of the Fronde, but was restored to favour by king Louis xiv, 1660, and received a small lucrative sinecure. Wr. *Alaric* (see below) and stage-plays 'to tickle the populace', though he ranged himself with the champions of correctness and the Unities (q.v.).

-ii. Madeleine (1608-1701): Fr. novelist; sister of above; the more talented member of the literary partnership, which was dissolved by the brother's death. The *maison de Sophie*, as their Paris house was known in Precious (q.v.) circles, became the centre of a regular Saturday reunion, more serious in tone, perhaps, than the normal *salon* of the period; and the hostess had her reward in the appreciation and adulation of her contemporaries, such as Conrart, Boileau, and Segrais; in the esteem of her own sovereign and of foreign princes, including queen Elizabeth of Engld. and queen Christina of Sweden; and in the increasing esteem of critics as eminent as Victor Cousin, Brunetière and Ste-Beuve, who recognize the acclamation of mlle. de Scudéry as 'la première fille du monde' and 'la merveille' of the *Grand siècle* of Louis xiv. The contrast between sister and brother is as remarkable at least as her unconsciousness of it; it is related that, in 1647, she made an attempt to free herself from his domination, and to live independently as a teacher; but the attempt, if it was made, fell through, and she was content to publish many of her bks. either anonymously or under her brother's name. Georges de S. was probably capable of better work than his *Alaric*, 1664, which was one among the many so-called epic poems (see s.v. Chapelain, e.g.), designed in the precious style of mannered conceits (q.v.) to indue the old form with modern dress. But whatever part Georges may have taken in stimulating his sister's gifts, and even in collaborating with her, it is with Madeleine de S. that literary history is primarily concerned. She was free from his vanity and self-consciousness. She was the first champion of women's rights; the first emancipated woman, who neither forfeited her charm of sex nor her sweetness of disposition. She owned to a passion for conversation, and she possessed a genius for correspondence; and it has been remarked (Koerting, *Französ. Roman im 17ten Jahrh.*, i, 405) that she preserved in all her works an even level of composition, a ' stagnation ' at the highest point of her achievement. Mlle. de S. was writing all her life, in verse as well as in prose. In the long list of her works, romances take first rank; and of the romances the 2 most important are *Artamène ou le Grand Cyrus*, 10 vols., 1649-53, and *Clélie*, 10 vols., 1656-60. What is the secret of the extraordinary success of these books? In the first place, it lay (and lies) in the instinct, derived from genius, which mlle. de S. displayed in hitting off the taste and needs of aristocratic literary society in the splendid age of Louis xiv. The *Grand Cyrus* was the longest novel in that era of long novels, long speeches, and long *ambages* of adventure and plot; its *ed. pr.* contained 6,670 closely printed pages, and it is as true to-day as it was when mme. de Genlis wr. her bk. *De l'Influence des Femmes sur la littérature française*, 1811, that ' these everlasting conversations, which, in the works of mlle. de Scudéry, suspending the march of the story, seem to us intolerable, were far from displeasing '. Secondly, though mlle. de S. admittedly based her history on the *Cyropædia* of Xenophon and on Herodotus, a fascination of the *Grand Cyrus* for contemporaries, and, indeed, for posterity, lay in the recognition of real personages under the disguise of hist. characters. A trustworthy key supplies names to nearly all the chief participants; among them may be mentioned: Cyrus, the great Condé; Sapho, the author; Therpandre, Malherbe (q.v.); Théodaras, Conrart (q.v.); Calliorates, Voiture (q.v.); the mage of Sidon, Godeau (q.v.); Cléomire, the marquis of Rambouillet (q.v.), and so forth; while the sieges and battle-scenes reproduced with remarkable accuracy events of the recent civil war. In *Clélie*, too, the 73 characters in the novel had each a prototype in modern life; among them may be mentioned: Hamilcar, Sarrazin (q.v.); Scaurus, Scarron (q.v.); Herminius, Pellisson (q.v.), etc.; the characters in this romance being selected, not from the aristocracy, as in the *Grand Cyrus*, but from middle-class recruits to the precious (q.v.) society. A feature of *Clélie*, which lent itself later to some ridicule and more abuse, was the coloured ' Map and Geographical Description of the *Pays de Tendre* ', a country watered by the stream of Inclination, with the city of New Friendship on its frontier, and other towns and villages round about; at a distance from Inclination are the wastes of Oblivion leading past the borders of lake Indifference to the shoreless sea of *Inimitié*; it was a pretty fancy, said to have been

suggested by Chapelain (q.v.), and obviously borrowed from the allegories of the *Romance of the Rose* (q.v.) and its descendants. Mlle. de S.'s earlier novel was *Ibrahim*, 1641 (dramatized by her brother, 1643), and her last novels were *Almahide, or the Queen Slave*, 8 vols., 1660, and *Mathilde d'Aguilar*, 1667, both in the school of Moorish fiction founded in Spain by G. P. de Hita (q.v.). Ménage (q.v.), her contemporary, expressed the judgment of his age when he wr. of mlle. de S.: ' Il y a mille choses dans les romans de cette savante fille qu'on ne peut trop estimer. Elle a pris dans les Anciens tout ce qu'il y a de bon, et l'a rendu meilleur, comme ce Prince de la Fable qui changeait tout en or '. But what a far cry it is, as Mr. Walkley has suggested in *The Times* newspaper, from the reticences of the *Pays de Tendre* to the frankness of some modern playwrights and novelists.

Secundus, Johannes (1511-36): Dutch Latinist; his name was latinized from Jan Everaerts. Wr. *Basia* (' Kisses '), love-poems in various Lat. metres, displaying not merely rare dexterity of composition and melody, but real sincerity of feeling; without falling into the gaping abyss of indecency. The *Basia* attained a just popularity, and afforded models of expression for the exercises in love-poetry in Engld. in the 17th cent.

Sedaine, Michael Jean (1719-97): Fr. dramatist; philosophe (q.v.). Wr. *le Philosophe sans le savoir*, 1765—a title which recalls some of Molière's—and *la Gageure imprévue*, 1768, both in prose. The former is the better play of the 2, and entitles S. to the high praises which he has earned as a writer of domestic drama, akin to the serious intention of the *comédie larmoyante* (q.v.) of his age. The philosopher of the piece is the heavy father of many stage-plays, whose aristocratic lineage is at war with his commercial career on the subject of the point of honour involved in the institution of the duel: a good dramatic situation, illustrating the fashions of the time.

Sedley, Charles (1639-1701): Engl. poet; baronet; ' rich as well as accomplished ', we are told (*C.H.E.L.*, viii, 215), he ' outlived his outrageous youth to become the friend and champion of William iii '. Those who are curious about the ' outrageous youth ' in the merry reign of king Charles ii may consult Pepys (q.v.) in his *Diary*, 1 July, 1663, 18 Feb., 1666-7, 23 Oct., 1668, and other entries; also Johnson (q.v.), *Lives of the Poets*, s.v. lord Dorset. The poetry consisted of 5 plays, and of occasional verses, collected, 1701; 2 specimens of these are contained in Palgrave's (q.v). *Golden Treasury of Songs and Lyrics* (nos. 81 and 98), and partake, with the rest, of the light yet half-serious grace of Lovelace (q.v.) and the courtly wits.

Seeley, John Robert (1834-95): Engl. historian; K.C.M.G., 1894. Wr., 1865, *Ecce homo*, a work in controversial theology, which, publd. anon., created a great stir in its day of ritual discussion. S.'s most important hist. work was *The Expansion of Engld.*, 1883, which owed something to the researches of Dr. Wm. Cunningham (born, 1849) into *The Growth of Engl. Industry and Commerce*; prof. of modern history at Cambridge, 1869.

Segrais, de, Jean Renaud (1624-1701): Fr. minor poet; secretary, 1672, to mme. de La Fayette (q.v.), and lent his name for the title-pages of her novels; transld. Virgil's *Æneid* and *Georgics* into Fr. verse, substituting elegance for sentiment, and wr. light verse of his own, impenetrable by any ray of human feeling. Wr., too, collection of short tales *les Divertissements de la princesse Auréliane*, 1656, which enjoyed some vogue. A vol. of anecdotal *Segraisiana* ('où l'on trouve quantité de particularitez remarquables touchant les Personnes de la Cour et les Gens de son tems') was issued at Amsterdam, 1723.

Ségur, de, Louis Phillippe (1753-1830): Fr. historian; diplomatist; *comte* by rank; ambassador at the court of the empress Catherine ii (q.v.), and a prominent figure in the imperial circle of letters and illuminism at Petrograd.

Seguro de Tordesillas, el (Span.): 'The Pledge, or Truce, of Tordesillas'; title of a Span. chronicle (s.v. *Cronica*), of the epoch of king John ii (q.v.) of Castile, relating a political episode of the year 1439, in which count Haro (Pedro Fernandez de Velasco) was entrusted with the honourable post of umpire between the parties to the truce. The *Seguro* was first publd. at Milan, 1611, and Ticknor (i, 177) came to the conclusion that 'few historical works can challenge such absolute authenticity'.

Selden, John (1584-1654): Engl. jurist; a man of profound learning, who also took part in public life; M.P. (in the Long Parliament) for the univ. of Oxford. S. is best known as the author of *Table Talks*—the title, of course, is Luther's (q.v.) *Tischreden*,—'being his sense of various Matters of Weight and High Consequence; relating especially to Religion and State', as the bk. was sub-titled in the *ed. pr.*, 1689, for which Richard Milward, S.'s amanuensis, was responsible. The charm and light of this wit and wisdom (*scintillæ juris*, in a later happy phrase) are undeniable; 'on the whole', says Hallam (*Lit. Europe*, ii, 522) 'they are full of vigour, raciness, and a kind of scorn of the half-learned, far less rude, but more cutting than that of Scaliger' (q.v.). Less well-known now, but of great importance, was the Lat. treatise by S., 1640, *de jure naturali et gentium juxta Disciplinam Ebræorum*. 'The object of the author' (*op. cit.*, 513), 'was to trace the opinions of the Jews on the law of nature and nations, or of moral obligation, as distinct from the Mosaic law; the former being a law to which they held all mankind to be bound. This theme had of course been untouched by the Greek and Roman philosophers, nor was much to be found upon it in modern writers. His purpose is therefore rather historical than argumentative; but he seems so generally to adopt the Jewish theory of natural law that we may consider him the disciple of the rabbis as much as their historian. His book, however, . . is among the greatest achievements in erudition that any English writer has performed'. Another very learned Lat. work is S.'s *de Diis Syris*, 1617, recently republd. His *Mare Clausum*, written 1618, but not publd. till 1636, was a reply to Grotius (q.v.), in *Mare Liberum*, 1609, on the right of Engld.

to exclude the fishermen of Holland from the seas which she asserted to be her own. Grotius retired, contented. *Fleta*, 1647, was a yet more strictly professional work, and the Selden society conserves the name of this ornament of the bar.

Selkirk, Alexander (1676-1721): Engl. sailor; deserted on the island of Juan Fernandez, 1704-9; enters lit. as the prototype of *Robinson Crusoe*, 1719, by Defoe (q.v.), who was not personally acquainted with S.

Sempere, de, Hyeronimo (16th cent.): Span. romancer. S. was caught at the flood of the chivalric convention started by *Amadis* (q.v.), and wr., 1554, 2 bks. of 'the celestial and pious chivalry of the Fragrant Rose', transporting the forms of that class of lit. into the region of religious allegory, with Christ as Knight of the Lion, Satan of the Serpent, and so forth; an extravagant and violent extension of the type.

Sénancour, de, Etienne Pivert (1770-1846): Fr. sentimental (romantic) novelist. Wr. variously for a livelihood, but is chiefly known as the author of *Obermann*, 1804, and, later, was relieved from want by the efforts of Villemain and Thiers (qq.v.). S. anticipated in *Obermann* the note of vague, lyrical aspiration which was manifest in the Romance (q.v.) movement of 1830, and his fame was postponed till about that date, when his admirers tended to exaggerate it. Mainly, the merit of this piece of sentimental, egoistic fiction is that it expressed the spirit of the times, and contained something of Rousseau's savage-worship, of Chateaubriand's moral disquiet, and of the roving genius of Goethe's *Wilhelm Meister* (see s.vv.). It was what the Germans calls a *Tendenz*-piece; not so much a novel with a purpose as a novel of purpose; the fateful romance of human striving against a destiny too big for fulfilment. Byron and Lamartine were in it, too, and it appealed a little too irresistibly to the wilful melancholy and cultivated disillusion of a self-analytical generation. This is the key to M. Arnold's (q.v.) admiration, in his *Stanzas in memory of the author of 'Obermann'*, where he compares the message of S. with that of Wordsworth and of Goethe for relief from 'the hopeless tangle of our age'. In a more strenuous time, it is legitimate to conjecture that S. succeeded in this bk. in giving literary expression to a consciousness, not wholly of his own mind, but assimilated from deeper thinkers of his time.

Seneca, Lucius Annæus (4 B.C.-65 A.D.): Rom. moralist; playwright; born at Cordova, in Spain; became a prominent figure at the imperial court, and tutor to Nero, afterwards emperor. S.'s influence over his pupil was 'for a long time almost unbounded; and, when Nero became emperor at the age of 17, Seneca became practically the administrator of the empire'. He amassed a huge fortune, perhaps 'without absolute dishonesty; but there can be no doubt that in indulging the weaknesses and passions of Nero, Seneca went far beyond the limits, not only of honour, but of ordinary prudence' (J. W. Mackail, *Lat. Lit.*, 172-3). True, he paid the penalty of a favourite; his fortune was sequestrated, and he committed suicide at his pupil-tyrant's bidding, 'with that strange mixture of helplessness and heroism with which the orders of the master of the world were then accepted as a sort of inevitable law of nature' (*ibid.*). We must recall in this connection that S.'s moral philosophy was largely, even predominantly, Stoic; 'and, if a violent death must be faced, the Stoicism which called death an actual good was the best way of making terms with a painful situation' (A. D. Godley, 1856-1925; public orator at Oxford; in *Engl. Lit. and the Classics*, 241). With S., the philosopher, we are not here further concerned, save to note that his *Naturales Quæstiones*, though totally without scientific value, were used as a textbook of physical science in the Middle Ages, and that, as a moral writer, 'though infected with the rhetorical vices of his age, his treatises are full of striking and often gorgeous eloquence, and in their combination of high thought with deep feeling have rarely, if at all, been surpassed' (Mackail, *op. cit.*, 174). But S., the philosopher, was also S., the tragic dramatist; at any rate, he wr. 9 plays on topics of Gk. mythology—*Hercules* (2), *Troades*, *Phœnissæ*, *Medea*, *Phædra*, *Agamemnon*, *Œdipus*, and *Thyestes*,—which were intended to please Nero's circle at his quieter literary evenings, and which, so far as we know, were never put on the stage. And 'Seneca's tragedies are penetrated through and through with the philosophy of Seneca the prose-writer. . . We may say broadly that all Seneca's tragedies talk in the vein of the Porch' (Godley, *ibid.* 242).

Now, this would matter very little if Nero, in 65 A.D., had been able to compel the plays as well as the playwright to commit suicide. But those plays, though 'they have no life, no dramatic insight or movement', still live in the sense that they 'are, historically, the chief source from which our own Elizabethan tragedy, as well as those of other European countries, was originated. For generations they were, for good and evil, the model which European dramatists followed' (*The Legacy of Rome*, 334); and the writer (prof. Mackail, again) quotes Mr. F. L. Lucas, *Seneca and Elizabethan Tragedy*: 'His (Seneca's) work is little remembered, still less regarded, now. But if you seek his memorial, look round on the tragic stage of England, France, and Italy'. Similarly, sir S. Lee writes (*Fr. Renaissance in Engld.*, 427): 'The Latin writer, Seneca, deserves to be reckoned the father of tragedy in England. It was under his exclusive inspiration that *Gorboduc* (see s.v. Sackville) was written in 1560'.

Is Europe proud of this paternity of her tragic drama? 'The worst technical fault in these tragedies', says Crutwell (*Hist. Rom. Lit.*, 375), 'is their violation of the decencies of the stage', and the fact that they were never staged is really no sufficient condonation. Moreover, 'the gross, the animal—it is scarcely even the sensuous—predominates all through these tragedies' (*ibid.*). Considering the circumstances of their orig., this feature is not surprising, but it is strange to reflect that 'no classical writer is so important in the history of the modern drama'; that modern dramatists—chiefly through

Garnier, q.v.—did not go back behind Seneca to the Gk. tragedians (chiefly Euripides) who had treated the same themes, but delighted in the Senecan rhetoric, horror, and declamation; that the Ghost (see s.vv. Kyd and Shakespeare) was a Senecan stock-character; that Corneille and Victor Hugo (qq.v.) recall Seneca with vivid insistence; that Ben Jonson (q.v.), himself largely Senecan, apostrophized S. equally with Æschylus and Euripides in the verses which he prefixed to the First Folio of Shakespeare; and that 'many a distinctive phrase of Senecan tragedy seems indeed to be interwoven with Shakespeare's dramatic speech' (sir S. Lee, *William Shakespeare*, 19). Proud or not, we cannot refuse the evidence to the direct influence of S. on European tragedy. The descent of modern comedy from Roman Plautus and Terence, and, through them, from Gk. Menander, follows simple and straightforward lines, which need no further explication; but S.'s violence, rhetoric, bloodshed, and his hardly differentiated characters, seem a strange source from which to trace the tragic drama of Italy, France and Engld. Yet in its origins, at any rate, and even a little way into Racine and Shakespeare, we have to accept this literary *provenance*: 'Every tragic scene which the Italians of the Renaissance set forth upon the boards of Rome or Florence, or Ferrara, was a transcript from Seneca. Following this lead, our English scholars went to school with Seneca beneath the ferule of Italian ushers' (J. A. Symonds, *Shakspere's Predecessors*, 175). 'Seneca cannot be too heavy, nor Plautus too light. For the law of writ and liberty, these are the only men', declared Polonius in his rescript for drama; *Hamlet*, ii, 2; and the words prove how heavily S. lay on the tradition of the tragic stage. (See, too, s.v. Machiavelli, whose moral teachings rendered more appropriate the part of the villain-hero). But these were not to be the only men for ever. Imagination, fancy and faëry were to win their way through the older stage-conventions, and plays founded on the liberty of *fantasia* were to oust, or, at least, to modify, the rule of knowledge of the ancients, consulted at several removes. (See, too, s.v. Jonson). The dead hand of S. has been lifted from the stage which he dominated so long, through those 9 tragedies composed for the edification of Nero in the 1st cent. 'There is nothing of the Senecan tradition in Mr. Galsworthy; and we look for it in vain in the plays of Mr. Bernard Shaw', wr. Mr. Godley at the close of his essay on Senecan tragedy (*op. cit.*, 247); and we may add, there is no trace of him in the master of both, H. Ibsen (q.v.), the second founder of European drama.

Senior, Nassau William (1790-1864): Engl. essayist; writer on economics; prof. of political economy at Oxford univ., 1825-30 and 1847-52; wr. the *Report* of poor-law commission, 1833-4. Apart from his more technical work, in which S. takes high rank among Engl. economists between Ricardo and J. S. Mill (qq.v.), he wr. valuable *Essays on Fiction*, 1864, *Hist. and Philosophical Essays* (posth.), 1865, and *Biographical Sketches*, 1863.

Sepulveda, de, Juan Ginés (1490-1573): Span. historian. Opposed Las Casas (q.v.) on the controversial question of the Indians in South America.

Sepulveda, de, Lorenzo (16th cent.): Span. romancer. Publd., Antwerp, 1551, a *Romancero* (q.v.), or collection of art-ballads, which included contributions from a writer disguised as ' Caballero Cesareo ', and plausibly identified with Pero Mexia (q.v.).

Sergardi, Lodovico (1660-1726): It. satiric poet. Wr. satires in Lat. verse, which are described as the last literary sensation of the 17th cent. in Italy *fin de siècle*.

Ser Giovanni (fl. 1378): It. writer of ' novelle ', after the pattern of the *Decameron*. His collection of 50 tales, related through 25 days by a monk and a nun in love, was entitled *Il Pecorone* (*ed. pr.*, Milan, 1558) and was intersected with popular lyric poems, racy of Florentine life and passion. The prose and verse are both pleasant, though not without traces of a mannered preciousness affecting the *bourgeois* inspiration. The subjects of the tales are varied, including hist. matters, and the first ' novella ' of the fourth day became the source of Shakespeare, *The Merchant of Venice*. Giovanni Fiorentino is always known and spoken of with his title-prefix *ser*.

Serres, de, Olivier (1539-1619): Fr. writer on agriculture. S. was a convinced Protestant, but an even better convinced follower of the maxim of Voltaire (q.v.) in *Candide* : ' il faut cultiver nôtre jardin '. He cultivated his ' garden ' on his property at Pradel for 30 years, during which he prepared his famous *Théâtre de l'Agriculture et Ménage des Champs*, 1600, which became a classic work on the subject. S.'s statues in France are perhaps as numerous now as his readers.

Settle, Elkanah (1648-1724): Engl. ' city poet ', by appointment to that now extinct office, 1691. If S. were extinguished with his office, Engl. lit. would not be poorer. He is identified with ' Doeg ' in part ii. of Dryden's (q.v.) *Absalom and Achitophel* :

Spiteful he is not, though he wrote a satire,
For still there goes some thinking to ill-nature,

and so on, through several paragraphs. The occasion for this attack was the production at court of some turgid plays by S. (*Cambyses*, 1666 ; *Empress of Morocco*, 1671, etc.), which temporarily interrupted Dryden's lead in drama. S. replied in *Absalom Senior*, 1682.

Seume, Johann Gottfried (1763-1810): Germ. descriptive writer. S. had an adventurous career, which included service in N. America among the troops sold to Engld. by count Fredk. ii of Hesse. He deserted on his return in 1783, and, after further military experience in Prussia and Russia, spent some years of comparative ease in literary activity at Leipsic. Wr., 1803, his well-known *Spaziergang nach Syrakus* (' Walk to Syracuse '), describing an actual walk (Dec., 1801 to Sept., 1802) to Sicily and back through Austria, Italy, Switzerld. and France. S. undertook another walk to Russia, Finland, and Sweden, narrated in *My Summer of 1805*, 1807. He left incomplete an interesting autobiography.

Sévigné, de, Marie (1626-96): Fr. letter-writer ; ' perhaps the most famous and remarkable of all letter-writers in literature ' (Saintsbury, *Fr. Lit.*, 320). *Née* de Rabutin-Chantal, orphaned at 7 years old, Marie was brought up by her uncle, de Coulanges, abbé of Livry ; was edu. partly by Ménage and Chapelain (qq.v.) ; frequented the *salon* of the precious (q.v.) set at the Hôtel de Rambouillet (q.v.) ; beautiful, vivacious, satirical, *spirituelle* ; was m., 1644, to the marquis de S., who was unfaithful and unloving ; he was killed in a duel, 1651, leaving mme. la Marquise with 2 children, Charles and Françoise. The latter was m., 1668, to the comte de Grignan, an elderly widower, and became the chief recipient of her mother's letters. Mme. de S. resided chiefly in Paris (Hôtel Carnavalet, 1677), or at her country-seat, les Rochers, near Vitré, or at Vichy, which she visited for her rheumatism ; she died of small-pox, at Grignan, in Provence, of which her son-in-law was governor and where she contributed largely to the expenses of his office. With the priceless gift of a lively imagination, which helped to idealize her absent daughter, mme. de S. turned her correspondence with mme. de Grignan into a brilliant commentary on men and things, whether her headquarters were fixed in the social surroundings of courtly Paris, or in the provinces, or at her favourite spa. Her tastes were cultivated and well-laid—she read Quintilian and Tacitus,—and definite enough not to be tedious, and to secure the personal touch which redeems letter-writing from bookishness. Though never gushing or sentimental, she was always essentially feminine ; brimming with wise affection, even with wise prejudices and preferences ; Racine, for instance, failed to appeal to her, and she had the courage to avow it ; Corneille and Molière enchanted her, and to Nicole and Pascal she extended admiration and friendship at once (see s.vv.). Her letters form an invaluable collection of hist. documents of the 17th cent. ; we follow in them the daily routine of a clever woman of the world, who knew everyone worth knowing, who guarded her highly-cherished intimacy, who had a mind and a fortune of her own, both of which she spent on worthy objects, who was just sufficiently disillusioned with life to be able to test its resources intellectually, and whose intellect was yet kept sweet by homely and natural affections. To these qualities of a great letter-writer mme. de S. was fortunate to add the opportunities derived from the habits of her times and from the circumstances of her own life ; and she brought to the task which she discharged so spontaneously a keen imaginative faculty which illuminated every incident and its reflection.

Seward, -i. Thomas (1708-90): Engl. divine ; canon of Lichfield, where he used to entertain Dr. Johnson (q.v.), at one time his pupil ; joint-editor of the plays of Beaumont and Fletcher (q.v.).

-ii. Anna (1747-1809): Engl. misc. author ; daughter of above ; known as the ' Swan of Lichfield ' ; wr. *Letters from Hell*, and other minor works ; a friend of Boswell (q.v.), to whom she supplied material for his *Life* of Johnson ; a prominent member of the circle, which included R. L. Edgeworth,

T. Day (qq.v.), and E. Darwin (q.v.), whose *Botanic Garden* was written at her instance, and whose biography she wr. A.S. appointed sir W. Scott (q.v.), who visited her, 1807, her literary executor, and he publd. her poetical works, etc., with a memoir, 1810, Her letters were issued in 6 vols., 1811.

Shadwell, Thomas (1642-92): Engl. poet; dramatist; both in a minor key. Wr. comedies. *Sullen Lovers* (after Molière, q.v.), 1668; *The Miser*, 1672, etc. The real interest of S. in lit., so far as it is still real, is derived, like that of Settle (q.v.), though in a higher degree, from his relations with Dryden (q.v.). S. was the 'Og' of part ii of *Absalom and Achitophel*, and wr. *The Medal of John Bayes* in reply to the greater poet. S. was great enough, however, in the estimation of contemporaries, to succeed Dryden as poet-laureate (q.v.), 1688.

Shaftesbury, Anthony Ashley Cooper, 3rd earl of (1671-1713): Engl. moral philosopher; pupil and patron of Locke (q.v.); 'introduced a new tendency in the moral philosophy of the modern period', in the sense that 'an involuntary impulse unites the individual with the whole race, just as naturally as the instincts lead to the propagation of the species and care of the young' (Höffding, *Brief Hist. Modern Philosophy*, E.T., 102). These ideas, which owed something to Bayle (q.v.), whose acquaintance S. made during his residence in Holland, were developed by Hutcheson (q.v.). Wr. *Inquiry Concerning Virtue*, 1699, and collected his philosophical writings, 1711, as *Characteristics of Men, Manners, Opinions and Times*. The technical meaning of 'moral sense' is commonly ascribed to S.'s teaching.

Shairp, John Campbell (1819-85): Engl. (-Scot.) critic; poet; prof. of poetry at Oxford univ., 1877-87. Wr. the monograph on Burns (q.v.) in 'Engl. Men of Letters', and edited the journal of Dorothy Wordsworth (q.v.), wr., too, *Aspects of Poetry*, 1881, and other studies, and a vol. of original verse, *Kilmahoe and other poems*, 1864.

Shakespeare, William (1564-1616): Engl. dramatist, poet; the greatest name in the history of Engl. lit., and, by common consent, among the few greatest men of letters in ancient and modern times; yet essentially a product of his own age, a Renaissance-man, an Elizabethan, an Englishman, a Warwickshire man, with a constant tug to his birthplace at Stratford-on-Avon. Wordsworth said of Milton (see s.vv.), 'Thy soul was like a star, and dwelt apart': there was nothing star-like in S. in his life-time; nor is it very helpful to appreciation to recall that Swinburne (q.v.) said, 'Without him, day were night in earth', and M. Arnold (q.v.): 'We ask and ask—Thou smilest and art still, Out-topping knowledge'. These sayings, typical of many in the vast bibliography of S., drawn from every civilized country in the world, remove S. too far from his surroundings, and from the warm, comfortable, human sympathy which informs all his poetic genius. He is more like the Bible (q.v.) in his nearness to us than like the sun or a mountain in his remoteness from us; and, though we must

not question the poets' metaphors, we may still guard our rights in the greater poet. Or, at least, before we enjoy any part of the libraries written about S., we must learn, first, to enjoy S., and to find what Seeley (q.v.) in another context calls, 'the moral underlying the flourishes of rhetoric'. 'The idol is the measure of the worshipper', said the wise American critic, J. R. Lowell, and it is for us to test this universal S.-worship by trying to measure the idol; otherwise, we become mere idolaters, repeating incantations at second hand.

But, lest we seem to assume too much in writing of a universal S.-worship, let us set down as briefly as possible some of the stages in his posth. fame. It was Ben Jonson (q.v.), his contemporary, who said as early as 1623 that 'He was not for an age but for all time', and that all the theatres of Europe owed him homage, and Milton (q.v.) in 1630 who called him 'Dear son of memory, great heir of fame'. Dante had to wait longer for Boccaccio's praises (see s.vv.). Pope and Johnson (qq.v.) edited S., and Wm. Dodd's *Beauties of Shakespeare*, 1752, was one among many tributes of 18th cent. admirers. L. Theobald's edn., 1734, showed the way to E. Malone (1741-1812), James Boswell, the younger (1778-1822), and hosts of others in textual commentary, which has not ceased for 200 years; and Hazlitt, Coleridge, Lamb at the beginning of the 19th cent., Collier, Halliwell-Phillips, Furnivall, Dowden, A. C. Bradley, C. H. Herford, sir S. Lee (S.'s biographer), sir I. Gollancz, M. H. Spielmann (in iconography), and hosts of others again, have continued S. study into the 20th.* It may reasonably be said that every writer on Engl. studies has added a brick to the temple. Passing over S.'s interpreters on the stage, who, though most vital of all to his art, belong properly to the history of the theatre, we turn to S. abroad, where the extent of his reputation is even more illuminating to our inquiry. Lessing (q.v.) was the first great Germ. to place S. as a dramatist above the dominant figures of Corneille and Racine (qq.v.), and to compare him not disadvantageously with Sophocles. This was in 1759; and though Engl. criticism, as noted above, was already moving to like conclusions, there is no doubt that the enlightened work of Wieland, Goethe, Schlegel, Tieck (qq.v.), and their contemporaries and successors in Lessing's wake, were pre-eminent in establishing S. as the supreme master of Romance (q.v.). Not only was much of the best of Coleridge's critical work founded on the Germ. studies, in which he and Carlyle (q.v.) led the way in Engld.; not only did Wordsworth write in 1815: 'The Germans only of foreign nations, are approaching towards a knowledge of what he (S.) is. In some respects they have acquired a superiority over the fellow-countrymen of the poet'; but S. became, virtually, a Germ. classic, whose one defect, as Heine (q.v.) remarked, was that he was an Englishman, and who profoundly influenced

* We may without discourtesy omit Thos. Bowdler (1754-1825), whose *Family Shakespeare*, 10 vols., 1818, survives chiefly in the term 'bowdlerize'.

the course of the most romantic national lit. in modern Europe. The Fr. vogue for S. was later than the Germ., owing, no doubt, to the rules of the classical drama. Voltaire (q.v.) was in Engld., 1726-9, and his appreciation of S. was only checked by his subservience to the Cornelian conventions. Ducis (q.v.) was an early translr., and, with the growth of the romantic movement in France, Hugo, Stendhal, G. Sand (qq.v.) and others prepared the new standards of taste which are manifest, e.g. in such a bk., as *l'Histoire litteraire du peuple anglais*, 1894, by J. J. Jusserand. Baretti (q.v.) commenced the Ital. appreciation of S., manifest, e.g., in Manzoni (q.v.), and S. has also made way among the countrymen of Calderon (q.v.). His widest vogue, however, outside Engl. and Germany, was in Russia before the Revolution, where Karamzin, Pushkin, Lermontov, Turgenev, and other great authors were at one in extolling and expounding his genius. A line is due to Kraszewski, the Polish poet, and plays of Shakespeare have been acted in the vernaculars of Greece, China, Japan, Bengal and other countries of India.

Having cited these witnesses, with more regard to their number than to their evidence, we are now better qualified to inquire into the grounds of the universal S.-worship, and to try to formulate a reply without recourse to vague flourishes of rhetoric, however eloquent and sincere.

Who was S., in the first instance ? The leading *Life* is that by sir S. Lee, originally contributed to the *Dict. Nat. Biog.*, of which its author succeeded sir L. Stephen (q.v.) as editor, and first publd. in bk. form, 1898. 6 edns. of that bk. were issued before 1915, when it was re-written and enlarged, and the new edn., too, has been reprinted. The watchful eye of this biographer since the last decade of the 19th cent. might seem enough for the poet's fame, but the 20th cent., resuming its studies, interrupted in every country by the Great War, has returned more keenly to S.-study, perhaps with an obscure sense that S. presides over a surer League of Nations than any which was called into being in Geneva. So, we read in an invaluable little bk., publd. at Oxford, 1924, and written by Mr. E. I. Fripp under the title of *Master Richard Quyny, Bailiff of Stratford-upon-Avon and Friend of William Shakespeare*, that ' the biography of Shakespeare has suffered from idle rumour and imperfect research. The idle rumour we owe mainly to Restorationist gossips and anecdotists who had little understanding of the poet or his age. The imperfect research is chiefly that of the late Mr. Halliwell-Phillipps, which, however praiseworthy as pioneerwork, was very limited and often misleading in its conclusions '. Mr. Fripp refers to sir S. Lee only 4 times in foot-notes, and on each occasion to disagree with him. He states definitely, on evidence ' which is not small and is continually growing ', that ' Shakespeare had an excellent schooling under Oxford graduates, that his father and mother were people likely to be interested in his education, that his father was a man of remarkable abilities and independence of judgement, . . .

and well able to use his pen ; that Stratford and the neighbourhood contained not a few residents with a claim to learning and eager to send their sons to the university, and that Shakespeare on leaving school entered an attorney's office, . . . and served in this invaluable capacity, with growing knowledge of men and motive and impartiality of judgement, for some nine years before (on his master's retirement) he joined the players '. Thus, at a stroke, we are released from the uncritical tradition of the illiterate Stratford poet, all but destitute of polished accomplishments, as well as from the mental perversities of ' its accompanying fables of the Baconian, Oxfordian and Derbian authorship ' of S.'s plays, to which the late sir E. Durning Lawrence and lord Sydenham of Combe succumbed. ' Equally baseless ', continues Mr. Fripp, ' is the " second-best bed " and the " dark lady " scandal '. 'W.H.', in the dedication of S.'s *Sonnets*—let us clear the undergrowth out of the way—is William Hall (' W. H. *All* happinesse . . . wisheth ' is the only ' cryptogram ' in the case !) who procured, or appropriated, the MS. for T. T.(horpe) ; but, more important than these diversions of the middlemen, is the fact that ' evidence is wholly wanting that Shakespeare " left " Stratford and his wife and children. The facts confirm the natural supposition of his moral sanity ',—a significant phrase in S.-criticism, at which reference may be made to an essay on *The Normality of Shakespeare illustrated in his treatment of Love and Marriage*, by prof. C. H. Herford (Engl. Association, Pamphlet no. 47, 1920 ; written in 1916). ' From first to last he was, whatever else, a Stratford man ; and he probably '—with this reasonable conjecture we close our quotations from Mr. Fripp—' returned to his native town and home every summer or autumn, for months at a time, and there prepared for the coming Christmas season, writing happily and swiftly in the midst of his family and friends and a passionately loved environment '.

With this saner approach to S.'s life ; with nothing abnormal or even unlikely to explain away, or to invent worse unlikelihoods to confuse counsel ; with this return to a straightforward record (unfortunately, but naturally, incomplete) of a busy man of many parts in a busy and parti-coloured age ; oscillating between his calling to the stage and his recall to his happy home, ambitious to excel in both callings, to lead his company of actors in London or the provinces, and to take a leading share in the concerns of his paternal town ; kindly, shrewd, industrious, quick, observant, much as Chaucer (q.v.), a similar Englishman, had been before him, and dowered with the crowning gift of genius, which is a ray that pierces where other rays are turned back, so that ' a few hours spent over Plutarch's *Lives* brought into being in Shakespeare's brain the true aspects of Roman character and Roman inspiration ' (Lee, *op. cit.*, 636), we are now better able to approach S.'s writings, which lend such intense interest to every light let in on his life.

We may select one or two threads, and use them if we can, as clues to the pattern of the design. S. never wr. a pref. : he was much too busy writing plays ; but the pref. of Spenser (q.v.) to the *Faerie Queen* is not inappropriate to our present purpose. 'The general end of the book ', Spenser assured Ralegh (q.v.), was ' to fashion a gentleman or noble person in virtuous and quiet discipline '. To fashion a gentleman—by example and contrast,—let us hold on to this thread for a moment, and take another in our hand. Among the excellent Germ. critics of S. was K.E. Vehse (1802-70), who wr. that S. 'was the first to rest his compositions on a purely human basis. Shakespeare, the untaught and un-learned poet' (we may correct Vehse on this point), 'was the first who displayed energetically the modern spirit of worldly knowledge, which is the direct converse of the spirit of the Middle Ages '. In other words, S. included in his human types, as part of their habitual equipment, the larger qualities painfully acquired by the rebels from medieval conventions. Next, take what Bacon (q.v.) wr. in his *Pref. to the Great Instauration* : ' I have not sought nor do I seek either to enforce or to ensnare men's judgments, but I lead them to things themselves and to the concordances of things, that they may see for themselves what they have, what they can dispute, what they can add and contribute to the common stock '. Note once more the opposition to the medieval spirit, the escape from ecclesiastical authority,—the appeal from convention to ' things themselves ', through the knowledge of which men were to ' add to the common stock ', and to increase the resources of human happiness. S.'s plays reflected this equipment and philosophy. Was not he who ' out-topped knowledge ', and without whom ' night were day ', great because of his humanity ? because he first and chiefly reflected the strivings of his age,—an age of geographical expansion and political self-consciousness, of wide intellectual libera-tion, of keen individualism displayed in the heroic endurance of physical peril and dis-comfort for the sake of enlarging the frontiers of knowledge, or for the sake of mere adven-ture and experience and for the right of calling oneself a man ; of feeling, at midnight under the stars, on a strange sea bounded by new shores, the sense of imperious manhood surging to generous self-expression ? He used the stage as a vehicle for the expression of individual consciousness. He wr. us free of the dead hand of Seneca (q.v.). His plays were character-plays, and his characters had free play. They worked out their own redemption, unassisted by the State and undistracted by the Church. From the stern rigours of the North (as at Elsinore in *Hamlet*) to the soft languors of the South (as at Verona, in *Romeo and Juliet*), he ranged with confidence and liberty. From the ' missing link ' in the chain of human evolution, the formless monster of the Caribbean sea, to the choicest product of a luxurious civilization, he ranged with like certainty of touch. What greater contrast could there be than this between Caliban and Cleopatra, between the untutored savage on the new-discovered island, wrought from the tales brought home by mariners scarce

crediting all they saw, and the queen of Egypt in her glory, surpassing the most splendid shows of Elizabeth's pageant-loving Court ? Yet S. is at home with both (cf. *Tempest*, ii, 2, and *Antony and Cleopatra*, v, 2). The sole problem which occupied him was the problem of men's conduct in the affairs of life. The subject of all his plays, and his own position towards that subject, is contained in Hamlet's apostrophe to Rosencrantz :

What a piece of work is a man ! how noble in reason ! how infinite in faculty : in form and moving how express and admirable ! in action how like an angel ! in apprehension how like a god ! the beauty of the world ! the paragon of animals !—(*Hamlet*, ii, 2).

Men ask for S.'s philosophy of life. They have it here. They ask what religion he professed, what code of morals he practised, how he was equipped for his task. The answer is here. He enfranchised the reason of man, from the undeveloped mutterings of Caliban to the subtlest utterance of Wolsey or Mark Antony. He transformed medieval woman from Dante's Madonna-like Beatrice or Tasso's languishing Leonora to quick types of living feminity ; Dame Quickly up to Desdemona. He mixed high and low on his stage, and shifted his times and places, with the practical manager's con-tempt for the rules of Aristotle and his com-mentators. (See s.v. Unities). He found his way from rhyme to blank verse, from euphuism (q.v.) to unaffected eloquence. He was always free to go his own way, from the pleasant upland pastures of Warwickshire to the theatres and taverns of London, and home again, when he had rung the curtain down, to the civic neighbourliness of Stratford-on-Avon.

The rest must be sought in the plays and poems. S. was so much a man of the Renais-sance that he took his treasure where he found it, not caring for proof or plagiary or for any probability save the dramatic. So, he completed what others had begun, and arrived where others had shown the way Amyot (q.v.) had translated Plutarch's *Lives*, Guevara (q.v.) had written of *Ten Emperors* ; S. put Rome on the stage. Montaigne (q.v.) had discoursed on *que sçais-je* ? Hamlet personated doubt. Machi-avelli (q.v.) had discussed kingly power ; king Lear showed forth its vanity. When every one of S.'s dramas has been analysed down to its last grain of pre-Shake-spearean ingredients, S.'s method is still unexplored. He patched (in purple) other people's plays (see, for a signal example, s.vv. Ur-Hamlet and Kyd)* ; he composed a sonnet-sequence in the Ronsard-Wyatt (see s.vv.) tradition. But while he poached and patched and followed precedent, he was always adding ' the majestic imagination, penetrating psychology, and rich verbal music of William Shakespeare '. For S.'s method with his sources was to make acting plays of bookish

* In a fascinating art. on 'Shakespeare's Hand-writing' by Wm. Thompson (*Quarterly Review*, April, 1925), the suggestion is made that S.'s colla-boration with Fletcher (q.v.) late in his career was partly, at least, motivated by writer's cramp, which would explain, too, the partial illegibility of the signatures to S.'s will.

plots. How he did it remains S.'s secret, for all genius is ultimately insoluble. The most we can do is to tabulate below the obvious list of his source-books, and to warn the intelligent reader that, when all the debt to Italy and Ovid, to Holinshed and Plutarch has been computed, and when all the hints have been expanded, by a direct study of S.'s works, into an appreciation of his mind and art, we are still but beginners in S.-knowledge. 'After God', it has been reverently said, 'Shakespeare has created most'; and prof. A. C. Bradley writes, in a bk. which every S.-student should read and ponder (*Shakespearean Tragedy*, 206, n.1): 'Nature plays such strange tricks, and Shakespeare almost alone among poets seems to create in somewhat the same manner as Nature'.

SHAKESPEARE'S WORKS

[Note : *s.* = source ; *Sh.* = Shakespeare ; *b.* = between ; *c.* = *circa*, about.]

Title.	Date of Composition.	Source, etc.
Titus Andronicus	*b.* 1584 and 1589	*Sh.* part-author ; *s.* unknown.
Comedy of Errors	1589-91	*s.* Plautus (Roman playwright).
Two Gentlemen of Verona	*c.* 1590-92	*s.* Montemayor (q.v.).
King Henry vi (parts 1, 2, 3)	1591-2	*s.* Holinshed ; *Sh.* part-author.
Venus and Adonis	1593	*s.* Ovid, *Met.* x.
Midsummer Night's Dream	*c.* 1593-95	*s.* Chaucer, *Knight's Tale.*
King Richard ii	1593	*s.* Holinshed ; Stowe's *Annals.*
Rape of Lucrece	1593-94	*s.* Ovid, *Fasti*, ii ; Chaucer, etc.
King Richard iii.	1594	*s.* Holinshed (based on sir Thomas More's *Richard iii*).
Love's Labour Lost	*c.* 1593-94	Euphuistic ; quasi-historical.
King John	*c.* 1595	*s.* 'The Troublesome Raigne of John, king of England' (1591).
Romeo and Juliet	*c.* 1596 (1st draft, 1591)	*s.* Arthur Broke's poem (1562) after Bandello (1554).
King Henry iv (parts 1 and 2)	(1) 1596-97 ; (2) 1598-99	*s.* Holinshed and chronicle-plays.
Merchant of Venice	*c.* 1596	*s.* Ser Giovanni (q.v.) and other Ital. novelists ; Marlowe, *Jew of Malta.*
Taming of the Shrew	*b.* 1594 and 1601	*Sh.* part-author ; *s. Arabian Nights*, etc.
Troilus and Cressida	*c.* 1599 (1st draft) *c.* 1602 (2nd rev.).	*s.* Chaucer, Caxton, Lydgate.
Much Ado about Nothing	1599	*s.* Ariosto ; Bandello.
King Henry v	1599	*s.* Holinshed.
As You Like It	1599	*s.* Lodge, *Rosalynde.*
Merry Wives of Windsor	*c.* 1600	*s.* Ser Giovanni and other Ital. novelists.
Hamlet	*c.* 1601	*s.* Saxo, *Hist. Danica* (12th cent.), through Belleforest's *Hist. Tragiques* ; Kyd (q.v.).
Julius Cæsar	*c.* 1601	*s.* North's *Plutarch's Lives.*
Twelfth Night	1601-2	*s.* Bandello ; Belleforest.
All's Well that Ends Well	*c.* 1602	*s.* Boccaccio, *Decameron.*
Measure for Measure	*c.* 1603	*s.* Whetstone, *Promos and Cassandra* (1578).
Othello	1604	*s.* Cinthio (q.v.).
King Lear	1605	*s.* Holinshed, and old plays.
Macbeth	1603-6	*s.* Holinshed ; King James i, *Demonology* (1599).
Pericles	*c.* 1607-8	*Sh.* part-author (?) ; *s.* Gower, *Confessio Amantis.*
Antony and Cleopatra	1607-8	*s.* North's *Plutarch's Lives.*
Coriolanus	*c.* 1608-10	*s.* North's *Plutarch's Lives.*
Cymbeline	*c.* 1609-10	*s.* Holinshed, Boccaccio.
Sonnets	1609 (*ed. pr.*)	Partly auto-biog., partly sonneteering-vogue.
Winter's Tale	1610-11	*s.* Greene, *Pandosto* (novel 1588); Ovid, *Met.* xi.
Tempest	1610-11	*s.* unknown ; various ; Montaigne's essay 'of Cannibals'.
King Henry viii	*c.* 1612	*Sh.* part-author ; *s.* Holinshed, etc.
Timon of Athens	unknown	*Sh.* part-author (?) ; *s.* North's *Plutarch.*

N.B.—It should be remembered that Shakespeare need not have read all the *books* mentioned. There were pamphlets and even oral traditions covering much of the story-matter at his disposal.

Shebbeare, John (1709-88): Engl. political writer; tory; surgeon by profession. Wr. *Letters to the People of Engld.*, 8 parts, 1756-70, for the sixth of which he was fined and pilloried, having already been imprisoned, 1754, for the political reflections in his novel, *Marriage*. He had literary tussles with Smollett (q.v.) and others, and regained royal favour in the reign of king George iii. ' His highest praise is, that he still remains readable ' (*C.H.E.L.*, x, 389).

Sheffield, John (1648-1721): Engl. statesman; patron of letters; third earl of Mulgrave; created marquess of Normanby, 1694, and duke of Buckingham and Normanby, 1703 (to be distinguished from Geo. Villiers, q.v., duke of Buckingham, created 1623). Wr. an *Essay on Poetry*, and turned Shakespeare's *Julius Cæsar* into 2 plays better adapted to the tastes of his generation; acquainted with Dryden and Pope (qq.v.); buried in Westminster Abbey. The present edifice of Buckingham Palace stands on the site of his mansion.

Sheffler, Johann (1624-77): Germ. mystic poet; converted, 1653, to the Roman church, in which he became priest; known as Angelus Silesius, from his saintly character and his native province respectively. S. may be said to have transferred the pantheistic mysticism of Böhme (q.v.), his fellow-countryman, and of his friend Frankenberg (q.v.), Böhme's disciple, to the region of poetry, thus discovering new powers for that art. Besides hymns of great merit, S. wr. a vol. of sacred verse called the *Cherubinische Wandersmann*, in which, through a series of musical couplets, he poured out the rapture of his soul in a wonderful vision of the oneness of the inner and the outer worlds: ' I am as great as God; he is as small as I '—' Nought is but I and thou; if we twain are no more, God is no longer God, nor Heaven roofs us o'er'— ' For me there is no death, though every hour I perish, Yet every time I find a better life to cherish '; these verses and verses like these complete the mystical view of preachers such as Tauler (q.v.) and anticipate the penetration of later thinkers. In another vol. of verse, called *Sacred Pastorals*, S. succumbed to the same fault as Spee (q.v.), so common in Renaissance writers, of confounding pagan imagery with Christian ritual.

Shelley, -i. Percy Bysshe (1792-1822): Engl. poet; one of the group of ' inheritors of unfulfilled renown ' (the phrase is his own), who enhanced immeasurably the glory of Engl. letters in a single decade, 1814-24. This group, like the elder group of Wordsworth (1770-1850), Coleridge (1771-1834) and sir W. Scott (1772-1832), consisted of 3 poets: Byron (1788-1824), Shelley (1792-1822), and Keats (1795-1821; see s.vv.); and it will be observed that the lifetime of the older group, the youngest of whom died at 60, included and overlapped at both ends the lifetime of the younger group, the eldest of whom died at 36. Another point of difference between the 2 groups, which is of significance to what they made, consists in their relations to the Fr. Revolution, which affected so profoundly men's thought and action far beyond the boundaries of France for more than a generation. Those relations are admirably traced, so far as our country is concerned, by prof. E. Dowden (1843-1913) in his *French Revolution and English Literature* (Kegan Paul, 1897), to which students should refer. Here we may briefly remark that the longer lifetime of the elder poets acted as a determining factor. It is true that, as prof. Herford writes (*C.H.E.L.*, xii, 57), ' The revolution, which had profoundly disturbed the elder poets, had, for the younger, already become history; the ideas and aspirations which Wordsworth and Coleridge first embraced and then did battle with, and which Scott consistently abhorred, had passed into the blood of Byron and Shelley, and kindled humanitarian ardours even in the artist Keats '. But the greater distance is not the whole of the story. The younger poets, though remoter from the facts, were closer to the results, and S. particularly devoted himself to singing those results into a semblance of practical counsel for a distracted world. He seemed to know that his time was short: all time was short in the presence of the eternities and the immensities which he contemplated—' the eternal law ', as he wr. in *Epipsychidion*,

By which those live, to whom this world of life
Is as a garden ravaged;

and his own brief span he regarded as but a conscious moment in which to repair the ravage of the past. By this intenser participation, this more constant political pre-occupation with the prospects, not of a nation, but of mankind, we may explain, more completely than by any personal considerations, the salient facts in the biography of S. Those facts are familiar to-day: how he ' stood up single-handed against fagging ' at Eton; how he wr., 1811, a pamphlet on *The Necessity of Atheism* containing such heady doctrine as:

' A husband and wife ought to continue so long united as they love each other; any law which should bind them to combination for one moment after the decay of their affection would be a most intolerable tyranny ';

now he was sent down by the authorities of Univ. Coll., Oxford, for privately printing and circulating 75 copies of this juvenile essay; how he married Harriet Westbrook in the same year, and left her in 1814, precisely because his affection had decayed; how he came into contact with W. Godwin (q.v.), the social writer, a perilous friend of headstrong youth, and what sparks were struck out of that contact: the spark of a visit to Ireld., 1812, and an *Address to the Irish People*, publd. at Dublin; the spark of *Queen Mab*, 1813, in which his ' Godwinian creed is proclaimed from the mouths of legendary personages, inspired, as in their loose irregular verse, by the mythical epics of Southey ' (q.v.; *C.H.E.L.*, xii, 59); and the spark struck by Mary, daughter of Godwin and Mary Wollstonecraft, who had inherited views on free-love and its rights from both her reforming and non-conforming parents. Too much has been written round these facts (which include Harriet Shelley's suicide, 1816), in too many letters, memoirs, and biographies; there has been

Tom (1775-1817), son of Richard Brinsley S., above ; wr. *Carwell, or Crime and Sorrow*, and other novels.

-vii. **Helen Selina** (1807-67) : Anglo-Irish poet ; daughter of above ; the Helen of *Helen's Tower* by lord Tennyson (q.v.) ; m. (1) commr. Blackwood, 1825, and became mother of first marquess of Dufferin and Ava, who wr. her *Life*, and (2) earl of Gifford, 1862. Wr. a comedy, *Finesse*, produced at Haymarket Theatre, 1863, and *Songs, Poems and Verses*, publd. posth., 1894.

-viii. **Caroline Elizabeth Sarah** (1808-77) : Anglo-Irish poet ; sister of above (second of the 3 daughters, who were known as the 3 beauties, of Tom and Caroline S.) ; m. (1) hon. George Norton, 1827, from whom she separated, 1836, and who died, 1875, and (2) sir William Stirling-Maxwell (ninth bt. ; 1818-78 ; historian of Span. art). Mrs. Norton, as she is still commonly known, was a very popular contributor to the keepsakes, albums, and other periodicals of the day ; she was also a pioneer in the cause of better legislation for the protection of married women. She wr. several novels, and her best remembered work in verse is *The Lady of La Garaye*, 1862. She is supposed to be the orig. of the heroine of *Diana of the Crossways*, by G. Meredith (q.v.).

Sherwood, Mary Martha (1775-1851) : Engl. moral writer ; *née* Butt ; m., capt. Henry S., 1803 ; went with her husband to India, where she took much interest in the care of soldiers' orphans. Mrs. S. is chiefly remembered as the author of the *History of the Fairchild Family*, an edifying narrative, publd. in 3 parts, 1818-42-47 ; her *Susan Gray*, 1802, was her first successful tale.

Shirley, James (1596-1666) : Engl. dramatist ; wr. a number of plays, and is chiefly rememberable (1) for the brief, impressive ode, which closed his *Contention of Ajax and Ulysses for the Armour of Achilles*, 1659 :

The glories of our blood and state
Are shadows, not substantial things ; . . .
Only the actions of the just
Smell sweet, and blossom in their dust ;

(2) for the death of his wife and himself on the same day, Oct., 1666, ' being in a manner overcome with affrightements, disconsolations, and other miseries ', caused by the Great Fire in London in that year.

Shorter, Dora Sigerson (d. 1918): Irish poet ; *née* Sigerson ; m., 1896, Clement K. Shorter ; wr. *The Fairy Changeling*, 1897 ; *Ballads and Poems*, 1898 ; *As the Sparks Fly Upward*, 1904, and other vols, of verse, much praised by G. Meredith (q.v.) and other competent critics. Her subjects were largely taken from Irish folklore.

Shorthouse, Joseph Henry (1834-1903) : Engl. novelist ; wr., among novels, *John Inglesant*, 1881, which he described as ' a philosophical romance '. It is set in the 17th cent., and is suffused by a cloistral glow, which attracted High Churchmen 200 years afterwards. Hailed at first as a work of genius, *John Inglesant* has gradually lost hold on the affections of the reading public ; and ' probably few critics would now commit themselves to the view that either it or any of its successors is destined to take a place among the classics

of English literature ' (Walker, *Lit. Victorian Era*, 512). Fewer still, after an art. in the *Quarterly Review*, July, 1925, which showed that S.'s novel is largely a mosaic of contemporary memoirs and letters.

Sibilet, Thomas (1512-89) : Fr. critical writer. Wr., 1548, *Art Poétique français*, one of many treatises on poetics which owed much to Ital. example, but of greater interest as anticipating (or coinciding with) the tastes and principles of the Pleiad (q.v.), just before the critical manifesto written by Du Bellay (q.v.).

Sidgwick, Henry (1838-1900) : Engl. philosopher ; m., 1876, Eleanor Balfour (sister of the first earl of Balfour), president of Newnham coll., 1892. Wr. *Methods of Ethics*, 1874 ; *Principles of Political Economy*, 1883 ; *Elements of Politics*, 1891, etc., and is accounted a follower of J. S. Mill (q.v.). S. was twice president of the Society for Psychical Research.

Sidney, Philip (1554-86) : Engl. soldier-poet ; knt., 1583 ; a typical product of the Renaissance, who satisfied in a supreme degree the exacting conditions of that ennobling apprenticeship. (1) He satisfied the condition of birth. His grandfather, sir Wm. S. (d., 1554) had attended king Henry viii at the Field of the Cloth of Gold, and was granted the castle of Penshurst, in Kent, where S. was born. His father, sir Henry S. (1529-86) was 3 times lord-deputy of Ireland and was president of Wales, 1571-5. His mother was a daughter of John Dudley, duke of Northumberland, executed, 1553, in connection with the lady Jane Grey plot, and sister, accordingly, to Robert Dudley, earl of Leicester, queen Elizabeth's notorious favourite, and a constant friend to his brilliant young nephew. Further, S.'s only sister was Mary, countess of Pembroke (1561-1621), whose gifts and charm were nearly equal to his own. (2) He satisfied every condition of personal qualities. His contemporary, sir Fulke Greville, first baron Brooke (1554-1628), who wr. S.'s *Life* (publd., 1652), said : ' Though I lived with him and knew him as a child, yet I never knew him other than a man, with such staidness of mind, lovely and familiar gravity, as carried grace and reverence above greater years '. He was the trusted friend of artists, statesmen and kings, including Hubert Languet (1518-81), the Fr. Huguenot humanist, with whom he maintained an intimate correspondence on an equal intellectual level ; Tintoretto (1518-94) and Paul Veronese (1528-88), Ital. painters ; and prince Wm. of Orange (1533-84), whose proverbial silence yielded to S.'s fascination. Hakluyt (q.v.) dedicated to him his *Voyages* ; Spenser (q.v.) his *Shepherd's Calendar* ; Giordano Bruno (q.v.) 2 of his learned vols., and more than 200 admirers were represented in a bk. of poems, issued in his memory. (3) He satisfied the condition of adventure. He travelled widely in Europe in his youth, visiting France, Germany, Austria, Poland, Italy, etc., and, apart from this intellectual restlessness, which began to alarm his uncle Leicester at home, S. wanted to join sir Humphrey Gilbert on the fateful expedition to Newfoundland, and he received a grant of land in America by letters patent which, by the sober testimony of sir S. Lee, were 'well fitted to be enrolled in the courts of Faërie'. Finally, he met his death from a wound received at the battle of Zutphen in the Low Countries, where his Protestant ardour led him to fight Spain before the Armada, and there is authentic warrant for the gallant tale about the bottle of water and 'thy necessity greater than mine'. (4) He satisfied the condition of love. His *Astrophel and Stella* sonnets, addressed to lady (Penelope) Rich (q.v.), daughter of the first earl of Essex, were Petrarchan in form and sentiment; Stella was the Laura of the Engl. Petrarch, who followed the example of Ronsard (q.v.) and the rest of the Fr. Italianates, and directly showed the way to the *Amoretti* of Spenser and the sonnet-sequences of other Tudor singers, including Shakespeare himself, and, in a later age, Rossetti and G. Meredith (see s.vv.). (5) He satisfied the condition of scholarship. He was one of the most widely-read men of his time; he wr. an *Apologie for Poetrie*, in reply to Gosson (q.v.), which is comparable with the older Renaissance essays by Minturno, du Bellay (qq.v), and others, and with the later *Defence of Poetry* by another Engl. poet, Shelley (q.v.).

We might pursue in greater detail the likeness of S. to the ideal courtier, described by Castiglione (q.v.) in his famous treatise. But we must pass over the full incidents of a life too short for the fulfilment of the renown of which contemporaries and posterity agree in recognition. S. accompanied queen Elizabeth to Kenilworth, where sir S. Lee conjectures that John Shakespeare of Stratford-on-Avon brought his son, William, to the brilliant pageant, which was remembered in *A Midsummer Night's Dream*; he flirted with the pedants of the Areopagus (q.v.), and with Harvey's (q.v.) schemes for classical Engl. metres; he quarrelled with the earl of Oxford, leader of a rival clique, and, falling under the queen's displeasure, retired to the home of his sister; he returned to court, 1581, the year in which Languet died; he married the daughter of sir Francis Walsingham, and was employed in various capacities before he added a hero's death to a courtier's life.

While living in retirement at his sister's, S. wr. the pastoral romance, *Arcadia* (ed. pr., 1590), the third and fourth edns. of which, 1598-9, contained S.'s *Sonnets*, his *Astrophel and Stella*, and his *Apologie for Poetrie*. It was inscribed 'to my dear lady and sister, the countess of Pembroke', and was described by the author as an 'idle work', in the sense of a bk. written in an interval of idleness; for in truth, as sir S. Lee writes (*Great Englishmen of the 16th Cent.*, 96), 'the work is far more serious than the deprecatory pref. suggests. Sidney's pen must have travelled with lightning speed. Whatever views may be entertained of the literary merits of his bk., it amazes one by its varied learning, its wealth of episode, and its exceptional length'. Probably, S., in the *Arcadia* (see, too, s.vv. Pastoral, Arcadia) sought to satisfy by his pen the ambitions which were forbidden to his sword, and to claim his part in the adventures of Ralegh (q.v.), Humphrey, and Drake, Partly, too, the *Arcadia* proposed a fresh solution of the current problem of a prose style by connecting the problem of style, more consciously than by Lyly's Euphuism (see s.vv.), with the problem of conduct. If courtiers would live 'romantic' lives, the Court would speak the language of romance; in other words, if the old ideals of chivalry could be adapted to the new age of commerce, exploration, and foreign conquest, an heroic tongue could be fashioned for their expression. To this ideal world S. was content to retire from the jealous perplexities of Court life, till he exchanged the fabled rivers of Arcady for the streams of Paradise, hardly more remote from his fancy, or less clearly visualized in his faith.

The *Arcadia* is a work of fiction, in which the plot is obscurely elaborated, the style is affected and in places repellent, and the pastoral element is partly a protest against what Languet had described in one of his letters to S. as 'the troubles that hamper and engross all that live within the circle of government'. Yet, these defects apart, it possesses a distinct claim on our attention. It marks the beginning of Engl. fiction, with its love plot and female characters, which Richardson and Fielding (qq.v.) were to develop, and the 19th cent. was to consummate. It added to the resources of the Engl. language, or, rather to the equipment of its inheritors, and, chiefly, it served to help the dramatic genius of the age, then just preening its wings to soar. As prof. Courthope reminds us: 'The pale and almost bodiless phantoms which floated vaguely before the imagination in the romance, touched by the magic wand of Shakespeare and his contemporaries, acquired colour, beauty, poetry, life. The gentle pastoral landscape of a non-existent country reappeared in the ideal forest of Arden, in the enchanted island of Prospero, in a Bohemia bordered by the sea'. Nor was the debt confined to hints of 'sentiment and landscape'. The story and plot were utilized for the purposes of drama, and an indirect tribute was paid to the influence of S.'s *Arcadia* by Beaumont and Fletcher (qq.v). in their *Cupid's Revenge*, and by Shakespeare in *King Lear*, *As You Like It*, *Twelfth Night*, and other plays.

Sieyès, de, Emmanuel Joseph (1748-1836): Fr. revolutionary writer and statesman; *comte* by rank (Napoleon i's creation). Wr. 3 pamphlets, 1788-89, one of which, *Qu' est-ce que le Tiers État?* was the keystone to the edifice of the Fr. Revolution. S.'s subsequent story belongs to history, not to lit., and we can only glance here at his authorship of the *Constitution of the Year 8*, which was finally shaped by Buonaparte, and which issued in the triple Consulate of Buonaparte, Ducos, and S. himself.

Siguenza, de, José (1545-1606): Span. theologian. Wr. a *History of the Order of San Geronimo*, 1595-1605, including a life of the saint.

Silesian Schools: Germ. poetry in the 17th cent. received its first stimulus from Silesia, and to this circumstance it is due that the name of the province was given to 2 successive and partly contemporary movements. The designation is not very happy, since Saxony and several northern cities, e.g., Königsberg the Great, were among the military and naval officers, the artizans, technicians and handicraftsmen, who helped effectively to impose modern ideas on medieval Moscow. Thus, the S. was one of the factors in the Europeanizing of Russia in the 17th cent., and one of its means was the drama. In 1672 the Protestant pastor of the S. was a certain Gregori, who started a theatre; his repertory included university-dramas, biblical plays, and ballets, and a performance was given before the emperor Alexis in 1674.

Slowacki, Julius (1809-49): Polish poet; dramatist. Wr. *Balladina* and *Lilla Veneda*, tragic dramas, described as half-fantastic and half-legendary, and plays founded upon episodes of Polish history in 17th and 18th cents.; also a *Queen Mary Stuart, William Wallace, Beatrice Cenci*, and others. S., who spoke of a 'fatal force' in his poetry, applied it to satiric epic in the manner of Byron's (q.v.) *Don Juan*, and his *Beniowski* is 'a comic museum of national curiosities of his own period. No work of Polish poetry is such a complete encyclopedia of national and international, literary and social, religious and philosophical problems and subjects of interest in the revolutionary period of the nineteenth century. . . He does not spare his fellow-writers on the Polish Parnassus, . . . and even challenges, in a powerful passage, the great Mickiewiez (q.v.) himself, whose fame he always envied' (Dyboski, *Periods of Pol. Lit. Hist.*, 102-3).

Smedley, Francis Edward (1818-64): Engl. novelist; wr. *Frank Fairlegh*, 1850, *Lewis Arundel*, 1852, *Harry Coverdale's Courtship*, 1855; intimate friend of Edmund Yates (q.v.).

Smiles, Samuel (1812-1904): Scot. biographer; moralist; successfully combined these 2 parts in his vols. on *Self-Help*, 1859, *Character*, 1871, *Thrift*, 1875, and *Duty*, 1880, which sought to teach those virtues by examples of men who had practised them assiduously and to their own advantage. The lesson was addressed to the 'hands' lately released from slavery in the factories and admitted to the possession of heads, containing both brain and tongues. The intention, excellent so far as it went, of Dr. S. (he received the LL.D. at Edinburgh univ., 1878) was to direct the exercise of these functions into channels likely to increase the industrial prosperity of Engld.; to this aim he returned in his *George Stephenson*, 1857; *Industrial Biography*, 1863; and *Lives of the Engineers*, 1877. In 1891, he wr. a history of the publishing-house of *John Murray*, and his other works included *Life of a Scotch Naturalist*, 1876, and minor biographic sketches. It is not without significance in retrospect that *Self-Help*, which was transld. into 17 languages, and achieved an immense success, appeared in the same year as Darwin's (q.v.) *Origin of Species*. It was essentially a bk. of the 19th cent., promoting the progressive development of mankind, and seeking to turn the new resources and opportunities to the service of man and God. The didactico-moral tone was unavoidable, and the note of individualism was firmly struck; but, as the thought of the age matured, and the industrial consciousness was strengthened, it was seen

that the keys of prosperity were not solely in the keeping of the industrious apprentice of the John Halifax type (see s.v. Craik), but depended partly on conditions shut out from the view of a generation which deemed that universal peace would follow the Universal Exhibition of 1851. Thus, the spirit of the age moved away—though a partial reaction may perhaps be due—from the constant perception of S.: 'I take Individual Character to be the highest embodiment of the human being,—the noblest heraldry of Man. It is that which signifies him, which elevates him in the scale of mankind, which forms the conscience of society, and creates and forms its best motive power'.

Smith, Adam (1723-90): Scot. political economist; edu. at univ. of Glasgow, where Hutcheson (q.v.) was a tutor; went to Balliol coll., Oxford, 1740, but found, like Gibbon (q.v.), little good to say of that univ., and returned, 1751, to the chair of logic in Glasgow; visited France, 1764-6, with a pupil, the third duke of Buccleugh, and met Hume (q.v.) and others in Paris, where he was received in the circle of the Physiocrats (q.v.), 'and learned highly to esteem Quesnay (q.v.); came home to Kirkcaldy, and wr. *The Wealth of Nations*, 1766, which virtually founded the science of political economy, and has maintained its primacy ever since, esp. during the unchallenged rule of the principle of free trade. It is not within the scope of this dict. to discuss the contents of S.'s great work, and we must note the statement of Mr. J. H. Millar (*P.E.L.*, ix, 289), that, 'if we attempt to extricate his purely economic teaching, we shall find that there is scarcely a point associated with the name of Smith in which Hume has not anticipated him'. But the praise follows on the next page in loyally unstinted measure, worthy of S.'s reputation : 'Only by a genius such as Hume's could the merits of *The Wealth of Nations* have been thrown into the shade', and Hume did not write the bk. which would have done so. We may test S.'s work, we are told, 'by comparison either with prior and contemporary work in the same department, or with work subsequent in date; and in either case the result is a triumph for Adam Smith'; and, we may add, for the infinitely painstaking method of the Scot. genius in research and exposition.

Smith, Alexander (1830-67): Scot. essayist; poet. Wr. *War Sonnets*, 1855, with S. Dobell (q.v.); *Dreamthorp* (essays), 1863, etc. S. belonged to the Spasmodic (q.v.) group, but is chiefly rememberable to-day for his pleasant vein in prose criticism.

Smith, George (1824-1901): Engl. publisher; son of the senior partner in the form of Smith and Elder, originally, 1816, East India agents, and founder of a famous publishing-house (Smith, Elder & Co.). S. was generous in his encouragement to new writers, and in his promotion of large enterprises. Among the former may be mentioned C. Brontë (q.v.), *Jane Eyre*, 1848, and Thackeray (q.v.), *Esmond*, 1851; among the latter, the *Cornhill Magazine*, 1859; the *Pall Mall Gazette* (q.v.), and the *Dict. of National Biography*, 1882 (see s.v. sir L. Stephen).

Smith, Goldwin (1823-1910): Engl. historian; visited America during the Civil War, and espoused the cause of the Northern States; resigned, 1866, the chair of Modern History in Oxford univ., which he had held since 1859, and settled in the United States and, later, at Toronto, where he turned his great gifts to controversial and journalistic uses, which had no permanent value. Wr. *Lectures on Modern History*, 1861; *England and America*, 1865; *Three English Statesmen*, 1867; *Cowper* ('English Men of Letters'), 1880; *Bay Leaves, Translns. from the Latin Poets*, 1893, etc.

Smith, -i. Horace (1779-1849): and
    -ii. James (1775-1839): Engl. humourists; brothers. Wr., 1812, *Rejected Addresses*, a vol. of famous parodies of contemporary poets; H.S.'s share included Scott, Byron and Moore; J.S.'s, Wordsworth, Coleridge and Crabbe. The bk. made a great hit, beside which the subsequent independent writings of the 2 brothers have not maintained a place.

Smith, James Elimalet (1801-57): Scot. divine; known as 'Shepherd Smith', after his organ, *The Shepherd*, founded, 1834; essay writer to the *Family Herald*, founded, 1843.

Smith, Sydney (1771-1845): Engl. divine; canon of St. Paul's, 1831; well-known and much-liked as a wit, and was an influential figure in literary and political circles, esp. at Holland House. Wr. *Plymley Letters*, 1807, in defence of Catholic emancipation, and was joined with Jeffrey (q.v.) and others in starting the Whig *Edinburgh Review*, 1802.

Smith, William (1813-93): Engl. scholar; knt., 1892; educational editor in the publishing-house of J. Murray (q.v.); edited *Quarterly Review*, 1867-93, and brought out permanently useful dictionaries of biography, antiquities, etc.

Smollett, Tobias George (1721-71): Scot. novelist, surgeon. The disappointment, even resentment, which S. felt at the failure of a tragedy, *The Regicide*, 1739, which he brought from Scotld. to London in the expectation of fame and fortune as a youth, is said to have embittered his life, which was marred by quarrels and controversies and one experience of imprisonment for libel. He travelled as a ship's surgeon, and was a proficient master of naval matters and sea-characters, depicted in his novels, and staged in his one successful play, *The Reprisal, or The Tars of Old Engld.*, a comedy, Drury Lane, 1757. S. was a busy misc. writer and translr.: his *History of Engld.*, frequently reprinted, is now the best known survivor of those activities, which included versions of *Gil Blas, Don Quixote*, and the works of Voltaire (q.v.). Many of those enterprises were undertaken in collaboration, and S. ranks among the early compilers of compendiums of popular information. His novels, which have permanent value, are *Roderick Random*, 1748; *Peregrine Pickle*, 1751; *Ferdinand Count Lathom*, 1753; *Sir Launcelot Greaves*, 1762; *History and Adventures of an Atom*, 1769; and *The Expedition of Humphrey Clinker*, 1771. The best of these were the first and second, but they are all undeniably coarse-grained, and Sterne (q.v.), who met S. in Italy, was not unfair in

describing him as 'Smelfungus' in the *Sentimental Journey*. Historically, however, S. is more significant. 'He is richer in types than Fielding' (q.v.), says the writer of ch. 2 in *C.H.E.L.*, x, 'and it needs only a mention of his naval scenes and characters to raise memories of a whole literature, which, receiving an impetus from the naval battles won after Smollett's death, has persisted even after the disappearance of wooden ships. The picaresque novel in general, which burst into activity soon after the publication of *Roderick Random*, was under heavy obligations to Smollett, and nowhere more so than in its modern example, *Pickwick*. Dickens, indeed, who was a great reader of Smollett, was his most eminent disciple'. The writer holds that S. 'will continue to be read by those who are not too squeamish or too stay-at-home to find in him complete recreation'.

Snorri, Sturluson (1178-1241): Icel. historian; critic; son of Hvamm-Sturla (Sturla of Hvamm), founder of the Sturlung house in Iceld., and uncle, accordingly, to Sturla (q.v.), who celebrated the annals of that house in the *Sturlunga Saga*. (See, too, s.v. Saga). There is a resemblance which cannot be gainsaid, though there are obviously many *mutanda*, between the fortunes of the Sturla family in Iceld. and those of the Medici (q.v.) family in Florence; human nature is the same in North and South, in the 13th cent. and the 16th; and 'this family'—which might be either—'was one of the most ambitious, and did as much as any to spoil the old balance of the Commonwealth. . . . The strange thing about them is that, with all their dangerous, showy qualities, they produced some of the finest literature: "out of the eater came forth meat". Snorri, son of Sturla, was for a long time one of the most persevering and successful capitalists of that time, making his fortune, greedily, by all available means; he is also great in Icelandic prose literature' (W. P. Ker, *Sturla the Historian*, Romanes Lecture, Oxford, 1906). Snorri's extant works consist of (i) a treatise in prose on ancient myths and modern poetry, known as the prose *Edda* (q.v.), first ascribed to S. by Arngrim (q.v., and see s.v. O. Worm), and described by the same competent authority as a bk. 'that has very little to learn from any renaissance or revival of learning'; and (ii) sagas in prose 'Lives of the kings of Norway', commonly known as *Heimskringla*, after the title in the abridgement contained in the famous MS., now in Copenhagen, the *Codex Regius* (q.v.). Snorri is not answerable for the mis-description by the scholars in the 17th cent. of all the poetic contents of that MS. as, comprehensively, *Edda* (the Elder): this was due to the theory then current that S.'s treatise on poetry, interspersed as it was with illustrations from the verse of Old Iceld., was an epitome of an older work. (See s.vv. Edda and Magnus Olafsson). S.'s *Edda* was nothing of the kind. It was a study of how to write poetry, which should be faithful to the romantic qualities in Icelandic myth, and which should yet be faithful to reject a belief in the mythical deities. It is almost modern in its rational tone towards the gods; tolerant, humorous ironical ; and is characterized (Ker, *op. cit.*) as ' a handbook of the Art of Poetry, written in the thirteenth century by a man of liberal genius '. S.'s *Kings' Lives*, chiefly of Olaf Tryggvason and the later St. Olaf, and probably founded on a lost work by Ari Thorgilsson (1067-1148), surnamed The Wise, are in the true heroic vein, worked by the writers of the Sagas, and perfected by S.'s nephew a few years later. How much of the *Heimskringla* is genuine Snorri is a problem which critics are computing with more and more credit to S. ; and it is good to be able to claim by name an author in the early 13th cent. for heroic prose, founded on historic fact, of so high an order of excellence. One incident, at least, in the *Heimskringla*, the narrative of the last sea-fight of king Olaf, beats Grenville and his Revenge (see Saintsbury, *P.E.L.*, ii, 344n). Snorri was murdered by one Arni Beiskr (' bitter ').

Society of Jesus : Religious Order of Jesuits, founded in Paris by Loyola, 1534, and confirmed by Bull of pope Paul iii, 1540 ; the first general of the Order was Loyola, succeeded in 1556 by Lainez, whose organizing ability ably supplied the place of the founder's enthusiastic initiative. The S.J. has been named the brain of the Holy See : without specific marks or duties, its members from an early date permeated the system of the Roman Church ; and their chief activity was displayed, not in politics, or the pulpit, or the confessional, but, more subtly, in the school-room. From the start, their zeal as crusaders was directed to missionary effort at home, and the schools which they founded were many and successful. As an educational influence, accordingly, the S.J. is a recognized force in the history of culture in Europe, and is associated with the employment of Lat. as a vehicle of instruction to a very late date. Their free schools and free bks., apart even from their system and methods of instruction, mark an important departure in educational practice, and in France, particularly, the original home of the Jesuits, founded to resist the disintegrating forces of the Reformation, they were reputed the best schoolmasters till as recently as 1901, when the Associations Bill of Waldeck-Rousseau became law. We are not concerned with the record of the Society in theological doctrine or in its missionary activity, nor with the causes (chiefly, perhaps, the lack of men of Loyola's stamp) which led to the expulsion, one by one, of its branches, from the great Catholic countries of Europe. But lit. is necessarily interested in the political philosophy of members of the order, such as Mariana (q.v.), who upheld the right of regicide against the anti-Machiavellism of Gentillet (q.v.) and Huguenot jurists such as Duplessis-Mornay (q.v.).

Solis, de, Antonio (1610-86): Span. dramatist ; divine ; historian. Born at Alcalá, and edu. at Salamanca, S.'s literary development followed the order of his biography. On taking orders in 1667, that is to say, S. ceased to write for the stage, in which he had shown himself an apt disciple of Calderon (q.v.) with touches of Gongora (q.v.) in his style, and devoted himself to the duties of his office as chronicler

of the Indies. His plays include *Gitanilla* (' The little Gypsy '), partly indebted to Cervantes and Montalvan (qq.v.), and partly utilized by Rowley and Middleton (qq.v. ; in *The Span. Gypsy*, and by Longfellow in *The Span. Student* ; a dramatic masque on Orpheus and Eurydice ; and *Amor al uso* (' Love à la Mode '), adapted by T. Corneille and Scarron (qq.v.). As historian, S. compiled, 1684, an admirable *History of the Conquest of Mexico.*

Solorzano. See s.v. **Castillo Solorzano.**

Soloviev, Vladimir (1853-1900) : Russ. moralist, theologian, critic, and poet ; a thinker *sui generis*, rare in the annals of timid Russ. philosophy. His adherence to the Slavophils in preference to the Westernizers (the names carry their own connotation ; see s.v. Russ. lit.) was neither blind nor extreme : ' What sort of East is thy desire ', he asks his country in a poem *ex Oriente lux* ; ' the East of Xerxes or of Christ ? ', and he was never in doubt to his own election for the side of Christ. S. did not succeed in completing the greater works which he planned : a transln. of Plato, a commentary on Holy Writ, and others ; but he wr. a treatise on ethics, *National Problems in Russia, Spiritual Principles*, etc., and a Fr. work on the *Russ. Church and the Universal Church.*

Somervile, William (1675-1742): Engl. poet ; was not ' ashamed to follow the example of Milton, Philips, Thomson, and all our best tragic writers ', in the employment of unrhymed verse in preference to rhymed. This citation from the pref. to *The Chace*, 1735, by S. is interesting as evidence of the vogue of Philips and Thomson (see s.vv.) and of the novelty of blank verse in the mid-18th cent. S. was a writer on sport and rural subjects : his invocation is famous,

> to the Chace, the sport of kings ;
> Image of War, without its guilt.

Sonnet : A lyrical poem, described by Geo. Gascoigne (q.v.), in his *Notes of Instruction for Verse*, 1575, as consisting ' of fourteen lines, each line containing ten syllables. The first twelve do rhyme in staves of four lines by cross metre, and the last two rhyming together do conclude the whole '. Gascoigne observed how ' some think that all poems, being short, may be called *sonets*, as indeed it is a diminutive word derived from *sonare* ' (to sound) ; but, omitting this evidence to laxity in constructing a S. in the 16th cent., it is not possible to improve the above definition of the S., now more than 350 years old. It may be amplified in places, however. And, first, 350 years is scarcely half the lifetime of the S., which is indigenous to Europe (there is no precedent for it in Gk. or Roman metrical schemes), and which took its rise as a *canzone*, or song of one stanza, in the amorous verse of Sicilian and Tuscan troubadours. The leading early formal sonneteer was Petrarch (q.v.), but there were sonnets in Ital. poetry before Petrarch ; and, out of many examples transld. by D. G. Rossetti (q.v.) in his *Early Ital. Poets*, we many select 2: (1) by Guido Guinicelli (q.v.), (2) by Dante (q.v.) himself, in which ' the wise man ' of the second verse is this same Guinicelli. These sonnets run :

I.

He that has grown to wisdom hurries not,
 But thinks and weighs what Reason bids
  him do
And after thinking he retains his thought
Until as he conceived the fact ensue.
Let no man to o'erweening pride be wrought,
 But count his state as Fortune's gift and due.
He is a fool who deems that none has sought
The truth, save he alone, or knows it true.
Many strange birds are on the air abroad,
 Nor all are of one flight or of one force,
 But each after his kind dissimilar :
To each was portioned of the breath of God,
Who gave them divers instincts from one
  source.
  Then judge not thou thy fellows what
  they are.

II.

Love and the gentle heart are one same thing,
 Even as the wise man in his ditty saith :
 Each, of itself, would be such life in death
As rational soul bereft of reasoning.
'Tis Nature makes them when she loves : a
  king
Love is, whose palace where he sojourneth
Is called the Heart ; there draws he quiet
  breath
At first, with brief or longer slumbering.
Then beauty seen in virtuous womankind
Will make the eyes desire, and through the
  heart
 Send the desiring of the eyes again ;
Where often it abides so long enshrin'd
 That Love at length out of his sleep will
  start.
  And women feel the same for worthy men.

The reader will observe that Gascoigne's definition (1575) is correct as to the 14 lines and the 10 syllables. But he is wrong as to the rhyming of these sonnets, written nearly 3 cents. before his day. He states that the rhyme scheme of the S. is *abab, bcbc, cdcd, ee*, whereas these pioneer Ital. specimens, accurately represented by Rossetti, are rhymed : *ababab* (or, *abba abba*), *cde, cde*. The difference is obvious : the old native Ital. S. consists of 2 parts, an octave (8 lines) and a sestet (6 lines) ; the Gascoigne S. consists of 3 quatrains (4 lines) and a couplet (2 lines). There is a corresponding difference in the distribution of the thought. The Petrarchan S. raised it through the octave, and then let it sink slowly to rest in the sestet : an up and down movement from exaltation to tranquillity ; the concluding couplet in the later S. led to a more pointed close, of which we may cite an example from Sonnet i of Spenser's (q.v.) *Amoretti* :

Leaves, lines, and rhymes, seek her to please
 alone,
Whom if ye please, I care for other none.

The S. was transported from Italy to France, chiefly by Du Bellay (q.v.), one of the 7 stars of the Pleiad (q.v.). Marot (q.v.) had preceded him in a tentative way, but sir S. Lee (*Fr. Renaissance in Engld.*, 203) quotes and confirms a contemporary testimony :

Ce fut toi, Du Bellay, qui des premiers en
 France
D'Italie attiras les Sonets amoureux.

Note the epithet *amoureux*. Ronsard (q.v.) called his sonnets simply *Amours* ; and it was the Troubadour tradition combined with a love-idealism derived from Plato (q.v.) which stamped the S. as the form most appropriate for those sequences of lyrical poems about love, associated often with one object, which were composed so lavishly in Tudor times by Sidney, Spenser, Shakespeare, and other greater and lesser masters, and which Rossetti, E. B. Browning, G. Meredith (qq.v.) and others continued in Engl. poetry till a recent day. Milton and Wordsworth (qq.v.) both availed themselves of this form of lyric verse, but they followed precedent by extending it to other topics than love. Meanwhile, the love-sonnet, whether single or catenated, was always, or nearly always, dominated by the conventions of its kind. The 'ideal' love of Petrarch for Laura was transferred from Italy to France, and from Italy and France to Engld., and governed more closely than readers are commonly aware the personal sentiment of the imitative poet. 'With this key Shakespeare unlocked his heart' is found, on examination, to be an incomplete statement of the fact. With the sonnet-key Shakespeare unlocked the lyrical treasuries of Alamanni, Sannazzaro (qq.v.) and other Ital. love-poets, of Ronsard, Du Bellay, and other Fr. love-poets, whom Wyatt and Surrey (qq.v.) in Engld. had ransacked before him. We may give some figures in this connection. It is computed that Ronsard wr. 709 sonnets out of a total of 1,396 poems. Between 1590 and 1610, says sir S. Lee, 'more sonnets were penned in England than in all the ages that followed'. These figures are impressive, but it is clear that the later writers would be very much under the influence of their precursors, and the evidence of exact scholars is more and more conclusive in this direction. The S. is still a lure for lyric poets. Its brevity and the concentration of its interest render it particularly alluring, and there are probably more indifferent or poor sonnets than there are similar failures in any other kind of poetry. 'Many generations of poets in all European countries', writes prof. Courthope (*History Engl. Poetry*, vi, 210), 'have used it for various purposes, and, in its most conventional form, I have often had occasion to show how its amorous conceits reflect the decay of medieval chivalry. But great representatives of the Classical Renaissance, Michael Angelo and Milton, had turned it to account for the expression of philosophical, religious, or political thought ; and Wordsworth, following in their track, made it the vehicle for still more complex moods. . . . Wordsworth's Sonnet is, as a rule, kept strictly within the traditional Italian lines. He avoids the three loose quatrains with the rhyming couplet at the close, used by the Elizabethan poets ; and generally maintaining the compact rhyming structure of the first eight lines, finds his liberty in the distribution of the six closing ones'. A careful student of poetry will discover that the lyric verse-form established in Italy in the 13th cent. was re-founded in Engld. in the 19th.

Sorel, Albert (1842-1906) : Fr. historian. Wr. valuable and monumental works on the

Diplomatic History of the Franco-Prussian War, 1875; the *Eastern Question in the 18th Century*, 1878; and *Europe and the Fr. Revolution*, 4 vols., 1885-92.

Sorel, Charles (*c.* 1597-1674): Fr. novelist; historiographer of France; facile misc. writer; chiefly memorable for his experiment in realism, *Histoire Comique de Francion*, 1622, and for his attempt, a generation before Molière and Boileau (qq.v.) to prick the bubble of the Precious (q.v.) affectation: S.'s *Berger Extravagant*, 1627, was the *Précieuses ridicules* of Molière (q.v.) in respect to pastoral preciosity; S. was indebted for it to some extent to Cervantes (q.v.), *Don Quixote*. But S. lacked the art which his insight required, and his *Francion*, 'the ancestor of *Gil Blas*, is a date, not a work' (Lanson, *Hist. Lit. fr.*, 189): its significance in literary history 'centres in the fact that it was the earliest French novel of manners' (Koerting, *Gesch. des Franz. Romans im 17ten Jahrh.*, ii, 65).

Sotheby, William (1757-1833): Engl. translr. Wr. *Poems*, 1790, and won a deserved reputation for his version of Virgil's *Georgics*, 1800. Transld., too, the epics of Homer, and Wieland's (q.v.) *Oberon.*

Soto, de, Luis Barahona (*c.* 1548-95): Span. poet; wr. heroic poem 'Part i of Angelica', in 12 cantos (there was never a Part ii), commonly known as *Lagrimas* (Tears) *de Angelica*, designed as a continuation of the *Orlando Furioso* of Ariosto (q.v.). Wr. also lyric verse, and some translns. from Ovid. S. was extravagantly praised by the major poets of his own country, esp. by Cervantes (q.v.); in the famous chapter of *Don Quixote*, in which so many books of chivalry were committed to the flames, the curate rescued *Angelica* on the ground that 'its author was one of the famous poets of the world, let alone Spain'. Posterity does not ratify this friendly judgment.

Sottie (Fr.): Generic name of a type of Fr. farce, the subject-matter of which was described by Sibilet (q.v.) as 'badinage, tomfoolery, and all kinds tending to laughter and fun'. The 'Sots' was an alternative name of the 'Enfants sans Souci' (q.v.), the dramatic society which dealt in 'satyre françoise'.

Soulié, Frédéric (1800-47): Fr. novelist; wr. *Mémoires du Diable*, 1837, *Romans historiques de Languedoc*, 1836-38, and other tales, decidedly of the second order of merit, in the vein of Sue (q.v.).

Soupirs et Flammes (Fr.): 'Sighs and Flames'; epithet employed somewhat contemptuously by Corneille (q.v.) to describe a type of tragic drama associated with Racine (q.v.), and even more with Quinault (q.v.) and other *doucereux* ('sweeteners'), whose interest was centred in the ruling passion of love, and who treated it in a tone of stateliness and gallantry. The correct line is:
'le commerce rampant de soupirs et de flammes'.

Southerne, Thomas (1660-1746): Engl. playwright. Wr. *The Fatal Marriage*, 1694, and *Oroonoko* (against the slave-trade), 1696, which achieved lasting success.

Southey, -i. Robert (1774-1843): Engl. poet and misc. writer; poet-laureate (q.v.), 1813, when the appointment was declined by sir W. Scott (q.v.); edu. Westminster, from which he was expelled for protesting against flogging (in *The Flagellant*, a school publication, 9 parts, March and April, 1792, esp. part 5), and Balliol coll., Oxford, where he made acquaintance with S. T. Coleridge (q.v.), to whom he owed much more than he gave; m. Edith (d., 1837), one of the 3 Fricker sisters at Bristol, another of whom was Mrs. Coleridge, and joined his brothers-in-law in their dream of a state of equal liberties on the Susquehanna (see s.v. Coleridge); travelled in Spain and Portugal, and wr. romantic-epic tales in fulfilment of his ambition to 'render every mythology the basis of a narrative poem'. Since he possessed a keen sense of colour and a power of telling a story, these tales, though little read to-day, have more merit than their neglect suggests; in order of publication, we may note: *The Fall of Robespierre: a Drama*, act i by Coleridge, acts ii and iii by S., 1794; *Joan of Arc*, epic, 1798; *Thalaba* (Arabia), metrical romance, 1801; *Madoc* (Paraguay), 1805; *Curse of Kehama* (India), 1810; *Roderick, the Last of the Goths*, 1814 (Bilderdijk, q.v., transld. this romance into Dutch, 1823-4). Others vols. of poetry followed; but we may quote prof. Vaughan (*P.E.L.*, x, 77) to the effect, that 'the merits of these poems naturally carry with them the corresponding defects. They are too long; the sentiment is often obvious, sometimes misplaced; the colour is not seldom laid on too thick. The poet, in fact, is throughout too much of the showman, deliberately manipulating his resources so that no single effect shall be lost upon the spectators'. Among his shorter poems may be mentioned, for the sake partly of a fading reputation, *Lodore, The Old Woman of Berkeley* and the *March to Moscow*. S. wr., too, some prose-works of outstanding value, esp. a *Life of Nelson*, 1813 (and frequently reprinted) and *History of the Peninsular War*, 3 vols., 1823-32. He edited the works of Chatterton (q.v.), and was particularly kind, and in a position to be kind, to poets less happily circumstanced than he: his vol. of verses by John Jones, a servant (*Attempts in Verse*, 1831) has recently been republd. by Mr. Humphrey Milford as *The Lives and Works of the Uneducated Poets*, an essay which formed S.'s introduction to the 1831 vol., and it is eloquent of the big poet's charity to his humble brethren. S., too, was a very competent translr.: he brought home from his early travels, not only the history of the Peninsular war, but a transln. of the *Cid* (q.v.), 1808, and versions of *Amadis* (q.v.) and *Palmerin*; and his letters, too, possess considerable interest.

-ii. Caroline Anne (1786-1854): Engl. poet; *née* Bowles; m., R.S. (above) as his second wife, 1839, at the close of a long friendship and correspondence. R.S. had encouraged her facility in writing narrative verse: *The Widow's Tale*, 1822, etc.

Spagnolo, J. P. See s.v. **Mantuan.**

Spanish Literature: The effective history of Span. lit. is contained between the years 1492 and 1700. 1492 is the simultaneous date of the capture of Granada and the overthrow of the

Moors in Spain under the Catholic sovereigns, Ferdinand and Isabella; of the quickening of national and religious sentiment by the expulsion of the Jews (Spain's deep debt to Moorish and Hebrew culture is not immediately in question); and of the discovery of America by Columbus. 1700 is the date of the death of king Charles ii, the last of the Habsburg monarchs, and of the accession of the duke of Anjou, grandson of king Louis xiv of France, as king Philip v of Spain, in the diminished dignity of which title he was confirmed by the treaty of Utrecht, 1713, after the War of the Span. Succession. Note that king Alfonso v of Aragon (uncle to Ferdinand the Catholic) had become Alfonso i of Naples by conquest in 1443, thus supplying a source for the Italian influence which was poured into Span. lit. at the turn of the 15th-16th cent. Thenceforward, to the beginning of the 18th cent., when Fr. influence entered with the Fr. king, and a brand-new Span. Academy was founded, 1714, on the model of the *Académie française*, there is unfolded a roll of great writers who accompied and enhanced the imperial glory which was Spain.

Before examining more closely this period of 200 years, with its preliminary 50 years' apprenticeship to Neapolitan culture, something must be said of the lit. prior to the close of the 15th cent. It is not necessary to go back to the successive conquests of the Peninsula by the Romans, the Goths, and the Arabs; nor exactly to evaluate the Span. contribution of Seneca (q.v.), Lucan, Martial and Quintilian to the Silver Age of Latinity. Gothic Spain (460-711 A.D.) likewise left marks on the country; and deeper and more permanent marks were scored by the Moorish conquerors, and by the Hebr. doctors who accepted their domination. We might recall the famous names of Ibn Gabirol (Avicebron), of Ibn Roshd (Averroes), and of Moses ben Maimon (Maimonides), among the teachers and forerunners of Duns Scotus, Aquinas, and the Scholastic philosophers in general (see s.vv.). But, important though the individuals were, it is legitimate in a brief survey of the harvest of Span. lit., as distinct from its seedtime, to remark how much more important was the inspiration of the early epochs than their achievement. The legends of the wars against the Moors, the contact with Arab civilization, the fighting tradition of the past, and the unity of aim between the Church and the State, were a few features of those stirring centuries; and their experiences bit very deeply into the consciousness of literary and artistic Spain. The Spaniard of the golden age was what his forefather had made him: a devout Catholic, an adventurous warrior, and a proud and an ardent patriot. His triumph, when it came, was a heady matter. Internally, his country was unified by the joint reign of Isabella of Castile (1474-1504) and Ferdinand of Aragon (1479-1516); externally, it presented a united front by its expulsion of alien elements in the name of the holy mother church. But no treatment, however harsh, of its ancient Moorish foe could eradicate Arab science and philosophy, or Eastern folk- and aphoristic lore, from the civilization of Spain;

and no persecution, however rigid, could expel Jew. blood from Span. veins. Frequently, the jealous eye of prejudice, seeing evenly with the lynx eye of the Inquisition, detected the strain of Hebr. orig. in one or another Span. author; and imputed as blame what was properly reputable as fame. Thus, the author of *Celestina* (q.v.), the prototype of modern realistic fiction, was probably of Jew. descent, to name one instance among many; and generally it may be said that the swift decline of Span. letters after the cardinal year 1700 was due in large part at least to the illusions fostered by Church and State during the preceding centuries: Cervantes' *Don Quixote*, for example, is from one point of view a line-upon-line manifesto against the illusion of chivalry. It would be relevant to inquire at this point if the policy of the Inquisition towards Span. lit. was positively repressive, or if it was a more or less accurate expression of what Spaniards wanted; if they got the lit. that they deserved, in other words; and if the sufferings of Ponce de Leon (q.v., himself of suspected Hebr. orig.) and other pious men at the hands of the Holy Office, and the all-devouring Index itself, were with or against the consent of the true conscience of Spain. But it would be difficult, if not impossible, to frame an exact conclusion to such inquiry; and we must be content to register the general statement hazarded above.*

The chief literary monument of early Span. lit. is the *Poema del Cid* of the 12th cent.: a *chanson de geste* in celebration of Ruy (Rodriguez) Dias de Bivar, of the 11th cent., *el Cid* (= seyd = lord) *Campeador* (= a champion), hero of the siege of Valencia, 1092-94; in his lifetime, a formidable foeman on the side of Spain against the Arabs; after his death, a symbol of the victory of patriotism and Christianity against their enemies; and, we may add, after his apotheosis, a type of the 'will to power', as delineated on the tragic stage of Corneille. This epopee, doubtless surviving as the last and fittest of earlier exercises, is composed in the Castilian romance-dialect and in the spirit of Castile, which were to become the Span. language and the Span. national spirit, in ascendancy over the co-existing dialects, Gallician and Asturian (the Catalan language is distinct in the independent lit. of Catalonia); in the same way that the dialect of the Île de France became the Fr. language in ascendancy over Limousin, etc. (See s.v. Fr. lit.).

The chivalric legends of the Cid were reinforced by the composition of songs and chronicles. One of the most important of the latter, by its contents and example, was

* The above paragraph was written before the publication of *Luis de Leon: A Study of the Spanish Renaissance*, by Aubrey F. G. Bell, a leading authority on the lit. of the Peninsula (Oxford, 1925). The Intro. to this work should be consulted, esp. § ii, 'Spain and the Reformation'; but it is difficult to concur with the author's conclusion: 'The effect of the Inquisition was thus, at least to some minds, not repression of thought but the utmost freedom in its expression' (unless he is referring to the minds of the Inquisitors), or to accept his special plea that, 'apart from a few Hebrew scholars, it would be difficult to give a single name of a well-known man of letters or science who suffered seriously at the hands of the Spanish Inquisition' (p. 56).

conditions of life will supply out of their realized resources the magnificent inspiration which was drawn from the enterprise of the State and the majesty of the Church. There are still giants in the path for another Don Quixote to slay, still illusions for the intellect to prick, still castles for the imagination to build. Two centuries of comparative silence may prove the ample preparation for a fresh epoch of world-literature on the classic soil of noble Spain.

Spasmodic Poets (Engl.): Nickname invented by W. E. Aytoun (q.v.) in *Firmilian, A Spasmodic Tragedy*, 1854, to characterize a group of poets, among whom the chief offenders were S. Dobell and Alex. Smith (qq.v.). P. J. Bailey (q.v.) is commonly included in their company, but his style was not spasmodic. What Aytoun condemned, we are told, ' was the confusion and inequality and extravagance of their work, its passion piled on passion, its thought disjointed from thought, the rant and fustian of the style, the lavishly sprinkled and over-wrought metaphors ' (Walker, *Lit, Victorian Era*, 513), and the description can hardly be bettered. There is a certain unreality and difficult straining after effect in the writings of these poets, which should not obstruct appreciation of their genuine worth, and *Firmilian*, unlike less kindly parodies, was not designed for such obstruction. It is pointed out that Tennyson's (q.v.) *Maud* would be spasmodic, if that name were not a nickname.

Spedding, James (1808-81): Engl. biographer; close friend of Carlyle, E. Fitzgerald, Tennyson (qq.v.) and others; edited the *Works* (7 vols., 1857-9) of F. Bacon (q.v.), and publd. his *Life and Letters*, 7 vols., 1861-74.

Spee, von, Friedrich (1591-1635): Germ. sacred lyrist; Jesuit; count (*Graf*) by rank. His religious poetry, collected under the title of *Trutz-Nachtigal* (*i.q.*, Bar-Nightingale, ' because ', as he wr., ' despite all nightingales its note is sweet and comely '), is of a high order of piety and poetic craft; and, though S. was not acquainted with the new gospel of poetry according to Opitz (q.v.), he was likewise moved by Renaissance models to aim at artistic versification. His main fault was a defect of this quality of foreign culture; in his eclogues and pastorals he transferred with frigid effect the scenery and persons of pagan mythology to the ritual and spirit of Christian worship. But his work was full of promise in a bleak time.

Speed, John (*c*. 1552-1629): Engl. cartographer; historian. Wr. a *History of Great Britain*, 1611, and publd. valuable maps of county and larger areas. S.'s tastes were clearly defined, and, though brought up to the tailoring trade, he became the friend and equal of antiquaries such as sir Henry Spelman (d. 1641) and others. Wr., too, *A Cloud of Witnesses, confirming . . . the Truth of God's most holie Worde*, 1616.

Spence, Joseph (1699-1768): Engl. scholar; prof. of Poetry at Oxford, 1728, in succession to T. Warton (q.v.). Wr. an essay on Pope's (q.v.) transln. of the *Odyssey*, which introduced him to the poet, whose circle he frequented. S. compiled notes of the conversation at Pope's villa, and his anecdotes were known

to and used by Johnson (q.v.) and other biographers. They were publd., 1820, as Spence's *Anecdotes*, and form a permanent record of the literary intimacies of the 18th cent.

Spener, Jakob (1635-1705): Germ. pietist; was preacher successively in Dresden and Berlin, and assisted in the foundation of Halle univ. Wr., 1675, *Pia desideria*, or ' The heart's longing for the blessed improvement of the evangelical church '. The aim of S. and of the pietistic movement in Germany, as a whole (see s.v. Pietism), was to bring out the best elements from the results of the Reformation, and to let the Thirty Years' War bury its dead.

Spenser, Edmund (*c*. 1552-99): Engl. poet; it may be recalled that Tasso's (q.v.) dates were 1554-95, and that Shakespeare (q.v.) was born in 1564. By contemporaneousness, accordingly, S. belonged exactly to the period of the Renaissance (q.v.) in Europe; and, almost more than any other Engl. poet, he acclimatized its fruits in his own country. Lamb (q.v.) called him the poets' poet, and this epithet, like many another from the same mint, has been proved by experience; Keats (q.v.), for example, was essentially Spenserian; he went through the *Faerie Queen* ' as a young horse through a spring meadow, ramping '. True, in his sonnet, *On sitting down to read ' King Lear '* again, Keats recanted his loyalty to S.

O golden-tongued Romance with serene lute ! . . .

Shut up thine olden pages, and be mute,

he bade S., in the near presence of a greater master. But he had passed through his apprenticeship to the poets' poet, and was destined to hand on what he had learned to the Pre-Raphaelite Brotherhood and to Tennyson (see s.vv.). We omit from this record the signs of more formal, or technical, Spenserianism which occurred in the 17th and 18th cents., and which provoked the warning of Dr. Johnson (q.v.), in no. 121 of his *Rambler*, ' On the Dangers of Imitation, and the Impropriety of imitating Spenser '. This kind of imitation was confined to the Spenserian stanza, and to S.'s taste for archaic Engl. diction, which, while wholly appropriate to his own search for native words in lieu of aureate Latinisms (see s.v. Latin), became redolent of Wardour Street, when selected at second-hand, as in Shenstone's *School-mistress*, e.g. (see also s.vv. Beattie, Croxall; the whole topic of technical Spenserianism is discussed, with novel ingenuity, by Dr. Harko G. de Maar, *Hist. of Modern Engl. Romanticism*, i; Oxford, 1924. On S., generally, reference should be made to Courthope, *Hist. Engl. Poetry*, ii, ch. ix, and *C.H.E.L.*, iii, ch. xi, by the same author; to R. W. Church, *Spenser*, ' English Men of Letters ', 1879; to sir S. Lee, *Great Englishmen of the 16th Cent.*, ch. v; and to *Edmund Spenser: An Essay on Renaissance Poetry*, by prof. W. L. Renwick, 1925). There is more than ample meaning in Lamb's epithet for S., without examining the debased Spenserianism of partly or wholly burlesque-poets, or even the imitative allegories of a poet like

James Thomson (q.v.), who stated, in his advertisement to *The Castle of Indolence*, 1748 (an exquisitely melodious poem), that ' this poem, being writ in the manner of Spenser, the obsolete words, and a simplicity of diction in some of the lines, which borders on the ludicrous, were necessary to make the imitation more perfect '. It is not from deliberate exercises of this kind, significant of S.'s influence though they are, that he earned the title of poets' poet. It belongs to him as much for the sake of the older poets who made him as for that of the younger poets whom he made, esp. in the 19th cent. He was a poets' poet, not merely because he was to serve as a model to poets to be, but because his own poetry was founded on past models. He learned from Richard Mulcaster, his headmaster (at Merchant Taylors', 1561-86 ; highmaster of St. Paul's, 1596-1608 ; d., 1611) ' the theory of the new poetry : to cultivate the mother tongue by the importation of the best learning and the imitation of the best models, wherever these were to be found. The Italians saw that the Romans had drawn from the Greeks ; the French, that the Italians had drawn from Greeks and Romans ; the English, that the French had drawn from Greeks, Romans and Italians ' (Renwick, *op. cit.*, 30) ; and, plainly, S. might draw from the Fr., Ital., Gk. and Roman, and might build on these foundations an adequate poetry in his mother-tongue, For it was the mother-tongue which was his chief care : ' so we find him setting out, with an academic solemnity which it would be crude to call pedantic and stupid to dislike—setting out not only as a disciple, but challenging, to prove his mother-tongue capable and himself a master ' (*ib.*, 33).

This, is, summarily, the whole of S. He was always a bookish poet. Though, like Ariosto (q.v.) at Garfagnana, S. spent part of his life in a provincial governorship in Ireland, where his castle at Kilcolman was fired by rebels in 1598, ' he differed from the great European poets who preceded or immediately succeeded him, in that he made no attempt to represent in his verse the dominant moving spirit in the world about him '. He made an attempt, very brilliantly successful, to create the utterance of his country's poetic lips. ' Had we *The English Poet* ', says prof. Renwick (*op. cit*, 93), ' the critical treatise which Spenser wrote before he published *The Shepheardes Calender*, we should probably find, under the heading of Elocution, a theory of linguistic development equivalent to that of the Pléiade ' (s.v. Pleiad) ; and, apart from probabilities, we know that the method of S. was that of a close student of letters, resolute to wrest from the noblest models the matters and manner of great Engl. poetry. ' Almost as a schoolboy he began to translate into English the poetry of France ', as Chaucer (q.v.), his master, had done before him. ' Before he went to Cambridge he prepared for a London publisher metrical translations of poems by Du Bellay, and he also rendered into seven English sonnets an ode of Petrarch from the version of Clement Marot ' (sir S. Lee, *op. cit.*, 160 ; see s.vv.). And he went beyond transln. ; he assimilated. In his epistle to G. Harvey (q.v.), dedicating the eclogues of the *Shepherd's Calendar*, S. wr. : ' So flew Theocritus, as you may perceive he was already full fledged. So flew Virgil, as not yet well feeling his wings. So flew Mantuan, as not being full somd. So Petrarque. So Boccace. So Marot, Sanazarus, and also divers other excellent both Italian and French poets. . . . So finally flyeth this our new Poet, as a bird whose principals be scarce grown out, but yet as one that in time shall be able to keep wing with the best '. And, though Harvey, in his lonely Areopagus (q.v.), objected that S. had been too bold in anglicizing the shepherds of Theocritus, Virgil and Sannazzaro (qq.v.), yet S. persevered on his way of assimilation and reproduction. His function was always that of the new poet, the poet destined to create utterance ; and having tried his wings, like Virgil, on a flight over *pascua, rura*, he reserved his mature power for *duçes* :

Lo ! I, the man whose Muse whilom did mask,*
As time her taught, in lowly Shepherd's
    weeds,
Am now enforced, a far unfitter task,
For trumpets stern to change mine oaten
    reeds,
And sing of Knights' and Ladies' gentle deeds ;
Whose praises have slept in silence long,
Me, all too mean, the sacred Muse areeds
To blazon broad amongst her learned throng :
Fierce wars and faithful loves shall moralize
    my song.

The Faerie Queen : Proem, i.

Thus, S. consciously conformed with the precepts of the treatises on poetics, in which Ital. and Fr. critics had expounded, for the information of new poets, the whole practice and theory of the ancients. He went, like his masters, from pastoral to epic verse, and his sole departure was to ' moralize ' his theme for the edification of the court of Gloriana (queen Elizabeth). So, in a dedicatory epistle to sir Walter Ralegh (q.v.), prefixed to *The Faerie Queen*, S. wr., in the same sense as to Harvey : ' The general end of all the book is to fashion a gentleman or noble person in vertuous and gentle discipline ' : Castiglione's (q.v.) end, it will be observed, and the general end of the movement known as the Renaissance. ' In which ', he went on, ' I have followed all the antique Poets historical ', among whom he mentions by name Homer, Virgil, Ariosto and Tasso.

It is not fanciful to suggest, though the scale of this art. compels us merely to throw out the suggestion, that the true analogue of S., by comparison with whom his place in lit. is most fully to be understood, is not Chaucer, Ariosto, or another, but the statesman, Machiavelli (q.v.). We are not discussing moral principles or æsthetic achievements : S. was a puritan, Machiavelli was—Machiavellian ; but in aim and purpose and object, the 2 men were moved by one idea. *Il Principe* was the prince to be, the ruler adapted out of old models to the conditions of new times, as S. was deliberately and consciously the new poet, expressing in the language of the present the qualities deposited in the past.

* ' As not yet well feeling his wings ' (*supra*).

33

Each sought to found the discipline of *virtue*, —the essential Renaissance idea ; and poetry, to S., like statecraft to Machiavelli, was not merely a profession, but a passion. ' All his energy ', says prof. Renwick (*op. cit.*, 182), ' was transformed into poetry '. His ' faith in the native land and the mother tongue was but an aspect of the larger faith in poetry. He wrought for the future, in the faith that devotion would be rewarded with immortal fame ' :

For deeds do die, however nobly done,
And thoughts of men do, as themselves, decay ;
But wise words, taught in numbers for to run,
Recorded by the Muses, live for aye.
The Ruines of Time.

We must break off here, with a brief list of the titles and dates of S.'s chief works. These comprised : *The Shepheardes Calender* (12 eclogues for the 12 months), 1579 ; *The Faerie Queene Disposed into twelve Books fashioning xii Morall Virtues*, books i, ii, iii, 1590 (1589) ; books iv, v, vi, 1598 (the last 6 books were not completed) ; *Complaints* (minor poems), 1591 ; *Amoretti and Epithalamion* (love-sonnets, q.v., and marriage-hymn), 1595 ; *Colin Clouts Come Home Againe* (including *Astrophel*, S.'s lament for sir Philip Sidney, q.v.), 1595, and *Foure Hymnes*, 1596. Mention is likewise due to S.'s prose *View of the State of Ireland*, written in 1596, *ed. pr.*, 1633.

Speroni, Sperone (1500-88) : It. critic ; playwright. Wr. *Dialogo delle Lingue*, 1543, mainly concerned with poetic diction, in which Bembo (q.v.) and others were represented as interlocutors. The dialogue, followed by similar treatises by Minturno and Castelvetro (qq.v.), was instrumental in recommending the use of the vernacular speech in place of Lat., and was transferred to the armoury of Du Bellay and the Pleiad (see s.vv.) in France.

Spieghel, Henrik Laurens (1549-1612) : Dutch poet ; leading member of the Eglantine (q.v.), and valued host of the younger writers.

Spielhagen, Friedrich (1829-1911) : Germ. novelist, the direct successor of Gutzkow (q.v.) in fiction. Wr., 1860, *Problematische Naturen*, with its title taken from Goethe's aphorism : ' There are problematical natures, never suited to any environment in life, and satisfied with none ' ; *In Reih' und Glied*, 1866, with its hero (like Meredith's, q.v., in *The Tragic Comedian*) modelled on the social reformer, F. Lassalle ; *Sturmflut*, 1876, and many more. S. was a novelist with a purpose, which fitted in with the social movements of his day, and he belongs to the same class of writers as Mrs. Gaskell (q.v.), for example, in her *Sylvia's Lovers*, 1863 : the background of industrial unrest is the same.

Spinoza, Benedict (Baruch) (1632-77) : Dutch philosopher ; of Jew. parentage and Port. extraction ; his grandfather, Abraham d'Espinosa, merchant, left Oporto for Amsterdam, 1593, fleeing from religious persecution, bringing with him his son, Michael, whose second wife (d., 1638) became the mother of B.S. He was edu. at a Hebr. school, where one of his teachers was rabbi Manasseh ben Israel, later (1655) delegate to Cromwell as to the re-admission of Jews into Engld. Grotius (q.v.), the

jurist, and Rembrandt, the painter, were among the friends of his boyhood, and it may be noted that S. was born in the same year as J. Locke (q.v.). Span. and Port. were the common languages of his home, and S. knew but little Dutch. A much more serious matter was his difficulty in learning Lat., which the Jews of that period disliked on account of its associations with the R.C. Church. S. contrived to get lessons from an ex-Jesuit physician, and these studies, which his tutor extended into the realm of modern philosophy, including Descartes (q.v. ; d., 1650) proved his undoing in his own religious community. On the death of Michael S., 1654, B.S. practised the trade of a grinder of lenses, which led Heine (q.v. ; himself a Jew) to remark at a later date : ' All our modern philosophers, though often perhaps unconsciously, see through the glasses which Baruch Spinoza ground '. In 1566, after 2 years' independence, S. found himself still less in sympathy with the habits of the little refugee community, which, in turn, was anxious to dissociate itself from the scandal of including a free-thinker in its fold. On 27 July in that year, the authorities of the Synagogue at Amsterdam pronounced the ban of excommunication on S. in a very complete form, and from that day, as M. Arnold (q.v. ; he quotes the terms of the ban) wr., ' they remained children of Israel, and he became a child of modern Europe ' (*Essays in Criticism*, i ; ' Spinoza and the Bible '). Dr. A. Wolf, in his *Life* (A. and C. Black, 1910), remarks acutely that, ' if Judaism alone had been concerned, the whole thing might have been ignored ', and that the action of the Synagogue was intended to impress the civil authorities quite as much as to expel S. : ' The ban against Spinoza was the due paid to Cæsar rather than to the God of Israel '. However this may be, his harsh experience (he took to grinding lenses at Ouwerkerke) led the young philosopher ' to inquire whether there was anything which was truly good, and which could be communicated, and by which alone, everything else being set aside, the mind might be affected ' ; and this search for the *summum bonum* occupied the rest of his too short life : in his *Tractatus Theologico-politicus*, 1670, his *Ethica* and *Tractatus Politicus* (unfind.), posth., 1677, and other writings and letters. The contents of S.'s philosophy must be sought from more special sources ; e.g. from *Spinoza : His Life and Philosophy*, by sir F. Pollock, bt. (second edn., 1899), from *Benedict Spinoza*, by prof. Alex. Gunn (Melbourne Univ. Press, 1925), or from Auerbach's (q.v.) novel, called after S., or from Renan's (q.v.) bicentenary address, delivered at The Hague, 1877, and re-issued in his *Nouvelles Etudes* (Paris, 1884), or, more briefly, from ' The Maker of Lenses ', in *Dreamers of the Ghetto*, by I. Zangwill (Heinemann, 1898). Translrs., editors, and commentators have been busy with S. for nearly 3 cents., and modern Spinoza-study may be dated from Lessing, Mendelssohn and Jacobi (see s.vv.), 1780. Goethe and Hegel (qq.v.) continued the study in Germany ; Coleridge (q.v.) transported it to Engld., and discussed it with Wordsworth (q.v.), as we learn from the droll anecdote of the (Fr.) spy-mania at the time of the Revolution, when the friends were overheard, ' behind a bank at the seaside (our favourite seat) ' in Somersetshire, talking of ' one *Spy Nozy* ' (Spinoza), and fell under grave suspicion accordingly ! (See Coleridge, *Biog. Literaria*, ch. x). Shelley (q.v.) began a transln. of the *Tractatus Theo.-Pol.*, and Byron (q.v.) was to have written a pref. to it, but the plan was interrupted by Shelley's death. A bronze statue of S. was unveiled at The Hague, 14 Sept., 1880, and ' the names of men illustrious in philosophy and literature in England, France, and Germany, men otherwise separated from one another in their occupation, pursuits, and beliefs, were inscribed side by side on the roll of supporters. Thus he would have desired to be commemorated. . . . Wealth in vital ideas is the real test of a philosopher's greatness, and by this test the name of Spinoza stands assured of its rank among the greatest ' (sir F. Pollock, *op. cit.*, 381).

Spitteler, Carl (1845-1924) : Swiss poet ; awarded Nobel prize for lit., 1919. S. was a late offshoot of the Ital. Renaissance (q.v.), and his great work, his diploma-piece, as it may be called, *Prometheus and Epimetheus*, 1881, was designed in the gorgeous colours and on the large canvas of Ariosto (q.v.). He practised journalism and novel-writing, but was fortunate in having sufficient means to be free to devote himself to poetry, even though its recognition was long delayed. One novel, *Lieutenant Conrad*, became popular in Switzld., but S.'s fame rests securely on his epic poem in 5 bks., *der Olympische Frühling* (' Spring on Olympus '), in which, in the words of prof. J. G. Robertson, ' once again after a long span of time, we have in European literature an epic in the noble style, and moreover, an epic of the gods of Greece. Transformed, transfigured, rejuvenated, these old gods pass once more across the stage of Western Europe ; once more the marble museum gods of classic learning, the shadow gods who had faded before Heine's bleeding Nazarene are forgotten : the old Olympians come back into our world in radiant, buoyant life '.

Sprat, Thomas (1635-1713) : Engl. divine ; bp. of Rochester, 1684 ; one of the founders of the Royal Society, whose history he wr., 1667 : fellowship of the R.S., he said, entailed ' a close, naked, natural way of speaking ; positive expressions ; clear senses ; a native easiness ; bringing all things as near the mathematical plainness as they can '. S.'s own sermons illustrated these qualities of prose style, which introduced a harder and a firmer pattern, more akin to contemporary Fr. example, into the decaying colours of Elizabethan gorgeousness.

Staal, de, Marguerite Jeanne (1684-1750) : Fr. memoirist ; *née* Cordier, but was known by her mother's maiden name as mlle. Delaunay ; m. baron de Staal, 1735. Mme. de S. was, briefly, the St.-Simon (q.v.) of Sceaux (q.v.) ; in other words, she composed the memoirs (*Mémoires*, 1755) of the ' court ' of the duchesse de Maine (q.v.), where the duc de Maine, the illegitimate son of king Louis xiv, was the nominal head of the ' party of the bastards ', in opposition to the court of the duc d'Orleans, regent of France during Louis xv's minority, of which S.-Simon was the chronicler. Mme. de S., whose devotion to the Sceaux faction earned her 2 years' imprisonment in the Bastile, wr. a vivid and valuable account of her times.

Staël, de, Anne Louise Germaine (1766-1817) : Fr. critic and novelist ; romanticist (see s.v. Romance) ; *née* Necker (q.v., and see s.v. Gibbon ; it is a pardonable confusion to say, with a writer in *The Times Lit. Supp.*, 12 Feb., 1925, that mme. de S. ' might have been Gibbon's daughter ') ; m., i, 1786, the baron de Staël-Holstein, Swed. ambassador at Paris ; ii, monsieur de Rocca, a man much younger than herself ; is always known by her first husband's style and name. Her mother had intended her to marry Wm. Pitt (1759-1806), son of the earl of Chatham, but she rebelled, and ' to marry M. de Staël was the nearest possible approach to marrying no one ' (*Times, ib.*). She was the more free for love and passion, and the Comte de Narbonne preceded B. Constant (q.v.) in her attachments. Introduced at her parents' house and in her mother's *salon* to the most progressive and intellectual society in Paris, on the eve of the Revolution, mme. de S. greeted its advent with delight, and made her own *salon* a meeting-place for the supporters of a political constitution *à l'anglaise*. From 1792 to 1795, she was obliged to seek refuge at Coppet, on the lake of Geneva, where her child (Narbonne's son) was born. She paid a visit, too, to Engld., mingling with the Fr. refugees at Juniper Hall ; but she returned to Paris after the Terror, and re-opened her *salon*, where she received Constant and Chénier, and other distinguished leaders of thought. A fresh term of exile at Coppet intervened, and ' by the waters of Leman she sat down and wept ', and wr. her book, *de l'Influence des Passions*. Whether inspired by Narbonne or Constant, it was to Constant's arms and his associates that at last she returned to Paris, where her house became the centre of an anti-Bonapartist cabal. In Oct., 1802, she had to quit France. She visited Germany and Italy, finally settling again at Coppet, where friends came to her from all quarters. In 1807, she again visited Germany, and in 1810 was placed under stricter surveillance by Napoleon's orders, and was forbidden to receive her friends. Two years later, she escaped to Petrograd, and went on to Sweden and Engld. After the fall of the Fr. Empire, she returned to Paris, where she died. We may quote *The Times* art. again for a graphic account of the 16 years with Constant, during which ' the ill-assorted lovers astonished Europe by the varied pageant of their broken hearts. Like the pagan poet and his mistress, each found it impossible to live with—or without—the other '. But Lesbia in this instance was even more vocal and lyrical than her Catullus.

Mme. de S. would have been a great writer in any age ; in the times in which she lived, she was enabled to wield immense influence. She was essentially a daughter of the Paris *salons* ; wherever she went, she created that atmosphere ; and, herself a brilliant talker,

she preferred the conversation of a clever man
to the view of Vesuvius and the bay of Naples.
In possession of these innate faculties, she
was readily amenable to cosmopolitan
experience, and hence was peculiarly fitted to
derive the best and the most from her surroundings in Germany and other countries.
Further, the *salon* atmosphere in the last years
of the 18th cent. was a political atmosphere,
and the daughter of Necker and his wife was
versed in politics from childhood. Of all the
clever women who took part (so often, a fatal
part) in the transition from Fr. political
idealism to Fr. political experiment in the
Revolution and the Empire, mme. de S. was
one of the cleverest and of the foremost.
She combined the worldly common-sense
of Voltaire (q.v.) with Rousseau's (q.v.)
love of ideas; and her romantic proclivity,
which found personal expression in her foolish
but happy second marriage, was fed by her
literary appreciation of Goethe's *Werther* in
her youth and of Scott's poems and novels in
later life. Both tastes—the moral in politics,
and the romantic in morals—were satisfied
by the writings of Kant (q.v.), of whose
thought she was a lucid and brilliant exponent.
Mme. de S.'s writings include: *Sur la Paix
intérieure*, 1795 (political); *de l'Influence
des Passions sur le Bonheur des Individus et
des Nations*, 1796 (Rousseauan); *de la
Littérature considerée dans ses rapports avec
les constitutions sociales*, 1800 (year 8); *Delphine*, 1802, *Corinne*, 1807 (novels); *de
l'Allemagne* (1810, edn. destroyed by order of
the Fr. police; publd., London, 1813); *Considérations sur la Révolution Française* and
Dix Années d'Exil (posth., 1818, 1821). Of
these, the most significant are, i, the treatise
on lit. and social institutions, ii, the 2 novels,
iii, the vol. on Germany, and, iv, the considerations of the Fr. Revolution. We shall
discuss them briefly according to their subjects.
Taking (i) and (iii) together, mme. de S.,
with a conspicuous originality which looked
back to the researches of Montesquieu (q.v.)
and others on climatic and other influences on
national character, argued that the value of
lit. is to be measured by its increasing
perfection, according to certain standards of
liberty, glory, virtue. This theory of perfectibility, which is the keystone of the arch of
her critical doctrine, has been praised and
assailed by different schools of thought.
Briefly, we may say that prof. Saintsbury,
whom no gleaner in the vast plains of European lit. can mention without honour and
respect, is at the head of the opponents, and
Taine (q.v.) of the supporters of the theory.
It is our business here to explain it, not to
judge it. Plainly, it proceeds from the
mental attitude of the *philosophes* (q.v.),
and conceals the danger inherent in *à priori*
views of mistaking proof for fact and of fitting
evidence to the verdict. To evaluate literary
productions by their progressive conformity
to standards of moral or social perfection
is to risk confutation by the facts of history;
and mme. de S.'s 'gradual march of the human
spirit' (*l'esprit humain* was always marching
in the 18th cent.) might be pulled up short by
the vision of some stray spirit of antiquity far

in advance of modern attainment. We are
back here at the old dispute of the Ancients
and Moderns (q.v.), and at the old jump over
the Middle Ages. Christianity, according to
mme. de S., marks a forward movement from
Attic perfection to the greater perfection of the
age of Louis xiv; but Christianity in this
scheme leaps its medieval activities. Here
we must leave the argument: it may be
remarked, however, that mme. de S. was the
first to follow, to whatever dubious goals, the
critical sign posts in the field which she
investigated. Her study of 'social constitutions' led her to her brilliant differentiation between national, and even racial, types;
and especially to the distinction between
the literatures *du Midi* (of the South) and *du
Nord* (of the North): Homer, on one side,
with the Gks., Romans, Italians, Span.,
and 17th cent. France; and, on the other side,
Engld., Germany, Scandinavia. Here, too, the
theory is countered by the facts that Dante,
the stern moralist, was Ital., and that *Romeo
and Juliet*, the drama of southern passion,
was an Engl. play; but here, again, the
exceptions do not disprove the rule, so long
as we recognize that such 'rules', like those
of grammar itself, are merely generalizations
from experience, and cannot bind human
practice. They are extraordinarily serviceable
and illuminating in the study of facts, which,
without such aids, is likely to be incoherent
and indeterminate. From these preliminary researches, mme. de S. proceeded in (iii),
the special study of Germany, 1810, to apply
her principles to a northern lit., and to evaluate
it as a foreigner for her own people. She
discussed in this great work 'Germany and
the manners (*moeurs*) of the Germans', 'Literature and the Arts', 'Philosophy and Morals',
and 'Religion and Enthusiasm'; reaching,
in the last two divisions, the foundations of
what is called romantic criticism (s.v. Romance),
and discovering that the *Nord* is romantic and
the *Midi* classical by disposition and descent.
'Romantic literature alone', she wr., 'is
still capable of perfectibility (*d'être perfectionée*),
because, having its roots in our own soil, it
alone can grow and gain fresh vigour; it
expresses our religion; it recalls our past;
it avails itself of our personal impressions by
which to stir our emotions'. Theory or no
theory, this perception is profoundly true,
and mme. de S.'s *Allemagne*, with its immense
debt to A. W. Schlegel (q.v.), her guide,
philosopher and friend in Germany, is one of
the pivotal works of criticism in lit. At the time
of its appearance, as we have shown, the Fr.
imperial authorities impounded it, and it was
first publd. in Engld.; it did not suit Napoleon's
supremacy to encourage comparative studies
of national powers and performances. We
may mention, as contemporary evidence to
mme. de S.'s influence in Engld., a remark
in the *Quarterly Review*, Oct., 1814, with
reference to the new distinction between
classic and romantic: 'Mme. de Staël has
made the British public familiar with these
expressions'.

Passing to (iv), we have to remark that mme.
de S. learned her politics and her religion in
Germany, and even became a disciple of

Rousseau through the discipleship of the Germ. writers whom she taught her countrymen to appreciate. Her own transition from Voltaire to Chateaubriand (qq.v.), from 1778 to 1830, was across the bridge built by Schiller, Kant and Goethe ; and it has been acutely said that mme. de S.'s Germany was arrested at a brief moment of activity : it was the Germany of the Liberation (1814), not of Fredk. the Great nor of Bismarck. As a novelist (ii), mme. de S. has herself been famous as 'Corinne'. Her heroines are the spiritual daughters of la nouvelle Héloïse (s.v. Rousseau), and are types of their author's love of love, as displayed in her relations with Narbonne, Constant and her second husband. The novels are admirable in their descriptive matter, esp. in their Ital. scenes, and they introduced into fiction the new character of the femme incomprise (q.v.). Her brilliant wit and originality will always command admiration, and it is well to remember, with prof. Vaughan (P.E.L., x, 417), that 'still more important is the debt that France owes to her openness of mind, to the zeal with which she strove to break down the "Chinese wall", which, as she complains, had been built up between France and the rest of Europe'.

Stagnelius, Erik Johan (1793-1823): Swed. poet. His collected works were publd. at Stockholm, 1824-26, and the young poet has been compared with Shelley (q.v.) in more than the fate of short life. Like Shelley, he was moved by the spirit of the generation of revolutionary romance, and commanded brilliant powers of lyrical expression. His physical weakness compelled an intellectual seclusion, which led to a vein of melancholy and mysticism in his poetry ; but, apart from his dramatic experiments, which were not successful, S. gave ample promise (and some performance) of high gifts and deep thought.

Stanhope, Philip Dormer. See Chesterfield, earl of.

Stanley, Arthur Penrhyn (1815-81): Engl. divine ; historian ; dean of Westminster, 1864 ; son of Edward S., bp. of Norwich, 1837-49 ; edu. at Rugby, under Arnold (q.v.), whose Life he wr., 1844 ; travelled to the east, 1862, with prince of Wales (king Edward vii) ; conducted Anglican ceremony at the marriage of the duke of Edinburgh and grand duchess Marie at Petrograd, 1874, and stood high in the favour of queen Victoria. S. was always liberal in respect to the ecclesiastical controversies of his time, supporting Jowett and Colenso (qq.v.), and defending Essays and Reviews, 1860, in the Edinburgh Review. His writings were not all theological. Apart from the biography of Arnold (above), he publd. Lectures on the History of (1) the Eastern Church, 1861 (2) the Jewish Church, 1863 (3) the Church of Scotland, 1892 ; Sinai and Palestine, 1855 ; Memorials of (1) Canterbury, 1854, (2) Westminster Abbey, 1867 ; and his style, like his personality, was charming.

Stanyhurst, Richard (1547-1618): Engl. scholar ; chiefly remembered for his transln. into Engl. hexameter verse of the Æneid, i-iv, of Virgil (q.v.): a meritorious enterprise very clumsily achieved.

Starter, Jan Janszen (1594- c. 1625): Dutch dramatist and poet. Born in London of Brownist stock, and transld. some Engl. songs into Dutch, writing others in his native tongue to Engl. airs. Became a member of the Eglantine (q.v.), and wr. plays and misc. verse with considerable musical skill.

Stebbing, Henry (1799-1883): Engl. divine ; rector of St. Mary Somerset, London, 1857 ; editor of the Athenæum (q.v.) from an early issue in 1828 ; wr. Lives of the Italian Poets, 1831, and other works.

Steele, Richard (1672-1729): Engl. (of Irish descent) essayist ; playwright ; politician ; knt., 1715 ; contemporary with Addison (q.v.), with whom he was associated in founding the Spectator, 1711 ; had previously founded the Tatler, 1709-11, in which, as 'Isaac Bickerstaff', he carried on 188 out of 271 issues ; M.P. Wr., The Funeral, a comedy, Drury Lane, 1701 ; The Lying Lover, Drury Lane, 1703, and other plays ; took various parts in public affairs, and figures prominently in the memoirs of the period. It is worth noting that no. 49 of the Tatler contained the famous compliment to a woman, 'to love her was a liberal education', applied by S. to lady Elizabeth Hastings. Swinburne (q.v.) described it as 'the most exquisite tribute ever paid to a noble woman'.

Steevens, George (1736-1800): Engl. critic ; assisted Johnson (q.v.) in his Lives of the Poets, and publd. various edns. of Shakespeare's (q.v.) works, with commentaries ; a controversial and clever writer, characterized by Gifford (q.v.) as 'the Puck of commentators'.

Steevens, George Warrington (1869-1900): Engl. journalist, whose early death interrupted the promise contained in his Dialogues of the Dead, 1895. S. wr. for the National Observer (s.v. Henley), the Pall Mall Gazette (q.v.), and the Daily Mail in its early days, and proved a brilliant war-correspondent in South Africa.

Steffens, Henrik (1773-1845): Dan. philosopher ; born in Norway, edu. in Denmark, and Germ. by descent and sympathy. S. and Schack v. Staffeld (q.v.) 'did for their country not only what Coleridge did for England, but what he proposed to do' (sir E. Gosse, Lit. Northern Europe, 157). S., in other words, was a missionary of Dan. culture, which had its chief missionstation at Jena (q.v.), where S. drank in deep draughts of romanticism from the works of Hardenberg, Schelling (qq.v.) and others. In Copenhagen, in 1803, his lectures on religion, art and philosophy helped to break the fetters of neo-classicism, and to inspire the young and ardent Denmark of Oehlenschläger (q.v.) and his successors. S. wr. novels in Dan. and Germ., and publd., 1840-45, an autobiography in 10 vols., full of interesting reminiscences of the Romantic movement. It is as an influence rather than as a writer that S. is a significant name in the history of culture in the North, and his meeting with Oehlenschläger was as epoch-making in its day as the meeting of Navagero with Boscan (qq.v.)—Italy with Spain—in 1526.

Steinhöwel, Heinrich (1412-82): Germ. fabulist ; physician at Ulm. Transld. Boccaccio's Decameron, and made collections and redactions

general usage till 1698, and many of the tunes still hold their own, despite the gibe of the first earl of Rochester (1641-1711):

> Sternhold and Hopkins had great qualms,
> When they translated David's Psalms,
>   To make the heart right glad:
> But had it been king David's fate
> To hear thee sing and them translate,
>   By God, 'twould set him mad.

(Quoted by lord Ernle, *Psalms in Human Life*, 149).

Stevenson, Robert Louis (1850-94): Scot. poet; essayist; novelist; son and grandson of eminent pioneers in engineering (Robert S., 1772-1850, and Thomas S., 1818-87; a paper on Thomas S., father of R.L.S., is included in the latter's *Memories and Portraits*, and references to his father and grandfather will be found in ' Random Memories ' in *Across the Plains*). It is difficult not to conclude that, in the generation or more which has elapsed since the death of S. at Samoa, in romantic surroundings, and after a brave struggle through a short life of invalidism, pity for his fate and admiration for his courage have conspired to exalt his fame to a level superior to its merits. He did some very charming work: nothing perhaps more permanently charming than the papers chosen and arranged by his constant friend, sir Sidney Colvin (who supervised, 1894-8, the Edinburgh edn. of S.'s works, 28 vols., and, later, publd. S.'s *Letters*), in *Across the Plains*, 1892. One or two quotations from those papers may help to convey the particular spell which S. exerted:

' None can care for literature in itself who do not take a special pleasure in the sound of names '.

' Pathos must be relieved by dignity of treatment. If you wallow naked in the pathetic, like the author of " Home, sweet home ", you make your hearers weep in an unmanly fashion '.

' It seems as if certain sorts of follies, like certain sorts of grain, were natural to the soil rather than to the race that holds and tills it for the moment '.

' In youth, like Moses from the mountain, we have sights of that House Beautiful of art which we shall never enter '.

' To miss the joy is to miss all. In the joy of the actors lies the sense of any action '.

' What an art it is, to give, even to our nearest friends ! and what a test of manners, to receive ' !

We must forgo longer extracts, but even these brief specimens of S.'s style and thought serve to show how intimate and genial, and how fully reasoned withal, was the note which he struck in the Engl. essay, descended through F. Bacon and Lamb (qq.v.). Other vols. of his essays included *Virginibus Puerisque*, 1881, dedicated to his friend, W. E. Henley (q.v.), containing the admirable paper, ' Ordered South ', and, in the title-paper, some excellent sentences on marriage, which tempt to further quotation:

' In all that concerns eating and drinking company, climate, and ways of life, community of taste is to be sought for. It would be trying, for instance, to keep bed and board with an early riser or a vegetarian '.

' I have always suspected public taste to be a mongrel product, out of affectation by dogmatism '.

' The word " facts " is, in some ways, crucial; I have spoken with Jesuits and Plymouth Brethren, mathematicians and poets, dogmatic republicans and dear old gentlemen in bird's-eye neckcloths; and each understood the word " facts " in an occult sense of his own '.

' To marry is to domesticate the Recording Angel '.

It is curious that S., in his romances (*Treasure Island*, 1883; *The Strange Case of Dr. Jekyll and Mr. Hyde*, 1886; *Kidnapped*, 1886; *The Black Arrow*, 1888; *The Master of Ballantrae*, 1889; *Catriona, a Sequel to Kidnapped*, 1893; *Weir of Hermiston*, left unfind., posth. 1896; in collaboration with his stepson, Lloyd Osbourne: *The Wrong Box*, 1889; *The Wrecker*, 1892; *The Ebb Tide*, 1894; and posth., completed by sir A. Quiller-Couch, *St. Ives*, 1897) was much more concerned with adventure than with love, despite the ease and grace of his talks (above) to girls and boys about to fall in love. But they are tales of adventure mostly of a rare excellence, and, among them, *Treasure Island* is now a boys' classic, and *Weir of Hermiston*, though a fragment, justifies the comparison of the aim of S. with that of sir W. Scott (q.v.). He wr., too, in a remarkably full life, 2 fine vols. of poetry: *A Child's Garden of Verse*, 1885, and *Underwoods*, 1887, besides *Ballads* and *Songs of Travel*. The children's poems are described by prof. Saintsbury (*C.H.E.L.*, xiii, 215) as ' perhaps the most perfectly natural book of the kind '; and ' The House Beautiful ', ' The Celestial Surgeon ' and the ' Requiem ' in *Underwoods*, inscribed on his own grave, and ending, ' Home is the sailor, home from the sea, And the hunter home from the hill ', are lyrics of real sensuousness and simplicity. These do not exhaust the list of S.'s writings (he wr. some plays with Henley, e.g.), but they illustrate effectively the promise and achievement of a writer who had to make his home abroad, and whose inevitably self-centred existence was reflected in the mirror which he held up, with hardly a speck to sully either the manfulness of the spectator or the wistful beauty of the spectacle.

Stjernhjelm, Jorge (1598-1672): Swed. poet and philologer; the ' father ' of Swed. poetry; pupil of Buræus (q.v.). In an excess of patriotism, not to be charged against his learned tutor, S. discovered in Old Norse the parent of all other languages, but his *Treasury of Gothic Speech*, 1643, and other works in humanistic scholarship have considerably more value than this rash generalization would suggest. S. wr., too, on geometry and philosophy; but his chief claim to renown rests now, as in his lifetime, on his Swed. poems, which included masques for the court of queen Christina (q.v.), and *Hercules*, 1658, which ' made the classical hexameter one of the national metres of Sweden ' (Sandys, *Hist. Class. Schol.*, iii, 338), and ' really gave Sweden her first true pattern of words and measures poetically handled ' (Elton, *P.E.L.*, viii, 361).

Stoke, Melis (14th cent.): Dutch rhyming chronicler; clerk in the employ of counts

Floris v and William iii. Wr. *Riming Chron-icle of Holland*, of which 3 MSS. are preserved in Royal Library at The Hague. Part i of his work ran to about 3,300 verses, and part ii to 10,000 ; S. drew on his own experience and that of eye-witnesses for events subsequent to the death of Floris v.

Stolberg, zu, -i. Christian (1748-1821): Germ. poet and translr.; count. Joined the Hain (q.v.) a few months after its foundation in 1772, and was particularly welcome for his personal acquaintance with Klopstock (q.v.). Transld. plays of Sophocles and wr. original lyric verse.

-ii. Friedrich Leopold (1750-1819): Germ. poet and translr.; count; brother of above, and, like him, a member of the Göttingen poets' union. Effected translns. from Homer, Plato, and Ossian (qq.v.). Gifted with more poetic sensibility than his elder brother, S. was the chief contributor to the *Poems* which they publd. jointly, 1779. His taste was formed in the spirit of Klopstock, and he aimed at a revival of the knightly virtues of medieval Germany. There was more than a touch of what we in Engld. now call pre-Raphaelitism in his attitude towards life and lit. In 1800 he was converted to the Roman Catholic Church, and alienated his old friend Voss (q.v.), who was suspicious of the later developments of the romantic movement. S.'s works were misc., and included a life of Alfred the Great, translns. from Æschylus and others, as well as odes, hymns, and ballads.

Storm, Theodor (1817-88): Germ. novelist and poet; a disciple, in the latter branch, of Eichendorff (q.v.). His best-known tales are *Aquis submersus*, 1877 ; *Renate*, 1878 ; and other so-called chronicle-stories.

Story-within-a-Story: A convention of fiction, the name of which is self-explaining. It flourished in the palmy days of long-winded romances, characteristic, mainly, of Fr. fiction in the 17th cent. (see s.v. Scudéry, e.g.), and it survived into the 18th cent. precursors of the modern novel (q.v.). From these precursors, Marivaux (q.v.) and others, it passed to Smollett (q.v.) and even to Dickens (q.v.), in whose *Nicholas Nickleby* (see ch. vi) we have perhaps its last notable example. The direct converse of this convention is the story-without-a-story, i.e., the story which is a succession of adventures more or less loosely linked together by a common character or common characters ; obvious examples of these are the *Decameron*, *Tales of my Landlord* (s.vv. Boccaccio, Scott) and sir A. Conan Doyle's *Sherlock Holmes*.

Stow, John (1525-1605): Engl. antiquary; a tailor by trade, and much indebted for the encouragement of his tastes to archbishop Parker (q.v.). Edited the works of Chaucer (q.v.), and old chronicles of Engl. history with rare skill and accuracy, and publd., 1598, *A Survey of London*, re-edited by H. Morley (q.v.), 1876. S. spent his private means on antiquarian research, and was granted by king James i the inadequate recognition of letters patent, 1604, authorizing him to collect from 'our loving subjects their voluntary contributions and kind gratuities '.

Straparola, Giovanfrancesco (16th cent.): It. writer of ' novelle '. His vol. of tales, entitled *Piacevole Notti* (' Pleasing Nights '), proved very popular in a Venetian edn., 1550 ; frequently reprinted ; transld. into Fr. at early date, and (recently, again, by W. G. Waters) into Engl. S.'s tales take a high place in the large company of their fellows including and since Boccaccio (q.v.), by their distinctive charm, pathos and true feeling ; they possess, too, the rarer and negative quality of not revolting the reader by cold indecencies. That they are moral in any positive sense of an aim at morality cannot be stated ; they would not be warm Ital. ' novelle ', if it were so ; but the writer, otherwise unknown, was very plainly a story-teller by instinct and not a hunter after salacious appeals.

Strauss, David Friedrich (1808-74): Germ. theologian and critic ; a disciple in hist. method of the school of Niebuhr and Sybel (qq.v.); applying it to his theological studies more temperately than L. A. Feuerbach (q.v.), a contemporary polemical writer. S.'s chief work was his *Leben Jesu, kritisch bearbeitet*, 1835, transld. as *The Life of Jesus, critically examined*, by George Eliot (q.v.), 3 vols., 1846 ; other works, hardly less famous, in the same sphere of Christian doctrine, were the *Christliche Glaubenslehre*, 1840-41, a study in the hist. development of Christianity and in its conflict with modern science ; *das Leben Jesu für das deutsche Volk*, 1864, etc.; including letters, exchanged with Renan (q.v.), a worker in the same field. S. wr., too, monographs on Voltaire, U. v. Hutten, Frischlin (qq.v.), and others, and he has been the subject in turn of a large number of critical writings in Germany, France and Engld., where, apart from George Eliot and other translators, S. supplied the model to R. Browning (q.v.) for his verse-picture of the Germ. prof. in *Christmas Eve :*

I felt at once as if there ran
A shoot of love from my heart to the man—
That sallow, virgin-minded studious
Martyr to mild enthusiasm,
As he . . . stood, surveying his auditory
With a wan, pure look, well nigh celestial,—
Those blue eyes had survived so much.

Straussfedern (Germ.): Title, meaning, lit., ostrich-feathers, of an album, or keepsake, publd. periodically at Berlin by Nicolai (q.v.) towards the close of the 18th cent., and containing a collection of light stories of a realistic tendency. The first author was Musäus (q.v.), who died, 1787, and was succeeded in the editorship by J. G. Müller, the youthful Tieck (qq.v.) and others.

Stricker, der (13th cent.): ' The Weaver ' (? of plays); South-Germ. wandering player, otherwise unknown by name. Wr., and invented character of, *Pfaffe Amis* (' Papa Amis '; see s.v. Amis), the Middle-High-German forerunner of Till Eulenspiegel and the Pfarrer of Kalenberg (qq.v.): a rascally priest of burlesque adventures and horseplay. His wit illustrated by examples the proverbial philosophy, *mundus vult decipi, ergo decipiatur* ; or, in scriptural parlance, treat a fool according to his folly. Wr., too, collection of fables to which he gave the title of *die Welt* (' the World ').

Strickland, Agnes (1796-1874): Engl. hist. writer. Wr. *Lives of the Queens of Engld.* 1840-8, and *of the Queens of Scotld.*, 1850-9. These works, in which her sister, Elizabeth S., collaborated, enjoyed a considerable repute, but did not rise much above a mediocre level.

Strindberg, August (1849-1912): Swed. novelist; dramatist; a devoted disciple of the so-called Naturalist school (see s.v. Nature; it was a one-sided view of nature which Zola and his school affected), and a follower of Nietzsche (q.v.) in his doctrine of the will to power. The coarse cleverness of S. and his very considerable gifts of style in prose cannot be disputed, but the whole tendency of this class of lit. is alien to present sentiment and sympathies, and it is perhaps unfair to judge it after the event of what was partially described as the 'Euro-Nietzschean' war. S.'s chief novels are *Tschandala* and *By the Open Sea* (with its superman-hero, Borg): his chief plays, a 'sexual trilogy'—*The Father, Miss Julia* and *The Creditors*.

Strode, William (1602-45): Engl. poet; dramatist; divine; canon of Christ Church, Oxford, 1638, and Public Orator to the univ., 1639. Wr., among other verse, some of which is still unedited, an allegorical play, *The Floating Island*, which, with music by H. Lawes (see, too, s.v. Milton) was played before king Charles i and his court at Oxford, 1636.

Strozzi, Alessandra Macinghi (1407-71): It. letter-writer. Wr. 72 familiar epistles to her sons in exile from Florence, valuable for their picture of domestic manners. With Alberti's *Famiglia* and the *Cortegiano* of a later date, they help to complete our knowledge of Florence (q.v.) in the 15th cent.

Strozzi, Palla (14th-15th cents.): It. humanist. Was instrumental in bringing Chrysoloras (q.v.) to Florence, where he employed his wealth and influence in promoting Gk. studies, and in improvement of the univ. Vespasiano gives S. credit for procuring many MSS. from Greece and Constantinople, including Aristotle's *Politics*, not previously known. He intended to found a public library, but was exiled from Florence by his rival, Cosimo de ' Medici (1434), and retired to Padua, where he occupied his stately leisure with the same learned and enlightening pursuits.

Strype, John (1643-1737): Engl. ecclesiastical historian; divine; collected valuable library of Tudor MSS., and wr. *Lives* of Cranmer, archbishop Parker (q.v.), Whitgift, and others. S.'s industry was matched by his length of days, but he walked contentedly in the plains of scholarship.

Stubbs, William (1825-1901): Engl. historian; bp. of Oxford, 1889. Wr. *The Constitutional History of Engld.*, 3 vols., 1874-8; the standard authority on the subject.

Stuñiga, de, Lope (15th cent.): Span. poet. S.'s name was given to a *Cancionero* (q.v.), *ed. pr.* 1872; it contained representative pieces by about 40 poets, and opened with 2 poems by S. himself. His father (Iñigo Ortez de S.) is represented in the *Cancionero* of Baena (q.v.). S. was a cousin of Quiñones, the hero of the 'Passo honroso' (q.v.), and was one of the 9 knights who defended the pass.

Sturla (*c.* 1214-84): Icel. historian; *saga* (q.v.)-writer; grandson of Sturla of Hvamm, founder of the Sturlung house, and nephew of Snorri (q.v.). Wr. the *Sturlunga Saga* (or *Islendinga Saga*, ' Icelandic memoirs ') edited by Vigfusson and York Powell, 2 vols., Oxford, 1879; and the *Hákonar Saga*, or life of Hacon (q.v.) Haconsson, king of Norway (died, 1263). We need not inquire too closely into the facts in dispute among scholars as to how much of the Sturlung chronicle was written by Sturla himself. Saintsbury, *P.E.L.*, ii, 345, writes with pontifical authority: ' To the historian who takes delight in literature, and does not care very much who made it provided it is made well, what has been called " the singular silence " as to authorship which runs through the whole of the early Icelandic literature is rather a blessing than otherwise. It frees him from those biographical inquiries which always run the risk of drawing nigh to gossip, and it enables him to concentrate attention on the literature itself '. We shall not rush in where Saintsbury fears to tread. Sturla wr. the *Sturlunga Saga*, the contemporary chronicle of a series of dramatic happenings *quorum pars magna fuit*, and modern readers may enjoy his work as ' the completion of Icelandic prose. It is hardly a metaphor to say that it is the mind of Iceland, expressing itself in the best way at the end of the old Icelandic life. Sturla's work is the Icelandic habit of thought and vision applied to the writer's own experience, whereas in the heroic Sagas it had dealt with things of a former age '. And, as to the methods of the Saga, whether of old times or new: ' The beauty of it in both cases is its impartiality. But this is naturally more remarkable and surprising in the later than in the earlier history. Sturla had been in the thick of it all himself, in many moss-trooping raids and forays; he had seen his kinsmen cut down; he had been driven to make terms with their chief enemy; it was his own daughter who was snatched out of the fire, where her young bridegroom lost his life. But there is nothing in history to show that he takes a side. He follows the custom of the old Sagas, which is, to let the characters alone and never allow the showman to come forward with his explanations and opinions ' (prof. Ker, q.v., *Sturla the Historian*; Romanes Lecture, Oxford, 1906. The same writer, in his *Epic and Romance*, 269-274, Macmillan, 1908, a singularly fascinating bk., contrasts this Icel. reticence, which was part of Carlyle's (q.v.) attraction to Iceld.—the strong, silent man point of view —with the method of the sieur de Joinville (q.v.), an exact contemporary with S., in his *Vie de Saint Louis*. This little study in comparison is well worth attentive reading. The misfortunes of the Sturlungs brought S. to Norway in 1263, after the submission of Iceld. to the Norse. He was coldly received by king Magnus at Bergen—' the last court-poet face to face with the last king-patron ' (Vigfusson and Powell, *Corpus Poeticum Boreale*, i, 260),— but won the king's favour by his verses, and wr. the life of king Hacon, Magnus's father, then in Scotld., from which he was not to return. Hacon (q.v.) was a great king, with a romantic monarchical succession, and S.

proved a great biographer ; ' he makes as good use as Froissart could have made of the memories of older men ' (Ker, *ibid.*), and employs the same masterly Iceld. prose, which constitutes the imperishable glory of this unique branch of lit. If S. marks the close of the classical age of Iceld., at least it is a master who closes it ; and it was to S.'s *Hákonar Saga* that Ibsen (q.v.) went 600 years after for his drama of *Kongsemnerne* (' rival kings ') or *The Pretenders*. But ' after Sturla, and after the fall of the commonwealth of Iceland [1262], although there were still some interesting biographies to be written, it may be reckoned that the heroic strain is exhausted '. (Ker, *Epic and Romance*, 268).

Sturm, Johannes (1507-89) : Germ. humanist and educational reformer. Born near Cologne ; studied at Lyons ; was headmaster of Strassburg school, 1538-1581. S.'s school had a European reputation, and was imitated in other Germ. cities ; boys of all nationalities were among its pupils, but S. was spared the consequent confusion of tongues by his rigid and almost exclusive devotion to the Lat. language as the means and end of a liberal education. Even in his own day this method led to excessive verbalism, but S.'s reputation as a scholar and as a friend of the great men of his time stood very high. He wr. text-books and Lat. treatises : *On the right way of opening schools of letters for boys*, 1538, and *Classical Letters* to his form-masters, 1565.

Sturm und Drang (Germ.) : Storm and Stress ; descriptive name of a period in Germ. life and letters, extending, as closely as possible, from 1765 to 1790. These frontiers include the ' Fragments towards a German Literature ' (*Fragmente zur deutschen Litteratur*, 1767) of Herder (q.v.) at one end, and the *Don Carlos*, 1787, of Schiller (q.v.) at the other ; a nearer delimitation is fixed by the *Götz von Berlichingen*, 1773, of Goethe (q.v.) and the ' Robbers ' (*Räuber*), 1781, of Schiller. The name, Sturm und Drang, which has since passed into universal acceptance, and which is eminently characteristic of similar periods in other literatures, e.g. in France after 1830, was transferred to the whole from a part, otherwise of little significance. This was a drama (a wild love-story placed in the surroundings of the American War of Independence), entitled *Wirr-Warr*, or *Sturm und Drang*, by Klinger (q.v.), 1776. The more technical name of *Geniezeit* (the period of genius ; see s.v. Lavater for a description of genius) is applied in histories to the epoch. The true father of the Sturm und Drang was Rousseau (q.v.), whom Schiller (the Schiller of *Don Carlos* and the *Räuber*) apostrophized in his grave in these terms : ' Socrates was undone through sophists ; Rousseau suffers, Rousseau falls through Christians ; Rousseau, who turns Christians into men '. The intense, concentrated contagion of Rousseau's idealism and fervour in young Germany during the closing quarter of the 18th cent. is comparable with nothing in modern literary history, except, possibly, the rapture of Petrarch (q.v.) by the spell of the golden age of Rome. It was the summons to freedom, the recall to nature, the sudden, impetuous revolt against trammel, and rule,

and school ; the intoxicating gospel of individualism ; which worked like madness in the blood of men who might differ in all respects save in a common resolve to find a name and a shape for the immensity that momentarily filled them. To found a pantisocracy on the Susquehanna—that bright dream of the three young poets, Coleridge, Southey, Lovell (qq.v.), who married the three sisters Fricker in or about 1795,—this was conceived in the very spirit of the Sturm und Drang, the object of which was to go back and to go forward ; to go back, with Herder's *Fragmente*, from the channels to the wells of poesy ; to go forward, with the greater and lesser geniuses—Heinse, Gerstenberg, Lenz, Klinger (qq.v.), and the rest—to a new art and a new world and a new brotherhood of man. It was mostly thunder on a precipice ; sonorous phrases and insecure feet : the account of it may be read in Goethe's *Wahrheit und Dichtung* ; but out of that twenty years' display of the sheer force of natural man came the classical thought of Germ. genius ; came the maturity of Goethe and Schiller, and the critical philosophy of Kant (q.v.), and all the wonders of the imagination which marked the beginning of the 19th cent. in northern Europe. Sturm und Drang is the tempestuous sense of being young in a time of creation, not of criticism any more : ' bliss was it in that dawn to be alive, And to to be young was very Heav'n ' (Wordsworth, *Prelude*, xiv ; of the Revolution-era in France), and if Rousseau was the father of the movement, Shakespeare may be said to have been its sponsor.

Suard, Jean Baptiste Antoine (1733-1817) : Fr. journalist ; dramatic censor ; elected to the Fr. Academy (q.v.), 1774. S. was proscribed during the Reign of Terror, but, later, returned to Paris. His wife (1739-1794), *née* Panckoucke (q.v.) was a well-known hostess (s.v. *salon*) in the epoch of the *Encyclopédie* (q.v.).

Sublime (Rhet.) : Technical term for a quality of style in lit. (prose or poetry), defined by the Gk. author of a famous treatise ' on the Sublime ' as ' a certain distinction and excellence of language ' (Sandys, *Hist. Class. Schol.*, i, 289), or ' a certain consummateness and eminence of words ' (Saintsbury, *Hist. Crit.*, i, 155) ; leading to ' not persuasion but transport ' (*ecstasy*) ; derived from 5 sources, viz. ' grandeur of conception ' (Sandys) or ' command of strong and manly thought ' (Saintsbury), ' intensity of emotion ' (Sandys) or ' vehement and enthusiastic passion ' (Saintsbury), ' appropriate employment of figures of thought and speech ' (Sandys) or ' skilfulness with figures ' (Saintsbury), ' nobility of verbal expression ' (Sandys) or ' of phrase ' (Saintsbury), and ' dignity and elevation of composition ' (Sandys) or ' of *ordonnance* ' (Saintsbury). Of these 5 sources the first 2 are the chief, and can be reached, not by art, but only by accustoming the mind to large ideas, since ' sublimity is the echo of greatness in the soul '. Moreover, in avoiding faults of art, such as tumidity, bombast, etc., success can only be attained by knowledge, since ' judgment in words is the final fruit of long experience ' ; and in a Ruskinian passage, which now closes the treatise, the Gk. author despairs of the Sublime in his own day, since 'what wastes and consumes men of talent in this age is the apathy in which, with few exceptions, we pass our lives, working and striving merely for applause and pleasure, never to do what is useful and what would secure praise which is worth having and worth our effort '.

This remarkable treatise of antiquity, of which the above is but the briefest summary, and which combines Hebraism with Hellenism in a striking illustration of the Sublime out of the first ch. of Genesis by 'the legislator of the Jews ', differs from all earlier (and, indeed, many later) treatises on rhetoric (the elements of style), by its insistence on the *mind* which informs the words and on the *soul* which inspires the style. Remarkable in contents, it is also remarkable in its history. Its author is unknown ; its date is settled only by internal evidence, and is probably the 3rd cent., A.D. ; and it was lost to Europe till the middle of the 16th cent., when it was transld. by Robortello (q.v.), working on a MS. in the Vatican, which ascribed the treatise to Dionysius (of Halicarnassus) *or* (Cassius) Longinus (died, 273). Robortello, by design or inadvertence, gave the author as Dionysius Longinus, and this ascription was continued till 1808, when a later scholar, Amati, discovered the mistake. Another MS. in Florence describes the treatise as anon. The Gk. title of the treatise is περὶ ὕψους, i.e., concerning height (or eminence), and ' the Grand Style ' discussed by M. Arnold (q.v.) in his lectures on translating Homer is as near an Engl. equivalent as can be found. But date, authorship and rendering are matters minor to the influence in Europe of this truly magnificent essay in criticism, which was written in order to supply a more adequate account of the subject than was contained in an earlier treatise on the Sublime by a certain Cæcilius, of Sicily, who was probably a Jew by religion. (The ' Jewish legislator ' reference may be a Cæcilian fossil). ' Longinus on The Sublime '—to give the ascription accepted from 1554 to 1808, was transld., 1674, by Boileau (q.v.), with an admirable pref., which he followed up by less admirable *Réflexions sur Longin*, and it captured Fr. taste from that date, Fénelon (q.v.) even preferring Longinus to Aristotle as critic. From France his reputation crossed to Engld., where Pope (q.v.), following Boileau, wr. in his *Essay on Criticism* :

Thee, bold Longinus ! all the Nine inspire,
And bless their critic with a poet's fire.
An ardent judge who, jealous in his trust,
With warmth gives sentence, yet is always just :
Whose own example strengthens all his laws ;
And is himself the great Sublime he draws.

Pope and Swift (q.v.) jointly wr. a treatise on *Bathos, or the Art of Sinking in Poetry ;* Dryden (q.v.) was a whole-hearted Longinus-man (see particularly his pref. to *Troilus and Cressida) ;* Addison (q.v.) was another (see particularly *Spectator*, no. 412); Akenside, Young, Goldsmith (qq.v.) and others yield rich spoils to careful students of ' Longinus ', whom Gibbon (q.v.) pronounced to be ' one of the noblest monuments of antiquity ', and ' almost doubted which is the most sublime : Homer's battle of the gods or Longinus' apostrophe upon it '. Casaubon (q.v.) called

the treatise ' a golden book ', and Saintsbury says that Longinus ' stands alone. We must skip 1500 years and come to Coleridge before we meet any critic entirely of his class, yet free from some of his limitations. His work remains towering among all other work of the class, the work of a critic at once Promethean and Epimethean in his kind, learning by the mistakes of all that had gone before, and presaging with instinctive genius much that was not to come for centuries after '. (See also s.v. Longinus).

Suckling, John (1609-42) : Engl. poet ; knt., 1630, after inheriting large estates in Norfolk from his father, sir John S. (d., 1627), and travel on the continent, where he may have seen military service under king Gustavus Adolphus of Sweden. Returned to the gayer court of king Charles i, and played at soldiering in Scotld., where he fitted out a troop with gorgeous clothes but less conspicuous courage ; was prominent, too, at other kinds of play, including the stage and the card-table, and was the inventor of the game of cribbage. As a man of letters, S. is remembered for his ballads and songs, contained in *Fragmenta aurea*, posth., 1646.

Sue, Eugene (1804-59) : Fr. novelist ; began with sea-fiction, based on his experiences as an army doctor, in which capacity he was a witness of the sea-fight of Navarino, 1827. Later, S. was infected by the example of Dumas *père* (q.v.), and his best-known romances are the *Mystères de Paris*, 1843, and *le Juif errant*, 1849. Both these books, esp. ' The Wandering Jew ', were crammed full of sensation and horror, and won a world-wide audience. S. was a prolific writer, decidedly of the second class.

Sulzer, Johann (1720-79) : Germ. critic. Wr. *Universal Theory of the Fine Arts*, which prof. Saintsbury describes as ' a painful compound of Dictionary and Bibliography ' (*Hist. Crit.*, iii. 150), but which was in its day a useful and a valiant attempt to systematize the point of view represented by Bodmer, Baumgarten (qq.v.) and other teachers of æsthetics.

Sumarokov, Alexander (1727-77) : Russ. dramatist ; ' to his own Russians ' writes Brückner, S. ' was really Corneille, Racine and Voltaire ' (*Gesch. d. Russ. Lit.*, 79) ; and even a more perspicacious posterity, while it would write Champistron (q.v.) for Racine, admits that S. rendered great services to the nascent Russ. stage, first in Petrograd, 1756, and then in Moscow, 1761. That his tragedies, adapted from the Fr. (in one instance from *Hamlet*) were more than strings of declamation divided into acts, with a childish respect for the rules of the game, as laid down by Boileau (q.v.), no one pretends to-day ; nor is much more value to be attached to his so-called comedies. S. was personally convinced that he had solved the problem of Tredjakovsky (q.v.), and had created the examples of lit. of which his rival had formulated the theories. He tried all kinds, except the novel, for which there was no Aristotelian authority ; but though he failed in all, by the standards of originality and taste, he considerably advanced the capacities of Russ. lit. and its readers' response to its appeal.

Superman (Engl.); (Germ. **Übermensch**): Ideal type of politico-philosophical being, constructed by hero-worship out of visions of the millennium. Periods in history immediately dominated by the mastery of a great man (e.g., Napoleon, esp.) have proved prolific in superman-literature, of which the conception of the philosopher-king in Plato's (q.v.) *Republic* may be taken to be the starting-point. Actually, the term *Übermensch* was first used by the Germ. visionary, Nietzsche (q.v.); but as hero-worship is a constant source of literary (chiefly, dramatic) inspiration, and as literary dreams of the millennium have been dreamed by seers in every age, the S. is to be found in lit. before the invention of his name, and of the perilous doctrines associated with the Germ. prophet. In a somewhat too special study of *The Superman in Modern Literature* (by Leo Berg; transld. by C. Field from the Germ.; Jarrold, *n.d.* [1916]), we are told that 'the cradle of the Superman stands on the threshold of the modern period, and he grows in and with modern literature' (84). But as the same writer reminds us, there were already Supermen at the time of the Renaissance (q.v.): powerful princes, inspired artists, noble humanists, whose sense of individuality was so consuming that they seem to embody the dreams of later Superman speculation. Petrarch's (q.v.) *virtù*, for example, may be said to descend by links, historically traceable, to the *Kultur* of the state founded by Prussia in Imperial Germany after 1871. For the state is the individual writ large, and hero-State-worship is even more powerful a fertilizer of Superman-politics than hero-Individual-worship of the Carlylean pattern (s.v. Carlyle). Thus, Petrarch (q.v.), 'the first modern man', as he was called by Renan (q.v.), prophet of the *intelligence supérieure*, raised *virtù* to a national cult, and may thus be entitled, proleptically, a Superman-philosopher *in petto*. The revival of learning, inaugurated by Petrarch, led to the Reformation associated with Luther (q.v.), and similar visions of perfectibility produced the *quasi*-Supermen of the Reformation. Not merely Faust (q.v.), who dared to investigate all knowledge, and not merely the Prospero of Shakespeare, creating a human being out of Caliban, but kings and rulers, absolutists and benevolent despots, ascended out of the turmoil of religious warfare. 'Had there been no Luther', says one authority, 'there would never have been a Louis xiv' (J. N. Figgis, *From Gerson to Grotius*, Cambridge, 1907); and in another place he says, 'It is impossible to understand Machiavelli without comparing him with Nietzsche'. This statement, literally true, as students of Machiavelli (q.v.) will be aware, brings back the doctrine of the Superman from the visionaries of the 19th cent., right through the Machiavellian statesmen-rulers, or super-princes, to the Lutheran Reformation and the Petrarchan Humanism. And, between the 14th cent. and the 19th, with all its fatal legacy to the 20th, lies a long series of gradations, which belong to the study of politics rather than to that of pure lit. In that field we must note the individualistic philosophy, which Napoleon's career taught by example, and which found expression in Kierkegaard's (q.v.) theology and in Carlyle's hist. method. The figure of Bismarck in the middle of the 19th cent. reaffirmed the Napoleonic legend, and was bound up with principles of Prussian thought going back to Frederick the Great and beyond. It was as a great man, rather than as a Teuton maker, that Goethe referred to Frederick as an inspiring influence on Germ. lit.; and the great, silent man of history was reinforced by romanticist heroes (see s.v. Romance), potent authors of their own fate, or majestic victims of their own temperament, Wagner (q.v.), Ibsen (q.v.) and Nietzsche continued the romantic tradition, and adapted the strong-man idea, immanent even in the Arthuriad (s.v. Arthur), to the circumstances and hopes of their own day. The 'Superman' of Dostoievsky (q.v.), or of Ibsen, or of a half-a-dozen Ibsenitish dramatists on the assimilative soil of Germany, is the would-be redeemer, or deliverer, whose panacea will cure humanity of all its ills. The degradation of this noble idea was due to the vanity and self-esteem of Superman-writers, each of whom laid the flattery to his soul that he was the chosen and anointed one. It was due, too, to an eagerness to anticipate the privileges of the redemption before its pains; to a relaxation of moral and social sanctions before the new era of morality had begun, and to a premature self-abandonment by the 'artistic temperament' to alleged rights of free-thought and of free-love. And, on the philosophic side, the theory of the 'will to power' was patronized by the Prussian State, as its strength and its ambition were matured; so that a link was forged between Nietzsche and Treitschke (q.v.), though no 2 men ever taught doctrines more dissimilar. Like other literary conventions, the convention of the S. has been exposed. He, too, like the Arcadian (s.v. Arcadia), is within us; no force from outside can impose him, or can perfect the race before its time. Our times are in other hands.

Surrey (Henry Howard) **earl of** (c. 1516-47): Engl. poet; K.G., 1542; son of Thomas H., third duke of Norfolk; cousin to queen Anne Boleyn; brother-in-law to the duke of Richmond, who was a natural son of king Henry viii. These exalted relationships were not altogether to a man's advantage in Tudor times, and S.'s distinguished career as soldier and poet was twice interrupted by imprisonment in the Tower, and ended at the scaffold on Tower Hill. Like Sidney (q.v.), he united in his person the best qualities of the perfect courtier of Castiglione (q.v.); and he shares with sir Thomas Wyatt (q.v.), his contemporary, the credit of the naturalization in Engl. poetry of Fr. and Ital. Renaissance models and ideas, thus forging an essential link between Chaucer and Spenser. S. was more conservative than Wyatt, or, at least, more sure-footed in his departures from tradition. He was a deeply careful student of Chaucer, and his extension of the resources of the Engl. language and metres was based on a thorough knowledge of its true genius and capacities; it was a development rather than a departure, and S. was thus competent to innovate more successfully

and more sympathetically than Wyatt. Much
of his exquisite love-verse was firmly founded
on the chivalric code (see s.v. Woman),
which had served Petrarch (q.v.) and his
successors ; and, though Puttenham (q.v.)
incorrectly states that S. had ' travelled into
Italy ', he says of S., more correctly even than
of Wyatt, that he had ' tasted the sweet and
stately measures and style of the Italian
poesy '. Style, indeed, is the just word ;
it was the gift of S. to Engl. poetry, at the time
of its urgent need ; and his undoubted debt to
Petrarch and Alamanni, among the Italians,
to Marot and Saint-Gelais, among the Fr.
(see s.vv.), was fully acquitted by his skill in
the manipulation of his own language and its
powers of poetic harmony. More brilliantly
than Wyatt, S. made the sonnet (q.v.) an
Engl. measure.*   He borrowed from foreign
example the hint of narrative blank verse
(q.v.) ; whether from Alamanni (teste, sir
S. Lee), or from Molza (teste prof. Courthope),
or from Trissino (teste Warton), or from the
blocks of decasyllabic verses occurring here
and there in the 2 prose Canterbury Tales of
Chaucer. The precise incidence of the obligation is less important than the fact that S.
employed this masterly metre, as Molza had
employed it before him, for the transln. of
Virgil, Æneid, ii and iv, and he handed it on for
noble purposes to a line of Engl. poets. This
claim alone would give S. a high place in the
history of Engl. lit., which he adorned in well-
nigh solitary grandeur in the barren period
before the Elizabethan harvest ; but his poetic
merits, independent of their origins, likewise
entitle him to esteem ; and, among many odes
and poems, lyrical, satirical, elegiac, which his
versatile but careful art created, most critics
agree in selecting as the supreme example of his
skill the lines on the death of the duke of Richmond, written in captivity, 1546, which are
conspicuously free from all taint of the artificiality almost inseparable from Petrarchan love-
poetry in his age, and which seem to blend the
personal lament with a universal threnody at
the passing of a type—the type of chivalry—
which had served its day.

Surtees, Robert Smith (1802-64) : Engl. sporting
novelist ; son of an antiquary (Robert S.,
1779-1834), after whom the Surtees Society
was named. R.S.S. started, 1831, the New
Sporting Magazine, in which he publd. his
sketches of ' Mr. John Jorrocks ', the grocer in
the field, issued as Jorrocks' Jaunts, 1838 ;
wr., too, Handley Cross, Ask Mamma, Mr.
Sponge's Sporting Tour, etc. A part of the
success of these novels was due to the illustrations by sir John Leech.

Suso, Heinrich (1300-1365) : Swiss (Germ.)
mystic ; his name was Latinized from Seuse.
Pupil of Eckhart (q.v.) ; father of poetic
mysticism ; wr., Little Book of Everlasting

<hr>

* The foregoing paragraph was in type before I saw
Edmund Spenser : An Essay in Renaissance Poetry,
by prof. W. L. Renwick (E. Arnold, 1925), from p. 70
of which excellent book I may now quote : ' The most
obvious weakness of English poetry between Chaucer
and Spenser is weakness of style.   Spenser could not
but . . . see that any superiority that Surrey
had over Wyatt was largely that Surrey was able to
mould his English to the sonnet form, where Wyatt
could only cramp his '.   See, too, s.v. Spenser,
supra.

Wisdom, a dialogue between Christ and a servant
of philosophy.

Sverre (died, 1202) : Norse king ; ' one of the
most remarkable adventurers who have ever
come forward as Saviours of Society ' (W. P.
Ker, q.v., Sturla the Historian, Romanes
Lecture, Oxford, 1906). S.'s ' rugged regiment ' of followers were known as Birki-
beinar (birchen-legs, from their birch-bark
gaiters), and at last by terror and repute he
established his rule in the land. S.'s interest
in lit. is, that he dictated his life to an abbot,
and the Saga (q.v.) of the Life of king Sverre
is a stepping-stone from Ari to Snorri (qq.v.).
S. wr., too, a kind of political testament, assert-
ing the doctrine, as he had asserted the practice,
of the divine right of kings, which became
binding on his successors. His immediate
successor was his grandson, Hacon (q.v.)
Haconsson, whose life was written by Sturla
(q.v.) in the Hákonar Saga, and whose rivalry
for the throne with duke Skule was a favourite
dramatic topic, right down to Ibsen (q.v.).

Svobodová, Ružena (1868-1920) : Czech novelist ;
skilful delineator of feminine types, in a series
of tales : Shipwrecked, On Sandy Soil, etc. ;
which owe a part of their inspiration to Russia,
especially to Gogol (q.v.). S.'s last bk. was
The Paradise, which she left unfind., but which
gives a charming picture, tinged with melancholy, due to failing health and the Great
War, of her home and early life in Southern
Moravia.

Swedenborg, Emanuel (1689-1772) : Swed.
mystic philosopher ; originally Svedberg ;
ennobled, 1719. S. belongs to the history of
philosophy and religion, which his followers
enhanced with the New Jerusalem Church,
founded, 1787, rather than to that of lit., but
he was essentially a religious poet, outside his
learned works in Lat. prose. Among these,
his Opera philosophica et mineralogica, 1734,
and his subsequent work on the animal kingdom
form real and serious contributions to science.
In 1743, S. visited London, where he died
(and was buried in Ratcliffe highway). We
must omit from this brief survey of a many-
sided genius the degree of seriousness in his
treatment of angelic visions, sympathetic
affinities, and other revelations of the unseen,
contained in his Arcana cœlestia . . . detecta,
or ' Secrets of Heaven . . . revealed ', 1749-
56. S., like Linnæus (q.v.), his contemporary,
Bergmann, the chemist, and Celsius, is one of
the great men of Sweden in the 18th cent., and,
though only secondarily a man of letters, he
has a place in the history of the thought upon
which lit. depends.

Swanwick, Anna (1813-99) : Engl. scholar ;
president of Queen's Coll. for Women, London,
and a founder of Girton Coll., Cambridge ;
effected translns. from Gk. and Germ., and is
esp. memorable for her version of Goethe's
(q.v.) Faust, 1850-78.

Swift, Jonathan (1667-1745) : Anglo-Irish
satirist ; divine ; born in Dublin, though a
Yorkshireman by descent ; cousin to Dryden
(q.v.) ; resided partly in Engld., partly in
Ireld., where he became dean of St. Patrick's,
Dublin, 1713, and is commonly known by his
diaconal title. S. was a posth. child, and,
though sent duly to school and coll. in Ireld., his

boyhood was wild in behaviour and poor in circumstances, and the future learned author of *The Battle of the Books* took his degree only by special grace. His mother, a distant relative to lady Temple, procured him a post at Moor Park, in the household of sir Wm. Temple (q.v.) whose secretary S. became. There he met Esther Johnson (1681-1728), a natural daughter of Temple, the ' Stella ' of S.'s after-life, and possibly at last his wife (documentary evidence is lacking). Temple died, 1699, and, though his relations with S. had been once or twice interrupted, he appointed S. to edit his papers and left him £100. But the sun never shone on S., either in Engld. or Ireld., and neglect, and want, and a growing hate of his kind embittered a disposition, warped, naturally, perhaps, by his mother's widowhood before his birth. However that may be, the darkness deepened, deepened to insanity at last. His relations with ' Stella ', to whom he wr. letters, sometimes twice a day, in the ' little language ', as he called it, of a big man's love, and with ' Vanessa ' (Miss Vanhomrigh ; died, 1723), to whom, and of whom, he wr. his poem *Cadenus and Vanessa*, belong to lit. for the sake of the letters and the poetry ; they belong to lit. inalienably, too, for the sake of Thackeray's (q.v.) essay on S. in his vol. of *Engl. Humourists.* ' In a note in his biography ', says Thackeray, ' Scott says that his friend, Dr. Tuke, of Dublin, has a lock of Stella's hair, enclosed in a paper by Swift, on which are written, in the dean's hand, the words, *Only a woman's hair* '. What a conjunction of talents : Swift, sir Walter Scott, Thackeray ! ' Did you ever hear ', continues the youngest of them, ' or read four words more pathetic ? Only a woman's hair : only love, only fidelity, only purity, innocence, beauty ; only the tenderest heart in the world stricken and wounded, and passed away now out of reach of pangs of hope deferred, love insulted, and pitiless desertion. . . . And yet to have had so much love, he must have given some, Treasures of wit and wisdom, and tenderness, too, must that man have had locked up in the caverns of his gloomy heart, and shown fitfully to one or two whom he took in there. But it was not good to visit that place. People did not remain there long, and suffered for having been there. He shrank away from all affection sooner or later. Stella and Vanessa both died near him, and away from him. He had not heart enough to see them die. He broke away from his fastest friend, Sheridan (q.v.) ; he shrank away from his fondest admirer, Pope (q.v.). He was always alone—alone and gnashing in the darkness, except when Stella's sweet smile came and shone upon him. When that went, silence and utter might closed over him. An immense genius : an awful downfall and ruin. So great a man he seems to me, that thinking of him is like thinking of an empire falling. We have other great names to mention—none I think, however, so great or so gloomy '.

Let us leave the gloomy dean to his memories, and deduct from Thackeray's estimate of him the parts due to what Mr. Charles Whibley calls the ' expression of Victorian prejudice '

(*Jonathan Swift*, Cambridge, 1917). Let us remember that S. kept faith with his friends ; that he fought abuses in high or low places with equal spirit and courage ; that, in London, ' when service might be rendered, he forgot himself and the claims of party ', and that, in Ireld., ' he extended his literary patronage to all the sad poets and faded blue-stockings of Dublin ' (Whibley, *ib.*), and so we shall temper the charges of misanthropy and cynicism. We have to turn from the man to his writings, which, almost always anon., include *The Battle of the Books* (1697), publd., 1704, with *The Tale of a Tub*, both extraordinarily brilliant in their satire on the shams and pedantry of scholars and theological, and both intimately connected with the *Phalaris* controversy, which is narrated s.v. Bentley ; they include the *Journal to Stella* and the poetic *Cadenus and Vanessa*, to which reference has been made ; *Drapier's Letters*, 1724, which by their courage and force prevented the introduction into Ireld. of the so-called ' Wood's Halfpence ', a currency said to be worth less than its face-value, coined for Ireld., 1722, under a patent, revoked, 1725, which was granted to the duchess of Kendal and sold by her to a Wolverhampton copperfounder named Wood ; they include, among many pamphlets and ephemeral publications, all recognizable by the *sæva indignatio* which was inscribed on his tomb, next his Stella's, in St. Patrick's, Dublin (*ubi sæva indignatio ulterius cor lacerare nequit*), the immortal work, *Gulliver's Travels*, 1726, which should be read with his *Directions to Servants*, 1728. *Gulliver*, of course, is a classic of the imaginary voyage class of lit., descended from Lucian through Rabelais (q.v.) ; it is also a classic of the nursery, delighting children by its giants and midgets ; but ' from all predecessors who describe an inverted Utopia under the form of a journey, Swift differs by his motive. . . . The disenchanted idealism of the whole book gives it some unity ' (*P.E.L.*, viii, 282), and the same author (prof. Elton) says that, ' crowning the accomplishment of the purely prose genius in English, Swift stands apart from his environment, like an *Agonistes* of the older drama '. S.'s works were edited, with a *Life*, by sir W. Scott, 19 vols., 1814, which is still the basis of later edns. ; Forster, q.v., wr. a *Life*, which he left unfind. ; the *Life* by rt. hon. sir H. Craik was first issued, 1882, and there are valuable monographs by sir L. Stephen, q.v., and J. Churton Collins (1848-1908).

Swinburne, Algernon Charles (1837-1909) : Engl. poet ; an incomparable melodist, who owed his mastery of lyrical and dramatic verse to his worshipful master, V. Hugo (q.v.), the object, hardly second to Shakespeare, of his constant and undiscriminating devotion. S., who left Oxford without taking a degree, succumbed, on his settlement in London after a period of travel abroad, to the sensuous spell of the Pre-Raphaelite Brotherhood (q.v.) ; and some aspects of his genius are well summarized in *C.H.E.L.*, xiii, 129 : ' In the childlike frankness of his denunciation of kings and priests he rivalled the outspokenness of Shelley (q.v.), whose lyric copiousness and variety he even surpassed. But, while Shelley, of the masters of English song, came nearest to him in point of time and the spirit of his verse, the cadences of his music were also founded upon the Elizabethans and Milton, and no influence moulded his phraseology so completely as the sacred literature, biblical and liturgical, of the religion whose professors were the object of his tireless invective '—a veritable triumph of the literary influence of the Bible (q.v.). S.'s work, ' as a whole ', says the same writer, ' suffers from the paucity of its contents ; his rapid genius was too easily satisfied with returning to the same themes over and over again, and reaffirming them with increased emphasis but little variety. But, in metrical skill, and in the volume of his highly decorated language, he had no rival among English poets '. As to the ' paucity of contents ', we need only add that S. arrived in a period of exhaustion : he pressed the Tennysonian note of beauty, extracted from Keats, so far that poets after S. tended to react into the violence of the barrack-room and the public-house. We need not enumerate his publd. poems, from the 2 plays, *The Queen Mother* and *Rosamund*, of 1860, to *The Duke of Gandia*, 1908 ; he was always essentially a sea-poet (not inappropriately, as the son of an admiral): ' I will go back to the great sweet mother, Mother and lover of men, the Sea ', he wr. in *The Triumph of Time*, contained in his *Poems and Ballads*, 1866, which he dedicated to Landor (q.v.) in the following quatrain :

The sea gives her shells to the shingle,
The earth gives her streams to the sea :
They are many, but my gift is single—
My verses, the first-fruits of me.

The collected edn., 1904, of S.'s *Poems* is in 6 vols., and of his *Tragedies*, 1905-6, is in 5 vols. He wr., too, a large amount of literary criticism, or more precisely, of dithyrambic eulogy of his favourite authors ; chiefly, *William Blake*, 1868 ; *George Chapman*, 1875 ; *A Study of Shakespeare*, 1880 ; *A Study of Victor Hugo*, 1886 ; *A Study of Ben Jonson*, 1889 ; *The Age of Shakespeare*, 1908, etc. He wr. a pamphlet, *Under the Microscope*, 1872, in reply to Buchanan's (q.v.) attack on Rossetti and himself as the ' Fleshly School ' (q.v.) ; and, since there was a kind of feeling among Victorians that S.'s poetic love of liberty corresponded to some defect in patriotism, we may quote 3 lines from his *England : an Ode :*

All our past proclaims our future : Shakespeare's voice and Nelson's hand,
Milton's faith and Wordsworth's trust in this our chosen and chainless land,
Bear us witness : come the world against her, England yet shall stand.

S.'s last years were spent at Putney with his friend and biographer, T. Watts-Dunton (q.v.).

Sybel, von, Heinrich (1817-95) : Germ. historian ; disciple of Ranke (q.v.), and precursor of Treitschke (q.v.).

Sylvester, Joshua (1563-1618) : Engl. poet ; chiefly rememberable for his spirited verse transln. of Du Bartas (q.v.), *La Semaine* (*His Divine Weekes and Workes*), 1605-7, to which Milton (q.v.) was much indebted.

Symonds, John Addington (1840-93) : Engl. critic ; deeply versed in Ital. studies ; mostly lived abroad, owing to ill-helath. Wr. studies of *The Renaissance in Italy*, 7 vols., 1875-86, of which prof. Saintsbury says (*Hist. Crit.*, iii, 552) : : ' From some little acquaintance with literary history, I think I may say that there is no better historical treatment of a foreign literature in English. One can never help wishing that the author had left half his actual subject untouched, and had completed the study of Italian literature '. It is the vols. dealing with the lit. of the Renaissance which have been laid under contribution in this dict., and the present writer gratefully records his humble concurrence with prof. Saintsbury's judgment. S. wr., too, vols. on Dante and Walt Whitman, transld. the *Autobiography* of Cellini (q.v.), and, apart from some vols. of original verse, was an accomplished translr. of the Ital. poetry which he interpreted so well. The affinity between S. and Pater (q.v.) is a commonplace of Engl. literary history in the 19th cent., but S.'s ' mind, like his style, was very much more irregular and undisciplined than Mr. Pater's ' (Saintsbury, *loc. cit.*).

Systeme de la Nature (1770) : Fr. bk. in 2 vols., ascribed to d'Holbach (q.v.), but more probably of multiple authorship, including d'Holbach, Diderot (q.v.), and others. It comprised a more complete presentment of the principles of materialism applied with ruthless logic to the regions of metaphysics and theology ; it reduced conscience to a function of sensation, and asserted the determinism of physical laws over the exploded determinism of divine laws. As such, the work was of great importance in the development of nihilistic thought along the lines which politically, led direct to the Fr. Revolution ; and it ranks as a manifesto of the *philosophes* (q.v.). It was publd. under ascription to a certain Mirabaud (q.v.), a deceased dummy in that school.

Syttendemai-Poesi (Norse) ; ' Seventeenth of May Poesy ' : Generic name of a class of poetry busily composed in Norway on the occasion and in celebration of the Declaration of Independence and the proclamation of king Christian of Norway, 17 May, 1814. The separation from Denmark and the constitution of a *storthing* (parliament) at Oslo (Christiania) were greeted with eager popular enthusiasm, which found its literary expression. ' This poesy, of course, was intensely patriotic, taking the form of odes to Eidsvold, hymns to Old Norway, and defiance to the world at large. It is tedious, and sometimes laughable if read now ; but then it had its significance, and was the inarticulate cry of a young, unsatisfied nation ' (sir E. Gosse, *Lit. Northern Europe*, 4 ; and see *s.v.* Wergeland).

Szafarjik, Pavel Josef (1795-1861) : Czech antiquary ; wr. part i of *Slavonic Antiquity*, 1837, in 2 vols., which ranks as a monument of scholarship, and was transld. into several languages. S. did not complete this work with the second part, and later research has corrected or upset some of his conclusions in what he publd. ; but he admirably prepared the way for future workers in a field, which he explored with great diligence, and in which he made effective discoveries. See, too, *s.v.* Palacký.

T

Tafur, Pero (*c.* 1410-*c.* 1484): Span. travel-chronicler. Wr. 'Journeys and Voyages in diverse parts of the world', *ed. pr.*, 1874. T.'s travel-book is interesting rather than valuable, and it is due to his gossiping personality and fresh curiosity that he may be described as the first Cook's tourist in literary history.

Tahureau, Jacques (1527-55): Fr. poet. T. died so young, and so shortly after the rise of the constellation of the Pleiad (q.v.) that it is hardly correct chronologically, though poetically it is reasonable, to speak of him as a satellite; certainly, he had rare affinities with the muse of Ronsard (q.v.) and the views of Du Bellay (q.v.), and is to be accounted a member of their school. He wr. 3 vols. of sonnets, odes, and love-verse in the modern Fr. forms, and it is noted as exceptional that he married the lady who figured as the *admirée* of his poetry. T. was spoken of as 'the French Catullus', and the epithet 'sugred sonnets' which Meres (q.v.) applied to Shakespeare was used by Vauquelin (q.v.) of T., and may stand to characterize his gift.

Taine, Hippolyte (1828-93): Fr. critic, philosopher, historian, and most often an amalgam of the three. Wr. 2 vols. *de l'Intelligence*; 5 vols. of *History of English Literature* (i-iv, 1856-64; v, 1869; transld. into Engl. by H. van Laun, 1873; cheap edn., 4 vols., Chatto, 1906); 2 vols. *de la Philosophie de l'Art*, and (with minor works of travel, etc.), 7 vols. of *Origines de la France Contemporaine* ('Ancien Régime', 'Révolution', 'Empire'), composed after the war of 1870. The essays on La Fontaine and Livy should also be mentioned. T., who acknowledged himself in graceful language a pupil of Ste. Beuve (q.v.), outran his master as a theorizer, and may fairly be said to have ridden his theories too hard. There was too much philosophizing about psychology in his criticism, too much mechanics in his history. His detractors quote from the Pref. to his *Engl. Lit.*, 'Vice and virtue are products, like vitriol and sugar; and every complex phenomenon arises from other more simple phenomena on which it hangs'. It is a fascinating but dangerous doctrine; and Saintsbury (*Hist. Crit.*, iii, 441) straitly says, that, to T., 'The man of letters, be he Shakespeare or Voltaire, Dante or Cervantes, was simply a made-up prescription'. But Saintsbury was always a sturdy opponent of the influence-of-the-epoch theory of lit., and his 'only adequate judgment' on T.'s *Engl. Lit.*, that it is 'positively and utterly worthless', is warped by his impatience of that doctrine. T.'s great work on Engl. lit. should not be read without outside knowledge of the subject, but it forms an invaluable supplement and stimulus to knowledge, and illustrates certain general ideas as to character, race, environment and type, which, though Procrustean in places, fit his subject in other places extraordinarily well. He illuminates his theme at every step, and his bk. thoroughly merits the high repute (within limits) which it enjoys. The work

on *Contemporary France*, which T. took over from Tocqueville (q.v.), is also solid and suggestive; though here, too, as critics point out, T.'s attitude is that of a physician studying an interesting case, or of a naturalist examining insect-life under the microscope.

Talavera, Ferrant Sanchez (fl. *c.* 1407-*c.* 1440): Span. poet. The collection of Baena (q.v.) has preserved 16 of T.'s poems, including an elegy on the death of admiral Ruy Diaz de Mendoza.

Talfourd, Thomas Noon (1795-1854): Engl. dramatist and critic; M.P.; judge; knt. T. conferred his greatest service on Engl. letters by piloting the copyright Act through the House of Commons, 1837-42. Wr. *Ion*, 1835, a tragedy on Gk. dramatic lines, which was successfully produced on the stage, and was followed by *The Athenian Captive* and *The Massacre of Glencoe*. T. was an early admirer of Wordsworth (q.v.), and was appointed literary executor to C. Lamb. (q.v.), whose *Letters*, 1837, and *Memorials*, 1848, he piously and skilfully publd.

Tallemant des Réaux, Gédéon (1619-92): Fr. memoirist; a frequenter at one time of the Hôtel de Rambouillet (q.v.). Wr., *c.* 1660, anecdotal series of *Historiettes*, dealing with the main personages, 376 in all, of society and lit. from the reign of king Henry iv till his own day. The memoirs, or reminiscences, are of considerable interest and entertainment, and are very frequently quoted.

Tamayo y Baus, Manuel (1829-98): Span. dramatist. Wr. a *Joan of Arc* (after Schiller, q.v.), 1847, and a *Virginia* (after Alfieri, q.v.), 1853. T.'s *Drama nuevo*, 1867, is perhaps the best-known of his plays, which were always clever and conscientious. His successor on the modern Span. stage was José Echegaray (born, 1832).

Tannhäuser, The (fl. *c.* 1270): Germ. Minnesinger (q.v.); a wandering singer and player ('Spielmann'), known to posterity by this title, which passed into the legend immortalized by Wagner (q.v.); the fame of his light-of-love adventures made him the hero of he fabled Venusberg. The T. belonged to the degeneracy of Minnegesang, or more precisely, to its transition into folksong, and his songs of love and satire, combine the effects of the Fr. *pastourelle* with those of Germ. village-verse.

Tansillo, Luigi (1510-68): It. poet. Born at Naples; wr. dramatic, didactic and lyrical verse of no particular distinction in merit.

Tarrega, Francisco Augstin (*c.* 1554-1602): Span. dramatist; resident at Valencia. Wr. *la Enemiga favorable* ('The friendly Foewoman'), mentioned with approval by Cervantes (q.v.; *Don Q.*, i, 48).

Tasso, -i. Bernardo (1493-1569): It. poet. Wr. *Amadigi di Francia* (Amadis of Gaul) in 100 cantos (57,000 verses), interesting historically on 2 grounds: (1) it marked the influence of Ariosto's (q.v.) more brilliant experiment, though itself the continuation of a tradition, in romantic epos, and (2) it departed from the

34

Pentateuch was publd., 1535, and had considerable success in advance of Christian iii's Bible (s.v. Pedersen); and his most notable contribution to homiletics was his collection of sermons, 1539, intended mainly for the instruction and edification of the lower orders of the Protestant clergy.

Taylor, Henry (1800-86): Engl. dramatic poet; employed at the Colonial Office, 1824-72; K.C.M.G., 1872. Wr. *Isaac Comnenus* (see s.v. Du Cange), 1827, *Philip van Artevelde*, 1834, and other plays, besides some prose-works of criticism and reflection. The *Artevelde* play was very successful, not on the stage, but in literary circles, where T. became a kind of 'lion', and roared sometimes a little sarcastically. As to the failure of *Philip* on the stage, 'if the apparently growing taste for psychological plays were some day to unite itself with a taste for literature, the case might be altered', writes prof. Saintsbury (*C.H.E.L.*, xiii, 112), who adds that T. was 'pushed from his stool, almost before he was fairly settled on it, by Tennyson, who used quite different forms and methods, and by Browning, who partly used the same, but added many others, and wielded them with much greater power'. This obstruction by the greater masters is true, but the comparative oblivion which has overtaken T. has also been ascribed to lack of inspiration and vitality in his dramas. (See Walker, *Lit. Victorian Era*, 270).

Taylor, -i. Isaac (1730-1807): Engl. engraver; illustrated, among other notable books, Richardson's (q.v.) *Sir Charles Grandison*, 778; portrait-painter; secretary of the Society of Arts.

-ii. Isaac (1759-1829): Engl. engraver; son of above; settled at Ongar as nonconformist divine, and publd. a series of manuals for children.

-iii. Isaac (1787-1865): Engl. engraver; philosophic writer; son of above. T.'s skill in his hereditary craft was admired by Rossetti (q.v.) but he turned his attention to lit., chiefly in the domain of theology, where he acquired considerable repute. Wr. *Elements of Thought*, 1823; *Natural History of Enthusiasm*, 1830, his masterpiece, and others, including *History of the Transmission of Ancient Books to Modern Times*, 1827; *Home Education*, etc.

-iv. Ann (1782-1866; m. Joseph Gilbert, 1813) and **Jane** (1783-1824): Engl. engravers; writers for children, both separately and in collaboration; daughter of Isaac T. ii (above), and sisters, accordingly, of Isaac T. iii. Wr., together, *Original Poems for Infant Minds*, 1804, and similar vols. of verse, including Jane T.'s 'Twinkle, twinkle, little Star', which achieved, and retain, a well-earned popularity.

-v. Isaac (1829-1901): Engl. philologer; divine; canon of York; son of Isaac T. iii (above). Wr. *The Alphabet*, 2 vols., 1883; *Words and Places*, 1864, and cognate treatises in philology and archæology. Wr., too, an interesting account of *The Family Pen: Memorials, Biography and Literature of the Taylor Family, of Ongar*, 2 vols., 1867.

Taylor, Jeremy (1613-67): Engl. divine; bp. of Down, 1661; a master of Engl. prose, who has been compared both with Spenser and Shakespeare, for a style described as uniformly magnificent. Wr. the *Liberty of Prophesying*, 1646; the *Great Exemplar* (a life of Christ), and other works, and chiefly *Rules and Exercises of Holy Living*, 1650, and of *Holy Dying*, 1651. The following excerpt will illustrate T.'s mastery of Engl. prose:

'In sickness the soul begins to dress herself for immortality. And first, she unties the strings of vanity that made her upper garment cleave to the world and sit uneasy. First, she puts off the light and fantastic summer-robe of lust and wanton appetite. Next to this, the soul by the help of sickness knocks off the fetters of pride, and vainer complacencies. Then she draws the curtains, and stops the light from coming in, and takes the pictures down, those fantastic images of self-love, and gay remembrances of vain opinion, and popular noises. Then the spirit stoops into the sobrieties of humble thoughts, and feels corruption chiding the forwardness of fancy and allaying the vapours of conceit and factious opinions. Next to these, as the soul is still undressing, she shakes off the roughness of her great and little angers and animosities, and receives the oil of mercies and smooth forgiveness, fair interpretations and gentle answers, designs of reconcilement and Christian atonement, in their places.

'I have seen the rays of the sun or moon dash upon a brazen vessel, whose lips kissed the face of those waters that lodged within its bosom; but being turned back and sent off, with its smooth pretences or rougher waftings, it wandered about the room and beat upon the roof, and still doubled its heat and motion. So is sickness and a sorrow entertained by an unquiet and discontented man.

'Nothing is more unreasonable than to entangle our spirits in wildness and amazement, like a partridge fluttering in a net, which she breaks not, though she breaks her wings'.

Note how the metaphor is sustained, and worked out; and how marked is the advance in power and richness in the use of the instrument of style since the days of the obvious verbal conceits (q.v.) and antithetical clauses of earlier experimentation. Note, too, the debt to the Engl. Bible (q.v.) in the build of the sentences and the vocabulary, in the very epoch of Bunyan (q.v.). T. has properly been characterized as the Chrysostom among Engl. theologians.

Taylor, John (1680-1653): Engl. poet; born in Gloucester; known as the 'Water Poet', from his trade as a London Waterman, who, after a spell in the navy, kept inns at Oxford and in London. He collected his *Works*, 1630; and 'the manner in which he published his books, which were separately of little bulk, was to print them at his own cost, make presents of them, and then hope for "sweet remuneration" from the persons whom he had thus delighted to honour' (Southey, q.v.: *The Uneducated Poets*, edited by J. S. Childers, Oxford, 1925). Southey adds: 'This mode of publication was not regarded in those days so close akin to mendicity as it would now be deemed '. T.'s poems have little intrinsic merit, but their personal interest as human documents is not inconsiderable; and he 'lived in an age when kings and queens condescended to notice him, nobles and archbishops admitted him to their table, and mayors and corporations received him with civic honours ' (ibid.).

Taylor, John Edward (1791-1844): Engl. newspaper proprietor; founded, 1821, the *Manchester Guardian*, which has maintained at a steady level of efficiency the liberal opinions and moral principles of its founder.

Taylor (Philip) Meadows (1808-76): Engl. novelist; entered the service of the nizam of Hyderabad, and did eminent work in civil and military capacities. Wr. successful Anglo-Indian novels: *Confessions of a Thug*, 1839; *Tara*, and others; and a *Story of my Life*, edited posth. by his daughter, 1877.

Taylor, Tom (1817-80): Engl. dramatist; journalist; edited *Punch*, 1874-80; prof. of Engl. lit. at London univ., 1845. Wr. a large number of plays, including *Still Waters run Deep*; *Our American Cousin*, etc.; an industrious but not a first-rate man of letters.

Taylor, William (1765-1836): Engl. critic; commonly called ' of Norwich ', as a leading member of a literary group in that then stronghold of radicalism; under that territorial designation, the subject of a monograph. *William Taylor von Norwich* by George Herzfeld (Berlin, 1897), which surveys from both ends the work of ' the most industrious and useful middleman between England and Germany—he can hardly be called an interpreter—until Carlyle appeared ' (Elton, *Engl. Lit.*: 1780-1830, ii, 405). Transld. Bürger's (q.v.) *Lenore*, with its immense temporary vogue, 1790; Lessing's *Nathan der Weise* and Goethe's *Iphigenie*; and in the *Monthly* and *Critical* reviews soon became (Elton, *ibid.*) ' an acknowledged arbiter on all things German'. His chief work was an *Historic Survey of German Poetry*, 1828-30, which Carlyle reviewed adversely in the *Edinburgh Review*, but which, even with its faults and despite its brief reputation, was a valuable guide to a field awaiting cultivation.

Tchehov. See Chekhov.

Tegnér, Esaias (1782-1846): Swed. national poet. ' The Tyrtæus of Sweden ' (Sandys, iii, 349); ' Sweden had produced no really great poet before Tegnér ' (Boyesen, *Essays on Scandinavian Lit.*, 236). ' He is the glory and boast of Sweden, and stands first among all her poets living or dead ' (Longfellow, *Prefatory Remarks* to his transln. of T.'s *Children of the Lord's Supper*). In this connection, sir E. Gosse (*Lit. Northern Europe*, 105) makes an illuminating remark: ' Between Tegnér and Runeberg ' (q.v.), he writes, ' the natural link is wanting. The link properly consists, it appears to me, in Longfellow, who is an anomaly in American Literature, but who has the full character of a Swedish poet, and who, had he been born in Sweden, would have completed exactly enough the chain of style that ought to unite the idealism of Tegnér to the realism of Runeberg '. (See, too, s.v. Scand. Lit., Sweden). It is not inconsistent with Longfellow's and Boyesen's tributes that

sir E. Gosse should remark (*op. cit.*) that the practical result of T.'s ' productions was to paralyse poetry in Sweden for half a century '; for T.'s genius was essentially conservative, and his brilliant success in combining native themes with the best models of foreign style certainly made his successors' problems more difficult. In T.'s verse Swed. neo-romanticism (s.v. Phosphorus), a somewhat hectic phenomenon, was converted to a saner idealism, which postponed for a while the realistic movement, afterwards consummated in Runeberg. These are matters interesting to critics, who like to appoint leaders to schools and schools to leaders, sometimes even on à priori grounds. Of T. it may safely be said, that, though deliberately academic, in the sense that he consciously used an exalted, rhetorical style, he was first and above all a poet; and his poetry conquered the disadvantages of his peasant's origin and clerk's apprenticeship. He browsed among books from an early age; Macpherson's (q.v.) *Ossian* and Homer were his chief delights, and he was fortunate in entering the univ. of Lund, in which he afterwards became prof.; later, 1824, he became bp. of Wexiö. It must be owned that a vigorous hedonism tempered his pastoral utterances, and that the melancholy or morbid elements in Swed. romance (Phosphorism) were routed by T.'s outspoken joy in life and frankly sensuous Hellenism. An excellent Christian, he was a more excellent pagan. He was a keen supporter of the Gothic League (q.v.), which aimed at effecting for Scand. that revival of local interest and colour, which Scott (q.v.) effected for his own country; but T. was too good a scholar to neglect the classical manner of Goethe and Schiller (qq.v.) in Germany. Not in vain did he fill the chair of Gk. at Lund; and, while his *Children of the Lord's Supper* recalls Goethe's *Hermann und Dorothea*, and his *Axel* is Byronic, his whole outlook on art is closely akin to that of the Schiller of *Wallenstein* and *Wilhelm Tell*. So much for the making of T. It remains to say that he was mostly self-made, on bold, large, generous, splendid lines; and that his best-known poem is the *Frithjof's Saga* of 1820-5 (the first 9 cantos appeared in *Iduna*, the organ of the *Gothic League*, 1821). This ancient Scand. tale of Ingeborg, Frithjof, Björn, and King Ring, modernized its national theme in much the same fashion as Tennyson (q.v.) modernized the tales of Arthur (q.v.), and it raised T. at once to the position of leading Swed. poet. It was transld. into almost every language: 18 times separately into Engl., and 18 times into Germ. before 1878; a new Engl. transln. in the original metres, by C. D. Locock, was publd. by G. Allen and Unwin in 1924. The work deserves even greater popularity than it has enjoyed. T.'s main characteristic was buoyancy,—a certain boyishness of spirit, which no worldly experience corrected. An unfortunate attachment in later life, against which he struggled in failing health, upset his mental balance for a time; it need only be mentioned here in connection with his poem, *Hypochondria*, which alone contradicts his wholesome doctrine that poetry is ' the health of life ', and that ' a poetry the duty of editing her literary remains, through Crashaw (q.v.), a mystic among Engl. poets, to J. A. Froude (q.v.), in the 19th cent., who ranked her in renown with Cervantes (q.v.). Leon deemed her inspired : ' I can hardly doubt that the Holy Ghost is speaking through her in many passages ' ; and Kelly, the historian of Span. lit., writing in our own day (*Lit. espagn.*, 255f.), says : ' She is a true miracle of genius, who takes her place in literature beside the most perfect masters. St. Ignatius of Loyola and St. Theresa are respectively the brain and the heart of the Catholic reaction ' ; and he cites the eulogies of Crashaw, Jeremy Taylor, and Dr. William Law (qq.v.). To this testimony nothing need be added, save to note the devotion of her spiritual child San Juan de la Cruz (s.v. Yepes), and to add the titles of T.'s writings : ' The Way of Perfection ' (*Camino de Perfeccion*), ' The Interior Castle ' (*Castillo interior*), ' The Mercy of God ' (*de la Misericordias de Dios* ; ranking as her autobiography), and ' Thoughts on the Love of God ' (*Conceptos del Amor de Dios*). To these should be added her letters (4 vols., Madrid, 1793), addressed to men and women in public and private life. As a leader of spiritual thought, St. T.'s name stands as high to-day as ever.

Tersteegen, Gerhard (1697-1769) : Germ. mystic ; a sweet singer of Pietism (q.v.), whose poems and example had great influence even beyond the limits of his humble Westphalian home.

Terza-rima (It.) : Three-line stanza. Descriptive name of the metre employed by Dante (q.v.), in his *Divina Commedia*, which starts as follows :

Nel mezzo del cammin di nostra vita
  Mi retrovai per una selva oscura,
  Chè la diretta via era smarrita.

Lines 1 and 3, it will be observed, rhyme. The first line of the second stanza rhymes with line 2 of the first :

Eh quanto a dir qual era è cosa dura.

Line 2 starts a fresh rhyme taken up by lines 1 and 3 of the third stanza, and line 3 of the second stanza repeats the -ura rhyme of stanza 1, line 2, and stanza 2, line 1. Thus, the rhyme-scheme of this metre is : *aba, bcb, cdc, ded, efe, fgf, ghg*, and so on. No poet of eminence adopted the metre in Italy (see Fazio degli Uberti, Frederigo Frezzi, and Matteo Palmieri), and it was employed variously in the succeeding centuries for didactic and satiric verse, and for burlesque.

Testi, Fulvio (1593-1646) : It. poet ; count by rank ; at first, a follower of the Petrarchists and Marinists, but shook himself free from their influence under the spell of Chiabrera (q.v.). T., like other court-poets in Italy, suffered from the patronage of the d'Este princes, now dukes of Modena, and always capricious in their favours. He died in prison, ' on the eve of release ', said the reigning duke, and his only crime seems to have been a desire to quit the ducal service. T. anticipated history by expecting Italy's salvation from Savoy, and some of his odes are stately and yet vivacious,— among them, *Ruscelletto orgoglioso*, the swollen rivulet, with its natural and applied meanings. Leopardi (q.v.) described T. as the Horace *manqué* of a barbarian generation. The praise is excessive, but he was undoubtedly

a lyric writer of fine powers,—finer than the thought which informed them.

Texeda, de, Geronimo (fl. 1627) : Span. pastoralist ; teacher of Span. in Paris, where he publd. a ' new version ' of the *Diana* of Montemayor (q.v.), largely founded on G. G. Polo (q.v.).

Thackeray, William Makepeace (1811-63) : Engl. novelist ; by common consent, one of the leading novelists of the 19th cent., and, as the author of *Vanity Fair* (20 parts, Jan., 1847-July, 1848 ; revised edns., 1853, 1863) and *Esmond* (*The History of Henry Esmond, Esquire*, 3 vols., 1852), one of the great novelists of Europe. T.'s life was written by Mr. Lewis Melville, 2 vols., 1910, and the bibliography of his writings occupies pp. 145-376 of vol. ii of that work. It is not possible, obviously, to contract those 230 pp. to the scale of the present bk., or to do more than to note that the first collected edn. of T.'s works was publd. in 22 vols., 1867-9, with 2 supplementary vols., 1885-6. An edn. in 13 vols., with biographical introductions by Anne Thackeray (lady) Ritchie, T.'s daughter (author of *The Story of Elizabeth*, 1863 ; *Old Kensington*, 1873, etc.), was issued, 1898-9 ; Mr. M. H. Spielmann, historian of *Punch*, publd. the *Hitherto Unidentified Contributions of W. M. Thackeray to ' Punch '*, 1899 ; Mr. Lewis Melville edited the *Works*, 20 vols., 1901-7 ; prof. Saintsbury, in 17 vols., 1908 ; lady Ritchie added *Chapters from Some Memoirs*, 1894 ; and, among other monographs, letters, and essays, we may mention *Thackeray*, in ' English Men of Letters ', 1879, by A. Trollope (q.v.), himself a novelist of high standing. And, with all this claim on biography and research, T. was only 52 when he died.

Born at Alipur, nr. Calcutta, where his father, Richmond T., died in 1815, T. was brought home to Engld. at an early age by his mother, Anne, *née* Becher, and his step-father, major Carmichael-Smyth, who is said to be delineated in colonel Newcome. He went to Charterhouse, 1822-8, which figures in several of his books, and read for a few months with his step-father in Devon (Clavering and Chatteris in *Pendennis* have been identified with Ottery St. Mary and Exeter), before proceeding to Trinity Coll., Cambridge. There he formed intimate friendships with Tennyson, E. Fitzgerald (qq.v.), and others ; and thereafter his versatile gifts—he might have earned his living by pencil as well as pen—were employed unrestingly in London. An early loss of fortune threw him on his own resources, and he wr., and drew, and lectured (on both sides of the Atlantic : *Engl. Humourists of the 18th cent.*, and *The Four Georges*), pouring his brilliant talents into *Fraser's Magazine*, *Punch*, *Cornhill* (which he edited, 1860-2 ; see s.v. G. Smith), and other periodicals. Prose and verse came with almost equal readiness ; and particular mention is due to *The Yellowplush Correspondence* (*Fraser's*, 1837-8), *Jeames's Diary* (*Punch*, 1845-7), *The Book of Snobs* (*Punch*, 1846-7), and the burlesque *Novels by Eminent Hands*, parodying G. P. R. James, Bulwer Lytton (qq.v.), and others. But posterity has wisely decided to remember T. chiefly, even solely, as a novelist ; and, more wisely than his contemporaries in the 19th cent., it has decided not to compare or to contrast him with his companion-novelist, Dickens (q.v.), with whom he once quarrelled and was never very intimate. This juxtaposition of *pairs* always strikes contemporary opinion more directly than posterity. Goethe and Schiller (qq.v.) formed one such pair; Tennyson and Browning (qq.v.) formed another; Dickens and Thackeray, a third; and Victorian dinner-parties and debates were often posed with the problem,—which do you prefer: Dickens or Thackeray? Tennyson or Browning? To these questions the best reply was given by the great chancellor, Bismarck, with reference to Goethe and Schiller: 'Thank God, the Fatherland possessed both good fellows'; and it is not as better or worse than Dickens or another, but as good *per se*, that T. is esteemed as a novelist. He wr. *Vanity Fair*, 1848; *Pendennis*, 1850; *Esmond*, 1852; *The Newcomes*, 1855; *The Virginians* (continuing *Esmond*), 1859; *Lovel the Widower*, 1861; *The Adventures of Philip*, 1862; and *Denis Duval* (unfind.), 1864. These novels fall into 2 groups, with one predominant in each. *Esmond* is supreme in the class of 18th-cent. romances, to which *The Virginians*, its sequel, belonged, and *Denis Duval* was to belong; and *Vanity Fair* is supreme in the class of novels of contemporary manners, which include the rest of his fiction. The predominance of *Esmond* is undisputed. It is the finest picture we possess of social life in the age of queen Anne. Beatrix, its heroine, is pourtrayed, or is suffered to pourtray herself, in all her woman's variability; and the plot was contrived to arouse genuine passion and emotion. Further, the writing afforded the fullest opportunities for T.'s mingled grace and humour; for the reflective, infinitely kindly, clear-sighted, sometimes stern, but always warm and human moralizing, which marked his leisurely style. The story of col. Henry Esmond, in the service of queen Anne, is an hist. novel of a very rare type of excellence. But *Vanity Fair* is even greater. The final test of a good novel is its character-value. In this great novel, that test may be freely applied. The different types of selfishness delineated in the George Osbornes, senior and junior, appeal powerfully from their acts to the imagination which represents them. Note, too, the study of Becky Sharp, the most sympathetic adventuress who ever lived in an Engl. novel. Her whole career is a failure. Amelia, for all her tears, is not worsted at the end: George's compromising letter becomes the *billet doux* of his widow's second marriage; sir Pitt goes back to his good Jane; Rawdon Crawley, the too fond husband, rises to manhood at the crisis, and is redeemed by his love of his son. Nothing ignoble comes to greatness, nothing good suffers enduring hurt, nothing remediable but has its opportunity. So, too, in the other greater novels: we recall type after type stamped with the impress of truth to character. 'This was decided by Becky Sharp'; 'that is the Jos Sedley fallacy'; 'by this road Dobbin was undone'; 'Colonel Newcome would have acted so'; 'that is an entry from Blanche Amory's diary': almost unconsciously we store these gathered experiences in our minds,

and start our judgment of action with the gain of a fresh set of precedents. Further, it was T.'s talent, and the good fortune of his readers, to adorn his narrative with little essays—little sermons, in the Horatian sense—, which are pleasant in themselves, and which help us across the bridges of the long periods covered by his tales. These sermons are sometimes called cynical; but, in fact, they are more exactly ironical (see s.v. irony); the maker looks at his creation, and he cannot always say that it is good. 'The puppets of his stage', it has been well said (*C.H.E.L.*, xiii, 301), 'possessed a higher value for themselves than for the impartial spectator',—the *spectator ab extra*, who, as the most Addisonian (s.v. Addison) of novelists, built his art on the foundations laid by the inventor of the *Spectator* in the 18th cent., and belongs at last to the Augustan company of Horace (q.v.) himself:

Spectatum admissi risum teneatis, amici?

Thebes: a Gk. episode in the romantic matter of Antiquity 'matière de Rome la grant'; see Bodel). Based on the *Thebaid* of Statius, the Roman epicist of the first cent., A.D., familiar as stace to European romance. The medieval version was effected by an anon. poet in the 12th cent. in the manner of Benoît (q.v.). Boccaccio in his *Teseide*, Chaucer in the *Knight's Tale*, Lydgate (qq.v.), and others, were redactors and continuators of the Theban legends.

Theobald, Lewis (1688-1744): Engl. critic; poet. Wr. *Shakespeare Restored; or a Specimen of the many Errors as well committed as unamended by Mr. Pope in his late Edition of this Poet*, 1726 (see s.v. Pope), for which the assailed editor avenged himself (1) by making T. the hero of his *Dunciad*, 1728, and (2) incorporating the best of T.'s corrections in the next edn. of his Shakespeare. T.'s own edn. of Shakespeare was publd., 7 vols., 1733, and has earned him the title of 'the Porson of Shakespearean Criticism' (J. Churton Collins, *Essays and Studies*, 263; endorsed by sir S. Lee, *William Shakespeare*, 577). 'It may be said with simple truth that no poet in our own or any language owed so great a debt to an editor as Shakespeare owes to this man'.[*] The restitution of T.'s fame must blacken, *pari passu*, the reputation of Pope, in regard to his gibbeting T. in the *Dunciad*. T.'s *Double Falsehood: a Tragedy*, 1727, was wrongly ascribed by him to Shakespeare, and his other poems and plays are of little value. But he was a considerable scholar, in Gk. as well as in Engl. studies; and 'the proper monument of Theobald', writes prof. Collins (*op. cit.*, 315), 'is not that cairn of dishonour which the sensitive vanity of Pope, . . . and the obsequious parrotry of tradition on the part of subsequent writers, have succeeded in accumulating. It is the settled text of Shakespeare'.

Théophile de Viau (1596-1626): Fr. poet; commonly called by his first name. Wr. misc. lyric verse and some experiments in

---

[*] The famous emendation of *Henry V*: II, iii, 17: 'His nose was as sharp as a pen and a table of green fields', to 'His nose was as sharp as a pen and a' babbled of green fields', appeared in *Shakespeare Restored*.

tragic drama : e.g., *Pyrame et Thisbé*, c. 1625, which started the precious (q.v.) vogue ; the former more successful than the latter. T. is interesting as a link between, say, Bertaut and Voiture (qq.v.), the lyric and the precious schools of writers ; and his life, too, is interesting as an illustration of the hazards of the times. He suffered exile as a Huguenot, but recanted in 1619 ; his *Parnasse satirique* involved him in a charge of atheism, and he was condemned to the stake in 1623 ; after long litigation, the sentence was changed to banishment, in which he died. A typical example of his style is the conceit (q.v.), or *pointe*, in his *Pyramus* play, of the dagger, the blood-stain on which was represented as a conscious blush at its own crime :

Le voilà, ce poignard, qui du sang de son maître
S'est souillé lâchement : il en rougit, le traître.

Thibaut iv (1201-63): Fr. lyric poet ; count of Champagne, king of Navarre ; imitator of the Provençal Troubadours, whose qualities of formal excellence were united in his verses with the vigour and freshness of the Northern *trouvères* (see s.vv.). T.'s important rank as feudal prince, and his relations both to North and South, rendered his court particularly appropriate for the fusion of the gifts of the *langue d'oïl* and *langue d'oc* ; and his *chansons* and dialogues of love are of real value in the development of lyric poetry.

Thiele, Just Mattias (1795-1874): Dan. literary critic. Wr. biography of Thorwaldsen, the eminent Dan. sculptor, and publd., 1818-23, a valuable prose-collection of Dan. folk-tales. T.'s original plays and poems have not survived their contemporary reputation.

Thierry, -i. Augustin (1795-1856): Fr. historian ; philosopher ; a disciple at first of St. Simon (q.v.) and later of Comte (q.v.). T. was early inspired by the romantic revival of medievalism : the *Martyres* of Chateaubriand (q.v.) and the *Ivanhoe* of Scott (q.v.) occupied his waking dreams. He wr. at first for noted newspapers (the *Courier* and the *Censeur européen*), but soon devoted himself to history, and continued to write despite the blindness which presently overtook him. His chief works are a *History of the Norman Conquest in Engld.*, 1825, and *Récits des Temps Mérovingiens*, 1840 ; the latter an admirable example of T.'s gifts of exploration in untravelled fields.

-ii. Amedée (1797-1873): Fr. historian ; brother of above. Wr. *History of Gaul*, 1840-47, and other works, more pedestrian in manner.

Thiers, Louis Adolphe (1797-1877): Fr. historian and statesman ; contemporary with Guizot (q.v.), and more forcible in more capacities than he. T.'s chief works were his *Histoire de la Révolution française*, 1823-27, which contributed powerfully to make his reputation, and the *Histoire du Consulat et de l'Empire*, 1845-62, which he worked at through many years, and which amply sustained his fame. T. is justly credited with fostering what is known in Fr. political history as the Napoleonic legend, and he certainly helped to create the atmosphere in which Napoleon iii was crowned. But he was never an ardent Imperialist, and it

fell to T. after 1870 to negotiate the terms of peace with Prussia, and to become president of the new Republic ; a post which he held till 1873.

Thirty Years' War (1618-48): Religious war between emperor Ferdinand ii and the Protestant princes of Germany, who supported the claim of Frederick v to the Imperial throne. France and Sweden (under Gustavus Adolphus) were involved, and the war was ended by the Treaty of Westphalia. The literary importance of the war was its devastating effect on the progress of the Renaissance in Germany ; the rising drama and poetic revival were broken short, and the true awakening was postponed till the 18th cent.

Thomas à Kempis (1380-1471): Germ. mystic. Born of humble parentage (his family name was Hämmerlein or Hamerken, Latinized to Malleolus=little hammer) at Kempen (near Cologne), whence his now universal designation was derived. T. attended the grammar school at Deventer (q.v.), and thus had the good fortune 'gradually to win his way to familiarity with men illustrious for their piety and probity' (early Lat. life of T.), i.e., members of the Brethren of the Common Lot (q.v.), and so obtained a place in the *Fraterhuis* ('brother-house'). Later, in 1406, T. became definitely attached to the Augustinian Order at the Convent of Mount St. Agnes, near Zwolle, where he rose to canon, 1412, and officiated as sub-prior till his death. T. wr. disciplinary works for novices in the cloister, lives of the most eminent of the brethren, mostly from personal acquaintance, and Christian mystical treatises, of which the most important and the most famous is the *de Imitatione Christi*, as to T.'s authorship of which, disputed at certain periods, no doubt is now entertained (one candidate was J. Gerson, q.v.). The 'heart-piercing' (Hallam's word) quality of this great bk., which is most striking in its original fervid Lat. than in any of the many languages into which it has been often transld., is admitted by generations of pious readers, and by Protestants hardly less than by Catholics. Its unworldliness is its most obvious characteristic ; the wholly happy acquiescence of à Kempis in the bliss of a cloistral seclusion, as remote from Dutch art as from German politics, which was at the same time filled with the presence and the business of God. Mrs. Meynell (q.v.), a mystic poet of our own day, Roman Catholic by creed, expresses the mood of the *Imitation of Christ* in her lines *To the Beloved* :

Darkness and solitude shine, for me.
For life's fair outward part are rife
The silver noises ; let them be.
It is the very soul of life
Listens for thee, listens for thee.

The darkness and solitude shone for T. in his cell, and the silver noises of the world outside did not distract his eager ear, listening from his very soul for the silence to which his life returned. Of T.'s significance to progressive thought no less than to mystic lit., let a higher authority pronounce : 'The reader may ask with astonishment, Shall this quiet mystic, wholly immersed in the contemplation of divine things, this recluse, obedient, rigidly catholic monk, shall he be placed in the ranks of those who paved the way for the Reformation ? We boldly answer in the affirmative. . . . Between the childlike, humble Thomas, and the heroic, independent Luther, there is a deep inward affinity, and in the whole character of the former there exist reformatory elements in no inconsiderable measure ' (Ullmann, *Reformers before the Reformation*, E.T., ii, 155, 157). The disciple of the Brethren of the Common Lot was bound to approach Biblical study from a directly human point of view.

Thomas, Antoine Léonard (1732-85): Fr. *philosophe* (q.v.). Wr. *Essai sur le caractère, les moeurs, et l'esprit des femmes dans les différents siècles*, 1772 ; an ambitious but not an arresting piece of research-work in the positivist vein of thought ; and *Éloges* (Praises) of great contemporaries in eloquent prose.

Thomasius, Christian (1655-1728) : Germ. philosopher and publicist ; ' the first journalist in Germany ; . . . his name must be heard in every history of the European liberation ' (Elton, *P.E.L.*, viii, 325-6); held a chair at Leipsic univ., where he startled tradition, in 1687, by delivering a lecture in the Germ. language ; his subject was the imitation of the Fr., which he sought for the first time to establish on a sound basis of national consciousness. His innovations, which included courageously a campaign against the witchcraft superstition, led to his retirement from Leipsic to Halle, where he was instrumental in converting the leading high school into a univ. T. founded the first Germ. monthly review, entitled ' Free-spirited, amusing and earnest, but reasonable and legitimate Thoughts or Monthly Talks on all topics, especially on New Books ', known briefly as the *Teutsche Monate*, and devoted, like all his brave wisdom, to the dissemination of liberal and rational teachings in the best spirit of the Aufklärung (q.v.), or reconstruction of national idealism after the Thirty Years' War (q.v.).

Thompson, Francis (1859-1907) : Engl. poet. Wr. *Poems*, 1893 ; *Sister Songs*, 1895 ; *New Poems*, 1897 ; a friend of Meredith, Patmore and Mrs. Alice Meynell (qq.v.), and much praised by these and other discriminating judges. Perhaps we may quote the opinion of a master in another craft, well-qualified by his Pre-Raphaelite sympathies to appreciate a disciple of Rossetti (q.v.); speaking of *The Hound of Heaven*, sir Edward Burne-Jones said : ' Since Gabriel's *Blessed Damozel* no mystical words have so touched me. Shall I ever forget how I undressed and dressed again, and had to undress again—a thing I most hate—because I could think of nothing else ? ' What was the quality of this poem, which, in those homely words, disturbed the great painter's toilet : ' In that incomparable poem ', said the *Athenæum* (q.v.), 9 Jan., 1909, ' are expressed once for all the experiences of what, in religious language, used to be called a " converted soul " ; and its value is their reality. It is no analysis of profligacy by some pulpiteer, complacent and patronizing, telling people what they ought to feel, and how they may be helped, if only they will take his advice. It is the vital utterance of a soul whose very gift of love has seduced it from the " first and only

fair " ; the cry of the passion-torn worshipper of beauty, who passes through an *inferno* of varied disillusionment before he turns to revere the source of it all. The poem is not merely splendid and sonorous, profound and religious. It is " the general confession " of all those who have sinned rather by excess of passion than defect of love ' ; and it is almost impossible to avoid the pleasure or recalling the sonorous and magnificent opening to that ode :

> I fled Him, down the nights and down the days ;
> I fled Him, down the arches of the years ;
> I fled Him, down the labyrinthine ways
> Of my own mind ; and in the mist of tears
> I hid from Him, and under running laughter.
>   Up vistaed hopes I sped ;
>   And shot, precipitated
> Adown Titanic glooms of chasmèd fears,
>   From those strong Feet that followed,
>   followed after.

Nor was T. less mighty in his simplicity than in his magnificence. His *Poems on Children* are delightful, and in the authentic spirit of Wordsworth (q.v.) :

> She went her unremembering way,
>   She went, and left in me
> The pang of all the partings gone,
>   And partings yet to be. . . .

> Nothing begins and nothing ends,
>   That is not paid with moan ;
> For we are born in other's pain,
>   And perish in our own.

T. is one of the really few instances of a great poet, who, like Crashaw (q.v.) perhaps, whom he partly resembles, has missed the full fame which he deserves.

Thompson, William (? 1785-1833) : Engl. economist ; wr., 1824, *Inquiry into Principles of Distribution of Wealth*, which, in contents and date, is the true foundation of scientific socialism, in advance of the Germ. teachings of K. Marx (1818-83) and F. Lassalle (1825-64). T. was acquainted with Bentham (q.v.). The lit. of socialism does not concern pure letters, but it should be remarked that what Marx added to T. was the mass-fact method, which has been acclimatized in Engld. since his day by the economic writings of Sidney and Beatrice Webb. The Marxian theory was due to (and as wrong as) that of T. and other fallacious thinkers (e.g. Sismondi, q.v.), but T.'s method was accurate, exhaustive, and new in its department : ' The main moral improvement ', he wr., ' to be expected from the system of mutual co-operation will be produced by the altered circumstances of the community '. This was Rousseau's (q.v.) view of the natural man perverted by wrong institutions, and it formed the basis of Robert Owen's experiments in socialism. The great word, ' capitalism ', by the way, which now signifies the socialistic wrong order of society, was invented by Louis Blanc, the Frenchman (1811-82), in 1840.

Thoms, William John (1803-85): Engl. antiquary ; introduced the word ' folk-lore ' into Engl. ; founded *Notes and Queries*, 1849 ; edited Stow's (q.v.) *London* ; publd. *Early Prose Romances*, 1827-8 ; *Lays and Legends*, 2 vols., 1834 ; *Gammer Gurton's Famous Histories*, 1846, and *Gammer Gurton's Pleasant*

Stories, 1848, (gammer=old wife ; *Gammer Gurton's Needle* was an old play).

Thomson, James (1700-48) : Scot. poet ; resided after 1736 at Richmond, Surrey, in the congenial neighbourhood of Pope (q.v.) and his circle. T. disputes (or shares) with David Mallet (dramatist ; died, 1765 ; joint-author of the masque, *Alfred*, 1740), the authorship of the famous patriotic stanzas, *Rule, Britannia*, which occur as a song in that play (Act iii., Sc. v.). T. A. Arne (1710-78) composed the music for it, 1753, and the balance of probability is in favour of T.'s sole authorship of the ode, since its sentiment recurs in his blank-verse poem, *Liberty*, 5 parts, 1734-6, dedicated to Frederick, prince of Wales, and in a shorter poem, *Britannia*. The national verses in *Alfred* point this sentiment in their final form, and deserve the popularity they enjoy. As a playwright, T. was not successful, or, at least, did not win permanent success : his tragedies include *Sophonisba*, 1739, *Agamemnon* and *Coriolanus*, and were all alike composed in blank verse. His *Castle of Indolence*, publd., 1748, was composed in Spenserian stanzas ; and, 'being writ', as its own advertisement stated, 'in the manner of Spenser, the obsolete words, and a similarity of diction in some of the lines, which border on the ludicrous, were necessary to make the imitation more perfect. And the style of that admirable poet, as well as the measure in which he wrote are, as it were, appropriated by custom to all allegorical poems writ in our language ; just as in French the style of Marot has been used by the politest writers of the age of Louis xiv '. This statement is more interesting historically than *The Castle of Indolence* is valuable poetically. The treatment of Spenser (q.v.) as the Marot of antique diction was a convention of the 18th cent., and was particularly the contribution of J. Philips (q.v.) to the poetry of his age. We need not discuss it here, save to note that the concentration of Spenser's imitators on his measure and the diction (esp. the obsolete words), with a faint peep of the 'ludicrous' under the 'simple', was to miss the spirit of romance, which awaited a later and a less technically inspired revelation. This leads to the remark, that T.'s *magnum opus*, *The Seasons*, (4 bks., in blank verse ; *Winter*, 1726, *Summer*, 1727, *Spring*, 1728, *Autumn*, 1730 ; now always arranged in their natural order), though containing romantic threads, and though expressly excepted by Wordsworth (q.v.) from his attack on poetic diction, was yet thoroughly in accord with the conventions of verse in the 18th cent. True, as sir E. Gosse points out (*Thomson*, Muses Library, Introduction), 'Coleridge's *Hymn in the Valley of Chamounix* follows, so closely as only genius in its audacity can follow, the *Hymn* of Thomson ', and, 'in the movement of his *Alastor*, Shelley paid his ancestor of *The Seasons* the splendid compliment of direct imitation ' (see s.vv.) ; true, too, that Milton's metre, replacing the heroic verse of Dryden and Pope, could not but evoke notable echoes of the Miltonic approach to nature, and that Virgil (q.v.)—the Virgil of the *Georgics*—was behind both T.'s *Seasons* and the *Cyder* of Philips ; still, T.'s 'obedience to the conventional

diction of poetry was in no sense reluctant ' (*C.H.E.L.*, x, 98), and, poet of nature though he is, he is is yet a poet of ' nature methodized ', whose ' temperate rhapsodies are among the digressions of *The Seasons* ' (*ib.*).

Thomson, James (1834-82) : Scot. poet ; friend of Charles Bradlaugh (1833-91), the freethinker, to whose *National Reformer* (founded, 1862), T. became a contributor, after his discharge from the army as an assistant schoolmaster ; visited America, and wr. miscellaneously till 1784, when *The City of Dreadful Night* was publd., March-May, in the *National Reformer*. Despite its unconventional provenance, it attracted the attention of great folk, and George Eliot (q.v.) wr. T. a letter of admiration for the ' distinct vision and grand utterance in the poem '. It was publd. in bk. form, 1880, with other poems, by Messrs. Reeves and Turner, under T.'s familiar initials, B.V., which stood for Bysshe Vanolis,—the first in token of his admiration for Shelley (q.v.), the second for Novalis (see s.v. Hardenberg). But T., though he had made some good friends (Meredith and P. B. Marston, qq.v., among them), had gone down hill during those years. He had quarrelled with Bradlaugh ; and, as Mr. Bertram Dobell, who introduced T. to his publishers, writes in a Memoir prefixed to the 1895 edn., 2 vols., of his *Poetical Works* : ' Thomson had one great failing which marred all his prospects and destroyed both his mental and bodily health. This was his craving for alcoholic stimulants '. We need not dwell on this aspect, but it goes some way to explain what prof. Walker (*Lit. Victorian Era*, 591) acutely analyses as the absence of evolution from T.'s philosophy : ' His pessimism was founded on the conviction that there was no hope for humanity any more than for himself, and that the appearance of progress was a mere illusion '; and ' there is nothing in English literature more gloomy and depressing' than *The City of Dreadful Night* and one or two companion-pieces. ' It is impossible to withhold from these pieces the tribute of deep admiration for the masterly execution ; but yet the thought forces itself upon the reader that it is *not* good to be here. ' These *tours de force* of melancholy were not the whole of T.'s poems, however. There are bright poems, such as *Sunday up the River* and *Sunday at Hampstead*, which, to one reader at least, recall the lyric magic of Heine (q.v.), some of whose songs T. skilfully transld.

Thorarensen, Bjarni (1786-1841) : Icel. poet ; an early champion of the national sentiment of Iceld. in the 19th cent. T.'s genius was primarily lyrical, and expressed itself in love-songs and patriotic odes, in which he was esp. responsive to the inspiration of courage, conflict and the all-conqueror, death.

Thoresen, Magdalena (1819-1903) : Norse poet and novelist ; *née* Kragh. Fru T.'s stepdaughter was married to Ibsen (q.v.) ; it was to Ibsen's rival, Björnson (q.v.), however, that Fru T.'s genius was most akin, and each owed something to the other. Her lyric and dramatic verse need not detain us here. It was her *Tales* of 1863 which won her the place she still occupies as a pioneer of the ' return to nature ' in Norway—a return in no patronizing vein to a nature not garnished for idealists. Other stories and vols. of stories followed, and one of Fru C.'s best works was her *Pictures from the Land of the Midnight Sun*, 2 vols., 1884, 1888. She lived to see the triumph of the literary methods which she helped so powerfully to introduce.

Thorild, Thomas (1759-1808): Swed. critic and poet. T. founded, 1784. a critical journal, 'The New Examiner', heralding the romantic revolt from the Fr. classicism which king Gustavus iii (q.v.) sought to naturalize in Sweden. The revolt was likewise inspired by Fr. models ; it was a new battle of Rousseau against Voltaire (see s.vv.) ; and T.'s Voltairean adversary was Kellgren (q.v.), who opened the columns of his own 'Stockholm Post' to the interchange of satire, sally, and critical fireworks. T. (whose original name was Thoren) had to quit Sweden, 1793, in consequence of the political disturbances after the king's assassination.

Thormódur Torfason, or Torvesen. See s.v. **Torfæus.**

Thóroddsen, Jón (1819-68): Icel. poet and novelist ; of the same type and generation as Bjarni Thorarensen and Jonas Hallgrimsson (qq.v.). T.'s chief merit resides in his prosetales, *Boy and Girl, Man and Woman*, etc., by which he is properly remembered as the founder of the modern novel in Iceland.

Thott, Birgitta (1610-62): Dan. scholar. Transld. the works of Seneca (q.v.), 1658, and added thereby a monument to Dan. prose, and a testimony at the same time to the capacity of women for serious labour and erudition. She laboured to establish this proposition, and was accounted among the foremost representative scholars of her own time.

Thou, de, Jacques Auguste (1553-1617): Fr. historian. Wr. a 'history of his times' in Livian Latin.

Thümmel, von, August (1738-1817): Germ. romance-writer. T. was affected by the influence of Wieland (q.v.) in the direction of a light-hearted use of any material that lay to hand. He wr., 1764, an amusing prose-epic *Wilhelmine*, or 'The Married Pedant' ; and, 1791-1805 (10 vols.)' A Journey to the Meridian Provinces of France in the Year 1785-1786 ', in which a learned Germ., seeking to brush away the dust and cobwebs of too much reading, is recommended a tour in France to open the pores of his impressions ; the pores are opened too wide, and another physician recommends the return-journey to cure him. The influence of Sterne (q.v.) is obvious.

Tickell, Thomas (1686-1740): Engl. poet ; friend of Addison (q.v.), to whose *Spectator* he became a contributor ; transld. bk. i of Homer's *Iliad* at the same time as Pope (q.v.), thus causing a quarrel between Pope and Addison ; edited Addison's works, 1721, and wr. in vol. i of that edn. a much-admired *Elegy* on his constant friend.

Tieck, Johann Ludwig (1773-1853): Germ. romanticist ; by common consent, a leader of that great and pregnant movement (s.v. Romance). T.'s long life of literary activity included several periods and changes, which it will be necessary, briefly, to trace. At the outset, however, it is at once useful and just

to affirm his claim to the title (Haym, *Rom. Schule*, 64) of 'the Matador of Romanticism ', in whose works (Wernaer, *Romanticism . . . in Germany*, 109) 'the romantic mood can be best studied '. He derived from the pioneers of *le lyrisme* in France the distinction of reviving landscape-poetry. The pregnant word 'Waldeinsamkeit' was coined by him for Rousseau's (q.v.) disciples in Germany, and signifies the deeply-felt appeal of 'forest solitude ', or the lonesomeness of tree-impressionism. The moon, too, was his (cf. Brandes, *Main Currents*, E.T., ii, 142), by reason of his special manipulation of moonlit scenery. To T., again, is owed the song most frequently quoted for its revelation of the faith and aims of the Romanticists (*Kaiser Octavianus*, prologue):

> Mondbeglänzte Zaubernacht,
> Die den Sinn gefangen hält,
> Wundervolle Märchenwelt,
> Steig' auf in der alten Pracht.

Only a Coleridge could translate it : roughly, its meaning runs :

> Witch'ry of the moonlit night,
> That doth hold our senses fast,
> Realm of faery, wondrous-bright,
> Rise in glory of the past.

T. helped to revive that 'Märchenwelt' ; he continued the Shakespeare transln. which A. W. Schlegel (q.v.) so well began ; and he developed with genuine delight the tricksy forms of romantic Irony (q.v.). But, romantic though T.'s life-work was in retrospect, he was not always or uniformly a romanticist. He began to write as a hack to Nicolai (q.v.), the Berlin bookseller and publisher, who was so sturdy a champion of the rational Aufklärung (q.v.) ; in this capacity T. contributed to the 'almanacs' and 'keepsakes' through which the young blood of the 'Sturm und Drang' (q.v.) was being poured. His chief work in this kind was a novel in letters, *William Lovell*, 1705-06, founded on the *Paysan perverti* of Restif (q.v.). It showed the influence of T.'s favourite readings in Goethe's *Götz* and Schiller's *Räuber* ; but as a German's study of an Englishman (Lovell) in Paris (which T. had not visited) at the time of the Revolution it does not show much else. His satiric drama, 1797, *der gestiefelte Kater* ('Puss in Boots '), though its pantomime was mainly concerned with lit., was a more considerable piece of work altogether, and helped to form his style in fancy and irony. T.'s next productive period was subject to a large extent to the influence of his friend Wackenroder (q.v.), who died in 1798. This gentle and glowing spirit pervaded his new novel *Franz Sternbald*. The hero, derived from Goethe's *Wilhelm Meister*, with affinities to Jean Paul Richter's *Titan*, is supposed to be a pupil of Dürer, the painter, and he and his friend are represented fulfilling a plan, never realized by T. and his friend Wackenroder, of wandering on foot from Nuremberg through Holland and Italy. Sternbald just wanders, with no other aim or end, but with a profusion of art, and scenery, and friendship, and women, and lyricism ('a truer knight of the moon than Franz Sternbald is not to be found ', Brandes, *op. cit.*, 145) ; but his fate and temper have been romanticized, and between *Lovell* and *Sternbald*, says J. G. Robertson (*Hist. Germ. Lit.*, 423), runs 'the line that separates Sturm und Drang from Romanticism'. Once the frontier was passed, T. plunged without looking back; and he brought a successful suit against the son of Nicolai for an unauthorized re-issue of his *juvenilia*. The loss of Wackenroder was compensated by the new friendship of Hardenberg (Novalis), and the works of T.'s maturity included 3 vols. of folk-tales; some original and redacted fairy-tales; 2 legend-dramas, *The Holy Genoveva*, 1799, and *Emperor Octavianus*, 1804; a transln. of *Don Quixote*, and a collection, entitled *Phantasus*, of his more purely romantic writings. A journey to Italy, 1804-06, was followed by a long period of ill-health, and T.'s former inclination to the doctrines of the brothers Schlegel and their circle was never completely resumed. He revised the transln. of those plays of Shakespeare which Schlegel had abandoned owing to some business dispute, though the hard work on them was actually done by T.'s daughter, Dorothea (b. 1799), and by count von Baudissin (q.v.). In 1819, T. settled definitely at Dresden, where he accepted office at the Court theatre, 1825; in 1841, he was honoured by a command to Berlin, at the court of king Frederick William iv of Prussia. The novels of his later years, some of which showed considerable skill in the management of hist. fiction, have an interest of their own in Germany, but are intrinsically far less important than the works of his Romantic period, which, whether praised or blamed by Romance-enthusiasts or their opponents, are admitted on both sides to be supreme in their kind. He may be dismissed as a moonstruck visionary, or as 'a German Lake poet'; but his solid contribution to the development of the movement can neither be dismissed nor minimized. Carlyle (q.v.) was aware of it, and transld. some of his *Märchen*, and a later age has noted an affinity between T. and the Transatlantic Hawthorne.

Tiedge, Christoph August (1752-1841): Germ. poet. Wr., 1800, a one-time famous didactic poem *Urania*, in which he was stirred by the teachings of Kant (q.v.) to recommend a belief in immortality, which he expressed in smooth-flowing verses with the sentimentalism, enthusiasm, and ease of a shallow but earnest nature. It was popular-philosophy in verse, and did not long survive its first audience.

Tifernas, Gregorio (*c.* 1415-66): first teacher of Gk. in France. Resided at Paris, 1456-60, when he withdrew to Venice.

Tillier, Claude (1801-44): Fr. novelist; literary disciple of Voltaire (q.v.), and accounted a major prophet in Germany. T.'s chief work of fiction was *Mon Oncle Benjamin*, 1843, which, for some cause, never fully explained, became the type of Fr. novel in Germ. eyes.

Timoneda, Joan (d., 1583): Span. bookseller (*i.q.*, publisher); purveyor of dramas. T.'s value resides in his labours as a busy collector of dramatic writings; and, while he transld. and adapted for the primitive Span. stage of his day the *Amphitryo* and *Menæchmi* of Plautus, a *Cornelia* from the *Negromante* of Ariosto (q.v.), and other pieces, including an *auto* (q.v.)

of the Lost Sheep, he also served the cause of the theatre by editing the 'comedies' and 'pastoral interludes' which Rueda (q.v.) had successfully produced in the market-places of the bigger Span. towns. But, in effect, T. was a mere jobber in letters ('pour Timoneda la littérature est une speculation'; Kelly, *Lit. espagn.*, 233), and at the best may be described as an inferior Hardy (q.v.).

Tiraboschi, Giralomo (1731-94): It. lit. historian; ducal librarian at Modena; wr. *Storia della letteratura italiana*, which is still the standard work on the subject, and is to be mentioned with all respect. The method is somewhat confused between chronology and kinds, and the trees are sometimes lost in the wood, but the work is a national possession.

Tirant lo Blanch (Span.): 'Tirante the white'; Catalan (see s.v. Catalonia) chivalric romance, 'Book of the Valorous and Strong knight Tirant lo Blanch'; 1490. The authors are said to be Johannot Martorell (books i-iii) and Johan de Galba (bk. iv); a Castilian version appeared in 1511, and an Ital. in 1538. It has its place in Cervantes (q.v.), in the famous ch. (i, 6), where the curate found in it 'a treasure of content, a mine of diversion. . . . Truly, friend, by right of style', he says, 'this is the best book in the world. In my opinion, this author is deserving, since he didn't with open eyes write nonsense fit to send him to the galleys for life. Take him home and read him and you'll see that I speak truth'.

Tocqueville, de, Alexis (1805-59): Fr. historian; trained as an advocate, but left the bar to travel in America on a mission of inspection of penal institutions. In the result, T. exceeded his brief, and brought home his *magnum opus* on *Democracy in America* (part i, 1835; part ii, 1839). This work is still a classic of history, and its merits are admirably stated by J.'s continuator, James (visct., 1914) Bryce (1838-1922; wr. *Holy Roman Empire*, 1862, and frequently reprinted; *American Commonwealth*, 3 vols., 1888): 'To de Tocqueville America was primarily a democracy, the ideal democracy, fraught with lessons for Europe and above all for his own France. What he has given us is not so much a description of the country and the people as a treatise, full of exquisite observation and elevated thinking, upon democracy, a treatise whose conclusions are illustrated from America, but one in a large measure founded, not so much on an analysis of American phenomena, as on general views of democracy, which the circumstances of France had suggested' (i, 4). Wr., too, *l'Ancien Régime et la Révolution*, 1850, and had contemplated a more extensive work on the lines of the *Origins of Contemporary France* by Taine (q.v.), when his weak health was closed by death.

Tode, Johann Clemens (1736-1806): Dan. novelist and miscellanist. Wr. plays, lyric verse, and popular philosophy with equal facility and success, and is chiefly known as the author of a light and rather brilliant novel, *Love's Need*.

Tolstoy, Leo Nikolayevich (1828-1910): Russ. novelist; nihilist (s.v. Nihilism); later, mystic* (s.v. Mysticism), altruist, and reformer; count by birth; by common consent, one of the masters of European lit. Vogüé (*Roman Russe*), writing in T.'s lifetime, declared: 'If the most interesting books are those which faithfully interpret the life of a fraction of humanity at a given moment of history, then our century [the nineteenth] has produced nothing more interesting than the works of Tolstoy. I do not hesitate to say that this writer is one of the greatest masters, among those who will be cited as witnesses for the age'. And, remarking on T.'s pursuit of the initiatory thought behind the visible act, Vogüé characterizes the master as 'an English chemist with the soul of a Buddhist Hindoo'; analysis and introspection combined. Variations of this eulogy would not add to its force; but M. Arnold (q.v.), it may be noted, writing at about the same date (*Fortnightly Review*, 1887; *Essays in Criticism*, ii), referred to T. as 'a great soul and a great writer', whose work in religion as well as in imaginative lit. 'is more than sufficient to signalize him as one of the most marking, interesting, and sympathy-inspiring men of our time'. And each concluded by echoing the appeal addressed to T. by Turgenev (q.v.) on his death-bed (1883): 'Great master of our Russian tongue, come back to your literary labours', from the lure of self-perfection and social reform. T. lived about five-and-twenty years after Vogüé's and Arnold's critiques, but he was not to be called back. The main facts of his biography are well-known, and they are important to a knowledge of his writings. At least, the central episode, that, 'in the midst of his great and glorious artistic career, he suddenly abjured literature and art, denounced worldly possessions, and said that truth was to be found in working like a peasant' (Baring, *op. cit.*, 198), has struck the imagination of mankind, as much by its seeming contrast ('in reality there was no inconsistency', *ibid.*) with T.'s earlier convictions as by its expression of the prevailing character of the racial temperament of Russia.

The seeming contrast is external only. T. was a nobleman by birth, he was nurtured in affluent circumstances, and he was dowered with literary genius. For many years, about 50, in fact, he accepted these gifts and endowments. He had not sought them, nor did he reject them; he was content to try to fulfil himself under the condition of possessing them. But the attempt miscarried; the fulfilment was inadequate to the capacity, and T.'s inner sense of failure destroyed his contentment with outward surroundings. 'I grew to hate myself', he wr.; and not in

* Critics differ as to the element of mysticism developed by T. in later life. 'Tolstoy hated the supernatural, and was alien to all mysticism' (Baring, *Russ. Lit.*, 'H.U.L.', 212). 'An aristocrat by birth and education, a gallant soldier, a sportsman, a man of fashion, a country gentleman, a historian, an economist, a philosopher, a theologian, and a mystic —these are many parts to fill, but he has filled them all and in a most striking fashion' (G. Drage, *C.M.H.*, xi, 651). Much depends on our definition of mysticism (q.v.), but we may concur with Vogüé (*Roman Russe*, 338) that, thought T. deemed the name of mystic inapplicable to a man who founded his paradise on earth, yet 'our language does not furnish us with any other expression suitable to his case'.

those circumstances nor under those conditions was he likely, he believed, to win 'that content surpassing wealth, The sage in meditation found'. So, still tentatively and imperfectly, for the weight of custom is heavy to throw off, T. tried in those later years to follow the longer road to truth. The goal was the same throughout, 'and there is something solemn and great', comments Mr. Baring (*op. cit.*, 201), 'about his having met with death at a small railway station' on his way to a monastery. Similarly, T. was true to the racial temperament throughout. The untranslatable quality, *ochaïania*, from which he suffered, and which he represented in suffering humanity, is a disease (and faculty) of the Russ. genius. The nearest Engl. rendering is despair; the Germ. *Weltschmerz* is nearer to it; but the one is too narrow and the other too diffuse to carry the meanings of intellectual fatalism, of moral anarchy and asceticism, which the Russ. word conveys. It was this restless search for the unattainable, which he insisted upon founding on earth, which drove T. to his extreme of renunciation through all the circles of despair (or wanhope, to use the old Engl. word) from nihilism to mysticism. Of course, the critics have been busy with him. He was open to attack for the incompleteness of his material sacrifices. Associations drew him in one direction, and aspirations in another; he might have done more wisely to use the gifts which he despised; his death at a roadside station was not a full realization of the ideals which he had formulated. Mr. Baring, for instance, comparing T. with Dostoievsky (q.v.)*, says that the former theorized on what the latter practised (see *Landmarks of Russ. Lit.*, 157, and *op cit.*, 211-13), and cleverly quotes in illustration of the thesis a quatrain from a ballad by G. K. Chesterton:

'We eat the cheese—you scraped about the rind,
You lopped the tree—we eat the fruit instead.
You were benevolent, but we were kind,
You know the laws of food, but we were fed'.
There is justice in this view; but it is probably juster to T. to consider his social and moral aims in the light of Wordsworth's (q.v.) desire to 'build social upon personal liberty', and to find that structure
Not in Utopia, subterranean fields,
Or some secreted island, Heaven knows where
But in the very world, which is the world
Of all of us—the place where, in the end,
We find our happiness, or not at all.
This, with whatever addition of mystic communion with nature, is the key to Meredith's (q.v.) musings on Earth; it is the key, too, to the symbolism of G. F. Watts's picture of 'Hope', and T. belongs to the same company

* 'The two are comparable not only in size but also in kind. They were both masters of the *psychological* novel. They were both passionately interested in the essential problems of life, death, and God, and both endeavoured to create a system of moral and social philosophy on a religious foundation. For the literary historian they are of greater interest as novelists than as moralists; but even apart from their imaginative work they were both (though in an unequal degree) great writers, and Tolstoy the greatest master of non-narrative Russian prose' (prince Mirsky, *Mod. Russ. Lit.*, 42).

of seers. Even more logically than they, up to the limit of his physical capacity and circumstances, he conformed his action to his vision. And, the man, Tolstoy, is his works; they are neither more nor less interesting than he. In fiction, he wr. *War and Peace*, 1865-72, an epic panorama of the Napoleonic wars, 1805-15, as majestic as St. Simon's (q.v.) *Mémoires* in its manipulation of crowds and courts, as revealing as Dostoievsky's novels in the intimacies of life in Russia, and the more stirring in its pictures of war because T. himself had been an officer in the Crimea; *Anna Karenina*, 1875-6, the novel of his own times, the *Odyssey* to the *Iliad* of *War and Peace*, with its wonderful psychological studies of the heroine and Vronsky, her lover, and Constantin Levin, the new incarnation of prince Bezukhov from *War and Peace*, and essentially the hero of the new fiction, intellectual, melancholy, nihilistic, the 'bourgeois Hamlet' of Russ. conditions; *Resurrection*, with its hero, prince Nehludov, a pale reflection of T. himself; *The Kreutzer Sonata*, 1889; *The Death of Ivan Iljich*, 1884, a rarely moving human document; the brilliant Caucasian story of *The Cossacks*; the quiet study of *Domestic Happiness*. These do not exhaust the list, but they illustrate the diversity of T.'s themes. The novels must be read, in order to illustrate the harmonious accompaniment of his style. In social ethics, he wr. *What is to be done?* a significant title in Russ. letters, already made famous by Chernichevsky (q.v.). In self-analysis, autobiography, and reminiscences: *Childhood, Boyhood, and Youth, My Religion, My Confession,* (all introspective), and the fascinating *Memories of Sevastopol*. His dramas need not detain us: the peasant-play, *Power of Darkness* is the best; but we must recall the educational handbooks which T. deemed it his duty to prepare at one period of his multifarious activities, and his original treatises on art from the point of view of Tolstoyan ethics. It is a wonderful record of life and thought, unique in the 19th cent., and only conceivable under the conditions of the Russ. genius, which, in this supreme manifestation, triumphed over the obstacles of authority, to which smaller men succumbed. T.'s immunity from prosecution was 'the first great victory of the liberty of individual thought over official tyranny in Russia' (Baring, *op. cit.*, 208); and we may trace in his works the gradual evolution of the five commandments of his creed, against anger, adultery, oaths, violence, war, and their sanction in the deepest springs of human conduct. Thus, we shall better appreciate the fine estimate of Mr. Geoffrey Drage (*C.M.H.*, xi, 652): 'His portraits of emperors, statesmen, generals, noblemen, officials, merchants, and peasants, form a gallery which no historian of this epoch can neglect. Ever independent in thought and action, all his writings show an independent spirit full of profound ideas and profound convictions. In his own words, the heroine of his story, whom he loves with all his heart, and whom he desires to represent in all her beauty, is Truth'. Truth-teller, Truth-lover, and Truth-seeker: 'his marvellous fulness and

exactness of observation, his fanaticism for truth, his skill in plastic, sensuous, artistic expression, his intimate mastery of the psychology of normal mankind, help to explain the extraordinary significance of Tolstoy's work far beyond the frontiers of his own country, and give him his place among the greatest epic writers of all ages' (Brückner, *Gesch. d. Russ. Lit.*, 364).

Tomando ora la espada, ora la Pluma (Span.): 'Wielding at one time the sword, at another the pen'; from the third eclogue of Garcilasso (q.v.) de la Vega, and since proverbial as a description of the life of many gallant Span. soldier-poets, and of such Englishmen in the same company as sir Philip Sidney (q.v.) and Rupert Brooke.

Torfæus, Thormodus (1640-1719): Dan. historian; philologer; Latinized from Thormódur Torfason or Torvesen. Wr., 1711, *Historia rerum Norvegicarum*, a distinguished piece of research-work, and was notable as a collector of MSS. for the King's Library at Copenhagen. In this capacity he procured the priceless vellums of bp. Brynjolf (q.v.) from Iceland, including the *Codex Regius* (q.v., and s.v. Edda, iii).

Torres-Naharro, de, Bartolomé (*c.* 1480-*c.* 1531): Span. poet; dramatist. T.-N. was born at Torres, near Badajoz, on the Port. frontier, and seems to have been a soldier captured by Algerian pirates, who took holy orders after his ransom. At any rate, he resided in Rome, where he sought the patronage of pope Leo x and of card. Giulio de Medici, afterwards pope Clement vii. This was about 1512. Later, perhaps in consequence of an obscene satire on the papal court ('The gallants and courtesans of Rome'), T.-N. repaired to Naples under the protection of Fabrizio Colonna, and dedicated his first-fruits of poetry, *Propalladia*, 1517, to the great Span. patron of letters, the marquis of Pescara, husband of Vittoria Colonna (q.v.). T.-N.'s poems are of less importance than his 8 plays or *comedias*, which seem to have been represented at private theatres in Italy before they were put in print, but which, so far as we know, were not enacted in Spain. They were reprinted frequently, however, despite a partial ban by the Inquisition, due to their free tone in religious matters, and N.'s influence on the stage was quiet and steady, in conformity with the artistic principles at which he aimed and the cultivated public to whom he addressed himself. The admixture of Ital. with Span. in his plays was not surprising in the work of a Spaniard resident in Rome and Naples; more deterrent from wide popularity was his occasional employment of Span. dialect forms, which would have interested an educated audience assembled in a great man's house, but would have been caviare to the multitude. Still, within their limits, T.-N.'s comedies mark a big step in the development of the Span. drama; and it is highly interesting to note that he worked out for his own guidance a sound theory of his art. He adopted from Horace (q.v.) the division of a play into 5 parts, but he called those parts, or resting-places, not acts but days (*jornadas*), in recollection probably of the days' portions allotted to the old Fr. mystery-plays (see Ticknor, i, 267); he preferred to restrict his *dramatis personæ* to not less than 6 or more than 12; and one or two of his plays observe unconsciously all the unities (q.v.). T.-N. was a skilful, even an elaborate, metrist; and it is to be added that he classified the future drama of Castile into 2 kinds: 'dramas founded on knowledge and dramas founded on fancy' (*comedia a noticia* and *comedia a fantasia*); an *introyto* ('prologue') served to introduce each play. Adopting T.-N.'s own classification, we may distinguish, as the best of his dramas, *a noticia*: the *comedia Soldadesca* (recruiting), *comedia Tinellaria* (servants' hall); and as the best *a fantasia*: the *comedia Trofea*, in which Apollo and Fame appear in behalf of the contemporary king Manuel of Portugal, and *comedia Ymenea*, which marks a genuine advance, and introduces us to the 'point of honour', so famous later, in Vega (q.v.), and to the *gracioso*, or comic servant, whom Vega even claimed to have invented. It may be added that T.-N.'s distinction between the play of learning and of fancy persisted in literary criticism. It is seen in the glib remark of Polonius (*Hamlet*, ii, 2) as to 'the law of writ and the liberty', or the classical and romantic stages, and, again, in Milton's distinction in *l'Allegro* between 'Jonson's learned sock', and 'Shakespeare, Fancy's child'.

Torres y Villarroel, de, Diego (*c*. 1693-1770): Span. scholar; poet; nugatory in both capacities, which he exercised in the period of decadence after the War of the Span. Succession; prof. at Salamanca univ. Wr. a sort of autobiographical confessional, *Vida, Ascendencia . . . y Aventuras*, 1743-58.

Tory, Geoffrey (1480-1533): Fr. scholar, printer, and bookseller; prof. of philosophy at Bordeaux and elsewhere; publisher and bookseller in Paris, where he was appointed printer-royal to king Francis i. Eminent engraver, miniaturist, and designer of types and woodblocks. T. issued, 1529, a vol. on taste in books, choice of words, and national fashions, entitled *Champ-Fleury*, and was associated with Rabelais, H. Etienne, Dolet (qq.v.) and others, in the linguistic reforms which were so prominent an aspect of the Renaissance in France.

Toscanaggiamento (It.): Tuscanization; epithet applied to the transition in the early 13th cent. of Sicilian song to the Ital. mainland, and esp. to Florence (q.v.), with the consequent modification of dialect which the verse underwent.

Tottel, Richard (died, 1594): Engl. printer from 1553; member of Stationers' company from its foundation, 1556. Publd. legal works, and, among others, the transln. of the *Æneid* by Surrey (q.v.) and *Songes and Sonnettes, written by the ryght honorable Lorde Henry Howarde, late Earle of Surrey, and others*, known as *Tottel's Miscellany*, 1557. This famous collection, which was reprinted 8 times during the reign of queen Elizabeth, and which is the source of some of the best poetry of the age, was partly compiled by Grimald (q.v.). Considerable credit is due to T. for his enterprise in this respect; his *Miscellany* helped to break down the privity of lovers' confidences

and conceits, and thus to raise the standard by widening the appeal of such writings.

Toulouse: town in southern France, famous for the aftermath of Provençal lit. (q.v.) in 14th cent. See s.v. Floral Games.

Toussain, Jacques (*c*. 1698-1547): One of the 2 first Fr. readers in Gk. in the Corporation of the Royal Readers (q.v.). Loyola, Calvin, and, possibly, Rabelais (qq.v.) were among his pupils.

Town: There was a lit. of the town, as distinct from the lit. of the court (q.v.), from a very early period of the Middle Ages; indeed, if its first manifestations are identified with anti-court lit., it may be traced right back through European history. Whoever were the anon. writers, who from the first quarter of the 13th cent. composed burlesques and satires on courtiers and courts, it is certainly as legitimate to assume that they were beginning to feel their own feet outside the charmed circle of the court-convention as it is historically correct to regard them as the source and orig. of the light *bourgeois* poetry which existed side by side with the love-lore and romance of the courts of Northern France and of Provence. The Lat. verse which was written round the name and fame of bp. Golias (q.v.) in the *Carmina Burana*, in the satires ascribed to Map (q.v.), and elsewhere, was town verse in the sense that it expressed a reaction from and a criticism of the standards which the scandalous bp. had used. A similar criticism and reaction marked the more distinctly *bourgeois* poetry of the Fr. *fabliaux* (s.v. Fable), which flourished *c*. 1250-1350; and the coarse but wholesome tone which characterized this type, even in its best examples, led to the brilliant delineation of popular views and characters in the Reynard (q.v.) cycle of romance, in the second part of the Rose (q.v.) -romance, and in many of the tales of Chaucer (q.v.). The contrast between Villon (q.v.) and Froissart (q.v.) brings into more striking prominence the clash of town and court, or, as we may call it, of realism and idealism, in the 14th cent.; and, as the *bourgeois*, or burgher, elements of society became more independent and self-respecting, the tone of revolt and reaction gradually disappeared from town-literature, and it assumed its right place as an independent and fruitful inspiration. This change is seen in the institution of the Floral Games (q.v.) at Toulouse, and in the analogous shifting of the centre of poetic composition in Germany from the Minnesinger (q.v.) of the courts to the Meistersinger (q.v.) of the town-guilds, which started in the 14th cent., and reached the height of its new vogue in the 16th, when such distinct branches of civic wit as the Grobian, Eulenspiegel, 'Fastnachtspiele', Folly-books (qq.v.), and other cycles of jest, had arisen in the self-conscious German townships, and had communicated their influence to other countries. In Italy, it is to be noted, where chivalry never found a secure foothold, this contrast of town and court hardly existed; the most progressive court-life in Italy was identified with civic interests, and the policy of rulers like the Medici (q.v.) at Florence was directed, by means of pageants, gifts, and constitutional measures, to making

material derived by medieval story-tellers from pagan antiquity (the 'matière de Rome la grant', in the classification of that material by Bodel, q.v.). The Trojan tales were the more interesting because medieval aggrandizers of the rulers of their own countries sought to prove such rulers' descent from a hero of the Trojan War. Thus, Brutus, a great-grandson of Æneas himself, was claimed as the progenitor of the Britons (see s.v. Geoffrey of Monmouth, who invented this genealogy in the 12th cent.). The appeal of Troy, accordingly, was patriotic as well as romantic; and the tales of the Trojan war descended in a Lat. version (s.v. Homer) ascribed to 'Dictys' and 'Dares' (from the Gk. and Trojan points of view respectively), 2 reputed writers of about the 6th cent., A.D. On their versions and others was based the first romantic redaction of the theme by a clerk, Benoît (q.v.), of Sainte-More, near Tours, completed about 1160 in over 30,000 lines, entitled *Roman de Troie*, and dedicated to queen Eleanor, wife of Henry ii. This poem exhibits all the features of medieval romance; the names are the names of antiquity, the manners are the manners of 12th cent. France. Calchas is a Christian bp.; Hector is loved by Morgan the fay. Next to Benoît as authority on Troy came Guido (q.v.), a Sicilian, whose *Historia*, ostensibly based on Dares, appeared in 1287. Other versions had appeared in the meantime, and there were ample source-books for Gower, Boccaccio, Chaucer and Lydgate when they came to use the tales. Caxton's *Recuyell of the Historyes of Troye* was the first Engl. printed book (1474).

Troy, as a first chapter in Engl. history, to which dignity Geoffrey (*supra*) had elevated it, began to be dropped from the history-books. in the 16th cent. Polydore Vergil (q.v.), did not avail himself of it, and was abused by Engl. antiquaries in consequence, and it is rather a fascinating speculation whether Milton (q.v.), if he had written his epic poem on the Arthuriad, as he had at one time contemplated, would have introduced the Roman orig. of British kings: there is no doubt he liked the fable for its story-value. Recently, prof. G. S. Gordon, of Oxford, has pleaded for its restoration to Engl. history-books. 'It is the historians and schoolmasters', he writes, 'who have betrayed us. The contempt of history for fiction may be overdone. A myth like this of Troy, infectious, pervasive, European, cannot reasonably be dismissed like a bad answer in a class of history. However absurd it may have been, it has claims on the historian because it was officially believed. From whatever angle we regard these things, we must conclude that they have been too hastily ejected from all footing in our histories'.

Tschudi, Aegidius (1505-72): Germ. hist. writer. Wr. *Helvetische Chronik* ('Swiss Chronicle'), which Schiller (q.v.) used as a source-book for his drama of Tell.

Tuke, Samuel (died, 1674): Engl. playwright; an original F.R.S.; created bt., 1664. Transld. comedies of Calderon (q.v.) and others, including *los Empeños de seis Horas* (as 'The Adventures of Five Hours') of Coello (q.v.), 1663, which was adversely criticized by Dryden (q.v.),

but when seen by Pepys (q.v.) on its first night, 8 Jan., 1663, was adjudged to be 'the best, for the variety and the most excellent continuance of the plot to the very end, that ever I saw, or think ever shall; and the house, by its frequent plaudits, did show their sufficient approbation'.

Tullin, Christian Braumann (1728-65): Dan. poet; born, like Holberg (q.v.) in Norway; wr. lyrical poetry of a high order of excellence. T. went for his models, not to Klopstock (q.v.), the high-priest of Germ. resonance, who was at that time resident in Copenhagen, but to J. Thomson, E. Young, and Pope (of the *Windsor Forest* style; see s.vv.), thus helping to lay the foundations of national romanticism in Denmark.

Tupper, Martin Farquhar (1810-89): Engl. poetaster; F.R.S., 1845. T.'s versified *Proverbial Philosophy*, 1838, enjoyed an enormous vogue at home and in America, but has long since passed into oblivion.

Turgenev,* -i. Ivan Sergievich (1818-83): Russ. novelist; poet. The praises of T. have been sung in a diminishing scale of affirmation, since the greater fame of Tolstoy and Dostoievsky (qq.v.) rose and eclipsed that of T. His voice has been found too soft, his distance from Russia too far, for the complete satisfaction of the aspirations of the younger generation of his countrymen. A partly political bias has been imported into the literary criticism of T., and his posth. reputation has suffered in much the same way and from much the same causes as Tennyson's (q.v.); and it may safely be left to the equal restitution of time. Fr. critics have always appreciated T., who spent many years in Paris and made many friends. Flaubert (q.v.), for instance, and G. Sand (q.v.) claimed him as a master. Henry James, too, was a great and a discriminating admirer. In the opinion of Taine (q.v.), T. was one of the most perfect artists whom the world has possessed since Sophocles. 'Europe', wr. *The Athenæum* (q.v.), when he died, 'has been unanimous in according to Turgenev the first rank in contemporary literature' (8 Sept., 1883); and, while disputes as to primacy are not to be settled within a century of an artist's death, it is well to recognize one ground of dispute in the rival claims of artistry and ideas as the basis of enduring greatness. T.'s claim rests finally on the former; and it was his sense of the supreme right of art which inspired his death-bed letter to Tolstoy (they had not always been friends): 'Come back, my friend, to literary labours', back from the lure of social ideals. 'Dear friend, great writer of our Russian soil, grant me this prayer'. Yet ideas too were not lacking. T., too, had his aspirations for public welfare and for the future. Born in a comfortable station, bred amid the peace of broad acres, edu. at good schools, and versed in Kant and Hegel (qq.v.) at Berlin, T. vowed himself early in life to fight the battle of the serfs, whose emancipation was won in 1861. In this holy war, he wr. in an autobiographical fragment,

* The family name is also transliterated Tourguénief, Tourguenev, etc.

' I swore never to make peace. This was my oath of Hannibal, and I was not the only one to take it in those days. I went to the West in order the better to carry out my oath '. He went to the West in order to cure the ills of the East ; but though he announced himself a Westernizer, his temperament was too contemplative and artistic to give this epithet its technical force in the politics of the day. (See s.v. Russ. lit. : Westernizers v. Slavophils). ' Russian writers ', says Vogüé acutely, ' in consequence of the conditions that are manufactured for them as well of the particular bent of their genius, never openly attack ; they neither argue nor declaim. They depict without inferring, and make their appeal to pity rather than to indignation ' (Roman Russe, 163). This was Gogol's method in Dead Souls (how sad a country is Russia, exclaimed Pushkin when he read it) ; this was to be Dostoievsky's method in The House of the Dead ; and this method, less vigorous and autocratic than that of Peter (q.v.) the Great in an earlier crusade against Russ. orientalism, was precisely suited to the genius of T. It is possible that the ' conditions ' which Vogüé speaks of bent the ' genius ' in the direction which it took ; and that Russ. realism (q.v.) is less an instinct of the national temperament than an artistic compromise with necessity ; that a detailed exposition of actual facts, that is to say, was chosen as the line of least resistance against the censorship which lay in wait for explicit opinions. Certainly, T.'s experience recommended the production of pictures of Russ. life rather than a plea for the reform of the conditions. He had publd. in a Petrograd review the ' Sketches of a Sportsman ' (1847-51), which were to found his name as a man of letters. Gogol's ' Farmhouse Evenings ' supplied the model for the kind, which R. Jeffries (q.v.) in this country represents by his Gamekeeper at Home. In other words, they are redolent of the soil, true vignettes of life in a world as yet not revealed to common vision. In their tone of natural sensibility they descend straight from the Igor (q.v.) lay, that old source of all Russ. poetry. They are innocent and inoffensive in execution, affording no chance to the censor's vigilance. But his vigilance was aroused none the less. Was it desirable in the interests of official Russia to pourtray so faithfully and so charmingly conditions of existence and types of being which appealed so instantly to pity ? The emancipation principle was in the air, though 10 years were still to elapse : the mere representation of serfdom by a writer as accomplished as T. was itself a special plea for abolition. The ' Sportsman's Sketches ' had to pass, but an article by T. on Gogol, who died in 1852, gave the censor his looked-for opportunity. T. called Gogol ' a great man ' ; it did not suit the censorship that such an opinion should be expressed ; it was not a description, but a conclusion ; and conclusions brought penalties in their train. T. was put under arrest for a month, and was remanded to meditate on his own estates. Like Pushkin's exile to the Caucasus, T.'s exile to the country may have saved him from worse political complications.

From this date he devoted himself to pure letters. He wr. 3 principal novels, A Nest of Gentlefolk, 1859 (it might be rendered ' A Haunt of Ancient Peace ') ; Fathers and Sons (1862, just after the emancipation law), and Virgin Soil, 1876. These fixed the type of the hero of Russ. fiction, who may best be described in the words of Vogüé (op. cit., 193), as ' at times hurried into nihilism by the vertigo of a too rapid intellectual growth, but more often educated, melancholy, rich in ideas and poor in acts, always getting ready to act, tormented by a vague and generous ideal of public good. . . . This bourgeois Hamlet, honest, cultivated, of tranquil intelligence and feeble will, freshly home from foreign travel with scientific theories for improving the land and bettering the condition of the peasantry ', confronts us in all the great Russ. novelists. Lermontov and Gogol make us acquainted with him ; Dostoievsky and Tolstoy immortalize him, but his features were moulded in imperishable lines by T.'s art and love of beauty. The very name of Nihilist to describe him was coined or made current by T. The Nihilist of T. is the type of Russ. youth, ' who bows to no authority, and recognizes no principle of conduct as an article of faith, whatever degree of reverence he claimed by such principle '. Philosophy of this kind was in the Russ. blood, derived from long-ago Oriental forbears ; but if Raskolnikov in Dostoievsky's Crime and Punishment is the supreme example of the type, repeated in Goncharov's (q.v.) Oblomov, Bazarov in T.'s Fathers and Sons, whose death-scene ranks among the grandest passages in all the records of fiction in Europe, was the first full-dress model from which he was drawn. And T.'s women ? ' For him, the corner-stone of the social system was the jeune fille de province, brought up without constraint, in a modest environment, immovably straight, loving, not romantic, less intelligent than a man, but more decided ' (Vogüé, ib., 194) ; and this type, too, is fixed in Russ. fiction ; T. handed it finished from Gogol to Tolstoy. T.'s mastery of form was as dexterous and complete in his smaller as in his larger works ; his Dream Tales and Prose Poems at the end of his life were as perfect in their kind as the Sportsman's Sketches at the beginning. Between the 2 came Rudin, 1856, On the Eve, 1860, Smoke, 1867, A Lear of the Steppes, Torrents of Spring, Clara Milich (founded on a famous Paris drama of real life), etc. ; and, whatever temporal deduction may be made from the sum of T.'s fame, he has recorded for all time the atmosphere of a certain epoch, and is ' the prose Virgil of Russian literature ' (Baring). His use of the Russ. language is described by prince Mirsky (Modern Russ. Lit., 29) as ' beautiful, caressing. His prose, at its best, produces an almost physical effect of intoxicating beauty. His language is very much his own creation. He broke away from all literary traditions, from the neat analytical style of Pushkin and Lermontov, as well as from the exuberant eloquence of Gogol. Compared with what came before him, his style is cunningly and consistently colloquial, elaborately natural, and laboriously unliterary. It is inimitable and perfect as long as he keeps it fresh and renewed. It becomes insipid and stale as soon as the suspicion of a cliché arises. When he speaks of Nature and Landscape he almost invariably keeps it fresh. But in the direct description of sentiment he very often sinks into the rut of self-imitation. His pitfalls are the false-beautiful and the languid '.

-ii. Nicholas Ivanovich (1784-1845): Russ. historian ; elder cousin to above ; implicated in the Decembrist rising of aristocratic liberalism, 1825, and spent his years of exile in Paris. Wr. a monograph on taxation, 1817, and a valuable history of his own country.

Turgot, Anne Robert Jacques (1727 81): Fr. statesman ; *philosophe* (q.v.). Into the conflicts between T.'s philosophy and orthodoxy on the one part, and between his statemanship and philosophy on the other, we are not here further concerned than to note that he was originally destined for the Church, but abandoned the prospect of rich emoluments ' in order not to be reduced to wearing a mask on his face all through his life ' ; he lived to become controller-general of finances for a brief term, 1775-76, when king Louis xvi dismissed him and encountered not long afterwards the fate of Revolution from which T.'s reforms might have saved the Fr. State. T.'s ardent labours in the cause of social regeneration and financial reform made him a friend of Diderot (q.v.) and his circle, and enrolled him as an able contributor to the *Encyclopedia* (q.v.). While carefully avoiding extremes of opinion, T. was sympathetic to the views of the Physiocrats (q.v.), and wr., 1766, a work on ' Wealth ', which was influential in its own day, and to some extent anticipated A. Smith (q.v.). Like many of the *philosophes*, T. was greater as a thinker than as a writer, and we owe much of our knowledge of him to *Vie de Turgot*, 1786, by his younger contemporary, Condorcet (q.v.). T. was the earliest translr. of Macpherson's (q.v.) *Ossian* into Fr., and effected translns., too, from Pope, Tasso, and others.

Turnebus, Adrian (1512-65): Fr. scholar ; Royal Reader in Gk. from 1547 (see s.v. Corporation), in succession to Toussain (q.v.) ; in the opinion of Montaigne (q.v.), the best and most erudite scholar of his age or for ages past. Wr. 30 bks. of Lat. *Adversaria* on passages in Gk. and Lat. classics, and was well-known as editor.

Tusser, Thomas (*c.* 1524-80): Engl. poetaster. Wr. *Hundred Good Points of Husbandry*, 1557, which contained many excellent sayings which passed into proverbial wisdom.

Tyard, Pontus de (1521-1603): Fr. poet ; bp. of Châlons ; student at the collège de Coqueret, and the sixth star of the Pleiad (q.v.), Dorat (q.v.) being the seventh. T. was a little senior to the original 5 members included in Ronsard's (q.v.) brigade, and had written his earliest bk. prior to Du Bellay's (q.v.) famous *Défense* ; it was entitled *Erreurs Amoureuses*, and T. has been credited with first introducing the sonnet (q.v.) into Fr. verse, an honour really due to St.-Gelais (q.v.). His poetry reached a standard, however, equal to the aims of the Pleiad, and he was also notable as a writer on theological and philosophical subjects, and for public work outside

lit. In some respects T.'s career recalls the more familiar record of M. Arnold (q.v.), esp. in the early exhaustion of his poetical vein.

Tyndale, William (? 1484-1536): Engl. Biblical scholar ; a leader of the Protestant Reformation (q.v.). ' Living in the notable reign of Henry viii, when the power of Rome was supreme in England ', writes Mr. F. G. Jannaway (*The Bible, and How it Came to us*, 24), ' it is remarkable that such an age could have produced a man with such traits of character as those possessed by ' T. His transln. from the Lat. of Erasmus's (q.v.) *Manual of the Christian Soldier* early involved him in a controversy, in the course of which he vowed, almost in the words of Erasmus, that the day would soon dawn when a ' boy that driveth the plough should know more of Scripture than the great body of the clergy then knew ; yea, even more than the Pope himself ' : a bold prophecy, which did not serve to recommend his constant scheme for providing an Engl. version of the New Testament, when he laid it, 1523, before bp. Cuthbert Tunstall (1474-1559) of London. So he went to Hamburg, 1524, and visited Luther (q.v.) at Wittenberg, and pursued his lonely task at Cologne and Worms. Even so, he met resolute opposition from the authorities at home, when he tried to introduce some copies of his completed work. He sent his Bibles across concealed in bales of merchandise, and they were circulated to some extent till an Act of Parliament was passed *ad hoc*, prohibiting the use of this ' false ' transln. T. completed the New Testament, 1525, the Pentateuch, *c.* 1530, and the bk. of Jonah, 1531, and his version, free and easy in places, and not without touches of humour, is exact, scholarly, and learned, and forms the foundation of the Engl. Bible (q.v.) to this day (see, too, s.v. Coverdale). T. publd., too, treatises on Justification by Faith and *The Obedience of a Christian Man*, which was approved by king Henry viii, but forfeited the king's favour by his opposition to Wolsey and the royal divorce, and was involved, further, in a polemic with sir Thos. More (q.v.). The end was inevitable : on 6 Oct., 1536, T. was strangled and burnt at the stake, with the prayer on his lips, ' Lord, open the king of England's eyes ! ' King and people are both immensely indebted to this scholar-victim of the Word of God.

Tyrwhitt, Thomas (1730-86): Engl. scholar. T.'s contributions to classical scholarship, which were considerable, are detailed in Sandys' monumental *History* of that faculty (iii, 419): they include a critical edn. and Lat. transln. of Aristotle's treatise on poetics ; an *ed. pr.* from a MS. in Florence of a speech of Isaeus, 1785, etc. ; and ' it was partly in recognition of his own earlier work that, in 1786, he received from Brunck (1729-1803 ; famous Strasburg Hellenist) the flattering assurance that England was " le pays de l'Europe où la littérature grecque est la plus florissante " '. T. brought his great gifts to bear with equal measure on the lit. of his own country. He took part, 1782, in the Chatterton (q.v.) inquiries ; he wr. *Observations upon Skakespeare*, 1766, and his *Canterbury Tales of Chaucer, to which are added an Essay on his language and* *versification, and an Introductory Discourse, together with Notes and a Glossary,* 5 vols., 1775-8, was a work of the highest importance to medieval studies in the 18th cent. T., says prof. Ker (*C.H.E.L.*, x, 241), 'is the restorer of Chaucer. . . . The art of the grammarian has seldom been better justified, and there are few things in English philology more notable than Tyrwhitt's edition of Chaucer'.

Tytler, -i. William (1711-92): Scot. historian; writer to the signet; discovered the *Kinge's Quair* of king James i (q.v.) of Scotld., and publd. the *Poetical Remains* of that royal author, 1783.

    -ii. Alexander Fraser (1747-1813): Scot. historian; son of above; judge of session as lord Woodhouselee, 1802; prof. of History at Edinburgh univ. Wr. *Elements of General History*, 1801, and other useful works.

    iii. Patrick Fraser (1791-1849): Scot. historian; son of above. Wr. *Life of the Admirable Crichton* (i.e., James Crichton, 1560-85; the epithet, Admirable, was affixed by sir Thomas Urquhart, q.v., 1652), 1819; *History of Scotland*, 1828-43, a work which long held the field for its accuracy and research, and other works, including the art. on Scotland in seventh edn. of the *Encyclo. Brit.*, 1839. T. was a friend of sir W. Scott (q.v.), and of sir Archibald Alison (1792-1867), author of a *History of Europe*, 1833-42, and (sequel) 1852-9.

U

Ubeda, de, Francisco Lopez (fl. 1605): Span. novelist; physician at Toledo. Wr. the *Picara Justina,* a female rogue-novel of no great merit; he intended to write a sequel, marrying Justina to Guzman (see s.v. Aleman), but the project was never carried out. The theory that U. was the pseudonym of Andreas Perez (q.v.) has been abandoned by recent scholars.

Udall, Nicholas (1505-56): Engl. playwright; scholar; headmaster of Eton coll., 1534-41, and of Westminster school, 1554-6; transld. portions of the Lat. works of Erasmus, q.v., and wr., chiefly, *Ralph Roister Doister,* 1540, a comedy in doggerel verse, after the model of Plautus, which may have been acted by the Eton boys while U. was still headmaster, and which forms, with Sackville's (q.v.) Senecan tragedy, *Gorboduc,* the starting point of Engl. drama; it was printed, 1566. There is no extant record of his composing an epilogue to the Westminster Plautine or Terentian play, still performed annually by the king's scholars at that school.

Uhland, Johann Ludwig (1787-1862). Germ. poet; born and died at Tübingen, where his father was secretary to the univ.; head of the so-called Swabian School of later Romanticists; 'the classic of the Romantic movement' (*Klassiker der Romantik*), according to D. F. Strauss (q.v.). Omond (*P.E.L.,* x., 333) has a pregnant phrase in this connection. After Heine (q.v.), he says, 'Uhland became impossible', so effectually did Heine, like Cervantes, bore a hole in 'the very crown of the German Romantic movement'. U.'s vogue may almost be said to be confined to his own country. He expressed exactly the sentiments (i) of Germany (1805-15) struggling to be free from the yoke of Napoleon, (ii) of Swabia looking back on her heroic past (or, of Germany looking back at her heroic past through the legendary lore of U.'s beloved Swabia). He avoided the extravagance and voluptuousness of the more fervid singers of the dawn, and so has been criticized at home for lack of 'das Träumerische und Schwärmerische' (Kluge, *Deutsch. Nat. Lit.*, 231); but 'the extravagances of a movement are not its hall-marks. Uhland is dreamy and sentimental, within bounds of reason' (Omond, *op. cit.*, 296), and he has left for permanent delight many stirring national lyrics, infused, like Tennyson's (q.v.) in a later day, with a conservative-passionate belief in 'freedom slowly broadening down'. 'Ye have crushed the foreign hordes', he wr., 'but have kindled no inner light; Free men ye cannot be called, Till ye shall have *established* the Right' (wenn ihr das Recht nicht *festgestellt*); and 'das Recht', or 'das teure Recht', was the constant theme of his patriotic muse. U.'s plays, *Ernest, Duke of Swabia,* and *Ludwig, the Bavarian,* are not much remembered to-day; far more unforgetable are his ballads and folksongs, some of which Longfellow transld., and among the best known of which are— *Klein Roland, Abschied, der gute Kamerad, der Wirtin Töchterlein, Schäfers Sonntagslied, das Schloss am Meere, Es zogen drei Burschen, das Gluck von Edenhall,* etc. Notable, too, and characteristic of his resolve to found the new Germany on the old, were his *Life of Walther v. der Vogelweide* (1822), and other critical writings, both before and after his appointment (1830) to a chair in his native univ. U.'s definition of romantic scenery is worth quoting: 'Eine Gegend ist romantisch, wo Geister wandeln', and the, *Geister,* or spirits which accompanied him, as he roamed through the ancient kingdoms of Romance (q.v.), kneeling in prayer by his side, or crossing the stream with the same ferryman, were the spirits evoked by his intense love of the countryside most familiar to him, and beckoning his countrymen to repopulate Germany with their genial presences. What the Lake district in England was to Wordsworth (q.v.), such was Swabia to U., whose songs and ballads, of pure and gentle lineage, are an expression and a source of Germ. idealism.

Ulenspiegel. See **Eulenspiegel.**

Ulloa, de, Luis (17th cent.): Span. dramatist; poet. Wr., 1659, a play *Alfonso viii* (his love-story with the Jewess of Toledo, which Diamante, q.v., later dramatized), and religious and other poems, publd. posthly., 1674, by his son.

Ulrich von Liechtenstein (c. 1200-76): Germ. poet; caricaturist of the court-epos. Wr. *Frauendienst* ('Service of Women'), 1255, a more or less mock-chivalric poem on the profane, as opposed to the divine side of the cult of *Minne*, or love-worship; (*Frauen-minne* was profane-love, or love of women; *Gottesminne* was divine love, or love of God, in the old nomenclature of Teuton chivalry; see s.v. Minnesinger). U. is typical of the passage, remarkably rapid in retrospect, from the full flower of Arthurian knightly idealism to the realism of the guild-poets (s.v. Meistersinger), and of the conflict introduced by contact with hist. facts and personages from peasant life.

Unities (Rhet.): A theory of rules governing dramatic composition, definitely formulated in France in the 17th cent., and formally accepted as binding on Fr. classical drama in 1640. The 3 Unities were those of Place, Time, and Action; the scene of a play was to be confined within spatial limits seizable by the intelligence of the audience; the duration of the action was to be limited, as nearly as possible, to the period required for its presentation; and the action was to be single, not multiple,— a tale, or romance, that is to say, was not to be sliced into segments, and presented in 5 acts on the stage, but a single dramatic conflict or tragic action was to be worked out through its stages to its conclusion. It will be seen that the theory of the Unities was based on the commands of commonsense: 'les règles du théâtre', said Aubignac (q.v.), 'ne sont pas fondées en autorité, mais en raison'; and the reason to which they appealed was that of the ordinary man, sick to death of the exactions on his patience and credulity of the heroic and chivalric romances and their long-winded interpreters, and anxious to be convinced by the plausibility of what he saw as well as to be thrilled by its horror or charmed by its beauty. The promulgation and acceptance of the rules in France (their orig. is discussed below) are, at bottom, a matter of Fr. history; of the history of drama in France, and must be considered in that light. The history is continuous till the production of the *Cid* (q.v.) of Corneille (q.v.), and can be grasped in its entirety. The drama of the Fr. Renaissance followed precisely the same lines as were followed by the drama of the Renaissance in Italy; first, Lat. translns. from the Gk. tragedians and Senecan (s.v. Seneca) plays founded on the same models; then came the plays in the Fr. language: Jodelle (q.v.), the playwright of the Pleiad (q.v.), Grévin, Garnier, Montchrétien (qq.v.), and the rest, all Senecan in method, and stilted in execution. The change came in 1599, when the Hôtel de Bourgogne, the headquarters of a feeble dramatic society known as the Confrérie (q.v.) de la Passion, was leased to Valleran Lecomte, whose playwright (or playwriting hack) was Alexandre Hardy (q.v.). Hardy was the first to treat the subjects of antiquity, whether classical or Biblical, as dramatic material and no longer as poetic themes. He, far more than Jodelle, who commonly bears the palm, was the founder of the Fr. classical theatre. But with the lease from the Confrérie went the stage-furniture of the Hôtel de Bourgogne. This is an all-important consideration. Lecomte was not in a financial position to scrap the 'plant', or properties, which he had acquired; and Hardy's task was that of a carpenter rather than of a playwright; he had to dovetail the action into the scenery provided. 'On this miserable stage of the Hôtel de Bourgogne, by the meagre light of candles, the contrast between the reality indicated and the image presented proved too striking: it was observed that the forest was a tree, and the sea a basin; it raised surprise that Germany and Denmark, or even the Place Royale and the Tuileries were only separated by a few planks, and that in a single hour the hero had grown thirty years older. This did not seem reasonable or credible. The romantic extravagances of the tragicomedies delighted the senses; but the inadequacy of the scenic illusion repelled. Though the employment of successive in place of simultaneous stage-furniture was not altogether unknown, its use was not understood. The Unities offered a solution which attracted the ordinary man; the imitation corresponded to to the reality, and thus sustained the illusion. In this true sense, they represented the *minimum* of convention, irreducible in a representation of life. . . . Thus, the acceptance of the Unities was a victory of realism over imagination; and that is why it was established in France, and not in Spain or England' (Lanson, *Hist. de la Lit.*, *fr.*, 421-22). It was a victory for the erudite critics, whose gradual domination of the Fr. stage may be traced from the early days of the Renaissance; circumstances hastened the adoption of the rules, but they were imposed, not by force from without, but by consent and necessity from within. It was not a bloodless victory, but the blood flowed after the event; the Unities had already won the day, when the battle over Corneille's *Cid* was stopped by his election to the Academy, 1647, and by his acceptance, 1660, of the principles which he was held to have violated in that play, 1636 (or Jan., 1637), and of which he had been thoroughly ignorant at the date of his *Mélite*, 1629. In fact, the formal adoption of the Unities between 1630 and 1640 was merely the work, in no department ever achieved without rancour and dispute, of substituting a written constitution for an undocumented working arrangement. Unconsciously, Hardy and others had been feeling their way towards the Unities, but it was not till 1631 that Mairet (q.v.) formulated the classical theory as a definite code in a pref. to his *Silvanaire*. In 1634, his *Sophonisbe* was the first 'regular' tragedy ever produced on the Fr. stage; and it is interesting to remark that its subject was the same as that of the *Sophonisba* of Trissino (q.v.), the first 'modern' tragedy in a vernacular tongue. Prefaces and treatises were multiplied; Chapelain (q.v.) was an important convert to the theory of the Unities, and he converted Richelieu, 1635; and Richelieu's jealousy of Corneille gave rise to the battle of the *Cid*. With that, the controversy was ended, and the rules became a condition of classical tragedy on the Fr. stage; stated in Boileau's (q.v.) formula:

Qu'en un lieu, qu'en un jour, un seul fait accompli

Tienne jusqu'à la fin le théâtre rempli.

It remains to ask : where did the rules come from ? Briefly, they were expanded from the Unity of Action laid down by Aristotle (q.v.) in his *Poetics* (vii). The course of expansion is traced very clearly by sir J. E. Sandys, *Hist. Class. Schol*, ii, xi. It began with Vida (q.v.), whose *Ars poetica*, was based on Horace (q.v.). The middle years of the 16th cent. in Italy were filled with editions, translns., commentaries, and adaptations of the Aristotelian and Horatian treatises ; the names of Trissino, Castelvetro, Cinthio, and others, should be consulted in this context. The Unity of Time first emerged in the treatise of Cinthio, 1543 ; that of Place, in Castelvetro, 1570 ; and the grand edn. of Aristotle was that of Vettori (q.v.), 1560. Thus, there was ample material to occupy the critics and playwrights of Spain (Cervantes *pro*, and Lope *contra* the rules), Engld., and France, when they came into their inheritance of the Ital. Renaissance. In France, as has been shown, the problem was solved *ambulando*. The generation which had been taught by Malherbe and J. L. de Balzac (qq.v.) to select its words with fastidiousness, which had been trained by Descartes (q.v.) to think logically and rationally, which Hardy had accustomed to dramatic action incompatible to a large extent with the poetic stage-properties of the Hôtel de Bourgogne, and which, finally, had acquired an Academy (q.v.) of social standing and aristocratic prestige, was thoroughly prepared to welcome the formulation of the principles to which all its trained instincts had steadily tended. Out of Aristotle, through the Lat. Horatian scholars and Hellenists of Italy, the Unities were recommended by the humanists to the playwrights, and were accepted by those in Paris in the 17th cent., because the audience which they addressed had been educated to require the satisfaction of rational and realistic standards of taste. The rule of the U. was observed in France till the 19th cent., and it exactly suited the dramatic genius of Racine (q.v.). Manzoni (q.v.) in Italy anticipated Victor Hugo (q.v.) in Paris in preferring the unregulated dramatic tradition of Shakespeare (q.v.), and Stendhal (q.v.) defended this looser and less rigid position in his essay on *Racine et Shakespeare*, 1822. It is interesting, indeed, important, to note that Stendhal's remarks in this contest were directly lifted from an essay in the *Rambler*, 1749-50, where Dr. Johnson (q.v.) argued that the U. were not essential to a ' just drama ', and that an appeal was always open ' from criticism to nature ', i.e., from the regulating critics to the natural course of dramatic events. For this distinction between dramas founded on *noticia* (knowledge) and *fantasia* (imagination), or on ' the law of writ ' (written rules) and ' the liberty ' (see s.v. Torres-Naharro, e.g.) runs through the whole history of drama, and the U. were merely codified in one chapter of that history as an expression of a prevailing convention.

Urbino, duke of. See **Frederick of Montefeltro.**

Urfé, d', Honoré (1568-1625) : Fr. novelist ; author of *Astrée*, a kind of heroic-pastoral romance, decadent rather than elevated by its departure from the type in the choice of places and (possibly) characters from real life. D'U.

set his Arcadia (q.v.) at the foot of his garden : on the banks of the Lignon, which flowed past his estate ; and this obvious clue has led to a less probable identification of Astrée herself with Diâne de Châteaumorand, d'U.'s brother's widow, whom he married in 1600 ; of Céladon, Astrée's lover, with the author ; of Euric with king Henri iv, and so forth. But the theory of a *roman-à-clef* (q.v.) is of more than doubtful correctness ; d'U.'s marriage with his sister-in-law was a matter of convenience rather than of affection, and Céladon became a stock name for a passionate lover ; he is banished by Astrée in the novel, and is saved by nymphs from an attempt to drown himself in the Lignon ; he resists the approaches of Galatea, and awaits, through various adventures of ideal shepherds, knights, and nymphs, refreshed at the fountain of love, the revocation of the sentence of exile. The romance was issued in 5 parts (i, 1607 ; ii, 1612 ; iii, 1619 ; iv and v, 1627), and is obviously the offspring—through the Fr. transln. (1582, and, again, 1613) of the *Diana* of Montemayor (1542)—of the Ital. pastoral (q.v.) of Sannazzaro, Tasso, and Guarini (see s.vv.). The *Amadis* (q.v.) influence was also marked in the lengthy machinery of adventure. It was the Span. model which admitted real names and places in the midst of the pastoral illusion, and d'U.'s extension of this licence and his more or less unvarnished prose-narrative, contrasted with the heroic-poetic tone of the purer pastoralists, suggest that he aimed at representing the life of the Fr. aristocracy of his day under a thin disguise of fiction. To this extent, d'U.'s *Astrée*, to which he added an imitation of the *Diana* and a vol. of ' moral epistles ', marks an advance in the cultivation of realism. It is said that, in 1624, an ' academy of true lovers ' was formed in Germany to live the *Astrée* life, which was certainly near enough to real conditions to supply hints to mme. de Rambouillet (q.v.) in organizing fashionable society into a source of precious (q.v.) lit. Hence, largely, the great popularity which the novel achieved.

Ur-Hamlet (Germ. prefix *ur-* means primordial) : Term commonly used by Shakespearean scholars to designate a conjectured *Hamlet*-play, available in Shakespeare's (q.v.) time but since lost, on which his great tragedy was founded. There is no reference in the term to such well-known sources of *Ur-H.* and *Hamlet* as the tales of Saxo or even Belleforest (see s.vv.) : the *Ur-H.* definitely means the acting-drama which must have been extant when Shakespeare wr. his *Hamlet*. The play is lost, and its author's name is lost with it. That authorship is now ascribed, in an ascending scale of proven affirmation, to Thomas Kyd (q.v.), Shakespeare's predecessor, and author of *The Spanish Tragedy*, which has obvious affinities in its plot and characters with the more famous play. It ' anticipates with some skill ', says sir S. Lee (*Shakespeare*, 1915, p. 357), ' the leading motive and an important part of the machinery of ' *Hamlet*. ' The most distinctive scenic devices of Shakespeare's tragedy manifestly lay within the range of Kyd's dramatic faculty and experience. . . . Kyd may justly be credited with the first invention of a play of *Hamlet* on the tragic lines which Shakespeare's genius expanded and subtilized '. The full argument in support of this conclusion will be found in § iv of the Introduction to the Oxford edn. (1901) of *The Works of Thomas Kyd*, by prof. F. S. Boas, who reproduces the chief findings of Germ. specialists on a topic particularly suited to their genius for patient research. Boas regards the problem as so complex that no short and simple solution is to be found. But he holds that Kyd wr. a *Hamlet*, conveniently described as the *Ur-Hamlet*, probably in 1587 ; and it was not printed ; that it was revived in 1594, 1596 and 1602 ; and that its acting-versions between 1587 and 1602 had been pulled about by the various companies of players, in order to suit their requirements. Thus, Shakespeare, coming to the plot in 1602, was not dependent on Kyd's primitive *Hamlet*, but on an improved and popularized stage-version, which had stood the test of the theatre. This version is represented in the First Shakespearean quarto, and a Germ. play, *der Bestrafte Brudermord* (' The Avenged Fratricide '), 1710, which has puzzled commentators on account of its insertions from Shakespeare's *Hamlet*, is merely another version of the lost stage-play utilized by Shakespeare 15 years after Kyd wr. his *Hamlet*. Accordingly, to cite the conclusion of prof. Boas : ' Generations of critics have sought to find a completely satisfying interpretation of the work. They have failed to do so—even the greatest of them —and failed inevitably. For the *Hamlet* that we know is not a homogeneous product of genius. It is—unless evidences external and internal continue to mislead us—a fusion, with the intermediate stages in the process still partly recognizable, of the inventive dramatic craftsmanship of Thomas Kyd, and the majestic imagination, penetrating psychology and rich verbal music of William Shakespeare '. A critical edn. of the existing play, breaking up the fused parts, so far as they are still recognizable, into *Ur-Hamlet* and Shakespeare's *Hamlet*, would be an interesting exercise.

Urquhart (**Urchard**), **Thomas** (1611-60) : Scot. scholar ; knt., 1641 ; ' the last and greatest of the great translators of the larger Elizabethan period ' (*C.H.E.L.*, vii, 256), in virtue of his version of the masterpieces of Rabelais (q.v.),

1653, 1664, 1693 ; the post. vols. being edited and continued by P. A. Motteux (1663-1718), a Fr.-Engl. scholar. A native tendency to extravagance of diction led U. ' to exaggerate the peculiarities of his original ; and this exaggeration has undoubtedly passed into the usual English estimate of Rabelais himself ' (*ib.*). But U. successfully combined the right blend of jargon and learning, and very little, if any, injustice to Rabelais was done by his Elizabethan translr.

Urrea, de, Geronimo (1513-c. 1574) : Span. poet ; wr. chivalric romance, *Don Clarisel, ed. pr.*, 1879, and transld., 1555, the *Chevalier délibéré* of La Manche (q.v., and see s.v. Acuña).

Urrea, de, Pedro Manuel (c. 1486-c. 1535) : Span. poet ; created count d'Aranda, 1488. U., who went to Rome in 1516 as Castilian ambassador to king Ferdinand, had previously proved himself a singer of no means powers in Italianate and sacred subjects. His *Cancionero* was publd., 1513, and included a versified rendering of act i of the prose-dialogue *Celestina* (q.v.), which added lustre to the famous piece. In 1514, U. wr. a prose *Penitencia de Amor*, in obvious imitation of the *Celestina*, but without its realism and sordidness ; U.'s romance was virtually an attempt to re-write the dialogue on the purer lines of the chivalric convention, as displayed, e.g., in San Pedro's (q.v.) *Carcel de Amor*.

Usque, Abraham (16th cent.) : Port. Biblical scholar ; born at Lisborn ; Jew ; fled from the Inquisition to Ferrara, where he established himself as a printer. Publd. the so-called Ferrara Bible, 1553, freely utilized by Valera (q.v.) some years later, and other works in Hebr. and Span. lit. It was an excellent Span. version, which passed the censors of the Inquisition as well as the Jew. authorities. U. was also known (in Lisbon) as Duarte Pinel, and the two names, though of the same person, are mistaken as names of distinct persons by Ticknor (i, 41n.).

Uz, Johann Peter (1720-96) : Germ. poet ; the most inspired of the Prussian or Anacreontic (see s.v. Anakreontiker) school, and the most deserving of the name of ' the German Horace ', to which they all aspired. Wr. *Lyric Poems*, 1749 ; *Theodicée*, 1755, and other philosophic verse, and operettas after the pattern of Zachariä (q.v.).

V

Vadé, Jean Joseph (1719-57) : Fr. poet. Wr. clever and humorous verse, light drama, parodies, etc., all of real merit. His *Fileuse* achieved conspicuous success, and his *Trompeur Trompé* was not overlooked in the *Mariage de Figaro* of Beaumarchais (q.v.), 1784.

Vair, du, Guillaume (1556-1621) : Fr. orator and moral philosopher ; ambassador to Engld., 1596 ; first president to the parliament of Provence ; bp. of Lisieux, 1617 ; a great political leader, on the side of peace and the royal authority, and a formidable opponent of the League. Several of his speeches, as publd.,

are models of eloquence, in the Ciceronian style, and he wr., too, a treatise ' on French eloquence, and the causes why it has remained so low ', which was a plea for more freedom in public life. This links on with his greater work in moral philosophy, and with his reflections from his own experience of high office in the judicature and the church. V. transld. Epictetus, and revealed his own system as a combination of Stoicism and Christianity. V.'s chief discourses were : *On the Moral Philosophy of the Stoics ; On Constancy, and Consolation in Public Calamities ;* and (politico-philosophical) *Exhortation to the Civil Life* and *Discourse on the Salic Law.* Justice and charity, and a meekness rare in his age, raised the works of this early moralist, who was also a speaker and a statesman, to a high level of influence and dignity ; and his point of view is emphasized by his more strictly religious writings, which included *Meditations* on Job, Jeremiah, and Isaiah.

Vajanský, Svetozár Hurban (1847-1916): Slovak poet and novelist. 'The modern Slovak novel is chiefly his creation', says Chudoba (*Short Surevy Czech Lit.*, 140) ; and, though V. to some extent compromised artistic truth with patriotic feeling, or even with propagandism for his country, his novels—*The Withered Branch, Root and Offshoots*, etc.,—give a vivid picture of Slovakian society in the period immediately prior to the establishment of the Republic.

Valdés, de, Juan (died, 1541): Span. moralist ; a reformer, if not actually a Protestant, in his religious views ; 'not a noisy propagandist, but rather a suave and discreet director of souls ' (Kelly, *Lit. espagn.*, 223) ; edu. at Alcalá (q.v.) ; entered service of emperor Charles v (q.v.) ; became chamberlain to pope Clement vii at Rome, and was afterwards attached to the household of card. Ercole Gonzaga at Naples, where his influence affected the fair Guilia Gonzaga, sung by Ariosto and B. Tasso (qq.v.) and other poets of the day. V.'s works, with one exception, were publd. posth., and that exception was publd. anon. They included commentaries on the epistle of St. Paul to the Romans and on the first epistle to the Corinthians ; a *Dialogue between Mercury and Charon*, in the manner of a satire by Lucian, defending the actions of the emperor down to 1528 (the year, accordingly, at which it may be dated), esp. in reference to his dispute with king Francis i of France, and attacking the ecclesiastical policy of king Henry viii of Engld. *in re* the divorce of queen Catherine of Aragon, the emperor's aunt ; a dialogue between ' Lactantius ' (*i.q.*, the author) and and unnamed archdeacon at Valladolid, justifying the sack of Rome, 1527, and anti-cipating Napoleon in its discussion of the emperor's possible surrender to the Reforma-tion (see s.v. Charles v). Both these dialogues are models of pure Span. prose, a quality which is still more characteristic or V.'s *Dialogo de la Lengua* (on language), written *c.* 1535, *ed. pr.*, anon., Madrid, 1737, thus missing the genera-tion to whom it was addressed. There are 4 interlocutors in this dialogue (2 Span. and 2 Ital.), and the objective is a search for the pure wells of Castilian undefiled. Posterity, says Fitzmaurice-Kelly (*op. cit.*, 224) has almost invariably endorsed V.'s verdicts, and he is 'incontestably the best prose-writer (*prosateur*) of his epoch. . . . As a stylist V. comes very close to his great successor ', Cervantes (q.v.), who, with his common good taste, is to be accounted among V.'s admirers.

Valdés, Juan Melendez. See s.v. **Melendez Valdés.**

Valdivielso, de, José (*c.* 1560-1638): Span. poet ; divine ; chaplain to the archbishop of Toledo. Wr. a very long and very dull sacred epopee of *The Life, Excellences and Death of the Most Glorious Patriarch . . . St. Joseph*, 1604,

which had considerable success ; *Twelve Sacramental Autos and some Divine Comedies*, 1622 ; and *Part i of a Spiritual Song-book* (see s.v. *Romancero*), 1612, ' which affords the same admixture of intimacy and devoutness to be found in the *Noble Numbers* of Herrick ' (q.v. ; Kelly, *Lit. espagn.*, 324).

Valencia: Town and district in S.E. Spain ; the univ. of V. was founded, 1499, and Bernardo Fenollar, who was one of its professors, was editor of the second bk. ever printed in Spain. (The first, a little grammar of no pretension dates from Barcelona, q.v., 1468). This was printed in 1474, and consisted of a collection of prize-poems at the poetical contest of that year at V., held in honour of the Madonna. Four of these poems were in the conquering Castilian tongue, thus showing, that, in the 15th cent., the independence of the Valencian dialect, so closely allied with Provençal (q.v.), had already been threatened with decay ; and this process was quickly consummated. March and Roig (qq.v.) had been among its chief practitioners ; and Villena (q.v.), though he used the Castilian, belonged territorially to V.

Valera, de, Cipriano (*c.* 1531-1625). Span. Biblical scholar ; left the monastery to become a Protestant ; lived at Gueva, and afterwards in Engld. Publd., London, 1596, a Span. version of the New Testament, and the Bible complete, Amsterdam, 1602. In this work he was assisted by another reformer, Cassiodoro de Reyna, and both availed themselves of a transln. issued at Ferrera, 1553, by the Port. scholar, A. Usque (q.v.).

Valera, de, Diego (*c.* 1412-87): Span. chronicler ; knight and soldier. Wr. *Cronica de España*, 1482, ' abbreviated ' —from the *Cronica general* of Alfonso The Wise (see s.vv.)—' by command of the Most Powerful Donna Isabella queen of Castile ' ; commonly known as the *Valeriana*. This work, in the latter portions of which the chronicler was also a participant, fully conscious of the merits of his part, was frequently reprinted, and has a pleasant and fluent style,

Valera, Juan (1824-1905): Span. novelist ; diplomatist. V., who represented Spain at Washington, Brussels and Vienna, publd. a vol. of *Poesias*, 1858, and of *Cartas* (letters) *Americanas*, 1889 ; but his chief work was his novel *Pepita Jiménez*, 1874, ' from which is dated the attention paid abroad to contem-porary Spanish fiction ' (Kelly, *Lit. espagn.*, 435), and which was particularly praised by so fastidious a critic as Patmore (q.v.). Other novels, *el Comendador Mendoza*, 1877, *Doña Luz*, 1879, etc., followed from V.'s busy pen. It was V.'s happy combination of gay treat-ment and grave subject which won Patmore's admiration.

Valerius, Johan David (1776-1852): Swed. poet ; represented the reaction from the Voltairean conventions at the court of king Gustavus iii (q.v.), and shone particularly in the lighter forms of lyric verse, *vers de société*, etc. V. was one of the most popular and widely-read poets in Sweden in the first quarter of the 19th cent., and women particularly were enthusiastic admirers of his elegant and pleasant muse.

Valla, Giorgio (*c.* 1430-99): It. Latinist. Native of Piacenza ; cousin to L. Valla (*infra*).

Transld., 1498, Aristotle's (q.v.) *Poetic* into Lat.; an important, if not a scholarly, piece of work, as it remained for some years the only text available to the nascent scholarship of Italy.

Valla, Lorenzo (1407-57): It. humanist and philologist; reformer. Born at Rome, where he remained till he was 24; became private secretary to king Alfonso of Aragon and Sicily, 1435, and quickly justified his appointment at the anti-papal court by his bitter and critical attacks on the papacy. He was already known by his Lat. dialogue *de Voluptate* (1431), of which Pastor, the Catholic historian, writes, 'no one has better expressed the programme of the radical heathenizing party', but in which Symonds, the modern humanist, says, 'Valla proclaims the fundamental principle of science, and inaugurates a new criterion of ethics'. There are 3 parties to the dialogue, Lionardo Bruni, who sustains the part of Stoicism, Antonio Beccadelli, that of Epicureanism, and Niccolo Niccoli, that of the true good, or medieval asceticism. The victory goes to Niccoli, but V. is plainly on the side of Beccadelli, who is the 'lark' to Niccoli's 'nightingale'. The treatise is extremely outspoken, esp. in its condemnation of monasticism (Stoicism) and the virtue of continence. But views of this sort in that age would necessarily be expressed with too much literalness and extravagance, and the objection of the Church to such a challenge as 'What nature has formed and created cannot be other than holy and admirable' is as obvious and inevitable as the challenge itself was novel and bold. It struck the note of rebellion, and of a return to the Paganism, or Naturalism, of Cicero (q.v.) in his philosophic writings; and it helped to found lines of advance in modern thought which even yet has not reached its goal. Thus recommended to Alfonso, V. lost no time in his new post. In 1440 he issued his famous pamphlet on 'Constantine's Donation', which called in question the temporalities of the Holy See, and personally abused pope Eugenius iv. Every weapon in the papal armoury was raised and launched against V., who, secure at Naples, continued his task as critic and assailant. The accession of pope Nicholas v reversed the attitude of Rome, and V. was appointed prof. of Rhetoric (1450), and apostolic writer to that humanist pope. In Rome, he assisted in the transln. of Gk. classics into Lat., which was the great scheme of Nicholas, and effected excellent versions of Herodotus and Thucydides. He further was vigorously engaged in the lit. of polemics which disgraced the scholarship of this age, and was as noisy in his invective as Poggio and the rest. Far more important was his work *de Elegantiis Latinæ Linguæ*, which passed through 59 editions in 66 years, was paraphrased by Erasmus (q.v.), and was epoch-making in the history of style: 'if those have done most for any science who have carried it farthest from the point whence they set out, philology seems to owe quite as much to Valla as to anyone who has come since' (Hallam). V.'s humanistic and critical work, it may be added, was confined to the Lat. language and to composition in prose.

Valladolid, de, Juan (15th cent.): Span. poet; also known as Juan Pocta; attached to the court of king Alfonso v (q.v.) of Castile, whom he accompanied to Naples, and was later patronized by queen Isabella. V. is said to have been the son of the town-crier, and was not represented in the courtly anthologies (s.v. *Cancionero*) of the age, but has a place in an obscene collection of 'works of jest provoking laughter' (*obras de burlas provocantes a risa*). He is only known by half-a-dozen pieces of coarse texture and polemical tone.

The town from which the town-crier's son took his name is famous in Span. history, and acquired a univ. in the 14th cent.

Valmore, Marceline Desbordes (1787-1859): Fr. poet; led a curiously vagabond existence, 'constantly unmaking and remaking her nest', in the words of Ste.-Beuve (q.v.). Her first profession was the stage, she married an actor, and only began to write when her singing-voice failed. There was more music than thought in her poetry, but she takes rank with the few great women who were poets in France (see s.v. Labé). Her friends included most of the leading men of letters of the day, and for a time she held a brilliant little *salon* in Paris.

Vanbrugh, John (1664-1726): Engl. writer of Restoration (q.v.) comedies, but more justly famous as the architect of Blenheim palace, the Clarendon building at Oxford, Castle Howard, Haymarket theatre, etc.; herald; knt., 1714. Keeping strictly to our province of lit., V.'s plays are not very memorable, and, as Jeremy Collier (q.v.) did not fail to point out, they were very immoral. Wr. *Æsop*, 1697, from *Esope* of Boursault (q.v.); *The False Friend*, 1702, from Lesage (q.v.), and others: 'his originality consisted in breathing the spirit of Middleton or Massinger into the works of his French and English contemporaries', but 'his plays can add nothing either to our knowledge of life or to our æsthetic experience' (Dobree, *Restoration Comedy*,152-3).

Vandal, Albert (1853-1910): Fr. historian. Wr. valuable works on the relations of king Louis xv of France and empress Elizabeth of Russia; on the relations of emperor Napoleon with emperor Alexander of Russia; and on *l'Avènement de Bonaparte*.

Van Laun, Henri (1820-96): Dutch teacher of Fr. in Engld. Transld. Taine (q.v.), *Hist. Engl. Lit.*, and made other valuable contributions to Fr. studies.

Varchi, Benedetto (1503-65): It. book-smith. Wr. works in Lat. and vernacular, on love, poetry, etc.; of no importance, except as cumulative evidence to the industry of scholarship in his day.

Varnhagen, von Ense, Karl August (1785-1858): Germ. miscellanist; m. Rahel Levin (1771-1833), a Jewess; their *salon* in Berlin became a centre of Germ. Romanticism. Heine (q.v.) frequented it about 1822, and it was a recognized focus of Goethe-worship; V. founded his style on Goethe's, and devoted several bks. to the master's memory. A much-prized bk. by V. was his *Rahel: a Memorial Volume for her Friends*, 1834.

Vasari, Giorgio (1511-74): It. biographer of artists, and himself a painter and an architect.

V.'s interesting, anecdotal work (he has been called 'the Herodotus of art') covers the lives of the chief painters, sculptors and architects of his own country since Giotto (d. 1337).

Vauban, de, Sebastian le Prestre (1633-1713): Fr. economist (political statistician); military engineer; marshal of France; *marquis* by rank. V.'s name, illustrious in military history, is obscured in lit. by the fact that his writings on economic subjects were in advance of his times. He wr. 2 works, *Oisivetés* ('Recreations'), in which he collected facts and figures, and *Project de la Dîme Royale*, 1707, in which he drew some conclusions as to the existing economic condition of the Fr. people, and proposed the imposition of a single tax (the *dixme*) on all classes of the population. The last years of the reign of king Louis xiv were not hospitable to independent inquiry and outspoken comment of this kind. V. incurred the king's displeasure, and his investigations, which, properly followed up, might have averted some of the evils of revolution at the century's end, led to no practical result.

Vaugelas, sieur de, Claude Favre (1585-1650): Fr. philologer; lexicographer; the oracle of correct diction at the Hôtel de Rambouillet (q.v.), and an original member of the Fr. Academy (q.v.). Wr., 1647, *Remarques sur la Langue française*, a collection of rulings, with a pref., in which V. displays his aim as a continuation in method and principle of the work of Malherbe (q.v.). The Academy was well advised in entrusting to V. the execution of the plan for a Dict. suggested by Chapelain (.q.v.). The first editor worked at it till his death, and the *Dictionnaire de l'Académie*, when it finally appeared in 1694, bore the impress of his consistent devotion to the cause of purity in grammar and vocabulary. V. also issued a transln. of Quintus Curtius.

Vaughan, Henry (1625-95): Engl. (Welsh) poet, commonly known as the Silurist, owing to the association of the Silures in ancient times with his birthplace in Brecknockshire, where he practised the medical profession. Wr. several vols. of verse and prose, mainly devotional, of a curiously uneven excellence, but rising in places to the height of his best-known poem, 'They are all gone into the world of light', which first appeared in part ii of *Silex Scintillans*, 1655 (part i, 1650). V.'s *Retreat* must have been familiar to Wordsworth (q.v.) when he wr. his *Immortality* ode; and V's *Vision* ('I saw Eternity the other night') has its place in every good anthology.

Vaughan, Robert Alfred (1823-57): Engl. congregational divine. Wr. *Hours with the Mystics*, a classical work on its own subject 1856.

Vaumorière, sieur de; Pierre d'Ortigues (1610-93): Fr. novelist; a favourite member of the Precious (q.v.) circle. Wr., 1656-62, *le Grand Scipion*, a title founded on the *Grand Cyrus* of Scudéry (q.v.), a tale of love, war, and politics; *Agiatis*, 1685, a tale of the Spartan wars; and some minor works. V.'s next most important masterpiece was his completion (vols. 8-12) of the *Faramond* of La Calprenède (q.v.), which critics entitled to pronounce judgment agree in regarding as the most

excellent example of a sequel by another hand to be found in the annals of lit.; the similar example of Baro (q.v.) in this period is far inferior in performance, since he had the advantage of Urfé's notes.

Vauquelin de la Fresneys (1536-1606): Fr. poet; follower of the Pleiad (q.v.), though his submission to its principles did not prevent him from composing mystery-plays after the medieval pattern. Wr. satires and pastorals, and an *Art poétique*; commenced, 1574, publd., 1605. The 3 bks. in about 1200 lines of this Fr. poetic treatise on poetry are interesting more for the sake of the opportunity which V. enjoyed of testing the Pleiad criticism by its productions than for any merit of their own.

Vauvenargues, de, Luc de Clapiers (1715-47): Fr. philosopher; soldier; *marquis* by rank; retired to Paris, as infantry captain, 1744. There he found consolation for his enforced inactivity by intercourse with Mirabeau (q.v.), the elder, and other kindred spirits, touched to expression as moralists and reformers by the new philosophy and the new freedom of approach to nature, which were in the air. V. laid his homage on the altar of Voltaire (q.v.), who accepted it with genuine humility; it was a foretaste of the triumph he was to enjoy in 1778, but in 1745 it was an unexpected triumph, which did credit to the worshipper as well as to the hero. V.'s ill-health, his unscientific training, and his too early death prevented him from writing works of lasting value; he publd., 1746, *la Connaissance de l'Esprit Humain*, which was read in after-years by the light of J. J. Rousseau's (q.v.) writings, with enhanced admiration for its enlightened sense of the functions of natural passions; he 'had begun to teach the culture of emotional instincts in some sayings of exquisite sweetness and moderation, as that "Great thoughts come from the heart"; but he came too soon, and, alas for us all, he died young, and he made no mark' (Morley, q.v., *Rousseau*, ii, 33).

Vavasseur, François (1605-81): Fr. lexicographer. Wr. histories of Constantinople; edited Villehardouin and Joinville (qq.v.); Lat. glossaries; works on coinage, etc.

Vedel, Anders (1542-1616): Dan. philologer. Transld., 1579, the Lat. *Historia Danica* of Saxo (q.v.), which had been first issued, 1514, by Pedersen (q.v.), thus laying the foundations of vernacular prose. V. was appointed historiographer, and commissioned to continue Saxo's chronicle, but neither he nor his successor, Krag, succeeded in making much headway; and V.'s more memorable work consists in his collection, 1591, of the first collection (roughly, 100) of hist. Dan. ballads. (See s.v. Ballad). This work, continued by Syv and Grundtvig (qq.v.), marks an important step in Dan. national lit. and study of the past.

Vega Carpio, de, Lope Felix (1562-1635): Span. dramatist; poet; miscellanist; called by Cervantes (q.v.; Pref. to *Comedias*, 1614) 'el monstruo de naturaleza' (that prodigy of nature), an estimate which the verdict of 3 centuries sees no cause to abate. Prodigious, certainly, was the amount of V.'s literary

almost to the height of heroism in the hapless tenacity of his self-preservation '.

Vergara, de, -i. Francisco (*c.* 1484-1545): Span. humanist. Wr., 1537, a Gk. grammar (the first in Spain), which Scaliger (q.v.) highly praised.

   -ii. Juan (1491-1557): Span. humanist; brother to above; disciple of Erasmus; associated with card. Ximenes (q.v.) at Alcalá on the Gk. text of his polyglott Bible.

Vergerio, Pietro Paolo (*c.* 1370-*c.* 1445): It. humanist. Studied at Padua; ranks as pioneer of New Learning; wr. (1392) *de ingenuis moribus* (equivalent to, on a gentleman's education), in which the principles of humanistic education were for the first time clearly laid down, and based on study of Latinity; an ardent Ciceronian; learned Gk. from Chrysoloras (q.v.) at Florence; became papal secretary, and was selected to compose Chrysoloras' epitaph, still legible on a pantry-ceiling of the hotel Insel at Constance, where he died (1415). V. went from Constance to Hungary, where he transld. the *Anabasis* of Arrian.

Vergil, Polydore (*c.* 1470-*c.* 1555): It. humanist; resident in Engld. as deputy-Papal collector; friend of More, Linacre (qq.v.), and their circle. Wr. Lat. history of Engld. in 26 bks., first publd. at Basle, 1534, and remarkable on several grounds. It displayed an animus against card. Wolsey, due to causes personal to V., which, being admitted to the dignity of history, was perpetuated by succeeding historians till a comparatively recent date, and partly blackened Wolsey's fame. At the same time, V.'s work was distinguished by a real effort at sifting evidence, and at establishing relations between causes and effects; he placed the study of Engl. history on scientific lines, and, inaccurate and prejudiced though he frequently is, he is an important writer in his class and generation. His services were employed by king Henry vii, and he thus became a pioneer of the Ital. Renaissance in his adoptive country.

Vergniaud, Pierre Victurnien (1753-93): Fr. revolutionary orator; victim of the guillotine. V. is the chief representative of the eloquence of the Girondins (q.v.).

Verlaine, Paul (1844-96): Fr. poet; 'for a time the most indubitable poet that France in one of her vacant interlunar periods has possessed' (Saintsbury, *P.E.L.*, xii, 56); a contributor to the *Parnasse* (q.v.), and a follower of Baudelaire (q.v.) in his attention to prosody and form. V.'s vicious life is of no purpose to lit. to-day, though it inspired some legends of former days, and helped to obtain for his pearls in the mud an admiration not wholly due to intrinsic merit. V.'s works include *Fêtes Galantes*, 1869; *Sagesse*, 1881; *Amour*, 1888; *Poèmes Saturniens*, 1890, etc.: poetry wholly musical, partly mystical, partly melancholy, and all suffused by that tone of audacious passion with which Wilde (q.v.) was shocking Engl. readers a few years afterwards. The epithet 'symbolist' has been attached to the type of writing associated with V. and with Mallarmé (q.v.), and the epithet may be taken as descriptive of the forced and artificial effects attained by their

muse. Something, no doubt, was due to the example of the American poet, E. A. Poe; but the wholesome taste of unprepossessed readers is disposed to reject a large part of the symbolism as decadent in tone and unintelligible in expression.

Verne, Jules (1823-1905): Fr. novelist. Wr. a number of bks., which very successfully combined popular science with romantic adventure, and did not aim beyond that mark. V., whose method was vulgar, in its literal sense, succeeded in anticipating some of the wonders of later discovery, though some of his marvels have been passed in their turn. His works, which are widely read and have been frequently transld., have always fascinated young people, and include *A Journey round the World in 24 Days*, *A Journey to the Centre of the Earth*, etc.

Verner, Karl Adolph (1846-96): Dan. philologist. V.'s father was a Germ. of Saxony, but his mother was a Dane, and most of his life was spent in univ. circles at Copenhagen. 'Verner's law', which regularizes the exceptions to 'Grimm's law' of consonantal relations (see s.vv. Grimm, Rask) is a part of the science of comparative philology.

Verri, Alessandro (1741-1816): It. novelist; translr.; count by rank; wr. a romance round the life of Sappho, the Lesbian poet, with some fine versions of her poetry, and *Roman Nights*, 1792-1804, imaginery conversations between the greater Romans, which proved a work of enduring popularity. V.'s romantic tendency was displayed by his transln. of *Hamlet*. V. and his brother, **Pietro** (1728-97), who wr. treatises on happiness and similar works, were members of the circle which publd. the periodical called *il Caffe* (see s.v. Beccaria), against whose loose and Gallicizing views Baretti (q.v.), among others, protested.

Versailles: Seat, near Paris, of the kings of France; particularly illustrious in the reign of king Louis xiv (say, from 1661, when the king took the helm of State, to 1715). The memoirs of Saint-Simon (q.v.) are the best contemporary evidence to the lustre and splendour of the Bourbon court in the *grand siècle* of the *roi Soleil*, when V. was the arbiter of taste and fashion to all the civilized world. The palace was entered by the mob, 1789, in the reign of Louis xiv's second successor, his great-grandson, Louis xvi, and is now, with its wonderful gardens, one of the show-places of the Fr. Republic.

Vespasiano da Bisticci (1421-98): It. biographer; 'the last of medieval scribes and the first of modern booksellers', as Sandys (*Hist. Class. Schol.*, ii, 95) and Symonds (*Ital. Renaissance*, ii, 221) concur in calling him, and, as such, an immediate precursor of the new era of Printing (q.v.). V. spent 14 years in collecting a library for the then duke of Urbino, consisting of all the Gk. and Lat. authors so far available, all 'written with the pen', for the mechanism of the press was beneath the ducal dignity. V. was agent, too, to other courts, and employed a staff of skilled copyists for supplying the requirements of his patrons. V., who is interred among the mighty in S. Croce, wr. a delightful and valuable vol. of *Lives of*

Illustrious Men, being intimate biographies of 103 scholars and patriots of the 15th cent., whom he had met and esteemed.

Vettori, Piero (1499-1585): It. Latin-Hellenist; Petrus Victorius. His scholarship was so eminent that Sandys (ii, 135) writes, 'the sixteenth century, for Italy at least, may well be called the *saeculum Victorianum*'. His work was almost exclusively editorial, and the main texts to which his talents were devoted were those of Aristotle and Cicero. V. lived at Florence during the greater part of his long life, where he occupied chairs of learning, besides taking part in diplomatic missions and the inevitable political frays. Medals were struck in his honour, and his portrait was painted by Titian. V.'s commentary on Aristotle's *Poetic* appeared in 1560, and is important in the development of the theory of dramatic Unities (q.v.).

Veuillot, Louis (1813-83): Fr. journalist; pamphleteer; converted, 1838, to the Church of Rome, of which he became an ardent propagandist and an eager and a convinced adherent. Edited *l'Univers* from 1843; it was suspended, 1861-67; and attacked with brilliant and mordant wit all the supporters of Gallicanism and opponents of papal infallibility. V.'s works, which had considerable vogue, include *Libres Penseurs, Dialogues Socialistes, Molière et Bourdaloue*, etc.

Viau, de, Théophile. See s.v. **Théophile.**

Vicente, Gil (c. 1485-1557): Port. dramatic poet; founder of the Port. theatre, as a follower of Enzina (q.v.), and, at a later stage of his career, of Torres-Naharro (q.v.). Of V.'s 42 pieces, which, in the elastic nomenclature of early drama, may be entitled comedies, tragi-comedies or pastoral plays, 14 were written in Port., 11 in Castilian (Span.), and the rest in that mixed dialect between the two (a species of macaronic, q.v.), which Enzina had invented. The causes of V.'s use of the Span. language (a phenomenon quite common in his age; see s.v. Resende, e.g.) may quite briefly be conjectured, as (i) the example of Enzina in that class of writings, and (ii) the marriage, 1500, of king Manuel of Port. with Isabella, daughter of the Catholic sovereigns, Ferdinand and Isabella, of Spain. However this may be, V.'s plays, 'taken together, are better than anything else in Portuguese dramatic literature' (Ticknor, i, 254). The first was a monologue recited by V. at court on 8 June, 1502, memorable as the earliest dramatic representation ever made in Portugal. It won the approval of the queen-mother, and was followed by half-a-dozen religious pastorals, or eclogues, in the manner of Enzina, and called *autos* (q.v.), or acts—of the 4 seasons, of the sibyl Cassandra, of the ship of glory, of fame, etc. Later, came plays, miscalled *comedias*, founded on the chivalric romances (among them, an *Amadis de Gaula*), and evincing, with a crude appreciation of plot and scene, a genuine gift of lyrical expression. Slight as these early experiments in drama were, they were not without influence on the later masters, Vega and Calderon (qq.v.).

Vico, Giovanni Battista (1668-1774): It. scholar; of sufficient eminence to have been included (in a vol., 1884, by prof. Flint) in the series of 'Philosophical Classics', by which Messrs. Blackwood edified an earlier generation, and to be mentioned by Sandys (*Hist. Class. Schol.*, iii, 55) as a scholar who had maintained, about 1730, 'that "Homer" was a collective name for the work of many successive poets', though V.'s views 'were at this time unknown to Wolf' (q.v., and see s.v. Homer). V.'s works were definitively publd. at Milan, 1835-7, and were chiefly written in Lat. on topics of jurisprudence and rhetoric. His *Principles of a New Science*, 1725, was written in Ital., and anticipated some of the Germ. philosophy of history, the more precise articulation of which tended to obscure his brilliant work.

Victorian (Engl.): Descriptive epithet of a period of Engl. lit. (and less frequently, of other forms of art-expression), extending approximately from 1840-90,—the half cent. included in the long reign (1837-1901) of queen Victoria. Writing within a generation of the close of that reign, it is not easy to say how far the meaning of the epithet will have changed in substance or shade when the Victorian age has been adjusted in the perspective of historians. But an entry is due to it here, (1) because bks. on the subject have been written by prof. H. Walker (*The Literature of the Victorian Era*; 1086 pp.; Cambridge, 1910), Mr. G. K. Chesterton (*Victorian Age in Literature*; 'H.U.L.'), and others; (2) because Mr. Lytton Strachey, in his *Eminent Victorians* and *Queen Victoria*, has founded a school of criticism in the matter; and (3) because even now it should be possible, and, if possible, it is desirable, to purge the epithet of some of its grosser marks of depreciation.

What we see quite clearly in the age is that it arose out of the setting of the sun of revolution in France. It arose as an age of reaction against violence and extremes: Byron and Shelley (qq.v.) were dead, and Wordsworth (q.v.) was declining into silence and acquiescence. If it is true, as Walker (*op. cit.*) says, that 'the years 1825 to 1840 show a comparatively meagre list of remarkable works', it is equally true, that, in 1842, Tennyson (q.v.) had opened the new era with his lyrics of compromise ('You ask me, why, tho' ill at ease'; 'Of old sat Freedom on the heights' 'Love thou thy land with love far-brought'), which exactly corresponded with, and partially anticipated, the essential Victorian note in politics, morality and social practice. Tennyson sought, and taught his generation to seek, 'sober-suited Freedom', 'settled government', 'precedent', 'the storied Past', 'Reverence, herald of knowledge', 'gradation'; and to avoid 'the falsehood of extremes', 'crude imaginings', 'raw Haste'. He saw that this counsel, though wise, was 'hard to shape in act', and it was perhaps from the contrast between the counsel and the action, displayed in many departments of public thought and its expression, that Engld. earned on the Continent a reputation for hypocrisy; or, rather, to be more exact, for speaking and writing more slowly and even more gravely than she acted, and simulating (or really feeling) surprise at being judged by her acts instead of by her utterances. We went on

36

extending our Empire, increasing our wealth, opening out new markets for our trade, preparing the way for democracy, making physical discoveries, and, generally, gathering the fruits of Disraelism in politics and Darwinism in science (Disraeli, 1804-81; Darwin, 1809-82), while all the time, or most of the time, we were affecting the detachment of a ' Grave mother of majestic works, From her isle-altar gazing down '. After all, say the iconoclasts of the 20th cent., the altar was heaped high with living sacrifices, which the grave mother had accepted without demur.

It may be that this taint of insincerity, of an incomplete grasp of the movements of the age, will continue to be attached to the epithet, V., as applied to the lit. of that epoch, and that Tennyson's *Poems* of 1842 will be more and more regarded as setting the tone for the succeeding 50 years. It may be, too, that the age was defective in the Gk. or Fr. sense of proportion, and that Stopford Brooke (q.v.) was right, when he wr. in 1894, a few months after Tennyson's death : ' There has been no ingratitude so great in the history of humanity as the ingratitude of Europe to France, and Tennyson represented with great vividness this ingratitude in England '. The Victorian age, we may almost say, forgot France, omitted her, and passed her by. Partly, it was Nelson's tradition, and the scare of ' Boney ' which survived in early Victorian nurseries (see, e.g., *Cranford*, ch. v, by Mrs. Gaskell, q.v.; but she recollected it from *c.* 1805); partly, it was a prudish distrust of Nature (q.v.) in relation to art, and the shocked idea of Paris as a city of illicit pleasures ; partly too, it was the gravitation of the Court to Germany, and the Germanizing influence of Carlyle (q.v.); but, anyhow, there was this prevailing forgetfulness of the most cultivated nation in Europe. M. Arnold (q.v.) was aware of it, and his invitation to a rigid Cobdenite generation to ' Hellenize a little with Free Trade ' was an economic variant of his moral rebuke to British Philistinism (q.v.). Swinburne and G. Meredith (qq.v.) raised their voices in devotion to the Fr. Hellas ; but the one was not ' proper ' to his age, and the other was imperfectly intelligible. The fact remains that the V. note in Engl. lit. grew in force without adequate appreciation of the truism stated by Saintsbury at the close of the epoch, that ' no literary historian or critic who combines seriousness with intelligence has ever denied that the first half of the century is emphatically and for all time identified with that movement (the 1830 movement ; see s.vv. Hugo, Lyrisme) in France '.

We may leave this aspect of the matter there. In effect, the Francophobe bias of the chief Victorian poets and novelists proved myopic—nearsighted. They walked in blinkers to that extent, and it is not fanciful to say that Arthur in the *Idylls of the King* would have gained in virile and truly romantic qualities, and would have lost in mawkish and monkish traits, if Tennyson had followed Malory (q.v.) to the ' old French books ', which, with sundry new ones, a nation apprenticed to lit. neglects at dire peril to its own

soul. So much we concede to the depreciators, merely noting that their own sense of Europe is sometimes a bit defective. Beyond this, sound criticism in the future is not likely to ask our grandchildren to go. The epithet, V., will not be permanently (and is hardly even now) synonymous with timidity, narrowness, shame, dubiety, stiffness, stuffiness, and the rest of the characteristics symbolized by the stuffed birds in old Timothy Forsyte's house on the Bayswater Road, in Mr. John Galsworthy's brilliant *Forsyte Saga* (*To Let*, ch. iv). It will be judged by the Oxford Movement (q.v.), started in 1841, with the publication of the famous Tract 90 (see s.v. Keble); by the Christian Socialism of Maurice (q.v.), of which C. Kingsley (q.v.) became the robust exponent in letters ; by the starker, unhyphenated Socialism of W. Morris (q.v.); by the fearless curiosity of experience exemplified by R. Browning (q.v.) in verse and by Meredith in fiction ; by the descent of the quest for truth and beauty through the art and poetry of the Pre-Raphaelite Brotherhood (q.v.); and by the big lines and generous design on which our fathers and grandfathers built the heritage which we are administering to-day.

Vicuna, de, Juan Lopez (17th cent.): Span. scholar. Publd., 1627, *Obras en verso del Homero espagnol* (the poetical works of the Span. Homer), by whom he meant, and was understood to mean, his friend L. de Gongora (q.v.), who had died earlier in that year. V. spent 20 years in the collection of these works, and much gratitude is due to him for his diligence and appreciation.

Vida, Marco Girolamo (*c.* 1480-1566): It. Latinist; earliest in the line of 16th-cent. critics. Born at Cremona, but spent his life in Rome and its neighbourhood. Wr. Lat. poem, *de arte poetica* (transld. into Engl. verse by Chr. Pitt, *c.* 1740, and included in Chalmers' *British Poets*), the pioneer-piece of the ' follow Virgil ' rescripts for practitioners of the poetic art, praised by Pope (q.v. ; *Essay on Criticism*, 705), bedecked with the critical ' tags ' dear to the 17th and 18th cents., and esp. noteworthy for its recommendation of the use of high-sounding words for their own sake, which influenced the Fr. school of criticism (see s.v. Pleiad), and for its praise of ' onomatopoeia ', or of the employment of words conveying their sense through their vocal sound. Wr., too, Lat. poems (in *Georgics* style) on silkworms and chess, and, at instance of pope Leo x, a *Christiad*, or sacred Lat. epic (1527), in the vein of the *de partu Virginis* of Sannazzaro (q.v.). Boileau (q.v.) and Pope ascribed to V., for his reconstruction in modern verse of the rules of composition first formulated by Aristotle and Horace, and the rhetoricians of antiquity, a critical authority equal to that of his ancient masters ; and Cremona, his birthplace, was regarded as a kind of second Mantua, the birthplace of Virgil (q.v.).

Vidalin, Pall Jonsson (1667-1727): Icel. jurist; poet ; antiquary. V.'s labours on old juristic works were not fully appreciated till about 1850 ; but he is properly recognized as one of the founders of the study of ancient Icel. law. (See s.v. Arngrim).

Vieusseux, Jean Pierre (1779-1863): It. man of letters; founded, 1821, the *Antologia* at Florence, a well-known review which attracted many famous contributors and enabled its editor to form a literary circle. Leopardi (q.v.) entered the circle on a brief visit to that city.

Vigfússon, Gúdbrandr (1828-89): Icel. scholar; edu. Copenhagen; came to Oxford, 1866, and lectured on Icel. lit. at the univ. from 1884; a standard authority on the *sagas* (q.v.) and folk-lore of his native country.

Vigny, de, Alfred Victor (1797-1863): Fr. poet, novelist, playwright; *comte* by rank; soldier by profession, but retired about 1828 into a ' tower of ivory ', as men said, the epithets being descriptive of the pure and unbroken reserve in which V. elaborated the expression of his pensive and sombre genius. He was one of the Romantic founders of Fr. lit. (see s.vv. *Lyrisme*, Romance), accessible to the influences of Scott (q.v.), Klopstock (q.v.), and the less immediate sources of new feeling, and approaching music and language with that reverence for variety and sound which was characteristic of the romantic revival. ' Long live England and Germany ! ' cried a contemporary journalist (cited in Lanson, *Lit. fr.*, 939 n. 3); ' long live brute and savage Nature, revived in the poetry of de Vigny, Lefèvre, and V. Hugo '. And it is to be noted that Hugo (q.v.) himself found inspiration and leading in V.'s verse. The earliest and perhaps the best was the lyric-narrative *Moïse* (Moses), 1822, which exhibited all the Romantic passion for natural scenery and all the Romantic instinct for vocabulary. *Eloa* followed, 1824, the *Poèmes antiques et modernes*, 1826, in which year appeared V.'s great hist. novel, *Cinq-Mars*, of the period of Louis xiii. An adaptation of Shakespeare's *Othello*, 1829, led to V.'s *Chatterton*, 1835, by common consent the high-watermark of the Romantic theatre (see s.v. Hugo for some plays below that mark). Later in life, V. returned to lyric verse, and the *Mont des Oliviers* in his vol. of *Destinées*, 1864, recalled—likewise in a Biblical theme—the beauty of his earlier work.

Villalobos, de, Francisco (c. 1473-c. 1549): Span. moralist, physician; a minor type of the learned doctor exemplified in sir Thomas Browne (q.v.). V. was a converted Jew, who became physician successively to king Ferdinand and the emperor Charles v; his *Summary of Medicine*, 1498, anticipated the *Secrets of the Philosophy of Medicine*, 1739, of Lopez (q.v.) de Corela. V.'s work was composed in *arte mayor* (q.v.) verses, and V. continued to write poetry at intervals. He transld., 1515, the *Amphitryon* of Plautus, and wr., 1524, a commentary on bks. i and ii of Pliny's *Nat. Hist.* But V.'s chief work was his *Libro titulado los Problemas* (Bk. entitled The Problems), 1542, which deals with topics as remote from one another as the planets and flattery, in the pleasant, discursive vein of an educated miscellanist. With this vol. was issued, too, the *Tractato de las tres grandes*—(Treatise of the 3 chief—), in which V. left his readers to fill in the missing word; ' Nuisances ' is the most likely light. The 3 nuisances are

talkativeness, argumentativeness, and much laughing, and the shrewd old physician enjoyed himself hugely in his disquisition on these themes of social and physical morality.

Villamediana (c. 1582-1622): Span. poet; disciple of Gongora (q.v.); Juan de Tarsis, second count of V. by rank; attached to the Span. court; served in Italy, where he met Marino (q.v.), and was thus infected with the virus which led to Gongorism; returned to Spain, 1617; banished, 1621; returned again in the same year, and was assassinated on the following 21 Aug.; it is said, at the instigation of king Philip iv, of whose consort, queen Isabella, daughter of king Henry iv of France, V. was reputed to be the lover. Wr. fables, *Phaethon* and *Phœnix*, in the manner of his master; court-masques; stinging satire; and other verse; all in the *estilo culto*.

Villanelle: Descriptive name of a class of medieval Fr. verse, developed in the 14th cent. out of models supplied by the Troubadours of Provence. Each stanza consists of 3 lines, with one of two refrains closing each.

Villani, -i. Giovanni (14th cent.): It. historian. Wr. *Cronica* of Florence (q.v.), which he left unfind. at the time of his death from the plague, 1348. V.'s qualifications for this work consisted in his intimate knowledge of the public life of the city, but he was hampered by the lack of critical training, and much of the early portion of his narrative is undistinguishable from legend. In his shrewd comments on the Florentine democracy of his own day, V.'s style as chronicler affords a remarkable contrast with that of his greater Fr. contemporary, Froissart (q.v.). By trade, V. was a merchant-banker, who came to grief through his loans to foreign sovereigns, among whom was the king of Engld.

    -ii. Matteo, brother of above, and continuator of the *Cronica*.

    -iii. Filippo, son of Matteo V.; author of a Lat. biographical work, *de Florentiœ famosis civibus*, in which it is noted that the section on Dante was an abridgement from Boccaccio's (q.v.) life of that poet.

Villasandino, de, Alfonso Alvarez (c. 1350-c. 1428): Span. poet. Baena (q.v.) gave V. the chief place in the collection which he made for the delectation of king John ii (q.v.), admitting as many as 244 of his pieces into that anthology, and speaking of him as ' the mirror, crown, and king of Spanish poetry '. The praise, though repeated by Santillana (q.v.) and other contemporaries and near posterity, is far in excess of V.'s merit. Kelly (*Lit. espagn.*, 90) calls him a ' coarse Galician '; and, though he was a facile versifier with a good mastery of the technique of his art, his inspiration was poor and his taste retrograde and artificial.

Villaviciosa, de, José (1589-1658): Span. poet; divine. Wr., 1615, *la Moschea*, a mock-heroic poem of the battle of the flies and ants, imitated from the *Mosquaca*, 1521, of Folengo (q.v.), who went back, of course, to the *Batrachomyomachia* of pseudo-Homer. V.'s poem, which seems to have been a unique effort of his ecclesiastical career, was eclipsed by the *Gatomachia* (cats' battle) of Vega (q.v.).

Villaviciosa, de, Sebastian (17th cent.): Span. dramatist; in the school of Vega (q.v.). Wr., in collaboration with Zavaleta (q.v.) *la Dama Corregidor*, which was adapted by Montfleury (q.v.) in his *la Femme juge et partie*.

Villayzan, de, Geronimo (1604-33): Span. dramatist ; of greater promise than performance, as was natural to the shortness of his life. His best-remembered play is *A gran daño gran Remedio* ('A great Remedy for a great Wrong ').

Villegas, de, Alonso (1534-*c.* 1604): Span. poet. Wr., 1554, *Comedia Selvagia*, in imitation of the *Celestina* (q.v.), act i of which V. believed to be the work of Cota (q.v.).

Villegas, de, Antonio (d., *c.* 1551): Span. poet ; his collection of verse, *Inventario*, was issued posth., 1565, and contained some pleasant 10-line pieces called *comparaciones*, because each closes with a poetic simile ; contained, too, longer pieces in the older courtly style, notably a *Pryamus and Thisbe*, which Kelly (*Lit. espagn.*, 205) characterizes as a ' detestable paraphrase '. A prose tale, entitled *Story of the Abencerraje and the fair Xarifa* (q.v.), which is also found in the vol., is probably not the work of V., though the theory that it forms a pendant to the *Diana* of Montemayor (q.v.) is equally untenable.

Villegas, de, Estevan Manuel (1589-1669): Span. poet ; a writer of precocious talent, who disappointed his early promise. Publd., 1618, a vol. of verse, in which he figured on the title-page as *sol matutinus*, the morning sun, at whose rising the stars disappeared from the sky, the stars in question being understood to refer to Vega (q.v.) and his contemporaries. V.'s work included some admirable translns. from Anacreon and Catullus, and he consoled his later years of disillusion by translating the *Consolations* of Boethius, 1665. The middle years of V.'s life were troublous and unproductive. Though his own verse is a model of limpid simplicity, V. devoted one of his elegies to the praise of the Gongoristic *Phaethon* of Villamediana (q.v.).

Villegas, de, Pedro Fernandez (1453-*c.* 1536): Span. poet ; archdeacon of Burgos. Transld. the *Inferno* of Dante (q.v.) into Span. verse, with an elaborate commentary. V.'s brother, **Gerónimo**, transld. some of the satires of Juvenal.

Villehardouin, de, Geoffroy (*c.* 1157-1213): Fr. historian ; born at Villehardouin, in the district of Troyes, whence his contemporary, Chrétien (q.v.), derived his surname ; was appointed marshal of Champagne, and was sent as ambassador to Venice with 5 other barons to negotiate the passage of the Fourth Crusade ; was present at the capture of Constantinople, and dictated his ' memoirs ', 1207-12. These are now known as the *Conquête de Constantinople* ; and, in the shape of a prose-chronicle which they assumed, they form the first hist. work of monumental significance in European lit. A *chanson de geste* in prose, V.'s work is precisely not a *chanson* because it is written in prose ; and with this departure in style, history, as a separate branch of letters, was separated from the narrative verse-romance. Moreover, V. had been a statesman before he lived to dictate his memoirs ; the political aspect of events interested him more than romantic narration.

His statesmanship was governed by the conception of feudal honour ; to offend against that was to threaten the foundations of society ; and he had a nice taste for adventure as an end in itself, as well as a means to other ends. So far, he shared Chrétien's point of view. But his title to the rank of the first historian of modern times rests on the directness of his method, on his brief and pithy characterizations, on his true hist. design, his perspective, and his reserve of judgment.

Villemain, Abel François (1790-1870): Fr. critic ; statesman ; orator ; with Cousin and Guizot (qq.v.), one of the ' triumvirate of the Sorbonne ', who, in the years before 1828, used their professorial chairs as tribunes of political influence. V.'s chair, after a brief period as assistant lecturer in history to Guizot, was that of rhetoric (Fr., *éloquence*), 1816 ; and, like his colleagues in history and philosophy, he aimed by wide generalizations and sweeping views of the past, at a popularization of knowledge rather than at original research. He had acquired from mme. de Staël (q.v.) the partly perilous doctrine of social forces in lit., and he tracked these through the lit. of his own country in the Middle Ages and in the 18th cent. (*Cours de littérature française*, from his lectures of 1827-30). Similar gifts were displayed in his minor critical writings ; but V., on the whole, is the least eminent of the Sorbonne trio. He was twice minister of Public Instruction, and became a peer of France ; and in 1832 he was elected perpetual secretary to the Fr. Academy (q.v.), of which he had been a member since 1821.

Villena, de, Henry (1384-1434): Span. scholar ; nobleman. Don Enrique de Villena, or de Aragon, sometimes wrongly entitled marquis de Villena (a dignity sold by his grandfather to the Crown), was a scion of the royal families of Aragon and Castile, and divided his time between the two courts, without consolidating his position at either. His ambitious and unfortunate career is less immediately to our purpose than his place in the literary annals of his country ; and even in that department his fame would seem to transcend his performance. His first work was a bk. of the *Trabajos* (labours) *de Hercules*, 1417 (*ed. pr.*, 1482), full of learned allegory and mythology, in a sustained style of archaic prose ; his composition of festive verses on the occasion of the cornation of king Ferdinand i of Aragon, 1414, is now discredited. V.'s next most important work was a prose treatise on the art of carving (*Arte eisoria*, or *Tractado del Arte de cortar del Cuchillo*), 1423, *ed. pr.*, 1766 (Madrid): ' it is not likely ', says Ticknor (i, 326, n.31) ' soon to come to a second edition ', and we may leave it at that. More valuable were V.'s translns. from Virgil (*Æneid*) and Dante, in which he was a pioneer at the dawn of Ital. culture in Spain, though his Latinity was poor. He wr., too, an *Arte de Trobar*, a kind of *ars poetica*, dedicated to Santillana (q.v.), of which only fragments survive. Against this meagre achievement is to be set the exalted estimation in which don Enrique was held by contemporaries and posterity. His learning, which included the rare knowledge of Gk., as well as Hebrew,

Arabic, Provençal, and other tongues, ' surrounded him with an aureole of mystery and awe ' (Kelly, *Lit. espagn.*, 82), and king John ii (q.v.) ordered his library to be burned after his death, on the ground, commonly held, that he dabbled in magical arts. ' No one reads Villena now ', adds Kelly (*ibid.*), ' but he will never be forgotten, for legend assures him a place in literary history '. And, apart from his legendary estimation, V.'s fame is secure as a patron of letters in Barcelona (q.v.), where he revived and extended the floral games borrowed from Toulouse (q.v.).

Villena, de, marquis ; duke of Escalona (*c.* 1660-*c.* 1730): Span. statesman ; founder and original director of the Royal Academy (q.v.) of Spain. V., who was a descendant of don Enrique (*supra*), and whose family name was Pacheco, took part in the War of the Span. Succession, 1702-13, and was employed in various viceregal offices. King Philip v of Spain, as a Bourbon brought up at Versailles, lent a ready ear to V.'s suggestion that Madrid should institute an academy on the model of the great *Académie française* ; and the necessary charter was granted on 3 Oct., 1714. The director set on foot the dict. (s.v. *Diccionario*), which, after the same model, was the new Academy's earliest enterprise ; and V. was succeeded in his office by his son. The date of his death is variously stated as 1725 and 1738.

Villoison, de, Jean Baptiste d'Ansse (1750-1805): Fr. Hellenist. Distinguished at an early age by his devotion to and eminence in classical studies ; publd., 1773, a critical edn. of Apollonius's *Homeric Lexicon*, and, 1778, an edn. of Longus's *Daphnis and Chloe*, (see s.v. Gk. fiction), with valuable notes. Travelled extensively in Near East, and resided at Venice, Strassburg, Göttingen, and other centres of learning, including Weimar, as the guest of the duke. V.'s chief work was in connection with the newly-discovered MS. of *Iliad* (Codex Venetus A), with the marginal *scholia* of Alexandrian critics, which he transcribed and edited with diligence, enthusiasm, and unique scholarly equipment. (See s.v. Homer). Retired to Orleans after the expulsion of nobles from Paris during the Fr. Revolution ; was subsequently recalled, and appointed to the chair of Gk. in the Collège de France (1802).

Villon, François (born, 1431): Fr. poet ; born at Paris, died in obscurity at a date unknown after 1463. François, properly de Moncorbier (or, maybe, Corbier, Corbueil, or des Loges) was brought up by one Guillaume de Villon, a chaplain, whose surname he assumed. He attended the univ. of Paris, graduating as bachelor, 1449, and master, 1452, but even in his student-days he preferred the rowdy to the studious, and the wine-parlour to the lecture-room. In 1455 (the date and time are stated : 5 June, at dusk), V. was attacked and wounded by a priest, Philippe Sermaise, whom he stabbed fatally in self-defence. The quarrel is said to have been about a woman. This ' accident ' drove him from Paris, to which he returned in Jan., 1456, under cover of letters of pardon, drawn in his favour in 2 names. In the following Dec., V. and 5 companions in a more serious delinquency scaled the walls of the college of Navarre, and stole a sack of gold coin. Paris knew him no more. In 1461 he is discovered in the prison of Meung-sur-Loire (the Meung of Jean of that ilk, the author of the greater part of the *Romance of the Rose*, q.v.), where he had spent the summer on a diet of bread and water, at the instance of the bp. of Orleans. The bishop's salutary discipline was remitted by king Louis xi in the course of general amnesty, and the pardon was extended to cover the old misdemeanour, so that V. returned to Paris. A fresh felony had more serious consequences. V. was arrested, tortured, and condemned to be hanged ; the sentence was commuted to banishment, 1463, and V. passes out of sight at that time. This, in outline, was the *life* of V. The question is, what was his *work* ? It was the life of a common thief and bravo ; it was the work of a great poet. Modern Fr. poetry begins with V., and for the sake of a few hundred lines of rarest sentiment and imagination, the bad man of R. L. Stevenson's (q.v.) mordant essay is reckoned among the world's good writers. Is there a paradox in this ? Stevenson answered, yes ; and his brilliant but inadequate characterization of V. makes the poet a monster of insincerity. The charge is untrue, and, even worse than untrue, it is unintelligent. For to the complete understanding of V.'s poems, a knowledge of his age is indispensable. He spent his brief and troubled life in a changing city under a changing sky. The Middle Ages were crumbling around him ; the Renaissance was being prepared out of reach ; and V.'s supreme merit lies in his artist's instinct for reconciling both appeals. It was merely a temporary truce which he patched up between the spirits of two ages ; he employed the technical apparatus of Jean de Meung and Eustache Deschamps (qq.v.)—the *ballade*, the *testament*, and the rest,—but he converted them to new uses. He renewed the exhausted lyric forms with the breath of an intensely sincere feeling. His body lingered in the Middle Ages ; his feet trod the narrow alleys on the seamy side of medieval Paris ; his hands supplied his needs whence they could ; but his intellect pressed forward to the Renaissance ; and this perpetual conflict between experience and aspiration, this eternal debate between the flesh and spirit of the poet, is the key to the seeming inconsistency and the alleged insincerity of his life and work. That ' human ending to night-wind ',—' Mais où sont les neiges d'antan '— : what is it but the cry of medieval mortality projected into the lyrical capacity of a Heine or Verlaine (qq.v.) ? V.'s tears in laughter were the twin signs of the transition from Froissart to Rabelais (qq.v.). He could tune a courtly *ballade* to gain a day's wage from king René of Anjou or prince Charles of Orleans, but he did not deceive himself as to the permanence of courts or kings. The dim shadows of dead queens were gone with the snows of yesteryear ; and, conventional as this note was in the reflective vein of medieval singers (see s.v. Death), V. was conscious of the rise of a new order, not of chivalry, but of humanity, heralding a truth

Vindiciæ contra Tyrannos—Visin   566

which he would not live to hear. The *Petit Testament* of V. consists of 40 stanzas of 8 verses (rhymed as *ab, ab, bc, bc*) and the *Grand Testament* of 173 ; a selection of *rondeaux* and *ballades* are included in the last as an integral part of its composition. These comprise the most famous poems : the *Ballade des Pendus*, the *Ballade des Dames du temps jadis*, the verses which D. G. Rossetti (q.v.) transld. as ' His Mother's Service to our Lady ', and others. V. has not wanted detractors, but year by year recognition grows ; and from Marot to Swinburne (qq.v.), great poets have been eager to acclaim him. We may quote the *envoi* to Swinburne's eulogy :

Prince of sweet songs made out of tears and fire,
A harlot was thy nurse, a god thy sire ;
Shame soiled thy song, and song assoiled thy shame.
But from thy feet now death has washed the mire,
Love reads out first at head of all our quire,
Villon, our sad, bad, glad, mad brother's name.

Vindiciæ contra Tyrannos (1579): Anon. Lat. treatise on political philosophy, formerly ascribed to Languet (q.v.), but now more commonly to Duplessis-Mornay (q.v.). In this treatise and in the *Franco-Gallia* of Hotman (q.v.) ' are to be found the ideas at the bottom of all theories of popular rights until the eighteenth century ' (Figgis, *Divine Right of Kings*, 113). It postulates the contract between the governor-king and the governed people, which reappears in Locke (q.v.), though, unlike Locke, the author of the *V.c.T.* assumes a prior contract between God on the one part and king and people on the other ; an idea which is to be traced to the political theory at the root of the conception of the Holy Roman Empire in its departure from the Papacy. ' It is hard ', says Figgis (*op. cit.*), ' to overestimate the resemblance between the ideas of Locke and the author of the *Vindiciæ* ', which exercised considerable influence on subsequent political philosophy.

Vinet, Alexander (1797-1847): Fr. (-Swiss) critic ; held chairs of lit. at Basle and at Lausanne, and ' carries his Chair too much with him ', in the opinion of Saintsbury (*Hist. Crit.*, iii., 591), who does not dispute, however, the essential gravity and ingenuity of V.'s judgment and expression. Thus, he cites one such *aperçu*: ' Only one poet has a greater range of metaphor than Hugo, and that is Humanity '. Wr. *Chrestomathie française* (3 vols., 1829-30): *Histoire de la lit. fr. au xviii* Siècle* (2 vols., 1853) ; *Études sur Pascal* (1848) ; *Moralistes de la lit. fr. des xvi* et xvii* Siècles* (1849), etc.

Vinje, Aasmund Olafsson (1818-70): Norse poet ; characteristic of the return to early Norse legend and myth, which distinguished his greater contemporaries, Björnson and Ibsen (qq.v.), in their first periods. V.'s chief poem in this kind was *Storegut*. In his lyrical gift, V. was akin to Heine (q.v.) the chief object of admiration by Norse poets at this date.

Vireli: Descriptive name of a class of medieval Fr. verse, which flourished in Northern France in the 14th cent., and was indebted to Troubadour models from Provence. The spelling *virelai*, which is common, was due to the false analogy of *lai* (lay, or song). The v. consisted of several stanzas, with repetitory rhymes and refrains so popular in the verse of that age.

Virgil: Publius Vergilius Maro (70-19 B.C.) : Rom. poet ; in some respects the most powerful single influence on modern lit. among the Ancients. V. was born in Mantua and died at Naples. His chief extant works, written uniformly in hexameter verse, are 10 *Eclogues*, *c.* 38 B.C., 4 *Georgics*, *c.* 31 B.C., and the *Æneid*, in 12 bks., publd. posth. by V.'s executors, Varius and Tucca, 19 B.C., and left unfind. by V. The minor poems attributed to him are partly of doubtful authorship. *Cecini pascua, rura, duces* (I have made pastoral, rural and epic poetry) was V.'s own account of his writings in the epitaph which he composed for himself, referring to the 3 sets of poems enumerated above. But the *duces*, according to a well-authenticated tradition, he would have left unsung, for his final instructions were that the MS. of the *Æneid* should be destroyed. Happily, his executors thought otherwise, but it is of interest, even after 20 centuries, to try to fathom V.'s intention. It is known that he wanted to spend another 3 years at its completion, and there are certain points in the *Æneid*, as we have it, at which, quite apart from some unfind. verses (' pathetic half-lines ', as they have been termed), even the ordinary reader perceives that revision might have led to improvement. A greater critic than the ordinary reader, prof. Garrod of Oxford, suggests a deeper cause for V.'s instruction to his executors. V., he says, ' is for ever being carried out of his own intention. . . . He is for ever lifting the veil of the romance of life,—and it falls again. He is for ever about to give us something greater in art than the rest of antiquity can show, and for ever just missing his supreme effect '. Thus, V.'s failure, if the word must be used, ' is of the order which sanctifies ', and is to be traced to a Celtic element in his blood, which was in conflict with the Roman : ' in his poetry we have the first appearance in literature of the romantic spirit '. This passage, so sensitive in its interpretative faculty, should be read in the light of the *The Study of Celtic Lit.*, by an earlier prof. of Poetry in Oxford, M. Arnold (q.v.), with its prefatory quotation from Ossian (q.v.) : ' They went forth to the war, but they always fell '.

Yet another occupant of that Oxford chair discovered romance in V.'s *Æneid*. ' The fountain-head of romanticism ', Mackail calls it (*Lat. Lit.*, 99), and the romantic history of the poet after death is a part of the romance of his poetry. His tomb at Naples became an object of pilgrimage, which St. Paul himself was believed to have visited. St. Augustine passionately admired him, and as passionately repented his worship of the pagan poet (*Confessions*, i, 20-22). V.'s likeness was set among the carven seers in the cathedral of Zamora, and in the cathedrals of Limoges and Rheims the Christmas appeal was made : ' O Maro, prophet of the Gentiles, bear thou thy witness to Christ ' ! He was accounted a

Magician in the Middle Ages (see Comparetti, *Virgil in the Middle Ages*, transld. by E. F. M. Benecke, 1895), to whose writings men repaired for a *sors Virgiliana*,—a verse chosen at random, as from the Bible, from which to read human fate. His *Æneid* was to Italy in Christian centuries as the *Nibelungenlied* (q.v.) to dwellers on the Rhine, or the *Iliad* to ancient Greece. He 'waited on the extreme verge of the Dark Ages to take Dante by the hand, and lead him, as the type of human reason, through the realms of Hell and Purgatory', to the portals of Paradise itself (Symonds, *Ital. Renaissance*, ii, 47 ; see, too s.v. Dante). 'The glory of the Latin race', Dante called him ; 'the honour of all science and all wit' ; 'the sea of wisdom' ; '*divinus poeta noster Virgilius*'. Nor, though the magic has faded, has admiration failed in later centuries. In one of the ingenious tables which adorn *The Foreign Debt of Engl. Lit.*, by prof. T. G. Tucker, of Melbourne (Doll, 1907), we are shown how V. is linked up with Homer and Theocritus, and down with Tasso, Spenser, Milton, Voltaire (*Henriade*), and with the rise of pastoral poetry and Arcadia (q.v.) in Europe (and see s.v. Sannazzaro). From the long list of his translrs. and editors we may select Gawin Douglas (1553), Dryden (1697), C. Pitt (1740), Heyne (1767-73), Voss, Conington and James Henry (1796-1876).

On what does this unique reputation rest,—this reputation of a pagan poet among the Christian prophets or among the miraclemen of the Middle Ages ? Chiefly, perhaps, on the so-called Messianic *Eclogue* iv and on *Æneid* iv and vi. If we turn back to prof. Garrod's essay, we find the following helpful comment on *Æneid* iv, 457-68,—the description of Dido's desolation after the failure of her final appeal to Æneas :—'In the shrine of Sychæus she hears strange voices, and Sychæus himself seems to call her. Above the calling of her dead husband there sounds the incongruous hooting of owls, and withal there ring in her ears the prophecies of older prophets. She dreams that she is some Manad, whom Æneas drives before him in frenzy, "and for ever she seems to be being left alone, to be setting forth ever upon some endless uncompanioned pilgrimage, and ever where no soul is to be seeking her Tyrians". To say ', adds the professor, 'that there is nothing else like that in Roman poetry is to speak idly : *for there is nothing else like it—so profound in psychology, so romantically mystical, so subtly overpowering—in all literature* ' (our itals.). In order to give the sounds, we quote the transld. passage in V.'s language :

Agit ipse furentem
In somnis ferus Æneas ; semperque relinqui
Sola sibi, semper longam incomitata videtur
Ire viam, et Tyrios deserta quaerere terra.

Note, here, *ferus* as the epithet for Æneas, in place of the conventional *pius*. This paradox of character is a part of the alleged 'failure' of V.,—a failure greater than many poets' successes. Note, too, the devices of style, which afforded a model to later poets, and esp. in recent times to Tennyson (q.v.), a lover of language hardly inferior to his Roman master : *furentem*, *ferus* ; semper sola sibi ;

longam incomitata ; *videtur viam* ; *Tyrios deserta terra* ; and the subtler resources of verbal music in these verses. And, further, to the praise of V.'s style, we may quote what was said of it by F. W. H Myers (q.v. ; *Collected Essays*, 115), a competent critic : 'What is meant', he asks, 'by the vague praise so often bestowed on Virgil's unequalled style ? ' And he answers that it is practically this, that V. 'has been perhaps more successful than any other poet in fusing together the expressed and the suggested emotion ; that he has discovered the hidden music which can give to every shade of feeling its distinction, its permanence, and its charm ; that his thoughts seem to come to us on the wings of melodies prepared for them from the foundation of the world '. It is difficult to get nearer than this to the secret of a charm and a spell, which have worked authoritatively in European poetry from Dante to Tennyson—from the 19th to the 19th cent. Other reputations fade ; V.'s has been undimmed since his death, and never has it shone more brightly than in the ages and empires of the last thousand years. There is hardly a great poet in all that period who would not at once associate himself with the tribute of the youngest in the long succession :

'Thou that singest wheat and woodland,
    tilth and vineyard, hive and horse and herd ;
All the charm of all the Muses often flowering
    in a lonely word ; . . .
Thou that seest Universal Nature moved by
    Universal Mind ;
Thou majestic in thy sadness at the doubtful
    doom of humankind ;
I salute thee, Mantovano, I that loved thee
    since my day began,
Wielder of the stateliest measure ever
    moulded by the lips of man '.

Virués, de, Cristobal (*c.* 1550-*c.* 1615) : Span. poet ; dramatist ; soldier ; wounded at the battle of Lepanto, and commonly known as captain V. ; much praised by Vega and Cervantes (qq.v.), on account of his writings for the stage. Five plays of his were included in his *Tragical and Lyrical Works*, 1609, and are supposed to have been acted between 20 and 30 years previously. Four of these are wild and extravagant, and repellent in their violent mortality : in the *Atila furioso*, e.g., more than 50 persons are killed in the course of the play ; the others are, *la gran Semiramis, la cruel Cassandra*, and *la infelice Marcela*. More merit attaches to his *Elisa Dido*, which is rather Gk. than Virgilian in form and treatment. V. claimed the invention of the division of a play into 3 acts (see s.v. Carpajal), a technical innovation to which some importance was given. He had distinct lyrical gifts, displayed in his dramatic choruses, and also in his narrative poem *el Monserrate*, 1587, the subject of which was taken from a legend of the Span. church in the 9th cent.

Visin, von, Denis Ivanovich (1745-92) : Russ. dramatist ; Germ. by descent (his name is variously written Fon-Visin and Wisin) ; known by a pardonable exaggeration as 'the Molière of Russia'. Certainly, V. owed to Molière a large part of the influences which formed him, and which came to happy expression in his 2 comedies, *The Brigadier*, 1766, and *The Young Squire*, 1782. The tone of both plays was satiric ; in this respect, V. was faithful to the example of his mistress, the empress Catherine ii (q.v.), and on the stage he was brilliantly successful. V.'s *Letters from France* and other prose-works carried his satiric vein ever further, and they possess the further interest of a disciple criticizing his foreign masters.

Visscher, -i. Roemer (1547-1620) : Dutch poet ; more celebrated for his hospitality to poets, as a leading member of the Eglantine (q.v.), or Amsterdam Chamber of Rhetoric, than for his own contribution to the art, which consisted chiefly of 2 vols. of aphorisms and epigrams. V. was a substantial merchant, whose house became a centre of literary activity, directed to the advancement and enhancement of the dignity of Dutch letters.

   -ii. Tesselschade (1594-1649) : Dutch poet ; daughter of above ; her elder sister was Anna V. (1584-1651), and ' it is surprising to what an extent the subtle influence and personality of these 2 sisters, and esp. of the younger, pervades the whole history of the great age of Dutch literature, associated with the names of Brederoo, Vondel, Cats, Hooft, and Huyghens ' (qq.v. ; *C.M.H.*, iv, 718). T. wr. lyric poems, which were much admired, and transld. Tasso's (q.v.) epic into Dutch verse.

Vitelli, Cornelio (15th cent.) : It. humanist. Invited to Oxford, 1475, where he was the first public teacher of Gk ; his pupils included Linacre and Grocyn (qq.v.).

Vitéz, Joannes (15th cent.) : Hungarian humanist. Chancellor to king Matthias Corvinus (q.v.) ; card. archbp. of Grau. Acquired copies of MSS. from Florence, and was a pioneer of the new learning in his own country.

Vittorino dei Ramboldini (1378-1446) : It. humanist and teacher. Born at Feltre ; ranks as founder of educational methods based on ideas generated by revival of learning. Entered univ. of Padua, where Vergerio (q.v.) was teaching ; learned Gk. from Guarino (q.v.) at Venice ; engaged in teaching at both cities ; finally settled at Mantua (1425), at the invitation of marquis of Mantua to undertake the education of his sons. There V. ' created a school of a type previously unknown ' (*C.M.H.*, i, 557) ; ' a school whose spirit, curriculum, and method justify us in regarding it as a landmark of critical importance in the history of classical education ' (Woodward, *Vittorino*, 24). The basis of study was the Lat. classics, taught as life and lit. rather than as grammar and learning. Gk. classics were also employed, with composition and recitation in both languages. Sports, in the form of outdoor activities, formed a departure from medieval tradition, and the lighter arts of society, including social manners, were deemed worthy of inclusion in this curriculum of humane studies. The Gk. training of mind and body was, doubtless, the source of V.'s method, but he imparted a new and deeper meaning to education as a preparation for complete living, and the contrast with the ecclesiastical theory of school-training, in ' La Giocosa ' or the ' pleasant house ', as his

school was called, was thorough and remarkable. His pupils included noble and humble ; several became famous scholars, e.g. Federigo da Montefeltro, Nicholas Perotti, George of Trebizond, Lorenzo Valla, and G. A. de'Bussi, afterwards bp. of Aleria—truly an imposing list even for the leading schoolmaster of the age.

Vivès, de, Juan Luis (1492-1540) : Span. humanist and educationist. Quitted Spain for the freer air of Paris, and, later, of Louvain (q.v.), where he met Erasmus (q.v.), and found a community of his countrymen, who were likewise attracted by the new learning at the univ., founded in 1426. Under these stimulating influences V. abandoned his youthful tendency to the obscurantist schools, and threw himself whole-heartedly into the cause of humane studies. He visited Engld., 1522-25, residing at Oxford, where, at Wolsey's invitation, he lectured in Corpus Christi on Latinity ; became tutor to princess Mary, daughter of king Henry viii and queen Catherine of Aragon, and dedicated to his pupil a Lat. treatise *on the Education of a Christian Woman*; incurred royal displeasure by siding with the queen against her divorce, and returned to Bruges as lecturer and tutor. Wr., 1531, a Lat. educational work *de Disciplinis*, in 3 parts : corrupt arts ; methods of teaching ; arts : the whole forming a consistent work, tracing the consecution of studies from their foundation in psychology to the details of their acquisition ; the high calling of the teacher is exalted out of the degradation of its decline in scholasticism, and V. ranks as an inspiring exponent of the ideals of the revival of learning, reconciling the paganism of Ital. humanists with the Christianity of Germ. reformers. Wr., 1538, *de animæ vita*, ' on the life of the soul ', in which the principles of modern empirical psychology, or of the philosophy of the emotions, were not obscurely anticipated.

Vives de Canesmas, Carlos Boyl (*c.* 1560-1621) : Span. dramatist ; resident at Valencia.

Voiture, Vincent (1598-1648) : Fr. precious (q.v.) letter-writer. V. was the son of a wine-merchant at Amiens, and never sought to conceal his orig. His admittance to the *salon* of the marquise de Rambouillet (q.v.), and his dominance in the proceedings of her *chambre bleue*, were triumphs due solely and wholly to his wit, his *esprit*, his gallantry, and the serious qualities of the intellect which fed his superficial brilliancy. V. became chamberlain to the king, and filled other offices at court, and his literary works, so called, consist of letters and occasional verses, valuable in their kind and style, but more celebrated in his own day than in ours. (See, too, s.v. Benserade for V.'s sonnet on Urania). V. was an original member of the Fr. Academy (q.v.), and was an eager disciple of the school of Morisco-Spanish romance, founded in Spain by G. P. de Hita (q.v.).

Volder, William (1493-1568) : known by scholar's-names of Fullonius and Gulielmus Gnapheus : Dutch Latinist ; schoolmaster ; was imprisoned and banished for his Protestant sympathies, and ended his days among the Reformers in Switzerland. Was chief writer of academic drama (see esp. s.v. Lat.), of the type devised by wise schoolmasters on the homœopathic principle of combining entertainment with instruction and warning. Availing himself of the parable of the Prodigal Son, V. wr. Lat. play, *Acolastus*, 1529, Terentian in scheme and Scriptural in moral; it had an immediate and a fairly permanent success; was transld. into Engl. (1540, by John Palsgrave), and served as model to a long series of dramatic variants on the justification of old heads against young blood.

Volksbuch (Germ.): Folktale; popular tale; of romantic, native, or hist. orig. The type flourished, like the *Volkslied* (q.v.), chiefly in the 16th cent., when the courtly tradition of lit. had broken down, and the self-conscious burghers required amusement and relaxation of a less specialized and exacting kind. In length the V. approximated to the Ital. *novella* rather than to the Fr. *roman*, to which it is otherwise closely akin, in its adventurous and amorous interest. Some 'folk-books' were founded directly on romantic material; Griselda, e.g., reappears, and the mermaid tales have obvious affinities with the Lohengrin (q.v.)-cycle. A similar revival awaited some of the heroes of old Teuton story. But the most popular works of the 16th cent. went home to actual occurrences nearer to the time and thought of the day; esp. this feature characterized the *Volksbücher* founded on bedevilment, witchcraft, alchemy, and the like; on superstitions, that is to say, which formed so lively a part of the belief and experience of the townsfolk. Thus, Dr. Faust, the Wandering Jew, Till Eulenspiegel, Pfaffe Kahlenberg, and others, had each a more or less credible hist. setting, and appealed to men and women with the force of events of which they had heard, or in the like of which they might even have taken part. They seized the imagination, not of Germany alone, but of all Europe, as demonstrated, for example, by the after-history of the Faust (q.v.) legend.

Volkslied (Germ.): Folksong; popular song, mostly hist. in subject, which flourished in N. Germany, and Switzerland from 14th to 16th cent. (See also s.v. Ballad). The authors are almost invariably unknown; the songs, which celebrated local victories in arms over a national foe or for the vindication of popular rights, passed into the possession of the people as a whole; they are, accordingly, democratic, or, more properly, demotic, in tone, with the point directed against unsocial tendencies: the cruel lord, the harsh stepmother, and so forth; sacred themes and episodes of old romance were also admitted; and the native Teutonic sympathy with natural objects in their sentimental aspect is already apparent in these early lyrics. The V. rose at the time when Minnegesang (s.v. Minnesinger) was forfeiting its appeal, owing to the growth of civic life; and it afforded a more spontaneous outlet for the new national consciousness than the rule-bound exercises of the Meistersinger (q.v.). Printed vols. of collected *Volkslieder* date from the beginning of the 16th cent., and attracted in the 19th cent. the critical sympathy of poets as eminent as Uhland and Lilienkron (qq.v.); see esp. s.vv. Brentano and Arnim for the *Wunderhorn*, or cornucopia, of 1806-8.

Vollenhove, Johannes (1631-1708): Dutch poet; imitator of Vondel, who was tenderly attached to him. Visited London as embassy chaplain, 1674, and wr. verses on the great fire. V.'s poems are best known through anthologies, as his imagination was inferior to his fluency.

Volney, de, François Chasseboeuf (1577-1820): Fr. early romanticist (see s.v. Romance); *comte* by rank. Wr., 1791, *Ruines*, a curious medley of sentimental melancholy, provoked by the contemplation of the past, and of visionary faith in reason, progress, and the termination of tyranny and priestcraft. V. may briefly be described as a lover of antiquity plunged into the epoch of the Fr. Revolution.

Voltaire (1694-1778): Fr. poet, philosopher; the representative man of letters of the 18th cent. in France. 'Let there be light! and Voltaire was', declares C. Mendès (q.v.); and V.'s progress across his age leaves the impression of a trail of advancing light, extinguishing the accepted creeds of the 17th cent. Thus, his writings are the expression of his age in action; and, before going further, it is appropriate to submit a tentative list of those writings, necessarily incomplete, in which attention should be called to the break of subject *c.* 1755: the significance of this change will be manifest at a later stage:—

i. Tragedies: *Œdipe*, 1718; *Brutus*, 1730; *la Mort de César*, 1731; *Zaïre*, 1732; *Alzire*, 1736; *Mahomet*, 1742; *Mérope*, 1743; *Sémiramis*, 1748; *l'Orphelin de la Chine*, 1755; *Tancrède*, 1760; *les Scythes*, 1767; *les Guèbres*, 1769; *Sophonisbe*, 1774; *Irène*, 1778.

ii. Comedies: *l'Indiscret*, 1725; *l'Enfant Prodigue*, 1736; *la Prude*, 1747; *l'Écossaise*, 1760; and a few others.

iii. Epopee: *la Henriade*, a serious glorification of king Henri iv of France, written in youth, and first issued, 1723; *la Pucelle*, a burlesque-epic on the subject of Joan of Arc and after the manner of Ariosto (q.v.), 1762; and minor pieces.

iv. Tales, chiefly Oriental; otherwise, novels with a purpose, disguised under an eastern veil: *Zadig*, 1748; *Babouc*, 1746; *Memnon*, 1747; *Micromegas*, 1752; *l'Ingénu*, 1757; *le Taureau Blanc*, 1773; and, preeminently, combining all the several purposes of the rest, *Candide*, 1758.

v. History and Philosophy: *Lettres Anglaises*, 1734; *Discours sur l'Homme*, 1738 (cf. Pope, q.v., *Essay on Man*); *Siècle de Louis xiv*, 1751; *Essai sur les Moeurs*, 1753 (-58); *Loi Naturelle*, 1756; *Désastre de Lisbon*, 1756; *Pauvre Diable*, 1758 (these last 3 in verse); contributions to the Encyclopedia (q.v.) 1751 and onwards; *Traité sur la Tolérance*, 1763; *Dictionnaire Philosophique*, 1764; *Commentaire des Délits et des Peines*, 1766 (a commentary on Beccaria, q.v.); *Examen Important de milord Bolingbroke*, 1767; *le Cri du Sang Innocent*, 1775; *la Bible enfin expliquée*, 1776; *Lettre à l'Académie sur Shakespeare*, 1776; and many others, including an infinite number of letters, tracts, broadsheets, etc., many issued anon., and repudiated by their author, who has earned the title of a journalist of genius. Space, too, must be found in this rubric for the brilliant *Diatribe du docteur Akakia*, 1752, provoked by V.'s rupture with the king of Prussia (see below), and launched against a certain Dr. König, then president of the Berlin Academy.

The above list, lengthy though it is, has many omissions in each division, and no reference is made to V.'s more specialized scientific writings. The main point to note, as was remarked, is the deepening of the philosophic, hist., and sociological studies, about the year, 1755 ; say, at the date of the earthquake of Lisbon and of V.'s poem upon it, 1756. For the oriental tales, which we have ventured to describe as novels with their purpose disguised under an eastern veil, of which *Candide* was the most famous, were as much social, moral, or political tracts as the ' Cry of Innocent Blood ', 1776, itself. It will be recalled that Rabelais (q.v.) hid his serious meaning under a torrent of badinage ; and the new birth of humanitarianism, which foreran the Fr. Revolution, encouraged a prudence of expression, such as was commended for the sake of their own safety to the free-thinkers of the Renaissance (q.v.) proper. V., in his fiery youth, had tasted the rigours of the Bastille ; nearly all his days, he was an exile from his own country ; many of his bks. were only smuggled into Paris ; and he lived to avail himself of anonymity and of the thin disguise of fiction and foreign skies. In this resource, it will be recognized that he had the example of Montesquieu (q.v.), whose *Lettres persanes* appeared in 1721 ; and, less immediately, the *roman-à-clef* (q.v.) of a previous generation of Fr. novelists had been utilized for somewhat similar ends.

If we turn from V.'s works to his life, we shall find the same break at 1755 ; and, if we turn from his life and works to his age, we shall find that the 18th cent. in France is divided at much the same point, between the death of Louis xiv, 1715, and the Revolution of 1789. Even in the accidents of chronology, V. was the personality of his age.

V.'s full name was François Arouet ; **he** assumed his famous surname at about 18 years of age, in the same way that Molière (q.v.) took his. The ingenuity which has resolved Voltaire into an anagram of a-r-o-v(u)-e-t-, l[e]-i(j [eune]) is more creditable than credible. Arouet *père* was a notary at Châtetet, and to the venerable duc de Saint-Simon (q.v.), V. was always ' the son of an advocate whom my father and I employed '. He left college with his future in his eyes and on his tongue ; both retained their sparkling brilliance till old age. In 1714, he met Ninon (q.v.) d'Enclos, and the aged beauty attracted the attractive youth, and left him a legacy to buy bks. Bks. and life (the life of the world) were the twin objects of V.'s heart's desire, and he seized his opportunities with both hands open. Eleven months in the Bastille, 1717, to cool the heat of his satire, gave him leisure for reflection, which he spent on his tragic ' Œdipus ' and on his heroic ' Henriad ' of early France. By 1724, he was already talked about as a poet, and a welcome guest at the houses of the great. In 1725, he was again in the Bastille, at the instance of a chevalier de Rohan, whom V. had challenged to a duel after the chevalier had had him horse-whipped for impertinence after a supper-party at the duc de Sully's. It was all highly aristocratic ; the notary's son had won his way to exalted tables, and, having won it, his views on Fr. society and government were necessarily coloured by his experience. His release was made conditional on his exile, and V. spent the next 3 years in Engld., where he met everyone he should, dedicated *Zaïre* to Bolingbroke (q.v.), and formulated his instincts into dogmas. ' England did not create Voltaire ', says a Fr. critic ; ' she instructed him ' ; and ' his pride in his trade (*son amour-propre d'écrivain*) was restored by seeing Newton buried in the Abbey, Prior charged with diplomatic missions, and Addison included in the ministry '. V. returned to Paris in 1729, with a sheaf of MSS. under his arm, and innumerable projects in his head. His Engl. *Lettres philosophiques* were issued in Fr. in 1734 (*Lettres Anglaises*), and the Paris bookseller was sent to the Bastille. V. escaped to the château de Cirey, the residence of his *belle Émilie*, mme. de Châtelet. The busy days which that lady protected, and the happy life which they led together, must be sought from other sources ; in 1740, V. was back in Paris, and a comedy for the marriage of the dauphin brought him the king's vagrant favour : in 1746, he was elected to the Academy (q.v.), and was appointed historiographer royal and gentleman-of-the-bedchamber. His dismissal, or retirement, was due to the king's mistress, mme. de Pompadour, whom V.'s bitter tongue had offended, and he paid visits to Sceaux (q.v.), to king Stanislas of Poland at Lunéville, and, again, to Cirey ; always writing, always abundantly. In 1749, mme. de Châtelet died, and V. set up house in Paris. Fortune had favoured his speculations, and he was now a man of great wealth, and of immense esteem in society and letters. *Zaïre*, his only ' tender tragedy ', with its conflict of Christian birth revealed to the willing bride of an Eastern lover, had raised him to the height of dramatic fame, and he had sustained it as poet, novelist, and historian.

We come now to an interlude in V.'s life, which is at the same time a remarkable chapter in the history of 2 nations : the Prussian episode, or the Franco-Prussian *entente*. Frederick ii (the Great) had been king of Prussia since 1740, and in 1743 V. had visited his capital on a diplomatic mission, when the king sought (with characteristic duplicity) to charm the ambassador and defeat the embassy. In July, 1750, after the death of mme. de Châtelet, and not unwilling to show the king of France that his court was not the only court in Europe, V. went at last to Potsdam as the honoured guest of the Prussian despot. His letters of this period are enchanting, and visitors to Potsdam will be familiar with the solid monuments of that airy *intermezzo*, when a Fr. poet was Prussian court-chamberlain, with a gold cross and a lavish salary, and played with exquisite grace the Goethe (q.v.) to Potsdam's Weimar. The end

came, about 2 years afterwards; it had
something to do, first, with a contract for
exchequer-bills and privy dealings with the
contractor, a certain Hirschel; and, secondly,
with Maupertius (q.v.), and a certain König's
candidature for the Berlin Academy: a trivial
piece of jealousy on Parnassus, but, as king
Frederick remarked, 'a squeezed orange is only
fit to throw away'. V. withdrew from
Prussia's hospitality, and, not being wanted
in France, he found a refuge in Switzerld.
He bought an estate at Geneva, which he
called *les Délices*, and another near Lausanne,
1755. 'He would go to no more Kings.
The Kings should come to him. . . . Now
began the reign of the philosopher, and the
apotheosis of the " patriarch " ' (Lanson,
Hist. Lit. Fr., 697).

V. had put his faith in princes, and they had
failed him; his faith in God, which is the
ancient consolation, was prejudicially affected
by the social evils that cried aloud around him,
by the hypocrisy that stalked by noon-day, and
by his personal experience of disillusion. Why
should genius languish in the Bastille? Why
should love miss its earthly crown? Why
should poverty be a crime? And was not this
attitude, too, precisely the reflection of his
times? In and near 1755, had not the subjects
of king Louis xv at least a glimmering perception of the guillotine that was to fall
on his successor? Was there not a weariness
of taxation, of warfare, even of glory? Had
philosophy, political and moral, no higher
good to show forth than Bourbonism-without-
end? History answered these questions, very
shortly after V.'s death, in the Revolution of
1789; but the generation before the revolutionaries prepared the way for the people.
Paris was Voltairean before it was Revolutionary; and, despite the triumph of 1778, when
all Paris did honour to the patriarch, V.
might have said with G. Meredith: 'what a
dusty answer gets the soul, When hot for
certainties in this our life'. He attacked
religion, they say; they said it persistently
in the 19th cent., when mysticism (q.v.),
re-animate in romance (q.v.), and trailing
strange properties from Germany, had restored
the deeper communion between creatures and
their Creator. The 20th cent., which has
witnessed the fate of militarism super-imposed
on romanticism, and which has attended the
close of the slowly-dying principles of medieval
thought, may hold V. guiltless of the worse
consequences of his unbelief. He attacked
religion, it is true: on the stage in *Œdipe*,
Zaïre, *Mahomet*, and in countless poems,
treatises, tales, and letters, including the
criticism of Fr. institutions in the famous
Lettres Anglaises. But he attacked abuses in
religion: this is the important distinction;
abuses in religion, justice, politics, law, whenever and wherever he encountered them. His
freelance was never in couch; he was indecently
indifferent to the conventions of St.-Simon,
and nothing is more illuminating than to
compare V.'s *Siècle de Louis xiv* with the great
duke's *Mémoires* of the same period. It was
at Ferney, on the Fr. frontier, where he
settled finally in 1760, that philosophy overtook V. He had nothing more to fear from
any man. The patriarch of Ferney was
inviolable. If he had died between 1740 and
1750, he would be remembered as the Byron of
France. As it is, Byron (q.v.) is an aspect
of the Voltaire of Engld. For V.'s position
at the top of affairs, above the need of money,
the favour of kings, the smiles of friends, the
popularity of crowds, raised him to an eminence
from which he could survey the past, present,
and future. He pleaded, *écrasez l'infâme*,
' crush the foul thing ', credulity, or religion;
but he was likewise the author of the saying
si Dieu n'existait pas, il faudrait l'inventer, ' if
God did not exist, it would be necessary to
invent him '; and V., in his advocacy of the
cause of the oppressed, had Christian virtues
if not Christian dogmas. And the last scene in
Paris, when the old man, with his youthful
fortune in his eyes, at last came into his own, and
the whole theatre rose to do him honour at
the production of his last tragedy, *Irene*,
stands out in literary history as a triumph of
mind over matter. Yet, finally, great as V.
was, and significant in his age and country,
he was too impatient and hot-foot a writer
to achieve supremacy in any kind. Where
V. is unsurpassed is in his irony, his brilliance,
his audacity, which illumined everything that
he touched. He was a bitter enemy: he was
jealous of dead Montesquieu; he quarrelled
with living Rousseau and Buffon (qq.v.);
fools he could not tolerate, and, somehow,
he saw more than any one else. But he was a
great genius, a great friend, a great benefactor.
He created the utterance of the lips for those
who were to overthrow the *ancien régime* of
France; the whole country became Voltairean,
and had to become Voltairean before it could
become free. The modern world began with
V. 'He cleared away the obstacles which
dammed back the rapidly rising flood, but his
hand was only the most active and unerring of
many engaged in the same task; and even
unassisted the impatient stream would have
overflowed and borne away the impediments in
its course' (*C.M.H.*, viii, 14). This is true;
but V., like Xenophanes of old, did not merely
mock and destroy: a builder of ruins he was,
' but, after the winnowings of generations, a
wide and deep repute still remains to him;
nor will any diminution which it may have
suffered be without compensation, for, with
the fading of old prejudices, and with better
knowledge, his name will be regarded with
increased liking and respect ' (sir E. Hamley,
Voltaire, 203). And we, remembering who
have come after him, remembering Renan
(q.v.) and the rest, may fitly apply to V. the
lovely lines of Mrs. Meynell's poem:

We know, we know how all too bright
    The hues are that our painting wears,
And how the marble gleams too white;—
    We speak in unknown tongues, the years

Interpret everything aright,
And crown with weeds our pride of towers,
    And warm our marble through with sun,
And break our pavements through with
        flowers,
With an Amen when all is done.

And the church, which refused burial to V.'s
bones, will not refuse him the Amen to-day.

Vondel, van den, Joost (1587-1679): Dutch poet and dramatist; shares with Grotius (q.v.) the chief place in Holland for her contribution to European lit. Born at Cologne, during the flight of his parents as religious refugees from Antwerp to Utrecht, and, finally, to Amsterdam, where V. was brought up to his father's trade as a hosier, later carried on by his wife, while V. devoted himself to the profession of letters, then unremunerative. He was a man of deep piety, and, like Grotius, his friend, suffered by his espousal of the cause of Barneveldt, who was executed, 1619, in the name of religion. Later, 1641, V. was converted to the Church of Rome. His long life was saddened towards its close by the defalcations of a son, to whom he had transferred his business, and he took a clerkship in the *Mont de Piété* at Amsterdam. No brief record is adequate to the admitted 'Laureate of Amsterdam, when that city was the heart of the Netherlands and the Netherlands stood at the very centre of the movements of Western Europe, responsive to all that took place from Sweden to Spain, from Turkey to England, and looking out over the seas, of which her control was just beginning to be disputed, to the Indies, East and West' (Grierson, *P.E.L.*, vii, 26). The self-education of the hosier's son in Fr., Germ., Ital., and, later, in Lat. and Gk.; his intense and ardent imagination, quickened by and quickening the patriotism which was concentrated in Amsterdam; the divine faith and human tenderness which he drew from his harsh experience of life; his happy marriage, and devoted friendship to men and women of the type of Tesselschade Visscher (q.v.); his inspiration, his renunciation, his genius—the evidence from his biography must be sought in fuller records than this; and elsewhere, too, must be sought the complete investigation of V.'s literary affinities with Du Bartas, Crashaw, and Milton (qq.v.). Here we note that V. began as a translr., and won renown as a lyrical poet, esp. in the field of satire. Barneveldt's judicial murder inspired one great satiric poem, and the doctrine of the damnation of unbaptized infants inspired another (*Decretum Horribile*); he wr. of God, love, children, and nature, in verse of rare delicacy and sweet music; but, as Milton finally chose the classical epic as the medium for the message which he had to deliver, so V. finally chose the classical drama for the expression of what he had to say on the topics of politics and religion, so close to the hearts of his countrymen. He was associated with Hooft (q.v.) in a transln. of the *Troades* of Seneca (q.v.), and it was in the Senecan vein that his first considerable tragedy, *Palamedes*, 1625, was composed. The tragic event of 1619 had supplied its motive, but it brought its author no profit, save of fame, and a fine, in lieu of worse penalty. The quarrels of the Eglantine (q.v.) were by this time at an end; V. was now the leading poet in the new Amsterdam Chamber which had emerged out of the dramatists' revolt; and he was invited, 1637, to write the opening play for its theatre. In the previous year he had transld. into Dutch the Lat. tragedy of Grotius, *Sophonisba*. His Academy-play was a clever adaptation of the story of the fall of Troy to the circumstances of modern Amsterdam, and it was notable for the beauty of its choric songs (V.'s lyrical gift was always stronger than his dramatic), and for the deepening note of Catholic thought, which aroused the suspicions of the clergy, confirmed, a few years later, by the poet's conversion. This drama was entitled *Gysbrecht van Amstel*. It was followed by a series of plays, mostly founded on Biblical subjects—Joseph, Saul's sons, Solomon, Jephtha, David, etc.—and, chiefly, by *Lucifer*, 1654, which is unique for several reasons. In it, V.'s dramatic talents found their best and their noblest expression. The comparative freedom which Lucifer enjoyed from set circumstance and tradition left the dramatist free to invent situations and characters; and the entire play moves more homogeneously than any other from V.'s pen. Prince Maurice's action against Barneveldt—that deeply-felt crime of his own times—and Cromwell's contemporary rebellion lent the poignant appeal of present sympathy to the old tale of angelic revolt and mutinous pride in heaven. Lucifer himself, Belial, Beelzebub, Raphael and Michael, are finely imagined and boldly drawn; but the drama, unlike the epic, precluded the appearance of the true Protagonist, the Lord of Heaven himself; and to that extent was at a disadvantage. But the choric songs of the angels provided a feature superior to any which epos could supply. The comparison with Milton is inevitable; but critics incline strongly to the conclusion that the English epic was but little indebted to the Dutch drama. Their common debt to Du Bartas and even to Grotius (qq.v.) is more obvious; and there were a tenderness and a human note in V. which were not in the range of Milton's sublimity. V. wr. many plays after *Lucifer*, but none of them touched quite the same high level; and, summarily, we may say of this now almost wholly neglected genius that he applied the dramatic art of the Renaissance (including its Unities, q.v.) to the dramatic matter of the Mystery- and Morality-play, in the manner of the homely burghers of Amsterdam. The result of this unique combination is somewhat rigid and sometimes unheroic, though V. attained to a height of lyric genius and of piety (in the sense of the Roman *pietas*, which was duty and pity as well) hardly to be matched in the lit. of Europe.

Vos, Jan (*c.* 1620-87): Dutch dramatist; glazier. Wr. melodramatic plays on the subjects of Medea and Titus Andronicus (he may have been acquainted with Shakespeare's tragedy), which failed in the final effort at the close of the golden age of Dutch lit. (q.v.) to lift the old happy-go-lucky plays of the Chambers of Rhetoric (see s.v. Rederijkers) into the classical atmosphere of the formal Academy (see s.v. Eglantine).

Voss, Johann Heinrich (1751-1826): Germ. poet and translr. Born in poor circumstances; subvented by friends, and assisted by Boie (q.v.) to Göttingen (q.v.), where he quickly became the life and soul of the poets' club known as the Hain (q.v.), devoted to spread the gospel of Germ. poetry according to Klopstock (q.v.). Married Boie's sister, and succeeded, 1775, to the editorship of the *Musenalmanach*, the organ of the Göttingen brotherhood; lived in later life at Jena and Heidelberg. V. was less a poet than a father of poets to-be, and his comparative non-success as a writer of songs and odes was compensated by his reform of the idyl. The last Germ. experiments in that form had come from the pen of S. Gessner (q.v.), to whom Crabbe (q.v.) might have posed his question (*Village*, i, 15):

If Tityrus found the Golden Age again,
Must sleepy bards the flattering dream prolong,
Mechanic echoes of the Mantuan song?

V.'s idyls of the countryside, though Theocritean in form, were realistic in treatment, and if his peasants did not sweat visibly, like Crabbe's, at least they wore no such 'tinsel trappings' as Gessner's. His best-known idyls are *The 70th Birthday*, 1781, and *Luise, a rural poem in three idyls*, 1783-84; the latter esp., for its influence, more obvious to Goethe than to V., on the greater poet's *Hermann and Dorothea*. By freeing the poetry of the countryside from the conventions of the Renaissance pastoral (q.v.) and associating it with the manner of the Gk. epic, V. conferred on modern lit. better service than he knew, and invented a *genre* of poetry of which Wordsworth's *Michael* and Meredith's *Love in the Valley* are in the direct line of descent. The romantic development of V.'s tastes, which led to his quarrels in later life with F. L. Stolberg (q.v.), was displayed in his choice of authors for transln. In this field his most notable work was his Homer (q.v.) in Germ. hexameters (*Odyssey*, 1781; *Iliad*, 1793), and his last labours were devoted to Shakespeare, in which he was assisted by his sons.

Vossius, -i. Gerard John (1577-1649): Dutch scholar. Rector, 1615, and prof. of eloquence, 1622, at Leyden univ.; prof. of history, Amsterdam, 1631 (see s.v. Saumaise); member of the Muiderkring (q.v.); declined similar post at Cambridge, 1624; canon of Canterbury, 1629. His learned Lat. works covered a wide range of studies, so that he is honourably known as the leading 'polyhistor' of his times. Wr., 1606, a treatise on rhetoric, which had considerable influence, and which he followed, 1647, by treatise on poetics, somewhat after the example of J. C. Scaliger (q.v.); his work in this department marked a real advance in the comparatively recent science of literary criticism (q.v.). Wr. also on the history of Gk. (1624) and Lat. (1627) lit., treatises which maintained their rank for at least 2 centuries; a Lat. grammar (1607), and philological treatises of profound erudition, including *Aristarchus*, 4 vols., 1635, and 9 bks. on good and bad Latinity, of which 4 were issued in 1645, and the remaining 5 posth. in 1685.

-ii. Isaac (1618-89): Dutch scholar; second son of above. Born at Leyden; appointed to chair of history, Amsterdam, at the early age of 15; left in 1649 for Sweden, where he taught Gk. to queen Christina; visited France and Engld., where he entered the Anglican Church, and was appointed prebendary at Windsor, 1673; his library was offered to the Bodleian, but the purchase fell through, despite the efforts of Evelyn and Bentley (qq.v.). V. was an industrious editor, but is better esteemed as a misc. scholar, of wide and welcome acquaintance and correspondence.

Vrchlický, Jaroslav (1853-1912): Czech poet and translr.; a voluminous and versatile writer, reminding us, by his metrical facility and readiness to attempt any form of verse from a madrigal to an epic (*Bar Kochba*), of Hardy (q.v.) in France or Lope de Vega (q.v.) in Spain. V. held the chair of modern lit. at the Czech univ. at Prague, and was admirably qualified for his post. His translns. included, in part or whole, Dante, Petrarch, Ariosto, Tasso, Calderon, Carducci, Camoëns, Byron, Shelley, Victor Hugo, Tennyson, Goethe, Schiller, Ibsen, Michiewiez, and Persian and Chinese poets: truly an astounding output, which, with his original writings, fills about 250 vols. A gifted selection may establish his fame in the present century.

W

Wackenroder, Wilhelm Heinrich (1773-98): Germ. Romanticist. Intimate friend of Tieck (q.v.), with whom he planned a journey to Rome, the Mecca of art, subsequently rendered imaginatively in Tieck's romance of the *Wanderings of Franz Sternbald*, issued, 1798, in the shadow of W.'s early death. Tieck felt the bereavement severely; for the gentle, almost feminine influence of W. was of the utmost value to the more robust and more professorial (and, therefore, less sensitive) talent of his friend. W.'s chief original work, of which about one-seventh has been computed as Tieck's contribution, was entitled *Heart-outpourings of an art-loving cloister-brother*, 1797. The title was cumbrous; but it expressed very exactly the contents of this pathetic human document, which thinly disguised the author's personal experience of the conflict between the music in his soul and the material duties proposed to his right-hand. 'Art is a seductive, forbidden fruit; whoso shall taste its inmost sweetest savour, he is irrevocably lost for the active living world'; and the hero, Joseph Berglinger, is none other than W. himself. His posth. work was entitled *Phantasies about art for friends of art*, but in this instance it is computed that about half the bk. is by Tieck, who proved himself a loyal friend and editor; W.'s fame in Germ. letters is inseparable from Tieck's.

Wade, Thomas (1805-75): Engl. poet. Wr. *Poems*, 1825; *Woman's Love*, a romantic drama, 1828; *The Jew of Arragon*, a tragedy, 1830, which 'was damned by an audience which would not tolerate the championship of the Jews' (Walker, *Lit. Victorian Era*, 286); and *Mundi et Cordis . . . Carmina*, a collection of poems, 1835, displaying a close study of Keats and Shelley.

Wagner, Heinrich Leopold (1747-79) : Germ. dramatist. Wr. tragedies of middle-class life, true forerunners of the problem-plays of the present day, but marked by the violence and explosiveness of the Sturm und Drang (q.v.) movement. The best known is 'The Infanticide' (*die Kindermörderin*), a revolting drama of seduction, desertion, and murder; the more notable, because W. owed to Goethe (q.v.), his constant model, the design for the Gretchen-scene.

Wagner (Wilhelm) Richard (1813-83) : Germ. musician, poet, and critic; lived in Paris, 1839-42, where he composed *der fliegende Holländer*, but produced it in Dresden, where he lived till 1849, composing *Rienzi*, *Tannhäuser*, 1845, and *Lohengrin*, 1850. In that year, W. moved to Switzerld., in order to escape prosecution for revolutionary activities, and publd. his critical writings, including the masterly *Oper und Drama*, 1851. The *Ring* trilogy of the Nibelungen, succeeded by *Rheingold*, occupied W. for many years, 1853-70, and was first represented as a whole at Bayreuth, 1876. *Tristan und Isolde*, 1865, was a dramatic expression of the philosophy of Schopenhauer (q.v.), and was followed by the *Meistersinger*, 1868, and *Parsifal*, 1882. Music, even Wagnerian, is outside the scope of the present vol., but, in Saintsbury's words, 'the re-knitting of the connection of Apollo's two arts—poetry and music—so long severed from each other by nothing so much as by the frivolity and mindlessness of the older opera itself, is a phenomenon in the history of literature far too important to escape notice here' (*P.E.L*, xii, 232).

Waldis, Burkard (1490-1556) : Germ. moral fabulist; Lutheran convert. Wr. *Esopus*, 'quite newly made and composed in rhyme withal 100 new fables'. Like Steinhöwel (q.v.) in the previous cent., W. cast a wide net, and went outside the old bestiary (q.v.) for his tales, which were directed with a convert's zeal to edification.

Wallace, Alfred Russel (1823-1913) : Engl. philosopher; O.M., 1908. Born at Usk, and started life as assistant to his brother, a land surveyor; travelled in S. America, 1848-52, and publd. *Travels on the Amazon and Rio Negro*; resumed his travels, 1854, visiting Malay archipelago and other countries, and brought back valuable collection of specimens; publd. *The Malay Archipelago*, 1869; *Geographical Distribution of Animals*, 1876; *Island Life*, 1880. W. and Darwin (q.v.) first met in 1854, and were associated on 1 July, 1858, in the communication to the Linnean Society of a joint paper consisting of an essay by W., ' on the tendency of Varieties to depart indefinitely from the Original Type ', and of Darwin's outline of the law of Natural Selection, sketched by him in 1842, and read by Lyell and Hooker in 1844. The idea thus formulated by Darwin ' flashed suddenly ' upon W. in the Moluccas in Feb., 1858, and he posted an outline of his views to Darwin forthwith; the story of this equal division of the honours of discovery is one of the pleasantest *personalia* of scientific research.

W. was a pall-bearer at Darwin's funeral, 1882, and the central figure at the jubilee celebration at the Linnean Society in 1908. Wr., too, *Miracles and Modern Spiritualism*, *The Wonderful Century*, and other works; was first Darwin medallist and a Fellow of the Royal Society.

Wallenberg, Jakob (1746-78) : Swed. poet. Wr. a tragedy, *Susanna*, in the Fr. neo-classic school of drama; wr., too, a prose travel-narrative. Both these pieces are far better than the average of their kind of the same date and place, and lead to regret at W.'s early death.

Wallin, Johan Olof (1779-1839) : Swed. poet; divine; won successive prizes at the Swed. Academy in his youth, and became archbishop in his old age. The brilliancy of W.'s career is indisputable, but his poetry, though talented and versatile, displayed no marked originality. It combined some good features of both epochs : the neo-classic age of Gustavus iii (q.v.) and the romantic reaction which overtook it. Like most compromises, however, the result is not wholly satisfactory. W.'s hymns earned him the title of ' the Harp of David ', and he wr., too, secular lyric verse, idylls, drinking-songs, and didactic pieces.

Walpole, Horace (1717-97) : Engl. letter-writer, novelist, virtuoso; fourth son of sir Robert W. (1676-1745), prime minister of Engld., and first earl of Orford), to whom he was always devoted, though father and son differed much in tastes, character, and even appearance; succeeded, 1791, his insane and bankrupt nephew as fourth earl of Orford, but made merely a formal use of the title; edu. at Eton, with, among others, T. Gray (q.v.), with whom he travelled on the Grand Tour, 1739, quarrelled, and made friends again; M.P., 1741-68; acquired Strawberry Hill, Twickenham, 1747, which he transformed into a minature Gothic castle, and spent a lifetime in adorning, displaying, and employing as a centre of society and the arts; set up a printing-press in it, and collected *objets de vertu*, which were sold, 1842, for £33,450 11s. 9d. Among W.'s best known writings were *Anecdotes of Painting in England*, 1762, which is said to have ' prevented the publication of a complete and trustworthy history of English painting' (H. B. Wheatley, *C.H.E.L.*, x, 254); *Historic Doubts on the Life and Reign of Richard iii*, 1768; *The Mysterious Mother*, a *Tragedy*, 1768, and *The Castle of Otranto*, a *Gothic Romance*, 1764, first masked as a transln. from a 16th cent. Ital. original. The vogue of this novel is past, but it enjoyed contemporary success and immense posth. influence : ' in spite of glaring defects ', says prof. Vaughan (*C.H.E.L.*, x, 60-1), ' of which it is hard to suppose that the author was not in some degree aware, an entirely new turn is here given to the novel (q.v.), and elements are brought into it which, at a later time and in hands more skilful, were to change it out of all knowledge. The bk. was written in conscious reaction against the domesticities and the sentiment of Richardson (q.v.). It was a deliberate attempt to divert fiction from the channel along which it had hitherto flowed; . . . to substitute for the interest of the present that of the past, the work of experience by that of the mysterious and supernatural'. W. thus ranks as the founder of the novel of terror, the *Schauerroman*, as Germ. romanticists entitled it, and is reckoned among the fathers of modern fiction. But his permanent fame rests securely on his *Letters*. These, which number several thousands, and which were addressed most frequently to sir Horace Mann (1701-86), a friend of 45 years' standing, among 160 correspondents (see also s.v. mme. Deffand), constitute a permanent monument, biographical and hist. at once, and are not merely invaluable as a record of 60 busy and interesting years, but are matchless, too, in personal interest and in literary art and charm. 'This world is a comedy to those who think, a tragedy to those who feel', is one of the many epigrams which occur in the letters to Mann : it is typical of the tone of the writer,—a little artificial, a little melancholy in its reflection ; the considered judgment of a man of varied tastes on a definite orbit of social life, who could see everyone and know everything, but who preferred to be an object rather than the subject of curiosity. The *Correspondence* was collected by P. Cunningham, 9 vols., 1857-9, and by Mrs. Paget Toynbee, 16 vols., 1903 ; Macaulay's (q.v.) *Essays* contain a bitter art. on W.'s *Letters* to Mann (from *Edinburgh Review*, Oct., 1833) ; a far more sympathetic and temperate judgment is that of A. Dobson (q.v.) in his *Horace Walpole : A Memoir*.

Walter, John (1739-1812): Engl. printer ; founder of *The Times* newspaper. W. bought a 'logotype', or whole-word printing, process, 1782, and set it up in premises which he had acquired in Printing-house-square ; started a *Daily Universal Register*, 1785, and changed its name to *The Times*, 1788. He was succeeded by his second son, **John W.** (1766-1847), who was succeeded in turn by his eldest son, **John W.** (1818-94).

Walther von der Vogelweide (c. 1170-1228) : Germ. Minnesinger (q.v.) ; 'the greatest lyric poet of the middle ages' (Robertson, *Germ. Lit.*, 120) ; 'the master of medieval lyric' (Biese, i, 159) ; 'the mouthpiece of the half-inarticulate, all-suggesting music that is at once the very soul and the very inseparable garment of romance' (Saintsbury, *P.E.L.*, ii, 258). The critics, it will be seen, agree as to the supremacy of W. in the delightful region of chivalric love-lyric in early 13th cent. Germ. poetry. Little is known of W.'s life, except that he was of noble family, but himself was poor ; that he lived in stirring times, and spent many years in travel, moving from castle to castle, and winning a welcome by his art. He wr. 'Sprüche' (maxims), as they were called ; political, or, rather, patriotic poems, esp., in the dynastic crises of 1197 and 1204. He spent some time at Vienna (his language is South-German), and was entertained, too, by the hospitable count of Thuringia, at whose court he met Wolfram (q.v.) of Eschenbach. The poets of his own country honoured him as the 'nightingale' of their craft ; and his surname 'of the Birds'-meadow' is not more poetical than his poems. Apart from the 'Sprüche' and from some religious musings, W.'s fame

rests securely on his 'Frauenminne', the profane branch of the noble numbers of the love-lyrists. In one sense, he naturalized the art of Minnesong ; though it was imported from Provence, the immigrant became indigenous under his hands. But while he nationalized it in one sense, he made its appeal universal in another. It was no longer Troubadours' love-song, according to the rules of its kind ; it was the outpouring of the heart of man. It was the worship and wonder of spring-tide :

> When the flowerets from the grass are springing,
> Just as if they laugh'd up to the sun,
> On an early morning in the May,
> And the little birds begin their singing,
> At the best that ever they have done,
> How delicious may our life be. Nay,
> 'Tis very half of Heaven. . . .

This, surely, is no other than the birthtime of poets' wonder. Perhaps the best-known of W.'s lyrics is his lovely *Unter der Linden* (Under the lime-tree). There is (or has been) a habit of comparing W. in Germany with Petrarch (q.v.) in Italy 100 years after, as lyric poets of extraordinary inspiration. The comparison, which is common, is inept ; but there is this likeness in their difference that each brought to poetry a naïve enthusiasm, Petrarch for learning, W. for observation, which freshened the founts of inspiration, and proved a potent influence on the lit. of his country.

Walton, Izaak (1593-1683) : Engl. essayist, biographer. Wr. excellent and valuable *Lives* of John Donne, 1640, R. Hooker, 1665, George Herbert, 1670 (qq.v.), and others, but is chiefly memorable for his work *The Compleat Angler*, 1653, second edn., 1655, and often reprinted, which stands at the head of a class of bks. particularly characteristic of the Engl. genius, and is still, and deservedly, a prime favourite. It is partly in dialogue, partly in verse, and its pleasant, humorous and kindly writing calls up the scenes and atmosphere of the quiet life of a rural fisherman, which W. enjoyed at Farnham and Winchester.

Wandering Jew : Germ. popular tale, or, at least, popularized in Germany during the 16th cent., when the *Volksbuch* (q.v.) flourished. The tragic figure of the shoemaker of Jerusalem, Ahasuerus, who had witnessed the Passion of the Saviour, and had repulsed Him from the threshold of his house, whence there fell on him the curse, never to rest from wandering, in that he had withheld the boon of rest, was alleged to have been seen in Hamburg in 1547, on the authority of Paul v. Eitzen, bp. of Schleswig. A certain Chrisostom Dudulæus wrought in Germ. his 'Wonderful Report' of the *ewige Jude*, whose fame was already current ; on this account was based an Engl. ballad, 1612, and later versions, down to that of Goethe (q.v.). Like the contemporary tale of Faust (q.v.), the moral of the W.J. is the inadequacy of exceptional exemption from the conditions of time and space to confer true happiness.

Warburton, William (1698-1779) : Engl. divine ; bp. of Gloucester, 1759. W.'s fame, such as it is, in lit. depends on his association with men greater than himself, and chiefly with Pope (q.v.), whose literary executor he became, 1744. W. had supplied Pope with notes on Bentley's (q.v.) *Milton* a few years before, with a view to inclusion in the *Dunciad*, and was a warm admirer of the *Essay on Man*. W.'s own writings included *The Divine Legation of Moses*, part i, 1737, part ii, 1741, a work still of some interest, though the controversies which it aroused have lost their zest, and an edn. of Shakespeare, 8 vols., 1747, in which ' such improvements as he introduced are mainly borrowed from Theobald ' (q.v.), or another (sir S. Lee, *William Shakespeare*, 579 ; Lee describes W. as ' a blustering divine of multifarious reading ').

Ward, Adolphus William (1837-1924) : Engl. scholar ; master of Peterhouse, Cambridge, 1900-24 ; president of Royal British Academy, 1911-3 ; knt., 1913. Wr. *Hist. of Engl. Dramatic Lit. to the death of Queen Anne*, 2 vols., 1875, and other works ; edited Marlowe's (q.v.) *Doctor Faustus*, 1878 ; Crabbe's (q.v.) *Poems*, 3 vols., 1905-6, etc. ; and was closely associated with the editorship of, and a frequent contributor to, the great Cambridge co-operative hist. works, planned by lord Acton (q.v.) : *C.M.H.*, *C.H.E.L.*, and *C.H.British Foreign Policy*.

Ward, Edward (Ned) (1667-1731) : Engl. coffee-house (q.v.)-journalist ; a tavern-keeper in London ; wr. *The London Spy*, 1698-1709, a coarse, dull account of the lower strata of society in his day, which possesses some hist. value for the sake of its observation, and some literary interest for its anticipation of sensational journalese in style.

Ward, Mrs. Humphrey. See **Arnold, Mary Augusta.**

Ward, William George (1812-82) : Engl. theologian ; Roman Catholic. Wr. *The Ideal of a Christian Church*, 1844, whence his nickname, Ideal Ward ; edited *Dublin Review*, 1863-78.

Warner, William (died, 1609) : Engl. poet ; wr. *Albion's England*, a metrical history, 1586, from Noah to the Norman Conquest, extended, 1606, to the reign of king James i ; Meres (q.v.) praised W. extravagantly, but his fame has not survived.

Warren, John Byron Leicester, third baron de Tabley (1835-95) : Engl. poet ; wr. a considerable amount of lyrical and dramatic verse of a high order, under the main influences of his age, those of Rossetti, Swinburne and Tennyson (qq.v.) His poetry suffered from neglect in his life-time, whether publd. under the name of ' George Preston ', ' William Lancaster ', or his own ; and, except for one or two slight spurts of popularity, it has never made its way to the reading public. Perhaps there was a surfeit of the kind. Yet lord de T. has many claims on the affection and gratitude of admirers, whose circle might well be extended ; and his accurate and intimate birdlore and botany were transmuted into beautiful figures of speech. His *Poems Dramatic and Lyrical*, 1893, contained the florilegium of his earlier vols., and was followed by a second series, 1895, under the same title, and by *Orpheus in Thrace*, posth., 1901.

Warren, Samuel (1807-77) : Engl. novelist ; wr. *Passages from the Diary of a late Physician*,

1830 ; *Ten Thousand a Year*, 1839 ; *Now and Then*, 1847 : all still readable.

Wartburg : Germ. castle in the hills of Thuringia, twice famous in literary history : (1), in 1206-07, when a poetic contest is said to have been held between the singers at the court of the landgrave Hermann of Thüringen, who included Walther (q.v.) von der Vogelweide, and a legendary Heinrich von Ofterdingen (see s.v. Hardenberg) ; the tradition may be true, but a 14th-cent. anon. poem (*Wartburgkrieg*) which purports to contain the compositions is probably apocryphal ; and (2) in 1521, when Luther (q.v.) found refuge with the reigning lord after the Diet of Worms.

Warton, -i. Thomas (*c*. 1688-1745) : Engl. scholar ; prof. of Poetry at Oxford, 1718-28 ; attracted to medieval studies by his taste for Gothic architecture at Windsor and Winchester (the transition of ' Gothic ' to 'romantic ' passed through architecture to lit. ; see s.v. Romance) ; applied himself to the study of Spenser (whose revival was an introduction to the romantic point of view) and Milton : ' it was indirectly from Warton that Pope got his knowledge of *Comus* and *Il Penseroso* ' (*C.H.E.L.*, x, 238). Wr. *Poems on Several Occasions* (posth., 1748), which ' contain some rather amazing borrowings from Milton's volume of 1645 ' (*ibid.*) as well as a *Runic Ode*, paraphrased from O. Worm's (q.v.) *Death-Song of Ragnar*, or, more precisely, from the reference thereto by sir William Temple (q.v.).

 -ii. Joseph (1722-1800) : Engl. critic ; elder son of above ; wr. early poems, showing a genuine feeling for nature, and essays on Pope, 1757, whose works he edited, 1797. Transld. Virgil (q.v.) into Engl. verse (with C. Pitt), 4 vols., 1753. J. W.'s *Odes on Various Subjects*, 1746, included a poem, *The Enthusiast*, said to have been written in 1740, which is ' perhaps the earliest deliberate expression in Engld. of the feeling in which the Romantic movement originated ' (Courthope, *Hist. Engl. Poetry*, vi, 379) ; and prof. Courthope goes on to point out, as evidence to a continuity in that movement, ' how the somewhat grotesque aspirations of *The Enthusiast* anticipate the Rousseau-inspired resolutions of the lover in *Locksley Hall* ; ' e.g., J. W.'s—

' With simple Indian swains that I may hunt, The boar and tiger through savannahs wild ' . . .

 -iii. Thomas (1728-90) : Engl. scholar ; brother of above ; prof. of Poetry at Oxford, like his father before him, 1757-67 ; Camden prof. of Ancient History, Oxford, 1785-90 ; poet-laureate (q.v.), 1785 (see s.v. Rolliad). T.W., the younger, as he is called, was busy with bks. all through his life, which, though shorter than that of his brother, was more productive, and recalled more closely his father's career. Like T.W. the elder, he was a Spenserian and Miltonian, writing *Observations on the Faerie Queene*, 1754, and editing Milton's *Poems on Several Occasions*, 1785. He edited Theocritus, 1770 ; publd. an inquiry into the authenticity of the ' Rowley ' poems (see s.v. Chatterton), 1782, and publd. original verse at the beginning and end of his active life, *The Pleasures of Melancholy*, 1745 ; *The*

Triumph of Isis, 1749; *Poems,* 1777 : collected, 1791, and edited, with memoir by R. Mant, 2 vols. 1802. A Warton lecture in his honour was founded by the British Academy. This compliment is due to T. W.'s *History of Engl. Poetry* (11th to 17th cent.), 3 vols., 1774-78-81 ; re-issued, 1824-40-71. It is a compilation of great interest even at this day, when prof. Courthope, likewise in his time a prof. of Poetry at Oxford, has written on more scientific lines and with the resources of another 100 years a *History of Engl. Poetry,* 6 vols., 1895-1910. Perhaps the later historian's tribute to the earlier will be appropriate in this place : ' His reading was wide, his scholarship sound, his taste fine and dis- criminating ; and though he had no pretensions to be called a great poet, his verse is at least marked by genuine poetic sensibility. Unfor- tunately, he set about his work in the spirit of an antiquary, and in the patience, the industry, and the accuracy, required for this branch of knowledge, he was inferior to men who could not compare with him in capacity as a literary critic ', (Courthope, *op. cit.,* i, Pref.).

' Viewed on the whole, the two Wartons may be regarded as the conscious and critical pioneers of the Romantic Movement in English Poetry. . . But neither was possessed of native poetical genius, and the enchanted horn which they had discovered, hung before the Castle of Romance, remained to be sounded by two poets of more powerful inspiration ' (i.e., Collins and Gray, qq.v. ; *ibid.,* vi, 385).

' **Was uns alle bändigt, das Gemeine** ' (Germ.): ' Commonness, our universal bondmaster ' ; from Goethe's (q.v.) memorial verses to Schiller (q.v.) ; the verse supplied a text to M. Arnold (q.v.), writing on the topic of British Philistinism (see s.v.) in pref. to *Essays in Criticism,* i :

' What example could ever so inspire us to keep down the Philistine in ourselves, what teacher could ever so save us from that bondage to which we are all prone, that bondage which Goethe, in those incomparable lines on the death of Schiller, makes it his friend's highest praise (and nobly did Schiller deserve that praise) to have left miles out of sight behind him—the bondage of *was uns alle bändigt, das Gemeine ?* '

Watson, Thomas (*c.* 1557-1592): Engl. scholar ; pronounced by the enthusiastic Meres (q.v.) to be the equal of Petrarch, Theocritus and Virgil, but found in perspective to have been a diligent and keen student of those and other excellent models, and to have made a real contribution to the progress of Engl. studies in his day. W.'s patron in letters was the statesman, sir Francis Walsingham, father- in-law of sir P. Sidney (q.v.), and W.'s works included Lat. versions of the *Antigone* of Sophocles, 1581, and the *Aminta* of Tasso (q.v.), 1585. Wr., too, *Hekatompathia,* or ' The Passionate Centurie of Love ', 1582, con- sisting of ' sonnets ', as he called them, in 18 verses each, founded on Fr. and Ital. models, and affording models to Shakespeare and later sonneteers (see s.v. Sonnet). Transld. Ital. madrigals, etc. ; wr., in Lat. and Engl., an eclogue on Walsingham's death, 1590, and was the ' Amyntas ' of Spenser's (q.v.) *Colin Clout,*

1595, in virtue of his own Lat. pastoral *Amyntæ Gaudia,* 1592.

Watts, Isaac (1674-1748): Engl. hymn-writer. Wr. *Horæ Lyricæ,* 1706 ; *Hymns,* 1707, and similar works, collected in a uniform edn., 1810. W. is the author of about 600 hymns, including, ' God, our help in ages past ', and other famous specimens.

Watts-Dunton (Walter) Theodore (1832-1914): Engl. poet ; novelist ; critic ; associated for many years with the *Athenæum* (q.v.), in which ' a great mass of valuable criticism is still and, it may be feared, will remain, buried ' (*C.H.E.L.,* xiii, 144). Wr. art. on *Poetry* in *Encyclopedia* (q.v.) *Brit.,* and on *The Renascence of Wonder in Poetry*—the phrase has become classical—in Chambers' *Encycl. of Engl. Lit.* Wr. *The Coming of Love and Other Poems,* 1897, and *Aylwin,* a romance, 1899. Late in life, W.-D. made a home in Putney with Swinburne (q.v.), and his *Letters* are of permanent interest.

Webbe, William (16th cent.): Engl. critic. Wr. *Discourse of Engl. Poetrie,* 1586, full of interesting contemporary information ; a friend of Spenser (q.v.).

Webster, John (*c.* 1580-*c.* 1625): Engl. tragic dramatist ; contemporary with Shakespeare (q.v.), and closely associated with that medley of plays and playwrights which is known as the Elizabethan theatre. Individual author- ship is often lost in that medley. The essential thing was to produce a play, suitable to one or other of the companies which were keeping court and town amused, and any writer would patch another's play, adding scenes or lines to suit his purpose, so that a dozen or more authors—Ben Jonson and Marlowe (qq.v.) among them—were all participants in this business of play-production, in which Shake- speare stands out as the supreme master.

In this crowd of playwrights and their plays, W., declares Swinburne (q.v.), ' stands nearer to Shakespeare than any other poet stands to Webster ; and so much nearer as to be a good second. It is only with Shakespeare ', he adds, ' that Webster can ever be compared in any way to his disadvantage as a tragic poet ' ; and, while admitting the primacy of Marlowe as a founder and pioneer, Swinburne holds that W. is superior in his power of construction and his dramatic subtlety of detail. It is not easy to justify all these praises from what is known definitely as W.'s original work. He colla- borated with Dekker (q.v.). in two comedies *Westward Hoe* and *Northward Hoe,* and with others in other plays and masques ; but his independent fame reposes on his tragedies, founded on real events or on tales in the popular Ital. story-repertories : *The White Devil, Appius and Virginia,* and *The Duchess of Malfy,* which all belong to his central period, *c.* 1608-18. The first of these is famous for its trial-scene ; all three for their depth of tragic potency, and a single line in the last, spoken by Ferdinand, brother of the murdered duchess, when he enters after her strangulation, is truly Elizabethan for its much riches in a small room : ' Cover her face ; mine eyes dazzle ; she died young '.

But, undoubtedly, great as these plays are in power and expression and dramatic conception, it is true that as Taine remarks (*Hist. Engl. Lit.*, E.T., ii, 2): ' No one has equalled Webster in creating desperate characters, utter wretches, bitter misanthropes, in blackening and blaspheming human life, above all, in depicting the shameless depravity and refined ferocity of Italian manners'. His thoughts, adds the historian, ' seem incessantly to be haunting tombs and charnel-houses ', a descriptive phrase due to W. himself who makes the duchess of Malfy speak to her murderer of his ' dismal preparation, this talk fit for a charnel '.

W.'s genius was never likely to find imitators or to found a school. He belonged, it is legitimate to say, to the Elizabethan decadence, which was almost contemporaneous with its flowering-time. He possessed intensely the imagination of that age, but he employed it in the study, not in the open air, and thus his love of curious lore acquired more than a tinge of morbidity. A buccaneer crossed with an antiquary and gifted with rare dramatic talent, is, perhaps, a final account of W.

Weckherlin, Georg Rudolf (1584-1653): Anglo-Germ. poet and diplomatist. Born at Stuttgart, m. an Englishwoman, and died in London; appointed, 1644, ' secretary for foreign tongues ' to Parliament, after nearly 20 years' experience as an under-secretary of State ; was succeeded by Milton (q.v.). W. wr. Engl. verse of merit, but his main work in poetry was achieved in his native tongue, which he familiarized, in advance of Opitz (q.v.) with Fr. Renaissance models and metres ; his *Odes and Songs*, 1619, marked a real departure in Germ. poetry, and was associated with the aims of the Heidelberg (q.v.) circle.

Weigel, Valentine (1538-88): Germ. Catholic mystic.

Weise, Christian (1642-1708): Germ. poet, playwright, and novelist ; rector of the gymnasium at Zittau. It is a matter of common consent that W.'s aims were more valuable and progressive than his achievement ; his principles are interesting, but his execution fell short. He wr. upwards of 100 dramas, mostly of the school-play type and standard, but is said to have been so fully aware of the importance of realism in dialogue as to have listened to and reproduced the conversation of washerwomen and others. Wr., too, some satire-romances in the *Simplicissimus* key (see s.v. Grimmelshausen), though a long way below that masterpiece, and lyric verse after Opitz (q.v.) patterns, but marked by true feeling.

Weisse, Christian Felix (1726-1804): Germ. playwright. Friend of Lessing (q.v.) at Leipsic, and exceptional in that circle by the fortune of his long life. It did not follow the dramatic pattern which Lessing would have laid down for it. In the hope of beating the Englishmen (and one Englishman esp.), W. wr. some Shakespearean tragedies, of which the most frequently acted were his *Richard iii* and *Romeo and Julia*. But his tastes governed his abilities, and he made his name by the composition of a class of play which is known in Germany as ' Singspiel ', a kind of musical comedy or light opera, derived from Gottssched's (q.v.) pattern of the pastoral, and so

claiming a long descent, but introducing rococo to the Germ. stage. W. delighted several generations of children by his sprightly periodical, the *Kinderfreund*.

Welhaven, Johan Sebastian Cammermeyer (1807--73): Norw. poet ; critic. wr., 1834, a sonnet-sequence, *Norges Daemring* (' Norway's Twilight '), which was an eloquent and noble plea for sane and reasonable patriotism, as the sure foundation of national art and morals. It was a plea *con* as well as *pro* ; the object which W. attacked was the noisy demonstrative nationalism of the *Sittendemai* (q.v.) variety, associated, as that name shows, with the ' 17th May ' anniversary of the declaration of the Independence of Norway from Denmark, 1814. Twenty years had cooled the ardour and tempered the spirit of those frenzies. Their chief representative in W.'s day was his contemporary, Wergeland (q.v.), whom he survived and surpassed. For he was critic and scholar as well as poet, and succeeding in establishing at Christiania standards of taste and principles of learning, which compensated for the loss occasioned by the national breach with Copenhagen and its traditions.

Wellekens, Jan Battista (1658-1724): Dutch painter and poet. Transld. Tasso's *Aminta*, 1715, and tried to anticipate the era of piscatorial art connected, e.g., with Josef Israëls.

Wells, Charles Jeremiah (1800-79): Engl. poet ; wr. *Stories after Nature*, 1822, reminiscent of Boccaccio (q.v.), and *Joseph and his Brethren*, 1824, a drama, issued under a pseudonym, which achieved no success. Many years later, Rossetti and Swinburne, qq.v., induced W. to reissue it, 1876, and it has justified its resurrection. W. enjoyed for a few years the friendship of Keats (q.v.).

Wergeland, Henrik Arnold Thaulov (1808-45): Norw. poet, patriot ; for some years the central figure of the so-called ' 17th of May ' (s.v. *Sittendemai*) frenzy in Christiania, associated with the anniversary of the declaration of the independence of Norway, 1814. W.'s early farces led the young nationalists to hail him as a Holberg (q.v.) free of Dan. taint ; but he wisely directed his talent to happy, popular airs and verses which took his countrymen's ears and hearts by storm. But as 1814 receded on the horizon, a critical reaction set in, and Welhaven (q.v.), in his ' Norway's Twilight ' (*Norges Daemring*) appealed for moderation both in literary and political transports. It must be added that W.'s ambitious drama on *Creation, Man and the Messiah*, 1830, made him an easy prey to censure. Norse letters at this period were in flux, or, more exactly, were winning their release from the year-long tyranny of Copenhagen, and W. profited by advice. Before the date of his early death, he had regained his hold on public taste, though the first raptures were never repeated. Such pieces, however, as his *Jan van Huysums Blomerstykke* (flower-piece), in which he unfolded the flowers in the painter's picture to all kinds of symbolical meanings, and moved still life with human passion, have real and permanent value ; and a word is due to the efforts of the patriot-poet and liberator to plead the cause of Jews in Norway, in two idyls (*Jew, Jewess*), 1842, 1844. His last and in some respects his greatest poem was *den engelske Lods* ('the English Pilot'), 1846.

Werner, Friedrich Leopold Zacharias (1768-1823): Germ. dramatist; the one considerable representative of drama among the Romanticists, whose lyrical and introspective mood was opposed inherently to such form of expression. W.'s Romantic tendency was temperamental; and it is not unfair to the school which fathered Fr. Schlegel's (q.v.) *Lucinde* and Schleiermacher's (q.v.) condonation of it to include in the evidence of W.'s tendency his wild and dissolute habits of life. These have otherwise no interest for lit., but it was characteristic of the Romantic movement again (see s.v. Romance) that W. should have sought and found peace after storm in the bosom of the Roman Catholic church. He became a priest and a popular preacher: the rake turned monk, with a streak of insanity in both. W.'s dramatic model was Schiller (q.v.), but his ineradicable mysticism and symbolism recall the style of Tieck (q.v.). His first play was *The Sons of the Valley*, in 2 parts, each 4 acts long, treating of the fall of the knights-Templar; he scored a more popular success by his *Martin Luther, or The Sanction of Force*, 1807, and a more academic success by his romantic tragedy *Wanda*, which Goethe (q.v.) produced at Weimar. This was followed by an *Attila*, 1809, and in the next year occurred W.'s conversion and a long visit to Rome. In 1814, he publicly recanted in a half-allegory, half-drama, entitled *The Sanction of Un-force*, in repudiation of his *Martin Luther*, and he wr., too, a *Holy Kunegunde* and a *Mother of the Maccabees*. Perhaps his best piece of all was a one-act so-called 'fate-drama' (q.v.), entitled *February 24th*, which opened a series of such spell- or fate-plays on the Germ. stage.

Wernher der Gärtner (13th cent.): Germ. poet; indicates the transition of the courtly romance to the realistic art-poetry of the town-guilds. Wr. *Meier Helmbrecht*, a Germ. tale of village life, and the first of its kind (c. 1240); the peasant aspires to be a knight, and the impoverished knight has become a robber. In this picture of social conditions, W. was faithful to the times in which he lived, and to the state of Upper Bavaria in his day; and his verse-tale is remarkable in its age for its rejection of the romantic lore of Arthur and the grail in favour of a simple, moving story reflected from actual life.

Wernicke, Christian (1665-1715): Germ. (East-Prussian) epigrammatist; Dan. minister in Paris, where he learned useful lessons of literary art and criticism. These he turned to good account by his attacks (chiefly in notes appended to his bks. of epigrams) on the so-called Second Silesian School (q.v.) of poetasters who were grouped round Hoffmannswaldau (q.v.) at Hamburg, and were writing opera *libretti*, etc. The storm which W. was mainly instrumental in rousing cleared the air of many affectations, and helped to open a new era of Germ. lit.

Wesley, -i. Samuel (1662-1735): Engl. poet; divine.

-ii. Samuel (1691-1739): Engl. poet; schoolmaster; eldest son of above.

-iii. John (1703-91): Engl. hymn-writer; brother of above; soon after 1738, 'began his wonderful journeys, which lasted almost to his death. During the half-century, he preached forty thousand sermons, and travelled (it is said) a quarter of a million miles' (*C.H.E.L.*, x, 364). Publd. 23 collections of hymns during the same period, and left *Journal* of hist. interest and literary value.

-iv. Charles (1707-88): Engl. hymn-writer; brother of above, whom he 'equalled in devotion, if not in tireless health' (*ibid.*); settled at Bristol, 1739-56; composed several thousand hymns, of which 500 are still in use. Two sons of C.W. were well-known musicians.

Of the Dissent (methodist) founded by the brothers Wesley and their younger contemporary at Oxford, George Whitefield (1714-70), this is not the place to speak, save to observe, under the safe conduct of the Cambridge historian cited above, that 'the new influence which passed over Engl. religion had its effect, gradual and much contested, upon English literature also. The age of Wesley and Whitefield introduced what may be called a new romanticism in religion, just as the Lake School, half a century later, may be said to have destroyed the classic tradition of the older poetry'. MM. Légouis et Cazamian (*Hist. Lit. angl.*) write on this point (pp. 893-5): 'A more open disposition towards the poetry of the heart, a more spontaneous faculty for vision and emotion under the laws of mystical imagination, a rekindling of thought and of the psychological being as a whole, were requisite before Wordsworth and Coleridge (qq.v.) could write, and win acceptance. What measure of idealistic warmth is found in romanticism borrowed something from the new heightening of the religious mood. Thus, the action of Methodism was comparable to that of Christian Socialism in the nineteenth century (see s.v. C. Kingsley), and it was partly due to that cause that the French Revolution did not catch on in England'.

Wessel, Johannes Hermann (1742-85): Dan. playwright; born, like Holberg (q.v.) in Norway, but counted Dane in literary history, since the political severance of Norway did not occur till 1814; with Holberg, too, and Ewald (q.v.), W. is one of the fathers of the Royal Theatre in Copenhagen. W.'s greatest triumph was 'to kill the French classical drama in Denmark by a single happy stroke of ridicule' (Millar, *P.E.L.*, ix, 350). The story is best told by sir E. Gosse, *Lit. of Northern Europe*, 145 foll. and it bears re-telling. Shortly after the foundation of the Royal Theatre in Copenhagen (1748) Dan. lit. was tending to transfer its imitative allegiance from the high and mighty line of Klopstock (q.v.) to the 'stilted and beperiwigged chivalry' of Voltaire's (q.v.) heroic alexandrines. It was a taste peculiarly unsuitable to the homely burgesses of Copenhagen, who vexed their theatrical intelligences with the romantic complexities of such topics as *Love without Hope, Love without*

Reward, Love without Fortune, etc. Through all these mock-heroic vapourings, W., in 1772, drove the clean sword of satire by his drama, *Love without Stockings*; and '*Zaire and Zarine* and all the other fantastic absurdities', writes Gosse, ' faded away in a roar of universal laughter'. W. added little of note in the remaining years of his short life to this brilliant burlesque-tragedy, which relieved the national theatre of Denmark from an insupportable burden of Gallicism.

Westerbaen, Jacob (1599-1670): Dutch poet. His poetry, collected in 1657 in 5 vols. of *Love-Poems, Heroic Poems, Miscellany, Ockenburg* (where he lived) and *Farrago Latina*, is of second rank throughout; and W.'s fame was undoubtedly increased by his fortunate marriage with the widow of Barneveldt, of unhappy fate, whose judicial murder in 1619 had so profoundly stirred public opinion. She was 11 years older than he, and belonged to the nobility of the Netherlands, whereas W. was the son of a rope-maker. His wife died in 1648.

White, Gilbert (1720-93): Engl. naturalist; born and died at Selborne, in Hants, and is known as White of Selborne by as clear a territorial title as any enjoyed by a landowner. The title is derived from W.'s *Natural History and Antiquities of Selborne*, written in letters, 1769-87, and publd. by his brother, Benjamin W. (1725-94), 1789. This famous and justly esteemed work has attracted more and more attention since the standard edn. was issued, 2 vols., 1877, by Thos. Bell (1792-1880), sometime secretary of the Royal Society and president of the Linnean Society.

White, Henry Kirke (1785-1806): Engl. poet; son of a Nottingham tradesman. The promise of his early verse was brought to the notice of Southey (q.v.), and a fund was raised to send him to Cambridge, where he died of overwork. His *Christiad*, a fragment, is the best-known of his posth. *Remains*, 1807.

White, Joseph (Maria) Blanco (1775-1841): Span. theologian; poet; Irish by descent on his father's side; Engl. by residence and adoption. W. was edu. at the univ. at Seville, and entered into holy orders in the Catholic church, but quitted Spain, the priesthood, and, temporarily, Christianity, 1810, when he migrated to London. There he was received by leaders of society such as lord and lady Holland and sir Humphry Davy, and edited, 1810-14, *el Español*; for which service to the Engl. cause in Spain he was rewarded with a civil pension. In 1814, W. removed to Oxford, and signed the 39 Articles; in 1815, he was in residence at Holland House, in a tutorial capacity, and began to write for Campbell's *New Monthly Magazine*. W. collected these contributions, 1822, as *Letters of Leucadio Doblado*, and was busy for some time with pamphleteering, transln. (Paley's, q.v., *Evidences*), etc. Later, 1826, W. returned to Oxford, received the signal distinction of hon. M.A., and a fellowship at Oriel Coll., where he joined the little group of intellectuals known as the Noetics (see s.v. Oxford Movement), His friends at this period included Whateley (to whose son he afterwards became tutor at Dublin), J. S. Mill, Newman (qq.v.), and others, and it

was probably the happiest time of his ' long remonstrant struggling life ' (Tuckwell, *Pre-Tractarian Oxford*, 257). W.'s deep emotions found poetic expression at times, and his sonnet *Night and Death*, 1828 (the closing line is : ' If Light can thus deceive, wherefore not Life ? '), was lavishly, even extravagantly, praised by S. T. Coleridge and Leigh Hunt (qq.v.). W.'s was a mobile and attractive personality, and ' his progress from the Roman to the Anglican, and from the Anglican to the Unitarian fold ; his letters, pamphlets, and articles on Spain, which despite his Irish blood was in effect his mother-country ; and his later ties with the Tractarians, form a singular Odyssey ' (Elton, *Survey of Engl. Lit.*, 1780-1830, ii, 267).

White, William Hale (1831-1913): Engl. novelist ; philosopher. Transld. the *Ethics* of Spinoza (q.v.), 1883, with an elaborate pref., and parallel passages adduced from Bruno (q.v.) : altogether, a valuable work ; wr., too, an essay, unfind., on *The Amendment of the Understanding*. It is, however, not as Hale White, the philosopher, but as Mark Rutherford, the novelist, that W., in his long life, won more permanent renown ; and the distinction between the two was kept as clear as that between C. L. Dodgson and Lewis Carroll (q.v.). Mark Rutherford, then, White's other self, wr. a series of novels, which are gradually winning their way to the appreciation of discriminating judges. They include : *The Autobiography of Mark Rutherford*, 1885 ; *Mark Rutherford's Deliverance*, 1886 ; *The Revolution in Tanner's Lane*, 1887 ; *Miriam's Schooling*, 1890 ; *Catherine Furze*, 1893 ; *Clara Hopgood*, 1896. Some of these deal, it will be seen, with the same personages, and all of them deal with life in the same key,—the subdued, stoical key of middle-class, middling-thoughtful, Engl. petty provincial society. It is not an inspiriting note : the selected stratum was too sober and austere for exaltation ; and W. was scrupulously exact in not exceeding its emotional content. But it provided the student of Spinoza and Wordsworth (for W. publd. one or two essays on Wordsworth's, q.v., text and mind) with a fund of aphorisms, and good counsel, and exquisitely economical observation. W., as a novelist, has been compared to his advantage with George Eliot (q.v.): he possessed an equal power of delineation, but avoided, as greater masters do not always avoid, excessive sentiment and moralizing.

Whitehead, William (1715-85): Engl. poet ; wr. tragedy, *The Roman Father*, 1750, *Creusa, Queen of Athens*, 1754, and a comedy, *The School for Lovers*, 1762. W.'s appointment, 1757, to the office of Poet Laureate (q.v.), declined by T. Gray (q.v.), was a topic for satire by C. Churchill (q.v.) and others, but he rendered it notable by some genuinely patriotic verse.

Wickram, Georg (16th cent.): Germ. miscellanist. Wr. *Rollwagenbüchlein*, 1555, *lit.* ' Wheel-carriage-booklet ', a curious 16th cent. example of the railway-literature so common to-day ; also wr. vernacular prose-redactions of some of the romance-cycle stories, e.g., *The Gold-thread*, and *The Mirror of Young Boys*, which combined a courtly origin with a popular appeal.

Wiclif, John (*c.* 1320-84): Northern Engl. theologian, reformer and controversialist. Like R. Rolle (q.v.), a Yorkshireman and Oxonian, but in complete contrast with the slightly older writer's mystic temperament. W. was master of Balliol, when ' from all parts of England, and from foreign countries too, youths were flocking to Oxford, where a new intellectual world opened itself to them ' (*C.H.E.L.*, ii, 50); later, vicar of Fillingham and rector of Lutterworth (*c.* 1374), where he died and was buried, though his remains were disinterred, 1428, and thrown into the river Swift. With the controversies, in which public opinion was largely on W.'s side, and with the heresies, e.g. on transubstantiation, on which not even his powerful patron, John of Gaunt, would support or protect him, and which explain the animus displayed even after 100 years, we are not here concerned. W. was a great philosopher, a great public man, and likewise a great popularizer of knowledge, in which connection we are reminded (*C.H.E.L.*, *ibid.*) that ' no place was more democratic than a medieval university : thither all classes came, and the ideas which were born in a lecture-room soon passed to the distant villages of the north. When Wiclif threw himself upon a wider public than that of the university, he was, after all, only carrying a little further that desire to popularize knowledge by thought which was common to all medieval teachers ',—particularly, we may add, since he chose with deliberate significance to write in Engl. as well as Lat. ' In abuse of his opponents ', we read, ' he maintains the sturdy tradition of controversy that still survives in Milton's prose. The style is rugged and vigorous ; the thought logical and packed close. . . . Wiclif, almost alone in his generation, had the reasoning power to go to the root of the matter, and the moral courage not only to state fearlessly what, rightly or wrongly, he found to be the source of evil, but to insist on basic reform '. In this connection, it should be recalled that W. has been described, in virtue of his treatise *de officio Regis*, as ' more modern than Luther and a deeper thinker '.

But a reformer of ecclesiastical and social abuses in the 14th cent. (and even in later cents.) had a difficult row to hoe, and W. did not escape trial and forfeiture. The Peasants' Revolt was an awkward commentary on his opinions, and the ' poor priests ' who walked in his ways and followed his teachings were quickly merged in the sect of the Lollards (street-preachers, street-corner idlers or lollers ; cf. Germ. *lollen*. The derivation from *lollium*, tares, is fanciful), who flourished continuously, till they, too, were merged in the Reformers of the 16th cent., though an Act *de haeretico comburendo*, enjoining burning them, was passed as early as 1401.

We turn from these activities of the *doctor evangelicus*, and from the learned writings which accompanied them, to W.'s vernacular transln. of the Bible (see s.v.), his chief part in which was vouched for by John Hus, the Bohemian reformer (executed 1416) and by the archbishop of Canterbury, 1412, in a letter to the pope. The evidence to his inspiration of the whole undertaking is practically overwhelming ; and, though the brothers, Nicholas and John Purvey, are named as his collaborators, W. was ' the originator, and in part the author, of the first complete Bible in the English language ' (*P.E.L.*, iii, 412), — veritably, a great achievement by the leading reformer before the Reformation (q.v.). W.'s name is also spelt Wyclif, Wycliffe.

Wieland, Christoph Martin (1733-1813) : Germ. poet, translr., and romancer. If the Gk. quality of *eutrapelia*—flexibility, accessibility, impressionableness—is as praiseworthy as M. Arnold (q.v.) would have us believe, then W.'s value is as high as the task of placing him is difficult. In an age addicted to schools of taste, W. attached himself to no master. He was brought up in a God-fearing home, and was entertained, 1752, at Zurich by Bodmer (q.v.), who believed that he had found in the youthful pietist the future wearer of the mantle of Klopstock (q.v.). Twenty years later, in 1772, when Klopstock's veritable disciples had founded their union of the Hain (q.v.), they celebrated the event by burning Wieland's portrait and his works : ' some one cried, " Wieland ", ' wr. Voss (q.v.), ' and we drained our glasses to the toast, Perish the corrupter of morals '. Yet another 8 years, and Goethe (q.v.) was writing to Lavater (q.v.) : ' As long as poetry is poetry, gold gold, and crystal crystal, Wieland's *Oberon* will be beloved and admired as a masterpiece of poetic art '. The blame and the praise alike strike us as excessive to-day. W.'s service to Germ. lit. consists in this very pliability to impressions by which he alienated the extremists. It was not as a challenge to the high and mighty line of Klopstock's *Messias* that W. flirted with the graces of irony, elegance, and levity ; nor was it as a professed romanticist that he turned from divine to human love. He happened to read and to admire certain bks. and writers successively at different times in his life, and his happy gift of assimilation lent varying expression to the talents which he ceaselessly exercised. As a young man, he wr. an *anti-Ovid*, 1752, a Biblical play, and a work on Christian sensibility, in which he exalted the poorest hymn-tune above the most charming fancy of an Anacreonticist (s.v. Anakreontiker). When he moved to Biberach from Zurich, he traversed Horace's travel-maxim, and changed both his mind and his sky. In the library of a worldly count von Stadion, W. browsed on the Illuminist lit. of Engl. deists and Fr. encyclopedists, and discovered that Shaftesbury and Rousseau (qq.v.) were at least as readable as Klopstock. He read Cervantes (q.v.), and straightway wr., 1764, *The Victory of Nature over Enthusiasm (Schwärmerei), or The Adventures of Don Sylvio von Rosalva*, in which the hero was cured by an experience of quixotic disillusion of seeing a naiad in every bush and a dryad in every pond. The romance had an immediate success, and was transld. into Fr., 1769, and again, 1771, under the title of *Don Quichotte Moderne*. An anon. Engl. version was issued in 1773, entitled *Reason Triumphant over Fancy*; *exemplified in the Singular Adventures of Don Sylvio de Rosalva. A History in which every Marvellous Event occurs Naturally. Don Sylvio* was followed by *Agathon*, 1766-67, a Gallic romance with a Gk. background, in which the moralizing of Richardson (q.v.) and the cynical hedonism of Voltaire (q.v., esp. *Candide*, 1759) were combined to overthrow the simple pieties of the soulful hero; under the Hellenic dress of Agathon, the Platonist, Hippias, the sophist, and the seductive Danae (sketched from the typical court-mistress of the 18th cent.), the everlasting forces which mould character were thinly disguised; and thus, though the Gk. interest of the second romance is as tepid as the Span. interest of of the first, W. certainly founded the psychological novel in Germany. Through these years W. was composing a quantity of light stories and airy verse, among which may be selected for mention *Idris*, an Ariosto-like love-fantasy, which was the piece selected for the pyre by Voss (q.v., and see above), *The New Amadis*, and *Musarion, or The Philosophy of the Graces*, a poem in praise of Epicureanism. Further, by his transln. of 11 of Shakespeare's plays into prose, and of *Midsummer Night's Dream* into the metres of the original, W. conferred an immense benefit on Germ. letters.

Meanwhile, in 1769, W. ceased residence at Biberach to become prof. of philosophy at Erfurt univ., and his immersion in more serious studies wrought another change in his writings. The first result was a politico-didactic romance, *The Golden Mirror, or The Kings of Scheschian*, in which theories of reform were imbedded in oriental fiction, and this led to an invitation from the widowed duchess of Saxe-Weimar for W. to become tutor to her sons. At Weimar (q.v.), accordingly, where all the great men of letters were gravitating, W. spent the second half of his long life, 1772-1813. There he edited the *Deutsche Mercur*, 1773-89, which had as model the *Mercure de France*, and in which he publd. most of his literary work, including *The Abderites*, a satirical romance, exposing the stupidities of Germ. provincial life under the guise of ancient Abdera. The only remaining work of note which posterity cares to remember is the verse-romance, *Oberon*, 1780, which retold the old tale of Huon (q.v.) of Bordeaux with reminiscences of the *Midsummer Night's Dream*, in the poetry of which, as we have seen, W. was saturated. 'Once more, saddle me, Muses, the hippogriff, for a ride to old realms of romance ',—it starts, and we are off on the wings of fantasy to the enchanted country of the elf-king, of Titania, of the caliph: if we do not echo Goethe's eulogy to-day, at least we recognize that W. saved Germany from the worse effects of that outburst of pious senti-mentalism in which the worshippers of Klop-stock would have stifled the 'airy fairy' voices to which his ears were sealed. W. tempered soulfulness by worldliness, and peopled the Teuton forest with new graces. In one of his latest works W. wr.: 'What need we fear from light ? What can we hope from darkness ? If diseased eyes are not able to bear the light, we must try to heal them ;'

and this fearless love of the light became the passionate cry of liberal-hearted Germany.

Wiele, van der, Johannes Stalpert (1579-1630): Dutch poet and divine. Wr. sacred verse on the saints and martyrs of the Catholic church, and a ' Treasury of Sacred Song for the Festivals of the Holy Year ' (a kind of *Christian Year* before Keble, q.v., for Roman Catholics), which has enjoyed a permanent vogue, in whole or in selections, for the sake of its simple piety and popular tunes.

Wilberforce, William (1759-1833): Engl. phil-anthropist; theologian; helped to found Bible Society, 1803; wr., 1797, *A Practical View of the Prevailing Religious System of Professed Christians in the Higher and Middle Classes in this Country contrasted with the Real Christianity*, the pragmatic portion of which dealt with ' the present state of Christianity in this country, and its importance to us as a political community '. For W. was a busy M.P., and leader of the Abolitionists (see, too, s.v. Clapham Sect, and cf. *Wilber-force*, by R. Coupland, Oxford, 1923; a very brilliant biography). W.'s bk. had a great success, 7,500 copies being sold between April and August, 1797, and it was transld. into Fr., Germ., Ital., Span. and Dutch. W.'s son, **Samuel W.** (1805-73) was bp. of Oxford, 1845-69, and took a prominent part in opposing *Essays and Reviews*, 1860 (see s.v. B. Jowett).

Wilde, Oscar O'F. W. (1856-1900): Engl. (Irish) poet; dramatist; wit; a founder, in a lighter variety, of the cult of beauty which Pater (q.v.) represented in its more serious aspect of æsthetic philosophy; lectured on his cult under that name in U.S.A., 1882, and was caricatured for its excesses in the lighter vein by sir W. Gilbert (q.v.) in *Patience*, 1884. Wr. *Poems*, 1881, characterized by heavy perfumes of literary ornamentation, but displaying considerable skill and emotional quality; drawing-room dramas, brilliant but fatiguing in their cleverness and smartness of dialogue, and occasionally original in situa-tion: *Lady Windermere's Fan*, 1892; *A Woman of No Importance*, 1893; *The Impor-tance of being Earnest* 1895; *Salomé*, Paris, 1893; transld. from the Fr., 1894. W. was imprisoned, 1895-7, for an offence under the Criminal Law Amendment Act, and wr. *De Profundis*, publd., 1905 (MS. deposited at British Museum, not to be inspected before 1960), and *The Ballad of Reading Gaol*, 1898: ' the product of his tragic overthrow, and well worth all that he had previously written ' (*C.H.E.L.*, xiv, 159).

Willem (13th cent.): Dutch fabulist. Wr. *Roman van den vos Reinaerde*, a romance of Reynard the fox, which marks an important step in the redaction of the ancient bestiary (q.v.) from its orig. in India, through Æsop and his Fr. adapters, to Caxton, La Fontaine (qq.v.) and modern times. (See also s.vv. Fable, Reynard). Little is known of W., though he tells us that he made many bks. (' viele bouke maecte '), except that he was born in Flanders, probably between Ghent and Antwerp, where he is most familiar with the place-names. The date of his romance is generally agreed at 1250; at least, it has the authority of J. Grimm (q.v.), against alternative conjectures ranging back to 1170. A Lat. transln. of the *Roman* was effected about 1275, and served to popularize it more widely. A *Reinhaert ii*, expanded from W.'s poem, appeared in Dutch, 1375, and a prose version in the following cent. originated the Dutch folk-book, *Reinke de Vos*, whence came the Germ. *Reineke Fuchs*, which was honoured later by Goethe (q.v.), 1792.

William ix (1076-1127): Count of Poitiers and duke of Aquitaine ; one of the earliest of Fr. Troubadours (q.v.). Wr. poems in various keys, esp. a moving lament at leaving his child and country on his departure to the Holy Land.

William of Malmesbury (*c.* 1090-*c.* 1142): Anglo-Norman historiographer. Wr. Lat. *de gestis regum Anglorum* and other works, in a style which dated W.'s departure from the method of the chroniclers in the direction of a more systematic arrangement and a more literary form. W. included the legendary history of king Arthur (q.v.) in his tales of the *gesta* of England's kings.

Wilson, John (1785-1854): Scot. essayist. Wr., under the *nom-de-guerre* of Christopher North, *Noctes Ambrosianæ* in *Blackwood's Magazine*, 1822-35, James Hogg (q.v.) figuring as the Ettrick Shepherd of that once very popular *pot pourri* of criticism, philosophy, current topics, etc. There was an exuberance about W., derived from his high animal spirits and athletic prowess, which carried him successfully over places of very uneven judgment ; and the same qualities served him in good stead as prof. of Moral Philosophy at Edinburgh univ.

Wimpheling, Jacob (1450-1528): Germ. scholar ; educationist. Founded school of new learning at his birthplace, Schlettstadt in Alsace, repeating in the south the work of Hegius and Langen (qq.v.) in north Germany. Wr., 1497, *Guide for the German Youth*, and 1500, *Adolescentia*, a landmark in the history of educational theory ; both in Lat. His works enjoyed very wide circulation, and W. takes a high place in the ranks of Germ. humanists at the brief period before their bifurcation by the Reformation ; he was really the leader of the elder party, and not less truly a patriot and a man of culture because he disliked the tone of the younger humanists at Erfurt univ.; thus 'more akin to Reuchlin, who was his pupil, than to Hutten on the one part or Luther on the other. (See s.vv.). W. is also memorable as writer of a play, *Stylpho*, 1470, produced at Heidelberg, in the first dawn of the Lat. Christian 'comic' drama ; and he wr. a vol., *Germania*, on the early history of his country.

Winckelmann, Johann Joachim (1717-68): Germ. Hellenist. 'Severely limiting himself to the study of Greek culture and antiquities, he drew from his own intellectual interest a fulness of passionate life which Rousseau and Goethe alone among the writers of their century can be said to have approached' (Vaughan, *P.E.L.*, x, 195). It is clear from this estimate, which is a commonplace of literary histories ('he has been well compared with old navigators who discovered unknown continents', J. G. Robertson, *Hist. Germ. Lit.*, 275), that the value of W.'s work lies in its influence on his age as much as, if not more than, in its intrinsic merit. W. was the son of a shoemaker, and every step in his progress in knowledge was marked by an effort of self-sacrifice. He had a year's study under Damm (q.v.) at Berlin, and contrived to continue his education at Halle, Jena, Dresden, and in Italy (after he had joined the church of Rome). It was on his return from that pilgrimage of culture, which he undertook like an old scholar of the Renaissance, but with a difference, to which we shall return, that W. was brutally assassinated at Trieste by an Ital. thief to whom he had displayed some gold medals. The difference, was, that the Germ. scholars of the 15th cent. (Reuchlin, for instance, q.v.) went to Italy to sit at the feet of foreign humanists, who should instruct them in Lat. and Gk. letters ; W., first among new humanists, went to seek the origins of art in the monuments of Rome and Greece. Not the style of Cicero and Virgil, but the hidden causes of that style in the Gk. sense of proportion and the Gk. instinct of design, were the secrets which W. went to wrest from marble, and coin, and gem. No Gk. exile from the East, such as Reuchlin's tutor, Argyropoulos (q.v.), could teach W. these aspects of humanism (q.v.), or speed Greece again across the Alps. The lessons were more patiently acquired by foot-rule, compass, and spade ; and, when acquired, they were applied to a revelation of art as a factor in civilization. W.'s 3 important bks. were *Thoughts on the Imitation of Gk. Works in Painting and Statuary*, 1755 ; *History of the Art of Antiquity*, 1764 ; and *Monumenta Antichi Inediti*, 2 vols., 1767-68. In the first bk. occurs the dictum : 'The common mark of excellence of Greek masterpieces is a noble simplicity and a calm grandeur' (*eine edle Einfalt und eine grosse Stille*), words which helped to alter the mind of Europe ; for 'a transformation in our attitude towards life, and in our general view of the world', wr. another Germ. critic (Paulsen, *Kant*, E.T., 17), 'always shows itself first in the æsthetic field'. W.'s dictum, taken up by Lessing (q.v.) in his unfind. treatise on the Laocoon (q.v.) -group, and correlated with the kindred speculations of Herder (q.v.) in the moral sphere, brought into the attenuated classicism of the day a genuine and a vital energy, and corrected by the same token of ordered purpose the exuberance of the romantic revolt (s.v. Sturm und Drang). The triumph of the new romantic movement (s.v. Romance), esp., in Germany and Engld., owed as much as it owned, and even more than it knew, to the antiquarian enthusiasm of the poor shoemaker's murdered son. When Wordsworth (q.v.) wr. in 1814, 'the Gods approve the depth, and not the tumult, of the soul' ; when Keats (q.v.) wr. in 1819 his *Ode on a Grecian Urn*, these poets were indebted to W. for the perception, new in his day, but sanctioned since its early close by authorities in wider fields than he could cultivate, that Romance may teach Hellenism a strange beauty, and Hellenism teach Romance a difficult truth. (See s.v. Hellenism ; Winckelmann 'is the last fruit of the Renaissance, and explains in a striking way its motive and tendencies'. Pater, *Renaissance*, xvi). W. has not been without honour. His birthday, 9 Dec., has frequently been the occasion for the publication of papers on subjects akin to those which occupied his genius in his lifetime, in Rome, Berlin, and other cities; Goethe, F. A. Wolf, Heyne and Herder (s.vv.) being among fellow-countrymen who have commemorated him in the past.

Winther, Christian (1796-1876): Dan. poet. W. is to be characterized as the first of a new line of Dan. poets, rather than as the last of the line of which Oehlenschläger was the first. The novelty of W.'s lyrical genius consisted in his power of bringing out the inner heart of song from the simplest and most commonplace themes. He made poetic the life of peasants: more poetic, perhaps, than it really was; yet not more poetic than it appeared to an idealist. And so W. came nearer a core of truth, Wordsworthian in its natural magic, than any other romantic disciple of the Germ. school of Dan. poetry had attained. In this instance it is most emphatically to be regretted that the Dan. language is so little known outside of Denmark.

Wiseman, Nicholas Patrick Stephen (1802-65): Card. archbishop of Westminster, 1850; born in Seville; exercised an influence on the development of the Oxford Movement (q.v.); a founder of the *Dublin Review*; wr. *High Church Claims*, 1841; *Fabiola, or The Church of the Catacombs*, a tale of the 3rd cent., 1854; and was well-known as a lecturer on art and lit. W. is said to be represented in R. Browning's (q.v.) poem, *Bishop Blougram's Apology*.

Wolcot, John (1738-1819): Engl. satirist; wr. under *nom-de-guerre* of Peter Pindar, but the *guerre* was always a guerrilla, of the *Rolliad* (q.v.) and minor kinds of political and literary pasquinade. 'The great fair of literature is incomplete without its merry andrews and street performers; and of these, in the time we are reviewing, Peter Pindar is the most amusing and vociferous, and when we wish for the relief of being vulgar we can listen to him' (Elton, *Survey Engl. Lit.*: 1780-1830, i, 33). The vulgar relief is not sought to-day, or is found in contemporary vulgarians, though its vogue at the end of the 18th cent. is, so far, the last echo of the Renaissance type of ink-slinging and slanging. W. Gifford (q.v.) replied to Wolcot in a like *Epistle*, 1800. W., whose works extend to 5 vols., had a fertile facility in many kinds, but a command of none: he claimed for himself

A desultory way of writing,
A hop and step and jump mode of inditing
My great and wise relation Pindar boasted.

Wolf, Friedrich August (1759-1824): Germ. scholar; edu. at Nordhausen under Fabricius (q.v.) and at univ. of Göttingen, where on 8 April, 1777, he entered his name for matriculation as *studiosus Philologiæ*. There was then no faculty of philology at Göttengen (nor, indeed, at any Germ. univ., though some isolated students of that faculty are reported at an earlier date from Erlangen); but W. carried his point, against the somewhat indifferent contempt of the rector of the univ., Heyne

(q.v.). In 1784, he was appointed prof. of philosophy and pedagogy at Halle, where (and whence, by Halle's influence) he helped to refound humanistic studies. Goethe (q.v.) attended some of his lectures, unknown to W., and bears testimony to their exceptional stimulation. W.'s bks. are of the best educational kind, which arise out of teaching, and include many brilliant edns. of Gk. and Lat. authors, as well as the world-famous *Prolegomena to Homer*, 1795. The story of this great work belongs primarily to scholarship, and to the history of Homeric study in modern Europe from Boccaccio downwards (see s.v. Homer); it was a work of supreme importance, contemporary with the transln. of Homer by Voss (q.v.), with his illustration by Flaxman, and with the *ed. pr.* of the *Scholia* by Villoison (q.v.), whose labours had facilitated W.'s. After the Fr. occupation of Halle, 1806, W. retired to Berlin. 'His greatest work', says sir J. Sandys (*Hist. Class. Schol.*, iii, 60), 'is to be found, not in the books that he produced but in the pupils that he stimulated to be the future leaders of classical learning in Germany during the first half of the nineteenth century'; and Sandys calls him 'the eponymous hero of all the long line of later scholars'.

Wolf, Hieronymus (1516-80): Germ. scholar and schoolmaster. Pupil of Melanchthon (q.v.); headmaster of Augsburg school, 1557-80; edited Demosthenes and other Gk. writers.

Wolfe, Charles (1791-1823): Engl. poet; wr. *The Burial of Sir John Moore* (at Corunna), 1817, 'one of those "windfalls of the muses"', for which one can only give the muses thanks' (*C.H.E.L.*, xii, 138). The authorship, which has been disputed, is indubitable, but the poem is unique in W.'s poetic achievement. It was originally a metrical paraphrase of the prose account of the episode in Southey's (q.v.) *Annual Register*, and it has lent itself to parody, esp. by Barham (q.v.). But it is a fine, stirring poem, which posterity does not let die.

Wolff, Elizabeth (Betje) (1738-1804): Dutch novelist and poet; *née* Bekker. (See also s.v. A. Deken). Betje Bekker was the youngest of 7 children, and lost her mother very early in her life. The loss was deeply felt, and doubtless partly accounts for her one-day elopement at the age of 17, an indiscretion cruelly misrepresented by her eldest brother, Laurence, and powerfully affecting all her outlook on life. In 1759 she was married to 'dominie' Adrian Wolff, a preacher, with whom she had corresponded on philology and poetry; her husband was 30 years older than she, and while there was great intellectual sympathy between them there was no real love; and Betje was thrown back more and more on the consolations of her wide and deep learning, and on the friendships which she enjoyed. The most intimate of these was contracted in 1776, a year before her husband's death, with Agatha Deken (q.v.), and it lasted till the end of her life. In her last poem *To a Friend* she expressed her tender desire to die before Agatha, and in fact predeceased her by a few weeks. After Wolff's death, the two women set up house together at Rijp, and commenced the literary collaboration which added so considerably to the fame of Dutch letters. Later, they settled at Trévoux, in France, in consequence of political disturbances, and followed with the utmost interest the course of revolution in that country. They had left their joint fortune in the care of a friend who went bankrupt, and in 1798 they returned to comparative poverty at the The Hague. Their first work in collaboration was called *Letters on Various Topics*, 1780; next came, 1781, *Economic Songs*; and, in 1782, their successful and really great novel, *Sara Burgerhart*. It was reprinted 1783, 1786, 1836 (twice), 1858, 1879, 1886, and 1891; transld. into Fr., by mme. de Charrière (q.v.), 1787, and into Germ., 1796. The first edn. bore the legend *Niet vertaald* ('not translated'), in token of the originality of the work, and in illustration to subsequent generations of the universal foreign element in Dutch lit. (q.v.) at this date. The story is told in letters, after the model of Richardson (q.v.), whose influence on Continental fiction was so strong; but it was true Dutch in its characters and treatment, and true Betje in a large part of its inspiration, notably in the drawing of 'brother Benjamin' in the unamiable likeness of her own brother Laurence. Another novel in 8 vols., *Willem Leevend*, followed in 1784-5, but met with less success than it merited, perhaps on account of its length. Some translns. and minor works were added to the record of a literary partnership unique in the history of Dutch lit.

Wolff, von, Christian (1679-1754): Germ. philosopher; 'the first to give a detailed exposition of modern philosophy in the German language' (Hoffding, *Hist. Phil.*, E.T., 132). W.'s 'importance consists in the fact that he reduced modern philosophy to an inclusive system that could be taught and learned in the universities, and by this means banished the Aristotelian school-philosophy from the German universities' (Paulsen, *Kant*, E.T., 15). His importance to lit. lies in the fact that his discipleship to Leibniz (q.v.) and his popular exposition of the national point of view in life and thought made him a leader in the movement of Aufklärung (q.v.), or Enlightenment, or re-construction, which ensued on the Thirty Years' War. This movement reached its zenith in 1740, a cardinal year in W.'s life. In the recently-founded (1694) univ. of Halle, W. incurred dismissal, 1723, at the instance of king Fred. Wm. i of Prussia, whose contempt for learning was a byword, and to the joy of the reactionary pietists (s.v. Pietism), whose separation from the rationalists corresponded to the similar departure of Reformation from Renaissance (s.vv.) in an earlier century. The joy and the monarch died in 1740, when Frederick ii (q.v., the Great) recalled W.

Wolfram von Eschenbach (*c.* 1170-*c.* 1220): romancer; 'the greatest poet in modern European literature before the dawn of the Renaissance' (Robertson, *Hist. Germ. Lit.*, 90); 'with the one exception of Dante, no medieval poet has treated so deep and portentous problems as this honest, hardy, sinewy Franconian, whose mental physiognomy reminds one of Dürer's famous knight riding fearlessly in the company of death and the devil' (Francke, 93); 'there is something of the Shakespearean essential force in this unbridled, overleaping, overflowing spirit' (Biese, i, 117); 'he surpasses all his contemporaries in coherency of arrangement, in Christian depth and purity of thought, and in moral seriousness' (Kluge, 47). The unanimity of the historians of Germ. lit., as the foregoing brief extracts show, in their praise of W., is due chiefly to the merits of his Percival (q.v.) -poem, by which he extended the resources of the Arthur (q.v.) -cycle of romance. W. tells us that he could neither read nor write; he was a poor Bavarian knight (Eschenbach is a village in Bavaria), who enjoyed, like many of his contemporaries, the patronage and hospitality of count Hermann of Thuringia; but his illiteracy, while it freed him from the conventions of romance, did not exclude an intimate acquaintance with the great Fr. romance-writers, and chiefly with Chrestien (q.v.) of Troyes. W. composed lyrical verses, but his masterpieces were court-epics, viz. *Parzival*, 1205-15; *Titurel*, a fragment, completed *c.* 1260 by another hand; and *Willehalm* (William of Orange), fragment, 1216. The first 2 are Arthurian; the third belongs to the Charlemagne (q.v.) romance-cycle. The greatest of these is the first, which is not merely poetically important on account of W.'s skill (whether original, or leaning on an unknown predecessor) in associating the ideal of chivalry with the holy grail (q.v.), and in developing the romantic qualities of a knightly quest; but this beautiful poem, in octosyllabic couplets, is notable, too, for its deep psychological insight. Percival's fight against *Zwifel* (modern Germ. *Zweifel*), or Doubt, has a moral meaning for all time; 'If Doubt is neighbour to the heart, The soul must always sorely smart', sings W., and in the conquest of *Zwifel* by *saelde* (modern Germ. *Seligkeit*, blessedness) through the adventures of body and soul, lies the permanent spiritual power of this early court-epic of Teuton chivalry.

Wolzogen, von, Caroline (1763-1847): Germ. novelist; *née* von Lengefeld, sister to Charlotte, wife of Schiller (q.v.); m., first, v. Beulwitz, second, 1796, her cousin Wilhelm v. Wolzogen. Wr. *Agnes von Lilien*, a novel, which was issued anon. in Schiller's *Horen*, and the reception of which was partly the cause of the breach of friendship between Schiller and the brothers Schlegel. Frau v. W.'s chief work was her *Life of Schiller*, her brother-in-law, from family reminiscences, letters, and Körner's papers, publd. 1830, and still authoritative.

Woman: A complete treatise on the place of woman in modern lit. cannot be attempted in a small compass, but a few directions may be given to intending students of the subject.

1. We may remark a gradual development of the natural woman out of the conventional woman. 'In the old chivalric poetry and fiction', says Courthope (*Hist. Engl. Poetry*, ii, 224), 'no more than three types of women are represented, the insipid idol of male worship who shows "mercy" and "pity" to her lover according to the regulation pattern

of the *Cours d'Amour* ; the fickle mistress like Cressida, who is inconstant to one lover, and so violates the code of chivalry ; and the unfaithful wife of the class of Guinevere or Iseult '. All these descended from the old *romans* (see s.v. Romance), where the love-passion always obeyed the rules of Ovid (q.v.), and action was always regulated by the requirements of chivalric court-manners. This was the woman of Europe's May-time, the atmosphere of which is preserved in the Arthur (q.v.) -vol. which Malory (q.v.) redacted from Fr. bks. : ' For it giveth unto all lovers courage, that lusty month of May, in something to constrain him to some manner of thing more in that month than in any other. . . . Therefore, all ye that be lovers call unto remembrance the month of May '.

But May was not perpetual in Europe. Writers more directly in the shadow of the Church, with its feminist teachings based on the Fall of Man, and its compensating feminism of the Madonna, had to abandon to her fate in satire the woman incarnate, and to concentrate their instinctive mother-love and lady-worship on a more rarified and sublimated pattern of womanhood. The code of chivalry was screwed up for this purpose. There was an ideal, chaste woman of the troubadours, who differed from the woman of the romancers in that her earthly lover sought no consummation of his worship. She pointed the way to heaven, and was then most spiritually present when corporeally remote. This Beatrice-woman of Dante (q.v.), who has been called the last of the troubadours, was an abstraction from the flesh : ' True love in this differs from gold and clay, That to divide is not to take away ' (Shelley, q.v., *Epipsychidion*, a Dantesque poem). She satisfied her lover by her upward lure, ' to make the candle ready for the flame ', as Dante wr. (*Par.* xxx, 54), in one of his homely metaphors, which strike with such impelling keenness on the awful sublimities of his theme. For the flame was no other than ' the Love which moves the sun and the other stars ' (*Ibid.*, xxxiii, 145).

Naturam expellas furca, tamen usque recurrit, and woman, so large a part of nature, was no exception to this truism. The Humanists implemented the troubadours, and Boccaccio (q.v.) says sir W. Raleigh (*Some Authors*, 3) ' might be called the escape from Dante '. He found the way prepared for him by older satirists and story-writers, by Jean de Meun in the second part of the *Romance of the Rose* (q.v.), and by street-corner singers of easy penmanship, who were quicker to see woman's foibles than her virtues. He was assisted, too, by common observation, in the last resort the inspiration of all lit. Conditions of life in Florence in the 14th cent., as in other Ital. city-states, due, partly, merely to the Southern sun, partly to social causes arising out of the celibacy and domestication of the clergy, tended, in the towns at any rate, to derogate from the austerity of women's virtue. Thus Boccaccio, composing his tales as a relief from the prevailing gloom at Florence, occasioned by the outbreak of plague, had everything in his favour,—human nature, local conditions, personal experience. All wrought together to

inspire him to write, in the *Decameron*, the first novel of psychology in modern Europe. The Boccaccian woman was neither Martha nor Madonna, neither an idol nor a thing of scorn ; she moved level with her lover on the lower planes of sensuous enjoyment.

2. This extraction of the natural woman from the conventional was assisted by normal events. Women themselves were finding expression in the parti-coloured life of the dawning Renaissance. Far away in Engld. there was nothing strange in Chaucer's (q.v.) gallery of portraits, which carried women's release from conventional treatment to a still higher degree of accuracy in character-delineation. The educationists (Vittorino, q.v., for example), who contributed so large a share to the spread of reason and reform, provided for women as well as men in their programmes and curricula, and, though the effort to unseal the fount of learning for the benefit of gentlewomen had very clear and strict limitations, the list of great women of the Renaissance—we may mention lady Jane Grey, queen Margaret of Navarre, queen Elizabeth, the countesses of Pembroke and Bedford, and lady Ann Bacon, mother of the great chancellor—stands to show the true capacity of women as scholars, authors and patrons.

In this respect there is a curious parallelism (just worth noting, since it helps to illuminate a complicated theme), between the 14th-15th and the 17th-18th cents. in social history as reflected in letters. Puritanism helped in the latter era to revive what we may call the stricter Fall-of-Man view of women. The Folly (q.v.) -lit. of the earlier period, with its gross wit directed against marriage and the dignity of the female partner to it, is matched in the later period by the Restoration (q.v.)-comedy, equally gross and even more witty, and quite as licentious in its attitude towards matrimony. And this decline of the respect for womanhood from the older Renaissance heights was caused by the austerities of men like Calvin and Knox, who had disinterred from the Middle Ages the old ecclesiastical contempt. Milton (q.v.) is not guiltless in this respect, and the feminist excesses which marked the suffrage campaign in Engld. at the beginning of the present century, were partly at least to be traced to the retrogression of liberalism in social practice during the 18th and early 19th cents. Milton's views on divorce were partly accountable for the hunger-strikes.

3. Prior to the Puritan reaction, however, woman in the mirror of letters continued to find her place in the sun, and the next great phase after Boccaccio, who was the first feminist writer in Europe, occurred, as might be expected, in dramatic lit., and even in the unreal world of the pastoralists. Among the latter, Montemayor (q.v.), in Portugal, wr., in his *Diana Enamorada*, what Courthope (*Hist. Engl. Poetry*, ii, 218), describes as ' the first work of European fiction that treats of the subject of hopeless love and female self-sacrifice, afterwards so fully developed by the Elizabethan dramatists. It blends something of the ideal atmosphere of romances like

Amadis de Gaul with the manners of modern life, and anticipates that taste for complication and intrigue which afterwards gave rise to the plots of the Spanish playwrights'. Among the former, we are reminded by Kelly (*Lit. espagn.*, 310), that, before Lope de Vega (q.v.), 'la femme jouait un rôle secondaire, sentimental ailleurs. Lope la plaça dans sa véritable cadre, comme le principe même du motif dramatique'. There were other beginnings in the Peninsula. The tragicomedy of *Celestina* (q.v.), just at the end of the 15th cent., contained rudimentary female characters, and a more than rudimentary nurse-confidante, who were to contribute to the new feminism; and the *Amadis* (q.v.)-cycle itself, long-winded and conventional though it was, contained the germ of the Rochester and Jane Eyre story of *le beau ténébreux* and his adoring female. Next in order, though the process was horizontal, not vertical, in distribution, sir Philip Sidney (q.v.), in *Arcadia*, borrowed and expanded the resources of living women in pastoral fiction. We come at last near to Shakespeare when we read (Courthope, *ibid.*, 226), that the common original of Sidney's female page, Diaphantus, and of Shakespeare's Viola is the Felismena of Montemayor.

4. The inhibitions of the Church, which invented (1) the sublimated woman of unearthly complexion, who attained her heaven in the *Divina Commedia*, and (2) the somewhat soiled and bedraggled Eve of satire, fable, and angry-timid priests, were very slowly disused in European lit. But prof. Herford reminds us in an essay on *The Normality of Shakespeare illustrated in his treatment of Love and Marriage* (Engl. Association pamphlet, 47; 1920) of the return to sanity by the Engl. master-playwright, and of the lines which he set for future practice. He avoided both the older perils: 'if he did not view women with the shy chivalry which, in his portrayal of them, so seriously limited the humour of Scott, he shows something of the same reluctance to make them the butts of ridicule. His women have in the highest degree the feminine accent, but they give little clue, in comparison with his men, to the qualities on which satire in all ages has fastened'.

This excellence having been reached, woman's place in lit. was more secure. The rest might show variations from the normal, as in the instance of the Germ. Romanticists (see s.v. Schlegel, e.g.), the Fr. blue-stockings (see s.v. Rambouillet, e.g.), and other feminities duly reflected from the social in the literary mirror. But in fiction and on the stage, woman had cast away her shackles; she re-appeared for the first time since Chaucer (and, less modestly in Boccaccio), in her guise as she was. Engl. lit. takes credit for a large share in this emancipation. Perhaps it was partly climatic; but, however that may be, we note the testimony of E. Dale (*National Life and Character in the Mirror of Early Engl. Lit.*, Cambridge, 1907; 285), who, writing of Cressida in Chaucer, says: 'In the flesh she is the outcome of the atmosphere of the Provençal Courts of Love, a woman in love with love; and yet, with all her frailty, how far superior she is to the exotic and sensual southern type from which her creation sprang! The difference is just that between the English ideals of womanhood and those of Italy and Provence'. We may point to a like difference between the women of G. Meredith and Flaubert (qq.v.).

5. A discussion of the contribution to the treatment of W. in European lit. made by Ibsen (q.v.), and his successors in other countries, would bring us too close to present times to be either profitable or conclusive. Love, the proper bond between the sexes, in its natural and supra-natural manifestations, has inspired philosophers and poets, novelists, dramatists and moralists. Mr. E. V. Lucas, in 1908, collected, under the name of *Her Infinite Variety* a feminine portrait-gallery. He limits his choice to Engl. authors, but, in a sense, they include all the rest; and these portraits, teaching by examples, show how wide is the range of inspiration which the theme of W. has given to men of letters. And, finally, Ruskin's (q.v.) dictum may be cited and pondered: 'Shakespeare has no heroes; he has only heroines'.

Wood, Anthony à (1632-95): Engl. historian; resident at Oxford; wr. *History and Antiquities* of the univ., 1674; and *Athenæ Oxonienses*, 1691-2, an extremely useful biographical dict. 'of all the Writers and Bishops who have had their education in the university of Oxford'. W. was expelled from Oxford, 1693, on account of an alleged libel in that work on the first earl of Clarendon.

Wood, Ellen (1814-87): Engl. novelist; *née* Price; m., 1836, and is always described as Mrs. Henry Wood. Wr. about 30 popular novels, including *East Lynne*, 1861; *The Channings*, 1862; *Mrs. Halliburton's Troubles*, etc. Mrs. W. conducted a magazine known as the *Argosy*.

Wordsworth, William (1770-1850): Engl. poet; poet-laureate (q.v.), 1843, on the death of Southey (q.v.); by common consent, despite some early obloquy, which is now justly forgotten, one of the few greatest poets whom Engld. or Europe has produced. Evidence to this proposition might be adduced from S. T. Coleridge (q.v.) downwards to J. S. Mill (q.v.); we prefer, writing in and for the 20th cent., to seek our evidence from more recent sources, and would summon as witness prof. Garrod, prof. of Poetry at Oxford, 1925, who holds that W., 'in his best poetry, has left to us work of a unique quality; work which supplies a more powerful aid to the imaginative life than is secured to us in the poetry of far greater poets. . . . Among the commonplaces of life, environed by custom and the casual cares of the world, still to live imaginatively,—this is not easy, and this, more than other poets, Wordsworth helps us to do' (*Wordsworth: Lectures and Essays*, 141).

Several influences went to form this unique genius. We may enumerate (1) the fortune of his long life. Though W. could not have foreseen that he was to live through the busy 80 years, which included the Fr. Revolution, the battles of Trafalgar and Waterloo, the Reform Act of 1832, the first 13 years under queen Victoria, and the industrial and educational movement culminating in the Great

Exhibition, 1851, yet his work was invested with a sense of tranquillity and space, so that expression became a function of design, as if he were confident through all that he would survive to see the rough places made smooth. (2) There was the influence of his early surroundings. He was born at Cockermouth, in Cumberland, and was edu. at the grammar school at Hawkshead. His career at St. John's coll., Cambridge, did not impress him deeply, and he went on from the univ. to a series of tours in France and Germany. Thence he came back before the century's end with an obvious sense of relief. He settled at Grasmere, 1799, setting up house with Dorothy W., his sister, and, 3 years later, Mary, *née* Hutchinson, joined the idyllic ménage as his wife. Children and friends arrived, and, in 1813, W. moved his household to Rydal Mount, Grasmere, where, like a poet in a fairy-tale, he lived till he died. (3) There were his early years in France. He went there in 1790, just before he took his degree, and again in 1792, just after that event. There he met Michel Beaupuy (1755-96), a Republican general and a paladin of the Revolution, whose soldierly chivalry and political idealism recall from his early grave our Engl. hero, general Gordon (1833-85). There, too, he fell in love with Annette Vallon, and became the father of Caroline (1792-1862), who, by her marriage with Jean Baptiste Baudouin gave Fr. descendants to W. in the female line. (See prof. G. M. Harper, *William Wordsworth : His Life, Works, and Influence*, 2 vols., 1916, supplemented by E. Legouis, *William Wordsworth and Annette Vallon*, Dent, 1922). These ardours of fame, love and liberty were keeping W. in France too long. There was a rumour of a risk that he would throw in his lot with the revolutionaries. His guardians—for his parents had died young—became angry and alarmed, and summoned him home. But the memory of those months proved permanent. Action had invaded contemplation, overflowing its banks with a torrent of long desire. The means awaited formulation, but already the end was clear : ' My heart was all given to the people, and my love was theirs ' (*Prelude*, ix, ' Residence in France ', 123-4). (4) There was the influence of friendship. In 1795, commenced the friendship with Coleridge (q.v.), which was deep enough to suffer the test of estrangement for a period of two years, and which was the fastest element in the brotherhood known to subsequent critics as the Lake (q.v.) school of poetry. To W.'s peaceful home in the Quantocks came C. Lamb, H. C. Robinson, Southey, De Quincey, Hazlitt (qq.v.), and others, including John Thelwall (1764-1834), social reformer and ' friend of the people ', who achieved imprisonment in the Tower. An echo of W.'s Fr. experience, of Thelwall's presence, and of local gossip, caused a Government spy to be sent down. Sir George Beaumont, a Leicestershire magnate, was another of W.'s friends, whose pictures and lands formed topics for some of his verse, and twice in 30 years W. visited sir W. Scott (q.v.) in Scotland. (5) We have to reckon with the Germ. influence. It was in Coleridge's

company that the Wordsworths spent a winter in Germany, 1798-9, visiting, among others, Klopstock (q.v.). Germ. thought, with which Coleridge was familiar, in Kant, Hegel, Winckelmann and Lessing (see s.vv.), who were all (except the last) alive, made a powerful appeal to W., in the country in which they wr.

Meanwhile, these formative influences had already found urgent expression. *Lyrical Ballads*, anon., 1798, containing 4 poems by Coleridge, including *The Ancient Mariner*, had been publd. before the Germ. journey ; and the second edn., in 2 vols., 1800, bearing W.'s name on the title-page, contained, besides additional poems, the famous *Pref.*, which is a manifesto of the Romantic movement (see s.v. Romance). The value of that *Pref.* is vouched for by no less an authority than prof. Saintsbury (*Hist. Crit.*, iii, 200), who writes, that, ' in no instance, save perhaps that of the Pléiade and Du Bellay's (qq.v.) *Défense et Illustration*, did a protagonist of the new poetry take the field in prose so early and so aggressively as did Wordsworth in his Preface to the second edition of *Lyrical Ballads*. In none, without exception, was such an attack so searchingly criticized and so powerfully seconded, with corrections of its mistakes, as in the case of the well-known chapters of the *Biographia Literaria* in which Coleridge examines Wordsworth's examination ' ; and, after characterizing the *Ballads* as the ' first sword ', and the *Preface* as the ' first horn ' in the campaign, Saintsbury adds that W.'s critical writings provide ' a bundle of documents unequalled in interest ', in its own class, since Dante (q.v.). We need not pause here to estimate the respective contributions of W. and Coleridge to this vol. We discuss it s.v. Coleridge (see p. 106, col. 1), where we show that Coleridge ascribed the chief share to W., who accepted that incense, with much besides. Perhaps the fairest statement is to say, that Coleridge did more to clarify the theory, and W. to exemplify the practice of the reforms in poetic diction which they initiated in common. Together, with Blake (q.v.), they ' took up and developed, with finer insight, those harmonies between man and external nature which Rousseau had been the first vividly to perceive ' (prof. Herford, *The Age of Wordsworth*, xvii). This is the key to W.'s poetry,—this harmony between man and external nature. To this problem he addressed himself in the years after 1798, and esp. in the golden decade, 1798-1808, between which dates, as M. Arnold (q.v.) was perhaps the first to point out, W.'s chief productive period lay. Such a harmony had been aimed at in ardent youth,—in his fiery experience in France, 1790-2 ; the same harmony he sought in peace, by the tranquil home-fires of nearly 60 years, recollecting his emotions in tranquillity, and purging the active in the contemplative life. A disciple of Rousseau (q.v.), even of Godwin (q.v.), he employed a ' finer insight ' than his masters, and took Plato's (q.v.) ' longer road ' to their goal. It was not enough, in his long, quiet years, to try to make all Frenchmen happy ; it was not enough to make all men happy by grants of franchise and equality ; these were mere palliatives of an evil the roots of which had not been grasped. Equal nature smiled at such expedients, unless those who employed them recognized them, not as ends in themselves, but as means to the common end beyond the confines of one country or even of one species of creation. Joy, as a quality of function—the performance of function proved by joy—was nature's way through all her manifestations. The proper study of mankind was *not* man, whether Frenchman, or Englishman, or another, but all nature, of which human nature is a part. So, alike in thought as in diction—in diction, secondarily to thought,—W. broke away from the 18th cent., and the philosophy of Boileau and Pope (qq.v.). He overran the boundaries which they had set to the curiosity and expatiation of mankind. The landscape-gardener's formal scenery could not satisfy him any more than the strict limits of the heroic couplet. The language of the Ancients (see s.v. Classicism) was as inadequate to his muse as the illusory happiness of Arcadia (q.v.) was below the ambit of his vision ; even Paradise was not lost to this new Milton :

Paradise, and groves
Elysian, Fortunate Fields—like those of old
Sought in the Atlantic main—why should they be
A history only of departed things,
Or a mere fiction of what never was ?
For the discerning intellect of Man,
When wedded to this goodly universe
In love and holy passion, shall find these
A simple produce of the common day.

We may trace the expression of this faith, and its sanction derived from, and consecrating, common sights, up and down the pages of W.'s poems :—

(1) One impulse from a vernal wood
May teach you more of man,
Of moral evil and of good
Than all the sages can.

(2) And 'tis my faith that ev'ry flower
Enjoys the air it breathes. . . .
If this belief from heaven be sent,
If such be Nature's holy plan,
Have I not reason to lament
What Man has made of Man ?

(3) To me the meanest flower that blows can give
Thoughts that do often lie too deep for tears.

(4) Alas ! what differs more than Man from Man !
And whence that difference ? Whence but from himself ?
. . . He whose soul
Ponders this true equality, may walk
The fields of earth with gratitude and hope ;
Yet, in that meditation, will he find
Motive to sadder grief, as we have found,
Lamenting ancient virtues overthrown,
And for the injustice grieving, that hath made
So wide a difference between Man and Man.

From these more didactic, sometimes even pedestrian, strains, W. soared on the wings of his interpretative faculty—interpreting nature to man—into the spaces of transcendental thought. His epical invocation was as clear as it was bold :

Of Truth, of Grandeur, Beauty, Love, and Hope,
And melancholy Fear subdued by Faith ;
Of blessed consolations in distress ;
Of moral strength, and intellectual power ;
Of joy in widest commonalty spread ;
Of the individual Mind that keeps her own
Inviolate retirement, subject there
To Conscience only, and the law supreme
Of that Intelligence which governs all—
I sing.

And he never looked back from his high purpose. Securely, effortlessly, he bore his readers up to the rare region of his song, till alone, among Engl. poets, he had solved the problem of the romanticists, to which even Novalis (q.v.) was unequal. That problem was stated by J. Joubert (q.v.), W.'s contemporary, in the following crystal-clear words : ' The true science of metaphysics consists, not in rendering abstract that which is sensible, but in rendering sensible that which is abstract ; apparent, that which is hidden ; imaginable, if so may be, that which is only intelligible ; and intelligible, finally, that which an ordinary attention fails to seize '. So, W. rendered the transcendental mood,—

In which the heavy and the weary weight
Of all this unintelligible world
Is lightened ; that serene and blessed mood
In which the affections gently lead us on,
Until, the breath of this corporeal frame
And even the motion of our human blood
Almost suspended, we are laid asleep
In body, and become a living soul :
While, with an eye made quiet by the power
Of harmony, and the deep power of joy,
We see into the life of things.

It is for this supreme appeal from the seen to the Unseen, from appearance to Reality, from understanding to Faith, from the inductive to the imaginative Reason, that men go back to W., and accompany him humbly through some arid stretches of verse to the heights where he walks unerringly in the serene light of impassioned knowledge. For W., imprisoning the gleams escaped from the soul of the universe, conveys in unfaltering language a poetic revelation fuller than any other. ' He never brought to perfection ', says a recent critic (Lascelles Abercrombie, *The Idea of Great Poetry*, 114), ' the whole life of his idea of things. But he came very near it once, and perhaps this partial achievement of Wordsworth's is the greatest thing in modern poetry ; it is surely the loftiest. Is there, outside Milton and Dante, anything really comparable with the *Ode on the Intimations of Immortality* ? ' And W. Pater (q.v.), an older critic, says : ' It is the contact of these thoughts, the speculative boldness in them, which constitutes, at least for some minds, the secret attraction of much of his best poetry—the sudden passage from lowly thoughts and places to the majestic forms of philosophical imagination, the play of these forms over a world so different, enlarging so strangely the bounds of its humble churchyards, and breaking such a wild light on the graves of christened children '.

We stop here. The present generation, and future generations presumably, are too busy, and too much stocked with great poetry, to read W. entire. They seek him, and will seek him, in selections, though M. Arnold's (q.v.) selection in the *Golden Treasury* series does much less than justice to the poet. Readers are unwise if they shrink from the discipline of W.'s long, psychological poems : *The Excursion*, 1814, in 9 bks. of blank verse, which was written as part ii of *The Recluse*, originally drafted in 3 parts, part i of which exists only in a fragment (*The Recluse*, posth., 1888), and part iii of which was never begun ; and *The Prelude*, in 14 bks. of blank verse, composed *c.* 1799-1805, and publd. posth., 1850 ; and students of *The Prelude* are recommended to start on that voyage of discovery, the rewards of which are rich, by reading prof. E. Legouis, *La Jeunesse de Wordsworth*, 1896 (E.T., Dent, 1897), which went back from the old man to the youth, and founded W.-criticism on fresh and forward lines. The shorter poems may be taken up anywhere, never, however, omitting the Immortality *Ode*, which W. himself singled out for special honour, tabulating it in capital type at the end of his minor pieces, in every collected edn. of his works, in token of its cardinal position. It will be helpful in reading the shorter poems, if their fullest significance is to be seized, to remember always the poet's ambition to ' build social upon personal liberty '. We should not be too much afraid of what M. Arnold called, with half a sneer, the ' Social Science Congress ' frame of mind ; it does not detract from enjoyment of W.'s poetry to recall that D. Masson (q.v.) included the poet in 1860, among the makers of *Recent British Philosophy*. At least, it assists understanding to realize that W. was always seeking the plan and purpose in the natural scheme, the unity reconciling the variety, the One harmonizing the many, the joy vindicating God to man. Even *Peter Bell*, which Shelley (q.v.) laughed at so immoderately, amid the more foolish cachinnation of lesser men, is more readable if we remember (1) the contemporary interest in the psychology of crime, and (2) that Peter Bell's ' primrose on a river's brim ' typified, to W., ' a lasting link in nature's chain, from highest heaven let down ' (*The Primrose of the Rock*). Lastly, there is the poet's bibliography, and the constant appeal of his lofty verse from the time of the Napoleonic Wars to that of the Great War, 1914-18. Among those who have written bks., or articles on W., apart from the names mentioned above, are sir L. Stephen, sir W. Raleigh, lord Houghton, F. W. H. Myers, A. H. Clough, J. A. Symonds, E. Dowden, W. Bagehot, Swinburne, J. Wilson, S. A. Brooke, J. C. Shairp, J. H. Shorthouse, A. Ainger, E. Caird, A. de Vere, and many others ; and there was a Wordsworth Society from 1879-86.

Worm, Ole, (1588-1654): Dan. scholar ; philologer. Wr. *Monumenta Danica*. W. was a busy collector of Iceld. MSS., many of which passed into the possession of Arne Magnússon (q.v.). The MS. of the *Edda* (q.v.) of Snorri (q.v.) is still known as *codex Wormianus*. See, too, s.vv. sir William Temple and Thomas Warton.

Wotton, Henry (1568-1639): Engl. poet ; diplomatist ; ambassador at Venice ; knt., 1603. Wr. *The State of Christendom, . . . Secret Passages and Hidden Mysteries of the Times*, publd. posth., 1657, and is the author of many witty sayings : among them, the definition of an ambassador, a man sent *ad mentiendum Reipublicæ causa*. W. is best remembered as the author of graceful verse, publd. in *Reliquiæ Wottonianæ*, 1651 ; two of his poems are included by Palgrave (q.v.) in the *Golden Treasury* : ' How happy is he born and taught That serveth not another's will ', and *Elizabeth of Bohemia* (' Ye meaner beauties of the night ').

Wouwer, van der, Jan (1574-1612): Dutch scholar ; his name is latinized as Wowerius. Born at Hamburg ; studied at Leyden univ. under Lipsius and Scaliger ; wr., 1604, Lat. treatise on *Polymathia*, the earliest attempt at an ordnance-survey of the field of scholarship, which he left incomplete. W. figures in a Rubens picture (in the Pitti palace) seated at a table with his friend Philip Rubens (q.v.), brother of the artist, with their teacher, Lipsius, between them.

Wyatt, Thomas (*c.* 1503-1542): Engl. poet. Son of a diplomatist, and entered royal service at early age ; lover of queen Anne Boleyn ; knt., 1536 ; served king Henry viii on several important embassies, on the last of which he contracted his fatal illness ; was twice imprisoned in the Tower, but on each occasion regained the king's confidence. W.'s place in Engl. lit. is important as a link, largely forged by Fr. assistance, between Italy and Engld. in the chain of the Renaissance ; he and Surrey (q.v.) are the most considerable poets in the period from Chaucer to Spenser (qq.v.), and it may briefly be said, with at least very approximate justice, that they familiarized poetic Engld. with the art of Alamanni and Marot (qq.v. ; Alamanni, it should be recalled, was Fr. by residence), and preserved their influence in Engl. verse even after it had been largely superseded in their own country by the greater genius of Ronsard (q.v.). To W.'s study of Fr. models is owed the long-due departure from Chaucerian metres and from the allegorical tradition ; W. aimed at variety, elasticity, and gaiety, and, though he achieved these less successfully than Surrey, he stood plainly in the forward line. He introduced the sonnet (q.v.) into Engl., seeking his patterns from Petrarch and Sannazaro through Saint-Gelais and his contemporaries (see s.vv.) ; he wr. lyric poems after Marot's models, not without an incidental debt to Skelton (q.v.), and was particularly happy in his naturalization of the rondeau (q.v.) ; the latest poems of his short life were satires, after Alamanni, on the vanities of courtiers. It is not possible to ascribe to W. a large share of formal originality and invention ; but his boon to Engl. poetry was considerable : he used his material skilfully ; and he had the further advantage of being an accomplished musician (as Castiglione, q.v., required of the perfect courtier), so that his ear was trained to the harmonies which he sought, and his invocation of the muse was more than conventional (cp., e.g., the lyric verses, *Address* *to his Lute*). His originality lay in a spontaneous, almost a rebellious, lyrical virility and intensity, contrasting with the elegant quietism of the Continental poets. He sought his own ideas out of the experience and emotion of his own personality : love and duty, and the duty of love, as regulated by the code of chivalry, did not exhaust the inspiration of W.'s muse. Like Alamanni once more, he rendered into vernacular verse the penitential *Psalms* ; and he fully merited the praise conveyed in the stately elegy of his friend and fellow-poet. Surrey :

A tongue that served in foreign realms his king,
  Whose courteous talk to virtue did inflame
Each noble heart: a worthy guide to bring,
  Our English youth by travail into fame.

Wycherley, William (1640-1716): Engl. dramatist (see s.v. Restoration comedy) ; spent 5 years in Paris as a youth, and was the only Englishman to be admitted to the still famous Hôtel de Rambouillet (q.v.). Thus, he came very early under the influence of Molière (q.v.), whose new, bright method in comedy had struck sparks out of his inflammable material. But he missed Molière's humanity, whether by the tug of his Puritan orig. or of the Elizabethan tradition of the Engl. stage : there is more of Webster (q.v) than of wit in W.'s harsh, cold, brutal satire. Evelyn (q.v.) wr. of him :

As long as Men are false and Women vain,
Whilst Gold continues to be Virtue's bane,
In pointed Satire *Wycherley* shall reign ;

and the revival of one of his plays in London in 1924 supports this view of his immortality. He was *taboo* for his ' plain dealing ' during the 19th cent., but, while his misc. verse is not likely to find new readers, his 4 comedies should be read and may be staged. According to what W. said to Pope (q.v.), whom he fawned on late in life, these plays were composed several years earlier than they were actually publd. The conjectural dates are given in brackets, and are interesting in so far as they gave W. primacy among the comedians of the Restoration in Engld. : *Love in a Wood*, 1671 (1659) ; *The Gentleman Dancing Master*, 1672 (1662) ; *The Country Wife* W.'s masterpiece—1675 (1663), and *The Plain Dealer*, 1677 (1666).

Wyss, Johann Rudolf (1746-1820): Swiss romancer. Wr. national anthem, ' Rufst du, mein Vaterland ', and *The Swiss Robinson, or The Shipwrecked Swiss Preacher and his Family*, the last and best of the Robinsonaden (q.v.), familiar in Engld. since 1820 as *Swiss Family Robinson*.

X

Ximenez de Cisneros, Francisco (1437-1517): Span. scholar and divine ; card. Founded, 1508, a coll. at Alcalá, to which he attracted the great Span. humanist, Lebrixa (q.v.), who took charge of the Gk. text of X.'s projected polyglott Bible, printed 1514, but not licensed for publication till 1520. It is not necessary here to examine the public career of X. in relation to the history of Spain ; but Ticknor (i, 432ff.), who notes that he ' had for a long period united in his own person the office of Civil Administrator of Spain with that of Grand Inquisitor ', does not acquit him of responsibility for the injury to the cause of Span. humanism and learning which ensued from the ecclesiastical policy of the emperor Charles v (q.v.).

Y

Yates, Edmund (1831-94): Engl. novelist ; journalist ; founded *The World* newspaper, 1874. Wr. *Broken to Harness*, 1864 ; *The Black Sheep*, 1867, etc. ; wr., too, some plays, which were produced in London, and was dramatic critic for several years to the *Daily News*.

Yepes, de, Juan (1542-91): Span. mystic ; martyr ; son of a nobleman, whose family ' abhorred ' him ; entered Carmelite monastery at Medina del Campo as Juan de Santa Matia, and is now known as the Ecstatic Doctor, San Juan de la Cruz ; beatified, 1674 (the topic of a masterly vol. *Saint Jean de la Croix et le problème de l'Expérience mystique*, by Dr. Jean Baruzi ; Paris, Alcan, 1925. See, too, s.v. Mysticism). In 1567 (the exact date was 14 Aug.), Teresa (q.v. ; saint) arrived at Medina del Campo. She was more than twice Juan's age, ' and there was something of the relation of spiritual mother to child in the friendship which instantly sprang up between them '. It was a burning, devastating friendship. Crashaw (q.v.), our Engl. mystic, has reproduced something of the flame to which this prophetess set fire. Juan followed Teresa, 1568, into the monastery which she founded, and was seized, 1577, by the envoys of the Inquisition, and thrown into prison at Toledo. His physical tortures do not concern us ; lit. is interested in the fact that Juan's literary remains still survive, partly unedited, in Spain, and that his *Subida*, or ' Ascent of Mount Carmel ' and ' Dark Night of the Soul ' (*Noche escura del Alma*) reveal him as a poet of rare fire, melody and spiritual purity. His poetry exercised a direct influence on *The Unknown Eros* of Patmore (q.v.) ; and we may concur with sir E. Gosse in regretting that ' the only thing Spanish ecclesiastics in the sixteenth century could think of doing with this wholly orthodox and harmless mystic was to lock him up in a privy and scourge him at intervals ' (*Sunday Times*, 22 Feb., 1925).

Yonge, Charlotte Mary (1823-1901): Engl. novelist; disciple of Keble (q.v.), to whose influence may be ascribed the High Church tone in her fiction, the bulk of which was voluminous, and the profits from which were devoted to religious objects. Her best-known novels are *The Heir of Redcliffe*, *Heartsease*, and *The Daisy Chain*.

Young, Bartholomew (16th cent.): Engl. scholar; transld. the *Diana* by Montemayor (q.v.) into Engl., the version being used by Shakespeare (q.v.) in *The Two Gentlemen of Verona*.

Young, Edward (1683-1765): Engl. poet; chiefly famous at home and abroad—and esp. abroad—for his poem *The Complaint, or, Night Thoughts on Life, Death, and Immortality* (commonly known, shortly, as *Night Thoughts*), 9 parts, 1742-5. Letourneur (q.v.) transld. it into Fr., 1769, in the period when Rousseau (q.v.) was moving his fellow-countrymen by similar meditations; the influence of Y. on this movement is examined by Texte: *Rousseau et les Origines du cosmopolitisme litt. : Rélations littéraires de la France et de l'Angleterre au 18ᵉ siècle*, 1895, and Germany, too, responded to it in her romantic mood. ' *Night Thoughts* ', says prof. Saintsbury, *C.H.E.L.*, x, 160, ' is hard reading, nowadays, even for the most catholic lover of poetry; and the rest of Young, even *The Universal Passion*, is harder '; and where that voracious reader fails in appetite, less catholic lovers quickly reach satiety. As a satirist, Y. anticipated certain tones and notes in Pope (q.v.). Taine (q.v.), a Frenchman, rightly says that, though Y. has brilliant flashes of imagination, and said beforehand not a little of what Chateaubriand and Lamartine (q.v.) were to discover, yet we see much more quickly ' that he makes the most of his grief, strikes attitudes, and

studies effects '. The most valuable Engl. study of Y. is G. Eliot's (q.v.) *Worldliness and Other Worldliness* (*Westminster Review*, 1857; reprinted in her ' Library Edition,' vol. x), where she discovers in his ' disposition to see a rebuke or warning in every natural object, the " pedagogic fallacy ". It is this pedagogic tendency ', she opines, ' this sermonizing attitude of Young's mind, which produces the wearisome monotony of his pauses '.

Young Germany : Generic name of a literary movement in Germany, near the beginning of the 19th cent., which was practically still-born. The yoke of the Austrian prince Metternich (q.v.) which was laid on Germany after 1814, disappointed the brighter hopes of the Romanticists, fostered through the Napoleonic period (1806-13, between the Battles of Jena and Leipsic) and led to the reaction of Y.G. The Paris July Revolution (1830) revived the hopes of the liberal post-Romantics, who had long affected a conviction of the superiority of France to Germany, in lit. as well as in politics. For the ' Young German ' movement was political, as much as, or even more than, literary; and its weapon in writing was the newspaper rather than the bk. As a purely literary ' arrival ', Y.G. made its first appearance in 1834, when a vol. of lectures on æsthetics by a don at Kiel (L. Weinburg, 1802-72) was expressly dedicated ' Dir, junges Deutschland, . . . nicht dem alten '. In the following year, a review was planned under the title, *Das junge Deutschland*, but it came to nothing. On 10 Dec., 1835, the Germ. Parliament, obediently to Austrian dictation, issued a decree suppressing the writings ' of the school of literature well known under the name of Young Germany '. It was, however, little more than a ' name ', for its greatest adherent, Heine (q.v.), who was banned among others in that ukase, was much greater than the ' school ' in which he was included.

Yriarte, de, Tomas. See s.v. **Iriarte.**

Z

Zachariä, Justus Friedrich Wilhelm (1723-77): Germ. poet. At first an adherent of Gottsched (q.v.) at Leipsic, Z. presently joined the deserters under the standard of the *Bremer Beiträge* (q.v.). His poetic work was mainly in the manner of light burlesque, and had no permanent vogue; his best was a mock-heroic, *The Renommist*, 1744, treating of student-life with more refinement than earlier crudities.

Zagoskin, Michael Nicholayevich (1789-1852): Russ. dramatist and novelist; a minor figure in both capacities. Z.'s plays were, artistically, on the level of *Pathelin* (q.v.), or little above it; his novels, though commercially successful, enjoyed a purely transient popularity. The best known was *Zury Miloslavsky*, 1829, a story of Russia in 1612, in a vein of sentimental patriotism, which had not much to do with history and even less with the mantle of Scott (q.v.). It was followed by a novel of 1812, and Z.'s flickering reputation was gradually extinguished by his own hand.

Zamora, Antonio (fl. 1720): Span. dramatist; collaborated sometimes with Cañizares (q.v.), and was at all times addicted to the imitation of Vega, Molina, (qq.v.), and others. About 40 of his plays survive.

Zapata, de, Luis (c. 1532-c. 1599): Span. poet; spent 13 years in writing an heroic poem *Carlos famoso*, publd., 1565, which dealt minutely with the reign of the emperor Charles v (q.v.), and which would have been much better written in prose. It contains 40,000 verses, and was mentioned with esteem by Cervantes in the chapter on Don Quixote's library.

Zappi, -i. Giovanni Battista (1667-1719): It. poet; of Imola; an original member of the Arcadia (q.v.) Academy, in which he bore his shepherd's crook under the name of Tirsi Leucasio, but he was capable of rising to higher flights of lyric verse, and wr. several excellent sonnets. In these he was surpassed by

-ii. Faustina, née Marutti, his wife, whose poems on the death of her son and her series on Portia and other Roman heroines 'sound strangely alive amidst the multitudinous strummings and flatulent pipings of the average Arcadian' (Elton, *P.E.L.*, viii, 397).

Zarate y Castronovo, de, Fernando (17th cent.) : Span. dramatist. Wr., among other plays in the vein of L. de Vega (q.v.) *la Presumida y la Hermosa* ('The Haughty Fair'), of which Molière (q.v.) availed himself in *les Femmes savantes*.

Zarzuela (Span.) : Generic name for a class of dramatic compositions, performed to a musical accompaniment. The name is said to have been adopted from the title of one of the royal palaces near Madrid, where such performances enjoyed the patronage of Ferdinand, card. archbishop of Toledo, brother to king Philip iv (q.v.) of Spain, in the 17th cent. Lope de Vega (q.v.) had produced an eclogue, (' The Forest without Love ') *Selva sui Amor*, at court, in 1630, in which all the parts were sung. This innovation was followed 30 years later by Calderon's (q.v.) *Púrpura de la Rosa* ('Stain on the Rose '), 1660, a full-length drama, which was sung throughout, on the occasion of the marriage of the princess Maria Theresa with king Louis xiv of France. In this form of entertainment the Span. Court was paying the compliment of imitation to the methods of Lully and Quinault (qq.v.) at the court of the royal bridegroom. The aid of music and singing became more and more usual after this date as a concomitant of drama, and the *zarzuela*, or musical play, whether in one act or three acts, is mainly associated with the name of the dramatist Candamo (q.v.) ; from that point it was but a short step to the introduction of Ital. opera in Madrid, which occurred in a tentative form in 1705. (See, too, s.v. Opera).

Zasius, Ulrich (1461-1534) : Germ. jurist ; prof. at Friburg ; ranks with Budæus and Alciati (qq.v.) as a founder of humanistic method in jurisprudence.

Zavaleta, de, Juan (17th cent.) : Span. dramatist. Wr., among other plays of little account, one on the Roman emperor Commodus, which led him, after he was struck with blindness in 1664, to proceed to write a life of the same emperor. Neither play nor life proved successful ; and Z. is chiefly remembered by the record of his personal ugliness.

Zayas y Sotomayor, de, Maria (*c.* 1590-*c.* 1650) : Span. novelist. Wr., 1637-47, *Novelas amorosas y exemplares*, which are more amorous than exemplary. One of them, 'Judge of his own Cause ', became the fourth tale introduced by Scarron (q.v.) into his *Roman comique* (for the other 3, see s.v. Castillo Solorzano). Scarron, again, went to Z. for the title and story of his *Précaution inutile*, which descended through Molière (q.v. ; *l'Ecole des Femmes*) and Sedaine (q.v. ; *la Gageure imprévue*) to Beaumarchais (q.v. ; *Barbier de Seville*). Ticknor (iii, 143n.) describes this tale (*el Prevenido engañado*) as ' one of the most gross I remember to have read ' ; and the author's defence must be left to the zeal of her imitators in France.

Zedlitz, von, Joseph Christian (1790-1862) : Germ. poet and threnodist ; baron by rank. Wr. lyric verses, collected in 1832, ballads, dramas, and a charming, fanciful narrative tale in verse,

Waldfraülein, 1843. Z.'s best work, however, consisted in his *Totenkränzen*, (Threnodies, *poèmes funèbres*, lit. wreaths for the dead), collected in 1827. These were metrical poems, in Ital. romance-lyric stanzas, commemorative of such men and women as Wallenstein, Goethe, Canning, Napoleon, Byron, Tasso, Petrarch and Laura, Romeo and Juliet.

Zeno, Apostolo (1668-1750) : It. writer of melodrama (in the correct sense of musical plays) ; critic and historian ; founded and edited the *Giornale de' Letterati* in Venice, and was appointed court-poet at Vienna, 1718-28, when he retired in favour of Metastasio (q.v.), to whom, in the field of operatic drama, Z. stands as a kind of John the Baptist. His association of opera with lit., though frigid and mechanical, was inspired by good sense and good taste.

Zepeda, de, Joaquin Romero. See s.v. **Cepeda.**

Zesen, von, Philip (1619-89) : Germ. Renaissance purist. Founded a society at Hamburg, the object of which was to provide native equivalents for foreign words, even for the proper names of classic lore. The members of his society assumed the names of flowers, according to the fanciful fashion of the prophets of Allah as Opitz (q.v.). Z. wr. romantic novels in the dreariest stage of subjection to foreign types of gallantry and adventure.

Zeyer, Julius (1841-1901) : Czech poet ; edu. mainly in Germany ; lived as tutor in Russia , later in Prague, France or Italy, ' or wherever his literary tastes and melancholy heart called him ' (Chudoba, *Czech Lit.*, 128). This roving romanticism was reflected in Z.'s writings, which included a Carlovingian epic poem ; heroic verse-tales of his own country, *Vyszehrad* ; an autobiographical novel, *Jan Maria Plojhar* ; the romance of a young Slovak in Paris, 'The House of a Drowning Star ' ; and travel-tales and scenes, burrowed out from personal observation and from his wide, desultory, constant studies of old or distant lit. Z. cultivated a style correspond ing with his romantic and exotic tastes, and it is too remote, perhaps, from commoner standards to maintain the appeal which he made to the younger minds of his own generation.

Zhukovsky, Vasili Andreevich (1783-1852) : Russ. poet ; like Pushkin (q.v.), of Eastern orig. on his mother's side ; ' he opened the door of Russian literature on the fields of German and English poetry ' (Baring, *H.U.L.*, xcix, 52) ; ' that he was the veritable initiator of romanticism, no critic would deny ; he first brought the new gospel from Germany, and was faithful to it for half a century. . . . He preludes most of the themes which Pushkin was to resume, in the same tone and on the same instrument ; he was the Perugini to Pushkin's Raphael ' (Vogüé, *Roman Russe*, 34). Apart from Z.'s services, obviously considerable, to Russ. lit., in extending its sources of foreign inspiration from France to Engld. and Germany, he was one of the ablest, if not the ablest, translr. who has ever practised that exacting art. He commenced with Gray's (q.v.) *Elegy* in 1802, and ended with the *Odyssey* in 1848, and was equally successful in both. (It is said that he visited

Stoke Poges in 1839, and revised his version with more poignant local colour. It should be added that Z.'s cast of mind and melancholy Russ. temperament were particularly suited to the tone of the *Elegy*). A barditus (q.v.) -ode for the Slav heroes of Austerlitz, 1806, and a ballad, *Ludmila*, 1808, adapted from Bürger's (q.v.) famous *Lenore*, increased Z.'s great reputation, which he maintained at a high level by a fairly constant flow of poetry, sentimental, thoughtful, elegiac, including further translns. from Schiller, Uhland (qq.v.), and others. Brückner's eulogy may be added to those cited above: Z., he writes (*Gesch. d. Russ. Lit.*, 165), 'was the most original translator in the world's literature. His versions became new poems; and Russian poetic expression was perfected by him in a measure far surpassing that of Karamsin in the realm of Russian prose'. Z.'s patriotic odes helped to procure him the post of tutor to the czarevich, afterwards Alexander ii.

Ziegler und Kliphausen, von, Heinrich Anselm (1653-97): Germ. romance-writer; of the 'twopenny-coloured' type of gallant and Oriental fiction, founded on Span. models. His chief work was the *Asiatische Benise*, an eastern tale of heroism, villainy, and tropical amorousness.

Zimmermann, Johann Georg (1728-95): Germ.-Swiss essayist; physician to the king of Engld. at Hanover. Wr. treatises on *Solitude* and *National Pride*, as well as conversations, etc., with king Fredk. (q.v) the Great.

Zinegref, Julius Wilhelm (1591-1635): Germ. poet; a leader of the Heidelberg (q.v.) group of Renaissance pioneers, whose work was so grievously interrupted by the Thirty Years' War (q.v.). Edited poems of Opitz (q.v.) with appendix of selected pieces by himself and other Heidelbergers. Wr. patriotic verse, and vol. of *Apophthegms*, 1626.

Zinzendorf, von, Graf N. L. (1700-1760): Germ. mystic poet; Catholic hymn-writer, akin in genius, to Spee (q.v.).

Zola, Emile (1840-1903): Fr. novelist. By temperament and manner, Z. belongs emphatically to the romanticists (s.vv. Lyrisme, Romance); his sweeping pen, his characterization of types, his profusion, his colour, his mass-formation, even his exaggeration, stamp him indelibly of the school of Hugo (q.v.). One critic even goes so far, and we may 'follow him with confidence, as to define Z.'s novels as 'sociological epopees', analogous to and comparable with the humanitarian epopees of Hugo's *Légende des siècles* (see Lanson, *Lit., fr.*, 1081). Thus, *Germinal*, 1885, is the epic of the miner of the North; *l'Assommoir*, 1877, is the epic of Paris industrialism; and there were the epopees of the Franco-Prussian war (*la Débâcle*, 1892), of *Rome*, 1896, *Paris*, 1898, and of natural selection, (*Fécondité*, 1889). This is the Zola of the romantic tradition. There was the other Zola of the realist revolt, who broke away with Flaubert (q.v., and see s.v. Gautier) from the imaginary into the natural world, and who wedded the romantic style to the realistic matter by depicting imaginatively what he saw and heard and smelt and touched. To

this realistic influence is to be added the scientific doctrine of writers like Taine (q.v.). Z. was ridden by philosophic theories. We recall from Taine's pref. to his *Hist. of Engl. Lit.* the famous sentence (quoted s.v. Taine), 'Vice and virtue are products, like vitriol and sugar; and every complex phenomenon arises from other more simple phenomena on which it hangs'. This kind of writing went straight to Z.'s head. In the realm of science he found his precise texts in such bks. as C. Bernard's (q.v.) *Experimental Medicine*; and Z. himself wr. a *Roman experimental*, 1880, in which he formulated this theory of fiction. The sociological experiment was worked out in the series of novels described as *l'histoire naturelle et sociale d'une famille sous le second Empire*, and known by the name of the family under the microscope and scalpel as the Rougon-Macquart series, 1871-93. It is bad Taine and bad Hugo; bad science and bad fiction, because an imperfect amalgam of both; and, necessarily almost, the products of vice occupied him more than those of virtue. Verne (q.v.) merely popularized science; Z. attempted to vindicate it in fiction, and there is little chance that his bastard art will survive the psychology of the present cent., which is sifting and assimilating the bold generalizations of the 19th. The best in Z. is his temperament, a poetic one, which carries his readers forward as on a flood; and, perhaps, the best expression of his poetic temperament was his espousal, absolute and without regard to consequences, of the cause of Dreyfus, 1897, in a crisis which rent France in twain.

Zorrilla, José (1817-93): Span. poet. Z.'s life was notable for his residence in Mexico, 1855-66, at the court of the unhappy emperor Maximilian. He wr. his reminiscences, 1880, but is chiefly remembered for the sake of his verse on national themes; *Cantos del Trovador*, 1841, etc.

Zschokke, Johann Heinrich (1771-1848): Germ.-Swiss novelist; settled in Switzld., at the age of 25, and wr. stories, *Bilder aus der Schweiz*, 1824-26, on the model of the Waverley Novels. Another well known 'after' bk. by Zschokke is his *Goldmacherdorf*, 1817, after Pestalozzi (q.v.). Perhaps the best of a very fertile but not very original pen was *Abällino*, or 'The Great Bandit', 1794, an interesting novel of the Sturm und Drang (q.v.) period in Germany.

Zurita, Geronimo (1512-80): Span. annalist; historiographer of Aragon, 1548. Wr. 1562-80, *Annals of the Crown of Aragon*, 6 vols., of considerable merit; esp. in the novel perception of hist. method as applied to documentary research at home and abroad, and the study of travel-records. Z. was excellently trained, and is ranked with Morales (q.v.) as one of the two 'fathers of Spanish history' (Ticknor, iii, 171).

Zurita y Haro, Fernando Jacinto (17th cent.): Span. novelist; of nugatory importance; also described as de Zarate. Z. wr. one of those silly show-tales of the worst period of the *cultismo* (q.v.) affectation, the point of which was the total omission of one vowel. No *a* was used in his dull story, *Meritos disponen Premios*, 1654. (See, too, s.v. Alcala y Herrera).

A GENERAL SKETCH OF EUROPEAN LITERATURE
IN THE CENTURIES OF ROMANCE

Chap.	I.	Story-Matters and Story-Writers	Chap.	VI.	Europe at School
„	II.	The Age of Dante	„	VII.	Europe at Large
„	III.	The Fourteenth Century	„	VIII.	The Maturity of Romance
„	IV.	1374 to 1492	„	IX.	The Age of Milton
„	V.	The Transit through 1492	„	X.	The Watershed of 1637

The Journal of Education says : . . . "The other and nobler way, of which Goldsmith (with all his shortcomings) and Hallam set the example, and which Mr. Laurie Magnus has followed, gives us something different from a 'cram' book or a book of reference. The student is led by his guide to the summit of hills that command a great stretch of plain : he views the country spread out as a map before him, and places that he has passed through or will visit in days to come are seen in their right relations to each other. To attempt this kind of conspectus is incomparably the more difficult task, and success in it seems to require the wide knowledge and power of generalization of a Lord Acton. Mr. Laurie Magnus would doubtless disclaim the ambition to rival 'the cultivated mind of Europe incarnate in its finest characteristics', but he has performed a very arduous feat with a skill that, to one reader at least, has pleasantly recalled Viscount Bryce's memorable description of Acton's conversation".

C.H.H., whose initials reveal a distinguished authority on the subject, writes in the *Manchester Guardian :* "Mr. Magnus has conceived his task on large lines. . . . Continental culture through the centuries has moved to vast and complex rhythms of its own, only fitfully and in fragments caught up into our island music, and it is the merit of Mr. Magnus's sketch to have made these larger rhythms in outline clear. . . . The sketch of the age of Dante in the second chapter is an admirable synthesis. . . . The Renaissance is unfolded in a series of vivid delineations and portraitures, lightly but significantly touched. Some of them, such as Petrarch, Montaigne, Cervantes, could not well be bettered within their compass, . . . and there is no lack of acute and curious observation by the way, in which even the well-read may find it worth their while to glean. . . . The wealth of knowledge, though never that of a specialist, is very remarkable".

Prof. George Saintsbury writes in the *Observer :* "This book of Mr. Magnus's is, for its subject, just the sort of book upon which to set training college students, while it ought to do not a little good to the superior shepherds—perhaps to some of the chief pastors themselves. . . . Here you get a view of the whole body to be compared with a view of the other whole. . . . A very difficult thing to construct ; a thing almost impossible to construct without some gaps or weak points here and there ; but a thing very well worth attempting, and, in this example, a thing very fairly and usefully done ".